T0191501

Lecture Notes in Computer Science 1308

Edited by G. Goos, J. Hartmanis and J. van Leeuwen

Abdelkader Hameurlain   A Min Tjoa   (Eds.)

Database and Expert Systems Applications

th International Conference, DEXA '97
oulouse, France, September 1-5, 1997
roceedings

Springer

Springer
Berlin
Heidelberg
New York
Barcelona
Budapest
Hong Kong
London
Milan
Paris
Santa Clara
Singapore
Tokyo

Series Editors

Gerhard Goos, Karlsruhe University, Germany

Juris Hartmanis, Cornell University, NY, USA

Jan van Leeuwen, Utrecht University, The Netherlands

Volume Editors

Abdelkader Hameurlain
Université Paul Sabatier, Lab. IRIT
118 Route de Narbonne, F-31062 Toulouse, France
E-mail: hameur@irit.fr

A Min Tjoa
Technische Universität Wien, Institut für Softwaretechnik
Resselgasse 3/188, A-1040 Wien, Austria
E-mail: tjoa@ifs.tuwien.ac.at

Cataloging-in-Publication data applied for

Die Deutsche Bibliothek - CIP-Einheitsaufnahme

Database and expert systems applications : 8th international
conference ; proceedings / DEXA '97, Toulouse, France, September
1 - 5, 1997 / A. Hameurlain ; A Min Tjoa (ed.). - Berlin ; Heidelberg
; New York ; Barcelona ; Budapest ; Hong Kong ; London ; Milan ;
Paris ; Santa Clara ; Singapore ; Tokyo : Springer, 1997
  (Lecture notes in computer science ; Vol. 1308)
  ISBN 3-540-63478-9

CR Subject Classification (1991): H.2, H.4, H.5.2, I.2.1, I.2.4-5, H.3, J.1

ISSN 0302-9743
ISBN 3-540-63478-9 Springer-Verlag Berlin Heidelberg New York

© Springer-Verlag Berlin Heidelberg 1997
Printed in Germany

Typesetting: Camera-ready by author
SPIN 10545874   06/3142 – 5 4 3 2 1 0   Printed on acid-free paper

Preface

The Database and Expert Systems Applications (DEXA) conferences are intended as a platform for the exchange of ideas, experiences, and opinions among theoreticians and practitioners and for defining requirements for the future systems in the areas of database and artificial intelligence technologies.

The scope of the papers covers the most recent and relevant topics of database and AI systems. The sessions are primarily devoted to object-oriented databases, active and temporal aspects, integrity constraints, multimedia databases, uncertainity handling, federated databases, digital libraries, learning issues, deductive databases, and knowledge based systems. This volume contains 62 papers selected by the programme committee from a total of 159 submissions, which is an acceptance rate of 39%.

DEXA `97 is the 8th annual conference after Vienna, Berlin, Valencia, Prague, Athens, London, and Zürich. This year the DEXA takes place at the University Paul Sabatier / IRIT in Toulouse, France.

We would like to express our thanks to all institutions actively supporting this event, namely to:

Institut de Recherche en Informatique de Toulouse IRIT, France
Universite Paul Sabatier UPS
AFCET - French Computer Society
Austrian Computer Society
GI (Gesellschaft fur Informatik)
FAW - University of Linz, Austria
Swiss Informaticians Society

Many persons contributed numerous hours to organize this conference. The names of most of them appear on the following pages.

Special thanks go to R. Löw (Technical University of Vienna), G. Wagner (FAW, Linz), J.P. Arcangeli, P. Bazex, S. Bonneau, M. Cailloux, P. Maurice,C. Ravinet, J.M. Thevenin (all from the Institut de Recherche en Informa-tique de Toulouse IRIT/ CNRS - INPT - UPS, France), and to the panel chair H. Afsarmanesh (University of Amsterdam, The Netherlands). We are very indebted to all members of the PC and others who have reviewed very carefully the submitted papers.

July 1997

A. Hameurlain (PC Chair)
IRIT, Université Paul Sabatier, France

A M. Tjoa (PC Chair)
Technical University of Vienna, Austria

List of Referees

E. Andonoff
R. André-Obrecht
J.P. Arcangeli
N. Aussenac
N. Benharkat
P. Bessiere
P. Besnard
J.P. Bodeveix
P. Bosc
M. Bouzeghoub
M. Bras-Grivart
H. Briand
L. Brunie
M. Cart
C. Cayrol-Testemale
M. Cayrol
L. Chaudron
J.P. Cheylan
Y. Chiaramella
L. Cholvy
C. Chrisment
R. Cicchetti
M.O. Cordier
R. De Caluwe
J. Desachy
T. Dkaki
A. Doucet
B. Dousse
J.L. Durieux
Y. Duthen

B. Espinasse
H. Farreny
L. Feraud
A.M. Filali
P. Gallinari
C. Gaspin
J.L. Golmard
G. Goncalves
R. Gerraoui
A. Guenoche
A. Herzig
P.H. Joly
G. Juanole
L. Lakhal
X. Lemaitre
C. Liming
R. Laurini
P. Marquis
L. Mascarilla
P. Meseguer
F. Morvan
J. Mothe
N. Mouaddib
G. Nachouki
J.C. Nicolas
G. Padiou
G. Pasi
G. Piatetsky-Shapiro
J.M. Pinon
J.M. Saglio

M. Schneider
F. Sedes
J.C. Sibertin-Blanc
A. Rauzy
M. Rusinovitch
J.M. Thevenin
M.L Vendittelli
J.L. Verdegay
L. Vieu

Conference Committee

Program Committee

General Chairperson
V. Marik, Czech Technical Univ., Czech Republic

Panel Chairperson
H. Afsarmanesh, University of Amsterdam, The Netherlands

Conference Program Chairpersons
A. Hameurlain, IRIT, Universit Paul Sabatier, France
A M. Tjoa, Technical University of Vienna, Austria

Program Committee Members

H. Afsarmanesh	University of Amsterdam, The Netherlands
H.J. Appelrath	University of Oldenburg, Germany
K. Bauknecht	University of Zurich, Switzerland
P. Bazex	IRIT, Universit Paul Sabatier, France
T. Bench-Capon	University of Liverpool, UK
B. Bhargava	Purdue University, USA
J. Bing	NRCCL Oslo, Norway
J. Bubenko	Royal Institute of Technology, Sweden
L. Camarinha-Matos	New University of Lisbon, Portugal
S. Christodoulakis	University of Crete, Greece
B. Croft	University of Massachusetts, USA
W.S. Cellary	University of Economics at Poznan, Poland
J. Debenham	Univ. of Technology, Sydney, Australia
P. Drazan	RIKS Maastricht, The Netherlands
D. Dubois	CNRS, IRIT, Univ. Paul Sabatier, France
J. Eder	University of Klagenfurt, Austria
T. Eiter	Technical University of Vienna, Austria
G. Gardarin	INRIA, France
S. Ghandeharizadeh	University of Southern California, USA
F. Golshani	Arizona State University, USA
G. Gottlob	Technical University of Vienna, Austria
I. Hawryszkiewycz	Univ. of Technology, Sydney, Australia
S. Jajodia	George Mason University, USA
M. Kamel	Naval Postgraduate School, USA
N. Kamel	City University of Hongkong, Hong Kong
Y. Kambayashi	IMEEL, Japan
G. Kappel	University of Linz, Austria
D. Karagiannis	University of Vienna, Austria

M.A. Ketabchi	Santa Clara University, USA
M.H. Kimk	KAIST, Korea
W. Klas	University of Ulm, Germany
E.P. Klement	University of Linz, Austria
J. Kouloumdjian	LISI-INSA, Lyon, France
P. Kroha	Technical Univ. of Chemnitz, Germany
J. Lazansky	Czech Technical Univ., Czech Republic
T.W. Ling	University of Singapore, Singapore
V. Lum	Chinese Univ. of Hong Kong, Hong Kong
R. Marty	IFA, Switzerland
A. Mendelzon	University of Toronto, Canada
J. Mylopoulos	University of Toronto, Canada
E. Neuhold	GMD-IPSI, Germany
T.W. Olle	T.W. Olle & Associates, UK
G. Ozsoyoglu	University Case Western Research, USA
G. Pangalos	University of Thessaloniki, Greece
M. Papazoglou	Queensland Univ. of Technology, Australia
B. Pernici	Politecnico di Milano, Italy
G. Pernul	University of Essen, Germany
H. Prade	CNRS, IRIT, Univ. Paul Sabatier, France
G. Quirchmayr	University of Vienna, Austria
I. Ramos	Technical University of Valencia, Spain
N. Revell	Middlesex University, UK
C. Rolland	University Paris I, France
N. Roussopoulos	University of Maryland, USA
R. Sacks-Davis	RMIT, Australia
M. Scholl	CNAM&INRIA, Paris, France
A. Sernadas	University of Lisbon, Portugal
M. Shahabi	University of Southern California, USA
A. Sheth	University of Georgia, USA
J.C. Smith	University of British Columbia, Canada
H. Sonnberger	European University Institute, Italy
R.B. Stanton	ANK, Australia
M. Takizawa	Tokyo Denki University, Japan
K. Tanaka	Kobe University, Japan
Z. Tari	RMIT, Australia
S. Teufel	University of Zurich, Switzerland
H.W. Thimbleby	Middlesex University, UK
C.H. Thoma	Ciba-Geigy, Switzerland
R. Traunmüller	University of Linz, Austria
K. Vidyasankar	Memorial Univ. of Newfoundland, Canada
S. Zdonik	Brown University, USA

Organizing Committee

J.P. Arcangeli	Institut de Recherche en Informatique de Toulouse (IRIT), France
P. Bazex	Institut de Recherche en Informatique de Toulouse (IRIT), France
S. Bonneau	Institut de Recherche en Informatique de Toulouse (IRIT), France
M. Cailloux	Institut de Recherche en Informatique de Toulouse (IRIT), France
R. Löw	Technical University of Vienna, Austria
P. Maurice	Institut de Recherche en Informatique de Toulouse (IRIT), France
C. Ravinet	Institut de Recherche en Informatique de Toulouse (IRIT), France
J.M. Thvenin	Institut de Recherche en Informatique de Toulouse (IRIT), France
G. Wagner	FAW, University of Linz, Austria

Important Note
on a Paper Published in the
DEXA'96 Conference Proceedings

One of the most important cornerstones of scientific publishing is the correct citation of all ideas and articles used for the development of the original contribution made by the author(s) of an article. Plagiarism is a serious breach of the trust that should exist between scientific colleagues, and authors have a natural right to expect that others will respect and suitably credit their work.

In the DEXA'96 proceedings, the article:

Wiertzyk, V.I., Ramaswamy, V.: Real-time transactions scheduling in database systems. Proc. DEXA'96, LNCS 1134, pp. 633–643. Berlin: Springer 1996

contains basic ideas and verbatim passages from the following article without listing it among the references:

Ulusoy, O., Belford, G.G.: Real-time transaction scheduling in database systems. Information Systems 18, December 1993

Due to the flood of articles in the database area, the similarities between these two papers were not detected by the referees.

We sincerely regret this fact and offer our apologies to O. Ulusoy and G.G. Belford for the situation described above.

A Min Tjoa
On behalf of DEXA

Table of Contents

Invited Lectures (1)

Modelling I

Object-Oriented Databases I

Active and Temporal Aspects I

Modelling II

Object Oriented Databases II

Active and Temporal Aspects II

Images

Integrity Constraints

Multimedia Databases

Invited Lectures (2)

Deductive Databases and Knowledge Based Systems

Allocation Concepts

Data Interchange

Digital Libraries

Transaction Concepts

Learning Issues

Optimization and Performance

Query Languages

Maintenance of Materialized Views

Federated Databases

Uncertainty Handling and Qualitative Reasoning

Software Engineering and Reusable Software

Remarks

Connecting Databases to the Web: A Taxonomy of Gateways

Gerald Ehmayer[1], Gerti Kappel[1], and Siegfried Reich[1]*

Department of Information Systems, Johannes Kepler University of Linz,
A-4040 Linz, AUSTRIA,
E-Mail:{gerald,gerti,reich}@ifs.uni-linz.ac.at

Abstract. The increasing popularity of the World-Wide Web (WWW) has resulted in a growing interest of companies to make use of the Internet for marketing, selling and presentation purposes. Moreover, with evolving Intranets, there is also a rising demand in using the Web for core business applications. Given the fact that databases are used in many business areas as information repositories, the idea of combining easy to use user interfaces as provided by the World-Wide Web browsers with state-of-the-art data management facilities as supported by today's database management facilities appears to be promising. However, there exist a variety of different technical solutions for connecting databases to the Web, each of them having its strengths and weaknesses with respect to criteria of the individual application domains.
This contribution presents a taxonomy of concepts underlying database and World-Wide Web connectivity and demonstrates for each type of application which solutions might be chosen.

1 Introduction

Since 1993, the World-Wide Web [1] has really been taking off due to its easy use and platform independent user interface providing basic support for multimediality. Databases, on the other, support consistent multi-user management of distributed multimedia information and have been in use in a range of business areas for years. Consequently, interfacing between these technologies appears to be very promising: large amounts of data can be re-used, information can be handled in a consistent way on a large distributed scale; at the same time, easy to use interfaces that are also broadly available facilitate the users' access to information. Categorising these "middleware" components [17] for Web to database connectivity is the subject of this contribution.

The paper is structured as follows. Section 2 investigates the requirements for database to Web connectivity. Then Section introduces the various approaches to connect databases to the Web; we present the fundamental components and describe how they can be combined in order to create different types of architectures. Section 4 summarises these concepts and shows to which type of application they can be applied. We finish in Section 5 with a conclusion.

* This work has been supported by the Austrian Fonds zur Förderung der wissenschaftlichen Forschung (FWF) under grant No. J01330-TEC.

2   Integration Requirements

This section introduces a number of different — partially controversial — criteria for interfacing databases from Web browsers. In particular, we describe "high-level" requirements rather than pure technical specifications. This is expressed by naming the criteria "performance" rather than "number of transactions per second".

It has to be kept in mind that not all applications demand all requirements. A simple information kiosk at a railway station, which informs users about current train timetables, may not impose high demands on concurrency control. On the other hand, an airline reservation system which has to ensure that each seat in a plane is only booked once makes great demands on exact concurrency control but requires a less multimedia user interface. Therefore, there is no *ideal* gateway but rather a number of solutions each with its strengths and weaknesses with respect to specific criteria.

The identified requirements for interfacing databases from the World-Wide Web are as follows:

- Harmonised user interface: whereby we mean, that the user interface allows the integration of different types of data within the client. For instance, results of database queries can be presented together with static text and images within the same browser.
- Interactive Web model [22]: interactivity of Web pages stands for the possibility to change the content as a re-action to a user's input. By that, false or ambiguous inputs can have already been dealt with at the client's side and the server load could be reduced. We refer to *immediate* reaction rather than to reactions in sort of a server's answer to a client's request. The focus is for example on Java applets or JavaScript pages rather than on clickable maps. This level of interactivity is also referred to as *highly* interactive as opposed to interactive.
- Consistency and integrity: data manipulation of course has to be done in a way that ensure the consistency and integrity of the data. Problems with using WWW browsers as frontends arise mainly because of the stateless nature of the Hypertext Transfer Protocol (HTTP) [2] and the fact that the browser is not closely integrated with the database system, i.e., the database does not know about the browser.
- Performance [19]: the performance to be expected from the different solutions may vary and would not really allow a comparison due to the differences in database architectures [1]. We therefore only investigate general bottlenecks or deficiencies of the various approaches.
- Scalability [7]: scalability can be measured by the size of the database as well as the number of simultaneous users the system is able to deal with. There is a relationship between the requirements performance and scalability.

---

[1] For databases per-se there exist a variety of benchmarks. For an overview see for instance [6].

- Openness [23]: openness refers to the ease of integrating new tools into the system, such as new databases, new browsers or re-use a different language for accessing the database. Platform independence is also closely related to this criterion.

3 A Multitude of Different Approaches

Having identified criteria for comparison and measurement we now present the different approaches connecting databases to the Web. We first describe the components involved in these approaches.

The browser. The browser represents the user interface component. The World-Wide Web browsers such as Netscape, Mosaic and Microsoft Explorer load documents encoded in the Hypertext Markup Language (HTML). The browsers of the Hyper-G/HyperWave system [13], called Amadeus and Harmony, use their own format called Hyper-G Text Format (HTF) [11]. A conversion from HTF to HTML with minimal loss is possible; thus, users can use ordinary Web browsers to access Hyper-G servers (but can not make use of the additional functionality provided by Hyper-G).

The server. The World-Wide Web server is a system process understanding HTTP (HyperText Transfer Protocol, [2]) requests from browsers and serving them HTML documents. The server is also responsible for invoking Common Gateway Interface (CGI, [15]) programs, dealing with Server Side Includes (SSI), and ensuring access restrictions. From now on when the term "server" is used, it refers to a World-Wide Web server.

The protocol. The application protocol being used for communication between browser and server is the HyperText Transfer Protocol (HTTP). HTTP is a stateless, extensible protocol so there exists the possibility to modify it.

The external application. Using the CGI as a middleware component means that the actual programming of the database connectivity has to be done by use of a programming language. Different solutions are possible. Very common are scripting languages such as *Perl* (especially *oraperl* and *dbperl*), *Tool-Command-Language (TCL)*, *JavaScript*, and others, as well as the compiling languages *C* and *Java*. Of course, any language can be used.

The external viewer. External viewers are those components that are platform dependent and are not part of the browser itself. A player for video or audio files for example might fall into this category. The browser loads the external viewer according to the specified type of file [18]. With the external viewer launched the control of the session (and consequently the data) is handed over by the browser to the viewer. So-called *plug-ins* offer a similar (platform dependent) solution with better integration.

The database. The database can be of any type, i.e. hierarchical, relational, object-oriented or object-relational, though currently most solutions work for SQL compliant databases. The database management system ensures well known database functionality such as persistence, multi-user support, concurrency, transactions, recovery, distribution, and so forth.

In developing gateways between the Web and databases, all of the components introduced above might be modified or used. Changes to one or several of these components of course have different implications: modifying the browser for instance would require all potential users to install a new browser, consequently this approach contradicts the criterion of openness (and would be difficult to be asserted anyway).

The subsequent sections describe different approaches of implementing database to Web connectivity. For each of the approaches we present the general architecture, explain the components involved and point out advantages and disadvantages with respect to the criteria mentioned above.

3.1 CGI — Common Gateway Interface

The Common Gateway Interface (CGI, [15]) is a standard for external gateway programs to interface with servers. The current version is CGI/1.1. The CGI approach is perhaps the best known approach of adding services to the WWW. Figure 1 shows the architecture of this approach. A browser requests an executable to be started at a server site. This external application then performs the database access, taking the given input parameters and delivers the result back to the server, which forwards it to the browser. The program takes the user's input as if it where standard input and simply writes to standard output which is propagated by the server. This approach allows arbitrary languages to be chosen, i.e. one might use for example *oraperl* for making accesses to *Oracle* databases using the Perl language; or one could use *C* with embedded SQL statements.

Fig. 1. WWW access to Databases using CGI

The main advantages of the CGI approach lie in the freedom of choice of a programming language as well as that any existing database can be re-used — given the fact that there is a programming language that can be applied for implementing the access.

There are essentially two problems associated with the usage of CGI: firstly, the server load can be heavy as each invocation of the CGI program starts a new server process and, secondly, transaction management is insufficient. The former can be improved by using a single, always active session to communicate with the database [10]. The latter problem is due to the stateless nature of the HyperText Transfer Protocol. Imagine a browser sending data to a server which in turn invokes the CGI executable, which then opens a new session in the database and processes the request. At this point a variety of concurrency problems may occur. For instance, a browser's reload request can not be identified by the server since it can not know that the second request refers to a previous one. Or imagine a browser's crash: as there is no direct connection from database to browser the database will keep the session alive although the browser crashed long ago.

Approaches to circumvent the stateless nature of HTTP include modifications of HTTP or setting of so-called cookies[2]. For example, in [3], HTTP is modified so that each time a connection between the browser and the server is established a session number is appended. Thus, the session and consequently user, password and current status can be verified. If there is no action in a session within 10 minutes the server assumes a time-out and performs a rollback of the whole session (and all enclosed transactions).

The placement of a so-called *cookie* is a mechanism that stores the client's state persistently at the client. The state information then can be reloaded and session information be generated for the database request. Following this approach, *Mengelbier* [14] proposes a modification to Netscape's cookie specification which consists of additional session information stored in the cookie.

3.2 SSI — Server Side Include

Another very popular approach of connecting databases to the Web, for instance taken by Netscape's LiveWire, is to use a server which *knows* how to cope with database commands. These commands are either embedded as comments within HTML or they are included in special tags, which are ignored by the browser; the server then performs the database access when serving the documents to the browser. As the access functions are included on the server's site this mechanism is called *Server Side Include (SSI)*. Figure 2 shows the general architecture of this approach, Figure 3 gives a sample HTML file using LiveWire.

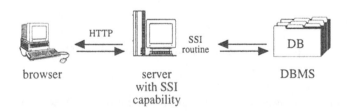

Fig. 2. WWW access to Databases using SSI

As stated above, the functions are included in the HTML documents as either comments or predefined — and therefore server specific — tags. Figure 3

---

[2] Cookies are a general mechanism which browser and server side connections (such as CGI scripts) can use to both store and retrieve information maintained by the browser side of the connection. This state object is called a cookie.

demonstrates part of an HTML file where a connection to a database is made. A simple SQL query is issued and the results are placed in local variables which then can be processed. Note, that **database** is a reserved keyword and resembles to a connection object. Only one connection to a database at a time is possible.

```
<HTML>
...
<SERVER>
database.connect(...)
result = database.cursor("select name, age from Person")
name1 = result.name
age1 = result.age
document.writeln(name1 + ", " + age1 + "<BR>")
result.next() // fetches next record
name2 = result.name
...
</SERVER>
</HTML>
```

Fig. 3. Example of Server Side Include

Concerning transaction management, similar problems as described above for the CGI approach arise. The connection only exists during the parsing phase of the processing of the HTML file. Additionally, there is no standard — as is with the CGI specification — for accessing databases with Server Side Includes; a dedicated server is needed. Therefore this approach is less open as it demands direct server to database connectivity and a predefined data manipulation language. Basing the SSI middleware on standards such as Open Database Connectivity (ODBC) allows connections to all relational databases supporting this protocol. Netscape's LiveWire for instance supports direct SQL connections to Oracle, Sybase, and Informix databases, and ODBC connections to all databases supporting ODBC.

The main advantage of this approach is a potentially better performance as the server directly invokes the database. However, this is implementation specific. At the same time, scalability might be a problem as the server could easily become a bottleneck by having to handle both, WWW and the database service.

3.3 Databases "speaking" HTTP

Following the approach of Server Side Includes the logical next step is to fully integrate server and database. The result is a database which *understands* HTTP-requests. Since the language spoken on the Web is HTML, all database manipulation has to be expressed in HTML and subsequently parsed by the database's interface.

The main advantage of this approach is that the database is called directly from the browser, therefore concurrency and transaction management can be better handled; yet, HTTP remains stateless. At the Dept. of Information Systems we are currently running a project which implements exactly this mechanism. The prototype is called InterAGGS (short for *I*nternet *A*pplications *G*ateway for *GemSt*one[3]) and has implemented an HTTP server as a process in the GemStone object-oriented database management system [4]. Figure 4 shows the principal architecture of this approach.

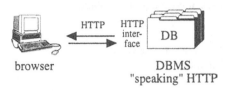

Fig. 4. Database "speaking" HTTP

Being similar to the approach of Server-Side-Includes (SSI) this approach suffers the same problems. The database itself could be a potential bottleneck by having to serve both ordinary WWW requests as well as data processing. Also openness is not given as the HTTP interface is database specific and thus the database is fixed. Real interactivity of Web pages is still not possible.

3.4 Direct Access from Browser to Database Using Java

Since the development of JDBC (Java Database Connectivity) and the support of Java by browsers, a new possibility of connecting to databases from within the WWW has been established.

So-called *Client Side Includes* allow, together with standardised interfaces database access for applets. The components as used within the following sections can be run with every Java/JavaScript enabled browser. Figure 5 illustrates the components and their interactions. The general architecture could also be implemented using *plug-in* technology (for plug-ins see below section 3.6).

The approach is based on the idea that a browser loads a dedicated program (the so-called *applet*), either via the Web or also locally, and the applet then performs the actual database manipulation. Thus, the server is no longer needed for database access as, once the applet has been loaded, the session control is with the browser.

There are many advantages of to approach. On the one side, full transaction management and concurrency control can be offered [20,21]. The platform

---

[3] Find more details on InterAGGS at http://www.lech.priv.at, as well as on the GemStone HTTP interface at http://gd.tuwien.ac.at/ go.

independence of Java and the support by browsers ensure availability on hetero-geneous platforms at the same time guaranteeing basic integration with existing HTML data. Basic interactivity of the Web model is also given. Besides, Java allows fancy user interfaces and animations to be programmed.

Additionally, performance might benefit from this approach as the client can be programmed to already compute basic plausibility checks, by that disburden-ing the database. Last but not least, JDBC is designed in order to allow access to multiple databases, by that easing the integration of different databases, both relational as well as object-oriented ones[4].

Figure 5 shows how browsers can — once they have loaded an applet — di-rectly communicate with the database. Due to security restrictions, Java applets currently (version 1.0.2) can only establish connections to the server they have been loaded from. Thus, the server process as well as the database have to be running on the same physical machine though they will be different processes.

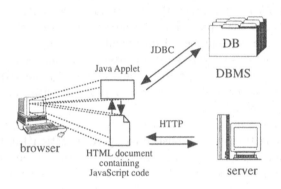

Fig. 5. Direct Access to Databases using JDBC

The integration between Java and HTML is still to be solved. So far, pro-gramming Java applets for accessing databases has lacked the possibility of for-matting output as the Java applet was not intimately integrated with the HTML code; i.e., applets could not access attributes of HTML forms. Recently, Netscape has added features to JavaScript that allow communication and data exchange between applets and JavaScript [8]. By that it is possible to implement transac-tions spawning over several HTML pages and at the same time using HTML for presenting the data.

The applet provides a collection of methods to connect to and access databas-es. These methods are matching a well selected subset of the JDBC standard and implemented for example by a reusable database controller class. The following figure shows portions of an example implementation:

---

[4] However, currently mostly relational databases support JDBC, a fact which seems bizarre considering Java's object-oriented nature.

```
public int getConnection(String alias, ...);
public int commit(String alias);
public int rollback(String alias);
public int executeQuery(String alias, String cursor, String
sql_statement);
public int next(String alias, String cursor);
public String getValue(String alias, String cursor, String
attribute_name);
public Date getDate(alias, cursor, attribute_name);
```

Fig. 6. Java Methods for Database Connection

JavaScript code embedded within HTML documents allows the calling of the applet's methods and integrate the results into the HTML source. When an HTML document is loaded, the script commands are performed by the browser before starting the HTML interpreter; the actual database control though, is with the applet. Because the applet remains persistent within the browser's environment, it can serve any number of documents with only one connection to the database: transactions spawning several pages can thus be realised. For database access the native database protocol could be used by the JDBC driver (not HTTP). For security critical applications a protocol with cryptography support could be implemented.

The JavaScript programmer is able to identify a connection by its alias, specified when the connection was established (see getConnection() in Figure 7). This allows the creation of more than one connection at a time, even to different databases. This strategy can also be used to enable HTML documents to control single transactions such as database queries. The method *executeQuery()* allows the programmer to issue identify by a cursor. Numeric return values of methods are used to indicate success or failure of methods.

In general, the approach using Java works fine for smaller programs; however, considering large distributed applications, maintaining the Java applets as well as the HTML pages extended with JavaScript might be difficult. Similar experiences are reported in [9] who argue that integration between applets and browsers is still inadequate and that workarounds with JavaScript are unsatisfactory and clumsy.

3.5 External Viewers for Accessing Databases

The approach of using an external viewer is based on the idea of using the type information of the document being loaded and launching an external viewer which then deals with the data. Figure 8 shows the principal architecture. A browser requests a document from a server; the document is of a specific (non HTML) type thus telling the browser to launch an external viewer, i.e., a specific database client. The control is handed over from the browser to the external viewer which in turn performs the database access. This approach requires the

```
<HTML>
<APPLET CODEBASE="..." NAME="dbAccess"> ...
</APPLET> ...
<SCRIPT language="JavaScript">
document.dbAccess.getConnection(al, "gemstone.ifs.uni-linz.ac.at")
cn = document.dbAccess.cursor("select name from person")
...
document.writeln("<B>" +
document.dbAccess.getValue(al, cn, "name") + "</B><BR>")
document.dbAccess.next(al, cn)
...
</SCRIPT>
...
</HTML>
```

Fig. 7. Talking to Java Applet from JavaScript

database command to be embedded in a document which then can be loaded by a simple mouse click; the browser has to be configured in order to deal with the document.

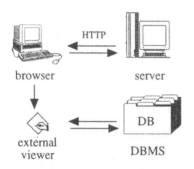

Fig. 8. Accessing a Database Using an External Viewer

Using a dedicated viewer, this approach fully satisfies transaction management and concurrency control. Additionally, there are performance benefits in using this configuration: the server merely answers the browser's request by delivering a MIME encoded document; the browser itself does not really deal with the document either as it invokes an external viewer. The price to pay however lies in the missing integration of Web and database data. Furthermore, there is an installation overhead as the external viewer has to be installed at every site.

3.6 Extending the Browser's Capabilities with Plug-ins

So-called *plug-ins* are programs that extend the capabilities of browsers in a specific way, for instance to allow the playing of video files from within the browser. Manufacturers of browsers define an API that allows software developers to implement native support for new or additional data types.

Implementing plug-ins is very similar to using an external viewer the main difference being that the plug-in avoids the need for another viewer to be launched and thus the control stays with the browser. Plug-ins are, however, platform specific and also have to be installed at every browser.

3.7 Proxy-based Services

Basing additional services on a proxy is a very common approach in the Web's world of adding further functionality.

This approach makes use of the Web's basic design by using so-called *HTTP proxy servers* in order to access databases. The basic idea is to re-direct the browser's request via a proxy server. This server then can perform the database access and deliver the result to the browser. The database manipulation commands have to be embedded in the HTML documents, the proxy server recognises them by parsing the browser's request. Figure 9 demonstrates the principal architecture of this approach.

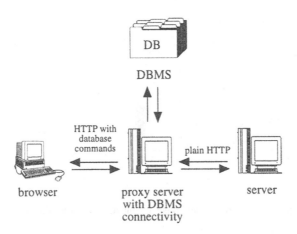

Fig. 9. Using a Proxy for WWW Database Connectivity

A sophisticated example for this approach can be found in [5]. The user requests a document from a server. A proxy-server queries a link database and returns the originally requested document enriched with the additional links to the browser.

From a requirement's point of view this approach resembles very much the Server-Side-Include advance. Interactivity of Web pages, up-to-date information as well as scalability are equally satisfied. Additionally, performance is well balanced by using a different server for database connectivity; besides, the Web allows any server to be a proxy as long as it talks HTTP, so different choices of database solutions are possible. However, transaction management and concurrency can not be ensured by this approach.

3.8 Database Connectivity in HyperWave

This section describes the approach taken by HyperWave, formerly called Hyper-G [13]. HyperWave uses a gateway server as an intermediate component between server and database. Using such a three-tier architecture allows the connection to multiple databases, keeping them alive as long as necessary and the implementation of caching mechanisms to reduce database access.

Figure 10 shows the components of this architecture. The SQL gateway server is responsible for parsing incoming SQL statements, connecting to the database and formatting the result. It also allows the author to specify several SQL statements and a MIME type attribute for presentation.

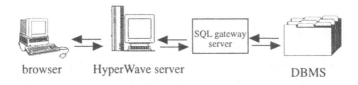

browser   HyperWave server   DBMS

Fig. 10. Three-Tier Approach in HyperWave

The gateway server is able to reduce the number of connections to the database, thereby reducing response time and licensing costs. Caching and already open connections can improve performance for recurrent and successive queries respectively. Only in environments with concurrent database access and permanent updates, would caching and data consistency have an impact. In comparison to the two-tier architecture (such as for instance the SSI approach), the three-tier architecture allows for the usage of both, a server and a gateway server in order to achieve higher scalability in a distributed environment.

4 Summary of Concepts

Table 1 gives an overview of the different concepts as well as to what degree they fulfill the requirements stated in section 2.

As can be seen from the table that two approaches — JDBC and HyperWave — have excellent properties with respect to most criteria. This means that either of these two technologies is well suited well for almost any database to Web

Table 1. Different Approaches and their Properties (- = no support, + = basic support, ++ = full support)

	CGI	SSI	DB w. HTTP	JDBC	Ext. Viewer	Plug-in	Proxy	HyperWave
Harmonised UI	++	++	++	++	-	+	++	++
Interactivity	-	+	+	++	-	++	-	++
Consistency	-	+	++	++	++	-	+	++
Performance	+	+	+	++	++	+	++	++
Scalability	++	+	+	+	++	++	++	++
Openness	+	-	-	++	-	+	+	+

integration. Additionally, by supporting Java, HyperWave also allows to make use of the client side include approach based on Java applets.

The great variety of different possible approaches demonstrates though, that also other solutions for database to Web integration are possible and reasonable. It basically depends on the application domain. For instance, simple querying of existing data, such as product data, can easily be done with the all available CGI approach. And, for smaller applications, also Server-Side Includes work very well.

5 Conclusion

In this contribution we have identified the requirements for World-Wide Web to database connectivity. We have presented the principal components for building different types of architectures and we have described the various approaches.

In conclusion there are two major lessons we have learned. Firstly, the most promising solutions which allow not only querying but also editing and collaboration suffer from the intermix of control code and formatting instructions; this mainly is due to the stateless nature of the HyperText Transfer Protocol as well as the insufficient Java to HTML integration; secondly, there is a constant change in the availability and the properties of tools. We will subsequently briefly describe these two points.

The increasingly important requirement for collaboration on the Web requires the application developer to make use of a variety of different tools which results in quite complicate configurations and architectures. In particular, considering the collaborative aspect, most of the configurations are workarounds of the stateless nature of HTTP. The integration between applets and browsers is still inadequate and workarounds with JavaScript are unsatisfactory and clumsy.

The question to be asked therefore is whether we should consider a stateful HTTP version. This could be realised as a separate protocol which could be used by browsers for all applications where transaction semantics is necessary. For "ordinary" browsing HTTP would be used; for collaboration on the Web a stateful HTTP would be used.

Additionally, from a software engineering point of view, particularly the CGI as well as SSI approach have the disadvantage that — as the result of the request should be processable by the browser — the output has to be encoded in HTML. As a consequence, algorithmic program code as well as SQL statements are mixed up with formatting code, consequently making debugging and maintenance difficult. Approaches such as using style sheets for HTML documents [12] proposed by the W3C do not really help in solving this issue, however, style sheets would help in abstracting the actual layout from the element type. Still, due to the nature of HTML a lot of layout information has to be provided, e.g. break-line or horizontal rule. Interestingly in this respect is the approach taken by [16] to develop a cross language variable substitution scheme between HTML and SQL. The implementation of course, results in a proprietary system, a fact which does circumvent the criterion of openness.

The second main lesson learned is that there is a permanent coming and going of products and versions thereof which really require a generalised middleware architecture for Web to database connectivity such as that implemented in HyperWave. It is simply not sufficient to see vendors moving towards multiple platform support, the 16 supported platforms for Netscape Navigator serving as prominent example. This is very valuable in general, though, from a database point of view, a commonly agreed architecture with well defined protocols and interfaces would be more desirable. A generalised and commonly available protocol for accessing databases could for example be one component of this architecture.

References

1. Tim Berners-Lee, Robert Cailliau, Ari Luotonen, Henrik Frystyk Nielsen, and Arthur Secret. The world-wide web. *Communications of the ACM*, 37(8):76–82, 1994.
2. Tim Berners-Lee, Roy T. Fielding, and Henrik Frystyk Nielsen. Hypertext transfer protocol — http/1.0. Technical report, Internet RFC 1945, May 1996.
3. Michael Björn and Ryosuke Hotaka. A WWW gateway for interactive relational database management. In *AusWeb95 — The First Australian WorldWideWeb Conference, Ballina*, May 1995.
4. P. Butterworth, A. Otis, and J. Stein. The GemStone object database management system. *Communications of the ACM*, 34(10):64–77, 1991.
5. Leslie Carr, Gary Hill, David De Roure, Wendy Hall, and Hugh Davis. Open information services. In *Fifth International World Wide Web Conference, Paris*, May 1996.
6. Akmal B. Chaudhri. An annotated bibliography of benchmarks for object databases. *SIGMOD RECORD*, 24(1):50–57, March 1995.
7. Hugh Charles Davis. *Data Integrity Problems in an Open Hypermedia Link Service*. PhD thesis, University of Southampton, U.K., Faculty of Engineering and Applied Science, Department of Electronics and Computer Science, November 1995.
8. Danny Goodman. *JavaScript Bible*, chapter LiveConnect: Scripting Java Applets and Plug-ins, pages 425–444. IDG Books Worldwide, Inc., Chicago, 1996.
9. Kaj Grønbæk, Niels Olof Bouvin, and Lennerth Sloth. Designing dexter-based hypermedia services for the world wide web. In *Proceedings of Hypertext '97, Southampton, U.K.*, pages 146–156, 1997.

10. Stathes P. Hadjiefthymiades and Drakoulis I. Martakos. Improving the performance of cgi compliant database gateways. In *Sixth International World Wide Web Conference. Santa Clara*, 1997.

11. Frank M. Kappe. Hyper-G text format (HTF). version 2.11. Technical report, IIG (Institute for Information Processing), May 1995.

12. Håkon W. Lie and Bert Bos. Cascading style sheets, level 1. a W3C recommendation available at http://www.w3.org/pub/www/tr/. Technical report, W3C, 1996.

13. Hermann Maurer. *Hyperwave™: The Next Generation Web Solution*. Addison-Wesley, 1996.

14. Magnus Mengelbier. Extended persistent client state http cookies. Technical report, Temple University, School of Business and Management. Available as http://www.sbm.temple.edu/~magnus/ext_cookie_spec.htm, 1996.

15. NCSA — The National Center for Supercomputing Applications. *The Common Gateway Interface, Version 1.1. Available as http://hoohoo.ncsa.uiuc.edu/cgi/*.

16. Tam Nguyen and V. Srinivasan. Accessing relational databases from the world wide web. In *SIGMOD '96, Montreal Canada*, pages 529–540, June 1996.

17. Louis Perrochon. W3 "middleware": Notions and concepts. In *Fourth International World Wide Web Conference, Boston, MA. Workshop "Web Access to the Legacy Data"*, December 1995.

18. J. Postel. Media type registration procedure. Technical report, Internet RFC 1590. Updates RFC 1521 MIME (Multipurpose Internet Mail Extensions), 1994.

19. Kim Pyung-Chul. A taxonomy on the architecture of database gateways for the web. Technical report, Database Laboratory, Dept. of Information Communications Engineering. Chungnam National University, Korea. Available as http://grigg.chungnam.ac.kr/~uniweb/documents/taxonomy/text.html, 1996.

20. Ulrike Sommer and Peter Zoller. "Online-Datenbanken", Internet — von der Technologie zum Wirtschaftsfaktor. In *Deutscher Internetkongress 97, Düsseldorf*, pages 333–341, 1997.

21. Sun Microsystems. *Java Database Access, Specification. Available as http://splash.javasoft.com/databases/*, 1997.

22. P. Vanouplines and P. Nieuwenhysen. Highly interactive WWW services: a new type of information sources. In *20th International Online Information Meeting, London*, pages 367–377, December 1996.

23. Uffe Kock Wiil and John J. Leggett. The HyperDisco approach to open hypermedia systems. In *Proceedings of Hypertext '96, Washington D.C.*, pages 140–148, 1996.

Multimedia Federated Databases on Intranets :
Web-Enabling IRO-DB

Georges Gardarin

Laboratoire PRiSM URA CNRS 1525
Université de Versailles-St Quentin
45 avenue des Etats-Unis
78035 Versailles Cedex - FRANCE
email : (1) <firstname>.<lastname>@prism.uvsq.fr

Abstract. *Integrating semantically heterogeneous databases requires rich data models to homogenize disparate distributed entities with relationships and to access them through consistent views using high level query languages. In this paper, we first survey the IRO-DB system, which federates object and relational databases around the ODMG data model. Then, we point out some technical issues to extend IRO-DB to support multimedia databases on the Web. We propose to make it evolve towards a three-tiered architecture including local data sources with adapters to export objects, a mediator to integrate the various data sources, and an interactive user interface supported by a Web browser. We show through an example that new heuristics and strategies for distributed query processing and optimization have to be incorporated.*

Key words. *Interoperable database, Federated database, Object-oriented database, Remote data access, Schema integration, Multimedia, Web, Query processing.*

1. Introduction

Object-oriented multidatabase systems (also referred to as federated databases or heterogeneous databases) represent the confluence of various trends in computer science and technology [1], among them object-orientation [2], distributed databases, and interoperability. Recently, the Internet has become the major vehicle in networking industry for information access and dissemination. The Web as a service on top of the Internet or Intranets focuses on transparent navigation and hypermedia document oriented information access. Thus, today there is a need to integrate the object-oriented multidatabase technology within multimedia Web-based systems, both for Intranet applications and Internet services. This paper discusses the integration of multimedia and Web techniques within the IRO-DB federated database system.

While much of the early work in federated databases concentrated on relational technology [3], some projects have been developed at the beginning of the 90's based on object models. Pegasus [4] was one of the first developed at HP Lab. It is centered around a global object model to which local objects (e.g., tables from a relational DB) are mapped. The global model is close to the object-relational one and the query language is SQL3+, an adapted version of SQL3. Started in 1993, the IRO-DB Esprit project [5] has developed a similar approach, but based on the ODMG "standard" [6].

IRO-DB supports an interactive schema integrator workbench to design integrated views of the federated database, and to automatically generate mappings to exported schemas. IRO-DB also focuses on relationship traversal and complex objects handling through collection support. This paper first gives an overview of the IRO-DB system architecture and describes some of the main components of the system.

Recently, a new generation of heterogeneous database systems has appeared in research. This generation typically focuses on a better support of multimedia objects and an integration with web-based technology. Some of the most well known projects are Garlic of IBM Almaden [7], Tsimmis of Standford University [8], Information Manifold of AT&T [9], and Disco from INRIA [10]. While some of these projects model data as labeled graphs with more or less typed nodes (Tsimmis), most still use object-relational (IM) or pure object models (Disco, Garlic). As with relational systems which have been extended to support object technology (e.g., Oracle 8 or Informix), we believe that operational federated object-oriented database systems can be extended to support multimedia objects and Web technology.

This paper first describes the IRO-DB object-oriented federated database system. Developed by a consortium of European partners, IRO-DB is now operational and an application was recently demonstrated. Thus, the difficulty is now to extend it to support multimedia objects, such as geographical data and images, and to make it Web-enabled. In the next section, we survey the IRO-DB architecture and main components. In the third section, we try to isolate the main issues to address for extending it to support Web technology with multimedia database servers. We propose a three-tiered architecture and discuss some query processing issues. In conclusion, we summarize the contributions of this paper and our future plans.

2. The IRO-DB Project

IRO-DB is an object-oriented federated database system. A version is currently operational. It interconnects a relational system INGRES, and three object-oriented DBMS : O2, Matisse and Ontos. In this section, we briefly describe the main system features and some key components.

2.1 Project Overview

IRO-DB (Interoperable Relational and Object-Oriented DataBases) is an ESPRIT project developed in Europe from 1993 to 1996. The novelty of the IRO-DB architecture is to use the ODMG'93 standard [6] as a common object model supporting the ODL definition language and the OQL query language to federate various object-oriented and relational data sources. The IRO-DB architecture is clearly divided into three layers, thus facilitating the cooperative development of the project in several research centers. The local layer adapts local data sources to the ODMG standard ; the communication layer efficiently transfers OQL requests and the resulting collections of objects ; the interoperable layer provides schema integration tools, security management, transaction management, object management, as well as a global query processor.

Accordingly, IRO-DB follows an architecture with three layers of schemas, i.e., with *local schemas*, *import/export schemas*, and *interoperable schemas* (also referred to as *integrated views*). A local schema is a local database schema, as usual. An export schema describes in ODMG terms the subset of a database that a local system allows to be accessed by cooperating systems. IRO-DB does not support a global unique integrated schema, but allow application administrators to define *integrated views*. It consists of a set of derived classes with relationships together with mappings to the underlying export schemas.

2.2 System Layer Descriptions

The architecture of the system is organized in three layers of components as represented in figure 1.

At the *interoperable layer*, object definition facilities stand for specifying integrated schemas, which are integrated views of the federated databases. We fully support the ODL view definition language, with many to many relationships. An interactive tool called the *Integrator Workbench (IW)* is offered to help the database administrator in designing integrated views. Views and export schemas are stored in a data dictionary. Object manipulation facilities include an embedding of OQL in the OML/C++ user language and modules to decompose global queries into local ones (global query processor) and to control global transactions (global transaction management). Object definition and manipulation facilities are built upon the integrated object manager (IOM).

The *communication layer* implements object-oriented Remote Data Access (OO RDA) services through the Remote Object Access (ROA) modules, both on clients and servers. Integration of the ROA protocol within the interoperable layer is provided through the object manager, which is able to manipulate collection of any types. Thus, it is possible to invoke OQL/CLI primitives to retrieve collections of objects stored on the local site. OQL/CLI primitives include connection and deconnection, preparation and execution of OQL queries with transfer of results through collections of objects, plus some specific primitives to import at the interoperable layer the exported ODMG schemas, as well as a primitive to perform remote method invocation.

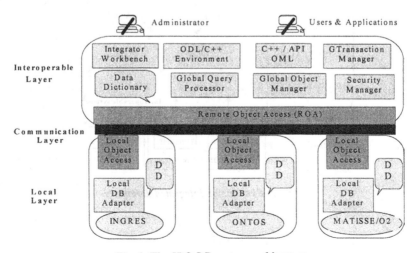

Fig. 1. The IRO-DB system architecture.

The *local layer* is composed of Local Database Adapters (LDA). A local database adapter provides functionalities to make a local system able to answer OQL queries on an abstraction of a local schema in term of ODMG schema (export schema). As an export schema only describes locally implemented types, only locally available functionalities are available for querying through OQL. That means for example that methods and access paths cannot be invoked with simple LDA whose does not know how to export complex ODMG schemas. In that case, only flat objects without relationships are handled at the local layer for relational systems. Of course, if the local system supports the full ODMG model, all syntactically correct ODMG queries are acceptable.

2.3 Main System Components

The Integrator Workbench
The integrator workbench generates from a graphic interface the ODL description of an integrated view, plus some mapping definitions using OQL and C++ method profiles. Integration is done one exported schema after the other. At first, two exported schemas are displayed using a graphical view of the object model. Classes are represented as nodes. Two types of arcs are used to represent relationships and generalizations linking class nodes together. Attributes and methods are directly linked to the class they belong to using aggregation arcs. A naïve schema integration is first perform by union of the two graphs. Then, integration is performed under the direction of the database administrator, which specifies similarities between the export schemas.

For example, with the CIM test-bed application that has been developed to demonstrate the system [11], we integrate two databases as represented in figure 2. Site 1 manages parts and manufacturers. Site 2 manages parts. The G::PART integrated view is a class with a one-to-many relationship referencing manufacturers, i.e., G::MANUF. The integrator workbench generates the view definition in ODL and the mapping to the import schemas given in figure 3.

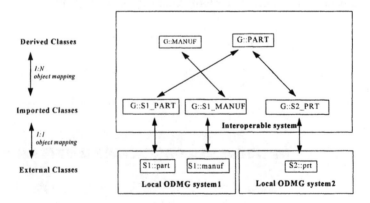

Fig. 2. Example of integrated databases.

Interface PART
    (extent   parts
    keys   part_id) {
    attribute String   part_id;
    attribute Date   upd_date;
    attribute   String   description;
    relationship   Set <MANUF> manufs
                       inverse MANUF::parts ; }
Mapping PART {
    origins   sorig, iorig;
    def_ext   select PART(sorig : s_inst, iorig : i_inst)
                  from s_inst in s_parts, i_inst in i_prts
                  where s_inst.part_id = i_inst.prt_id;
    def_att   part_id as this.sorig.part_id;
    def_att   upd_date as this.sorig.upd_date;
    def_att   description as this.sorig.description;
    def-rel   manufs as
              select me
              from me in manufs
              where (this.sorig = me.sorig.part) or (this.iorig = me.iorig.part);

Fig. 3. Definition of a derived class.

The Global Query Processor

The *Global Query Processor* goal consists in processing queries against an integrated schema. It is responsible for decomposing the query in order to identify the necessary object transfers and consequently the sub-queries that should be sent to local databases. It is composed of three components described below. Their complete description is presented in [12].

• *Translator*. It manages OQL queries expressed against derived classes and translates them in equivalent OQL queries expressed against imported schemas. The intuitive principle of translating a query expressed on derived classes consists in replacing all derived class extent names by their mapping definition. The translation process uses the derivation specification of each class available in the repository. If there are several layers of derived classes, the query is translated recursively, until it refers to imported classes only.

• *Optimizer*. The optimizer task consists in improving the query processing performance. For that, it applies a set of rules to minimize the object transfers and the communication cost between the IRO-DB client and the local databases. At first, a cost model was designed for the optimizer using a calibrating approach [13]. Although some ODBMSs were calibrated, the cost model was finally not used and heuristics were used. First, rules are applied to flatten the query as much as possible. Next, selections (i.e., restrictions and projections) are moved down the tree. Finally, caching rules are used to avoid transferring objects already in the client cache.

• *Decomposer*. The query decomposer identifies sub-trees which refer to mono-site queries and generates the OQL corresponding sub-queries. The query decomposer generates an execution plan composed of two distinct parts : (i) the set of sub-queries executed on local DBMS, (ii) the synthesis query corresponding to the part of the query tree to evaluate globally.

The Global Object Manager

The *Global Object Manager* ensures virtual object management for the imported and derived objects. It allows objects creation and access and guarantees their identity at the interoperable layer. The Object Manager imports objects from external database systems and combines them into a uniform representation by creating surrogate objects. In IRO-DB the management of imported classes differ from the management of derived class. The instantiation of an imported class is not necessary for the evaluation of an OQL query. On the contrary, for all queries that return derived objects as opposed to structured values, it is mandatory to create derived objects since they do not exist in other remote databases. The instantiation of a virtual class is done by its constructor method.

The Remote Object Access

The Remote Object Access component is implementing the CLI interface for OQL queries on TCP/IP. It provides a set of commands to manage contexts, connections, export schemas, statements, results and transactions. We have modified the standard CLI interface to handle OQL queries in place of SQL, but also and mainly to handle collections of objects in place of tuples. Thus, primitives to handle object descriptions have been added. Iterators have been introduced and standard OML primitives to cross a collection through an iterator have been added.

An ad-hoc protocol derived from FAP has been implemented to support the transfer primitives, using XDR for encoding. Commands are bundled into messages by the ROA and unbundled on the server by the LOA. An object is transfered as a structure of values with a tag giving the type of each attribute. Similar objects are organized in collections (list, set, bag and array) both on the server site and the client site, according to the query result type. Collections of similar objects are packed in pages for improving the transfer rate.

The Local Database Adapters

The role of local database adapter (LDA) is to execute received OQL queries on top of the local database and to send back results through the Local Object Access module (LOA). It accesses to the local data dictionary containing the definition of the export schema referenced by the query. Then, it translates the OQL query to a set of local queries. On top of relationnal systems, complex OQL queries are generally translated to several SQL queries. Assembling the results in collections is one of the most difficult task. To populate the dictionary from a local database schema, each LDA provides an *export schema builder*. This is a tool reading the relevant part of the local database schema and building an ODMG counterpart.

Although we design a generic adapter for ODMG databases, we quickly discovered that each ODBMS interface is specific. Thus, except the common libraries which are those of the relational LDA, the object LDAs have no common modules. The O2 LDA is mainly implementing a dynamic OQL on top of O2. Each OQL query is translated into a selection of object identifiers and then into some accesses to the relevant object attributes or methods. The MATISSE LDA is very specific ; it interprets OQL queries using the MATISSE C API. The ONTOS LDA is quite similar, but with a different target language.

3. Extending IRO-DB to Support Web Multimedia Databases

In this section, we discuss how we plan to extend IRO-DB to the Web, as a mediator supporting object-relational queries on integrated views of multiple data sources, the query being issued from Web browsers. Due to the multimedia nature of the Web, multimedia servers also have to be supported. As an example, we discuss the case of an image server.

3.1 Integrating the Web

Integrating a federated database system to the Web first means accessing it through browsers and Http servers. Web client access is currently dominated by browser software from Netscape and Microsoft (Explorer) providing graphical user interfaces. One major characteristic of such navigators is that their functionality can be easily extended and adapted to specific application needs. There are at least four approaches to extend a browser : (1) **Scripts** written in a script language (e.g., JavaScript) included in Html pages and interpreted by the browser, (2) **Applets** written in Java that are small applications whose intermediate code is included in Html documents to be interpreted by browsers, (3) **Plugs-in** written in any language, compiled and loaded on demand then linked to extensible browsers, (4) **ActiveX controls,** a technology provided by Microsoft, which are persistent modules loaded from the server and integrated to windows browser through the DCOM Microsoft technology.

Among these approaches, it is hard to predict which will become dominant in the future. However, it seems already that scripts are limited to data entry, plugs-in are too heavy to manage, and ActiveX controls are Microsoft dependent. Thus, Java applets seems to be the best technology for integrating IRO-DB functionality with browsers.

On the server side, the interest of DBMS vendors is to provide suitable frameworks to their customers, which allow for the easy creation or adoption of information services for the Web. Currently, there are four approaches to develop Web servers for database applications : (1) **CGI (Common Gateway Interface)** is the mechanism for a user to invoke a program that sends output Html formatted data back to the client. The program can invoke a database manager, e.g., through an ODBC SQL interface or a specific one. For example, the Oracle Web product is based on a CGI interface to process queries and return formatted results. (2) **Server APIs** are specific interface to the server. The Netscape API includes a Database Connectivity Library for direct SQL connectivity to most relational databases, including Oracle, Informix, Sybase and ODBC for DBMS independent connections. The Microsoft API includes dbWeb, an application able to process queries from a Web browser and handles the communication between the browser, an ODBC data source, and a Web server to display the results on an outgoing Web page. (3) **Java-based server APIs** use the Java programming language to create applets on the client side that run programs on the server side. The so-called JDBC (Java Database Connectivity) API proposed by SunSoft makes available a standard interface to any Java applet or application. JDBC is based on the X/OPEN SQL Call Level Interface (CLI), the basis of ODBC. JDBC is available on top of ODBC, which means that any relational database is accessible through JDBC. The protocol used to access a relational database from JDBC is some variation of the ISO Remote Data Access (RDA) protocol, depending from the database server. (4) **ActiveX server tools** are pushed by Microsoft. They are written in Visual Basic or Visual C++ and run under the control of ActiveX browser objects.

Integrating the Web also means being able to access multiple data sources from the interoperable layer runtime, hereafter referred to as the *mediator*. A mediator aiming at database integration should support most database servers in an efficient way using Web technology. It should also be able to integrate loosely formatted files, such as Html files. As introduced above, the JDBC API, which can be plugged on any type of formatted data, seems to be currently the best approach for relational data sources in the Web context. There are plans to support object-relational and object databases. However, JDBC does not yet supports multimedia data or semi-structured files. Thus, it has to be extended with specific data types, as images, texts, Html documents, etc. We further detail this point in the communication layer section.

Finally, for mediating between various databases on the Web, a three-tiered architecture, as represented in figure 4, seems to be well suited. The user will contact the mediator home page. Through Java applets, global queries will be formulated and sent to the mediator using HTTP-CGI or Java to Java protocols (e.g., RMI). The mediator will then decompose the query in local sub-queries sent to local sources through JDBC for formatted databases, and through some extensions of it for multimedia databases.

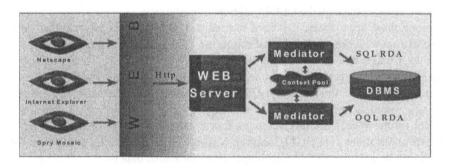

Fig. 4. A three-tiered mediator architecture.

3.2 Local Support for multimedia sources

The ODL and OQL languages are the local description and manipulation languages provided by LDAs in IRO-DB. ODL is similar to CORBA IDL, but with the notion of extents and relationships. Is that sufficient to describe and manipulate multimedia objects ? Let us consider for example an Html file with references to images. Html documents are generally loosely formatted. They are often retrieved using keywords. Keywords can be modeled by a method returning a ranked array of, for example, 10 keywords. References (i.e., HREF) to images can be modeled through 1-1 relationships. Images are generally in Graphical Interchange Format (GIF) or in Joint Photographic Experts Group (JPEG) format. The only available function on such data types is display. Thus, in that case, ODL is sufficient to describe an image.

However, in the case of an image DBMS, content-based queries are possible. In many image systems, pick lists are available for query support. Pick lists gives values for typical features, such as colors, textures, shapes, etc. [14]. Other operations, such as rotate, clip (to select an image region), overlay to check if two images intersect, are possible. Thus, a description of an image can be specified using ODL as given in figure 5.

Query processing is more difficult, as queries in multimedia servers are not exact match queries. Often, a search expression involves uncertainty and fuzziness, with comparison operators like "SIMILAR TO" in conditions. Such predicates have to be defined as operations at the type level in ODL. Sophisticated techniques have been developed for similarity measurement ; they generally compute a measure from 0 to 1. Returning this measure to the mediator is not sufficient as the query processor does not know how to interpret and combine such numbers. Visual query languages as QBIC supports such fuzziness [7], but mediators do not. This is an open problem.

```
Interface image
{ attribute
photoid int ;
content array[1024,1024] int ;
operation
array[10] picklist(image) ;
image rotate (image, angle) ;
image clip (region) ;
boolean overlay (image, image) ;
integer similar (image, image) ; }
```

Fig. 5. A simplified definition of an image database.

A typical query on a database federating employees with their pictures defined as images is then :

```
SELECT Clip(Rotate(I,90),"area")
FROM Employees E, I in E.Pictures
WHERE E.age() > 50 and I.similar("Bandit") > 0.8 ;
```

It retrieves all employees older than 50, which look like the bandit picture. Each resulting picture is rotated of 90° and cut using the clip function to fit in the screen. Processing such a query assuming that employees are handled by some objet-relational database server and that images are managed by a multimedia server is a difficult task that we further investigate below.

3.3 Extending the Communication Layer

The IRO-DB communication layer provides facility to communicate from the mediator to the local adapters. With Java, JDBC can be used to query and update relational databases as explained above. However, JDBC has several shortcomings. First, it is based on SQL and does not support objects yet. An OQL version seems to be in preparation. Second, it does not support global transactions. Integration to transactional monitors is hard to develop. Thus, we plan to replace the IRO-DB communication layer by JDBC to which some extensions will be incorporated. For multimedia servers, it is not obvious that JDBC will be the right choice. We might then use specific communication protocols based on RMI for example, the Java remote method invocation protocol.

3.4 Extending the Interoperable Layer

The IRO-DB interoperable layer includes design help components and query processing components. Both have to be extended as briefly indicated below.

3.4.1 The Integrator Workbench

The Integrator Workbench should support new data types and new mapping functions from one data type to another. For example, integrating two sets of images, one in GIF, the other in JPEG, requires the knowledge of this data types and of a conversion function from JPEG to GIF. This seems to be feasible by integrating libraries of components in the Workbench. More difficult will be the integration of semi-structured data types, such as Html files. Semi-structured type templates should be abstracted from files and integrated in the workbench. The less specific will be the type templates, the less integration will be feasible.

3.4.2 The Query Processor

In IRO-DB, the query processor does not integrate cost-based optimization as stated above. It just applies simple heuristics as push selection first. This strategy could give bad results in a multimedia context. For example, using the query given in the example above, the optimizer might generate two sub-queries, respectively sent to the employee database and to the picture database, as follows :

    (Q1) SELECT E.Images
         FROM Employees E
         WHERE E.age() > 50
    (Q2) SELECT I, res = Clip(Rotate(I,90),"area")
         FROM I in Pictures
         WHERE I.similar("Bandit") > 0.8 ;

and a synthesis query run on the mediator :

    (Q3) SELECT res
         FROM E in Q1 E, I in Q2
         WHERE I = E.Images.

This will be a very bad plan, as every image will be compared to the bandit on the multimedia site and many will be transferred on the net. Avoiding bad plans clearly requires clever heuristics or even a full object cost model [15]. Some operations (e.g., clip) are only possible on certain sites. Thus, algorithms that use the source descriptions to generate executable query plans are required [16]. Also, transforming function expressions and knowing operation costs is not an obvious task. A general framework for this problem is proposed in [17].

3.4.3 The Object Manager

The IRO-DB object manager only handles the basic data types of OQL. This is insufficient on the Web, with multimedia objects. A question is : should it handle all data types imported from local databases ? If yes, the object manager has to be extensible. Every manipulated data type should be integrated at the level of the object manager. Thus, when exporting a new type, the LDA will have to supply it to the object manager of the mediator. Except if a portable and transferable language is used everywhere (e.g., Java), this is impracticable. One (poor) solution is to restrict the set of available data types. For example, BLOBs could be used to transfer images. Another (rich) solution is to develop all abstract data types in Java and to download the bytecode where needed. Sending methods should then be taken into account by the query optimizer, as sending bytecode might be costly.

4. Conclusion

In this paper, we describe the IRO-DB federated object-oriented database system architecture. IRO-DB federates relational and object-oriented databases through an object-oriented data model with an associated object query language derived from the ODMG proposal. The overall aim of the project — the provision of building blocks for federated database management — has been recognized worldwide as one of the most important challenges in database research and development at the beginning of the 90's. The project develops suitable object-oriented generalizations of the SQL Access Group protocols extended with object-oriented features for the exchange of complex objects. It takes into account relevant industrial data interchange standards or proposals, such as the OMG architecture and the ODMG model. IRO-DB is a joint effort in Europe, which integrates components developed by various partners. The system is currently operational and a demonstrator CIM application is available.

Our goal is now to extend IRO-DB to make it Web-enabled and to support multimedia data sources. Through this paper, we isolate some of the difficulties to do so. It appears that rewriting the system in Java and using Java packages to support multimedia types and to access databases will help solving many problems. However, it is insufficient. As demonstrated, query optimization has to be re-considered. User interface objects have to be developed as applets and template data types have to be plug in to support semi-structured files. Further, the management of metadata has to be improved to support a large number of data sources, with quick structural changes. However, we do not believe that developing a new data model is necessary as the ODMG data model is sufficient to support references as relationships and complex objects as collections. SQL3 provides the same features. We hope that these two models will converge to a unique one sufficient for most Intranet/Internet federated database applications.

5. Acknowledgments

The authors would like to thank all the IRO-DB participants, and specially Béatrice Finance and Peter Fankhauser for providing good basis for this paper.

6. References

1. Bukhres O.A., Elmagarmid A.K. Ed., "Object-Oriented MultiBase Systems", Book, Prentice Hall, 1995.
2. Bouzeghoub M., Gardarin G., Valduriez P., "Object Technology", Book, Thomson Press, London, 1997.
3. Sheth and J.A. Larson, "Federated Database Systems for Managing Distributed, Heterogeneous, and Autonomous Databases", ACM Computing Surveys, 22(3):183--236, September 1990.
4. Rafi, P.DeSmedt, W. Kent, M. Ketabchi, W. Litwin, M-C Shan. "Pegasus : A system for seamless integration of heterogeneous information sources", IMS International Conference, Vienna, Austria, 1991.
5. Gardarin G., Gannouni S., Finance B., Fankhauser P., Klas W., Pastre D., and Legoff R., "IRO-DB : A Distributed System Federating Object and Relational Databases", In O. Bukhres and A. Elmagarmid Editors, Object-oriented Multibase Systems, Prentice Hall, September, 1995.
6. Catell Ed., "Object Databases: The ODMG-93 Standard", Book, Morgan & Kaufman, 1993.
7. Carey et. al., Towards Heterogeneous Multimedia Information Systems, In Proc. of the RIDE Workshop on Research Issues in Data Engineering, pp. , Taipeh, March 1995.
8. Garcia-Molina H., Hammer J., Ireland K., Papakonstantinou Y., Ullman J., and Widom J.,"Integrating and Accessing Heterogeneous Information Sources in TSIMMIS." In Proceedings of the AAAI Symposium on Information Gathering, pp. 61-64, Stanford, March 1995.
9. Kirk T., Levy Alon Y., Sagiv Y. and Srivastava D., "The Information Manifold", Proceedings of the AAAI Spring Symposium on Information Gathering in Distributed Heterogeneous Environments, Stanford, March, 1995.
10. Tomasic A., Rashid L., Valduriez P., Scaling Heterogeneous Distributed Databases and the Design of DISCO," in the Proceedings of the 16th Intl. Conf. on Distributed Computing Systems, Hong Kong, 1995.
11. Ramfos A., Fessy J., Finance B., Smahi, V., "IRO-DB : a solution for Computer Integrated Manufacturing Applications", 3rd Intl. Conf. on Cooperative Information System, CoopIS-95, Vienna, Austria, Pp. 125-136, May, 1995.
12. Finance B., Fessy J., Smahi V., "Query Processing in IRO-DB", 4th Intl. Conf. on Deductive and Object-Oriented Databases, DOOD'95, Proceedings. Lecture Notes in Computer Science, Vol. 1013, Springer, Singapore, Pp. 299-318, December, 1995.
13. Gardarin G., Sha F., Tang, Z.H., "Calibrating the Query Optimizer Cost Model of IRO-DB, an Object-Oriented Federate Database System", 22nd Intl. Conf. on Very Large Data Bases, VLDB'96, Mumbai (Bombay), India., Morgan Kaufmann, Pp. 378-389, September, 1996.
14. Khoshafian S., Brad Baker A., "MultiMedia and Imaging Databases", Book, Morgan & Kaufman, San Fransisco, 1996.
15. Gardarin G., Gruser O., Z. Tang, "A Cost Model for Clustered Object-Oriented Databases", 21st VLDB Conference, pp. 323-334, Zurich, Switzerland Sept. 95.
16. Levy A., Rajaraman A., Ordille J., "Querying Heterogeneous Information Sources Using Source Descriptions", in Proc. Of the 22nd International Conference on Very Large Data Bases, pp. 251-262, Mumbai, India, Sept. 1996.
17. Naacke H., Gardarin G., Tomasic A., "Leveraging Mediator Cost Models with Heterogeneous Data Sources", in Proc. French National Workshop on Advanced Databases, BD3, INRIA Ed., Grenoble, September 1997.

A Terminological Canonical Data Model for Cooperating Heterogeneous Geographical Information Systems

Tarek Branki[1,2] and Bruno Defude[2]

[1] Laboratoire d'informatique Paris Nord, Université Paris13, Avenue J. B. Clément
93430 Villetaneuse France, Branky@etna.int-evry.fr
[2] Computer science department, Institut National des Télécommunications, 9, Rue
Charles Fourier 91011 Evry cedex-France, Bruno.Defude@int-evry.fr

Abstract. The best way to make cooperate heterogeneous GIS (Geographical Information Systems) is to integrate them through a federated architecture. This last one necessitates in its first step the definition of a Canonical Data Model (CDM). The GEOgraphical COOPerative Model (GEOCOOPM) we have defined belongs to the family of terminological systems also known as description logics. We develop, in this paper, a precise syntax and semantic of Geocoopm and demonstrate the following: (1) First, Geocoopm gives a semantic to the spatial dimension. (2) It also permits the definition of heterogeneous data types (maps, numerical data, spatial data). (3) Geocoopm can represent various transformations on these data.(4) Finally, it provides a great facility for a good organisation of data and transformations using the subsumption function which enables building many hierarchies of data and transformations. This is a first step towards the schema integration process. We provide many examples to illustrate our claims.

1 Introduction

This paper addresses the problem of *cooperation* between *heterogeneous Geographical Information Systems* (GIS). Cooperation means for us the capacity to share data or /and mathematical models [3] [2] and to work together with a goal well defined. The term heterogeneity covers several points grouped together in the context of GIS in two classes:

- data heterogeneity due to several differences:
  - Differences in types: maps, images, numerical data ...
  - Differences in formats: raster or vectorial format for data.
  - Differences in syntax: Different representation models [17, 7, 8] Arc/info, Smallworld, Geoconcept, ...
  - Differences in semantic: vegetation feature, erosion feature ...
  - Differences in spatial referential.

---

[3] We replace all along this paper the term model by the term transformation in order not to be confused with data model.

- transformations heterogeneity due to their representation and their function ability (storm transformation, erosion transformation ...)

Problems concerning distribution and federation have been well studied within the scope of relational [15] and object-oriented database management systems (DBMS). On the other hand, very few works have been accomplished for GIS.

The main differences between GIS and classical DBMS are essentially the presence of transformations, the consideration of spatial attributes and an unclear separation between data (extension) and schema (intension). On an architectural point of view, a federation of heterogeneous GIS enabling to realize this cooperation, can be defined as a federation of heterogeneous DBMS through a loosely coupled architecture or a tightly coupled architecture [15]. We have decided to choose a tightly coupled architecture which provides transparent access to heteregeneous sources.

A federated architecture inevitably requires, in a first step, the definition of a *canonical data model* (CDM) common to all of the GIS. It should enable the representation of different data and transformations and the achievement of this cooperation.

The GEOCOOPM (GEOgraphical COOPeration Model) that we have defined [6] is a canonical data model which belongs to the family of terminological systems also known as description logics. In these languages everything is defined in terms of concepts (unary relations) and roles (binary relations between concepts) which are automatically classified into two taxonomies using the subsumption function. Afterwards, these hierarchies will make easier schema integration. Generalization and specialization relations which are deduced automatically by the model will represent some of interschemas properties to discover in schemas comparison step [16, 14]. Consequently, in the general architecture, we are interested in the definition of a CDM in a future context of schema integration.

The paper is organized as follows. We express, in Section 2 the main model's features, then we give an informal presentation of Geocoopm. In Section 3, we formally introduce our model: syntax of different data types and transformations and then an associated declarative semantic. In Section 4, we focus on the subsumption relation and its application on data and transformations. We compare in Section 5 our work with related work. Finally, we summarize, in Section 6 our contribution and outline our future research actions.

2 Informal Presentation of the Model

The GEOCOOPM model (GEOgraphic COOperative Model) that we have defined is the concern of semantic models. It is inspired by Navathe's research work for the Candide model [14, 3]. It has a rich semantic and has the properties of terminological logics [5] (models that come from works achieved in artificial intelligence in knowledge bases area [4] as KL-ONE [4] family).

---

[4] We mention as examples Back, Classic ...

In our Geocoopm model, everything is represented in terms of concepts and roles.

Concepts can easily represent different heterogeneous data types (numerical data, spatial data ...). A data is assimilated to unary relation.

As for roles, they permit to easily model transformations [5] because they are assimilated to n-ary relations. Furthermore, roles allow representing attributes [6] as a binary relation between concepts.

Subsumption and classification give an organisation to data and make easier, afterwards, the integration of these data.

Several geographical data models exist in literature [7, 17, 13] but in our opinion, never a canonical data model for geographical information with powerful classification mechanism has been proposed.

The Geocoopm CDM can define spatial data (e.g: lake, farmland, school ...), numerical data (e.g: rainfall records ...), cartographical data (e.g: layer hydrographic lines and points ...) and transformations that handle these data (e.g: erosion transformation, vegetation transformation ...).

2.1 Spatial Data

These are all data representing the most primitive spatial objects as lake, highway .... They are defined from both the constructors previously stated and the universal concept *Anyspatial-data*.

For instance, a set of *Lake* objects with attributes such as: the name of the lake whose type is string, the surface of the lake whose type is real, the attribute specifying its geometry, will be represented by the following *lake* concept:

```
lake :< And (Anyspatial-data, all(lake-name, string), all( surface, real),
       all(lake-geo, geometry))
```

Anyspatial-data specifies a declaration of a spatial data.

Lake-name, surface, lake-geo are attribute-roles and *string, real* and *geometry* are basic concepts.

2.2 Numerical Data

These ones are simply structured data which represent numerical samples, records .... A numerical data is then represented like a spatial data except that it is specified by the universal concept *Anynumerical-data*. Thus, all of numerical data are compared and classified with each other and not with the other types of data (spatial, ...).

If we take for example the numerical data *Ice* with attributes *Ice-ref, Ice-speed-melting, speed-erosion, calotte-ice-speed-formation* it will be represented by:

```
Ice :< And (Anynumerical-data, all(Ice-ref, integer),
       all(Ice-speed-melting, real), all(speed-erosion, real),
       all(Calotte-ice-speed-formation, real))
```

---

[5] We say, in that case, in indiferent manner, transformation-roles or transformations.
[6] We say, in that case, in indifferent manner, attribute-roles or attributes.

2.3 Cartographical Data

These data are the most represented data in GIS. In several cartographical data models, they are defined through:

- simple layers which are in fact only abstractions (equivalent to schemas in DBMS) of what will represent maps as characteristics,
- or more complex layers that are superpositions of simple layers.

Cartographical data are concepts defined by the universal concept *Anymaplayer-data* and are composed of spatial concepts defined previously. They have also their own attributes (meta-attributes) so as resolution of the map, its orientation ...which are, in that case, abstract in the universal concept anymaplayer-data.

Let a layer [10] be described in Arc-Info by:

```
Layer hydrographic lines and points
 arcs : drainage lines
  attributes :type(intermittent, channel),
  stream hierarchy, river mile index
 points : wells, gage stations
  attributes : type
```

It will be translated into Geocoopm as:

```
drainage-line :< And (Anyspatial-data, all(stream-hierarchy, string),
                all(river-mile-index, integer), all(geo-drainage, geometry)
                all(type,value-domain {intermittent, channel})

well :< And (Anyspatial-data, all(type, string), all(geo-well, geometry))

gage-station :< And (Anyspatial-data, all(type, string),
                all(geo-gage-station,  geometry))

Layer-hydrographic-lines-and-points :< And (Anymaplayer-data,
                        all(has-drainage-lines, drainage-line),
                        all(has-wells, well),
                        all(has-gage-stations, gage-station))
```

where *has-drainage-lines, has-wells* and *has-gage-stations* are attributes.

The three first declarations indicate that *drainage-line, well* and *gage-stations* concepts are spatial data having attributes defined above. Moreover, the last declaration expresses the fact that the layer *hydrographic-lines-and-points* is a cartographical concept that accepts as attributes [7] spatial concepts *well, gage-station* and *drainage-line*. It is clear that separation between spatial data and cartographical data enables a greater independence of each other. In fact, cartographical concepts are necessary because they are directly involved in transformations and spatial data are also needed because they are the basic spatial objects. Hence, both concepts must exist separately.

---

[7] We remark that point and line are abstract to the single concept geometry.

2.4 Transformations

They specify set of operations which take in heterogeneous data types and produce data of a certain type.

In Geocoopm, a transformation is represented by a role with n concepts.

Example: an *Erosion* transformation which needs numerical data so as *slope-length* and *slope-angle* and cartographical concepts so as *soil-map* and *vegetation-cover* is described by:

```
Erosion:< In-Data(slope-angle,slope-length, soil-map, vegetation-cover)
          And Out-Data (soil-erosion)
```

Slope-angle, slope-length, soil-map, vegetation-cover and *soil-erosion* are cartographical and numerical concepts.

3 Formal Presentation of the Language

We present in this section the syntax and the semantic we have developed for Geocoopm. This language has a syntax which comes under the syntax of clausal languages in the sense of logic programming. Its semantic is completely inspired by description logics and particularly by the terminological system Back.

3.1 Syntax

Let $\mathcal{K}$ be a set of constants symbols (values, class names, instance names), $\mathcal{C}$ a set of concepts symbols (basic concepts: string, real, geometry, integer, anymaplayer-data ...), $\mathcal{A}$ a set of attributes (attribute-roles) symbols and $\mathcal{T}$ a set of transformations (transformation-roles) symbols. Terms are of four kinds: object names (values, class names, instance names), concepts, attributes and transformations. The syntax of formation of terms is the following (k represents an integer, v a constant, V_i a value, R an attribute and C and C_i denote concepts):

```
constant    : v
basic-concept: String | Integer | Real | Geometry | Nothing |
            Anyspatial-data | (universal concept for spatial data)
            Anynumerical-data| (universal concept for numerical data)
            Anymaplayer-data | (universal concept for cartographical data)

set         : Value-domain{V1,..Vn} | (set of values)

basic-role  : Anyrole | role-name

concept     : constant | basic-concept | set |
            Not(C)        | (negation)
            And(C1,...,Cn)| (conjunction)
            All (R, C)    | (universal quantification)
            Some(R, C)    | (existential quantification)
```

```
                Atleast(k,R)  | Exactly(k,R) | (numerical restrictions)

role            : basic-role                          |
                  In-data(C1,.....,Cn-1) And Out-data (Cn)|
                  R and DOMAIN(C)  | (restriction of the definition set)
                  R and RANGE(C)   | (restriction of the target set )
```

3.2 Declarative Semantic

A semantic gives an interpretation to the whole model.

Basic concept interpretation domains are as follows:

- the domain $\mathcal{N}$ of integers for the concept Integer.
- the domain $\mathcal{R}$ of real numbers for the concept Real.
- the domain $\mathcal{S}$ of strings for the concept String.

The interpretation domain of the geometry concept is defined below.

Definition1: Let I, J be two intervals of $\mathcal{R}$, we call a plane denoted by $\wp$ the cartesian product of I and J i.e $\wp = I \times J$ [8]. Let (x,y) and (x_i, y_i) (for i=1,...n) be elements of $\wp$.

The concept Geometry represents spatial objects which are:

- points interpreted by (x,y) belonging to $\wp$,
- or lines (segments) interpreted by $((x_1, y_1), (x_2, y_2))$ (origin point of the segment and extremity point of the segment) belonging thus to $\wp \times \wp$,
- either polygons or polylines interpreted by { $((x_1, y_1), (x_2, y_2))$, $((x_3, y_3),$ $(x_4, y_4))...$} (all the segments composing the polygon or the polyline) belonging therefore to the powerset $\mathcal{P}(\wp \times \wp)$.

Consequently, the interpretation domain of the concept geometry is the following: $\mathcal{G} = \wp \bigcup (\wp \times \wp) \bigcup (\mathcal{P}(\wp \times \wp))$

We can then define the declarative semantic of Geocoopm.

Let $\mathcal{L}$ be the language built from sets $\mathcal{K}$, $\mathcal{C}$, $\mathcal{A}$ and $\mathcal{T}$.

Definition2: an interpretation $\mathcal{I}$ is of the form $\mathcal{I}(\mathcal{D},\text{I})$

- $\mathcal{D}$ a non-empty set called domain of $\mathcal{I}$.
- I is a function which associates
  - For each constant of $\mathcal{K}$ an element of the domain $\mathcal{D}$,
  - For each concept of $\mathcal{C}$ a subset of instances in $\mathcal{D}$,
  - For each attribute of $\mathcal{A}$ a subset of pairs (instance, value of this attribute) of $\mathcal{D} \times \mathcal{D}$,
  - For each transformation t of $\mathcal{T}$ a subset of n-tuples $(c_1, ...,c_n)$ de $\mathcal{D}^n$ where n is an integer superior to 1 and such as $c_n = t(c_1, ..., c_{n-1})$ (C_n is the result of the function t applied to parameters $C_1, ... C_{n-1}$) and,
  - for each value V_i and (for $i = 1...n$), for each concept C and C_i (for $i = 1...n$), for each attribute R and for each integer k :
- I[Nothing] = $\emptyset$

---

[8] We are only interested in 2-D space.

- $I[\text{Value-domain}\{V_1, \ldots V_n\}] = V_i$ avec $i = 1, \ldots n$
- $I[\text{Anyrole}] = \bigcup_{n=1}^{\infty} \mathcal{D}^n$
- $I[\text{And}(C_1, C_2, \ldots C_n)] = \bigcap_{i=2}^{n} I[C_i]$
- $I[\text{Not}(C)] = \{\ x \in \mathcal{D} \ / \ x \notin I[C] \ \}$
- $I[\text{All}(R,C)] = \{\ x \in \mathcal{D} \ / \ \forall\ y \in \mathcal{D},\ (x,y) \in I[R] \Rightarrow y \in I[C] \ \}$
- $I[\text{Some}(R,C)] = \{\ x \in \mathcal{D} \ / \ \exists\ y \in \mathcal{D},\ (x,y) \in I[R]\ \&\ y \in I[C] \ \}$
- $I[\text{Atleast}(k,R)] = \{\ x \in \mathcal{D} /\ |\ \{\ y \in \mathcal{D}/\ (x,y) \in I[R]\ \}|\ \geq k\ \}$
- $I[\text{Exactly}(k,R)] = \{\ x \in \mathcal{D} /\ |\ \{\ y/\ (x,y) \in I[R]\ \}\ |\ = k\ \}$
- $I[\text{R and DOMAIN}(C)] = \{\ (x,y) \in \mathcal{D} \times \mathcal{D} \ / \ (x,y) \in I[R]\ \&\ x \in I[C]\ \}$
- $I[\text{R and RANGE}(C)] = \{\ (x,y) \in \mathcal{D} \times \mathcal{D} \ / \ (x,y) \in I[R]\ \&\ y \in I[C]\ \}$
- $I[\text{In-data}(C_1, \ldots C_{n-1}) \text{ and Out-data } (C_n)] = \{\ (x_1, \ldots, x_n) \in \mathcal{D}^n \ / \ x_i \in I[C_i]$
  $\&\ \forall\ (x_1, \ldots, x_{n-1}, y_n) \in \mathcal{D}^n \Rightarrow x_n = y_n\}$

and I must verify the following properties:

- Interpretation of all basic concepts (anymaplayer-data, ..., geometry ...,
  values) are pairwise disjoint.
- Union of interpretation of these concepts gives $\mathcal{D}$.

I corresponds to the interpretation of concepts and roles in terminological
logics with certain differences:

- Introduction of several basic concepts whose most important is the Geometry
  concept which enables representing the spatial dimension.
- Use of three universal concepts (Anymaplayer-data, Anyspatial-data, Anynu-
  merica l-data) in order to be able to classify separately data types. In terminological logics, we only handle one universal concept.
- Introduction of transformations as n-ary predicates. In description logics ,
  only binary roles are present.
- Use of sets of values which are only present in certain terminological systems
  such as Back.

Definition3: A terminology T is a set of declaration of concepts and roles generally without cyclic definition.

4 Subsumption

The subsumption relation is the main property in terminological formalisms
because it can formalize clearly the specialization link between concepts and
between roles. The advantage of the subsumption relation is that its definition
is based on the declarative semantic.

Definition4 [11]: A concept C_1 is subsumed by a concept C_2 in a terminology
T if and only if for each domain $\mathcal{D}$ and for each interpretation I defined on $\mathcal{D}$,
we have : $I[C_1] \subseteq I[C_2]$.

Each terminological system owns in its kernel a subsumption algorithm which
determines if a concept subsumes another one.

Several cases of subsumption can be mentioned. The most trivial case occurs
when a concept is explicitly introduced in the description of another.

Example :

```
Altitude-Water := And(Altitude, Water)
```

The cartographical concept Altitude subsumes the cartographical concept Altitude-Water. In the same manner, the cartographical concept Water subsumes the cartographical defined concept Altitude-Water.

A less trivial case occurs when the subsumption algorithm detects relations which are implicit. This case is represented by the following example:

```
Shopping-street := And(street, All(shop, geometry))
```

```
Financial-street := And(street, All(bank, geometry))
```

```
Minimal-business-shopping-area := And(area,
                    Exactly(1, contain and Range(shopping-street)),
                    Exactly(1, contain and Range(Financial-street)))
```

Without appearing in its description, the *Minimal-business-shopping-area* concept is subsumed by all areas composed of at least two streets.

In a similar manner, we can define the subsumption relation between transformations.

Definition5: A transformation T_1 is subsumed by a transformation T_2 in a terminology T if and only if for each domain $\mathcal{D}$ and for each interpretation I defined on $\mathcal{D}$, we have : $I[T_1] \subseteq I[T_2]$.

We can then deduce if a transformation T_1 is a sort of transformation T_2.

Theorem1 : Let T_1 and T_2 two transformations defined respectively in domains $X_1 \times X_2 \ldots \times X_n$ and $Y_1 \times Y_2 \ldots \times Y_n$. T_1 subsumes T_2 in a terminology T if and only if for each domain D and for each interpretation I defined on D, X_i subsumes Y_i for each i= $1 \ldots n$.

A simple example will be :

```
Water-pollution-transfo :< In-data(Water-layer, Water-pollution-data)
                    and Out-data(Water-pollution-layer)
```

```
Sea-pollution-transfo :< In-data(Sea-layer, Sea-pollution-data)
                    and Out-data(Sea-pollution-layer)
```

Cartographical concepts *Water-layer* and *Water-pollution-layer* subsume respectively *Sea-layer* and *Sea-pollution-layer* concepts and numerical concept *water-pollution-data* subsumes *Sea-pollution-data* concept. Consequently transformation *Water-pollution-transfo* subsumes transformation *Sea-pollution-transfo*.

In Geocoopm, subsumption is at the root of the classification algorithm which organizes concepts and transformation-roles into four hierarchies (one for each data type : spatial, numerical and cartagrophical and another for transformations) reflecting their generality level in comparison with their intensional definition.

In this way, at the time of introducing a new concept (respectively a transformation-roles), this one will be placed above the concepts (respectively the transformation-roles) which it subsumes and below the ones that subsume it.

Classification is the only operation which enables to correctly locate a new concept or a new transformation in one of the four hierarchies.

5 Related Works

A few works have been achieved by database and GIS community concerning cooperation of heteregeneous GIS. The most related work to ours has been done by Alonso et al. in [2] which resolves the problem of interoperability by using a loosely coupled architecture. Alonso et al. implement a layer on top of each GIS enabling the construction of large geographical transformations in a cooperative environment. The user who wants to cooperate must describe all his objects, projects and transformations in his level of cooperation whenever he needs them.

Abel et al. analyse in [1] the integration of GIS with other systems. They show how to use a classical database architecture(e.g a three level architecture) and a federated database architecture to resolve the incompatibilities between systems in terms of differences in external, conceptual and internal schemas.

In another context, Laurini presents in [9] several problems of measurement errors occuring in distributed geographical databases in either layer or zonal fragmentation. He proposes an algorithm of geometrical linking of federated geographical databases in the case of zonal fragmentation. Our work is situated in another level. It is more oriented towards layer fragmentation than zonal one. Besides, it takes into account transformations and consequently cooperation, and considers the heterogeneity in a more general context. Both problems are different but have some common points.

6 Conclusion

The model Geocoopm we defined fits well to the stated problem. Geocoopm can clearly represent heterogeneous data (maps, numerical data ...). It can be extended to other data types such as images, graphics .... The definition of a map which is made by superposition of layers correspond exactly to concepts in description logics just as transformations are well represented by roles. Besides, the subsumption relation will facilitate schema integration. To our knowledge, there exists no CDM combining the concepts of terminological languages with GIS or spatial databases.

The definition of Geocoopm is in fact, the first step of the federation process. The next crucial step we are interested is the schema integration. It will be necessary to see how to use at best Geocoopm's features in order to achieve this integration. In reality, the presence of spatial attributes and the thin separation between data and schemas will complicate the task of integration. As our model generates automatically data and transformation generalization hierarchies, it is certain that our strategy of integration will be a semi-automatic approach and therefore, certain conflicts [12] would be partially solved.

References

1. D. J. Abel, P. J. Kilby and J. R. Davis. The systems integration problem. *International Journal of Geographical Information Systems*, Volume 8, Number 1, pages 1-12, 1994.

2. G. Alonso and A. El Abbadi. Cooperative modelling in applied geographic research. *International Journal of Intelligent and Cooperative Information Systems*, Volume 3, Number 1, pages 83–102, 1994.

3. H. W. Beck, S. K. Gala and S. B. Navathe. Classification as a query processing technique in the CANDIDE semantic data model. In *Proc. IEEE CS Intl. Conf. on Data Engineering*, pages 572–581, Los Angeles, February 1989.

4. R. J. Brachman. What's in concept: Structural foundations for semantic networks. *International Journal Man–Machine Studies*, pages 127–152, 1977.

5. R. J. Brachman, D. L. Mc Guiness, P.F. Patel-Schneider, L. A. Resnick and A. Borgida. Living with CLASSIC: When and how to use a KL–ONE like language. *Principles of Semantic Networks: Explorations of the Representation of Knowledge*, pages 401–456, 1991.

6. T. Branki and B. Defude. A terminological canonical data model for cooperating heteregeneous geographical information systems. Technical report, National Institute of Telecommunications, 1997.

7. M. Egenhofer. SpatialSQL: A query and presentation language. *IEEE Transactions on Knowledge and Data Engineering*, Volume 6, pages 86–95, 1994.

8. R. H. Guting. An introduction to spatial database systems. *VLDB Journal*, Volume 3, Number 4, pages 357–399, 1994.

9. R. Laurini. Raccordement géométrique de bases de données géographiques fédérées. *Ingénierie des Systèmes d'Information*, Volume 4, Number 3, pages 361–388, 1996.

10. S. Morehouse. ARC/INFO: A geo-relational model for spatial information. In *Seventh Proceedings on Digital Representation of Spatial Knowledge*, pages 388–397, Washington D. C, March 1985.

11. B. Nebel. Computational complexity of terminological reasoning in BACK. *Artificial Intelligence Magazine*, Volume 34, Number 3, pages 371–383, 1988.

12. C. Parent, S. Spaccapietra and T. Devogele. Conflicts in spatial database integration. In *Ninth International Conference on Parallel and Distributed Computing Systems*, Dijon, France, September 1996.

13. M. Scholl and A. Voisard. Thematic map modelling. In *First International Symposium, SSD'89*, pages 167–190, Santa Barbara, California, July 1989.

14. A. P. Sheth, S. K. Gala and S. B. Navathe. On automatic reasoning for schema integration. *International Journal of Intelligent and Cooperative Information Systems*, Volume 2, Number 1, pages 23–50, 1993.

15. A. P. Sheth and J. A. Larson. Federated database systems for managing distributed, heteregeneous and autonomous databases. *ACM Computing Surveys*, Volume 22, Number 3, pages 183–236, 1990.

16. S. Spaccapietra and C. Parent. View integration: a step forward in solving structural conflict. *IEEE Transactions on Knowledge and Data Engineering*, Volume 6, Number 2, pages 258–274, 1994.

17. M. F. Worboys and P. Bofakos. A canonical model for a class of areal spatial objects. In *Third International Symposium, SSD'93*, pages 36–52, Singapore, June 1993.

An Extensible Approach to Reactive Processing in an Advanced Object Modelling Environment

Leung-Chi Chan[1] and Qing Li[2]

1. *Independent Consultant, Kowloon, Hong Kong. Email: mchan@netvigator.com*
2. *Department of Computing, The Hong Kong Polytechnic University, Hung Hom, Kowloon, Hong Kong. Email: csqli@comp.polyu.edu.hk*

ABSTRACT

This paper describes a new approach for supporting reactive capability in an advanced object-oriented database system called ADOME-II. Besides having a rich set of pre-defined composite event expressions and a well-defined execution model, ADOME-II supports an extensible approach to reactive processing so as to be able to gracefully accommodate dynamic applications' requirements. In this approach, production rules combined with methods are used as a unifying mechanism to process rules, to enable incremental detection of composite events, and to allow new composite event expressions to be introduced into the system declaratively. Methods of supporting new composite event expressions are described, and comparisons with other relevant approaches are also conducted. A prototype of ADOME-II has been constructed, which has as its implementation base an ordinary (passive) OODBMS and a production rule base system.

1. Introduction

Next generation information systems (NGISs) and their applications such as CSCW, OISs, DSSs, and spatial/temporal information systems require integrated data and knowledge management [WL92, Rup94, PF94, Rom90]. In these applications, data objects are no longer just passive entities but can be active and dynamic (i.e., they can exhibit active and dynamic behaviors). In addition, application semantics are seldomly restricted to merely traditional data-level semantics, but often amount to knowledge-level semantics, ranging from specific integrity constraints to more general problem-solving rules. To better understand, and to more adequately accommodate, the requirements of NGISs, we have developed ADOME - an ADvanced Object Modeling Environment which utilizes extended object-oriented techniques [LL93, LL94, CCL95]. Putting it simply, ADOME is a common data/knowledge storage manager that takes care of storing, manipulating, and retrieving data objects, rules and procedures. Its underlying architecture (see Figure 1) is characterized by a direct integration of a rule base with an OODBMS, through a versatile bridging mechanism based on a generalized notion of roles [LL93, LL94]. In this approach, roles effectively serve as "mediators" for bridging the gap between data base and knowledge base semantics. A prototype system of ADOME has already been implemented, which supports a set of operations that facilitate dynamic object-rule bindings as well as general role (and rule) manipulations [CCL95].

This paper describes ADOME-II, the sequel of ADOME, which extends ADOME

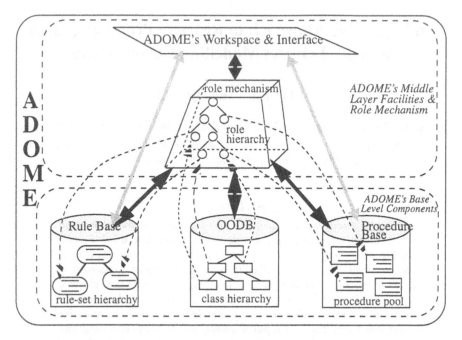

Fig. 1. ADOME's Role-centered Architecture for Supporting Data and Knowledge
Integaion

with a flexible and comprehensive reactive mechanism. The purpose is to better support the *active* aspects of NGIS applications such as CSCW, where operations are often
realized through cooperative activities [LL96]. In particular, with ADOME's comprehensive integrated data and knowledge management facilities, not only the Condition-
Action (or IF-THEN) rule paradigm is readily supported, but also the reactive processing in the form of Event-Condition-Action (ECA) rules [Day89] can be integrated into
the system in an extensible manner. As demonstrated by ADOME-II, such (re)active
database capabilities can be naturally devised in ADOME through devising an event
mechanism on top of it, enabling a wider range of applications and systems (employing ECA rules) to be accommodated within the same framework. The objective of this
paper is thus to describe in detail the approach we have taken for developing ADOME-
II's reactive mechanism.

The rest of the paper is organized as follows. Section 2 presents the event and rule
model of ADOME-II, along with the associated rule and event language, and execution semantics of rules and events. In section 3, the operational aspect is elaborated
where an approach to supporting rule execution and composite event detection is
described; we also compare some other approaches which are relevant to our work. We
discuss in section 4 some implementation details of ADOME-II. Conclusions and
future research directions are given in section 5.

2. A Flexible Event & Rule Model

We first provide in this section, an overview of the basic facilities, semantics, and
mechanism of supporting reactive capabilities in ADOME-II in order to provide a necessary context for our subsequent discussions; more details are reported in [CL96].

2.1 Modeling Events as Objects

In ADOME-II, event occurrences are modelled as objects and classified into event types [CL96]. By modeling events as objects, event parameters can be conveniently stored as properties of event occurrences. A distinctive feature of our model is the support of the non-redundant event propagation, which is more general than inheriting events or rules along a class hierarchy in other systems like ODE [GJ91], SAMOS [GD94] and NAOS [CCS94]. Event propagation is useful in cases where subset/superset event type relationships are desirable. For example, to trigger a statistical rule that gathers the statistics of every database update operations, it is sufficient to associate the rule to the event type *[update]* and relevant objects in order to achieve the purpose. There is no need to associate the rule to events of every kinds of update operations which is inefficient and difficult to maintain. The algorithm to enforce the non-redundancy of event propagation are detailed in [Cha96].

While primitive events are the basis of reactive modeling, it is the composite events that allow complex situations to be specified [CKA+94]. Here, the set of composite events are not fixed: through an extensible approach, the set of composite event operators can be extended without affecting other database components and applications. An extensible and declarative approach to detecting composite events (using production rules), are described in section 3.

2.2 Rule-Object & Event-Rule Association

To allow rules to be freely shared among objects, we require that a rule (which is a Condition-Action pair in ADOME) can only be activated when the three components: events, objects, and the rule (condition-action pair) itself, are associated or bound together explicitly. In other words, association of a rule with an object establishes the fact the rule is applicable on the object. On the other hand, associating an event type to a rule specifies the moment for the rule to be triggered.

A notable difference of ADOME-II with other ECA rule systems lies in the treatment of relationships of objects, rules and events. Many ECA rule systems only support a 1:1 relationship mapping between events and rules. Even when 1:M mappings are allowed between events and rules, the relationship cardinality between objects and rules is still 1:M at most. Our model is more flexible in that M:M mappings among events and rules are supported. In our model, an event e can be bound to a rule r without the knowledge of other events, leading to a more *decentralized* form of sharing.

3. Extensible Approach To Reactive Processing

There are a number of recent active object-oriented database that have very rich composite event specification languages, for instances, Sentinel [CKT+95], ODE [GJS92a, GJS92b], and SAMOS [GD93, GD94]. While their event expressions have many common (or equivalent) features with each other, their event detection mechanisms are often quite different. As there is little consensus on a minimal and sufficient set of event operators and it is possible that new event operators may be needed when emerging requirements are identified, we therefore present in this section an extensible and uniform approach to processing rules and events.

3.1 Framework for Supporting Reactive Processing

Within the framework we supported the following core reactive functionalities: *com-*

posite event detection, rule activation, evaluation of rule condition and execution of rule actions, rule scheduling and conflict resolution. Our approach is distinguished from others by the use of production rules as a unifying mechanism for supporting all of these functionalities. Composite event detection is done by a set of event detection rules (see section 3.3). When an event occurs, its associated rules are triggered through the execution of its specialized internal rules, namely rule-triggering production rules (denoted as **TR**). On the other hand, a set of wrapper production rules (denoted as **WR**) are used to decide when to execute application rules. Figure 2 shows the steps involved in executing the three kinds of production rules: **TR**, **WR**, and **EDR**, the latter denotes event detection rules. By adopting production rules, existing techniques for incremental and efficient evaluation of production rules can be reused.

repeat
    while EDR ∪ TR ≠ ∅ **do**
        R ← First rule in EDR ∪ TR;
        Execute R and remove R from EDR ∪ TR;
    end-while
    if WR ≠ ∅ **then**
        R ← First rule in the WR;
        if (R.EC-coupling-mode = IMMEDIATE) **then**
            Execute R and remove R from WR;
        else
            if (Event Pre-Commit occurred) **then**
                Execute R and remove R from WR;
        end-if
        Re-order WR;
    end-if
until EDR = ∅ ∧ TR = ∅ ∧ WR = ∅;

TR: set of pending rule-triggering production rules;

WR: set of pending wrapper production rules, initially WR = ∅;

EDR: set of pending event detection rules;

Fig. 2. Event & Rule Processing Cycle

3.2 Supporting Rule Triggering, Activation & Execution

The stages of rule triggering for execution and the roles played by different rules at different stages can be summarized as follows:

1. An application rule is triggered by an event occurrence of type E. The rule-triggering production rule of an event type E is responsible to trigger the application rule, and it has the form shown below:
   Rule TR:
   Condition: *An event of type E occurred*
   Action: *Triggers rule(s) associated with E*
   The rule TR above eventually gets executed after an event of type E occurs. As the result of the execution, an entry is created in the rule agenda for the associated application rule(s).

2. The wrapper production rule for each triggered rule in the agenda monitors the state and E-C coupling mode of the triggered rule. As soon as the condition of the wrapper rules is satisfied, the triggered rule is logically considered activated and scheduled for execution. The actual scheduled rule is, however, the wrapper rule of which an action is to execute the triggered rule:

Rule Wrapper-Immediate:
Condition: *rule R is triggered* ∧ *R is enabled*
Action: *if (R.Condition) then R.Then-Action else R.Else-Action, Remove
agenda entry*

Rule Wrapper-Deferred:
Condition: *rule R is triggered* ∧ *R is enabled* ∧ *event Pre-Commit occurred*
Action: *if (R.Condition) then R.Then-Action else R.Else-Action, Remove
agenda entry*

3. Wrapper rules are scheduled according to their priorities, each of which is determined by the priority of the application rule a wrapper rule wraps. Those with the same priority have their order of execution resolved by their time of activation, i.e. the relative time of condition satisfaction. Deterministic rule execution is thus guaranteed.

4. When a wrapper rule is executed, its actions are executed. The actions of a wrapper rule are to execute an application rule and remove the application rule's entry from the agenda. The application rule is represented in the procedural construct if...then...else... of the production rule system. The reasons to wrap an application rule in a single procedural construct are: firstly, the application rule's condition will not be evaluated more than once which ensures that the time of condition evaluation is precise, and that side-effects of condition evaluation can be more predictable; secondly, variables that record the results of condition evaluation can be passed to actions of the same rule.

As seen above, much of the reactive functionalities of ADOME-II are supported by reusing the similar functionalities of the production rules. Therefore, we are able to capitalise on their rich functionalities and avoid duplication of efforts.

Supporting Composite Event Detection
The set of composite event operators supported by ADOME-II is similar to Snoop's , the semantics of these operators can be found in [Cha96]. The focus here is on the approach of implementing composite event detection.

Two fundamental steps are required to detect composite events: monitoring over the conditions of occurrence of composite events, and signaling the occurrence when the conditions are met. Signaling an occurrence of a composite event is achieved by creating an instance of the appropriate event class. Monitoring the conditions of occurrence of composite events is done by event detection production rules, or simply event detection rules. For each composite event type, there is at least one such rule in which the condition of occurrence is embedded. A condition of an event detection rule is a set of first-order predicates and functions on event types, event instances and their properties. Actions are functions and method invocations. It is possible for several event detection rules to cooperate to detect occurrences of a single event type. The pattern of such cooperation is totally under the control of event detection rules---usually in the form of state transitions of an event occurrence.

3.3   Incremental Composite Event Detection with Production Rules
All composite events here are detected in the recent context, but we have outlined methods to detection composite events in other contexts as well [Cha96]. Each composite event is detected by a set of event detection rules. Each event detection rule is

locally visible to an event type and is composed of a condition part and action part. The condition is expressed in predicates (with the extension that functions and methods are allowed in logic formula and object properties can be referred to in the dot notation). In the following subsections, the methodology of detecting all pre-defined event expressions is described.

Logical and Sequence Events Detection Rules

Logical events are events composed of logical event expressions. Conjunction event expressions and other logical event expressions can be transformed into corresponding event detection rules in a straightforward manner. For instance, the conjunction event expression below specifies that a conjunction event E will occur only if E is enabled, and both $E1$ and $E2$ occurred, and they both satisfy invariants on triggering objects and parameter context requirements.

$E = And(E1, E2)$
Condition : $Enabled(E) \wedge Occurred(E, E1, x1) \wedge Occurred(E, E2, x2) \wedge Same\text{-}Object(x1,x2)$
Action : $E.Raise(x1,x2)$

The critical predicate in the above rule is the '*Occurred*' predicate which specify the event occurrences of interest. When the condition of rule is satisfied, the occurrence of event E is signaled by calling the method *Raise()* of event type E with constituent event occurrences. To detect the general case, that is, $E = And(E1,...,En)$, the event detection rule can be extended accordingly.

The sequence event detection rule (as well as some others) is constructed from that of the conjunction event expression with additional auxiliary predicates. Note that due to the similarity with the conjunction event detection rule, their common sub-expressions can be shared and evaluated once.

$E = Seq(E1, E2)$
Condition : $Enabled(E) \wedge Occurred(E, E1, x1) \wedge Occurred(E, E2, x2) \wedge Absolute\text{-}Follows(x1, x2) \wedge Same\text{-}Object(x1, x2)$
Action : $E.Raise(x1, x2)$

The event detection rule for a disjoint sequence event expression are constructed by replacing the predicate '*Absolute-Follows(x1, x2)*' by '*Disjoint-Absolute-Follows(x1, x2)*'.*Disjunction, Aperiodic*, *Within* and *Not* events can be detected in similar fashion and thus omitted here, they are detailed in [Cha96].

3.4 Temporal Event Detection Rules

Temporal events require references to time. To enable time to be referenced in the same model as that of the database, we separate the generation and detection of time changes and use an object to model the system clock, which is used for all time references in event detection rules.

It is essential that time detection can be done efficiently. To this end, the temporal event detection rules detect the change in time attribute values of the system clock object in decreasing grain size. For example, to be informed when the moment "12:00 1 Jan 1997" is reached, it is required to detect when the year reaches 1997, followed by detecting when January is reached and so on until the smallest required time granularity is reached (in this example, it is the minute).

Cumulative Event Detection Rules

The *Aperiodic** event shown below employs intermediate event occurrences. Here intermediate event occurrences are used to accumulate event occurrences. There are four detection rules used for detecting the event. Rules 1a and 1b perform initialization when the event $E1$ occurs. Rule 2 accumulates occurrences of $E2$ and rule 3 terminates the detection process and signals the occurrence of the event.

$E = Aperiodic^*(E1, E2, E3)$

Rule 1a:

 Condition : *Enabled(E) ^ Occurred(E, E1, x1) ^ ~ (Occurred-Any-Intermediate(E, x) ^ Same-Object(x1, x)) ^ ~ (Occurred(E, E3, x3) ^ Absolute-Follows(x3, x1) ^ Same-Object(x1, x3)))*

 Action : *x ← E.Raise-Intermediate(x1), x.obj = Triggering-Object(x, x1)*

Rule 1b:

 Condition: *Enabled(E) ^ Occurred(E, E1, x1) ^ Occurred-Any-Intermediate(E, x) ^ Same-Object(x1, x) ^ ~ (Occurred(E, E2, x2) ^ Follows(x2, x1) ^ Same-Object(x2, x1) ^ ~ (Occurred(E, E3, x3) ^ Absolute-Follows(x3, x1) ^ Same-Object(x3, x1)))*

 Action : *x.ts = x1.te, x.te = x1.te*

Rule 2:

 Condition : *Enabled(E) ^ Occurred-Any-Intermediate(E, x) ^ Occurred(E, E2, x2) ^ Follows(x2, x) ^ Same-Object(x2, x) ^ ~ (Occurred(E, E3, x3) ^ Absolute-Follows(x3, x) ^ Same-Object(x, x3))*

 Action : *x.Add-Constituent-Event(x2), x.obj = Triggering-Object(x, x2)*

Rule 3:

 Condition : *Enabled(E) ^ Occurred-Any-Intermediate(E, x) ^ Occurred(E, E3, x3) ^ Absolute-Follows(x3, x) ^ Same-Object(x, x3)*

 Action : *x.Add-Constituent-Event(x3), x.te = x3.te, x.obj = Triggering-Object(x, x2), x.state = MATCHABLE*

Feasibility of Evaluating Event Detection Rules

All the event detection rules can be evaluated by common production rule systems with appropiate object-extensions, for instance, CLIPS[Cli93]. They can be evaluated efficiently in principle (though the actual performance depends on implementation) because the number of event detection rules of an event type is constant, and the number of condition elements in an event detection rule is also proportional to the number of its arguments. Hence, there is no risk of exponential explosion of rules or condition elements. Also, the event detection rules can be evaluated incrementally. This is because predicates on event occurrences are evaluated only when a new occurrence is created (or deleted, if the predicates contain a negation on the event occurrence), or when attributes of event occurrences are changed. Functions and methods are re-evaluated only when their arguments are changed. Therefore, by examining all event detection rules, it is concluded that event detection rules can be evaluated incrementally.

4. Implementation

As mentioned, an implementation prototype of ADOME has already been built on top of an OODBMS called ITASCA [Ita94] and an expert system shell called CLIPS (C Language Integrated Production System) [Cli93], using a mixture of LISP and C++ to integrate both of them [CCL95]. Our philosophy of implementing the ADOME (and ADOME-II) prototype is to reuse as much as possible the underlying existing components while attaining acceptable performance and extensibility. Therefore, roles, rules and events are implemented as first class objects managed by the DBMS. Further, events and rules processing are performed by special purpose production rules supported by CLIPS. The complexity of implementation is thus greatly reduced and the reactive module is made extensible [Cha96].

The functional modules of the system kernel that realize the loosely coupled architecture are shown in Figure 3 (where the newly introduced and developed modules are enclosed by dotted lines). The *Object Access Interfaces* and *Cache Manager* together

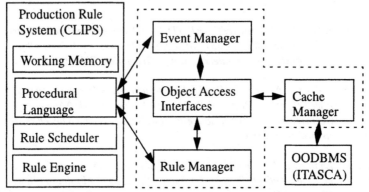

Fig. 3. Functional Modules of the System Kernel

enable database objects accessible not only by production rules but also by the procedural language of the production rule system. The *Object Access Interfaces* also generate events on object operations. The *Event Manager* comprises the generation of abstract events, detection of composite events, rule triggering and definition and manipulation of events. The *Rule Manager* provide various operations on rules such as definition, activation/deactivation, and association with events and objects. It also supports queries on rules.

Currently, the *Object Access Interfaces* and the *Rule Manager* are completed. The only component of the *Event Manager* which is to be completed is the translation of some of the event detection rules into CLIPS production rules. In the current prototype, the triggered rules can be executed according to their E-C coupling modes (immediate and deferred) and the rule scheduling policy (rule priority and time of activation). The condition and action part of a rule can be any valid function of the procedural language interface, which includes the functions exported by the ADOME-II system.

5. Concluding Remarks

This paper has described ADOME-II, the sequel of ADOME which is a common data/ knowledge storage manager we have developed, in response to the need of accommodating those next-generation information systems (NGISs) and their applications requiring such capabilities. Our design is motivated by i) there are applications which involve different kinds of, and hence different ways of handling, application rules, some of which are better modelled by the Condition-Action (or alternatively, data-driven paradigm) while others by the ECA (or called event-driven paradigm), and ii) an event mechanism can easily be built on top of a data-driven system such as ADOME, through utilizing the production rule engine already available.

We have devised a rule and event model that adequately supports the aforementioned capabilities. In this model, events and rules (and procedures) are modelled as "first-class" objects and they are classified, stored and processed in ADOME-II in a coherent "object-oriented" way. Through the use of dynamic association mechanism and various categories of events, rules can be shared among objects of different roles/ classes and without repeating their triggering events, thus providing pseudo data-driven rule capabilities in addition to event-driven rule capabilities.

Due to ADOME's loosely-coupled characteristics and our stepwise fashion of devising (re)active capabilities onto it, the resultant system (viz. ADOME-II) allows us to best utilize the fully retained underlying rule base facilities which are general-purpose and more powerful than those supported in active databases. In this approach, production rules combined with methods are used as a unifying mechanism to process rules, to enable composite events to be detected incrementally, and to allow new composite event expressions to be introduced into the system in a declarative manner. Compared with other relevant work, our ADOME-II system is consequently more *declarative and extensible*. Such extensibility is critical for a system to be able to evolve gracefully in accommodating dynamic NGIS applications' requirements.

The semantically-rich rule and event model is implemented using a unifying mechanism based on production rules combined with methods. In this approach, all major reactive functionalities are implemented by using predicates, functions and methods in production rules. The system not only benefits from the extensibility and declarativeness of production rules, but the efficient condition evaluation of production rules is also readily reused for composite event detection. Further, we are also able to reuse the advanced facilities of the production rule engine, namely rule scheduling and conflict resolution.

Apart from implementation, further work is to apply the prototype to some advanced information system applications such as cooperative problem-solving in an organizational environment [LL96], and data object integration in a distributed data/ knowledge base environment where (re)active rules are frequently utilized.

Acknowledgement: This research has been supported, in part, by UGC research grants council of Hong Kong Government, under grants HKUST 183/93E and HKPU 354/108.

REFERENCES

[CM94] S. Chakravarthy, D. Mishra, Snoop: An Expressive Event Specification Language for Active Databases, Data & Knowledge Engineering, vol. 14, pp. 1-26, 1994.

[CKA+94] S. Chakravarthy, V. Krishnaprasad, E. Anwar and S.-K. Kim, "Composite events for active databases: semantics, contexts and detection", Proc. 20th Int Conference on Very Large Data Bases, pp. 606-617, 1994.

[CKT+95] S. Chakravarthy, V. Krishnaprasad, Z. Tamizuddin, and R. Badani, ECA Rule Integration into an OODBMS: Architecture and Implementation," IEEE Intl Conference on Data Enginerring, pp. 341-348, 1995.

[Cha96] L. C. Chan, "Extending an Advanced Object Modeling Environment with Versatile Rule Sharing and Reactive Capability," Master Thesis, Computer Science Department, The Hong Kong University of Science and Technology, August 1996.

[CCL95] L.C. Chan, K.W. Chiu and Q. Li, "A Versatile Bridging Mechanism with an Experimental User Interface for an Expert OODBMS," Technical Report HKUST-CS95-35, Department of Computer Science, Hong Kong University of Science & Technology, May 1995.

[CL96] L.C. Chan and Q. Li, "Devising a Flexible Event Model on Top of a Common Data/ Knowledge Storage Manager," Proc. of 6th Workshop on Information Technologies and Systems (WITS' 96), pp. 182-191, Dec. 1996.

[Cli93] CLIPS User Guide and Reference Manuals. Software Technology Branch, Lyndon B. Johnson Space Center, 1993.9

[CCS94] C. Collet, T. Coupaye and T. Svensen, "NAOS: Efficient and Modular Reactive Capabilities in an Object-Oriented Database System," Proc. 12th International Conference on Very Large Databases, pp. 132-143, 1994.

[Day89] U. Dayal, "Active Database Management Systems", Proc 3rd International Conference on Data and Knowledge Bases, pp 150-169

[GD93] S. Gatziu and K. Dittrich, "Events in an Active Object-Oriented Database System," Proceedings of the First International Workshop on Rules in Database Systems (RIDS '93), pp. 23-39, August 1993.

[GD94] S. Gatziu and K. Dittrich, Detecting Composite Events in Active Database Systems using Petri-Nets," Proceedings of the Fourth International Workshop on Research Issues in Data Engineering (RIDE-ADS '94), pp. 2-9, February 1994.

[GJS92a] N. Gehani, H. Jagadish, and O. Shmueli, "Event Specification in an Active Object-Oriented Database," Proc. ACM SIGMOD International Conference on Management of Data, pp. 81-90, June 1992.

[GJS92b] N. Gehani, H. Jagadish, and O. Shmueli, "Composite Event Specification in an Active Object-Oriented Database: Model & Implementation," Proc. International Conference on Very Large Databases, pp. 327-338, August 1992.

[GJ91] N. Gehani and H. Jagadish, "ODE as an Active Database: Constraints and Triggers," Proc. 17th International Conference on Very Large Databases, pp.327-336, September 1991.

[Ita94] ITASCA User Manual, ITASCA System Inc., 1994.

[LL93] Q. Li, and F.H.. Lochovsky, "An Approach to Integrating Data and Knowledge Management in Next Generation Information Systems," Proc. Int'l. Workshop on Next Generation Information Technologies and Systems, Israel, 1993, pp. 59-66.

[LL94] Q. Li and F.H. Lochovsky, "Roles: Extending Object Behavior to Support Knowledge Semantics," Proc. Intl. Symp. on Advanced Database Technologies and Their Integrations, Japan, 1994, pp.314-322.

[LL96] Q. Li and F.H.. Lochovsky, "Advanced Database Support Facilities for CSCW Systems," Journal of Organizational Computing & Electronic Commerce, 6(2), 1996, pp.191-210.

[LPS91] Q. Li, M. Papazoglou and J.L.Smith, "Dynamic Object Models with Spatial Applications" Proc. Int'l. Conf. on Computer Systems and Applications (COMPSAC), IEEE, 1991.

[Rom90] G.-C. Roman. "Formal Specification of Geographic Data Processing Requirements", IEEE Trans. on Knowledge and Data Eng., 2(12), pp. 370-380, 1990.

[Rup94] W. Rupietta, "An Organization & Resources Model for Adapting Office Systems to Organizational Structures", Proc. DEXA, pp. 346-350, 1994.

[Per90] B. Pernici, "Objects with roles," Proc. ACM Conf. Office Inf. Sys., 1990, pp. 205-215.

[PF94] J.D. Palmer and N.A. Fields, "Computer-Supported Cooperative Work", IEEE Computer, Vol. 27 No. 5, pp. 15-17, 1994.

[WC96] J. Widom and S, Ceri (Eds.), "Active Database Systems—Triggers and Rules for Advanced Database Processing," Morgan Kaufmann, San Francisco, California, 1996.

Constructing the Functional Model

John Debenham

Key Centre for Advanced Computing Sciences, University of Technology, Sydney,
PO Box 123 Broadway, NSW 2007, Australia.
debenham@socs.uts.edu.au

ABSTRACT

The problem of constructing the functional model for knowledge-based systems is discussed. The functional model is derived from a specification of the system transactions and from the conceptual model. The conceptual model is a representation of the system expertise using a uniform formalism. In this formalism data, information and knowledge are all represented in the same way. This formalism incorporates two classes of constraints which apply equally to data, information and to knowledge. The transactions are specified by identifying those items in the conceptual model which are directly associated with updates and queries. The functional model shows how the knowledge in the conceptual model should be employed to deliver the transactions. Using a broad definition of 'best', the problem of deriving the best functional model is shown to be NP-complete. A sub-optimal algorithm for deriving solutions to the functional model construction problem is given.

1. INTRODUCTION

The problem of implementing the functional model of a knowledge-based system to achieve optimal performance is described in [1]. This problem is NP-complete; a sub-optimal algorithm operates in polynomial time when the knowledge-based system to not heavily constrained [op.cit.]. Here the problem of deriving the functional model from the conceptual model of a knowledge-based system is discussed. This problem is also NP-complete. A sub-optimal algorithm is given for solving this problem.

The *conceptual model* is a representation of the data, information and knowledge in an application. The terms 'data', 'information' and 'knowledge' are used here in a rather idiosyncratic sense. The *data* in an application are those things which are taken as the fundamental, indivisible things in that application; a data thing can be represented as a simple constant or variable. The *information* is those things which are "implicit" associations between a set of data things. An *implicit* association has no succinct, computable representation. An information thing can be represented as a tuple or predicate. The *knowledge* is those things which are "explicit" associations between a set of information things or data things. An *explicit* association has a succinct, computable representation. A knowledge thing can be represented either as a set of programs in an imperative language or as a set of rules in a declarative language.

The first step in a design methodology for knowledge-based systems is the construction of a *requirements model* which specifies *what* the system should be able to do [2]. The requirements model will not be described here. The second step in that design methodology is the construction of a *conceptual model* [3]. The conceptual model inherits the specification of *what* the system should be able to do by links from the requirements model [4]. In general the conceptual model may be redundant. The third step in that design methodology is the construction of a "functional model". The *functional model* is a representation of a "sufficient" set of rules that can support the system transactions. The functional model is "functional" in the sense that it shows how those rules may be employed to deliver the transactions specified in the requirements model. The functional model is *not* redundant. The functional model is derived from the conceptual model and from a specification of the system transactions. Using a broad definition of "best", the problem of deriving the best functional model is NP-complete.

2. KNOWLEDGE AND RULES

The conceptual model is a representation of "knowledge" and the functional model is a representation of "rules"; the relationship between knowledge and rules is now described. *Knowledge* is an "explicit" association between a set of information things or data things. A *rule* is a *functional* "explicit" association *from* a set of information things or data things called the *body to* a single data or information thing called the *head*. Thus a rule is knowledge. For example, if "the sale price of parts is the cost price marked up by a factor determined by the type of part" is analysed as being an explicit association between "part/cost-price", "part/sale-price", "part/type" and "type/mark-up" then it is knowledge. For example, if "if the cost price of a part is known and the type of that part is known then the sale price of that part is its cost price marked up by a factor associated with that part's type" is analysed as being a functional association *from* "part/cost-price", "part/type" and "type/mark-up" *to* "part/sale-price" then it is a rule. This rule can be represented on a "dependency diagram" as shown in Figure 1. A *dependency diagram* for a rule is a graph; each thing in the head or body is represented by a node that is labelled with the predicate associated with that thing, and a directed arc is drawn from each body node to the head node. In a rule all the tuples of the head predicate can be derived, using the rule, from the tuples in the body predicates. A rule may be defined using a declarative language such as Horn clause logic. Rules are defined using Horn clauses here. A dependency diagram can be constructed for rules defined using any "if...then" formalism; thus the relevance of what follows is not restricted to systems implemented in logic.

Rules have a functional, "if...then" form. Knowledge does not necessarily have a functional form. Each chunk of knowledge may be interpreted as one or more rules. For example the raw chunk of knowledge "the sale price of parts is the cost price marked up by a factor determined by the type of part" could be interpreted as one, or all, of the following functional forms:

$$\text{part/sale-price}(x, y) \leftarrow \text{part/cost-price}(x, z), \text{part/type}(x, w),$$
$$\text{type/mark-up}(w, u), \ y = z \times u$$
$$\text{part/cost-price}(x, z) \leftarrow \text{part/sale-price}(x, y), \text{part/type}(x, w),$$
$$\text{type/mark-up}(w, u), \ y = z \times u$$
$$\text{type/mark-up}(w, u) \leftarrow \text{part/type}(x, w), \text{part/cost-price}(x, z),$$
$$\text{part/sale-price}(x, y), \ y = z \times u$$

In general, a single dependency diagram can not represent knowledge; dependency diagrams represent functional interpretations of knowledge. In §3 the conceptual model is described; it is expressed in terms of a formalism called "items". In that formalism each chunk of raw knowledge is represented as a single item. The conceptual model [3] represents only the system expertise; it does *not* represent the transactions that the system will be required to deliver. The conceptual model does *not* identify those functional interpretations of the knowledge items that are necessary to deliver the required system functionality. In §4 the functional model is described. The functional model represents the required functional interpretations and the system

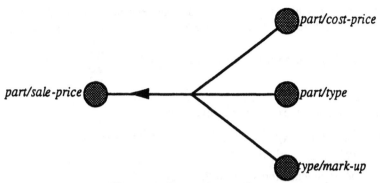

Figure 1 Dependency diagram

transactions. The functional model is derived from the conceptual model and from a specification of the system transactions.

3. CONCEPTUAL MODEL

The conceptual model is expressed in terms of items. Items are a uniform formalism for representing raw chunks of knowledge. Items represent the data and information things in a conceptual model as well as the knowledge. Each item incorporates two classes of constraints. Constraints for knowledge are thus included in the conceptual model [5]. The key to this uniform representation is the way in which the "meaning" of an item, called its *semantics*, is specified. Items may be viewed either formally as λ-calculus expressions or informally as schema [3]. The λ-calculus view is used here; it provides a sound theoretical basis, but it is *not* intended for practical use.

Items have a *name* which by convention is written in italics. The *semantics* of an item is a function which *recognises* the members of the *value set* of that item. The value set of a data item at a certain time τ is the set of labels which are associated with a population that implements that item at that time. The value set of an information item at a certain time τ is the set of tuples which are associated with a relational implementation of that item at that time. Knowledge items have value sets too. Consider the rule "the sale price of parts is the cost price marked up by a factor determined by the type of part"; suppose that this rule is represented by the item named *[part/sale-price, part/cost-price, part/type, type/mark-up]*, then the value set of this item is the set of eight-tuples associated with [part, sale-price, part, cost-price, part, type, type, mark-up] at that time. This approach to specifying semantics extends to complex, recursive knowledge items too.

Items are named triples; they consist of the item's semantics, value constraints and set constraints. A *value constraint* is an expression which must be satisfied by any member of the item's value set. A *set constraint* is a structural constraint on an item's value set; for example, a constraint on the size of the value set. Some items have "components". Items which do not have components are called "basis items"; basis items represent simple data things. Given a value set D_A, a *basis item A* will have the form:

$$A[\ \lambda x \bullet [J_A(x)] \bullet,\ \lambda x \bullet [K_A(x)] \bullet,\ (L)_A\ ]$$

where $J_A(x) = \text{is-a}[x:D_A]$, K_A is an expression which is satisfied by the members of the value set and L is a set constraint on the value set such as the cardinality constraint "< 100" meaning that the value set has less than 100 members. A non-basis item A is defined as follows. Given a set of n items $\{A_1,..., A_n\}$ the *components* of A, given an n-tuple $(m_1, m_2,..., m_n)$, $M = \displaystyle\sum_{i=1}^{n} m_i$, if:

- S_A is an M-argument expression of the form:
$$\lambda y_1^1...y_{m_1}^1...y_{m_n}^n \bullet [S_{A_1}(y_1^1,...,y_{m_1}^1) \wedge \quad ...... \quad \wedge S_{A_n}(y_1^n,...,y_{m_n}^n) \wedge$$
$$J_A(y_1^1,...,y_{m_1}^1,...,y_{m_n}^n)] \bullet$$

- V_A is an M-argument expression of the form:
$$\lambda y_1^1...y_{m_1}^1...y_{m_n}^n \bullet [V_{A_1}(y_1^1,...,y_{m_1}^1) \wedge \quad ...... \quad \wedge V_{A_n}(y_1^n,...,y_{m_n}^n) \wedge$$
$$K_A(y_1^1,...,y_{m_1}^1,...,y_{m_n}^n)] \bullet$$

- C_A is an expression of the form:
$$C_{A_1} \wedge C_{A_2} \wedge ... \wedge C_{A_n} \wedge (L)_A$$
where L is a logical combination of:
  - a *cardinality constraint*;
  - "Uni(A_i)" for some i, $1 \le i \le n$, a *universal constraint* which means that "all members of the value set of item A_i must be in this association", and
  - "Can(A_i, X)" for some i, $1 \le i \le n$, where X is a non-empty subset of $\{A_1,..., A_n\}$ - $\{A_i\}$, a *candidate constraint* which means that "the value set of the set of items X functionally determines the value set of item A_i.

then the named triple $A[\, S_A, V_A, C_A]$ is an n-adic *item* with *item name* A, S_A is called the *semantics* of A, V_A is called the *value constraints* of A and C_A is called the *set constraints* of A. For example, the information item named *part/cost-price*; could be defined as:

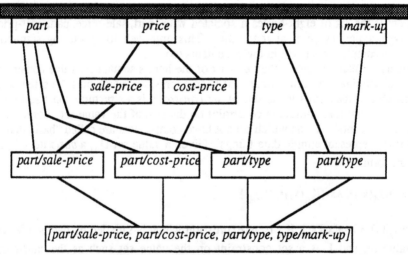

Figure 2 Simple conceptual map

part/cost-price[$\lambda xy \bullet [S_{part}(x) \wedge S_{cost\text{-}price}(y) \wedge costs(x, y)] \bullet$,

$\lambda xy \bullet [V_{part}(x) \wedge V_{cost\text{-}price}(y) \wedge ((x < 1999) \rightarrow (y \leq 300))] \bullet$,

$C_{part} \wedge C_{cost\text{-}price} \wedge (Uni(part) \wedge Can(cost\text{-}price, \{part\})_{part/cost\text{-}price}$]

The knowledge item *[part/sale-price, part/cost-price, part/type, type/mark-up]* could be defined as:

[part/sale-price, part/cost-price, part/type, type/mark-up][

$\lambda w_1 w_2 x_1 x_2 y_1 y_2 z_1 z_2 \bullet [S_{part/sale\text{-}price}(w_1, w_2) \wedge S_{part/cost\text{-}price}(x_1, x_2)$

$\wedge S_{part/type}(y_1, y_2) \wedge S_{type/mark\text{-}up}(z_1, z_2)$

$\wedge ((w_1 = x_1 = y_1) \wedge (y_2 = z_1) \rightarrow (w_2 = z_2 \times x_2))] \bullet$,

$\lambda w_1 w_2 x_1 x_2 y_1 y_2 z_1 z_2 \bullet [V_{part/sale\text{-}price}(w_1, w_2) \wedge V_{part/cost\text{-}price}(x_1, x_2)$

$\wedge V_{part/type}(y_1, y_2) \wedge V_{type/mark\text{-}up}(z_1, z_2)$

$\wedge ((w_1 = x_1) \rightarrow (w_2 > x_2))] \bullet$,

$C_{part/sale\text{-}price} \wedge C_{part/cost\text{-}price} \wedge C_{part/type} \wedge C_{type/mark\text{-}up} \wedge$

(Uni(*part/sale-price*) $\wedge$ Uni(*part/cost-price*)

$\wedge$ Can(*part/sale-price*, {*part/cost-price, part/type, type/mark-up*})

$\wedge$ Can(*part/cost-price*, {*part/sale-price, part/type, type/mark-up*})

$\wedge$ Can(*type/mark-up*, {*part/sale-price, part/cost-price, part/type*})

)*[part/sale-price, part/cost-price, part/type, type/mark-up]*]

which appears rather clumsy, but this item represents the expertise in at least three different rules, *and* it contains two types of constraint. These constraints are not included in most other knowledge representation formalisms.

The *conceptual model* is a collection of items and a *conceptual map* that shows the name of each item and the relationship of each item to its components. A simple conceptual map is shown in Figure 2.

4. FUNCTIONAL MODEL

The *functional model* is a representation of the system transactions and a "sufficient" set of rules that can support the system transactions [6]. Each rule represented in the functional model is an interpretation of a knowledge item in the conceptual model. Each rule is defined in terms of predicates and may be represented using a dependency diagram; where each predicate corresponds to an information item in the conceptual model. The functional model also represents the system transactions. The system transactions are represented by identifying the "input predicates" and the "query predicates". The *input predicates* are those predicates that can accommodate the system inputs and whose tuples may be actually stored in a relational database. The *query predicates* are those predicates that are used directly to service the identified queries. The functional model is represented as a "functional diagram". A *functional diagram* is a graph that shows, on one diagram, the dependency diagrams for all of the rules so that each predicate is shown just once. For example, Figure 3 shows a functional diagram for a functional model with eight rules; three output predicates are shown on the left, and four input predicates are shown on the right. The transaction predicates are identified in the functional diagram using large arrows. The set of input predicates and the set of query predicates need not be disjoint. The definition of a

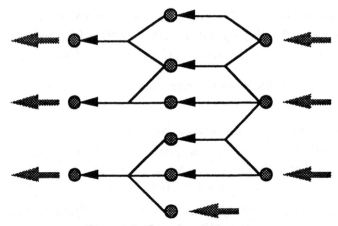

Figure 3 Functional diagram

functional model given above uses the term 'sufficient'; a *sufficient* set of rules is one that enables a complete set of tuples for each query predicate to be deduced from the tuples in the input predicates, and which is minimal in the sense that no rules can be removed without destroying this property.

The functional model is derived from the conceptual model and from a specification of the system transactions. The conceptual map shown in Figure 2 contains only one knowledge item, namely *[part/sale-price, part/cost-price, part/type, type/mark-up]*. At least three rules can be derived from that single knowledge item. If four system transactions are to derive *part/sale-price* and to accept inputs for *part/cost-price*, *part/type* and *type/mark-up* then the knowledge required to support these four transactions is the particular rule represented on the dependency diagram shown in Figure 1. Each knowledge item in the conceptual model will contribute at most one rule to the functional model.

We assume that the conceptual model is complete in the sense that it contains sufficient knowledge to deliver the required functionality. In other words, we assume that the specification of the system transactions leads naturally to the identification of items in the conceptual model that can accommodate those transactions directly. The *input items* are those items that can accommodate the system inputs and whose value sets may be stored in a relational database in the final implementation [7]. The *output items* are those items that can accommodate the system queries. The input items and the output items together are called the *transaction items*.

Suppose that the transaction items have been identified in the conceptual model. The problem of constructing the functional model is decomposed into:

- the problem of selecting a set of knowledge items from the conceptual diagram, and
- for each item selected, the problem of identifying a particular "if-then" interpretation (as defined by the candidate constraints)

so that the resulting rules can support the system transactions [8] [9]. A *selection* is set of rules that enables the value sets of the output items to be deduced from the value sets of the input items. The problem of constructing the functional model is "to choose the selection of least complexity". The *complexity of a selection* is the sum of the complexities of the rules in that selection. It is assumed that an item cannot have negative complexity. This additive definition of complexity of the items in a selection is quite reasonable because any least complex selection will contain at most one rule with any specified predicate as its head. Potential head predicates are identified by the item candidate constraints. Three complexity measures for rules are:

- The *trivial measure*, by which the complexity of any rule is unity.
- The *domain measure*, by which the complexity of any rule is its number of components.
- The *relation measure*, by which the complexity of any rule is an estimate of the time to retrieve a tuple from that rule's value set if it were stored as a relation.

These simple measures make no attempt to capture the structure of the rule. They make no attempt to measure the complexity of a rule's definition. A solution to the functional model construction problem is a selection of least complexity.

5. PROBLEM COMPLEXITY

The functional model construction problem is NP-complete. The functional model construction problem remains NP-complete if this problem is restricted to circuitless sets of items with non-recursive semantics.

Proof

The proof is by reduction to the "Optimum solution to AND/OR graphs" problem [10].

An AND/OR graph can be transformed into a set of items so that the problem of finding the optimum solution to the AND/OR graph is thus transformed into a restriction of the functional model construction problem.

Given an AND/OR graph, proceed as follows.

Each AND construct of the form $A \leftarrow (B_1 \wedge B_2 \wedge ... \wedge B_n)$, with n arcs, is replaced by an item $[A, B_1, B_2,...,B_n]$ with n components with set constraint:

$Can(A, \{B_1, B_2, .., B_n\})$

and the complexity of this item is the sum of the weights of the arcs flowing from the AND node "A".

Each OR construct of the form $A \leftarrow (B_1 \vee B_2 \vee ... \vee B_n)$, with n arcs, is replaced with n items $[A, B_1], [A, B_2],.., [A, B_n]$ with set constraints:

$Can(A, \{B_1\})$

. . . .

$Can(A, \{B_n\})$

respectively, and the complexities of these n items are the weights of the corresponding arcs flowing from the OR node "A".

The semantics of the items which have been constructed in the proof above are required to functionally determine the component A in terms of the other components. Subject to this requirement the item semantics can have any form. The items that have been constructed represent rules. The functional diagram of these rules does not contain a circuit.

The (unique) item which is not in the body of a candidate constraint in any other item is the (single) output item. The set of items which are not the subject of a candidate constraint are the set of input items. Thus an optimal solution to the given AND/OR graph will transform to a solution of the functional model construction problem for this set of items. The functional model construction problem remains NP-complete for circuitless sets of items with arbitrarily simple semantics.

6. CONSTRUCTING THE FUNCTIONAL MODEL

In §5 the functional model construction problem was shown to be NP-complete. The solution to the functional model construction problem is the selection with least complexity. The complexity of a selection is the sum of the complexities of the rules in that selection. Thus, each rule contributes its own complexity to this sum just once no matter how many times it is used by the other rules in the selection.

An alternative notion of complexity is now introduced. Consider the functional diagram, for any particular rule in a selection there will be a finite number of paths from its head node to the transaction query nodes in the functional diagram [11]. This finite number is the *rule weight* of that rule. The *tree complexity* of a selection of rules is defined to be the sum, over all the rules in that selection, of the products of the rule complexities and the corresponding rule weights. The problem of finding the selection with least tree complexity is not the functional model construction problem. It is the *tree cover problem* which may be solved in polynomial time. In a functional diagram, if X is a set of nodes and U is the set of identified input nodes, then the selection that supports X on U and is the solution to the tree cover problem is denoted by T[X , U]. Algorithm A finds T[Q , U]. The algorithm marks all nodes either "active" or "passive", and either "visited" or "unvisited". All rules are marked either "chosen" or "not chosen". This Algorithm systematically marks each node x on the functional diagram with the tree complexity of the selection T[{x} , U].

ALGORITHM A.

1. Construct the *combined diagram* consisting of the dependency diagrams of all rules that can be derived from the items in the conceptual map so that each predicate name occurs on one node only

2. In the combined diagram, mark all rules "not chosen". Mark the set of nodes U "active" and "visited", and mark all other nodes "passive" and "unvisited", and mark the set of nodes U with zero cost.

3. **while** there are nodes in Q marked "unvisited"

   do for all rules with "active" body predicates and "unvisited" head predicates, calculate the sum of the rule cost and all its body predicate costs, mark the rule with the least such sum as being "chosen", mark the head predicate of that rule with this sum, mark the head predicate of that rule "active" and "visited", mark each body predicate of that rule "passive" as long as that body predicate is not also a body predicate in another rule whose head predicate is marked "unvisited".

   endwhile

4. T[Q , U] will be the set of rules marked "chosen". The tree complexity of this selection, comp(T[Q , U]), will be the sum of the costs marked on the set of query nodes Q.

The correctness of Algorithm A follows from the observation that *if* the active nodes are marked with T[{x} , U], *then* the cost marked on the head predicate of the rule chosen in step 2 of the Algorithm must be T[{x} , U] for that predicate. If it is possible to support the set Q on the set U then the Algorithm will terminate with each node in Q marked "visited". Algorithm A systematically "builds across" from the input predicates towards the query predicates. Algorithm A does not attempt to "look ahead" to incorporate any nodes which might offer a significant cost saving.

The complexity of Algorithm A depends on the amount of inter connectivity in the combined diagram. If a combined diagram has the property that each predicate is a body predicate in at most k rules, for some fixed constant k, then the time complexity for Algorithm A is a linear function of the number of rules in that combined diagram. In general, it may be shown that the time complexity will be a quadratic function of the number of rules in the combined diagram.

Algorithm B finds reasonably intelligent solutions to the functional model construction problem in polynomial time. The algorithm starts with the solution to the tree cover problem. Then it adds nodes to that solution, in the order of the cost savings that they offer individually, provided that this cost saving is positive. Algorithm B. The algorithm is phrased in terms of Algorithm A.

ALGORITHM B.
1. Construct the *combined diagram* consisting of the dependency diagrams of all rules that can be derived from the items in the conceptual map so that each predicate name occurs on one node only
2. Initialise X to be the set, Q, of query nodes. Let U be the set of update nodes.
3. <u>while</u> there is a node, c, in the combined diagram, for which the expression comp(T[X , U]) - comp(T[X , U ∪ {c}]) - comp(T[{c} , U]) is positive (this node is called a *critical point*)
   <u>do</u> choose the node, c, for which the above expression is greatest <u>and</u> find all nodes on direct paths from c to X in the calculation of T[X , U ∪ {c}] <u>and</u> add these nodes to the set X
   <u>endwhile</u>
4. The solution is T[X , U] when step (2) terminates. The set X contains the incorporated nodes.

Algorithm B implements the method described above because if the expression given in step 2 is positive then at least two paths must go from {c} to the set X in the graph T[X , U ∪ {c}].

In Algorithm B, if c lies on T[X , U] then the expression quoted in step 2 will always be positive. In fact, the value of this expression will be a multiple of comp(T[{c} , U]). Thus, if all critical points lie on T[Q , U] then no new nodes will be added to the graph and the critical points will all be incorporated into the set X, one at a time, starting with those "nearest" the query nodes. On the other hand, if, at any stage, a node c is added which does not lie on T[X , U] then the result of applying one iteration of step 2 in Algorithm B will change the graph by adding node c and all nodes on all paths from c to U to the set X.

The complexity of Algorithm B depends on the proportion of nodes in the combined diagram which are critical. It is quite realistic to assume that this will be bounded by a quadratic function of the number of trees in the combined diagram, n. In which case, the time complexity of Algorithm B will be bounded by a cubic or quartic function of n, depending on the bound for the solution to the tree cover problem given in Algorithm A. If, in any iteration in Algorithm B, the critical point chosen in step 2 is already in the tree T[X , U] then the computation for that particular iteration is greatly reduced.

7. CONCLUSION

Dependency diagrams are an appropriate representation for rules but not for raw chunks of knowledge. A uniform representation has been proposed in which each chunk of raw knowledge is represented as a single item. The conceptual model is defined using this uniform representation. The problem of deriving the functional model has been shown to be NP-complete in the context of a broad definition of a "best" selection of rules. A sub-optimal algorithm for deriving solutions to the functional model construction problem has been given.

REFERENCES

[1]   J.K. Debenham and V. Devedžić, "Designing Knowledge-Based Systems for Optimal Performance", in proceedings Seventh International Conference on Database and Expert Systems Applications DEXA'96, Zurich, Switzerland, September 1996, pp728-737.

[2]   J.K. Debenham, "Unification of Knowledge Acquisition and Knowledge Representation", in proceedings International Conference on Information Processing and Management of Uncertainty in Knowledge Based Systems IPMU'96, Granada, Spain, July 1996, pp897-902.

[3]   J.K. Debenham, "Knowledge Simplification", in proceedings 9th International Symposium on Methodologies for Intelligent Systems ISMIS'96, Zakopane, Poland, June 1996, pp305-314.

[4]   R. Capobianchi, M. Mautref, M. van Keulen and H. Balsters, "An Architecture and Methodology for the Design and Development of Technical Information Systems", in proceedings 9th International Symposium on Methodologies for Intelligent Systems ISMIS'96, Zakopane, Poland, June 1996, pp511-520.

[5]   J.K. Debenham, "Constraints for Knowledge Maintenance", in proceedings AAAI Spring Symposium in Artificial Intelligence in Knowledge Management, Stanford, California, March 1997.

[6]   A Motro and S. Goullioud, "Knowledge Organisation for Exploration", in proceedings Sixth International Conference on Database and Expert Systems Applications DEXA'95, London, September, 1995.

[7]   H. Katsuno and A.O. Mendelzon, "On the Difference between Updating a Knowledge Base and Revising It", in proceedings Second International Conference on Principles of Knowledge Representation and Reasoning, KR'91, Morgan Kaufmann, 1991.

[8]   F. Lehner, H.F. Hofman, R. Setzer, and R. Maier, "Maintenance of Knowledge Bases", in proceedings Fourth International Conference DEXA'93, Prague, September 1993, pp436-447.

[9]   J.K. Debenham, "Understanding Expert Systems Maintenance", in proceedings Sixth International Conference on Database and Expert Systems Applications DEXA'95, London, September, 1995.

[10]   S. Sahni, "Computationally Related Problems", SIAM Computing, Vol 3, No 4, 1974, pp 262-279.

[11]   S. Even, "Graph Algorithms", Computer Science Press, 1979.

Horizontal Class Partitioning in Object-Oriented Databases

Ladjel Bellatreche[1] and Kamalakar Karlapalem[1] and Ana Simonet[2]

[1] University of Science and Technology
Department of Computer Science
Clear Water Bay Kowloon, Hong Kong
email : {ladjel, kamal}@cs.ust.hk
[2] TIMC-IMAG Laboratory
Faculty of Medicine La Tronche 38706 France
email : asimonet@imag.fr

Abstract. The Horizontal Fragmentation (HF) is a process for reducing the number of disk access to execute a query by reducing the number of irrelevant objects accessed. In this paper, we present horizontal fragmentation based on a set of queries, and develop strategies for two versions of HF: *primary* and *derived*. Primary horizontal fragmentation of a class is performed using predicates of queries accessing this class. Derived horizontal fragmentation of a class is the partitioning of a class based on the horizontal fragmentation of another class.

1 Introduction

The methodology for distributed database design consists of data fragmentation and data allocation. Data fragmentation is the process of clustering data from a class by grouping relevant attributes and objects accessed by an application into class fragments. Data fragmentation enhances performance of applications as it reduces the amount of irrelevant data to be accessed and transferred among different sites in a distributed system. The decomposition of a class into class fragments also permits concurrent processing since a query can access fragments of a same class simultaneously [12]. The problem of data fragmentation in the distributed relational database systems has been recognized for its impact upon the performance of the system as a whole [6], [15] and [16]. The object-oriented database (OODB) environment supports an object-oriented data model which is built around the fundamental concept of an object, and includes features such as encapsulation, inheritance, class composition hierarchy, etc., complicate the definition of horizontal class fragmentation, and then we can not apply the techniques used in the relational model [15] and [16] in a straightforward manner. In the object-oriented environment, the fragmentation is a process which breaks a class into a set of class fragments. A class can be fragmented horizontally or vertically. A horizontal class-fragment is a nonempty proper subset of objects, while a vertical class-fragment is defined by a nonempty proper subset of attributes [3].

1.1 Related Work

The issues involved in distributed design for an object database system are presented in [11], and the authors suggested that the techniques used in relational model [13] can be extended to object databases. However, they do not present an *effective* solution. In [9, 10], the authors developed representation schemes for horizontal fragmentation, and presented a solution for supporting method transparency in OODBs. Ezeife et al. [8] presented a set of algorithms for horizontally fragmenting the four class models: classes with simple attributes and methods, classes with complex attributes and simple methods, classes with simple attributes and complex methods and classes with complex attributes and methods. They used the algorithm developed by [16]. However, the number of minterms [16] generated by this algorithm is exponential to the number of predicates. The authors do not discuss the derived horizontal class fragmentation object-oriented environment. Bellatreche et al. [3] studied the vertical fragmentation problem for a model of class with complex attributes and methods.

1.2 Data Model

In this paper, we use an object-oriented model with the basic features described in the literature [1, 5]. Objects are uniquely identified by object identifiers (OID). Objects having the same attributes and methods are grouped into a class. An instance of a class is an object with an OID which has a set of values for its attributes. Classes are organized into an inheritance hierarchy by using the specialization property (isa), in which a subclass inherits the attributes and methods defined in the superclass(es). The database contains a root class which is an ancestor of every other class in the database. Two types of attributes are possible(simple and complex) : a simple attribute can only have an atomic domain (e.g., integer, string). A complex attribute has a database class as its domain. Thus, there is a hierarchy which arises from the aggregation relationship between the classes and their attributes. This hierarchy is known as class composition hierarchy which is a rooted directed graph (RDG) where the nodes are the classes, and an arc between pair of classes C_1 and C_2, if C_2 is the domain of an attribute of C_1. An example of such a RDG is given in figure 1. The methods have an signature including the method's name, a list of parameters, and a list of return values which can be an atomic value (integer, string) or an object identifier (OID).

The main contributions of this paper are:

1. Study of the impact of queries on the horizontal fragmentation.

2. Development of two algorithms (primary and derived) to achieve the horizontal class fragmentation.

3. Confirmation of the conjecture that some fragmentation techniques presented for the relational approach can be generalized and applied for the object-oriented model [11].

The rest of paper is organized as follows : section 2 presents some definitions used in specifying the problem of horizontal fragmentation, section 3 presents the primary algorithm, section 4 introduces the derived algorithm, and section 5 presents conclusions.

2 Basic Concepts

Before describing the horizontal class fragmentation algorithm, some definitions are presented.

Notation: If a_i is an attribute of the class C_i, then:
- $a_i : C_i$ denotes a single valued attribute.
- $a_i : Const(C_i)$ denotes a multi-valued attribute.

Definition 1. A query in object-oriented database models has the following structure [5]: $q =\{$Target clause; Range clause; Qualification clause$\}$.

1) *Target clause* specifies some of the attributes of an object or the complete object of the class that is returned. That is, v or $v.a_i$, where v denotes the complete object, and $v.a_i$ denotes attribute a_i of object v.

2) *Range clause* contains the declaration of all object variables that are used in the qualification clause. It is denoted as: v/C where C is a class.

3) *Qualification* clause defines a boolean combination of predicates by using the logical connectives: $\wedge$, $\vee$, $\neg$. We denote the cardinality of a qualification clause $|qc|$ as the number of simple predicates it contains.

Example 1. The query q for retrieving the name of all projects whose cost is greater than \$70000 and located at "Hong Kong" is formulated as:
$q = \{v.Pname; v/ \text{ Project}; v.Cost() > \$70000 \wedge v.Location = \text{"Hong Kong"}\}$.

Definition 2. (Simple predicate) Banerjee et al. [2] define a *simple predicate* as a predicate on a simple attribute and it is defined as :
attribute_name $< operator >$ *value*, where operator is a comparison operator $(=, <, \leq, >, \geq, \neq)$ or a set operator $(contained-in, contains, set-equality, etc.)$. The value is chosen from the domain of the attribute.

Since some object-oriented systems, such as Orion, and extensions of relational systems such as PostQuel, allow usage of methods in queries [5], we extend the definition of simple predicate defined by [2] to:
Attr_Meth $< operator >$ *value*, where Attr_Meth is an attribute or a method, operator is as defined obove. The *value* is chosen from the domain of the attribute or the value returned by a method. A query that involves only simple predicates will be called *simple query*, such as $\{Cost () > \$70000\}$.

Definition 3. A path P represents a branch in a class composition hierarchy and it is specified by $C_1.A_1.A_2....A_n$ (n ≥ 1) where :
- C_1 is a class in the database schema
- A_1 is an attribute of class C_1
- A_i is an attribute of class C_i such that C_i is the domain of the attribute A_{i-1}

of class C_{i-1}, $(1 < i \leq n)$. For the last class in the path C_n, you can either access an attribute A_n, or a method of this class which returns a value or set of OIDs. The length of the path P is defined by the number of attributes, n, in P. We call the last attribute/method A_n of P the *sink* of the path P.

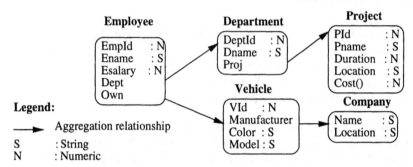

Fig. 1. The Class Composition Hierarchy of the class Employee

Definition 4. (Component predicate) A component predicate p_j $(1 \leq j \leq n)$ is a predicate defined on a path. A query that involves component predicate(s) will be called a *component query*.

3 Primary Horizontal Class Partitioning Algorithm

Horizontal Class Partitioning (HCP) varies according to the type of queries (simple or component). We will first discuss HCP for simple queries(primary horizontal class fragmentation), and then HCP for component queries(derived horizontal class fragmentation).

We assume that the class C_i to be fragmented. Let $Q = \{q_1, q_2, ..., q_l\}$ be a set of queries defined on class C_i, and each query q_j $(1 \leq j \leq l)$ is executed with a certain frequency. There are two types of queries that can be defined on a class C_i: simple queries S and component queries E, note $S \cup E = Q$. These component queries are defined on other classes in the class composition hierarchy but they have attributes or methods of C_i as their sinks. For example, the predicate Pname = "Database" is a simple predicate for the class *Project*, where as it is a component predicate for classes *Department* and *Employee*.

Primary Algorithm

Step 0 : Determine the predicates Pr used by queries defined on the class C. These predicates are defined on set of attributes A and the set of methods M. Let $|Pr| = n$, $|A| = r$ and $|M| = m$ represent the cardinality of Pr, A and M, respectively.

Step 1 : Build the predicate usage matrix of the class C. This matrix contains queries as rows and predicates as columns. The value(q_i, p_j) of this matrix equals 1 if a query q_i uses a predicate p_j; else it is 0.

Step 2 : Construct the predicate affinity matrix which is square and symmetric, where each value $aff(p_i, p_j)$ can be : 1) Numerical, representing the sum of the frequencies of queries which access simultaneously p_i and p_j($1 \leq i, j \leq n$), 2)

Non numerical, where the value " $\Rightarrow$ " of $aff(p_i, p_j)$ means that predicate p_i implies predicate p_j, value " $\Leftarrow$ " means that predicate p_j implies predicate p_i, and the value " $*$ " means that two predicates p_i and p_j are "similar" introduced in [14] in that both are used jointly with a predicate p_l.

Step 3 : In this step, we apply the algorithm described in [14] to group the predicates to form clusters where the predicates in each cluster demonstrate high affinity to one another. The partitions of the graph generates a set of subsets $\mathcal{P}$ = $\{P_1, P_2, ..., P_s\}$ of predicates.

Step 4 : In this step, we optimize the predicates contained in each subset by using predicate implication. We obtain a set of subsets $\mathcal{P}' = \{P'_1, P'_2, ..., P'_\alpha\}$ $(\alpha \leq s)$ of optimized predicates.

Step 5 : For each subset P'_i of $\mathcal{P}'$ resulting from step 4, we enumerate the attributes and the methods $Attr\_Meth$ not used by P'_i. For an $Attr\_Meth_j$ of $Attr\_Meth$, let w_j be the number of predicates defined on it $\{p_{i1}, p_{i2}, ..., p_{iw_j}\}$. We split P'_i into w_j subsets P'_{ik} $(1 \leq k \leq w_j)$, where each P_{ik} contains the predicate(s) of P'_i plus p_{ik}. We repeat this step until each subset P'_i uses all the attributes and methods. From the set $\mathcal{P}$, we build the attribute/method usage matrix which is an $(\alpha * (r + m))$ matrix and contains the subsets of predicates as rows and attributes A and methods M as columns. Each value (i, j) of this matrix is equal to 1 if $Attr\_Meth_j$ is used by a predicate of P'_i; otherwise it is 0.

Step 6 : If the predicates in each subset refer to the same attribute or method we link them by an OR connector, otherwise we use an AND connector to generate the class fragments. The final number of horizontal fragments will be equal to the number of subsets obtained step 4 plus one, including the fragment defined by the negation of the disjunction of all predicates previously defined, that we call **ELSE**.

Step 7 : Our algorithm may give rise to overlapping fragments. This step consists of refining these fragments in order to obtain non overlapping fragments.

Example 2. In Figure 1, we give the class composition hierarchy of a class *Employee*. The class Employee has two complex attributes: Dept, and Own, and three simple attributes: EmpId, Ename and Esalary which represent respectively the identifier, the name and the salary of an employee. We assume that the class *Project* will be fragmented and let the set of queries defined on this class:

$q1$:$\{v.\text{PId}; v/ \text{ Project}; v.\text{Duration} \leq 3 \wedge v.\text{Cost()} > 7000\}$.
$q2$:$\{v.\text{Pname}; v/ \text{ Project}; v.\text{Duration} \leq 4 \wedge v.\text{Cost()} > 7000\}$.
$q3$:$\{v.\text{Dname}; v/ \text{ Department}; v.\text{Proj.Duration} = 2 \wedge v.\text{Proj.Cost()} \leq 7000 \wedge v.\text{Proj.Location} = \text{"Hong Kong"} \}$.
$q4$:$\{v.\text{Esalary}; v/ \text{ Employee}; 5 \leq v.\text{Dept.Proj.Duration} \leq 6 \wedge v.\text{Dept.Proj.Cost()} \leq 7000 \}$.

We notice that q_1 and q_2 are simple and q_3 and q_4 are component and their sinks are in the class *Project*. The predicate usage matrix of the *Project* class is shown in figure 2. Let $p_1, p_2, ..., p_7$ the predicates used by the queries q_1, q_2, q_3, q_4 be: p_1 : Duration ≤ 3, p_2 : Duration ≤ 4 , p_3 : Duration $= 2$, p_4 : $5 \leq$ Duration ≤ 6 , p_5 : Cost() > 7000, p_6 : Cost() ≤ 7000, p_7 : Location $=$ "Hong Kong". The attributes used by these predicates are, Duration and Location which will be renamed by a_1 and a_2, respectively, and there is one method used by these predicate: $Cost()$ which will renamed as m. We notice that: $p_1 \Rightarrow p_2$, $p_3 \Rightarrow p_1$, $p_3 \Rightarrow p_2$, p_1 and p_2 are similar, and p_3 and p_4 are similar. We also add the access frequency column which shows the number of accesses to a predicate for a specific period for each query as shown figure 2.

$$
\begin{array}{c c c c c c c c c}
 & p_1 & p_2 & p_3 & p_4 & p_5 & p_6 & p_7 & acc \\
q_1 & 1 & 0 & 0 & 0 & 1 & 0 & 0 & 20 \\
q_2 & 0 & 1 & 0 & 0 & 1 & 0 & 0 & 35 \\
q_3 & 0 & 0 & 1 & 0 & 0 & 1 & 1 & 30 \\
q_4 & 0 & 0 & 0 & 1 & 0 & 1 & 0 & 15
\end{array}
$$

Fig. 2. Predicate Usage Matrix

The value associated with two predicates in figure 3 represents the sum of the frequencies of the queries which access simultaneously these two predicates.

$$
\begin{array}{c c c c c c c c}
 & p_1 & p_2 & p_3 & p_4 & p_5 & p_6 & p_7 \\
p_1 & 20 & \Rightarrow, * & \Leftarrow & 0 & 20 & 0 & 0 \\
p_2 & \Leftarrow, * & 35 & \Leftarrow & 0 & 35 & 0 & 0 \\
p_3 & \Rightarrow & \Rightarrow & 30 & * & 0 & 30 & 30 \\
p_4 & 0 & 0 & * & 15 & 0 & 15 & 0 \\
p_5 & 20 & 35 & 0 & 0 & 55 & 0 & 0 \\
p_6 & 0 & 0 & 30 & 15 & 0 & 45 & 30 \\
p_7 & 0 & 0 & 30 & 0 & 0 & 30 & 30
\end{array}
$$

Fig. 3. Predicate Affinity Matrix

We now apply step 3 of the PA to this matrix. Figure 4 shows three partitions of predicates $P_1 = \{p_1, p_2, p_5\}$, $P_2 = \{p_3, p_6, p_7\}$, $P_3 = \{p_4\}$.

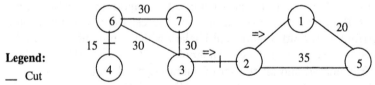

Legend:
— Cut

Fig. 4. Predicate Sets Generated by Primary Algorithm

The subset P_1 will be refined into $P'_1 = \{p_2, p_5\}$ because $p_1 \Rightarrow p_2$. After the optimization step, we obtain three subsets: $P_1 = \{p_2, p_5\}$, $P_2 = \{p_3, p_6, p_7\}$, $P_3 = \{p_4\}$.

$$
\begin{array}{c c c c}
 & a_1 & a_2 & m \\
s_1 & 1 & 0 & 1 \\
s_2 & 1 & 1 & 1 \\
s_3 & 1 & 0 & 0
\end{array}
$$

Fig. 5. Attribute/Method Usage Matrix.

In the attribute/method usage matrix in figure 5, we remark that the subset P_2 uses all the attributes and methods, but the subset P_1 does not use the attribute a_2, we notice that there is one predicate defined on a_2 (Location = "Hong Kong"), therefore, we split P_1 into P_{11} (see Step 5 of PA) where: $P_{11} = \{p_2, p_5, p_7\}$. Similarly, the subset P_3 will be split into: $P_{31} = \{p_4, p_5, p_7\}, P_{32} = \{p_4, p_6, p_7\}$. Then we obtain four subsets of predicates: $P_{11} = \{p_2, p_5, p_7\}$, $P_2 = \{p_3, p_6, p_7\}$, $P_{31} = \{p_4, p_5, p_7\}$ and $P_{32} = \{p_4, p_6, p_7\}$, each defining a horizontal class fragment.

Finally, generating the horizontal fragments:

$Project_1$ given by clause cl_1 : (Duration ≤ 4) $\wedge$ (Cost() > 7000) $\wedge$ (Location = "Hong Kong").

$Project_2$ given by clause cl_2 : (Duration $= 2$) $\wedge$ (Cost() ≤ 7000) $\wedge$ (Location ="Hong Kong").

$Project_3$ given by clause cl_3 : ($5 \leq$ Duration ≤ 6) $\wedge$ (Cost() > 7000) $\wedge$ (Location = "Hong Kong").

$Project_4$ given by clause cl_4 : ($5 \leq$ Duration ≤ 6) $\wedge$ (Cost() ≤ 7000) $\wedge$ (Location = "Hong Kong").

$Project_5$ given by clause cl_5 : ELSE.

Complexity of Primary Algorithm The complexity of the primary algorithm is from steps 2 and 5, and that is $O(l*n^2)$ and $O(\alpha*(r+m))$, respectively. We note that n, l, α, r, and m represent the number of predicates, number of queries, number of fragments, number of attributes used by the queries, and the number of methods used by queries, respectively. Therefore, the complexity of our algorithm is: $O[l*n^2 + \alpha*(r+m)]$.

4 Derived Horizontal Class Fragmentation Algorithm

If the set of queries Q defined on C_i contains one or more component queries, then there should be some other class $C_j(j \neq i)$ in the class composition hierarchy which[3] is horizontally fragmented by the primary algorithm. Therefore, we can also horizontally fragment the class C_i based on the horizontal fragmentation of the class C_j. Such a fragmentation is known as *derived horizontal class fragmentation(DHCF)* [9].

4.1 Implicit object join

In order to support query predicates on complex attributes, object-oriented query languages usually use path expressions in which each attribute of a class C_i whose domain is a class C_j specifies an implicit join between C_i and C_j. Now we extend the definition of selection operation used in the relational model [7] to that on a path.

---

[3] There is a path from the class C_i to the class C_j with length $g(g \geq 1)$

Definition 5. (Selection operation) Let $P = C_1.A_1.A_2...A_n$ be a path; a selection operation is defined as : $\sigma_{<selectioncondition>} (< C_1 >)$, where the symbol σ is used to denote the selection operator, and the selection condition is a qualification clause (Definition 1) specified on the attributes and methods of the class C_n in the path P. The class resulting from the selection operation has the same attributes and methods as C_1 which satisfies a condition defined on attributes and methods of C_n.

Definition 6. Let two classes C_i and C_j in a path P (C_j is the domain of an attribute a_k of C_i). We define $fan\text{-}out(C_i, a_k, C_j)$ as the average number of C_j objects referred to by an object of C_i through attribute a_k. Similarly, the sharing level, $share(C_i, a_l, C_j)$, is the average number of C_i objects that refer to the same object of C_j through attribute a_l [4]. We define $FAN(C_i, C_j)$ and $SHARE(C_i, C_j)$ as the average of $fan\text{-}out(C_i, a_k, C_j)$ and average of $share(C_i, a_l, C_j)$, over all the objects of class C_j and class C_i, respectively.

4.2 Algorithm

The inputs of the DHCF algorithm are the class C_i to be fragmented, and we assume that class C_j in the class hierarchy has been horizontally fragmented by PA into α fragments $\{F_1, F_2, ..., F_\alpha\}$. Note that each fragment $F_k (1 \leq k \leq \alpha)$ is defined by a qualification clause qc_k. The steps of the DHCF algorithm are :
1) For each clause $qc_k (1 \leq k \leq \alpha)$ determine its predicates $\{p_{k1}, p_{k2}, ..., p_{k|qc_k|}\}$. We recall that the $|qc_k|$ represents the cardinality of the qualification clause qc_k.
2) For each predicate $p_{kl} (1 \leq l \leq |qc_k|)$, determine the name of its attribute or method denoted by A_{kl}.

We can define the fragments defined by the DHCF algorithm as follow:
$f_k = \sigma_{\phi_{m=1}^{|qc_k|} <p_{km}>} (C_i)$ where ϕ is a logical connectives ($\wedge$, $\vee$) used in clause qc_k.

Example 3. We assume that the *Employee* class will be derived fragmented based on the horizontal fragments of the *Project* class. Let $Project_i (1 \leq i \leq 5)$ and $Emp_j (1 \leq j \leq 5)$ be respectively the project and employee class fragments. $Project_1$: (Duration ≤ 4) $\wedge$ (Cost() > 7000) $\wedge$ (Location = "Hong Kong"). In $Project_1$ there are three predicates p_{11} : $Duration \leq 4$, p_{12} : $Cost() > 7000$ and p_{13} : $Location = $ "$Hong Kong$", then Emp_1 is defined as:

$$Emp_1 = \sigma_{(E_1 \wedge E_2 \wedge E_3)} (\text{Employee}), \text{ where:}$$
$E_1 = (Employee.Dept.Proj.Duration \leq 4)$, $E_2 = (Employee.Dept.Proj.Cost() > \$7000)$ and $E_3 = (Employee.Dept.Proj.Location = "Hong Kong")$.
With the same technique we can determine others horizontal class fragments of Employee, i.e., Emp_2, Emp_3, Emp_4, Emp_5.

4.3 Correctness of the Derived Horizontal Fragmentation Algorithm

The fragments defined by primary horizontal fragmentation algorithm satisfy the correctness rules of completeness, reconstruction and disjointness [14].

However, the fragments defined by the derived horizontal fragmentation can overlap and thus do not satisfy the disjointedness property. We now present an algorithm called non_overlap described in figure 6. The inputs for this algorithm is the class C_i which is derived horizontal fragmented based on the horizontal fragmentation of class C_j. In order to know the overlapping instances of the class C_i, we check whether the fan-out(C_i, C_j) for each object instance of class C_i could be greater than 1. To do that, for each instance, we look in the class composition schema for the type of its complex attributes; if all these complex attributes are single valued, then fan-out(C_i, C_j) is 1. Otherwise, even if there is one complex attribute which is multi-valued the fan-out(C_i, C_j) could be greater than 1. Note that rigorous checking of whether two derived horizontal fragments are overlapping or not would require examining each object instance of class C_i. In case there is a multi-valued object-based instance variable, we execute the non_overlap algorithm. We note that this algorithm ensures the disjointedness property. In order to facilitate the maintenance of the database, we create a table with three columns: the first column contains the OID(s) of the instance(s) eliminated by non_overlap algorithm, the second contains the fragment which includes these instances, and the third column contains the name of the fragment(s) from which these instances were eliminated. We call this table overlap catalog. The overlap catalog facilitates the identification and management of objects which belong to more than one horizontal fragment.

begin

 For each *overlapping* instance I_j do

  For each fragment that contains I_j do

   Compute the queries access frequency to I_j

   Take the fragment with *maximal access frequency*, which is called F_i

   For each fragment F_l $(l \neq i)$ do $F_l = F_l - I_j$

end

Fig. 6. The non_overlap algorithm

5 Conclusion

In this paper, we have studied the role of queries in the horizontal fragmentation in the object-oriented model, which has not been addressed adequately by researchers. We have proposed two horizontal fragmentation algorithms: primary algorithm and derived algorithm. We have established the complexity of the *primary horizontal fragmentation* which is $O(l * n^2)$, (n and l represent the number of queries and their predicates, respectively) and there better than earlier work. The fragments defined by the *derived horizontal algorithm* can overlap, then we have proposed a method in order to eliminate overlapping instances. We are now evaluating the performance of our algorithm and studying the impact of the update queries defined on the resulting fragments.

References

1. M. Atkinson, F. Bancilhon, F. DeWitt, K. Dettrich, D. Maier, and S. Zdonik. The object database system manifesto. *in Proceeding of the first International Conference on Deductive, Object-Oriented Databases*, pages 40–57, 1989.

2. J. Banerjee, K Kim, and K. C. Kim. Queries in object oriented databases. *in Proceedings of the IEEE Data Engineering Conference*, February 1988.

3. L. Bellatreche, A. Simonet, and M. Simonet. An algorithm for vertical fragmentation in distributed object database systems with complex attributes and methods. *in International Workshop on Database and Expert Systems Applications (DEXA'96), Zurich*, pages 15–21, September 1996.

4. E. Bertino and C. Guglielmina. Path-index: An approach to the efficient execution of object-oriented queries. *Data & Knowledge Engineering*, 10:1–27, 1993.

5. E. Bertino, M. Negri, G. Pelagatti, and L. Sbattella. Object-oriented query languages: The notion and the issues. *IEEE Transactions on Knowledge and Data Engineering*, 4(3):223–237, 1992.

6. S. Ceri, M. Negri, and G. Pelagatti. Horizontal data partitioning in database design. *Proceedings of the ACM SIGMOD International Conference on Management of Data. SIGPLAN Notices*, 1982.

7. R. ElMasri and S. B. Navathe. *Fundamentals of Database Systems*. Benjamin Cummings, Redwood City, CA, 1994.

8. C. I. Ezeife and K. Barker. A comprehensive approach to horizontal class fragmentation in distributed object based system. *International Journal of Distributed and Parallel Databases*, 1, 1995.

9. K. Karlapalem and Q. Li. Partitioning schemes for object oriented databases. *in Proceeding of the Fifth International Workshop on Research Issues in Data Engineering- Distributed Object Management, RIDE-DOM'95*, pages 42–49, March 1995.

10. K. Karlapalem, Q. Li, and S. Vieweg. Method induced partitioning schemes in object-oriented databases. *in 16th International Conference on Distributed Computing System (ICDCS'96), Hong Kong*, May 1996.

11. K. Karlapalem, S.B. Navathe, and M. M. A. Morsi. Issues in distributed design of object-oriented databases. In *Distributed Object Management*, pages 148–165. Morgan Kaufman Publishers Inc., 1994.

12. S. J. Lim and Y. K. Ng. A formal approach for horizontal fragmentation in distributed deductive database design. *in the 7th International Conferences on Database and Expert Systems Applications (DEXA'96), Lecture Notes in Computer Science 1134, Zurich*, pages 234–243, September 1996.

13. S.B. Navathe, S. Ceri, G. Wiederhold, and Dou J. Vertical partitioning algorithms for database design. *ACM Transaction on Database Systems*, 9(4):681–710, December 1984.

14. S.B. Navathe, K. Karlapalem, and M. Ra. A mixed partitioning methodology for distributed database design. *Journal of Computer and Software Engineering*, 3(4):395–426, 1995.

15. S.B. Navathe and M. Ra. Vertical partitioning for database design : a graphical algorithm. *ACM SIGMOD*, pages 440–450, 1989.

16. M. T. Özsu and P. Valduriez. *Principles of Distributed Database Systems*. Prentice Hall, 1991.

Incremental Inheritance Model for an OODBMS

Mohammed Benattou and Lotfi Lakhal

LIMOS
Université Blaise Pascal Clermont-Ferrand II
Complexe Scientifique des Cézeaux
63177 Aubière cedex
France.

Abstract. The semantics of inheritance presented in this paper is based on the incremental modification mechanism that is formalized by the generator associated with class, modification function, and the building inheritance operators. The model is based upon an intuitive explanation of the proper use and purpose of inheritance, and is essentially dedicated to dynamic (i.e. run-time) inheritance of properties, for OODBMS. A simple typing of inheritance is derived by Cook's constraint, that defines the conditions of the validity of generator derivation. We show by using the subtyping relation defined in the O2 OODBMS, the correctness of the proposed model (i.e. the Cook's constraint is respected). And therefore, the integration of our incremental model in O2 is valid.

1 Introduction

Inheritance allows objects of different structures to share properties (methods or attributes) related to their common parts. Several authors have tried to define a semantic of inheritance. Cardelli [10] identifies inheritance with subtype relation; McAllister and Zabith [22] suggest the boolean classes system for knowledge representation; Minsky and Rozenshten [23] use the concept of regulatory laws for message passing to characterize inheritance. In OODBMS [4], the semantics of inheritance is based on subtyping ($\leq$) : the system checks whether the inheritance definition is legal, that is if there is no subtyping violation. Although the subtyping relationship provides static type-checking, it does not allow a formalization of the inheritance mechanism corresponding to the form of inheritance used in object-oriented programming [12]. Inheritance is not subtyping [13] but an intricate mechanism, featuring dynamic binding together with some clever naming conventions (pseudo-variables *self* and *super*). Inheritance is a mechanism for incremental modifications [12, 18].

This paper develops a formal model for the management of the inheritance mechanism. This model is built on the incremental modification principle, based upon an intuitive explanation of the proper use and purpose of inheritance, and is essentially dedicated to dynamic inheritance of properties, for OODBMS. The incremental inheritance mechanism allows to construct a new class by modifying one of the existing superclasses. We formalize this mechanism by the specification of the modification function and the definition of the building operators. In order to formalize multiple inheritance, we propose an extension of the incremental model of single inheritance to multiple inheritance with dynamic conflicts resolution at run-time.

Type theory defines the condition of the validity of generator derivation. A simple typing of inheritance is derived by Cook's constraint [13]. Unfortunately, this constraint is not respected, when we use the subtyping rule for functional type defined by L. Cardelli [10] (contravariance [11] $\alpha \longrightarrow \beta \leq \alpha' \longrightarrow \beta'$ iff $\alpha' \leq \alpha$ and $\beta \leq \beta'$). This problem is caused by the interaction between recursion and subtyping [1, 3, 13]. C. Lecluse and P. Richard et F.Velez [21] use "covariance specialization" ($\alpha \longrightarrow \beta \leq \alpha' \longrightarrow \beta'$ iff $\alpha \leq \alpha'$ and $\beta \leq \beta'$)) as the subtyping rule for method types in the O2 DBMS. This approach gives a less restrictive type system, but is safe [21], more natural, flexible and expressive [11]. We show that the proposed model respects the Cook's constraint, when we use the subtyping relation ($\leq$) defined in the O2 DBMS. And therefore, the integration of denotational method for dynamic message evaluation using the incremental inheritance mechanism [6, 7] in O2 is valid.

This paper is organized as follows: Section 2 describes the basic concepts of records, *self-reference*, and generator used in the fixed-point theory to analyze *self-reference* definitions. Section 3 introduces the formal model for single inheritance based on W. R. Cook's works. Section 4 presents the incremental model for multiple inheritance with conflict resolution. Section 5 shows by formal validation the correctness of our model, using the O2 type system.

2 Self-reference and generator

Self-reference occurs when a structure is defined in term of itself. This technique is frequently used in programming languages: recursive procedures, functions and datatypes. In the object-oriented paradigm, self-reference, which is syntactically standarized by the pseudo-variable *self*, that enables to refer to a property (method or attribute) of the object where the message is sent. The pseudo-variable *self* represents recursion or *self-reference* [18]. The fixed-point semantics provides the mathematical setting for the analysis of recursive programs [12, 18]. At run-time, we consider an object as a record [13, 18] where fields (attributes or methods) contain values. The record-based model proposed by L. Cardelli [10] constitutes the basic model for our framework. We extend it to object databases, in particular we focus on the values taken by the fields of a record at run time.

Definition 1. A record S is a finite mapping from a set of labels to a set of values. A record with labels $x_1, x_2, ..., x_n$ and values $v_1, v_2, ..., v_n$ is written $[x_1 \longmapsto v_1, x_2 \longmapsto v_2, ..., x_n \longmapsto v_n]$. All labels which are not in the list are mapped to $\perp$. The domain of a record S is defined by $\text{Dom}(S) = \{ x \setminus S(x) \neq \perp \}$ ($S(x)$ represents the value of the property x in S, $S(x) = \perp$ where x is assumed to be mapped to an undefined value in S).

In classical object-oriented programming languages such as Smalltalk [17], the value encapsulated in an object is an atom or a tuple of other objects. In our model this value can be represented by: (i) basic values: atom, object identifier; (ii) set values: if $v_1, v_2, ..., v_n$ are values then $\{v_1, v_2, ..., v_n\}$ is a set of values; (iii) tuple values: if $x_1, x_2, ..., x_n$ are labels and $v_1, v_2, ..., v_n$ are values then $[x_1 \longmapsto v_1, x_2 \longmapsto v_2, ..., x_n \longmapsto v_n]$ is a tuple of values.

Class Person
    tuple(name, firstname, address, SsSystem)
    method Display = display(self.name,
        self.firstname,self.address, self.SsSystem).

Class Student
    Inherit Person
    tuple(SsSystem, department)
    method Display = (super.Display,
        display(self.department))

Class Employee
    Inherit Person
    tuple(SsSystem, department, salary)
    method Display = (super.Display,
        display(self.department, self.salary))

Class StudentEmployee
    Inherit Student Employee
    method Display = (super.Display)

Fig. 1. Example of a multiple inheritance schema

A class generates objects with similar properties. A class can be represented as a function that creates objects. In object-oriented approach objects communicate by message passing. Objects may send, receive and send messages to themselves and thus, classes must provide means of *self-reference* [18]. The concept of generator is introduced to refer to the function whose least fixed point specifies the meaning of recursive definitions. The generator of a class is a function of the form (in λ-calcul [5]): $\lambda self.Body$ where *self* may occur freely in body. An object is defined as the fixed-point of the generator associated with its class [12]. We use the example given in figure 1 to illustrate the concept of generator and the creation of objects. The generator of class *Person* is defined as follows:

$$Person = \lambda n,f,a,g.\lambda self.[name \longmapsto n, firstname \longmapsto f, address \longmapsto a,$$
$$SsSystem \longmapsto g, Display \longmapsto display(self.name, self.firstname, self.address,$$
$$self.SsSystem)]$$

Let *o* be an object of the class *Person* such that: *o = new Person(Dupont, Durant, 12 alberto street, general)*. The object *o* is created by the fixed-point of the generator of class *Person* as follows:

$o = Fix(Person(Dupon, Duran, 12\ alberto\ street, general))$
$\quad = [name \longmapsto Dupont, firstname \longmapsto Durant, address \longmapsto 12\ alberto\ street,$
$\quad\quad SsSystem \longmapsto general, Display \longmapsto display(Dupont, Durant, 12\ rue$
$\quad\quad\quad\quad alberto, general)]$

3 Incremental model of single inheritance

In single inheritance, the incremental mechanism of inheritance allows to construct a new class by modifying one of the existing superclasses. This section gives the formal aspects of an incremental model of single inheritance.

3.1 Wrappers

The modification is expressed as the addition or replacement of the properties by redefinition of the existing methods. The concept of wrapper is introduced to describe a modification function. By the way, each subclass defined by inheritance is associated with the function of modification "wrapper", specifying the modifications given by the declaration of this new subclass. A wrapper is naturally expressed as a function of the form : $\lambda self.\lambda super.Body$, where the parameter *self* is like the *self-reference* in a generator of class, *super* is used to refer inherited properties. A wrapper contains just the information in the subclass definition and has explicit access to the original properties in the superclasses. Let us now consider the second class definition of figure 1. *Student* class is defined by the single inheritance, the wrapper of *Student* is defined as follows:

$StudentWrapper = \lambda n,f,a,s,ds.\lambda self.\lambda super.[SsSystem \longmapsto s, department \longmapsto ds,$
$Display \longmapsto (super.Display, display(self.department))]$

3.2 Single inheritance mechanism

The incremental model of inheritance allows to construct a new subclass by modifying one of the existing superclasses. The process which allows to built the inheritance record is achieved by the three following stages: (i) specification of the modification function from the new subclass (ii) modification of the superclass by the wrapper function (iii) addition of the inherited properties of the superclass.

The modification function specifies the changes given by the declaration of the new subclass. The wrapping operator allows us to compute the new modification record by mapping the wrapper function onto the generator record of the superclass.

Definition 2. Let $\mathcal{R}$ be a set of records, and let f be a modification function defined on $\mathcal{R}$, and S be a record of $\mathcal{R}$ f: $\mathcal{R} \longrightarrow \mathcal{R}$
$$S \longrightarrow f(S).$$
The wrapping operator $\odot$ used to express the modification of the record S by f is defined as follows: f $\odot$ S = f(S).

Thus, the *Student* class in figure 1 is defined by the modification of *Person* class. The *StudentWrapper* function defining the modification function is applied to the generator of *Person* class. The result of this application is a new record modification, where any change specified by the *StudentWrapper* may replace the corresponding properties in the *Person* generator. In this case, the behavior of *Display* method is redefined by the modification operator.

$StudentWrapper \odot Person = \lambda n,f,a,s,ds.\lambda self.[SsSystem \longmapsto s, department \longmapsto$
$ds, Display \longmapsto (display(self.name, self.firstname, self.address, self.SsSystem),$
$$display(self.department))]$$

The inheritance record is computed by combining the generator record of superclass with the new modification record. The following definition formalizes the combination of two records.

Definition 3. Let S1 and S2 be records. The left-combination of records $\oplus_L$ is defined as follows:

$$(S1 \oplus_L S2)(x) = \begin{cases} S1(x) \text{ if } x \in Dom(S1) - Dom(S2) \\ S2(x) \text{ if } x \in Dom(S2) - Dom(S1) \\ S1(x) \text{ if } x \in Dom(S1) \cap Dom(S2) \end{cases}$$

The idea of $\oplus_L$ is the composition of two records where the left one wins in the case of conflict. The building process of inheritance record is formalized by the following definition.

Definition 4. Let f be a modification function defined on $\mathcal{R}$ and let S be a record of $\mathcal{R}$. The single inheritance operator $\triangleright$ is defined by:
$$f \triangleright S = (f \odot S) \oplus_L S$$
$$= f(S) \oplus_L S.$$

In the example given in figure 1 the class *Student* is defined by the single inheritance of the class *Person*. The generator of *Student* class is defined by the single inheritance operator $\triangleright$ as follows:

$Student = StudentWrapper \triangleright Person$
$\qquad = (StudentWrapper \odot Person) \oplus_L Person.$

The new record created by the modification is combined with the generator record of *Person* class by the operator $\oplus_L$. The result of inheritance should be a new record definition that is a new generator. We deduce the generator of *Student* class.

$Student = StudentWrapper \triangleright Person$
$\qquad = \lambda n,f,a,s,ds.\lambda self.[name \longmapsto n, firstname \longmapsto f, address \longmapsto a,$
$SsSystem \longmapsto s, department \longmapsto ds, Display \longmapsto (display(self.name,$
$self.firstname, self.address, self.SsSystem), display(self.department))]$

4 Incremental model of Multiple inheritance

The incremental multiple inheritance mechanism is an extension of the single inheritance mechanism. It allows to define a new subclass by modification of several superclasses. This section formalizes the incremental multiple inheritance mechanism.

4.1 Multiple inheritance and conflicts

Multiple inheritance is a generalization of single inheritance that allows multiple parents to be involved in the construction of the child. Despite its theoretical power as a concept and its usefulness in software development, this inheritance model encounters many difficulties because of conflicting properties (conflicts happen when one property can be inherited by several paths), semantic problems [26] and the complexity of linearization algorithms [9].

In object-oriented programming languages, the ways of solving conflicts differ with respect to several parameters [14] (at compile-time or run-time, the kind of answer given to the user, the number of inherited occurrence, ...). Indeed, there are two strategies to solve conflicts depending on whether they request an interaction with the users or not. The first alternative includes explicit designation naming (C++ [29]), renaming (Eiffel [24]), exclusion (CommonObject [25]). In second strategy the conflicts are solved dynamically and transparently by the system: CommonLoops [8], LOOPS [27], and ClOS [28] exemplify such techniques. In OODBMS, there are several solutions to such ambiguities. In the O2 [21], the system solves the name conflict by renaming the conflicting properties. Furthermore, intervention from the user is required to solve some conflicting cases [2]. There are other OODBMS which support multiple inheritance such as Orion [19], Antos, Objectstore [20] and Versant. As oposit to O2, Orion automatically solves ambiguities, the system maintains an ordering among the superclasses which desambiguates inheritance of methods. In Antos (C++) system, conflicts are solved dynamically: in the event of name conflict, earlier base class attributes overrides the others. In Objectstore and Versant the conflict resolution is very similar to C++.

None of these systems make the difference between name and value conflicts. Name conflict occurs when distinct properties share the same name. And conflict with different values of the same property (the property is unique) is called value conflicts [14, 16]. The most appropriate way of solving the name conflict is by disambiguating (renaming for explicit designation) [16]. The complete name is generated, which guarantees the uniformity and univocity of naming, such that any property can be designated by its name and its class definition. The value conflict is solved by a linearization algorithm that gives a total order on the inheritance hierarchy H (*precedence list* [28]). If x is the conflicting property, then the value of x is taken in the first conflicting class of the list containing x. At the time of writing, the incremental monotonous algorithm P_{ima} looks like a serious successor to the classical algorithms (P_1 et P_{clos}). More detail about linearization techniques can be found in [14, 15, 16].

4.2 Multiple Inheritance Mechanism

The incremental multiple inheritance mechanism is a generalization of single inheritance. The incremental inheritance process of multiple inheritance allows to build the record of a C class generator defined by direct superclasses inheritance $C_1, C_2, ..., C_n$ (C1 is called a direct superclass of C2 if C2 inherits from C1 and if there is no C3 such that C2 inherits from C3 and C3 inherits from C1). Let $GC_1, GC_2, ...GC_n$ be the generators associated with the classes $C_1, C_2, ...C_n$. The construction of the record generator of class C is achieved as follows:

1. Computation of the new record combination of $GC_1, GC_2, ...GC_n$ using the $\oplus_C$.
2. Specification of wrapper function of C.
3. Modification of the new combination record by the wrapper function.
4. Addition of inherited properties by the $\oplus_L$ operator.

The aim of the new record combination is to return to the single inheritance case. However, the combination of records sets the problem of conflicting properties.

Definition 5. Let x be a property, and let S_1 and S_2 be two records. x is called a conflicting property of S_1 and S_2 if $x \in \text{Dom}(S_1) \cap \text{Dom}(S_2)$.

We distinguish between two kinds of conflicts : name and value conflicts. In the example given in figure 1, we consider the classe *EmployeeStudent* defined by multiple inheritance. The *department* property defined in *Student* and *Employee* is an instance of a name conflict, each instance of *EmployeeStudent* can be bound to two distinct departments: for example developer in the computing department and student in the department of mathematics. On the other hand, the *SsSystem* property defined in *Person* and redefined in *Student* and *Employee* is the same property but takes different values (general in *Employee* class and student's in *Student* class). In fact the redefinition of a property in a subclass redefines only some aspects in this one. It does not concern the semantic aspect but rather the behavior aspect.

Definition 6. Let x be a property of a record S. The set of the super-records of S defining x denoted by $Def(x,S)$, is defined as follows :
$Def(x,S) = \{ S'/ S < S'$ et $x \in Dom(S') \}$ ($<$ is the inheritance relation)

The consequence of the definition 6 is the values conflict. Indeed, if x is a conflicting property of two records S_1 and S_2, and if $Def(x,S_1) \cap Def(x,S_2) \neq \emptyset$, then there exist a super-record S of S_1 and S_2 defining x. So x of S_1 and S_2 is a redefinition of x of S. And because the redefinition of a property concerns only the value conflict [16], the property x presents a value conflict between S_1 and S_2. In the case of $Def(x,S_1) \cap Def(x,S_2) = \emptyset$, we impose a name conflict by lack of additional semantics that may provide from definitions of the x property in S_1 and S_2 (property aspects : type, set of possible values, constraint,...). We now define the combination of records with conflict resolution.

Definition 7. Let H be a hierarchy of records, and let S_1 and S_2 be two records. We define $\oplus_C$ as a combination operator on records with conflict resolution (name and value) as follows: $(S_1 \oplus_C S_2) := \text{Comb\_Reso\_Conf}(S_1, S_2)$.

The function $\text{Comb\_Reso\_Conf}(S_1, S_2)$ gives the combination of two records S_1 and S_2 with conflict solving:
$\text{Comb\_Reso\_Conf}(S_1, S_2) := \lambda S_1, S_2.\lambda x.$

$$
\begin{bmatrix}
\text{if } x \in Dom(S_1)\text{-}Dom(S_2) \text{ then } S_1(x) \\
\text{else if } x \in Dom(S_2)\text{-}Dom(S_1) \text{ then } S_2(x) \\
\text{else if } x \in Dom(S_1) \cap Dom(S_2) \\
\qquad \text{then if } Def(x,S_1) \cap Def(x,S_2) \neq \emptyset \\
\qquad\qquad \text{then if } Pos(S_1,Precedence\_list(H)) < Pos(S_2,Precedence\_list(H)) \\
\qquad\qquad\qquad \text{then } S_1(x) \\
\qquad\qquad\qquad \text{else } S_2(x) \\
\qquad\qquad\qquad fi \\
\qquad\qquad \text{else } Rename(S_1,x), Rename(S_2,x) \\
\qquad\qquad fi \\
\text{else } \bot \\
fi
\end{bmatrix}
$$

The function $Precedence\_list(H)$ gives the priority list of records hierarchy H given by P_{ima}. The function $Pos(S, Precedence\_list(H))$ gives the position of the record S in the priority list. The function $Rename(S,x)$ renames the property x in the record S by S_x. In the example given in figure 1, the generator of the *Employee* class is built by the single inheritance operator (see 3.2).

$Employee = EmployeeWrapper \rhd Person$
$\qquad = \lambda n,f,a,g,de,p.\lambda self.[name \longmapsto n, firstname \longmapsto f, address \longmapsto a,$
$SsSystem \longmapsto g, department \longmapsto de, salary \longmapsto p,$
$Display \longmapsto (display(self.name, self.firstname, self.address, self.SsSystem),$
$display(self.department, self.salary))]$

There are three conflicting properties between *Student* and *Employee*: the department property is an instance of name conflict, and the properties *Display* and *SsSystem* give value conflicts. The Precedence_list of inheritance hierarchy schema shown in figure 1 gives:

$Precedence\_list(H)= (StudentEmployee, Student, Employee, Person)$.
In this order the body of the *Display* method and the value of the *SsSystem* attribute are chosen in *Student* class.

$Student \oplus_C Employee = \lambda n,f,a,s,ds,de,p.\lambda self.[name \longmapsto n, firstname \longmapsto f,$
$\qquad address \longmapsto a, SsSystem \longmapsto s, Student\_department \longmapsto ds,$
$\qquad Employee\_department \longmapsto de, salary \longmapsto p, Display \longmapsto (display$
$\qquad (self.name, self.firstname, self.address, self.SsSystem),$
$\qquad display(self.Student\_department, self.Employee\_department))]$

As in single inheritance, the modification in multiple inheritance is expressed by the wrapper function, where the pseudo-variable *super* is used to refer to direct superclasses. The definition of wrapping operator must be extended to provide multiple inheritance.

Definition 8. Let $\mathcal{R}$ be a set of records, and f a modification function defined on $\mathcal{R}^n$ and let $S_1, S_2, S_3, .., S_n$ be records of $\mathcal{R}$. The wrapping $\odot$ operator is defined as follows: $f \odot (S_1, S_2, S_3, .., S_n) = f(S_1 \oplus_C S_2 \oplus_C S_3 \oplus_C ....S_n)$

In the example given in figure 1, the class *StudentEmployee* is defined by multiple inheritance of class *Student* and *Employee*. The wrapper of the *StudentEmployee* class is defined as follows:

StudentEmployeeWrapper $= \lambda$n,f,a,s,ds,de,p.λself.λsuper.
   $[Display \longmapsto (super.Display)]$

The wrapping operator $\odot$ changes the generators of *Student* and *Employee* by modifying the inherited behavior properties (redefine Display method).

StudentEmployeeWrapper $\odot$*(Student,Employee)* $= \lambda$n,f,a,s,ds,de,p.λself.
   $[Display \longmapsto (display(self.name, self.firstname, self.address,$
     $self.SsSystem), display(self.Student\_department,$
     $self.Employee\_department))]$

The building process of multiple inheritance record is formalized by the following definition.

Definition 9. Let $\mathcal{R}$ be a set of records, and f a modification function defined on $\mathcal{R}^n$ and let $S_1, S_2, .., S_n$ be records of $\mathcal{R}$. The multiple inheritance $\triangleright_C$ operator is defined as follows:
$$f \triangleright_C (S_1, S_2, ..., S_n) = (f \odot (S_1, S_2, ..., S_n)) \oplus_L (S_1 \oplus_C S_2 \oplus_C ... \oplus_C S_n)$$
$$= f(S_1 \oplus_C S_2 \oplus_C ... \oplus_C S_n) \oplus_L (S_1 \oplus_C S_2 \oplus_C ... \oplus_C S_n).$$

StudentEmployee = *StudentEmployeeWrapper* $\triangleright_C$ *(Student,Employee)*
= *(StudentEmployeeWrapper* $\odot$*(Student,Employee))*$\oplus_L$*(Student* $\oplus_C$ *Employee)*
= *(StudentEmployeeWrapper(Student*$\oplus_C$*Employee))*$\oplus_L$*(Student* $\oplus_C$ *Employee)*.

StudentEmployeeWrapper $\odot$ *(Student,Employee)* =
   StudentEmployeeWrapper(Student$\oplus_C$*Employee)*

The generator of the class *StudentEmployee* is defined by the multiple inheritance operator $\triangleright_C$:

We deduce the *StudentEmployee* generator:
StudentEmployee $= \lambda$n,f,a,s,ds,de,p.λself.$[name \longmapsto n, firstname \longmapsto f,$
   $address \longmapsto a, SsSystem \longmapsto s, Student\_department \longmapsto ds,$
   $Employee\_department \longmapsto de, salary \longmapsto p, Display \longmapsto (display$
   $(self.name, self.firstname, self.address, self.SsSystem),$
   $display(Self.Student\_department, self.Employee\_department))]$

5 Correctness of the model

The semantics of inheritance presented in this paper is based on the incremental modification mechanism that is formalized by generators associated with classes and wrappers. A type theory defines conditions on the validity of the construction of new generators. A simple typing of inheritance is derived by Cook's constraint [13]. This constraint is not verified when we use the subtyping rules defined in object-oriented programming [1, 3, 13]. In this section, we show that when we use the subtyping relation ($\leq$), defined in the O2 DBMS then our incremental model of inheritance applied to O2 DB schema respects the Cook's constraint. And therefore, the integration of our incremental model in O2 is valid.

Definition 10. Let GC be a generator of class C, and suppose that GC has type of the form t $\longrightarrow$ t. Let $a_1, a_2, ..., a_n$ be distinct attributes of GC defined by types $t_1, t_2, .., t_n$ and $m_1, m_2, m_3, ...m_k$ be distinct methods of GC defined by signatures $s1, s_2, s_3, ..., s_k$. The type of generator GC is defined as follows: $\tau(\text{GC}) = t = [a_1 : t_1, ..., a_n : t_n, m_1 : s_1, ..., m_k : s_k]$.

Theorem 11. *Let C and C' be two classes of an O2 DB schema. Let GC and GC' be two generators of C and C' defined by the incremental model of inheritance. If C < C' (i.e C is a subclass of C') then $\tau(\,GC) \leq \tau(GC')$.*

Lemma 12. *If x is a property defined in the class C with type t then x:t belongs to GC the generator of class C.*

Proof : Let x:t be a property of type t defined in C. If x:t is not in the super-classes of C, then x:t is not a modification of a superproperty since it is not a redefinition. Therefore it is added to GC 's properties with the $\oplus_L$ operator.
If x:t is a redefinition then there exists at least one super-generator GC' that holds the definition of x. Let t' be a type of x in GC'. The generator GC is built by inheritance: GC =(WC $\odot$ GC') $\oplus_L$ GC. Since the property x:t is a redefinition, x:t belongs to WC "Wrapper" of C. The operation (WC $\odot$ GC') = WC(GC') replaces x:t' in GC' by x:t in C, but it does not change the type of x:t in C. Therefore x:t belongs to WC(GC'), and we have x:t of (WC $\odot$ GC') and x:t' of GC'. As a result, x:t belongs to(WC $\odot$ GC') $\oplus_L$ GC' therefore x:t belongs to GC. $\square$

Proof of theorem 11: By hypothesis C < C', therefore $\sigma(\text{C}) \leq \sigma(\text{C'})$. If the incremental model of inheritance is used, we have GC and GC' representing respectively the generators of C and C'. We must prove that τ (GC) $\leq \tau(\text{GC'})$. GC is either built using single inheritance (in this case the problem is reduced to the Cook constraint verification), or using multiple inheritance (and then other generators than GC' are used in the construction of GC). The latter case is more complex ; the conflicts must be dealt with separately.

single inheritance:
We know that C' is the only superclass of C such that GC = (WC $\odot$ GC') $\oplus_L$ GC'. Proving that: $\tau(\text{GC}) \leq \tau$ (GC') is equivalent to proving that for each x:t' in GC', x is defined in GC with the type t and t $\leq$ t'. Within the O2 DB schema, if the property x of C' has not been redefined in C, then x:t' is in C' and therefore in GC' (lemma 12), and x is only added via the operator $\oplus_L$ to the GC generator. The property x keeps the same type t' in GC. Within the

O2 DB schema, if the property x:t' of C' is redefined in C by x:t, then x:t' in GC' and x:t in GC (lemma 12). The O2 DB schema respects the contrevariant typing rules, i.e. if x:t' of C' has been redefined in C with x:t, therefore $t \leq_{st}$ t' for the attribute x. If x is a method, where t'= sign(x) in C' and t= sign(x) in C, therefore $t \leq_m$ t' [21]. Thus $\tau(GC) \leq \tau(GC')$. $\square$

Multiple inheritance:

When multiple inheritance is used, classes other than C' appear in the construction of the generator GC. Let $C_1, ..., C_k, C', C_{k+1}, ..C_n$ be the direct superclasses of C. The generator of GC is defined using multiple inheritance as follows:

$$GC = WC \triangleright_C (GC_1, ..., GC_k, GC', GC_{k+1}, ..GC_n)$$
$$= (WC \odot (GC_1, ..., GC_k, GC', GC_{k+1}, ..GC_n)) \oplus_L (GC_1 \oplus_C ...GC_k \oplus_C GC' \oplus_C$$
$$GC_{k+1}... \oplus_C GC_n)$$
$$= WC(GC_1 \oplus_C ...GC_k \oplus_C GC' \oplus_C GC_{k+1}... \oplus_C GC_n) \oplus_L (GC_1 \oplus_C ...GC_k \oplus_C$$
$$GC' \oplus_C GC_{k+1}... \oplus_C GC_n)$$

We want to prove that $\tau(GC) \leq \tau(GC')$ even if the construction of GC involved the modification of classes other than C'. Let x:t' $\in$ C'. Therefore we have x: t' $\in$ GC' (lemma 12). We must deal with two separate cases:

First case: We suppose that x:t' is not a conflicting property of the classes $C_1, ..., C_k, C', C_{k+1}, ..C_n$. If x:t' is not redefined in the class C, then x:t' belongs to $(GC_1 \oplus_C ...GC_k \oplus_C GC' \oplus_C GC_{k+1}... \oplus_C GC_n)$. It is simply transfered to GC using the $\oplus_L$ operator; its type does not change. If x:t' is redefined by the type t in the class C, then x:t belongs to GC (lemma 12). And since, the O2 DB schema respects the contrevariant typing rules, we have $t \leq t'$.

Second case: We suppose that x:t' $\in$ C' is a conflicting property. We must again deal with two subcases: x presents a name conflict or values conflict.

If x:t' of the C' presents a name conflicts then there exist j and h in [1..n] such that x belongs to $C_{j_1}, C_{j_2}, .., C', ..C_{j_h}$ and $j_k < j_{k+1}$ for all k in [1..h]: $x:t_{j_1} \in C_{j1}, x:t_{j_2} \in C_{j2}, ..., x:t' \in C', ..., x:t_{j_h} \in C_{j_h}$.

The name conflict is solved by the $\oplus_C$ combination operator. Indeed, the property x is renamed in the conflicting generators. We have:
$C_{j_1}.x : t_{j_1} \in GC_{j_1}, C_{j_2}.x : t_{j_2} \in GC_{j_2}, ..., C'.x : t' \in GC', ..., C_{j_h}.x : t_{j_h} \in GC_{j_h}$.
The renamed properties are simply transfered to the generator GC with the $\oplus_L$ operator. therefore x:t' of C' becomes C'.x: t' in the generator GC' and is transfered to the generator GC with the $\oplus_L$ operator. We find C'.x:t' $\in$ GC, its type does not change. In the case of name conflict, x cannot be redefined in C (if this case occurs, then there is a conception error) and therefore an exception should be raised to warn the programmer.

If x:t' of C' presents a values conflict then there exist j and h in [1..n] such that x belongs to $C_{j_1}, C_{j_2}, ..., C', ..., C_{j_h}$ and $j_k < j_{k+1}$ for all k in [1..h]: $x:t' \in C_{j_1}, x:t' \in C_{j_2}, ..., x:t' \in C', ..., x:t' \in C_{j_h}$

Indeed, the property x has the same domain (the same type and the same set of values) in the conflicting classes. Therefore the property x in GC is the property of the class that has the priority (the priority is computed by the linearization algorithm). Whichever may be this class the property x with type t' is generated by $(GC_1 \oplus_C ...GC_k \oplus_C GC' \oplus_C GC_{k+1}...\oplus_C GC_n)$. If x is redefined in C by the type t, then x:t belongs to GC (lemma 12) and since O2 DB schema respects the contrevariant typing rules, we have t $\leq$ t'. If x has not been redefined in C then x:t' is transfered to GC by the $\oplus_L$ operator. The property x keeps the same type t' in GC in this case. Thus, we have proved that for all x:t' in GC', x:t belongs to GC and t $\leq$ t'.

Conclusion : If GC is the generator of the class C and GC' is the generator of the class C' and if C inherits from C' then $\tau(C) \leq \tau(C')$.

6 Conclusion

In object oriented pradigm, objects communicate by the message sending. The message evaluation process, is the result of the function that takes a message, and searches the message selector, in the class or superclasses of the object receiving the message, using somehow the inheritance mechanism. The incremental model of inheritance presented in this paper allows to build a generator of each class from the generators of the superclasses. The result is a function that allows the creation of objects. It contains the proper properties. The inherited properties, where the name conflicts are solved by renamming based on the explicit designation, and the values conflict by linearization mechanism. The complete method body is built by the modification (redefined properties). The proposed model should be used for dynamic (i.e at run-time) message evaluation. The message is directly evaluated on the the generator of the object class where the message is sent. We have shown that the proposed model respects the Cook's constraint, when we use the subtyping relation ($\leq$) defined in the O2 DBMS. And therefore, the integration of dynamic method for message evaluation using the proposed model in O2 DBMS is valid.

References

1. M. Abadi and L. Cardelli, "On subtyping and matching". ECOOP'95 Proceedings 1995, pp 145-167.
2. M. Adiba, C. Collet, "Objets et bases de données le SGBD O2". Edition Hermès, 1993.
3. R. M. Amadio and L. Cardelli, "Subtyping recursive types". ACM Transactions on Programming Languages and Systems, 15(4), 1993, pp 575-631.
4. M. Atkinson, F. Bancilhon, D. Dewih, K.Dittrich, D. Maier, S. Zdonick, "The Object-Oriented Database System Manifesto". DOOD'89 Proceedings, 1989, pp 25-42.
5. H. P. Barendregt, "The Lambda Calculus Its syntax and semantics" volume 103 of studies in Logic and The foundations of Mathematics. North-Holland, 1981.
6. M. Benattou, L. Lakhal, "Héritage incrémental: Modèle, Méthode, Validation". Ingénierie des systèmes d'information, 4(5), 1996, pp 637-661.

7. M. Benattou, L. Lakhal, "Incremental Inheritance Mechanism and its Message Evaluation Method". BIWIT'97 Proceedings 1997, IEEE Computer Society Press (to appear).

8. D. G. Bobrow, K. Kahn, G. Kiczales, L. Masinter, M.Stefik, F.Zdybel, "Common-Loops : Mergin Lisp and Object-Oriented Programming". OOPSLA'86 Proceedings, 1986, pp 17-29.

9. G. Bracha, W. Cook, "Mixin based inheritance", OOPSLA'90 Proceedings, 1990, pp 303-311.

10. L. Cardelli, "A semantics of multiple inheritance". Information and Computation, 76, 1988, pp 138-164.

11. G. Castagna, "Covariance and contravariance: conflict without a cause". ACM Transaction On Programming Language and System, 17(6), 1995, pp 805-843.

12. W. R. Cook, J. Palsberg, "A Denotational Semantics of Inheritance and its Correctness". OOPSALA'89 Proceedings, 1989, pp 433-443.

13. W. R. Cook, W. L. Hill, P. S. Canning, "Inheritance Is not Subtyping". ACM Symposium On Principales of Programming languages, 1990, ACM, pp 125-135.

14. R. Ducournau, M. Habib, M. Huchard, M.L. Mugnier, "Monotonic Conflict Resolution Mechanism for Inheritance". OOPSALA'92 Proceedings, 1992, pp 16-24.

15. R. Ducournau, M. Habib, Huchard M., Mugnier M.L. "Proposal for a monotonic multiple inheritance linearisation". OOPSLA'94 Proceedings, 1994, pp 164-175.

16. R. Ducournau, M. Habib, Huchard M., Mugnier M.L, Napoli A. "Le point sur l'héritage multiple". Technique et Science Informatique, 14(3), 1995, pp 309-345.

17. A. Goldberg, D. Robson, "SMALLTALK-80 : the language and its implementation". Adison-wesley, 1983.

18. A. V. Hense, "Denotational semantics of an object-oriented programming language with explicit wrapper". Formal aspect of computing, 1993, (5), pp 181-207.

19. W. Kim, N. Ballou, H. Chou, J. F. Garza and D. Woelk, "Features of the Orion Object-Oriented Database System". Object-Oriented Concepts, Databases and Applications, W. Kim and F. Lochovsky (Ed), ACM Press, New York, 1989, pp 251-282.

20. C. Lamb, G. Landis, J. Orenstein, D. Weinreb, "The objectStore System". CACM, 34(10), 1991, pp 50-63.

21. C. Lecluse, P. Richard, F. Velez, "O2 An Object-Oriented Data Model". SIGMOD Proceedings, 1988, pp 424-433.

22. D. McAllester R. Zabih. "Boolean classes". OOPSLA'87 Proceedings, 1987, pp 482-493.

23. N. Minsky D. Rozenshtein. "A Law-based approch to object-oriented Propgramming". AMC Conf. OOPSLA'87 Proceedings , 1987, pp 417-423.

24. B. Meyer, "Object-oriented Software Construction". Prence Hall, 1988.

25. A. Snyder "Encapsulation and inheritance in object-oriented programming languages". OOPSLA'86 Proceedings, 1986, pp 38-45.

26. A. Snyder, "Inheritance in Object-oriented Programming Languages". (Eds), Inheritance hierarchie in knowledge representation and programming languages, Wiley, London 1991, pp 153-171.

27. M. Stefik and D. G. Bobrow. "Object-oriented Programming: Themes and Variation". The AI Magazine, 6(4), 1986.

28. G. L. STeele Jr, "Common Lisp: the language". Second Edition Digital Press 1990.

29. B. Stroustrup. "Multiple Inheritance Fot C++". EUUGS'87 Proceedings, 1987.

A Clustering Technique for Object-Oriented Databases

Jean-Yves Gay* and Le Gruenwald **

* Institut des Sciences de L'Ingenieur, Génie Informatique, 6317 Aubière Cedex, FRANCE
** The University of Oklahoma, School of Computer Science, Norman,Oklahoma 73019, U.S.A.

Abstract- This paper proposed a new clustering technique for an object-oriented database mangement system. The technique is dynamic and employs a reduced set of statistics to minimize statistics collection overhead. Clustering is done automatically by using several evaluation criteria and requires less knowledge from the user by using fewer user's hints than other techniques. The technique also allows the user to tune the clustering process through a reduced set of parameters. Simulation experiments based on the HyperModel benchmark showed that the proposed clustering technique outperformed the two existing techniques, ORION and CACTIS.

1.Introduction

Data clustering is among those techniques that can be used to improve the performance of an object-oriented database management system (OODBMS). When data cannot fit in the main memory, they are stored on the hard disks. Without any clustering technique, accessing two related objects mostly requires two disk I/Os because these two objects are not stored in the same page. Because of the slowness of hard disks which require some milli seconds to perform a random access, the performance of the OODBMS is very poor. On the contrary the main memory can perform very quick random access (some nano seconds). Thus it is very important to store related objects close to each other in order to have a maximum of relevant information when a page is loaded from the disk to the main memory.

Most implemented clustering techniques for OODBMS are static: O2 [2], CACTIS [10], ORION [11]. Objects are clustered at creation time and their placement is never reconsidered if the user does nothing. Recently proposed techniques are dynamic: STD [4], CK [5], Amadeus [8], Eos [9]. Objects are clustered at creation time and reclustered when a modification of clustering criteria or an object update is done. Some of the static and dynamic techniques use statistics to reflect the evolution of the object's usage: CACTIS , STD, Amadeus. The main drawback is the statistics storage size which becomes prohibitive for very large databases. Some of the existing clustering techniques require user's hints to specify the object placement: O2, Eos, ORION. The other techniques provide a set of parameters to tune the clustering process which are very hard to fix.

We propose a new clustering technique which is dynamic, uses a reduced set of statistics and requires fewer user's hints than other techniques. The user can tune the clustering process through a reduced set of parameters. We perform simulations to compare our clustering technique with two other techniques: CACTIS [10] and ORION [11]. The rest of the paper is structured as follows. Section 2 presents our clustering technique. Sections 3 describes the simulation results, and Section 4 concludes the paper.

2.The New Clustering Technique

There are five major parts of our technique: statistics collecting, storage size determination, bad clustering detection, new clustering determination, and object clustering and reclustering.

2.1. Statistics collecting

Three kinds of statistics are collected during an unspecified period until a bad clustering is detected: statistics used for the reclustering algorithm, statistics used to determine the objects which should be reclustered, and statistics used by the buffering process.

A.Statistics used for the reclustering algorithm
A.1 statistics about inter-class relationships

[6] has shown that CK [5] has good clustering capabilities because it uses several criteria in its algorithm. In our technique we examined the three kinds of relationships as in CK: equivalence, version and configuration. The main drawback of CK is that the information used is given by the user and thus cannot reflect the actual use of objects as accurately as statistics gathered during run-time. For each class, we stored the number of times each examined relationship is crossed. In order to limit their size, these statistics are relative to classes and not to object instances.

A.2 statistics about the read/write access

When objects are mainly read accessed, to increase object locality, they should be duplicated and stored close to the objects which are using them. This is the reason why we collected a second kind of statistics: each time an object of a class is accessed, we store the type of access (read or write). To limit the size of the statistics, information stored is relative to classes and not to object instances. If the number of read accessed objects is greater than the number of write accessed objects, then the class access type is called *READ*; otherwise the class access type is called *WRITE*. Because we use statistics that are true with a given certainty, and because it is important that the class access type does not change for each reclustering, the class access type is set to *READ* only when $\#reads/\#writes > (1+\varepsilon)$ and set to *WRITE* only when $\#writes/\#reads > (1+\varepsilon)$. In other words, the class access type is changed only when the difference between the number of reads and the number of writes becomes sufficient. One part of ε is a function of the quality of the statistics (see 2.3) and the other part is a user parameter (see 2.4).

B.Statistics used to determine the objects which should be reclustered

We have to determine which objects should be reclustered to increase the database performance with as little overhead as possible. Thus we collected statistics of the number of times an object of a class is accessed and only the *m* most reached objects are reclustered. m is set by the user (see 2.4). These statistics are relative to object instances.

C. Statistics used by the buffering process

The number of chunks read in the memory buffer and the total number of chunks read both in memory and disk are collected each time a chunk is read when an object in it is reached via a studied relationship.

2.2. Determination of the Size of the storage unit

[7] has shown that the size of the clustering unit called a chunk has a significant influence on the quality of clustering. The size should be markedly higher than the average size of objects. To avoid having a fragmented disk, the storage unit size is set. The user's hints are required to set this parameter as follows:

let c_i $i=1,...,n$ be a class of the database.
s_i $i=1,...,n$ the size of the class c_i.
m_i $i=1,...,n$ the estimated number of instances of the class c_i.

The storage size is given by the formula :

$$storage\_size = (average\ object\ size) \times (average\ number\ of\ object\ in\ a\ chunk)$$

$$where\ average\ object\ size = \frac{size\ to\ store\ all\ the\ objects}{total\ number\ of\ objects} = \frac{\sum\limits_{i=1}^{n} s_i \times m_i}{\sum\limits_{i=1}^{n} m_i}$$

2.3. Bad clustering detection

Statistics are collected during a time which is a function of the quality of the clustering. A period ends when a bad clustering is detected. Two conditions must be true.

- the ratio between the number of chunks read in the memory buffer and the total number of chunks accessed has to be lower than a threshold T_{buffer}: $\dfrac{number\ of\ chunks\ read\ in\ the\ buffer}{total\ number\ of\ chunks\ read} \leq T_{buffer}$. This condition determines the quality of the clustering process.

- the evolution of the statistics must be sufficient, that is the number of chunks accessed is greater than a threshold T_{evol}.

A. The value of T_{buffer}

The value of T_{buffer} is a function of many parameters such as the use of the objects in the database, the size of the memory buffer, the quality of the clustering performed by the reclustering algorithm, and the size of the storage unit. It is too difficult to find a function to set T_{buffer} accurately. This is the reason why we adopted a floating threshold as follows. Let $ratio_n$ be the measured value of the ratio when a reclustering is needed and $ratio_s$ the value of the ratio of the previous reclustering. The variation of T_{buffer} is given by the following algorithm :

If $ratio_n \approx T_{buffer}$ **then**
         increase T_{buffer} by δ
else   /*$ratio_n < T_{buffer}$ */
         If $ratio_n < ratio_s$ **then**
                 decrease T_{buffer} by δ

The decrease value δ of T_{buffer} is a parameter set by the user at the beginning and remains the same afterwards. T_{buffer} is decreased when the new organization of the objects on the disk is not better than the old one. In this case it is not necessary to require a so good ratio and to perform a reclustering each time T_{evol} objects have been reached: the new organization of the objects cannot be better with such use of the objects and thus it is a wasted reorganization. T_{buffer} is increased when the measured ratio is equal to the required one. This happens when the number of objects reached is greater than T_{evol}. In this case the organization of the objects on the disk slowly becomes bad and we can hope that a reclustering will markedly improve the future ratio between the number of objects read in the memory buffer and the total number of objects read both in memory and disk.

B. The value of T_{evol}

The value of T_{evol} is a function of the number of classes in the database and of the precision of the collected statistics. This precision is determined by estimating a binomial distribution with a normal distribution [3]. We study the problem with an example: assume a class has 64.4% read access and 35.6% write access. We want to assert that objects of this class are write accessed with a probability $p=64.4\% \pm C_\alpha$ with certainty $(1-\alpha)$. C_α is the confident interval of p with the certainty $(1 - \alpha)$.

Let X be a random variable, where $X = \begin{cases} 1 & \text{if the object is write accessed} \\ 0 & \text{else} \end{cases}$

Let f_n be a measure of p for a sample size of n.

$$f_n = \frac{s_n}{n} = \frac{x_1 + x_2 + ... + x_n}{n} \qquad \text{where } x_i = \begin{cases} 1 \text{ if } WRITE \\ 0 \text{ else} \end{cases} \text{ is a realisation of } X$$

We will test the assumption $P_p=\{P(X=WRITE)=p\}$ against $\{P(X=WRITE)\neq p\}$. We want the probability to reject $\{P(X=WRITE=p\}$ to be less than α. We notice: $Pp(Tn \neq p) < \alpha$

According to [3], when $n \geq 50$, $nf_n \geq 10$, $n(1-f_n) \geq 10$ then a binomial distribution can be rounded with a normal distribution $N(np, \sqrt{np(1-p)})$.

The test becomes :
$$\begin{cases} F = \dfrac{S}{n} \\ \overline{R} = [p \pm t_\alpha \dfrac{\sigma}{\sqrt{n}}] \end{cases} \text{with } P(Z > t_\alpha) = \dfrac{\alpha}{2}; Z \text{ is } N(0,1)$$

F is the random variable associated with f.

$\overline{R}$ is called the complement of the reject interval, so it is the confidence interval.

$$p = f_n \pm C_\alpha \qquad \begin{aligned} where \quad & C_\alpha = t_\alpha \sqrt{\dfrac{f_n(1 - f_n)}{n}} \\ and \quad & f_n = \dfrac{x_1 + ... + x_n}{n} \end{aligned}$$

by using statistic tables we can determine t_α which is a function of α and then determine C_α.

With the values of our example we have: $f_n = 64.4\%$ and $n = 137 + 248 = 385$
we set $(1 - \alpha) = 90\%$
we obtain : $t_\alpha = 1.65$ and then $C_\alpha = 0.04$, i.e. 4%
Thus we can conclude that with 90% confidence, the portion of objects which are *WRITE* accessed is between 60.4% and 68.4%.

In our situation we want to know the best sample size n. Thus we have to solve the opposite problem. We have to determine:

1 - what level of confidence we want to have (the value of $1 - \alpha$)

2 - what maximum C_α we want to permit.

The value of n is : $n = \dfrac{f_n(1 - f_n) * t_\alpha^2}{C_\alpha^2}$ given with the above formula

Because we do not know n, we do not know f_n. This value can be set to $1/2$. [3] stated that the function $n(f_n)$ is highest when $f_n = 1/2$.

Then the formula becomes: $n = \dfrac{t_\alpha^2}{4C_\alpha^2}$

E.g. : Supposing that we want to be sure that our estimation is true at 90% and with an interval of 5%.

$C_\alpha = 0.05 \quad \alpha = 1 - 0.9 = 0.1$ and $f_n = 0.5$

we determine t_α by using statistical tables: $t_\alpha = 1.65$, and then we calculate $n = 273$. We need a sample of 273 values.

To obtain the value of T_{evol} we have to multiply n by the number of classes in the system. It is evident that all the statistics of all the classes are not the same, some are more precise, some are less. T_{evol} only guarantees an average precision of the statistics. For example, with the values of the previous example ($n = 273$). If there are 10 classes in the system, a sample size of 2730 is required. Thus $T_{evol} = 2730$.

2.4. New clustering determination

When a bad clustering has been detected, we have to calculate the quality of the statistics for all classes. In other words we have to calculate the size of the confident interval of the statistics for each class. At the end of the period, we know f_n, the real value of n and we can set α. It may be too expensive to calculate C_α for each value of f_n, so we set $f_n = 0.5$. We cannot perform reclustering with classes on which statistics are not good enough. If the calculated C_α is too big, it means that not enough statistics regarding the class have been collected. Thus current statistics are kept to be added with those that will be collected during the next period and no reclustering is performed with the objects of this class (see *step 1* in Figure 1).

We deal with two kinds of configurations of the statistics about the inter-class relationship. When one relationship is crossed more often than the other two, objects are reclustered following this relationship (see *step 5* in Figure 1). The problem is different when the numbers of times the two major relationships are crossed are similar. In this case which one is greatest, considering the uncertainty of the statistics ? May be the "smallest" one will be the "greatest" one during the next period. It is why in this case we take into account the variation of the statistics to anticipate the future object usage: if the relationships a and b have been used with almost the same frequency during the period but if the variation with the former period of the usage of a is big, maybe in the future period, a will be the most used relationship (see step 4 in Figure 1).

Procedure Clustering_Determination
    for class in all classes **do**
//step 1
        quality1 := compute the quality of the statistics about the kind of relationships
        if quality1 > C_α **then**   *//not enough statistics*
          add_statistics();   *//old and new statistics are merged*
        else
//step 2
          quality2 := quality of the statistics about the kind of access (R or W)
          //is the class mainly read accessed or write ?
          class.old_type_access := class.type_access;
          if (class.#access[READ]/class.#access[WRITE] > 1+quality2+γ) **then**
            class.type_access := READ;
          else
            if (class.#access[WRITE]/class.#access[READ] > 1+quality2+γ) **then**
               class.type_access := WRITE;
            endif
          endif
//step 3
          first_relation_ship := max({equivalence,version,configuration});
          second_relation_ship:=max({equivalence,version,configuration}\
                                          first_relationship);
          if (second_relationship's evolution $\geq \beta_1$*first_relationship evolution) and

```
                (first_relationship's evolution ≥ quality1 + γ) and
                (abs(class.#access[first_relationship] - class.#access[second_relationship])
                  < β₂) then
//step 4
                    class.major_relationship := type of second_relationship;
                    if major_relationship <> old_major_relationship then
                        class.old_major_relationship = class.major_relationship;
                        if class.type_access = READ then
                            for obj in m more reached objects of class do
                                recluster_object(obj);
                        endif
                    endif
                else
//step 5
                    if (first_relationship's variation > quality1 + γ) then
                    class.major_relationship := type of first_relationship;
                        if major_relationship <> old_major_relationship then
                            class.old_major_relationship = class.major_relationship;
                        if class.type_access = READ then
                        for obj in m more reached objects of class do
                            cluster_object(obj);
                        endif
                    endif
                endif
            endif
        endif
    endfor
```

Fig. 1- Clustering Determination Algorithm

Below we provide explanations for the parameters used in the clustering algorithm determination : γ, β_1, β_2 and m.

γ is used to avoid statistic variations and set by the user. The higher γ is, the less hazardous statistics variations will disrupt the clustering process. It is beneficial to set a high value when special operations are performed (occasional operations such as a backup).

The values of β_1 and β_2 are functions of the desired anticipation about the way to cluster objects following one relationship. The lower β_1 is, the higher the anticipation is. The higher β_2 is the higher the anticipation is. The values of β_1 and β_2 should be adjusted by the user as a function of the use of objects in the database. In a transitional period (when the use of the objects is evolving) it may be beneficial to have a strong anticipation.

The number m of the most reached objects is a function of the desired response time. The more objects are reclustered, the more overhead there is. m allows flexible activity of the clustering process and is set by the user.

2..5. Object clustering and reclustering

The *cluster_object* procedure is called when an object is created or updated or when an object has to be reclustered. It is similar to the one presented in [5] and reformulated in [6], but is modified to integrate object duplication for configuration and equivalence and to be used for clustering and reclustering.

- *step 1*: the algorithm builds a list of all candidate chunks. A candidate chunk is a chunk that owns an object in relation with the object to (re)cluster according to the major relationship: equivalence, version, configuration.
- *step 2* : if the object to (re)cluster is an equivalence or a configuration, it is stored in the first candidate chunk that has enough space left to store it if the main access type is *WRITE*, or is duplicated in each candidate chunk when the main access type is *READ*. If there is no chunk with enough space left, a new chunk is created when the object is clustered or the chunk is splitting when the object is reclustered.

step 3 : As stated in [6] when the main relationship is *VERSION*, the problem is more difficult. For each candidate chunk, the algorithm evaluates a cost. If a *by_reference* attribute is not placed in the chosen chunk, the system needs to dereference it at run-time, thus an effort is made to place the instance on the same chunk as the sources of its inherited attributes, taking into account their access frequencies. The cost of storing a target object in chunk p, modeled by *ref_lookup(p)*, is incremented by *weight(p)*, which is a function of the access frequency of structural relationships for chunk p. Inherited *by-copy* attributes can be either copied into a candidate chunk or be looked up at run-time. Thus there are two cost variables : *copy-storage(p)* to model the cost of storage and *copy_lookup(p)* to model the cost of *by-reference* implementation. To determine a candidate chunk, the algorithm needs to transform the lookup and storage cost into the same scale for comparison. The lookup cost *Lookup_cost* is represented by $P_{hit}*C_{buf}+(1-P_{hit})*(C_{os}+P_{io}*C_{io})$ where P_{hit} is the probability of buffer hit, P_{io} is the probability of doing I/O during buffer replacement, C_{io} is the cost of I/O, C_{buf} is the cost of searching through buffer and C_{os} is the cost of getting a free page from the operating system. The storage cost *storage_cost* is represented by *lookup_cost*scale_factor* where *scale_factor* is determined by the user [5]. When a chunk has been chosen, the object is either stored in it if there is enough space left, or the chunk is splitting by using the split procedure that partitions a weighted graph into two sub-graphs each of which fits into one chunk. Related objects are connected in a weighted graph in which nodes represent relationships among objects. Arcs are associated with weights given the frequency access to the different relationships.

3.SIMULATION RESULTS

We compared our technique with CACTIS[10] and ORION [11] using the simulation model proposed in [6] and the HyperModel benchmark [1]. We measured query response time and the number of I/Os required during database reorganization and object clustering (called clustering I/O overhead). Due to space limitation, in this Section we report only some of the simulation results.

3.1. Effect of the number of objects in the database

The clustering I/Os overhead is almost constant with our clustering technique whereas the increase is exponential with ORION and CACTIS. This is due to the fact that the number of objects reclustered each time a bad clustering is detected is limited to the most accessed ones in our technique whereas the reclustering concerns all objects in the database with CACTIS or ORION. With an initial set of 200 objects, the clustering I/Os overhead of our technique is 11 times better than that of CACTIS and 31 times better than that of ORION. With an initial set of 800 objects our method is 57 times better than CACTIS and 131 times better than ORION.

Figure 2 shows that response time obtained with our method increases linearly with the number of objects and that our method totally outperformed ORION and CACTIS, especially with a high number of objects, since response time increases exponentially with these two methods. With an initial set of 400 objects, our method is 54 times better than CACTIS and 273 times better than ORION. With an initial set of 800 objects our method is 344 times better than CACTIS and 1000 times better than ORION. The good performance obtained is due to a very little clustering overhead incurred in our method compared to those in CACTIS and ORION.

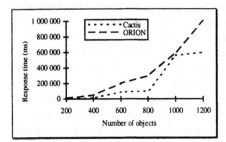 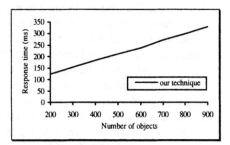

Fig. 2- Response time v.s. number of objects

3.2. Effect of the read/write ratio

The simulation experiments show an increase of the clustering overhead for all the three techniques. The lower the read/write ratio is, the more objects are created, and thus the higher the number of objects in the database is. Response time decreases linearly with the read percentage for our method whereas it increases with CACTIS and ORION. With a read percentage of 78 %, the response time of our technique is 109 times better than that of CACTIS and 437 times better than that of ORION. With a read percentage of 24%, the ratios are respectively 490 and 1366. The increase of performances of our technique when the read/write ratio decreases is due to the fact that the number of transaction I/Os decreases too. For CACTIS the number of transaction I/Os also decreases but is compensated by the increase of the clustering overhead.

4.CONCLUSIONS

This paper proposed a new clustering technique that offers several innovative features. First the size of the statistics is really reduced compared with those proposed in existing methods. The required storage size of our technique is linear with the number of objects whereas those introduced in other techniques are not. Second we developed a replication strategy which is adaptable for each class of objects. Objects are duplicated only when they are read accessed to increase object locality. Third our technique is flexible and can be tuned to avoid big overhead when the OODBMS is overloaded. Fourth, the clustering process can be tuned by using a reduced set of statistics which is easier to set compared with those required in existing techniques. The simulation results have shown that our technique performs much better than CACTIS and ORION in terms of query response time.

References

[1] T.L. Anderson, A.J. Berre, M. Mallison, H.H. Porter III, B. Scheider, *"The HyperModel Benchmark"*, International Conference on Extending Database Technology, March 1990, pp 317-331

[2] Veronique Benzaken, *"An Evaluation Model for Clustering Strategies in the O2 Object Oriented Database System"*, The Third International Conference on DataBase Theory (ICDT'90), December 1990.

[3] R. Berthuet, *"Cours de Statistiques"*, CUST, Clermont-Ferrand, France, 1994.

[4] Frederic Bullat, Michel Schneider, *"A dynamic clustering strategy for object oriented databases"*, CUST, Clermont-Ferrand , 1996.

[5] Ellis E. Chang, *"Effective Clustering and Buffering in an Object Oriented DBMS"*, University of California, Berkeley, Computer Science Division, Technical Report, No. UCB/CSD 89/515, June 1989.

[6] Jérôme Darmont, Le Gruenwald, *"A Comparison Study of Clustering Techniques for Object-Oriented Databases"*, Information Sciences Journal, December 1996.

[7] Carsten Gerlhof, Alfons Kemper, Christoph Kilger, Guido Moerkotte, *"Partition-Based Clustering in Objects Bases : From Theory to Practice"*, 4th international conference on Foundation of Data Organization and Algorithms, 1993, pp 301-316.

[8] Yvon Gourhant, Sylvain Louboutin, Vinny Cahill, Andrew Condon, Gradimir Starovic, Brendan Tangney, *"Dynamic Clustering in an Object-Oriented Distributed System"*, 1992.

[9] Olivier Gruber, Laurent Amsaleg, " *Object Grouping in Eos"*, Workshop on Distributed Object Management, August 1992, pp 117-131.

[10] Scott E. Hudson, Roger King, *"Cactis : A Self-Adaptative, Concurrent Implementation of an Object Oriented Database Management System"*, ACM Transaction on Database Systems, Vol.14, No. 3, September 1989, pp 291-321.

[11] Won Kim, Jorge F. Garza, Nathaniel Ballou, Darrel Woelk, *"Architecture of the ORION Next-Generation Database System"*, IEEE Transactions on Knowledge and Data Engineering, Vol. 2, No. 1, March 1990, pp 109-124.

Design and Implementation of TEMPO Fuzzy Triggers

**Tarik Bouaziz‡, Janne Karvonen,
Antti Pesonen and Antoni Wolski**

Technical Research Centre of Finland (VTT)
VTT Information Technology
P.O. Box 1201, FIN-02044 VTT, Finland

```
e-mail: <first name>.<last name>@vtt.fi
http://www.vtt.fi/tte/projects/tempo/
```

Abstract

Fuzzy triggers are database triggers incorporating fuzzy concepts. The approach leads to the application of approximate reasoning to trigger-based decision making. In C-fuzzy triggers, fuzzy rules may be specified in the trigger condition part. The C-fuzzy trigger model is presented, and an implementation thereof in the TEMPO Server—a prototype active database system—is described. The performance test results are included.

Keywords: Active databases, approximate reasoning, fuzzy triggers.

1 Introduction

In various application domains of information technology a phenomenon of data explosion may be observed. For example, in the field of industrial process management, the data explosion effect is caused by the improved data acquisition techniques: more and more process variables are reported at higher and higher frequencies. In a needs survey performed in 1993 [JP93] a peak acquisition rate required for a major power station installation was about 5 000 measurements per second, and the requirements have been growing since then. In the presence of data explosion one needs powerful means to extract useful information from the flooding data. In time-critical environments like manufacturing process management and control, the speed of data evaluation is also of great importance. As we see it, providing the right information at the right time becomes a new challenge of next generation database systems. The goal may be achieved by improving the active capabilities of database systems. In this paper, we present an implementation of a new type of database triggers using fuzzy inference in making the decisions. The results of this work are applicable to other environments suffering from data explosion—ranging from corporate databases to World Wide Web.

The work presented in this paper was originally driven by the requirements of an industrial application: a paper machine drive control system. A paper machine is equipped with tens of high-power electric motors. Process measurements data is stored in a database which is fed by sensors. There is a need to analyze the data and

---

‡ The work has been carried out within the ERCIM Fellowship programme (ERCIM Human Capital and Mobility Programme).

to provide useful information to the end user, in a timely and appropriate manner, in order to prevent failures of the drive system. To achieve this, in the TEMPO project, we have proposed a technique of *fuzzy triggers* [BW96]. In this paper, we focus on a concrete implementation of the concept.

To our best knowledge, no attention has been paid until now on integrating imprecision and/or uncertainty within database triggers. There are many approaches through which this integration can take place [BW96, BW97]. The TEMPO approach focuses on a seamless integration of fuzziness within database triggers. There are three design criteria which we strive to satisfy in TEMPO.

The first goal is to enhance the expressive power of triggers to capture the expert knowledge which is imprecise, incomplete or vague. This knowledge is more easily expressed using fuzzy rules which allow fuzziness in the antecedents and/or consequents [Zad84, Zad89]. Indeed, many experts have found that fuzzy rules provide a convenient way to express their domain knowledge. In industrial applications, linguistic terms such as *low, medium, high, large, small*, etc. are widely used since they convey more information than crisp values would do [Men95].

The second goal is to extend the (exact) reasoning inherent to triggers and to integrate it with the approximate reasoning more tightly. This makes fuzzy triggers a powerful mechanism to capture both approximate and exact reasoning characterizing real-world problems. Approximate reasoning deals with inference under imprecision and/or uncertainty in which the underlying logic is approximate rather than exact [Zad75, GKB+84]. It should be noted that in our daily life most of the information on which our decisions are based is linguistic rather than numerical in nature. In this perspective, approximate reasoning provides a natural framework for the characterization of human behavior and suitable for decision making.

The third goal, a practical one, is to find an easy way to add a fuzzy trigger capability to an existing active database system since we have previously developed such a system [WKP96]. Also, a possibility to use an existing fuzzy inference engine is highly recommended since it reduces the implementation effort.

This paper is organized as follows: Section 2 illustrates the main features of the model of implemented fuzzy triggers. Section 3 presents selected topics of the implementation of the TEMPO Server prototype. We show performance test results in Section 4. Then, we conclude in Section 5.

2 TEMPO Fuzzy Triggers

In this section we briefly describe a trigger model incorporating approximate reasoning (fuzzy inference) in the process of the evaluation of the condition part of an ECA trigger. We are calling such triggers *C-fuzzy triggers* (or Condition-fuzzy ECA triggers). For a more detailed presentation of this one and other fuzzy trigger models, see [BW96, BW97]. The C-fuzzy trigger model is based on the concepts of the linguistic variables, the corresponding terms and the rule set function.

2.1 Linguistic Variables

A linguistic variable is a variable whose values are words rather than numbers [Zad89]. It has a name and a term set which is a set of linguistic values (terms) defined over the definition domain of the linguistic variable. Each term is defined by its corresponding membership function.

Example: Let us consider the linguistic variable *temperature*. Its term set *T(temperature)* could be *T(temperature) = {low, normal, hot}* where each term is characterized by a fuzzy set in a universe of discourse *U = [0, 300]*. We might interpret "low" as "a temperature below about 100°C," "normal" as "a temperature close to 120°C" and "hot" as "a temperature above about 130°C". These terms can be characterized as fuzzy sets whose membership functions are shown in Figure 1. Each element u ∈ U belongs to a fuzzy set F with a degree of membership $\mu_F(u)$ ∈ [0, 1]. For example, if the current temperature is 90°C then the membership degree to the fuzzy subset *low* is equal to 0.5.

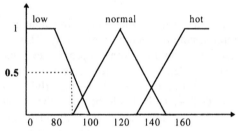

Figure 1. Membership functions of the linguistic variable temperature.

The domain of a linguistic variable is defined using a *linguistic type*. For example, we assume that the above linguistic variable is of the linguistic type called *Temperature* which can be defined as follows[1]:

```
CREATE LING TYPE Temperature float (
     low        TRAPEZOID (0, 0, 80, 100),
     normal     TRAPEZOID (90, 120, 120, 150),
     hot        TRAPEZOID (130, 160, 300, 300)
)
```

2.2 Rule Set Functions

A fuzzy logic rule takes the form of *if-then* statement such as "if X IS A then Y IS B" where X and Y are linguistic variables, A and B are terms. The *if* part of a fuzzy *if-then* rule is called the *antecedent* (or premise), whereas the *then* part is called the *consequent*. The antecedent part of a fuzzy rule is a conjunction and/or a disjunction of *fuzzy propositions* such as (X IS A) where *X* is a linguistic variable representing a database value, fuzzyfied using the term A.

---

[1] The syntax of the language RQL/F used in these examples is based on SQL. The full syntax of the language elements can be found in the extended version of this paper in ftp://ftp.vtt.fi/pub/projects/rapid/tempo-design.ps.

A *rule set* is a series of *if-then* statements, grouped in a structure called *a rule set function*. The idea behind it is to utilize the expressive power of fuzzy rules and to take the advantages of the fuzzy inference by incorporating the rule set as a function call in the trigger condition part. Formally, the rule set function is defined as follows:

$$RSF : \{R \times S_i\} \to D$$

where R is a set of fuzzy rules in which the consequent linguistic variable should be the same one occurring in all the fuzzy rules in R. S_i refers to the current state of the database. The range of RSF, D, is a domain (universe of discourse) of the output linguistic variable. Thus, RSF yields a value which can be used in a regular comparison predicate evaluating, in turn, to *true* or *false*.

Example: Let us consider a rule set function which monitors the speed and the temperature of a motor. Each fuzzy rule in the rule set traduces the occurrence of an alarming condition. Let us assume the default alarm value is "a_none" which is considered as an output when none of these rules is fired (no alarm). We are interested in specifying rules leading to other alarm values. The rule set may be defined as follows:

```
CREATE RULE SET ControlAlarm (temperature Temperature, speed Speed)
    Severity DEFAULT a_none(
        IF temperature IS normal AND speed IS high THEN a_low,
        IF temperature IS high AND speed IS very_high THEN a_high,
        ...)
```

The rule set `ControlAlarm` monitors the temperature and the speed parameters of a motor. The rule set expresses the conditions when the operator should be alarmed. In order to simplify the syntax, the output linguistic variable does not appear explicitly in the example shown above (only its type is specified as "Severity").

2.3 C-fuzzy Triggers

A C-fuzzy trigger is a regular ECA trigger which includes, in its condition part, a function call to a rule set. The execution semantics of a C-fuzzy trigger is based on the execution model of regular ECA trigger as shown in [WC96], p. 17. In its simple form, the *rule processing algorithm*, which characterize the execution model, repeatedly executes three consecutive calculations performed when an event occurs:

1. detecting an event and finding a relevant trigger,
2. evaluating the condition and
3. executing the action if the condition is true.

Our approach of incorporating fuzzy inference into triggers requires only the modification of the second calculation step of the above rule processing algorithm. The condition contains a rule set function call which takes place during the condition evaluation. The following three calculation steps are included in the evaluation of each rule set function call:

2.1 *Fuzzification:* the fuzzification is the process of converting crisp input data to fuzzy sets. The linguistic variables in the antecedent part of the rules are evaluated, i.e. the corresponding source data are mapped into their membership functions and truth values then fed into the rules. We are assuming no fuzzy values need to be stored in the database.

2.2 *Inference:* The most commonly used fuzzy inference method is the so-called *Max-Min inference method* [Lee90], in particular in engineering applications [Men95]. The Max-Min inference method is applied to the rule set, producing a fuzzy conclusion.

2.3 *Defuzzification:* the result of the fuzzy inference is a fuzzy set. The defuzzyfication step produces a representative crisp value as the final output of the system. There are several defuzzification methods [Lee90, Men95]. The most commonly used is the *Centroid (Center-of-gravity) defuzzifier* which provides a crisp value based on the center-of-gravity of the result (the output fuzzy set). The Center-of-gravity method yields to a crisp function value which is then applied to the comparison predi cate.

Example: Let us assume that, when the returned defuzzified value of the rule set function is between two and three, then a medium-level alarm is raised. A corresponding trigger can be defined as follows:

```
CREATE TRIGGER Trig_alarm_medium INSERT ON motor
    WHEN (ControlAlarm(temp, speed) > 2 AND
          ControlAlarm(temp, speed) <= 3)
    (MediumTempAlarm@TempAlarms)
```

If the condition is satisfied, the action specified as `MediumTempAlarm@TempAlarms` is executed. Note that the action part contains a call to an external procedure, i.e. the action of a trigger is executed outside the database. This feature is significant for control room applications of complex industrial processes (e.g. a paper mill or a power plant).

3 TEMPO Fuzzy Trigger Implementation

The TEMPO Server has been written in C++ and it runs both in the Unix (HP-UX) and Windows NT environments. Its object model comprises of 147 C++ classes. The *Client/Server* and *Server/Action Server* protocols have been implemented using the Socket API. For in-process multithreading, the libraries of Win32 API (for Windows NT) and the DCE-compliant *pthread* package (for Unix) were used. A free demonstration package of TEMPO Server for Windows NT (and Windows 95) is available for downloading from our web site (http://www.vtt.fi/tte/projects/tempo/). The following subsections present selected topics of the implementation.

3.1 Architecture Overview

The TEMPO Server is a prototype active database system equipped with C-fuzzy triggers. It has been designed for maintaining rapidly changing temporal data acquired from an industrial process. The requirements of such environments have been analyzed in a previous case study [WKP96] which have led to the development of RapidBase—an active time series database system. TEMPO Server has been built by extending RapidBase. In terms of external characteristics, the RQL language of RapidBase has been extended with constructs to define database objects related to rule set processing: linguistic types and terms, rules and rule sets. The trigger syntax has been modified to include rule set calls in the trigger conditions (predicates). The syntax of the resulting language, RQL/F, is demonstrated in the examples appearing in this paper.

In the true spirit of contemporary database systems, all the objects of newly introduced database types may be maintained dynamically by the user: they can be created, dropped or modified at any time. In the same time, the referential integrity constraints among the objects are maintained by the system.

Figure 2 depicts the essential components of the TEMPO Server. All the parts shown are comprised within a single operating system process. The server process maintains network connections to client programs submitting RQL/F requests and connections to programs responsible for executing triggers actions (such programs are called *Action Servers*). Following the RapidBase operation model, TEMPO Server supports external trigger actions of arbitrary semantics. The unit of concurrency control and recovery is a single RQL/F command.

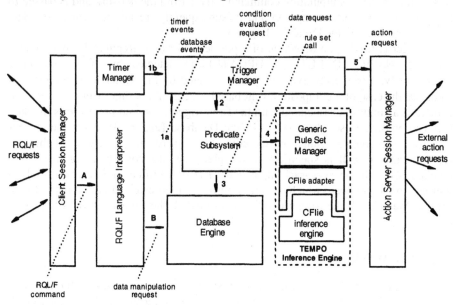

Figure 2. General architecture of the TEMPO Server.

Brief descriptions of the TEMPO components are given below:

- The *Managers* are entities responsible for maintaining, persistently, certain objects. The requests to create and modify such objects are directed, to the managers, by the *RQL/F Language Interpreter* (the requests are not shown in the picture).

- The *Database Engine* is a low-level main-memory-based data manager maintaining database table objects and indices.

- The *Predicate Subsystem* provides services to create pre-compiled predicates of the complexity allowed by the RQL/F language. The predicate objects themselves are managed either by the interpreter (if they are related to data manipulation commands) or by the Trigger Manager (if they are a part of a trigger definition).

- The *TEMPO Inference Engine* comprises a generic component and a specific third-party fuzzy inference software (CFlie[2]).

As compared to RapidBase, the Inference Engine is the only entirely new component. Of the other components, only two had to be modified: the Predicate Subsystem—to be able to make use of the rule set objects, and the interpreter—to accept the new language syntax.

3.2 Run-time Trigger Processing

The arrows shown in the figure illustrate the advancing of the run-time trigger processing. A data manipulation command arrives from the network and is passed to the interpreter for processing (A) and it, subsequently, results in elementary data requests executed by the Database Engine (B).

A trigger is fired upon detection of a pre-defined event. Regular database events (of type INSERT, DELETE or UPDATE) are detected by the engine (1a). Alternatively, a triggering event may be generated by the Timer Manager (1b), as would be the case of a composite-event based trigger, like a timer trigger [WKP96]. If there is a condition associated with the fired trigger, a stored predicate is invoked (2). The predicate uses the services of the Database Engine (3) to get the current data for the predicate evaluation, including the data for the evaluation of the rule set. If a rule set call is specified, in the predicate, the corresponding rule set is invoked (4) with the necessary input data. The defuzzified rule set call result is returned to the predicate which, in turn, returns the predicate evaluation result to the Trigger Manager. If the trigger condition is satisfied, the trigger action is requested (5).

3.3 Predicate Subsystem

The Predicate Subsystem of the TEMPO Server consists of a set of hierarchical, tree-like *predicate objects*, which are used for evaluating the predicates of RQL/F queries and trigger conditions. Fuzzy inference is fully encapsulated within these objects. Any predicate can contain a rule set call as a sub-expression anywhere in the tree structure. From the point of view of the system, a rule set call is simply an expression that returns a floating-point value. The return value can then be used in other predicate expressions, e.g. in a comparison. The arguments to the rule set call

---

[2] Originally developed as *Flie* at Institute of Robotics, ETH, Zurich, Switzerland; converted to C at Lab. for Concurrent Computing Systems, Swinburne Univ. of Technology, Hawthorn, Australia.

can be any expressions, e.g. column values, constants or even other rule set calls. The fuzzification of the argument values and the defuzzification of the result value are handled inside the Inference Engine. The Predicate Subsystem only needs to pass the crisp argument values to the Inference Engine and call the proper rule set function.

3.4 Inference Engine

TEMPO Inference Engine consists of two main modules: *Generic Rule Set Manager* (GRSM) and the *CFlie inference engine*. GRSM is responsible for storing and maintaining rule set objects by creating, modifying and deleting them. The CFlie inference engine is the software module that implements the inference method. We chose CFlie because of its speed and simplicity. However, CFlie can be easily replaced with some other inference engine package, since the GRSM is implemented in such a way, that it fully hides the underlying engine implementation from other parts of the system.

4 Performance

The performance of the fuzzy trigger system was measured using two kind of tests: i) performance of the TEMPO Inference Engine alone and ii) the total throughput of the TEMPO Server in trigger-intensive processing. The selected metrics allow us to asses the applicability of the approach to real life applications. The tests were run in a 133 MHz Pentium PC with 32 MB of main memory. The operating system was Windows NT 4.0. The database size was tailored to the size of available main memory so no page faults were occurring.

In the first test, the speed of the inference process was evaluated by way of full load of inserts to a database table, each causing a fuzzy trigger firing. The performance of the TEMPO Inference Engine was isolated from the overall performance of the system by running the tests with two trigger configurations. In the first case, only one trigger was used. In the second case, two identical triggers were used. No action requests were generated. The Inference Engine performance was calculated by dividing the speed difference of the two cases by the number of inserts. In both cases, five test runs with 10 000 inserts to a database table were used. To find out the non-fuzzy condition evaluation time, similar tests with normal triggers, without fuzzy predicates, were also performed.

With the rule set of eight rules, each consisting of two premise predicates and one conclusion predicate, one fuzzy condition evaluation took approximately 0,45 ms. With 64 rules the corresponding result value was 0,55 ms. With non-fuzzy triggers, one condition evaluation was approximately 0,1 ms (Fig. 3a).

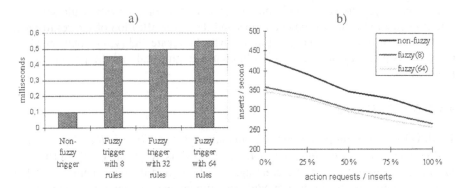

Figure 3. Results of a) the TEMPO Inference Engine performance, b) the TEMPO Server throughput performance.

The speed difference between non-fuzzy and fuzzy condition evaluation can be clearly seen. It is caused by a start-up overhead of the rule set processing. However, it should be noted that the number of rules in a rule set has only a slight effect on the performance.

In the second test, the full TEMPO Server throughput was measured (Fig. 3b). In addition to the condition evaluation time of a trigger, also the overhead caused by the insert request processing and action request transmission were taken into account. Three kind of tests were performed: i) with normal, non-fuzzy trigger, ii) with a fuzzy trigger using a rule set of 8 rules and iii) with a fuzzy trigger using a rule set of 64 rules. Five test runs with 10 000 inserts were used with each of the above cases. Among the test cases, the relative amount of inserts causing action requests, was varied.

The difference between non-fuzzy and fuzzy trigger throughput is notable. It can be explained with the speed difference of the condition evaluation of non-fuzzy and fuzzy triggers (see Fig. 3a). Increasing the relative amount of action requests from 0% to 100% of inserts, decreases the maximum insertion speed by approximately 25% in both non-fuzzy and fuzzy trigger tests. It is worth noting that the number of rules in a rule set has only infinitesimal effect on the overall performance.

5 Conclusions

We have investigated a seamless approach of integrating fuzzy logic rules with a traditional active database server. We have also demonstrated a feasible implementation of the proposed C-fuzzy trigger model. The performance results enforce our confidence in the approach as a way to alleviate the data explosion problem in data-intensive industrial applications. The benefits and the application domains of C-fuzzy triggers are summarised in [BW96] with some open research problems.

References

[BW96]   Bouaziz T. and Wolski A. *Incorporating Fuzzy Inference into Database Triggers.* Research Report No TTE1-2-96, VTT Information Technology, Espoo, Finland, November 1996.

[BW97]   Bouaziz T. and Wolski A. *Applying Fuzzy Events to Approximate Reasoning in Active Databases.* In Proceedings of the IEEE International Conference on Fuzzy Systems, Barcelona, Spain, July 1-5, 1997.

[GKB+84] Gupta M.M, Kandel, A., Bandler, W. and Kiszka, J. (Eds.). *Approximate Reasoning in Expert Systems.* Elsevier Science Publishers, North-Holland, 1984.

[JP93]   Jokiniemi, J. and Palomäki, A. *Real-Time Databases: A Needs Survey.* Research Report No. J-15, Lab. for Information Processing, VTT, Helsinki, February 1993, 13 pp.

[KY96]   Klir G.J. and Yuan B. (Eds.). *Fuzzy Sets, Fuzzy Logic, and Fuzzy Systems: Selected Papers by Lotfi A. Zadeh.* In Advances In Fuzzy Systems-Applications and Theory, Volume 6, 1996, 821 pages.

[Lee90]   Lee C.C. *Fuzzy Logic in Control Systems: Fuzzy Logic Controller-Part I and II.* In IEEE Transaction on Systems, Man, and Cybernetics, Vol. 20, No. 2, March/April 1990, pp. 404-435.

[Men95] Mendel J. M. *Fuzzy Logic Systems for Engineering: A Tutorial.* In Proc. of the IEEE, Special Issues on Engineering Applications of Fuzzy Logic, Vol. 83, No. 3, March 1995, pp. 345 - 377.

[PBW96] Pesonen, A., Bouaziz, T., and Wolski, A. *Case Study: Applying Fuzzy Triggers to a Drive Control System.* Research Report No. J-6/96, VTT Information Technology, Espoo, Finland, August 1996.

[WC96]   Widom J. and Ceri S. *Introduction to Active Database Systems.* In Widom J. and, Ceri S. (Eds.), "Active Database Systems: Triggers and Rules For Advanced Database Processing", Morgan Kaufmann, 1996, pp. 1-41.

[WKP96] Wolski A., Karvonen J., and Puolakka A. *The RAPID Case Study: Requirements for and the Design of a Fast-Response Database System.* Proceedings of the First Workshop on Real-Time Databases (RTDB'96), March 7-8, Newport Beach, CA, USA, pp. 32-39. (also at ftp://ftp.vtt.fi/pub/projects/rapid/case.ps).

[Zad75] Zadeh L.A. *Fuzzy Logic and Approximate Reasoning.* In Synthese, 30, 1975, pp. 407-428. (also in [KY96]).

[Zad84] Zadeh L.A. *The Role of Fuzzy Logic in the Management of Uncertainty in Expert Systems.* In [GKB+84], pp. 3-31.

[Zad89] Zadeh L.A. *Knowledge Representation in Fuzzy Logic.* In IEEE Transactions on Knowledge and Data Engineering, 1(1), 1989, pp. 89-100.

Supporting and Maintaining Derivations:
A Declarative Active Approach

Mohammad Said Desouki, Ana Simonet, Michel Simonet

Laboratoire TIMC-IMAG
Faculté de Médecine de Grenoble
38706 La Tronche cedex - France
e-mail: Said.Desouki@imag.fr,(Ana,Michel).Simonet@imag.fr

Abstract. Derivations in object-oriented databases are supported currently by means of imperative methods or by using deductive or even active rules. As imperative languages are difficult to analyze in order to extract dependencies, derivations are never maintained and attributes are calculated each time they are requested. Deductive rules, inherited from the relational model, are a declarative manner to express derivations, but they do not provide a maintenance mechanism. Active rules can be used to maintain derivations, but they are event-oriented whereas derivations are naturally data-oriented. We propose to join the advantages of both the declarative expression of the deductive approach and the automatic maintenance of the active approach. We aim at defining a declarative language to express mono-valued, multi-valued and recursive derivations in an object-oriented database context, and maintaining these derivations using a dependency graph.

1 Introduction

Attribute derivation in object-oriented database systems is the mirror of procedural attachment in knowledge base systems, which has deductive and active aspects [4]. Procedural attachment is purely procedural, hence its name. It uses imperative programming languages, or sometimes it calls external procedures [12]. However, the advantages of declarativity are known: programming facility and productivity, simple semantics, and ease of parallel processing, optimization and analysis [10]. Language analysis is particularly important in a derivation context. In fact, the values of some attributes are interdependent. For example, the salary of a person depends on his grade. It is necessary to know the dependencies between the derived attribute and the other attributes, in order to maintain the value of the derived attribute during the database life cycle. When a value is dynamically modified, it is necessary to assume the coherence of the values depending on it. The simplest strategy to preserve coherence is to never store the calculated value; thus the base is always coherent because the value is calculated each time it is requested. However the price to pay is the computation time at each access.

Deductive rules are a declarative manner to express derivations, but they do not provide a maintenance mechanism. The deduced facts are the logical consequences of the database facts using the specified deduction rules. Deductive rules are mainly used to define views and complex computations and to respond to queries, but their results are not materialized, i.e., they are calculated every time they are requested. This avoids the maintenance of the derived relations, which is considered a difficult task. Also, the integration of these rules in the object oriented model creates some impedance mismatch problems [11].

Another possible choice consists in storing the calculated value, and providing the user with a mechanism to specify the necessary actions to be taken after each modification in order to preserve coherence. Usually this is done using active or ECA (Event Condition Action) rules. An active rule specifies actions to be automatically carried out in response to some specific event when a certain condition is satisfied [6]. Active databases still lack theoretical foundations [5]; the consistency of a set of rules, the coherence of the fired rules, and the termination of the execution phase are not assured. Recently, many research [9] has been done to establish theoretical foundations and appropriate semantics to active databases. Also, some research [1] has been done into providing static analysis techniques for predicting whether a given rule set is guaranteed to terminate, and whether rule execution is confluent. However, derivations are naturally data-oriented, i.e. the values of derived attributes are expressed as functions of values of other attributes, whereas active rules are event-oriented. It follows that many active rules are needed to express a simple dependency relationship which can be encoded in a simple derivation formula.

The most adequate solution is to maintain coherence automatically using derivations, without asking the user to specify additional rules. When a value is calculated, it is stored, but when some values on which it depends have been modified, it is marked to be recalculated at its next access. We aim at following this solution by defining a simple declarative language for derivations, in order to extract dependencies easily and automatically. We then use a dependency graph to represent dependencies and to maintain the coherence of the database automatically. Our approach combines the advantages of both declarative expression of deductive rules and automatic processing of active rules in an object oriented database context. Our language has a high abstraction level, and it is completely integrated within the object model. Mono-valued, multi-valued and recursive derivations are possible and all derivations are maintained automatically. We try to design a dependency model which preserves the database consistency regarding derivation tools in an active way.

2 Related Work

A derived attribute is an attribute whose value is calculated using the values of some other attributes. As the value of a derived attribute is always derivable from the attributes on which it depends, it is usually considered that this value does not need to be stored. It is calculated at each read access, even if nothing has been changed in the database. This may be reasonable if derivations are simple, but in some fields such as molecular biology, some useful calculations may need a considerable time to be computed, hence the interest of storing the calculated value. However, storing the calculated value will require that it be maintained at each modification of the values on which it depends. Storing and maintaining may be the right strategy when the number of "read" operations is significantly grater than that of modifications, which is often the case in usual database applications. In such situations, the computation time to maintain derivations will be negligible compared to that of attribute calculations.

In works which follow the procedural attachment approach, a method is associated with each derived attribute to deduce its value. As the logic of the method used to make the derivation is hidden from the model, operations of analysis and extraction of the dependencies are impossible. An example of such a situation is the calculation of the attribute Tax:

    class PERSON
    attributes
            Name : STRING;
            Salary : REAL;
            Tax : REAL Calculate_Tax(Salary);

where $Calculate\_Tax$ is called each time the attribute Tax is accessed even if the attribute $Salary$ has not been changed.

When derivations become more complex (e.g., recursive derivations), it is interesting to use deductive rules. In some systems, such as $Peplom^d$ [3], the body of a method may be a deductive rule. For example, the $Ancestors$ attribute may be calculated by the following rule:

    Ancestors(X) :- this.Parents(X)
               | this.Parents(Y) & Y.Ancestors(X)

Many authors [2] claim that merging update features in a declarative language is the most critical problem of deductive databases. They define updates as *logic + control*, and agree on the need to introduce some form of control in deductive rules without moving to the all-procedural solution of object oriented languages.

In ECA models, derivations are expressed as active rules where events are modifications and actions are updates. One rule is needed for each modification. It specifies the update operation to perform given this modification. For example, to express a dependency between the attributes x, y, z and w where $x = y*z+w$, three active rules are needed:

    $ON(ModificationOf\ y)$
    $IF(True)$
    $DO(Modify\ x\ by\ x = y*z+w);$
    $ON(ModificationOf\ z)$............................
    $ON(ModificationOf\ w)$............................

PARDES [7] is a data-driven oriented active database model which extends the ECA model by adding data driven rules which can express derivations in a simpler manner. Derivations are translated into a dependency graph which is used to infer the actions to be taken on each event. For example, the derivation:

    $Order\_Price := sum(Quantity * Price)$

is used to update the attribute $Order\_Price$ when the attribute $Quantity$ or

Price is modified or when a new item is created or removed from the *order* class. It constitutes an interesting extension of active databases but it is limited to simple arithmetic derivations.

3 The Derivation Language

We aim at defining a derivation language with well determined semantics and a high abstraction level. A simple way of expressing relations between attributes or derived data is to give a set of formulas (assertions or invariants). Although these specifications are simple, they are a natural way to define dependencies between data.

A computational assertion is a relation between attributes which has the form of an integrity constraint, because it is not only used to derive values, but also to maintain the derived values. It expresses that an attribute is derived in a certain way and that the defined relationship is always verified. An assertion can access all the (known) attributes of the concerned object. We consider two kinds of assertion: simple and conditional.

A simple assertion is an equality between the derived attribute and an arithmetical or logical or set expression among attributes or values with the possibility of using path expressions to access the attributes of other object levels.

$$attribute = expression\_of(attributes)$$

For example, the *Tax* attribute in a class *PERSON* is maintained using a simple assertion: $Tax = Salary * 0.025$.

```
class PERSON
attributes Name : STRING;
           Salary : REAL;
           Tax : REAL calc stored;
           Brothers : SetOf PERSON;
           Parents : SetOf PERSON;
           Children : SetOf PERSON;
```

When the value of *Tax* is consulted, if it is not up to date the calculation is fired and the new value is stored. Also, when *Salary* is modified, the attribute *Tax* is marked to be recalculated the next time it is consulted.

As an example of multi-valued derivation consider the calculation of the attribute *Cousins* in the same class *PERSON*:

$Cousins = Parents.Brothers.Children$

Here we use a path notation to denote the set of children of the brothers of the parents of the concerned object person.

A recursive derivation is a derivation of an attribute from an other attribute where the two attributes have the same domain and their values are related by some recursive rule. One example of recursive derivation is the derivation of the attribute *Ancestors* which can be specified by:

$Ancestors = Parents\ UNION\ Parents.Ancestors$

The two usual logical rules used to specify the calculation of *Ancestors* in ordinary systems are replaced here by a simple set formula. In fact, one distinctive feature of our approach is that it supports all the functionalities of deductive databases [8] without providing any theorem proving computational model in the database management system. However, it is capable of deducing additional information from the database by applying assertions.

To express all deductive computations we must provide conditional choice between many different computations, because some derivations have many forms of calculation where each form depends on one special condition.

A conditional assertion is a structure combining many simple assertions each of which is preconditioned.

$$Attribute = Precondition_1 : expression_1$$
$$Precondition_2 : expression_2$$
$$................$$
$$Precondition_n : expression_n$$
$$[otherwise : expression_{n+1}]$$

For example, the calculation of the attribute $Fact$:

$$Fact =$$
$$(Value = 0) : 1;$$
$$(Value = 1) : 1;$$
$$OTHERWISE : Value * Previous.Fact.$$

In a conditional assertion, the choice of assertions depends on preconditions. A precondition is a logical formula in normal conjunctive form. A special and optional precondition named *otherwise* may be specified at the end of a conditional assertion to take into account the cases which are not covered by the preconditions.

To assure the coherence, the preconditions of a conditional assertion must be mutually exclusive (disjointed). The verification of disjunction of these preconditions is performed at compile time to ensure that one assertion is available to calculate an attribute at a given moment. The special precondition *otherwise*, if it is specified, assures the completeness; if not the completeness is verified at compile time by verifying that the preconditions cover the domains of all its attributes.

An assertion is invoked when the value of the concerned attribute is consulted and it is unknown, or when it must be recalculated because the attribute is marked, for example because one of the attributes which it depends on has been modified. In both cases, the computation is fired only when the value is requested.

4 The Dependency Graph

Assertions are used to derive some attribute values from other values. The relationships between attributes, as expressed by these assertions, are coded into a dependency graph. This graph is constructed from the assertions at compile time. Each attribute is connected to the attributes which are used in its assertion.

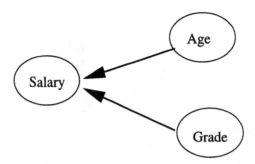

Fig. 1. Dependency between *Salary*, *Age*, and *Grade*.

When an attribute is modified, all the attributes whose derivation depends directly or indirectly on this modified attribute are marked to be calculated the next time they are consulted. Thus, the graph determines automatically the transitive closure of an update operation, i.e., all necessary modifications resulting from this update. Thus, the active processing which is ensured in active databases by rules specifying the necessary updates to perform when a modification occurs, is ensured here by the automatic propagation of modifications through the graph.

The strategy of materialization of derivations is semi-consistent, i.e., modifications resulting from updates are not executed immediately. Each modification is executed at the next access or consultation of its value. The use of a dependency graph makes the control mechanism minimal in the sense of the number of modifications, i.e, there is no redundancy. Marking attributes, instead of firing calculations immediately, minimizes computations, because even if several successive modifications have been performed only one calculation will be fired at the next read access operation. To avoid infinite cycles of updates in the dependency graph, an attribute may not be derived directly or indirectly from its own value.

4.1 Definitions

The dependency graph for a set of attributes is a directed graph such that:

- The nodes of the graph correspond to the set of all attributes that are calculated using an assertion or used in the body of an assertion.
- The edges of the graph correspond to a precedence relation that exists between the attributes appearing on the right hand side and the attribute on the left hand side of a computational assertion.

Thus all the attributes used in an assertion are connected to the derived attribute. Hence, the dependency graph contains the edge $a \longleftarrow b$ if there exists an assertion $a = expression(..., b, ...)$.

If an attribute b is used in the assertion of an attribute a, we say that a *depends on* b, which is denoted by $a \longleftarrow b$. Thus, in an assertion

$$a = expression(b_1, b_2, ..., b_n)$$

we have:

Furthermore, when $a \longleftarrow b$, subsequently, a depends indirectly on each attribute which b depends on. The concept of dependency is recursively applied to each assertion and its attributes: $a \longleftarrow b \longleftarrow c \longleftarrow ... \longleftarrow z$.

4.2 Dependency Graph Construction Algorithm

The algorithm consists in building an elementary dependency graph DG_i for each assertion D_i of an attribute $a_{i,0}$, and then merging all the DG_i in a unique dependency graph DG.

Input: A set of assertions D_i where each D_i is the computational assertion used to calculate the attribute $a_{i,0}$. Note that the dependencies of the conditions used in the conditional assertions are taken into account in the *expression_of*, and $a_{i,0} \neq a_{j,0}$ where $i \neq j$: there is only one assertion per attribute.

$$D_1 : a_{1,0} = expression\_of(a_{1,1}, a_{1,2}, ..., a_{1,K_1})$$
$$D_2 : a_{2,0} = expression\_of(a_{2,1}, a_{2,2}, ..., a_{2,K_2})$$
$$...$$
$$D_n : a_{n,0} = expression\_of(a_{n,1}, a_{n,2}, ..., a_{n,K_n})$$

Output: The dependency graph.

1. For each assertion D_i, $1 \leq i \leq n$, do
2.   Create the $a_{i,0}$ node in the dependency graph DG_i
     //The derived attributes.
3.   For $a_{i,j}$, $1 \leq j \leq k_i$, do
       3.1. Create the $a_{i,j}$ node in the dependency
            graph DG_i //The other attributes.
       3.2. Create an arc from $a_{i,j}$ to $a_{i,0}$ in DG_i
     End-For
   End-For
4. //Merging the dependency graphs DG_i in the final
     graph DG:
   If a node $a_{i,0}$ in DG_i = a node $a_{j,l}$ in DG_j
   where $l \neq 0, i \neq j$ then:
     Merge DG_i and DG_j by having the incoming
     arcs of $a_{i,0}$ point to $a_{j,l}$ and
     delete $a_{i,0}$
   End-If

4.3 Extending the Dependency Graph for Indirect and Recursive Dependencies

An indirect dependency is a dependency between the derived attribute and an attribute at another object level. It is expressed using the path notation to access attributes in other object levels. This is necessary because some attributes are also objects and have themselves attributes. For example, in the derivation:

$$Cousins = Parents.Brothers.Children$$

we specify the attribute *Cousins* of an object *Person* as the attribute *Children* of the persons which are in the attributes *Brothers* of the persons which are in the attribute *Parents* of the first person.

Constructing a dependency graph for such a dependency is not a straightforward task. It is not sufficient to specify that the attribute *Cousins* depends only on the attribute *Parents* which is at the same level. If we did so, the attribute *Cousins* must be recalculated only when the attribute *Parents*, is modified. If we consider that the attribute *Parents* (which contains two persons) will be modified if one of the attributes of one of the two persons is modified, then the attribute *Cousins* must be modified even if one of the *Parents*, for example, has changed his *Car*.

The required dependency graph to make here is that the attribute *Cousins* depends on the attribute *Parents* at the same object level (i.e., it depends on the *Parents* oids), but it also depends on the attribute *Brothers* of each object in *Parents* at another object level, and on the attribute *Children* of each object in *Brothers* at a third object level.

Encoding these dependencies into the current dependency graph at compile time is impossible, because we can only access one object level. That is why we have to extend the dependency graph.

A recursive dependency is a dependency encoding a recursive derivation. The derived attribute depends on itself recursively but at other object levels. This does not create cycles, but as for the indirect dependencies, it is impossible to encode the recursive dependency in the current dependency graph.

The Extended Dependency Graph. The extended dependency graph for a set of attributes is a directed graph such that:

- The nodes of the graph correspond to the set of all the attributes that are calculated using an assertion or used in the body of an assertion, and the set of reference nodes which correspond to path expressions.
- The edges of the graph correspond to a precedence relation that exists between the attributes, or the paths appearing on the right hand side and the attribute on the left hand side of an assertion.

Thus we have added to the graph a special kind of node which are the reference nodes. These nodes encode the path expressions in the assertions into the dependency graph. This extended graph is generated at compile time. It remains valid until the first calculation of the concerned derived attribute is completed.

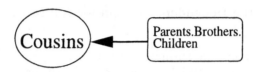

Fig. 2. The extended dependency graph for *Cousins*.

After the first derivation, the path expressions will be resolved and the graph will be turned into a normal dependency graph. When resolving a path expression, the corresponding reference node is replaced by a node for each attribute in the path expression (cf 4.4).

Extended Dependency Graph Construction Algorithm .

Input: A set of assertions D_i
$D_1 : a_{1,0} = expression\_of(a_{1,1}, a_{1,2}, ..., a_{1,K_1})$
$D_2 : a_{2,0} = expression\_of(a_{2,1}, a_{2,2}, ..., a_{2,K_2})$
$\quad ...$
$D_n : a_{n,0} = expression\_of(a_{n,1}, a_{n,2}, ..., a_{n,K_n})$

Output: The extended dependency graph.

1. For each assertion D_i, $1 \leq i \leq n$, do
2.   Create the $a_{i,0}$ node in the dependency graph DG_i
3.   For $a_{i,j}$, $1 \leq j \leq k_i$, do
        3.1. Create the $a_{i,j}$ node in the dependency
            graph DG_i
        3.2. Create an arc from $a_{i,j}$ to $a_{i,0}$ in DG_i
    End-For
   End-For
4.   For each path expression $path_{i,j}$, $1 \leq j \leq k_i$, do
        4.1. Create a $path_{i,j}$ reference node in
            the dependency graph DG_i
            //The reference nodes.
        4.2. Create an arc from $path_{i,j}$ to $a_{i,0}$ in DG_i
    End-For
   End-For
5. //Merging the dependency graphs DG_i in the final
    graph DG:
   If a node $a_{i,0}$ in DG_i = a node $a_{j,l}$ in DG_j
   where $l \neq 0, i \neq j$ then:
      Merge DG_i and DG_j by having the incoming
      arcs of $a_{i,0}$ point to $a_{j,l}$ and
      delete $a_{i,0}$
   End-If

4.4   Materializing Dependencies

The dependency graph is created at compile time and it specifies the relation between the attributes occurring at different object levels. But the dependency graph is not actually instanciated until execution. It is instanciated at run time when objects are created and thereafter attributes are attached.

The dependencies of the same object level (e.g., Age) are simply materialized by instanciating the corresponding graph when an object (e.g., PERSON) is accessed or manipulated. One general graph is needed and it is used to maintain dependencies between all the objects. The materialization of other dependencies (recursive and indirect) is delayed until the first calculation of their attributes. When this is done, an instance of the dependency graph is created for the concerned object, and the attributes (objects) used in the computation are attached to this dependency graph. Thus, there is in this case one dependency graph per object, and it is nothing more than a connection of the differents attributes by edges expressing their dependencies. In general, the indirect and recursive dependencies are dependencies between objects rather than dependencies between attributes, because they concern different object levels.

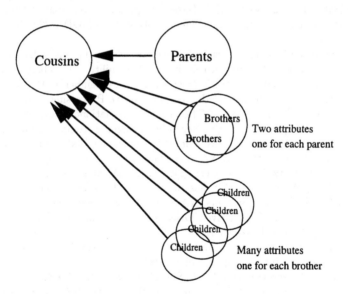

Fig. 3. The final dependency graph of *Cousins*.

5   Conclusion

We have presented a declarative approach to express derivations in an object-oriented database, which has taken advantage of both deductive and active approaches. The assertion language has a high abstraction level, it is simple, clear and expressive. Each assertion has a unique interpretation, and thus clearly determined semantics. The coherence problem does not arise, because there is one assertion per attribute, and when many assertions are used in a conditional assertion the disjunction of the preconditions is verified to ensure that the computation will be performed by only one assertion. In these assertions, the reasoning completeness is also verified to ensure that there is always an assertion to perform the derivation. Our approach maintains database consistency through a dependency graph. Modifications are propagated through the graph when values are updated. Finally, since dependencies are explicit, it is easy to analyze applications, to determine, for example, all possible effects of a single modification in the database.

References

1. A. Aiken, J. M. Hellerstein, J. Widom: Static Analysis Techniques for Detecting the Behaviour of Active Rules. ACM Trans. on Database Systems, Vol.20, No. 1, March 1995.
2. F. Cacace, S. Ceri, S. Crespi-Reghizzi, L. Tanca, R. Zicari: Integrating Object-Oriented Data Modeling with a Rule-Based programming paradigm. Proceeding of the ACM Conference on the Management of Data (SIGMOD), 225-236, Atlantic city, May 1990.
3. P. Dechamboux and C. Roncancio: Peplom: an Object Oriented Database Programming Language Extended with Deductive Capabilities. Database and Expert Systems Applications DEXA-94, LNCS (856), 2-14, September 1994.
4. M. S. Desouki and M. Simonet: Deductive and Active Processing in Database and Knowledge Base Systems. Proc. of The Second International Baltic Workshop on DB and IS, Workshops in Computing Series by Springer, Estonia, Talinn, June 1996.
5. M. S. Desouki, A. Simonet, and M. Simonet: Processing Deductions in an Active Fashion. Proc. of the 7th Int. DEXA Workshop, 23-29, Zurich, September 1996.
6. K.R. Dittrich, S. Gatziu, A. Geppert: The Active Database Management System Manifesto: A Rulebase of ADBMS Features. Proc. of the 2nd International Workshop on Rules in Database Systems, RIDS '95, Athens, September 1995.
7. O. Etzion, PARDES A Data-Driven Oriented Active Database Model. SIGMOD RECORD, Vol. 22, No. 1, March 1993.
8. G. Gardarin and E. Simon: Les systèmes de gestion de bases de données déductives. Technique et Science Informatiques, vol 6, 1987.
9. G. Gottlob, G. Moerkotte, and V. S. Subrahmanian: The PARK Semantics for Active Rules. Proc. of the 5th Int. Conf. on EDBT, LNCS 1057, March 1996.
10. J.W. Lloyd: Practical advantages of declarative programming. In Proc. of the Joint Conference on Declarative Programming, GULPRODE'94, 1994.
11. J. D. Ullman: A Comparison of Deductive an Object Oriented Database Systems. Deductive and Object Oriented Database DOOD'91, eds. C.Delobel, M. Kifer, Y. Masunaga, 263-277. Springer, LNCS 566, 1991.
12. T. Winograd. Frame Representation and the Declarative Procedural Controversy. Reading in knowledge representation, 357-370, edited by Brachman and Levesque, Morgan Kaufman publisher, California, 1985.

Modeling Histories in Object DBMS

Marie-Christine Fauvet, Jean-François Canavaggio, and Pierre-Claude Scholl

Laboratoire Logiciels, Systèmes et Réseaux, IMAG
Université de Grenoble, BP 72, 38402 St Martin D'Hères cedex (France)
Tel. +33 4 76 82 72 83, Fax. +33 4 76 82 82 87
e.mail: {FirstName1-FirstName2.Name@imag.fr}

Abstract. Temporal DBMS offer concepts and functionalities related to data timestamping and history management. Analyzing the numerous approaches in this field demonstrate a significant lack of unification of the main results, thus postponing the emergence of commercial products. This problem is about to be solved for the relational approach, e.g. through the definition of the TSQL2 language. However, there is still much to be done in the context of object DBMS. This paper proposes an historical model integrating the main functionalities needed by an object DBMS to cope with the data historical dimensions.

Key words: temporal databases, data history, temporal query object language, O_2.

1 Introduction

In conventional DBMS the use of temporal values is often limited, particularly with respect to their structure and the granularity of their definition. Furthermore, with these systems, a database state represents a snapshot of the reality as defined by the last update. When the need for maintaining data evolution arises, their history has to be managed at the application level, thus increasing data and programs complexity. Temporal DBMS aim at overcoming this lack of capabilities. The numerous studies in this field show the richness of the necessary concepts and the variety of proposals and experimentations [23,20]. However a significant lack of unification of the main results is observed, thus postponing the emergence of commercial products. The publication of a consensus glossary of the main temporal concepts [13] and the definition of the TSQL2 language [21] are examples showing that this problem is about to be solved for relational DBMS. However, there is no comparable results in the context of object data models.

The TEMPOS project[1] (Temporal Extension Model for Persistent Object Servers) investigates the feasability of a temporal server through the implementation of a prototype on top of the O_2 DBMS [8]. In this paper, we present preliminary results of the TEMPOS project: they include the definition of a multigranular temporal data model which gathers in an unified way the necessary concepts to model time and data histories. This model is formalized through the functional specification of type hierarchies and associated functions. It is validated through the implementation of O_2 classes.

---

[1] TEMPOS is part of the STORM project [1] which aims at extending object DBMS to deal with structural, temporal and active features of multimedia data.

This paper is organised as follows. In section 2 we briefly survey related works in the context of object oriented models. Section 3 describes our historical model based upon three views: attribute evolution status, history updating modalities and history representations. Section 4 presents history operations, illustrated on a classical example through typical temporal queries. Section 5 reports on the prototype development. Section 6 concludes the paper and sketches future work.

2 Related work

In the object oriented approaches (see [20] for a survey), temporal dimensions can be defined at the object level (e.g. TMAD [14], OSAM/T [22]) or at the attribute level (e.g. TOOSQL [16], OOTempSQL [6], TF-ORM [10], T-Chimera [2]) or at both levels (e.g. TIGUKAT [12], OODAPLEX [26]). Some of these studies support only a single time dimension (valid or transaction time), others support bitemporal time. Depending of the system, timestamp values may be instants, intervals or instant sets, and histories are seen as temporal functions or sequence of snapshots.

Most studies adopt a discrete model of time. Durations, instants and intervals (also termed periods) are the basic data types that can be manipulated directly through classical operations (order relations, arithmetic operations). Most proposals offer only a fixed set of standard time units (year, month, day, hour, minute, second). In OSAM/T [22], TIGUKAT [12], OODAPLEX [26], new time units can be implemented at the application level by adding specialized classes which include conversion methods.

All works aim at extending existing DBMS according to one of the three following architectures [24]:
− The temporal functionalities are integrated into the system. This should be the best solution from both the user point of view (homogeneity and facility of use) and the performance point of view (optimization and representation techniques). But it may be difficult or impossible to achieve, depending on the considered host DBMS.
− A temporal server (as in TMAD) groups the temporal services and acts as an interface between the application programs and the DBMS (see also [7,25]). This is transparent to the user who sees the whole as a temporal DBMS, but this solution may result in less efficiency, the temporal server being implemented above the DBMS.
− Application programs directly use a temporal library made of specific functions (as in TF-ORM [15]). Even if a good performance can be achieved, usability is not always the best, depending on the level of abstraction of the offered primitives.

Our objective is to investigate the feasability of a temporal server through the implementation of a prototype on top of the O2 DBMS. As a first step, we define a set of temporal types dedicated to the management of simple and complex temporal values and temporal relationships, and in particular of histories. The main guidelines of our approach are the following: to provide an extensible set of basic temporal types allowing to express temporal values with respect to any chosen calendar and to manage any necessary time units. To provide a specific history type constructor to render reasoning on histories independent of any particular internal or external representation. To provide a taxonomy of updates based upon an analysis of the various ways in which continuous or discrete phenomena can be observed.

3   Main features of the historical model

3.1   Model of time

We adopt a discret linear time model in which time is represented in a multi-granular way (see for instance [25]): based on an extensible set of temporal units this model takes into account the multiple levels of granularity at which time is observable. It comprises a variety of temporal types including instant, duration, interval and D-sequence (i.e. sequence of discontinuous intervals formalizing the notion of coalesced temporal element [13]). These types are provided with a rich set of operations which are independent of the units being involved. Because of space limitations, we do not further describe here this time model [11,5].

3.2   Temporal characteristics of objects and attributes

The *evolution status* of an attribute characterizes its behaviour in time and the way it is observed. An attribute is *constant* if it must not change in time, else it is *mutable*. A mutable attribute can be *historical* or *fugitive*: it is *historical* if its successive values are meaningful and thus recorded, whereas it is *fugitive* if only its most recent value is meaningful. An object is historical if at least one of its attributes is historical. It is constant if all of its attributes are constant. An object is fugitive if none of its attributes is historical and if at least one of its attribute is fugitive.

The *history* of an historical attribute includes whatever has to be kept from its evolution. It is a set of snapshots taken during the entity life at the instants considered to be relevant by the application. A *snapshot* is defined here as a temporal relation between a state and a timestamp representing the instant at which this state is observed. In order to differentiate these two kinds of values, we respectively term them *structural* and *temporal* values. In the following, a snapshot is said to be an I_snapshot, an X_snapshot or a D_snapshot respectively if the observation moment is an instant, an interval or a D_sequence.

The *temporal dimension(s)* of an historical attribute gives the meaning of its snapshots. The most noteworthy distinction is between *valid* and *transaction time* [13]: in the former case, temporal values date property changes in the (application) real world, whereas in the latter, they date database changes.

The *time unit* of an historical attribute gives the granularity at which its snapshots are observed. The *temporal domain* of an historical attribute is the definition domain of the associated histories seen as temporal functions. A temporal domain may evolves in time through specific updating operations[2].

---

[2] The temporal domain of an attribute is a subset of the entity lifespan. This allows to describe situations where a property is temporarily undefined. For instance, during the time an employee is off duty, all properties related to his work are undefined.

3.3   History updating modalities

An history is built from a succession of updates which provide the data reflecting the evolution of the corresponding attribute or some corrections on already recorded snapshots. Obviously, the recorded snapshots do not necessarily concern all instants of the temporal domain, their timestamps being chosen by the user according to a periodicity specific to the nature of the attribute. The structural values of the attribute at instants not described by such updates are defined according to several modalities presented below.

We say that a snapshot is *effective* when its structural value is given by an update operation. The *effective (temporal) domain* of an history is the set of corresponding timestamps. When the purpose of an update operation is to indicate that the structural value is missing in the reality, the value is said to be *absent*. Conversely, the *potential domain* of the history is the difference between the domain and the effective domain[3]. Related snapshots are said *potential* to stress the fact that their structural value is not necessarily absent and can be defined by a *temporal interpolation* according to the set of effective structural values.

We differentiate four kinds of historical attributes depending on the intended interpretation of their potential values:
— *Discrete* historical attribute: their potential values are always considered as absent (e.g. the history of the daily amount of books sold in a bookstore).
— *Regular* historical attribute: in this particular case of discrete attribute, the potential domain is empty. The temporal domain is dynamically defined by the update operations (e.g. the history of successive deposits on a bank account).
— *Stepwise* historical attribute: structural values are stable between two update operations (e.g. the history of a bank account balance).
— *Interpolated* historical attribute: potential values are defined by a temporal interpolation function (e.g. the history of a physical continuous process).

When the temporal dimension is the transaction time, historical attributes are, by nature, stepwise attributes.

3.4   History representations, chronicles

Any sequence of snapshots is called a *chronicle*. The temporal domain of a chronicle is implicitly given by the snapshots it is made of. A chronicle can be interpreted as a regular history. On the other hand history representations are based upon chronicle representations.

We specialize several kinds of chronicles. An I_chronicle is a sequence of I_snapshots in chronological order. An X_chronicle is a sequence of X_snapshots (with mutually disjoint intervals) in increasing order with respect to the relation *precedes* on intervals[4]. In a *canonical* X_chronicle the intervals are maximal, i.e two consecutive X_snapshots timestamped by contiguous intervals have different structural values. A D_chronicle is a sequence of D_snapshots with mutually distinct structural values.

---

[3] In the same way, [18] differentiates *time points* and *data points*. They correspond to our potential and effective domains.

[4] [I..J] precedes [K..L] $\iff$ J < K

The representation in *intention* of an history consists of its temporal domain, the chronicle of its effective snapshots and its interpolation function. In the cases of regular, discrete or stepwise attributes, this function is built in the system, whereas for interpolated attributes, it is explicitly given by the user.

The representation in *extension* of an history enumerates the complete set of its snapshots according to its temporal domain. It is thus a chronicle built from an appropriate interpretation of the potential snapshots according to the kind of associated historical attribute.

4 Operations on histories

The model includes a set of high level primitives on histories: they allow the user to reason on histories independently of their possible representations and they alleviate the burden of navigation through objects implementing histories. These operations, taken from several contexts, are adapted to our model and validated, through their facility of use in typical examples [11] and their implementation in the prototype. We illustrate here two kinds of operations: temporal extensions of the relational algebra adapted to the object context (see for instance [23,9]); iterators on sequences (see for instance [3,17]) adapted to histories and taking advantage of the chronological order. For each operator, we give a functional specification followed by some queries in the OQL language extended by the operators. Each query is preceded by a comment stating the type of the result.

4.1 A modeling example

We illustrate our approach on a simple standard example about employees working in a general store organized in several departments (figure 1). An employee is identified by his first name. At any time, he lives at some unique address, belongs to only one department and earns an unique (monthly) salary. Each department is identified by its name; at any time, the department staff (non empty set of employees) is managed by a single employee.

```
class Employee <
    name: Constant(string),              class Department <
    address: History(day,string),            name: Constant(string),
    salary: History(month,real),             manager: History(day,Employee)
    hireDate: Fugitive(Instant(day)),        staff: History(day,{Employee}) >
    assignment: History(month,Department)>
```

Fig. 1. classes Employee and Department

Attributes name in the classes Employee and Department are constant. Hire-Date is a fugitive attribute: it may change in case of correction, but only its most recent value is meaningful. Its type is Instant at the granularity of day. Attributes address, salary and assignment in the class Employee and attributes manager and staff in the class Department are historical attributes (granularity: month or day). For the sake of simplicity, we consider here only the valid time dimension and we assume that all historical attributes are stepwise. The temporal domain of attributes address, manager and staff is defined statically as $[0..\infty[$. An employee can be temporarily on leave; thus, the temporal domain of attributes salary and assignment is defined dynamically, so as to represent employee's actual working time. TheEmployees and TheDepartments are the persistent roots of classes Employee and Department.

4.2 Notations

In the examples the following notations are used: Nil denotes an absent value; <T1, T2, ..., Tn>, [T], {T} and T1 $\longrightarrow$ T2 denote type constructors, respectively, tuples, sets, sequences and functions. T1(T2) denotes an instance of type T1 parametrized by type T2; u being a time unit, Instant(u), Interval(u) and D_sequence(u) denote the restrictions to unit u of the corresponding types. History (u, T) (resp. Chronicle (u, T)) denotes an history (resp. chronicle) type: u is the observation unit and T is the structural value type. In order to describe function values, we use the lambda notation, λx1,x2,... • E where the symbol λ introduces the parameter names x1,x2,.. and the symbol • introduces the expression E defining the function.

4.3 Projection, temporal restriction, natural temporal join

History projection: Let T be a tuple type, N be the set of its attribute names, X be a non empty subset of N, h be an history of type History(u, T). Then h[X] denotes the projection of history h with respect to X, i.e. the history deduced from h by projection of each of its snapshots with respect to X. The type of the result is Chronicle(u, T[X]).

R.1 : *For each employee give his name and the history of his assignments (department name).*

> { *type:* {<*name : string, assign : Chronicle (month, string)*>} }
> select tuple (name : e.name, assign : e.assignment[name]) from e in TheEmployees

History temporal restriction: Applying a *temporal restriction* operator to an history h yields a chronicle made of snapshots selected in h according to a predicate P. The symbol Γ is used to denote this operator. We particularize two forms of temporal restrictions:

> _ Γ_{if} _: History(u,T), (T $\longrightarrow$ boolean) $\longrightarrow$ Chronicle(u,T)
> { h Γ_{if} P = {<I,v> | <I,v> $\in$ h $\wedge$ P(v)} }
> _ Γ_{in} _: History(u,T), {Instant(u)} $\longrightarrow$ Chronicle(u,T)
> { h Γ_{in} F = {<I,v> | <I,v> $\in$ h $\wedge$ I $\in$ F} }

R.2 : *For each employee give his name and his assignment history restricted to the period [1-1990...12-1996]*

> { *type:* {<*name: string, assign: Chronicle (month, Department)*>} }
> select tuple (name: e.name, assign: e.assignment Γ_{in} [@'1-1990'..@'12-1996'])
> from e in TheEmployees
> { *The expression [@'1-1990'..@'12-1996'] denotes the interval bounded by the two instants '1-1990' and '12-1996'.* }

R.3 : *For each employee give his name and his address history while living elsewhere than in Paris.*

> { *type:* {<*name: string, adr: Chronicle (day, string)*>} }
> select tuple (name: e.name, adr: e.address Γ_{if} λa • a $\neq$ 'Paris')
> from e in TheEmployees

History temporal join: The *natural temporal join* of two histories h1 and h2 of types History(u, T1) and History(u, T2) is a chronicle of type Chronicle(u, <T1, T2>). Its snapshots are built from the snapshots of h1 and h2 timestamped by a same instant. We differentiate the internal and the external join, respectively noted by the symbols $*_\cap$ and $*_\cup$, depending on whether the resulting history temporal domain is the intersection or the union of the given history temporal domains.

- $*_{\cap-}$: History(u, T1), History(u, T2) $\longrightarrow$ Chronicle (u, <T1,T2>)
  $\{\ h1 *_\cap h2 = \{<I,<v1,v2>> \mid <I,v1> \in h1 \wedge <I,v2> \in h2\}\ \}$
- $*_{\cup-}$: History(u, T1), History(u,T2) $\longrightarrow$ Chronicle (u, <T1,T2>)
  $\{\ h1 *_\cup h2 = h1 *_\cap h2$
  $\cup \{<I,<v1, Nil>> \mid <I,v1> \in h1 \wedge I \in TDom(h1) \setminus TDom(h2)\}$
  $\cup \{<I,<Nil, v2>> \mid <I,v2> \in h2 \wedge I \in TDom(h2) \setminus TDom(h1)\}.\ \}$
  { *h being an history, TDom(h) is the temporal domain of h.* }

R.4 : *For each employee having been working in the Toys department, give his name and his address history while he was assigned to the Toys department.*

The idea is to build for each employee the temporal join of his address and assignment histories, the latter being restricted to the time he is assigned to the Toys department.

{ *type:* {<*name: string, sal: Chronicle (month, string)>*} }
select tuple (name: e.name,
$\qquad$ sal: (e.address $*_\cap$(e.assignment Γ_{if} λd • d.name = 'Toys'))[address])
from d in TheDepartments, e in flatten (SDom (d.staff)) where d.name = 'Toys'
{ *h being an history SDom(h) is the set of structural values belonging to h's snapshots. SDom(d.staff) is a set of sets of employees; flatten (SDom (d.staff)) is a set of employees.* }

R.5 : *When did Gaston earn more than Zoé?*

To illustrate the external join, we choose here to retain the instants at which Gaston earns more than Zoé, both being known (not Nil) or the instants at which Gaston's salary is known and Zoé's one is unknown.

{ *type:* {*Instant(month)*} }
select Tdom ((g.salary $*_\cup$z.salary),
$\qquad$ Γ_{if} λ <sg,sz> • sg $\neq$ Nil $\wedge$ (sz $\neq$ Nil $\wedge$ sg > sz $\vee$ sz = Nil))
from g in TheEmployees, z in TheEmployees
where g.name = 'Gaston' and z.name = 'Zoé'

4.4 Iterators on sequences

We apply here some basic sequence iterators [17] to histories. They provide a good way to deal with the succession in time of structural values. Such iterators are: **Map**, the pointwise application of a function to the elements of a sequence; **Selection** of the elements satisfying a predicate; **TheCouples** which builds the sequence of consecutive couples in a given sequence; **LeftPart** and **RightPart** which split a sequence S into two parts L and R according to a predicate P (S = L & R) so that R's first element is the first element of S (from left to right) satisfying P.

R.6 : *Give Zoé's assignment history since the first time she has been assigned to the Toys department.*

{ *type: Chronicle (month, Department)* }
select RightPart (X_Hist (e.assignment), λx • SV(x).name = 'Toys')
    { *h being an history, X_Hist(h) is the canonical X_Chronicle representing h in extension. SV(x) is the structural value of the snapshot x.* }
from e in TheEmployees where e.name = 'Zoé'

R.7 : *Give the name of the employees who moved from Paris to Grenoble.*

The idea is to work on the sequence of consecutive couples of snapshots of each employee's address history and to select the couples made of a first element with Paris as address and a second element with Grenoble.

{ *type: {string}* }
select e.name from e in TheEmployees
where RightPart (TheCouples (X_Hist (e.address)),
                λ<i1, i2> • SV (i1) = 'Paris' ∧ SV (i2) = 'Grenoble') ≠ ∅

TheCouple is applied to the X_chronicle deduced from an employee address history, so as to work on couples of consecutive snapshots timestamped by intervals RightPart is used to find the first couple corresponding to the employee's appropriate move.

5 Prototype development

A prototype on top of the O_2 DBMS [4] is under development. It consists of several components: a temporal library of classes implementing in O_2 the temporal model, divided into three parts respectively dedicated to time units, time types and history types; and a pre-processor of TempOQL [5], a temporal extension of the OQL language. Application programs can use temporal facilities either through TempOQL or directly through method calls, for instance in O_2C. The time unit library is composed of classes describing units (instances of standard ones are built in the prototype). For each couple of comparable units a special class describes the most appropriate conversion methods. The various components are parametrized so as to let the DBMS manager update the library by adding or deleting units. Specific tools will be developed later to make this task easy.

In TempOQL, temporal types are primitive and temporal values are expressed in a quasi natural way with some necessary syntactic tags (@ for instants, # for durations): for example, @"5/3/96", @"5/3/1996", @"March 5 1996", are instances of instant expressions in the American standard, #"3 mois, 2 jours" is an instance of duration expression in French. The language is parametrized so as to admit several standards. The interpreter handles a set of formats for each temporal type and translates temporal expressions into corresponding OQL queries made of calls to the appropriate temporal value constructors. Currently, we are in the process of implementing the history classes and the corresponding extensions to OQL. The next step will be to define the external form of the data definition and manipulation languages, and to implement them.

6 Conclusion

In this paper, we have presented an historical model unifying the various temporal concepts and functionalities recognized as necessary to extend a persistent object server. According to a discrete model of time, data can be timestamped by simple or complex temporal values with respect to an extensible set of time units. Time values are manipulated through a rich collection of functions organized in a hierarchy of temporal types. *Snapshots* are the basic temporal association reflecting the distinction between data temporal and structural dimensions. Bitemporal dimensions are modeled with history snapshots. The historical model differentiates two temporal characteristics: the attribute evolution status (*constant, historical* or *fugitive*) models the way an attribute is observed; the history updating mode (*regular, discrete, stepwise, interpolated*) models the way historical attributes updates are to be interpreted. The model supports several kinds of history representations through the simple notion of *chronicle*. The type hierarchy offers high level operations which aim at encompassing the natural complexity of temporal expressions. This model is currently validated by a prototype running on top of an object DBMS. This implementation is crucial to identify inaccuracies and to support experimentations, in particular in order to work out a query taxonomy, prerequisite to language and method design.

We plan to study implementation strategies and to design appropriate management tools. Once the model will be stabilized, we shall address issues about optimization and efficient storage structures.

Acknowledgments: the authors wish to thank Marlon Dumas for his active participation since he joined the project.

References

1. M. Adiba. STORM an object-oriented, multimedia DBMS. In K.Nowsu, editor, *Multimedia Database Management Systems*, chapter 3, pages 47–88. Kluwer Academic Publishers, 1996.
2. E. Bertino, E. Ferrari, and G. Guerrini. A formal temporal object-oriented data model. In *Proceedings of Advances in Database technology - EDBT '96 5th International Conference on extending database technology, LNCS 1057*, Avignon, France, March 1996. Springer Verlag.
3. R. Bird and P. Wadler. *Introduction to functional programming*. Prentice Hall, 1988.
4. J.-F. Canavaggio. Une bibliothèque temporelle pour un SGBD. In *les actes des deuxièmes journées des jeunes chercheurs, GDR - PRC Bases de données - Pôle modélisation et environnements de développement*, pages 117–130, Paris, Janvier 1996.
5. J.F. Canavaggio and M. Dumas. Manipulation de valeurs temporelles dans un SGBD à objets. In *actes du 15ème congrès INFORSID*, Toulouse, juin 1997.
6. T.S. Chang and S.K. Gadia. An object-oriented model for temporal databases. In Snodgrass [19].
7. L. Console, B. Pernici, and P. Terenziani. Towards the develoment of a general temporal manager for temporal databases : a layered and modular approach. In Snodgrass [19].

8. O. Deux. The story of O_2. *IEEE Transaction on Knowledge and Data Engineering*, 2(1), March 1990.

9. D. Dey, T. M. Barron, and V. C. Storey. A complete temporal relational algebra. *The VLDB Journal*, 5(3), august 1996.

10. N. Edelweiss, J. Palazzo, and B. Pernici. An object-oriented temporal model. In *Proceedings of the CAISE'93 Conference, LNCS 685*, Paris (France), june 1993. Springer Verlag.

11. M.-C. Fauvet, J.-F. Canavaggio, and P.-C. Scholl. Expressions de requêtes temporelles dans un SGBD à objets. In *Actes des 12èmes Journées Bases de Donnéees Avancéees*, pages 225–250, Cassis, France, août 1996.

12. I. A. Goralwalla and M. T. Ozsu. Temporal extensions to a uniform behavioral object model. In Springer Verlag, editor, *Proceedings of the 12th International Conference on the Entity-Relationship Approach - ER'93, LNCS 823*, 1993.

13. C.-S. Jensen, J. Clifford, R. Elmasri, S. Gadia, P. Hayes, and S. Jajodia (editors). A consensus glossary of temporal database concepts. *ACM SIGMOD Record*, 23(1), March 1994.

14. W. Kafer and H. Schoning. Realizing a temporal complex-object data model. In *Proc. of the ACM SIGMOD Conference*, California, June 1992.

15. J. Palazzo, N. Edelweiss, E. Arruda, A. Laender, and J Cavalcanti. Implementation of an object-oriented temporal model. In *Proceedings of the 6th International Conference on Database and Expert Systems and Applications (DEXA)*, London (UK), september 1995.

16. E. Rose and A. Segev. TOOSQL a temporal object oriented query langage. In *Proceedings of the 12th International Conference on the Entity-Relationship approach, LNCS 823*, Arlington, Texas, December 1993. Springer-Verlag.

17. P.-C. Scholl, M.-C. Fauvet, F. Lagnier, and F. Maraninchi. *Cours d'informatique - Langages et Programmation*. Collection Manuels Informatique. Masson (Paris), Septembre 1993.

18. A. Segev and A. Shoshani. A temporal data model based on time sequences. In Tansel et al. [23].

19. R. T. Snodgrass, editor. *ARPA/NSF International Workshop on Infrastructure for Temporal Databases*, Arlington, Texas, June 1993.

20. R. T. Snodgrass. Temporal object-oriented databases: a critical comparison. In W. Kim, editor, *Modern database systems. The object model, interoperability and beyond*, chapter 19. Addison Wesley, 1995.

21. R. T. Snodgrass, editor. *The TSQL2 temporal query language*. Kluwer Academic Publishers, 1995.

22. S. Su and H.-H. Chen. A temporal knowledge representation model OSAM/T and its query langage OQL/T. In *Proc. of the 17th VLDB International Conference*, Barcelona, September 1991.

23. A. U. Tansel, J. Clifford, S. Gadia, S. Jajodia, A. Segev, and R. T. Snodggrass, editors. *Temporal Databases*. The Benjamins/Cummings Publishing Company, 1993.

24. C. Vassilakis, P. Georgiadis, and A. Sotiropoulou. A comparative study of temporal dbms architecture. In *Proceedings of the 7th International Workshop on Database and Expert Systems and Applications (DEXA)*, Zurich (Switzerland), september 1996.

25. X. S. Wang, S. Jajodia, and V. S. Subrahmanian. Temporal modules : an approach toward federated temporal databases. *Information Systems*, 82:103 – 128, 1995.

26. G.T.J. Wuu and U. Dayal. A uniform model for temporal and versioned object-oriented databases. In Tansel et al. [23].

Activity Threads: A Unified Framework for Aiding Behavioural Modelling

Bernard Faure[1]   Maguelonne Teisseire[2]   Rosine Cicchetti[1,3]

[1] IUT Aix en Provence - Département Informatique
Avenue Gaston Berger, 13625 Aix en Provence Cedex 01 FRANCE
Tel: (33) 04 42 93 90 43 - Fax: (33) 04 42 93 90 74
E-mail: faure@alpha.iut.univ-aix.fr
[2] LIRMM UMR CNRS 5506 - ISIM - Univ. Montpellier II
[3] LIM - Univ. de la Méditerranée

Abstract. Modelling dynamics is a difficult and errorprone task and designers are provided with few aid when abstracting behaviour. For aiding designers when describing behaviour, analysis techniques could be developed for detecting some modelling defects or possible critical situations. Such controls are strongly required, however they cannot filter all possible anomalies. For complementing them, we propose a method for exhibiting and giving back to designers "what is actually expressed" in their specifications. The representation mechanism which is defined for supporting the method is called thread of activity. Threads provide an interesting vision of behaviour highlighting possible modelling defects.

1 Introduction

Modelling dynamics is a difficult and errorprone task and designers are provided with few aid when abstracting behaviour. In fact, conceptual approaches give general modelling principles and representation tips and do not offer behavioural control capabilities [4,8,9,15–17]. In contrast, controlling behaviour has been addressed in different fields, including expert systems, deductive and active databases, software and real-time system specifications [2,3,5,10,12,19]. For aiding designers when describing behaviour, analysis techniques, adapted or inspired from evoked research work, could be developed for detecting some modelling defects or possible critical situations. Such controls are strongly required, however they cannot filter all possible anomalies.

For complementing them, we propose a method for exhibiting and giving back to designers "what is actually expressed" in their specifications. The underlying idea is close to aided systems paraphrasing users' queries for a validation concern. The general principle of the method is to extract, from the high level representation of dynamics, all authorized behaviours for the application, and to present them in a simple and natural way. With this method, the designer is provided with a mechanism for checking if "what he intended specifying is well captured" and if "what is captured in specifications was actually intended".

The representation mechanism which is defined for supporting the method is called thread of activity. Activity threads capture the required functionalities of the modelled application. To illustrate its feasability, we experiment our approach with two very different conceptual models: OMT [16] and IFO_2[18], but in this paper we focus on the experimentation with IFO_2.

The paper is organized as follows. In section 2, we introduce activity components and threads and explain how they can be used for aiding behavioural modelling. In section 3, we give the algorithms for exhibiting threads from IFO_2 specifications. An outline of related work is given in section 4.

2 Activity Instruments

A functionality of the modelled application is intended for reacting to particular environment stimuli and reaching a given objective. It is a set of tasks, probably scheduled in a complex way and possibly including, apart from the initial stimuli, additional interactions with the environment. It could be merely performing some tasks in a sequential way as soon as an event occurs. But it could also include iterations, choices or concurrency.

Our approach for exhibiting actual behaviours captured in specifications places emphasis on application functionalities. Such functionalities are reconstituted from dynamic schemas by using the concept of **threads of activity**. A thread models how reactions and interactions with the environment are organized for meeting requirements of a given functionality. In fact, for each relevant external stimuli, a thread describes what must be done and when. Considering a thread taken in isolation, various controls can apply and reveal defects. Moreover, a comparative examination of activity threads makes it possible to highlight interactions between different functionalities to be enhanced. Thus undesirable side effects could be located within dynamic specifications.

2.1 Activity components and threads

Threads of activity are built from activity components or units which could be either basic or complex. A basic component represents "anything which could happen" during the application life, i.e. an event or the triggering of an operation. Events could be either external, temporal or internal and an operation is whatever code which could be either set or instance oriented. Events and operations have parameters. *Evt* stands for the set of external and temporal events in specifications and *Op* groups the operations and internal events.

For building complex components, four constructors can be recursively applied to basic components. These constructors are the following:

- sequence: $\bullet(c_1, c_2, \ldots, c_n)$ represents the ordered triggering (or occurrence) of components $c_1, \ldots, c_n$;
- set: $\circ(c_1, c_2, \ldots, c_n)$ stands for the triggering (or occurrence) of components $c_1, \ldots, c_n$, in any order;
- alternative: $\mid (c_1, c_2, \ldots, c_n)$ symbolizes an exclusive choice between $c_1, c_2, \ldots, c_n$;
- concurrency: $\parallel (c_1, c_2, \ldots, c_n)$ represents concurrency between components.

An instance of a component is an authorized behaviour. It stands for the scheduled execution of all nested operations, possibly suspended while waiting for some events. It concerns a set of objects corresponding to parameters of events and operations in the thread.

An activity component, being either basic or complex, could combine two additional features: it could be optional (or necessary) and multiple (or simple). This means that a component could have no instances or several ones. When a multiple component is embedded in a higher level component, it could have various instances for each instance of the higher level component. The optional feature of a component is denoted by using brackets (instead of parenthesis if the component is complex) and its possible multiple feature by using: $*$.

Example 1. As an illustration throughout the paper, we consider the classical example of a trading company, selling some goods to customers and buying them from suppliers. In this context, let us consider the following situation: when a customer orders a particular product, if he is a new customer, the associated object must be created. Then the considered order must be captured (by invokating the method *Init_Order*). The order could be dealt in two different and exclusive ways. If the ordered product is available, it could be delivered (by performing the operation *Delivering*) or else a supplier request must be triggered. This situation could be described through the following activity component:

$C_1 = \bullet(Order\_Receiving, [Init\_Customer], Init\_Order, | (Delivering, Supplier \_Request))$. □

An activity thread is defined as an activity component, having arbitrarily nested components. Since it models all the authorized behaviours for a given functionality, an activity thread is supposed to be required, during the application life, by some external stimuli and to reach a given objective.

An activity thread is an activity component, $T.struct = const(c_1, c_2, \ldots, c_n)$, such that the following requirements are met:

1. *Initiality:* if $const \in (|, \|)$ then $\exists c_i$ such that $c_i \in Evt$, or c_i satisfies the initiality property; if $const = \bullet$ then $c_1 \in Evt$ or c_1 satisfies the initiality property; if $const = \circ$ then $\forall i = 1 \ldots n$, $c_i \in Evt$ or c_i satisfies the initiality property;

2. *Propagation:* if activity propagation reaches an embedded component c_{ij} then its higher-level component c_i has been necessarily reached before. Furthermore, if $const_{c_i} = \bullet$ then $\forall k = 1 \ldots (j-1)$, c_{ik} has been reached; if $const_{c_i} = |$ then $\nexists c_{ik}$, $k \neq j$ such that c_{ik} is reached.

3. *Termination:* an instance of T is either infinite or it terminates in one or several components, called terminal, standing for the functionality goal.

Of course when exhibiting threads from a dynamic schema, we make use of the introduced properties. In particular cases, the method cannot build any thread from a schema, because of the initiality property. This situation reveals deadlocks between activity components which can be located within specifications. Useless elements in specifications are also detected and the designer is alerted.

2.2 Which lessons learn from activity threads

In this section, we examine how taking advantages of activity threads for improving specification and controlling application dynamics, or in other words, which lessons can a designer learn from activity threads for understanding better the specified behaviour, and solving possible problems.

Examining external or temporal events When included in an activity thread, external or temporal events could play different parts: originating the propagation in the thread; simulating the reaction of the environment in response to a previous action of the application; or introducing a delay in propagation.

Any external or temporal event embedded in a low level component of an activity thread would result in a temporary suspension of activity. When the considered event is temporal, the activity is likely to be resumed. But if it is external, it can exist instances either temporarily or definitively uncompleted if the event never occurs. From a modelling viewpoint, such external events must be carefully examined and the designer is invited to precise whether uncompleted instances are acceptable, and if not, he must specify how managing such a situation (likely by introducing a suitable delay before choosing another alternative).

Dealing with optional components When an activity thread includes an optional component, authorized instances of the thread can or not encompass an instance of this component. Optional components can be used not only for constraining the triggering of an operation or more generally, of a component, but also for filtering relevant occurrences of events.

When a terminal component is embedded in an optional higher level component, instances of the considered thread could be uncompleted, if the condition of the high level component does not hold. In fact, for these instances, the functionality does not reach the desired goal. Uncompleted instances could reflect an intended failure of the functionality (for example, orders from "bad customers" can be rejected and nothing is done after), but they could also reveal defects in modelling. Thus the designer is alerted and if he does not accept uncompleted instances, he must pay particular attention to triggering conditions: can conditions hold during the application life? And in which acceptable delay?

Managing simple and multiple components In the simplest case, all components of an activity thread are simple. Thus each instance of a thread represents a "one-shot" execution (possibly organized in a complex way) of various operations which could be suspended for waiting for some events.

A multiple component could be used for two different reasons. Firstly it could express iteration of operation triggering or more generally component triggering. This means that for each instance of the higher level component, the embedded component is repetitively executed. Another reason for using multiple component is to combine several instances of a precedent component in the thread for dealing them together.

Multiple component must be carefully examined because they can originate non terminating instances. In fact, for each multiple component, a termination condition must be specified and a maximum number of iterations could be an additional guard. However in some cases, multiple components do no alter termination of thread instances. This happens when they combine several instances, having different objects as parameters, and originated by different occurrences of an event (or a combination of events). Such components introduce a variable granularity in handled parameters. Even if instances of these components are guaranteed to be finite, a synchronization condition is strongly required. If it does not exist, the multiple feature of the component is useless: once a single instance is built, propagation goes on in the thread.

We have briefly examined how designers can take advantages of threads. In the following section we explain how building threads from conceptual schemas elaborated with IFO$_2$.

3 Activity threads in IFO$_2$

The IFO$_2$ model [13,18] is an extension of the semantic model IFO [1]. It provides a uniform framework for both structural and behavioural modelling. For abstracting dynamics of application, it adopts an event-oriented philosophy. Before describing how threads of activity are captured from behavioural schemas, we propose an overview of this dynamic model.

3.1 The IFO$_2$ dynamic model: an illustrated overview

In IFO$_2$, any relevant fact is represented as an *event*. Events are identified and characterized by parameters (objects reacting or invoked when the considered events occur). IFO$_2$ events can be basic or complex.

The IFO$_2$ basic types can be *simple*, *abstract* or *represented*. Simple types represent the invocation of some method specified for a structural object type. The abstract event type symbolizes external or temporal events, stemming from the outside world. It is also used to represent internal events which are interesting only through their consequences by triggering other events. Finally, the represented type provides an original facility for reusing parts of specifications. Actually, it stands for another type, described elsewhere which can be used without knowing its precise description.

For expressing event synchronizations, we adopt a constructor-based approach. Event *composition* reflects the conjunction of events of different types. *Sequence* is similar to composition but includes a chronological constraint between the occurrences of the component events. *Grouping* expresses conjunctions of events of a common type, and *union* stands for event disjunction.

Example 2. Figure 1 illustrates the basic types corresponding to the creation operation *Init_Order* modelled through a simple type, the external events of *Order_Receiving* are represented with an abstract type. The represented type *Delivering* is introduced for reusing the complex type *Delivery*. When a delivery is performed, the stock and the customer accounts are updated. Then the order is completed. For capturing the described situation, a sequence type *Delivery* is specified as depicted in Figure 1. □

Causality links between events are expressed by using functions. More precisely, event types are interconnected by functions through the fragment concept. A fragment describes the system reactions in a given situation, and this description focuses on a principal type called *heart*. Functions of event fragments express general conditions for event chaining since they can combine the following features: *simple* or *complex*, i.e. an event of their type origin triggers one or several events of their target; *partial* or *total*, i.e. an event of their type origin can or must trigger an event of their target; and *deferred* or *immediate*, if there is a delay or not between the occurrences of the origin and target events.

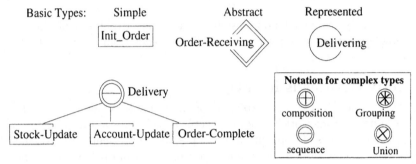

Fig. 1. Event Types Examples

In addition, we make a distinction between *triggering* and *precedence functions*: the fact that an event of the fragment heart triggers the occurrence of other events is different from the fact that an event is preceded by the occurrence of other events.

The partial views provided by fragments are grouped together within an *event schema* which offers an overview of the behaviour. More precisely represented types are related to fragment hearts by means of IS_A links. These links introduce a behavioural hierarchy and multiple inheritance is possible. Thus the behaviour part, modelled through a fragment, can be reused as a whole.

Example 3. The IFO$_2$ schema, in figure 2, represents an overall and simplified reaction of the application for dealing with customers' orders. The fragment of heart *Order_Receiving* depicts what happens when a customer orders a product. When such an event occurs, it could trigger the operation *Init_Customer* and then it necessarily triggers *Order_Management* which is an alternative between two represented types *Supplier_Request* and *Delivering*. The latter stands for the complex type *Delivery* and the former symbolizes a simple type *Requiring*, supposed to send an order to a supplier. *Requiring* is heart of a fragment and it possibly triggers a method for creating a new model of product. *Requiring* is reused in the last fragment of the schema through an IS_A link and a represented type *Being_Required*. This fragment describes what is done when an external event *Reception* occurs (the supplier delivers the requested product). Let us notice that a precedence function is used for capturing the causality link between *Being_Required* and the external event type. The latter triggers a represented type *Being_Delivered* which stands itself for *Delivery*. □

3.2 Extracting activity threads

In this section we present the algorithm defined for extracting threads of activity from IFO$_2$ schemas. Its general principles are the following. Threads are built all along a navigation through the IFO$_2$ schema. Once a fragment is reached, through a single type which is triggered (or several), all possible components reflecting the underlying behaviour are built. When a cycle is detected between fragments the corresponding component is marked as multiple. The result of this navigation is a graph of components which does not encompass concurrency constructors. The latter are introduced when rewriting the graph in form of a thread, since in IFO$_2$, concurrency is captured by specifying different fragments. The different notations used in the algorithm description are the following: an event schema is a directed acyclic graph $G_{Se} = (S_{Se}, L_{Se})$ where S_{Se}, including $S_{Se-entry}$ the set of entries (not caused by another event type), stands for the set of root types (i.e. which are not components of a complex type) and L_{Se}, the set of links between these types, is the disjoint union of the fragment function set and the set of IS_A links.

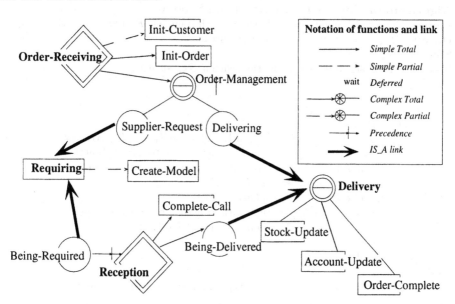

Fig. 2. A Schema Example

Algorithm of Thread Extraction from Fragment:

Input: G_{Se} an event schema IFO$_2$.

Output: For each fragment F in G_{Se}, Ω_F the set of local activity threads.

Step 1:
1. For each fragment F in the schema G_{Se}: $F_{entry} \leftarrow \emptyset$; $\Omega_F \leftarrow \emptyset$.
2. For each $Te \in S_{Se-entry}$ in the fragment F: *Append Te to F_{entry}*

Step 2:

Iterate
1. For each fragment F in the schema G_{Se}, such that $F_{entry} \neq \emptyset$ do:
   For each $T \in F_{entry}$: *Append $Thread(T)$ to Ω_F*
2. For each fragment F in the schema G_{Se}: $F_{entry} \leftarrow \emptyset$
3. For each thread ω of Ω_F built at Step 2.1, for each event type $T \in \omega$ such that $\exists T_1, \ldots, T_n$, event types respectively in fragments $F_1, \ldots, F_n$, related to T by an IS_A link and which are not target of a triggering function:

If $\nexists\ const(T_i, \omega_i') \in \Omega_{F_i}{}^1$ then: *Append* T_i to F_{i_entry}.
  End Iterate
End

Thread is a procedure applying to a type and building all the possible activity threads by navigating from this type through its fragment:
If T is source of n functions having $T_1, \ldots T_n$ as targets
$Thread(T) \leftarrow \bullet(T, Thread_R(T_1), \ldots Thread_R(T_n))$ else $Thread(T) \leftarrow T$.
$Thread_R$ is specified in the following way: if T is target of:
. a simple and partial function, then $Thread_R(T) \leftarrow [Thread(T)]$
. a complex and total function, then $Thread_R(T) \leftarrow Thread(T)*$
. a complex and partial function, then $Thread_R(T) \leftarrow [Thread(T)]*$
else $Thread_R(T) \leftarrow Thread(T)$.

Algorithm of Thread Extraction from Schema:
Input: The set of fragment threads Ω_F for each fragment F in an event schema G_{Se}.
Output: $\Omega_{G_{Se}}$ the set of schema activity threads.
Step 1: $\quad \Omega_{G_{Se}} \leftarrow \emptyset$
Step 2: $\quad$ For each fragment F in the schema G_{Se} such that $\exists\ Te \in F$ and $Te \in S_{Se-entry}$:
  For each $\omega \in \Omega_F$:
    Iterate
      For each $T \in \omega$:
        If T is directly related by an IS_A link to $T_1, \ldots, T_n$, event types in fragments $F_1, \ldots, F_n$ which are not target of a triggering function:
          if T is a complex type with at least a represented type:
          $Replace(T, \omega, \bullet(Flat(T), \| (F_1, \ldots, F_n)))$
          else $Replace(T, \omega, \| (F_1, \ldots, F_n))$
        else if T is a complex type with at least a represented type:
          $\quad\quad Replace(T, \omega, Flat(T))$ else $Delete(T, \omega)$.
    End Iterate
    Append ω to $\Omega_{G_{Se}}$
End
Flat rewrites a type according to basic types and activity thread constructors.

Example 4. The IFO$_2$ schema, in figure 2, captures a single thread C. It is built from the activity components extracted from each fragment in the schema.
$C = \bullet(Order\_Receiving, [Init\_Customer], Init\_Order, | (\bullet(Stock\_Update, Account\_Update, Order\_Complete), \bullet(Requiring, \| (Create\_Model, \bullet(Being\_Required, Reception, Complete\_Call, Being\_Delivered, Stock\_Update, Account\_Update, Order\_Complete)))))$. Among critical situations detected all along this construction, let us notice the event *Reception* which can cause uncompleted instances due to its external feature (a customer's order could never be satisfied).□

4 Related work
Since our method is intended for complementing verification techniques, an outline of such controls is particularly interesting.

---

^{1} *const* is one of the four constructors defined for the activity threads, Section 2.1.

Behaviour verification problems have been addressed in different fields, including expert systems, deductive and active databases, software and real-time system specifications. Approaches proposed in these various fields share some commun concerns, in particular the problem of termination when processing rules or executing programs[3,19].

Z. Manna and A. Pnueli propose a specification and verification approach for concurrent reactive programs by using $\forall$-automata [10,11]. They are interested in controlling fundamental program properties: initialization, consecutivity, termination, justice and fairness. This approach is adapted to real-time systems in [12]. Closer from our research context, verification techniques are proposed for analysing the behaviour of distributed systems [6,7]. They are inspired from dataflow analysis, originally proposed as a technique for determining program properties [14]. Based on state transition diagrams, these techniques provide an automatic detection of state unreachability and deadlock between concurrent processes, caused by communication anomalies. The proposed method does not reveal all the synchronization errors but it is really useful for preliminary understanding of process behaviour and a non-expensive detection of anomalies far from trivial. Another approach is proposed in [2]. It refers to active DB behaviour. The defined techniques analyse a set of ECA rules for verifying their processing termination, confluence and observable determinism.

5 Conclusion

In this paper, we present a method for aiding behavioural modelling by adopting a paraphrasing-like approach. The representation mechanism supporting the approach is the concept of thread of activity. We explain how exhibiting threads from dynamic schemas elaborated with IFO$_2$. All along the thread construction, consistency controls can apply for revealing defects or possible critical situations which are yielded to designers.

However a graphic presentation of possible branches in threads (comparable to workflow) would offer a more clear cut vision of threads for users. Other perspectives of the presented work are various. First of all threads could be seen as an interesting mechanism for comparing dynamic conceptual models. Furthermore, evoked controls can be refined and aid provided to users can be improved, for instance by suggesting solutions when critical cases are detected. Finally threads of activity can be seen as an intermediary model for the "design" step of application development. It could be the basis for refining specifications and aiding users, which are no longer designers but application programmers, when detailing implementation features such as transaction specifications.

References

1. S. Abiteboul and R. Hull. IFO: A Formal Semantic Database Model. *ACM Transactions on Database Systems*, 12(4):525–565, December 1987.
2. A. Aiken, J.M. Hellerstein, and J. Widom. Static Analysis Techniques for Predicting the Behaviour of Active Database Rules. *ACM Transactions on Database Systems*, 20(1):3–41, March 1995.

3. E. Benazet, H. Guehl, and M. Bouzeghoub. VITAL: A Visual Tool for Analysis of Rules Behaviour in Active Databases. In *Proocedings of the Rules in Database*, Lecture Notes in Computer Science, Athens, Greece, September 1995.

4. G. Booch. *Object-Oriented Design with Applications*. Benjamin/Cumming Company, 1991.

5. S. Chakravarthy, V. Krishnaprasad, E. Anwar, and S.K. Kim. Composite Events for Active Databases: Semantics, Contexts and Detection. In *Proc. of Conf. VLDB*, pages 606–617, Santiago, Chile, September 1994.

6. S. C. Cheung and J. Kramer. Tractable Flow Analysis for Anomaly Detection in Distributed Programs. In *Proceedings of the 4th European Software Engineering Conference*, pages 283–300, 1993.

7. S. C. Cheung and J. Kramer. Tractable Dataflow Analysis for Distributed Systems. *IEEE Transactions on Software Engineering*, 20(8):579–593, 1994.

8. P. Coad and E. Yourdon. *Object-Oriented Analysis*. Yourdon Press Computing Series, 1990.

9. P. Loucopoulos and R. Zicari. *Conceptual Modeling, Databases and CASE: An Integrated View of Information Systems Development*. Wiley Professional Computing, 1992.

10. Z. Manna and A. Pnueli. Specification and Verification of Concurrent Programs by ∀-Automata. In *Proc. of the Temporal Logic in Specification Conference*, volume 398 of *LNCS*, pages 124–164, Altrincham, UK, April 1987.

11. Z. Manna and A. Pnueli. The Anchored Version of the Temporal Framework. In *Proocedings of the Linear Time, Branching Time and Partial Order in Logics and Models for Concurrency Conference*, volume 354 of *Lecture Notes in Computer Science*, pages 201–284, 1989.

12. J. S. Ostroff and W. Murray Wonham. A Framework for Real-Time Discrete Event Control. *IEEE Transactions on Automatic Control*, 35(4):386–397, April 1990.

13. P. Poncelet, M. Teisseire, R. Cicchetti, and L. Lakhal. Towards a Formal Approach for Object-Oriented Database Design. In *Proc. of the Int. Conf. VLDB*, pages 278–289, Dublin, Ireland, August 1993.

14. J.H Reif and A. Smolka. Dataflow Analysis of Distributed Communicating Processes. *International Journal of Parallel Programming*, 19(1):1–30, 1990.

15. C. Rolland and C. Cauvet. *Trends and Perspectives in Conceptual Modeling*. in [9], 1992.

16. J. Rumbaugh, M. Blaha, W. Premerlani, F. Eddy, and W. Lorensen. *Object-Oriented Modeling and Design*. Prentice-Hall, 1991.

17. I. Sommerville. *Software Engineering*. Addison-Wesley, 1991.

18. M. Teisseire, P. Poncelet, and R. Cicchetti. Towards Event-Driven Modelling for Database Design. In *Proc. of the Int. Conf. VLDB*, Santiago, Chile, September 1994.

19. J. Widom and S. Ceri. *Active Database Systems. Triggers and Rules for Advanced Database Processing*. Morgan Kaufmann Publishers, 1996.

Linking Object-Oriented Conceptual Modeling with Object-Oriented Implementation in Java

Oscar Pastor, Emilio Insfrán, Vicente Pelechano, Susana Ramírez

Departament de Sistemes Informàtics i Computació
Universitat Politècnica de València
Camí de Vera s/n
46071 Valencia (Spain)
{opastor | einsfran | pele}@dsic.upv.es

Abstract

Nowadays, if we want to obtain a sound and correct final software product it is very important to be able to properly join modern OO programming environments, which are built for the new Internet architectures, with the OO methodologies produced over the last few years in order to deal properly with the Conceptual Modeling process.

Our contribution to this objective is the OO-Method [Pas96, Pas97-1] proposal. OO-Method is an OO Methodology that allows analysts to introduce the relevant system information by means of a set of graphical models to obtain the conceptual model through a requirement collection phase, so that an OO formal specification in OASIS [Pas95] can be generated at any given moment. This formal specification acts as a high-level system repository. Furthermore, a Java software prototype, which is functionally equivalent to the OASIS specification, is also generated in an automated way. This is achieved by defining an execution model that gives the pattern to obtain a concrete implementation in the selected target software development environment. A CASE workbench [Pas97-1] supports the methodology.

1 Introduction

Software technology has undergone, over the last few years, considerable transformation. One of the main reasons for this transformation is the emergence of the object-oriented (OO) model as a software production paradigm that covers all the traditional analysis, design and implementation steps. We have OO methodologies [Boo97, Rum91], OO databases, OO programming languages, etc.

However, we consider that there is still not a clear understanding of what an object is. Or, better explained, everyone understands perfectly what his/her objects are. The problems come from the fact that often objects in conceptual modeling are not the same as in programming or database environments. Consequently, ambiguities appear everywhere. The OO approach is still a loosely defined term, even if some salient features constitute a minimum basis (complex objects, object identity, methods, encapsulation, inheritance)

The source of this confusion can be found in the lack of a standard and universal formal approach for the OO model. Many attempts have been made in the OO logic area [Jun91, Kif96] and research continues. OO logic attempts to provide a unified logical formalism for modeling objects and other aspects of the OO paradigm [Dub94]. However, the situation reached with the relational model, from the formal point of view, has not yet been reached in the OO model.

In this context, Inter/Intranet architectures and web environments are starting to be widely used, and this has been announced as a software computing revolution. The common software development environment for such an environment is claimed to be a Java-based one. Of course, Java [Arn96, Kra95, Tit95] is presented as an OO programming language.

At the same time, continuous efforts are being made in the area of OO conceptual modeling, especially in terms of OO methodologies that have their corresponding CASE workbench [Boo97,Pas97] in order to provide reliable and productive software production environments.

The lack of a precise connection between the conceptual modeling world and the software development tools in web environments is, in our opinion, one of the most interesting problems. We have to close this *gap* to be able to properly design and implement organizational systems using three-tiered architectures based on simple and easy-to-use client stations, web servers and database servers.

Our contribution to this state of the art is presented in this paper. With our OO-Method proposal, we provide an OO methodology that covers the phases of Analysis and Design obtaining a specification in a formal and OO specification language called OASIS. It acts as a high-level data dictionary, where all the relevant system information is captured. A Java prototype, including both static and dynamic properties, is obtained in an automated way starting from the OASIS specification.

The static properties are represented in a relational database schema and the dynamic properties are represented by generating *Java applets* and web interfaces that include the dynamic behaviour of the component system classes.

The main features of this approach are the following:

1. The formal system specification is obtained in an automated way from the graphical information introduced during the OO-Method analysis process.

2. The Java implementation is also obtained in an automated way from the formal system specification. This is done implementing a precise mapping between formal specification concepts and Java components.

We have divided the paper into the following sections: after the introduction, in section 2, we present the most important OO-Method features. In section 3, we give a quick overview on the actual proposals related to Java development environments. Next, in section 4, we explain how the OO-Method analysis models are translated to a Java environment. This is done by determining the exact architecture of the concrete execution model implementation, developed in Java, which is attached to the conceptual model (built in the OO-Method analysis step). We finish this paper with conclusions and a list of references.

2 The OO-Method Proposal

OO-Method is an Object-Oriented Software Production Methodology based on two essential models: the *conceptual model* and the *execution model.*

The software production process in OO-Method starts with the conceptual modeling step where we have to determine the relevant system properties without being worried about any implementation details. Once we have an appropriate system description, a well-defined execution model determines all the implementation-dependent properties of the final software product in terms of user interface, access control, service activation, etc.

The conceptual model describes the Information System within a well-defined OO framework using three complementary point of views:

- **Object Model**: is a graphical model where system classes including attributes, services and relationships (aggregation and inheritance) are defined. Additionally, agent relationships are introduced to specify who can activate each class service.

- **Dynamic Model**: is another graphical model to specify valid object life cycles and interobjectual interaction. We use:

  - *State Transition Diagrams* to describe correct behaviour by establishing valid object life cycles. By valid life, we mean a right sequence of states that characterizes the correct behaviour of the objects for every class.

  - *Object Interaction Diagram:* represents interobjectual interactions. We define two basic interactions:

    - *Triggers*, which are object services that are activated in an automated way when a condition is satisfied.

    - *Global interactions*, which are transactions involving services of different objects (interobjectual transactions).

- **Functional Model**: is used to capture semantics attached to any change of an object state as a consequence of an event occurrence. We specify declaratively how every event changes the object state depending on the involved event arguments (if any) and object's current state. We give a clear and simple strategy (classification of attributes [Pas96]) for dealing with the introduction of the necessary information. This is a contribution of this method that let us to be able to generate a complete OASIS specification in an automated way.

From these three models, a corresponding formal and OO OASIS [Pas95] specification is obtained using a well-defined translation strategy. The resultant OASIS specification acts as a complete system repository where all the relevant properties of the component classes are included.

Once all the relevant system information has been collected, the *execution model* accurately states a pattern used to implement object properties in any target software development environment. The phases of the process can be seen in Fig. 1.

At this point, we give an *abstract view* of an execution model for dealing with the task of implementing the conceptual model. According to the execution model, a prototype, which is functionally equivalent to the OASIS specification, is built in an automated way. The *code generation strategy* is independent of any concrete target development environment.

A CASE Tool [Pas97-1] that provides an operational environment that simplifies the analysis, design and implementation of Information Systems from an object-oriented perspective supports OO-Method. The contribution of this CASE environment is its ability to generate code in well-known industrial software development environments (Java, Visual C++, Delphi, Visual Basic and

PowerBuilder) from the system specification. It constitutes an operational approach to the ideas of the *automated programming paradigm* [Bal83]: collection of system information properties, automated generation of a formal OO system specification, and a complete (including static and dynamics) software prototype which is functionally equivalent to the quoted system specification.

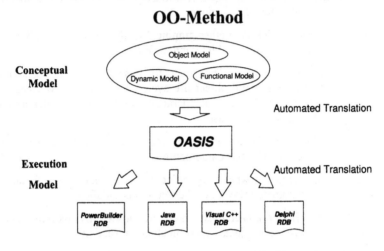

Fig. 1. Phases of OO-Method.

3 Java as a Software Development Environment

Nowadays the Internet and Web technology have become the new frontier for application developers. In this context, Java is playing an important role due to its promising features: architecture independence, portability, multithreading, soundness, security and so on. That means that new needs arise: Java tools, methodologies, CASE tools supporting Java code generation, etc.

Most of the products developed in this area are RAD-oriented, visual development tools (Symantec's Café, Borland's Latté, Visual J++, IBM's Visual Age for Java, etc.). In the methodology field there are some well-known analysis/design CASE tools for example Rational's ROSE/Java, Platinum's Paradigm Plus, and Forté that provide the developers with *limited support* to fully implement Internet/Intranet applications. These proposals share a common weakness: when the development step is reached, the conceptual modeling efforts are unclear, mainly because it is not possible to produce an accurate code that is functionally equivalent to the specification of the system requirements. We should be able to produce code which includes statics and dynamics in an interactive way from the very beginning of the requirement specification step, and not generate only static templates for the component system classes as most OO CASE tools do.

OO-Method solves these problems allowing analysts and designers to build conceptual models of information systems following a methodology that is oriented to generating Internet/Intranet applications based on Java in an automated way.

4 Implementing an OO Conceptual Model in a Java Environment

In this section, we explain how to implement an OO Conceptual Model in an Internet/Intranet development environment. We use Java as a programming language and a relational database [Pas97-2] as a *persistent object repository* as illustrated in Figure 2. For this purpose OO-Method uses an abstract execution model based on the conceptual model. The generation process is carried out binding the execution model and the specific features of the selected programming environment, in this case Java. First, we present the basic features of the OO-Method execution model and then we explain the actual Java implementation of this execution model by showing the set of Java classes that make up the prototype.

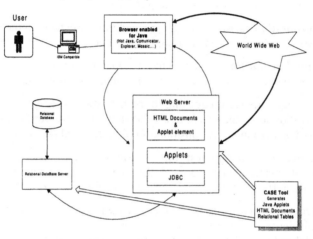

Fig. 2. Global Architecture of the proposed prototype in Java.

4.1 The OO-Method Abstract Execution Model

The OO-Method execution model is a pattern to be used to implement all the system properties collected during the analysis phase, in any target software development environment. The code generation process will use this execution model as a guide to implement the conceptual model in the selected target environment.

This execution model has three main steps:

1. **access control**: first, as users are also objects, the object logging in the system has to be identified as a member of the corresponding object society.

2. **object system view**: once an object is connected, it must have a clear representation of which classes it can access. In other words, its object society view must be clearly stated, exactly determining the set of object attributes and services that it can see or activate.

3. **service activation**: finally, after being connected and having a clear object system view, an object will be able to activate any available service in its worldview. Among these services, we will have event or transaction served by other objects or system observations (object queries).

Any service execution is characterized as the following sequence of actions:

1. **object identification**: as a first step, the object acting as server has to be identified. This object existence is an implicit condition for executing any service unless if we are dealing with a new[1] event. At this point, the object attribute values , which characterize its current state, are retrieved.

2. **introduction of event arguments**: the rest of the arguments of the event being activated must be introduced.

3. **state transition correctness**: we have to verify in the object State Transition Diagram (STD) that a valid *state transition* exists for the selected service in the current object state.

4. **precondition satisfaction**: the precondition associated to the service that is going to be executed must hold if not, an exception will arise.

5. **valuation fulfilment**: once the precondition has been verified, the induced event modifications take place in the persistent object system.

6. **integrity constraint checking in the new state**: to assure that the service activation leads the object to a valid state, we must verify that the (static and dynamic) integrity constraints hold in this final resulting state.

7. **trigger relationships test**: after a valid change of state, the set of rules condition-action that represent the internal system activity have to be verified. If any of them hold, the corresponding service will be triggered.

The previous steps guide the implementation of any program to assure the functional equivalence between the object system description collected in the conceptual model and its reification in a programming environment.

4.2 An Architecture for Implementing the Execution Model in Java

The strategy adopted in our work is based on the development of Java applets that implement the full functionality of the system modeled.

The architecture of an OO implementation in Java that corresponds to an OO Conceptual Model is shown in Figure 3.

The components are the following classes:

- **System** class
- **Menu_Page** class
- **Parameter_Request** class
- set of **Analysis** classes (those detected in the analysis phase)
- **Database** class

---

[1] *Formally, a new event is a service of a metaobject that represents the class. The metaobject acts as object factory for creating individual class instances. This metaobject (one for every class) has as main properties the class population attribute, the next oid and the quoted new event.*

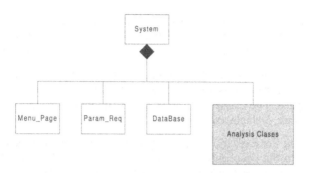

Fig. 3. Class Diagram of the Java Prototype

The **System** class is the main class of the architecture. This class is composed of the Menu_Page, the Parameter_request, the set of Analysis classes and the Database class. The System class implements the three main steps of the execution model:

- control user access to the system looking for the existence of an authorized object in the database. This way of accessing control allows any system object to be an active user of the object society according with the agent relationships defined in the conceptual model.

- create a new Menu_Page instance (this page will show a typical web menu page in the client browser) with as many options as classes are visible to the connected user. When the user selects one of them, the services that the user is able to activate in that class are shown.

- manage the activation of services requested by an user. For this purpose the System instance creates a new **Parameter_Request** object to capture all the required argument values for the quoted service activation.

We have as many **Analysis** classes in the Java prototype as system component classes are in our source Conceptual Model.

A **Database** class instance acts as a *bridge* between the relational database storage of the Analysis class objects and their corresponding Java objects managed by the user's web browser. The main features of this object include services to *retrieve* and *update* the database according to the object activity during the application execution.

All the classes described above have attributes and methods (services) that support the whole execution model.

4.3 Linking an OO Conceptual Model to an Implementation in Java

In order to better understand the architecture and behaviour of the previous component classes of the Java Execution Model, we introduce a Rent-a-Car case study as a brief example:

"A company is involved in the rent of vehicles without drivers as a principal activity. These vehicles are bought at the beginning of the season and usually sold when the season is over. When a customer rents a car, a contract is generated and it

remains open until the customer returns the vehicle. At that time, the total amount to be pay or refunded to the customer (in the case of surety) is calculated. After this step, the car is ready to be rented again".

First, we construct the Conceptual Model (object, dynamic and functional models) identifying the classes and specifying their relationships and all the static and dynamic properties. The classes identified in this problem domain are the following: Contract, Customer, Vehicle and Company.

Based on the Execution Model proposed above, the architecture of the Java applet attached to the conceptual model is shown in Figure 4. In this figure, we are representing a *particular Class Diagram* for the Rent-a-car case study where the System class has every analysis class as components.

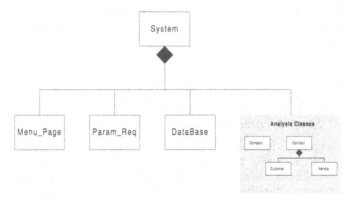

Fig. 4. Class diagram for the Java prototype of the *Rent-a-car* case of study.

Next, we are going to describe an illustrative scenario for the Rent-a-Car prototype generated. This scenario will show the interaction between Java objects and their behaviour when a user enters into the object system.

When a client loads the main HTML page that calls the Java applet, an instance of the *System* class is created and *User* identification is required (see Fig. 5).

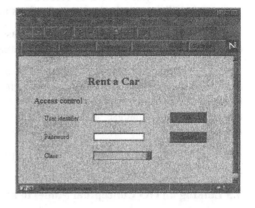

Fig. 5. A User Access Control Page.

After a *User* connects to the *Rent-a-Car* system, a menu page with an option for every class will appear (see Figure 6). If the user clicks in a class option, a new menu page associated with the selected class will be generated (including one option for every class event or transaction offered to the system user).

Fig. 6. Rent a Car option page.

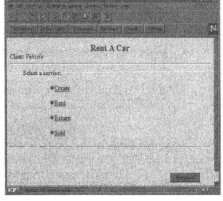

Fig. 7. Car Class Services Menu Page.

In our example, when the user selects the *Car* class, the service list offered by this class is shown, as can be seen in Figure 7.

Every service option activation will generate a new request parameter page, as can be seen Figure 8. This page will ask the user for the parameters needed to execute the event/transaction. The *Ok control button* has a code associated to it that will call to a class method that implements the effect of the event on the object state. This method will check the state transition correctness and method preconditions. If this checking process succeeds, the object change of state is carried out according to the functional model specification. We finish the method execution by verifying integrity constraints and trigger condition satisfaction in the *new state*. Object state updates in the selected persistent object system became valid through the services offered by the Database object.

Fig. 8. Parameter Request Page for the *Create* Service of the *Car* Class.

This execution model assures the functional equivalence between the conceptual model and its reification in a Java-programming environment. This feature opens up the possibility of creating a CASE tool which could generate Java applications starting from a conceptual model.

5 Conclusions and Future Work

Advanced web applications will depend on object technology to make them feasible, reliable and secure. To achieve this goal, well-defined methodological frameworks must be introduced properly connecting OO conceptual modeling and OO software development environments. OO-Method provides such environment. The most relevant features are the following:

- an operational implementation of an automated programming paradigm where a concrete execution model is obtained from a process of *conceptual model translation*

- a precise object-oriented model, where the use of a formal specification language as a high-level data dictionary is a basic characteristic

All of this is done within the next-generation web development environments, making use of the Inter/Intranet architectures an using Java as software development environment.

Research work is still being undertaken to improve the quality of the final software product that is generated including advanced features such as user defined interface, schema evolution or optimized database access mechanisms.

References

[Arn96] Arnold K., Gosling J. *The Java Programming Language*. Sun MicroSystems. Addison-Wesley, 1996.

[Bal83] Balzer R. et al. *Software Technology in the 1990s: Using a New Paradigm*. IEEE Computer, Nov. 1983.

[Boo97] Booch G., Rumbaugh J., Jacobson I. *UML. v1*. Rational Software Co., 1997.

[Dub94] Dubois E., Du Bois Ph., Petit M., Wu S. *ALBERT: A Formal Agent-Oriented Requirements Language for Distributed Composite Systems*. Proc. CAiSE'94. Workshop on Formal Methods for Information System Dynamics, pags: 25-39, University of Twente, Technical Report 1994.

[Jun91] Jungclaus R., Saake G., Sernadas C. *Formal Specification of Object Systems*. Eds. S. Abramsky and T. Mibaum Proceedings of the TapSoft's 91, Brighton. Lncs. 494, pags. 60-82, Springer-Verlag. 1991.

[Kif96] Kifer M. *Deductive and Object Data Languages: A Quest for Integration*. DOOD96. pags: 187-212. 1996.

[Kra95] Kramer D. *The Java Platform*. Sun MicroSystems. Addison-Wesley. 1995.

[Pas95] Pastor O., Ramos I., Canós J. *Oasis v2: A Class Definition Language*. Proc. DEXA95, Springer-Verlag. 1995.

[Pas96] Pastor O., Pelechano V., Bonet B., Ramos I. *An OO Methodological Approach for Making Automated Prototyping Feasible*. Proc. DEXA96. Springer-Verlag. September 1996.

[Pas97-1] Pastor O., Insfrán E., Pelechano V., Romero J., Merseguer J. *OO-METHOD: An OO Software Production Environment Combining Conventional and Formal Methods*. CAiSE97. June 1997.

[Pas97-2] Pastor O., Insfrán E., Quiles G., Barberá J. *Object-Oriented Conceptual Modeling Techniques to Design and Implement a Sound and Robust Oracle Environment*. European Oracle Users Group EOUG'97. 1997.

[Rum91] Rumbaugh J., Blaha M., Permerlani W., Eddy F., Lorensen W. *Object Oriented Modeling and Design*. Englewood Cliffs, Nj. Prentice-Hall. 1991.

[Tit95] Tittel E., Gaither M. *60 Minute Guide to Java*. IDG Books WorldWide, Inc. 1995.

Toward a Unified Data Model
for Large Hypermedia Applications

Bing Wang

Computer Science Department, University of Hull, Hull, HU6 7RX, United Kingdom

Abstract. The major problem in using the current hypermedia mechanisms to support large applications is that the node and link structure is too simple to reveal the semantic connections among documents, and in particular, it is difficult to maintain consistency among them. This paper discusses a unified data model (HyperDB) on the basis of the database approach for supporting large hypermedia applications. The HyperDB modelling techniques can be served as both the semantic analysis tool to capture semantics of a hypermedia application and the conceptual data modelling tool to define a hypermedia structure which can be supported by a database system.

1 Introduction

Hypermedia, a flexible way to organize document, makes it easy for us to arbitrarily link document components. However, because of this highly free style link structure, it also causes a serious problem for the large hypermedia application design, this is the well-known problem in hypertext research — *the dis-orientation of the user navigating in the hyper-space*. To avoid users being lost in the hyper-space, we need to reduce unnecessary links and to provide structural links to organize document structure. The proposed data model described in this paper provides users with a framework to well organize documents and semantic relationships among them.

The research presented in this paper is the further improvement of the previous research[13, 14, 12]. In particular, it combines the advantages of the current model based hypermedia approaches and provides a unified data model which is more suitable for the large hypermedia applications. The remainder of this paper is organized as follows: section 2 reviews several related researches. Section 3 discusses the formal definitions of *HyperDB*. Section 4 describes the design strategies and system modules, and in the final section, we will briefly summarize the major benefits of HyperDB approach and its future development.

2 Related Research

The history of using databases to support hypertext or hypermedia applications can be tracked back ten years ago[1]. In the early 1990s, the research of using databases to support hypermedia focused mainly on the aspect of how to use relational databases to support hypertext machines. During this time, the researches have realized the importance of using database facilities to model and support the complex object definition[3]. A typical example of such approach is the *HyperBase* developed by Schutt and Streitz in 1990[7]. One of the important results of this research is that database system can model hypertext application structures but relational database is not efficient in modelling complex objects which exist in most hypermedia applications. The *Intermedia* approach[10] and Lange's prototype further demonstrated that a commercial object oriented database can be used to easily model and support hypertext applications[5]. The *Intermedia* research compared in particularly relational and object oriented approaches in order to find out which is the best and the most suitable for supporting hypermedia structure[10]. The conclusion is that the information exchange between the hypermedia applications and the database is through the message sending and simplified by using the object oriented database approach. Our research in 1993 also supports this result[11].

The HDM(Hypertext Design Model) is the early approach for defining a general purpose model for authoring-in-the-large[2]. The concepts and methodologies used in the HDM approach is quite similar to our research published in 1991[13] and 1992[4]. The aim of the HDM approach is to support high level specification of the existing or to-be-developed applications and application development. The most important contribution of HDM is that HDM used a data modelling view to analyse a hypertext application and to use a possible database to maintain or support the modelling results. Thus, HDM links the application structure and the actual data model together. To further develop those concepts used in HDM, Schwabe, etc[9] proposed an object oriented hypermedia design model called OOHDM[8]. The aims of OOHDM is the same as those of HDM but the former is constructed in an object oriented way. As a design method, OOHDM approach focuses only on how to structurally represent a hypermedia application. It lacks the description of how to link the defined structure with the data structure which can be supported by the existing database systems.

In the recent hypermedia research, one of the important trends is to use hypertext ideas to implement an open hypermedia system. This is to link different tools in a hypertext style. Such example is the HyperDisco which provides an extensible object oriented hypermedia platform supporting intertool linking, concurrency control and other features. Its objectives are to provide a platform to integrate existing tools and to extend integrated tools to handle multiple processes[15]. The major problem of the current open hypermedia approach is that it lacks the fundamental mechanisms to illustrate how to link heterogeneous tools. The same problem exist in OOHDM approach as well. Our objective is not to repeat a design for a similar functional tool. We need to consider theoretically the mechanisms of how to describe the relationships between a hypermedia application structure and the corresponding supporting tools. This is why HyperDB comes out.

3 A Unified Hypermedia Application Design Model

HyperDB takes both the advantages of the hypermedia system to freely construct an application and the database system to conceptually model and support the application structures. In this section, we will firstly discuss the possible constraints of a semantic hypermedia data model in order to clearly define an application structure. Then, we will illustrate the basic constructors and the application structure schema definition of HyperDB for supporting a large hypermedia based application environment.

3.1 Hypermedia Constraints

For a semantic hypermedia data model, it has an important component. That is the semantic constraint. A semantic constraint defines two semantics. Firstly, it defines the semantic restriction among building blocks. Secondly, it defines the possible results when certain operations are executed on the data model. Thus, we have the *inherent constraints*[1] and the *operational constraints*.[2]

1. *Constraints for the Node Structure*

   The semantic constraints for the node structure are definitions to describe properties of the node structure. They belong to inherent constraints. The current node structure is too simple to capture semantics of an application structure. This is because a node mainly acts as a container for chunks of data. It is difficult to simply split a document into several or a number of parts. The early research has already shown such node structure is impossible to support complex applications[3]. However, recent researches also showed that we can add more semantics to the node[6]. But, the result of such enhancement is that the application structure is forced to match the pre-defined data structure. Still, the relationships between the application structure and supporting data model are vague. The basic data types defined in HyperDB is such an attempt to enrich the inherent properties of the conventional hypermedia data model and to close the gap between the supporting data model and the corresponding application structure.

2. *Constraints for the Link Structure*

   The link defines the operational constraints of a hypermedia data model. It captures the dynamic information of the data model. Although some researches introduced several complex link types such as structured link, zoom link and so on, the semantics of link structure is still very simple. They only functionally connect nodes. This is the main reason why users are easy to become lost in the hyper-space due to the poor semantics supported by links and why users always find the current hypermedia systems can not provide enough facilities to represent a complex document structure. It is difficult for

---

[1] It is the definition of the nature of a building block and cannot be violated in a data model.

[2] They are rules for explicitly define the results of the operations.

current link structure to reveal semantic meanings of an application structure. This is because the link structure cannot capture intro- and interrelationships between documents or among components of documents. The
HyperDB illustrated below introduce the new concept of hypermedia link
structure. The link type in the HyperDB will take two roles for both linking
nodes and representing semantics between nodes.

There is always a conflict between free link and the fixed document structure.
Hence, there is a trade-off inbetween. The purpose for us to introduce hypermedia
constraints is to illustrate that such conflict can be reduced to the lowest level
by providing a single and unified supporting mechanism, that is, the node and
link types of the hypermedia system are also the building blocks of the semantic
data model which can be supported by a database system. That is the HyperDB
approach illustrated below.

3.2   HyperDB Basic Constructor Types

The basic constructors of HyperDB are the major building blocks for constructing a hypermedia application structure. Our focus is that the constructor should
have both the functionalities of hypermedia to classify and organize the application structure and the those of the database to model the application structure
and capture the application semantics. We have three constructors. They are
node constructor, composite node constructor and *schema constructor.*

node constructor Node constructor is the most basic data type of HyperDB
and it is both the information container and the semantic constructor. A node
constructor is a complex object type. The information within the node can be
different types such as text, audio, video and image. We firstly define the media
type of the information stored in a node:

$$Multimedia ::= text \mid audio \mid video \mid image$$

The visible part of a node in HyperDB is the multimedia information stored
in a database and it has a system created identity. The node constructor of
HyperDB is to organize the multimedia information to semantically represent
an application structure. A given set [ComponentID] is used to represent the
system generated unique identities.

Components
  id : *ComponentID*
  media_part : $\mathbb{P}$ *Multimedia*

The node of HyperDB has the basic function as those of the conventional node.
The source and destination of a link is a multimedia data.

Node _____

source, destination : Components

$\exists\, m : \mathbb{P}\, Multimedia \bullet source.media\_part \in m \wedge destination.media\_part \in m$

The HyperDB approach is different from the conventional approaches in the aspect of constructing nodes in a semantic way. This is the abstract schema of the node constructor. In HyperDB, a node is built on the basis of existing components.

Node_Constructor _____

node : Node
new_media_part : Components
new_id' : ComponentID
super_sub : $\mathbb{P}(Components \times \mathbb{P}\, Components)$

---

dom super_sub = 1

ran super_sub = $\{node.source.id\} \cup \{node.destination.id\}$

$\exists\, c : Components \mid c = new\_media\_part \bullet (c.media\_part = \{\} \Rightarrow$
$(c.id = node.source.id \vee c.id = node.destination.id) \wedge$
$(new\_media\_part = (c.media\_part \cup node.source.media\_part) \vee$
$new\_media\_part = (c.media\_part \cup node.destination.media\_part)))$
$\vee$
$(c.media\_part \neq \{\} \Rightarrow new\_media\_part.media\_part = c.media\_part \wedge$
$new\_id' = new\_media\_part.id \cup ComponentID)$

The above node constructor schema expresses two significant semantic meanings. Firstly, a new node can inherit attributes from other nodes. This is described by the *super-sub* function which links a node with several other nodes. In this case, all the multimedia information of the sub-node can be the same as that of the super node. That is, object identities (component identities) are the same as those of super nodes. No new multimedia information is created and the multimedia information of the sub-node is the combination of the source and destination from the super node. On the other hand, if the created node inherits nothing from the existing nodes, a new multimedia part and the corresponding component identity are generated. Secondly, an isolated node cannot exist without any semantic meanings. A node should be at least a super or sub-node. If it is not an inheritable node, it must be a component node defined in composite node constructor.

composite node constructor We believe that complex and composite node structures are the basic constructors to define the structure of an application. We further give the definition of the composite node constructor which makes the existing node as the component part of another node.

```
┌─ Composite_Node_Constructor ─────────────────────────
│ Node_Constructor
│ composite_parts : ℙ Multimedia
├──────────────────────────────────────────────────────
│ ∃ n : Node | n = node • composite_parts = n.source.media_part∪
│ n.destination.media_part
└──────────────────────────────────────────────────────
```

A composite node is not a new created node since it is only a container to hold other nodes. That is why there is no new corresponding identity generated for a composite node. The methodology of the HyperDB approach is to avoid the complexity of using the object oriented approach to model every possible object. The HyperDB approach uses a simple mechanism to treat component information only as an unique and fundamental object. Two constructors defined above are used to structurally define the application structure. Finally, to abstract the node type of the HyperDB approach, we have the the following type definition of the HyperDB node type.

$$Node\_Type ::= InheritableNode \langle\!\langle Node\_Constructor \rangle\!\rangle$$
$$| \; CompositeNode \langle\!\langle Composite\_Node\_Constructor \rangle\!\rangle$$

This Z type definition uses free type structure of Z to recursively define that a node type of HyperDB can be either an inheritable node or a composite node. *InheritableNode* and *CompositeNode* are two free type constructors which can be used to refer two node constructors in the schema calculation.

schema constructor The schema of an application is the designer's abstract view of the application structure. In the hyperDB approach, it is a mechanism to represent how components are related with one another. As the main purpose of the HyperDB approach is to use the powerful database facility to model an application structure, we propose the concept of the schema constructor which gives the user a database's view to analyse and model an application without losing the functionality of hypermedia. To get more semantics of an application schema, we need to use schema operators to combine or integrate different schemata. A given set [**ObjectType**] is used to represent all the possible data type supported by a database system.

```
┌─ Scheme_Constructor ─────────────────────────────────
│ Node_Constructor
│ Composite_Node_Constructor
│ node_object : Node_Type ↣ ObjectType
├──────────────────────────────────────────────────────
│ ∀ nodes : ℙ Node_Type • ∀ n : nodes • ∃ o : ObjectType;
│ N₁ : Node_Constructor; N₂ : Composite_Node_Constructor |
│ n = InheritableNode N₁ ∨ n = CompositeNode N₂ • o = node_object n
└──────────────────────────────────────────────────────
```

The above schema precisely defines that for all nodes defined by a user they must belong to the existing node types which have the corresponding object types associated. Thus, all the nodes to abstract the application structure can be also presented by the abstract data types supported by a database system. However, the node type definitions of HyperDB only illustrate intra relationships within a node. To further describe semantic connections among nodes, we need link types to specifically define relationships between node types.

3.3 HyperDB Link Types

In order to specify functions of links in the HyperDB approach, we classify links into two different types. The first is the navigation link and the second is the relationship connection. There are two reasons for such distinction. Firstly, we want to simplify the link structure and specify the exact semantic connection between nodes. Secondly, we want to describe the semantic relationships among the application components at the node type level, i.e, the schema level to abstract semantic meanings. Most current hypermedia approaches mix these two different link types and their focus is on the user's level link of how to organize an application structure. This increases the difficulty to describe those complex relationships between and within application structures.

1. *Navigation Link Type*

   A navigation link type is purely a functional link to link instances of a node type. In the HyperDB approach, an instance link is a non-semantic link. That means it only physically links two instances. In the prototype design, this is just a browsing function defined on the source and the target of nodes.

   Navigation_Link

   $target_1, target_2 : Node\_Type$
   $navigation\_link : \mathbb{P}(Multimedia \times Multimedia)$

   $\forall nodes : \mathbb{P}\, Node\_Type \bullet \exists n_1, n_2 : nodes;\ N_1 : Node\_Constructor;$
   $N_2 : Composite\_Node\_Constructor \mid n_1 = InheritableNode\ N_1 \vee$
   $n_1 = CompositeNode\ N_2 \vee n_2 = InheritableNode\ N_1 \vee n_2 =$
   $CompositeNode\ N_2 \bullet N_1.node.source.media\_part = target_1 \wedge$
   $N_2.node.destination.media\_part = target_2$
   $\Rightarrow target_1 = navigation\_link\ target_2$

   ---

2. *Connection Type*

   A connection between node types is a high level relationship type which specifies a user's defined semantics between node types. We need a specified relationship exactly represent a semantic meaning between two node types. This is achieved by the connection type defined by the following schema.

   Node_Type_Connection

   $connection : \mathbb{P}(Node\_Type \times Node\_Type)$

   $\forall node\_types : \mathbb{P}\, Node\_Type \bullet \exists n_1, n_2 : node\_types;$
   $N_1 : Node\_Constructor;\ N_2 : Composite\_Node\_Constructor \mid$
   $n_1 \neq InheritableNode\ N_1 \vee n_2 \neq CompositeNode\ N_2 \bullet n_1 \mapsto n_2$

The above schema expresses that if two node types are not inheritable and composite node types, there must be a named semantic relationship defined between them. This further implies that no isolated node types exist in the hyper-space. This is the advantage of the HyperDB approach since every defined node type has specific purpose for its existence. If a node type is an isolated one, it is not allowed to be existed in HyperDB.

In this section, we discuss node type constructors and their corresponding formal definitions. Our purpose is to illustrate the internal structure of a node type, in particular, the different semantic connections among the defined node types and how node types are related in order to represent an application structure. These formal definitions only describe the static properties of the node types of the HyperDB approach. Particularly, the schema definitions illustrate the inherent constraints of the node types. For the limited length of this paper, we are not going to discuss their formal Z specification here. There are seven types of operations.

4 Implementation

In the following paragraphs, we will briefly discuss the design strategies and system structure as the main purpose of this paper is to illustrate the data model of the HyperDB approach.

- An Open System
  An open hypermedia system is such one which can provide a supporting mechanism to integrate and link the existing applications. In the HyperDB approach, this is driven by a schema definition of the application. We develop a formal language on the basis of Z specification to define node types and relationships. This is a database meta-schema definition language which describes the type level information of nodes and relationships. When an application is defined, the structural information is captured by this language and stored in a database. On the other hand, the HyperDB approach also supports the second meaning of the open hypermedia system which is the same schema definition shared by a group of users. Since the HyperDB structure is a unified data structure, the corresponding prototype should support a distributed information sharing. That is, a group of users can use the same schema definition but the actual information stored in the database may be different.
- An Object Oriented System
  The second feature of the HyperDB prototype is its object oriented design. C++ provides us with a strong object oriented supporting mechanism to implement the object oriented model. This is revealed by the class definitions to abstract both functions and behaviours of similar operations and definitions. We defined three major classes to describe the displaying, defining and manipulating nodes, links and relationships. These three classes further act as the super classes to define specific sub-classes for manipulating node and

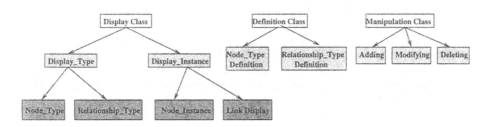

Fig. 1. HyperDB class structure

link information. To naturally organize these classes, we propose a concept — *manager* to link these classes in the source code design stage. A manager is a functional independent module. Our approach has two advantages. Firstly, we separate the interface from the database. This means that we do not need to re-design the interface when a database is changed, and *vice versa*. Secondly, it is easy for us to extend and re-use the functionalities of the prototype. By using the manager concept to construct the prototype, we can simplify the system structure. We use a single window to display all information which are useful to users.

5 Conclusion

Our focus in this paper is on using the powerful database facilities to maintain and store multimedia information without losing the flexibility of hypermedia to view information and navigate in the hyper-space. It addresses the mechanism of how to combine both advantages of hypermedia and database systems to define and maintain a hypermedia application structure which has been rarely discussed. The major contribution of this work is the formal specification to describe the internal structure of the unified data model. Thus, it offers a sound basis for the next generation of hypermedia and integrated information system design. Our next plan is to establish the communication between different platforms in order to achieve a real open hypermedia network supporting environment for large hypermedia applications.

References

1. P. K. Garg. *Information Management in Software Engineering: A Hypertext Based Approach.* PhD thesis, Computer Science Department, University of Southern California, USA, 1989.

2. Franca Garzotto and Paolo Paolini. Hdm — a model-based approach to hypertext application design. *ACM Transactions on Information Systems*, 11(1):1–26, January 1993.

3. F. G. Halasz. Seven issues: Revisited. *Hypertext'91 Keynote Talk*, December 18, 1991.

4. P. Hitchcock and B. Wang. Formal approach to hypertext system based on object oriented database systyem. *Information and Software Technology*, 34(9):573–592, September 1992.

5. D B Lange. Constructing a hypertext based program development environment using a commercial oodbms, September 2 1991. Paper Submitted for OOPSLA'91.

6. Nitin Sawhney, David Balacom, and Ian Smith. Hypercafe: Narrative and aesthetic properties of hypervideo. In *Hypertext'96*, pages 1–10, Washington DC, USA, March 16-20 1996. ACM Press.

7. H A Schutt and N A Streitz. Hyperbase: A hypermedia engine based on a relational database management system. In *Proceedings of the First European Conference on Hypertext*, pages 95–108, France, November 1990.

8. D. Schwabe and G.Rossi. The object oriented hypermedia design model. *Communication of the ACM*, 38(8), 1995.

9. Daniel Schwabe, Gustavo Rossi, and Simone D.J. Barbosa. Systematic hypermedia application design with oohdm. In *Hypertext'96*, pages 116–128, Washington DC, USA, March 16-20 1996. ACM Press.

10. K E Smith and S B Zdonik. Intermedia: A case study of the differences between relational and object-oriented database systems. In *OOPSLA'87 Proceedings*, pages 465–542, October 4-8 1987.

11. B Wang. *Integrating Database and Hypertext to Support Documentation Environments*. PhD thesis, Computer Science Department, University of York, Heslington, York, Y01 5DD, U.K, 1993.

12. B. Wang. The design of an integrated information system. In Roland R. Wagner and Helmut Thomas, editors, *Database and Expert System Applications (DEXA'96), Lecture Notes in Computer Science No. 685*, pages 479–488, Zurich, Switzerland, September 1996. Springer-Verlag.

13. B. Wang and P. Hitchcock. *InterSect*: A general purpose hypertext system based on an oriented database. In Dr. Ing. D. Karagiannis, editor, *Database and Expert Systems Applications (DEXA'91)*, pages 459–464, Berlin, Germany, August 1991. Springer-Verlag.

14. B. Wang, T. Holden, and P. Wilhelmij. A rule-based approach for controlling data modelling. In J.G.Chen, F.G.Attia, and D.L.Crabtree, editors, *The 6th International Conference on Artificial Intelligence and Expert System Applications*, pages 109–114, Texas, USA, December 1994. I.I.T.T International.

15. Uffe Kock Wiil and John J. Leggett. The hyperdisco approach to open hypermedia systems. In *Hypertext'96*, pages 140–148, Washington DC, USA, March 16-20 1996. ACM Press.

Managing the Global Behavior of Composite Objects

C. Oussalah, M. Magnan, and S. Vauttier

LGI2P / EMA - EERIE, Parc Scientifique G. Besse, 30 000 Nîmes - France
E-mail : {oussalah,magnan,vauttier}@eerie.fr

Abstract. Managing the global behavior of composite objects is a
complicated task which encompasses several aspects: the collaboration
of the behavior of the composite object with that of its components, the
management of its semantic integrity and the evolution of its behavior. In
this paper, a model is proposed for the specification, the representation
and the management of the global behavior of composite objects.

1 Introduction

Many object-oriented systems provide composition links to represent and
manipulate the structure of composite objects [7, 10]. But only few systems
provide adapted means to capture the behavior of composite objects.
Nonetheless, composite objects are assemblies of objects the interactions of which
must be appropriately defined and controlled to make them act as a whole.
Managing the global behavior of composite objects is a complicated task which
encompasses several aspects: the collaboration of the behavior of a composite
object with that of its components, the integrity management of the composite
object and the evolution of the behavior of a composite object.

Composite objects therefore need expressive and declarative models to
efficiently represent and manage their behaviors. Among the various models
which have been proposed to manage object behavior [4, 5], some models aims
to manage specifically the behavior of composite objects [1, 13]. However, these
models usually address only integrity maintenance problems. Moreover, even
though general behavior models can be applied to composite objects [4, 5],
they are not adapted to managing their global behaviors because they take into
account neither the semantics of the composition relationship nor the evolution
of the composite objects.

The COBALT (Composite Object Behavior AppLied Taxonomy) model is
therefore proposed to address the problems of the specification, representation
and management of the global behavior of composite objects. The specification
of the global behavior is performed thanks to *behavior diagrams* which provide
a high-level, easy to understand, visualization of behaviors. Behavior diagrams
can automatically be translated into object-oriented features which implement
the global behavior of composite object classes. For this purpose, *state objects*
and *behavior objects* are introduced in order to explicitly represent and manage

the global behavior of composite objects instead of burying it into the code of objects' methods.

The remainder of this paper is organized as follows. After introducing the composite object model that we use (§2), a model for the specification of the behavior of composite objects is proposed (§3). The way the global behavior of composite objects is represented (§4) and managed (§5) is then described. Finally, conclusions from this work are drawn (§6).

2 Composite Objects

A composite object is defined as the aggregation of a set of objects, called its components, which describe the parts of the composite object [1]. Each component can itself be a composite object. This hierarchical collection of objects is called a composition hierarchy. A composite object references its components through composition links. Thus, a composite object class (or composite class for short) is defined by its *local structure*, which describes the set of the attributes of the objects of this class and by its *global structure*, which defines these composite objects as variable assemblies of components. The following example, which will be used throughout this paper, describes a gas pump [2]. The objects of the composite class *Pump* are composed of a body, a tank, a motor, a clutch, a gun and a pair of displays showing the state of the pump and the volume of the gas. The definition of the class *Pump* is given below. The syntax is C++-oriented.

```
class Pump
isa CompositeObject
     private:
     //    Attributes
           company : string;
     //    Internal components
           the_body : Body;
           the_tank : Tank;
           the_motor : Motor;
           the_clutch : Clutch;
     public:
     //    External components
           the_gun : Gun;
           the_display (ident: string) : set(Display);
     //    Methods
           Pump create();
           void delete();
           void enable();
     end class;
```

Each component is referenced by a composition link. For instance, the link *the_body* defines a composition link towards objects of the class *Body*. Composition links can belong either to the interface (external components) or to the implementation of a composite class (internal components). Internal components are private to the composite object to which they belong and cannot be shared. External components in contrast can be accessed directly (they are visible) : they enrich the interface of the composite object with the functionalities of their own interfaces.

A component is known, from the point of view of the composite object, by the name of the composition link which references it. A composition path expression is therefore defined as the sequence of the names of the composition links which link the composite object and one of its components. If a composition link is multi-valued, its name is not sufficient to identify a component in a set or a list. An identifier must be provided to identify each component. For example, the expression *the_display('Message').display()* can be used in a method of the composite class *Pump* to send the message *display()* to the component referenced by the composition link *the_display* and identified by the identifier *'Message'*.

3 Specification of the Behavior of Composite Objects

The behavior of a composite object can be rather complex, even for a simple example such as a gas pump. Thus, before a customer can use the pump, it must be enabled. The volume display is reset and the message display says 'Welcome'. The motor is now started when the gun is taken out of the holster and the message display is changed to 'Dispensing gas'. Then, when the trigger of the gun is pressed, the clutch is engaged and the gas is delivered. In turn, when the gun is replaced in the holster, the clutch is released, the motor is stopped and the message display says 'Please...Wait'. The pump must then be enabled again.

The design and management of composite objects are all the more complex because they do not have to cope with a single monolithic entity but with the interactions of a set of objects that cooperate to act as a whole.

3.1 Global Behavior Taxonomy

The basic principle of the specification of the behavior of a composite object class is to distinguish in its description:
- its *local behavior*, which defines the basic functionalities which apply locally to the objects of this class,
- from its *global behavior*, which defines the functionalities and the management of these composite objects as wholes.

Local behavior is static because it is based on the attributes of the composite objects whereas global behavior is dynamic because it depends on their current global state and composition. Even if some work distinguishes static behavior from dynamic behavior of objects [4, 6, 8], none has specifically studied the dynamic behavior of composite objects.

The analysis of the global behavior of composite objects highlights three main problems when dealing with their aggregated and dynamic structures:
- *behavior collaboration*, which encompasses all the mechanisms used to define the functionalities of the whole by combining the individual functionalities of the components.

- *integrity management*, which includes all the actions that control and update the state of the composite object and its components, in order to maintain the consistency of the entity it embodies.
- *behavior evolution*, which groups the means that express the different states of the composite objects and their impact on the way they execute and manage their functionalities, in order to retain coherent behaviors.

Collaboration is used to define functionalities, the execution of which depends on the reception of messages (passive behavior). On the contrary, integrity management or behavior evolution are spontaneously handled by the composite objects as a reaction to the state changes they, or their components, are ordered to make (active behaviors) [9]. Indeed, external components are meant to be directly accessed. Nonetheless, to enforce the reuse of component object classes, component classes must not be programmed according to the composite classes they compose. Their definition must remain intrinsic: this is called *component class independence* towards the composite classes which reference them [13].

3.2 Behavior diagrams

This section presents the graphical formalism, the *behavior diagrams*, proposed for the specification of the global behavior of composite objects. Behavior diagrams are not intended to be an alternative to the formalisms proposed in the recent OO modeling methods. Indeed, a concensus seems to arise about the requirements to properly specify object behavior. For instance, both Fusion [2] and UML [15] use state diagrams and interaction diagrams. State diagrams are used to depict the object life cycles as sets of states and transitions and interaction diagrams describe a given functionality in terms of message exchanges between objects. Our behavior diagrams comply with this approach and are based on *state diagrams* as well as *collaboration* and *integrity diagrams* (two kinds of interaction diagrams). They should therefore be regarded as an extension of the existing formalisms in order to take into account the global behavior of composite objects. In particular, existing methods lack the means to easily express the relations between the state diagram of a composite object and those of its components. Moreover, they do not provide much support to express the behavior evolution.

State Diagrams. A top-down specification of the global behavior of composite objects is recommended. It starts with the definition of the different states of the composite object, which identify the different ways the composite object behaves, and their transitions. The state diagrams of a class (composite or not) is a graph in which the nodes represent the possible states of the objects of this class and the edges the transitions between these states. The labels of the edges identify those functionalities, the execution of which can change the state of the object, and eventually the conditions required to cross the transitions (Fig. 1).

Collaboration Diagrams. Behavior collaborations describe how the local functionalities of the composite object class and its component classes are

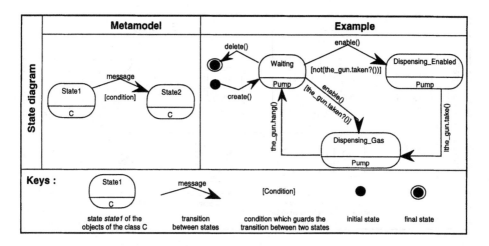

Fig. 1. State diagrams of the objects of the composite class *Pump*

combined to define the global functionalities of the composite object class. We have identified four types of collaborations:

- *percolation* [16] which implicitly defines the execution of the functionality invoked by the incoming message, as the result of executing this functionality locally on the composite object and all its components.
- *blind delegation* [11] which specifies that the message received by the composite object is forwarded to the first of its components (in terms of composition hierarchy) the class of which possesses a corresponding functionality.
- *explicit delegation* which, on the contrary, explicitly names the component to which the message is forwarded in order to ensure its priority over the other components which are able to handle the functionality.
- *explicit combination* (Fig. 2) which defines the execution of the message that is received by the composite object as the sending to the composite object and its components of a new set of messages which are combined by a high-level operator (sequence, parallelism, alternative, ...).

    Only one collaboration diagram may be associated with one functionality at a time in order to have only one way to execute an operation.

Integrity Management Diagrams. Integrity management diagrams specify the operations that have to take place after the execution of a functionality to maintain the consistency of a composite object. Integrity management diagrams apply to both the functionalities of the composite class and to interface functionalities of its component classes. Two kinds of integrity management are to be distinguished:

- *unconditional integrity management* which defines operations to be performed after the execution of a functionality to coordinate state changes of the components. Only functionalities of the component classes are concerned by such behaviors since they cannot rule the interactions of components within composite

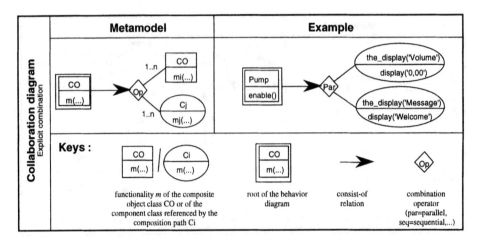

Fig. 2. A collaboration diagram of the objects of the composite class *Pump*

objects (component class independence) in opposition to the functionalities of composite classes which are designed on purpose to combine properly the behaviors of the component classes (thanks to behavior collaborations).

- *conditional integrity management* which specifies the invariants that must be maintained and the operations that restore them when they are violated. The roots of these behavior diagrams represent functionalities whose execution can violate the invariant. The invariants are expressed as condition labels on the 'imply' arrows (Fig. 3). The set of combined operations is executed only when the condition is true (the invariant is no longer enforced). Several behaviors of this kind can be attached to a functionality to express several invariants. Priorities may then be defined by the designer to express an evaluation order.

Behavior Diagram Interrelations. Once these different types of behavior diagrams have been described for a composite class and its component classes, correspondences between these scattered diagrams may be specified in order to completely define the global behavior of the objects of this composite class.

• *State hierarchization.* State diagrams are used to describe the life cycles of the objects whether they be composite objects or not. In order to correctly manage the global behavior of a composite object class, it is necessary to synchronize its state diagram with those of its component classes, this means to specify the states in which components are expected to be when a composite object of this class is in a given state. Thus, each node of the state diagram of a composite class can be zoomed and described in terms of the states of its component classes: this forms a state hierarchy which is parallel to the composition hierarchy. This information will be used during the management of the composite object behavior.

• *Behavior evolution.* The execution of a functionality may produce different behaviors depending on the current state of the object. The evolution of the

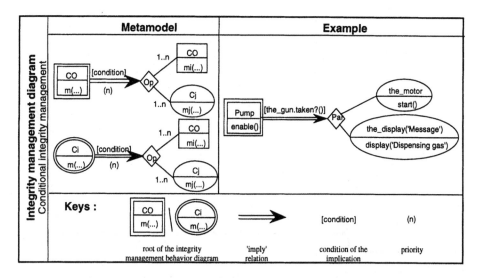

Fig. 3. An integrity management diagram of the objects of the composite class *Pump*

behavior of the composite objects has therefore to be specified according to the evolution of their state. State diagrams are then also used to express in which states the collaboration and integrity management diagrams are valid. Thus, the scope of a collaboration or an integrity management diagram can be restricted to one state by including the behavior diagram in a cell labeled with the name of the chosen state. The functionality call will result in the behavior described by the behavior diagram only if the composite object is in the corresponding state (activation state). The evolution of the behavior of the composite objects can thus be expressed by associating with a functionality more than one behavior. The execution of a functionality may also be forbidden in a given state in order to maintain the consistency of the composite object.

4 Representation of the Behavior of Composite Objects

The representation model relies on the concepts of *state objects* and *behavior objects* [12]. With each composite class is associated a set of state object classes which represent the different possible states of the objects of this composite class as specified by its state diagram. Each state object class references the set of behavior object classes defining the behavior of the objects of the composite class in this state (Fig. 4). The behavior object classes represent the behavior specified by the collaboration and integrity management diagrams and are referenced by the state object classes corresponding to their activation state. Three types of behavior objects are thus distinguished: collaboration, integrity management and evolution behavior objects, this latter type of behavior object being used to represent state transitions.

State object classes may also be associated with non-composite classes to

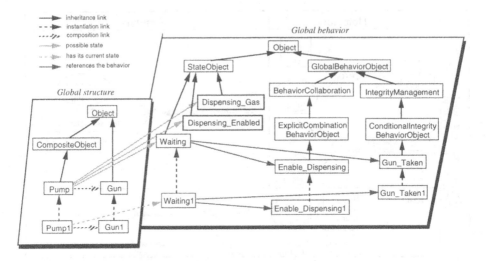

Fig. 4. State and behavior objects of the example of the class *Pump*

model their life cycles. Nevertheless, in this case, only evolution behavior object classes may be referenced by these state classes. Indeed, the global behavior of a composite object is only associated with the composite object in order to respect the component class independence principle.

At instance level, the system ensures the creation and the management of state and behavior objects. An instance of each state and behavior object class is created by the system. Any time, a composite object references the state object representing its current state. The behavior objects that are referenced by this state object define the global behavior which has to complete the local behavior defined by the methods of the class of the composite object.

The translating of the behavior diagrams into state and behavior objects can be automatically performed by processing the graphical formalism used.

5 Management of the Behavior of Composite Objects

Each message sent to a composite or component object is filtered by a controller object the task of which is to determine, depending on the state of the object and the states of its parent composite objects, the way the called functionality has to be performed. Each composite and component object references the state object that represents its current state and only those behavior objects that are referenced by this state object are valid. Therefore, when a message is sent to a composite or component object, the controller has to verify that the called functionality is not frozen, to execute the functionality and, finally, to manage the consequences of the execution of the functionality.

• In order to verify that the called functionality is not frozen, the controller examines the list of the frozen functionalities of the state objects associated with the receiver object and the composite objects of which it is part. If the functionality is frozen in one of these states, an exception is raised.

• If the receiver of the initial message is a composite object, in order to determine how the functionality has to be executed, the controller searches for any collaboration behavior object that manages to the called functionality in the state object currently referenced by the receiver object. If no collaboration behavior object is found, the look up of the functionality is handled classically by the method selection mechanism.

• Managing the consequences of the execution of a functionality consists in applying all the integrity management and evolution behavior objects currently valid for this functionality. The lookup of these behavior objects is carried out by examining the state objects referenced by the receiver object and by the composite objects of which it is a component. The consequence management mechanism may be decomposed into two levels:

- local mechanism: the controller examines the state object associated with the receiver object to search for integrity management and evolution behavior objects that define the actions that have to be performed after the execution of the functionality. Integrity management objects are applied before evolution objects in order to restore the consistency of the composite object before changing its state. Moreover, unconditional integrity management behavior objects are processed before conditional integrity management behavior objects since they define actions that must always be performed after the execution of the functionality.

- global mechanism: once the local mechanism has been applied on the receiver object, the consequences of the execution of the functionality have to be propagated to the composite objects of which the receiver object is a component in order that they in turn restore their consistency. The local mechanism is therefore recursively applied to all these composite objects by going up the composition links.

It should be noted that the execution of the action of a behavior object can involve the sending of a new set of messages which may in turn entail the processing of new behavior objects. These behavior objects are processed separately (new activation context) by applying the same management mechanism. In order to avoid infinite loops and therefore ensure termination [3, 18], the principle is adopted that a behavior object cannot be applied more than once during the management of a given functionality for a given object.

6 Conclusion

The management of the behavior of composite objects is addressed by providing a taxonomy of the behaviors which are used to describe the global behavior of composite objects. This taxonomy has led to the proposal of specification and representation models of composite object behavior. COBALT is being developed in C++, over the SGBDOO Versant [17], to implement the composite object model of a CAD framework. Moreover, the same approach is being applied to the extension of the current model to cope with the management of complex objects (objects linked by connection links, association links, etc.): it is founded on using the semantics of the relations between objects to organize the behavior of sets of objects automatically.

References

1. E. BLAKE and S. COOK. On Including Part Hierarchies in Object-Oriented Languages with an Implementation in Smalltalk. In ECOOP'87 Proceedings, 1987.
2. D. COLEMAN, P. ARNOLD, S. BODOFF, S. DOLLIN, H. GILCHRIST, F.HAYES and P. JEREMES. *Object-Oriented Development - The Fusion Method.* Prentice Hall, 1994.
3. U. DAYAL, E. HANSON and J. WIDOW. Active Database Systems. In W. KIM, editor, *Modern Database Systems*, Addison-Wesley Publishing Company, 1995.
4. S. DUCASSE, M. BLAY and A.M. PINNA. A Reflective Model for First Class Dependencies. In *ACM OOPSLA'95 Proceedings*, 1995.
5. A. GOLDBERG and D. ROBSON. *Smalltalk-80 : The Language and its Implementation*, Addison-Wesley, 1983.
6. R. GUETARI and F. PIARD. An Object-Oriented Method of Analysis, Specification and Design for Industrial Information Systems. In *6th IEEE Int. Conf. on Tools with Artificial Intelligence*, 1994.
7. M. HALPER, J. GELLER and Y. PERL. An OODB Relationship Model. In *Proceedings of the 1st International Conference on Information and Knowledge Management*, 1992.
8. T. HARTMANN, J. KUSH, G. SAAKE and P. HARTEL. Revised Version of the Conceptual Modeling and Design Language TROLL. In *Proceedings of the ISCORE Workshop*, 1994.
9. G. KAPPEL and M. SCHREFL. Modelling Object Behavior : To Use Methods or Rules or Both ?. In *DEXA'96 Proceedings*. LNCS, 1996.
10. W. KIM. *Introduction to Object-Oriented Databases.* MIT Press Cambridge, 1990.
11. H. LIEBERMANN. Delegation and Inheritance : Two Mechanisms for Sharing Knowledge in Object-Oriented Systems. In *Acte des 3èmes Journées Orientées Objet*, 1986.
12. M. MAGNAN, C. OUSSALAH and S. VAUTTIER. From Specification to Management of Composite Object Behavior. In *TOOLS USA'97 Proceedings*, Santa Barbara, CA, 1997.
13. M. MURATA and K. KUSUMOTO. Daemons: Another Way of Invoking Methods. *Journal of Object-Oriented Programming*, 2(2), 1989.
14. D. RAMAZANI and G. v. BOCHMANN. Extending OMT for the Specification of Composite Objects. In *Proceedings of TOOLS USA 96*, 1996.
15. RATIONAL SOFTWARE CORPORATION. *Unified Modeling Language.* Version 1.0, 1997.
16. J. RUMBAUGH. Controlling Propagation of Operations using Attributes on Relations, In *ACM OOPSLA'97 Proceedings*, 1988.
17. VERSANT OBJECT TECHNOLOGY. *VERSANT Reference Manual.* VERSANT Object Database Management System, Release 4.0, July 1995.
18. L. van der VOORT and A. SIEBES. Termination and Confluence of Rule Execution. In *Int. Conf. on Information and Knowledge Management*, November 1993.

Heuristic Clustering of Database Objects According to Multi-Valued Attributes*

Jukka Teuhola

Turku Centre for Computer Science (TUCS), University of Turku
Lemminkäisenkatu 14 A, FIN-20520 Turku, FINLAND

Email: teuhola@cs.utu.fi
Tel: +358-2-3338636   Fax: +358-2-3338600

Abstract. This paper studies clustering of objects on the basis of set-valued attributes, so that objects in the same cluster share as many attribute values as possible. Our primary application is clustering of objects participating in a many-to-many relationship. Since the precise optimum is computationally too hard to find, a relatively simple and fast heuristic is developed. The sets of attribute values are represented by non-unique, fixed-size signatures, which constitute the basis for clustering. Objects to be clustered are stored on the leaf pages of a binary tree, where each internal node contains a pair of signatures directing the search for a suitable leaf. The core of the method is a page splitting algorithm, which tries to combine two endeavours: enhance clustering and keep the tree balanced. In a random case, there is little chance for beneficial clustering. However, the dependencies and correlations between real-life objects enable us to achieve notable increase of performance.

Keywords: Clustering, Multi-valued attributes, Many-to-many relationships, Signature files, Page splitting, Object databases.

1   Introduction

Accessing singular objects from a database presents no performance problems to current database systems. However, accessing a large set of objects in a single transaction may be too inefficient, unless the objects are well clustered on disk. It is obvious that clustering remains an important issue in data storage, as long as slow rotating deviced are used. The difficult thing is choosing the right basis for clustering in each case. Alternative grounds are, for example:

1. *Content:* Objects may, for example, be sorted by the values of a given attribute.
2. *Structure:* Objects participating in a busy relationship may be good candidates for clustering.
3. *Usage:* Clustering may be based on gathered statistics of co-accessed objects.

---

* This work was supported by the Academy of Finland

The techniques for simple content-based clustering are well-known: the B-tree (with its variants) is most suitable for keeping objects physically in key order. *Multi-key clustering* is more difficult, but can be achieved to some degree with the *grid* organization [12], or *multidimensional trees* [2]. Mapping of multiattribute objects onto linear space was discussed in [9]. Theoretical results concerning multidimensional search structures can be found from [18]. In any case, these methods are restricted to a fixed number of dimensions.

Structure-based clustering is common in databases supporting complex data structures. In object databases, for example, we can distinguish clustering along class composition hierarchies, along class generalization hierarchies, and combinations of the two. The most natural candidates for clustering are *composite objects*, consisting of parent-child $(1 : M)$ relationships between objects and their components. This case has been studied already with the early hierarchical DBMSs, see [14]. General directed acyclic graphs were investigated in [1]. Other results from clustering in object databases have appeared e.g. in [3, 4, 16, 17].

Actually, any kinds of relationships may be important access paths; they need not be of PART-OF type, nor $1 : M$. It is just that objects in *many-to-many* $(M : M)$ relationships are much harder to cluster. The difficulties are embodied e.g. in the fact that CODASYL databases support this type of relationship only indirectly, via a common child of two $1 : M$ relationships. Clustering of multi-parent children (or shared subobjects) was considered in [15], but here we tackle the harder problem, namely clustering the components of $M : M$ relationships. Object databases usually support these relationships directly, so that one object contains a *reference set* to the related instances in the other class, and vice versa. These reference sets can as well be considered *multi-valued attributes*, which explains the title of the present paper.

The third main category of clustering, based on access statistics, is not restricted to the constructs defined in the schema. Objects of any type and content may be clustered together, if there is enough evidence of their co-usage [19].

2   Problem Definition

We first motivate the problem with a small example. A university database contains information about students, courses, and the relationship 'Pass' between the two (Fig. 1a). Two natural queries against this schema are: 1) retrieve the students who have passed a given course, and 2) retrieve the courses that a given student has passed. The $M : M$ relationship Pass can be represented as a confluence of two $1 : M$ relationships — actually it *must* be, if there is *intersection data*, such as date passed, grade earned, etc. (see Fig. 1b). However, without redundancy, the above two queries cannot be answered by just accessing the common child. Thus, the clustering of parents is essential.

If the relationship instances between students and courses were random, we would have poor chances of successful clustering. However, the situation is far from random: e.g. a student majoring in computer science will certainly take more courses on computer science than on, say, botany. Therefore, *subject* is the

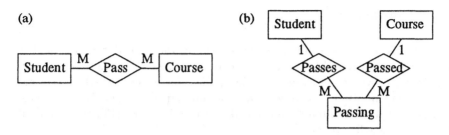

Figure 1. Two ER-representations of a many-to-many relationship: (a) direct, (b) via a shared subobject type.

common denominator for the two object types, and could be used as a basis of clustering. Unfortunately, the common link is not always so obvious.

The presented clustering task can be transformed into a more general problem of clustering based on a multi-valued attribute. The set of courses (references to courses) taken by a student can be considered an attribute of the student. If we cluster together such students, who have similar sets of courses taken, then we simultaneously support the access path from courses to students. The same approach applies to such multi-valued attributes that do not represent relationships. For example, take the object type 'car' with attribute 'colours' (allowing any number of them). If we cluster together cars which have similar sets of colours, then accessing by colour is enhanced.

Before formally defining the clustering task, we define some notations:

- $X = \{x_1, \ldots, x_n\}$ denotes the set of objects to be clustered,
- A = domain of values of the clustering attribute,
- $\text{Attr}(x_i) = \{a_{i1}, \ldots, a_{ik_i}\} \subseteq A$: values of the clustering attribute for x_i,
- $\text{Size}(x_i)$ = size of object x_i,
- P = page set,
- c = page capacity.

The optimization task can be expressed as follows: Define a page allocation function Page, where $\text{Page}(x_i)$ expresses the home page of x_i, such that the following expression is minimized

$$\sum_{a \in A} |\text{Pages}(\{x \in X | a \in \text{Attr}(x)\})|$$

where Pages is a generalization of function Page to set-valued arguments. In addition, the following constraint must be obeyed

$$\forall p \in P : \sum_{\text{Page}(x)=p} \text{Size}(x) \leq c$$

i.e. the page capacity must not be exceeded. Objects larger than a page can be handled by clustering only their headers.

In order to simplify the storage scheme, we restrict ourselves to the case where objects of different types are not stored on the same page.

3 Set Signatures

A *signature* is a fixed-size binary code describing the object from which it is calculated by some suitable (hashing) function. Access methods based on signatures have proved to be very useful in applications where stored objects are searched using multiple, possibly a variable number of criteria [5]. Examples include multivalued attributes and multikey access methods [13], text retrieval [11], and multimedia systems [6].

Research on signature techniques has mostly concentrated on organizing the signature files and improving the search effectiveness [7, 20]. Our purpose is quite different, namely clustering of the objects themselves, from which the signatures are calculated. Yet, the different goals are not orthogonal, at all. As we shall see, the signature tree suggested by Deppisch [7] is rather close to our constructions.

The first step to our clustering method is to map, for each object, the variable-size set of its attribute values (references) into a fixed-size signature. This is important because we want to ensure fast comparison of sets. Since we content ourselves with heuristic clustering, the mapping need not be 1:1, i.e. two distinct sets may map to the same signature. However, a high overlap of two signatures is a strong indication of the similarity of the actual sets.

A signature is defined as a fixed-size (k) bit vector, obtained by mapping $\text{Sig}(\{a_1,\ldots,a_n\}) = [b_1,\ldots,b_k]$, where $b_j = 1$ if there exists at least one a_i such that $\text{Hash}(a_i) = j$, otherwise $b_j = 0$. Simply stated, the attribute values are hashed to $1\ldots k$, and 1-bits are set to the hit positions. It is obvious that two attribute sets with a large intersection will map to very similar signatures. The opposite does not hold because, as in hashing, collisions do occur.

Ratio n/k in a way represents the *loading factor* of the signature. Any factor is possible, because the attribute sets are of variable size. However, a high loading factor reduces the usefulness of signatures for measuring the overlap of original sets. For reasons to be explained in the next section, we recommend that the average number of 1-bits in a signature (called its *weight*) is less than $k/2$. The maximum recommended loading factor is obtained from the condition $k(1 - (1 - 1/k)^n) \leq k/2$, which gives approximately $n/k \leq \ln 2 \approx 0.693$. Our clustering method is meant for relatively small values of n, otherwise the storage/processing penalty becomes too high. For example, $n = 100$ (on the average) implies $100/(0.693 \cdot 8) \approx 18$ bytes long signatures, which is very moderate. Of course, the more bits we can afford to 'invest' in signatures, the better they represent the original attribute sets, resulting in a better degree of clustering.

There are two main alternatives in the management of signatures:

1. *Static* signatures are calculated at object creation time, and stored with the object. Positioning of objects is *not* static; they may be moved e.g. in page splitting.
2. *Dynamic* signatures are updated when the underlying multivalued attribute changes. Dynamic signatures can be recalculated and need not be stored.

In our experiments (Section 6), we assumed static signatures, for simplicity.

4 Data Structure

A *binary tree* with the following characteristics (see also Fig. 2) will be built. Internal nodes contain two template signatures, called *attractors*. The data pages are stored as leaves, containing the actual objects. Given the signature of a new object to be inserted, the path from the root to a leaf is determined by choosing at each node the closer of the attractors. An example path is given in Fig. 2. The new object is inserted in the obtained leaf, if there is room. Otherwise, the leaf must be split and the tree extended.

From now on, we call the tree an *attractor tree*. The reader may notice an analogy with so called *evolutionary* (or *phylogenetic*) trees, used for representing the refinement of species in the history of evolution, see e.g. [8].

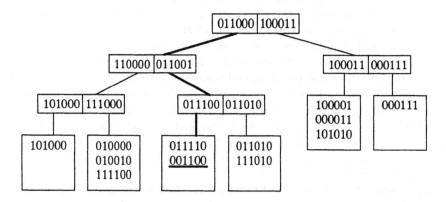

Figure 2. Attractor tree with data pages as leaves. A sample path for signature = 001100 is shown.

Two reasonable choices of measuring the distance between signatures are:

1. *Hamming distance*, expressing the number of differing bits (0/1 or 1/0),
2. k minus the number of common 1-bits.

We suggest the latter, because common 0-bits only imply similarity of the *complement* sets, which is usually not so relevant. The distance is obtained fast by determining the logical NAND of the arguments, and counting the 1-bits.

The attractors are determined at page splits. A new internal node is created at the end of an existing path. The node will point to the two new pages resulting from split. In principle there are no restrictions concerning the two attractors in a node — in practice they will be most different in the root, and gradually more similar down the tree. Also, there are no restrictions on the attractors on different paths of the tree. Even the *same* attractor may occur in multiple places.

The tree is not necessarily balanced. This may result from several (almost) equal attribute sets, or from collisions. In the worst case, the structure may degenerate into a linear list. Also the creation order may affect the balance; a random order is recommended.

The organization of internal nodes in secondary storage is not specified in detail here. For N pages, there will be $N - 1$ nodes, with $2(N - 1)$ attractors, consuming $2k(N - 1)$ bits memory. If k is moderate, large portions, if not all, of the internal nodes can be kept in main memory. Notice also that the tree is needed *only* when inserting new objects or reclustering old ones. Accessing objects for queries or updates takes place using object identifiers and their normal access paths, without touching the tree.

5 Page Splitting

The most important issue in promoting clustering is intelligent splitting of full pages, during the growth of the object set. There are two, often contradictory, endeavours in splitting, namely 1) optimal clusters, and 2) even split. By 'optimal' we mean here a division that minimizes the number of page accesses in queries with the clustering attribute as key. The problem is known to be similar to the Graph Partitioning Problem, and therefore NP-complete. Tsangaris and Naughton [16] applied Kernighan's heuristic graph partitioning algorithm [10], but even that is quadratic. A linear-time heuristic was suggested by Deppisch [7], where two relatively dissimilar *seeds* were first selected from the set of page signatures. The rest were then added one by one to the closer subset. Balancing of the split was accomplished in a brute-force way, possibly deteriorating the dissimilarity of the subsets.

We developed a splitting method which is linear in the number of objects, but emphasizes separation of clusters, at the cost of possible unbalance of the split. With a small addition to the basic algorithm (explained later), the overall loading factor is not compromised. The steps of the algorithm are as follows.

Algorithm A.

1. Initialize two *count vectors*, $P = [P_1, \ldots, P_k]$, and $Q = [Q_1, \ldots, Q_k]$, to zeroes. These will be used as the basis when deriving the attractors.
2. For each signature S of the page to be split, do: If $S \cdot P \leq S \cdot Q$, then $P = P + S$ and $Q = Q + \overline{S}$; else $P = P + \overline{S}$ and $Q = Q + S$. Here '+', '·' and '−' represent vector sum, inner product, and complement, respectively.
3. Determine the attractors (A and B) of the new pages: If $P_i \geq (\sum_{i=1}^{k} P_i)/k$, then $A_i = 1$ else $A_i = 0$. Similarly, if $Q_i \geq (\sum_{i=1}^{k} Q_i)/k$, then $B_i = 1$ else $B_i = 0$.
4. Split the page into two, by depositing each object to the half, whose attractor is closer to the signature of the object.

Note that S itself is added to the closer vector, and $\overline{S}$ to the other. This has a kind of 'pull-and-push' effect, enhancing separation of the subclusters. The closeness is measured by the inner product, so that each vector position has a weight, expressing how strongly the position 'belongs' to that attractor.

If the split is totally unbalanced, we attach the *same* attractor to both sons and deposit all objects to the right son. Hereafter, the left son is preferred in insertions, leaving the right son *frozen*. Repeated unsuccessful splits may generate a linear path of left sons, with frozen leaves as right sons. The following theorem gives a sufficient condition for balanced split.

Theorem 5.1. *Algorithm A splits a set of random signatures uniformly, if the proportion r of 1-bits in the signatures is less than $1/2$.*

Proof. Assume that we build two subsets of objects, starting from empty sets, and denote their (dynamically growing) sizes by p and q, corresponding to count vectors P and Q. From the algorithm we know that $\sum_{i=1}^{k} P_i = rkp + (1-r)kq$ and $\sum_{i=1}^{k} Q_i = (1-r)kp + rkq$ and so $\sum_{i=1}^{k}(P_i + Q_i) = k(p+q)$. If at some point, $p = wq$, where $w > 1$ (unbalance), it means that, when choosing between P and Q,

$$
\begin{aligned}
\text{Prob}(Q) - \text{Prob}(P) &= \frac{((1-r)kp + rkq) - (rkp + (1-r)kq)}{k(p+q)} \\
&= \frac{(w-1)(1-2r)}{w+1} > 0
\end{aligned}
$$

Since the signatures are random, this means that Q has a higher probability to be selected, until a balance is returned. The process thus controls itself by always favouring the smaller subset. This feature is sufficient to guarantee a uniform split in an average case. The situation is symmetric for $w < 1$. □

The validity of the theorem has been observed in a number of experiments. Although the signatures are not random in practice, there is usually sufficient variation, so that the self-balancing property is effective.

6 Experiments

We studied the behaviour of our clustering algorithm with both real-life and artificial test data. For space reasons, we report results from only two cases.

Our first experiment concerns the STUDENTS-COURSES relationship, with data extracted from our university database. We tried clustering of both object types: students according to the courses passed, and courses according to the respective students. The parameters were as follows:

- number of students = 18 532
- number of courses = 7 091
- number of student-course pairs = 690 879
- page size = 4Kbytes
- object size = 50 bytes + pointer array to the connected objects
- signature size = 100 bytes

We assume that the variable-size pointer array, as well as the related signature, are stored detached from the actual object, so that they need not be included in the object size, from the clustering point of view.

The algorithm has a special procedure for cases where splitting fails. In the implementation, we made a more general interpretation of a 'failure': if the smaller half has less than 20% of the objects, then the larger half is 'frozen', and considered as a well-clustered, 'final' set of objects.

After allocating the objects according to our heuristic algorithm, the clusteredness of students was measured by accessing students of each course in turn, and counting the number of page accesses. The same was done in the opposite direction. The results are given in Table 1.

Table 1. Results from clustering students and courses.

Clustered object type	Relationship accessed	#Accessed objects (aver.)	#Accessed pages (aver.)	Loading factor	Max depth
student	course-student	97.4	15.2	0.70	19
course	student-course	37.3	10.6	0.67	17

When accessing students of a given course, about 6.4 relevant students were obtained from each page. A random allocation to the 323 pages would give less than 1.2 relevant students per page, so a considerable advantage was obtained. The courses were not quite so well clustered — about 3.5 relevant courses were obtained from each accessed page, on the average. The loading factor tended to be close to 70%. The depth of the attractor tree was approximately $2 \log_2 P$, implying resonable balance.

As the second example case, we generated an artificial many-to-many relationship, say $A : B$, with various degrees of inherent clusteredness. This was accomplished so that A,B-pairs (actually their object identifiers) were taken randomly from a block-diagonal distribution (Fig. 3), with varying number of blocks. Duplicate A,B-pairs were eliminated. Thus, when the number of blocks is increased, the clusteredness increases and this should be captured by our clustering algorithm. A single block represents a random set of pairs, from which no benefit should be extractable. The case is symmetric, so it is sufficient to observe clustering of only one class (say A). The parameters were:

- number of A-objects = number of B-objects = 10 000
- number of A,B-pairs = 1 000 000
- page size = 4 Kbytes
- object size = 50 bytes + array of 100 pointers
- signature size = 100 bytes

The results are given in Table 2, showing a rapid reduction in the number of page accesses (when accessing all A's connected to a given B), as the number of diagonal blocks is increased, as expected.

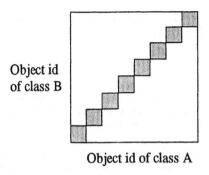

Object id
of class B

Object id of class A

Figure 3. Schematic illustration of the block-diagonal distribution.

Table 2. Clustering objects from a block-diagonally distributed relationship.

Number of diag. blocks	Accessed objects	Accessed pages	Loading factor	Percentage of frozen pages	Max depth
10	100	67.2	67.2	0	19
20	100	25.8	66.4	0	20
30	100	17.8	65.0	5.3	16
40	100	9.8	71.9	32.4	27
50	100	3.8	95.5	93.0	35

The loading factor rises close to 100%, due to the increase of frozen leaves. The increase of the tree depth indicates degeneration — it proved very difficult to reinforce the balance, without sacrificing the level of clustering.

7 Conclusions

Traditionally, database objects have been clustered by simple criteria. We suggested that objects could also be clustered according to multi-valued attributes and relationships. The latter case includes $M : M$ relationships and confluences of $1 : M$ relationships. Since the general multi-criteria clustering problem is NP-hard, we developed a simple and fast heuristic, based on fixed-size approximations (signatures) of variable-size sets.

The presented clustering approach is local in the sense that objects of only one class are clustered together. New object-based applications often contain composition and generalization hierarchies of several object classes, whose mixed clustering could bring additional benefit. Combining our intra-class clustering method with some hierarchical ordering is left for further work.

Our algorithm could also be used as a logical, hierarchical clustering method, where partitioning of subclusters is decided by some other rule than the restriction to physical pages. Typically, some kind of threshold for the variance within a cluster is applied. There are a large number of possible applications, mainly in the areas of artificial intelligence and information retrieval.

References

1. Banerjee, J., Kim, W., Kim, S-J., and Garza, J.F.: "Clustering a DAG for CAD Databases", *IEEE Trans. Softw. Eng.* **14**(11), 1988, 1684–1699.
2. Bentley, J.L.: "Multidimensional Search Trees Used for Associative Searching", *Comm. of the ACM* **18**(9), 1975, 509–517.
3. Chang, E.E., and Katz, R.H.: "Exploiting Inheritance and Structure Semantics for Effective Clustering and Buffering in an Object-Oriented DBMS", Proc. ACM SIGMOD, 1989, 348–357.
4. Cheng, J.R., and Hurson, A.R.: "Effective Clustering of Complex Objects in Object-Oriented Databases", Proc. ACM SIGMOD, 1991, 22–31.
5. Christodoulakis, S., and Faloutsos, C.: "Signature Files: An Access Method for Documents and Its Analytical Performance Evaluation", *ACM Trans. Office Inf. Syst.* **2**(4), 1984, 267–288.
6. Christodoulakis, S., et al.: "Multimedia Document Presentation, Information Extraction and Document Formation in MINOS: A Model and a System", *ACM Trans. Office Inf. Syst.* **4**(4), 1986, 345–383.
7. Deppisch, U.: "S-Tree: A Dynamic Balanced Signature Index for Office Retrieval", Proc. of ACM Conf. on Res. and Dev. in Inf. Retrieval, 1986, 77–87.
8. Gusfield, D.: "Efficient Algorithms for Inferring Evolutionary Trees", *Networks* **21**(1), 1991, 19–28.
9. Jagadish, H.V.: "Linear Clustering of Objects with Multiple Attributes", Proc. ACM SIGMOD, 1990, 332–342.
10. Kernighan, B.W., and Lin, S.: "An Efficient Heuristic Procedure for Partitioning Graphs", *Bell System Techn. J.* **49**(2), 1970, 291–307.
11. Lee, D.L., Kim., Y.M., and Patel, G.: "Efficient Signature File Methods for Text Retrieval", *IEEE Trans. Knowl. and Data Eng.* **7**(3), 1995, 423–435.
12. Nievergeld, J., Hinterberger, H., and Sevcik, K.C.: "The Grid File: An Adaptable, Symmetric Multikey File Structure", *ACM Trans. Database Syst.* **9**(1), 1984, 38–71.
13. Sacks-Davis, R., Kent, A., and Ramamohanarao, K.: "Multikey Access Methods Based on Superimposed Coding Techniques", *ACM Trans. Database Syst.* **12**(4), 1987, 655–696.
14. Schkolnick, M.: "A Clustering Algorithm for Hierarchical Structures", *ACM Trans. Database Syst.* **2**(1), 1977, 27–44.
15. Teuhola, J.: "Clustering of Shared Subobjects in Databases", Proc. Int. Conf. on Inf. Syst. and Manag. of Data (CISMOD), New Delhi, 1993, 175–188.
16. Tsangaris, M.M., and Naughton, J.F.: "A Stochastic Approach for Clustering in Object Bases", Proc. ACM SIGMOD, 1991, 12–21.
17. Tsangaris, M.M., and Naughton, J.F.: "On the Performance of Object Clustering Techniques", Proc. ACM SIGMOD, 1992, 144–153.
18. Willard, D.E.: "Multidimensional Search Trees that Provide New Types of Memory Reductions", *Journal of ACM* **34**(4), 1987, 846–858.
19. Yu, C.T., Suen, C-M., Lam, K., and Siu, M.K.: "Adaptive Record Clustering", *ACM Trans. Database Syst.* **10**(2), 1985, 180–204.
20. Zezula, P., Rabitti, F., and Tiberio, P.: "Dynamic Partitioning of Signature Files", *ACM Trans. Inf. Syst.* **9**(4), 1991, 336–369.

Object-Oriented Environment for Collaborative Software Design

Waldemar Wieczerzycki
Department of Information Technology
University of Economics
Mansfelda 4, 60-854 Poznań, Poland
e-mail: wiecz@kti.ae.poznan.pl.

Abstract. In the paper a new approach for modeling program variants is proposed, which is focused on both increasing the level of software reuse and supporting collaboration of programmers who work together. In this approach, a program is composed of a program body and a set of logically independent program contexts. During the program development, collaboratively working programmers address different contexts and do not conflict with each other. The programming environment supports awareness and communication mechanisms among them. During the program execution, only one context is active. It may, however, be changed dynamically at program run-time.

1. Introduction

It is increasingly recognized that software engineering is an engineering discipline concerned with the development of large software systems. These large system developments could not be accomplished without the cooperative working of several software engineers [2]. With the advent of computer supported collaborative software design (*CSCSD*), many process models of development with associated method and tool support have emerged [3, 5], but comparable models, methods and tools for large-scale software engineering design are lacking.

It is also increasingly recognized that large scale software should not be written from scratch, but rather assembled of existing universal pieces of code. Effective reuse of code is perhaps one of the most important factors in being able to deliver the right software product at the right time [1].

The reason that the object-oriented approach brings an interesting contribution to collaboratively written reusable software is that we can consider multiple clients and multiple implementations, not just one implementation as with subroutine libraries. If an object agrees to support certain functionality, it can be used polymorphically with other implementations of the same functionality.

A significant problem to date is that object-oriented languages and development approaches have not focused on articulating these interfaces on which both collaboration and reuse is based. Object encapsulation and class inheritance are not by themselves a solution to the problem. Is there a way that can more effectively and polymorphically support both collaboration in software design and reuse of code?

If we consider recent areas of software application, like computer aided design (*CAD*), software engineering (*CASE*), management (*CAM*), etc., we find out that they often require mechanisms to model slightly different object variants (versions). They might be modeled at the application level, however, it would be better to incorporate them into the programming language, thus increasing the level of polymorphism.

On the other hand, variants of program components (functions, data structures) support collaborative design of programs, since different designers may be easily assigned to different variants. Moreover, variants of program components support the design of generic and universal programs, which may be easily adapted to changing over the time user requirements and preferences, thus increasing the level of their reusability. To summarize, versioning embedded in programming languages might be a solution for large scale collaborative software design, typically oriented on reuse of existing components.

In [7] a new approach for modeling variants is proposed, which is focused mostly on increasing the level of software reuse. First, versioning concepts extending object-oriented programming language are described. Next, the approach is practically illustrated showing how the proposed concepts could be introduced into C++ language. A brief discussion concerning implementation issues is also given.

The approach mentioned above may also be useful in supporting collaboration among members of a software development group. It requires, however, some further extensions in the language itself and quite new mechanisms in the programming environment.

Briefly saying, the main goal of this paper is to show that an object-oriented language equipped with variants can increase the level of software reuse and support the collaboration of software designers in a very natural way, getting benefits from extended language semantics. The paper is structured in the following way.

In Section 2, the approach to incorporate variants into object-oriented languages is briefly reminded. Next, necessary extensions aimed at supporting collaboration are proposed. In Section 3 new mechanisms of the programming environment are described which support users' discussion and awareness during the software development process. A particular tool for final program generation is also proposed. Finally, in Section 4, conclusions and implementation remarks are given.

2. Programming Language

2.1. Basic Concepts

In the proposed approach [7] a program is composed of a *program body* and a set of logically independent *program contexts*. The program body contains global functions and global data structures. A particular global function, called the *main function*, is distinguished which starts and ends the program execution. Each program context contains exactly one variant of every class defined in the program and one variant of every non-global function, called a *context function*. It means that logically the number of both classes and context functions is the same in every program context.

During the program execution only one context is active. It may be, however, changed dynamically by a particular context switching command, which can be used only in the scope of global functions. Thus, at a particular moment of time the program is logically viewed as a sum of the program body and exactly one program context. It is illustrated in Fig. 1. The program is composed of its body and three contexts: Cx_1, Cx_2, Cx_3. The program body contains three global data structures: D_1,

D_2, D_3, and two global functions: F_1 (which is the main function), and F_2. Every context contains one variant of three classes: c_1, c_2, c_3, and one variant of two context functions: f_1 and f_2. Class c_1 is a root level class, while classes c_2 and c_3 are its direct subclasses. Context Cx_1 is an active one, which means that all references to context functions and classes from the program body are automatically re-addressed to Cx_1.

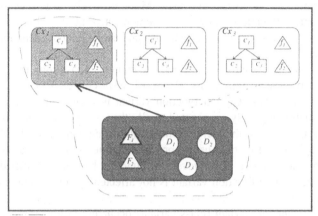

Fig. 1. Logical view of program structure

Variants of the same class/function belonging to different contexts need not be different. In order to avoid redundancy, the same variants are physically shared by program contexts. In case of classes, there are two possible levels of sharing: total and partial. Total class sharing is used when the class definition is exactly the same in two program contexts. Partial class sharing is used when the class definition is partially different in two program contexts, i.e. some class variables and/or methods are modified, while others remain unchanged. In the former case a single class is a unit of sharing, while in the latter case two units of sharing are used: a single variable and a single method.

In order to correctly resolve dynamic context switching the late binding technique is used and some restrictions on versioning are imposed. The late binding technique is commonly used in object-oriented languages: some of them (like Smalltalk [4]) use it widely, while other (like C++ [6]), for the sake of efficiency, constrain its scope only to virtual methods.

2.2. Extensions

Collaborative software engineering environments are dynamic and strongly interactive. Users develop their program progressively by adding new program components, frequently interacting with the programming environment and other users. Thus, the approach presented in Section 2.1 requires extensions, since originally it has been addressed to static environments, in which all contexts are fully defined before the compilation process [7].

A particular context, called *root context*, is distinguished. It is the only one which is defined from scratch. All other contexts are derived either from the root context or from another non-root context. Whenever a new context (a child) is dynamically derived, logical copies of all class and context function variants of its parent are associated with it. In other words, whenever a user derives his private context from a colleague's context, he logically inherits every program component accessible by his colleague. Inherited program component variants are called *implicit* variants. Afterwards, the child context may evolve independently of its parent, according to updates performed by the respective user. More precisely, a particular subset of classes and context functions may be re-implemented in the child context, thus introducing new class and function variants, which become independent and are called *explicit* variants.

The programming system keeps track of context derivation and stores links between shared program components. If one of users creates a new function (or a class), then in fact a single explicit function variant is created in the user's context, which is immediately logically propagated to all other contexts in which it appears as an implicit variant. Also further refinements of this function made by the function creator are propagated to other users, providing none of them has modified the function in a private context. If, however, the function has been modified by one of users, then the respective function variant is not affected by refinements made by the function creator.

If an implicit function variant (class variant) occurring in a user's context (i.e. a shared function variant) is not satisfactory, then he may modify it according to individual preferences, or select another variant, if available. In the first case, a new explicit function variant is introduced which is local (not shared) to the context accessed by the modifier, and a link to the original function variant is automatically broken. In the second case, the user browses all available explicit variants of the function and selects the one which is the most relevant. This operation replaces the link to the variant which no longer occurs in the user's context by a new link to the variant pointed by the user, which becomes implicit in the user's context. It is also possible to establish a link for a function which has been locally defined in the user's context. In this case, a local function variant is removed from the system and the context accessed by the user starts to share the selected function variant with the context in which it has been originally introduced, i.e. an explicit variant is replaced by an implicit variant in the user's context.

To summarize, when a non-shared function variant (class variant) is updated, then this update does not affect any other program context. The update operation introduces a new explicit function variant which replaces the previous one, thus the total number of function variants is preserved. When a shared implicit variant is updated, then this update also does not affect other program contexts. A link to the explicit variant is broken and a new explicit variant is introduced, thus the total number of variants is increased by one. Contrarily, an update performed on a shared explicit variant is propagated to all program contexts containing links to this variant. The number of variants is preserved and the links are not modified.

3. Support of Collaborative Software Development

The basic collaboration rule is that at a given time moment every user addresses exclusively at most one program context. This context is determined and dedicated to the user at the very beginning of his session, providing no authorization rule is violated, and the context selected is not accessed by any other user. Another possibility is to start user's session with the derivation operation which is never conflicting with operations of other users. By default, the user who derives a new program context is its owner and has unlimited access privileges.

As a consequence of the above rule, every user starting his session has an access to exactly one variant of every context function and every class, which has been already defined in the commonly designed program. Some functions and classes appear explicitly in the user's context, while other - implicitly. Since contexts addressed by different users are different and logically independent, it is not possible for the users to work simultaneously on the same piece of code. Even if they access the same class or context function, in fact they work on its isolated variants.

3.1. Users' Discussion

The most important elements of the collaboratively designed program are those which are common to all program contexts. Thus, it is natural that they have to be discussed and accepted by all team members. First, the contents and the implementation of a program body has to be discussed. Typically, the program body is created in the root context, at the beginning of program development, by a selected single person (e.g. the head of a team). When ready, the program body is logically copied to other users' contexts who derive them from the root. Afterwards, whenever further modifications in the program body are required, only one user may introduce them, providing that his intentions are known to others. The intentions are disseminated orally, if users work in the same room, or by available tele-conferencing tools, if they are physically distributed. Normally, the program body is locked after its creation, i.e. no updates are allowed. It may become unlocked for a single user, if all users with open sessions send explicit acknowledgments, and other users (who are not logged-on) have not set restrictions concerning inter-session modifications of the program body before the commitment of their recent sessions. Since the program body is monoversion and shared by all contexts, updates performed on it are immediately propagated to other contexts and displayed to other users, if required by them (cf. Section 3.2).

Second, a general program structure has to be accepted by all designers, i.e. the number of program modules, their names, the specificity of functions and classes comprised by modules. In practice it means that whenever a user wants to create a new program module, its header, which contains the name and comments concerning future contents, is displayed to other users. Similarly to modifications of the program body, an acknowledgment has to be sent by every on-line user.

Finally, every signature of a context function and every class interface must be acknowledged by all users. Since class signature contains the information on inheritance relationships, accepting it by all team members implies accepting modifications in the inheritance DAG. In the case of introducing a new context function or a class, the user sending his acknowledgment confirms that he is informed about the occurrence of a new program element, which is potentially useful for him. In the case of modifying a signature (or an interface) of an existing function (class), the user confirms his acceptance and the will to update all references to the modified function (class) in his context, in order to preserve its syntactical correctness.

3.2. Users' Awareness

Collaboratively working software designers need to be aware of what other people do, e.g. which program components have already been developed, in how many variants are they available, which components are currently under development, etc. To achieve this information, they do not want to browse the entire code of the program or to perturb their colleagues asking them questions. They would rather prefer to use particular programming system mechanisms, which can filter the whole information available and give them the most useful parts of it. In our approach, to fulfill these requirements, we use so called views, which work similarly to views commonly used in database management systems. Briefly speaking, a *view* is a sort of window which hides detailed and technical information concerning the code developed by other users, e.g. function implementation, and shows more abstract information, potentially useful to the view owner and adjusted to his preferences.

We distinguish two view types:
- a view based on exactly one context,
- a view based on more than one context.

A view based on a single context is used to look at the work of exactly one user, who is assigned to the program context on which the view has been created. Contrarily, a view based on more than one context, abstracts the information concerning the work of more than one user. There is one pre-defined view of this type, created automatically at the beginning of a user's session, which is based on all program contexts, including the one addressed by the user. It shows signatures and interfaces of all context functions and classes available, and the number of existing variants as well.

Views are implemented by special program contexts. Speaking more technically, a view is a read-only context which is derived directly from the context(s) on which it is based, after defining it by the user. In the simplest case, when a view does not hide any information, the corresponding context totally shares program components with its parent. In general, however, the corresponding context comprises only subset of elements contained in its parent, according the view definition, given to the system by the respective user. In such case, directly after context derivation (which initially is a logical copy of its parent), a selection mechanism is triggered which cuts off pieces of code not required by the user, and optionally transforms resting pieces to the form relevant to user's requirements.

Typically, a view contains signatures and interfaces of functions and classes included in the corresponding context, which have already been implemented and tested by a respective user. If required, a view may also contain information on functions and classes currently being developed. It is also possible to define a view that contains elements recently introduced, e.g. during last section or since a particular moment of time, elements that have been marked by their owner as important, comments put at the beginning of a class. method and/or context function definitions, etc.

Since views are read-only contexts, they can not contain any private data. Moreover, all elements included in a view are shared with a parent context(s). Thus, if a user working in the parent context introduces updates to objects visible in views, they are automatically propagated (possibly with some transformations, as given in view definitions) to respective views.

Contexts representing views are temporary. As mentioned before, the are created directly after their definition is presented to the system. They exist until the end of user's session, or even shorter, if the user explicitly deletes them. Although views are temporary contexts, their definition may be persistent and stored in the user's context. In such case, this definition is used by the system whenever the user opens his session, thus all views used during previous sessions may be automatically restored.

Views are illustrated in Fig. 2. User U_1, who accesses context C_{X1}, has defined two views V_2 and V_4 based on contexts C_{x2} and C_{x3}, respectively. User U_2, who accesses context C_{X2}, has also defined two views V_1 and V_5. View V_5 is defined recursively on view V_4. Finally, user U_3 has defined only one view, namely V_3, which shows the contents of context C_{x2} in a different way than view V_2 does.

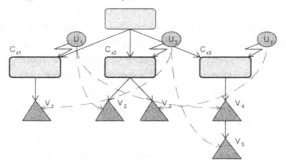

Fig. 2. Views based on contexts

3.3. Final Program Generation

The language and the programming system proposed up till now may, in general, support two different collaborative working styles. The first style emphasizes software reusability and genericity. Every designer develops a single context assigned to him which, in comparison to other contexts, corresponds to slightly different requirements, e.g. different hardware/software platforms, communication languages, user interfaces, provided functionalities, etc. Thus, the final program which encompasses all designers' contexts, can change its behavior without the need for source code modification (and re-compilation). It is sufficient to dynamically change the context at a program run-time.

One may say that in the case of the above working style designers divide their work somehow *horizontally*. On one hand, they share everything what is general enough and need not include the specificity of different alternatives, and, on the other hand, everybody develops individual variants of all program components which will support different program behavior, according to assumed alternatives. For example, in a program which provides communication with the user in three different national languages, all classes and functions which do not implement the user interface may be shared between contexts, while other have to be available in three different variants, corresponding to three different languages.

The second working style emphasizes collaboration of team members. Every designer develops a subset of classes and functions which are functionally related to each other, and might be considered as a subsystem (module) of the final software. In this style, an intersection between subsets of classes and functions assigned to different designers is empty, or it contains few elements only. In such situation, the final program generator should merge contexts addressed by all team members into a single one, not necessarily providing variants of functions and classes.

One may say that in the case of the above working style designers divide their work somehow *vertically*. They try to distinguish subsystems which comprise logically related classes and functions. The communication between different subsystems is limited, so they may work relatively independently of each other, providing that both a functionality and an interface of every subsystem is well defined and commonly accepted.

In practice, collaboratively working designers usually mix horizontal and vertical style, thus producing a code which comprises, on one hand, classes and functions developed individually (i.e. mono-variant) and, on the other hand, classes and functions developed in parallel by many people (i.e. multi-variant), which vary on implementation details. Thus, in the proposed approach, there is a need for a particular final program generator, which supports the integration of pieces of code that are partially mono-variant and partially multi-variant.

We assume that the generator takes as an input all program contexts created during the software development process (cf. Fig. 3), and produces as an output a subset of contexts which reflects common efforts of team members. The resulting program is composed of a context called the *main context* and a set of contexts called the *variant contexts*. The main context provides a default program behavior. It contains the program body, all mono-variant classes and context functions, and a single variant of every multi-variant class and function (considered as a default variant). Variant contexts provide alternative program behavior; they may be dynamically selected at program run-time. According to our approach (cf. Section 2), every variant context is self-contained, which means that it collects single variants of all program components, some of them are explicit (i.e. defined in the context), while other are implicit (i.e. shared with other contexts). There are also some program contexts, called *revision contexts*, which are not included in the final program. They reflect progressive nature of software development; they collect historical variants of program components which are actually useless in the final program, however, they have to be retained in the programming environment, because they may be useful in the near future, e.g. to perform roll-backs in software development, due to unsatisfactory assessment of the program by its users.

The main problem which has to be solved concerns the creation of the main program context. In the simplest case, if designers purely work according to the vertical style, the main context may be produced automatically, without any user intervention. There is no reason for hesitation on which variant to choose, because intersections between different pairs of contexts are always empty (cf. Fig. 4a).

Moreover, in such situation, the final program does not contain variant contexts, since every program element is available in only one variant.

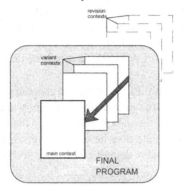

Fig. 3. Final program generation

The solution of the main context generation is not so straightforward when designers work according to the horizontal (or mixed) style. Now, users' intervention is required, in order to select a variant of a class/function which will appear in the main context, and variants which will appear in variant contexts. To achieve this, the final program generator might be integrated with a debugging tool which helps the user(s) to undertake proper decisions.

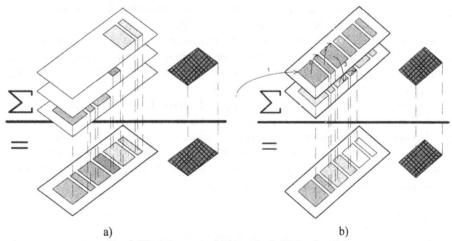

a)   b)

Fig. 4. Working styles: (a) vertical, (b) horizontal

The debugger starts tracing the program in a context, called the *initial context*, which has been pointed by the user (cf. step 1 in Fig. 4b). This context also becomes a *default context*, which means that its classes/functions are automatically moved to the main context being created, according to the thread of a program execution (cf. steps 2 in Fig. 4b). The default context is changed if one of the following events occurs:
- lack of a function (or a class method) called,
- unsatisfactory or erroneous behavior of currently traced function (method).

In the first case, if there is only one variant of a function/method called, switching between contexts is unambiguous and the context which provides the unique function/method implementation automatically becomes a new default context. Now, according to the rule presented above, if no special event occurs, this new context provides variants to the main context. If there is more than one variant of a function/method called, the user has to decide which context should become a default context.

In the second case (cf. step 3 in Fig. 4b), the program execution has to be rolled back at the beginning of the function/method currently traced. It is feasible, if the debugger makes a snap-shot of the data segment every time a new function/method is called. Thus, values of global data may be easily restored, while values of local data are just ignored. Now, again a new default context has to be selected in a similar way to the previous case.

4. Conclusions

First important advantage of the proposed approach is the support for collaboration among different team members working on the same software. The program itself contains components which are natural units of both work division between software designers and consistency checking. These components are logically independent during the software development process, thus conflicts between simultaneously working team members may be avoided. During the final program generation, which is substantially supported by particular mechanisms of the programming environment, these components are integrated, producing a code which reflects common efforts of team members. Depending on the chosen working style (horizontal/vertical), the emphasis is put either on designing disjointed pieces of code assigned to different team members, or on providing alternative implementation of the same pieces of code by different team members.

Second important advantage of the proposed approach is the increase of software reuse. The program itself contains different sets of versions of data and functions which correspond to different user requirements, e.g. different hardware/software platforms, communication languages, user interfaces, provided functionality, etc. Thus, in many cases the program behavior may be changed without the need for source program modification and re-compilation.

Bibliography

[1] Atkinson, B., Goldberg, A., Griss M., McCullough, R., Morisson, J.. Reuse: Truth or Fiction, *Proc. Int. Conf. OOPSLA '92, Panel Session* (1992).
[2] Boldyreff, C., Software Engineering Design: A Paradigm Case of Computer Supported Cooperative Work, in *Design Issues in CSCW* (D. Rosenberg, C. Hitchison , eds.). Springer-Verlag (1994).
[3] McDermid, J.A., Introduction and Overview, Part II: Methods, Techniques and Technology, in *Software Ingeneer's Reference Book*, (J.A. McDermid, ed), Butterworths, London (1990).
[4] Goldberg, A., Robson, D., Smalltalk-80: The Language and its Implementation, *Addison-Wesley* (1983).
[5] MIT-JSME, Computer Aided Cooperative Product Development, *Proc. of the MIT-JSME Workshop*, MIT, Cambridge, MA (1989).
[6] Stroustrup, B., The C++ Programming Language, *Addison-Wesley* (1991).
[7] Wieczerzycki, W., Software Reusability Through Versions, *Software - Practice and Experience*, Vol. 26(8), pp. 911-927, John Wiley & Sons (1996).

Refined Termination Decision in Active Databases

Sin Yeung LEE & Tok Wang LING
Department of Information Systems and Computer Science
National University of Singapore
Lower Kent Ridge, Singapore 0511, Singapore.
email : jlee@iscs.nus.edu.sg, lingtw@iscs.nus.edu.sg

Abstract Termination decision in trigger systems is important to make sure that any rule execution does not result in an infinite loop. In general, it is an undecidable task. Several recent works have been proposed to prove termination under certain situations. However, most of the existing methods only make use of the trigger conditions. The influence of the trigger actions to the trigger conditions is hardly considered. Among the few methods which consider both trigger actions and trigger conditions, they are usually based on some restrictive assumptions, and their trigger architecture may be limited to only certain model. In this paper, we will investigate how the relationship between trigger actions and trigger conditions can be captured in a more general trigger model. We will first introduce the concepts of activator and deactivator. These capture the relationship between the trigger actions of one rule with the trigger condition of another rule. Based on these, we propose a refined method to detect more termination situations than previous works.

1 INTRODUCTION

A new generation of database systems supports active rules for the detection of events occurring in the database and the triggering of induced actions [4, 7]. Whenever an event occurs, matching trigger rules are triggered, and their associated conditions are checked. If a condition is satisfiable, then the associated action of that trigger rule will be executed, which may in turn trigger other rules. This offers powerful means for integrity maintenance, replication management and more.

However, active rules are difficult to design and monitor. In particular, a set of rules may trigger each other indefinitely and the system cannot terminate. This non-termination decision problem makes developing even a small application system a difficult task. Hence, it is important to have some analysis methods on the set of trigger rules to predict its behavior in advance. Although it is undecidable whether the execution of any given set of trigger rules will finally terminate, it is beneficial to have tests to detect the subset of trigger rules which will terminate and those which may not terminate. With these tests, the rule programmers only need to verify a smaller subset of the trigger rules.

Most of the recent researches are based on the trigger graph method [1]. Based on the trigger graph, there are different approaches to handle this termination problem. The first approach investigates the rule conditions to determine termination. For example, consider the following two rules,

r1 : Ins $a(X,Y)$ If $X > 5 \wedge c(X,Y)$ Do Ins $b(X,Y)$, Del $c(X,Y)$
r2 : Ins $b(X,Y)$ If $X < 5 \wedge \neg c(X,Y)$ Do Ins $a(X,Y)$

If rule r1 is executed, according to its trigger condition, X should be greater than 5. In this case, the predicate in the trigger condition of r2, $(X<5)$, fails. Hence, r2 will not be executed. In this scenario, methods such as [6] conclude that the execution of r1 cannot trigger rule r2, hence, the cycle ≪r1,r2≫ can be terminated. However, there is a drawback. Predicates that can be updated during the trigger executions cannot be used. For example, we cannot make use of the predicates $c(X,Y)$ and $\neg c(X,Y)$ in r1 and r2 respectively as r1 deletes one tuple from c. Therefore, many terminating conditions is not detected.

Taking into account those predicates that can be modified by some trigger actions, another approach investigates the influence of some trigger actions on the trigger conditions. For instance, consider the following trigger rules:

r1 : Ins $a(X,Y)$ If $X>5$ Do Ins $b(X,Y)$,Del $c(X,Y)$

r2 : Ins $b(X,Y)$ If $c(X,Y)$ Do Ins $a(X,Y)$

Since the action of r1 deletes $c(X,Y)$, when rule r2 is triggered by rule r1, its condition, $c(X,Y)$, becomes unsatisfiable unless $c(X,Y)$ is re-inserted by some other events between the execution of rule r1 and r2. Hence, termination is proven. Note that other approaches [1, 5, 6] cannot decide this termination.

One of the major works that adopts this approach is [3]. It adds activation edges into a triggering graph. r1 has an activation edge to r2 if r2's trigger condition changes from false to true after the action of r1. However, [3] restricts the underlying-objects of the trigger system. In particular, all the updated objects are just simple variable. A sample trigger rule is as follows,

r1 : Mod A If $B=2$ Do Mod B to 3

However, when the method is applied to a real-life active DBMS, it may no longer be correct even when the update object is just a relation table. Consider the following,

$r1'$: Mod $a(X,I)$ to $a(X,I')$ If $b(X,Y) \wedge a(Y,2)$ Do Mod $a(Y,2)$ to $a(Y,3)$

[3] cannot even decide if $r1'$ is self-deactivating. The major difficulty is that now we have variables which can be instantiated to different values and give different rule instances. Equally difficult is to decide if a rule activates another rule. In other words, [3] may not be able to construct the activation graph correctly to determine trigger termination for complex trigger rules.

In this paper, we will first introduce the concept of *activator*. Rule r1 is an activator of r2 if r1's action may make the r2's condition from false to true. A decision algorithm will be given. To have a finer terminating decision, similar to [6], the trigger conditions of both rules are taken into consideration. Similarly, r1 is a *deactivator* of another rule r2 if it will definitely make the condition of r2 false in every triggering order. Decision algorithm will also be given. Using both activator and deactivator, we propose a rule reduction algorithm. The rule reduction algorithm will generate a subset of these rules which may be executed indefinitely. If the return subset is an empty set, then we conclude the trigger system can be terminated. We will give some examples and show how this new method can improve existing methods, and at least covers all the termination cases decided by [3].

The main contribution of this paper is to give a better decision on termination:

1. Our method detects termination cases which are not considered by [8, 5, 6]. These methods use only trigger conditions or trigger actions alone to decide trigger terminations, and

2. gives a more precise condition for activation/deactivation of trigger rules, which other methods such as [3] are lacking, and

3. is less restrictive. We do not require rules to be self-deactivated. In fact, we separate deactivator as a separate property to be investigated.

4. Based on all these improvements, we propose a rule reduction algorithm to reduce a given rule set. If the reduced set is an empty set, then termination is guaranteed.

2 TRIGGER ARCHITECTURE

2.1 Trigger rule specification

In this paper, we assume that the underlying database of the trigger system is of relational model. However, our proposed method is equally applicable when data types, inheritance, temporal feature are added such as in OODB database.

In this paper, each trigger rule takes the following form:

$rule\_name$: $trigger\_event$ If $trigger\_condition$ Do $action_1, \ldots, action_n$

Each trigger event takes one of the following forms:

Ins $table\_name(var\_list)$
Del $table\_name(var\_list)$
Mod $table\_name(var\_list)$ to $table\_name(mod\_var\_list)$

where var_list and mod_var_list are lists of distinct variables. In addition, variables that appear in var_list can also appear in mod_var_list. The trigger condition for each rule is a conjuncts of literals, negative literals and evaluable functions.

Each trigger action takes one of the following forms:

Ins $table\_name(expr\_list)$
Del $table\_name(expr\_list)$
Mod $table\_name(expr\_list)$ to $table\_name(mod\_expr\_list)$

where $expr\_list$ and mod_expr_list are lists of constants, variables or functions.

Any variable which appears in $expr\_list$ of any action must either appear in $trigger\_event$ or $trigger\_condition$. Those variables that appear in $trigger\_condition$ but not in $trigger\_event$ are called *local variables*. Throughout this paper, we refer $trigger\_event$ as $rule\_name.evt$ and $trigger\_condition$ as $rule\_name.cond$.

Example 2.1 The following trigger rule specifies that an increase of an employee salary should cause an increase of the salary of his/her manager by the same amount:

$incr\_salary\_rule$: Mod $emp(E\#,Sal)$ to $emp(E\#,Sal')$
    If $(Sal' > Sal) \wedge mgr(E\#,M\#) \wedge emp(M\#,MSal)$ Do
      Mod $emp(M\#,MSal)$ to $emp(M\#,MSal + Sal' - Sal)$ □

2.2 Trigger rule execution

In this paper, the trigger execution assumes the following abstract trigger architecture. The database maintains a set, Set_{evt}, of outstanding event instances, and a queue of rule instances, $Queue_{exec}$, to be evaluated. An event instance is a ground instance that takes the form,

    $action\ table\_name(constant\_list)$

and a rule instance is a copy of a trigger rule such that all of its non-local variables are fully instantiated, but none of its local variables are instantiated yet. If Set_{evt} is an empty set and $Queue_{exec}$ is an empty queue, then the execution is terminated. Otherwise, the trigger execution can be conceptually viewed as the concurrent execution of a consumer and a producer on Set_{evt} as follows,

1. (Consumer of Set_{evt}, producer of $Queue_{exec}$)

   An event instance e is selected from Set_{evt}, one or all, depending on the trigger model, of the trigger rules r is selected for the next step if there is a substitution unifier σ such that $(r.evt)\sigma = e$. The variables of rule r are instantiated by σ, and the resulting rule instance $r\sigma$ is inserted into the evaluation queue $Queue_{exec}$ for execution. The event e is now removed from Set_{evt}.

2. (Consumer of $Queue_{exec}$, producer of Set_{evt})

   One rule instance $r\sigma$ is selected from the evaluation queue $Queue_{exec}$. Its condition $(r.cond)\sigma$ is evaluated. Assume there exists a substitution unifier θ such that $((r.cond)\sigma)\theta$ is satisfied, then for each action event of rule r, evt_i, insert $((evt_i)\sigma)\theta$ into Set_{evt}. Remove $r\sigma$ from $Queue_{exec}$.

Intuitively, the consumer of Set_{evt} matches rules and instantiates the rule variables, and passes the rule instances to $Queue_{exec}$ for evaluation of their conditions. The producer of Set_{evt} then selects one ground rule and evaluates its condition to decide if the rule can be fired. If the condition succeeds, new events are generated.

Note that this abstract architecture of rule execution is general enough to cover several different trigger execution variations. For example, priority rules trigger model can be implemented if $Queue_{exec}$ is a priority queue.

3 ACTIVATOR AND DEACTIVATOR

3.1 Activator

Definition 3.1 A rule r1 is an *activator* of another rule r2 if there exists a database state such that r2.*cond* is unsatisfiable, but becomes satisfiable immediately after the execution of the actions of r1. □

Example 3.1 Consider the following two trigger rules defined as follows,

   r1 : Ins $a(X,Y)$ If $b(X,Y)$ Do Ins $c(X,Y)$
   r2 : Del $b(X,Y)$ If $c(X,1)$ Do Del $d(X,Y)$

Assume we have a database that contains only the tuples $\{b(1,1),b(1,2)\}$. Given a transaction $\{$Ins $a(1,1)$,Del $b(1,2)\}$, this transaction will trigger both trigger rules. Now, if we execute rule r2 first, its condition $c(X,1)$ fails. However, if we execute r1 first immediately before r2, the action of r1 inserts the tuple $c(1,1)$. Now rule r2 can be executed successfully. By Definition 3.1, r1 is an activator of r2. Note that an activator of r2 does not necessarily make the condition of r2 satisfiable for all database states. If the transaction is to insert $a(1,2)$, r1 still cannot make r2 executable. □

To decide if one rule r1 is an activator of rule r2, intuitively, we need to first assume that the condition of r2 is not true before r1 is executed. We then show that the updated database after the execution of r1 will make r2 satisfiable. To compute this, we can apply the differential calculus to simulate the database after the execution of rule r1. However, there is another important factor — the trigger condition of r1. Note that if r1 in the previous example is replaced by:

$r1'$: Ins $a(X,Y)$ If $(Y>5)$ Do Ins $c(X,Y)$

Now, rule $r1'$ can insert tuple $c(X,Y)$ only when $(Y>5)$. Hence, $r1'$ cannot insert the tuple $c(1,1)$ as $(1>5)$ is false. Indeed, the action of $r1'$ is irrelevant to the condition of rule r2. The satisfiability of the predicate $c(X,1)$ in the condition of r2 is not affected by the action of rule $r1'$. Hence, rule $r1'$ is not an activator of rule r2.

From the above discussion, it is beneficial to take the trigger condition into consideration. However, due to the non-deterministic nature of the execution order, we can only bring in predicates in the condition which are database-independent. They can be evaluable functions as well as predicates that are not updated by any trigger actions. In this paper, for simplicity, we shall only make use of evaluable function.

With these facts in perspective, we can now show an algorithm to decide if a rule r1 is an activator of another rule r2. The algorithm will do the following,

1. assume that the condition of r2 before execution of r1, A_{before}, is false, and
2. given a pre-condition A_{r1_ok} that rule r1 is executed,
3. the condition of r2 after execution of r1, A_{after} can become satisfiable.

This can be summarized in the following algorithm:

Algorithm 3.1
function is_activator(r1,r2:trigger_rule):boolean;
    rename all the variables of r1 so that they do not appear in r2.
    Let A_{before} be $\neg(r2.cond)$.
    Construct A_{r1_ok} as follows,
        Let A_{r1_ok} be $r1.cond$.
        Replace all the non-evaluable predicate in A_{r1_ok} by TRUE.
        Finally, simplify the expression.
    Construct A_{after} as follows:
        Let A_{after} be $r2.cond$.
        For each of the actions of r1 do
            if the action is an insertion: Ins $a(X_1,\ldots,X_n)$, then
                replace every occurrence $a(Y_1,\ldots,Y_n)$ in A_{before} by
$$a(Y_1,\ldots,Y_n) \vee (\ A_{r1\_ok} \wedge (Y_1=X_1)\wedge \cdots \wedge (Y_n=X_n)\ )$$
            if the action is a deletion: Del $a(X_1,\ldots,X_n)$, then
                replace every occurrence $a(Y_1,\ldots,Y_n)$ in A_{before} by
$$a(Y_1,\ldots,Y_n)\wedge \neg(\ A_{r1\_ok}\wedge (Y_1=X_1)\wedge \cdots \wedge (Y_n=X_n)\ )$$
            if it is a modification: Mod $a(X_1,\ldots,X_n)$ to $a(Y_1,\ldots,Y_n)$, then
                replace every occurrence $a(Z_1,\ldots,Z_n)$ in A_{before} by
$$[\ a(Z_1,\ldots,Z_n)\wedge \neg(A_{r1\_ok}\wedge (Z_1=X_1)\wedge \cdots (Z_n=X_n))\ ]\ \vee$$
$$(\ A_{r1\_ok}\wedge (Z_1=Y_1)\wedge \cdots \wedge (Z_n=Y_n)\ )$$
    if $A_{before}\wedge A_{after}$ is satisfiable, then return TRUE, else return FALSE.   □

Example 3.2 Take the following two rules:
    r1 : Ins $a(X,Y)$ If $(Y<5)$ Do Ins $b(X,Y)$, Mod $c(2,Y)$ to $c(2,Y+1)$
    r2 : Ins $d(U,V)$ If $c(U,3)$ Do Ins $d(U,V+1)$
To test if rule r1 is an activator for rule r2, we first perform the renaming step. However, since no variable appears in both r1 and r2, no renaming is required. Next we let A_{before} be $\neg c(U,3)$. A_{r1_ok} is simply $(Y<5)$. We then construct A_{after} as
$$[c(U,3)\wedge \neg((Y<5)\wedge (U=2)\wedge (3=Y))]\ \vee ((Y<5)\wedge (U=2)\wedge (3=Y+1))$$

The conjunction $A_{before} \wedge A_{after}$ can be evaluated as,
$$\neg c(U,3) \wedge \left[[c(U,3) \wedge \neg((Y<5) \wedge (U=2) \wedge (3=Y))] \vee \right.$$
$$\left. ((Y<5) \wedge (U=2) \wedge (3=Y+1)) \right]$$
which can be rewritten as,
$$\left[\neg c(U,3) \wedge c(U,3) \wedge \neg((Y<5) \wedge (U=2) \wedge (3=Y)) \right] \vee$$
$$\left[\neg c(U,3) \wedge (Y<5) \wedge (U=2) \wedge (3=Y+1) \right]$$
The first conjunct is unsatisfiable, whereas the second conjunct is satisfiable, says, when $c(2,3)$ is not in the database. Hence, rule r1 is an activator of rule r2. □

3.2 Variable Assignment and Deactivator

As described earlier, a deactivator always makes the trigger condition of its target trigger rule false in all possible cases. Hence, unlike the computation of activator, the decision of a deactivator requires to take all the possible triggering sequence into consideration. For example, consider the following four rules:

r1 : Ins $a(X,Y)$ If $(X=1)$ Do Del $b(X,Y)$
r2 : Del $b(X,Y)$ If TRUE Do Ins $c(X,Y)$
r3 : Del $b(X,Y)$ If TRUE Do Ins $c(Y,X)$
r4 : Ins $c(X,Y)$ If $b(X,Y)$ Do Ins $d(Y,X)$

If r1 triggers r2, which then triggers r4, the action of r1 — Del $b(X,Y)$, obviously makes r4 non-executable. However, when r1 triggers r4 via r3, r4 can remain executable. Note that the difference between triggering via r2 and via r3 is on the instantiation of the variables X and Y. Hence, in order to decide an deactivator, we shall introduce a notation called *variable assignment* to capture different variables instantiation along different execution sequence.

Definition 3.2 Given a trigger graph TG, a *path* of rules is in the form $\ll r_1, \ldots, r_n \gg$ such that there is an edge in the trigger graph from the rule r_i to r_{i+1} in the trigger graph for each i where $1 \leq i \leq n-1$. A path is a *simple path* if each rule is different. A cycle $\ll r_1, \ldots, r_n \gg$ is constructed from a path $\ll r_1, \ldots, r_n \gg$ and one extra edge $\ll r_n, r_1 \gg$. It is a *simple cycle* if the underlying path is a simple path. □

Definition 3.3 Given two rules r1 and r2 such that r1 has a simple path P, $\ll r1, \ldots, r2 \gg$ that leads to r2 in the trigger graph, a *variable assignment* $Va(\ll r1, \ldots, r2 \gg)$ of rule r2 with respect to rule r1 via the path P takes the form
$$\{y_1 := x_1, \ldots, y_n := x_n\}$$
where each y_i is the set of global variables used in rule r2, and each x_i is

1. a global variables used in rule r1, or
2. a constant, or
3. a function, or
4. a meta-constant _ , meaning no information.

The variable assignment captures the syntactic relations of the variables between the two rules. In other word, given that all the global variables of r1 are known, after a lists of activation along the simple path P, the value of the global variables in r2 can be obtained from this variable assignment. □

Example 3.3 Given the following rules:

r1 : Ins $a(X,Y)$ If $d(X,Z) \wedge d(Z,Y)$ Do Ins $b(X,Y),c(X,Z)$

r2 : Ins $b(X,Y)$ If $d(X,Y)$ Do Ins $c(Y,X)$

r3 : Ins $c(X,Y)$ Do Ins $d(X,Y)$

Va($\ll$r1,r3$\gg$) is $\{X:=X, Y:= \_ \}$. Now, if event Ins $a(1,2)$ triggers r1, which then triggers r2, the value of X in rule r3 has the same value as the X in rule r1, i.e. 1. The value of Y in rule r3, however, cannot be obtained from the global variables used in r1. If we consider a different path of activation, we can get a different variable assignment. Assume now rule r1 triggers rule r3 via rule r2. In this case, Va($\ll$r1,r2,r3$\gg$) is $\{X:=Y, Y:=X\}$. In other words, if r1 is triggered by the event Ins $a(1,2)$, we will expect when r3 is executed, X is instantiated to 2 and Y to 1. $\square$

To compute the variable assignment along a path, we first describe the composite operator $\cdot$ as follows,

Definition 3.4 The *composition* of two assignments $\{x_1:=y_1, \ldots, x_n:=y_n\}$ $\cdot$ $\{u_1:=v_1, \ldots, u_n:=v_n\}$ can be computed as follows,

1. Let V be $\{x_1:=y_1, \ldots, x_n:=y_n\}$
2. Replace any expression y_i in V by $\_$ if y_i uses at least one variable that is not found in u_j.
3. Replace every occurrence of u_i in each of the function/variables y_j in V by v_i.
4. Return V as the results of the composition. $\square$

Example 3.4 The composition $\{x:=y, y:=z+1, z:=u\} \cdot \{x:=5, y:=x+1, z:=2 \times x\}$ is $\{x:=(x+1), y:=(2 \times x)+1, z:= \_ \}$ $\square$

Algorithm 3.2 The following describes how to compute the variable assignment along a given path,

function Va ($\ll r_1, \ldots, r_n \gg$: path) : var_assignment;
    if $n=2$ then return $\{y_1 = x_1, \ldots, y_n = x_n\}$
        where each y_i is a global variable used in r_2, and x_i is the
        corresponding variable/constant/expression in the action of r_1.
    else return Va ($\ll r_1, \ldots, r_{n-1} \gg \cdot \ll r_{n-1}, r_n \gg$) $\square$

Definition 3.5 $(C)(\text{Va}(P))$, the application of a variable assignment $\text{Va}(P)$ which takes the form $\{x_1:=y_1, \ldots, x_n=y_n\}$ on a trigger condition C which uses variables $u_1, \ldots, u_n$, is a new trigger condition obtained by the following steps,

1. First, replace all the u_k in C which does not appear in any of the x_j by $\_$.
2. Next, we replace every variable u_i in C by y_j if u_i is indeed x_j, $\square$

Example 3.5 Apply $\{X:=Y, Y:=Z, U:= \_ \}$ on the condition $a(X,Z) \wedge b(U,Y)$ will generate a new condition, $a(Y, \_) \wedge b(\_ ,Z)$ $\square$

Definition 3.6 A rule r1 is an *deactivator* of rule r2 if

1. there is at least one simple path from r1 to r2 in the trigger graph, and
2. for every simple path P from r1 to r2, the execution of rule r1 will falsify the condition of rule r2 of the trigger instance triggered along the rule sequence P. $\square$

Example 3.6 Given the following rules:

    r1 : Ins $a(X,Y)$ If $(X > 5)$ Do Del $b(X,Y)$

    r2 : Del $b(X,Y)$ If $c(Y,X)$ Do Del $c(Y,X)$

    r3 : Del $c(X,Y)$ If $b(Y,X)$ Do Ins $d(X,Y)$

Suppose r1 is triggered by an event Ins $a(11,22)$, this will cause a deletion of tuple $b(11,22)$. This very deletion will trigger rule r2 to possibly trigger an action Del $c(22,11)$. Finally, when the deletion of $c(22,11)$ triggers rule r3, the condition $b(11,22)$ is evaluated. Unless $b(11,22)$ is re-inserted, the action of r1 makes the condition of rule r3 unsatisfiable. As the action of r1, Del $b(X,Y)$, causes the condition of rule r3 to become unsatisfiable, r1 is a deactivator of rule r3.   □

To decide if a rule r1 is a deactivator of another rule r2, we basically first capture the assertions resulted from the action of r1. We then prove that based on these assertions A, and regardless of the trigger sequence from r1 to r2, the condition of r2 has a contradiction with the assertions A. The following algorithm summarizes the idea,

Algorithm 3.3 This algorithm decides if a rule r1 is a deactivator of another rule r2,
function is_deactivator (r1,r2 : rule) : boolean ;
    If there is no simple path from r1 to r2 in the trigger graph, then return FALSE;
    Construct the database independent condition A_{r1_ok} as in Algorithm 3.1:
        Let A_{r1_ok} be r1.cond.
        Replace all the non-evaluable predicate in A_{r1_ok} by True.
        Finally, simplify the expression.
    Let A_{r1} be a formula initialized to True.
    For each actions of r1 do,
        If the action is an insertion of $a(x_1, \ldots, x_n)$, then
            let A_{r1} be $A_{r1} \wedge a(x_1, \ldots, x_n)$.
        If the action is a deletion of $a(x_1, \ldots, x_n)$, then
            let A_{r1} be $A_{r1} \wedge \neg a(x_1, \ldots, x_n)$.
        If the action is a modification of $a(x_1, \ldots, x_n)$ to $a(y_1, \ldots, y_n)$, then
            let A_{r1} be $A_{r1} \wedge a(y_1, \ldots, y_n) \wedge \neg a(x_1, \ldots, x_n)$.
    For each simple path P from node r1 to r2 do,
        If $A_{r1} \wedge A_{r1\_ok} \wedge (r2.cond)(Va(P))$ is satisfiable, then return FALSE.
    return TRUE;   □

Example 3.7 Refer to Example 3.6, we can prove that r1 is a deactivator of r3 by Algorithm 3.3. We first observe that the database independent condition of r1 is $(X > 5)$. The next step is to decide the set of assumption, A_{r1}. Since the only action of rule r1 is Del $b(X,Y)$, hence, A is $\neg b(X,Y)$. Now, there is only one simple path from r1 to r3 : «r1,r2,r3», hence, we only need to prove that $A \wedge (X > 5) \wedge (r3.cond) Va(\text{«r1,r2,r3»})$ is unsatisfiable. As r3.cond is $b(Y,X)$, and $Va(\text{«r1,r2,r3»})$ is $\{X := Y, Y := X\}$, the expression is simplified to be,

    $\neg b(X,Y) \wedge (X > 5) \wedge b(X,Y)$

It is clearly unsatisfiable. Hence, r1 is a deactivator for r3.   □

Theorem 3.1 Given a simple cycle «$r_1, \ldots, r_n$», if there exists a node r_i,
1. there is a deactivator r_j in the cycle which deactivates r_i, and
2. every activator in the entire trigger graph which may activate r_i is proven to execute finitely,

then, the cycle will terminate. ☐

Based on Theorem 3.1, the rule reduction algorithm can be formalized as,

Algorithm 3.4 (Graph Reduction)
procedure reduce_trigger_graph(var G : trigger_graph);
    Label every rule in G as "infinite";
    Repeat until no more change of G is possible:
        Change the label of rule r from "infinite" to "finite" if,
            there does not exist any edge $\ll r',r \gg$ in the trigger graph, (r' is not
            necessary different from r) such that r' is labeled "infinite",
        Or Every activator of r is labeled "finite", and,
            for all the possible cycle Γ that contains r,
                there is always a deactivator in Γ that deactivates r,
    Remove all the rules that are labeled as "finite",
    and their associated edges from G.
    This final graph is the reduced trigger graph. ☐

Theorem 3.2 If the reduced trigger graph is an empty graph, then the trigger system can always terminate. ☐

Example 3.8 Consider the following rules:
    r1 : Ins $a(X,Y)$ If $(X>2)$ Do Ins $b(X,Y)$
    r2 : Ins $b(X,Y)$ If $d(X,Y)$ Do Ins $c(X,Y)$
    r3 : Ins $c(X,Y)$ If $\neg b(X,Y)$ Do Ins $a(X,Y+1)$
In this example, there is only one cycle Γ, which is $\ll$r1,r2,r3$\gg$. We apply Algorithm 3.4 to decide if it can terminate. We first label all the three rules as "infinite". Now, since r1 can deactivate r3, and there is no activator which activates r3, we therefore label r3 as "finite". Subsequently, rule r2 and r1 will also be labeled as "finite". There is no further change of the labeling. Now since all rules are labeled as "finite", they are removed. The algorithm returns an empty graph. According to Theorem 3.2, the trigger system can always terminate. ☐

Example 3.9 If however, we make a slight change on the action of rule 2:
    r1' : Ins $a(X,Y)$ If $(X>2)$ Do Ins $b(X,Y)$
    r2' : Ins $b(X,Y)$ If $d(X,Y)$ Do Ins $c(Y,X)$
    r3' : Ins $c(X,Y)$ If $\neg b(X,Y)$ Do Ins $a(X,Y+1)$
Now there is still only one cycle Γ, $\ll$r1',r2',r3'$\gg$. However, there is no more deactivator in the cycle. In particular, $r1'$ is not an deactivator of rule $r3'$ now. Since no other deactivator exists in the cycle, no rule can be labeled as "finite", the trigger graph cannot be reduced further. In this case, we cannot determine if these three rules can always terminate. ☐

Clearly, every termination case detected by the activation graph method [3] can be detected by Algorithm 3.4. However, as our method
  1. handles predicate logics instead of prepositional logic,
  2. considers in addition the trigger condition of the activator, and
  3. is more flexible to allow trigger rules which are not self-deactivating.
We can detect more cases than what [3] can.

4 CONCLUSION

This paper has proposed a new method to termination analyze of active rules set. It investigates the co-relation between trigger conditions and the trigger actions. Based on it, we further analysis if the actions of a rule may falsify or possibly resatisfy the trigger condition of another rule. Using the concept of activator and deactivator, we propose a rule reduction algorithm, which detects many terminating condition that cannot be detected by existing methods. Our method improves upon existing methods such as [3, 6] by not relying on any restrictive assumption, and considers more information, in particular, the trigger actions and conditions to decide trigger termination.

References

[1] A.Aiken, J.Widom and J.M.Hellerstein, "Behavior of database production rules: Termination, confluence, and observable determinism", *Proc ACM SIGMOD International Conf on the Management of Data*, 59-68, 1992.

[2] E.Baralis and J.Widom, "An Algebraic Approach to Rule Analysis in Expert Database Systems", *20th VLDB Conf*, 475-486, Sept 12-15, 1994.

[3] E.Baralis, S.Ceri and S.Paraboschi, "Improved Rule Analysis by Means of Triggering and Activation Graphs", *RIDS'95*, pg 165-181.

[4] U.Dayal, "Active Database Systems", *Proc 3rd International Conf on Data and Knowledge Bases,* Jerusalem Israel, June 1988.

[5] A.P. Karadimce and S.D. Urban, "Conditional term rewriting as a formal basis for analysis of active database rules", *4th International Workshop on Research Issues in Data Engineering (RIDE-ADS'94)*, February 1994.

[6] A.P.Karadimce, S.D.Urban, "Refined Trigger Graphs: A Logic-Based Approach to Termination Analysis in an Active Object-Oriented Database", *ICDE'96*, pg 384-391.

[7] M.Stonebraker, G.Kemnitz, "The POSTGRES Next-Generation Database Management System", *CACM*, 34(10), 78-93, Oct 1991.

[8] L.van der Voort and A. Siebes, "Termination and confluence of rule execution", *Proc 2nd International Conf on Information and Knowledge Management*, Nov 1993.

A Time-Stamped Authoring Graph for Video Databases

Kohji Zettsu[1], Kuniaki Uehara[2], Katsumi Tanaka[3], and Nobuo Kimura[1]

[1] Kobe Research Center, Telecommunications Advancement Organization of Japan,
Kobe International Friendship Building, Chuo Kobe, 650 JAPAN
e-mail: {zettsu, kimura}@kobe-sc.tao.or.jp
[2] Research Center for Urban Safety and Security, Kobe University,
Nada Kobe, 657 JAPAN
e-mail: uehara@kobe-u.ac.jp
[3] Graduate School of Science and Technology, Kobe University,
Nada Kobe, 657 JAPAN
e-mail: tanaka@in.kobe-u.ac.jp

Abstract. This paper presents a "time-stamped authoring graph", which is a new video description model and retrieval method based on fragmentary descriptions of video contents (i.e., the authors' impressions or feelings) and their relationships. It can handle continuous video images better than existing description models, which tend to have problems in extracting parts of continuous video images and giving them precise descriptions. A video retrieval algorithm using a time-stamped authoring graph is explained, and the criteria for selecting or ranking the retrieved video images are discussed. The design and implementation of the prototype for video description and retrieval interfaces are also described and examined, with some examples.

1 Introduction

In order to store videos in a database and retrieve them on demand, they must be indexed for identification. There are two types of index: the first is a content-based index derived from characteristic data of video signals such as DCT (distributed cosine transfer) values, color constructions, and so on. The second is based on textual descriptions, which are expressions that can be recognized by humans such as keywords. Which type of index is used depends on the video retrieval algorithm.

Let us consider the retrieval of video images based on their textual descriptions. Currently, every videos stored in the database must be indexed with secondary information derived from the descriptions of its contents. Many description models have been introduced for retrieving the appropriate description of the video contents. Most use descriptions of the scenes or stories of video parts. In these description models, the more precisely each video part is described, the more accurately the retrieval request is satisfied. Therefore, they are designed to give precise descriptions of video parts that are carefully extracted from a continuous stream of video images. However, it is not easy to identify precisely a collection of video parts (i.e., video cuts).

In this paper, we present a new approach to indexing a video, using a video description model called a time-stamped authoring graph, and show how it handles the problems mentioned above. Section 2 presents our time-stamped authoring graph, and explains how a video is described by using the graph. Section 3 gives the retrieval algorithm. Section 4 discusses in more detail several factors for selecting or ranking retrieved videos. Section 5 describes the design and implementation of our description and retrieval system.

2 Time-stamped Authoring Graph

A time-stamped authoring graph is a new description model for describing a video. In Sect. 2.1, we compare the features of a time-stamped authoring graph with those of conventional description models. In Sect. 2.2, we explain how a video is described by the time-stamped authoring graph.

2.1 Features of a Time-stamped Authoring Graph

Many description models for describing video contents have been introduced. Most of them are based on time intervals [1][5]. Authors first select a part of a video defined by a time interval, and then describe the specified part by means of keywords and so on. That is, most description models assume that authors can precisely identify time intervals. When an author wants to retrieve certain video images, he/she searches for the description that best matches the request and retrieves the video part associated with the description. To increase the accuracy of retrieval, it is necessary to identify a video part as precisely as possible. Authors describe the stories or the meanings of video parts in strict form, using keywords, records [3], graphs [2][4], and so on. It might seem easy to retrieve the video parts by means of these description models, but actually, it is very difficult to extract video parts properly from continuous video images in such a way as to satisfy all kinds of requests, and then to describe those parts precisely even when they do not have sufficiently distinctive stories or scenes to be described effectively.

Our time-stamped authoring graph does not aim to describe a video by predefined video parts and precise descriptions of them. Instead, it describes a video by fragmentary expressions of the contents (i.e., the authors' impressions or feelings) at certain points of time in the video stream, and the relationships between those contents. Thus, it is not necessary to select the video part carefully and give a complete description of it. An author can start his/her description from anywhere in the video stream, and can describe the contents at any time he/she wants, using any expressions. This is the most significant feature of video description using a time-stamped authoring graph.

The second main feature is that it describes the relationships between time-stamped descriptions of video stream explicitly. Thus, it can express the relationship between video images that are widely separated in the video stream, using a label such as "cause-and-effect relationship." This makes it possible to retrieve video images by tracing link relationships.

2.2 Video Description

A time-stamped authoring graph represents a video by a undirected graph consisting of nodes and links. A node has a timestamp and an annotation (description). The annotation expresses the contents at the time in the video stream indicated by the timestamp (actually, it is the time code started from the beginning of the video stream). Any annotation related to the contents, such as impressions, feelings, or narrative, can be attached to the node. Each link represents the relationship between annotations of nodes.

The following steps explain how to describe a video by using a time-stamped authoring graph.

1. When the author thinks of some phrase or phrases expressing the contents at a point of time in the video stream, he/she writes them down, together with the timestamp. This becomes a node of the description graph. The author can create as many nodes as he/she wants. Some nodes may not have a specific timestamp pointing to the video contents described in the annotation, if the annotation describes bibliograhpic knowledge about the video stream. Examples of this are annotations about the acting cast, the background to the story, rumors, and so on. These nodes are treated as "nodes without timestamps."

2. Related nodes are them connected. The connections become links of the description graph. The author can create as many links as he/she wants. Links are divided into the following three types, according to the situations in which they are created.

    Commonsense link This type of link represents a relationship derived implicitly by the author's common sense. An example of a commonsense link is a link between the terms "Aladdin" and "Arabian Nights."

    Generalization link This type of link shows that the annotation of the node at one end of this link is a generalized expression of the one at the other end. An example of this relationship is the one between the terms "airplane" and "F15 fighter."

    Normal link Any other type of link is classified as a "normal link". This type of link is specified explicitly by authors or automatically created by the term co-appearance relationship described in Sect. 5.

Figure 1 shows an example of a time-stamped authoring graph. This graph describes a part of the preview video for the animation movie "Cyborg 009" (a very famous animation movie in Japan) produced by the Toei film company.

3 Video Retrieval

In this section, we explain the algorithm for retrieving video parts by using time-stamped authoring graphs. It will be recalled that the algorithm is designed to

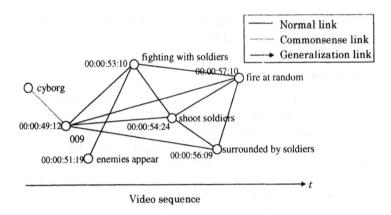

Fig. 1. Video description by time-stamped authoring graph

compare and contrast the given query and the label of a node in the graph, which is an annotation of the video cut, and then to retrieve the node most relevant to the query. Although queries and annotations are written in natural language, especially in Japanese, this is not a natural language processing task. That would be and extremely diffucult job, for which one would need to consider the semantic concepts associated with the words in a query [2].

3.1 Video Retrieval Algorithm

The actual retrieval algorithm is made up of three separate routines. The first of these retrieves a time-stamped authoring graph to determine the set of match nodes (see below for a defintion of match nodes). The second routine traverses the graph and extracts the minimal subgraphs whose nodes consist of the match nodes retrieved in the first routine. The third routine takes these findings one at a time, and for each generates a sequence of video cuts that provides an answer to the query.

3.2 Keyword Matching

The first phase of video retrieval is called keyword matching. Keywords are words in an annotation. The aim of keyword matching is to determinate the set of nodes $m(q_i)$ whose annotations are the same as or similar to the word q_i in a query Q, where i ranges over the length of the query, i.e., $Q = (q_1, \ldots, q_i, \ldots, q_n)$. These retrieved nodes are called match nodes. Keyword matching is done as follows:

1. Compare the keywords in each node with the words in a query. If the meaning of a keyword is the same as or similar to that of a word in the query, the node attached to the keyword is treated as a match node.
2. By tracing commonsense links and generalization links, determine the possible match nodes. In this step, if a node is connected to the match node by a commonsense link, the node is treated as a match node. If a node is

connected to its "immediate parent" node by a generalization link, the child nodes are also treated as match nodes.

After traversing the graph, all the match nodes are classed into subgroups according to the words in a query. For example, $m(q_1) = \{1, 4\}$, $m(q_2) = \{2\}$, $m(q_3) = \{6\}$. Furthermore, the match node list $\mathbf{m}(Q) = (m_{i_1}(q_1), \ldots, m_{i_n}(q_n))$ is generated, where $m_{i_k}(q_k)$ is one of the match nodes for word q_k. All the possible match node lists are generated and gathered into a set $\{\mathbf{m}_j(Q)\}$, where j ranges over the number of possible lists.

Figure 2 visualizes the keyword matching algorithm described above. Note that the video material is the famous Japanese animation movie "Cyborg 009. " In this movie there are nine protagonists. The last hero is named "Cyborg 009." Here we assume that the video retrieval query is "Cyborg is fighting with enemies." Annotations such as "fight soldiers"and "009" are assigned to nodes. Numerical values assigned to nodes are time-stamps for annotations.

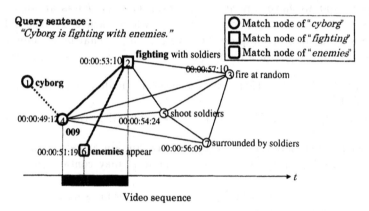

Fig. 2. Graph search algorithm

3.3 Traversal of a Graph

Next, for each match node list, the algorithm tries to identify the minimal subgraph in the graph, where each element of the list corresponds to at least one node of the subgraph. The minimal subgraph $s_i(Q) = (N_{s_i(Q)}, L_{s_i(Q)})$ for the match node list $\mathbf{m}_i(Q)$ is considered as a semantically good description for an answer to the query Q, since a video scene's full concept is defined in the graph as all the nodes that can be reached by an exhaustive tracing process, originating at its match nodes, together with the total sum of relationships among these nodes specified by generalization and commonsense links. Note that $N_{s_i(Q)}$ is the set of nodes in $s_i(Q)$ and $L_{s_i(Q)}$ is the set of links in $s_i(Q)$. This step is iterated so as to extract all possible minimal subgraphs for each match node list. We denote the set of minimal subgraphs $S(Q)$ for the query Q as follows: $S(Q) = \{s_i(Q)\}$.

3.4 Selection of Video Cuts

Finally, the algorithm takes these minimal subgraphs one at a time, and for each subgraph selects the corresponding video cut. That is, for each $n_j^{s_i(Q)} \in N_{s_i(Q)}$, the algorithm selects the sequence of video cuts according to the timestamp associated with the node $n_j^{s_i(Q)}$. For each $s_i(Q) \in S(Q)$, this step is also iterated until all the possible sequences of video cuts have been retrieved.

4 Criteria for Retrieved Video Cuts

As explained in the previous section, the retrieval process using our time-stamped authoring graph consists of three phases: (1) keyword matching, (2) traversal of a time-stamped authoring graph, and (3) selection of video cuts. In this section, we will describe criteria for selecting or ranking video cuts that are retrieved in the final phase.

Suppose that we have a minimal subgraph $G = (V, E)$ as an answer. This subgraph G should contain nodes $v_1, \ldots, v_n$, where each v_i corresponds to at least one word q_j in a given query $Q = \{q_1, \ldots, q_m\}$. That is, G should satisfy the following conditions for a query Q:

1. For each word q_j in Q, there exists at least one node v_i such that v_i contains the word q_j.
2. For any proper subgraph G' of G, G' does not satisfy the above condition 1.

It should be noted that the subgraph G may contain a node v that does not contain any word q_j in Q. Also, a certain node v_i may contain more than one word.

In considering a criterion for selecting or ranking answers to a query Q, the following factors will be important:

[Factor 1] The number of nodes in an answer should be minimum.
[Factor 2] The number of video cuts corresponding to an answer should be minimum.
[Factor 3] The number of "matching" nodes to the number of "non-matching" nodes in an answer should be minimum.

For example, let us consider the time-stamped authoring graph in Fig. 3. In this figure, we assume that each node v_i corresponds to a time t_i ($1 \leq i \leq 8$). That is, the timestamp value of node v_i is t_i. We also assume that each node v_i is associated with a set of keywords.

Suppose that we have the following queries Q_1 and Q_2:

$$Q_1 = \{q_1, q_2, q_3\} \tag{1}$$
$$Q_2 = \{q_2, q_4\} \tag{2}$$

For query Q_1, we obtain the two minimal subgraphs G_{11} and G_{12} as answers (see Fig. 4). In accordance with [Factor 1], we prefer G_{12} to G_{11}, since G_{12}

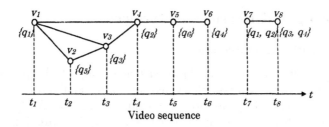

Fig. 3. Time-stamped authoring graph for query Q

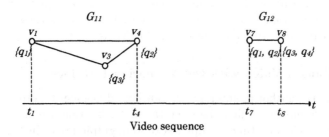

Fig. 4. Subgraphs for query Q_1

consists of fewer nodes. Also, if $|t_8 - t_7| < |t_4 - t_1|$, we prefer G_{12} to G_{11}, in accordance with [Factor 2]. For query Q_2, we obtain the two minimal subgraphs G_{21} and G_{22} as answers (see Fig. 5).

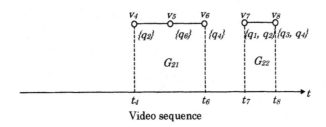

Fig. 5. Subgraphs for query Q_2

The graph G_{22} consists of only "matching" nodes, although G_{21} contains a non-matching node v_5. In accordance with [Factor 3], G_{22} is preferred to G_{21}.

As shown in the above example, we should consider several factors in order to establish a precise criterion for selecting or ranking answers. In line with these considerations, we will discuss the notions of the "recall" ratio and "precision" ratio for a query Q. However, further experimentation and research on this topic will be needed.

5 Authoring and Retrieval Interfaces

5.1 Design and Implementation

Because of the increasing need for digitized video images to be processed and shared over computer networks, the video authoring and retrieval interfaces were designed to be used by multiple users through the WWW (World Wide Web). Thus, the interfaces are implemented as Java applets running on WWW browsers. A Java applet is a small program written in the Java programming language that can run on most operating systems through WWW browsers or applet viewers (which are platform independent). The Java applet is also downloaded from the network server when it is executed. Thanks to these features of Java, anyone can work with these interfaces anywhere.

5.2 Describing a Video with the Authoring Interface

Figure 6 shows the authoring interface. An author adds nodes to a time-stamped authoring graph and draws links between the nodes by using the interface. The figure includes a part of a time-stamped authoring graph describing the preview video for the animation movie "Cyborg 009." The preview video lasts about 3 minutes. We have a description in a form of a time-stamped authoring graph, which has 115 nodes and 148 links. In this figure, points marked with squares are nodes with timestamps, and those marked with diamonds are nodes without timestamps. Solid lines, dotted lines, and arrows represent normal links, commonsense links, and abstract links, respectively.

Fig. 6. Authoring interface

5.3 Retrieving Video Cuts by using a Retrieval Interface

Figure 7 shows the retrieval interface. To retrieve desired video images, the user specifies his/her request through this retrieval interface, in the form of a sentence in natural language such as (I want to browse the scene in which) "Cyborg is fighting with enemies." Once the query sentence has been given, the retrieval interface returns video cuts related to the query sentence. Then, the user reviews those cuts if they are the desired ones.

Fig. 7. Retrieval interface

We tried retrieving video cuts by using the description graph of "Cyborg 009" (shown in Fig. 6). For the query sentence "a monster attacks (someone or something)", we got 5 cuts (shown in Fig. 7).

5.4 Automatic Link Generation

When an author wants to describe a video, it is a hard work for him/her to create a lot of links properly. What is worse, generation of all links by the author causes unwanted results on retrieval. To avoid these problems, the authoring interface should be able to generate links automatically to some extent.

In our authoring interface, we attempt to generate links automatically on the basis of "co-appearance relations" between keywords in annotations. If a pair of keywords is found in many nodes, it can be said that these keywords have a co-appearance relation with each other. Once this co-appearance relation is found, the authoring interface automatically generates a link between these nodes. Thus, generating links based on co-appearance relations expands implicit relationships between keywords to explicit relationships between nodes.

We tried creating the description graph which consists of nodes previously described in Fig. 6 and links generated from co-appearance relations between those terms that appear in more than three nodes. We got 48 links automatically generated against 115 nodes.

We also tried retrieving video cuts by using this description graph for the same query sentence in Sect. 5.3, and got almost the same results. This result demonstrates the effectiveness of the method for generating links automatically from the co-appearance relation.

6   Conclusion

We have presented a video description model and retrieval method based on fragmentary descriptions of video contents and their relationships. We compared the characteristics and advantages of our method with those of existing description models, and discussed the video retrieval process in detail, identifying items of concern. We proposed prototype interfaces for the description and retrieval of video images, and gave some examples.

In summary, the first important point is that a time-stamped authoring graph allows an author to describe a continuous video stream without considering how accurately he/she needs to extract parts of the video stream in response to various retrieval requests, and allows him/her to give them precise descriptions even without a detailed knowledge of all the stories or scenes. The second important point is that a user can retrieve video images that are related to the request. However, we must consider that some criteria are needed in order to evaluate how well a part of a video matches a request and identify the best-matched part. We are working on establishing such criteria.

Acknowledgements

We thank Toei film company for contributing the preview videos for animation movies.

References

1. Allen, J. F.: Maintaining Knowledge about Temporal Intervals, CACM, Vol. 26, pp. 832-843 (1983).
2. Kim, Y., Shibata, M.: Content-Based Video Indexing and Retrieval -A Natural Language Approach, IEICE Trans. Inf. and Syst., Vol.E79-D, No. 6, pp. 695-704 (1996).
3. Oomoto, E., Tanaka, K.: OVID: Design and Implementation of a Video-Object Database System, IEEE Transactions on Knowledge and Data Engineering, Vol. 5, No. 4, pp. 629-643 (1993).
4. Uehara, K., Oe, M., Maehara, K.: Knowledge Representation, Concept Acquisition and Retrieval of Video Data, Proc. of International Symposium on Cooperative Database Systems for Advanced Applications, pp. 527- 534 (1996).
5. Weiss, R. et al.: Content-Based Access to Algebraic Video, IEEE Multimedia, pp. 140-151 (1994).

An Approach to Spatio-Temporal Queries
– Interval-Based Contents Representation of Images – *

Masayoshi Aritsugi[1]   Toshimi Tagashira[2]
Toshiyuki Amagasa[1]   Yoshinari Kanamori[1]

[1] Department of Computer Science, Gunma University
1-5-1 Tenjin-cho, Kiryu 376 Japan
{aritsugi,amagasa,kanamori}@dbms.cs.gunma-u.ac.jp
[2] Toshiba Corporation
1-1-1 Shibaura, Minato-ku 105-01 Japan

Abstract. Contents retrieval from image sequences can be expressed with predicates on them. This paper introduces spatio-temporal predicates to be applied to image sequences. Numerous kinds of queries with spatio-temporal relations between objects, e.g., topological relations, direction relations, temporal relations, and combinations of them, are expressed with the predicates. We also show with examples how such queries are processed in a database storing interval data created by projecting objects appearing in image sequences on the x-, y-, or time-axis. A representation of spatio-temporal concepts is employed with primitive operations for illustrating the process in this paper.

1 Introduction

Contents retrieval of image sequences is seriously required in wide areas. A large number of image data such as remote sensing images, videos, and X-ray photographs are being collected. To manage such data efficiently, we usually attach keywords to them so that we can retrieve appropriate data volume by using the keywords. However, it is natural that such facilities are not always useful for every users.

One of potential solutions for the issue is to support *spatio-temporal queries* which can be applied to such image sequences. In the cases where users are aware of objects and their spatial and temporal relations appearing in the collected data, such queries can be a powerful tool to treat image sequences. What users have to do is to express spatio-temporal relations between objects, and they can get image sequences including the relations. The more general spatio-temporal queries are, the more various kinds of needs are satisfied in contents retrieval.

This paper introduces numerous kinds of spatial, temporal, and spatio-temporal predicates on objects appearing in image sequences. In [15] we have modeled an object appearing in image sequences with minimum bounding cuboids, each of which consists of a minimum bounding rectangle and a time interval. That is, all needed information is described by combining interval data, created by projecting objects on the x-, y-, or time-axis. Note that we assume that objects have already been detected and modeled with intervals properly. The predicates are based on the modeling presented in [15].

Also, this paper shows how the introduced spatio-temporal queries are processed with the interval data stored in a database. Interval-based representations

* This work was supported in part by the Ministry of Education, Science, Sports and Culture in Japan under a Grant-in-Aid for Scientific Research on Priority Areas (Grant-No. 08244101) and in part by Nihon Sun Microsystems K.K.

of objects in terms of spatial and/or temporal aspects are employed by many researches (e.g., [1, 11]). One reason why employing interval-based representation is that intervals are so general that the representing way can be applied to wide variety of areas. Therefore, we think that spatio-temporal queries and ways of processing of the queries described in this paper should be of interest to spatio-temporal database community in general.

The remainder of this paper is organized as follows. Section 2 describes an overview of the conceptual data model we use as a basis of the discussion in this paper. Section 3 introduces spatio-temporal queries, and shows with examples how to process the queries with interval data stored in a database. Section 4 compares our study with other work, and Section 5 concludes this paper.

2 Representation of Spatio-Temporal Concepts

In this section we describe briefly interval-based spatio-temporal representation of objects; a more detailed description including formal definitions of concepts can be found in [15].

We model an object appearing in an image with a minimum bounding rectangle (MBR). We do not think of how to detect objects: all objects should be modeled with MBRs properly. In the modeling, we assume that the status appearing in the image continues as it looks like by the time the next image is created. This assumption allows us to model an object with minimum bounding cuboids (MBCs) each of which consists of an MBR and the time interval.

Definition 1 *Given object O, let $Ox = (Ox.sp, Ox.ep)$ and $Oy = (Oy.sp, Oy.ep)$ be its intervals, created by projecting it on x- and y-axes, respectively. The minimum bounding rectangle of object O is defined as the domain (x, y) where*

$$Ox.sp \leq x \leq Ox.ep \wedge Oy.sp \leq y \leq Oy.ep \quad .$$

This is described as $(Ox, Oy; O)$ in this paper.
Definition 2 *Let the time interval in which $(Ox, Oy; O)$ is available be $Ot = (Ot.sp, Ot.ep)$. Let us define that the object's minimum bounding cuboid is the domain (x, y, t) where*

$$Ox.sp \leq x \leq Ox.ep \wedge Oy.sp \leq y \leq Oy.ep \wedge Ot.sp \leq t \leq Ot.ep \quad .$$

This is described as $(Ox, Oy, Ot; O)$ in this paper.
Figure 1 and 2 illustrate a minimum bounding rectangle and a minimum bounding cuboid, respectively.

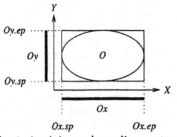

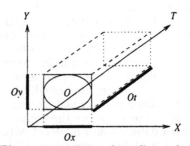

Fig. 1. A minimum bounding rectangle (MBR)

Fig. 2. A minimum bounding cuboid (MBC)

Incidentally, modeling objects with MBRs can support only approximate forms of objects. This drawback is not addressed in this paper, but can be found in [11, 12].

One of the features of our conceptual model is that we not only express time intervals in which an object appears but time intervals in which the object does not. These time intervals are called *real time intervals* and *null time intervals*, respectively [2]. In the representation, an object in a null time interval is modeled as a *null MBC* which consists of a *null MBR* with certain time interval. The null MBR and null MBC are described as $(\varepsilon, \varepsilon; O)$ and $(\varepsilon, \varepsilon, Ot; O)$, respectively.

To model dynamic changes of objects, including the objects' movement, expansion, contraction, appearance and disappearance, we introduce composite MBCs.

Definition 3 *Given an image sequence consisting of n images, each numbered as i $(1 \leq i \leq n)$. Given object O, the MBC O_{mbc_i} of which is $(Ox_i, Oy_i, Ot_i; O)$. The object's composite MBC is defined as*

$$\{O_{mbc_1}, O_{mbc_2}, \ldots, O_{mbc_n} | (\ldots ((Ot_1 \text{ meets } Ot_2) \text{ meets } Ot_3) \ldots \text{ meets } Ot_n)\}$$

where Ot_i meets Ot_{i+1} means $Ot_i.ep + 1 = Ot_{i+1}.sp$.

Figure 3 illustrates an example modeling object O with a composite minimum bounding cuboid.

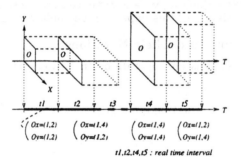

t1,t2,t4,t5 : real time interval
t3 : null time interval

Fig. 3. A composite MBC

We use Allen's relations between two intervals as a basis of all relations between intervals created by projecting objects on the x- or y-axis. We extended the relations as shown in Figure 4 [15]. The extended relations allow us to express direction relations and distances between objects easily. Note that this extension is natural and does not require anything of Allen's relations: the values $n1$ and $n2$ can be derived from the values of MBCs, which should already be stored in a database.

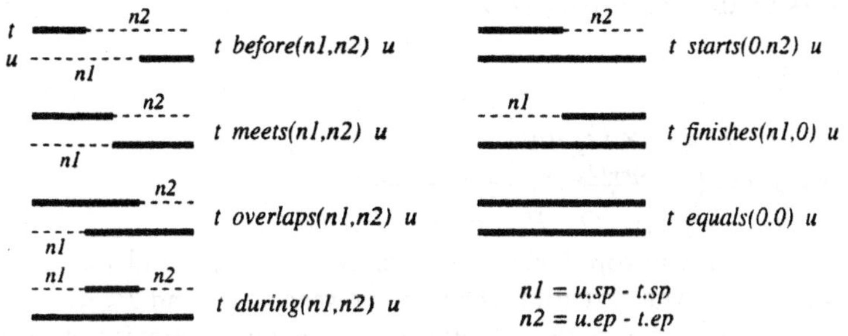

Fig. 4. Extended relations between two intervals

By using the extended interval relations, we can express spatial relations including topological and direction relations and distances between objects appearing in an image.

There are eight kinds of topological relations between MBRs [9], namely, Disjoint, Meets, Insides, Contains, Overlaps, Equals, Covered_by, and Covers. Direction relations between objects, for example, above, left-below and so forth, are defined by combining two interval relations: one is along x-axis, and the other is along y-axis. One of the features of our model is that the direction relation between objects can be defined even in the case where the topological relation between the two objects is Contains [15]. We defined two types of distances between objects: distance between the centers of gravity and shortest distance between two objects.

Spatio-temporal relations are expressed by combining the temporal interval relations and the spatial relations. Examples are shown in the following section.

3 Spatio-Temporal Queries

This section introduces temporal, spatial, and spatio-temporal predicates, and presents primitive operations for evaluating the predicates. For the sake of brevity, data concerning objects along x-, y-, and time-axes are considered in the following; however, the discussion of this paper can be applied to more complex data.

3.1 Basic Operations and Their Notations

First, the following symbols and operations are introduced to develop the discussion.

On Intervals
Let $t = (t_s, t_e)$ and $u = (u_s, u_e)$ be intervals.

- $t.sp = t_s$
- $t.ep = t_e$
- $t.dur = \begin{cases} t_e - t_s + 1 \ (t \neq \varepsilon) \\ 0 \qquad\qquad (otherwise) \end{cases}$
- $intersection(t, u) = \begin{cases} (max(t_s, u_s), min(t_e, u_e)) \ (t \cap u \neq \emptyset) \\ \varepsilon \qquad\qquad\qquad\qquad\qquad (otherwise) \end{cases}$
- $Re(t, u)$: the extended Allen's relation between t and u.

On MBRs
Let $O_{mbr} = (O_x, O_y; O)$ and $P_{mbr} = (P_x, P_y; P)$ be minimum bounding rectangles of objects O and P, respectively.

- $O_{mbr}.x = O_x$
- $O_{mbr}.y = O_y$
- $O_{mbr}.area = O_x.dur \times O_y.dur$
- $O_{mbr}.gravity = (\frac{O_x.sp + O_x.ep}{2}, \frac{O_y.sp + O_y.ep}{2})$
- $SR(O_{mbr}, P_{mbr}) = (Re(O_x, P_x), Re(O_y, P_y); O, P)$
- $TR(O_{mbr}, P_{mbr})$: the topological relation between O_{mbr} and P_{mbr}.
- $DR(O_{mbr}, P_{mbr})$: the direction relation between O_{mbr} and P_{mbr}.
- $Dist(O_{mbr}, P_{mbr})$: the distance between the centers of gravity of O_{mbr} and P_{mbr}.
- $SDist(O_{mbr}, P_{mbr})$: the shortest distance between O_{mbr} and P_{mbr}.

On MBCs

Let $O_{mbc} = (O_x, O_y, O_t; O)$ be a minimum bounding cuboid of object O.

- $O_{mbc}.x = O_x$
- $O_{mbc}.y = O_y$
- $O_{mbc}.t = O_t$
- $O_{mbc}.mbr = (O_x, O_y; O)$

On Composite MBCs

Let $O_{cmbc} = \{O_{mbc_1}, O_{mbc_2}, \ldots, O_{mbc_n} | (\ldots ((Ot_1 \ meets \ Ot_2) \ meets \ Ot_3) \ldots$
$meets \ Ot_n)\}$ be the composite minimum bounding cuboid of object O.

- $O_{cmbc}.r = \{O_{mbc_i} | O_{mbc_i}.x \neq \varepsilon \wedge O_{mbc_i}.y \neq \varepsilon \wedge 1 \leq i \leq n\}$
- $O_{cmbc}.n = \{O_{mbc_i} | O_{mbc_i}.x = O_{mbc_i}.y = \varepsilon \wedge 1 \leq i \leq n\}$

On Collections

Let o_i be an interval, an MBR, or an MBC, and C be a set of o_i, i.e., $\{o_1, o_2, \ldots, o_n\}$.
Suppose that the order of elements in C can be decided. Note that a composite
minimum bounding cuboid is a set of MBCs.

- $C.op = \{o_i.op | 1 \leq i \leq n\}$ where

$$op = \begin{cases} sp, \ ep, \ or \ dur & (o_i \ is \ an \ interval) \\ x, \ y, \ area, \ or \ gravity & (o_i \ is \ an \ MBR) \\ x, \ y, \ t, \ or \ mbr & (o_i \ is \ an \ MBC) \end{cases}$$

- $C/x = \begin{cases} o_x & (1 \leq x \leq n) \\ o_{n+x+1} & (-n \leq x \leq -1) \end{cases} (x \in integer)$

3.2 An Image Sequence

In the following discussion, we use an example of image sequences depicted in
Figure 5.

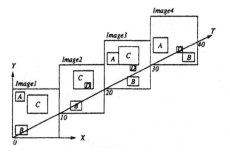

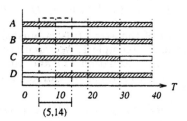

Fig. 6. The temporal relations.

Fig. 5. An example of image sequences

Four objects, i.e., A, B, C, and D, are modeled with MBRs in the example.
In the example, object A appeared in all images but image 2, with slightly
changes of the area the object occupies, while object C held from image 1 to
3 and disappeared in image 4. Object B moved from right side to left in the
space, while object D appeared from image 2 to 4 with slightly moving down.
When modeling the example with composite minimum bounding cuboids, the
data stored in a database are as follows.

$$A_{cmbc} = \{((1,3),(12,14),(0,9);A),(\varepsilon,\varepsilon,(10,19);A),$$
$$((1,4),(8,11),(20,29);A),((1,5),(4,9),(30,39);A)\}$$
$$B_{cmbc} = \{((1,4),(1,3),(0,9);B),((4,7),(1,3),(10,19);B),$$
$$((8,11),(1,3),(20,29);B),((11,14),(1,3),(30,39);B)\}$$
$$C_{cmbc} = \{((5,11),(8,13),(0,29);C),(\varepsilon,\varepsilon,(30,39);C)\}$$
$$D_{cmbc} = \{(\varepsilon,\varepsilon,(0,9);D),((9,10),(8,9),(10,19);D),$$
$$((9,10),(6,7),(20,29);D),((9,10),(4,5),(30,39);D)\}$$

3.3 Temporal Queries

Temporal queries are divided into the following three categories:
- About time intervals in which objects exist;
- About time intervals in which objects do not exist; and
- About Combinations of them.

As we described before, we treat time intervals not only in which objects exist but also in which objects do not exist. Therefore, we here discuss only those in which objects exist.

There are two kinds of temporal queries.

1. Using temporal relations between time intervals.
   ex. 1 *Which objects appear between five to fourteen seconds?*
   ex. 2 *Which objects exist during the interval from five to fourteen seconds?*
2. Using durations of time intervals.
   ex. 3 *Which objects exist continuously for more than or equal to 30 seconds?*
   ex. 4 *Which objects exist for more than or equal to 30 seconds in total?*

First of all, we get temporal data for processing temporal queries. To perform the queries described above, we pick up the following results from the example shown in Figure 5; that is, we extract real time intervals from the composite MBCs.

$$A_{cmbc}.r.t = \{((0,9);A),((20,29);A),((30,39);A)\}$$
$$B_{cmbc}.r.t = \{((0,9);B),((10,19);B),((20,29);B),((30,39);B)\}$$
$$C_{cmbc}.r.t = \{((0,29);C)\} \tag{1}$$
$$D_{cmbc}.r.t = \{((10,19);D),((20,29);D),((30,39);D)\}$$

The result of the extraction is illustrated in Figure 6.

For query example 1, we calculate the relations between each element of the sets shown in Equation (1) and time interval $(5,14)$. Equation (2) show the results, and from them we can get the answer of example 1 as objects A, B, C, and D.

$$Re(A_{cmbc}.r.t,(5,14)) = \{overlaps, after, after\}$$
$$Re(B_{cmbc}.r.t,(5,14)) = \{overlaps, overlapped\_by, after, after\}$$
$$Re(C_{cmbc}.r.t,(5,14)) = \{contains\} \tag{2}$$
$$Re(D_{cmbc}.r.t,(5,14)) = \{overlapped\_by, after, after\}$$

On the other hand, to answer example 2, we look for time intervals containing $(5,14)$ completely. According to Equation (2), we get the answer as object C. However, as shown in Figure 6, object B must be also included in the answer. This is because a time interval in which an object exists can be split into several time intervals when picking up the time interval from a composite MBC. To avoid this, we introduce the two operations, *append* and *merge*, as follows.

Definition 4 *Let $C = \{t_1, t_2, \ldots, t_n\}$ be a set of time intervals. Given a time interval t_{n+1} where $max(t_1, t_2, \ldots, t_n) = t_n \wedge t_n < t_{n+1}$, let us define operation append as follows.*

$$append(C, t_{n+1}) = \begin{cases} \{t_1, t_2, \ldots, t_{n-1}, (t_n.sp, t_{n+1}.ep)\} & (Re(t_n, t_{n+1}) = meets) \\ \{t_1, t_2, \ldots, t_n, t_{n+1}\} & (Re(t_n, t_{n+1}) \neq meets) \end{cases}$$

Then, we define operation merge as

$$merge(C) = C_n$$

where

$$\begin{cases} C_1 = \{t_1\} \\ C_i = append(C_{i-1}, t_i) \ (2 \leq i \leq n) \end{cases}$$

Applying *merge* to each of Equation (1), we get the following.

$$\begin{aligned} merge(A_{cmbc}.r.t) &= \{((0, 9); A), ((20, 39); A)\} \\ merge(B_{cmbc}.r.t) &= \{((0, 39); B)\} \\ merge(C_{cmbc}.r.t) &= \{((0, 29); C)\} \\ merge(D_{cmbc}.r.t) &= \{((10, 39); D)\} \end{aligned} \tag{3}$$

As a result, we get the answer of example 2 as objects B and C.

For query example 3, we apply *dur* to Equation (3), and thus get the answer as objects B, C, and D (see Equation (4).) Also, we can get the answer of example 4 as objects A, B, C, and D, by summing each of elements in Equation (4).

$$\begin{aligned} merge(A_{cmbc}.r.t).dur &= \{10, 20\} \\ merge(B_{cmbc}.r.t).dur &= \{40\} \\ merge(C_{cmbc}.r.t).dur &= \{30\} \\ merge(D_{cmbc}.r.t).dur &= \{30\} \end{aligned} \tag{4}$$

3.4 Spatial Queries

There are five kinds of spatial queries we think in this paper.

1. Using interval relations.
   ex. 5 *Which objects have the relation (meets, starts) with MBR ((5,11),(8,13))?*
2. Using topological relations.
   ex. 6 *Which objects have the relation Meets with MBR ((5,11),(8,13))?*
3. Using direction relations.
   ex. 7 *Which objects are left-below from MBR ((5,11),(8,13))?*
4. Using distances.
   ex. 8 *Which objects are 2cm away from MBR ((5,11),(8,13))?*
5. Using occupied areas.
   ex. 9 *Which objects occupy $20cm^2$?*

We first get MBRs for spatial queries (Equation (5)); that is, we eliminate time intervals from the composite MBCs.

$$A_{cmbc}.mbr = \{((1,3),(12,14);A),(\varepsilon,\varepsilon;A),((1,4),(8,11);A),((1,5),(4,9);A)\}$$
$$B_{cmbc}.mbr = \{((1,4),(1,3);B),((4,7),(1,3);B),((8,11),(1,3);B),$$
$$((11,14),(1,3);B)\} \tag{5}$$
$$C_{cmbc}.mbr = \{((5,11),(8,13);C),(\varepsilon,\varepsilon;C)\}$$
$$D_{cmbc}.mbr = \{(\varepsilon,\varepsilon;D),((9,10),(8,9);D),((9,10),(6,7);D),((9,10),(4,5);D)\}$$

For example 5, we examine relations between each of Equation (5) and MBR $Q_{mbr} = ((5,11),(8,13))$ as shown in Equation (6), and get the answer as object A.

$$SR(A_{cmbc}.mbr, Q_{mbr}) = \{(before, overlapped\_by; A, Q),(meets, starts; A, Q),$$
$$(overlaps, overlaps; A, Q)\}$$
$$SR(B_{cmbc}.mbr, Q_{mbr}) = \{(meets, before; B, Q),(overlaps, before; B, Q),$$
$$(finishes, before; B, Q),(overlapped\_by, before; B, Q)\} \tag{6}$$
$$SR(C_{cmbc}.mbr, Q_{mbr}) = \{(equals, equals; C, Q)\}$$
$$SR(D_{cmbc}.mbr, Q_{mbr}) = \{(during, starts; D, Q),(during, meets; D, Q),$$
$$(during, before; D, Q)\}$$

Example 6 are solved by obtaining topological relations between each MBR of Equation (5) and MBR Q_{mbr}. Topological relations are derived from combinations of interval relations along x- and y-axes (detailed descriptions can be found in [15]). From Equation (6), we get Equation (7). The answer for query example 6 is objects A and D.

$$TR(A_{cmbc}.mbr, Q_{mbr}) = \{(Disjoint; A, Q),(Meets; A, Q),(Overlaps; A, Q)\}$$
$$TR(B_{cmbc}.mbr, Q_{mbr}) = \{(Disjoint; B, Q),(Disjoint; B, Q),$$
$$(Disjoint; B, Q),(Disjoint; B, Q)\}$$
$$TR(C_{cmbc}.mbr, Q_{mbr}) = \{(Equals; C, Q)\} \tag{7}$$
$$TR(D_{cmbc}.mbr, Q_{mbr}) = \{(Covered\_by; D, Q),(Meets; D, Q),$$
$$(Disjoint; D, Q)\}$$

Example 7 are processed similarly by obtaining direction relations between each MBR in Equation (5) and MBR Q_{mbr}. The direction relations are shown in Equation (8), where, for example, $DR(A, B) = (<_x, >_y; A, B)$ means that A is in a negative direction along x-axis and in a positive along y-axis from the B's point of view (formal definitions can also be found in [15]). Therefore, *left-below* appeared in example 7 is expressed as $(<_x, <_y)$. According to Equation (8), the answer is objects A and B.

$$DR(A_{cmbc}.mbr, Q_{mbr}) = \{(<_x, >_y; A, Q),(<_x, =_y; A, Q),(<_x, <_y; A, Q)\}$$
$$DR(B_{cmbc}.mbr, Q_{mbr}) = \{(<_x, <_y; B, Q),(<_x, <_y; B, Q),(=_x, <_y; B, Q),$$
$$(>_x, <_y; B, Q)\} \tag{8}$$
$$DR(C_{cmbc}.mbr, Q_{mbr}) = \{(=_x, =_y; C, Q)\}$$
$$DR(D_{cmbc}.mbr, Q_{mbr}) = \{(>_x, <_y; D, Q),(>_x, <_y; D, Q),(>_x, <_y; D, Q)\}$$

Also, shortest distances can be obtained from Equation (5) as follows.

$$SDist(A_{cmbc}.mbr, Q_{mbr}) = \{1, 0, 0\}$$
$$SDist(B_{cmbc}.mbr, Q_{mbr}) = \{4, 4, 4, 4\}$$
$$SDist(C_{cmbc}.mbr, Q_{mbr}) = \{0\} \tag{9}$$
$$SDist(D_{cmbc}.mbr, Q_{mbr}) = \{0, 0, 2\}$$

The answer of example 8 is objects B and D, as shown in Equation (9).

For queries using occupied areas, we can use *area* operation. Equation (10) shows the result from applying the operation to Equation (5). The answer of example 9 is objects A and C.

$$A_{cmbc}.mbr.area = \{9, 0, 16, 25\}$$
$$B_{cmbc}.mbr.area = \{12, 12, 12, 12\}$$
$$C_{cmbc}.mbr.area = \{42, 0\} \tag{10}$$
$$D_{cmbc}.mbr.area = \{0, 4, 4, 4\}$$

3.5 Spatio-Temporal Queries

Spatio-temporal queries are those containing temporal and spatial conditions. The queries are divided into two types: queries about changes of objects and about relations between objects.

Changes of Objects

We discuss five kinds of changes of objects: expansion, contraction, movement, appearance, and disappearance.

Expansion and contraction concern the change of an object's area. Objects expanding and contracting can be formalized as follows.

– Expansion

$$\{O \mid O_{mbc_i}.mbr.area < O_{mbc_j}.mbr.area \land Re(O_{mbc_i}.t, O_{mbc_j}.t) = meets\}$$

– Contraction

$$\{O \mid O_{mbc_i}.mbr.area > O_{mbc_j}.mbr.area \land Re(O_{mbc_i}.t, O_{mbc_j}.t) = meets\}$$

These are performed along with Equation (10). For example, we can find the facts that object A expanded at $A_{mbc_3}.t.sp$ and $A_{mbc_4}.t.sp$, and contracted at $A_{mbc_2}.t.sp$.

We define movement of an object as that of the gravity of the object. Then, the following predicate is the query for moved objects.

$$\{O \mid O_{mbc_i}.mbr.gravity \neq O_{mbc_j}.mbr.gravity \land Re(O_{mbc_i}.t, O_{mbc_j}.t) = meets\}$$

Let us look at object B, for example. We get

$$B_{cmbc}.mbr.gravity = \{(2.5, 2), (5.5, 2), (9.5, 2), (12.5, 2)\}$$

and then, we disclose the fact that object B moved from left to right in the space.

Objects of which change is appearance or disappearance are expressed as follows.

$$\{O \mid O_{mbc_i}.mbr.x = \varepsilon \land O_{mbc_i}.mbr.y = \varepsilon \land O_{mbc_j}.mbr.x \neq \varepsilon \land O_{mbc_j}.mbr.y \neq \varepsilon$$
$$\land Re(O_{mbc_i}.t, O_{mbc_j}.t) = meets\}$$

$$\{O \mid O_{mbc_i}.mbr.x \neq \varepsilon \land O_{mbc_i}.mbr.y \neq \varepsilon \land O_{mbc_j}.mbr.x = \varepsilon \land O_{mbc_j}.mbr.y = \varepsilon$$
$$\land Re(O_{mbc_i}.t, O_{mbc_j}.t) = meets\}$$

Changes of Relations between Objects

Changes of relations between objects can be expressed by combining temporal predicates and spatial predicates. Here we consider some examples.

ex. 10 Which were the objects that first were away from and then touched object B?

Example 10 is written as follows.

$$\{O \mid TR(O_{mbc_i}.mbr, B_{mbc_j}.mbr) = Disjoint$$
$$\wedge TR(O_{mbc_{i'}}.mbr, B_{mbc_{j'}}.mbr) = Meets$$
$$\wedge Re(intersection(O_{mbc_i}.t, B_{mbc_j}.t), intersection(O_{mbc_{i'}}.t, B_{mbc_{j'}}.t))$$
$$= (before \vee meets)\}$$

ex. 11 Which were the objects that first were contained by object C and then touched object B?

This includes a relation between more than two objects. This can be expressed as follows.

$$\{O \mid TR(O_{mbc_i}.mbr, C_{mbc_j}.mbr) = Insides$$
$$\wedge TR(O_{mbc_{i'}}.mbr, B_{mbc_k}.mbr) = Meets$$
$$\wedge Re(intersection(O_{mbc_i}.t, C_{mbc_j}.t), intersection(O_{mbc_{i'}}.t, B_{mbc_k}.t))$$
$$= (before \vee meets)\}$$

ex. 12 Which objects moved from left to right in the space?

By looking an image itself as MBR $Q_{mbr} = ((0, 15), (0, 15))$, this example can be queried as follows.

$$\{O \mid DR(O_{mbc_i}.mbr, Q_{mbr}) = (<_x) \wedge DR(O_{mbc_{i'}}.mbr, Q_{mbr}) = (>_x) \wedge$$
$$Re(O_{mbc_i}.t, O_{mbc_{i'}}.t) = (before \vee meets)\}$$

4 Related Work

Allen defined time intervals as temporal entity primitives, and listed all possible temporal relations between two time intervals [1]. He also mentioned that indefinite and relative temporal knowledge could be expressed using time intervals. All representation of spatio-temporal concepts and queries on them in this paper are based on Allen's relations [15].

Spatial queries have been proposed so far, especially in geographical information system (GIS) [7]. Also, temporal queries have been proposed so far [13, 10, 14]. However, there has been, to our knowledge, little study on the combination of spatial and temporal queries. That is perhaps because geographical information is assumed not to be updated frequently, and temporal database researchers have not focused on spatial data so much. On the other hand, our study is to support contents retrieval of image data such as remote sensing images, videos, and X-ray photographs, as described in Introduction. To this end, predicates on both spatial and temporal aspects are indispensable.

Nabil et al. [9] defined 2D projection interval relationships for representing directional and topological relationships between two objects. They adapted

Allen's temporal intervals [1] and 2D-strings to produce the unified representation. They did not integrate temporal concepts into their work.

Claramunt and Thériault [4] integrated time into GIS. They introduced several kinds of changes of each object appearing in images, and proposed recording them along with the times of their occurrence as each object's versions. They proposed new temporal operators which can be integrated into TSQL [10]. However, they did not include spatio-temporal queries.

Chu et al. [3] introduced a semantic data model to manage medical image data, and presented a spatial evolutionary query language (SEQL). The language allows us to express spatio-temporal queries. Objects appearing in an image are connected with each other, making a semantic graph in their conceptual data model. The connections in the graph express relationships between objects and histories of patients. The user writes queries with the connections. In contrast, our conceptual model is based completely on intervals, and queries are expressed and processed with them.

The study by Day et al. [5] is probably the most similar to our own. These authors proposed a graphical data model for specifying spatio-temporal semantics of video data. In the model, MBRs are used not only to model objects, but to derive the relative spatial relationships between them. One point of difference between their study and the present one is that we model an object with a composite minimum bounding cuboid that consists of only interval data and, therefore, is a simple form, while they used a graph connecting MBRs.

Del Bimbo et al. [6] proposed a language, Spatio-temporal Logic, for the symbolic representation of the contents of image sequences. In this logic, objects are represented as MBRs, and spatial relationships between two objects are defined as combinations of Allen's interval relations along the x- and y-axes. Moreover, they supported visual querying. However, to support querying by visual sketch, they did not support to express the exact degree of time intervals in predicates. For example, predicate "object A was left from object B, then moved to right" can be expressed in their model. However, how long each of the situations was keeping cannot be expressed. On the other hand, since we use time intervals, not only real time intervals but null time intervals, those like the above example can be expressed in the framework of our study.

5 Conclusions

In this paper we have introduced numerous kinds of spatio-temporal queries, and also shown how to process the queries with interval data stored in a database. Objects appearing in image sequences are modeled with intervals, which are fully investigated in the world, and all queries are expressed and processed with the intervals.

The form of spatio-temporal queries introduced in this paper is not user-friendly. We have to design an easy-to-use spatio-temporal query language, integrate them into well-known query languages like SQL, or create tools to retrieve in various ways, say, to retrieve by drawing as an example of answer. We are currently developing R-tree based index management for interval-based representations of objects appearing in image sequences.

References

1. J.F. Allen, "Maintaining Knowledge about Temporal Intervals," *CACM*, 26(11), pp.832–843, Nov. 1983.

2. T. Amagasa, M. Aritsugi, Y. Kanamori, and Y. Masunaga, "Interval-Based Modeling for Temporal Representation and Operations," *Submitted for Publication*, 1997.

3. W.W. Chu, I.T. Ieong, and R.K. Taira, "A Semantic Modeling Approach for Image Retrieval by Content," *VLDB Journal*, 3(4), pp.445–477, Oct. 1994.

4. C. Claramunt and M. Thériault, "Managing Time in GIS An Event-Oriented Approach," *Proc. the International Workshop on Temporal Databases*, pp.23–42, Sep. 1995.

5. Y.F. Day, S. Dağtaş, M. Iino, A. Khokhar, and A. Ghafoor, "Object-Oriented Conceptual Modeling of Video Data," *Proc. 11th ICDE*, pp.401–408, 1995.

6. A. Del Bimbo, E. Vicario, and D. Zingoni, "Symbolic Description and Visual Querying of Image Sequences Using Spatio-Temporal Logic," *IEEE TKDE*, 7(4), pp.609–621, 1995.

7. M.J. Egenhofer, "Spatial SQL: A Query and Presentation Language," *IEEE TKDE*, 6(1), pp.86–95, 1994.

8. P. Ladkin, "Time Representation: A Taxonomy of Interval Relations," *Proc. the National conference on Artificial Intelligence*, pp.360-366, 1986.

9. M. Nabil, J. Shephred, and A.H.H. Ngu, "2D-Projection Interval Relationships: A Symbolic Representation of Spatial Relationships," *Proc. 4th International Symposium on Large Spatial Databases*, Lecture Notes in Computer Science 951, pp.292–309, Aug. 1995.

10. S.B. Navathe and R. Ahmed, "A Temporal Relational Model and a Query Language," Information Sciences, 49, pp.147–175, 1989.

11. D. Papadias and T. Sellis, "Qualitative Representation of Spatial Knowledge in Two-Dimensional Space," *VLDB Journal*, 3(4), pp.479–516, Oct. 1994.

12. D. Papadias, Y. Theodoridis, T. Sellis, and M.J.Egenhofer, "Topological Relations in the World of Minimum Bounding Rectangles: A Study with R-trees," *Proc. SIGMOD Conf.*, pp.92–103, June 1995.

13. R.T. Snodgrass, "The Temporal Query Language TQuel," *ACM TODS*, 12(2), pp.247–298, June 1987.

14. R.T. Snodgrass Ed., *The TSQL2 Temporal Query Language*, Kluwer Academic Publishers, 1995.

15. T. Tagashira, T. Amagasa, M. Aritsugi, and Y. Kanamori, "Interval-Based Representation of Spatio-Temporal Concepts," *The 9th Conference on Advanced Information Systems Engineering (CAiSE*97)*, Lecture Notes in Computer Science, June 1997 (to appear).

An Image Retrieval System Based on the Visualization of System Relevance via Documents

Nathalie Denos, Catherine Berrut, Mourad Mechkour

CLIPS
IMAG-Campus - BP 53
F-38041 Grenoble Cedex - France
E-mail: [Nathalie.Denos|Catherine.Berrut|Mourad.Mechkour]@imag.fr
Phone: (33) 4-76-63-57-23
Fax: (33) 4-76-44-66-75

Abstract. This paper describes a system for an image retrieval system in which relevance related and system-use related user strategies can be performed. The query supports, in addition to classical topical inputs, strategic parameters that can be set by the user, either directly or via the visualization of retrieved images that are organized with respect to which relevance criteria are verified. Typical retrieval situations are defined, that account for the dynamic aspect of a given retrieval session.

1 Introduction

Information retrieval systems aim at retrieving documents from a corpus, on the basis of a query expressing an information need. Documents are indexed with respect to their content or to features that are likely to be used for retrieval. A matching function defines the system's estimation of the *relevance* of a document to the query, on the basis of the document's index. The modeling of relevance is thus a major topic in information retrieval research.

Most of today information retrieval systems are dedicated to end-users, i.e the the information needs providers. It is well known that two users uttering the same query would not judge the same documents as relevant. At the root of this phenomenon are the numerous situation-related relevance factors that influence relevance judgments. Nonetheless, most information retrieval systems model relevance as a function that maps a given query to a set of documents, regardless of these variations.

1.1 Existing approaches

For a system to account for these situation-related variations, it has to adapt to the particular situation during the retrieval process. Today, two types of techniques are available: relevance feedback techniques, and strategy-based techniques.

Relevance feedback techniques [7,8] work out an iterative process where, given a set of retrieved documents, the user judges some of these documents as relevant, or non-relevant; the system computes a new query on the basis of this information and displays the corresponding set of retrieved documents. Grossly speaking, the new query is computed by adding or subtracting the terms (or modifying the weights of the terms) that appear in the relevant or non-relevant documents.

For this technique to actually improve the results, relevance judgments must be correctly performed throughout the entire set of retrieved documents (correct relevance detection by the user), which is hardly realized in the frequent case where the set of retrieved documents is both big and linearly presented.

Moreover, all the selected documents are treated in a uniform way to generate the new query, which assumes that documents are all judged relevant for the same reason; but relevance judgments are shown to be rooted in various sources (even if we restrict to document-related sources) [9,2].

Strategy-based approaches are based on a finite and small number of querying situations identified via a typology of users or needs [10]; the system implements one specific matching function per situation, called *search strategies* [6,3].

This technique assumes that it is possible to characterize a stereotypical retrieval situation in terms of a matching function, and that a given user in a given retrieval situation can be associated to a given element of the typology (or more directly to one of the search strategies). But relevance factors are so numerous and intricately intertwining that it is difficult to involve a sufficient number of them in the definition of a small set of types of situations. Moreover, in practice it is difficult for the system to determine which strategy to apply in which case.

1.2 Our approach

We propose to design a system in order for a user to elaborate his own search strategy. For this we lean, on the one hand, on the idea of parameterizing system relevance – that search strategies suggest, and on the other hand, on the iterative retrieval process – as relevance feedback suggests. System relevance parameters shall be tuned by the user iteratively to improve the query formulation.

For a user to be able to tune the system's parameters, the semantics of these parameters must be made clear to him. We develop a visualization of retrieved documents that allows the user 1) to establish connections between document characteristics and system parameters and 2) to handle the result with respect to precision and recall.

Our system offers two main features to allow the user to elaborate his own search strategy: an extended query language that includes strategic parameters and a structured visualization of the set of retrieved documents that allows the user to understand the system's interpretation of his query in an intuitive way.

The extended query language involves two types of strategic parameters: 1) semantic parameters, that specify not only terms – like in regular queries, but also the role these terms shall play in system relevance estimation – like specific properties of search strategies; 2) pragmatic parameters, that allow for the handling of both the set of retrieved documents (size of the result) and the way it is structured in the visualization. The pragmatic parameters are meant to let the user to obtain a better context for the detection of relevance, and to improve the formulation of his information need while understanding the system's interpretation of his query.

To sum up, our approach accounts, on the one hand, for two broad and generally neglected relevance factors: *diversity in the use of document-related relevance criteria* and *ease of detection of relevance*, and on the other hand for one frequently missing feature in systems: *the intuitive understanding of the system's interpretation of the query*.

The system presented here implements the underlying conceptual and formal models described in [4,5]. The corpus is a collection of images that we present in section 2. The query language, retrieval model and interaction with the user are formalized in section 3 and illustrated in section 4.

2 Application and problem statement

2.1 The data

The corpus is a set of 658 scanned photographs of Paris, that may be searched for their anecdotal, architectural, historical and/or esthetic interest.

Images are manually indexed according to six disjoint facets: *Author*, *Content* (symbolic content of the image), *Connotation* (subjective impression), *Morphology* (technical aspects: point of view of the photographer, spatial arrangement of components, lightening), *Gender* (type of the scene) , *Precisions* (contextual information about elements of the content). A tree-like thesaurus (*broader/narrower* relationships) is available for querying upon facet *Content*, although indexing terms are exclusively drawn from the set of maximal degree terms, i.e. the thesaurus narrowest terms, in order to ensure independence between terms, at least to a certain extent.

2.2 Querying needs

The goal is to design a system that provides a queryable access to this corpus, that benefits best from the multi-faceted indexing model. The system shall be usable for many different purposes (various retrieval situations) and by any type of users.

Users We want to avoid restrictions on the type of users (individual characteristics like formal education, knowledge of the field, intended use of the images retrieved, etc.). For instance, a journalist looking for an illustration for his paper stands in a very different retrieval situation from that of an architecture student searching for iconographic documentation on Paris buildings, either in general or with respect to a specific architectural feature. Each of these individuals will utter their queries in different ways, and will need a more or less focused result.

Media As soon as we regard images as *documents that support information* in broad, the classical text retrieval modeling assumption that "a topical match is enough", cannot hold anymore. Users need a more complex setting to express their needs because the needs can be expressed under the form of very different relevance criteria. As a consequence the system's relevance model must also be more complex. Another characteristic of images is that user relevance criteria are more likely to fall into the realm of subjectivity than for classical textual purposes. It is very likely that a user query a system in his own words, even if they do not fit the system's interpretation for these words. Hence, it is important that the system account for this necessity of clarifying its semantics for relevance estimation.

Types of search situations As a consequence of these two constraining features (users and uses are not restricted and documents are images), not only the system must model relevance in a complex *and* self explanatory way, but also it must be able to adapt to the various retrieval situations at hand. The prototype that implements this model is available via the World Wide Web to fit the assumption of a diversity of users and uses.

3 Relevance model

For each document, the system estimates its conformity to the query, which is a combination of relevance criteria. Then the system groups documents into classes depending on which criteria are verified, and it orders classes with respect to the number of criteria verified in each class.

3.1 Query language

A query is a combination of *facet-wise criteria*, that are in turn a combination of *elementary criteria*. Elementary criteria are associated with terms. In facet *Content*, any term of the thesaurus can be used as the basis for an elementary criterion. Hence, both indexing terms (the narrowest terms) and their broader terms can be used. For the other facets, only indexing terms are allowed, as no thesaurus is available.

Elementary relevance criterion An elementary criterion $\xi[t]$ is a function that maps a document D to a boolean value: $\xi[t](D) \in \{true, false\}$. We denote the ith elementary criterion of Q as ξ_i instead of $\xi[t_i]$. For each facet, there is a predefined set of *abstract elementary criteria* that specify the role that a given term shall play in the relevance estimation.

For facet *Content*, we can define three abstract elementary criteria (*Equal*, *Specific*, *Close*), given a term t and a document D, as follows:

- *Equal*[t](D): exists t' in D such that $t' = t$;
- *Specific*[t](D): exists t' in D that is a narrower term of t;

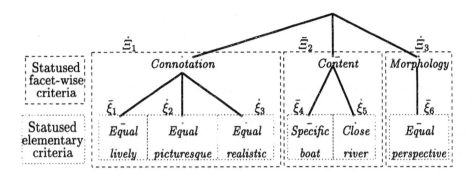

Fig. 1. Example of a query

- *Close*[t](D): exists t' in D and $\exists t''$ such that t' and t are narrower terms of t'', of degree $degree(t'') + 1$ and $degree(t'') \neq 0$.

For the other facets, as the thesaurus is flat, only the equality criterion can be defined.

Status of a criterion Each elementary criterion ξ_i is associated with a two-valued *status* –either *mandatory* or *optional*, that allows the user to handle the precision and the organization of the result (see later). If mandatory, the statused elementary criterion is denoted by $\bar{\xi}_i$, and if optional, by $\dot{\xi}_i$. As for the estimation of a document's conformity to the relevance schema, an optional criterion need not be verified for the document to be retrieved, whereas a mandatory one is necessarily verified.

Each facet-wise criterion, which is a set of statused elementary criteria, is also associated with a two-valued status –*mandatory* or *optional*, exactly in the same way as elementary criteria. $\bar{\Xi}_j = FacetName(\xi_1, \ldots, \xi_{N_j})$ denotes the jth mandatory facet-wise criterion, and $\dot{\Xi}_k = FacetName(\xi_1, \ldots, \xi_{N_k})$ denotes the kth optional facet-wise criterion.

Figure 1 demonstrates notations with respect to the query example *photographs featuring boats and rivers (or something close) in it, that preferably has a lively and possibly picturesque or realistic connotation, and preferably in a perspective view.*

A query can be fully described as follows: $Q = \{\dot{F}, \bar{F}, \dot{T}, \bar{T}\}$, where $\dot{F}$ (resp. $\bar{F}$) is the set of optional (resp. mandatory) facet names, and $\dot{T}$ (resp. $\bar{T}$) is the set of optional (resp. mandatory) elementary criteria. Both facet-wise criteria Ξ_j and elementary criteria ξ_i are *criteria*. To denote any of these two types of criteria, we use the letter X, and $\bar{X}$, $\dot{X}$ for mandatory and optional ones.

3.2 System relevance estimation

Set of retrieved documents Given a query Q and a corpus $\mathcal{D}$, the set of retrieved documents $Q(\mathcal{D})$ is the set of those documents D that verify all of the mandatory facet-wise criteria in Q. A document verifies a facet-wise criterion if it verifies all of the mandatory elementary criteria that it comprises: $Q(\mathcal{D}) = \{D \in \mathcal{D}, \forall \bar{\Xi} \in Q, \forall \bar{\xi} \in \bar{\Xi}, \bar{\xi}(D) = true\}$.

Relevance classes Visualization of documents is based on a classification of documents with respect to which optional criteria they verify. The classification has two layers following the structure of the query Q: it comprises a set of classes that refer to facet-wise criteria, and each class comprises a set of subclasses that refer to elementary criteria.

We denote each set of classes or subclasses as $\{C_\Sigma\}_{\Sigma \in \mathcal{S}}$. Let Ref be the reference set of documents for a given level (either class or subclass), and N_{opt} be the number of optional criteria $X_i, i \in [1..N_{opt}]$ for this reference set. $\mathcal{S}$ is the set all possible combinations of optional criteria, denoted by a N_{opt}-bit word with "1" for a selected optional criterion, and "0" for a non-selected one. For example with $N_{opt} = 3$, the combination where all optional criteria are selected is denoted by $\Sigma_{max} = 111$, and the combination where all optional criteria are not selected is denoted by $\Sigma_{min} = 000$. $\Sigma[j]$ denotes the jth bit of Σ:
$$C_\Sigma = Ref \quad \cap \quad \{D \in \mathcal{D}, \forall j \in [1..N_{opt}], (\Sigma[j] = 1 \implies \dot{X}_i(D) = true)\}.$$

For classes, Ref is the set of retrieved documents $Q(\mathcal{D})$ and the optional criteria are the optional facet-wise criteria that appear in the query Q. In figure 1, $N_{opt} = 2$ due to $\dot{\Xi}_1$ and $\dot{\Xi}_3$ (*Connotation* and *Morphology*). For subclasses, Ref is a given class, and optional criteria are the subset of the optional elementary criteria that belong to those facet-wise criteria that are selected in the reference class. With our example query, for class $C_{\Sigma_{min}} = C_{00}$ as a reference set, $N_{opt} = 1$ due to $\dot{\xi}_5$ (*river*), and for class $C_{\Sigma_{max}} = C_{11}$, $N_{opt} = 3$ due to $\dot{\xi}_2$, $\dot{\xi}_3$ and $\dot{\xi}_5$ (*picturesque*, *realistic* and *river*).

For a given reference set, the number of criteria is denoted by $N = N_{opt} + N_{mand}$, with N_{opt} (resp. N_{mand}) the number of optional (resp. mandatory) criteria.

Relevance degrees for classes For a given C_Σ, its *relevance degree* $d^o(C_\Sigma)$ is the number of optional criteria that are selected by Σ, i.e. $Card(\{i \in [1..N_{opt}], \Sigma[i] = 1\})$. The bigger the degree is, the better system relevance is, as the system assumes that all of the criteria inputed are preferably verified. Relevance degrees define a partial order on a set of classes or subclasses.

Visual relevance classes For relevance classes not to overlap in the visualization of the result, we define a set of visual relevance classes $\widehat{C}_\Sigma$ recursively on a given set of relevance classes C_Σ as follows:

$$\begin{cases} \widehat{C}_{\Sigma_{max}} = C_{\Sigma_{max}} \\ \widehat{C}_\Sigma = C_\Sigma \setminus \bigcup_{\{\widehat{C}, d^o(\widehat{C}) > d^o(\widehat{C}_\Sigma)\}} (\widehat{C}) \ for \ \Sigma \neq \Sigma_{max} \end{cases}$$

This definition applies at both class and subclass levels, and it ensures that sets of visual classes are disjoint. Furthermore, a document which belongs to different classes only appears in the visual class which has the higher relevance degree.

Q	37 answers					
Classes	C_{11}	C_{10}			C_{01}	C_{00}	
# answers	1	6			15	15	
Subclasses		c_{010}^{10}	c_{100}^{10}	c_{000}^{10}		c_1^{00}	c_0^{00}
# answers	1	1	1	4	15	3	12
# relevant	0	1	1	2	0	2	4

Q'	37 answers											
Classes	C_{11}	C_{10}					C_{01}	C_{00}				
Subclasses		$c_{0100100}^{10}$	c_{100100}^{10}	c_{000010}^{10}	c_{000100}^{10}	c_{000000}^{10}		c_{1101}^{00}	c_{1000}^{00}	c_{0010}^{00}	c_{0100}^{00}	c_{0000}^{00}
# answers	1	1	1	1	1	2	15	2	1	1	3	8
# relevant	0	1	1	1	1	0	0	2	0	1	3	0

Table 1. Running example: relevance judgments before (Q) and after (Q') Detail

Application to the running example Our example query produces four classes C_{11} (degree 2), C_{01} and C_{10} (degree 1), and C_{00} (degree 0) due to optional facets *Connotation* and *Morphology*. Each class comprises several subclasses: 8 for C_{11} and C_{10}, and 2 for C_{01} and C_{00}. In table 1 we detail subclasses for classes C_1 and C_{10} and we show the number of answers in each class and each subclass.

3.3 Interactive retrieval process

Visualization of the results according to ordered and qualified relevance classes is our method to improve information retrieval systems performance, having system conception essentially centered on the interactive aspect of the system use. From the user's perspective, a typical session is a loop with these three steps:

1. modify the query and launch retrieval ;
2. examine the results to detect relevance and evaluate one's satisfaction;
3. in case satisfaction is not reached or cannot be correctly evaluated, search for clues to improve the query and goto step 1.

A given set of criteria defines a set of potentially retrieved documents. Statuses allow changing the point of view on this set: with all criteria optional, the biggest possible set is retrieved, and changing some criteria to mandatory has the result focused on a particular subset where these criteria are verified.

We distinguish two types of query modifications: those that add, withdraw or change an existing criterion (*semantic modifications*) and those that modify statuses, leaving criteria unchanged (*pragmatic modifications*).

Typical non-satisfaction situations In table 2, we define four stereotypical problematic situations that a user may encounter during a session, and for each one, we briefly describe what is required for the user to keep on improving

Sit.	Problem	What the user wants	Actions
1	$Q(\mathcal{D}) = \emptyset$	Retrieve something	Loosen 1
2	$Q(\mathcal{D}) \neq \emptyset$ and no relevant documents	Check completeness Check semantics	Loosen 1 Loosen 2
3	Both relevant and non-relevant documents within a class	Separate relevant documents from non-relevant ones	Detail
4	Both relevant and non-relevant classes	Tidy up (suppress non-relevant classes, and rank relevant classes first)	Focus

Table 2. From problematic situations to query modifications

the result, and we associate four actions that correspond to query modification types that we define on a syntactical basis (meaning is given later). We denote the initial query as $Q = \{\dot{\mathbf{F}}, \bar{\mathbf{F}}, \dot{\mathbf{T}}, \bar{\mathbf{T}}\}$ and the result of the modification $Q' = \{\dot{\mathbf{F}'}, \bar{\mathbf{F}'}, \dot{\mathbf{T}'}, \bar{\mathbf{T}'}\}$.

Loosen 1 Some mandatory statuses must be changed to optional, and everything else remains unchanged: $(\dot{\mathbf{T}} \cup \bar{\mathbf{T}} = \dot{\mathbf{T}'} \cup \bar{\mathbf{T}'})$ and $(\dot{\mathbf{F}} \subset \dot{\mathbf{F}'}$ or $\dot{\mathbf{T}} \subset \dot{\mathbf{T}'})$.

Loosen 2 At least one abstract criterion must be changed to a *weaker* one with respect to the ordering: *Close* $\leq$ *Specific* $\leq$ *Equal*, and everything else remains unchanged: $((\dot{\mathbf{T}} \cup \bar{\mathbf{T}}) \setminus (\dot{\mathbf{T}'} \cup \bar{\mathbf{T}'}) = \{\xi_i[t_i]\})$ and $((\dot{\mathbf{T}'} \cup \bar{\mathbf{T}'}) \setminus (\dot{\mathbf{T}} \cup \bar{\mathbf{T}}) = \{\xi_i'[t_i]\})$ and $(\forall i, \xi_i'$ is weaker than $\xi_i)$.

Detail At least one elementary criterion must be added, and everything else remains unchanged: $(\dot{\mathbf{F}} = \dot{\mathbf{F}'})$ and $(\bar{\mathbf{F}} = \bar{\mathbf{F}'})$ and $(\dot{\mathbf{T}} \subset \dot{\mathbf{T}'}$ or $\bar{\mathbf{T}} \subset \bar{\mathbf{T}'})$.

Focus Some optional elementary statuses must be changed to mandatory, and everything else remains unchanged: $(\dot{\mathbf{F}} = \dot{\mathbf{F}'})$ and $(\bar{\mathbf{F}} = \bar{\mathbf{F}'})$ and $(\dot{\mathbf{T}} \cup \bar{\mathbf{T}} = \dot{\mathbf{T}'} \cup \bar{\mathbf{T}'})$ and $(\bar{\mathbf{T}} \subset \bar{\mathbf{T}'})$.

We show how the three types of actions given in the rightmost column of the table allow the user to pursue his goal, and we detail the technical aspects of these actions, with respect to the degree of involvement of user matters.

Situation 1: shortage (bad recall and precision) User analysis: An empty result means that all mandatory criteria never occur in conjunction in any document of the corpus. Although, a user may want to see documents that verify only a subset of the mandatory criteria, as it is well-known that relevance is a relative notion: considering that the corpus does not comprise as good documents as the user expected, the user shall revise his criteria for a document to be relevant. *System view:* At performing *Loosen 1*, N_{mand} will decrease, i.e. some or all of the mandatory criteria will be turned to optional and the set of retrieved documents shall increase. The first class will be empty but additional lower-degree classes will appear.

Situation 2: no relevant document (bad recall and precision) When documents are retrieved, but none of them is deemed relevant by the user, it can be for two different reasons.

User analysis 1: First, the user can agree that the retrieved documents fit well with his query terms, but other relevance parameters make him judge them irrelevant (for instance "boats" are "barges", that he does not like). The query can be loosened to retrieve other possibly more relevant documents. *System view: Loosen 2* modifies abstract criteria (semantic modification), or *Loosen 1* modifies statuses (pragmatic modification). As the following examples show, the user must be involved for the complete specification of the modification to perform. *User view: Loosen 1* The user can loosen the query in turning $\overline{Equal}[river]$ and $\overline{Equal}[boat]$ into optional criteria. Then additional classes of documents appear, that group on the one hand boats with anything but rivers, and rivers with anything but boats. This provides an overview of the corpus from the perspective of the need. He may find that "barges" are not that bad, compared to the other possibilities that the corpus offers. *Loosen 2* For instance, if the user only retrieves "barges", in changing the $\overline{Equal}[river]$ into $\overline{Close}[river]$, he may retrieve other types of boats in different but close contexts to rivers.

User analysis 2: Second, the user can find that the retrieved documents are not topically related to his need. In this case, query terms are probably misused and the user shall check their semantics via document indexes. To proceed to this verification term by term, the user needs classes that verify only one criterion. *System view:* A particular case of *Loosen 1* is turning all criteria to optional: $\bar{\mathbf{T}}' = \emptyset$. Then, the (1)-degree classes contain those documents that verify one criterion and only one, and the $(N-1)$-degree classes contain those documents that verify all criteria but one. *User view:* When misused terms are identified, the user shall search the thesaurus for more appropriate terms to express his need in conformity with the system's semantics.

Situation 3: bad average class-wise precision *User analysis:* When a user encounters both relevant and non-relevant documents within a single class ("mixed class"), he may be satisfied as he found relevant documents, or he may want to reorganize classes in order to separate relevant documents from non-relevant ones (increase the average *class-wise precision* with respect to this set of mixed classes). *System view:* In performing *Detail*, new criteria are added in such a way that the class is split. New criteria are optional by default, to preserve the previously retrieved set of documents: $\dot{\mathbf{T}} \subset \dot{\mathbf{T}}'$. They can be defined in the same way as in classical relevance feedback techniques, but as many terms are candidate for being added to the query the system alone is a little bit short-sighted. *User view:* The reasons why the user judges some documents relevant may not be expressible in the indexing model, which prevents from increasing class-wise precision. In the other case, the user can manually perform the selection of one or more terms via document indexes. If added to the query as optional criteria, the effects produced by each optional criterion can be examined in the new classes created.

Situation 4: bad global precision In our interactive framework, bad precision does not does not prevent the user from being satisfied, as opposed to classical systems evaluation: documents are grouped into classes that make the detection of relevance easy, even if the set of retrieved documents is large. A user may be satisfied when one class of documents is relevant, even if most classes are non-relevant.

User analysis: Nonetheless, a user may want to rank relevant classes first, and display as few non-relevant classes as possible. *System view:* The pragmatic modification to perform on the query is *Focus.* Let $\Sigma \neq \Sigma_{max}$ be the name of one relevant class. If the selected optional criteria in Σ are turned to mandatory criteria, this class will be ranked first. In case more than one class is judged relevant, the choice of which optional criteria to turn mandatory is more complicated. Moreover, it will not even be always possible to have relevant classes ranked first within the scope of our model. *User view:* If the reasons why classes are judged relevant are not expressible within the scope of the system's semantics, the user will see that he has to give up the idea to improve global precision.

3.4 Different modes for system use

The above analysis shows, for each problematic situation, the part of the query modification that can be performed by the system, and the part that requires the user's involvement. For an optimal query modification, the system shall be used in *manual mode.* But a help can guide the user towards a number of possible choices, or a completely automatic processing of query improvement can be implemented.

We define contextual help as a function that, given a situation defined by system parameters like N_{opt}, N_{mand}, the size of classes, and the relevance judgments collected, suggests a number of query modification patterns in which semantic parameters are to be filled up by the user. Such a mode requires a type of situation-related knowledge that is tightly connected to system parameters, which makes it less complex than pure user-related knowledge.

Although query modification depends on context and user advice (semantic modifications *Loosen 2* in situation 2 and *Detail* in situation 3) require the user most), it can be automated, using knowledge on abstract criteria for *Loosen 2*, and existing techniques for automatic query expansion for *Detail.* As for pragmatic modifications (*Loosen 1* in situations 1 and 2 and *Focus* in situation 4), a drastic choice can be made: that of changing all of the concerned statuses. Therefore we can define an automatic mode where the user would only produce feedback either on classes or on individual documents.

4 Example of a typical situation

In table 1, relevance judgments associated with our example query are shown according to classes and subclasses. Some pictures contain *representations* of boats, and not boats in real (sculptures, embroidery). The user finds these pictures relevant (situation 3) and wants to split subclasses accordingly (*Detail* modification). The index of a few of these relevant images allow him to express this criterion in the system's semantics, though he has to cope with the limitations of the indexing model: he adds to *Content* the terms *Sculpture, Embroidery* and *Allegory* as optional. After this *Detail* modification, classes remain unchanged, but subclasses in classes C_{10} and C_{00} isolate relevant documents from non-relevant ones (see table 1).

5 Conclusion

A prototype of our system has been implemented on top of the Object Oriented DB-MS O2 [1], and its interface can be any WWW-navigator with JAVA facilities. It allows to retrieve images on the basis of the described relevance criteria. The user-oriented relevance model encompasses system use purposes. For the time being, the interface is not really usable by an end-user; it has to be improved, especially for the representation of classes. So is the fact that only one class or subclass can be examined at a time: comparing classes would be a useful feature.

As this prototype implements a system relevance model that accounts for part of the wide variety of relevance factors –limited by what the indexing model tackles, it can be viewed as an experimental framework to experiment on users strategies for system use. Such experiments will be led, in order to guide the further implementation of contextual help and automatic query modification modes.

References

1. M. E. Adiba and C. Collet. *Objets et bases de données, le SGBD O2.* Hermès, 1993.
2. C.L. Barry. User-defined relevance criteria : an exploratory study. *Journal of the American Society for Information Science,* 45(3):135–141, 1994.
3. W.B. Croft and R.H. Thompson. The use of adaptive mechanisms for selection of search strategies in document retrieval systems. In *Third Joint BCS-ACM Symposium,* Cambridge, 1984.
4. N. Denos. Modelling relevance in information retrieval systems: a conceptual model based on user criteria for relevance, and a formalization. Rapport de recherche, CLIPS-IMAG, 1997.
5. N. Denos. *Modéliser la pertinence pour l'utilisateur d'un système de recherche d'information : modèle conceptuel, formalisation et application.* PhD thesis, Université Joseph Fourier Grenoble I, 1997. Forthcoming.
6. C.J. van Rijsbergen. *Information Retrieval.* Butterworths, second edition, 1979.
7. J.J. Rocchio Jr. Relevance feedback in information retrieval. In G. Salton, editor, *The SMART retrieval System–Experiments in Automatic Document Processing,* chapter 14, pages 313–323. Prentice-Hall, Inc., Englewood Cliffs, New Jersey, 1971.
8. Gerard Salton and M.J. McGill. *Introduction to modern Information Retrieval.* Mcgraw Hill Book Company, New York, 1983.
9. L. Schamber. *Annual review of information science and technology - volume 29,* chapter 1. Learned Information, Medford, N.J., 1994.
10. M. Smaïl. *Raisonnement à base de cas pour une recherche évolutive d'informations ; prototype Cabri-n - Vers la définition d'un cadre d'acquisition des connaissances.* PhD thesis, Université Henri Poincaré, Nancy, France, 1994.

ImageRoadMap:
A New Content-Based Image Retrieval System

Youngchoon Park   Forouzan Golshani

Department of Computer Science and Engineering
Arizona State University
Tempe, Arizona 85287-5406
{ycpark, golshani}@asu.edu

ABSTRACT

We introduce a new content-based image retrieval system, named ImageRoadMap, for retrieval by visual information. ImageRoadMap provides both computer vision capabilities and database management capabilities. We describe the architectural design of the system and its six main components: Image Processing Object, Image Database Object, Domain Management Object, Feature Extraction Object ,Visual Query Object, and Data Retrieval and Indexing Object. These objects are independent of one another and may be replaced by objects with equivalent or enhanced features.

The Image Database Object is responsible for management of actual image data, visual features and other data types. It performs similarity measurement and similarity based indexing. By utilizing Self-Organizing Feature Map (SOFM) and other indexing methods, spatial color distribution, dominant color set, number of objects and other visual features may be computed. Users of ImageRoadMap may present queries in several different ways depending on the characteristics and the nature of the query. Currently the system supports: Query by Example, Query by Color Contents, Query by Sketch, and Query by Concept.

1. Introduction

The recent growth of digital image data has increased the need for techniques which can classify, filter, and retrieve images, from the large image databases, based on similarity between the user's query image and registered (i.e. stored) images. An image database system goes beyond the traditional database systems by incorporating various modes of non-textual digital data [Furth95]. Image data are more voluminous than textual data, and require supporting methods for rapid and efficient storage and retrieval [Gong94]. Different visual query interfaces and processing techniques are required for image data handling. Image database systems need efficient visual features, image processing techniques, and similarity based indexing by using the various visual features and query types [Guttman84]. Image database systems are classified into two major categories by their indexing and retrieval techniques. One is the text based approach and the other is called the image property based approach.

The text-based approach uses a keyword or a sentence to index and retrieve images. In this approach, an existing database system can be used for the indexing and retrieval images. However automatic generation of descriptive keyword or text annotation corresponding to an image is almost impossible with respect to the current image processing and computer vision technology. As such, the process of image indexing must be done by human operator.

The image property based approach, also called content-based image retrieval, uses visual information extracted from of images, such as color histograms, scene complexities, texture and object shapes, for the indexing and retrieval of images. Content-based image retrieval systems find and retrieve a set of images from the database that satisfy the similarity criteria of the given query. These techniques require significantly different retrieval and indexing schemes compared to the text based image database systems and various image processing techniques.

The effectiveness of content-based image retrieval in an image database system depends on content representations, the types of queries allowed, and the search and retrieval methods. Two important considerations of a content-based image retrieval system design are selection of appropriate types of visual features and indexing methods in order to meet the performance requirements of image database applications. More detailed discussion about indexing methods and data structures can be found in [Ang93, Chang95, Guttman84, White96], and good explanation about visual features can be found in [Furht95, Smith96, Kevin96].

Because of their simplicity and robustness, color, texture, object shape, and spatial feature are frequently selected as part of the set of visual features. Visual features of an image can be considered as patterns. Patterns are constructed by one or more features, such as color, object shape, and spatial features. A pattern is often represented by a vector (called feature vector) or a tree. The degree of similarity is computed by comparing the pair of visual feature vectors or trees. Similarity measures are used to eliminate unnecessary comparison between the query image and database images, particularly during the database population stage. In search and retrieval process, once the target set is reduced to a small group of images, then similarity measures can be effectively used to discriminate among the resulting set.

A wide variety of visual features may be applicable in general purpose visual information management systems. However, application-dependent systems rely on a specific set of visual features. For instance, out of all visual features, object shape and spatial features are more important in medical image database system, whereas geographical information systems use texture and color as the dominant set of visual features. The problem is that there is no single mathematical or systematic model for selecting an appropriate set of features for visual information classification in the general case. However, certain features are more applicable to a large variety of applications. ImageRoadMap automatically extracts global visual features, such as color, texture, spatial feature and object shape from images.

In this paper, we focus on the architectural design of ImageRoadMap and its querying capabilities. ImageRoadMap has six major components. They are (1) Image Processing Object, (2) Feature Extraction Object, (3) Domain Management Object, (4) Visual Query Object, (5) Data Retrieval And Indexing Object, and (6) Image Database Object. Unlike other existing system models, ImageRoadMap provides a construction facility for user-definable domain knowledge bases. Through this facility, users can build special purpose image databases. In addition, ImageRoadMap uses a realistic and efficient approach to extract a set of general visual features such as color, texture, and spatial features automatically. Therefore, the system has all the necessities for a general-purpose image database system.

2. Related work

There are several notable research projects and systems on content-based image processing, including such topics as: the development of an effective set of visual features, visual query interface, and indexing methods.

QBIC (Query By Image Content) [Flickner95, Niblack93], developed at IBM, has three major components, namely, Database population, Feature Extraction and Query process. The database population module is responsible for image indexing and text annotation for extracted objects. The feature extraction module is responsible for computing of image and object features. The query process module creates, reviews the retrieval result and refines queries. QBIC uses a fully automatic, unsupervised segmentation method to extract an object from a restricted class of images, and uses a semiautomatic method for identifying objects. QBIC computes color, texture, shape, sketch of each object and image. It provides a variety of search tools such as keyword search, search by color percentages, and search by color layout. Keyword search can be combined with graphical search.

Virage, developed by Virage Inc., consists of: the Image Representation Layer which concerns raw image, the Image Object Layer which deals with the processed image, the Domain Object Layer which handles the user's features of interest , and the Domain Event Layer which is responsible for the user's events of interest for video. Virage system uses several image processing techniques such as smoothing and histogram modification to index images. Users can search images based on the general color distribution of the image, the spatial arrangement of the color regions in the image, the general shape characteristics of the objects in the image and textures in the image. One useful feature of Virage system is that the user can adjust the relative importance of the visual feature by changing weights.

The aim in the development of *VisualSEEk* [Smith96, Chang95] was to provide content based image and video retrieval for the World Wide Web. The system has relatively simple architecture compared with QBIC and Virage. In *VisualSEEk*, indexing images involves two steps. The first is region extraction which involves: manual or semi-automated extraction of region, fixed block segmentation of the images, and color segmentation. In VisualSEEk, users can construct a visual query with the selection of colors, textures, and assignments of characteristics of shape, size and spatial layout to region.

Chabot [Orgle96] integrates the use of registered text and other data types with content-based image analysis to perform "concept queries". The system uses the relational database management system POSTGRES for storing and managing the images and their associated textual data. Chabot's text-based concept query combined with content-based query improves the ability of image retrieval.

Other work related to this topic includes those presented in [Alex94, Khoshafian96].

3. The Architecture of ImageRoadMap

Content-based image retrieval systems may be considered as storage and retrieval systems where images are created, indexed, modified, searched and retrieved. Such systems must include capabilities expected from vision systems and databases. This section outlines the system architecture and its overall capabilities.

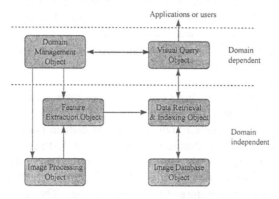

Fig.1. The Architecture of ImageRoadMap.

3.1 System Components

Figure 1 shows the overall architecture of ImageRoadMap and its major components. In the following we describe each module in more detail.

The *Image Processing Object* comprises a set of image processing operators. It does a variety of low level image processing operations including image file input and output. This object is used in both database population and retrieval stage. When a certain domain knowledge exists for the given image, the object performs appropriate image processing operations that have been selected by the Domain Management Object. When no domain knowledge is specified, it performs a set of operations by default. This object consists of the following sub-objects.

(1) Image File Manipulation Object : which performs input and output operations of image files.

(2) Color Processing Object: which is responsible for various color model conversions.

(3) Low Pass Filter Object: for performing image smoothing and noise elimination operations such as Gaussian filtering, median filtering, mean filtering, etc..

(4) High Pass Filter Object: to carry out image enhancement operations such as edge detection and low level feature extraction.

(5) Image Transform Object: for performing various image transform operations such as discrete cosine transform, wavelet, and FFT. [Smith96]

(6) Image Segmentation Object: to perform various image segmentation operations such as region growing, split and merge. When the concern of a query is the local properties of a collection of images, this object then extracts particular segmented regions of the images and forwards them to the feature extraction object.

(7) I/O Device Manipulation Object: which provides a rich set of interfaces between the database subsystem and various image acquisition facilities, such as the scanner.

The *Feature Extraction Object* produces a set of visual feature vectors. If there is some prior knowledge on an image, then the domain management object will select a set of feature extraction operations and define a set of important features for the image. Otherwise, this object extracts global visual features. This object used the following sub-objects:

(1) Global image statistics object: This object computes the global features of images such as color histogram, mean, standard deviation, spatial color distribution, object shape, spatial image formation, and dominant colors.

(2) Texture object: This object analyzes texture areas, when such a feature is present.

(3) Geometric feature object: This object extracts a visual feature vector for a geometric shape in an image.

(4) Spatial feature object: This object extracts spatial features such as relative location of objects and spatial color distribution.

The *Domain Management Object* manages domain knowledge (called meta-data) and assists the Image Processing and Feature Extraction objects. Domain knowledge is a user defined entity representing a physical property (or concept) that can contribute to the recognition of a visual feature. ImageRoadMap categorizes the given domain knowledge before further processing. The accumulated domain knowledge is used to perform indexing, feature extraction, and classification of image contents.

Generally, domain knowledge for image processing and feature extraction includes:
- important visual features and various threshold values,
- general color property including global color, and dominant color for a domain, and
- image processing and feature extraction strategies for a domain.

The *Visual Query Object* provides a rich set of visual query interfaces and handles not only alphanumeric expressions, but also other non-alphanumeric expressions, such as icons and pictures drawn by users. ImageRoadMap provides "query by example", "query by color content" and "query by sketch" as general visual query interface. A more discussion and examples are presented in the next section.

The *Data Retrieval And Indexing Object* is responsible for both database population (e.g, image insertion) and the retrieval process. This object performs similarity based indexing that eliminates unnecessary comparisons between stored images and the query image by using SOFM (Self-Organizing Feature Map) which performs adaptive pattern classification. This object consists of two sub-objects, namely, Indexing object and Retrieval object. The Retrieval object provides several types of pattern matching, including exact match, partial match, range, and partial.

The final object is the *Image Database Object* whose main component is an object-relational database system. It does storage and table management.

3.2 Querying and content retrieval in ImageRoadMap

For retrieving images, large image database systems must provide robust capabilities for interfaces for browsing and querying with high performance. Users resort to browsing when no precise query can be formulated. Some useful hints for the design of visual query interfaces can be found in [Smith96, Kevin96, Niblack93].

Generally, search in conventional database systems is based on exact matching. However, search in content-based image retrieval systems involves uncertainty. Uncertainty and fuzziness exists in content-based image database systems due to a number of reasons:

. In image retrieval systems, users may give weighting factors that reflect the relative importance of search attributes. In other words, the user specifies which visual features or attributes are more important than others.

. Content-based image database systems should support inexact search terms such as: "mostly blue", or "circular shape".

.. Support for proximity search may be necessary.

In the subsequent sections, we will describe ImageRoadMap's query modes, visual query interfaces and the related processing techniques. A user of ImageRoadMap has the choice of posing queries in any of the four usage modes, namely: Query by Color Content, Query by Example, Query by Sketch, and Query by Concept.

3.3 Query by Color Content

Many image database systems provide query by color content [smith96, Niblack93, Greg96]. Because of their insensitivity to noise and insensitivity to image resolution, color histograms are widely used in image systems (like QBIC [Flickner95], and *VisualSEEk* [Smith96]) for comparing images. An ordinary color histogram cannot model the spatial color distribution of pixels since images with similar histograms may have completely different contents. To solve this limitation, we have developed a new method, called a spatial color distribution model, that uses discrete cosine transform, image segmentation and image labeling. Instead of using pixel values, our method uses the DC values obtained from a Discrete Cosine Transform (DCT) to calculate a histogram. DCT works as follows. The image is divided into blocks of size 8x8. The DCT function transforms the image data representing the intensities of the pixels (i.e. the spatial domain) into a frequency domain represented by an 8x8 block of values known as DCT coefficients with one main value identified as the DC value . DCT is an important step in the process of image compression. In the simplest case, the DC value may be calculated by the following formula:

$$DCT(0,0) = \frac{1}{8} \sum_{x=0}^{7} \sum_{y=0}^{7} pixel(x,y).$$

DCT(0,0), called the DC coefficient, indicates the left-upper most component of the 8x8 DCT block. Suppose we divided an image into 25 DCT blocks, and suppose that after the application of DCT to all of the blocks, the resulting twenty-five DC coefficients (one DC coefficient per block) are as follows.

```
185 196 245 219 227
173 187 244 220 185
169 210 230 240 225
174 224 216 226 210
126 135 124 133 147
```

By using the technique of split and merge with $\tau1 = 10$ as a threshold value, followed by the labeling technique, we can have the following result. The split and merge technique is based upon a quad tree data representation whereby a square image segment is split into four regions if the original image segment is nonuniform in attribute. If cluster of neighboring squares are found to be uniform with respect to the mean value of DC coefficients and the threshold $\tau1$, they are merged into a single region composed of those adjacent blocks.

```
A A B C C    185 186 245 219 227
A A D C E    179 187 244 220 185
F G H H H    169 210 230 240 235
I J K K K    174 224 216 215 210
L L M M M    126 135 124 133 137
```

In the above example, 185, 186, 179 and 187 are merged because the differences of DC values form the mean value are less than the predefined threshold value of 10. These four merged microblocks are considered as a single block, named *homogenousblock*. Similarly, 219, 227, and 220 are merged too. The next step is measuring the size of *homogeneousblock*, and calculating the average DC value of the *homogeneousblock*. Another threshold value, $\tau2$, determines the minimum size of the cluster for merging. If the size of *homogeneousblock* is less than the threshold $\tau2$, the blocks will not be considered in spatial color distribution calculation. In this example, $\tau2$ is 2. Once the calculation of size measurement has been completed, the first-order moment that represents the center of object for each *homogeneousblock* will be computed. The values of x_{ij} and y_{ij} indicate the position of center of an object in the data structure. To manage the size of merged blocks and DC values associated with merged blocks, we will keep the data structure that is shown in Figure 2.

Average of DC			131		187		219		224		243	
Size	Center of X	P	5	x_{00}	P	4	x_{10}	P	4	x_{20}	P	4	x_{30}	P	3	x_{40}	P
	Center of Y			y_{00}			y_{10}			y_{20}			y_{30}			y_{40}	

Fig.2. Data Structure for representing the spatial color distribution.
The field *P* points to the next *homogeneousblock*

The following algorithm describes the spatial color distribution model extraction steps.

```
Input : image i, size = MxN
Output : Spatial color distribution for each dominant color
Data Structures : struct SCD_TBL {
                        integer average_DC_value;
                        integer size_of_homogenousblock;
                        integer center_x;
                        integer center_y;
                        integer pointer_to_next_ homogenousblock;
                }
                grid[mi][mj]; // keeping the DC coefficients
                labeled_grid[mi][mj] // keeping the labeled info
```

```
// the number of microclocks = (1/8)*M * (1/8) * N;
// compute the DC values for each microblock
FOR (mi=0;mi<(int)1/8M;mi++) {
        FOR (mj=0;mj<(int)1/8N;mj++)      {
                grid[mi][mj] = DCT(microblock[][]);
        }
}
// do split and merge where we use grid[][] rather than using image I
labeled_grid[mi][mj] = labeling(split_and_merge(grid[mi][mj]));
// using labeled_grid[][], calculate the size of homogenousblock
// and the first-moment
get size and the first moment by using connected component labeling
generate SCD vector for an image
```

Fig.3. Algorithm for spatial color distribution extraction

Comparison of two spatial color distributions are as follows.

Consider two images I and I', together with their spatial color distributions SCD_I and $SCD_{I'}$.

Let us assume SCD_I and $SCD_{I'}$ have the following values.

$SCD_I = <(ADC_0, s_{00}, x_{00}, y_{00}), (ADC_0, s_{01}, x_{10}, y_{10})...,(ADC_n, s_{nm}, x_{nm}, y_{nm})>$

$SCD_{I'} = <(ADC_0', s_{00}', x_{00}', y_{00}'), (ADC_0', s_{01}', x_{10}', y_{10}'),...,(ADC_n', s_{nm}', , x_{nm}', y_{nm}')>$

where, s_{nm} and s_{nm}' indicate the size of homogenousblocks. The two integers, n and m are index for homogenousblocks.

The distance between SCD_I and $SCD_{I'}$ may be calculated by using equation (1)

$$\Delta d_I = \sum_{i=0}^{n} \left\{ \left[a(ADC_i - ADC_i')^2 \right]^{\frac{1}{2}} + \sum_{j=0}^{m} \left[b(s_{ij} - s_{ij}')^2 \right]^{\frac{1}{2}} \right\} \qquad (1)$$

The error function (1) measures the Euclidean distance of color contents and spatial distribution of dominant colors of the two images. The two constants a and b are weighting factors.

Retrieval engine retrieves a set of images that are similar to the user's color content. The visual interface of color content based image retrieval is shown in Figure 4. Through the visual query interface, user can pick a certain color in the color picker dialog or can input real valued color values for each channel.

3.4 Query by example

One of the major problems in content-based image retrieval lies in the formulation of the visual query. ImageRoadMap provides a capability of "Query by example". User can select an image from the randomly generated images. User can change weights that specify the relative importance of the visual feature and refine the search result.. Figure 5 illustrates the similarity based index structure in ImageRoadMap. Figure 6 shows the visual query interface of "Query by Example". In this query interface, users can specify an interested region, too. In Figure 5, C_i in the Class Indexing Layer 1 indicates a class, (or called cluster). Each class holds a set of images that have similar visual features. The Class Indexing Layer 1 is a SOFM

[Kohonen86] with n classes. The Class Indexing Layer 2 consists n SOFMs. Each SOFM in the Class Indexing Layer 2 contains sub-classes for a class in the Class indexing Layer 1.

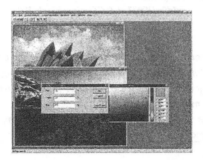

Fig.4. Visual query interface of "Query by Color Content"

In database retrieval, the Class Indexing Layer 1 will select a class that is closest to the given query (or an image). In fact, the Class Indexing Layer 1 will choose an appropriate SOFM in the Class Indexing Layer 2. The selected SOFM in the Class Indexing Layer 2 will point an image index table. Through this indexing scheme, we can reduce the amount of comparison in database search. Since SOFM models the normal distribution of visual features in a class, we can easily examine the database content.

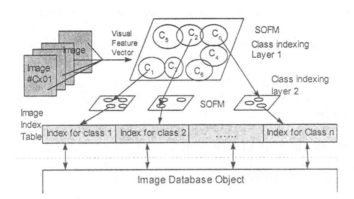

Fig.5. Similarity based index structure in ImageRoadMap

3.5 Query by sketch

ImageRoadMap makes use of a semi-automatic object shape extraction method. First, users must define a bounding box that contains an object. Currently extraction of overlapped objects, and multiple objects extraction are not allowed. Once a bounding box is specified, the adaptive thresholding [Niblack93] technique is applied to the bounded region. Thresholding is a method to convert color or gray scale image to binary image so that objects are separated from background.

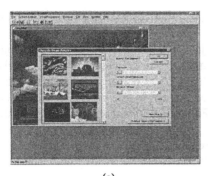 

(a)   (b)

Fig.6. (a) Visual query interface for "Query by Example" (b) Query results for "Query by Example". The black rectangle region is the weighted region.

The next step of shape analysis is contour tracing. However, if an extracted object contains holes or has geographically complex contour then contour analysis becomes complex and time consuming.

In ImageRoadMap, we use a new technique, called projection based contour analysis to get a set of general visual features for object shape such as chain code based contour representation, size of object, and compactness. Figure 7 shows the 12-directional chain code used in object shape representation.

Figure 8 illustrates the processing steps of projection based object shape representation. The proposed two projection methods are considered as signal transform functions. The methods transform a complex two-dimensional shape into a simple one-dimensional signal.

Fig.7. 12-directional chain code

In the first stage of object shape analysis, a user-defined bounded-region is converted into gray scale image. We assume that the background of bounded-region is distinguishable from an object. By utilizing the adaptive thresholding method, we can extract an object from the bounded-region.

Once we have an extracted object, two projection methods are applied to get the two projected images in the second stage. The PV projection counts the number of black pixels from the left to line L1 and from right to L1 along the Y axis. The PH projection counts the number of black pixels from the top to the line L2 and from the bottom to the line L2 along the X axis.

In the third stage, the contours of the AH and AV images are encoded by using 12 directional chain code. The encoding example is shown in Figure 8. In ImageRoadMap, we sample 32 points to represent the object shape from the contour of each projected image. Therefore, the number of total sampling points for an object region is 64.

In Addition, we use the size of object, and compactness to index an object. The size of an object is the same as the summation of the number of black pixels in thresholded image. Compactness is the measure of an object's closeness to circular shape. It is defined as the perimeter squared divided by the area. The compactness value will be minimal for a circular object. For each projected image, the compactness value will be computed.

The indexed objects can be retrieved by using "query by sketch" which was discussed previously and was presented in Figure 9.

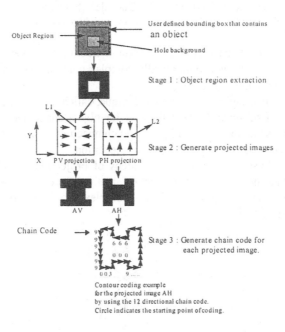

Fig.8. Object shape representation method in ImageRoadMap. Two projection methods are applied to the thresholded image. Two projection methods, called PV projection and PH projection are applied the both object region. The PV projection counts the number of black pixels from left to line L1 and from right to L1 along the Y axis. The PH projection counts the number of black pixels from top to the line L2 and from bottom to the line L2 along the X axis. In this example, the object contains a hole.

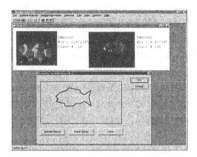

Fig.9. The example of "Query by sketch"

3.6 Query by concept

ImageRoadMap uses WordNet™ that is an electronic thesaurus developed by George Miller, to measure a similarity between user's textual query and the concepts stored in database. Figure 10 illustrates an example of database population based on concept. Figure 11 shows an example of concept based image retrieval. To retrieve a set of images by using concept, we use the first scene returned by WordNet™.

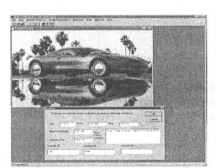 

Fig.10. Concept based database population **Fig.11.** Example of query by concept. Concept is "car and automobile"

4. Empirical issues and Performance observations

Currently, 1,148 images are registered in ImageRoadMap. To analyze the performance of the content based image retrieval capability, we use precision and recall that are defined as follows.

$$\text{Precision} = \frac{\text{Number of Relevent Images Retrieved}}{\text{Total number of Images Retrieved}} \quad (2)$$

$$\text{Recall} = \frac{\text{Number of Relevent Images Retrieved}}{\text{Total number of Relevant Images in the Solution Set}} \quad (3)$$

Precision measures how accurate the retrieval has been, whereas recall measures the completeness of retrieval. Both of these values are in the interval[0,1].

Example 1 : Query by example with region weighting.

In this query, ImageRoadMap retrieves a set of images containing a significant blue region(i.e., blue sky) that is located at the upper region. We investigated 1,000 images. Some of results is shown in the Figure 6. Spatial color distribution model based retrieval scheme retrieves 47 images with overall precision 0.74. While ordinary color histogram based retrieval scheme retrieves 63 images with an overall precision of 0.62.

Example 2 : Query by object shape-image that contains fish

In this query, ImageRoadMap retrieves a set of images that contain fish. We investigated 69 images. Retrieval scheme that uses projection based object shape representation retrieves 8 images with overall precision 0.68.

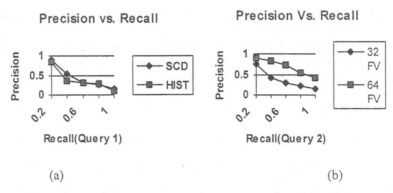

(a)   (b)

Fig.12. Retrieval Effectiveness. (a) comparison between ordinary histogram method and spatial color distribution for query 1. (b) comparison between 32 dimensional feature vector based indexing and 64 dimensional feature vector based indexing.

Figure 12 shows the results of query processing in terms of precision and recall. To analyze the performance of spatial color distribution, we made comparisons with an ordinary histogram bin based feature set [Niblack93]. Figure 12 (a) shows that our spatial color distribution model marks slightly higher precision values than the ordinary histogram. In Figure 12 (b), we show the performance of projection based image feature vector. By increasing the number of feature vector dimension, we get results.

The goal for both precision and recall is to be as close to 1 as possible. Recall and precision are influenced by the application and the indexing scheme. If many visual features are used in indexing, then recall will be favored because many images, particularly most of the relevant ones, will be retrieved. However, if domain oriented or unusual visual features are used in indexing, then precision will be favored. These two quantities are useful to determine whether the retrieval results are satisfactory. In Figure 12, for example query 1, the value of recall is 0.32, and the precision value is 0.61. An acceptable retrieval results for the sample query 2 is that the value of recall is 0.61 and the value of precision is 0.75.

5. Conclusion

Multimedia information systems, specifically image databases, must allow for creation, processing, storage, management, retrieval, transfer and presentation of images and their associated information. Image database systems sit at the confluence of two different fields, namely databases and computer vision. Other areas that contribute significantly are: image processing, signal processing and communication, artificial intelligence, and visual programming languages. The development of ImageRoadMap has certainly taken advantage of all of the above fields. However, in this presentation, we have focused only on two aspects that are more relevant to databases. They are: specialized indexing techniques and diverse query formulation paradigms. Another novel technique introduced is the spatial color distribution model. By using this technique, ImageRoadMap can process spatial queries. Projection based object shape analysis technique reduces the number of computations in contour analysis and simplifies the object shape analysis.

References

[Alex94]   Alex Pentland, Rosalind Picard, and Stan Selaroff, " Photobook : Tools for Content-Bases Manipulation of Image databases", SPIE PAPER 2185-05 Storage and Retrieval of Image and Video Databases II, San Jose, CA, Feb. 6-10, 1996

[Ang93]   Y.-H Ang, A.D.Narasimhalu, & S. Al-Hawamdeh. Image information retrieval systems. In C.H. Chen, L.F.Pau, & P.S.P. Wang, Editors, *Handbook of Pattern Recognition and Computer Vision*, pages 719-739. World Scientific, SINGPORE 1993.

[Chang95]   S.F Chang. Compressed domain Techaniques for Image/Video Indexing mainpulation, Special Session on Digital Library and Video on demand, I.E.E.E international Conference on Image Processing, Washington,D.C.,October 1995.

[Flickner95] M.Flickner *et al.* Query by image and video content: The QBIC system. *IEEE Computer*, 28(9):23-32, September 1995.

[Furht95]   Barko Furht, Stephen W. Smoliar, and Hongjiang Zhang, *Video and Image Processing in Multimedia System*, Reading , Pages 225-270, Kluwer Academic Publishers, 1995.

[Gong94]   Y.Gong et al. An image database system with content capturing and fast image indexing abilities. In Proceedings of the International Conference on Multimedia Computing and Systems, pages 121-130. 1994.

[Guttman84]   A.Guttman. R-trees: A dynamic index structure for spatial searching. In ACM Proc. Int. Conf. Manag. Data (SIGMOD), pages 47-57, June 1984.

[Kevin96]   Kevin Bowyer and Narendra Ahuja, *Advances in Image Understanding"*,pages , 301-332, IEEE Computer Society Press, Reading, 1996.

[Kohonen86]   Kohonen. T, Learning Vector Quantization for Pattern Recognition, Helsinki University of Technology TR No. TKK-F-A601. 1986.

[Niblack93]   W. Niblack, et al, The QBIC Project: Querying Image by using color, texture, and shape. In Storage and Retrieval for Image and Video Databases. SPIE Vol. 1908, 1993.

[Orgle96]   Viginia E.Ogle and Michael Stonebraker, "Charbot: Retrieval from a relational database of images", http://s2k-ftp.cs.berkeley.edu :8000/personal/ginger/chabot.html

[Pass96]   Greg Pass, Ramin Zabih and Justin Miller, Comparing Images Using Color Coherence Vectors, In Proc. The 4th International Multimedia Conference '96, pages 65 - 73. 1996.

[Smith96]   John R. Smith and S-F.Chang, VisualSEEk : a fully automated content-based image query system, The Forth ACM Multimedia Conference, Boston MA, pp 87-98, Nov. 1996.

[White96]   D.A. White and R. Jain, Similarity Indexing with the SS-tree, In. Proc. 12th IEEE International Conference on Data Engineering, New Orleans, Louisiana, Feb . 1996.

First Steps to a Formal Framework for Multilevel Database Modifications

Frank Buddrus[1], Heino Gärtner[2], and Sven-Eric Lautemann[1]

[1] Johann Wolfgang Goethe-Universität Frankfurt, Fachbereich Informatik, Datenbanken und Informationssysteme, Postfach 11 19 32, D-60054 Frankfurt am Main, Germany, {buddrus|lautemann}@informatik.uni-frankfurt.de
[2] Universität Bremen, Fachbereich Mathematik und Informatik, Arbeitsgruppe Datenbanksysteme, Postfach 33 04 40, D-28334 Bremen, Germany, gaertner@informatik.uni-bremen.de

Abstract. We propose a formal basis for operations which can be understood as implicitly used in many kinds of schema modifications. Approaches for view definition, schema evolution, and schema versioning all rely on operations which work either on instance, on schema, or on both levels. This paper discusses a basic set of these operations called *modification primitives* and describes their semantics on the basis of the Extended Entity Relationship (EER) Model in a Hoare-style notation. We focus on the structural part of the schema definition and outline our ideas for arbitrary manipulations of instances.

1 Introduction

Modern database applications call for flexible modeling concepts with a high degree of abstraction and the power to anticipate the requirements of an evolving environment. These aims have been addressed by research and developments in the area of database modeling languages and concepts [HK87, PM88]. Apart from the development of database modeling concepts, we see a parallel line of research efforts, which focus on the introduction of concepts for describing derived interfaces like views [AB91, MP96, SLT91, Sou95, Wie91], schema evolution [BKKK87, FMZ+95, Lau97, Mon93, Odb95, PÖ95, SLH90, SZ87, Zic92] and (on object level) database versions [CJ90] in the respective model. An interesting point is, that there seems to be a great need for such database modifications independent of the data model.

In this paper we present operations, called *modification primitives*, which can serve as a basis for arbitrary schema and database modifications. The idea is to develop a set of these modification primitives which have the potential to be the building blocks of higher level schema and database derivation operations as they are used in the definition of views or in schema evolution. We chose the EER-Model [Gog94], which is an extension of the well-known Entity Relationship model [Che76, BCN92], because it is semantically well founded and contains all features which are widely accepted to be desirable for the structural part of an object-oriented database [ABD+89]. Figure 1 shows an example of an EER diagram. *Components* i.e. entity-valued attributes are denoted by arcs from attributes to entities. *Type constructions* are depicted as triangles. The construction named *is* in our example has *House* as input type and *Church* and *Castle* as output types.

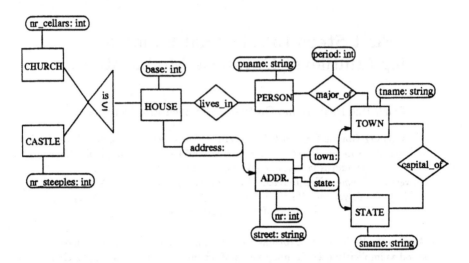

Fig. 1. Sample EER diagram of a community.

The paper is structured as follows: Section 2 introduces the basic concepts for describing a database. The following four sections deal with the modification primitives for names, types, and structural properties. In Section 7 we sketch our ideas for integrating integrity constraints, view definitions, and other predicate based derivation concepts in our framework. In Section 8 we conclude by comparing our ideas — as far as they are presented in this paper — with related research and by discussing the shortcomings and advantages of our framework.

2 Basic Definitions

Before explaining the basic modification primitives we have to deal with some preliminaries. Our understanding of a schema is an adaptation of the Extended Entity Relationship (EER) Model [EGH+92] and our notation is based on [Gog94].

Definition 1: Environment.
An Environment Z consists of a schema S and a database state DB.

$$Z = (S, DB)$$

Definition 2: Schema.
A schema S consists of a structural part, integrity constraints, and a set of names for the structural part.

$$S = (STRUCT, CONSTRAINTS, NAME)$$

where CONSTRAINTS is a set of formulas without free variables and

$$STRUCT = \{ENTTYPE, RELTYPE, ATTRIB, COMP, CONSTRUCT\}$$

where ENTTYPE, RELTYPE, ATTRIB, COMP, CONSTRUCT are finite sets describing the identifiers used for the respective objects. NAME is a pairwise disjoint set of strings. Furthermore we define a bijective function $name : STRUCT \rightarrow NAME$.

A semantic function μ maps the structural components to semantic objects. A given ENTTYPE *Person* may in a certain state be mapped to persons p_1, p_2, and p_3 thus

$$\mu[\text{ENTTYPE}](\text{Person}) = \{p_1, p_2, p_3\}$$

For details see [Gog94]. Furthermore we define

$$\mu(X) = \bigcup_{x \in X} \mu[X](x)$$

with $X \in \{\text{ENTTYPE, RELTYPE, ATTRIB, COMP, CONSTRUCT}\}$.

Definition 3: Database state.
A database state is defined by the instances of all structural parts of the schema.

$$DB = (\mu(\text{ENTTYPE}), \mu(\text{RELTYPE}), \mu(\text{ATTRIB}), \mu(\text{COMP}), \mu(\text{CONSTRUCT}))$$

Definition 4: Modification Primitive.
The modification primitive ω is the basic notion for modifying an environment. We distinguish the following operations:
- Add an element (α)
- Rename an element (β)
- Delete an element ($\bar{\pi}$)
- Retype an element (ρ)
- Select database elements (σ)

Thus

$$\omega : Z \to Z \text{ with } \omega \in \{\alpha, \beta, \bar{\pi}, \rho, \sigma\}$$

We state the semantics of our primitives in a Hoare-style notation [Bac86, GS94, LS87] but actually describe states by means of pre- and postconditions. Thus the description of our modification primitives will be of the following form:
{*precondition*}
$\qquad \omega[\mathcal{I}](p_1, \ldots, p_n)$
{*postcondition*}

Where $\mathcal{I} \in \text{STRUCT}$ is an index, e.g. $\bar{\pi}[\text{ATTRIB}]$ is the modification primitive to delete an attribute and p_i are the parameters to the operation. The precondition has to be valid in order to perform the operation ω. After the execution of ω we state that the postcondition is valid.

Definition 5: Schema Invariants.
Schema invariants are sets of predicates that a consistent schema must fulfill.

We are a bit permissive in that point, because we do not explicitly define a complete set of schema invariants (see e.g. [BM93]). There are different ways to ensure schema invariants. For example, if the deletion of an entity type must not lead to attributes without a source entity schema invariants can be used:
$\{\forall a \in \text{ATTRIB asource}(a) \neq \bot\} \subseteq SI$
$\{SI, \ldots\}$
$\qquad \bar{\pi}[\text{ENTTYPE}](e)$
$\{SI, \ldots\}$

Another way would be to ensure the predicate through the precondition of the respective modification primitive and thereby make the operation partial:
$\{\ldots, \forall a \in \text{ATTRIB} \; \text{asource}(a) \neq e, \ldots\}$
$\quad \bar{\pi}[\text{ENTTYPE}](e)$
$\{\ldots\}$

In the subsequent sections we describe the effects of the modification primitives.

3   Adding Elements

In this section we present the formal definitions for adding elements to an EER schema. The add primitive (α) is used to create new structures, i.e. entity types, relationship types, attributes, components, and compositions.

Entity Types

To achieve a small and orthogonal set of primitives, the creation of entity and relationship types does not allow the specification of attributes. Instead they have to be added later using $\alpha[\text{ATTRIB}]$.

$$\{SI, Z, ename \notin \text{NAME} = \{name_1, \ldots, name_m\}, E \notin \text{ENTTYPE} = \{E_1, \ldots, E_n\}\}$$
$$\quad \alpha[\text{ENTTYPE}](E, ename)$$
$$\{SI, Z, \text{NAME} = \{name_1, \ldots, name_m, ename\}, name(E) = ename,$$
$$\text{ENTTYPE} = \{E_1, \ldots, E_n, E\}\} \tag{1}$$

The comparison of pre- and postcondition of formula (1) shows that E has been added to the set ENTTYPE of entity types, $ename$ has been added to the set NAME of names and assigned to E by defining the value of $name(E)$.

Relationship Types

The roles of a relationship type R, i.e. the set of entity types involved in R must not be modified in our model, because of the following reason: if R does not contain any relationships $r \in R$ any modification can of course be done by simply deleting R and adding a new relationship type R' with the required roles, i.e. in this case no extra update primitive is required. If, on the other hand, relationships already exist for relationship type R, the addition of new roles to R would require an update of the stored relationships, i.e. the $\perp$ value would have to be set for the new entity in each $r \in R$ which is not allowed in the EER model by definition. A relationship must always include one entity for each of its roles. Therefore, all required roles of a relationship type R have to be specified when R is created. In the precondition of formula (2) operation LTS (ListToSet) is used to change the list of related entity types into a set.

$$\{SI, Z, rname \notin \text{NAME} = \{name_1, \ldots, name_m\},$$
$$R \notin \text{RELTYPE} = \{R_1, \ldots, R_k\}, LTS(< E_1, \ldots, E_n >) \subseteq \text{ENTTYPE}\}$$
$$\quad \alpha[\text{RELTYPE}](R, rname, < E_1, \ldots, E_n >)$$
$$\{SI, Z, \text{NAME} = \{name_1, \ldots, name_m, rname\}, name(R) = rname,$$
$$\text{RELTYPE} = \{R_1, \ldots, R_k, R\}\} \tag{2}$$

Attributes

$\{SI, Z, aname \notin \text{NAME} = \{name_1, \ldots, name_m\}, A \notin \text{ATTRIB} = \{A_1, \ldots, A_n\},$
$D \in DS, X \in \text{ENTTYPE} \cup \text{RELTYPE}\}$
$\quad \alpha[\text{ATTRIB}](A, aname, X, D)$
$\{SI, Z, \text{NAME} = \{name_1, \ldots, name_m, aname\}, name(A) = aname,$
$\text{ATTRIB} = \{A_1, \ldots, A_n, A\}, asource(A) = X, adest(A) = D,$
$\mu[\text{ATTRIB}](A)(X) = \bot\}$ (3)

Components

Analogously to the above given arguments for relationship types, modification of the source and destination entity types of a component and of input and output entity types of a construction are not allowed. Therefore, those have to be specified in the creation of a component or construction type.

$\{SI, Z, compname \notin \text{NAME} = \{name_1, \ldots, name_m\},$
$Comp \notin \text{COMP} = \{Comp_1, \ldots, Comp_n\}, E_{source}, E_{dest} \in \text{ENTTYPE},$
$csource(Comp) = \bot, cdestination(Comp) = \bot\}$
$\quad \alpha[\text{COMP}](Comp, compname, E_{source}, E_{dest})$
$\{SI, Z, \text{NAME} = \{name_1, \ldots, name_m, compname\}, name(Comp) = compname,$
$\text{COMP} = \{Comp_1, \ldots, Comp_n, Comp\}, csource(Comp) = E_{source},$
$cdestination(Comp) = E_{dest}\}$ (4)

Constructions

One of the general schema invariants SI specifies, that there must be no circles in the set of constructions. Predicate $path(E, E')$ tests if entity type E is an input of a construction that has entity type E' as output. Predicate $path^*(E, E')$ is the transitive closure of $path(E, E')$ and is required to check if a new construction can be added to an EER schema. This is forbidden by definition, if the new construction introduces a circle, i.e. if there exist two entity types E and E' such that $path^*(E, E')$ and $path^*(E', E)$. The formal definition of $path$ and $path^*$ looks like this:

$$path(E, E') := \exists Constr \in \text{CONSTRUCT} :$$
$$E \in input(Constr) \wedge E' \in output(Constr)$$
$$path^*(E, E') := \exists E_1, \ldots, E_m \in \text{ENTTYPE} :$$
$$E = E_1 \wedge E' = E_m \wedge \forall i \in \{1, \ldots, (m-1)\} : path(E_i, E_{(i+1)})$$

$\{SI, Z, constrname \notin \text{NAME} = \{name_1, \ldots, name_m\},$
$Constr \notin \text{CONSTRUCT} = \{Constr_1, \ldots, Constr_n\},$
$\{E_{inp\_1}, \ldots, E_{inp\_k}, E_{outp\_1}, \ldots, E_{outp\_l}\} \subseteq \text{ENTTYPE},$
$input(Constr) = \bot, output(Constr) = \bot,$
$\neg(\exists E \in \{E_{inp\_1}, \ldots, E_{inp\_k}\}, \exists E' \in \{E_{outp\_1}, \ldots, E_{outp\_l}\} : path^*(E', E))\}$
$\quad \alpha[\text{CONSTRUCT}](Constr, constrname, \{E_{inp\_1}, \ldots, E_{inp\_k}\}, \{E_{outp\_1}, \ldots, E_{outp\_l}\})$
$\{SI, Z, \text{NAME} = \{name_1, \ldots, name_m, constrname\}, name(Constr) = constrname,$
$\text{CONSTRUCT} = \{Constr_1, \ldots, Constr_n, Constr\},$
$input(Constr) = \{E_{inp\_1}, \ldots, E_{inp\_k}\}, output(Constr) = \{E_{outp\_1}, \ldots, E_{outp\_l}\}\}$ (5)

4 Renaming Elements

The rename primitive (β) can be used to change the name of a structural element. This is done by modification of the function *name* that maps STRUCT to NAME. The rename primitive works in the same way for each structural element X. It replaces the old name of X by the new one in the set of names and changes the value of $name(X)$ accordingly.

$\{SI, Z, newname \notin \text{NAME} = \{name_1, \ldots, name_m, oldname\}, name(X) = oldname,$
$X \in STRUCT\}$
$\quad \beta(X, newname)$
$\{SI, Z, \text{NAME} = \{name_1, \ldots, name_m, newname\}, name(X) = newname\}$ \hfill (6)

5 Deleting Elements

If structural elements are removed from an environment these operations do not only affect the schema but also the database part of the environment. These changes will be reflected by the respective μ-functions in the pre- and postconditions.

Attributes

The removal of an attribute has a quite straightforward definition and is depicted in Figure 2 for an attribute of a relationship type.

Fig. 2. Deletion of attributes.

However, conflicts with schema invariants can arise, if for example entity types without attributes are disallowed. This might also be the case, if the respective attribute is referenced in a constraint.

$\{SI, Z, [\text{NAME} = \{name_1, \ldots, name_m, aname\}, name(A) = aname,$
$\text{ATTRIB} = \{A_1, \ldots, A_n, A\},$
$\mu(\text{ATTRIB}) = \mu[\text{ATTRIB}](A_1) \cup \cdots \cup \mu[\text{ATTRIB}](A_n) \cup \mu[\text{ATTRIB}](A)\}$
$\quad \tilde{\pi}[\text{ATTRIB}](A)$
$\{SI, Z, \text{NAME} = \{name_1, \ldots, name_m\}, name(A) = \bot, \text{ATTRIB} = \{A_1, \ldots, A_n\},$
$\mu(\text{ATTRIB}) = \mu[\text{ATTRIB}](A_1) \cup \cdots \cup \mu[\text{ATTRIB}](A_n)\}$ \hfill (7)

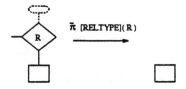

Fig. 3. Deletion of relationship types.

Relationship Types

Figure 3 shows the deletion of a relationship type. We assume, that the relationship type has no attributes.

$\{SI, Z, \text{NAME} = \{name_1, \ldots, name_m, rname\}, name(R) = rname,$
$\text{RELTYPE} = \{R_1, \ldots, R_n, R\}, \neg\exists A \in \text{ATTRIB} : R \in asource(A)\}$
$\quad \bar{\pi}[\text{RELTYPE}](R)$
$\{SI, Z, \text{NAME} = \{name_1, \ldots, name_m\}, name(R) = \bot, \text{RELTYPE} = \{R_1, \ldots, R_n\},$
$\mu(R) = \bot, participants(R) = \bot\}$ (8)

Entity Types

We assume, that the entity type has neither attributes, nor components, and is not member of any construction or relationship type.

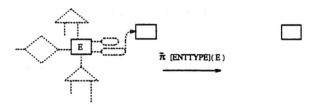

Fig. 4. Deletion of entity types.

$\{SI, Z, \text{NAME} = \{name_1, \ldots, name_m, ename\}, name(E) = ename,$
$\text{ENTTYPE} = \{E_1, \ldots, E_n, E\}, \neg\exists A \in \text{ATTRIB} : E \in asource(A),$
$\neg\exists Comp \in \text{COMP} : E \in csource(Comp),$
$\{E, set(E), list(E), bag(E)\} \cap cdestination(\text{COMP}) = \emptyset,$
$\forall r \in \text{RELTYPE} : E \notin participants(r), \forall c \in \text{CONSTRUCT} : E \notin input(c) \cup output(c)\}$
$\quad \bar{\pi}[\text{ENTTYPE}](E)$
$\{SI, Z, \text{NAME} = \{name_1, \ldots, name_m\}, name(E) = \bot,$
$\text{ENTTYPE} = \{E_1, \ldots, E_n\}, \mu(E) = \bot\}$ (9)

Fig. 5. Deletion of components.

Components

$\{SI, Z, \text{NAME} = \{name_1, \ldots, name_m, compname\}, name(Comp) = compname,$
$\text{COMP} = \{Comp_1, \ldots, Comp_n, Comp\}\}$
$\quad \bar{\pi}[\text{COMP}](Comp)$
$\{SI, Z, \text{NAME} = \{name_1, \ldots, name_m\}, name(Comp) = \bot,$
$\text{COMP} = \{Comp_1, \ldots, Comp_n\},$
$csource(Comp) = \bot, cdestination(Comp) = \bot\}$ ⠀⠀⠀⠀⠀⠀⠀(10)

Constructions

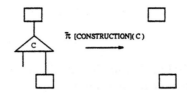

Fig. 6. Deletion of constructions.

$\{SI, Z, \text{NAME} = \{name_1, \ldots, name_m, constrname\}, name(Constr) = constrname,$
$\text{CONSTRUCT} = \{Constr_1, \ldots, Constr_n, Constr\}\}$
$\quad \bar{\pi}[\text{CONSTRUCT}](Constr)$
$\{SI, Z, \text{NAME} = \{name_1, \ldots, name_m\}, name(Constr) = \bot,$
$\text{CONSTRUCT} = \{Constr_1, \ldots, Constr_n\},$
$input(Constr) = \bot, output(Constr) = \bot\}$ ⠀⠀⠀⠀⠀⠀⠀(11)

6　Retyping Elements

The retype primitive (ρ) is used to change the type of attributes and components. In order to perform a reasonable update to the database part of the environment this primitive has to respect type convertibilities. For attributes we can specify convertibility in the form of tables. The type of a component is given by the entity of its destination. We assume one component c being type convertible to c' if a (transitive) input/output relation exists along constructions from the type of c' to the type of c.

Attributes

Given a type d and a type convertible type d', conversions can be applied using function *convert: $DS \to DS$* according to Table 1. The first table describes convertibility of basic data types, the second one convertibility of sorts of data types. Type convertibility is read from left to right (row entry to column entry). Here $\times$ indicates that retyping is allowed, — indicates that retyping is not applicable.

	int	float	real	string		d'	$\text{set}_{d'}\{\}$	$\text{bag}_{d'}\ \{\{\}\}$	$\text{list}_{d'}<>$
int	$\times$	$\times$	$\times$	$\times$	d	$\times$	$\times$	$\times$	$\times$
float	$\times$	$\times$	$\times$	$\times$	$\text{set}_d\{\}$	—	$\times$	$\times$	$\times$
real	$\times$	$\times$	$\times$	$\times$	$\text{bag}_d\ \{\{\}\}$	—	$\times$	$\times$	$\times$
string	—	—	—	$\times$	$\text{list}_d<>$	—	$\times$	$\times$	$\times$

Table 1. Type convertibility for simple and sorts of data types.

Type convertible attributes (indicated by the function *convertible: $DS \times DS \to$ boolean* as given by Table 1) can be retyped. Performing a retype primitive on an attribute the database part of the environment is modified by converting all data of the attribute concerned.

$$\{SI, Z, A \in \text{ATTRIB}, adest(A) = D, D, D' \in DS, convertible(D, D'),$$
$$\mu[\text{ATTRIB}](A) = \{(e_1, v_1), \ldots, (e_n, v_n)\}\}$$
$$\rho[\text{ATTRIB}](A, D')$$
$$\{SI, Z, A \in \text{ATTRIB}, adest(A) = D' \in DS,$$
$$\mu[\text{ATTRIB}](A) = \{(e_1, convert_{D,D'}(v_1)), \ldots, (e_n, convert_{D,D'}(v_n))\}\} \qquad (12)$$

Components

Components that are type convertible can be retyped. Performing a retype primitive on a component the database part of the environment is modified in the way that each data of the component concerned is changed to its input type regarding (transitive) construction relations with the new type.

$$\{SI, Z, Comp \in \text{COMP}, cdestination(Comp) = E_{dest}, \{E_{dest}, E'_{dest}\} \subseteq \text{ENTTYPE},$$
$$\mu[\text{COMP}](Comp) = \{(e_1, e_{d1}), \ldots, (e_n, e_{dn})\},$$
$$\exists Constr \in \text{CONSTRUCT} : E'_{dest} \in input(Constr), E_{dest} \in output(Constr),$$
$$\{(e_{d'1}, e_{d1}), \ldots, (e_{d'n}, e_{dn})\} \subseteq \mu[\text{CONSTRUCT}](Constr)\}$$
$$\rho[\text{COMP}](Comp, E'_{dest})$$
$$\{SI, Z, Comp \in \text{COMP}, cdestination(Comp) = E'_{dest}, \{E_{dest}, E'_{dest}\} \subseteq \text{ENTTYPE},$$
$$\mu[\text{COMP}](Comp) = \{(e_1, e_{d'1}), \ldots, (e_n, e_{d'n})\}\} \qquad (13)$$

7 Manipulating Instances

In this section we sketch our ideas for incorporating instance manipulations in our framework. There are basically two main issues to consider: (i) Restricting current instances, and (ii) generating new instances. This distinction resembles the separation of object generating and object preserving queries [MP96], however in our context object preservation is only feasible for the first case (i) because we want the $\mu(X)$ to be disjoint. The current instances can thus be restricted by an operation $\sigma_{add\_constraint}$:

$$\{SI, Z, \varphi \text{ is a constraint}\}$$
$$\sigma_{add\_constraint}(\varphi(X))$$
$$\{SI, Z, \text{CONSTRAINTS} = \text{CONSTRAINTS} \cup \varphi, \mu(X) = \{\mu(X) \mid \varphi\}\} \qquad (14)$$

The basic idea for other instance manipulations is to provide a mechanism σ_{trans} to encapsulate a query Q and define a type compatible iterator $\mathcal{I}$, which maps the results of the query $r(Q)$ to a target structure $\mathcal{T}$.

$$\{SI, Z, \sigma_{trans} \text{ is type compatible}\}$$
$$\sigma_{trans}(\mathcal{I}, Q, \mathcal{T})$$
$$\{SI, Z, \mu(\mathcal{T}) = \mu(\mathcal{T}) \cup \mathcal{I}(\mathcal{T}, r(Q))\} \qquad (15)$$

Consider for example the creation of entity type "MAJOR" which will hold all persons who are or have once been majors of a town with attributes "mname:string" and "townname:string". This type can easily be created according to (3) and (1). With the above introduced primitive σ_{trans} we can now populate our new entity type:

$\alpha[\text{ENTTYPE}](\text{major}, "\text{MAJOR}");$
$\alpha[\text{ATTRIB}](\text{mname}, "\text{mname}", \text{major}, \text{string});$
$\alpha[\text{ATTRIB}](\text{townname}, "\text{townname}", \text{major}, \text{string});$
$\sigma_{trans}(\mathcal{I}, Q, \mathcal{T})$

with

$\mathcal{I} = \forall i \in r(Q) \text{ new}[\mathcal{T}](\text{mname} \leftarrow i.1, \text{townname} \leftarrow i.2)$
$\mathcal{T} = \text{major}$
$Q = -[\text{pname}(p), \text{tname}(t) \mid (p : \text{PERSON}) \wedge (t : \text{TOWN}) \wedge \text{major\_of}(p, t)] -$

This example is of course only a rough sketch of our ideas to encapsulate queries. Especially the iterator has to be adapted, when query languages other than the one presented in [Gog94] are used.

8 Conclusion and Future Work

systems, multi database systems, schema evolution, views

In many application domains, schema updates have to be performed frequently to reflect changes in the application environment. This is especially true as databases are very long lived. Schema modifications are also an important means for multi-database systems, interoperability, and federated database systems. We have presented first steps to a formal approach to the specification of basic schema and database updates for the EER model.

The intension of our approach is to provide a solid base for concepts or procedures which rely on schema and database modifications. This is however not completely the case, so far. An important issue which needs to be incorporated in our framework is a way to propagate updates from a derived to an old environment, which would allow for instance updatable views. Another important point would be to extend the interface to the query language to support arbitrary complex query results. Finally, dynamic and temporal constraints need to be considered.

However, the approach presented in this paper provides an integrated way to handle schema and database updates and has therefore the potential to describe arbitrary complex schema and database modifications. Furthermore, a formal model is required to ensure a complete description and correct implementation of a system's behaviour regarding updates to schemas and databases.

We plan to extend the presented approach to complex schema updates each of which is composed of several of the basic updates presented here. The formal description supports the evaluation of such compositions, which are required for instance in software engineering environments. Moreover, a formal model will then allow an analysis and comparison of the semantics of schema update primitives of different systems.

References

[AB91]   Serge Abiteboul and Anthony Bonner. Objects and Views. In *Proc. Intl. Conf. on Management of Data*, pages 238–247. ACM SIGMOD, May 1991.

[ABD⁺89] Malcolm Atkinson, François Bancilhon, David DeWitt, David Dittrich, David Meier, and Stanley Zdonik. The Object-Oriented Database System Manifesto. In *Proc. of the 1st Int'l Conf. on Deductive and Object-Oriented Databases (DOOD)*, pages 40–57, Kyoto, Japan, December 1989.

[Bac86]   Roland C. Backhouse. *Program Construction and Verification*. Prentice Hall, London, 1986.

[BCN92]   Carlo Batini, Stefano Ceri, and Shamkant Navathe. *Conceptual Database Design – an Entity-Relationship Approach*. Benjamin/Cummings, Redwood, 1992.

[BKKK87] Jay Banerjee, Won Kim, Hyoung-Joo Kim, and Henry F. Korth. Semantics and Implementation of Schema Evolution in Object-Oriented Databases. In *Proc. of the ACM SIGMOD Int'l Conf. on Management of Data*, pages 311–322, San Francisco, CA, May 1987. ACM Press.

[BM93]   Elisa Bertino and Lorenzo Martino. *Object-Oriented Database Systems - Concepts and Architectures*. Addison-Wesley, Wokingham, 1993.

[Che76]   P. P. Chen. The entity relationship model - toward an unified view of data. *ACM Trans. on Database Systems*, 1(1):9, March 1976. Reprinted in M. Stonebraker, Readings in Database Sys., Morgan Kaufmann, San Mateo, CA, 1988.

[CJ90]   Wojciech Cellary and Geneviève Jomier. Consistency of Versions in Object-Oriented Databases. In *Proc. of the 16th Int'l Conf. on Very Large Databases (VLDB)*, pages 432–441, Brisbane, Australia, 1990. Morgan Kaufmann.

[EGH⁺92] Gregor Engels, Martin Gogolla, Uwe Hohenstein, Klaus Hülsmann, Perdita Löhr-Richter, Gunter Saake, and Hans-Dieter Ehrich. Conceptual modelling of database applications using an extended ER model. *Data & Knowledge Engineering*, 9:157–204, 1992.

[FMZ⁺95] Fabrizio Ferrandina, Thorsten Meyer, Roberto Zicari, Guy Ferran, and Joëlle Madec. Schema and Database Evolution in the O₂ Object Database System. In *Proc. of the 21st Int'l Conf. on Very Large Databases (VLDB)*, pages 170–181, Zurich, Switzerland, September 1995. Morgan Kaufmann.

[Gog94] Martin Gogolla. An extended entity-relationship model fundamentals and pragmatics. *Lecture Notes in Computer Science*, 767, 1994.

[GS94] David Gries and Fred B. Schneider. *A Logical Approach to Discrete Math.* Texts and Monographs in Computer Science. Springer-Verlag, New York, 1994.

[HK87] Richard Hull and Roger King. Semantic Database Modelling: Survey, Applications and Research Issues. *ACM Computing Surveys*, 19(3):201–260, 1987.

[Lau97] Sven-Eric Lautemann. A Propagation Mechanism for Populated Schema Versions. In *Proc. of the 13th Int'l Conf. on Data Engineering (ICDE)*, pages 67–78, Birmingham, U.K., April 1997. IEEE, IEEE Press.

[LS87] Jacques Loeckx and Kurt Sieber. *The Foundations of Program Verification (Second edition)*. John Wiley and Sons, New York, N.Y., 1987.

[Mon93] Simon Monk. *A Model for Schema Evolution in Object-Oriented Database Systems*. PhD thesis, Lancaster University, February 1993. 101 pages.

[MP96] Renate Motschnig-Pitrik. Requirements and comparison of view mechanisms for object-oriented databases. *Information Systems*, 21(3):229–252, 1996.

[Odb95] Erik Odberg. *MultiPerspectives: Object Evolution and Schema Modification Management for Object-Oriented Databases*. PhD thesis, Norwegian Institute of Technology, February 1995. 408 pages.

[PM88] Joan Peckham and Fred Maryanski. Semantic data models. *ACM Computing Surveys*, 20(3):153–189, September 1988.

[PÖ95] Randal J. Peters and M. Tamer Özsu. Axiomatization of dynamic Schema Evolution in Objectbases. In *Proc. of the 11th Int'l Conf. on Data Engineering (ICDE)*, Taipei, Taiwan, March 1995. IEEE Press.

[SLH90] Barbara Staudt Lerner and A. Nico Habermann. Beyond Schema Evolution to Database Reorganization. In *Proc. of the 5th Conf. on Object-Oriented Programming Systems, Languages, and Applications (OOPSLA)*, pages 67–76, Ottawa, Canada, October 1990. ACM Press.

[SLT91] Marc H. Scholl, Christian Laasch, and Markus Tresch. Updateable Views in Object-Oriented Databases. In *Proc. of the 2nd Int'l Conf. on Deductive and Object-Oriented Databases (DOOD)*, pages 189–207, Munich, Germany, December 1991. Springer-Verlag. Lecture Notes in Computer Science No. 566.

[Sou95] Cássio Souza dos Santos. Design and implementation of object-oriented views. *Lecture Notes in Computer Science*, 978, 1995.

[SZ87] Andrea H. Skarra and Stanley B. Zdonik. Type Evolution in an Object-Oriented Database. In *Research Directions in Object-Oriented Programming*, pages 393–415. MIT Press, 1987.

[Wie91] Gio Wiederhold. Views, Objects, and Databases. In *On Object-Oriented Database Systems*, pages 29–43. Springer, 1991.

[Zic92] Roberto Zicari. A Framework for Schema Updates in an Object-Oriented Database System. In François Bancilhon, Claude Delobel, and Paris Kanellakis, editors, *Building an Object-Oriented Database System – The Story of O₂*, pages 146–182. Morgan Kaufmann, San Mateo, California, 1992.

Versions of Integrity Constraints inMultiversion Databases

Anne Doucet and Sophie Monties

LIP6 - Université P. & M. Curie
Case 169, 4 place Jussieu
F-75252 Paris Cedex 5, France
{doucet,monties}@laforia.ibp.fr

Abstract. In earlier work, we proposed an integrity constraint mechanism intended to maintain consistency in multiversion databases [6, 5]. However, we did not consider versions of integrity constraints. This paper analyses the extension of this integrity mechanism, in order to express and manage versions of constraints. To make this extension possible, we address two issues. First, we inventory the properties of constraint versions. Second, we study two solutions to represent constraint versions.

1 Introduction

Versioning is a major need in a growing number of applications. To support these needs, several version models have been proposed [16, 2, 1, 13, 12, 14, 15]. A main issue in such models is to maintain consistency. The classical way to maintain consistency is to use integrity constraints, which are assertions that must be verified by the data at the end of each transaction. Defining the consistency of a set of versions or configurations is a difficult problem [10, 11, 3]. It implies to define the notion of consistency of a multiversion database state, which appears to be a problem in most version models [4]. In the *DataBase Version* (DBV) approach [4], each version of the multiversion database represents a state of the modeled universe, allowing to define a consistent database state [3]. We have extended our integrity constraint mechanism to take into account the new dimension introduced by versioning [5, 6]. Constraints in this model, denoted *mv-constraints*, allow to express consistency of each DBV and across DBVs.

Most of the time, integrity constraints in monoversion databases are defined in the schema. This representation offers an homogeneous (all elements of the schema are grouped) and global (data must respect the schema) vision of the database. Similarly, a single schema, containing both the data structure and the mv-constraints, is defined for all DBVs. However, a multiversion database reflects the evolution of the real world. Update transactions allow to pass the evolution of the entities on the database. The evolution of the rules which govern the real world are more complex to pass on. For instance, let C_1 an mv-constraint fixing to 10% the minimal percentage of fallow lands for French farmers. If an European decree changes the minimal percentage from 10 to 15%, C_1 has to be updated to reflect the real world. As a result of this update, all the French farmers having between 10 and 15% of fallow lands violate C_1. The database is no longer consistent, even if each DBV represents a state of the real world. The same problem arises when a new rule is added in the database.

Several solutions exist to avoid inconsistencies due to constraints updating. One consists in forbidding schema updates. But the set of mv-constraints might no longer represent the rules of the real world, which may change. A second solution authorizes mv-constraint updates. In this case, the database is no longer consistent with the schema. Neither of these two solutions is satisfactory. The rules in force in each real world state represented by a DBV are translated into mv-constraints. Handling versions of mv-constraints allows to update mv-constraints in a DBV without side effect on other mv-constraints of other DBVs. To satisfy the need of mv-constraint versions, several steps are necessary. The first step is to delimit the effects due to the change from one to several mv-constraint versions. The application field, the identification, the expression and the checking of an mv-constraint are different, whether it is versioned or not. The second step concerns the representation of mv-constraint versions. We focus in this paper on mv-constraint versions, and do not address the problem of schema versions and updates.

The paper is organized as follows: Section 2 shows the framework of this paper, Section 3 exposes the properties of the mv-constraint versions, Section 4 proposes two representations of them, and Section 5 concludes.

2   Multiversion databases

We briefly remind here the main principles of our method to define and manage mv-constraints in multiversion databases [5, 6]. We present the Data Base Version model, which is the framework of our work, and define consistency is this context. Then we present the checking process, based on a classification of mv-constraints, and describe consistency management.

The DBV approach

One of the main specificities of the DBV model [4, 8, 9] consists in separating the physical level, *what is managed by the system*, and the logical level, *what the user sees*. At the logical level, a multiversion database is seen as a set of *DataBase Versions* (DBVs). Each DBV represents a possible real world state. A DBV is identified by a DBV identifier and composed of object versions. As an object version can have the same value in several DBVs, the object version concept is split in two concepts. The *logical object version* represents the object version as it is seen by users in a given DBV, and the *physical object version* is used by the system to store the value of all the logical versions of this object having the same value. A database version is composed of one logical version of each object, identified by a pair (object identifier, database version identifier).

A DBV is created by logical copying, called *derivation*, of an existing DBV, and may evolve independently from the others. This means that a DBV may be updated or deleted without side effect on other DBVs. A *contents* and a *label* are associated with each DBV. The contents is composed of a version of each database object, and the label allows to represent the application semantics using *DBV attributes*. Figure 1 gives a very simplified example of a multiversion database for French agricultural production. Two classes describe the farmers and the fields:

class **Farmer** type tuple (name: string, address: string, owned: set(Field),

cultivate: set tuple (cultivation: string, %: int), fallow: int);

class **Field** type tuple (parcel_Nb:int, m2:int, cultivated_m2:int, cultivation:string);

The cultivate, fallow, m2 and cultivated_m2 attributes respectively represent the proportions of each cultivations and the percentage of the fallow lands of a given farmer, the area and the cultivated area of a field. The other attribute names state their semantics. Objects of class Farmer are denoted by $a_1, a_2, \ldots$, and objects of class Field by $t_1, t_2, \ldots$. The set of DBV identifiers is denoted by $\mathcal{D}$. The database state is composed of six DBVs, $DBV1$, $DBV2$, $DBV3$, $DBV4$,

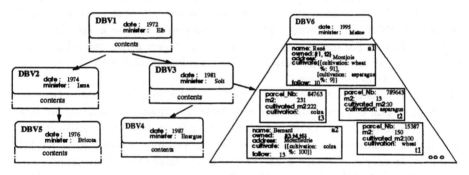

Fig. 1. A multiversion database with one of its DBV detailed

$DBV5$ and $DBV6$, labeled by the date of their creation and the name of the agriculture minister of the moment. A partial order, materialized by arrows, represents the derivation order among configurations. Figure 1 details the $DBV6$ contents, namely its logical object versions and their values. In 1995, farmer a_1 owns two fields (t_1 and t_2) on which he respectively cultivates 100 m^2 of wheat and 10 m^2 of asparagus.

Consistency in the DBV model is defined as follows. Each DBV represents a state of the real world and is thus similar to a monoversion database. Consistency of a DBV may be defined the same way as consistency of a monoversion database [7]. There are three ways of evolution of a multiversion database: updating a DBV, logically copying (deriving) a new DBV from an existing one, or deleting a DBV. Consistency of a multiversion database is defined as the consistency of its set of DBVs (of each DBV). But, if the model places no restriction on multiversion database evolutions, most applications need to establish links between DBVs, so that a DBV cannot evolve without taking into account some other DBVs. Such links are expressed by mv-constraints, which may concern DBV label and/or contents. Mv-constraints take into account this additional dimension. The definition of consistency must consider these links between DBVs:

mutual consistency of DBVs must be checked as well. The definition of consistency becomes: let T a transaction which transforms a multiversion database state E into a state E'. E' is consistent iff: (i) each DBV is consistent, (ii) DBVs are consistent between them and (iii) T is consistent [1].

Classification criteria

We present the classification of mv-constraints we use to elaborate specific checking methods taking into account the nature of the mv-constraints. This nature is defined with respect to three criteria, described below. Mv-constraints involve classes, objects, and database versions. These three *domains* influence the checking process, and are thus considered in the classification.

Scope The scope criterion allows to restrict the checking area of the constraint. Constraint checking requires the reading of one or several elements of each domain d (resp. mono d and multi d). For example, constraint C_1 (*At least 10% of the fields of a farmer must lie fallow*) is multi object, mono class and multi DBV. Indeed, all versions of all objects of class Farmer must be read to check it, and all DBVs are concerned. The scope criterion is used to adapt the checking to each case. For instance, constraints on one object across several database versions are not checked the same way as constraints involving all objects of one class in one database version.

Binding A constraint may involve one element of a domain d one at a time (intra d) or several elements simultaneously (inter d). Mono d constraints are intra d, whereas multi d constraints may be intra or inter d. Inter d mv-constraints link different elements of the same domain. For instance, constraint C_2 (*A field is owned by only one farmer at the same time*) is inter object (the values of the attribute **owned** of the objects of class Farmer are compared), intra class (only class Farmer is concerned) and intra DBV (comparisons are done in each DBV). Constraint C_3, (*The cultivated area of a field cannot increase, except if the area of the field has increased*) is multi intra object, mono class, multi inter DBV. The different versions of each object of class Farmer are compared, there is no link between these objects, but there is a link between the considered DBVs. The scope criterion selects the object versions involved by the mv-constraint, whereas the binding criterion focuses on dependencies between these object versions. Checking a multi intra d mv-constraint consists in checking a mono d mv-constraint on several (possibly all) elements of d, whereas several elements of d must be considered simultaneously to check a multi inter d mv-constraint.

Transition Transition mv-constraints, generalization of dynamic constraints in monoversion databases, control the transitions between multiversion database states. Both initial and final states of a transaction must be considered during checking process. Constraint C_4 (*If a farmer begins a new cultivation, the percentage of his fallow lands or of one of his other cultivation must decrease*) is a transition mv-contraint. Its checking implies to compare the farmer's cultivations in each DBV before and after the execution of the transaction. C_4 is a transition mv-constraint, multi intra object, mono class, multi intra DBV. Even if they involve several DBVs, constraints C_1, C_2 and C_3 are not transition mv-constraints.

---

[1] T transforms a consistent state into an other consistent state.

Only the final state of the multiversion database needs to be considered while checking them.

The position of an mv-constraint with respect to each of these criteria (scope, binding and transition) is called its *nature*.

Management of consistency in multiversion databases
We briefly present the formalism and the checking principles defined in [5].
Formalism An mv-constraint is a prenex first order logic formula completed by two operators, *pre* and *post*, used for transition mv-constraints. The left part of the formula is called the *prefix*, and the right part the *matrix*. The prefix contains quantified variables on classes (objects or database versions) or on paths of set type. The matrix is composed of atomic formulae[2] linked using logical operators. C_1 is expressed as follows: $\forall d \in \mathcal{D}$, $\forall x \in \text{Farmer}$, (x,d).fallow ≥ 10
Consistency checking Optimizing the mv-constraint checking process is essential. We propose three kinds of optimization. The first two kinds consist in determining the set of mv-constraints that might be violated by a transaction, and in reducing the checking field of the mv-constraint to the relevant database elements. The third kind of optimization is specific to multiversion database, and consists in defining a specific checking method for each nature of mv-constraints.

3   Mv-constraint versions

Updating constraints is possible in monoversion databases, but not in multiversion databases. Since versions of the real world can be stored, versions of constraints should also be stored. We discuss in this section the consequences on the application field, the nature, and the management of mv-constraints due to the introduction of versions of mv-constraints.

The application field of an mv-constraint having only one version is the whole multiversion database. In case of versions of mv-constraints, each version must be associated to distinct DBVs. Consider mv-constraint C_2, which limits the number of owners of a field. Let v_1 and v_2 be the values of two versions of C_2. v_1 restricts the number of owners of a field to one and v_2 accepts several owners if the area of the field is larger than 5000 m^2 per owners. Let t be a version of an object of class Field. The area of t is 20000 m^2 and it is owned by three farmers. t violates the value v_1 of C_2 and respects v_2.

This example shows that no more than one version of an mv-constraint can be applied to a single DBV. *The set of DBVs must be partitionned with respect to the versions of an mv-constraint.* This partition can be obtained by considering DBV labels or identifiers. In the previous example, the value of a version of C_2 is given by the date, which is an attribute of the label of the DBVs. Suppose that v_2 is created in 1981. Then v_1 is the value of C_2 for all DBVs preceding 1981, and v_2 is the valid value of C_2 for all other DBVs. This shows that the

---

[2] A term can be a variable, a constant, an object identifier, a database version identifier or a path. An atomic formula is composed of two terms separated by an arithmetic operator or comparator $(+,-,/,^*,<,>,\geq,\leq,=,\neq)$.

DBV partition can be based on a label property. The membership of a DBV to a partition subset is obtained with respect to this property.

The partition can also be obtained by considering the DBV identifier. Suppose that in 1996, a legislator wants to anticipate the effects of two different modifications of an existing law, expressed by an mv-constraint c_i. Two versions of the law are created, having respectively the values v_i and v_j. To represent these two situations, two DBVs, $DBV7$ and $DBV8$, are derived from $DBV6$. The only difference between these three DBVs is the value of c_i, which is respectively v_i in $DBV7$ and v_j in $DBV8$. The partition is obtained with respect to the DBV identifier. In all cases, a version of an mv-constraint is associated to each DBV. A consequence of this systematic association is the modification of the mv-constraint identifier. An mv-constraint is identified with its name (C_1 for instance). This identification is no longer sufficient. The DBV identifier (id_{DBV}) must be associated with the mv-constraint identifier (id_{mvc}). A version of an mv-constraint is identified by a couple $(id_{mvc},\ id_{\mathrm{DBV}})$.

We have shown the need of having a partition of the DBVs with respect to each mv-constraint. This modifies the links implied by mv-constraints between DBVs. The links between objects or classes are not concerned. We discuss now the consequences due to versions of mv-constraints on the classification with respect to the DBV domain.

Mono DBV mv-constraints A mono DBV mv-constraint, which implies only one DBV, becomes a version of the mv-constraint contained in the DBV. Versions of this mv-constraint associated with other DBVs have the value NIL. The expression of mono DBV mv-constraints is not modified. The DBV partition is composed of two subsets, the DBV to which the mv-constraint relates on the one hand, all other DBVs on the other hand.

Multi intra DBV mv-constraints In this case, several DBVs are concerned, but are not related. A multi intra DBV mv-constraint is checked in each DBV independently from the others. Mv-constraints are then duplicated (logical copy) in each DBV. A multi intra DBV mv-constraint c becomes a set of versions of a mono DBV mv-constraint: c is linked to each DBV. Each DBV DBV has its own version of c, identified by (c, DBV). This implies to modify the expression of mv-constraints. The formula contains a quantifier on the DBV identifier set, which indicates the scope of the mv-constraint. For instance, in the expression of C_1 ($\forall d \in \mathcal{D}, \forall x \in$ Farmer, $(x, d).\texttt{fallow} \geq 10$), $\forall d \in \mathcal{D}$ means that the formula concerns all DBVs. As a version of an mv-constraint is associated with each DBV, it is no more necessary to specify the DBVs to which it is applied. The quantifier is removed. The versions of C_1 are expressed as follows:

- $\forall DBV \in \mathcal{D}, (C_1, DBV) = \forall x \in$ Farmer, $(x, DBV).\texttt{fallow} \geq 10$

The partition of DBVs is obtained as follows. All DBVs having the same value of a version of a given mv-constraint form a subset. Thus, there is one subset per value. Updates of versions of mv-constraints have no side effect on other DBVs. For instance, if the minimal percentage of fallow lands for each farmers goes from 10 to 15% in 1995, only the versions of C_1 contained in DBVs ulterior to 1995 are updated.

Multi inter DBV mv-constraints As multi inter DBV mv-constraints define links between DBVs, it is not possible to translate them into mono DBV mv-constraints. The application field of a version of an mv-constraint is quite complex to define. Consider the following value val_1 of C_3: *If the cultivation is cereal, the cultivated area of the field cannot increase, except if the area of the field has increased or if the field is out of cultivation.* Let us consider three versions of object t_1 (of the class Field) contained in $DBVi$, $DBVj$ and $DBVk$:

DBVid	parcel_Nb	m2	c._m2	cultivation
$DBVi$	789643	13	0	fallow
$DBVj$	789643	13	5	asparagus
$DBVk$	789643	13	10	asparagus

$(C_3, DBVi) = (C_3, DBVj) = (C_3, DBVk) = val_1$

t_1 respects val_1 of C_3 in the three DBVs because t_1 is not a cereal cultivation.

The value of C_3 is updated in $DBVj$ and becomes val_2: *The cultivated area of a field cannot increase, except if the area of the field has increased or if the field was out of cultivation.*

Then, $(C_3,DBVi) = (C_3,DBVk) = val_1, (C_3,DBVj) = val_2$.

Now, t_1 violates val_2 when comparing $DBVj$ and $DBVk$. Depending on the version of C_3 which is considered, t_1 respects or violates C_3. Only one mv-constraint version has to be checked between two DBVs. In the previous example, the versions of C_3 have the same value in $DBVi$ and $DBVk$. val_1 is checked between these two DBVs. On the contrary, the values of the versions of C_3 are different in $DBVi$ and $DBVj$, and in $DBVj$ and $DBVk$. Thus, no version of C_3 is checked between these two pairs of DBVs, neither val_1 nor val_2.

When a version of an mv-constraint c is updated with a value val in a DBV, val is checked between all the DBVs having the same value val for the version of c. The consistency with respect to c does not need to be checked between DBVs having different values for the version of c. Updating a version of an mv-constraint c in a DBV has no side effect on other DBVs. However, it might imply modifications on the subsets of the partition associated to c.

4   Representation of mv-constraint versions

Constraints are usually defined in the schema, and the database is consistent if the data contained in the database respects the schema (i.e. verifies the structure of the classes and the constraints). In multiversion databases, there is generally a single schema valid for all database versions. Defining mv-constraints in the schema is no longer satisfactory as it is not possible to update mv-constraints. One must either forbid any schema modification (including mv-constraint modification) or accept some inconsistencies. Both cases are unacceptable, as they do not represent the real world evolution. We propose two main alternatives to solve this problem. One consists in representing the mv-constraints as part of a versionable schema. The second proposition represents mv-constraints as objects. In both cases, we study the consequences of these representations on the definition, the storage, the checking process and the update of mv-constraint versions. In the remainder of this section, we consider that only mv-constraints can be modified and versioned.

4.1 Mv-constraints represented in the schema

In most systems, constraints are defined in the schema. The main advantages of this representation is to provide independence between data and schema, and to give an homogeneous and global vision of the constraints. The consequences of this representation are the following:

Definition and storage: As mv-constraint versions are defined in the schema, the formalism presented in Section 2 is still valid. In the same way, storing versions of mv-constraints is quite similar to storing mv-constraint without version. The only difference is that each DBV owns its schema version which contains a version of each mv-constraint.

Consistency checking: The contents of a multiversion database $\mathcal{B}$ must respect the schema (structure and mv-constraints) of $\mathcal{B}$. The checking method presented earlier is still valid. Versions of mono DBV constraints are checked in each DBV of $\mathcal{B}$. Versions of multi inter DBV mv-constraints are checked in each subset of the partition associated to these mv-constraints.

Update: Updating a version of an mv-constraint c in a DBV DBV has no side effect on other DBVs. If c is mono DBV, the new value of the version of c is checked in DBV. If c is multi inter DBV, the partition associated to c is modified. The version of c is in another subset of the partition. The new value has to be checked in the relevant subset.

Version vision: Each DBV has its own schema which contains the structural part and the versions of mv-constraints. Each DBV is similar to a monoversion database. Schema and contents are independant. The structural part and the versions of mv-constraint are defined in a similar (global and declarative) way. The checking methods are easily adapted to versions of mv-constraints. Finally, checking versions of mono DBV mv-constraints is restricted to a DBV, while checking versions of multi inter DBV mv-constraints is restricted to a subset of a partition.

4.2 Mv-constraints represented in the contents

Representing mv-constraints as objects avoids the management of versions of schema. We describe the consequences of this representation on the definition, storage, checking process and update of mv-constraint versions.

Definition: Mv-constraints can be represented by one class with two attributes: **mv_constraint** and **nature** which respectively represent the formula and the nature of a mv-contraint. Both are of type string.

Storage: Mv-constraints are stored as objects.

Consistency checking: The principle described in Section 2 can still be used. However, a preliminary step is necessary: the two groups of objects, representing the entities of the real world and the mv-constraints, have to be separated. The DBV contents is no more homogeneous.

Update: Updates of versions of mv-constraints are performed by transactions. Updates of objects, reflecting a real world modification, and updates of mv-constraints, reflecting a rule modification are now performed the same way. This can lead to some confusions, and may generate inconsistencies.

Version vision: Representing mv-constraints as objects leads to the loss of independence between the schema and the contents of a multiversion database, and to the lack of homogeneity in its contents. The vision of mv-constraints spread out in the contents, is no more global. The main advantage of this representation is its easy implementation. Representing versions of mv-constraints in the schema requires a schema versioning mechanism, while this representation does not require a specific mechanism. The single schema is fixed and the mv-constraint versions are obtained through the object version mechanism. The definition, storage, checking, and update problems are directly solved.

The first representation has many advantages: the definition language is declarative and global, the schema and the contents are independent, and updates of mv-constraint and of object versions are performed differently. However, a schema version mechanism is necessary to implement the mv-constraint versions. In the second representation, the problems due to the schema versions are avoided and the implementation of the mv-constraint version is performed using the current object version mechanism. This representation has thus a simpler implementation.

5 Conclusion

We address the problem of versioning constraints. This work follows earlier work on integrity management in multiversion databases [5, 6], where versions of constraints were not considered. Considering versions of constraints is necessary to accurately represent the real world. The issue of defining the properties of mv-constraint versions and the issue of representing them are both addressed.

We inventoried five main properties of mv-constraint versions: (i)A version of an mv-constraint c is associated to each DBV DBV, and is identified by the pair (c,DBV). (ii)When the version of c contained in DBV is updated, its value is updated without side effect on other DBVs. (iii)If a DBV DBV' is derived from an existing DBV, DBV, (c,DBV') is a logical copy of (c,DBV). (iv)The set of DBVs having the same value v for a given version of c, makes up a subset of the partition associated to c. The value of c checked in or between DBVs contained in this subset is v. (v)The nature of c on the DBV domain is either mono DBV or multi inter DBV.

We have next studied two representations of mv-constraint versions and their respective consequences on the definition, the storage, the checking and the update of mv-constraint versions. Both solutions have advantages and drawbacks. Representing mv-constraints as objects is easier to implement, but it seems more judicious to choose the other representation. Indeed, representing mv-constraints in the schema allows to keep the independence schema-contents and to have a global vision of the mv-constraints.

As future work, we plan first to implement the integrity mechanism for multiversion database we have defined, in order to validate our work. A second objective is to integrate existing results on schema evolution and object migration, and to extend them to our context.

6 Acknowledgments

We thank Stéphane Gançarski for his fruitful comments on this work, and Mourad Sefrioui for his careful reading of this paper.

References

1. R. Agrawal and H. V. Jagadish. On correctly configuring versioned objects. *Proc. VLDB*, pages 367–374, Amsterdam, August 1989.
2. T.M. Atwood. An object-oriented DBMS for design support applications. *Proc. COMPINT*, pages 299–307, Montréal, September 1986.
3. C.M. Bauzer-Medeiros, W. Cellary and G. Jomier. Maintaining Integrity Constraints across Versions in a Database. *8th Brazilian Database Conference*, Campina Grande, Brazil, 1993.
4. W. Cellary and G. Jomier. Consistency of versions in object-oriented databases. *Proc. 16th VLDB*, Brisbane (Australia), 1990.
5. A. Doucet, S. Gançarski, G. Jomier, and S. Monties. Cohérence des Bases de données multiversion. *Proc. BDA'96*, Cassis (France), 1996.
6. A. Doucet, S. Gançarski, G. Jomier, and S. Monties. Integrity constraints for multiversion databases. *Proc. BNCOD'96*, Springer Verlag, Edinburgh (Scotland), 1996.
7. J. Gray and A. Reuter. Transaction Processing: concepts and techniques. Morgan and Kaufmann Publishers, ISBN 1-55860-190-2 – 1070 pages, 1993.
8. S. Gançarski and G. Jomier. Managing Entity Versions within their Context: a Formal Approach. Proc. DEXA'94, LNCS 856, pp. 400-409, September 1994.
9. S. Gançarski, G. Jomier and M. Zamfiroïu. A Framework for the Manipulation of a Multiversion Database *In : DEXA'95 International Conference, Workshop Proc.*, ISBN 3-901653-00-7, pp. 247–256. London (U.K.), 1995.
10. A. Gupta and S. Tiwari. Distributed Constraint Management for Collaborative Engineering Databases. *In : Proc. Second International Conference on Information and Knowledge Management* Washington, D.C. ACM, 1993.
11. A. Gupta and J.Widom. Local Verification of Global Integrity Constraints in Distributed Databases. *In : ACM SIGMOD Int. Conf. on Management Of Data*, pp 49-59, 1993.
12. R. H. Katz. Toward a unified framework for version modeling in engineering databases. *ACM Computing Surveys*, 22(4):375–408, December 1990.
13. W. Kim, E. Bertino, and J.F. Garza. Composite objects revisited. *ACM SIGMOD Record*, 18(2):337–347, June 1989.
14. W. Käfer and H. Schöning. Mapping a version model to a complex-object data model. *Proc. IEEE Data Engineering*, Tempe (Arizona), 1992.
15. G. Talens, C. Oussalah, and M.F. Colinas. Versions of simple and composite objects. In *Proc. 19th VLDB*, Dublin, 1993.
16. S. Zdonik. Version management in an object-oriented database. *International Workshop on Advanced Programming Environments*, pages 138–200, Norway, 1986.

Structuring the Process of Integrity Maintenance

Enric Mayol, Ernest Teniente

LSI Department, Universitat Politècnica de Catalunya
Jordi Girona Salgado 1-3, Edifici C6
E-08034 Barcelona - Catalonia
e-mail: [mayol | teniente]@lsi.upc.es

Abstract

Two different approaches have been traditionally considered for dealing with the process of integrity constraints enforcement: integrity checking and integrity maintenance. However, while previous research in the first approach has mainly addressed efficiency issues, research in the second approach has been mainly concentrated in being able to generate all possible repairs that falsify an integrity constraint violation.

In this paper we address efficiency issues during the process of integrity maintenance. In this sense, we propose a technique which improves efficiency of existing methods by defining the order in which maintenance of integrity constraints should be performed. Moreover, we use also this technique for being able to handle in an integrated way the integrity constraints enforcement approaches mentioned above.

1. Introduction

Database updating has attracted a lot of research during last years [Abi88]. Several problems may arise when updating a deductive database [TU95]. One of the most important problems is that of *enforcing database consistency*. A deductive database is called consistent if it satisfies a set of integrity constraints. When performing an update, database consistency may be violated. That is, the update, together with the current content of the database, may falsify some integrity constraint.

A well-known approach to deal with this problem is that of *integrity maintenance* [ML91, Wüt93, TO95, Dec96], which is concerned with trying to repair constraints violations by performing additional updates that restore consistency of the database. In this way, it is guaranteed that the state resulting from applying the update does not violate any integrity constraint and that it satisfies the update requested by the user.

In general, integrity constraints are very interrelated because they may have some predicates in common. These predicates may appear explicitly in their definition or implicitly because they participate in the definition of a certain derived predicate that appears in the integrity constraint definition. For this reason, integrity maintenance uses to be very complex since, for instance, repairs of an integrity constraint may correspond to violations of other integrity constraints; or since an already repaired integrity constraint could be violated again by the repair of another integrity constraint. This situation is aggravated by the fact that even simple integrity constraints can be violated through several updates and because often a multitude of repairs exist.

The methods proposed so far for integrity maintenance have been mainly concerned with the generation of a complete set of repairs of integrity constraints violations, but they have paid little attention to efficiency issues. Thus, for instance, when a constraint is repaired all other constraints are checked for consistency even though they were already satisfied prior to the repair and they could not be violated by the performed repair.

In this paper we propose a technique for determining the order in which integrity constraints should be handled to minimize the number of times that an integrity constraint must be reconsidered. This technique provides two important advantages. First, it minimizes the number of recomputations of testing whether a given constraint is violated. Second, it ensures that a repair of a certain integrity constraint is performed only when all repairs of other constraints that could induce a violation of it have been performed.

Our technique is based on the definition of a graph, the *Precedence Graph*, which explicitly states all relationships between repairs and potential violations of integrity constraints. Information provided by this graph is directly applicable to the methods we have proposed in the past for handling consistent updates in deductive databases [MT95, TO95] and it could be easily adapted to other existing methods.

A different approach to enforce database consistency is *integrity checking*; which is concerned with developing methods for checking whether a given update violates an integrity constraint [Oli91, GCMD94]. In this case, when a violation is detected, the transaction is rejected. Both integrity constraint enforcement approaches are reasonable. The correct choice of an approach for a particular integrity constraint depends on the semantics of the integrity constraint and of the deductive database.

Most of the existing methods are only concerned with handling one of the approaches in an isolated manner, without taking into account the strong relationship between the problems to be solved in both cases. As far as we know, the only proposal towards this direction is that of [CHM95] which presents a method that follows the integrity checking approach, but makes some exceptions by using certain constraints to suggest new updates.

To further contribute to enforcing database consistency, we also propose in this paper a technique for integrating the treatment of integrity checking and integrity maintenance. This technique is based on incorporating also in the Precedence Graph the information corresponding to the integrity constraints to be checked, and considering its relationship with constraints to be maintained.

This paper is organised as follows. Next section reviews basic concepts of deductive databases. Section 3, which is based on [Oli91, UO92], reviews the concepts of event, transition rules and event rules. In Section 4 we propose the Precedence Graph as a tool for structuring the process of integrity enforcement. In Section 5 we propose a mechanism to execute that graph. In Section 6 we relate our approach to previous work. Finally, in Section 7 we summarize our conclusions.

2. Deductive Databases

In this section, we briefly review some definitions of the basic concepts related to deductive databases [Llo87] and present our notation. A *term* is a variable symbol or a constant symbol. If P is an m-ary predicate symbol and $t_1, ..., t_m$ are terms, then $P(t_1, ..., t_m)$ is an *atom*. The atom is *ground* if every t_i ($i = 1, ..., m$) is a constant. A *literal* is defined as either an atom or a negated atom. A *fact* is a formula of the form: $P(t_1, ..., t_m) \leftarrow$, where $P(t_1, ..., t_m)$ is a ground atom.

A *deductive rule* is a formula of the form: $P(t_1, ..., t_m) \leftarrow L_1 \wedge ... \wedge L_n$, with $n \geq 1$, where $P(t_1, ..., t_m)$ is an atom denoting the conclusion, and $L_1, ..., L_n$ are literals representing conditions. Any variable in $P(t_1, ..., t_m)$, $L_1, ..., L_n$ is assumed to be universally quantified over the whole formula. A derived predicate P may be defined by means of one or more deductive rules. In this paper, we assume that all variables appearing in some condition of a rule appear also in its head.

An *integrity constraint* is a closed first-order formula that the deductive database is required to satisfy. We deal with constraints in *denial* form: $\leftarrow L_1 \wedge ... \wedge L_m$, with $m \geq 1$, where the L_i are literals and all variables are assumed to be universally quantified over the whole formula. More general constraints can be transformed into this form by first applying the range form transformation [Dec89] and then using the procedure described in [LT84].

For the sake of uniformity, we associate to each integrity constraint an inconsistency predicate Icn, with or without terms, and thus they have the same form as the deductive rules. We call them *integrity rules*. Then, we rewrite the former denial as: $Icn \leftarrow L_1 \wedge ... \wedge L_m$, with $m \geq 1$

A *deductive database* D is a triple (EDB, IDB, IC), where EDB is a set of facts, IDB a set of deductive rules and IC a set of integrity constraints. The set EDB of facts is called the *extensional* part of the database and the set of deductive rules and integrity constraints is called the *intensional* part.

We assume that deductive database predicates are partitioned into base and derived (view) predicates. A base predicate appears only in the extensional part and (eventually) in the body of deductive rules. A derived predicate appears only in the intensional part. Any database can be defined in this form [BR86]. We deal with *stratified* databases [Llo87] and, as usual, we require the database to be *allowed* [Llo87]; that is, any variable that occurs in a deductive rule has an occurrence in a positive condition of an ordinary predicate.

Example 2.1: The following example will be used throughout the paper:

Acc(Paul)	$Mem(x) \leftarrow Rec(x) \wedge Acc(x)$
Rec(Paul)	$Active(x) \leftarrow Part(x)$
Part(Paul)	
	$Ic1(x) \leftarrow Acc(x) \wedge Neg(x)$
	$Ic2(x) \leftarrow Active(x) \wedge \neg Mem(x)$
	$Ic3(x) \leftarrow Rec(x) \wedge \neg Part(x)$

This database contains four base predicates: Rec states that a person is recommended to be member of a club; Acc states that he/she is accepted as member; Part states that a person is participating in an activity; Neg states that a person has a negative report. Derived predicates are Mem and Active that state when a person is a member or has an active attitude in the club.

Notice that the database contains also three integrity constraints stating, respectively, that it is not possible to be a member and to have a negative report; that active people must be members; and, that a recommended person must participate in some activity.

3. The Augmented Database

The definition of the Precedence Graph, given in next section, will take into account a set of rules that define the difference between two consecutive database states. This set of rules, together with the original database D, form the Augmented Database [Oli91, UO92], denoted by A(D), which explicitly defines the insertions and deletions induced by a transaction T that consists of a set of base fact updates.

The concept of Augmented Database is based on the concept of *event*. For each predicate P in the underlying language of a given deductive database D, a distinguished *insertion event predicate* ιP and a distinguished *deletion event predicate* δP are used to define the difference of deducible facts of consecutive database states.

If P is a base predicate, ιP and δP facts (called *base event facts*) represent insertions and deletions of base facts, respectively. For this reason, we assume that a transaction T consists of a set of base event facts. If P is a derived predicate, ιP and δP facts represent induced insertions and induced deletions, respectively. If P is an inconsistency predicate, ιP represents a violation of the corresponding integrity constraint. For inconsistency predicates, δP facts are not defined since we assume that the database is consistent before the update.

The definition of ιP and δP depends on the definition of P in D, but is independent of any transaction T and of the extensional part of D. For each derived or inconsistency predicate P, the Augmented Database contains the rules about ιP and δP, called *event rules*, which define exactly the insertions and deletions of facts about P that are induced by some transaction T. Event rules are defined as follows:

$$\iota P(\mathbf{x}) \leftarrow P^n(\mathbf{x}) \wedge \neg P(\mathbf{x}) \qquad \delta P(\mathbf{x}) \leftarrow P(\mathbf{x}) \wedge \neg P^n(\mathbf{x})$$

where P refers to a predicate evaluated in the old state of the database, P^n refers to the predicate P evaluated in the new state of the database and $\mathbf{x}$ is a vector of variables.

The Augmented Database contains also a set of *transition rules* associated to each derived or inconsistency predicate P. These transition rules define the evaluation of predicate P in the new state (denoted by P^n) in terms of the old state of the database and the events that occur in the transition between both states.

Given a deductive database D, the Augmented Database A(D) consists of D, its transition rules and its event rules. Description and discussion of the procedure for automatically deriving an Augmented Database from a database can be found in [Oli91, UO92, several simplifications are also described.

Example 3.1: This example shows the Augmented Database of example 2.1

$Mem(x) \leftarrow Rec(x) \wedge Acc(x)$	(C_1) $\iota Ic1(x) \leftarrow Acc(x) \wedge \neg\delta Acc(x) \wedge \iota Neg(x)$
$Active(x) \leftarrow Part(x)$	(C_2) $\iota Ic1(x) \leftarrow \iota Acc(x) \wedge Neg(x) \wedge \neg\delta Neg(x)$
$Ic1(x) \leftarrow Acc(x) \wedge Neg(x)$	(C_3) $\iota Ic1(x) \leftarrow \iota Acc(x) \wedge \iota Neg(x)$
$Ic2(x) \leftarrow Active(x) \wedge \neg Mem(x)$	(C_4) $\iota Ic2(x) \leftarrow Active(x) \wedge \neg\delta Active(x) \wedge \delta Mem(x)$
$Ic3(x) \leftarrow Rec(x) \wedge \neg Part(x)$	(C_5) $\iota Ic2(x) \leftarrow \iota Active(x) \wedge \neg Mem(x) \wedge \neg\iota Mem(x)$
	(C_6) $\iota Ic2(x) \leftarrow \iota Active(x) \wedge \delta Mem(x)$
$\iota Mem(x) \leftarrow Rec(x) \wedge \neg\delta Rec(x) \wedge \iota Acc(x)$	(C_7) $\iota Ic3(x) \leftarrow Rec(x) \wedge \neg\delta Rec(x) \wedge \delta Part(x)$
$\iota Mem(x) \leftarrow \iota Rec(x) \wedge Acc(x) \wedge \neg\delta Acc(x)$	(C_8) $\iota Ic3(x) \leftarrow \iota Rec(x) \wedge \neg Part(x) \wedge \neg\iota Part(x)$
$\iota Mem(x) \leftarrow \iota Rec(x) \wedge \iota Acc(x)$	(C_9) $\iota Ic3(x) \leftarrow \iota Rec(x) \wedge \delta Part(x)$
$\delta Mem(x) \leftarrow \delta Rec(x) \wedge Acc(x)$	
$\delta Mem(x) \leftarrow Rec(x) \wedge \delta Acc(x)$	
$\iota Active(x) \leftarrow \iota Part(x)$	
$\delta Active(x) \leftarrow \delta Part(x)$	

Rules C_1 to C_9 define all possible ways of inserting facts about predicates Ic1, Ic2 and Ic3. These rules deserve special attention since they define all possible situations in which database consistency is violated by the application of some transaction.

4. Structuring the Process of Integrity Maintenance

Structuring the process of integrity maintenance is concerned with determining the order in which integrity constraints should be handled. This order is provided by the *Precedence Graph*, which explicitly states all relationships between repairs and potential violations of integrity constraints.

To obtain the Precedence Graph we only take into account syntactical information associated to the definition of each integrity constraint. Thus, we do not need to consider the contents of the EDB nor the transaction to be applied to the database. Therefore, we generate the Precedence Graph at definition time, and we delay to run time to test whether potential dependencies defined in the graph correspond to real violations.

We take advantage of assuming that the database is consistent before the application of a transaction T. Then, violations of database consistency due to the transaction T are only produced because some insertion event rule associated to an integrity constraint becomes true. Moreover, repairs of the constraint are defined by the violated insertion event rule, since a repair corresponds to an additional update that falsifies the effect of T on the corresponding event rule. For this reason, we refer to the insertion event rules of an integrity constraint as the *conditions* of that integrity constraint.

To state dependencies between integrity constraints more precisely, we consider the conditions associated to an integrity constraint instead of the own integrity constraint definition. Thus, the Precedence Graph will state all relationships between repairs and potential violations of these conditions.

Example 4.1: Conditions associated to integrity constraint Ic1 of example 3.1 are the following:

$$C_1 \leftarrow Acc(x) \wedge \neg \, \delta Acc(x) \wedge \iota Neg(x)$$
$$C_2 \leftarrow \iota Acc(x) \wedge Neg(x) \wedge \neg \, \delta Neg(x)$$
$$C_3 \leftarrow \iota Acc(x) \wedge \iota Neg(x)$$

Note that each condition describes a situation to be avoided to ensure that an update does not violate integrity constraint Ic1. Therefore, ensuring that no condition holds we guarantee that no integrity constraint is violated. In the following we will refer to each condition by its identifier C_i (i=1..n).

4.1 Events Dependency Graph

Several derived events and several conditions may be induced when applying a transaction consisting of a set of base event facts. For instance, in the previous example the application of the base event ιAcc may induce the derived event ιMem as well as conditions C_2 and C_3. Obtaining the Precedence Graph requires to determine which repairs of a condition are potential violations of other conditions. To determine this information, we need first to explicitly state the relationship between base events and their effect on derived events and conditions. Given the Augmented Database A(D), we can identify the following dependencies:

Definition 4.1 Let E be an event and C be a condition or a derived event. We say that *C directly depends on E* if there is a rule in A(D) with event C as head and such that E appears in its body. A direct dependence is positive (resp. negative) if E is a positive literal (resp. negative).

By considering together all direct dependencies between events and conditions we can build the Events Dependency Graph [Cos95], which explicitly states the relationship between the application of events on a database and their induced effect, and which builds the basis for the process of structuring integrity maintenance.

Definition 4.2 An *Events Dependency Graph* EDG for a set of events and a set of conditions, is a pair EDG = <Nod, Edg> where Nod is a finite number of nodes, Edg ⊆ (Nod x Nod) is a set of directed edges such that each node n ∈ Nod is labelled with a condition identifier or an event . Given two nodes v and v', there exists an edge e=(v,v') iff v' directly depends on v. Edges are marked positive (resp. negative) if the dependence is positive (resp. negative).

Example 4.2: Consider again the database D of Example 3.1. Fig.1 represents the Events Dependency Graph derived from the Augmented Database A(D). Black arrows correspond to positive edges, while grey arrows correspond to the negative ones.

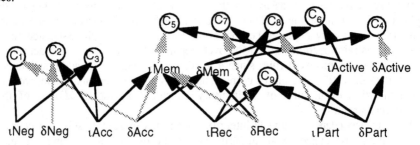

Fig.1. Events Dependency Graph of example 3.1

Definition 4.3 Let EDG be an Events Dependency Graph and v and v' two nodes in EDG. We say that:
- v *depends* on v' if EDG contains a path from v' to v.
- v *depends evenly* (resp. *oddly*) on v' if there is a path from v' to v in EDG containing an even (resp. odd) number of negative edges.

Dependencies between events and conditions allow us to determine potential violations and repairs of a condition. Intuitively, a potential violation of a condition C_i is an event that when applied to the database may induce an insertion of the inconsistency predicate associated to C_i. That is, C_i may become true due to that event. On the other hand, a potential repair of a condition C_i is a base event that when applied to the database may falsify C_i. This notion can also be generalized for derived events and we will refer to them as potential falsifiers. This information can be syntactically identified by considering the dependencies defined by the Events Dependency Graph.

Definition 4.4 Let E be an event and C_i a condition.
- E is a *potential violation* of C_i if C_i depends evenly on E.
- E is a *potential repair* of C_i if E is a base event and C_i depends oddly on E.
- E is a *potential falsifier* of C_i if E is a derived event and C_i depends oddly on E.

At definition time we can not ensure that an event will be a real violation of a certain condition at run time since the database must also satisfy other requirements that may be unknown at this moment. This is why we talk about potential violations. We talk about potential repairs and falsifiers since, in general, repairing a condition may require the application of more than one event.

Example 4.3: Consider again condition C_2 of Example 3.1. Event $\iota Acc(x)$ is a potential violation of C_2 because it could make C_2 true depending on the rest of literals of the condition. Event $\delta Neg(x)$ is the only potential repair of condition C_2.

It may happen that no potential repair exists for a certain condition. So, we distinguish between two different kinds of conditions. Checking conditions are those that have no potential repair; while conditions with some potential repair are called generation conditions. Each condition can be classified only into one of these two categories.

Definition 4.5 Let C_i be a condition. C_i is a *checking condition* if there is no potential repair associated to it. Otherwise, C_i is a *generation condition*.

Checking conditions of the example are C_3, C_6 and C_9. All other conditions are generation conditions.

4.2 Precedences Between Conditions

We are interested on minimizing the number of times that a condition should be reconsidered. For this reason, we should first deal with those conditions whose repairs may induce a violation of other conditions. The Events Dependency Graph does not tell us which conditions should precede which others, but it provides the basis for determining this information.

In general, a condition will have several potential repairs. Moreover, due to the multilevel structure of derived predicates, derived events must also be considered when determining precedences among conditions. Thus, some of the potential repairs may be meaningless since they are already implied by considering potential falsifiers. Therefore, we have to define first which are the meaningful events that must be considered to determine the precedence between two conditions. We call them meeting events and they are defined as follows:

Definition 4.6 Let C_i and C_j be two different conditions. A base or derived event E is a *meeting event* if one of the following conditions holds:
- it appears in the definition of both C_i and C_j.
- it appears in the definition of C_i and it defines a derived event that appears in C_j but not in C_i
- it defines a derived event that appears in C_i and another derived event that appears in C_j but not in C_i.

Intuitively, it can be seen that to determine the precedence between two conditions we have to consider only those events that participate on the definition of both conditions. This may be done either explicitly by considering the definition of the conditions or implicitly by taking into account the derived events they define and that appear in the definition of the conditions.

Example 4.4: Consider again the database example 3.1. The only meeting event for conditions C_1 and C_4 is $\delta Acc(x)$; while meeting events for conditions C_4 and C_7 are $\delta Rec(x)$ and $\delta Part(x)$.

Now, by taking into account meeting events we can identify precedences between conditions. Intuitively, condition C_i must precede condition C_j if there exists a meeting event that, depending on whether it holds or not, it may falsify condition C_i and satisfy condition C_j. That is, this event will be considered when generating a repair for C_i and this may induce a violation of C_j. Precedences are determined by considering dependencies provided by the Events Dependency Graph.

Definition 4.7 Let C_i be a generation condition and C_j a condition. We say that C_i *precedes* C_j if one of the following two cases holds:
- There exists a meeting event E such that E is a potential repair or falsifier of C_i and a potential violation of C_j.

- If there exists a derived meeting event E such that C_i depends evenly on E and C_j depends oddly on E.

Example 4.5: Consider the deletion event $\delta Rec(x)$. This event is a potential repair of C_7 and a potential violation of conditions C_4, C_5 and C_6. Then, event $\delta Rec(x)$ defines the following precedences between conditions:

$$C_7 \rightarrow C_4, C_5, C_6 \qquad \text{due to } \delta Rec(x)$$

4.3 Precedence Graph

By considering together all precedences between conditions we can build the Precedence Graph, which explicitly states all relationships among repairs and violations of conditions. In this way, it defines the order in which conditions should be handled to minimize the number of times that a condition must be reconsidered, which substantially increases efficiency of the integrity maintenance process. Moreover, the Precedence Graph is used to ensure that a repair of a certain condition is only performed when it is guaranteed that all repairs of conditions that could induce a violation of this condition have already been performed.

Definition 4.8 A *Precedence Graph* PG for a set C of conditions, is a pair PG=<Nod,Edg> where Nod is a finite number of nodes, Edg $\subseteq$ (Nod x Nod) is a set of directed edges such that each node n $\in$ Nod is labelled with a condition identifier and each edge is labelled with an event. There exists a directed edge edg = (n,n'), labelled with event E, if the condition labelling node n precedes the condition labelling node n' due to E.

Two types of nodes can be distinguished in a Precedence Graph. Nodes with no ongoing edges correspond to conditions which cannot be violated by repairs of other conditions. Nodes with no incoming edges correspond to conditions for which no repairs exist or such that their repairs may not violate other conditions.

In some cases, a Precedence Graph may contain cycles among certain conditions. For readability reasons, we group these cycles into a single node that contains a subgraph defining precedences between conditions of the cycle and the rest.

Example 4.6: Consider again the database of example 3.1. Precedences between conditions of this database are the following:

$C_5 \rightarrow C_2, C_3$	due to $\iota Acc(x)$	$C_7 \rightarrow C_4, C_5, C_6$	due to $\delta Rec(x)$
$C_1 \rightarrow C_4, C_5, C_6$	due to $\delta Acc(x)$	$C_8 \rightarrow C_5, C_6$	due to $\iota Part(x)$
$C_5 \rightarrow C_8, C_9$	due to $\iota Rec(x)$	$C_4 \rightarrow C_7, C_9$	due to $\delta Part(x)$

The Precedence Graph obtained by collecting and integrating all these precedences contains two cycles: $C_5 \rightarrow C_8 \rightarrow C_5$ and $C_7 \rightarrow C_4 \rightarrow C_7$. These cycles would be drawn as two different subgraphs.

The existence of cycles may indicate that the process of integrity maintenance does not terminate. However, it is important to note that the existence of a cycle between a set of conditions does not necessarily imply that dealing with conditions of the cycle should be performed forever. On the contrary, a cycle in the Precedence Graph does not correspond in general to an infinite loop at execution time.

If we analyse in more detail each obtained precedence, we can detect that some of them are never achievable at run-time since the requirements of each condition are incompatible. We refer the reader to the full version of the paper [MT97] where we propose some optimizations that allow us to eliminate unfeasible precedences, obtaining a more precise Precedence Graph.

We show in Fig.2 the optimized Precedence Graph. Nodes labelled with checking conditions are filled in grey to be differentiated from nodes labelled with generation conditions.

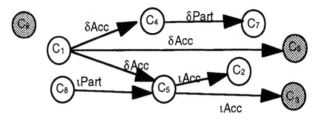

Fig.2. Final Precedence Graph of example 3.1

Note that, in this example, the optimization allowed to eliminate precedences that are responsible of cycles.

4.5 Joining Integrity Maintenance and Integrity Checking

In general, it may be interesting to distinguish between integrity constraints to be checked and integrity constraints to be maintained. In our method, the integration of both approaches can be performed by incorporating also in the Precedence Graph information related to the integrity constraints to be checked.

In fact, integrity constraints to be checked can be seen as a special case of constraints to be maintained where the repair action is to abort the transaction. That is, when one of these constraints is violated, possible repairs need not be taken into account. Therefore, all conditions associated to an integrity constraint to be checked correspond to checking conditions. In this way, the only relevant information to be taken into account when incorporating these conditions into the Precedence Graph is the information regarding their potential violations.

5. Execution of the Precedence Graph

Given an initial transaction T which may violate some of the conditions, the execution of the Precedence Graph is intended to obtain a new transaction T' that guarantees that all conditions remain not violated after the application of T'. T' will contain the updates belonging to T as well as the repairs considered for maintaining the conditions. In general, several transactions T'$_i$ may exist. Our approach is aimed at obtaining all of them. To specify the integrity maintenance process, we must define when and how each of these conditions should be processed.

The own structure of the Precedence Graph implicitly defines a non-deterministic order to take conditions into account: conditions for which all the predecessors have already been processed should be considered with priority since they can not be violated by repairs of other conditions. We will mark nodes of the graph to indicate candidate conditions to be processed at each step. A marked node states that its associated condition is potentially violated by the current transaction. Therefore, when a condition C_i is processed, the node is unmarked and, if it can be repaired, all conditions that are preceded by C_i due to that repair are marked.

Given a transaction T and a marked Precedence Graph G_T, we can obtain all the transactions TS$_i$ that maintain G_T. This is performed by means of the algorithm in Fig.3. Initially, marked conditions of G_T correspond to the conditions that may be violated by T.

```
Function Execute_Graph (T, GT):<set of transactions>
/* input: a transaction T and a marked Precedence Graph GT */
/* output: set of transactions TS that maintain GT */
begin
TS := Ø;
while GT is marked do
        C := Select_Next_Node(GT);
        if C is not a subgraph then
                GT := Remove_Mark(C, GT);
                violated := Check_Condition(C, T);
                if violated then
                        if C is a checking condition then Return(Ø);
                        else
                                RS := Compute_All_Repairs(C, T);
                                for each R ∈ RS do
                                        GT:= Add_New_Marks(GT, R);
                                        TR := T ∪ R;
                                        TS := TS ∪ Execute_Graph(TR, GT)
                                end for each;
                        end if;
                end if;
        else /* C is a subgraph */
                GT := Remove_Mark(C, GT);
                TSG := Execute_Graph(T, C);
                for each TG ∈ TSG do
                        R := TG - T;
                        GT := Add_New_Marks(GT, R);
                        TS := TS ∪ Execute_Graph(TG, GT)
                end for each;
        end if;
end while;
Return (TS);
end;
```

Fig.3. Algorithm to maintain Conditions of the Precedence Graph

Several functions have been considered in the definition of the previous algorithm. They are used for the marking and unmarking of nodes, selection nodes to be processed, checking whether a condition is violated and computing all repairs of a given condition. They exhibit the following behaviour:

- *Add_New_Marks (G_T, R):* given a marked graph G_T and a repair R, returns as a result the new marked graph which incorporates marks of all conditions that can be violated by R. This is done by considering which events in R are potential violations of which conditions in G_T.

- *Remove_Mark (C, G_T):* it unmarks node C from G_T and returns the new marked graph.

- *Select_Next_Node (G_T):* given a marked graph G_T it selects the next node to be processed. Nodes with unmarked predecessors are selected with priority. If there are different candidates to select, nodes corresponding to checking conditions are considered first. This helps to improve efficiency of the whole process since if this condition is violated, no other node will be considered.

- *Check_Condition (C, T):* given a condition C and a transaction T, it tests whether C is violated by T. To improve efficiency, this can be done by means of any arbitrary method for integrity checking.

- *Compute_All_Repairs (C, T):* given a condition C and a transaction T, it returns the set of all possible repairs of C. This function must take into account the translation of potential falsifiers into potential repairs.

Treatment of subgraphs is performed by means of a recursive call to the function Execute_Graph(T, G_T), where T is the current transaction and G_T corresponds to the subgraph defined by the selected node.

Example 5.1: Consider again the database of example 3.1 and its associated Precedence Graph shown in Fig.2. The following table summarizes the execution of the Precedence Graph given the initial transaction T = {ιNeg(Paul)}.

In each row, an 'V' shows the node selected at each step and an 'X' indicates that a node is marked. The column 'Transaction' indicates which events belong to the transaction T and each new inclusion into it is denoted in italic.

C_1	C_2	C_3	C_4	C_5	C_6	C_7	C_8	C_9	Transaction
V		X							ιNeg(Paul),*δAcc(Paul)*
		X	X	X	V				ιNeg(Paul),δAcc(Paul)
		X	X	V					ιNeg(Paul),δAcc(Paul)
			V	X					ιNeg(Paul),δAcc(Paul)
				V					ιNeg(Paul),δAcc(Paul),*δPart(Paul)*
						V			ιNeg(Paul),δAcc(Paul),δPart(Paul),*δRec(Paul)*

The integrity maintenance process finishes and the transaction T'={ιNeg(Paul), δAcc(Paul), δPart(Paul), δRec(Paul)} is obtained. Note that this is the only transaction that maintains database consistency in our example.

To maintain database consistency in this example, we have processed only 6 conditions. In particular, we should note that none of them has been considered more than once. On the contrary, if we had not taken into account the information provided by the Precedence Graph, 35 conditions would had been processed. The reason is that in the latter case, when a condition is repaired all other conditions must be checked again for consistency even though they were already false prior to the repair and they could not be violated by it. This important drawback is shared by all methods proposed up to now for integrity maintenance.

In fact, it is sufficient for us that only one integrity constraint is repaired to have a better performance than integrity maintenance methods proposed up to now. Even in this simple case, current methods must reconsider again previously processed constraints. The number of unnecessary constraints processed by these methods significantly increases when the complexity of the database, of the considered transactions and of the number of necessary repairs augments.

6. Relation with Previous Work

A significant amount of work has been devoted to the area of integrity checking to define the order in which derived predicates should be evaluated to optimize the test of whether a transaction violates an integrity constraint [Ple93, Sel95]. In this sense, several graphs that define this order have been proposed. Similar work has been performed in the area of active databases to explicitly state the relationship between the activation of rules for predicting termination and confluence of active rules [BW94, AHW95].

Work in these two areas is different from ours since we are aimed at determining the order in which integrity constraints should be handled and not the order of evaluation of predicates involved in an integrity constraint definition. In fact, this latter order is defined by our Events Dependency Graph which states the relationship between base events and their potential effect on derived events and conditions. However, as we have seen, this graph is not sufficient to determine the order of processing integrity constraints.

Work most related to ours has been proposed in the area of integrity maintenance. Methods proposed up to date in this area have paid little attention in efficiency issues. A significative exception is the work performed by Gertz [Ger93, Ger94].

Gertz proposes to carry out at definition time the analysis and the specification of reactions on constraint violations. He provides a declarative specification language for reactions on violations suitable to express several integrity constraints enforcement approaches and describes how to obtain, once the integrity constraints and their corresponding reactions have been specified by the designer, a dependency graph which expresses the relationship between repairs and potential violations of integrity constraints.

Several differences exist between Gertz's proposal and ours. The first one is related to the way of handling integrity maintenance. Gertz proposes the designer to explicitly specify reactions to integrity constraints violations, while we consider these reactions to be automatically generated from the definition of the integrity constraints. Thus, looking for dependencies between integrity constraints is more complex in our approach since they are not explicitly stated and have to be implicitly derived from the integrity constraints definition.

Another important difference refers to the expressiveness of the definition language considered in both proposals. Gertz's proposal is restricted to databases without deductive rules, thus considering only flat integrity constraints (i.e. constraints that are defined only by means of base predicates); and it is restricted also to integrity constraints in Implicative Normal Form (which does not allow negation in the body of a constraint). On the contrary, we handle deductive rules as well as non-flat integrity constraints and we allow negation to appear in the body of the rules and of the constraints (in fact, the only requirements we impose on the database are those of allowedness and stratification which are much more general than Gertz requirements). Thus, our technique can be applied in more cases than Gertz's technique. It is also worth to mention the additional complexity of our approach due to the fact that we have to take the definition of derived predicates into account.

Finally, if more than one dependency exists between two integrity constraints, Gertz forces to the designer to weight all possible reactions to indicate which reaction should be considered with priority. Thus, it is guaranteed that at execution time only one repair is considered for a concrete violation of an integrity constraint. On the contrary, we take into account all possible repairs of a given integrity constraint definition. Thus, we will be able to restore database consistency in cases where Gertz's approach is not able to do it since the designer may not have appropriately weighted the repairs of integrity constraints.

7 Conclusions

We have proposed a technique for improving efficiency of the integrity maintenance process. This technique is based on the definition and execution of a graph, the Precedence Graph, which explicitly states the relationship between repairs of an integrity constraint and potential violations of other integrity constraints.

The proposed technique contributes to improving efficiency of integrity maintenance in two different ways. First, it minimizes the number of recomputations of testing whether a given constraint is violated. Second, it ensures that a repair of a certain integrity constraint is performed only when all repairs of other constraints that could induce a violation of it have been performed.

Another contribution of the technique proposed in this paper is that it allows to take into account integrity constraints to be checked in addition to integrity constraints to be maintained. Thus, we have shown a possible way of integrating into a single method both integrity constraint enforcement approaches.

Acknowledgements

We are grateful to D. Costal, A. Olivé, J. A. Pastor, C. Quer, M. R. Sancho, J. Sistac and T. Urpí for many useful comments and discussions. This work has been partially supported by the CICYT PRONTIC program project TIC94-0512.

References

[Abi88]   Abiteboul, S. "Updates, a New Frontier", Int. Conf. on Database Theory (ICDT'88), Springer, 1988, pp.1-18.

[AHW95]   Aiken, A.; Hellerstein, J.M.; Widom, J. "Static Analysis Techniques for Predicting the Behavior of Active Database Rules", ACM Transactions on Database Systems, Vol. 20, N° 1, Mrach 1995, pp. 3-41.

[BR86]   Bancilhon, F.; Ramakrishnan, R, "An Amateur's Introduction to Recursive Query Processing", Proc. ACM SIGMOD Int. Conf. on Management of Data, Washington D.C., 1986.

[BW94]   Baralis, E.; Widom, J. "An Algebraic Approach to Rule Analysis in Expert Database Systems", Proc. of the 20th VLDB Conference, Santiago, Chile, 1994, pp. 475-486.

[GCMD94] García, C.; Celma, M; Mota, L.; Decker, H. "Comparing and Synthesising Integrity Checking Methods for Deductive Databases", Int. Conf. on Data Engineering (ICDE'94), Houston (Texas), 1994, pp. 214-222.

[CHM95]   Chen, I.A.; Hull, R.; McLeod, D. "An Execution Model for Limited Ambiguity Rules and Its Application to Derived Data Update". ACM Transactions on Database Systems, Vol. 20, N° 4, December 1995, pp. 365-413.

[Cos95]   Costal, D. "Un mètode de planificació basat en l'actualització de vistes en bases de dades deductives", PhD Thesis, Barcelona, 1995 (in catalan).

[Dec89]   Decker, H. "The Range Form of databases or How to avoid Floundering", Proc. 5th ÖGAI, Springer-Verlag, 1989.

[Dec96]   Decker, H. "An Extension of SLD by Abduction and Integrity Maintenance for View Updating in Deductive Databases", Joint International Conference and Symposium on Logic Programming (JICSLP'96), Bonn (Germany), 1996.

[Ger93]   Gertz, M. "On Specifying the Reactive Behavior on Constraint Violations", Informatik-Berichte 2/93, Institut für Informatik, Universität Hannover, 1993.

[Ger94]   Gertz, M. "Specifying Reactive Integrity Control for Active Databases", Research Issiues on Data Engineering: Active Databases (RIDE-ADS'94), Houston, Texas, 1994, pp. 62-70.

[Llo87]   Lloyd, J.W. "Foundations on Logic Programming", 2nd edition, Springer, 1987.

[LT84]   Lloyd, J.W.; Topor, R.W. "Making Prolog More Expressive". Journal of Logic Programming, 1984, No. 3, pp. 225-240.

[ML91]   Moerkotte, G; Lockemann, P.C. "Reactive Consistency Control in Deductive Databases", ACM Transactions on Database Systems, Vol. 16, No. 4, December 1991, pp. 670-702.

[MT95]   Mayol, E.; Teniente, E. "Towards an Efficient Method for Updating Consistent Deductive Databases", Basque International Workshop on Information Techlogogy (BIWIT'96): Data Management Systems, IEEE Computer Society Press, San Sebastian, Spain, 1996, pp. 113-122.

[MT97]   Mayol, E.; Teniente, E. "Structuring the Process of Integrity Maintenance (Extended Version)", Technical Report RR-97/29, 1997, Universitat Politècnica de Catalunya.

[Oli91]   Olivé, A. "Integrity Checking in Deductive Databases", Proc. of the 17th VLDB Conference, Barcelona, Catalonia, 1991, pp. 513-523.

[Ple93]   Plexousakis, D. "Integrity Constraint and Rule Maintenance in Temporal Deductive Knowledge Bases", Proc. of the 19th VLDB Conference, Dublin, Ireland, 1993, pp. 146-157.

[Sel95]   Seljée, R. "A New Method for Integrity Constraints Checking in Deductive Databases", Data & Knowledge Engineering, Vol. 15, 1995, pp. 63-102.

[TO95]   Teniente, E.; Olivé, A. "Updating Knowledge Bases while Maintaining their Consistency", The VLDB Journal, Vol. 4, Num. 2, 1995, pp. 193-241.

[TU95]   Teniente, E.; Urpí, T. "A Common Framework for Classifying and Specifying Deductive Database Updating Problems", International Conference on Data Engineering (ICDE'95), Taipei, 1995, pp. 173-182.

[UO92]   Urpí, T.; Olivé, A. "A Method for Change Computation in Deductive Databases", Proc. of the 18th VLDB Conference, Vancouver, 1992, pp. 225-237.

[Wüt93]   Wüthrich, B. "On Updates and Inconsistency Repairing in Deductive databases", Int. Conf. on Data Engineering, Vienna, 1993, pp. 608 - 615.

A Retrieval Mechanism for Semi-Structured Photographic Collections

Joemon M. Jose and David J. Harper

The Robert Gordon University
Aberdeen, UK, AB25 1HG.
{j.jose,d.harper}@scms.rgu.ac.uk

Abstract. In this paper, a new approach for retrieval from semi-structured photographic collections is described. We have developed a retrieval model based on the Dempster-Shafer theory of evidence combination. Basic concepts of the Dempster-Shafer theory are explained and the suitability of this theory for information retrieval is explored. A retrieval model for a semi-structured photographic collection is presented. Extensibility of this retrieval model for multimedia information retrieval is discussed. Integration of database and information retrieval concepts is a major requirement for semi-structured multimedia information retrieval and is accomplished in this model. A novel indexing scheme for photographic materials is described. We use spatial features, which are objects and their location, as photographic features. We have developed a multi-modal query interface for querying a photographic collection. A prototype system, Epic, has been implemented and is described in this paper.

1 Introduction

Due to the widespread use of photographs in everyday life, there is a need for storing, managing and retrieving photographs [Orn95]. A large amount of pictorial information is produced in domains like the newspaper industry, the advertising business and the publishing industry. Journalists may look for photographs that describe an event or concern a person. Advertising professionals and publishers may look for photographs that are most useful for conveying their ideas. A number of commercial as well as in-house photographic repositories support these large populations of desirous searchers [Caw93,FMBR95].

Most of these photographic or other similar multimedia repositories are semi-structured. By semi-structured, we mean that the data has no absolute schema fixed in advance, and its structure may be irregular or incomplete. As an example, a newspaper photographic collection may contain photographs, the report or story published along with that photograph, reporter's name, date, photographer's name etc. Searchers may need exact match retrieval based on some attributes of these documents (eg. photographer name) and inexact match retrieval for some other attributes (eg. story) or a combination of both. Moreover, to cater for the wide-ranging access requirements to a multimedia repository, we need to provide retrieval based on the content of the various media types [GR95]. Unfortunately, with the present state of image processing techniques, we cannot achieve large scale domain independent recognition of the content of images. However, a number of promising approaches indicate some results in fairly restricted domains [NBE+93,O'D93]. In the absence of a single ideal feature extraction technique and also considering multiple types of data and various access requirements, it is our contention that retrieval effectiveness can be improved if we combine or integrate different feature extraction and retrieval mechanisms [JH95].

Our approach is depicted in Fig. 1. A multimedia collection can be queried in a variety of ways. The idea is to match a query component with a corresponding component of the document (eg. image query with the image component of the document) and arrive at a similarity value. This activity will result in one or more similarity values for the documents in the collection. What we need next is a flexible and efficient method for combining these similarity values to arrive at a final score. This combination method should also have the power to combine exact (DB) and inexact (IR) match retrieval. We propose to use the powerful Dempster-Shafer method for combining evidence from multiple sources. We have developed a retrieval model based on the Dempster-Shafer approach which satisfies all the above requirements and this model is presented in this paper. The goal of this paper is to describe a new retrieval model that can be

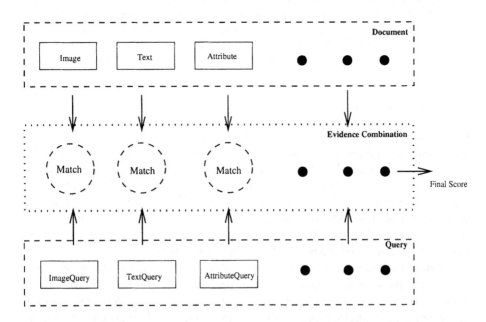

Fig. 1. Combining different retrieval mechanisms

used for multimedia information retrieval and also for database and information retrieval integration. To demonstrate the feasibility of our approach, we have applied this method to a collection of photographs. The outline of this paper is as follows. We will introduce the Dempster-Shafer theory followed by an exploration of the properties of this theory for information retrieval applications. After that, we will describe the application of this theory in photographic retrieval. Then, we will discuss the implementation of a prototype photograph retrieval system. Subsequently, we will discuss related work and conclude.

2 Dempster-Shafer Theory

Dempster-Shafer theory provides a framework for accumulation of evidence and its combination. The heart of this theory is Dempster's rule of combination: the combination of degrees of belief or support based on one body of evidence with those based on an entirely distinct body of evidence. This theory is a generalisation of the Bayesian approach, in which the commitment of a portion of belief to a proposition implies that the rest of belief is committed to the negation of the proposition. In the Dempster-Shafer formalism, commitment of a portion of the belief to one proposition does not imply commitment of the rest of its belief to its negation. In the absence of any evidence in support of the negation of a proposition, the remaining belief is assigned to the entire set and thus allows us to represent our uncertainty. In the following, the basic structures and the combination method of Dempster-Shafer theory are described [Sha76].

2.1 Frame of Discernment

The *frame of discernment*, denoted by Θ, is an exhaustive set of mutually exclusive elements that can be interpreted as hypotheses or propositions. The power set that contains all the subsets of Θ is denoted by 2^Θ and the elements of this power set are also considered as hypotheses.

As an example, consider a collection of documents containing three documents say d_1, d_2, d_3. Then, the possible propositions of interest would be: with respect to an information need, document $\{d_i\}, i = 1, 2, 3$ is relevant, documents $\{d_i, d_j\}, i, j = 1, 2, 3$, are relevant, and documents $\{d_1, d_2, d_3\}$ are relevant. Hence, in this case the frame of discernment $\Theta = \{d_1, d_2, d_3\}$ and the subsets of Θ corresponds to our propositions of interest.

When a proposition corresponds to a subset of a frame of discernment, we will say that the frame discerns that proposition.

2.2 Basic Probability Assignment

The Dempster-Shafer theory uses a number in the range $[0, 1]$ to indicate the degree of belief in a hypothesis or proposition given a piece of evidence. This number is the degree to which the evidence supports the hypothesis. And the impact of the distinct piece of evidence on the subsets of Θ is represented by a function called a basic probability assignment (*bpa*) or mass function, and is denoted by m.

Definition 1. If Θ is a frame of discernment, then a function $m : 2^\Theta \to [0,1]$ is called a *basic probability assignment* whenever

$$m(\emptyset) = 0 \text{ and } \sum_{A \subseteq \Theta} m(A) = 1.$$

The set $F = \{A | A \subseteq \Theta, m(A) > 0\}$ is called a focal element set and elements of this set are called focal elements of the mass function.

The quantity $m(A)$ is a measure of that portion of the total belief committed exactly to A, where $A \subseteq \Theta$, and the total belief is one. This portion of belief cannot be further subdivided among the subsets of A and does not include portions of belief committed to subsets of A. The quantity $m(\Theta)$ is a measure of that portion of the total that remains unassigned after commitment of belief to various proper subsets of Θ. Thus, the *bpa* assigned to Θ represents the 'uncertainty' of the evidence.

2.3 Belief Function and Belief Interval

In the Dempster-Shafer formalism, the total belief in a proposition A is represented by an interval, say $[B(A), P(A)]$. The lower value, $B(A)$ represents the support for the proposition A and sets minimum value for its likelihood. The upper value, $P(A)$, denotes the plausibility of that proposition and establishes a maximum likelihood. That is, $P(A)$ expresses how much we should believe in a proposition if all currently unknown facts were to support that proposition. Thus the true belief in that proposition will be somewhere in the interval $[B, P]$. The width of a belief interval can also be regarded as the amount of uncertainty with respect to a hypothesis, given the evidence. The quantity $B(A)$ includes degree of belief committed exactly to A and also to the subsets of A.

An understanding of belief functions and belief intervals is not necessary for the purpose of this paper. For more information see [Sha76].

2.4 Combination of Evidence

Mathematically, Dempster's rule is simply a rule for computing, from two or more belief functions over the same set Θ, a new belief function called their orthogonal sum. This rule corresponds to the pooling of evidence: if the mass functions being combined are based on entirely distinct bodies of evidence and the set Θ discerns the relevant interaction between those bodies of evidence, then the orthogonal sum gives degrees of belief that are appropriate on the basis of combined evidence.

Let m_1 and m_2 are two mass functions defined in the frame of discernment Θ. Then a new mass function, m, is defined as follows:

$$m(A) = \frac{\sum_{B \cap C = A} m_1(B) \star m_2(C)}{1 - \sum_{B \cap C = \emptyset} m_1(B) \star m_2(C)} \quad A, B, C \subseteq \Theta \qquad (1)$$

This is known as Dempster-Shafer evidence combination rule.

3 Exploration of Dempster-Shafer Theory

What is the suitability of Dempster-Shafer theory for information retrieval? In this section, we will answer this question by exploring certain aspects of the Dempster-Shafer theory.

In general, the Dempster-Shafer evidence combination is computationally expensive. Considering the need to retrieve from large collections like TREC, the application of the Dempster-Shafer combination method will involve serious computational effort. In the following, we will show how we can simplify the evidence combination method in a particular case where we have positive evidence for singleton hypotheses only. We will also analyse the behaviour of this combination function in some specific cases of uncertainty. Following that, we will show the power of Dempster-Shafer combination method for database and information retrieval integration.

Let us consider a frame of discernment with three hypotheses, i.e. $\Theta = \{d_1, d_2, d_3\}$. Suppose, m_1 and m_2 are two mass functions defined on Θ based on two distinct bodies of evidence. Then $m_1(\Theta)$ and $m_2(\Theta)$ represent the uncertainties in those bodies of evidence. Let us assume that the focal elements of these two mass functions are the singleton hypotheses and the frame Θ i.e., we have positive belief for $\{d_1\}, \{d_2\}, \{d_3\}$ and Θ only.

3.1 Simplification of the Combination Method

In this section, we will show the simplification of the combination method shown in equation (1).

The orthogonal sum $m_1 \oplus m_2$, say m, can be computed using the combination method in equation (1):

$$m(\{d_i\}) = \frac{m_1(\{d_i\}) \star m_2(\{d_i\}) + m_1(\Theta) \star m_2(\{d_i\}) + m_1(\{d_i\}) \star m_2(\Theta)}{1 - \sum_{\{d_k\} \cap \{d_j\} = \emptyset} m_1(\{d_k\}) \star m_2(\{d_j\})}$$

The denominator in the above equation is a normalising factor and is independent of $\{d_i\}$. Hence, the above equation can be written as,

$$m(\{d_i\}) \propto m_1(\{d_i\}) \star m_2(\{d_i\}) + m_1(\Theta) \star m_2(\{d_i\}) + m_1(\{d_i\}) \star m_2(\Theta) \quad (2)$$

Equation (2) can be used to compute combined degrees of belief and is computationally much less expensive than the Dempster-Shafer combination function given in equation (1). Thus, given distinct bodies of evidence that have positive impact on singleton hypotheses only, we can apply this simplified formula for evidence combination. The resulting mass values $m(\{d_i\})$ can be normalised by dividing each by $\sum_i m(\{d_i\})$. However, this is not necessary as relative belief values are sufficient for ranking retrieved documents.

The rule of combination shown in equations (1) and (2) is a rule for combining a pair of belief functions, but by repeatedly applying it, one can obviously combine any number of belief functions. The Dempster-Shafer combination is commutative ([Sha76], page 61, Theorem 3.3) and hence the order in which evidence is combined is not important.

3.2   Boundary Conditions

In this section, we will look into the behaviour of the theory in various cases of uncertainty.

In the case of complete confidence in a piece of evidence we have $m(\Theta) = 0$, and then m reduces to be a probability function.

If we have complete confidence in two bodies of evidence then equation (2) becomes:

$$m(\{d_i\}) \propto m_1(\{d_i\}) \star m_2(\{d_i\}) + 0 \star m_2(\{d_i\}) + m_1(\{d_i\}) \star 0 \qquad (3)$$

$$\text{i.e.,   } m(\{d_i\}) \propto m_1(\{d_i\}) \star m_2(\{d_i\})$$

That is, in the case of complete evidence, Dempster-Shafer based combination reduces to be a probability based combination method.

In the case where we have complete confidence in one piece of evidence, say in m_1 (i.e., $m_1(\Theta) = 0$.) then equation (2) becomes:

$$m(\{d_i\}) \propto m_1(\{d_i\}) \star m_2(\{d_i\}) + 0 \star m_2(\{d_i\}) + m_1(\{d_i\}) \star m_2(\Theta)$$

$$\text{i.e.,   } m(\{d_i\}) \propto m_1(\{d_i\}) \star m_2(\{d_i\}) + m_1(\{d_i\}) \star m_2(\Theta) \qquad (4)$$

In this case, the mass function for which we have complete confidence contributes more towards the combined belief.

If $m_1(\Theta) = m_2(\Theta) = \mu$ then equation (2) becomes:

$$m(\{d_i\}) \propto m_1(\{d_i\}) \star m_2(\{d_i\}) + \mu \star m_2(\{d_i\}) + m_1(\{d_i\}) \star \mu$$

$$\text{i.e.,   } m(\{d_i\}) \propto m_1(\{d_i\}) \star m_2(\{d_i\}) + \mu \star [m_2(\{d_i\}) + m_1(\{d_i\})]$$

In this case, the proposition with high belief will contribute more towards the combined belief.

With the above observations, we could conclude that the behaviour of the theory accords well with the general intuition on combining evidence.

3.3   DB and IR Integration

An integrated framework in which we can provide exact match and inexact match retrieval is an essential requirement for retrieval from semi-structured information repositories. Here, we will describe the power of the Dempster-Shafer combination method in handling exact match and inexact match retrieval in one computational framework.

We have seen above that in the case of complete confidence in one body of evidence, say in m_1 (i.e., $m_1(\Theta) = 0$.) the equation (2) reduces to the equation (4).

In equation (4), if $m_1(\{d_i\}) = 0$ then the combined belief $m(\{d_i\}) = 0$.

That is, if we have complete confidence in a body of evidence, then this combination mechanism will impose a filtering condition on the combined belief. We will have final belief only for those hypotheses which have positive belief based on complete evidence. Thus, for exact match retrieval we model mass functions without any uncertainty. Hence, when we apply equation (2) to combine evidences, the resulting mass function will provide belief for hypotheses which satisfy the exact match criterion.

This property makes the combination function in equation (2) more suitable for combining exact and inexact match retrieval. Moreover, like with handling vague queries in conventional database systems we could incorporate distance metrics for attribute-value queries.

We have seen the behaviour of the theory in situations where mass functions generate positive evidence for singleton hypotheses. In such situations, application of equation (2) for evidence combination reduces computational expenses. Now, we will show the application of this theory in a photographic retrieval situation where we model mass functions with focal elements as singleton hypotheses.

4 A Photographic Retrieval Model

In this section, we will explain our retrieval model, based on the simplified Dempster-Shafer theory, applied to the case of photographic information retrieval.

We have a photographic collection in which the photographs are stored along with various textual information. To simplify the discussion, and without loss of generality, we assume that a document in the collection has only two components, a picture component and a text component. Hence, we define a document as follows.

Definition 2. A *multimedia document* $\mathcal{M}$ is a structure $\mathcal{M} = \langle P, T \rangle$ where P is the photographic component of $\mathcal{M}$, and T is its textual component.

The various querying mechanisms are explained in the next section and for the sake of this discussion we assume that there are two types of querying: text and picture querying. Searchers can use either of these or both. Thus, a query can also be seen as a document: it also has two components, a picture query component and a text query component. Each query component is considered as a body of evidence and we create mass functions based on these. Then, these mass functions are combined to generate a final belief. Later, we will see how a searcher's uncertainty in the representation of a query component is dealt with.

In the following, we will explain how we obtain basic probability assignments based on different sources of evidence. It is assumed that a collection of N documents exists. Then, the frame of discernment is $\Theta = \{d_1, d_2, \ldots, d_N\}$. The corresponding proposition of interest is that *a document d_i is relevant to the searcher's information need.*

Next we will introduce our picture characterisation scheme and the corresponding querying mechanism. Following that, the individual retrieval models for pictorial matching and text matching are described. At the end of this section, we will show the evidence combination approach.

4.1 Photograph Indexing and Querying

One important aspect of designing access methods for picture collections is determining the sort of features that can be used for retrieval. We propose to use objects in the photograph and their locations as features for picture retrieval. We refer to these features as the spatial features from a photograph. In this section the spatial indexing and querying method is discussed along with a discussion of the usefulness of spatial features for retrieval.

Spatial Indexing. Commonly, images are characterised by associating with them a set of keywords or some attribute-value pairs [Mos94]. These keywords are assigned to the image manually and used for retrieval. However, this approach has all the drawbacks of the standard text retrieval systems that use manually assigned keywords for retrieval. Moreover, the problems would be exacerbated if one uses keywords to describe spatial relationships among objects in the image. This is because numerous spatial relationships are possible, even between two objects, and any particular relationship may be described in various ways.

This situation can be ameliorated by associating the keywords with the corresponding objects in the photograph instead of associating them with the entire picture. Then, the object and the corresponding location constitute an indexing feature.

Photographs can be seen as consisting of objects. These may be objects like people, buildings, automobiles, gardens, etc. The objects have certain locations in the image. Hence we can describe an image P as $P= \{(\lambda_1,\rho_1),(\lambda_2,\rho_2), \ldots \}$, where λ_1, λ_2, $\lambda_3,\ldots$ are the objects and ρ_1, ρ_2, $\rho_3,\ldots$ are their respective regions. These objects and their region are used as picture features and are known as spatial features.

Computing tools can be provided to extract these features with the minimum intervention from the user. To index an image, the indexer identifies objects and specifies the locations of these objects in the image. This is done by drawing a box (rectangle) around the object using the mouse. Then, the indexer describes this object by naming it. From these descriptions, the system automatically generates spatial features. In comparison with the keyword based retrieval approach, the user is performing minimal additional work by identifying the area in which objects appear in an image.

Why Spatial Indexing. We will describe briefly why we believe spatial indexing can be useful for effective picture retrieval. More detailed discussion on spatial features is available in [JH95].

Relatively few studies have been conducted into the kind of queries that users are likely to put to an image collection. Enser [Ens93] has done a study on user queries to the Hulton Deutch collection. He says, 'Sometimes the need to translate the client's mental image of his information need into a linguistic expression is facilitated by the identification of that need with a particular picture, or by the incorporation of the sketch, in those cases where the request is received by letter or fax'. If the user has a mental image of a need, we believe this can be more readily translated into a set of objects and their relative or absolute locations in a picture.

Lansdale et.al. [LSW96] have described the need for a spatially depicted interface for retrieval from visual repositories. Their initial experiments have shown that a spatially depictive interface to visual collections will enhance the retrieval effectiveness. Also, an interface that is expressive enough will give a searcher an opportunity to reflect on her information need and modify it as required.

Spatial Querying. If the spatial features are useful for picture retrieval then the question is "how do we use them for querying?". Spatial querying is described in here.

A query canvas of the size of a photograph is provided for spatial querying [JHH96]. Searchers can draw rectangles on this query canvas and label them. From these, the system automatically derives spatial query features.

As an example, consider a user who wants a photograph of a fountain with a tree behind it. Assuming that the user has a mental image of a photograph with a tree in one corner and a fountain in the middle, two boxes can be drawn on the query canvas: one in a corner and the other at the center. The box at the corner will be named as 'tree' and the one at the center will be named as 'fountain'. In this way, a user's mental image of the information need can be captured.

In addition to spatial querying, searchers can perform other types of data access such as retrieval based on attribute-value pair and similarity retrieval based on textual features. This is discussed in section 5.

4.2 Basic Probability Assignment based on the Photographic Component

In the spatial retrieval model, the aim is to match the characterisation of the spatial component of the query to the characterisation of the spatial component of the documents. The query is characterised by spatial features. Using these features as evidence, a belief is calculated that indicates support for the proposition of interest. To formalise these notions, the following definitions will be used.

Definition 3. A *region* ρ is a structure $\rho = \langle x, y, w, h \rangle$ where (x, y) is the origin of the rectangular area defining the region, and w and h are the width and height of the rectangular area.

Definition 4. A *spatial feature* ϕ is a structure $\phi = \langle \lambda, \rho \rangle$ where ρ is a region and λ is a label identifying the object associated with the region ρ.

Definition 5. A *picture* or spatial component P is a set $P = \{\phi\}$ where $\{\phi\}$ is a set of spatial features forming the characterisation of the picture.

Definition 6. Given two regions ρ_1 and ρ_2. Then the *distance* between the regions ρ_1 and ρ_2 is defined as

$$D(\rho_1, \rho_2) = 1-$$

$$\frac{\sqrt{(x_1 - x_2)^2 + (y_1 - y_2)^2 + ((x_1 + w_1) - (x_2 + w_2))^2 + ((y_1 + h_1) - (y_2 + h_2))^2}}{\Delta}$$

where Δ is a normalising factor depending on the dimension of the picture P.

The value of D is in the range $[0,1]$ where zero represents no similarity and 1 represents perfect similarity between the two regions. This distance measure takes into account the position as well as size of each region.

Using this measure we get a similarity value of one for two rectangles with the same origin and extent. This similarity value decreases as rectangles move apart and will be zero for two rectangles (points!) at the opposite corners of the space. This distance measure is used as spatial similarity.

Definition 7. Let λ_i and λ_j be the labels of two spatial features. Then, we can define a *picture indicator function* as follows

$$I(\lambda_i, \lambda_j) = \begin{cases} 1 & \text{if } \lambda_i = \lambda_j \\ 0 & \text{otherwise} \end{cases}$$

Definition 8. Let P_D be a picture document and let P_Q be a picture query and $\phi_q = \langle \lambda_q, \rho_q \rangle$ be a spatial feature in P_Q. Then, the *Spatial Filter Function* for ϕ_q is defined as

$$\mathcal{F}(\phi_q, P_D) = I(\lambda_q, \lambda_j) \star max_j D(\rho_q, \rho_j)$$

where $\phi_j = \langle \lambda_j, \rho_j \rangle$, and $\phi_j \in P_D$

When there are more than two instances of a same object in the photograph, this spatial filter function produces a similarity value for the closest object to the query feature. Hence, it avoids counting the same feature more than once and uses the highest similarity possible for a query feature.

Using the above definitions, we can define the evidence (or similarity score) for a document based on the spatial component as follows:

Definition 9. Let P_D be a picture document, and let P_Q be a picture query. Then, the similarity between P_D and P_Q can be defined as

$$\text{sim}(P_D, P_Q) = \sum_{\phi_i \in P_Q} \mathcal{F}(\phi_i, P_D)$$

By computing the similarity between spatial query component and the picture query component, we reach a positive similarity value for some documents in the collection and zero for the rest. The next step is to convert these similarity values into a mass function (*bpas*). Scores are normalised and converted into *bpas* by dividing each by the sum of all the scores.

A searcher is given an opportunity to specify his confidence, μ, in each component of the query. This confidence is interpreted as the searcher's certainty in that query representation. Then the resulting uncertainty in that query representation is $(1 - \mu)$. This uncertainty $(1 - \mu)$, can be propagated by assigning a belief $(1 - \mu)$ to the set of all documents (i.e. to the frame of discernment Θ). This means that the belief $(1 - \mu)$ could not be assigned to any smaller subsets of Θ based on the evidence at hand, but must instead be assumed to be distributed in some (unknown) manner among other focal elements of Θ. That is $m(\Theta) = 1 - \mu$. To make $\sum_i m(\{d_i\}) = 1$, we multiply each normalised score by μ. These resulting m values constitute the mass function or basic probability assignments based on the spatial query component. This process is shown in the table below.

Document	Score	Norm. Score	bpa
d_1	s_1	$n_1 = \frac{s_1}{S}$	$n_1 \star \mu = m(\{d_1\})$
d_2	s_2	$n_2 = \frac{s_2}{S}$	$n_2 \star \mu = m(\{d_2\})$
$\vdots$	$\vdots$	$\vdots$	$\vdots$
d_N	s_N	$n_N = \frac{s_N}{S}$	$n_N \star \mu = m(\{d_N\})$
Θ	0	0	$(1 - \mu) = m(\Theta)$
Sum	$\sum_{i=1}^{N} s_i = S$	1	1

4.3 Basic Probability Assignment based on the Textual Component

Here, the objective is to match the textual representation of the document with the textual component of the query. We take the textual query features as evidence, and calculate the belief in these propositions. Before explaining the computation, we need the following definitions.

Definition 10. A *text component* T is a set $T = \{\tau\}$ where $\{\tau\}$ is a set of text features (e.g. terms in a natural language document).

Definition 11. Let τ be a text feature. Then a (*inverse document frequency*) weight $w(\tau)$ can be associated with τ as follows

$$w(\tau) = \log \frac{N}{f(\tau)}$$

where N is the total number of documents in the document collection.

Definition 12. Let τ_i and τ_j be two text features. Then, we can define a *text indicator function* as follows

$$I(\tau_i, \tau_j) = \begin{cases} 1 & \text{if } \tau_i = \tau_j \\ 0 & \text{otherwise} \end{cases}$$

Using the above definitions, we could define the evidence (or score) for a document based on the text component of the query as follows:

Definition 13. Let T_D be a text document, and let T_Q be a text query. Then, the similarity between T_D and T_Q can be defined as

$$\text{sim}(T_D, T_Q) = \sum_{\tau_i \in T_Q} \sum_{\tau_j \in T_D} I(\tau_i, \tau_j) \star w(\tau_i)$$

This evidence is also normalised and the searcher's uncertainty in the representation of the textual query component is also taken into account by assigning it to the frame of discernment. A belief value is computed using the same procedure as used in the pictorial case explained at the end of the section 4.2.

4.4 Evidence Combination

Now the component matching functions have been designed for both the textual and the picture component, evidence coming from both matching processes will have to be combined in order to arrive at one overall relevance score for the document given a query. Since we have positive evidence for singleton hypotheses only, the simplified Dempster-Shafer evidence combination mechanism described in equation (2) is applied.

Using equation (2), a combined belief is computed and the documents are presented to the searcher in decreasing order of belief.

In our present approach, we compute mass functions for a query component. However, we could compute mass functions for individual query features and then evidence combination can be applied. This may increase computational cost considerably and hence has not been considered for implementation.

We can extend this retrieval framework for more than two query components. We can model mass functions for any type of query components in a similar way and then the evidence combination formula can be applied. We have extended this model for simple database queries and described briefly in the next section.

5 Implementation

We have demonstrated the practicability of our approach by building a prototype photograph retrieval system, called *Epic*, which is described briefly below. Our implementation is based on a client-server architecture and communication between the client and the server takes place using the HTTP protocol. In order to sustain our retrieval model we need to have an extensible server system. This permits us to add support for different media types and feature extraction and matching techniques. We also need to have an architecture that support the integration of exact and inexact match retrieval.

We have built a server system that satisfies these objectives. The server system is an extension of the *ECLAIR* framework [HW92] and is built on the principles of extensibility and reusability. The idea is to exploit the features of an object-oriented database management system by building a layer of IR framework on top of it. This allows us to utilise the features provided by an underlying database management system. We have redesigned and extended *ECLAIR* and a light-weight data model that supports the representation of semi-structured collections has been built into this framework. For the representation of indexing features we use an inverted index structure. The data model and this index structure support the integration of exact and inexact match retrieval achieved in our retrieval model.

The client side of the application, namely the user interface, has been built using the JAVA programming language, and a snapshot of this interface is shown in Fig. 2. The upper left part of the figure is a multi-modal query interface and the bottom left is a result viewer. A document viewer is at the right hand side of the interface. The query interface supports various sorts of query mechanisms and the result viewer provides a thumb view of the retrieved documents. A searcher can select documents from the result viewer and view them in the document viewer.

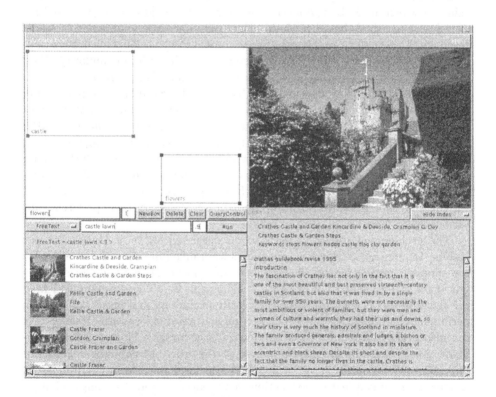

Fig. 2. Epic Interface

One component of the query interface is a query canvas where searchers can sketch spatial queries. It also has a text-based query interface where searchers can issue text queries. Searchers can also specify their confidence in each query component.

In the present implementation of the system we support simple database queries of the form " name=value". However, extending this interface for more complex queries is not considered to be a major problem, as we only need to add only the corresponding matching scheme in the server system. At present, a searcher can select a field name and specify their query term. The interface does not separate exact and inexact match queries but by assigning a confidence value of one the searcher is specifying a filtering condition which is equivalent to an exact match retrieval.

6 Discussion

Recently, integrated approaches to image retrieval have been discussed by many authors. In [OS95], the problem is approached from a database retrieval standpoint, in which an SQL-type mechanism is used to integrate content-based retrieval with attribute-based retrieval. They use information contained in hand-keyed database fields to supplement image content information. One drawback of this approach is that it cannot rank documents in the order of similarity. Also, the combination or filtering mechanism implemented using SQL is very rigid. WebSeer, a system being developed by Swain et al. [SFA97], uses information derived from analysing the image content to complement the textual information associated with an image and information derived from the image header. They have developed a form-based textual query interface for image searching on the web and they rank images based on their similarity value with the query. However, the final score is reached by an ad-hoc mechanism of combining similarities from various sources and then filtering on certain features. Moreover, searchers are not provided with an opportunity to specify their preference for various query features.

The problems identified in the systems discussed above are tackled in our system. Documents retrieved in our model are ranked in order of similarity. By the application of Dempster-Shafer theory we achieve flexible and efficient integration of various sources of evidence. As shown in Fig. 2, we have implemented the retrieval model for three types of feature extraction and matching. We can perform similarity retrieval based on textual features and/or spatial features. We can also perform attribute-based retrieval (exact match). Since the Dempster-Shafer combination function is commutative, the order of combining belief is not important. We could integrate a new retrieval mechanism into the framework as long as there is a feature extraction, representation and matching technique available. As an extension of this work, we are going to extend this retrieval model for colour and texture feature based retrieval.

What are the strengths of the retrieval framework discussed here in comparison to other approaches? First, we believe, this framework is a general one for multimedia information retrieval and can be extended to incorporate other media types and their corresponding feature extraction and matching techniques. Second, this framework allows the integration of exact and inexact match retrieval in one computational model.

Over the years, a lot of work has been done integrating database and information retrieval concepts. Most of this work has tried to exploit an existing database by building an IR system on top of it. A review of such work is available in [HW92]. The *ECLAIR* architecture described in the implementation section is one such approach. The *ECLAIR* architecture integrates the features of an object-oriented database management system with an IR framework. Our work is an extension of this work. However, in the original *ECLAIR* framework the integration of database and information retrieval aspects is not achieved in its retrieval model. In the retrieval framework discussed here, we can achieve the integration of exact and inexact match retrieval in one process. Schauble [Sch93] proposes an architecture for DB and IR integration. The major difference is that in our model we could achieve combination of evidence from multiple sources along with their specified uncertainty. This allows us to extend our system for any number of media and feature extraction techniques. However, we have not dealt with the problems arising from dynamic data. Motro [Mot88] discusses an approach to integrate vague queries into a relational database management system. They ranked documents in order of similarity and users are allowed to provide their own similarity metrics. In our retrieval framework users can also define their own matching mechanism (by extending the server framework). However, the major difference is that our integration mechanism is achieved in one computational framework.

Van Rijsbergen [vR92] discusses the inadequacy of the Bayesian approach for information retrieval applications in the context of the inherent uncertainty involved in various phases of retrieval. He further introduces the Jeffrey's conditioning for information retrieval applications. Jeffrey's conditioning provides a mechanism for revising probability measures in the light of uncertain evidence. Jeffrey's conditioning is a generalisation of the Bayesian approach by incorporating the passage of experience or a searcher's acquired knowledge during the course of retrieval. When the sum of uncertainties involved in the query representations is equal to one (i.e. $\sum_i \mu_i = 1$), our model satisfies Jeffrey's conditioning. However, in our model a searcher can express his uncertainty in a query representation independent of other query components. Moreover, Jeffrey's conditioning does not support exact and inexact match integration.

7 Conclusion

This work is grounded in the belief that progress in multimedia information retrieval can be made if different retrieval approaches can be combined or integrated in a flexible and efficient way. The Dempster-Shafer evidence combination mechanism provides a framework for achieving this goal. Since more and more multimedia collections are semi-structured in nature, we believe that it is time to develop a retrieval mechanism for semistructured repositories. We need to identify new features for providing effective retrieval for photographic collections.

Currently there is no single image processing technique that can be applied to images from diverse domains such as photographic collections. Therefore, there is need to develop and use semi-automatic techniques for image feature extraction. It is also very important to have a querying interface that exploits these image features for query representation.

The main contributions of our work are the following: we have proposed a new approach to multimedia information retrieval in which we combine multiple sources of evidence; and we have developed a retrieval model based on the Dempster-Shafer theory. This model provides a framework for retrieving information from semi-structured collections and integrates exact and inexact match retrieval. We have introduced a novel approach for picture retrieval which has the potential to provide more precise retrieval. A prototype system which is extensible and reusable has been built for photographic information retrieval.

Acknowledgements

We are grateful to Professor Keith van Rijsbergen for introducing us to the Dempster-Shafer theory. Discussions with Jan-Jaap IJdens at various stages of this work was highly beneficial. We would also like to thank David Hendry for his encouragement. Finally, thanks should go to the National Trust of Scotland. The work presented here has been supported by the Principal's Research Fund at the Robert Gordon University.

References

[Caw93]   A. E. Cawkell. Picture-queries and picture databases. *Journal of Information Science*, 19:409–423, 1993.

[Ens93]   P. G. B. Enser. Query analysis in a visual information retrieval context. *Journal of Document and Text Management*, 1(1):25–52, 1993.

[FMBR95] S. Flank, P. Martin, A. Balogh, and J. Rothey. Photofile: A digital library for image retrieval. In *Proceedings of International Conference on Multimedia Computing and Systems*, pages 292–295, Washington, D.C., 1995.

[GR95]   V. N. Gudivada and V. V. Raghavan. *IEEE Computer: Special Issue on Content-Based Image Retrieval Systems*, volume 28 of *9*. IEEE Press, September 1995.

[HW92]   D. J. Harper and A. D. M. Walker. ECLAIR: an extensible class library for information retrieval. *The Computer Journal*, 35(3):256–267, June 1992.

[JH95]   J. M. Jose and D. J. Harper. An integrated approach to image retrieval. *The New Review of Document and Text Management*, 1:167–181, 1995.

[JHH96]   J. M. Jose, D. J. Harper, and D. G. Hendry. A spatial feature based photograph retrieval system. In H. P. Frei, D. Harman, P. Schauble, and R. Wilkinson, editors, *Proceedings of the Nineteenth Annual International SIGIR Conference on Research and Development in Information Retrieval*, page 341. ACM Press, August 1996.

[LSW96]   M.W. Lansdale, S. A. R. Scrivener, and A. Woodcock. Developing practice with theory in HCI: applying models of spatial cognition for the design of pictorial databases. *International Journal of Human-Computer Studies.*, 44:777–799, 1996.

[Mos94]   J. Mostafa. Digital image representation and access. *Annual Review of Information Science and Technology*, 29:91–135, 1994.

[Mot88]   A. Motro. VAGUE: A user interface to relational database that permits vague queries. *ACM Transactions on Office Information Systems*, 6(3):187–214, July 1988.

[NBE⁺93] W. Niblack, R. Barber, W. Equitz, M. Flickner, E. Glasman, D. Petkovic, P. Yanker, C. Faloutsos, and G. Taubin. The qbic project: Querying images by content using color, texture, and shape. In W. Niblack, editor, *Proceedings of SPIE-93*, pages 173–187. SPIE, February 1993.

[O'D93]   M. H. O'Docherty. A multimedia information system with automatic content retrieval. Technical Report UMCS-93-2-2, Department of Computer Science, University of Manchester, Manchester M13 9PL, England, 1993.

[Orn95]   S. Ornager. The newspaper image database: Empirical supported analysis of users' typology and word association clusters. In E. Fox, P. Ingwersen, and R. Fidel, editors, *Proceedings of 18th SIGIR Conference*, pages 212–218, Seattle, July 1995. ACM Press.

[OS95]   V. Ogle and M. Stonebraker. Chabot: Retrieval from a relational database of images. *IEEE Computer*, 28(9):40–48, September 1995.

[Sch93]   P. Schauble. SPIDER: A multiuser information retrieval system for semistructured and dynamic data. In R. Korfhage, E. Rasmussen, and P. Willett, editors, *Proccedings of the sixteenth Annual Internatinal ACM SIGIR Conference on Research and Development in Information Retrieval*, pages 318–327. ACM Press, June-July 1993.

[SFA97]   M. J. Swain, C. Frankel, and V. Athitsos. WebSeer: An image search engine for the world wide web. In *IEEE Computer Vision and Pattern Recognition Conference (Submitted)*. http://www.cs.uchicago.edu/swain/pubs/CVPR97Sub.ps, June 1997.

[Sha76]   G. Shafer. *A Mathematical Theory of Evidence*. Princeton University Press, 1976.

[vR92]   C. J. van Rijsbergen. Probabilistic retrieval revisited. *The Computer Journal*, 35(3):291–298, 1992.

Encapsulating Multimedia Contents and a Copyright Protection Mechanism into Distributed Objects

Yutaka Kidawara[1], Katsumi Tanaka[2] and Kuniaki Uehara[3]

[1] Kobe Research Center, Telecommunications Advancement Organization of Japan,Kobe International Friendship Building,
Chuo Kobe 650, JAPAN
e-mail: kotaro@kobe-sc.tao.or.jp
[2] Graduate School of Science and Technology, Kobe University,
Nada Kobe 657, JAPAN
e-mail: tanaka@in.kobe-u.ac.jp
[3] Research Center for Urban Safety and Security, Kobe University,
Nada Kobe 657, JAPAN
e-mail: uehara@kobe-u.ac.jp

Abstract. We proposed an Encapsulated Multimedia Object (EMO) for the copyright protection. EMO as a Java applet is independent of computer hardware and operating systems. Also, it can control its view for each user. An EMO displays a complete image for a legal user. However, it displays an incomplete image for an illegal user. We developed a copyright protection prototype system by EMO and tested it. We found several useful features and also some limitations. Presently, we are re-designing the EMO and EMO database system. Also, we reported their concepts.

1 Introduction

Recently, much attention has been focused on the environment for creating, retrieving and delivering multimedia contents. Presently, several multimedia contents, such as still images, CG assets, video movies assets etc., can be delivered through the internet and/or CD-ROMs. Since these multimedia contents are digital data, they are easily duplicated and their copyright violated. This copyright protection problem for multimedia contents is one of the most serious problems in the multimedia industry. Conventionally, the delivering and the copyright management of multimedia contents has been centralized-controlled. For example, upon users' purchase requests, passwords are returned to the purchasing users. That is, the multimedia contents and the mechanism for copyright management have been completely separated. Recently, a new technology for copyright management has been developed, called " Information Hiding". For example, the technology of "water-marking" can provide permanently embedded copyright information in the data. In this paper, we will propose a new approach to cope with the copyright management for multimedia contents. Our main idea is to encapsulate original multimedia contents and its copyright protection mechanism into a form of "distributed object". For example, intuitively, a still image and its copyright protection method (including a user certification method) is encapsulated into a Java object. A downloaded object can autonomously solve its copyright management. This idea can bring the following additional functionalities which are needed to deliver and use multimedia contents.

- Providing multiple views of multimedia contents according to each user's status.
- Providing multiple index data for multimedia contents according to each user's status.

The major contributions of the present paper are summarized in the following.

The Concept of Encapsulation of Multimedia Contents and Management Methods We introduce the concept of "Encapsulated Multimedia Object (EMO)". Each EMO can have one of the following kinds of contents: a text, a still image, a motion image, a 3D image (such as VRML data). Each EMO contains its contents protection management mechanism including user certification and contents viewing management.

Implementation of EMOs as Java Applets We designed and implemented EMOs as Java applets. We will describe the implementation issues such as a Java applet as a copyright protection mechanism, user certification server, and their usefulness and current problems.

Possibilities of EMOs and EMO databases We will also consider the possibility of extending our current EMOs for other purposes as well as copyright protection. Also, we will describe some issues concerned with construction of EMO database management.

Section 2 describes the idea and the functionalities of the EMOs, especially for copyright protection. Section 3 describes the implementation issues of the EMOs. Section 4 will discuss the possibilities of extending our EMO concept. Section 5 is concluding remarks.

2 The Concept of Encapsulation of Multimedia Contents and Management Methods

2.1 Conventional copyright management

Most of the conventional copyright management methods have been based on centralized-control. That is, basically, a server manages the multimedia contents and controls their downloading. In general, the downloading procedure from a server to local computers through a network is described as follows.

1. A user connects to a server.
2. He/She selects his/her favorite multimedia content.
3. He/She issues a request to get the contents.
4. A server certifies the user and permits downloading.
5. He/She downloads it.
6. He/She uses it on his/her local computer.

It should be noted that the conventional method downloads a complete data after user certification process. After downloading, the distributor can not control the copyright of the sent data. Recently, information hiding technologies are used for multimedia. This technology is to embed information into an image signal and an audio signal [2][3]. They can not perceive without using a special method. The watermark is one of the information hiding technologies and is applied to an image data. Presently, some multimedia authoring tools support watermark technology to embed an author's copyright into his/her works. The watermarking technology can embed and can show his/her copyright. However, it does not protect from an illegal change and an illegal usage [1][4].

2.2 EMO basic concept

Using object oriented technology, the notion is of the object hiding its private data from other objects and the application programs. Encapsulating multimedia content into an object as private data, the content is hidden from other objects and their applications. This mechanism is very useful for enforcing restriction on illegal modification and to protect a multimedia content. EMO is based on this idea. It encapsulates multimedia contents, copyright information, server URL information and various methods into a single object. An image data is encapsulated into an EMO by a generating tool. A server stores EMOs and delivers them to users. If a user found his/her favorite EMO, he/she sends a user certification request to the server after downloading it . A server certifies the user and issues a usage permission. The EMO shows the complete data. If another user copies a document from the certified user which used the EMO, the EMO on the document checks the usage permission and shows "Unofficial copy" message on the complete image. Figure 1 shows our basic concept of a copyright management system by EMO.

2.3 EMO management method

The EMO encapsulates the original multimedia contents and their management methods into itself. An EMO can be downloaded by a conventional downloading procedure. When an EMO is used by an application software, the EMO calls its initializing method, user certification method and viewing-control method autonomously.

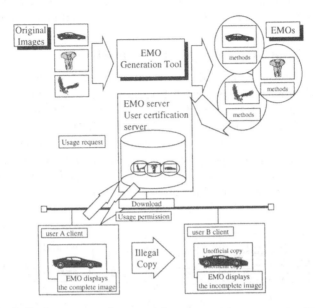

Fig. 1. Basic concept of a copyright management system by EMO

Initializing method After loading an EMO to an application software, the EMO calls its initializing method autonomously. This method opens the encapsulated multimedia contents, initializes several parameters and calls the permission check method. The method communicates to a user certification server through the network and checks the certified users.

Viewing-control This method controls the EMO's view in accordance with the user's permission. When the user is already certified, this method shows /plays a complete view of the EMO. On the other hand, if the user is not yet certified, it shows /plays an incomplete view of the EMO.

User certification request method This method sends user information and his local computer information to a certified server. Also, it requests user certification to the EMO server through the network. Accepting the user certification key from the server, the EMO gets its usage permission.

3   Implementation of EMOs as Java Applets

We believe that our notion of EMOs must run independently from computer hardware and operating systems. We selected Java language for this purpose because Java is secure, robust, portable and architecture-neutral. Also, Java can create "Applet" which is a portable program on the network. An applet is used for the small interactive program in an internet browser application. On the other hand, it is used as a mobile-agent [5] and a distributed object [6]. We implemented EMOs as Java applet, which work as new data management object.

3.1 Storing Image-data by Java class variables

Because the current Java language does not allow us to store Java applets on local clients, we used Java class variables to hold image-data. Figure 2 shows our implementation of EMOs by using the Java class variables. That is , an EMO (say EMO1 object) is implemented as an instance of an EMO class. Each EMO class can have only one instance. As shown in figure 2, the value of the class variable is realized as an instance of GraphicsClassBase class. Because of the limitation of the size of the value of a class variable, an instance of GraphicsClassBase class may be implemented as a set of instance of PixelNode class.

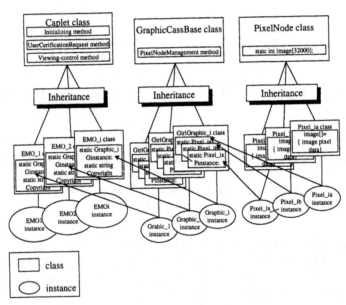

Fig. 2. A configuration of EMO as Java applet

3.2 Copyright protection mechanism

The Copyright protection of EMOs is realized by a combination of several methods, which are defined in the Caplet class as shown in figure 2. EMO creates the view from the encapsulated image data in the initializing method. And EMO communicates with a user certification server and checks whether he/she is certified or not. Although the usage-permitted EMO displays completely, a usage-prohibited EMO shows "Unofficial Copy" message on the encapsulated image. This mechanism is independent of the application. Each EMO checks the usage permission autonomously.

3.3 EMO generation tool

To create an EMO as a Java applet, Java programming knowledge is required. Moreover, the creator must write Java program code. We developed the EMO generation tool as a Java application. This tool transforms the original image data automatically to an EMO. We describe here the way to create an EMO by using our EMO generation tool.

1. A user select image data (such as GIF and JPEG) and describes its copyright and owner information.
2. The tool reads GIF and JPEG format image data and analyzes image data.
3. The tool generates a new subclass of Caplet class, and encapsulates the image data in its class variable.
4. The tool starts compiling the source code and generates an EMO_ith class.

Figure 3 shows our EMO generation tool.

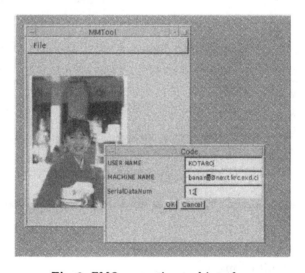

Fig. 3. EMO generating tool interface

3.4 Experiments

We tested some EMOs at several clients on the network(IBM PC, Macintosh, SUN, SGI etc.) under various applications. (Netscape, Cyberdoc, OpenDoc). Currently, the EMO mechanism is available at these environments. Presently, the EMOs are stored in a http server and hard-disks on local computer. Both the remote EMO and the local EMO can be used under various software applications just like the conventional image data. Figure 4 shows an example. This example uses four image objects on word processor software. It contains three certified EMOs and an uncertified EMO. The uncertified object shows "Unofficial copy" messages. On the other hand, the certified EMOs show their complete image. If other users copy this usage-permitted document, all EMOs showed autonomously "Unofficial copy" message on all the images. We tested the availability on various computers and several software applications. We can use these objects just like conventional data, and found that EMO was very useful for copyright management.

Fig. 4. An example EMO under the word processor application

3.5 Current limitations

We found current limitations as follows.

Each EMO can communicate with only a server that stores it. A local client computer downloads the Java applet from server and makes it run. This mechanism might be dangerous. An illegal applet might send a user's information to an other server. However, a Java applet is secure because Java restricts several functions from an applet. An applet can not read /write a client local disk and system resource information. Also, it can communicate with only the server that stores it. Because the SecurityManager class of a Java applet restricts them on several software applications. An EMO as a Java applet has the same restrictions. Therefore, all the necessary information for the user certification have to store in a server which the EMOs are stored.

An image data may consist of several Java class files. EMOs encapsulate an image data in several class variables. Since Java restricts the number of the class variables, massive image data may be separated over some Java classes. The Java compiler creates a Java class file for a Java class. As a result of this, an image data file change to some Java class files .

The size of an EMO is usually larger than an original image data. The size of an EMO class is larger than the size of the original image data. Analyzing an EMO class file, we found the size of a class variable initializing method is very large. The method is attached automatically by Java compiler. This method uses 4 steps to initialize a class variable and does not use a loop function. Therefore,the initializing method size is four times as big as any data we encapsulate.

4   Possibilities of EMOs and EMO databases

We tested the usefulness of the EMO as a Java applet. EMO is useful for protection of copyright. On the other hand, we also found several current limitations. We are now designing several extensions of EMOs and databases to extend the current EMO function.

4.1   Extended EMOs

We redesign current EMOs by encapsulating new items. Our extended EMO contains new indices for efficient retrieval. We call the new index "multi-level index". It consists of multiple levels of index information. Figure 5 shows the configuration.

Multi-level index Some users wish to retrieve impressively multimedia contents and other users may wish to retrieve multimedia contents simply by keywords. It is difficult for the computer and its software to understand the human intent. We designed the multi-level index for several kinds of retrievals including impressive retrieval. This index gives several attributes of information to the multimedia object. The multimedia object that we proposed, encapsulates these indices. A creator describes various indices at several levels and gives the different services according to the user level. For example, a creator can decide the price of each user level. A user can select the user level according to the user's purpose. A normal- level user can only read a copyright index in an EMO. However, a high-level user can read their detailed keywords and signal information. We design a copyright index as the normal-level index. It describes its copyright and the server URL information. Also, a creator can add free keyword index, an EMO distributive path information index and a signal-level index information as a high level index.

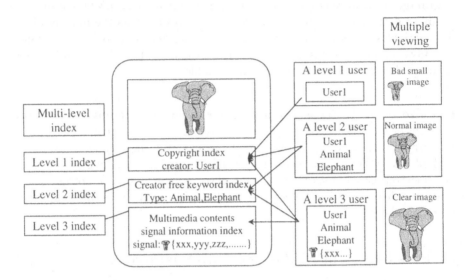

Fig. 5. Extended EMO with Multi-level index and Multiple viewing concept

Multiple-viewing Presently, we have already developed a simple viewing control function. Our copyright protection method is a simple viewing control. We are designing multiple-viewing methods as an extended function of EMOs. The multiple-viewing function is just like a multi-level index. A user can select his/her viewing method according to the user level. For example, a normal-level user can only a small image. A high-level user, however, can use a large and clear image.

4.2 EMO database

We are designing an EMO database. It stores many EMOs and retrieves EMO effectively. As we described, an EMO has multi-level indices and multiple views. The database also uses its function. An EMO database changes a retrieval method according to the user level. For example, a normal-level user can retrieve EMOs by simple keywords such as the copyright information and creator's name. A high-level user can retrieve impressively by many keywords and the contents specific signal information. An EMO database changes the function according to the user level. Figure 6 shows the concept.

5 Conclusion

We proposed the concept of the Encapsulated Multimedia Object (EMO) which can autonomously protect the copyright of the multimedia contents. Also, we implemented EMOs for copyright protection as Java applets and tested their

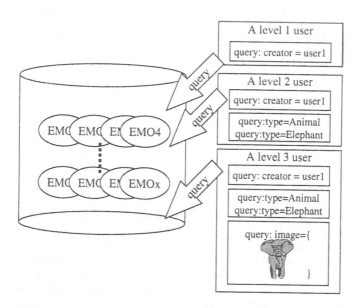

Fig. 6. The concept of EMO database

usefulness. An EMO is independent of the application and the computer hardware. It enables us to protect the copyright of the encapsulated multimedia contents. On the other hand, we found several limitations of the current EMOs. Presently, we are designing the extended EMOs and EMO databases. An extended EMO has the multi-level index to change services for users. Also, EMO databases can give effective retrieval services for each user. They can give a new facility for the multimedia creator as well as protecting their copyright.

References

1. Aucsmith,D.: Tamper Resistant Software: An Implementation, Proceedings of Information Hiding First International Workshop, pp.317-333, May - June (1996)
2. Cox,I.J.,Kilian,J.,Leighton,T. and Shamoon,T.: A Secure Robust Watermark for Multimedia, Proceedings of Information Hiding First International Workshop, pp.185-206, May- June (1996)
3. Gruhl,D., Lu,A. and Bender,A.: Echo Hiding, Proceedings of Information Hiding First International Workshop, pp. 295-315, May - June (1996)
4. Smith,J.R. and Comiskey,B.O.: Modulation and Information Hiding in Image, Proceedings of Information Hiding First International Workshop, pp.187-226, May - June (1996)
5. Aglets http://www.trl.ibm.co.jp/aglets/index.html
6. HORB http://ring.etl.go.jp/openlab/horb/index.html

A Priority-Driven Inheritance Scheme for Temporal-Spatial Structures in Multimedia Databases

Jisook Park[1], Yunmook Nah[2], and Sukho Lee[1]

[1] Dept. of Computer Engineering, Seoul National University, Korea
[2] Dept. of Computer Engineering, Dan-Kook University, Korea

Abstract. This paper presents an inheritance scheme for efficiently reusing previously defined temporal-spatial structures. In this scheme, temporal-spatial structures of multimedia data are defined within the database schema on the class level and can be inherited into all subclasses in a class hierarchy. This paper presents a model for defining, storing, and reusing temporal-spatial structures and proposes a priority-driven inheritance function regarding all combinations of possible temporal-spatial structures. Our scheme enables users to incrementally define the complex temporal-spatial structures of multimedia data without schema redefinition overhead.

1 Introduction

Recently, research and development for applications have been extensively reported [1,4,6,7,9,10]. Multimedia documents representation techniques have been studied to allow exchange of such documents on computer networks. As a result, the standard multimedia document architecture (ODA) / interchange format (ODIF) [2] and multimedia document retrieval system (MULTOS) [9] based on ODA were proposed. However, the MULTOS system is a structure-based document retrieval system rather than a database system, because it lacks object operations and its whole target is only document id retrieval.

Some of the new requirements for multimedia applications are well covered by object-oriented paradigm, resulting in some experimental DBMSs [6,9]. The major trends, however, put focus on how to store and retrieve monomedia data, such as text, images voice, etc. Some other requirements can be covered by extended object-oriented model. For example, an open data model for VODAK [1,7] is extended using new modeling primitives on the meta level. This system provides the facilities to define the basic concepts to execute time-dependent operations. But it dose not deal with the spatial aspects of multimedia data and cannot provide capability for reusing the temporal relationships.

Consequently, most existing models or systems have no consideration on how to reuse the previously defined temporal-spatial structures of multimedia data when a new structure is defined. If these facilities are provided, users can incrementally define the complex temporal-spatial structures without redefining overhead.

We focus on how effectively the temporal-spatial structures of multimedia data can be defined and reused. In this paper, temporal-spatial structures of multimedia objects are defined within the database schema on the class level and they are inherited into all subclasses in a class hierarchy. In order to support inheritance of temporal-spatial structures, it is required to define the meaning of the inheritance. In other words, given any two classes c and c' (c is a subclass of c'), if c has attributes which are related sequentially in time axis and c' has attributes which are composed in a space, the result structure of c after inheriting the structure of c' is ambiguous. This paper formally defines the inheritance of temporal-spatial structures by defining a priority-driven inheritance function which can be applied to any type of classes.

In the next section, our model, TSM(Temporal-Spatial Model), is briefly presented. Section 3 describes the concepts of temporal cohesion and spatial cohesion. We also explain how to assign temporal-spatial priorities between temporal-spatial structures using these concepts. Section 4 develops a priority-driven inheritance function regarding all combinations of possible temporal-spatial structures based on priorities defined in Sect. 3. Finally, conclusions and future research directions are discussed in Sect. 5.

2   Overview of TSM

This section gives an overview of TSM which is developed for representing, storing, and inheriting the temporal-spatial structure of multimedia data. Introductory example classes are also presented. TSM is extensively used for a prototype multimedia database system ALPHA [3,8].

2.1   Definition of Temporal-Spatial Structures

An *object* is any real-world entity that exists in time and space and has unique object identifier. An object has *temporal-spatial structure* which consists of a set of attributes and temporal-spatial relations between them. These temporal-spatial relations are divided into four groups: temporal sequence, spatial sequence, parallel, and spatial composition. All objects which have the same temporal-spatial structures may be grouped into a *class*. The temporal-spatial structure of a class can be represented by *extended domain types*.

Given the set B={Int, Real, String}, M={Text, Graphic, Image, Audio}, the set of class names C, and the tag set TS={s,sc,t,p}, the domain types for temporal-spatial structures as explained in [5] can be defined as follows:

- spatial composition: $sc[a_1 : d_1, a_2 : d_2, \cdots, a_n : d_n]$
    - describes relations of component objects within a space
- spatial sequence: $s< a_1 : d_1, a_2 : d_2, \cdots, a_n : d_n >$
    - describes sequential ordering of spaces

- temporal sequence: t$< a_1 : d_1, a_2 : d_2, \cdots, a_n : d_n >$
  - describes sequential ordering of objects in time
- parallel collection: p$[a_1 : d_1, a_2 : d_2, \cdots, a_n : d_n]$
  - describes parallel occurrence of objects in time
- random cases of the above: sc$\{d\}$, s$\{d\}$, t$\{d\}$
  - describe relations of component objects within a collection

Here, $a_1, a_2, \cdots, a_n$ are attributes and $d_1, d_2, \cdots, d_n$ are domain types. The tag *s* means *spatial*, *sc* means *spatial composition*, *t* means *temporal*, and *p* means *parallel*. Figure 1 shows example classes defined using the above domain types. The class *Person* has five attributes which are composed spatially and two attributes of the class *Student* will be shown sequentially in time axis. The attributes *audioProfile* and *papers* of the class *GraduateStud* will be presented simultaneously.

```
CREATE CLASS Person SUPER Object
sc[ name: String,
    birthDate: Date,
    addr: String,
    picture: Image,
    family: sc{Person} ]
CREATE CLASS Student SUPER Person
t< studentProfile: sc[deptName: String,
                      studNumber: Int,
                      friends: sc{Person} ],
    hobby: Video >
CREATE CLASS GraduateStud SUPER Student
p[ audioProfile: Audio,
   papers: t{Paper} ]
```

Fig. 1. Example Multimedia Classes

2.2 Inheritance of Temporal-Spatial Structures

TSM supports single inheritance, thus the classes form a hierarchy. The temporal-spatial structure defined for any class are inherited into all its subclasses recursively. Conversely, the temporal-spatial structure of any class can be constructed by combining its own structure with the structure inherited from its superclass. Section 3 and section 4 describe how they can be combined.

Figure 2 shows a tree representing the class hierarchy corresponding to Fig. 1. This tree has a number of nodes and arrows. There are three types in nodes; a square, a simple ellipse, and a bold ellipse. They represent a class, a simple attribute, or a composite attribute, respectively. A square and a bold ellipse have a tag indicating the temporal-spatial relations between component attributes.

The type of an arrow connecting two nodes describes the type of relationship between them. A simple arrow means an aggregation between a class and an attribute or between a composite attribute and an attribute. An arrowed bold line indicates a generalization between classes and an arrowed dashed line represents an association between an attribute and a class. Table 1 shows the logical constructors corresponding to tags used in a tree.

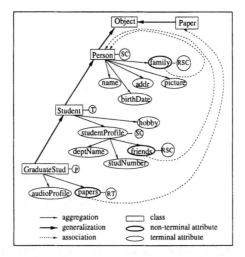

Fig. 2. The Class Hierarchy for Example Classes

Table 1. Logical Notations

Tag	Logical Constructor	Tag	Logical Constructor
T	$t[\ ]$	RT	$t\{\ \}$
S	$s[\ ]$	RS	$s\{\ \}$
P	$p[\ ]$	RSC	$sc\{\ \}$
SC	$sc[\ ]$		

3 Temporal-Spatial Priority

In this section, the concepts of temporal and spatial cohesion are introduced and temporal priority and spatial priority are defined based on these concepts. By using these two priorities, temporal-spatial priorities will be assigned between all combinations of temporal-spatial structures.

3.1 Temporal Priority

Given objects a and b which are related with a temporal-spatial relation R, we use the term $R(a, b)$ to denote the temporal-spatial structure of them.

Definition 1. *Duration* of an object o ($o \in O$, O is the set of objects) is the result of the following function D. Here, (t_1, t_2) denotes the valid interval of an object o in time axis.

$$D : o \rightarrow (t_1, t_2).$$

Definition 2. *Temporal coherence operator* denoted by $\cap_t$ is an operator applied between objects. The result of this operation represents an intersection of durations of operand objects. Given objects a and b ($a, b \in O$), the temporal coherence operator is defined as follows.

$$a \cap_t b = \mid t_2 - t_1 \mid, \quad \text{where } (t_1, t_2) \subset D(a) \text{ and } (t_1, t_2) \subset D(b).$$

Figure 3 shows how the temporal coherence operator can be applied to temporal-spatial structures in TSM. For example, objects a and b in Fig. 3.(a) are presented simultaneously, thus they have an intersection τ.

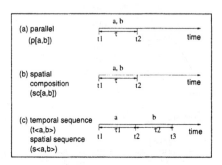

Fig. 3. Temporal Cohesion and Temporal Priority

Definition 3. *Temporal cohesion* assesses the tightness with which related objects are 'presented together' in time axis and is determined by the temporal coherence operation. Given $R(a, b)$ and $R'(a', b')$, if $a \cap_t b$ is larger than $a' \cap_t b'$, then the temporal cohesion of $R(a, b)$ is larger than that of $R'(a', b')$.

As described in Fig. 3, the temporal cohesion of parallel or spatial composition is larger than that of temporal sequence or spatial sequence.

Definition 4. *Temporal priority* is assigned as follows: the larger the temporal cohesion, the higher the temporal priority level. Given $R(a, b)$ and $R'(a', b')$, the difference and equivalence in temporal priority are represented as follows.

$$R(a, b) >_t R'(a', b'), \quad R(a, b) =_t R'(a', b').$$

The temporal priorities between the temporal-spatial structures in TSM are as follows.

$$p[a,b] =_t sc[a,b] >_t s{<}a,b{>} =_t t{<}a,b{>}$$

3.2 Spatial Priority

Definition 5. *Region* of an object $o \in O$ represents the scope of the object in a space $p \in P$ (P denotes the uncountably infinite set of spaces). Given o, region of o is the result of the following function R and is specified by the two positions $(x_1@y_1, x_2@y_2)$, upper-left corner and lower-right corner of o, in p.

$$R{:}o \rightarrow (x_1@y_1, x_2@y_2).$$

Definition 6. Given objects a and b ($a, b \in O$), *spatial coherence operator* denoted by $\cap_s$ is defined as follows.

1. $a \cap_s b = \phi$, $\quad if \not\exists R(a)$ or $\not\exists R(b)$,
2. $a \cap_s b = p$, $\quad if \exists p$ such that $R(a) \subset p$ and $R(b) \subset p$, $p \in P$,
3. $a \cap_s b = 0$, $\quad if \not\exists p$ such that $R(a) \subset p$ and $R(b) \subset p$, $p \in P$.

In Fig. 4, objects a and b in (a) belong to the same space p, $p \in P$ and a and b in (b) are located in different spaces, $p1$ and $p2$, with an interval ρ in time. Therefore, the result of (a) is p where both a and b are placed and the result of (b) is 0. In temporal sequence or parallel relation, the result is null because they have any object which have no region in a space.

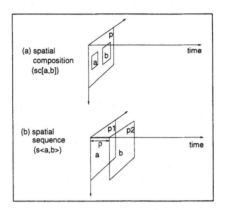

Fig. 4. Spatial Cohesion and Spatial Priority

Definition 7. *Spatial cohesion* assesses the tightness with which related objects are 'presented together' in spaces. Given $R(a,b)$ and $R'(a',b')$, the spatial cohesion of $R(a,b)$ is larger than that of $R'(a',b')$ in the following cases: 1) if $a \cap_s b$ is not null (i.e. p or 0) and $a' \cap_s b'$ is null, or 2) if $a \cap_s b$ returns a space p and $a' \cap_s b'$ returns 0.

Definition 8. *Spatial priority* is assigned as follows: the larger the spatial cohesion, the higher the spatial priority level. Given $R(a,b)$ and $R'(a',b')$, the difference and equivalence of spatial priority are represented as follows.

$$R(a,b) >_s R'(a',b'), \quad R(a,b) =_s R'(a',b').$$

The spatial priorities among the temporal-spatial structures in TSM are as follows.

$$\text{sc[a,b]} >_s \text{s<a,b>} >_s \text{t<a,b>} =_s \text{p[a,b]}$$

3.3 Temporal-Spatial Priority

Temporal-spatial priority is assigned by temporal priority and spatial priority in which temporal priority is given much weight. In other words, temporal priority is considered first. Spatial priority is considered if and only if the temporal priorities are the same.

Definition 9. *Temporal-spatial priority* indicates the relative importance of each temporal-spatial structure against the others. Given $R(a, b)$ and $R'(a', b')$, temporal-spatial priority is defined as follows ($>_{ts}$ and $=_{ts}$ are used to denote the difference and equivalence in temporal-spatial priority).

1. $R(a, b) >_{ts} R'(a', b')$, if $R(a, b) >_t R(a', b')$,
2. $R(a, b) >_{ts} R'(a', b')$, if $R(a, b) =_t R(a', b')$ and $R(a, b) >_s R'(a', b')$,
3. $R'(a', b') >_{ts} R(a, b)$, otherwise .

Table 2 shows the temporal-spatial priorities between the temporal-spatial structures in TSM.

Table 2. Temporal-Spatial Priorities between the Structures in TSM

	t<>	s<>	p[ ]	sc[ ]
t<>	$=_{ts}$	$<_{ts}$	$<_{ts}$	$<_{ts}$
s<>	$>_{ts}$	$=_{ts}$	$<_{ts}$	$<_{ts}$
p[ ]	$>_{ts}$	$>_{ts}$	$=_{ts}$	$<_{ts}$
sc[ ]	$>_{ts}$	$>_{ts}$	$>_{ts}$	$=_{ts}$

4 Inheritance of temporal-spatial structures

This section defines an inheritance function and a class structure generating function which can be applied to all combinations of temporal-spatial structures by using the temporal-spatial priority.

4.1 Class Structure with Inheritance

A temporal-spatial structure consists of attributes and their temporal-spatial relation. $A(c)$ and $TS(c)$ are used to denote the attributes and their temporal-spatial relation, respectively. For an example class *Professor*, $TS(c)$ and $A(c)$ are applied as follows.

CLASS Professor
sc[name:String, birthDate:Date, supervise:Lab, picture:Image]

$TS(\text{Professor}) = \text{sc}[\ ]$,
$A(\text{Professor}) = \{\text{name:String, birthDate:Date, supervise:Lab, picture:Image}\}$.

Now, we will define the inherited class structure using the inheritance function and will show the validity of this function.

Definition 10. *Inherited class structure* is the result of the following function ι_m. Given a set of classes C, $DT(C)$ denotes the set of domain types of C.
$$\iota_m: DT(C) \times DT(C) \to DT(C)$$
Given any c and $c'(c, c' \in C$, c is a subclass of $c')$, the function ι_m is applied as follows. Here, $name(a)$ denotes the name of an attribute a.

1. $\iota_m(DT(c), DT(c')) = TS(c)(A(c) \cup a)$,
   if $DT(c') >_{ts} DT(c)$, where $name(a) = name(c')$ and $DT(a) = \sigma_m(c')$,
2. $\iota_m(DT(c), DT(c')) = TS(c')(A(c') \cup a)$,
   if $DT(c) >_{ts} DT(c')$, where $name(a) = name(c)$ and $DT(a) = \sigma_m(c)$,
3. $\iota_m(DT(c), DT(c')) = TS(c)(A(c) \cup A(c'))$, otherwise .

The basic idea of the above function is as follows. In the first and second cases in which the temporal-spatial priorities of c and c' are different from each other, *the class structure having higher priority is defined as the domain type of a new attribute called c (the name of the higher class) in the class structure having lower priority.* Let us consider the classes Person and Student defined in Fig. 1. The priority of Person is higher than that of Student, therefore, the structure of Person is defined as the domain type of a new attribute, named *person* (beginning with lower-case letter), of Student as follows.

ι_m(DT(Person), DT(Student))
= t<person:sc[name:String, birthDate:Date, addr:String,
             picture:Image, family: sc{Person}] INHERITED,
     studentProfile: sc[deptName:String, studNumber: sc{Person}],
     hobby: Video >.

In the last case, the classes c and c' have the same temporal-spatial structure. Therefore, the result structure has the same temporal-spatial tag and contains a set of attributes c and c'.

The following theorem shows the validity of the function ι_m.

Theorem 1. The function ι_m is closed given a set of class names C and a set of domain types $DT(C)$.

Proof. Given C and $DT(C)$, we can prove the validity of ι_m by showing that $\iota_m(DT(C))$ will be also $DT(C)$. As explained Table 3, the temporal-spatial structures with tags are divided into four types and there are sixteen combinations for the four types. For all the sixteen cases, the results of the function $\iota_m(DT(C))$ are also $DT(C)$. For example, given two classes c and c', if c has 't<>' and c' has 'p[ ]', then the result will be 't< p[ ] >', because 'p[ ]' is higher than 't<>' in temporal-spatial priority. □

Table 3. The result of ι_m for the domain types in TSM

	t<>	s<>	p[ ]	sc[ ]
t<>	t<>	t< s<> >	t< p[ ] >	t< sc[ ] >
s<>	t< s< > >	s<>	s<p[ ] >	s< sc[ ] >
p[ ]	t< p[ ] >	s< p[ ] >	p[ ]	p[sc[ ]]
sc[ ]	t< sc[ ] >	s< sc[ ] >	p[sc[ ]]	sc[ ]

Definition 11. Given C and a class hierarchy rooted *Object*, *class structures* of C can be constructed by the following function σ_m.

$\sigma_m : C \to DT(C)$.

Given any two class names c and $c'(c, c' \in C)$, the function σ_m is applied as follows.

1. $\sigma_m(c) = DT(c)$, if c is a subclass of *Object*,
2. $\sigma_m(c) = \iota_m(DT(c), \sigma_m(c'))$, if c is a subclass of c' .

In the above definition, if c has no superclass except *Object*, then c has its own domain type as a class structure. Otherwise, that is, c has one or more ancestors, then the class structure of c can be generated by applying the function ι_m from c to *Object*, recursively.

4.2 Inheritance Examples

Now, we will show how automatically the structures for example classes defined in Fig. 1 can be generated by the function σ_m. At first, the class *Person* is a direct subclass of *Object*, thus it has no inherited structure. The structure of *Student* can be generated by combining its own structure with the structure inherited from *Person*, because it is a subclass of *Person*. As explained in Sect. 4.1, the structure of *Person* is defined as the domain type of a new attribute named *person* in the class *Student*. The structure of *GraduateStud* is also constructed by combining its own structure with the structure inherited from its ancestors *Student* and *Person*. The temporal-spatial priority of *GraduateStud* is higher than that of *Student*. Thus, the structure of *GraduateStud* is defined as the domain type of an attribute named *graduateStud* in the inherited structure as follows (See Fig. 5).

$\sigma_m(\text{GraduateStud}) = \iota_m(\text{DT}(\text{GraduateStud}), \sigma_m(\text{Student}))$
$= \iota_m(\text{DT}(\text{GraduateStud}), \iota_m(\text{DT}(\text{Student}), \text{DT}(\text{Person})))$
$= \text{t}<$ person:sc[name:String, birthDate:Date, addr:String,
     picture:Image, family:sc{Person}] INHERITED,
  studentProfile:sc[deptName:String, studNumber:Int,
      friends:sc{Person}] INHERITED,
  hobby:Video INHERITED,
  graduateStud:p[audioProfile: Audio, papers:t{Paper}] $>$

5 Conclusion

This paper proposed a priority-driven inheritance scheme to efficiently reuse the temporal-spatial structures of multimedia objects. In this scheme, temporal-spatial structures defined on the class level can be inherited into all subclasses in a class hierarchy. We proposed a priority-driven inheritance function regarding all combinations of possible temporal-spatial structures. In order to explain the semantics of inheritance, the concepts of temporal cohesion and spatial cohesion were introduced and the temporal-spatial priorities between temporal-spatial structures were defined using these concepts.

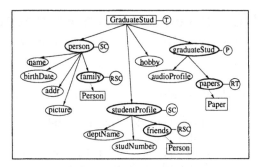

Fig. 5. The Inherited Class Structure

The proposed scheme enables users to define a new temporal-spatial structure incrementally by reusing the previously defined structures without schema redefinition overhead. Also, the system management overhead is reduced because the data duplication on the schema level is minimized.

The inheritance scheme is used for supporting inheritance in the prototype multimedia system ALPHA [3,8]. A further research is required for adapting the proposed scheme to the standardized data language like SQL3.

References

1. Aberer, K. and Klas, W., "Supporting Temporal Multimedia Operations in Object-Oriented Database Systems," in Proc. of Int. Conf. on Multimedia Computing and Systems, pp.352-361, May, 1994.
2. Campbell-Grant, I.R.(ed.), "Office Document Architecture (ODA) and Interchange Format Par 2: Document Structures," ISO 8613-2, ISO/IEC JTC1/SC18/WG3, Mar., 1988.
3. Lee, S., et. al, "Design and Implementation of the Multimedia DBMS ALPHA," Journal of Korea Information Science Society, Vol.22, No.2, pp.1181-1188, 1994.
4. Meghini, C., Rabitti, F., and Thanos, C., "Conceptual Modeling of Multimedia Documents," IEEE Computer, Vol.24, No.10, pp.23-30, 1991.
5. Nah, Y., Lee, S., Hwang, S., "Two-level Modeling Schemes for Temporal-Spatial Multimedia Data Representation," in Proc. of DEXA, pp.102-107, 1992.
6. Kim, W., Modern Database Systems, ACM Press, Addison-Wesley, New York, 1995.
7. Klas, W., Neuhold, E.j., and Schrefl, M., "Using an Object-Oriented Approach to Model Multimedia Data," Computer Communication, Vol.13, No.4, pp.204-216, 1990.
8. Park, J., Lee, S., Cha, J., and Nah, Y., "A Presentation Scheduling Scheme for Multimedia Databases," in Proc. of COMSAC'97, pp.21-23, 1996.
9. Woelk, D. and Kim, W., "Multimedia Information Management in an Object-Oriented Database System," in Proc. of VLDB, pp.319-329, 1987.
10. Woelk, D., Luther, W., and Kim, W., "Multimedia Applications and Database Requirements," in Proc. IEEE Computer Society Office Automation Sympo., pp.180-189, 1987.

Relational Database Reverse Engineering and Terminological Reasoning

Jacques Kouloumdjian   and   Farouk Toumani

Laboratoire d'Ingénierie des Systèmes d'Information
INSA Lyon, Bâtiment 501,
F-69621 Villeurbanne, FRANCE
koulou@lisiecrin.insa-lyon.fr

Abstract. Reverse engineering of relational databases has known an increasing interest due to the need to have a more effective use of databases whose semantics has become uncertain. For a reverse engineering to be efficient, realistic assumptions have to be made on the physical DB schema and the degree of involvement of the designer for providing knowledege on data and for validating results. This paper describes a method which exploits various sources for gathering information on data and proposes validation tools based on the use of terminological logics. Moreover no assumption on physical schemas is needed (unless 1rst normal form).

Keywords: Database reverse engineering, relational databases, conceptual models, data semantics elicitation, validation, terminological logics

1   Introduction

Database Reverse Engineering (DBRE) is part of the maintenance activity of information systems. It consists in restoring a database (DB) conceptual schema from an implemented system. It has known an increasing interest these last years since many applications have been developed without the help of CASE tools and/or design methods. Moreover even if documentation is available it is not always reliable. The lack of precise knowledge of data semantics hampers the effective utilization of data [14].

DBRE can be considered as an activity inverse to DB design. However it cannot be reduced to a schema translation from a physical model to a conceptual one because of *semantic degradations* that may have occurred during the DB design [12, 26]. Traditionally DB design is decomposed into four stages:

1. specifying users requirements on the application domain,
2. translating these requirements to a conceptual schema using some conceptual model,
3. converting the conceptual schema to a logical one expressed in an access data model,

4. finally implementing the logical schema into a physical schema by means of the data description language of a data base management system.

Each step involves new model and takes into account specific parameters and objectives with respect to previous stages. It can modify decisions made earlier. For example two entity-types in the conceptual schema may be implemented into the same record type for optimization reasons. The semantics of the application domain is therefore no more correctly reflected in the physical schema and reconstructing the conceptual schema from the database needs more information than simply the implementation description. Gathering this information is a crucial point in DBRE.

A number of papers have dealt with *relational* databases reverse engineering (see for example [18, 19, 15, 11, 7, 9, 16, 23, 25, 24, 28]) and it is now agreed that the DBRE process can be divided into two main stages [13]:

– DB semantics eliciting which is aimed at acquiring knowledge on data stored in the DB. This knowledge is expressed in terms of the relational model concepts (keys, functional dependencies, inclusion dependencies...) and depends on the assumptions made on DB schema (e.g. relations assumed to be in 3rd normal form).
– building a conceptual schema on the basis of knowledge gathered from various sources (data dictionary, application programs, data itself).

In this paper we will present issues appearing when reverse engineering relational DB and the answers that we have given in the DREAM [1] project. The main characteristics of the DREAM project are:

- The method is based on assumptions that are as realistic as possible: limited initial information on the data semantics, few restrictions on database implementation characteristics (e.g. attribute naming, normal form of relations).
- Original methods for eliciting data semantics have been proposed. They are based on the use of information contained in data dictionary, SQL statements and database extension.
- The interactions with human expert are precisely defined and his help is required mainly to validate the final schema: a completely automated process is not realistic and human expert has to be involved at one stage or an other, either to make decision on points left open by the RE process ot to check the correctness of the resulting conceptual schema.
- Inference techniques based on terminological logics are used on the conceptual schema for checking consistency of its description, reducing redundant parts and infering new properties when possible. To achieve these goals, the extracted data semantics is converted to a terminology equivalent to the extended ER schema to be checked. The formalism which is used is an extension (called TERM for Terminological Entity Relationship Model) of a terminological model (see Fig 1).

---

[1] Database Reverse Engineering Analysis Method

The rest of the paper is divided into two parts: 1) a description of DREAM method first, according to a set of criteria covering all the parameters which characterize RE methods and 2) the approach chosen for validating the final conceptual schema whose originality is to use terminological logics.

2 DREAM reverse engineering method

The method is aimed at covering all stages of *relational* DB reverse engineering [25, 24]. It is depicted on figure 1. The first stage is equi-joins and keys elicitation from data dictionary, programs, views and queries (possibly with user's help). This knowledge is then processed to produce an EER (Extended Entity Relationship) or a TERM schema. Finally validation takes place.

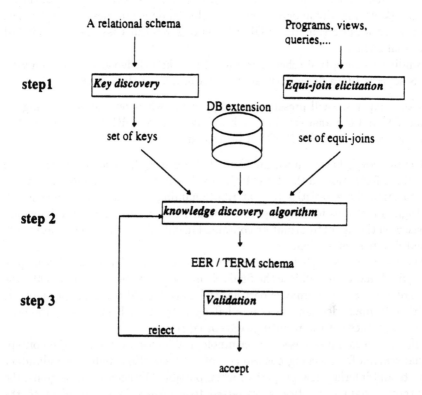

Fig. 1. The DREAM method

To show on what assumptions the method is based, we will use a framework recently described by Chiang et al [8] for design and evaluation of RE methods for relational DB. This framework defines a number of criteria that should be taken into account to clearly state assumptions, goals and limits of any method. These criteria are grouped into 3 families:

- *foundations (assumptions) of the method,*
- *the reverse engineering process itself,*
- *validation*

2.1 Foundation of DREAM method

This part is concerned with three questions:

- What kind of meaning do we attach to the conceptual schema to be built in the DBRE process?
  For example that could be the meaning intended by the original designer. More pragmatically in our case it is a possible conceptual specification for the physical schema.
- What target conceptual model are we to use?
  Ideally this model should have a good expressive power, support a correct representation of data base semantics and facilitate validation procedures. Entity-Relationship (ER) model and its extensions (EER) [11] are used most of time. We have chosen in DREAM, as final target model, an ER model extended with aggregation, generalization and specialization applied both to entity-types and relationship-types. An original point of the method is the definition of a formal model called TERM (for Terminological Entity Relationship Model), based on terminological logics, which is convenient for expressing (possibly n-ary) associations and which supports reasoning. It is aimed at checking some properties of the schema (consistency among others).
- What are the prerequisites on DB?
  We have made the following assumptions:

  - *no consistent naming of attributes.* Consistent naming allows semantic correspondences between attributes belonging to different relation schemas and is therefore a source of information on data semantics. However it is a strong assumption not often satisfied in real situations.
  - *availability of keys,* if data dictionaries provide the information. If not, key attributes can be suggested from equi-join analysis.
  - *no knowledge of inclusion dependencies.* In the project they are discovered from equi-joins and data analysis.
  - *no assumption on the normal forms of relations* (except 1NF). Most of research works in relational DB reverse engineering are based on the strong assumption that relations are in 3rd NF making it easier to establish correspondences between relation schemas and entity-types. However in physical schemas relations are often denormalized to 2nd or 1st NF for

optimization reasons. Dealing with 1NF relations is difficult and needs the discovery of functional dependencies between non-key attributes. As for key search, functional dependencies between non-key attributes can be discovered from equi-joins analysis in a more efficient fashion than systematic dependency search (as proposed in [6]for example).

2.2 RE process

The criteria associated to RE process express the ability of methods for an automatic recovery of data semantics and for its correct translation to a conceptual schema. They are threefold:

- *thoroughness of semantics acquisition techniques.* As already explained, directly deriving conceptual schema from physical representation [19, 15, 14] does not lead to a correct abstraction of real world. Additional semantics should be found and used. In DREAM this semantics is extracted from SQL queries (found in programs, queries and views) and from data base extension.
  We will explain the underlying idea on an example. Consider the SQL query:

  select ...
  from A, B
  where $A.a_i = B.b_j$

  from which the following equi-join can be derived:

  $A.a_i \bowtie B.b_j$

  For interpreting this equi-join, we must take into account:

  - The analysis of DB extension to refine the relationship between a_i and b_j . Let S_3 be the set of common values of attributes a_i and b_j, and S_1 and S_2 the sets of the values of a_i and b_j respectively. As an example, suppose that:

    $S_3 \equiv S_2$ and $S_3 \subset S_1$

    We can deduce an inclusion dependency $b_j \ll a_i$.

  - the role (key or non-key) played by a_i and b_j in A and B. In the example given above, if a_i and b_j are both keys respectively in A and B, an instance of B may be considered as instance of A in the conceptual schema and therefore B can be considered as a sub-type of A.

- *rules for deriving conceptual schema from semantics* . Constructing a conceptual schema from inclusion dependencies has been fairly well described in literature (see for example [14]). In [24] we give algorithms which take into account both inclusion dependencies and functional dependencies between non-key attributes.
- *performance efficiency* in terms of human expert involvement in the process (how much and when) and of automatization of the method. In DREAM human expert intervention is required only for decision making at precise points of the RE process: to decide which element "hidden" in denormalized relations and elicited by the method should be conceptualized and to validate the final conceptual schema.

2.3 Validation stage

An important point in a DBRE process lies in the validation of the conceptual schema derived from the relational one. The validation stage consists in two main points:

- *Checking the compliance of the conceptual schema with respect to the universe of discourse..*
  The help of human expert is required at this point.
- *checking the quality of the conceptual schema.*
  The quality of a conceptual schema is defined with respect to its consistency (i.e., no contradictory information) and its minimality (i.e., no redundancy of information).

The second kind of validation have been rarely dealt with in DBRE methods. This task is relatively simple if the knowledge used to derive a conceptual schema is provided by an expert and thus assumed to be correct. However, in practical situations the needed knowledge must be extracted from various and heterogeneous sources and often suffers from inconsistency and redundancy. This stresses the need for an automatic quality checking framework during the translation stage of DBRE process. Formalisms supporting inference processes are appropriate to such purposes. Terminological representations for knowledge appear to be adequate both for data modeling and reasoning on structures. They have been use in DREAM to check the consistency and the minimality of conceptual schemas as briefly presented in the next section.

3 Using terminological logics

Terminological logics are Knowledge Representation (KR) formalisms issued from the language KL-ONE. They deal with a structured representation of knowledge and reason with it. In such languages the universe of discourse is described by means of *concepts*, which are used to represent sets of individual, and *roles*, which are binary relations used to represent interrelationships between concepts.

Such description of the universe of discourse is called a *terminology*.

Terminological logics constitute an active field in KR area where many efforts have been devoted to the development of Terminological Knowledge Representation Systems (TKRS), e.g., KRYPTON [5], CLASSIC [4], BACK [22], LOOM [17]. At the core of the TKRS is the terminological formalism which is made up of a set of concepts and role constructs. The intended meaning of a concept or a role is then specified by providing expressions, called *concept (or role) descriptions*, formed by means of the constructs supported by the terminological formalism.

Example. The following concept description denotes concept *Student* as all the persons which are registred in a university.

$Student = Person \sqcap atleast(1, registred) \sqcap all(registred, University)$

The symbol $\sqcap$ is used to denotes concept conjunction and is intepreted as set intersection. the expression $atleast(1, registred)$ denotes the set of individuals who are registred and the expression $all(registred, University)$ denotes the set of individuals whose all registrations are in universities.

In a terminology, concepts and roles (called terms) are structured into hieararchies determined by the *subsumption* relation which is interpreted as set containment. For instance, the concept *Student* is subsumed by *Person* since it denotes a subset of persons which have some additional properties (registred in a university).

The hierarchical structure of terminologies constitute the base of the reasoning services provided by TKRS [10]. Reasoning with TL consists mainly in finding the right place of a term in the hierarchy of terms. This kind of reasoning, called *taxonomic reasoning*, is based on the comparison of terms descriptions and allow automatic verification of consistency (i.e., checking contradictory information) and minimality (i.e., remove redundancies) of descriptions and the detection of implicit knowledge in knowledge bases.

Taxinomic reasoning in DBRE

Taxonomic reasoning was acknowledged as very fruitful in a wide range of DB applications, e.g., DB design [1, 3], federated DB [27, 2] and semantic query optimization [20]. We were interested by the advantages of using a target model equipped with taxinomic reasoning ability in a DBRE process. To achieve this task we need to express conceptual schemas using terminological logics in order to benefit from reasoning services provided by terminological systems. The advantages of this approach are summarized below.

3.1 Construction and enrichment of conceptual schemas

The ability of terminological systems to make automatic classification is useful for the construction of conceptual schemas. Once a conceptual structure is produced during the translation process, it is automatically integrated at the right place in the conceptual schema under construction. This mechanism is very useful for taking into account new knowledge while the translation process is still running. A simple example is given on figure 3 where the new concept *Assistant* is integrated in an already existing hierarchy according to its description. It is classified as a sub-class of *Teacher* and *Reasearcher*.

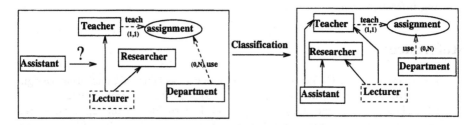

Fig. 2. Classification of a new concept

Furthermore, during the construction step the terminological system is able to detect implicit knowledge hidden in the descriptions, e.g. detection of subsumption relation between concepts or refinement of cardinatity constraints. Thus the resulting conceptual schema is enriched with the inferred knowledge.

3.2 Conceptual schemas validation

We are considering here the second type of checking reported in section 2.3.

- *Checking consistency of conceptual schemas.*
  The consistency of conceptual schemas is formally defined on the basis of the notion of consistency of a terminology which have been well studied in the context of terminological logics [21]. Therefore, checking the consistency of conceptual schemas can be automatically performed by the terminological system.
- *Refinement of conceptual schemas.*
  Redundancies, with respect to the hierarchies represented in the termonilogical system, are automatically removed from term descriptions. The resulting terminology is formed by term descriptions wich contain a minimum of specialization contraints with respect to their subsumer.

4 Conclusion

In this paper we have highlighted some of the key points of relational DB reverse engineering. One of them is data semantics discovery which should be based on all possible sources of information. SQL queries and programs in general have been until now rather poorly exploited for this purpose. We have shown how equi-joins detected in queries could help find dependencies in connection with database itself. Much attention has not been paid either to the quality of the conceptual schema resulting from the reverse engineering process and to its validation in general. We have proposed a formalism called TERM based on terminological languages. The equivalence between the EER schema and TERM schema has been established. Improvements of the results (such as consistency and minimality) are then conducted on TERM schemas taking advantage of existing inference tools.

References

1. S. Bergamaschi and C. Sartori. On Taxonomic Reasoning in Conceptual Design. *ACM Transaction on Database Systems*, 17(3):385–422, September 1992.
2. J.M. Blanco, A. Illarramendi, A. Goñi, and J. Bermúdez. Building a Federated Relational Database System: An Approach Using a Knowledge-Based System. *International Journal of Cooperative Information Systems*, 3(4):415–455, 1994.
3. A. Borgida. Description Logics in Data Management. *IEEE Transactions on Data and Knowledge Engineering*, 5(7):671–682, 1995.
4. A. Borgida, R. Brachman, D. MacGuiness, and L. Resnick. CLASSIC: A Structural Data Model for Objects. In *Proceedings of the ACM SIGMOD International Conference on Management of Data Portland, Oregon, USA*, pages 58–67, June 1989.
5. R.J. Brachman and H.J. Levesque. Tales from the Far Side of KRYPTON: Lessons for Expert Database Systems from Knowledge Representation. In L. Kerschberg, editor, 1st *International Conference on Expert Databases Systems, Charleston, USA*, pages 3–43, apr 1986.
6. M. Castellanos and F. Saltor. Extraction of Data Dependencies. In Kitahashi Jaakkola, Kangassalo and Markus, editors, *Proceedings of the 3^{td} European-Japanese Seminar on Information Modelling and Knowledge Bases, Budapest*, pages 400–420. IOS Press, Amsterdam, 1993.
7. R.H.L. Chiang, T.M. Barron, and V.C. Storey. Reverse Engineering of Relational Databases: Extraction of an EER Model from a Relational Database. *Data and Knowledge Engineering*, 10(12):107–142, 1994.
8. R.H.L. Chiang, T.M. Barron, and V.C. Storey. A Framework for the Design and Evaluation of Reverse Engineering Methods for Relational Databases. *Data and Knowledge Engineering*, 21(1):57–77, 1997.
9. K.H. Davis and A. Arora. Converting a Relational Database Model into an Entity-Relationship Model. In *Proceedings of the 6th International Conference on the Entity-Relationship Approach New-York, USA*, pages 243–256, November 1987.
10. F.M. Donini, M. Lenzerini, D. Nardi, and W. Nutt. The Complexity of Concept Languages. Technical Report RR-95-07, DFKI, Kaiserslautern, Germany, April 1995.

11. R. Elmasri and S. Navathe. *Fundamentals of Database Systems.* Benjamin/Cummings Publishing Compagny, Inc, Redwood City, California, second edition, 1994.

12. J-L. Hainaut. Database Reverse Engineering : Models, Techniques and Strategies. In *Proceedings of the 10th International Conference on the Entity-Relationship Approach San Mateo, California*, pages 729–741, October 1991.

13. J-L. Hainaut, C. Tonneau, M. Moris, and M. Chandelon. Schema Transformation Techniques for Database Reverse Engineering. In *Proceedings of the 12th International Conference on the Entity-Relationship Approach Arlington, Dallas, USA*, volume 823 of *Lecture Notes in Computer Science*, pages 364–375. Springer-Verlag, Berlin Heidelberg, 1993.

14. P. Johannesson. A Method for Transforming Relational Schemas into Conceptual Schemas. In *Proceedings of the 10th International Conference on Data Engineering Houston, Texas*, pages 190–201. IEEE Computer Society, February 1994.

15. P. Johannesson and K. Kalman. A Method for Translating Relational Schemas into Conceptual Schemas. In *Proceedings of the 8th International Conference on the Entity-Relationship Approach Toronto, Canada*, pages 279–293, October 1989.

16. K. Kalman. Implementation and Critique of an Algorithm which Maps a Relational Database to a Conceptual Model. In *Proceedings of the 3td International Conference on Computer Aided Software Engineering Trondheim, Norway*, volume 498 of *Lecture Notes in Computer Science*, pages 393–415. Springer-Verlag, Berlin Heidelberg, 1991.

17. R. MacGregor. Inside the LOOM description classifier. *SIGART Bulletin*, 2(3):88–92, June 1991.

18. H. Mannila and K-J Räihä. Algorithms for Inferring Functional Dependencies from Relations. *Data and Knowledge Engineering*, 12:83–99, 1994.

19. V.M. Markowitz and J.A. Makowsky. Identifying Extended Entity-Relationship Object Structures in Relational Schemas. *IEEE Transactions on Software Engineering*, 16(8):777–790, August 1990.

20. B.S. Navathe, A. Savasere, T. Anwar, H. Beck, and S. Gala. Object Modelling Using Classification in CANDIDE and its Applications. In A. Dogac, T. Ozsu, A. Biliris, and T. Sellis, editors, *Advances in Object-Oriented Database Systems, Proceedings of the of the NATOI Advanced Study Institute on Object-Oriented Systems, Izmir, Kusadasi, Turkey*, volume 130 of *Computing and Systems Sciences*, pages 435–476. Springer-Verlag, Berlin Heidelberg, 1994.

21. B. Nebel. Reasoning and Revision in Hybrid Representation Systems. volume 422 of *Lecture Notes in Computer Science*, page 300. Springer-Verlag, New York, 1990.

22. C. Peltason. The BACK System- An Overview. *SIGART Bulletin*, 2(3):114–119, June 1991.

23. J-M. Petit, J. Kouloumdjian, J-F Boulicaut, and F. Toumani. Using Queries to Improve Database Reverse Engineering. In *Proceedings of the 13th International Conference on the Entity-Relationship Approach Manchester, UK*, volume 881 of *Lecture Notes in Computer Science*, pages 369–386. Springer-Verlag, Berlin Heidelberg, October 1994.

24. J-M. Petit, F. Toumani, J-F. Boulicaut, and J. Kouloumdjian. Towards the Reverse Engineering of Denormalized Relational Databases. In *Proceedings of the 12th International Conference on Data Engineering New Orleans, USA*, pages 218–227. IEEE Computer Society, Feb 1996.

25. J-M. Petit, F. Toumani, and J. Kouloumdjian. Relational Database Reverse Engineering: a Method Based on Query Analysis. *International Journal of Cooperative Information Systems*, 4(2,3):287–316, 1995.

26. W.J. Premerlani and M. Blaha. An Approach for Reverse Engineering of Relational Databases. *Communications of the ACM*, 37(5):42–49, May 1994.

27. A.P. Sheth, S.K. Gala, and S.B. Navathe. On Automatic Reasoning For Schema Integration. *International Journal of Cooperative Information Systems*, 2(1):23–50, 1993.

28. O. Signore, M. Loffredo, M. Gregori, and M. Cima. Reconstruction of ER Schema from Database Applications: a Cognitive Approach. In *Proceedings of the 13th International Conference on the Entity-Relationship Approach Manchester, UK*, volume 881 of *Lecture Notes in Computer Science*, pages 387–402. Springer-Verlag, Berlin Heidelberg, October 1994.

Efficient Answer Extraction of Deductive Databases Modeled by HLPN

Kamel Barkaoui and Yasmina Maïzi

Laboratoire CEDRIC-CNAM, 292 Rue St Martin,
Paris Cedex 03, France.

Abstract. This paper proposes a model, called Deductive High-Level Petri Net (DHLPN), for which syntax and semantics are derived from High-Level Petri Nets (HLPN). This model serves as a means for capturing the behavior of deductive databases and for implementing an efficient recursive query evaluation. The efficiency of the proposed query evaluation technique lies in the fact that the order of generated tokens (ground predicates) is never greater than the initial set of tokens. We will compare this interpretation technique to the well known interpretation techniques that are magic-sets and envelopes. We will also show that it is possible to give a necessary and sufficient structural condition for the existence of query answers, not taking account of the extensional database.

1 Introduction

Much recent work has been focused on evaluating logic based programs and in particular, on the field of deductive databases. The major advantage of a deductive database is the ability to write queries and programs declaratively, using both facts and simple logical rules to represent knowledge. An important question arises: how should declarative queries be answered efficiently? In response to this, the resulting techniques have offered attractive solutions. The main feature of these strategies is to improve efficiency by restricting the computations to relevant facts. They all use information passing strategy in some form [3]. One of the most cited technique is the magic-set transformation and its variants[1][3][11] which have become the standard method for evaluating queries in deductive databases [14], due to its generality and efficiency. The magic-sets method is guaranteed to terminate, it does not duplicate work, and it focuses only on the portion of the database that is relevant to the query. In this paper, we present an evaluation method for which complexity is generally better than magic-set method, and identical in the worst case. This method, based on high-level Petri nets formalism can be applied to any stratified program and query. The motivation of this choice is that this formalism allows an easy exploitation of the control structure underlying logic based programs. We first propose a HLPN model, then we propose an efficient interpretation algorithm, that optimizes query evaluation in deductive databases, and for which the Bottom-up and Top-down strategies are naturally reconciled. We show that, contrary to magic-sets and envelopes methods, and given any extensional database size, the number of facts generated is limited to the extensional database size. The paper is organized as follows: in section 2 we introduce notations and preliminary definitions; section 3 presents the DHLPN's model; in section 4 we recall the basic principles of the magic-sets and envelopes optimization techniques; in section 5 we present the DHLPN based interpretation technique and compare it to the magic-sets and envelopes ones. In section 6 we state a necessary and sufficient existence condition for a query answer, based on a structural technique analysis of Petri nets that is T-invariant. Finally, section 7 contains our concluding remarks.

2 Preliminaries

Informally, a logic based program defining a deductive database is a 6-tuple of the form: $\prec$Pred,Const,Var, Funct $= \{f_0,.., f_m\}$, Fact $=\{fact_0,..., fact_n\}$, Rule$=\{r_0,...$, $r_i\}\succ$, whose arguments are respectively, a set of predicates, a set of constants, a set of variables, a set of functions, a set of initial facts and a set of first order logic formulas, eventually, with the presence of the numerical comparison operators (i.e. $=, \neq, \succ, \geq, \prec, \preceq$) [15]. These sets are assumed to be finite. Each logical program may be defined as follows :

1. A term is defined as follows:

- A variable or a constant symbol is a term.

- If f is an n-ary function symbol and $T_1,..., T_n$ are terms, then $f(T_1,..., T_n)$ is a term.

2. A literal is defined as follows:

- If p is an n-ary predicate symbol and $T_1,..., T_n$ are terms, then $p(T_1,..., T_n)$ (also written $p(\overrightarrow{T})$) is an atom.

- A literal is either an atom or a negated atom.

3. A definite clause(also rule) has the general form :

$$p(\overrightarrow{T}) \lor \neg q_1(\overrightarrow{T_1})\lor \neg q_2 (\overrightarrow{T_2})\lor ...\lor \neg q_n(\overrightarrow{T_n})$$

Written in a Prolog style as: $p(\overrightarrow{T})$:- $q_1(\overrightarrow{T_1})$, $q_2(\overrightarrow{T_2})$, ..., $q_n(\overrightarrow{T_n})$; read declaratively as $q_1(\overrightarrow{T_1})$ and $q_2(\overrightarrow{T_2})$ and ...$q_n(\overrightarrow{T_n})$ implies $p(\overrightarrow{T})$, where $p(\overrightarrow{T})$ is an atom and $q_1(\overrightarrow{T_1})$, $q_2(\overrightarrow{T_2})$, ..., $q_n(\overrightarrow{T_n})$ are literals. We refer $p(\overrightarrow{T})$ as the head of the clause and $q_1(\overrightarrow{T_1})$, $q_2(\overrightarrow{T_2})$, ..., $q_n(\overrightarrow{T_n})$ as the subgoals. The subgoals together are called the body of the clause. The commas in the body denote conjunction.

4. A program is a finite set of clauses. A Horn clause is one with no negative subgoals, and a Horn program is one with only Horn rules. A Datalog program is a function-free Horn program. For the purpose of this paper, we will only consider Datalog programs.

5. Following Prolog convention, Lower-case letters will generally denote predicate symbols, function symbols and constants; while upper-case letters will denote variables. The word "ground" is used as a synonym for "variable-free".

6. Certain predicates are defined by the rules, they appear as the head of one or more rules. These are called IDB (intentional database) predicates. Other predicates are not defined by rules, but by a stored relation, these are called EDB (extensional database) predicates.

7. A query is of the form ?-q(X_1, X_2, X_3,...,X_n) or ?-q($\vec{X}$), where q is an IDB predicate and each X_i is either a variable or a constant.

8. The Herbrand universe of a deductive database's program P is the set of all ground terms which can be formed using constants and function symbols appearing in P. The Herbrand base of P is the set of all ground atoms which can be formed by using predicate symbols from P, whose arguments are in the Herbrand universe. The Herbrand interpretation is an interpretation with the Herbrand universe as a domain. A Herbrand interpretation for P is a Herbrand model for P.

3 Deductive High-Level Petri Nets

The purpose of this section is to provide a brief presentation of Deductive High-Level Petri Nets (DHLPN). We recall, the graphical representation and algebraic definition of a deductive high-level Petri net. For more details, the reader is referred to [9].

3.1 Net Notations

Deductive high-level Petri nets are derived from high-level Petri nets: colored Petri nets [4][8]and Predicate Transition Nets (PrTN) [6]. DHLPN are bipartite digraphs, where the nodes called "places" represent the predicates and the nodes called "transitions" represent the rules. The set of places is denoted P and the set of transition T. As in PrTN, in our model, tokens are considered as structured objects carrying values similar to database tuples (i.e. facts); and transitions for which the firing can be controlled by imposing conditions over the token values. It has been shown that PrTN are a powerful tool for modeling first order logic programs in Expert systems. Indeed, it has been proved in [5] that each well formed formula in first order logic can be represented in a PrTN. Thus any logic based program using Horn clauses can be suitably modeled by a Predicate Transition Net. In a deductive HLPN formalism, according to some predicates, a fact is modeled by a valuated token, namely a color, in the corresponding place. Hence, the set of possible facts for a predicate defines the "color domain" of the corresponding place. The occurrence of a predicate in a rule is modeled by an arc which links the corresponding place to the corresponding transition, moreover, every arc is labeled by a color function to state the tokens to be used by the firing of the corresponding transition, with respect to a given color. Three types of arcs must be considered :

1. "transition output arcs" (out) are used for predicates that occur in the head of a rule; they are able to produce tokens (i.e. deduced facts) ;

2. "test arcs" (tst) are used for predicates that occur positively in the body of a rule; intuitively, a test arc (p,t) (where p ∈ P and t ∈ T), is equivalent to a double arc, (p,t) and (t,p), since it allows the test for the existence of some tokens, keeping the place marking invariable [2] [4] ;

3. "inhibitor arcs" (inh) deal with negative predicates appearing in the body of a rule, in order to express the testing for the absence of certain tokens (not necessarily all) in a given place.

In Deductive high-level Petri nets, We annotate the arcs by color functions. A color function is made up of tuples of basic functions defined on classes of colors. Sums of tuples are needed when predicates appear several times (either positively or negatively) in a rule. According to the type of arcs, we define three incidence functions named $W_{[out]}$, $W_{[tst]}$ and $W_{[inh]}$. In the following we introduce formally a deductive high-level Petri net, then illustrate it through an example.

Definition 1. Let U be a non empty finite set. A multi set b is a function $b \in [U \rightarrow \mathbb{N}]$. Intuitively a multi set contains all the occurrences of a given item. Each multi set over U is represented by the sum : $\sum_{u \in U} b(u) \cdot u$, where the integer $b(u)$ denotes the occurrences of u in the multi set over U. The set of all multi sets over U is denoted by Bag(U).

Definition 2. A deductive high-level Petri net is a tuple:
$$DHLPN = \langle P, T, C, W, \phi, M_0 \rangle, \text{ where:}$$
- P is a finite set of places (predicates)
- T is a finite set of transitions (rules). $P \cap T = \emptyset$.
- C is the family of finite nonempty color classes; $\forall x \in P \cup T$ C(x) denotes the color domain of x.
- $W_{[a]}$ with $a \in \{tst, inh, out\}$ is a $(P \times T) \cup (T \times P)$-indexed family of functions such that $\forall p \in P, \forall t \in T, \forall c \in C(t)$, $W_{[a]}(p,t)(c)$ and $W_{[a]}(t,p)(c)$ are multisets over C(p).
- ϕ is a predicate function defined by:
$\phi \in [C(t) \rightarrow \{True, False\}]$. By default $\forall t \in T, \phi(C(t)) = True$.
- M_0: $M_0(p) \in Bag(C(p))$ is the initial marking of p.

The DHLPN can be represented graphically like Colored Petri nets, by a graph denoted $\mathcal{N}G = \langle P, T, F \rangle$, where $F \subseteq (P \times T) \cup (T \times P)$ is the set of arc or flow relation. In this graph, places and transitions are drawn as circles and boxes respectively. An arc $(p,t) \in F$ is drawn from a place p to a transition t iff: $W_{[tst]}(p,t) \neq \emptyset$ or $W_{[inh]}(p,t) \neq \emptyset$. An arc $(t,p) \in F$ is drawn from a transition t to a place p iff: $W_{[out]}(t,p) \neq \emptyset$ or $W_{[tst]}(p,t) \neq \emptyset$.

Example 1. Consider the following nonlinear same-generation example [15]
(r_1) sg (X,Z) :- flat (X,Z).
(r_2) sg (X,Z) :- up (X,U), sg (U,V), flat (V,W), sg (W,Y), down (Y,Z).

The extensional database is EDB = {up(c,a); up(a,e); flat(a,b); flat(a,c); flat(d,a); flat(e,d); down(b,d); down(d,e)}

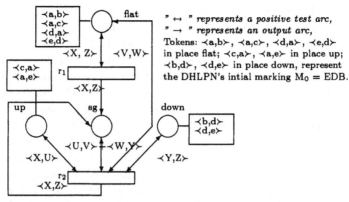

Fig. 1. The translation into high-level Petri net
of the non linear same generation example

3.2 Transition Enabling Conditions and Firing Rule

A "canonical model" for Horn programs is given by a unique least Herbrand
model. There exists a correspondance between this model and the DHLPN's
one. In the DHLPN model, the computation of the minimal Herbrand model
is achieved after successive firings of transitions. These firings produce deduced
facts in places, providing consequently the minimal Herbrand model in question.
The computation of deduced facts is ensured by a semi naive forward chaining
technique, taking into account the Petri net control structure and the arcs' labels
dependencies. According to the types of arcs, two transition enabling conditions
should be satisfied.

Definition 3. A transition $t \in T$ is enabled for a given marking M and for a given
color $c \in C(t)$ iff :
1. $\nexists$ t' | $\pi(t') < \pi(t)$, and t' is enabled.
2. $\forall p \in P$, $W_{[test]}(p,t)(c) \leq M(p)$, $\phi(c) = $ True and $W_{[inh]}(p,t)(c) > M(p)$, or
   $\forall p \in P$, $W_{[test]}(p,t)(c) \leq M(p)$, $\phi(c) = $ True; $W_{[inh]}(p,t) = \emptyset$.

Definition 4. The firing of an enabled transition t for a marking M gives a new
marking M' denoted: $M \xrightarrow{t} M'$ and defined by:
$$M'(p) = M(p) + W_{[out]}(t,p)(c).$$
Moreover we have: $\forall$ M, $\forall$ t, $M \xrightarrow{t} M' \Rightarrow M' \succ M$.

4 Magic-sets and Envelopes Optimization Techniques

One of the central problem in the implementation of deductive database systems
is designing the query optimizer [13]. In the presence of recursive queries, we
want to avoid infinite expressions and nested loops. The principal work done has
focused on the bottom-up evaluation such that the rewriting of program's rules
can mimic the top-down evaluation and ensure the finiteness of the bottom-up

evaluation, while avoiding irrelevant facts. There is an extensive literature on the subject of optimization techniques. One of the most well-known is the magic-sets transformation and its variants [1][3][11][12]. In[14], the author showed that there are still some very basic misconceptions about the magic-sets method and proposed a method based on envelopes, that in many cases may be better than the magic-sets one. We will not explain both methods in details; we will only give the most basic ideas of the two approaches, in order to compare our evaluation method to these previous ones. For more details the reader is referred to [14][3]. The magic-sets method computes "magic" predicates for the bindings of goals in a program's rule. These rules are rewritten using magic predicates so that only relevant facts to the query are generated. The rewriting is guided by a choice of Sideways Information Passing Strategy (SIPS) for each rule. A SIPS [3] is a decision on how to pass information sideways in the body of a rule while evaluating the rule. A SIPS specifies how bindings available in the head will be used, the order in which subgoals in the body will be evaluated and how bindings will be passed between predicates in the body. Given a SIPS, the first step of the rewritten method is to produce an adorned version, P^{ad} of a program P; then the second one consists on introducing magic predicates. P^{ad} is obtained using the bf adornment class. The later is a system of adornments that distinguishes between bound (b adorned) and free (f adorned) argument positions. For example the query goal (q) : ?- p(5, Y) can be adorned p^{bf} (5, Y), the subscript bf indicates that the first argument of p is bound and the second is free. EDB predicates are not adorned. Let us now consider the previous nonlinear same-generation example. Figure 2 gives the corresponding adorned program with respect to the query ?- sg (a, Z), and Figure 3 shows the corresponding magic program.

(r_0) ?- sg(a,Z)
(r_1) sg^{bf} (X,Z) : - flat (X,Z).
(r_2) sg^{bf} (X,Z) : - up (X,U), sg^{bf} (U,V), flat (V,W), sg^{bf} (W,Y), down (Y,Z).

Fig. 2. The adorned nonlinear same-generation program.

m-sg^{bf} (a).
m-sg^{bf} (U) :- m-sg^{bf} (X), up (X,U).
m-sg^{bf} (W):- m-sg^{bf} (X), up (X,U), sg^{bf} (U,V), flat (V,W).
sg^{bf} (X, Z) :- m-sg^{bf} (X), flat (X,Z).
sg^{bf} (X, Z) :- m-sg^{bf} (X), up (X,U), sg^{bf} (U,V), flat (V,W), sg^{bf} (W,Y),
　　　　　　　down (Y,Z).

Fig. 3. Magic program of the nonlinear same-generation example with a bf query.

Now if the query is sg(a,c), we get two adornments, one adornment bb for the head predicate and one adornment bf for the body predicate. In the new magic program with respect to the query sg(a,c), we have to create more rules according to the different ordering bb and bf, this magic program is shown in Figure 4.

m-sg^{bb} (a,c).

m-sg^{bb} (W,Y) : - m-sg^{bb} (X,Z), up (X,U), sg^{bf} (U,V), flat (V,W),
                down (Y,Z).

m-sg^{bf} (U) : - m-sg^{bb} (X,Z), up (X,U).

m-sg^{bf} (U) : - m-sg^{bf} (X), up (X,U).

m-sg^{bf} (W) : - m-sg^{bf} (X), up (X,U), sg^{bf} (U,V), flat (V,W).

sg^{bb} (X,Z) : - m-sg^{bb} (X,Z), flat (X,Z).

sg^{bb} (X, Z) : - m-sg^{bb} (X,Z), up (X,U), sg^{bf} (U,V), flat (V,W),
                down (Y,Z), sg^{bb} (W,Y).

sg^{bf} (X,Z) : - m-sg^{bf} (X), flat (X,Z).

sg^{bf} (X,Z) : - m-sg^{bf} (X), up (X,U), sg^{bf} (U,V), flat (V,W), sg^{bf} (W,Y),
                down (Y,Z).

Fig. 4. Magic program of the nonlinear same-generation example with a bb
query.

Even if the two columns of the query are bound, the resulting magic program
is complicated and its computation is less efficient than what expected. Thus,
in [14] a method that creates envelopes is proposed. Envelopes are similar to
magic-sets, in the sense that they restrict a query evaluation to the relevant
facts but not necessarily to the same relevant facts generated by magic-sets. The
restriction is obtained by dividing IDB predicates into factors corresponding to a
subset of columns of these predicates. A combination of an envelope and a magic
program on the previous same-generation example is represented in Figure 5.

m-sg^{bf} (a) :- fl-sg (a).

m-sg^{bf} (U) :- m-sg^{bf} (X), fl-sg (X), up (X,U), fl-sg (U).

m-sg^{bf} (W) :- m-sg^{bf} (X), fl-sg (X), up (X,U), sg^{bf} (U,V), flat (V,W),
                fl-sg (W).

sg^{bf} (X,Z) :- m-sg^{bf} (X), fl-sg (X), b2-sg (Z), flat (X,Z).

sg^{bf} (X,Z) :- m-sg^{bf} (X), fl-sg (X), b2-sg (Z), up (X,U), sg^{bf} (U,V),
                flat (V,W), sg^{bf}(W,Y), down (Y,Z).

Fig. 5. Combination of magic program and envelope with a bf query.

4.1 Comments

The program in Figure 3 has an unary magic predicate. If the size of the EDB
is n, then only $O(n)$ facts can be generated for that predicate; however there are
some cases when it could generate $O(n^2)$ facts . The program in Figure 5 based
on envelopes never generates more than $O(n)$ facts . Further more, the program
of figure 4 has a binary predicate m-sg^{bb}, so $O(n^2)$ facts may be generated for
m-sg^{bb}, when only $O(n)$ facts are generated for sg. The advantage of the program
obtained by combining envelope and magic sets is that the number of generated
facts for envelope predicates is no more than $O(n)$. However there are some cases,
depending on the EDB size, where the magic predicate m-sg^{bb} has only $O(n)$
facts, while the envelope program creates $O(n^2)$ facts. Thus the magic program

could be better. We will study in the following section the cases for which the proposed evaluation method, based on the DHLPN, does not generate more than $O(n)$ facts for IDB predicates while the previous methods generate $O(n^2)$ facts; and we will identify the cases where neither our approach nor the previous ones could generate less than $O(n^2)$ facts.

5 The Deductive HLPN Based Interpretation

In this section, we present a DHLPN based interpretation technique, for optimizing query evaluation in deductive databases. The proposed method is an optimized mixed bottom-up and top-down approach. It consists of performing a sequence of firing and reverse firing of DHLPN's transitions; taking advantage of a strategy similar to the sideway information passing strategy (SIPS). This strategy is such that the order of transitions in the firing sequence and the scanning of domains places focuses the computation on the facts relevant to the query. In the following, we will first give the method, then illustrate it through an example.

5.1 The Interpretation Skeleton for Query Evaluation

Given a deductive database D, a query ?- $q(\vec{A})$, and the corresponding adorned program P^{ad}; we built the corresponding deductive HLPN, with respect to arcs' dependencies and to the selected SIPS. The set of P^{ad} rules is split into recursive and non recursive ones. Let $r_r = \{r_{r1}, r_{r2},...,r_{rm}\}$ be the set of recursive rules and $r_n = \{r_{n1}, r_{n2},...,r_{nk}\}$ be the set of non recursive rules. The evaluation always starts with the set of non recursive rules. Each DHLPN's place domain is defined by the Cartesian product $(C_1 \otimes C_2 \otimes ... \otimes C_n)$, where n is the arity of the corresponding predicate. The algorithm scans all the places relevant to the query pushing the bound argument of the query into the arcs. The principal operations performed by the algorithm can be summarized in two steps. For each rule the following operations are performed.

Step1 : The first step consists of evaluating a rule of the non recursive set r_n. The algorithm identifies the partition relevant to q's evaluation. The q's bound argument is pushed in q's output arc $W_{[out]}$ (r_{ni}, q), where r_{ni} is q's input transition. The reverse firing of r_{ni} with respect to the bound argument color pushes this restriction to the first test arc belonging to $^\bullet r_{ni}$'s partition (i.e. all the r_{ni} input places sharing the same variables in color functions labelling the r_{ni}'s test arcs). Let $p_1, p_2, ..., p_n$, be the places belonging to this partition. If $C_1 \otimes C_2 \otimes ... \otimes C_k$ is p_1's domain then only C_1 is scanned giving a partial set of tuples that match. The bindings obtained for $C_1 \otimes C_2 \otimes ... \otimes C_k$, are propagated sideways to $p_2, ..., p_n$. The firing of r_{ni} with respect to the tuples that match stores in place q a subset of tuples that satisfy the query.

Step2 : The second step consists on evaluating a rule of the recursive set r_r. As in the first step the algorithm identifies the partition $^\bullet r_{ri}$ relevant to q's evaluation, and it performs the same operations as in Step1, the only difference here is that in q's partition q's place may occur several times. While propagating the bindings sideways; at each time we encounter place q, the algorithm has to scan place q and to perform Step1 in order to find all the tuples that match with the bindings. The propagation is finished when the last arc and place of the partition are treated. The recursive q's input transition r_{ri} is fired with respect to the tuples that match. A new set of tuples that satisfy the query is stored in place q.

Example 2. Let us consider the previous same generation example. In order to follow the appropriate SIPS we duplicate the test arc $W_{[tst]}$ (sg, r_2) giving an evaluation order of the arc's labels. The given query is ?- sg(a,Z); and $r_n = \{r_1\}$, $r_r = \{r_2\}$. Each tuple in place sg can be produced by $W_{[out]}$ (r_1, sg) or $W_{[out]}$ (r_2, sg). The set of tuples produced during the evaluation of the query is represented in Figure 6. In this figure, the firing of a transition r_i is denoted by an arc labelled r_i, the reverse firing by r_i^{-1}, the scanning of a place by S_c and the propagation of bound arguments from a color function to another one by S_{ips}.

Step 1: the following operations are performed :

?-sg(a,Z) $\xrightarrow{r_1^{-1}}$?-flat(a,Z) $\xrightarrow{S_c}$ flat(a,b), flat(a,c) $\xrightarrow{r_1}$ **sg(a,b), sg(a,c)**

Step 2: the following operations are performed :

?-sg(a,Z) $\xrightarrow{r_2^{-1}}$?-up(a,U) $\xrightarrow{S_c}$ up(a,e) $\xrightarrow{S_{ips}}$?-sg(e,V)

Since sg is a recursive predicate, we have to perform the two steps for evaluating ?-sg(e,V):

Step 1: ?-sg(e,V) $\xrightarrow{r_1^{-1}}$?-flat(e,Z) $\xrightarrow{S_c}$ flat(e,d) $\xrightarrow{r_1}$ sg(e,d)

Step 2: -sg(e,V) $\xrightarrow{r_2^{-1}}$?-up(e,U) $\xrightarrow{S_c}$ ∅. We return to the previous Step 2,

sg(e,d) $\xrightarrow{S_{ips}}$?-flat(d,W) $\xrightarrow{S_c}$ flat(d,a) $\xrightarrow{S_{ips}}$?-sg(a,Y) $\xrightarrow{S_c}$ sg(a,b), sg(a,c) $\xrightarrow{S_{ips}}$?-down(b,Z), ?-down(c,Z) $\xrightarrow{S_c}$ down(b,d) $\xrightarrow{r_2}$ **sg(a,d)**.

Fig. 6. The DHLPN's query evaluation behaviour

5.2 DHLPN Interpretation vs Magic-sets and Envelopes Methods

We have seen in subsection 4.1, that the optimizations offered by the magic-sets and envelopes techniques have not brought the expected results, since the answer of a query may generate $O(n^2)$ facts for intentional database predicates, starting from an EDB of size n. In fact, the rewriting complexity of those techniques depends on the EDB and on the type of the query. Indeed, answering a query ?-$q^{bb}(\vec{T})$, may generate a number of tuples that exceed the one generated by a query ?-$q^{bf}(\vec{T})$. The reason is that the rewriting proposed by those techniques can add a type of rules that derives IDB predicates after a Cartesian product, whereas such types of rules are not present in the original program. That is why the number of tuples generated can reach a size equal to $O(n^2)$. An illustration of this case is the rule deriving the magic predicate m-sg^{bb}(W, Y) in Figure

4. Since the DHLPN model that allows rules' interpretation does not modify the initial program structure, the DHLPN's evaluation never generates more than $O(n)$ facts if the EDB size is n, in the two cases (i.e. with bf and bb adornment). From the comparison, we can say that contrary to the previous techniques, the proposed algorithm in the DHLPN is monotonic in the sense that if we consider two queries q_1 and q_2 such that semantically $q_1 \subseteq q_2$ (i.e. the answers of q_1 are a part of answers of q_2 or all the answers of q_2); then the number of facts generated by q_1 is always less than or equal to the number of facts generated by q_2, which is not the case for the previous methods. Also, we can claim that if the number of free arguments in a given query is at most one, then the number of facts generated for the intentional database predicates is no more than $O(n)$. However, if the original program contains a rule that requires a Cartesian product for deriving an IDB predicate, then neither the previous techniques nor the DHLPN interpretation can avoid generating $O(n^2)$ tuples, where n is the size of the EDB.

6   T-invariant Technique

Net invariant technique is one of the various structural analysis techniques in Petri net theory. The idea is based on the fact that some behavioral information can be obtained through a linear representation. In this section, we propose to use a Petri Net structural technique analysis that is T-invariant. A similar approach applied to the modeling of logic programs was proposed in [10].

Let us consider a query $?\text{-}q(\overrightarrow{T})$ on a given DHLPN. We show that the existence of this query answer is closely related to the existence of particular T-invariant on the DHLPN. The existence condition is given by theorem 10.

Definition 5. A firing sequence $\sigma = t_1, t_2, ..., t_n$ is said to be executable from a marking M_0 if t_1 is firable from M_0, and t_2 from M_1, and so on for all transitions in σ. This can be denoted by any of the following ways :
$$M_0[\sigma \succ M_n$$
$$M_0[t_1, t_2, ..., t_n \succ M_n$$

Definition 6. The Parikh mapping of a firing sequence $\sigma = t_1, t_2, ..., t_n$ is denoted by $\bar{\sigma}$. It gives the number of each transitions' occurences in σ.

Definition 7. Let $?\text{-}q(\overrightarrow{T})$ be a query on a given DHLPN. The extended DHLPN with respect to this query is obtained by adding an output transition r_q for place q and an output transition r_{p*} for each IDB predicate denoted p^*. The set of these augmented transitions is denoted by T_q. Arc (q, r_q) and arcs of type (p^*, r_{p*}) are input arcs denoted $W_{[inp]}(p,t)$.

Definition 8. The incidence matrix A_q (m×n) of an extended DHLPN is defined as follows:
$$A_q[p,t] = \begin{cases} W_{[out]}(t,p) & \text{if } t \notin {}^{\bullet}T_q \\ -W_{[inp]}(p,t) & \text{if } t \in T_q \\ 0 & \text{otherwise} \end{cases}$$

Definition 9. An n-dimensional vector of integers X is called a T-invariant iff $A_q X = 0$. We denote by $X(i)$ the ith component of X.

Property 1. Let $q(\vec{T})$ be a query. If there exists a firing sequence such that $M_0[\sigma \succ M_0$ producing an answer for $q(\vec{T})$, then $A_q X = 0$, where $\bar{\sigma} = X$ and $X(r_q) \neq 0$.

Theorem 10. *Let DHLPN* $= \langle P, T, C, W, \phi, M_0 \rangle$ *be a deductive HLPN and* $q(\vec{T})$ *be a query. There exists an answer for* $q(\vec{T})$ *iff there exists a T-invariant* X *($A_q X = 0$) such that* $X \geq 0$, *$X(r_q) \neq 0$.*

Proof. The necessity is obvious by property 1. The sufficiency is proved as follows. Let X be a vector such that $A_q X = 0$ and $X(r_q) \neq 0$. Then one can exhibit a firing sequence σ such that $M_0[\sigma \succ M_0$, producing an answer for $q(\vec{T})$. Indeed, the occurrence order of σ's transitions is obtained with respect to their priority order. σ starts by firing output transitions of EDB predicates, then by output transitions of IDB predicates, and finishes with augmented transitions (T_q). Generally, σ is not unique.

Example 3. We use the previous same generation example: from the query ?-$sg(a,Z)$, we add two transitions, a transition r_q corresponding to the query, and a transition r_{sg} for the IDB predicate sg. The corresponding extended DHLPN is depicted by Figure 7. There have been several proposed methods for finding T-invariants of high-level Petri nets [7] unfortunately, these methods are of high complexity and applicable under some conditions on color functions admitting inverses. For our example, one can check that $X^T = \prec 1,2,1,1 \succ$ is a solution of $A_q X = 0$, and $X(r_q) = 1$.

$$
A_q X = \begin{array}{c} \\ \text{flat} \\ \text{up} \\ \text{sg} \\ \text{down} \end{array}
\begin{array}{cccc} r_1 & r_2 & r_q & r_{sg} \\ \end{array}
\left(\begin{array}{cccc}
0 & 0 & 0 & 0 \\
0 & 0 & 0 & 0 \\
<X,Z> & <X,Z> & -<a,Z> & -<X,Y> \\
0 & 0 & 0 & 0
\end{array} \right)
\left(\begin{array}{c} 1 \\ 2 \\ 1 \\ 1 \end{array} \right)
= \left(\begin{array}{c} 0 \\ 0 \\ 0 \\ 0 \end{array} \right)
$$

A corresponding firing sequence deduced from $X^T = \prec 1,2,1,1 \succ$ is $\sigma = r_1, r_2, r_2$, r_q, r_{sg}. This ordering is due to the following priority order $\pi(r_1) \prec \pi(r_2)$. r_q and r_{sg} can be fired simultaneously. One can check that we have $M_0[\sigma \succ M_0$. Indeed:

$$M_0 \xrightarrow{r_1} M_1 = M_0 + sg(a,b) + sg(a,c) + sg(d,a) + sg(e,d) \xrightarrow{r_2} M_2 = M_1 + sg(a,d) \xrightarrow{r_2} M_3$$
$$M_3 = M_2 + sg(c,d) + sg(c,e) \xrightarrow{r_{sg}} M_4 = M_3 - sg(d,a) - sg(e,d) - sg(c,d) - sg(c,e) \xrightarrow{r_q} M_5$$
$$M_5 = M_4 - sg(a,b) - sg(a,c) - sg(a,d) = M_0.$$

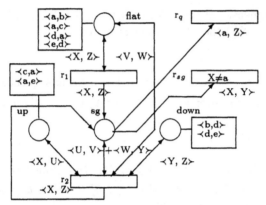

Fig. 7. The extended DHLPN wrt the query ?- sg(a,Z)

Remark. The answers of the query ?- sg(a,Z) correspond exactly to M_4(sg).

7 Conclusion

We proposed a special class of HLPN for modeling and interpreting logic based programs and especially deductive databases. We provided an efficient evaluation method for recursive query processing. The semi-naive algorithm used is a mixed Bottom-up Top-down approach. The advantage of this algorithm is that it can be applied to any stratified program translated into High-Level Petri Nets; it never generates infinite expressions and it ensures the finiteness of the query evaluation. Its main property is that it never generates more facts for intentional database predicates than the size of the given extensional database. Moreover, in the worst case our algorithm generates no more facts than magic-sets method or envelopes method. We also established a necessary and sufficient structural condition for query answer existence based on T-invariant computation, not taking into account the EDB. Our future work will consist of handling with complex queries in DHLPN. Some interesting results can be expected about control strategies for parallel processing of logic programs and deductive databases.

References

1. F. Bancilhon, D. Maier, Y. Sagiv, J. D. Ullman: Magic Sets and Other Strange Ways to Implement Logic Programs. Proc. ACM SIGACT- SIGMOD Symp. on Principles of Database Systems. (1986) 1-15.
2. K. Barkaoui , N. Boudriga , A. Touzi: A Transition Net Formalism for Deductive Databases Efficiently Handling Queries and Integrity Constraints Aspects. In Proc of the Int. Conf. on Database and Expert System Applications. Springer-Verlag. DEXA. Valencia. (1992).
3. C. Beeri, R. Ramakrishnan: On the Power of Magic. Journal of Logic Programming. (1991) 255-300.

4. S. Christensen: Coloured Petri Nets Extended with Place Capacities, Test Arcs and Inhibitor Arcs. Proc. 14th Int. Conf. on Application and Theory of Petri Nets. Chicago. (1992) 186-205.

5. H. J. Genrich, K. Lautenbach: Facts in Place: Transition nets. Lecture Notes in Computer Science, 64. Springer-Verlag.

6. H. J. Genrich: Predicate/ Transition Nets. In Advances in Petri Nets'86. Springer-Verlag (1987).

7. S. Haddad; J. M. Couvreur: Towards a General and Powerful Computation of Flows for Parametrized Coloured Nets. Proc 9th Int. Conf. on Application and Theory of Petri nets. (1988).

8. K. Jensen, G. Rozenberg (Eds): High Level Petri Nets Theory and application. Spring-Verlag. (1991).

9. Y. Maïzi, K. Barkaoui, J. M. Ilié: High-Level Petri Net Formalism for an Efficient Interpretation of Deductive Databases. Proc. fourth Maghrebian Conference on Software Engineering and Artificial Intelligence. Algiers. (1996).

10. G. Peterka, T. Murata: Proof Procedure and Answer Extraction in Petri Net Model of Logic Programs. IEEE Transactions on Software Engineering. Vol. 15, No.2. February (1989) 209-217.

11. R. Ramakrishnan: Magic Templates: A Spellbinding Approach to Logic Programs. Proc. Int. Conf. and Symp. on Logic Programming. (1988) 140-159.

12. J. Rohmer, R. Lescoeur, J. M. Kerisit: The Alexander Method: A Technique for the Processing of Recursive Axioms in Deductive Databases. New Generation Computing (1986) 273-285.

13. R. Ramakrishnan, D. Ullman: A Survey of Deductive Database Systems The Journal of Logic Programming. (1994).

14. Y. Sagiv: Is There Anything Better than Magic?. Proc. of the North American Conference on Logic Programming. Austin, Texas. (1990) 235-254.

15. J. D. Ullman: Principles of Database and Knowledge-Base Systems. volume 1, 2, Computer Science Press. (1988).

Modeling Negative and Disjunctive Information in Relational Databases

Rajshekhar Sunderraman

Dept. of Mathematics and Computer Science
Georgia State University
Atlanta, GA 30303-3083

Abstract. We present a generalization of the relational model of data in which disjunctive and negative information can be represented explicitly and manipulated. There are situations where the closed world assumption to infer negative facts is not valid or undesirable and there is a need to represent and reason with negation explicitly. We consider explicit negation in the context of disjunctive databases as there is an interesting interplay between these two types of information. *Disjunctive paraconsistent relations* are introduced as the main structure in this model. The relational algebra is appropriately generalized to work on disjunctive paraconsistent relations and their correctness is established.

1 Introduction

Two important features of the relational data model [2] for databases are its value-oriented nature and its rich set of simple, but powerful algebraic operators. Moreover, a strong theoretical foundation for the model is provided by the classical first-order logic [14]. This combination of a respectable theoretical platform, ease of implementation and the practicality of the model resulted in its immediate success, and the model has enjoyed being used by many database management systems. Even nonrelational systems are often described, for commercial purposes, as supporting relational features.

One limitation of the relational data model, however, is its lack of applicability to nonclassical situations. These are situations involving incomplete or even inconsistent information.

Several types of incomplete information have been extensively studied in the past such as *null* values [3, 5, 8, 11], *partial* values [6], *fuzzy* and *uncertain* values [4, 13], and *disjunctive* information [7, 9, 10, 16].

In this paper, we present a generalization of the relational model of data. Our model is capable of representing and manipulating positive disjunctive facts as well as explicit negative facts. We introduce *disjunctive paraconsistent relations*, which are the fundamental structures underlying our model. These structures are generalizations of *paraconsistent relations* [1] which are capable of representing definite positive and negative facts. A disjunctive paraconsistent relation essentially consists of two kinds of information: positive tuple sets representing disjunctive facts (one of which belongs to the relation) and negative tuples representing negated facts (tuples that definitely do not belong to the relation).

Disjunctive paraconsistent relations are strictly more general than paraconsistent relations in that for any paraconsistent relation, there is a disjunctive paraconsistent relation with the same information content, but not *vice versa*. We define algebraic operators over disjunctive paraconsistent relations that extend the standard operations over paraconsistent relations.

2 Motivation

Explicit negation occurs in everyday world where certain values cannot be given to some parameters. In current database systems, negation is implicitly assumed (using closed world assumption [15]) when a particular query has a null answer from the database. But this poses a problem. Consider the following relational database

suppliers			parts			supply	
SNUM	SNAME		PNUM	PNAME		SNUM	PNUM
s1	jones		p1	nut		s1	p1
s2	smith		p2	cam		s1	p3
s3	blake		p3	bolt		s2	p2
			p4	wheel		s3	p4

Consider the query "find all suppliers who do not supply part p1". Suppose there is a known list of suppliers, then the answer for the query would be { s2, s3 }. This may be a definite answer from the database (augmented with the CWA), but the answer has some indefiniteness because the database may be *incomplete*. Explicit presence of incomplete information in the form of *null values* complicates the problem further. Suppose the tuple (s3,null) is part of the supply relation. Then, we are uncertain whether to include s3 as part of the answer or not. Finally, a similar problem occurs when one allows disjunctive information (such as (s3,p1) OR (s3,p2)) as part of the database.

Definite negation can occur without explicit negation in current database systems. The use of functional dependencies provide this facility. Consider the functional dependency that each person can have only one social security number. Hence if we know the SSN for a particular individual then we can explicitly assume the negation of all other possible numbers as the person's social security number.

Sometimes it is important to explicitly include in the database certain negative information. Consider a medical database containing patient information. When a doctor needs to check whether a patient has diabetes, (s)he would be more comfortable with a negative answer generated by the system using definite information (of explicit negative data) than with a negative answer found using the closed world assumption.

We are not considering the use of negative information as an integrity constraint. Rather we are utilizing negative information in query processing to provide definite negation when needed. When a positive data is included in the database, which negates a previous explicit negative information, the new data may be allowed to be entered if the user wishes to enforce it.

In this paper, we consider explicit negation in the context of disjunctive databases. We extend the representation provided in [9] by introducing explicit negative facts. There is an interesting interplay between these two kinds of information. Negative facts tend to reduce the amount of incompleteness present in the disjunctive facts as seen by the equivalence $((P \vee Q \vee R) \wedge \neg P) \equiv (Q \vee R) \wedge \neg P$. After introducing disjunctive paraconsistent relations, we present operators to remove redundancies and inconsistencies. We also extend the standard relational algebra to operate on disjunctive paraconsistent relations. The information content of disjunctive paraconsistent relations is characterized in terms of paraconsistent relations which we briefly present in the next section.

3   Paraconsistent Relations

In this section, we present a brief overview of paraconsistent relations and the algebraic operations on them. For a more detailed description, refer to [1]. Unlike ordinary relations that can model worlds in which every tuple is known to either hold a certain underlying predicate or to not hold it, paraconsistent relations provide a framework for incomplete or even inconsistent information about tuples. They naturally model *belief* systems rather than *knowledge* systems, and are thus a generalisation of ordinary relations. The operators on ordinary relations can also be generalised for paraconsistent relations.

Let a *relation scheme* (or just *scheme*) Σ be a finite set of *attribute names*, where for any attribute name $A \in \Sigma$, $dom(A)$ is a non-empty *domain* of values for A. A *tuple* on Σ is any map $t : \Sigma \to \cup_{A \in \Sigma} dom(A)$, such that $t(A) \in dom(A)$, for each $A \in \Sigma$. Let $\tau(\Sigma)$ denote the set of all tuples on Σ.

Definition 1. A *paraconsistent relation* on scheme Σ is a pair $R = \langle R^+, R^- \rangle$, where R^+ and R^- are any subsets of $\tau(\Sigma)$. We let $\mathcal{P}(\Sigma)$ be the set of all paraconsistent relations on Σ.   ☐

Definition 2. A paraconsistent relation R on scheme Σ is called a *consistent paraconsistent relation* if $R^+ \cap R^- = \emptyset$. We let $\mathcal{C}(\Sigma)$ be the set of all consistent relations on Σ. Moreover, R is called a *complete paraconsistent relation* if $R^+ \cup R^- = \tau(\Sigma)$. If R is both consistent and complete, i.e. $R^- = \tau(\Sigma) - R^+$, then it is a *total paraconsistent relation*, and we let $\mathcal{T}(\Sigma)$ be the set of all total paraconsistent relations on Σ.   ☐

To reflect generalization of relational algebra operators, a dot is placed over an ordinary relational operator to obtain the corresponding paraconsistent relation operator. For example, $\bowtie$ denotes the natural join among ordinary relations, and $\dot{\bowtie}$ denotes natural join on paraconsistent relations. We first introduce two fundamental set-theoretic algebraic operators on paraconsistent relations:

Definition 3. Let R and S be paraconsistent relations on scheme Σ. Then, the *union* of R and S, denoted $R \mathbin{\dot{\cup}} S$, is a paraconsistent relation on scheme Σ, given by $(R \mathbin{\dot{\cup}} S)^+ = R^+ \cup S^+$ and $(R \mathbin{\dot{\cup}} S)^- = R^- \cap S^-$; and the *complement* of R, denoted $\mathbin{\dot{-}} R$, is a paraconsistent relation on scheme Σ, given by $(\mathbin{\dot{-}} R)^+ = R^-$ and $(\mathbin{\dot{-}} R)^- = R^+$. □

If Σ and Δ are relation schemes such that $\Sigma \subseteq \Delta$, then for any tuple $t \in \tau(\Sigma)$, we let t^Δ denote the set $\{t' \in \tau(\Delta) \mid t'(A) = t(A), \text{ for all } A \in \Sigma\}$ of all extensions of t. We extend this notion for any $T \subseteq \tau(\Sigma)$ by defining $T^\Delta = \cup_{t \in T} t^\Delta$. We now define some relation-theoretic operators on paraconsistent relations.

Definition 4. Let R and S be paraconsistent relations on schemes Σ and Δ, respectively. Then, the *natural join* (or just *join*) of R and S, denoted $R \bowtie S$, is a paraconsistent relation on scheme $\Sigma \cup \Delta$, given by $(R \bowtie S)^+ = R^+ \bowtie S^+$, and $(R \bowtie S)^- = (R^-)^{\Sigma \cup \Delta} \cup (S^-)^{\Sigma \cup \Delta}$, where $\bowtie$ is the usual natural join among ordinary relations. □

Definition 5. Let R be a paraconsistent relation on scheme Σ, and Δ be any scheme. Then, the *projection* of R onto Δ, denoted $\dot{\pi}_\Delta(R)$, is a paraconsistent relation on Δ, given by $\dot{\pi}_\Delta(R)^+ = \pi_\Delta((R^+)^{\Sigma \cup \Delta})$, and $\dot{\pi}_\Delta(R)^- = \{t \in \tau(\Delta) \mid t^{\Sigma \cup \Delta} \subseteq (R^-)^{\Sigma \cup \Delta}\}$, where π_Δ is the usual projection over Δ of ordinary relations. □

Definition 6. Let R be a paraconsistent relation on scheme Σ, and let F be any logic formula involving attribute names in Σ, constant symbols (denoting values in the attribute domains), equality symbol $=$, negation symbol $\neg$, and connectives $\vee$ and $\wedge$. Then, the *selection* of R by F, denoted $\dot{\sigma}_F(R)$, is a paraconsistent relation on scheme Σ, given by $\dot{\sigma}_F(R)^+ = \sigma_F(R^+)$, and $\dot{\sigma}_F(R)^- = R^- \cup \sigma_{\neg F}(\tau(\Sigma))$, where σ_F is the usual selection of tuples satisfying F. □

4 Disjunctive Paraconsistent Relations

In this section, we present the main structure underlying our model, the *disjunctive paraconsistent relations*. We identify several types of redundancies and inconsistencies that may appear and provide operators to remove them. Finally, we present the information content of disjunctive paraconsistent relations.

Definition 7. A *disjunctive paraconsistent relation*, R, over the scheme Σ consists of two components $< R^+, R^- >$ where $R^+ \subseteq 2^{\tau(\Sigma)}$ and $R^- \subseteq \tau(\Sigma)$. R^+, the *positive* component, is a set of tuple sets. Each tuple set in this component represents a disjunctive positive fact. In the case where the tuple set is a singleton, we have a definite positive fact. R^-, the *negative* component consists of tuples that we refer to as definite negative tuples. Let $\mathcal{D}(\Sigma)$ represent all disjunctive paraconsistent relations over the scheme Σ. □

Example 1. Consider the following disjunctive paraconsistent relation:
$supply^+ = \{\{< s1, p1 >\}, \{< s2, p1 >, < s2, p2 >\}, \{< s3, p3 >, < s3, p4 >\}\}$
$supply^- = \{< s1, p2 >, < s1, p3 >\}$. The *positive component* corresponds to the
statements s1 supplies p1, s2 supplies p1 or p2, and s3 supplies p3 or p4 and the
negative component corresponds to s1 does not supply p2 and s1 does not supply
p3. It should be noted that the status of tuples that do not appear anywhere in
the disjunctive paraconsistent relation, such as (s3,p1), is unknown. □

Inconsistencies can be present in a disjunctive paraconsistent relation if all
the tuples of a tuple set of the positive component are also present in the negative
component. In such a case, the tuple set states that at least one of the tuples
in the tuple set must be in the relation whereas the negative component states
that all the tuples in the tuple set must not be in the relation. We deal with this
inconsistency by removing both the positive tuple set and all its tuples from the
negative component. This is done by the **norm** operator defined as follows:

Definition 8. Let R be a disjunctive paraconsistent relation over Σ. Then,
$\mathbf{norm}(R)^+ = \{w | w \in R^+ \wedge w \not\subseteq R^-\}$
$\mathbf{norm}(R)^- = R^- - \{t | t \in R^- \wedge (\exists w)(w \in R^+ \wedge t \in w \wedge w \subseteq R^-)\}$ □

A disjunctive paraconsistent relation is called *normalized* if it does not contain
any inconsistencies. We let $\mathcal{N}(\Sigma)$ denote the set of all normalized disjunctive
paraconsistent relations over scheme Σ.

We now identify the following two types of redundancies in a normalized
disjunctive paraconsistent relation R:

1. $w_1 \in R^+$, $w_2 \in R^+$, and $w_1 \subset w_2$. In this case, w_1 subsumes w_2. To eliminate
   this redundancy, we delete w_2 from R^+.
2. $v \subseteq R^-$, $w \in R^+$, and $v \subset w$. This redundancy is eliminated by deleting the
   tuple set w from R^+ and adding the tuple set $w - v$ to R^+. Since we are
   dealing with normalized disjunctive paraconsistent relations, $w - v$ cannot
   be empty.

We now introduce an operator called **reduce** to take care of redundancies.

Definition 9. Let R be a normalized disjunctive paraconsistent relation. Then,
reduce(R) is defined as follows:
$\mathbf{reduce}(R)^+ = \{w' \mid (\exists w)(w \in R^+ \wedge w' = w - R^- \wedge$
$\qquad\qquad \neg(\exists w_1)(w_1 \in R^+ \wedge (w_1 - R^-) \subset w'))\}$
$\mathbf{reduce}(R)^- = R^-$ □

Example 2. Consider the following disjunctive paraconsistent relation: $R^+ =$
$\{\{< a >\}, \{< b >, < c >\}, \{< c >, < d >\}, \{< a >, < e >\}, \{< f >, < g >\}\}$
and $R^- = \{< b >, < i >\}$. The disjunctive tuple $\{< a >, < e >\}$ is subsumed
by $\{< a >\}$ and hence removed. In the disjunctive tuple set $\{< b >, < c >\}$,
$< b >$ is redundant due to the presence of the negative tuple $< b >$ resulting
in the positive tuple $\{< c >\}$ which in turn subsumes $\{< c >, < d >\}$. The
reduced disjunctive paraconsistent relation is: $\mathbf{reduce}(R)^+ = \{\{< a >\}, \{< c >\}, \{< f >, < g >\}\}$ and $\mathbf{reduce}(R)^- = \{< b >, < i >\}$ □

The information content of a disjunctive paraconsistent relation can be defined to be a collection of paraconsistent relations that are represented in the disjunctive tuples. The different possible paraconsistent relations are constructed by selecting one of the several tuples within a tuple set for each tuple set in the positive component. In doing so, we may end up with non-minimal paraconsistent relations or even with inconsistent paraconsistent relations. These would have to be removed in order to obtain the exact information content of disjunctive paraconsistent relations. The formal definitions follow:

Definition 10. Let $U \subseteq \mathcal{P}(\Sigma)$. Then,
normrep$_\Sigma(U) = U - \{R | R \in U \wedge R^+ \cap R^- \neq \emptyset\}$ □

The **normrep** operator removes all inconsistent paraconsistent relations from its input.

Definition 11. Let $U \subseteq \mathcal{P}(\Sigma)$. Then,

reducerep$_\Sigma(U) = \{R | R \in U \wedge \neg(\exists S)(S \in U \wedge R \neq S \wedge S^+ \subseteq R^+ \wedge S^- \subseteq R^-)\}$

□

The **reducerep** operator keeps only the "minimal" paraconsistent relations and eliminates any paraconsistent relation that is "subsumed" by others.

Definition 12. The information content of disjunctive paraconsistent relations is defined by the mapping **rep**$_\Sigma : \mathcal{N}(\Sigma) \rightarrow \mathcal{P}(\Sigma)$. Let R be a normalized disjunctive paraconsistent relation on scheme Σ with $R^+ = \{w_1, \ldots, w_k\}$. Let $U = \{< \{t_1, \ldots, t_k\}, R^- > | (\forall i)(1 \leq i \leq k \rightarrow t_i \in w_i)\}$. Then,
rep$_\Sigma(R) = $ **reducerep**$_\Sigma($**normrep**$_\Sigma(U))$ □

Note that the information content is defined only for normalized disjunctive paraconsistent relations.

Example 3. Consider the following disjunctive paraconsistent relation on a single attribute scheme Σ:
$R^+ = \{\{< b >, < e >\}, \{< c >, < d >\}, \{< e >, < g >\}\}$ and $R^- = \{< b >\}$
The process of selecting tuples from tuple sets produces the following paraconsistent relations:

$U = \{ < \{< b >, < c >, < e >\}, \{< b >\} >, < \{< b >, < c >, < g >\}, \{< b >\} >,$
$\quad < \{< b >, < d >, < e >\}, \{< b >\} >, < \{< b >, < c >, < g >\}, \{< b >\} >,$
$\quad < \{< e >, < c >\}, \{< b >\} >, < \{< e >, < c >, < g >\}, \{< b >\} >,$
$\quad < \{< e >, < d >\}, \{< b >\} >, < \{< e >, < d >, < g >\}, \{< b >\} >\}.$

Normalizing the above set of paraconsistent relations using **normrep** gives us:

$U' = \{ < \{< e >, < c >\}, \{< b >\} >, < \{< e >, < c >, < g >\}, \{< b >\} >,$
$\quad < \{< e >, < d >\}, \{< b >\} >, < \{< e >, < d >, < g >\}, \{< b >\} >\}.$

Finally, removing the non-minimal paraconsistent relations using the **reducerep** operator, we get the information content $\text{rep}_\Sigma(R)$ as follows:

$$\text{rep}_\Sigma(R) = \{< \{< e >, < c >\}, \{< b >\} >, < \{< e >, < d >\}, \{< b >\} >\}.$$

$\square$

The following important theorem states that information is neither lost nor gained by removing the redundancies in a disjunctive paraconsistent relation.

Theorem 13. *Let R be a disjunctive paraconsistent relation on scheme Σ. Then,* $\text{rep}_\Sigma(\text{reduce}(R)) = \text{rep}_\Sigma(R)$ $\square$

5 Generalized Relational Algebra

In this section, we first develop the notion of *precise generalizations* of algebraic operators. This is an important property that must be satisfied by any new operator defined for disjunctive paraconsistent relations. Then, we present several algebraic operators on disjunctive paraconsistent relations that are precise generalizations of their counterparts on paraconsistent relations.

Precise Generalizations of Operations

It is easily seen that disjunctive paraconsistent relations are a generalisation of paraconsistent relations, in that for each paraconsistent relation there is a disjunctive paraconsistent relation with the same information content, but not *vice versa*. It is thus natural to think of generalising the operations on paraconsistent relations, such as union, join, projection etc., to disjunctive paraconsistent relations. However, any such generalisation should be intuitive with respect to the belief system model of disjunctive paraconsistent relations. We now construct a framework for operators on both kinds of relations and introduce the notion of the precise generalisation relationship among their operators.

An n-ary *operator on paraconsistent relations with signature* $\langle \Sigma_1, \ldots, \Sigma_{n+1} \rangle$ is a function $\Theta : \mathcal{P}(\Sigma_1) \times \cdots \times \mathcal{P}(\Sigma_n) \rightarrow \mathcal{P}(\Sigma_{n+1})$, where $\Sigma_1, \ldots, \Sigma_{n+1}$ are any schemes. Similarly, an n-ary *operator on disjunctive paraconsistent relations with signature* $\langle \Sigma_1, \ldots, \Sigma_{n+1} \rangle$ is a function $\Psi : \mathcal{D}(\Sigma_1) \times \cdots \times \mathcal{D}(\Sigma_n) \rightarrow \mathcal{D}(\Sigma_{n+1})$.

We now need to extend operators on paraconsistent relations to sets of paraconsistent relations. For any operator $\Theta : \mathcal{P}(\Sigma_1) \times \cdots \times \mathcal{P}(\Sigma_n) \rightarrow \mathcal{P}(\Sigma_{n+1})$ on paraconsistent relations, we let $\mathcal{S}(\Theta) : 2^{\mathcal{P}(\Sigma_1)} \times \cdots \times 2^{\mathcal{P}(\Sigma_n)} \rightarrow 2^{\mathcal{P}(\Sigma_{n+1})}$ be a map on sets of paraconsistent relations defined as follows. For any sets $M_1, \ldots, M_n$ of paraconsistent relations on schemes $\Sigma_1, \ldots, \Sigma_n$, respectively,

$$\mathcal{S}(\Theta)(M_1, \ldots, M_n) = \{\Theta(R_1, \ldots, R_n) \mid R_i \in M_i, \text{ for all } i, 1 \leq i \leq n\}.$$

In other words, $\mathcal{S}(\Theta)(M_1, \ldots, M_n)$ is the set of Θ-images of all tuples in the cartesian product $M_1 \times \cdots \times M_n$. We are now ready to lead up to the notion of precise operator generalisation.

Definition 14. An operator Ψ on disjunctive paraconsistent relations with signature $\langle \Sigma_1, \ldots, \Sigma_{n+1} \rangle$ is *consistency preserving* if for any normalized disjunctive paraconsistent relations $R_1, \ldots, R_n$ on schemes $\Sigma_1, \ldots, \Sigma_n$, respectively, $\Psi(R_1, \ldots, R_n)$ is also normalized. $\qquad \square$

Definition 15. A consistency preserving operator Ψ on disjunctive paraconsistent relations with signature $\langle \Sigma_1, \ldots, \Sigma_{n+1} \rangle$ is a *precise generalisation* of an operator Θ on paraconsistent relations with the same signature, if for any normalized disjunctive paraconsistent relations $R_1, \ldots, R_n$ on schemes $\Sigma_1, \ldots, \Sigma_n$, we have $\mathbf{rep}_{\Sigma_{n+1}}(\Psi(R_1, \ldots, R_n)) = S(\Theta)(\mathbf{rep}_{\Sigma_1}(R_1), \ldots, \mathbf{rep}_{\Sigma_n}(R_n))$. $\qquad \square$

We now present precise generalisations for the usual relation operators, such as union, join, projection. To reflect generalisation, a hat is placed over an ordinary relation operator to obtain the corresponding disjunctive paraconsistent relation operator. For example, $\bowtie$ denotes the natural join among ordinary relations, $\widehat{\bowtie}$ denotes natural join on paraconsistent relations and $\widehat{\widehat{\bowtie}}$ denotes natural join on disjunctive paraconsistent relations.

Definition 16. Let R and S be two normalized disjunctive paraconsistent relations on scheme Σ. Then, $R \widehat{\cup} S$ is a disjunctive paraconsistent relation over scheme Σ given by $R \widehat{\cup} S = \mathbf{reduce}(T)$, where $T^+ = R^+ \cup S^+$ and $T^- = R^- \cap S^-$. and $R \widehat{\cap} S$ is a disjunctive paraconsistent relation over scheme Σ given by $R \widehat{\cap} S = \mathbf{reduce}(T)$, where $T^+ = R^+ \cap S^+$ and $T^- = R^- \cup S^-$. $\qquad \square$

The positive component of the union is the usual union of the respective positive components of the operands, whereas the negative component of the union is the intersection of the respective negative components of the operands. In the case of intersection the roles of union and intersection are reversed. The intuition behind this and subsequent definitions are derived from the belief system basis for disjunctive paraconsistent relations.

The following theorem establishes the *precise generalization* property for union and intersection:

Theorem 17. *Let R and S be two normalized disjunctive paraconsistent relations on scheme Σ. Then,*

1. $\mathbf{rep}_\Sigma(R \widehat{\cup} S) = \mathbf{rep}_\Sigma(R) S(\dot{\cup}) \mathbf{rep}_\Sigma(S)$.
2. $\mathbf{rep}_\Sigma(R \widehat{\cap} S) = \mathbf{rep}_\Sigma(R) S(\dot{\cap}) \mathbf{rep}_\Sigma(S)$. $\qquad \square$

Definition 18. Let R be a normalized disjunctive paraconsistent relation on scheme Σ, and let F be any logic formula involving attribute names in Σ, constant symbols (denoting values in the attribute domains), equality symbol $=$, negation symbol $\neg$, and connectives $\vee$ and $\wedge$. Then, the *selection* of R by F, denoted $\widehat{\sigma}_F(R)$, is a disjunctive paraconsistent relation on scheme Σ, given by $\widehat{\sigma}_F(R) = \mathbf{reduce}(T)$, where $T^+ = \{w | w \in R^+ \wedge (\forall t \in w) F(t)\}$ and $T^- = R^- \cup \sigma_{\neg F}(\tau(\Sigma))$, where σ_F is the usual selection of tuples. $\qquad \square$

A disjunctive tuple set is either selected as a whole or not at all. All the tuples within the tuple set must satisfy the selection criteria for the tuple set to be selected.

Definition 19. Let R be a normalized disjunctive paraconsistent relation on scheme Σ, and $\Delta \subseteq \Sigma$. Then, the *projection* of R onto Δ, denoted $\widehat{\pi}_\Delta(R)$, is a disjunctive paraconsistent relation on scheme Δ, given by $\widehat{\pi}_\Delta(R) = \mathbf{reduce}(T)$, where $T^+ = \{\pi_\Delta(w)|w \in R^+\}$ and $T^- = \{t \in \tau(\Delta)|t^{\Sigma \cup \Delta} \subseteq (R^-)^{\Sigma \cup \Delta}\}$, where π_Δ is the usual projection over Δ of tuples. □

The positive component of the projections consists of the projection of each of the tuple sets onto Δ and $\widehat{\pi}_\Delta(R)^-$ consists of those tuples in $\tau(\Delta)$, all of whose extensions are in R^-.

Definition 20. Let R and S be normalized disjunctive paraconsistent relations on schemes Σ and Δ, respectively with $R^+ = \{v_1, \ldots, v_n\}$ and $S^+ = \{w_1, \ldots, w_m\}$. Then, the *natural join* of R and S, denoted $R \bowtie S$, is a disjunctive paraconsistent relation on scheme $\Sigma \cup \Delta$, given by $R \bowtie S = \mathbf{reduce}(T)$, where T is defined as follows. Let $E = \{\{t_1, \ldots, t_n\}|(\forall i)(1 \le i \le n \rightarrow t_i \in v_i)\}$ and $F = \{\{t_1, \ldots, t_m\}|(\forall i)(1 \le i \le m \rightarrow t_i \in w_i)\}$. Let the elements of E be $E_1, \ldots, E_e$ and those of F be $F_1, \ldots, F_f$ and let $A_{ij} = E_i \bowtie F_j$ for $1 \le i \le e$ and $1 \le j \le f$. Let $A_1, \ldots, A_g$ be the distinct A_{ij}s. Then,
$$T^+ = \{w|(\exists t_1) \cdots (\exists t_g)(t_1 \in A_i \wedge \cdots \wedge t_g \in A_g \wedge w = \{t_1, \ldots, t_g\})\}$$
$$T^- = (R^-)^{\Sigma \cup \Delta} \cup (S^-)^{\Sigma \cup \Delta}.$$
□

Theorem 21. *Let R and S be two normalized disjunctive paraconsistent relations on scheme Σ_1 and Σ_2. Also let F be a selection formula on scheme Σ_1 and $\Delta \subseteq \Sigma_1$. Then,*

1. $\mathbf{rep}_{\Sigma_1}(\widehat{\sigma}_F(R)) = S(\dot{\sigma}_F)(\mathbf{rep}_{\Sigma_1}(R)).$
2. $\mathbf{rep}_{\Sigma_1}(\widehat{\pi}_\Delta(R)) = S(\dot{\pi}_\Delta)(\mathbf{rep}_{\Sigma_1}(R)).$
3. $\mathbf{rep}_{\Sigma_1 \cup \Sigma_2}(R \bowtie S) = \mathbf{rep}_{\Sigma_1}(R) S(\bowtie) \mathbf{rep}_{\Sigma_2}(S).$

□

6 Conclusions and Future Work

We have presented a framework for relational databases under which positive disjunctive as well as explicit negative facts can be represented and manipulated. There are at least two directions for future work. One would be to make the model more expressive by considering disjunctive negative facts. Work is in progress in this direction. A tuple set in the negative component would represent the fact that it is not true that one of the tuples within the tuple set is in the relation. A symmetric treatment of negative tuple sets would result in a more expressive model in which positive as well as negated disjuncts are represented. The algebraic operators will have to be extended appropriately. The other direction for future work would be to find applications of the model presented in this paper. Recently there has been some interest in studying extended logic programs in which the head of clauses can have one or more literals [12]. This leads to two notions of negation: *implicit* negation (corresponding to negative literals in the body) and *explicit* negation (corresponding to negative literals in the head). The model presented in this paper could provide a framework under which the semantics of extended logic programs could be constructed in a bottom-up manner.

References

1. R. Bagai and R. Sunderraman. A paraconsistent relational data model. *International Journal of Computer Mathematics*, 55(3), 1995.
2. E.F. Codd. A relational model for large shared data banks. *Communications of the ACM*, 13(6):377–387, June 1970.
3. E.F. Codd. Missing information (applicable and inapplicable) in relational databases. *SIGMOD Record*, 15(4):53–78, December 1986.
4. E. Gelenbe and G. Hebrail. A probability model of uncertainity in databases. In *Proceedings of the International Conference on Data Engineering.* IEEE Computer Society Press, 1986.
5. J. Grant. Null values in a relational database. *Information Processing Letters*, 6(5):156–157, October 1977.
6. J. Grant. Incomplete information in a relational database. *Fundamenta Informaticae*, III(3):363–378, 1980.
7. J. Grant and J. Minker. Answering queries in indefinite databases and the null value problem. In P. Kanellakis, editor, *Advances in Computing Research*, pages 247–267. JAI Press, Greenwich, CT, 1986.
8. T. Imieliński and W. Lipski. Incomplete information in relational databases. *Journal of the ACM*, 31(4):761–791, October 1984.
9. K.-C. Liu and R. Sunderraman. Indefinite and maybe information in relational databases. *ACM Transactions on Database Systems*, 15(1):1–39, 1990.
10. K.-C. Liu and R. Sunderraman. A generalized relational model for indefinite and maybe information. *IEEE Transactions on Knowledge and Data Engineering*, 3(1):65–77, 1991.
11. D. Maier. *The Theory of Relational Databases*. Computer Science Press, Rockville, Maryland, 1983.
12. J. Minker and C. Ruiz. On extended disjunctive logic programs. In J. Komorowski and Z.W. Ras, editors, *Proceedings of the Seventh International Symposium on Methodologies for Intelligent Systems*, pages 1–18. Lecture Notes in AI, Springer-Verlag, New York, June 1993.
13. K.V.S.V.N. Raju and A.K. Majumdar. Fuzzy functional dependencies and lossless join decomposition of fuzzy relational database systems. *ACM Transactions on Database Systems*, 13(2):129–166, 1988.
14. R. Reiter. Towards a logical reconstruction of relational database theory. In M. Brodie, J. Mylopoulos, and J.W. Schmidt, editors, *On Conceptual Modeling*, pages 191–238. Springer-Verlag, Berlin and New York, 1984.
15. Raymond Reiter. On closed world data bases. In Hervé Gallaire and Jack Minker, editors, *Logic and Data Bases*, pages 55–76. Plenum Press, 1978.
16. R. Sunderraman. Deductive databases with conditional facts. *Lecture Notes in Computer Science*, 696:162–175, 1993.

Query-Driven Data Allocation Algorithms for Distributed Database Systems*

Kamalakar Karlapalem and Ng Moon Pun

University of Science and Technology
Department of Computer Science
Clear Water Bay Kowloon, Hong Kong
email : kamal@cs.ust.hk

Abstract. The objective of a data allocation algorithm is to locate the fragments at different sites so as to minimize the total data transfer cost incurred in executing a set of queries. We develop a site-independent fragment dependency graph representation to model the dependencies among the fragments accessed by a query, and use it to formulate and solve data allocation problems for distributed database systems based on (*query-site* and *move-small*) query execution strategies. We show that an optimal solution can be achieved when the query-site query execution strategy is employed, and for the move-small query execution strategy we performed experimental evaluation about the effectiveness of a hill-climbing heuristic algorithm in achieving a near-optimal solution.

1   Introduction

A distributed database is a collection of data which belongs logically to the same system but is physically spread over the sites of a computer network. A typical user can access the complete database from any site, a distributed database system processes and executes an user's query by accessing the data from multiple sites. A major component of query execution cost is the data transfer cost. It is desirable to reduce the amount of data transfer which can be achieved by optimally allocating the data fragments to the sites of the distributed database system. Optimal allocation of fragments is a complex problem because of mutual interdependency between allocation scheme and query optimization strategy. We model the dependencies between the fragments and the amount of data transfer incurred to execute a query based on a query execution strategy as site independent fragment dependency graphs. We use these fragment dependency graphs to aid in coming up with an optimal or near optimal allocation of fragments. We call this approach to data allocation problem as query-driven data allocation in distributed database systems.

The data allocation problem, first addressed by Chu [4], and subsequently addressed by [6, 2, 11, 3], who developed and generalized the problem description. Apers [1] considered the allocation of the distributed database to the sites so as

---

* This research has been funded by RGC CERG grant HKUST 609/94E.

to minimize total data transfer cost. But the author solves the complete fragmentation and allocation problem. This curtails the applicability of this methodology when fragmentation schema is already defined and allocation scheme must be generated. There have been many linear programming formulations proposed for data allocation problem [7, 5, 10, 8, and others]. The main problem with these approaches is the lack of modeling of the query execution strategy.

The rest of the paper is organized as follows: section 2 describes the inputs to the data allocation problem, section 3 describes a cost model used to calculate the total data transfer cost incurred to execute a set of queries, section 4 describes two algorithms developed in this paper, section 5 describes experiments conducted to evaluate the effectiveness of a hill-climbing heuristic algorithm, and section 6 presents some conclusions.

2 Inputs for Data Allocation Problem

Consider a distributed database system with m sites, with each site having its own processing power, memory and a database system. Let S_α be the name of site α where $0 \leq \alpha \leq m - 1$. The m sites of the distributed database system are connected by a communication network. A link between two sites S_i and S_j (if it exists) has a positive integer C_{ij} associated with it giving the cost for a unit data transferred from site S_i to site S_j. If two sites are not directly connected by a communication link then the cost for unit data transferred is given by the sum of the cost of links of a chosen path from site S_i to site S_j. Let $Q = \{q_0, q_1, \ldots, q_{n-1}\}$ be the most important queries accounting for more than 80% of the processing in the distributed database system. Each query q_β can be executed from any site with a certain frequency. Let $a_{\alpha,\beta}$ be the frequency with which query q_β is executed from site S_α. These frequencies of executions of queries at all sites can be represented by a $m \times n$ matrix, A. Let there be k fragments (or database objects, or relations), named, $\{F_0, F_1, \ldots, F_{k-1}\}$. A query accesses one or more fragments.

Query Representation The main problem in deciding on the optimal allocation is the lack of a representational model of the dependencies among the fragments accessed by the query. We use the distributed query decomposer and data localization algorithms [9] to decompose a distributed query into a set of fragment queries. This decomposed query incorporates the dependencies between fragments. These dependencies model binary operations (like join, union) between the fragments that need to be processed in order to execute the distributed query. We estimate the sizes of the intermediate relations [9] generated after executing the unary and binary operations by making use of the database statistics (like, cardinality and lengths of tuples of the fragments/relations) available from the system catalog. Since we are incorporating distributed query processing, the query decomposition and data localization phases we eliminate access to irrelevant fragments and generate a concise decomposed query operator trees on fragments. In the distributed query optimization and execution phase optimal binary operation orderings are based on a query execution strategy, such as,

1. **[Move-Small]** If a binary operation involves two fragments located at two different sites then ship the smaller fragment to the site of the large fragment.
2. **[Query-Site]** Ship all the fragments to the site of query origin and execute the query.

Query Evaluation Each of the k queries on the distributed database are restructured and decomposed to generate an query operator tree.

Example 1. Consider the following query taken form [9] accessing relations E(Eno, Ename, Title), G(Eno, Jno, Resp, Dur), and J(Jno, Jname, Budget):

```
SELECT Ename FROM J, G, E
WHERE G.Eno = E.Eno AND G.Jno = J. Jno AND Ename <> ''J.Doe''
      AND J.Name = ''CAD / CAM '' AND ( Dur = 12 OR Dur = 24 )
```

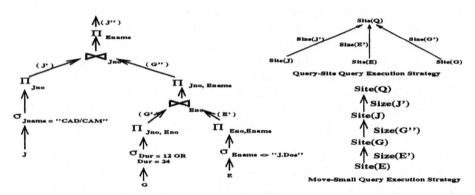

Fig. 1. Query Operator Tree and Fragment Dependency Graphs

The corresponding relational algebra tree after query decomposition and data localization is shown in figure 1. The intermediate relations generated after the query restructuring phase are J', G', E', G''', and J''. Assume that the size of G' is greater than the size of E', and the size of J' is greater than the size of G'''. By using the move-small query execution strategy it is preferable to transfer E' to the site where G' is located and also to transfer G''' to the site where J' is located, in order to minimize the total size of data required to be transferred to execute the query. In case of query-site query execution strategy, the intermediate relations J', G', and E' are all shipped to the site where the query is initiated. Based on these two query execution strategies the corresponding fragment dependency graphs that are generated are illustrated in figure 1. In a fragment dependency graph, the fragment-nodes (like Site(J), Site(G), etc.) represent the potential sites where the fragments are located. The query-node Site(Q) represents the site where the query is initiated (i.e., query site). There is a cost value attached to each edge of the graph corresponding to the amount of data that may be transferred if the fragments corresponding to the two nodes of the edge are located at different sites, or the location of the fragment and the query site are different sites. The fragment dependency graph models the execution strategy used by the query optimizer without fixing the locations of the fragments.

3 A Cost Model for Total Data Transfer

There are two aspects of the data transfer cost incurred to process a query that need to be modeled. The first aspect is the unit data transfer cost from one site to another. This is modeled as minimum cost path and the corresponding path from one site to another. We use an all-pairs shortest path algorithm to generate the cost matrix C, where $C_{i,j}$ is cost of transporting an unit of data from site S_i to site S_j. In order to find the best allocation of a fragment it is enough to know the size of data from every fragment that is required from every site. However, the problem is that the size of data from a fragment that is required from a site, varies with the locations of other fragments. The fragment dependency graph of every query models two types of data transfer cost. The first type is from the sites where the fragments are located to the site where the query is initiated. The second type is from the site where one fragment is located to the site where another fragment is located. In the first type, the size of data of a fragment required by every site does not vary with the location of other fragments. Let $r_{\beta,\gamma}$ (matrix R) be defined as size of data of F_γ needed to be transported to the site where q_β is initiated. Let there be a query q_β initiate from site S_α, $a_{\alpha,\beta}$ times (matrix A) in an unit time interval. And let q_β request fragment F_γ and each request require $r_{\beta,\gamma}$ amount of data transfer from the site where F_γ is located. Let $u_{\alpha,\gamma}$ (matrix U) be the amount of data needed to be transferred from the site where fragment F_γ is allocated to the site S_α where the queries are initiated. That is, $u_{\alpha,\gamma} = \sum_{\beta=0}^{k-1} a_{\alpha,\beta} \cdot r_{\beta,\gamma}$.

The second type of data transfer cost corresponds to the deeper levels of the fragment dependency graph. The data is transported from the site where one fragment is located to the site where the other fragment is located in order to perform binary operation involving two (or more different) fragments. In this case, the amount of data of a fragment required by a site varies with the allocation of other fragments. For each query we need to extract the information about how much data needs to be transferred from site where one fragment is located to the site where another fragment is located. Let $d_{\gamma,\gamma'}^{\beta}$ (matrix D^β) be the size of data of F_γ needed to be transported to the site where $F_{\gamma'}$ is located to process q_β. Then the amount of data that needs to be transported from the site where F_γ is located to the site where $F_{\gamma'}$ is given by, $d_{\gamma,\gamma'} = \sum_{\beta=0}^{n-1}(\sum_{\alpha=0}^{m-1} a_{\alpha,\beta})d_{\gamma',\gamma}^{\beta}$

Let $site(F_\gamma)$ denote the site where fragment F_γ is located. The total data transfer cost,
$$t = \sum_{\gamma=0}^{k-1}\sum_{\gamma'=0}^{k-1} c_{site(F_\gamma),site(F_{\gamma'})} \cdot d_{\gamma,\gamma'} + \sum_{\alpha=0}^{m-1}\sum_{\gamma=0}^{k-1} c_{site(F_\gamma),\alpha} \cdot u_{\alpha,\gamma},$$
where the first term gives the data transfer cost incurred to process the binary opera-

tions between the fragments located at different sites, and the second term gives the data transfer cost incurred to transfer the results of the binary operations of fragments to the site where the query is initiated. The objective in data allocation problem is to minimize t by altering the function $site(F_\gamma)$ (which maps a fragment to a site).

4 Algorithms for Query-Driven Data Allocation

The solution for allocation problem depends on the query execution strategy employed by the distributed database system to execute the query. In this section, we shall develop solutions for the allocation problem when *query-site* and *move-small* query execution strategies are used.

Query-Site Query Execution Strategy In this case, all the fragments are transferred to the query site, and the query is executed at the site of its origin. Let fragment F_β be allocated at $S_{\alpha'}$ then let $w_{\alpha',\beta}$ represent the cost of data transferred from F_β to site $S_{\alpha'}$. That is,

Let $x_{\alpha',\beta}$ be 1 if F_β is allocated at site $S_{\alpha'}$, and it is zero otherwise. The allocation problem is formulated as assign zero-one values to $x_{i,j}$ under the constraints,

1. $\sum_{\alpha'=0}^{m-1} x_{\alpha',\beta} = 1$ for all $0 \leq \beta \leq k - 1$.
2. $\sum_{\beta=0}^{k-1} x_{\alpha',\beta} \leq l_{\alpha'}$ for all $0 \leq \alpha' \leq m - 1$.

so as to minimize $\sum_{\alpha'=0}^{m-1} \sum_{\beta=0}^{k-1} x_{\alpha',\beta} \cdot w_{\alpha',\beta}$.

The first constraint ensures that each fragment is allocated to exactly one site, and the second constraint ensures that no site is allocated more fragments than the maximum number that can be allocated at that site. This problem can be mapped to a maximum flow minimum cost problem and an optimal mapping can be achieved.

Maximum Flow Minimum Cost Formulation The first step in translating allocation problem to a maximum flow minimum cut problem is calculate the cost of allocating a fragment to a particular site (i.e., $w_{\alpha',\beta}$).

In order to formulate the data allocation problem as a maximum flow minimum cut problem (see figure 2) we need to perform following steps:

1. Two nodes a source and a sink are created named, S and T respectively.
2. m nodes are created, each one corresponding to a site.
3. k nodes are created, each one corresponding to a fragment.
4. For each node S_i, a edge from S to it is created and the capacity and cost of the link are assigned as l_i and 0 respectively.
5. For each node F_i, a edge from it to T is created and the capacity and cost of the link are assigned to 1 and 0 respectively.

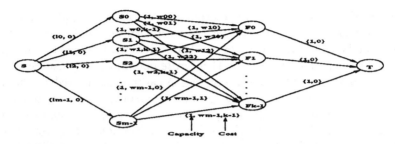

Fig. 2. Mapping *Query-Site* Data Allocation Problem as Max-flow Min-cut Problem

6. For every pair of nodes S_i and F_j, a edge from S_i to F_j is created and the capacity and cost of the link are assigned to 1 and $w_{i,j}$ respectively.

The problem is to find the maximum flow with minimum cost from S to T. It can be observed that the maximum flow in this case is k (i.e. the number of fragments in the distributed database system), since it is bounded by the sum of capacity of incoming edges to T. The sum of capacity of out coming edges from S must be bigger than k (the number of fragments) for all fragments to be allocated. This will be true if $\sum_{\alpha=0}^{\alpha=m-1} l_\alpha \geq k$. At the point of maximum flow, there must be exactly one incoming edge (say from node S_j) to F_i with flow equal to 1 and all other incoming edges (from nodes S_p) have flow equal to zero, for $0 \leq p \leq k-1$ and $p \neq j$. This is equivalent to allocating fragment F_i to site S_j. Since the capacity of flow from S to site S_i is assigned l_i, $0 \leq i \leq k-1$, no site will be allocated more than the maximum limit on the number of fragments allowed. The problem then is to achieve maximum flow from node S to node T with minimum cost. This is equivalent to assigning each fragment to a site while minimizing the total data transfer cost.

Move-Small Query Execution Strategy The general data allocation problem has been proved to be NP complete [6]. Finding the optimal solution by exhaustive search would require $O(k^m)$ in the worst case where k is the number of fragments and m is the number of sites. Therefore, a heuristic algorithm based on high climbing technique is developed in order to find a near optimal solution.

Hill-Climbing Algorithm for Data Allocation The initial solution generated by the max-flow min-cut formulation is refined by applying some operations on it. The objective for applying these operations is to reduce the total data transfer cost. There are two types of operations that are defined, namely, *migrate* - migrate fragments from its currently allocated site to newly allocated sites, and *swap* - swap the locations of one set of fragments with the locations of new set of fragments. These operations take into consideration the dependency between the fragments as modeled by fragment dependency graphs. These operations are iteratively applied till no more reduction is observed in the total data transfer cost.

The set of migrate and swap operations are as follows. migrate(F_i, S_j) — move fragment F_i to S_j. This operation can be applied to each fragment, and the fragment can be moved to any one of $m-1$ sites (it is not located at). Therefore, there can be maximum of $k*(m-1)$ *migrate* operations that can be applied during each iteration. The *migrate* operation can potentially reduce the data transfer cost involved in processing the binary operation over two fragments. Similarly, one can define operations, migrate2(F_i, S_j, F_p, S_q) and migrate3($F_i, S_j, F_p, S_q, F_r, S_t$). swap(F_i, F_j) — swap the location of fragment F_i with location of fragment F_j. This operation can be applied to each distinct pair of fragments. Therefore, there can be a maximum of $k*(k-1)/2$ *swap* operations that can be applied during each iteration. Since there is a limit on number of fragments that can be allocated at a site, by swapping fragments we maintain this constraint, and simultaneously explore if we can improve the allocation. Note that a migrate operation cannot be applied if the limit on the number of fragments that can be located at a site is exceeded. Similarly, one can define operations, swap2(F_i, F_j, F_p, F_q) and swap3($F_i, F_j, F_p, F_q, F_r, F_t$).

In the experiments that we have conducted, we noticed that *migrate* and *swap* operations are applied most often, followed by *migrate2* and *swap2* operations, and the least frequent occurrences were that of *migrate3* and *swap3* operations. This was the reason for us to define three different types of migrate and swap operations.

Example *We shall use the example presented in section 4 with the distributed database system using the move-small query execution strategy. The fragment dependency graph is as illustrated in figure 1. Let the fragment sizes are size(E') = 5, size(J') = 30, and size(G'') = 25. First, we shall use the top-level of the fragment dependency graph, i.e the edge from Site(J) $\longrightarrow$ Site(Q), to solve for initial allocation scheme by using maximum-flow minimum cut formulation. As there is only one query, we have the matrix $R = [\,0\ 0\ 30]$ with each element corresponding to relations E', G'', and J' respectively, and the matrix $A = [3\ 2\ 1]^t$ (i.e. a column vector) with each element corresponding to sites S_0, S_1, and S_2 respectively. Let the cost matrix for unit data transfer cost from one site to another be (the rows and columns correspond to sites $S_0, S_1,$ and S_2 respectively):*

$$ C = \begin{bmatrix} 0 & 2 & 5 \\ 2 & 0 & 3 \\ 5 & 3 & 0 \end{bmatrix} $$

After formulating the problem as maximum-flow and minimum cut problem and solving it we get the initial solution as: allocate fragment E at site S_0, allocate fragment G at site S_1, and allocate fragment J at site S_0. This allocation schema is represented as $\{S_0, S_1, S_0\}$ corresponding to the sites where the relations E, G and J are to be located respectively.

The matrix D^1 giving the amount of data needed from a fragment to be transported to site of another fragment derived from the fragment dependency graph (shown in figure 1) is:

$$D^1 = \begin{bmatrix} 0 & 5 & 0 \\ 0 & 0 & 25 \\ 0 & 0 & 0 \end{bmatrix}$$

The row and columns of matrix D^1 correspond to fragments E', G'', and J' respectively. Now we get the total amount of data that must be transported from the site where one fragment is located to the site where another fragment is located as (the rows and columns correspond to fragments E', G'', and J' respectively).

$$D = (3 + 2 + 1) \cdot \begin{bmatrix} 0 & 5 & 0 \\ 0 & 0 & 25 \\ 0 & 0 & 0 \end{bmatrix} = \begin{bmatrix} 0 & 30 & 0 \\ 0 & 0 & 150 \\ 0 & 0 & 0 \end{bmatrix}$$

The total data transfer cost for the initial allocation $\{S_0, S_1, S_0\}$ is $(2*30 + 2*150) + (2+1)*30 = 450$. The cost value in first parenthesis corresponds to the data transfer cost incurred in transferring E' to site where G is located, and transferring G'' to the site where J is located. The second cost value corresponds to the data transfer incurred in transferring the result J' to the query site.

We now apply the hill-climbing heuristic algorithm to improve upon the initial solution so as to further reduce the total data transfer cost if possible. Two operations were applied to improve the initial solution provided by the max-flow min-cut algorithm, namely, i) migrate(J, S_1) — which reduced the total data transfer cost from 450 to 180, and ii) migrate(E, S_1, G, S_0, J, S_0) — which reduced the data transfer cost from 180 to 150. The solution to data allocation problem generated by the hill-climbing algorithm is $\{S_1, S_0, S_0\}$ (i.e. allocate relation E at site S_1, relation G at site S_0, and relation J at site S_0) with the total data transfer cost incurred to execute the query as 150, which was the optimal solution found by exhaustive enumeration..

5 Experimental Evaluation

We conducted sixteen experiments with number of fragments ranging from 5 to 8, and number of sites ranging from 5 to 8. The ranges for number of sites and number of fragments were limited because of the time take taken to generate the optimal solution using exhaustive enumeration. Each experiment consisted of 100 allocation problems with number of sites and number of fragments fixed. Each allocation problem had between 10 and 20 queries, and each query had a fragment dependency graph. The communication network, the relation sizes, the link costs, and the structure of fragment dependency graph were randomly generated. Each allocation problem was solved by using hill-climbing algorithm and its solution was compared with the optimal solution generated by exhaustive search.

Table 1 presents the results for the 16 experiments which were conduected for varying number of fragments and sites. For each experiment 100 allocation

Table 1. Experimental Evaluation of Near Optimality of Hill-Climbing Algorithm

No. of Fragments	No. of Sites	No. of Optimal Solutions	Average Deviation (%)	No. of Solutions with Deviation in Range			
				(0, 5%)	[5%, 10%)	[10%, 20%)	[20%)
5	5	84	2.4	5	1	5	5
5	6	79	2.6	9	3	7	2
5	7	79	2.9	7	5	4	5
5	8	77	2.0	13	5	2	3
6	5	85	1.9	3	4	5	3
6	6	85	1.5	7	3	3	2
6	7	83	1.4	13	1	0	3
6	8	64	6.0	15	6	9	6
7	5	84	2.2	5	3	5	3
7	6	67	3.5	17	6	8	2
7	7	77	3.0	11	4	4	4
7	8	76	2.8	13	1	8	2
8	5	76	2.3	10	9	3	2
8	6	66	5.5	14	5	9	6
8	7	74	3.4	9	6	8	3
8	8	70	4.2	11	6	10	3

problems were randomly generated and solutions obtained. Table 1 shows the nature of solutions in terms of number of problems for which optimal deviations were obtained and the closeness measured by average deviation from the optimal solution to evaluate the goodness of near optimal solutions. From the experiments conducted, we note, (i) The hill-climbing algorithm generated optimal solution for large number of problems (on an average, for greater than 75% of problems). (ii) The average deviation of a near optimal solution from the optimal solution was on an average less than 5% in total data transfer cost. (iii) For a small percentage of cases about 5% the deviation of near optimal solution from optimal solution was greater than 20%. This is to be expected of a hill-climbing algorithm in that it wanders-off and finds a local optimal solution.

We conducted further experiments by considering different network topologies (like ring, star, fully connected, tree) and different query access patterns (like fewer access frequencies/site (5-10/unit time interval), to large access frequencies (like 100/unit time interval), and the results were similar to those shown in table 1. We have not included these results for the lack of space. The experimental results do imply that the hill-climbing algorithm can be used in practice to allocate fragments for distributed database systems.

6 Conclusions

The problem of non-redundant data allocation of fragments in distributed database system is addressed in this paper. A major contribution of this work is the development of a site-independent fragment dependency graph representation of data transfer costs incurred in executing a query by using a particular query execution strategy. We studied the data allocation problem for two popularly used query execution strategies, namely, query-site and move-small. We mapped the data allocation problem with query-site execution strategy as a max-flow min-cut problem and showed that it can be solved to generate an optimal solution. A hill-climbing heuristic algorithm was developed for the data allocation problem with move-small query execution strategy. We studied the effectiveness of this algorithm by conducting a set of experiments, which show that the hill-climbing heuristic algorithm generates the optimal solution for a large percentage of allocation problems. Moreover, the near optimal solution generated by the algorithm has on an average small percentage of deviation from the optimal solution in terms of the total data transfer costs incurred to process all the queries. Therefore, the query-driven data allocation algorithms can be used in practice allocating fragments in distributed database systems.

References

1. P. M. G. Apers. Data allocation in distributed database systems. *ACM Transactions on Database Systems*, 13(3):263–304, September 1988.
2. R. G. Casey. Allocation of copies of a file in an information network. In *Proceedings of Spring Joint Computer Conference, IFIPS,*, pages 617–625, 1972.
3. S. Ceri, G. Martella, and G. Pelagatti. Optimal file allocation for a distributed on a network of minicomputers. In *Proceedings of International Conference on Databases, Aberdeen*, pages 345–357, July 1980.
4. W. W. Chu. Optimal file allocation in a multiple computer system. *IEEE Transactions on Computers*, C-18(10), 1969.
5. D. W. Cornell and P. S. Yu. Site assignment for relations and join operations in the distributed transaction processing environment. In *Proceedings of International Conference on Data Engineering, IEEE*, pages 100–108, February 1988.
6. K. P. Eswaran. Placement of records in a file and file allocation in a computer network. *Information Processing*, pages 304–307, 1974.
7. B. Gavish and H. Pirkul. Computer and database location in distributed computer systems. *IEEE Transactions on Computers*, C-35(7):583–590, 1986.
8. X.-M. Lin, M.E. Orlowska, and Y.-C. Zhang. Database placement in communication networks for minimizing the overall transmission cost. *Mathematical and Computer Modelling*, 19(1):7–19, Jan 1994.
9. T. Ozsu and P. Valduriez. *Principles of Distributed Database Systems*. Printice-Hall Inc., 1991.
10. S. Ram and R.E. Marsten. A model for database allocation incorporating a concurrency control mechanism. *IEEE Transactions on Knowledge and Data Engineering*, 3(3):389–95, Sept 1991.
11. C. V. Ramamoorthy and B. Wah. The placement of relations on a distributed relational database. In *Proceedings of 1st Int. Conf. Distributed Computing Systems, Huntsville, Alabama*, September Oct, 1979, pp 642-649.

A General Multidimensional Data Allocation Method for Multicomputer Database Systems

Yu-lung Lo

Department of Management Information Systems
China Junior College of Industrial & Commercial Management
No. 56, Sec 3, Hsing-Lung Rd., Taipei, Taiwan 117, Republic Of China
Internet: ylo@ms12.hinet.net

Kien A. Hua

Department of Computer Science
University of Central Florida
Orlando, FL 32816-2362, USA
Internet: kienhua@cs.ucf.edu

Honesty C. Young

IBM Research Division
Almaden Research Center
San Jose, CA 95120-6099, USA
Internet: young@almaden.ibm.com

Abstract. Several studies have demonstrated that both the performance and scalability of a shared-nothing parallel database system depend on the physical layout of data across the processing nodes of the system. Today, data is allocated in these systems using horizontal partitioning strategies. This approach has a number of drawbacks. In recent years, several multidimensional data declustering techniques have been proposed to address these problems. However, these schemes are too restrictive, or optimized for a certain type of queries. In this paper, we introduce a new technique which is flexible, and performs well for general queries.

1 Introduction

It has been recognized that *shared-nothing* (SN) architecture [10] is most scalable to support very large database systems. In this architecture, *processing nodes* (PNs) consisting of one or more processors with local memory and dedicated disk drives are interconnected through a high-bandwidth communication network. Since in this model each PN processes the portion of the database on its disks, the degree of parallelism is determined by the physical layout of the data across the PNs of the system.

Essentially all of today's SN systems allocate their data using horizontal partitioning strategies. This simple approach has a number of drawbacks. For instance, if a range-select query whose predicate includes an attribute other than the partitioning attribute, then the entire space must be searched. In this case, the PNs will typically waste CPU cycles and I/O bandwidth only to determine that most of the data pages do not contain any relevant tuples. This type of problem is inherent with horizontal partitioning and cannot be easily addressed. A solution commonly used today is to speedup the search operations on all the PNs using local secondary indices. This approach, however, is not effective for range queries. In this case, many random accesses to the data file will occur across all the PNs. To address this problem, the relation can be partitioned using multiple attributes. Locally, each partition can be organized as a grid file. We will refer to this scheme as *multidimensional data partitioning* (MDP) technique (viewing horizontal partitioning methods as unidimensional).

In the early 80's, the *Disk Modulo* (DM) method was proposed by Du and Sobolewski [2]. More recent MDP techniques include *Field-wise Exclusive-or* (FX) [7], *Error Correcting Codes* (ECC) [4], another coding-theoretic approach [1], and *Hilbert Curve Allocation Method* (HCAM) [3]. Among these schemes, FX and ECC have restrictions on the number of available PNs which must be a power of 2. In addition, ECC has a restriction on the cardinalities of the attributes which must be power of 2 also. The approach proposed in [1] is less restricted. However, it still requires that the domain of each attribute is divided into the same number of ranges. HCAM and DM are very flexible. However, they are optimized for a certain type of queries.

In this paper, we will introduce a more general technique whose good performance is not susceptible to the type of the queries. Furthermore, our proposed technique is free of restrictions on the number of intervals for each dimension. Due to its generality, we will refer to this new technique as GMDA (*General Multidimensional Data Allocation*) in this paper.

The remainder of this paper proceeds as follows. In Section 2, we briefly review DM and HCAM. The proposed technique is presented in Section 3. In Section 4, we describe the simulation model, and give the simulation results. Finally, we state our conclusions in Section 5.

2 Existing Multidimensional Data Allocation Techniques

In this paper, we will only compare our scheme to HCAM and DM since they are less restricted than the other techniques, and are known to perform well [3, 2].

2.1 Hilbert Curve Allocation Method (HCAM)

HCAM is based on the idea of space filling curves [5]. A space filling curve visits all points in a k-dimensional space grid exactly once and never crosses itself. Thus it can be used to impose a linear ordering on the grid blocks of a multidimensional file scheme (Fig 1a). *Jagadish* suggested in [6] that this concept can be used to allocate a grid file [8] to the blocks of a disk system to minimize the disk access effort. In [3], *Faloutsos* and *Bhagwat* used Hilbert curve to design a data allocation strategy for multidisk (or SN) systems. In this scheme, the Hilbert Curve was used to traverse the grid blocks and assign each one to a disk unit (or PN) in a round-robin fashion (Fig 1b). This method was shown to provide good performance on square range queries [3].

2.2 Disk Modulo (DM) Allocation

We denote a grid block of a multidimensional file by its coordinate. For instance, let D_1 and D_2 be the domains of the partitioning attributes A_1 and A_2, respect-

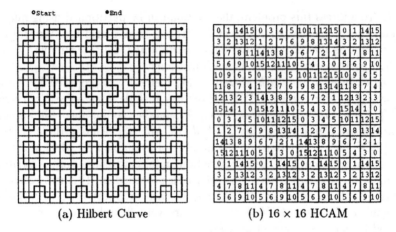

(a) Hilbert Curve (b) 16 × 16 HCAM

Fig. 1. An HCAM example

0	1	2	3	4	5	6	7	8	9	10	11	12	13	14	15
0	1	2	3	4	5	6	7	8	9	10	11	12	13	14	15
1	2	3	4	5	6	7	8	9	10	11	12	13	14	15	0
2	3	4	5	6	7	8	9	10	11	12	13	14	15	0	1
3	4	5	6	7	8	9	10	11	12	13	14	15	0	1	2
4	5	6	7	8	9	10	11	12	13	14	15	0	1	2	3
5	6	7	8	9	10	11	12	13	14	15	0	1	2	3	4
6	7	8	9	10	11	12	13	14	15	0	1	2	3	4	5
7	8	9	10	11	12	13	14	15	0	1	2	3	4	5	6
8	9	10	11	12	13	14	15	0	1	2	3	4	5	6	7
9	10	11	12	13	14	15	0	1	2	3	4	5	6	7	8
10	11	12	13	14	15	0	1	2	3	4	5	6	7	8	9
11	12	13	14	15	0	1	2	3	4	5	6	7	8	9	10
12	13	14	15	0	1	2	3	4	5	6	7	8	9	10	11
13	14	15	0	1	2	3	4	5	6	7	8	9	10	11	12
14	15	0	1	2	3	4	5	6	7	8	9	10	11	12	13
15	0	1	2	3	4	5	6	7	8	9	10	11	12	13	14

Fig. 2. A 16 × 16 DM example

ively. Then, (i, j) represents the grid block that covers the ith interval of D_1, and the jth interval of D_2. In DM, block $(X_1, X_2, ..., X_d)$, where $0 \leq X_i < N$, is assigned to PN $DM(X_1, X_2, ..., X_d)$ which is computed as follows:

$$DM(X_1, X_2, ..., X_d) = \left(\sum_{i=1}^{d} X_i\right) \bmod N,$$

where N is the number of PNs. A 16 × 16 DM example is given in Fig 2.

3 Proposed Technique: GMDA

The proposed technique, GMDA, is presented in this section. In this scheme, a grid block $(X_1, X_2, ..., X_d)$ is assigned to PN $GMDA(X_1, X_2, ..., X_d)$, where

$$GMDA(X_1, X_2, ..., X_d) = \left(\sum_{i=2}^{d} \lfloor \frac{X_i \cdot GCD_i}{N} \rfloor + \sum_{i=1}^{d} (X_i \cdot Shf\_dist_i)\right) \bmod N, \quad (1)$$

in which $Shf\_dist_i = \lfloor \sqrt[d]{N} \rfloor^{i-1}$, and $GCD_i = gcd(Shf\_dist_i, N)$. We note that the number of intervals on each dimension does not have to be identical.

In order to gain insight on the allocation patterns and properties of the proposed technique, in the following subsections we will examine GMDA in its procedural form.

3.1 Two-Dimensional Algorithm

In this subsection, we first describe the procedure for two-dimensional files. Given N PNs, we organize the data file as a two dimensional grid structure such that each dimension has exactly N intervals. The allocation of these grid blocks to the PNs is done as follows:

1. We compute the *shift distance*, $shf\_dist = \lfloor \sqrt{N} \rfloor$.
2. Mark the top most row as the *check row*.
3. PNs $0, 1, \cdots, N-1$ are assigned to the N grid blocks of this row from left to right. Go to the next row.
4. The allocation pattern for the current row is determined by circular left shift the pattern of the row above it by shf_dist positions.
5. If the allocation pattern of the current row is identical to that of the check row, we perform circular left shift on the current row one more position and mark it as the new check row.
6. If there are more rows to consider, repeat steps 4, 5 and 6 for the next row.

A 16×16 example is given in Fig 3 to illustrate this data allocation technique. In this case, the shifting distance is $4 (= \lfloor \sqrt{16} \rfloor)$. We observe that the mapping for each row is obtained by circular-left-shifting the row above it four positions; except that rows 4, 8, and 12 are obtained by circular-left-shifting rows 3, 7 and 11, respectively, five positions.

Row 0 →
0	1	2	3	4	5	6	7	8	9	10	11	12	13	14	15
4	5	6	7	8	9	10	11	12	13	14	15	0	1	2	3
8	9	10	11	12	13	14	15	0	1	2	3	4	5	6	7
12	13	14	15	0	1	2	3	4	5	6	7	8	9	10	11

Row 4 →
1	2	3	4	5	6	7	8	9	10	11	12	13	14	15	0
5	6	7	8	9	10	11	12	13	14	15	0	1	2	3	4
9	10	11	12	13	14	15	0	1	2	3	4	5	6	7	8
13	14	15	0	1	2	3	4	5	6	7	8	9	10	11	12

Row 8 →
2	3	4	5	6	7	8	9	10	11	12	13	14	15	0	1
6	7	8	9	10	11	12	13	14	15	0	1	2	3	4	5
10	11	12	13	14	15	0	1	2	3	4	5	6	7	8	9
14	15	0	1	2	3	4	5	6	7	8	9	10	11	12	13

Row 12 →
3	4	5	6	7	8	9	10	11	12	13	14	15	0	1	2
7	8	9	10	11	12	13	14	15	0	1	2	3	4	5	6
11	12	13	14	15	0	1	2	3	4	5	6	7	8	9	10
15	0	1	2	3	4	5	6	7	8	9	10	11	12	13	14

Fig. 3. 16×16 GMDA

The GMDA strategy for 2-dimensional files can be presented more formally as follows.

Algorithm 2D_GMDA:

Input: $Block[N][N]$ is an empty array representing the $N \times N$ grid blocks of the 2-dimensional file; N is the number of PNs.

Output: Each element of the array $Block[N][N]$ is assigned an integer value between 0 and $N - 1$. "$Block[i][j] = p$" denotes the assignment of PN p to the grid block $Block[i][j]$.

begin
    $Shf\_dist \leftarrow \lfloor \sqrt{N} \rfloor$;
    for $(j \leftarrow 0; j < N; j \leftarrow j + 1)$
        $Block[0][j] \leftarrow j$; /* No shift for row 0 */
    end-for
    $Check\_row \leftarrow 0$;

    for $(i \leftarrow 1; i < N; i \leftarrow i + 1)$
        if $(Block[Check\_row][0] = Block[i - 1][Shf\_dist])$
            /* current row has the same mapping as row $check\_row$ */
            for $(j \leftarrow 0; j < N; j \leftarrow j + 1)$
                $Block[i][j] \leftarrow Block[i - 1][(Shf\_dist + j + 1) \bmod N]$;
            end-for
            $Check\_row \leftarrow i$; /* set $Check\_row$ to current row */
        else
            for $(j \leftarrow 0; j < N; j \leftarrow j + 1)$
                $Block[i][j] \leftarrow Block[i - 1][(Shf\_dist + j) \bmod N]$;
            end-for
        end-if
    end-for
end

3.2   Handling Higher Dimensions

In this subsection, we extend the 2D_GMDA algorithm to handle three or more dimensions. For clarity, we first consider the 3-dimensional case. A cube with N^3 grid blocks can be seen as N 2-dimensional planes stacked up in the third dimension. Let's label these N planes 0 to $N - 1$. The allocation strategy for this cube is given in the following algorithm.

Algorithm 3D_GMDA:

Step 1: We compute the mapping for the first rows of all the 2-dimensional planes by considering these rows collectively as forming a plane along the third dimension. We apply the 2D_GMDA algorithm to this plane, except that the shifting distance is set to $\lfloor \sqrt[3]{N} \rfloor^2$.

Step 2: We apply the 2D_GMDA algorithm to each of the 2-dimensional planes using $Shf\_dist = \lfloor \sqrt[3]{N} \rfloor$ and the first row already computed in Step 1.

In a hypercube, a plane can be identified by specifying its coordinate. For instance, $(W = 0, X = x, Y = x, Z = 1)$, where '$x$' denotes the entire domain space of the respective dimension, represents a 2-dimensional plane. A set of planes are said to belong to the $(X_i \cdots X_j)$-family if any two of their X_i-coordinate, $\cdots$, X_j-coordinate are unspecified. For instance, the following planes belong to the (XYZ)-family:

$$(W = 0, \ X = x, \ Y = x, \ Z = 1)$$
$$(W = 3, \ X = 2, \ Y = x, \ Z = x)$$
$$(W = 2, \ X = x, \ Y = 3, \ Z = x)$$

Using these concepts, we can describe the mD_GMDA strategy as follows.

Algorithm mD_GMDA:

Step 1: We apply the 2D_GMDA algorithm to the plane denoted by $(X_0 = x, X_1 = x, X_3 = 0, X_4 = 0, \cdots, X_{m-1} = 0)$ using $Shf\_dist = \lfloor \sqrt[m]{N} \rfloor^{m-1}$.

Step 2: We apply the 2D_GMDA algorithm to each of the planes in the $(X_0X_1X_2)$-family whose first rows have been determined in Step 1. In this step, we use $Shf\_dist = \lfloor \sqrt[m]{N} \rfloor^{m-2}$.

Step 3: We apply the 2D_GMDA algorithm to each of the planes in the $(X_0X_1X_2X_3)$-family whose first rows have been determined in Step 2. In this step, we use $Shf\_dist = \lfloor \sqrt[m]{N} \rfloor^{m-3}$.

Step 4: We apply the 2D_GMDA algorithm to each of the planes in the $(X_0X_1X_2X_3X_4)$-family whose first rows have been determined in Step 3. In this step, we use $Shf\_dist = \lfloor \sqrt[m]{N} \rfloor^{m-4}$.

$$\vdots$$

Step $m-1$: We apply the 2D_GMDA algorithm to each of the planes in the $(X_0X_1 \cdots X_{m-1})$-family whose first rows have been determined in Step $m-2$. In this step, we use $Shf\_dist = \lfloor \sqrt[m]{N} \rfloor$.

---

4 Simulation Study

4.1 Simulation Model

The simulator used in our study is depicted in Fig 4. The *Query Generator* generates random queries. Whenever resources (i.e., PNs) become available, the *Scheduler* examines the queries in the *scheduling window* (see Fig 4), and selects queries for execution based on a *largest-fit-first* strategy.

We assumed that the arrival rates of the queries match the processing rate of the parallel system well. The *Executor* simulates the execution of queries, collects performance data, and informs the scheduler when resources become available.

The following system and workload parameters were used in our study:

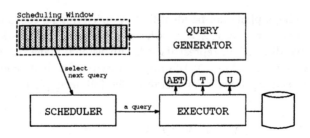

Fig. 4. Simulator

PARAMETER	VALUES
size of the scheduling window	20 queries
number of PNs	16, 32, 64, or 128
number of partitioning attributes	3
number of intervals on each dimension	number of PNs
sizes of grid blocks	varied (discussed shortly)
size of the relation	about 42 million tuples
processing power per PN	can process one tuple per time unit

We note that the size of the relation is maintained at about 42 million tuples for each simulation run. This is achieved by varying the sizes of the grid cells as follows:

SYSTEM SIZE	CELL SIZES
16 PNs	5,120 to 15,360 tuples
32 PNs	640 to 1,920 tuples
64 PNs	80 to 240 tuples
128 PNs	10 to 30 tuples

We intentionally made the ranges large enough to allow correlations among the attributes. Once the grid had been created, the cells were allocated to the PNs using DM, HCAM or GMDA.

Three metrics were used in our comparative study: *Average Execution Time* (*AET*), *Throughput* (*T*), and *System Utilization* (*U*). We note that *AET* does not include waiting time. *T* measures the average number of queries processed per one million time units. *U* is computed as the average of the utilizations of the N PNs in the system.

4.2 Performance on Partial Match Queries

A *partial match query* q is an n-tuple $\langle v_1, v_2, \cdots, v_n \rangle$, where v_i is either a value from the domain of the ith attribute or is unspecified, and where the number of unspecified attributes must be at least one [9]. If v_i is specified, it determines a single interval on the ith dimension of the grid space. We considered only queries that involve one or more of these partitioning attributes. The average execution times and the system throughputs of the three MDP schemes under this workload are given in Table 1 and Table 2, respectively. In these tables, the worst scheme

No.	HCAM	DM		GMDA	
of PNs	AET	AET	Saving	AET	Saving
16	148987.19	99957.06	32.91%	98494.75	33.89%
32	47388.84	23508.13	50.39%	23503.79	50.40%
64	13898.72	5673.18	59.18%	5660.81	59.27%
128	3786.01	1381.20	63.52%	1381.06	63.52%

Table 1. Average execution times under partial match queries

No.	HCAM	DM		GMDA	
of PNs	Throughput	Throughput	Improvement	Throughput	Improvement
16	7.31	10.00	36.75%	10.15	38.78%
32	25.72	42.54	65.42%	42.55	65.45%
64	96.60	176.27	82.47%	176.65	82.87%
128	361.89	724.01	100.06%	724.08	100.08%

Table 2. Throughputs per one million time units under partial match queries

is used as the reference to compute the savings and improvements achievable by the other two better techniques.

For the discussion of the experimental results, we define the *aspect ratio* of a query as the ratio of its dimensions. For instance, let's consider a 3-dimensional data file. A partial match query with two specified attributes will have an aspect ratio of $1:1:N$, where N is the number of intervals on the third dimension. We can view $n:n:n$ as a *cube* aspect ratio, $1:N:N$ as a *wide* aspect ratio, and $1:1:N$ as a *very wide* aspect ratio.

We observe in Table 1 and Table 2 that GMDA and DM perform comparably. They provide very significant improvement over HCAM. For our workload, the average saving in execution time ranges from 32.91% to 63.52%; and the improvement on system throughput is between 36.75% and 100.08%. The poor performance of HCAM is due to the fact that it is customized for cube-aspect-ratio queries. The shapes of partial match queries, however, have wider aspect ratios that seriously affect its performance.

The poorer performance of HCAM can be attributed to its low system utilization. The curves shown in Fig 5 are consistent with the results presented in Table 1 and Table 2. As we increase the number of PNs, the system utilization of DM and GMDA improves slightly while that of HCAM drops quite significantly.

4.3 Performance on Range Queries

A *range query* is similar to partial match queries, except that a range of values is specified for an involved attribute rather than just a single value. Furthermore, all the attributes can be specified. The results of these experiments are given in Table 3 and Table 4. We note that the performance of HCAM improves substantially over its own performance under partial match queries. This is due to fact that the aspect ratios of range queries tend to be less wide. In fact, HCAM outperforms DM by as much as 25.42% in term of average execution time, and

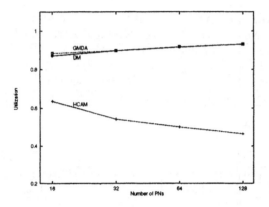

Fig. 5. System utilization under partial match queries

31.09% in terms of system throughput. Nevertheless, the proposed technique, GMDA, remains the performance leader. It provides savings on average execution time as high as 29.74%, and throughput improvements of up to 39.03%. The superiority of GMDA is due to the fact that it is the only scheme which can maintain the high system utilization (see Fig 6) in these experiments.

The curves for HCAM and DM slide downfards in Fig 5 and Fig 6, respectively. Only the system utilization of GMDA are consistently high; and the curves are rising in both of these figures. From this observation, we can conclude that only the proposed method is immune from the effect of the different aspect ratios of the various types of queries. This robustness property confirms our initial assessment that GMDA is more general than either DM or HCAM.

No. of PNs	DM AET	HCAM AET	Saving	GMDA AET	Saving
16	232687.77	209079.76	10.15%	186365.66	19.91%
32	94820.70	81719.62	13.82%	70608.43	25.53%
64	41023.70	32472.56	20.84%	29426.61	28.27%
128	19173.21	14299.63	25.42%	13470.33	29.74%

Table 3. Average execution times under range queries

No. of PNs	DM Throughput	HCAM Throughput	Improvement	GMDA Throughput	Improvement
16	4.47	4.85	8.58%	5.39	20.54%
32	10.88	12.37	13.67%	14.18	30.25%
64	25.03	30.90	23.45%	33.99	35.81%
128	53.40	70.00	31.09%	74.24	39.03%

Table 4. Throughputs per one million time units under range queries

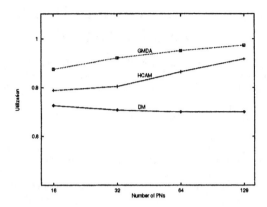

Fig. 6. System utilization under range queries

5 Conclusion

In this paper, we have introduced a general data allocation technique, GMDA, for multidimensional files in a shared-nothing environment. Our simulation results indicate that DM and HCAM experienced significant degradation in performance under range and partial match queries, respectively. Only GMDA is able to sustain the various types of queries. The robustness of GMDA can maintain good system utilization for both types of workloads.

References

1. Khaled A. S. Abdel-Ghaffar and Amr El Abbadi. Optimal disk allocation for partial match. *ACM Trans. on Database Systems*, 18(1):132–156, March 1993.
2. H. C. Du and J. S. Sobolewski. Disk allocation for cartesian product files on multiple disk systems. *ACM Trans. on Database Systems*, 7(1):82–101, March 1982.
3. C. Faloutsos and P. Bhagwat. Declustering using fractals. In *Proc. of the Int'l Conf. on Parallel and Distributed Information Systems*, pages 18–25, San Diego, California, January 1993.
4. C. Faloutsos and D. Metaxas. Disk allocation methods using error correcting codes. *IEEE Trans. on Computers*, C-40(8):907–914, August 1991.
5. C. Faloutsos and S. Roseman. Fractals for secondary key retrieval. In *Proc. of ACM Symposium on Principles of Database Systems*, pages 247–252, March 1989.
6. H. V. Jagadish. Linear clustering of objects with multiple attributes. In *Proc. of ACM SIGMOD Conf.*, pages 332–342, Atlantic City, New Jersey, May 1990.
7. M. H. Kim and S. Pramanik. Optimal file distribution for partial match retrieval. In *Proc. of ACM SIGMOD Conf.*, pages 173–182, Chicago, Illinois, June 1988.
8. J. Nievergelt, H. Hinterberger, and K. C. Sevcik. The grid file: An adaptive symmetric multikey file structure. *ACM Trans. on Database Systems*, 9(1):38–71, March 1984.
9. R. L. Rivest. Partial-match retrieval algorithms. *SIAM J. Computing*, 15(1):19–50, March 1976.
10. M. Stonebraker. The case for shared nothing. *IEEE Database Engineering*, 9(1):4–9, March 1986.

Distribution Object Oriented Databases:
An Allocation Method

Franck RAVAT[(2)], Marianne DE MICHIEL[(1)], Gilles ZURFLUH[(2)]

IRIT - University Paul Sabatier - 118, route de Narbonne 31062 Toulouse cedex

☎ : (33) 5 61 55 66 11 Poste 7435 - Email : mmichiel@univ-lr.fr, {ravat, zurfluh}@irit.fr,

(1) : L3I, University of La Rochelle

(2) : CERISS of University Toulouse I and URACOM / Alcatel Telecom

Abstract

In this article, we propose a solution for the distributed object oriented database design. Our work is based on a top-down approach. Notably, we concentrate on the allocation step that allows to place the object class fragments and the methods onto sites of the distributed system. In this aim, we defined an objective function that minimizes the storage and the communication costs. We completed this presentation by the proposal of a heuristic.

Key Words

Distributed object oriented databases, Allocation method, Storage and communication costs

1. Introduction

The computer and network developments allow to implement distributed computer systems adapted to needs of companies composed of geographically distant units. This aspect concerns the DataBase Management Systems (DBMS). A distributed DBMS is the software that allows the management of distributed databases (a collection of multiple logically interrelated databases distributed across a computer network [1][2]) and makes the distribution transparent to users [1].

The distributed DB design has been extensively studied [1] with the relational model. But, the object paradigm is recognized as adapted to represent the complex and multimedia data. Also, our objective is to propose a solution for the distributed object oriented databases (OODB) design. Our work is in the framework of the top-down approach [3] that allows to distribute the global conceptual schema of a DB to design the schemata of the local databases (cf. figure 1 showing the steps of our approach).

In this article, we study the distribution design step in an object oriented context. More particularly, we present the allocation step. This paper is organized as follows. In section 2, we define the framework of our study : the different steps of the distribution process and the previous works done in the area of the data allocation. In section 3, we present our objective function that proposes the data and processing allocation. The section 4 contains two examples of the allocation method use.

2. Context

The figure 1 represents the top-down approach to design distributed OODB. In the following sections, we explain the distribution design step in an object context.

2.1. Translation

The *translation* step consists in transforming a global schema into a formalism more adapted for the next operations. Indeed, after a class fragmentation, a method M does not necessarily apply itself on a fragment F, notably when all the attributes manipulated by M are not present in F. Moreover, it is very complex or impossible, to fragment a method body so as to describe the fragment behavior. To solve these problems, we propose to separate the static and dynamic components [4] [5] [6].

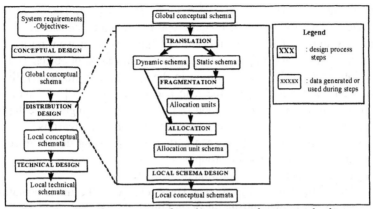

Figure1. : Distribution steps of an object oriented conceptual schema

• *The static schema* contains only classes and semantic links between these classes (inheritance links, association links and composition links).

• *The dynamic schema* allows us to represent the more significant methods (rule of 80/20) chosen for the fragmentation and allocation steps and the different links between them. Our model is an extension of the knowledge representation model called Shood [7][8][9] (developed at the university of Grenoble -France-). This schema regroups the two following concepts :

◊ *The method-classes:* Each method is represented by a method-class in which the attributes are the arguments, the body and the type of the method.

◊ *The semantic links:* An *inheritance link* between a method-class X and a sub-class Y indicates that the method Y overloads the method X. We define *a composition link* between a composed method-class X and a component method-class Y if the method represented by X invokes the method represented by Y during its execution and the Y method is not invoked by other methods. We define a *reference link* between two method-classes X and Y in order to indicate that the method X invokes the method Y but Y could be invoked independently of X.

2.2. Next steps : fragmentation and allocation

In [4][10], we defined a fragmentation process of static schema classes. This process specifies fragments by taking into account the object accesses (by the methods of the dynamic schema) and the access frequencies of these methods. This work extend the Navathe's work [11][12] defined for the relational model. The allocation step allows to place onto the distributed system sites the allocation units of the static and dynamic schemata (class fragments and methods). This step is detailed in this article.

2.3. Allocation: state of the art

Several work proposed a fragment allocation specific to the relational model. In the following table, we enumerate the significant work done in this area :

Authors	Criteria	Constraints
[13]	Costs of transaction processing and data transmissions	No fragment duplication
[14]	Total transmission cost	No constraint
[15][16]	Communication cost	Storage and availability constraints
[1]	Query processing and Fragment storage costs	Response time, Storage and Processing constraints

Blankinship and al. [17][18] extends the Apers work [14] by proposing an heuristic that take into account the distributed request optimization and the data allocation.

These methods do not integrate the allocation of applications as we want to do for an object schema. Some work propose solutions for the allocation of objects [19][20][21]. They take into account the object position in the aggregation graph [21], the access information on object groups [20], the read and write requests [19]. Some authors propose an allocation without duplication [21], while others integrate the duplication [20]. However, these work do not fit our needs for the following reasons :

- they concentrate on links between particular objects but do not integrate the concept of class fragments regrouping objects ;
- they do not integrate the allocation of methods ;
- they imply the knowledge of some costs relative to the implementation that are not always known during the design process ;
- they do not take account the object access requests.

So, we propose a solution that integrates the placement of objects and methods.

3. Our Allocation Method

Our aim is to place onto the distributed system sites two elements that have a strong interaction : fragments of the static schema and methods. We propose an allocation based on an objective function optimization. This function minimizes the communication and the storage costs and integrates some constraints. This allocation permits also the fragment and method duplications. The originality of our approach consists in locating at the same time data and processing (methods) while current allocation solutions do not integrate the processing placement [13], [14], [15], [16], [17] and [18].

3.1. Input data

We use 3 variables : NS (number of sites named S_1, ...S_{NS}), NF (number of fragments named F_1, F_2, ...F_{NF}) and NM (number of methods named M_1, M_2, ...M_{NM})

3.1.1. Different types of communication

We defined four communication types : Method-Site Communications (MSC), Method-Method Communications (MMC), Method-Fragment Communications (MFC) and Site-Site Communications (SSC).

These different communication types will be represented by means of matrices :

- *The matrix MSC* ; the specification of $[MSC_{ij}]_{NM*NS}$ follows the next rule :

$\forall$ i,j with $1 \le i \le NM$ and $1 \le j \le NS$,
    $MSC_{ij} = x$ if the method Mi is directly invoked x times from the site S_j ($x \ge 0$),

- *The matrix MMC* ; the specification of $[MMC_{ij}]_{NM*NM}$ follows the next rule :

$\forall$ i,j with $1 \le i \le NM$ and $1 \le j \le NM$, $MMC_{ij} = x$ if Mi invokes x times M_j ($x \ge 0$),

We make the assumption that it does not exist cycle of method invocations.

- *The matrix MFC* ; the specification of $[MFC_{ij}]_{NM*NF}$ is based on the following rule :

$\forall$ i,j with $1 \le i \le NM$ and $1 \le j \le NF$, $MFC_{ij} = 1$ if Mi manipulates directly F_j, 0 otherwise.

- *The matrix SSC* ; the specification of $[SSC_{ij}]_{NS*NS}$ is defined as follows :

$\forall$ i,j (i $\neq$ j) with $1 \leq i \leq$ NS and $1 \leq j \leq$ NS,
SSC_{ij}= smallest sum of the access costs of communication channels binding S_i and S_j
SSC_{ii} = 0 or local access cost to a byte of S_i

3.1.2. The methods

The type of the method (update or consultation) influences transfers to undertake. A consultation method manipulates only a copy of consulted fragments but an update method manipulates all the copies of the updated fragments.

3.1.2.1. Consultation

Within the framework of a method-fragment communication, all the fragments manipulated by a method may be transferred on the storage site of this method (for the execution of it). For a method-method communication, we consider only the transfer of the called method result to the site of the calling method. We use the same process for a site-method communication (method result onto the result display site).

3.1.2.2. Update

We split the update in a data consultation and a data modification. This modification consists in actualizing all the fragment copies manipulated by the method.

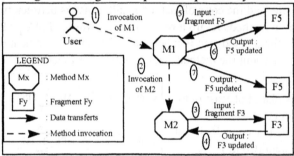

Figure2. : Example of data transfers during an update

In figure 2, the user invokes M_1. This method updates the duplicated fragment F_5 and invokes the method M_2 that manipulates F_3. The method M_1 consults the copy of F_5 that induces a minimum cost and updates the two copies of F_5.

To take into account the method type we define the following vector.

- *The vector MAJ* : $[MAJ_i]_{NM}$ indicates if a method is an update or not.

$\forall$ i with $1 \leq i \leq$ NM, MAJ_i = 1 if M_i is an update, 0 if M_i is a consultation.

3.1.3. Other input data

- *The vector RES* : The values of this vector are based on the number of objects "returned" by a method (selectivity) and the size of attributes "returned" by a method. The specification of $[RES_i]_{NM}$ follows the next rule:

$\forall$ i with $1 \leq i \leq$ NM, RES_i = x if the average size of the result of M_i is coded on x bytes

- The size of each fragment is given by the *vector $[TF_i]_{NF}$* :

$\forall$ i with $1 \leq i \leq$ NF, TF_i = x if the fragment F_i is composed x bytes.

- The *vector CS* gives the storage cost of a byte on the sites. $[CS_i]_{NS}$ is defined as:

> $\forall$ i with $1 \leq i \leq NS$, $CS_i = x$ if the storage cost of a byte on the site S_i is x.

3.2. Output data

- The fragment location is expressed by means of a matrix $[FS_{ij}]_{NF*NS}$:

> $\forall$ i,j with $1 \leq i \leq NF$ and $1 \leq j \leq NS$, $FS_{ij} = 1$ if F_i is placed onto S_j, 0 otherwise.

- The method location is expressed by a matrix $[MS_{ij}]_{NM*NS}$:

> $\forall$ i,j with $1 \leq i \leq NM$ and $1 \leq j \leq NS$, $MS_{ij} = 1$ if M_i is placed onto S_j, 0 otherwise.

3.3. Our allocation method

To place fragments and methods, we propose to minimize an objective function.

3.3.1. Preamble

3.3.1.1. Hypotheses

The following hypotheses specify the framework of the study :

- It does not exist a cycle in the method calls (or method invocations).
- Our function takes into account the costs of data transfers between a fragment site and a method site, and the costs of method result transfers between two sites.
- Only consultation methods return a result. In other words, if $MAJ_i = 1$ then $RES_i = 0$.
- In our projects, the method size is much smaller than the fragment sizes. Also, we do not take into account the method sizes to define our function.

3.3.1.2. Constraints

- Each method is placed at least onto a site of the system (Cont1)
- Each fragment is placed at least onto a site of the system (Cont2)
- Total size of fragments of S_j must be less than S_j capacity (Cont3).

> Cont1 : $\forall$ i $\in [1..NM]$, $\sum_{j=1}^{NS} MS_{ij} \geq 1$
>
> Cont2 : $\forall$ i $\in [1..NF]$, $\sum_{j=1}^{NS} FS_{ij} \geq 1$
>
> Cont3 : $\forall$ j $\in [1..NS]$, $\sum_{i=1}^{NF} FS_{ij} . TF_i \leq Capacité_j$

3.3.2. Cost function

This function evaluates different matrices FS or MS. Lowest cost matrices will constitute the output matrices that give the method and fragment allocations.

3.3.2.1. Additional information

- A communication cost between two sites S_i and S_j is dependent of the transferred data and the control information. This cost $Ccom_{ij}$ is given by the function:

> $\forall$ i,j with $1 \leq i \leq NS$, $1 \leq j \leq NS$, and $i \neq j$, $Ccom_{ij} = Cf_{ij} + x . SSC_{ij}$

- *Notation* : We use the next notations to simplify our objective function.

> $\forall [M_{ij}]_{max1*max2}$ a matrix, $\forall i \in [1..max1]$, $\forall j \in [1..max2]$,
>
> $\overline{M_{ij}}$ is defined as follows : $\begin{cases} \overline{M_{ij}} = 0 \text{ si } M_{ij} = 1 \\ \overline{M_{ij}} = 1 \text{ si } M_{ij} = 0 \end{cases}$

372

3.3.2.2. Fragment and method allocation : our proposition

• *Our objective function (ALLOC):* it minimizes communication costs between sites, and, storage costs of fragments and methods.

> ALLOC = min (STO + CC) under constraints Cont1, Cont2 and Cont3

• *Storage Cost (STO):* it is the sum of storage costs of each site. For a site S_s, the storage cost dependents on the storage cost of a byte (on S_s) and the size of a fragment present on S_s.

$$STO = \sum_{s=1}^{NS} CS_s \cdot \left(\sum_{j=1}^{NF} FS_{ij} \cdot TF_j \right)$$

• *Communication costs (CC):* This cost is dependent on a method call cost and on the frequency of these calls.

$$CC = \sum_{i=1}^{NM} \sum_{s=1}^{NS} CA_{is} \cdot MSC_{is}$$

◊ *The cost of Mi call from the site S_s (Ca_{is}):* Two cases can happen either Mi is on S_s or Mi is not on S_s. The local execution cost is not always the best. It cost may be more bad if all the fragments manipulated by Mi are present on another site that has itself a method copy. Thus, if Mi is present on S_s and on another site, we search the copy of Mi that induces a minimum cost. Autre$_{is}$ permit to search the method M_i present on a site different from S_s and whose its call implies a minimum cost.

$$CA_{is} = \begin{cases} Si\ MS_{is} \neq 0,\ Min(C_{is}, Autre_{is}) \\ Si\ MS_{is} = 0,\ Autre_{is} \end{cases}$$

$$Autre_{is} = \underset{\substack{j \in [1..NS] \\ j \neq s \\ MS_{ij} \neq 0}}{Min} (C_{ij} \cdot MS_{ij})$$

◊ *Communication costs induced by M_i allocated on S_j (C_{ij}) :* The execution of M_i placed onto S_j implies the access to fragments manipulated by M_i, and, the invocation of methods called by M_i.

$$C_{ij} = CD_{ij} + CI_{ij}$$

◊ *Direct costs (CD) :* this cost depends on the method type (update, consultation).

$$CD_{ij} = MAJ_i \cdot Cmaj_{ij} + Ccons_{ij} \cdot \overline{MAJ_i}$$

◊ *Direct access cost to fragments manipulated by the consultation method Mi allocated on S_j. ($Ccons_{ij}$) :* this cost integrates the transfers of the M_i result between S_j and S_s (site of M_i invocation). *resultat$_{ij}$* is the transfer cost of the Mi result between S_j and S_s and *Consul$_{ij}$* the cost relative to the fragment consultation by the method Mi of S_j. The local access cost (*cons_loc$_{ij}$*) depends on the number of bytes accessed locally by Mi and the access cost to a byte on S_j.

$$Ccons_{ij} = consul_{ij} + resultat_{ij}$$
$$resultat_{ij} = Res_i \cdot SSC_{js} + Cf_{js}$$
$$Consul_{ij} = cons\_loc_{ij} + cons\_non\_loc_{ij}$$
$$cons\_loc_{ij} = SSC_{jj} \cdot \left(\sum_{k=1}^{NF} MFC_{ik} \cdot FS_{kj} \cdot TF_k \right)$$

Cons_non_loc$_{ij}$ allows to determine the minimum access cost to fragments consulted by M_i and non present on S_j. For each fragment F_k, we search the site that has a F_k copy and that induces a minimum access cost to F_k by the consultation method M_i allocated on S_j.

$$cons\_non\_loc_{ij} = \sum_{k=1}^{NF} \left(\underset{\substack{l=1..NS \\ l \neq j \\ \overline{FS_{kj}} \cdot FS_{kl} \neq 0}}{Min} \left(MFC_{ik} \cdot \overline{FS_{kj}} \cdot FS_{kl} \cdot (Cf_{lj} + TF_k \cdot SSC_{lj}) \right) \right)$$

◊ *Access cost to fragments directly manipulated by an update method M_i allocated on S_j* : this cost is decomposed into an access cost to a copy of fragments being updated (Consul$_{ij}$),a cost of local update (maj_loc$_{ij}$ identical to cons_loc$_{ij}$) and a cost of non local update (maj_non_loc$_{ij}$).

$$Cmaj_{ij} = maj\_loc_{ij} + maj\_non\_loc_{ij} + Consul_{ij}$$

$$maj\_non\_loc_{ij} = \sum_{k=1}^{NF} \sum_{\substack{l=1 \\ l \neq j}}^{NS} \left(MFC_{ik}.FS_{kl}.\left(Cf_{lj} + TF_k.SSC'_{lj} \right) \right)$$

◊ *Indirect Cost (CI)* : To define these costs (cf. CA_{is}), we take into account the invocation cost of a method and data of the matrix MMC that indicate the different calls between methods as well as the frequencies of these calls.

$$CI_{ij} = \sum_{\substack{m=1 \\ m \neq i}}^{NM} MMC_{im}.CA_{mj}$$

4. Applications

In this section, we apply the formulae described in the previous sections. To decrease the complexity of our cost function, we propose different simplifications:
- The value of the constant cost (Cf) is very less than the variable cost. So, we propose to consider the constant cost as null.
- The value of local access costs is negligible in comparison with the data transfer cost. Also, we neglected local update, access and consultation costs.

4.1. Example 1 : a simple example where methods do not invoke another ones

4.1.1. Input data

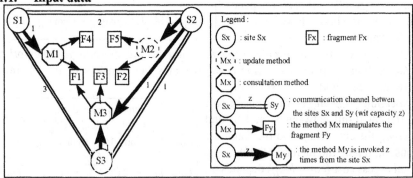

Figure3. : Input Data of the example 1

We propose to allocate 5 fragments and 3 methods on 3 sites (NS = 3, NF = 5, NM = 3). In figure 3, we present these different elements their interactions. We complete this representation with the next matrices :

- Information on fragments

	F1	F2	F3	F4	F5
TF	3000	200	5000	200	10

- Information on methods

	M1	M2	M3
RES	100	0	2000

	M1	M2	M3
MAJ	0	1	0

- Information on sites

CS	S1	S2	S3
	1	2	3

CAP	S1	S2	S3
	5000	1000	10000

- Information on the communications

MMC	M1	M2	M3
M1	0	0	0
M2	0	0	0
M3	0	0	0

MSC	S1	S2	S3
M1	1	0	0
M2	0	1	0
M3	0	1	1

SSC	S1	S2	S3
S1	0	2	3
S2	2	0	1
S3	3	1	0

MFC	F1	F2	F3	F4	F5
M1	1	0	0	1	0
M2	0	1	0	0	1
M3	1	0	1	0	0

4.1.2. Output matrices

The cost function would have to be applied on all the MS and FS matrices satisfying the 3 constraints. Since the method size is very less than the fragment size, we propose in a first part to place the methods on all the sites. After calculations, we will delete methods non used.

FS	S1	S2	S3
F1	1	0	1
F2	0	1	0
F3	0	0	1
F4	1	0	0
F5	0	1	0

In this section, we give only the matrix FS that minimizes our objective function.

4.1.3. Calculus details

- The matrix maj_non_loc :

Only, M2 is an update, thus the lines M1 and M3 are not filled. $maj\_non\_loc_{2,3}$ ($=TF_2.SSC'_{2,3} + TF_5.$ $SSC'_{2,3}$) indicates the transfer cost of the fragments updated by M2 (of S_3)and not placed onto S_3.

Maj_non_loc	S1	S2	S3
M1	x	x	x
M2	420	0	210
M3	x	x	x

- The matrix $Consul$

All the methods make at least a consultation. $Consul_{1,3}$ ($= TF_4.SSC'_{1,3}$) indicates for M_1 allocated on S_3 the transfer costs of fragments consulted by M_1 and not allocated on S_3.

Consul	S1	S2	S3
M1	0	3400	600
M2	420	0	210
M3	15000	8000	0

- The matrix $Cmaj$

Cmaj	S1	S2	S3
M1	x	x	x
M2	84	0	42
M3	x	x	x

- The matrix CI

CI	S1	S2	S3
M1	0	0	0
M2	0	0	0
M3	0	0	0

- The matrix CD

Direct access costs depend on the method invocation site, the method and the storage site of this one. To facilitate the comprehension, we propose to use three CD matrices (CD1, CD2 and CD3: one by site). In $CD1$ (Methods invoked from S1), if M_1 is placed onto S1 then $CD1_{1,1}=0$ (F_1 and F_4 placed onto S_1). If M_1 is located onto S_2, the cost changes because it is necessary to transfer the result of M_1 from S_2 to S_1.

CD1	S1	S2	S3
M1	0	3600	900
M2	x	x	x
M3	x	x	x

- The matrix *Autre*

Autre	S1	S2	S3
M1	900	200	300
M2	0	420	0
M3	6000	2000	10000

- The matrix CA

CA	S1	S2	S3
M1	0	200	300
M2	0	0	0
M3	6000	2000	0

4.1.4. Results

With the matrices FS and MS presented previously, we obtain the following results :

CC = 2000, STO = 27620, ALLOC = 29620 with M_1 on S_1, M_2 on S_2 and M_3 on S_3

4.2. Example 2

The input data matrices :

TF	F1	F2	F3	F4	F5	F6
	3000	200	5000	200	10	100

RES	M1	M2	M3	M4
	100	0	2000	500

CS	S1	S2	S3
	1	2	3

MAJ	M1	M2	M3	M4
	0	1	0	0

CAP	S1	S2	S3
	5000	1000	10000

MFC	F1	F2	F3	F4	F5	F6
M1	1	0	0	1	0	0
M2	0	1	0	0	1	0
M3	1	0	1	0	0	0
M4	0	0	1	0	0	1

MSC	S1	S2	S3
M1	1	0	0
M2	0	1	0
M3	0	1	1
M4	0	0	1

MMC	M1	M2	M3
M1	0	0	0
M2	1	0	0
M3	0	0	0
M4	1	0	0

SSC	S1	S2	S3
S1	0	2	3
S2	2	0	1
S3	3	1	0

We give now the FS matrix for which we obtain the minimum ALLOC function. After application of the allocation algorithm, we obtain the following placement : no method and no fragment on S_1, the M_2 method with F_5 and F_2 on S_2 and M_1, M_3, M_4, F_1, F_3, F_4 and F_6 on S_3.

FS	S1	S2	S3
F1	0	0	1
F2	0	1	0
F3	0	0	1
F4	0	0	1
F5	0	1	0
F6	0	0	1

5. Conclusion

The object of this article is to propose a solution for the distributed object oriented databases design. We focus on the distribution design step of a top-down approach. In the object context, we decompose this step into four sub steps. In this article, we proposed a solution for the data and processing allocation on the site of a distributed OODB. Current work do not integrate the processing placement in their allocation process. We therefore developed an original solution that proposes to allocate class fragments and methods. Finally, we illustrated our allocation method by two examples. Our allocation method minimizes the communication and the storage costs. Our objective function permits to allocate simultaneously static and dynamic components. It integrates the fragment and method duplications and 3 constraints.

To reduce the complexity of our solution, we developed an heuristic [5] that is not presented in this article. An extension to our work concerns the integration of new elements such as the load balancing cost. Indeed, to improve performances of a distributed system, the parallel executions allow to exploit the totality of resources offered by components of the system. Another extension could concern the integration of a method execution cost. The advantage of our solution is that this objective function is extensible.

Bibliography

[1] M. Özsu, P. Valduriez "Principle of distributed database systems" Ed. Prentice Hall, 1991

[2] G. Gardarin, P. Valduriez, "SGBD Avancés : Bases de données objets, déductives, réparties", Ed. Eyrolles, 1990

[3] S. Ceri, B. Pernici, G. Wiederhold "Distributed Database Design Methodologies" Proc. of the IEEE, Vol. 75, N° 5, pp. 533-546, May 1987

[4] F. Ravat "OD3 : contribution méthodologique à la conception de bases de données orientées objet réparties", Ph.D. thesis, University Paul Sabatier, France, September 1996

[5] F. Ravat "La fragmentation d'un schéma conceptuel orienté objet", Ingéniérie des systèmes d'information, Vol. 4, N° 2, pp. 161-193, 1996

[6] C. Ernst, A.Lapujade, F.Ravat, G.Zurfluh "Distributed Object Oriented Database Design: A Method and A Tool" IEEE BIWIT'97, July 97

[7] J. G. Escamilla de los Santos "Shood : un modèle méta-circulaire de représentation des connaissances", Ph.D. thesis of Institut National Polytechnique of Grenoble (France), Sept 1993

[9] G. T. Nguyen, D. Rieu " Multiple object representation" 20 Th. ACM Computer Science Conference, Kansas City Mars 1992

[8] D. Rieu, and al. "Représentation, sélection et combinaison de méthodes" VIII Journées Bases de Données Avancées 15-18 Sept. 1992

[10] F. Ravat, G. Zurfluh, "Class partitioning", Journal of Computing and Information (JCI) Vol.1, N°2, pp. 759-779, November 1995

[11] S. Navathe, C. Ceri, G. Wiederhold et J. Dou "Vertical partitioning algorithms for database design", ACM Transaction on Databases, Vol. 9 N° 4, pp.680-710, Dec 1984

[12] S. Navathe and al. " A mixed partitioning methodology for distributed database design" Technical Report TR 90-17, February 1990

[13] S. Ceri, and al. "Distribution design of logical database schemas", IEEE Transactions on software engineering, Vol. SE-9, n°4, pp. 487-503, July 1983

[14] P. M.G. Apers "Data allocation in distributed database systems", ACM Transactions on database, Vol. 13, n°3, pp. 263-304, Sept. 1988

[15] R. Mukkamala "Design of partially replicated distributed databases systems : an integrated methodology", Ph.D Thesis, Computer Science Department, University of Iowa, July 1987

[16] R. Mukkamala, S.C.Bruell, R.K. Shultz "Design of partially replicated distributed database systems: an integrated methodology", Proc. of ACM SIGMETRICS conference, Vol. 16, N° 1, pp. 187-196, 1988

[17] R. Blankinship, A. R. Hevner, S.b. Yao "An iterative method for distributed database design", VLDB'91, pp. 389-400, Sept 1991

[18] R. Blankinship "An iterative method for distributed database design", Ph.D. Thesis, University of Maryland, college park, 1991

[19] Y. Huang, O. Wolfson "Object allocation in distributed databases and mobile computers", Proc. of 10th international conference on data engineering, pp.20-29, 1993

[20] H. Min "An efficient storage protocol for distributed object databases", Conf. on parallel and distributed processing, pp. 606-610, 1993

[21] O. Gruber, L. Amsaleg "Object grouping in EOS", distributed object management edited by M. T. Özsu, U.Dayal, P. Valduriez, Morgan Kaufmann publishers, pp. 117-131, 1994

Annex

$Autre_{is}$: Call Cost of the method M_i allocated on a site different from S_s

Ca_{mj}: Invocation cost of M_m from the site S_j

$Ccons_{ij}$:Access cost to fragments directly consulted by the method Mi of S_j

CD_{ij} : Access Cost to fragments directly manipulated by the method Mi (direct costs)

Cf_{ij}: constant cost relative to the transfer of control information between S_i and S_j

CI_{ij}: Access Cost to methods Mj invoked by the method Mi (Indirect Costs)

C_{is}: Communication costs induced by a method M_i allocated on S_s

$Cmaj_{ij}$: Access cost to fragments directly updated by the method Mi

$cons\_loc_{ij}$: Cost relative to the consultation of fragments allocated on S_j by M_i

$cons\_non\_loc_{ij}$: Cost relative to the consultation of fragments non allocated on S_j by M_i

$consul_{ij}$:Cost of consultation by M_i of S_j

CS_s: Storage cost of a byte on the site S_s

FS_{js}: Binary variable that indicates if the fragment F_j is present on the site S_s

maj_loc_{ij}: Update Cost of fragments allocated on S_j (for the method M_i)

$maj\_non\_loc_{ij}$:Update Cost of fragments non allocated on S_j (for the method M_i)

MAJ_i / $\overline{MAJ}_i$: Mi is / is not an update

MFC_{ik}: Mi manipulates directly F_k

MMC_{im}: Number of invocations of the method M_m by the method Mi

MSC_{is}: Invocation number of Mi by S_s

Ms_{ij}: The method M_i is placed on the site S_j

Res_i: size of the Mi result

$resultat_{ij}$: Transfer cost of the Mi result from S_j (site of M_i) to S_s (of M_i invocation)

SSC_{ij} :access cost to a byte of S_i from S_j

TF_j: Size of the fragment F_j

A Meta Message Approach for Electronic Data Interchange (EDI)

C. Huemer*, G. Quirchmayr*, A M. Tjoa[+]

*Institute of Applied Computer Science and Information Systems, University of Vienna,
e-mail: {ch,gq}@ifs.univie.ac.at

[+]Institute of Software Technology, Vienna University of Technology,
e-mail: tjoa@ifs.tuwien.ac.at

Abstract. Still most of the current information systems are intra-organizational. Since products, services and production processes have become more information intensive, there is an increased need to transfer these information between organizations. Electronic Data Interchange (EDI) standards have been proposed to exchange these information between two independently operating information systems. All these standards have in common that they standardize business documents—which represent the relevant information—on instance type level. Since a data interchange between business partners is always based on a small subset of the standards, it is necessary to agree upon this subset. In our paper we present a concept for interchanging this agreement via EDI itself. The presented concept leads to a standardization on the meta level.

1 Introduction

Many years ago the industry discovered the great benefits of electronic information transfer. Various exchange formats, or so-called EDI standards, have been developed. Most of them were proprietary standards or at least restricted to either a certain branch (ODETTE) or a certain region (ANSI X.12). In 1987 the ISO published the syntax of UN/EDIFACT as an international and intersectorial valid standard [2,14]. As soon as the first directory of EDIFACT came out, companies started to build and sell their own EDI translation software and to use EDI messages for orders and invoices. Over the years, it became clear that it was rather difficult for a company to get started with EDI. A case study involving about 60 European organizations showed that most of these organizations were not able to derive the expected benefits from EDI [3]. So the implementation of EDI was slower than originally expected.

Although it is often stated that EDI is 80% business and only 20% technique [4], we feel that the technical aspects of EDI are quite underestimated. It is our opinion that the higher the complexity of EDI techniques the harder their integration into the business. A more efficient method of interchanging business data would therefore reduce the costs of implementation and only the benefit/cost ratio will be relevant when deciding whether or not to participate in EDI. The fact that 90% of the Fortune 1000 enterprises have invested in EDI, but less than 1% of the small and medium enterprises are involved in EDI, indicates that the current method of exchanging business data is not mature. Consequently, there is a growing need for new methods which will allow small and medium enterprises to participate in EDI.

It is easy to detect, that EDIFACT—as opposed to its intention—is not an international and branch-independent standard. International and intersectorial from a implementation point of view would mean that any message created by the sending application in the standard conform format will be automatically processable by the receiving application. This would require the following two conditions: First, both information systems must have the same understanding of the interchanged data. Second, the receiving application must be able to process any data that might be included in a standard message. Unfortunately, none of these conditions are fulfilled.

Business partners willing to exchange data electronically in a structured format have first to agree on the actual data they want to interchange. The format of these data is mainly determined by the semantics the involved information systems are able to process. Hence, business partners have to sit down, discuss how they are going to interchange files and implement these specifications within specific translation software. Consequently, a detailed functional agreement is needed for each business relationship. It follows that business partners—although using the international and intersectorial EDIFACT standard—in fact, use a corresponding proprietary standard for each business relationship. In this paper we present a concept for exchanging the functional interchange agreements between the business partners via EDI itself. Other concepts which address the problem of functional agreements include Open-edi [10], Business System Interoperation (BSI) [13], and Object Oriented edi [1].

2 Shortcomings of the Current EDI Standards

Although the advantages of EDI are well known, most of the SMEs are not able to participate in EDI. Legal aspects and security problems are some of the reasons. But there is also a substantial number of shortcomings in the information technology aspect of the current standards. The following problems are encountered [7,11,12]:

- Resulting structures are too complex and consequently too hard to read and to navigate.
- Multiple standards and different versions of each standard are in use.
- Semantics are not part of the EDI standard.
- Semantic interpretation of the standard is included in implementation conventions, which are different for each industry sector and/or geographical region.
- A detailed interchange agreement is necessary to establish an EDI relationship to a trading partner.
- Overhead in network costs and reduced processing efficiency due to segment tags and delimiters marking unused data.
- Standards are published only in English.
- Business Processes are not considered by the standards. Consequently, integrating EDI into the business processes of an organization is too hard to perform, especially for small and medium size enterprises.
- The current translation software is too inflexible. The process of retrieving EDI messages from a mailbox, translating it into a flat file, convert the flat file into a database import format and import this into the database of the business application is much too complex.
- A change request to an EDI standard is much too time-consuming due to the bureaucracy of the standard organizations.

3 The Meta Message Approach in Detail

The proposed method is based on an EDIFACT meta message, which allows the transmission of the format of the messages carrying the business data. Candidates for meta messages are the *Directory Definition Message* (DIRDEF), the *EDI Implementation Guideline Definition Message* (IMPDEF), and the *Functional Agreement Definition Message* (FAGDEF).

DIRDEF is a message developed by the UN. It allows the transmission of an EDIFACT Directory set or parts thereof in EDIFACT syntax [15]. IMPDEF is used to put the contents of a Message Implementation Guideline (MIG) into an EDIFACT message [5]. Nevertheless, both DIRDEF and IMPDEF are in some respect not optimal for our purpose. Therefore, we combine the best features of DIRDEF and IMPDEF and extend them by further concepts to create a new meta message—FAGDEF—which is best suited for our approach.

However, it is a global goal that our approach is independent of the specific format of a meta message. This means that we provide a generic approach which can easily be adapted to a specific kind of meta message. Consequently, we achieve a great flexibility in the sense that it is possible to accommodate the approach to future versions of existing meta messages as well as to new types of meta messages.

The message independent approach can be described as follows: The core component of our method comprises a tool for building functional agreements which we call *Functional Agreement Designer*. This tool allows the design of a meta message. Furthermore, mapping tables to the internal storage format of directories and functional agreements can be specified according to this design. Hence, each kind of meta message can be imported to derive functional agreements with the *Functional Agreement Designer*. These functional agreements can be based on subsets of existing messages and on wild subsets which manipulate the messages in a non standard conform way. Furthermore, functional agreement specifications can also incorporate concepts not covered by the standard, like fixed and optional components. For functional agreements including additional concepts which are disregarded by the standard we use the term 'exchange agreement'. It is obvious that also subsets of already defined exchange agreements can be established. Accordingly, the *Functional Agreement Designer* enables the adoption of a message design to the real business needs of the user's company. The self-created functional agreements can be translated into a meta message of any included meta message format. These meta messages can be transmitted electronically to the partner company. Furthermore, the message definition in the meta message format should be a valid input format to the EDI translation software. The translation software is used to map an instantiated EDI message carrying business data to the input format of the business application. If the business partner also uses an EDI translation software that is able to accept the meta message as input format, he will be able to handle messages in the format created by the initiating company. This means a consequent extension of the basic idea of EDI, because the functional agreement on the interchange structure between two companies will be based on EDI [8].

3.1 Functional Agreement Definition Message

As mentioned above, both DIRDEF and IMPDEF are not optimal for exchanging functional agreements in EDIFACT environments. DIRDEF allows to specify component usage just for one step down the component hierarchy. This means that it is possible to cite which segments are used in a message. But it is not possible to designate the usage of data elements within a certain segment of a message. Consequently, all segments of the same type are structured equally regardless of their position in a message. This might be sufficient for the standard specification, but is not adequate for the specification of exchange agreements between business partners. The same problem applies for codes assigned to a coded simple data element. DIRDEF does not provide a possibility to specify that in a certain position within a certain message one subset of codes is allowed and at a different position within a different message (or even in the same message) a different subset of codes is applicable.

In contrast, IMPDEF provides the concept of multi level component definitions. But unfortunately, this concept is equivocally implemented in IMPDEF. This is due to the fact that the position specific component specification is made totally independent to the general subdirectory definitions.

In addition to these problems the specification on the usage of a component is too general in the standard specification. The standard covers only two kinds of requirement designators to indicate that a component must be used or can be used in an interchange. But these are not sufficient to describe in detail the requirements of a component. On the one hand a component might be specified in the standard as conditional, but is required by the receiving application. This problem could be solved with DIRDEF and IMPDEF. But on the other hand more specific requirement designators are needed to denote the usage of components. A complete segment usage can be described by combinations of the following designators:

- Mandatory: The component must always be specified
- Conditional: The component could be specified. No specification means a null value for the corresponding field.
- Optional: The component could be specified. No specification means that a default value is applied for the corresponding data field
- Default: A default value for an optional data field.
- Fixed: A fix value specified which can not be updated in an interchange

Furthermore, the combination of requirement designator and maximum number of occurrences specified for a component is inadequate. In the EDIFACT standard definition only one designator and one number of occurrences can be specified. For example

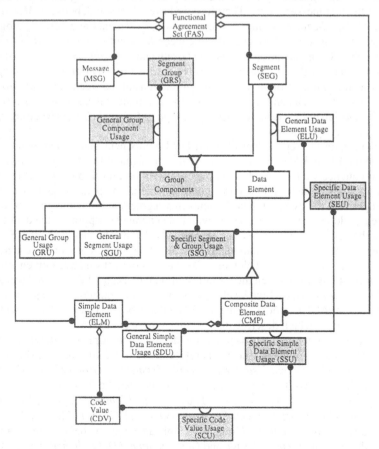

Fig. 1. OMT-Model of the FAGDEF Message

M 9 means that the component must be specified at least once, but can be specified up to 9 times. It is not possible to specify who many times a component must be included and how many times it could be stated. The combination of the various above mentioned requirement designators and a number of occurrences specified for each designator would be more appropriate for the specification of data fields to be interchanged. To overcome these problems, we define a new EDIFACT message which exactly meets the requirements of our objective. According to the overall goal we call this message *Functional Agreement Definition Message* (FAGDEF). A complete technical description of FAGDEF in style of an EDIFACT boiler plate is given in [9].

The basic technology used in FAGDEF is explained by means of the OMT diagram in Figure 1. The classes in the white boxes and their interrelationships of Figure 1 are derived from DIRDEF and IMPDEF. The class represented in grey boxes and their relationships to other classes are the result of two new main concepts in FAGDEF.

The first new FAGDEF specific concept is the explicit representation of segment groups. This concept is necessary, because of different treatment of the same group for fixed, optional, mandatory, and conditional usage. Accordingly, we establish the class *Segment Group* as first level component for message structures. Conceptually, the described message structure is identical to the structure of one fictitious segment group (Segment Group 0). This fictitious segment group covers all segments and segment groups of the first message level. Therefore we have a 1-to-n link between *Message* and *Segment Group*. Segment groups are composed of segments and further subgroups. Therefore, there is a n-to-m relationship between *Segment Group* and *Group Components*, which is a generalization of *Segment Group* and *Segment*. The general usage of a group component within a segment group is described by *General Group Component Usage*, which is a link attribute to the n-to-m relationship between *Segment Group* and *Group Components*. Depending on whether the component is a segment or a segment group, the specializations *General Segment Usage* or *General Group Usage* are responsible for the link specification.

The second main concept is that of multi level component definitions, which is also used in IMPDEF. In FAGDEF it was our goal to implement this feature unequivocally. As a consequence we have tried to keep a consistent relationship between the position specific multi level usage and the corresponding general component usage. This means, for example, that the usage of data elements in a segment at a specific position within a message should be specified in context with the general description of the data element usage in the corresponding segment. Conceptually this means that in IMPDEF the specific component usage is a relationship between the specific component usage of the above level and the component elements. By way of contrast we have implemented this feature as relationship between the specific component usage of the above level and the general component usage of the level in question. For this purpose we explicitly distinguish between FAGDEF meta segments which describe the general component usage and meta segments which describe the specific component usage.

At the first level of component usage we are faced with multiple specific derivations of the general group component usage. Therefore, there is a 1-to-n relationship between *General Group Component Usage* and *Specific Segment & Group Usage*. On the following levels we keep the relationship between the specific usage of the above level and the general usage of the same level. Thus, *Specific Element Usage* is a link attribute to the n-to-n relationship between *Segment Usage* and *General Element Usage*, and *Specific Simple Data Element Usage* is a link attribute to the n-to-m relationship between this *Specific Element Usage* and *General Simple Data Element Usage*. Finally, the specification of a subset of valid codes in *Specific Code Value Usage* is a link attribute to the n-to-m relationship between *Specific Simple Data Element Usage* and *Code Value.*

3.2 Software for the Meta Message Approach

This subsection covers a description of the *Functional Agreement Designer* which is a software tool to support our Meta Message Approach. Furthermore, we present the necessary interactions between the *Functional Agreement Designer* and the translation software to be able to exchange messages on the basis of self-designed functional agreements. The whole software needed to perform application-to-application data exchange is depicted in Figure 2.

The *Functional Agreement Designer* is composed of two core components, the *Meta Message Mapper* and the *Browser & Editor.* Both components are based on the *Directory Definition & Functional Agreement Set Database* which integrates the different components of the *Functional Agreement Designer.* The database of the *Functional Agreement Designer* contains information on meta message designs (*Meta Message Design Database*), on structures of EDIFACT standard directories, of subsets thereof, and of exchange agreements (*Directory & Agreement Structures Database*). Furthermore, it covers information on the mapping between the meta messages and the EDIFACT or functional agreement structures (*Mapping Table Definitions Database*). Furthermore, there must be a connection between the *Functional Agreement Designer* and the communication interface to be able to receive and send meta messages.

In order to browse through an EDIFACT standard directory or through an exchange agreement, it first has to be included into *Directory Definition & Functional Agreement Set Database.* This task is performed by the *Meta Message Mapper.* For this purpose the *Meta Message Mapper* must be aware of the design of the meta message. This design specification might be received by another meta message which is already known by the *Meta Message Mapper.* But it can also be designed from scratch with the *Meta Message Designer,* which is part of the *Meta Message Mapper.* The design of all included meta messages is stored in the *Meta Message Design Database.* Note that the functionality of the *Meta Message Designer* is identical to that of the *Browser & Editor.*

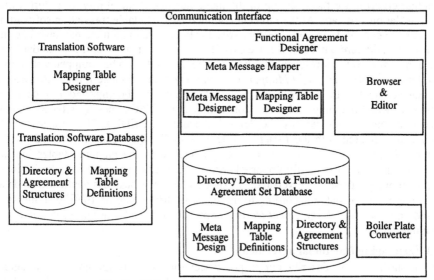

Fig. 2. Software for the Meta Message Approach

Afterwards mapping tables which describe how to transform 'conventional' messages (=the contents of a meta message) into the internal representation of the *Functional Agreement Designer* must be defined. This function—similar to that of specifying mapping tables in the translation software—is fulfilled by the *Mapping Table Designer*. After specification of the mapping tables, meta messages of an included type might be received electronically via the communication interface. According to the type and version of a meta message the appropriate mapping table is automatically loaded and the contents of the meta message is transformed into the format of the *Directory & Agreement Structures Database*. Received meta messages might include descriptions of EDIFACT standard directories, (wild) subsets of the standard directories, implementation conventions, or exchange agreements created by a business partner.

All directories and their derivations included in the *Directory & Agreement Structures Database* can be accessed via the *Browser & Editor*. The *Browser* is designed to navigate through the EDIFACT standard directories, subsets and exchange agreements in a very flexible and clearly arranged manner. It allows access at each level of the EDIFACT hierarchy (messages, segments, composite data elements and single data elements) and offers links between these levels [6]. The *Browser* also serves as a starting point for the Editor. By using the *Browser & Editor* it is possible to create subsets of standard directories, completely new messages and exchange agreements [9]. The results are stored in the *Directory & Agreement Structures Database*.

Although a stand-alone *Functional Agreement Designer* might be useful for the documentation of functional agreement definitions, its full power will only be reached if the designed specifications can be transferred to the translation software. Consequently, it is necessary to convert the definitions stored in the internal database into meta messages. For this purpose mapping tables can be specified with the *Meta Message Designer* to export the (wild) subsets and functional agreements into a meta message format (which must be included in the *Meta Message Design Database*). Note, that the expressiveness of the meta message should be at least as powerful as the expressiveness of the output alternative of the *Browser & Editor*, because otherwise self-created specifications might be lost.

Another criterion for the selection of the meta message is the ability to import it into the translation software. At the moment commercially available translation software is not flexible enough to import directory specifications given in a meta message into the translation software database. But we expect them to be open at least for standardized meta messages in the foreseeable future. May be they will also be equipped with a tool similar to our *Meta Message Mapper* to except any meta message format. If the meta message created by the *Functional Agreement Designer* can be imported into the translation software, mapping tables for 'conventional' EDIFACT messages based on created functional agreements can be defined. Accordingly, EDIFACT messages whose format was created with the *Functional Agreement Designer* can be received via the communication interface, translated in compliance with the mapping tables into an interface file, which is finally imported with the converter software into the business application's database. Vice versa, data exported from the business application's database might be translated according to the mapping tables into an EDIFACT message based on a *Functional Agreement Designer* specification, and sent via the communication interface.

3.3 Exchanging functional agreements

In this subsection we describe our proposed scenario for exchanging functional agreements which are based on the business needs of the business partners via EDI and the

384

subsequent exchange of messages based on these agreements. The description of this scenario should be read in conjunction with Figure 3 which depicts the overall process. The first step for the initiating business partner is to include the EDIFACT standard directories into the *Browser & Editor*. Hopefully, in the near future this can be done by receiving on-line a meta message from an EDIFACT reference database (1a). At the moment it is only possible to import them from the directory descriptions provided in ASCII formats via the *Boiler Plate Converter* (1b).

Now the initiating business partner develops an EDIFACT conform or wild subset (2a) or an exchange agreement (2b) on the basis of a standard version. The resulting exchange specification will include only those components which will actually be exchanged in the business transaction. Via the documentation tool the initiating business partner can print a documentation of the self-created functional agreement, which can be used as implementation guideline (3a, 3b). The functional agreement definition can be exported from the *Functional Agreement Designer* into a meta message (4a, 4b). In order to ensure that the business partner has the same understanding of the functional agreement the meta message must be sent to the responding business partner.

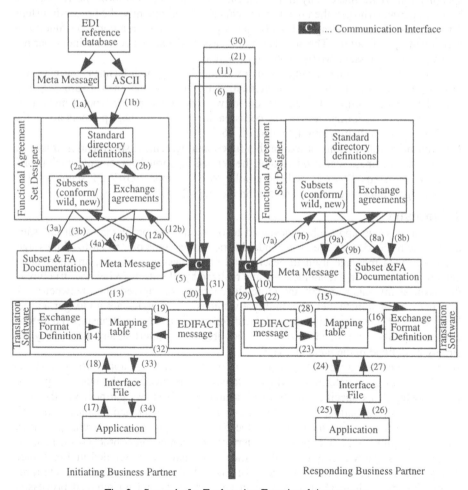

Fig. 3. Scenario for Exchanging Functional Agreements

Thus, the resulting meta message is passed to the communication interface (5), which is responsible for the transmission to the business partner (6).

The responding business partner receives the meta message via his communication interface and imports the functional agreement definition into his *Functional Agreement Designer* (7a, 7b). He is now able to verify the definition created by the initiating business partner via the *Browser & Editor*. If he detects any discrepancies, he can also adopt the functional agreement. Similarly to the originator, the responding business partner may print a documentation of the functional agreement (8a, 8b) and export the functional agreement definition into a meta message (9a, 9b).

If the responding business partner has made any changes to the functional agreement specification, he must inform the initiating business partner. Therefore, he passes the meta message including the new functional agreement specification to his communication interface (10) in order to transmit back to the originator (11). The initiating business partner receives the meta message via his communication interface and imports the adopted functional agreement specification into his *Functional Agreement Designer* (12a, 12b). Now, he can again verify and/or adopt the functional agreement specification. If he makes any improvements, he must again inform the responding business partner who can then react on the changes. Consequently, the processing steps 3 to 12 may repeat as along as both business partners agree on a common functional agreement specification. The agreement process will end when a business partner receives a meta message where no changes were made.

As soon as there is an agreement on the exchange format, both business partners will provide the functional agreement specification to their translation software (13, 15). Note that for this purpose the translation software must accept the type of meta message as valid input format. When this occasion arises both business partners are in the position to design their mapping tables (14, 16).

Now, business transactions based on this functional agreement specification might be processed. A business scenario based on the defined functional agreement which is presented in the steps 17 to 25 will be similar to a common EDIFACT scenario. The responding business scenario is depicted in the steps 26 to 34.

4 Summary

The meta message approach is designed to overcome the problems of current standards. The basic idea is to reduce standardization to one type of standardized message, namely a meta message used to describe all other messages. Hence, an interchange agreement is based on a meta message and realized by EDI itself. When the structure of the business messages are not any more standardized, but agreed upon between business partners by a meta message, multiple versions of a message are no longer a problem. An exact message structure is defined for each business relationship. Therefore, change requests to the standardization bodies are not so important any more. They can simply be defined in the meta message.

Business processes are partially reflected in the meta message approach. The sender application program determines which data can be produced by the business process implemented. This specification is made available to business partners via the meta message. Business partners verify whether or not the implemented business processes in their information system can process these data. The process of interchanging meta data will continue until an appropriate interface between business processes is reached. If a meta message will only cover those data types and codes included in a real interchange, the long and complex structure of EDIFACT is reduced to an absolute minimum. Therefore, there is no overhead in network costs and no reduced processing efficiency due to segment tags and delimiters marking unused data. Nevertheless, the problem of dispersed semantics is not solved by the meta message approach.

The process of determining a business relation specific interchange format also ensures that the involved business partners will have a common understanding of the semantic interpretation of included data types. The semantics of data types can be documented in free text fields of the meta message. Semantics are part of the interchange agreement, but not provided in a processable format.

The meta message approach makes high demands on future translation software. Tomorrow's translation software must be able to accept the format of a meta message as valid input format. It must be more flexible by allowing mapping tables to be the direct interface between the EDI message and application data structures. However, multilinguality is not explicitly covered by the meta message approach, but could be easily incorporated [6].

References

[1] AC.1; The next Generation of UN/EDIFACT - An Open-edi Approach using IDEF Models & OOT; June 1997; http://www.premenos.com:80/klaus/ooedi/

[2] Berge J.; *The EDIFACT Standards*; NCC Blackwell Limited; Oxford; 1991

[3] Bielli P.; *Social and Economic Impacts of EDI: Executive Summary*; Department of Information Systems;
Bocconi University; Milano;

[4] Emmelhainz M.A.; *Electronic Data Interchange: A Total Management Guide*; Van Nostrand Reinhold; New York; 1990

[5] Hage C.; *EDI implementation guideline definition message (IMPDEF)*;
http://www.chage.com/chage/edi/impdef/impdef6b.txt

[6] Huemer C., Tjoa A M.; *A Multilingual Browser for the UN/EDIFACT Communication Standard*; Proceedings of the 21th Euromicro Conference; Como, Italy; 1995; pp 748 - 753

[7] Huemer C., Quirchmayr G.; *The Dilemma of EDI - Problem Analysis of Current Standards*; Proceedings of the 7th Information Resources Management Association (IRMA) International Conference; Washington; May 1996; pp 101 - 107

[8] Huemer C., Quirchmayr G., Tjoa A M.; *Modelling Functional Agreements in EDIFACT Environments*; Proceedings of the IFIP/ICCC International Conference on Information Network and Data Communication; Trondheim, Norway; June 1996; pp 87 - 100

[9] Huemer C., Electronic Data Interchange (EDI): Standards, Shortcomings, Solutions; Ph.D. Thesis; Institute of Applied Computer Science and Information Systems, University of Vienna; February 1997

[10]International Organization for Standardization; *The Open-edi Conceptual Model*, ISO/IEC JTC1/SWG-EDI Document N222; 1991;
http://www.premenos.com:80/klaus/open-edi/concept.html

[11]Steel K.; *Matching Functionality of Interoperating Applications: Another Approach to EDI Standardisation*; ISO/IEC JTC1/SC30 IT11/7/94-108; September 1994

[12]Steel K.; *The ICARIS Project*; ECA 95; University of Melbourne, Department of Computer Science; 1995

[13]Steel K.; *Business System Interoperation*; University of Melbourne; Department of Computer Science; July 1996; ftp://turiel.cs.mu.oz.au/pub/edi/bsiintro.doc

[14]United Nations, Economic and Social Council; *UN/EDIFACT Syntax Rules*; ISO 9735; International Organization for Standardization; Geneva; 1987

[15]United Nations, Economic and Social Council; *Directory Definition Message (TAG 52.315)*; Trade Data Interchange Protocols; Geneva; 1993

Schemaless Representation of Semistructured Data and Schema Construction

Dong-Yal Seo[1], Dong-Ha Lee[1], Kang-Sik Moon[1], Jisook Chang[1],
Jeon-Young Lee[1], and Chang-Yong Han[2]

[1] Dept. of Computer Science and Engineering
Pohang University of Science and Technology
Pohang, Kyungbuk, 790-784, KOREA
[2] Data Warehouse Advanced Technology
Oracle Systems Korea, Ltd.
Youngdeungpo-Gu, Seoul, 150-010, KOREA

Abstract. We should consider semistructured data of which have a weak schema information in networked information world. To manage such semistructured data efficiently, this paper introduces a data model for semistructured data and operations for schema construction. We transform semistructured data into structured one by introducing schema construction methodology, compared to the former studies which are fully dependent on schemaless manipulations. For schema construction, we defined operations for building *IS-A/IS-PART-OF* relationships, collecting data objects to build a primitive class, and merging two data instances or classes.

1 Introduction

1.1 Motivation

In early stages of data processing such as inventory/account management systems, a centralized large database system was used as an information server. Through the database design (or real-world modeling) phase, DBA(Database Administrator) defines a well-structured schema. We perform data acquisition and creation after schema definition. For end-users, their role is to manipulate data via predefined schema. The schema is firm and end-users are not responsible for schema management.

As data sources and computing environment are distributed, abundant of information is provided by individual users and updated very quickly. Each end-user creates and updates his/her own information, like DBA. The WWW(World-Wide Web) is a typical domain of the examples. Every user creates his/her own documents and submitts in the WWW. How to manage those plenty of HTML documents and other web resources? We should always navigate through hyper-links or search by keywords because there is no absolute schema in the stored information. If we could define a schema on the set of web resources, not only we have a better structure of gathered information but also we can use a structured query language. Schema provides the well-structured view of stored data. It expresses data location, relationships among data objects, data categories, summarized concepts, and so on.

The data sets, where there is no absolute schema fixed in advance and whose structure may be irregular or incomplete, are known as *semistructured data*. Even though a data is created as a well-structured, i.e., schema-based, set of data, it becomes semistructured when the data comes out from its original structure. For example, a single record from a relational table is semistructured if we have no idea about the overall structure of the table and the relationships with other tables.

1.2 Problems and Approaches

Figure 1 shows the approaches of information processing based on the structural nature of data sources. Right side of the figure presents conventional data processing. Information itself has a rigid structure and is represented with a well-structured model, like relational or object-oriented. Users manipulate data with a schema which mainly provides an structural abstraction of stored data.

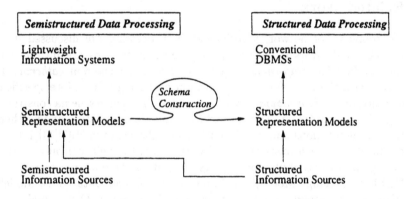

Fig. 1. Information Structures and Processings

Left side shows the processing of information with poor schema, i.e. *semistructured information* [12] (or even *unstructured* [3]). Semistructured information is represented with a lightweight model, which permits schemaless creation of data instances, and is stored in a lightweight storage. Stored information is manipulated with a lightweight query language, which can be used with incomplete schema information.

The studies on lightweight approaches much overlooked the importance of database schema. Although schemaless manipulation is convenient for users who want to retrieve data without deep knowledge of underlying structures, schema is indispensable for embedded SQL, API calls, or stored procedures. Schema gives firmness and conceptualized view.

In semistructured data processing, end-users represent data instances without complete knowledge of the predefined schema. (Or even without any schema information.) So data creation phase can be performed before schema definition phase. For semistructured data processing, we established the strategy, "*schemaless creation, schema-based manipulation*" which involves the following goals:

1. Provide a *representation model* for schemaless data instances. The model should be expressive enough to describe semistructured data instances from heterogeneous data sources.
2. Devise a mechanism for *schema construction* which can be applied to a schemaless pool of data instances. After applying schema construction procedures, we will have a rigid schema and manipulate the stored data with SQL.

The remaining parts of this paper is composed as follows. Section 2 presents related work and corresponding contributions. Section 3 and 4 address a data model for schemaless creation of data objects and operations for schema construction, the main contribution of this work, respectively. And finally, conclusion and directions for future work are discussed in section 5.

2 Related Work

General problems of networked information processing are discussed in [4]. Three conceptual layers of networked information systems are introduced as *information Interface*, *information dispersion*, and *information gathering*. Our work deals with the problems in information gathering layer. More specifically, we are interested in *data mapping problem* and we introduce schema construction operators for that problem. The importance and the motivation about schemaless data representations and manipulations are discussed in [1][3][11][12].

Schemaless data instances are usually described by their attributes and corresponding values. Attribute-value pairs were used for data representation in OEM(Object Exchange Model)[11], Labeled-Tree[3], and Data Forest Model[1]. Although not developed as a semistructured data model, O_2's *complex value* model[8] shows a good way of semistructured representation with attribute-value pairs. All the earlier models for semistructured data are similar to each other and their expressive powers are almost same.

TSIMMIS[3] project[7] introduces OEM and other related work[12] about the integration of heterogeneous information sources. OEM provides sets and nested substructures as well as atomic values like integers and strings by using attribute-value pairs[4]. Labeled-Tree model, has the same expressive power as the OEM, represents semistructured data as trees, i.e., the trees with a labeling of edges. Data Forest Model supports list type which is unable to be described in the OEM and the labeled-tree.

The former studies are mainly focused on lightweight approaches and the importance of database schema is too overlooked. The schema construction approach draws a distinction between our study and conventional methodologies in

---

[3] The Stanford-IBM Manager of Multiple Information Sources
[4] In [11], the term "level-value pair" was used instead of "attribute-value pair".

semistructured data processing. The problems on structuring[13] and typing[9] semistructured data are introduced recently.

The studies on subject-oriented programming[10] introduce a methodology for class compositions which deals with behaviors compared to our approach which deals with data.

3 Schemaless Creation of Data Objects

Objects are usually distinguished by their *types*, where type describes applicable *operations* and *properties*. Properties define either *attributes* of the object itself or *relationships* among objects. We mainly considered data objects from the viewpoint of properties.

3.1 Model Definition

Our data model describes schemaless data objects with a series of attribute-value pairs, called *AVPL(Attribute-Value Pairs List)*. An attribute-value pair is composed of two tuples, attribute and value. When we denote a set of AVPL, a set of attributes, and a set of values as D, A, and V, respectively, AVPL is defined as follows:

1. Single attribute-value pair is an AVPL

$$(a \in A) \land (v \in V) \longrightarrow \{(a,v)\} \in D$$

2. Union of two attribute-value pairs is an AVPL

$$D_1, D_2 \in D \longrightarrow D_1 \cup D_2 \in D$$

Attribute is an ordered collection of one or more variables, where each variable itself is also an attribute. When S denotes the set of strings, attribute is defined as follows:

1. Singleton attribute

$$s \in S \longrightarrow s \in A$$

2. Composite attribute (Attribute with multiple variables)

$$a_1, a_2, \ldots, a_n \in A \longrightarrow (a_1, a_2, \ldots, a_n) \in A$$

where $(a_1, a_2, \ldots, a_n)$ is an ordered sequence of attribute variables.

Value is an assignable instance, or a set of instances, to the corresponding attribute and its variables. *Assignment* of values to attributes are defined as follows:

1. Singleton attribute and value

$$a \longleftarrow v$$

where $a \in A$ and $v \in V$

2. Composite attribute and value

$$(a_1, a_2, \ldots, a_n) \longleftarrow (v_1, v_2, \ldots, v_n)$$

where $(a_1, a_2, \ldots, a_n) \in A$, $(v_1, v_2, \ldots, v_n) \in V$, and each v_i is assigned to a_i $(1 \leq i \leq n)$.

The domain of attributes includes primitive strings, references of values, set (or list) of values, and AVPL objects. Therefore, an AVPL object itself (or a set of AVPL objects) is also a component of other AVPL objects and allows nested structure.

When we denote a set (or type system) of values as V, types of values are defined as follows:

1. Primitive character strings

$$s \in S \longrightarrow s \in V$$

where S denotes a set of strings.
2. References to any type of values

$$v \in V \longrightarrow \&v \in V$$

where $\&v$ is the reference, i.e., identifier, of v and.
3. Set of any types of values (unordered)

$$v_1, v_2, \ldots, v_n \in V \longrightarrow \{v_1, v_2, \ldots, v_n\} \in V$$

4. List of any types of values (ordered)

$$v_1, v_2, \ldots, v_n \in V \longrightarrow < v_1, v_2, \ldots, v_n > \in V$$

5. AVPL objects

$$d \in D \longrightarrow d \in V$$

where D denotes a set of AVPL objects.
6. Null (empty value)
   Any attribute can be *null*valued, i.e., no value is assigned.
7. Identifier
   A self contained label, a string, which begins with '#'. Identifier is optional and used by other AVPL objects as a reference.

3.2 Expressive Power

All the atomic values are *strings* in AVPL. Other kinds of atomic types like *integer*, *float*, and *boolean* are not provided. Those types can be easily derived from a data source and users are free from atomic types.

We can represent table-structured values as well as references(identifiers), sets, lists,and nested structures. It provides table structures with a composite attribute (as table headers) and a corresponding list of composite values (as record tuples). Advanced semantics of object-oriented model, like *IS-A* relationship cannot be represented. Figure 2 is an example of AVPL object in tabular representation.

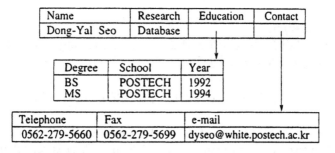

Name		Research	Education	Contact
Dong-Yal Seo		Database		

Degree	School	Year
BS	POSTECH	1992
MS	POSTECH	1994

Telephone	Fax	e-mail
0562-279-5660	0562-279-5699	dyseo@white.postech.ac.kr

Fig. 2. Tabular Representation of an Example AVPL Object

4 Schema Construction

4.1 Schema and Objects

Schema, in an OODB, defines classes and their relationships. And the relationships among classes imply the relationships among objects. Schema defines both structural and behavioral part of a class. In this work, we mainly focused on structural part.

To construct a schema from a pool of schemaless objects, we should build 1)a class from a set of instances, and 2)various relationships among those classes. At first, we will remind possible relationships among classes to define operations for constructing classes and their relationships. There are two relationships between obejcts, *IS-A* and *IS-PART-OF*. The former is the basis of the inheritance hierarchy and the latter is is the basis of the composition hierarchy.

A *type* is a collection of objects with the same structural and behavioral information in an object-oriented model. Type is implemented as a class and the class defines a *collection* relationship. Not only objects are created as instances of a class, a class could be created as a collection of instances.

One object can be described in more than two ways. In this case, those two descriptions must be merged into a single description because an object is unique in object-oriented world. So two descriptions can have an *equivalence* relationship.

4.2 Schema Construction Operations

1. *Creation of a class by Instance Collection*
   For the AVPL objects $S_1, \ldots, S_m$ and their attribute-sets $A_1, \ldots, A_m$, a class of AVPL objects $\mathcal{U}$ is constructed with *Object_Collect($S_1, \ldots, S_m$)* if

$$\mathcal{U} = \{S_1, S_2, \ldots, S_m\}$$

   where the attribute-set $\mathcal{U}_A$ of $\mathcal{U}$ is $\mathcal{U}_A = A_1 \cup A_2 \cup \cdots \cup A_m$ For all attributes $a \in \mathcal{U}_A$, if there is any AVPL object $S_i(1 \leq m)$ where a is not in A_i, the value of a is *NULL*.

2. *Merging*

   (a) *Object Merging*

      For two AVPL objects S and T, a new AVPL object U is constructed with *Object_Merge(S, T)* if

$$U = \{w | (w \in S \cup T) \wedge \exists \hat{a}(\hat{a} \in S \wedge \hat{a} \in T)\}$$

      where the attribute-set of U is the same as $S \cup T$ and $\hat{a}$ is a common(shared) attribute-value pair of S and T. w is an attribute-value pair.

   (b) *Class Merging*

      For two classes of AVPL objects S and $\mathcal{T}$, a new class of AVPL objects $\mathcal{U}$ is constructed with *Class_Merge(S, T)* if $U \in \mathcal{U}$ is constructed with *Object_Merge(S, T)* and $\mathcal{U}$ is constructed with *Object_Collect($U_1, U_2, \ldots, U_m$)* where $S \in \mathcal{S}$, $T \in \mathcal{T}$, and $U_i \in \mathcal{U}$ for $1 \leq i \leq m$.

3. *Composition (IS-PART-OF Relationship)*

   (a) *Object Composition*

      For two AVPL objects S, T, a new AVPL object U is constructed with *Object_Compose(S, T)* if

$$U = (S - t) \cup \hat{T}$$

      where $t \in S$ and $t \in T$. $\hat{T}$ is T itself or a reference to T. The attribute-set of U is the same as S.

   (b) *Class Composition*

      For two classes of AVPL objects S and $\mathcal{T}$, a new class of AVPL objects $\mathcal{U}$ is constructed with *Class_Compose(S, T)* if $U \in \mathcal{U}$ is constructed with *Object_Compose(S, T)* and $\mathcal{U}$ is constructed with *Object_Collect($U_1, U_2, \ldots, U_m$)* where $S \in \mathcal{S}$, $T \in \mathcal{T}$, and $U_i \in \mathcal{U}$ for $1 \leq i \leq m$.

4. *Inclusion(IS-A Relationship)*

   For two sets of AVPL objects $\mathcal{U}$ and $\mathcal{V}$, a new relationship, $\mathcal{U}$ is a subset of $\mathcal{V}$, can be constructed with *Class_Include(U, V)* if

$$\mathcal{U} \subseteq \mathcal{V}$$

   where attribute-sets $\mathcal{U}_A$ and $\mathcal{V}_A$ of $\mathcal{U}$ and $\mathcal{V}$, respectively, has relationship of $\mathcal{V}_A \subseteq \mathcal{U}_A$.

5. Trivially we can define additional operations, such as *destruction*, *splitting*, and *exclusion*, from the inverse of the above defined operations.

    Figure 3 explains the operations *Object_Merge()*, *Object_Compose()*, and *Object_Collect()*. Other operations like *Class_Merge()* or *Class_Compose()* can be implemented by using *Object_Merge()* or *Object_Compose()* with *Object_Collect()*, respectively. *Object_Compose()* in Figure 3 means composition by reference value.

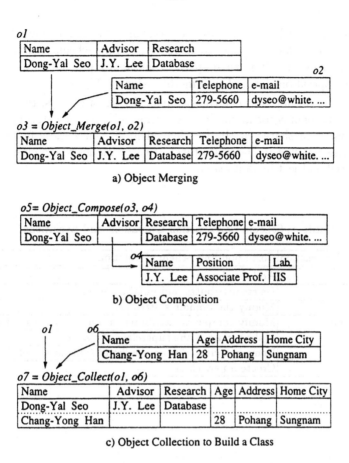

o1

Name	Advisor	Research
Dong-Yal Seo	J.Y. Lee	Database

o2

Name	Telephone	e-mail
Dong-Yal Seo	279-5660	dyseo@white. ...

o3 = Object_Merge(o1, o2)

Name	Advisor	Research	Telephone	e-mail
Dong-Yal Seo	J.Y. Lee	Database	279-5660	dyseo@white. ...

a) Object Merging

o5= Object_Compose(o3, o4)

Name	Advisor	Research	Telephone	e-mail
Dong-Yal Seo		Database	279-5660	dyseo@white. ...

o4

Name	Position	Lab.
J.Y. Lee	Associate Prof.	IIS

b) Object Composition

o1   *o6*

Name	Age	Address	Home City
Chang-Yong Han	28	Pohang	Sungnam

o7 = Object_Collect(o1, o6)

Name	Advisor	Research	Age	Address	Home City
Dong-Yal Seo	J.Y. Lee	Database			
Chang-Yong Han			28	Pohang	Sungnam

c) Object Collection to Build a Class

Fig. 3. Example of Schema Construction Operations

4.3 Schema Consistency

When the user runs a schema construction procedure using above mentioned operations, schema evolution takes place in the pre-existing schema. In database world, it is very important to keep schema consistency. We introduce several effects of schema construction operations on the existing schema hierarchy and map the consequences of the effects on the taxonomy of the schema-modification operations listed in [2]. In fact, the schema construction operations might heavily affect static structure of classes.

For example, *merge* operation could be considered as *attribute adding* operation in schema evolution taxonomy if the class to be merged has relationships with other classes. Thus, if the invariants properties of the inheritance hierarchy cannot be preserved, the operation that breaks schema consistency rules should be rejected[5].

We chose schema evolution taxonomy of ORION data model based on the

---

[5] Refer [6] for more about schema invariants.

comparisons in [6]. Table 1 shows the taxonomy of schema modifications in an object-oriented database and their corresponding schema construction operations. It means that we can map the consistency problems by our schema construction operations into schema modification problems.

Because we did not consider the behavioral part of objects, the reader will not find any taxonomy for methods. We neither address the category of default value attributes or shared attributes defined in [2], since these functions only have valuable meaning in classical object-oriented model where class definition always precedes object instantiation.

Table 1. Schema Construction Operations and Evolutions

Schema Construction	Corresponding Schema Evolution
Merge	Add attributes
Split	Delete attributes and build a new class
Compose	Modify the domain's attributes
Decompose	Modify composite attributes into noncomposite attributes
Include	Make a class S the superclass of class C
Exclude	Remove a class S from the list of superclasses of class C
Collect	Create a new class

5 Conclusion and Future Work

We introduced a new model of database processing where objects are created before schema definition. We defined a type system for semistructured data instances, and the operations for the construction of structural schema from a set of schemaless data instances.

In our data model, a schemaless data instance is created as a description which contains a list of user-defined attributes and their corresponding values. For schema construction, we defined operations for building *IS-A* and *IS-PART-OF* relationships, collecting objects to build a class, and merging two objects or classes to make a larger one. Operations can be applied in both object-level and class-level.

Our approach is suitable for the applications where we collect and manage semistructured data instances, which are not created as instances of predefined schema. Database system for collected HTML documents is a good application of our work. HTML documents have significantly less structure than the examples in this paper and it is more difficult to extract the attribute-value pairs needed to construct the schema.

References

1. Abiteboul, S., Cluet, S., Milo, T.: Correspondence and Translation for Heterogeneous Data. *Proceedings of the '97 ICDT*, Delphi, Greece (1997) 352-363
2. Banerjee, J., Kim, W., Kim, H., Korth, H.: Semantics and Implementation of Schema Evolution in Object-Oriented Databases. *Proceedings of the '87 ACM SIGMOD*, San Francisco, CA (1987) 311-322
3. Buneman, P., Davidson, S., Hillerbrand, G., Suciu, D.: A Query Language and Optimization Techniques for Unstructured Data. *Proceedings of the '96 ACM SIGMOD*, Montreal, Canada (1996) 505-516
4. Bowman, C., Danzig, P., Manber, U., Schwartz, M.: Scalable Internet Resource Discovery: Research Problems and Approaches. *Communications of the ACM.* **37**(8) (1994) 98-107
5. Bowman, C., Danzig, P., Hardy, D., Manber, U., Schwartz, M.: The Harvest Information Discovery and Access System. *Proceedings of the Second International World Wide Web Conference*, Chicago, Illinois (1994) 763-771
6. Tsichritzis, D., ed.: *Object Management.* Centre Universitaire d'Informatique, University of Geneva (1990)
7. Chawathe, S., Garcia-Molina, H., Hammer, J., Ireland, K.: The TSIMMIS Project: Integration of Heterogeneous Information Sources. *Proceedings of IPSJ Conference*, Tokyo, Japan (1994)
8. Bancilhon, F., Delobel, C., Kanellakis, P. eds.: *Building an Object-Orient System: The Story of O2.* Morgan Kaufmann, San Mateo, CA (1992)
9. Nestorov, S., Abiteboul, S., Motwani, R.: Inferring Structure in Semistructured Data. *Proceedings of the Workshop for the Management of Semistructured Data (in Conjunction with '97 ACM PODS/SIGMOD)*, Tucson, Arizona (1997) 42-48
10. Ossher, H., Kaplan, M., Harrison, W., Katz, A., Kruskal, V.: Subject-Oriented Composition Rules. *Proceedings of the OOPSLA '95*, Austin, Texas (1995) 235-250
11. Papakonstantinou, Y., Garcia-Molina, H., Widom, J.: Object Exchange Across Heterogeneous Information Sources. *Proceedings of the 11th IEEE International Conference on Data Engineering*, Taipei, Taiwan (1995) 251-260
12. Quass, D., Rajaraman, A., Ullman, J., Widom, J.: Querying Semistructured Heterogeneous Information. *Proceedings of 4th International Conference on Deductive and Object-Oriented Databases*, Singapore (1995) 319-344
13. Seo, D., Lee, D., Lee, K., Lee, J.: Discovery of Schema Information from a Forest of Selectively Labeled Ordered Trees. *Proceedings of the Workshop for the Management of Semistructured Data (in Conjunction with '97 ACM PODS/SIGMOD)*, Tucson, Arizona (1997) 54-59

M-ary Commitment Protocol with Partially Ordered Domain

Iwao Shimojo, Takayuki Tachikawa, and Makoto Takizawa

Dept. of Computers and Systems Engineering
Tokyo Denki University
Ishizaka, Hatoyama, Saitama 350-03, JAPAN
E-mail {gan,tachi,taki}@takilab.k.dendai.ac.jp

Abstract. Distributed applications are realized by the cooperation of multiple processes. A group of the processes have to make consensus to do the cooperation. The processes exchange the values with the other processes to make consensus. The processes are referred to as consent if each process takes one value which satisfies a consensus condition. A dominant relation among the values is defined to show what values the processes can take after taking a value in the consensus protocol. Each process decides what value to be taken after taking one value by using the dominant relation. In this paper, we discuss how to make consensus in a group of multiple processes by using the dominant relation.

1 Introduction

In distributed applications like groupware [1], a group of multiple processes cooperate to realize some objective. The processes have to make consensus in order to do the cooperation. The processes make consensus if they take a value which satisfies a consensus condition by exchanging values with each other.

Only two values, i.e. 1 (commit) and 0 (abort) can be taken in the two-phase commitment (2PC) protocol [2, 6, 10]. In the 2PC protocol, the process taking 1 can take 1 or 0 although the process taking 0 can only take 0. Hence, we name it a *binary* commitment. After notifying other processes of 1, the process is *uncertain* [11] where the processes have to wait for the decision of the coordinator process. Here, the process may block if the coordinator is faulty. In more general consensus protocols, the processes may take more kinds of values and, after taking some value v, the process can take one value which depends on v. Takizawa *et. al.* [14, 15] discuss a *dominant* relation $\preceq$ in which the domain D is partially ordered. That is, a value v_1 in D *dominates* v_2 ($v_1 \preceq v_2$) if the process can take v_2 after taking v_1. There are two kinds of groups, i.e. *homogeneous* and *heterogeneous* ones. In the homogeneous group, one dominant relation holds for all the processes. In the heterogeneous group, a dominant relation is defined for each process. That is, even if one process takes a value v' after taking v, another process might not take v' after v. Each process has to learn the dominant relations of other processes by obtaining the values taken by the processes.

In this paper, we discuss an m-ary commitment protocol with the ordered domain composed of multiple values $v_1, \cdots, v_m$. The protocol is obtained by extending the 2PC protocol. We also discuss the decision process based on the dominant relation in the heterogeneous group.

In sections 2, we discuss the dominant relation. In section 3, we present the basic consensus protocol. In section 4, we discuss the decision logics of consensus protocols. In section 5, we discuss the m-ary consensus protocol.

2 *M-ary* Commitment

2.1 Two-phase commitment

The two-phase commitment (2PC) protocol [2, 6, 11] in distributed database systems [10] is used to realize the *atomic commitment* [6, 11], i.e. transactions either update all or none of the database systems. There is one *coordinator* process p_0 in the 2PC protocol [2, 6]. If a transaction would commit, p_0 sends a *Prepare* (1) message to all the *participants*, i.e. server processes $p_1, \ldots, p_n$. Otherwise, p_0 sends *Abort* (0). Each p_i sends 1 to p_0 if p_i could commit. Otherwise, p_i sends 0 to p_0 and then aborts. If p_0 receives 1 from every process, p_0 sends *Commit* (1) to $p_1, \ldots, p_n$. If p_0 receives 0, p_0 sends *Abort* (0) to all the processes sending 1. Here, it is noted that p_0 may send 0 even if p_0 receives 1 from all the processes. For example, if the application process p_0 in the client receives an interrupt signal from the user after sending *Prepare*, p_0 sends 0. On receipt of 1 and 0, p_i commits and aborts, respectively. The commitment protocols make the following assumptions:

1 No participant process can change the value after notifying the others of 1 or 0 until receiving the decision from p_0.
2 The decision logic is based on the atomic commitment, i.e. *all-or-nothing* principle.
3 The coordinator p_0 makes a global decision by using the values obtained by the processes. Even after all the processes take 1, p_0 may make a decision 0.
4 0 dominates 1. The processes sending 0 abort unilaterally without waiting for the decision from p_0. The processes sending 1 may abort if the decision of p_0 is 0.
5 Every process is not autonomous, i.e. it obeys the global decision of p_0.

p_i is *uncertain* [11] after taking 1 until receiving the decision from p_0. The uncertain process p_i may block if p_0 is faulty because all p_i can do after sending 1 is wait for the decision from p_0.

2.2 Dominant relation

We discuss how each process can take values in a group G of multiple processes $p_1, \ldots, p_n$. A domain D is a set of possible values to be taken by the processes in the group G. In the consensus protocol, each process p_i first takes an initial value v_{i0} in D $(i = 1, \ldots, n)$. p_i takes a value v_{i1} in D using $\langle v_{10}, \ldots, v_{n0} \rangle$ and notifies the other processes of v_{i1}. p_i obtains a new tuple $\langle v_{11}, \ldots, v_{n1} \rangle$ after exchanging the values with the other processes. This step is named the first *round*. Thus, p_i takes a value $v_{i,j+1}$ in D based on $\langle v_{1j}, \ldots, v_{nj} \rangle$. This step is the $(j+1)$th round. Finally, the protocol terminates at the mth round if $\langle v_{1m}, \ldots, v_{nm} \rangle$ satisfies a consensus condition M.

For example, one person can go swimming after saying "I would like to go skiing" but another person cannot. Thus, values $v_{i,j+1}$ which p_i can take at the $(j + 1)$th round depend on the jth value v_{ij}. For every pair of values x and y in D, x *precedes* y in p_i ($x \rightarrow_i y$) iff p_i can take y after taking x. $x \rightarrow_i y$ is transitive. x and y are *equivalent* in p_i ($x \equiv_i y$) iff $x \rightarrow_i y$ and $y \rightarrow_i x$. $x \rightarrow y$ and $x \equiv y$ iff $x \rightarrow_i y$ and $x \equiv_i y$, respectively, for every p_i.

[Example 1] Here, let H, K, and W show "I would like to go to hot spring, go skiing, go swimming," respectively. If p_i can take H after K, $K \rightarrow_i H$. $K \rightarrow_i W$ if $K \rightarrow_i H \rightarrow_i W$. □

[Definition] For every pair of values x and y in D and every process p_i, y *dominates* x in p_i ($x \prec_i y$) iff $x \rightarrow_i y$ but $y \nrightarrow_i x$. □

$x \preceq_i y$ iff $x \prec_i y$ or $x \equiv_i y$. $x \preceq_i y$ means that p_i can take y after x. $x \prec y$ and $x \preceq y$ iff $x \prec_i y$ and $x \preceq_i y$ for every p_i, respectively. Let $\pi_i(x)$ be $\{y \mid x \preceq_i y\}$. If there are multiple values in $\pi_i(x)$, p_i takes the highest priority value in $\pi_i(x)$. A value y_1 is referred to as *more privileged* than y_2 for x ($y_1 \Rightarrow_i^x y_2$) if $x \preceq_i y_1$, $x \preceq_i y_2$, and $y_1 \preceq_i y_2$. For example, suppose that $K \preceq_i H$, $K \preceq_i W$, and $H \preceq_i W$. H is more privileged than W. p_i prefers H than W after taking H. Suppose that neither $v_1 \preceq_i v_2$ nor $v_2 \preceq_i v_1$. p_i can specify which one is more privileged, v_1 or v_2. p_i takes v_i which is the most privileged in $\pi_i(x)$. Each value y in $\pi_i(x)$ is given priority for x, i.e. $pr(y,x)$. If $y_1 \Rightarrow_i^x y_2$, $pr(y_1, x) < pr(y_2, x)$. Suppose that p_i taks y after x, i.e. $x \preceq_i y$. p_i can take x again if $y \preceq_i x$. Here, if p_i takes y again, the decision process is indefinitely iterated. Hence, if p_i takes y just after x, $pr(y, x)$ is decreased by one.

For every pair of values x and y in D, $x \cup_i y$ means the least upper bound (*lub*) of x and y on $\preceq_i$. That is, $x \cup_i y$ shows a value z such that (1) $x \preceq_i z$ and $y \preceq_i z$, and (2) there is no value w such that $x \preceq_i w$, $y \preceq_i w$, and $w \preceq_i z$. $x \cup_* y$ is a value z where (1) $x \cup_i y \preceq_i z$ and (2) there is no w such that $x \cup_i y \preceq_i w \preceq_i z$ for every p_i. For example, suppose that $a \preceq_i c$ and $b \preceq_i c$ in p_i while $a \preceq_j d$, $b \preceq_j d$, and $d \preceq_j c$ in p_j. $a \cup_i b$ is c and $a \cup_j b$ is d while $a \cup_* b = c$. For every tuple $\langle v_1, \ldots, v_n \rangle \in D^n$, $\cup_*\langle v_1, \ldots, v_n \rangle$ shows a value x such that $v_i \preceq_i x$ for every p_i and there is no value y such that $v_i \preceq_i y \preceq_i x$ for every p_i. The greatest lower bounds (*glb*) $\cap_i$ and $\cap_*$ are defined in the similar way as $\cup_i$ and $\cup_*$.

D includes a special *bottom* value $\bot$ where $\bot \preceq_* x$ for every x in D. D also includes λ which denotes that p_i does not decide which value p_i takes. Values in D which are not λ are *proper*. $\top$ denotes the *top* of D if $x \preceq_* \top$ for every x in D. $\top$ means some value which satisfies the requirement of every process. A proper value x is *minimal* and *maximal* in p_i iff there is no proper value y such that $y \prec_i x$ and $x \prec_i y$ in D, respectively. After p_i had taken minimal x, p_i can take any value in D. Once p_i takes maximal x in D, p_i can take no value. For example, a process taking 0 aborts independently of the others in the 2PC protocol. A process taking 1 aborts if some process takes 0. Hence, $1 \prec 0$. 1 is minimal and 0 is maximal.

The group G is *homogeneous* iff $\preceq_i = \preceq_j$ for every pair of processes p_i and p_j in G. G is *heterogeneous* iff $\preceq_i \neq \preceq_j$ for some pair of p_i and p_j. For example, some p_i can take H after K but p_j cannot in Example 1. Here, $\preceq_i \neq \preceq_j$.

2.3 Examples

Lattice-based domain Let A be a set $\{a_1, \ldots, a_m\}$ of primitive values. We assume that there is no dominant relation among every pair of primitive values in A. A domain D is obtained from A as follows:

1 For every primitive value x in A, $x \in D$.

2 For every pair of x and y in D, $x \cdot y \in D$ and $x \mid y \in D$.

Here, $x \cdot y$ and $x \mid y$ mean that each process takes x and y, and x or y, respectively. We assume that every value v in D is normalized in a disjunctive normal form: $v = v_1 \mid \ldots \mid v_h$ $(h \geq 1)$ and $v_i = x_{i1} \cdot \ldots \cdot x_{il_i}$ $(i = 1, \ldots, h, l_i \geq 1)$ where $x_{ij} \in A$. D also includes λ.

For every proper values x_1, x_2, y_1, and y_2 in D, there are the following axioms on $\preceq \subseteq D^2$:

1 $x_1 \preceq y_1 \cdot y_2$ if $x_1 \preceq y_1$ or $x_1 \preceq y_2$,

2 $x_1 \preceq y_1 \mid y_2$ if $x_1 \preceq y_1$ and y_2,

3 $x_1 \cdot x_2 \preceq y_1$ if $x_1 \preceq y_1$ and $x_2 \preceq y_1$, and

4 $x_1 \mid x_2 \preceq y_1$ if $x_1 \preceq y_1$ or $x_2 \preceq y_1$.

For every proper value x in D, $\sim x$ means that each process does not take x. $\sim (x \mid y) = (\sim x) \cdot (\sim y)$ and $\sim (x \cdot y) = (\sim x) \mid (\sim y)$. In this paper, we assume that $\sim a_i$ means $a_1 \mid \ldots \mid a_{i-1} \mid a_{i+1} \mid \ldots \mid a_m$. In addition, $\perp$ means $a_1 \mid \ldots \mid a_m$ and $\top$ means $a_1 \cdot \ldots \cdot a_m$.

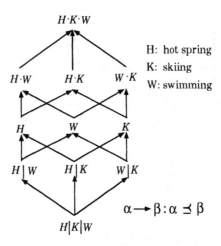

H: hot spring
K: skiing
W: swimming

$\alpha \longrightarrow \beta : \alpha \preceq \beta$

Fig. 1. Lattice domain D

[**Example 2**] $A = \{H, K, W\}$ in Example 1. For example, $K \cdot W$ means that a person p_i would like to go to a place where p_i can ski and swim. $H \mid K \mid W$ is $\perp$. $H \cdot K \cdot W$ is $\top$. A person saying $H \mid K \mid W$ can change the opinion to any proper value in D. On the other hand, a person saying $H \cdot K \cdot W$ cannot change the opinion. We assume that each person p_i takes a value in a form α_i, $\alpha_1 \mid \ldots \mid \alpha_k$, or $\alpha_1 \cdot \ldots \cdot \alpha_k$ for primitive values $\alpha_1, \ldots, \alpha_k$ in A. Hence, $D = \{H, K,$

W, $K|W$, $W|H$, $H|K$, $H|K|W$, $K \cdot W$, $W \cdot H$, $H \cdot K$, $H \cdot K \cdot W$, λ}. Fig. 1 shows a Hasse diagram of the lattice $\langle D, \preceq, \cup, \cap \rangle$ where each directed edge $\rightarrow$ denotes $\preceq$. For example, $H \cdot W \cup H \cdot K$ and $H \cdot W \cap H \cdot K$ are $H \cdot K \cdot W$ and H, respectively.

Each person p_i may have its own dominant relation $\preceq_i$ $(\supseteq \preceq)$ in the heterogeneous group. For example, suppose that p_i can take K after saying H. That is, $H \preceq_i K$ in p_i. $H \preceq_i W \cdot K$. However, $H \preceq_j K$ does not hold in p_j. Here, if p_i takes H and p_j takes $W \mid K$, p_i and p_j can make consensus on K. □

Preference based domain Let us consider an example of the weekly scheduling of the meeting. A day schedule is composed of three slots, i.e. A for 9:00 - 10:30am, B for 10:30 - 12:00am, and C for 13:30 - 15:00. Each slot in a week is identified in a form xy where x shows a day, i.e. $x \in \{Mon., Tue., Wed., Thu., Fri.\}$ and $y \in \{A, B, C\}$. For example, $Wed.A$ shows a meeting slot for 9:00 - 10:30 on Wed. Suppose that three persons A, B, and C would like to have a meeting in some slot of Mon., Wed., and Fri. Each person has the following preferences;

- A prefers a meeting as early as possible.
- B prefers a meeting in a later slot at the beginning of a week.
- C prefers a meeting in a later slot of Wed., Fri., and Mon.

Fig. 2 shows Hasse diagrams of the dominant relations of A, B, and C.

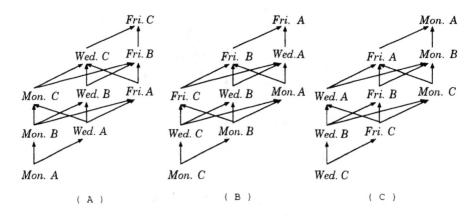

Fig. 2. Preference based domain D

2.4 Non-blocking condition

In the 2PC protocol, the process taking 1 is *uncertain* [11] because the global decision may be 0. The uncertain process p_i blocks if the coordinator p_0 is faulty before sending the decision to the processes and all the operational processes are uncertain. We extend the blocking concept in the 2PC protocol to the domain partially ordered in the dominant relation.

Suppose that the processes p_1 and p_2 notify the others of H in Fig. 1. Here, if p_3 is faulty after notifying p_1 of the value v, p_1 and p_2 can take values dominating v since p_1 can tell p_2 about v of p_3. If p_3 is faulty before the notification, neither p_1 nor p_2 know of v. Hence, p_1 and p_2 block, i.e. wait for the value of p_3 since H is not maximal. p_3 may have taken a value not dominated by H. Next, suppose that p_1 takes $H \cdot K \cdot W$ and p_2 takes H. Since $H \cdot K \cdot W$ is the top $\top$ and $H \preceq H \cdot K \cdot W$, p_1 and p_2 can make consensus $H \cdot K \cdot W$ even if p_3 is faulty. After p_3 recovers from the fault, p_3 can ask p_1 or p_3 of the consensus value. It is sure that p_1 can take $H \cdot K \cdot W$ since $H \cdot K \cdot W$ is maximal.

[**Definition**] A process p_i is *uncertain* if p_i takes a value which is not maximal and p_i does not make consensus yet. □

A process p_i taking the maximal value x is *certain* since p_i cannot change x. The uncertain process may take another value.

Suppose that p_j is faulty and an operational process p_i is uncertain. Let v be $\sqcup_*\langle v_1, \ldots, v_{j-1}, v_{j+1}, \ldots, v_n \rangle$. That is, every operational process can take v. If p_j is sure to be able to take v, all the operational processes make a consensus v. Otherwise, they have to wait for the recovery of p_j, i.e. p_i blocks and cannot take a value dominating v_i. Even if all the operational processes cannot make consensus, they do not block if the following NB condition is satisfied.

[**Non-Blocking (NB) condition**] The protocol is *non-blocking* if

(1) all the processes, whether or not operational, can take an upper bound of the values taken by all the operational processes in the group, or

(2) all the operational processes can take values which satisfy the consensus condition. □

3 Basic Commitment Protocol

3.1 Procedure

The processes $p_1, \ldots, p_n$ in a group G exchange values at each round until they make consensus by using a following *protocol*.

[**Basic protocol**][Fig. 3]

1 Each process p_i takes an initial value v_{i0}. p_i notifies all the processes in G of v_{i0}. $j := 0$.

2 p_i obtains $v_{1j}, \ldots, v_{nj}$. p_i makes a local decision $v_{i,j+1} = F_{ij}(v_{1j}, \ldots, v_{nj})$. F_{ij} is a *local decision* function. p_i notifies all the processes of $v_{i,j+1}$.

3 A global decision $v = GD(v_{1j}, \ldots, v_{nj})$ is obtained by using a *global decision* function GD. If the *termination* condition $M(v_{1j}, \ldots, v_{nj}, v)$ holds, p_i obtains v. Otherwise, $j := j + 1$ and go to step 2.

4 p_i obtains the global decision v. p_i makes the final local decision $d_i = LD_i(v_{1j}, \ldots, v_{nj}, v)$. LD_i is a final local decision function. □

3.2 Coordination schemes

There are two points on the coordination among the processes $p_1, \ldots, p_n$ in the group G. The first point is which process makes a global decision. In the centralized decision, every participant p_i obeys the decision made by the coordinator p_0. In the distributed decision, every p_i makes the consensus decision by itself. The other point is how to deliver values taken by the processes to the other

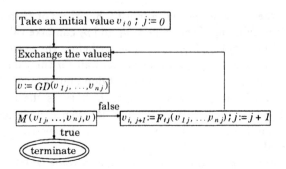

Fig. 3. Basic protocol

processes in G. In the centralized delivery, every p_i first sends messages to p_0 and then p_0 forwards the messages to all the processes in G. On the other hand, every p_i sends messages to all the processes in the distributed delivery.

The protocol with the centralized decision and delivery is *centralized*. The 2PC [6] and 3PC [11] protocols are centralized. Here, every p_i first sends a value v_i to p_0. On receipt of $\langle v_1, \ldots, v_n \rangle$, p_0 decides a value $v = GD(v_1, \ldots, v_n)$. p_0 sends v to p_1, ..., p_n.

The *distributed* protocol adopts the distributed decision and distributed delivery. In the distributed protocol [9, 12], each p_i sends v_i to $p_1, \ldots, p_n$. On receipt of the values, p_i makes the consensus decision by itself. If p_i cannot make the consensus, p_i obtains $v_i' = F_{ij}(v_1, \ldots, v_n)$ and sends v_i' to $p_1, \ldots, p_n$. Thus, every p_i has to send a message m to all the other processes. In the one-to-one network, p_i has to issue n transmission requests of m. At each round, $n(n-1)$ messages are transmitted.

4 Decision Logics

4.1 Local decision

At the end of the $(j+1)$th round, p_i gets $v_{i,j+1}$ in D which satisfies the dominant relation $\preceq_i$ with $\langle v_{1j}, \ldots, v_{nj} \rangle$. Here, $v_{i,j+1}$ is obtained by the *local decision function* F_{ij}, i.e. $v_{i,j+1} = F_{ij}(v_{1j}, \ldots, v_{nj})$ where $v_{ij} \preceq_i v_{i,j+1}$. p_i has its own F_{ij}. Let S_i be a sequence of the values $v_{i0}, v_{i1}, \cdots, v_{i,j+1}$ taken by p_i.

In the homogeneous group, each p_i can estimate what value another process takes since every process has the same dominant relation. If p_i and p_j take values x and y, respectively, p_i and p_j can take a value $v = x \cup y$. However, in the heterogeneous group, p_i cannot estimate the values to be taken by another p_k since $\preceq_i \neq \preceq_k$ and p_i does not know of $\preceq_j$. By recording the values taken by p_j, p_i can learn some part of $\preceq_j$. Here, $\preceq_{ik}$ is a subset of $\preceq_j$ which p_i knows. p_i receives a value v_j' at the next round after receiving v_j from p_j. On receipt of v_j', p_i can know that $v_j \preceq_j v_j'$ holds in p_j. Here, let $\pi_{ij}(x) \ (\subseteq \pi_j(x))$ be a set of values $\{y \mid x \preceq_{ij} y\}$ which p_i knows dominates x in p_j. Here, $\pi_{ii}(v) = \pi_i(v)$ for p_i. Each time p_i obtains $\langle v_1', \ldots, v_n' \rangle$ after p_i has $\langle v_1, \ldots, v_n \rangle$, p_i includes v_j' in $\pi_{ij}(v_j)$ $(j = 1, \ldots, n)$.

We discuss which value p_i takes after obtaining $\langle v_1, \ldots, v_n \rangle$. Here, let π_i be $\pi_{i1}(v_1) \cap \cdots \cap \pi_{in}(v_n)$.

(1) If $\pi_i \neq \phi$, p_i takes the most privileged value x in π_i such that $v_j \preceq_j x$ for every p_j.

(2) If $\pi_i = \phi$, p_i finds one value x in $\pi_{ii}(v_i)$ which is the most privileged. □

Each time p_i takes a value x for v_i, the priority of x in $\pi_i(v_i)$ is decreased, i.e. $pr(x, v_i) = pr(x, v_i) - 1$. Hence, it is resolved that the same value is taken indefinitely. Here, suppose that p_i obtains $\langle v_{1j}, \ldots, v_{nj} \rangle$ at the jth round. If $\pi_i = \phi$, i.e. $\cup_* \langle v_{1j}, \ldots, v_{nj} \rangle = \lambda$, p_i cannot take a value at the next step. Here, p_i sends $\pi_i(v_{ij})$ so that every other process p_k can obtain $\pi_{ki}(v_{ij}) = \pi_i(v_{ij})$. p_i receives $\pi_k(v_{kj})$ from p_k. Then, p_i tries to obtain $\cup_* \langle v_{1j}, \ldots, v_{nj} \rangle$ again by using $\pi_{ki}(v_{kj})$ obtained here. If one value $v_{i,j+1}$ is obtained, p_i sends $v_{i,j+1}$ to all the processes. Otherwise, some process takes the most privileged value, i.e. may go back to the previous value. In this paper, a process p_i whose value is different from the majority of $v_{1j}, \ldots, v_{nj}$ is selected. p_i takes the most privileged value x and sends x to $p_1, \ldots, p_n$. Then, (1) is executed again. If π_i is still ϕ, another process is selected. After every process is selected, if no value is obtained, the protocol terminates.

4.2 Global decision

After obtaining the values $v_1, \ldots, v_n$, the global consensus value v is globally decided by using the global decision function GD. For every $\langle v_1, \ldots, v_n \rangle \in D^n$, $GD(v_1, \ldots, v_n)$ gives a value v in D. If $v_j \preceq_j v$ for every p_j, every process p_i can change v_i to v. Unless $v_i \preceq_i v$, p_i cannot change the value to v. For example, suppose that there is a transaction T manipulating three database systems A, B, and C, which take values 0, 1, and 1, respectively, in the 2PC protocol. If $GD(1, 0, 1, 1) = 0$, B and C can change the values to 0, i.e. can abort. On the other hand, suppose that $GD(1, 0, 1, 1) = 1$. A cannot commit because A aborts already although B and C can commit. In Fig. 1, suppose that the global decision $H \cdot K$ is obtained where p_i takes $H \mid W$. Since $(H \mid W) \preceq (H \cdot K)$, p_i can obey $H \cdot K$. Yahata and Takizawa [15] discusses kinds of global decisions.

In the binary commitment decision of the 2PC protocol, 1 is obtained as the global decision only if all the processes take 1. If some process takes 0, 0 is obtained. The binary commitment decision can be extended to the m-ary domain $D = \{d_1, \ldots, d_m, \perp, \lambda\}(m \geq 2)$. In the m-ary commitment, the process takes one value among m (≥ 2) values while either 1 or 0 is taken in the binary one. $GD(v_1, \ldots, v_n) = v$ if $v_i = v$ for every p_i. Otherwise, $GD(v_1, \ldots, v_n) = \cup_* \langle v_1, \ldots, v_n \rangle$. $\cup_* \langle v_1, \ldots, v_n \rangle$ means a value which every p_i can take after taking v_i. If $\cup_* \langle v_1, \ldots, v_n \rangle = \lambda$, nothing is decided.

5 M-ary Commitment Protocol

We extend the binary commitment protocol to the m-ary commitment protocol.

5.1 Binary commitment protocol

First, the 2PC protocol is described in terms of the domain D, the decision logics, and the dominant relation. In the commitment protocol, suppose that 1 means *commit* and 0 means *abort*. Hence, D includes two values 1 (*commit*) and 0 (*abort*), i.e. $D = \{0, 1\}$.

The protocol terminates at the 2nd round. At the 1st round, every process p_i takes an initial value $v_{i0} \in D$ and sends v_{i0} to the coordinator p_0. Then, p_0 takes v_{01} but p_i takes the same value v_{i1} as v_{i0} at the 2nd round. Here, $v_{00} \preceq v_{01}$ but $v_{i0} = v_{i1} \preceq v_{01}(i \geq 1)$. That is, only p_0 can change the value but no participant can. In the centralized protocol, v_{01} is the global decision. Every process taking 0 *aborts* unilaterally, i.e. without waiting for the global decision. On the other hand, processes taking 1 may commit or abort up to the global decision. Hence, $1 \preceq 0$. 0 is maximum and 1 is minimum.

The final local decision is $LD_i(v_0, v_1, \ldots, v_n, v) = v$ because the process taking 1 obeys the global decision. That is, the processes taking 1 are not autonomous.

5.2 Centralized protocol

We extend the binary commitment so that each process p_i can take more than two values, i.e. $v_1, \ldots, v_m(m \geq 2)$, λ, and $\perp$. That is, $D = \{v_1, \cdots v_m, \lambda, \perp\}$ where $\perp$ may be one value v_j. In the 2PC protocol, p_i may not be able to send the value even if p_i receives *Prepare* from the coordinator p_0, e.g. p_i is too heavy-loaded to take a value. In such a case, p_i can send λ or p_i can be considered to take λ if no reply of *Prepare* is received in some time units. The global decision GD is the m-ary commitment one. We assume that the group G is heterogeneous.

First, we present the centralized protocol to realize the m-ary commitment. There is one coordinator p_0 and participants $p_1, \ldots, p_n$.

[**Basic centralized protocol**]

1 First, p_0 takes a value v_0 and sends $\langle v_0, \lambda, \ldots, \lambda \rangle$ to $p_1, \ldots, p_n$. $j := 0$.

2 On receipt of $\langle v_0, v_1, \ldots, v_n \rangle$ from p_0, each p_i takes one value v_i in D by using the local decision F_{ij} as discussed before and sends v_i to p_0. In addition, p_i may send λ to p_0 if p_i could not decide whatever to take. p_i may send $\perp$ to p_0 if p_i could take any value in D. $j := j + 1$.

3 p_0 obtains $\langle v_1, \ldots, v_n \rangle$ where each v_i is obtained from p_i at step 2.
   - If $v_0 = v_1 = \cdots = v_n(= v)$, p_0 makes the global decision v and sends v to $p_1, \ldots, p_n$.
   - If $v_i = \cup_* \langle v_0, v_1, \ldots, v_i, \ldots, v_n \rangle \neq \lambda$ for some p_i, p_0 makes the global decision v_i and sends v_i to $p_1, \ldots, p_n$
   - If $v_0' = \cup_* \langle v_0, v_1, \ldots, v_n \rangle \neq \lambda$ and $v_0' \neq v_j$ for every p_i, p_0 takes v_0' where $v_0 \preceq v_0'$ and $v_i \preceq v_0'$ for every i. Then, p_0 sends $\langle v_0', v_1, \ldots, v_n \rangle$ to $p_1, \ldots, p_n$ and go to 2.
   - If $\cup_* \langle v_0, v_1, \ldots, v_n \rangle = \lambda$, p_0 terminates and sends the global decision λ to $p_1, \ldots, p_n$.

4 On receipt of the global decision v from p_0, if v satisfies the final local decision LD_i, p_i takes v. Otherwise, p_i takes v_i. □

From $\langle v_0, v_1, \ldots, v_n \rangle$ at step 3, $v_i \preceq v_0$ for every p_i. On receipt of $\langle v_0, v_1, \ldots, v_n \rangle$, p_i takes a value v_i' by the local decision function F_{ij}. Here, $v_i \preceq v_i'$ and $v_0 \preceq v_i'$. Here, if v_i' is maximum, p_i makes the final decision v_i' and terminates after sending v'_i. Otherwise, p_i has to wait for the next decision value from p_0. Here, p_i is *uncertain*. At step 3, p_0 makes a consensus decision v if $v = v'_0 = v_i$ for every p_i. p_0 sends v to all the processes and terminates. This decision corresponds to the *commit* in the 2PC. On receipt of v, each p_i takes v as the final consensus value. If $v_i \neq v_j$ for some pair of p_i and p_j, p_0 takes a new value v'_0 after receiving $v_1, \ldots, v_n$. p_0 finds the least upper bound v of $\langle v'_0, v_1, \ldots, v_n \rangle$. If some p_i takes v $(\neq \lambda)$, i.e. $v_i = v$, p_0 makes a consensus decision v. p_0 sends v to $p_1, \ldots, p_n$. It corresponds to the *abort* in the 2PC. If $v \neq v_i$ for every p_i, p_0 sends $\langle v, v_1, \ldots, v_n \rangle$ to $p_1, \ldots, p_n$ and step 2 is iterated.

Suppose that p_0 is faulty at the jth round after each p_i sends v_i before sending the reply v'_0 to all the processes. If p_i receives no reply in some predetermined time units, p_i detects that p_0 is faulty and invokes the following termination protocol to make consensus among the operational processes. Here, suppose that each p_i takes a new value v'_i after receiving $\langle v_0, v_1, \ldots, v_n \rangle$.

[**Termination protocol**]

  1 p_i sends *StateReq* with v'_i to $p_1, \ldots, p_n$.

  2 Suppose that p_k receives *StateReq* from p_i. If p_k had received no reply from p_0, p_k sends the value v'_k to p_i. If p_k had received some reply v'_0 from p_0, p_k sends the reply $\langle v_0, v_1, \ldots, v_n \rangle$ back to p_i.

  3 p_i makes the decision by the *termination* rule if p_i receives the replies of *StateReq* from all the operational processes. □

[**Termination rule**]

  1 If p_i receives a maximal value v from some process, p_i takes v as the global decision.

  2 If some operational p_i still takes λ, p_i makes a consensus decision of the maximal value. Otherwise, p_i waits for the recovery of p_0. □

Next, suppose that p_i recovers from the fault. Suppose that p_i records the local state in the log L_i. p_i invokes the following recovery protocol.

[**Recovery protocol**]

  1 p_i restores the state from L_i.

  2 If p_i is uncertain, p_i asks other processes in the same way as the termination protocol.

  3 If p_i had taken λ or the maximal value, p_i makes the consensus decision on the maximum value. □

5.3 Example

Let us consider the example as shown in Fig. 1. Suppose that there are three processes A, B, and C. Here, suppose that A can take a value W after H, i.e. $H \prec_A W$. That is, A can change the value to "go swimming" after saying "go to hot spring". A, B, and C initially take H, $H|K$, and $W|K$, respectively, and exchange the values. After the first round, every process obtains the tuple $\langle H, H|K, W|K \rangle$ of the initial values. Here, $\pi_A(H) = \{H, W, H \cdot W, H \cdot K, W \cdot K, H \cdot W \cdot K\}$, $\pi_B(H|K) = \{H|K, H, K, H \cdot W, H \cdot K, W \cdot K, H \cdot W \cdot K\}$, and $\pi_C(W|K) = \{H \cdot K, W \cdot K, W \cdot H, W, K, H \cdot W \cdot K\}$. Since A knows about $\preceq_A$, A can obtain $\cup_*\langle H, H|K, W|K \rangle = W \cdot K$. However, neither B nor C can obtain $W \cdot K$ because they know nothing about $\preceq_A$. If B takes H, every process cannot obtain the global decision because $\cup_* \langle W \cdot K, H \rangle = H \cdot W \cdot K$. If B knows about $\preceq_A$, B can take K, $H \cdot K$, $W \cdot K$, or $H \cdot W \cdot K$ so that all the processes take the value to which they can change.

Suppose that B takes H and C takes W. After the second round, every process obtains $\langle W, H, W \rangle$. In addition, B and C know "$H \prec_A W$" on receipt of the values and stores it in $\pi_{BA}(H)$ and $\pi_{CA}(H)$, respectively. Here, B finds that the global decision could not be obtained. At the third round, B takes K by the backward decision. Then, every process obtains the global decision $K \cdot W (= \cup \langle H, H|K, K|W \rangle)$.

6 Concluding Remarks

This paper has discussed the general framework of consensus protocols where the values to be taken by the processes are partially ordered by the dominant relation. The dominant relation $\preceq_i$ is defined for each process p_i in the heterogeneous group. p_i decides which value v_i' p_i takes after taking v_i so that $v_i \preceq_i v_i'$. We have also presented the m-ary commitment protocol obtained by extending the 2PC protocol, where each process takes m (≥ 2) kinds of values. We have shown the blocking condition in the m-ary commitment. The protocol can be adopted to the groupware applications.

References

1. Barborak, M., Malek, M., and Dahbura, A.: The Consensus Problem in Fault-Tolerant Computing, *ACM Computing Surveys*, Vol.25, No.2, pp.182-184,198-199(1993).
2. Bernstein, P. A., Hadzilacos, V., and Goodman, N.: *Concurrency Control and Recovery in Database Systems*, Addison-Wesley, pp.222-261(1987).
3. Birman, K. P., Schiper, A., and Stephenson, P.: Lightweight Causal and Atomic Group Multicast, *ACM Trans. on Computer Systems*, Vol.9, No.3, pp.272-314(1991).
4. Ellis, C. A., Gibbs, S. J., and Rein, G. L.: *Groupware*, Comm. ACM, Vol.34, No.1, pp.38-58(1991).
5. Fischer, J. M., Lynch, A. N., and Paterson, S. M.: Impossibility of Distributed Consensus with One Faulty Process, *Journal of ACM*, Vol.32, No.2, pp.374-382(1985).
6. Gray, J.: Notes on Database Operating Systems, An Advanced Course, *Lecture Notes in Computer Science*, No.60, pp.393-481(1978).
7. Lamport, L.: *Time, Clocks, and the Ordering of Events in a Distributed System*, Comm. ACM, Vol.21, No.7, pp.558-565(1978).
8. Lamport, L. and Shostak, R.: The Byzantine Generals Problem, *ACM Trans. Programming Languages and Systems*, Vol.4, No3, pp.382-401(1982).
9. Nakamura, A. and Takizawa, M.: Causally Ordering Broadcast Protocol, *Proc. of IEEE ICDCS-14*, pp.48-55(1994).
10. Ozsu, M. T. and Valduriez, P.: *Principle of Distributed Database Systems*, Prentice-Hall(1990).
11. Skeen, D. and Stonebraker, M.: A Formal Model of Crash Recovery in a Distributed System, *IEEE Computer Society Press*, Vol.SE-9, No.3, pp.219-228(1983).

12. Tachikawa, T. and Takizawa, M.: Selective Total Ordering Broadcast Protocol, *Proc. of IEEE ICNP-94*, pp.212−219(1994).
13. Turek, J. and Shasha, D.: *The Many Faces of Consensus in Distributed Systems*, *Distributed Computing Systems*, IEEE Computer Society Press, pp.83-91(1994).
14. Yahata, C., Sakai, J., and Takizawa, M.: Generalization of Consensus Protocols," *Proc. of the 9th IEEE Int'l Conf. on Information Networking (ICOIN-9)*, pp.419-424(1994).
15. Yahata, C. and Takizawa, M.: General Protocol for Consensus in Distributed Systems, *Proc. of DEXA(Lecture Notes in Computer Science*, No. 978, *Springer-verlag)*, pp.227-236(1995).

Metadata for a Digital Library of Historical Documents

María José Aramburu Cabo and Rafael Berlanga Llavori

Department of Computer Science, Universitat Jaume I, Castellón SPAIN

{aramburu,berlanga}@inf.uji.es

Abstract. The main purpose of this paper is to present a new object oriented data model for structured documents and their temporal features. We first characterise historical documents as those participating into a set of applications where temporal aspects of documents are specially relevant. Then, we describe a formal temporal data model for historical documents, which relies on two specially suited type systems. One expresses the flexible structure of document classes. The other allows defining metadata. In this way, metadata becomes a central feature, which is introduced into the data model by means of metaclasses. Finally, we discuss which are the novel uses of metadata in a digital library of historical documents.

1 Introduction

Digital libraries have become an active area of research that involves physical aspects like mass storage and remote access mechanisms, as well as logical aspects, like the organisation and retrieval of the electronically stored information. New proposals for digital libraries approach to the storage of books, newspapers, periodicals, patents, medical records, manuals and so on [Fox95] [Ara97a]. In many aspects, the success of these proposals is subject to the way in which the stored documents are catalogued and how this information is used when retrieving them. In this context, descriptive information about an information resource is termed metadata. Among others, the most usual metadata supported by current systems are *authors*, *title*, *publisher*, *subject*, *date*, *type*, *resource*, *contributor*, *role*, *ISBN* and so on [Wei95]. Once these items are stored together with the information to which they refer, they are indexed and employed during document retrieval.

In this work, we have amplified the scope of metadata to describe two additional features about documents: their logical organisation and their temporal dimensions. Both features are developed in the following section. The final aim of this work is to provide a temporal database model to support all this metadata and show how it can be used during document retrieval. The resulting system should allow users of digital libraries to obtain enhanced benefits from their repositories.

1.1 Historical Documents

We regard historical documents as those that keep information related with the time in which they are created and that will also be useful at the future. In this group, we can find newspapers, periodicals, patents and so on. In order to assist their storage and retrieval, we define a model for historical documents that is outlined below.

Firstly, we consider the complex structure of documents. For each class of documents a generic structure is defined. By means of an original type system for documents which complements usual object oriented type systems in two senses: it allows for ordered tuples and provides union of types. These requirements have been already treated by previous works in several ways [Chr94][Özs95]. By another hand, despite the fact that documents do not evolve, three different time dimensions can be identified for historical documents:

1. Documents can be grouped by types whose features may change along time. This can be understood as some kind of schema or type evolution. Per example, newspapers regularly change their layout and organisation.

2. Every document has been published or edited at a given time. Their features will agree with the type definition that is current at that time. Following with the previous example, we see that every newspaper is dated and logically, its layout corresponds with the current definition of its type at that date.

3. The last dimension of time refers to the time in which the users of a document consider that its contents are valid or up-to-date. Per example, in a newspaper, the weather broadcast will be valid for the two following days whereas news about a trial will be valid during the whole trial process.

All the information that defines the organisation and temporal dimensions of historical documents falls into the scope of metadata. In this paper we discuss how to represent metadata and how to apply it to document manipulation and retrieval. When integrating metadata and documents into a single data model, a two-level architecture necessarily arises. At the upper layer metadata represents information about the documents stored in the lower layer. This constitutes the main novelty of the proposed data model. The remainder of the paper is organised into three sections. Section 2 defines a data model for historical document databases. Section 3 analyses the use of the metadata in this data model. Finally, section 4 summarises the conclusions.

2 A Data Model for Historical Documents

In this section, we present a formal data model for historical documents as previously defined. Within an object-oriented data model, we make use of metaclasses to include time features and behaviour describing the history of document types and objects. The section is organised as follows. Section 2.1 describes the type systems on which the data model relies. Then, sections 2.2, 2.3 and 2.4 define metaclasses, classes and objects respectively. Section 2.5 examines the class inheritance relationships. Finally, section 2.6 defines the database schema and instance.

2.1 Type Systems

The proposed data model relies on two different type systems, namely: $\mathcal{MTS}$ and $\mathcal{DTS}$. The former is intended to define metadata types, whereas the latter is intended to describe document types. This separation into two systems is produced because the documents and their metadata exhibit quite different syntax notations. In the remainder of the paper, the set of all the object unique identifiers is denoted by *OI* and the set of all the document class names by *CI*.

$\mathcal{MTS}$ Type System

The type system $\mathcal{MTS}$ follows the syntax below:

$$\tau := \mathcal{ATOMIC} \mid time \mid interval \mid [A_1:\tau_1,.., A_n: \tau_n] \mid \{\tau\}$$

where the type group $\mathcal{ATOMIC}$ contains all the atomic types such as *integer*, *real*, *char*, *string*, etc., *time* is the type that designates the domain of time instants, *interval* is the type that designates the domain of time intervals, $[A_1:\tau_1,.., A_n: \tau_n]$ is the tuple constructor and $\{\tau\}$ is the set constructor.

The value domains of the atomic and structured types adopt the usual semantics given in the complex value data model [Abi95]. At this respect, to obtain the domain of a $\mathcal{MTS}$ type τ, the function $dom(\tau)$ is defined. Further, the value domain of the type *time* is defined as in [Ber96]. Thus, $dom(time)$ is a set of values isomorphic to the set of natural numbers. Time intervals are then interpreted as sets of consecutive time instants, over which the set-theoretic operators (i.e. $\cap$, $\cup$ and $\subseteq$) are used to define the basic temporal relationships. Formally, these domains can be stated as follows:

$$dom(time) \equiv \mathcal{TIME} = \{0, 1, 2, 3, 4, 5, 6, .., now, ...\}$$

$$dom(interval) \equiv \mathcal{INT} = \{[x, y] \mid x, y \in \mathcal{TIME}, x \leq y\}$$

$\mathcal{DTS}$ Type System

The syntax of the $\mathcal{DTS}$ types is as follows:

$$\tau := \mathcal{RAWDATA} \mid \mathcal{CLASS} \mid (\tau_1 \mid ...\mid\tau_m) \mid \tau+ \mid \tau* \mid \tau? \mid [\mid\mid A_1:\tau_1,.., A_m:\tau_m \mid\mid]$$

Here, each type of $\mathcal{RAWDATA}$ is a multimedia type such as *text*, *picture*, *graphic*, etc. Each type of $\mathcal{CLASS}$ is a class name from *CI*. Both sets of types comprise the set of basic data types in terms of which the structured types are defined as follows:

1. The constructor '|' expresses the *union of types* and gives the range of data types, $\tau_1,..., \tau_m$, that some component can take.

2. The option suffix '+' expresses that the component is expected to appear at least once, '*' indicates that the component can appear zero or more times and '?' expresses that the component can appear once or zero times.

3. The tree-like structure is formed with *nested ordered tuples* using the attribute names A_i as the node concepts.

Observe that the type system $\mathcal{DTS}$ brings up great similarities with the Data Type Definition language of SGML. Indeed, they both are mainly aimed to express the document generic structure in flexible terms by means of a grammar based syntax.

The type system $\mathcal{DTS}$ is intended to represent all the historical document types. This means that each document type has associated a time interval on which it can be used. Consistently, the values generated for each historical type must also be time-dependent. At this respect, $\{\tau\}_t$ will denote the set of *legal values* of a $\mathcal{DTS}$ type τ at a given time instant t. This function is the temporal version of the function *dom* defined for the type system $\mathcal{MTS}$.

2.2 Metaclasses

From a conceptual point of view, a metaclass is a class of classes. In other words, a metaclass abstracts the common structural and operational properties of a set of classes. Thus, a metaclass can be defined as a 5-tuple:

$$MC = \langle id, meta\_type, c\_meth, min\_type, o\_meth \rangle$$

where *id* is the metaclass's identifier, *meta_type* is a $\mathcal{MTS}$ type, *c_meth* is a set of method signatures defined over the type system $\mathcal{MTS}$, *min_type* is a $\mathcal{DTS}$ type and *o_meth* is a set of method signatures defined over $\mathcal{DTS}$ types.

The state of a class represents its metadata, which is defined in the metaclass's component *meta_type*. By the other hand, the behaviour of a metaclass is defined by the set of methods *c_meth*. Among others, these comprise creating instances and checking their consistency. At the same time, each metaclass induces a class hierarchy with only a root that has associated the type *min_type* and the set of methods *o_meth*. In this way, all the classes of a metaclass share a common minimal type and behaviour.

Due to the nature of the applications at hand, the basic behaviour of the whole data model can be stated at the metaclass level. Notice that most of the main operations involved in a digital library are reduced to the insertion of new documents and the retrieval of the stored ones. It is by this reason that, in the remainder of the paper, the operational part of the data model is omitted.

Finally, we assume that metaclasses cannot form hierarchies, that is, the populations of metaclasses are totally disjoint. This assures that the object populations do not participate in different class hierarchies. It is worth mentioning that this invariant is specially relevant to our applications since document bases for digital libraries need to handle very different kinds of data (e.g. multimedia, structured documents, etc.) that must be arranged in disjoint class hierarchies.

Example 1: In previous works [Ara96][Ara97a], after analysing and modelling a digital library of historical documents, four metaclasses were distinguished: *document*, *publication*, *periodical* and *multimedia* data. The primary metaclasses are the *document* and the *multimedia* ones, because they support both the simple document types (e.g. *article*, *section*, etc.) and the indexed multimedia data types (e.g. *text*, *picture*, etc.) respectively. Further, the metaclass *publication* groups all the document classes that have been published at a given time, whereas the metaclass *periodical* groups all the document classes that are periodically published. Table1 summarises the relevant metadata that define each of these metaclasses.

Apart from the usual metadata associated to these documents (e.g. *Volume*, *ISBN*, *Period*, etc.), a set of system-maintained metadata is included as well. Thus, documents include an attribute called *Rev-ref* to maintain the inverse references to their container objects. Multimedia data also includes this attribute. Moreover, multimedia data is indexed by a key called *Index* which is related with its contents.

Metaclass/ Metadata	*document*	*publication*	*periodical*	*multimedia*
meta-type (*MTS*)	Authors:{*string*} Contrib:{*string*} Purpose:*string*	Publisher:*string*	Name:*string* Period:*time* ISSN:*string* Editor:{*string*}	Format:*string*
min_type (*DTS*)	Rev-ref:{*CLASS*}	Date-P:*date* ISBN:*string* Site: *string**	Number:*integer* Volume:*integer*	Rev-ref:{*CLASS*} Index:*ATOMIC* Contents:*RAWDATA*

Table 1: Sample of Metadata for the four predefined metaclasses.

2.3 Classes

As earlier mentioned, historical document types may evolve along time. Particularly, document classes are supposed to change as new metadata and compositions for them need to be supported. This property lead us to define time-dependent semantics for classes, inheritance and the database schema.

We define a class signature as the following 5- tuple:

$C = \langle id, lifespan, type, history, mc \rangle$, where:

1. *id* is the class identifier,

2. *lifespan* is a value of INT that indicates the valid time of the class,

3. *type* is a value from {historic, static} that indicates if the class evolves,

4. *history* is a 4-tuple as follows:

$$(h\_type=(\tau_1@i_1,.., \tau_n@i_n), \quad c\_state =(v_1@j_1,..,v_k@j_k),$$
$$i\_ext = (p_1@i_1,.., p_n@i_n), \quad m\_ext = (p^*_1@i_1,.., p^*_n@i_n))$$

where $\tau_1 .. \tau_n$ denote DTS types, $v_1.. v_k$ denote MTS values, $p_1.. p_n$, $p^*_1.. p^*_n$ are sets of object identifiers from OI, and, $i_1.. i_n$ and $j_1,..,j_k$ are time intervals from INT. Here, the component *h_type* expresses the history of the *C*'s type. The component *c_state* represents the history of the class's state. Finally, *i_ext* contains the proper population and *m_ext* contains the extended one. The intervals of these series must meet each other so that they are disjoint and their composition coincides with the *C*'s lifespan. Notice that the intervals of *h_type*, *ext* and *p-ext* form the same temporal sequence.

5. *mc* is the metaclass to which the class *C* belongs.

As a metaclass instance, a class must to be a *consistent instance*. Therefore, all the historical states of a class must be values compatible with the type of its metaclass. Formally, provided that *M* is the metaclass to which a class *C* belongs, the following condition must hold:

for each $(v@i) \in C.history.c\_state, v \in dom(M.meta\_type)$

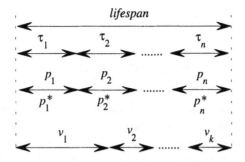

Fig. 1. Example of temporal evolution of the class's type, state and population.

Example 2: The following class definition can be considered to represent the evolution of the class of short papers of a document database:

Doc = ⟨*id*= *short_paper*, *lifespan*=[1, 100], *type*= historic,

 history = (

 h_type=

 ([|| *title*:*string*, *body*:*section*+, *ref*:*string** ||]@[1, 30],

 [|| *title*:*string*, *abstract*:*text*, *body*:*section*+, *ref*:*string** ||]@[31, 50],

 [|| *title*:*string*, *keywords*:*string*+, *body*:*section*+, *ref*:*string** ||]@[51,100]),

 c_state= ((*authors*={'J.Smith'}, *contrib*={ }) @ [1, 100]),

 p_ext =({ *i*#1, *i*#4, *i*#5,*i*#6} @[1,30], {*i*#3,*i*#7}@[31,50], {*i*#10,*i*#11}@[51,100])),

 mc = *document*⟩

The following functions serve us to simplify the notation of the forthcoming definitions. The function *type*(*c*, *t*) is defined to access the historical type of a class with name *c* at the time instant *t*. The function *lifespan*(*c*) returns the life-span of a class with name *c*. Finally, the function $\pi^*(c, t)$ returns the population of member objects of a class with name *c* at the time instant *t*.

2.4 Objects

Unlike classes, the objects of the data model do not evolve along time. Especially, neither object updates nor migrations are allowed in a digital library of historical documents. However, as described in the introduction, objects present two time dimensions: the edition time and the valid time. The former is a time instant that serves to attach each object to its type whereas the latter represents the time interval on which the object is viewed as up-to-date or valid. Regarding the above considerations, an object signature can be associated with the following 5-tuple:

 O = ⟨*oid*, *e_time*, *v_time*, *value*, *c_id*⟩

where *oid*∈ *OI* is the object identifier, *e_time* is a time instant, *v_time* is a time interval, *value* is a value from the *DTS* type system, and *c_id* is the name of the most specific class to which the object *O* belongs at time *e_time*.

Definition (Object Consistency) An object *O* is said to be consistent if

 O.value ∈ { *type*(*O.c_id*, *t*) }$_t$ with *t* = *O.e_time*.

Example 3: Given the example of section 2.3, the following object declaration shows an instance of the class *short_paper*:

Doc = ⟨ *oid* = *i*#21, *e_time* = 40, *vt* = [10,41],

    v = (*title*="Object-Orientation..", *abstract*=*i*#24, *body*={*i*#134, *i*#211, *i*#56}, *ref*={ }),

    c_id = *short_paper*⟩

Aggregation hierarchies of objects are now subject to a set of constraints over the two time attributes above defined. Firstly, the *e_time* component of an object *o* and its parts must be equal. That is because the historical type of *o* must be compatible with the historical types of its aggregates. At the other hand, the *v_time* attribute of an object *o* must cover all the valid times of the objects referenced by *o*. These temporal constraints need to be considered when defining the consistency of a set of objects, which is done below.

The following definition uses the function *ref(o)*, which takes as input an object *o* and returns the set of objects identifiers referenced by *o*. Further, I(*O*) denotes the set of identifiers of the objects in *O*.

Definition (Consistent Set of Objects) A set OBJ is a consistent set of objects if the following conditions hold:

1. for all objects *o*∈ OBJ, *o* is a consistent object,
2. for each pair *o*, *o'*∈ OBJ, such that *o.oid* = *o'.oid* then *o.e_time* = *o'.e_time*, *o.v* = *o'.v* and *o.vt* = *o'.vt*,
3. for all objects *o*∈ OBJ, each identifier in *ref(o)* must be contained in I(OBJ),
4. for each pair *o*, *o'*∈ OBJ such that *o'.oid*∈ *ref(o)*, *o.e_time*= *o'.e_time*,
5. for each pair *o*, *o'*∈ OBJ such that *o'.oid*∈ *ref(o)*, *o'.v_time* ⊆ *o.v_time*.

Conditions 1, 2 and 3 are adaptations of the definition given in [Ber96]. Condition 1 accounts for the consistency of isolated objects, condition 2 accounts for object identity and condition 3 accounts for referential integrity. Conditions 4 and 5 are the temporal constraints about the aggregation hierarchy of objects previously described.

2.5 Inheritance

Class hierarchies allow users to define inheritance relationships between classes. In our data model, a class can only be related to others via inheritance if its lifespan occurs during the lifespan of its superclasses. Moreover, due to class evolution, this relationship does not necessarily hold during the whole life-span of the subclass. Figure 2 illustrates an example of time-varying inheritance relationship between the proceedings of a workshop and the journal that publishes it as a special issue. In this case, the proceedings has been edited in two different journals during its lifespan.

A *class hierarchy* is here defined as the tuple ⟨*Cl*, ≤$_{IS-A}$⟩, where *Cl* is a set of class names and ≤$_{IS-A}$ is a ternary relationship formed with pairs of classes from *Cl* and time intervals from *INT*. Each tuple ⟨*c*, *c'*, *i*⟩ from ≤$_{IS-A}$ is interpreted as the fact that *c* is a subclass of *c'* during the time interval *i*. Accordingly, the following condition must be true for this relation: *i* ⊆ *lifespan(c)* ⊆ *lifespan(c')*.

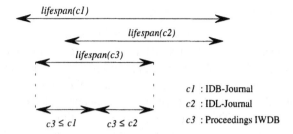

Fig. 2. Example of temporal relationships for class inheritance.

Like the relation $\leq_{IS\text{-}A}$, the subtype relationship, denoted with $\leq_t$, is a ternary relation formed by pairs of types from $\mathcal{DTS}$ and time instants from $\mathcal{TIME}$. Both relationships $\leq_{IS\text{-}A}$ and $\leq_t$ must be consistently related each other to form consistent class hierarchies. The following definitions define such constraints between both relations.

Definition (int-well-formed CH) A class hierarchy $\langle C\mathcal{l}, \leq_{IS\text{-}A}\rangle$ is *intentionally well-formed* iff for each $\langle c, c', i\rangle \in \leq_{IS\text{-}A}$ holds $\langle type(c, t), type(c', t), t\rangle \in \leq_t$ for all $t \in i$.

Definition (ext-well-formed CH) A class hierarchy $\langle C\mathcal{l}, \leq_{IS\text{-}A}\rangle$ is *extensionally well-formed* iff for each $\langle c, c', i\rangle \in \leq_{IS\text{-}A}$ holds $\pi^*(c, t) \subseteq \pi^*(c', t)$ for all $t \in i$.

2.6 Historical Document Databases

This section joins together all the preceding definitions to formulate what we understand for a historical document database. Following other object-oriented database models, we distinguish between the schema of the database (set of classes) and its instance (set of objects). The former includes the definitions of metaclasses, which induce the disjoint class hierarchies and the common structure for the states of their classes. Thus, the signature for a database schema can be defined as follows:

$$Schema = \langle \mathcal{MCl}, \mathcal{Cl\text{-}Def}, \leq_{IS\text{-}A}\rangle$$

where $\mathcal{MCl}$ is a set of metaclass definitions, $\mathcal{Cl\text{-}Def}$ is a set of consistent class definitions which forms a intentionally-well-formed class hierarchy under the inheritance relationship $\leq_{IS\text{-}A}$. By the other hand, an instance base of the above database schema is a consistent set of objects OBJ as defined in section 2.4. Additionally, the class hierarchy formed by the schema must be extensionally-well-formed with respect to OBJ.

3 The Roles of Metadata

The preceding sections have defined a database for historical documents. Whose aim is to support digital library applications involving this kind of documents. This is why the description of its data model has been focused on incorporating metadata, which is one of the prime features of digital libraries. This section discusses which are the roles of metadata within a digital library that uses the proposed database model. Mainly, these roles concern with the insertion and retrieval of historical documents.

3.1 Document Insertion

Metadata can be applied when inserting documents in two senses. Firstly, the definition of the generic structure of a document class serves to validate the specific structure of document objects. Thus, the logical references contained within an object state must preserve the aggregation relationships at the class level. Secondly, the values of temporal document attributes can be automatically deduced from the values of certain meta-attributes. This is the case of the valid time (*v_time*), which can be deduced by default from either the date of publication (*date-P*) or the set of valid times of the objects that a document refers to. This constitutes a way of propagating upwards or downwards the temporal attributes of documents through the object aggregation hierarchy. To sum up, supporting all these metadata into the data model helps to enforce the integrity of the database. Section 2.4 has defined formally these constraints. A set of predefined *c-methods* associated to the schema metaclasses is in charge of checking and enforcing such constraints. So, the definition of metadata at class level, assists the overall instantiation process.

3.2 Query Formulation

In [Ara97a], a Document Retrieval Language (DRL) is proposed to retrieve and relate historical documents accordingly to a set of temporal and structural conditions. This language is based on the standard ODMG [Cat93], which is extended to support temporal predicates (e.g. before(d_1, d_2), during(d_1, d_2) and so on), predicates about the structural relationship between documents (e.g. contains(d_1, d_2)) and predicates about textual contents (e.g. contains_text(d, t)). This language can be extended to accept queries on metadata. From the formal data model designed in section 2, it follows that every class in the base is an instance of some metaclass. Consequently, we can apply our DRL to retrieve the metadata encapsulated in class objects. Per example, the query below can be used to know the classes of Periodical that are published yearly and that contain the class Review among their components. Knowing the generic structure of a document class facilitates the formulation of query conditions. Similarly, due to the evolution of document classes, users may need to know the valid definition of the involved classes at the time in which the database is going to be projected.

> select c from Periodical as c
> where c.period= 1year and c contains_type Review

When processing this query, the evaluation module must notice that Periodical is not a class, but a metaclass. In this way, the variable c will take as domain the set of classes that are instances of the corresponding metaclass. This facility allows users to query the database schema prior to formulate any demands for documents. It is also possible to draw up queries that combine conditions over the data and the metadata of some class. This feature increases the expressiveness of the query language, at the same time that allows users to specify more complex retrieval conditions, taking profit of the metadata stored in the base. Per example, the next query asks for all the documents published by *John Smith* during 1995 with the purpose of being a bibliography. Considering that there may exist several types of documents with this purpose, a nested query should appear in the clause from as follows:

> select d from (select c from Document c where c.purpose = 'bibliography') as d
> where d.author= 'John Smith' at [1/1/1995, 31/12/1995]

To evaluate this query, the nested query must be first solved to obtain a set of classes satisfying it. The union of the instances in any of these classes will constitute the domain over which the variable d will range. The clause at affects to both queries.

4 Conclusions

In this paper, a new approach to the design of a digital library of historical documents has been proposed. The paper presents such a library as a temporal object-oriented database of historical documents that also supports metadata, which takes an outstanding role in current digital libraries. The difference with other proposals is that our model integrates and, at the same time, differentiates between metadata and the rest of document attributes and contents. Instead, current digital libraries only deal with metadata attributes (e.g. keywords, title, etc.), ignoring the rest of information of the stored documents. At the other hand, current object-oriented data models do not support metadata as here described. The use of metadata in our approach has permitted enhancing previous document applications in several senses. Firstly, we store and project the global contents of the documents with their original organisation. Secondly, a temporal dimension (v_time) has been added to facilitate the specification of temporal relationships between the documents to be retrieved.

5 References

[Abi95] Abiteboul, S., Hull, R. and Vianu, V. *"Foundations of Databases"*. Addison Wesley Publishing Company, 1995.

[Ara96] Aramburu, M.J. and Berlanga, R. *"Object Oriented Modelling of Periodicals"*, 7th Workshop on Database and Expert System Applications, Zurich, 1996.

[Ara97a] Aramburu, M. and Berlanga, R. *"An Approach to a Digital Library of Newspapers"*. To appear in Information Processing & Management, Sp. Issue on Electronic News, 1997.

[Ber96] Bertino, E. Ferrari, F. and Guerrini, G. *"A Formal Temporal Object-Oriented Data Model"* Proc. of the International Conference on Extending Data Base Technology, Avignon. LNCS No. 1057, Springer Verlag, March 1996.

[Cat96] Cattell, R.G.G., Ed. *"The Object Database Standard: ODMG-93 Release 1.2."* San Francisco: Morgan Kaufmann Publishers 1996.

[Chr94] Christophides, V., Abitebul, S., Cluet, S. and Scholl, M. *"From Structured Documents to Novel Query Facilities"*. Proc. of the ACM SIGMOD, Minnesota, 1994.

[Fox95] Fox, E.A., Akscyn, R.M., Furuta, R. and Legget, J. *"Digital Libraries"*. Communications of ACM, 38(4), 22-103, 1995.

[Özs95] M. T. Özsu et al, *"An Object-Oriented Multimedia Database System for a News-on-Demand Application"*, Multimedia Systems, No. 3, 1995.

[Wei95] Weibel, S. *"Metadata: The Foundations of Resource Description"*. D-Lib Magazine. http://www.dlib.org. July 1995.

Assembling Documents from Digital Libraries[*]

Helena Ahonen, Barbara Heikkinen, Oskari Heinonen, and Pekka Kilpeläinen

University of Helsinki, Department of Computer Science
P. O. Box 26, FIN–00014 University of Helsinki, Finland

Abstract. We consider assembling documents using, as a source, a digital library containing SGML documents. The assembly process contains two parts: 1) finding interesting fragments, and 2) constructing a coherent document. We present a general document assembly framework. First, we describe a system for tailoring control engineering textbooks. Its assembling facilities are rather restricted but, on the other hand, the quality of documents produced is high. Second, we address the problem of filtering and combining interesting information from a large heterogeneous document collection. The methods presented offer various ways to find the interesting document fragments. Moreover, the elements found in the fragments are mapped to generic elements, like sections, paragraph containers, paragraphs and strings, which have known semantics. Hence, even arbitrary compositions can be formatted and printed.

1 Introduction

In an on-going research and development project called Structured and Intelligent Documents (SID) [1] we study *document assembly* in its different aspects. By document assembly we mean computer-aided construction of a new document using several existing document sources. Assembly is usually an interactive process (Figure 1) within which an author or editor uses various tools to find appropriate sources and to configure the intended document. The process consists of two parts: 1) finding the interesting document fragments and 2) constructing a coherent document from these fragments.

One application area we have considered is assembling educational material from digital libraries. A digital library may contain, for instance, textbooks, articles, exercise collections, and simulations. This kind of a library can be used in multiple ways. The publisher can print customized textbooks for various school branches and levels. Additionally, teachers can form tailored compositions of WWW or CD-ROM delivered material—e.g., summaries, slides and tests—for their own classes. Students could also use the digital library directly for problem-oriented learning, as a data bank, or as an active textbook with computer-assisted learning features.

Recently, several publishers and universities have launched their own services for delivering customized textbooks [10,11,3]. All the approaches seem to have

---
[*] This work was supported by the Finnish Technology Development Centre (TEKES). Authors' e-mail: *{hahonen, bheikkin, oheinone, kilpelai}@cs.helsinki.fi.*

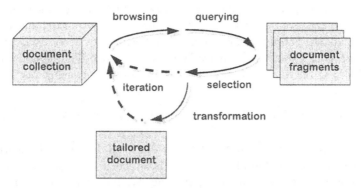

Fig. 1. Assembly process.

a fairly static set of document fragments that can be combined to form a book, and their user interfaces simply allow the user to choose a selection of these parts. We claim that dynamic compositions are needed, and to achieve this, we have decided to use Standard Generalized Markup Language (SGML) [6] for the management of the material. Haake et al. have introduced the Individualized Electronic Newspaper [5] which also uses SGML as the document presentation format. Their approach, although somewhat similar to ours, concentrates on gathering and presenting news-like material according to readers' profiles while our goal is more general: a coherent assembled customized SGML document.

SGML is a metalanguage for defining document structures. The logical structural parts, *elements*, of an SGML document are marked up by start and end *tags*. The set of element names and the permitted structures of the elements are given in the *document type definition* (DTD) that is essentially a context-free grammar, in which the right-hand sides of the rules are regular expressions. A DTD can be used to facilitate structured queries and various transformations needed, e.g., to produce multiple output formats. SGML representation defines only the syntax of the structures: any semantics, e.g., how the elements should be formatted for printing, has to be attached by some application.

Although one of the strengths of SGML technology is to allow several representations and formats to be generated from the same documents, multiuse of documents by dynamic assembly of structure elements is still an unsolved problem, and hardly any techniques or tools exist. The necessity of assembly is, however, clearly seen and considered to be of great importance [8,9].

In this paper we present a general document assembly framework. First, we describe a system for tailoring control engineering textbooks. Its assembling facilities are rather restricted but, on the other hand, the quality of documents produced is high. Second, we address the problem of filtering and combining interesting information from a large heterogeneous document collection. The method presented offers various ways to find the interesting document fragments. Moreover, the elements found in the fragments are mapped to generic elements, like sections, paragraph containers, paragraphs and strings, which have known semantics. Hence, even arbitrary compositions can be formatted and printed.

The rest of the paper is organized in the following way. Section 2 describes the system for tailoring textbooks via a WWW user interface. The general framework is introduced in Section 3. Finally, Section 4 gives some conclusions.

2 System for Tailoring Textbooks via WWW

One of our project partners, the Finnish National Board of Education, has started to create a new digital library that is intended to contain various educational material related to control engineering. We have participated in converting textbooks into SGML, and we have also implemented a system for tailoring new specialized textbooks using the material. The following section presents the structure of the documents and how it can be used in assembling. Section 2.2 describes the system architecture.

2.1 Structure of the Documents

The first components of our digital library are three textbooks on control engineering. The books, originally prepared using MS Word[1], contain many equations and technical pictures. Creating a structured SGML version required laborious conversion steps using tools such as MathType[2], DynaTag[3], OmniMark[4], and FrameMaker+SGML[5].

The major hierarchical structure elements of a book are chapters, sections, subsections and paragraphs. We have used as a basis for our document type definition the Book DTD of the ISO 12083 standard [7] extended with element types for exercises, answers, examples, formulas, definitions and clauses. The book is enriched with internal supplementary information. Manual seeding, based on information from the authors, was necessary to classify the fragments of the material into appropriate categories. Each text paragraph is classified according to the level (vocational, college, university), the branch of specialization (metal industry, process industry, data communications, civil engineering, etc.) and the didactic form of the contents (introductory, base material, advanced, applied, summary, auxiliary, examination).

The categorization is represented in the text paragraphs and their superstructures as SGML attributes. Attribute values are propagated from the upper levels of the structure, if not overridden in the element. Figure 2 is an example of the supplementary information attached to the markup of the material.

The shown chapter was authored by Jari Savolainen (author=aJS). It is recommended for students at the college level (level=b). The content of the

---

[1] MS Word is a trademark of Microsoft Corporation.
[2] MathType is a trademark of Design Science, Inc.
[3] DynaTag is a trademark of Inso Corporation.
[4] OmniMark is a trademark of OmniMark Technologies Corporation.
[5] FrameMaker+SGML is a trademark of Adobe Systems Incorporated.

422

```
<CHAPTER id="c4" author="aJS" level="b">
  <TITLE>S&Auml;&Auml;T&Ouml;LOHKOT TAAJUUSTASOSSA</TITLE> ...
  <SECTION id="c4.1" level="b" content="BB" branch="unspec">
    <TITLE>Impedanssi-kompleksinen vastus</TITLE> ...
    <EXAMPLE id="c4ex1" level="c" content="CC" branch="unspec">
      <FIGGRP id="c4fg2"><FIG entity="c4f2"><CAPTION>Impedanssin
        sis&auml;lt&auml;m&auml; ...</CAPTION></FIGGRP>
      <P><KEYWORD freq=1>kokonaisimpedanssi</KEYWORD>
        Laske sarjakytkenn&auml;n kokonaisimpedanssi U = 5 V</P>
      <ANSWER><P><KEYWORD freq=1>kokonaisimpedanssi</KEYWORD>
        Kokonaisimpedanssi on sarjaankytkettyjen impedanssien summa.
        <EQ id="c4df13"><EQBODY entity="c4d13"></EQ></P> ...
```

Fig. 2. An example of internal supplementary information.

section 4.1 is base material (content=BB). The example of the section is directed at students at the university level (level=c) and it contains advanced material (content=CC). Keywords and their frequencies are listed explicitly. Formulas are in external entity files (attribute *entity* of element *eqbody*) in MIF format. They can also be represented in picture formats, e.g. TIFF. Using the added markup, we can easily extract, e.g., base material for college level students, or exercises for university level students. Search features of existing commercial SGML browsers such as DynaText[6] or Panorama Pro[7] support this kind of querying.

2.2 System Architecture

We have built a system that gives teachers a possibility to order customized control engineering textbooks. An overview of the system can be seen in Figure 3. An order is processed as follows.

1. **Order.** The client fills in an HTML form and submits it.
2. **Processing of order.** The order form is processed. The composition of the assembled document is created based on the input from the client and some heuristic rules. The table of contents is returned to the client. If the client confirms the order, the specification of the composition is submitted to the assembly process.
3. **Assembly.** According to the input for the assembly, which is represented by a list of file names, the assembly process retrieves the desired texts and images from the SGML collection and composes the new textbook. Thereafter, the textbook is formatted and the page layout is manually checked. Finally, a PostScript file is submitted to the printing house.
4. **Printing.** The printing house produces the textbooks and delivers them to the client.

---

[6] DynaText is a trademark of Inso Corporation.
[7] Panorama Pro is a trademark of SoftQuad, Inc.

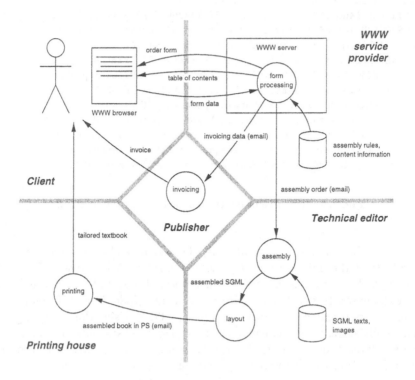

Fig. 3. Overview of the system.

As a user interface for the teachers we use an HTML form (Figure 4). The form contains a table of contents for each of the three books. The fragments that can be used for selection are chapters, sections, subsections, and, in some cases, author-defined sequences consisting of several paragraphs.

The columns in the table of contents are (from left to right):

1. **Choice.** By checking choice buttons the user selects corresponding structures of the books. The user can select whole chapters, or just some sections, subsections, or predefined paragraph sequences.
2. **Title or beginning of text.** Original chapter, section or subsection title, or the beginning of the text of the paragraph sequence.
3. **Page count.** Length of the part.
4. **Content.** For example, 'johdanto' (introductory), 'perusaines' (base material), 'soveltava' (applied).
5. **Level.** For example, 'ammattioppilaitos' (vocational).

The rightmost column indicates the lowest school level for which the part is recommended. At the moment this knowledge is only given to the teacher as a hint; it is not used in any automated way. As the digital library does not contain any branch-specific material yet, we have not utilized the values of the *branch* attribute.

Fig. 4. Order form.

The six choice buttons above the table are shortcuts. They enable the user to select multiple items by one click. The first button selects all the material, and the others select all parts of the named content (e.g., 'johdanto'), respectively. This selection approach could be extended to other attributes as well.

As the selections have several dimensions, it is not at all obvious, how all the choices should be presented to the client; the order form becomes easily too complicated. One solution would be to offer pre-defined assemblies as a starting point: some fragments would be pre-selected but the user could change the selections.

In order to achieve sensible results, the assembly has to utilize heuristics which guarantee the inclusion of all necessary fragments. For example, if only some sections of a chapter are selected then also the title of the chapter and the introductory paragraphs are included.

If the ordered books are delivered on paper, the problem of predictability arises (since attributes and heuristics are used). Hence, the teacher should be able to check the contents of the result. At the moment, after the teacher has submitted the form, the ordering system immediately returns the table of contents for the assembled textbook, as well as the number of pages and the price of the order. We also assume that the teacher has a paper copy of all the original books, when he/she selects the fragments to be included. Instead of the table of contents, the whole assembled textbook could be sent to the client, e.g., by email.

After the confirmation of the order, a list of file names is submitted to the assembly process. The assembly retrieves the required files and concatenates them to form one SGML document. As the DTD of all the assembled textbooks is the same as the original, it is possible to create, using FrameMaker+SGML, the formatting layout nearly automatically. Due to some problematic cases, e.g., improper page breaks, a manual inspection is still needed. Finally, the textbooks are produced by a printing house. In our system a preprinted cover page is used, on which the personalized headings are printed. The printing house delivers the books to the client.

3 General Assembly Framework

A tailoring system presented in the previous section produces high quality textbooks, but its applicability is restricted to fairly small document collections. Whereas, when large and heterogeneous digital libraries are concerned, the user should be offered more flexible ways to filter information and construct meaningful combinations.

3.1 Selection of Interesting Document Fragments

As we have seen, in the current system the user selects chapters and sections by marking them up in the table of contents. This is not feasible if the document collection is large. Hence, our new system under development allows four ways to select elements to be included in the assembly.

The first one is a rather standard search that will include full-text search with conditions on the structure and attribute values. For instance, within our control engineering library, the user might want to create a collection of exercises for college students majoring in data communications.

The second way is based on the Scatter/Gather clustering [4]. The user-controlled iterative clustering process forms a classification of the material, and gives the user an extracted view of the documents. This is especially invaluable when the user is dealing with an unfamiliar collection of documents; traditional query models do not help the user to achieve a simple overview. The user can further select the appropriate clusters for reclustering, and in this way narrow down the retrieval space.

The third possibility is to browse the document collection by navigating in the tree structure and selecting the desired elements manually. Reasonable use of this selection usually necessitates that the two above-mentioned selection methods have already been used to reduce the document collection.

The fourth possibility is to start from the elements selected so far, and let the system search for similar or related elements in the collection. Similarity of two elements can be estimated, for example, by the amount of the same words they contain.

In the current system the user can only prune the existing books: mixing the sections of different books is not possible, and even within one book it is not possible to change the order of sections. This kind of modifications are, however, often desired. Hence, in the new system the user is allowed to modify the set of selected documents in order to obtain a final textbook. The modifications include rearranging the elements, moving or copying selected fragments to be part of an existing element, and replacing an element either by its parent or children elements. As the result of the selection phase, an ordered list of document fragments, with the original internal tree structures, is returned.

3.2 Constructing a Coherent Document

In our textbook tailoring system, all the documents share a common DTD, and also the resulting textbook is of the same type. Thus, the overall structure of the new document is known, and we can also utilize the formatting declarations of the original documents. This is not the case in general. The source documents may have differing structures, and an arbitrary composition of their fragments does not belong to any known document class. Therefore, no formatting rules are available, i.e., the documents cannot be browsed or printed in the formatted form.

When constructing a useful SGML document, two points have to be considered: 1) what is the document type definition of the new document, and 2) how the application programs, e.g. formatters, can process the document. Given a set of document fragments, each of which is a valid SGML element according to its DTD, the following steps are taken.

1. The elements of the fragments are classified and generalized.
2. A new document type definition is constructed.
3. A new document is constructed using the generic elements.
4. Formatting rules for the assembled document are constructed.

The aim of the element classification is to map every element to some generic element with well-known semantics. We have defined a set of generic elements that often appear in texts. We also give them element declarations and simple semantics, e.g., how the element should be printed.

All the fragments are traversed once to collect the set of element names, and for each element, the set of elements it contains as well as the average length of its content. Thereafter, each element found is mapped to some generic element: *Section*, *Paragraph container*, *Paragraph*, or *String*. Mapping is done bottom-up using the rules in Table 1. First, all short elements are classified as *Strings*. Second, *Paragraphs* are identified. After that, all the remaining elements are classified as *Sections*, and finally, all *Sections* that do not contain any other *Sections* are remapped to be *Paragraph containers*.

Generic element	Conditions
String	Contains ordinary text and/or other *Strings*; length of the content is less than 100 characters.
Paragraph	Contains ordinary text and/or *Strings*; length of the content is more than 100 characters.
Paragraph container	Contains *Strings* and/or *Paragraphs* (at least one *Paragraph*).
Section	Contains *Strings*, *Paragraphs*, *Paragraph containers* and/or *Sections* (at least one *Paragraph* or *Paragraph container*).

Table 1. Recognition rules for element classification.

Some elements, like tables and figures, do not match well any of the generic elements. These elements are preserved as such, as well as the elements they contain. The elements can be identified using simple heuristics, e.g., in tables the proportion of tags compared to the text content itself is high, and the DTD usually gives enough hints for recognizing figures and formulas.

Construction of the new DTD is straightforward: it expresses essentially nothing more than the inclusion relationships of the generic elements, e.g., a section is allowed to contain paragraphs but not vice versa (see Figure 5). *Text* refers to SGML character data.

```
Document -> (Section | Paragraph_container | Paragraph | String)*
Section -> (Section | Paragraph_container | Paragraph | String)*
Paragraph_container -> (Paragraph | String)*
Paragraph -> (String | Text)*
String -> (String | Text)*
```

Fig. 5. Grammar of the new DTD.

If some element structure is left unclassified, its original definition is added to the DTD. Additionally, the element has to be contained in the definition of the parent. For instance, if a *Table* has occurred within a *Paragraph container*, the definition for *Paragraph container* is changed to:

```
Paragraph_container -> (Paragraph | String | Table)*
```

The actual assembly process composes a valid SGML document from the fragments. After classification we have an ordered list of fragments containing classified elements. The root elements of the fragments may be *Sections*, *Paragraph containers* or *Paragraphs*. (*Paragraph* is the smallest fragment size allowed.)

First, a new document root is constructed for the new document. Our intended top-level structure contains a list of *Sections*, possibly preceded by a couple of *Paragraphs* or *Paragraph containers*. Hence, *Paragraphs* and *Paragraph containers* located between two *Sections* in the fragment list have to be combined by generating a new *Section*. If the generated new *Section* is too large, the *Paragraphs* may be joined in order to get several smaller *Sections* [2]. Additionally, the desired number of top-level *Sections* can be given as a parameter. If the number of *Sections* and generated *Sections* exceeds this threshold, some consecutive *Sections* have to combined. The *Sections* to be combined can be chosen by considering the similarity of consecutive *Sections*, based, e.g., on the amount of words in common.

The formatting rules can be constructed in a straightforward manner. The generic elements have their formatting rules that are independent of the documents assembled, whereas an unclassified element is output using the rules attached to the original document. The formatting of generic elements is based on the following principles. *Strings* are inline elements (no newline at the end). The font of ordinary text is normal, whereas marked *Strings* are emphasized using, e.g., boldface or italics. *Paragraphs* have a newline at the end. *Sections* have some vertical space at the beginning, and if a *Section* has a *String* element in the beginning, it is interpreted as a title and hence output using boldface and large font. *Sections* are numbered automatically.

The mapping of elements into generic elements, which have simple formatting rules, can be compared to the conversion of some structured form to an HTML format: the complexity of the structure is reduced. Opposite to HTML, the new document still has a hierarchical structure. Moreover, the old element name can be stored to each element as an attribute name. Hence, the original structure can be reconstructed.

4 Conclusions

We have introduced a novel approach for assembling documents using, as a source, a digital library containing SGML documents. The assembly process contains two parts: 1) finding interesting fragments, and 2) constructing a coherent document.

We first presented a system for tailoring textbooks via WWW. In our system, the order of a client is processed as follows. The client fills in and submits an HTML form. The form is processed and the fragments to be included in the assembled book are selected automatically. The choice of fragments is dependent on the client's input and a few heuristic rules. The texts and images are retrieved from the digital library and the layout is created. Finally, the books are printed and delivered to the client. We have developed our assembly system together with a group of teachers, including the authors of the textbooks used. At the moment, the teachers are about to select sample assemblies of material. So far the results are encouraging: the teachers find the assemblies useful, even if the collection is still rather restricted.

The approach demonstrated with the current system will be developed further as part of a more general assembly environment. Since document collections concerned are assumed to be large, more advanced selection possibilities are included in the system. Additionally, flexible assemblies from several sources have to be supported. Our method has the following steps.

1. The user selects interesting document fragments by querying and browsing.
2. The elements of each fragment are mapped to well-known generic elements (section, paragraph container, paragraph, string).
3. A new document type definition is formed.
4. A new document is constructed from the generic elements.
5. The formatting rules are formed for the elements.

The approach presented is simple and easily implemented. Each of the above steps can be further developed to gather more of the semantics of the source documents. For instance, new generic elements, e.g. tables, can be recognized. Our aim is to improve the intelligence of the classification system, the DTD generation, the assembly heuristics and the formatting rules. However, as the primary goal is to present a compilation of information in an organized form with uniform and clear output, a rather simple method may actually work, at least in unanticipated situations, more reliably.

References

1. Helena Ahonen, Barbara Heikkinen, Oskari Heinonen, Jani Jaakkola, Pekka Kilpeläinen, Greger Lindén, and Heikki Mannila. Intelligent Assembly of Structured Documents. Report C-1996-40, Department of Computer Science, University of Helsinki, 1996.
2. Helena Ahonen, Barbara Heikkinen, Oskari Heinonen, and Mika Klemettinen. Improving the accessibility of SGML documents: A content-analytical approach. In *SGML Europe '97*, Barcelona, 1997. GCA.
3. Custom CourseWare. McMaster University Bookstore, 1997. URL: `http://bookstore.services.mcmaster.ca/home/ccw/ccw.html`.
4. Douglas R. Cutting, Jan O. Pedersen, David Karger, and John W. Tukey. Scatter/Gather: A cluster-based approach to browsing large document collections. In *Proc. of the 15th ACM/SIGIR Conference*, Copenhagen, 1992.
5. Anja Haake, Christoph Hüser, and Klaus Reichenberger. The individualized electronic newspaper: an example of an active publication. *Electronic Publishing — Origination, Dissemination and Design*, 7(2):89–111, June 1994.
6. ISO. *Information Processing — Text and Office Systems — Standard Generalized Markup Language (SGML), ISO 8879*, 1986.
7. ISO. *Information and documentation — Electronic manuscript preparation and markup, ISO 12083*, 1994.
8. W. Eliot Kimber. Re-usable SGML: Why I demand SUBDOC. In *SGML '96*, Boston, 1996. GCA.
9. John McFadden. Hybrid distributed database (HDDB) and the future of SGML. In *SGML Europe '96*, Munich, 1996. GCA.
10. Nelson Canada Power Pak. Nelson Canada, a Division of Thomson International, 1997. URL: `http://www.thomson.com/nelson/custom/custom.html`.
11. Primis. Primis Custom Publishing, a Division of McGraw-Hill, 1997. URL: `http://www.mhcollege.com/primis/`.

Two-Layer Transaction Management for Workflow Management Applications[†]

Paul Grefen, Jochem Vonk, Erik Boertjes, Peter Apers

Center for Telematics and Information Technology
University of Twente
{grefen,vonk,boertjes,apers}@cs.utwente.nl

Abstract

Workflow management applications require advanced transaction management that is not offered by traditional database systems. For this reason, a number of extended transaction models has been proposed in the past. None of these models seems completely adequate, though, because workflow management requires different transactional semantics on different process levels. In the WIDE ESPRIT project, a two-layer transaction management approach has been adopted to cope with this problem. The approach consists of a transaction model built from an orthogonal combination of two existing models and a transaction management architecture with two independent transaction managers. This architecture is integrated into the next generation of the commercial FORO distributed workflow management system.

1. Introduction

Workflow management applications require transaction management functionality that goes beyond the traditional simple transaction model provided by current database management systems. In particular, support for long running activities with relaxed notions of isolation and atomicity and complex process structures is required. As indicated by the large number of proposed transaction models, no single model can effectively cope with the broad set of requirements imposed by complex workflow management applications. On a high level of granularity in these applications, a relaxed notion of transactionality is required to allow cooperativeness between multiple workflow tasks. On a lower level of granularity, stricter transactional notions are required to model business transactions that may involve complex process structures and multiple actors but require atomicity and isolation semantics.

In the WIDE ESPRIT project, the approach has been taken therefore to use a combination of modified existing transaction models, instead of inventing yet another new model. The result is an orthogonal two-layer transaction model that supports both high-level and low-level workflow semantics. The two-layer model is supported by two independent transaction manager modules, each of which manages one layer of the model. These modules are implemented on top of a commercial DBMS. The resulting transaction management architecture is integrated into the next generation of the FORO workflow management system (WFMS) with specific attention to distribution aspects and platform independence.

[†] The work presented in this paper is supported by the European Commission in the WIDE project (ESPRIT No. 20280). Partners in WIDE are Sema Group sae and Hospital General de Manresa in Spain, Politecnico di Milano in Italy, ING Bank and University of Twente in the Netherlands.

This paper is organized as follows. In Section 2, we first give an overview of related work. In Section 3, we present the process model underlying the workflow model constructed in the WIDE project. Section 4 discusses the transaction model dealing with the requirements following from the process model. The functional design of the software architecture supporting the transaction model is next presented in Section 5, the implementation in the context of the FORO WFMS in Section 6. We conclude the paper with a short discussion and outlook on future work.

2. Related work

In the past decade, numerous extended transaction models have been proposed for long running transactions [El92]. Examples are nested transactions [Da91], sagas [Ga87], and contracts [Re95]. General frameworks have been constructed, like ACTA [Ch94], that provide a conceptual framework for extended transaction models. Various extended transaction models have been proposed for use in workflow management contexts [Lo93]. In WIDE, we do not aim at the specification of yet another transaction model, but at the combined use of concepts from existing models. In contrast to many other proposals, we aim at an industry-strength implementation of extended transaction support.

In the Exotica project [Al96], advanced transaction models are emulated by means of the Flowmark WFMS, thereby trying to remove the need for advanced transaction support. In WIDE, we aim at advanced transaction support that is orthogonal to workflow management functionality. Although the basic ideas are quite different between Exotica and WIDE, some aspects are common. This will be made clearer in the sequel of this paper.

In WIDE, we provide extended transaction management on top of a commercial DBMS platform. In [Ba95], the reflective transaction framework is presented that provides extended transaction support using transaction adapters. There are a number of important differences to our work. The reflective framework provides flexible transaction semantics through reflection, whereas we provide flexibility through a two-layer model with multiple levels in each layer. Further, the reflective framework uses a transaction monitor with an open architecture (Transarc's Encina), where we use a closed database platform (Oracle). Finally, the reflective framework aims at a prototype realization, where we aim at integration into a commercial product.

3. The WIDE workflow management process model

In the WIDE project, an extended workflow model and language are developed with advanced process primitives like multitasks, various join operators, exceptions, etc. [C96a]. Important for this paper is the fact that a *multi-level process model* is used (see [Gr97] for an ER-diagram of the model) that allows for hierarchical decomposition of workflow processes with flexible transactional semantics.

The top level of a process hierarchy is formed by a complete workflow process. The bottom level consists of individual tasks, i.e. process parts that are not further decomposed in the workflow specification. Usually, an individual task is performed by a single actor in a short period of time. In the process hierarchy, the higher levels are long-running processes with cooperative characteristics and therefore require re-

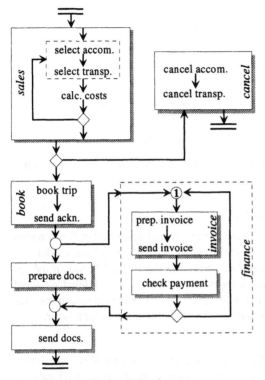

Figure 1: Example business process

laxed transactional semantics. The lower levels are relatively short-living processes requiring strict transactional semantics. The separation between the higher and lower levels is formed by the notion of *business transaction* in the workflow application. Process levels representing business transactions and their subprocesses have strict transactional semantics; their superprocesses have relaxed semantics.

In the WIDE model, the process levels above business transactions are represented by *non-atomic supertasks*. These supertasks do not behave strictly atomically, as this would imply the undoing of large amounts of work in case of an error. Also, they are not executed in strict isolation, as strict isolation would prevent the sharing of information as required in a workflow management environment. A rollback mechanism at this level is required though, to be able to undo a workflow to a certain point in case of errors. Rollback should offer application-oriented semantics, i.e. it should return a workflow to a state that is identical to a previous state from a business point of view, not necessarily from a database point of view.

The process levels associated with business transactions and below are represented by *atomic supertasks and tasks*. These supertasks should ideally be executed in strict atomicity and isolation. A rollback mechanism should offer complete undo to the pre-supertask state in case of critical errors. Besides normal atomic supertasks, *non-critical supertasks* need to be supported. Non-critical supertasks allow the definition of process parts that cannot cause critical errors and hence do not require rollback functionality.

The semantics of the two process layers are completely orthogonal: atomic supertasks are black-box "steps" in non-atomic supertasks. This means that changes can be made to one layer without affecting the other layer. There can be an arbitrary number of process levels in each of the two layers and each level can contain arbitrarily complex process structures. Consequently, application designers have a high level of freedom in structuring applications.

An example travel agency workflow process is shown in Figure 1 in a slightly adapted WIDE graphical workflow notation. In the figure, all boxes represent supertasks. Solid shadowed boxes represent business transactions, dotted boxes supertasks

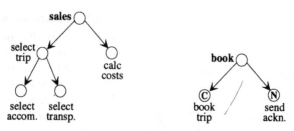

Figure 2: Example local transactions

above or below the level of business transactions. The ◊ symbol represents an or-split, the O symbol an and-split or and-join, and the ① symbol an or-join.

4. A two-layer transaction model

In the WIDE project, the two-layer workflow process model described in the previous section is mapped onto a two-layer transaction model. In this transaction model, the upper layer is formed by *global transactions* providing the relaxed transactional semantics of process layers above business transactions and the lower level by *local transactions* providing the strict transactional semantics of business transactions. Below, we first discuss the local transaction layer, then the global transaction layer.

4.1 Local transactions

The local transaction layer of the WIDE model is used to support business transaction semantics in workflow processing. Business transactions require strict ACID transaction properties. They differ from traditional 'flat' ACID transactions, as supported by most commercial DBMSs, from the fact that they have a hierarchic structure consisting of subtransactions and basic actions. For this reason, we have chosen a nested transaction model for the local transaction layer in WIDE, partly based on nested transaction models (see e.g. [Da91]). The WIDE model provides flexible commit-dependency between subtransactions and their parents.

An example local transaction is the subprocess 'sales' from the example workflow, as depicted in Figure 2. This local transaction models selling a trip by selecting accommodation and transport details for a customer and providing the price tag for this selection. The local transaction consists of two subtransactions 'select trip' and 'calc costs'. The first subtransaction consists of two basic tasks; the second is a basic task by itself. Note that the control flow as shown in Figure 1 is not relevant for the local transaction concept, only the process hierarchy is taken into account.

In a local transaction, we can have critical and non-critical subtransactions. A critical subtransaction determines the success of its parent transaction: if the subtransaction aborts, its parent cannot commit. The success of a non-critical subtransaction does not affect the success of its parent. Figure 2 shows local transaction 'book' from the example workflow. In this transaction, subtransaction 'book trip' is critical, 'send ackn.' is noncritical, i.e., a failure in sending a booking acknowledgment does not abort the entire booking transaction, whereas a failure in the booking itself does.

Local WIDE transactions also provide a notion of intra-transaction concurrency control, used to obtain a mechanism for regulating data access between concurrent subtransactions of a local transaction. Intra-transaction concurrency control is per-

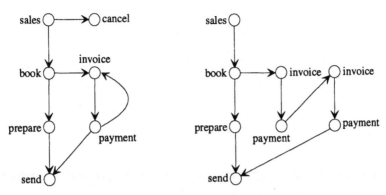

Figure 3: Global specification (left) and execution (right) graphs

formed on the granularity level of workflow data objects as defined in the WIDE information model [C96a], e.g. a workflow document or a folder containing multiple
documents.

4.2 Global transactions

The global transaction layer of the WIDE transaction model requires relaxed notions
of isolation and atomicity to cater for the needs of workflow processes above the
business transaction level. Rollback on the global transaction layer should have appli-
cation-specified semantics instead of the database-oriented semantics of the local
transaction model. In this relaxed transactional context, local transactions must be
black-box steps with respect to transactional semantics. For these reasons, we have
chosen a global transaction model that is heavily based on the saga transaction model
[Ga87], extended with a flexible mechanism for partial rollback.

A WIDE global transaction consists of a rooted directed graph of global transaction steps (local transactions). The graph is rooted as it can have only one starting
step. It can have an arbitrary number of ending steps, and it can contain cycles. The
graph represents the possible execution orders of the steps in the workflow process.
The global transaction of the example workflow is shown in Figure 3. It is easily obtained by projecting the process structure in Figure 1 onto the business transaction
structure.

Individual steps in the global transaction model conform to the ACID properties.
Isolation in the global transaction, however, is relaxed with respect to the ACID
model by making intermediate results in between steps visible to the context of the
global transaction (i.e. steps commit their results to the shared database).

As we can have or-splits and cycles in a global transaction specification, the specification graph and the execution graph of a global transaction are different in general:
paths that are not executed in an or-split are not in the execution graph and cycles are
replaced by the instantiation of the iteration. Figure 3 shows an execution graph of the
example specification graph. In this execution, the 'cancel' local transaction has not
been executed and the 'invoice-payment' iteration has been executed twice. To reason
about the dynamic properties of a global transaction in execution, the execution graph
is considered, not the specification graph.

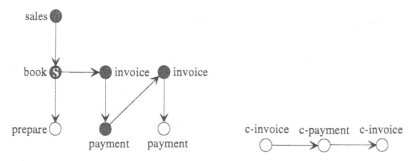

Figure 4: Partial execution graph (left) and compensating specification graph (right)

As in the saga model [Ga87], relaxed atomicity is obtained by using a compensation mechanism to provide rollback functionality. Rollback of global transactions is performed by executing compensating steps (local transactions) for the steps in the global transaction that have been committed (running, not-yet-committed steps can simply be aborted as they are atomic local transactions). Compensating steps are application-dependent and have to be specified by the application designer.

Complete rollback of a global transaction is often not desirable, as this may imply throwing away the results of a long workflow process. For this reason, we have introduced the notion of *savepoints* in global transactions. A savepoint is a step in a global transaction that is a safe place to begin forward recovery from. Unlike savepoints in the saga model [Ga87], global transaction savepoints do not require making checkpoints. Like the functionality of compensating steps, placement of savepoints in a global transaction is fully application-dependent.

An example of an execution requiring global rollback is shown in Figure 4. Here we see a partial execution of the specification graph in Figure 3. The grayed steps have been committed, two steps are being executed. Local transaction 'book' has been specified to be a savepoint. Now assume that running local transaction 'payment' raises an error that requires global rollback. Then all running local transactions are aborted (using the local transaction mechanism). Next, the execution graph needs to be compensated from the point where the error occurred until a savepoint is encountered (to the start of the graph if none is found). This means that compensation is performed by executing the dynamically constructed global transaction depicted in Figure 4. In this figure, the prefix 'c' for a local transaction indicates its compensating counterpart. Note that a very simple example is chosen for reasons of brevity. In general, compensating global transactions can have a complex structure.

5. A two-level transaction manager

The two-level transaction model outlined in the previous section is supported by a transaction manager architecture that is realized on top of the transaction service of a commercial DBMS. To provide portability, a high level of independence is required with respect to specific DBMSs. This implies making as few assumptions as possible about the transaction service of the underlying DBMS. To provide modularity in its construction and flexibility in its use, the overall transaction management architecture consists of independent global and local transaction management subarchitectures.

These two architectures are discussed on a functional level below. Their implementation in the context of the FORO WFMS is described in the next section.

5.1 Local transaction support

Local transaction support extends the basic 'flat' model of the underlying DBMS to the WIDE nested transaction model. As such, local transaction support can be seen as a transaction adapter as described in [Ba95]. A main difference between our situation and the situation described in [Ba95] is the fact that we deal with a closed DBMS architecture instead of a relatively open TP monitor architecture.

To be able to use the DBMS transaction management facilities in an effective and efficient way, each WIDE local transaction is mapped to a single DBMS transaction. A major issue in this mapping is the fact that possibly parallel subtransactions have to be mapped to a single sequential DBMS transaction. This results in database operations of multiple subtransactions being executed in an interleaved fashion.

Local transaction support handles abort of critical and non-critical subtransactions. If abort of a critical subtransaction leads to abort of the complete local transaction, this is easily performed by aborting the transaction on the DBMS level. If abort is limited to a subtransaction because a non-critical subtransaction is involved, partial rollback on the DBMS level is performed using the DBMS savepoint mechanism (distinguish these low-level DBMS savepoints from global transaction savepoints as discussed in Section 4.2). Interleaving of subtransactions as mentioned above complicates this situation, as it may lead to either the abortion of other subtransactions or the impossibility to abort a subtransaction.

Local transaction support provides simple mechanisms for intra-transaction isolation to allow the specification of parallel subtransactions operating on the same workflow data. The granularity of concurrency control is that of workflow objects, the scope is one local transaction.

5.2 Global transaction support

Global transaction support provides global transaction functionality as described in Section 4.2. Its main task is the construction of compensating global transactions when a global abort is requested, i.e. the construction of specification graphs containing compensating local transactions. Global transaction support uses local transactions in a black-box fashion, i.e. it sees global transaction steps the contents of which are completely irrelevant at the global transaction level. This ensures full independence from the underlying DBMS.

Global transaction support in WIDE bears some resemblance to the way sagas are supported in the Exotica project [Al96]. The main difference is the fact that Exotica is static (compile-time) in the construction of compensating structures, while WIDE is dynamic (enactment-time). WIDE allows cycles in process graphs, which requires analysis of the execution graph instead of the specification graph, implying dynamic compensation analysis. The introduction of global savepoints in the WIDE model provides additional flexibility in handling global aborts.

6. Implementation in the FORO architecture

In the WIDE project, the conceptual transaction management architecture outlined in the previous section is implemented on top of the Oracle DBMS and coupled to the FORO WFMS [Ce97] and an active rule management architecture [C96b]. The overall architecture is designed to be completely orthogonal with respect to transaction management, active rule management, workflow management, and data management. Distribution in the WIDE architecture is obtained through the use of a CORBA-compliant distributed object model [OM95], a client/server data management architecture, and a hierarchically distributed workflow server architecture [Ce97]. Independence from the underlying DBMS is obtained through an object/relation mapper, which maps object-oriented operations into relational primitives for the DBMS. The integration of extended transaction management with workflow and data management is shown in Figure 5. This figure clearly shows the independent subarchitectures.

6.1 Local transaction support

Local transaction management in WIDE is performed at a functional and a physical level to ensure maximum independence from the underlying DBMS. The functional level consists of a Local Transaction Manager (LTM) module and Local Transaction (LT) objects (see Figure 5). Each LT object is responsible for the functional management of a single local transaction. It manages the nested transaction structure and maps this to an abstract flat transaction model. The object is created dynamically by the LTM when the transaction starts. The LTM functions as a dispatcher of workflow events to the appropriate LT objects and of local transaction events to the workflow engine. Its main task is to keep both subarchitectures as independent as possible: through the use of the LTM, the workflow engine does not need to be aware of the existence of multiple LT objects. All transactional operations in the functional level are based on logical transaction identifiers. LTM and LT are fully independent from the underlying DBMS.

The physical level of local transaction support consists of the Local Transaction Interface (LTI) module. The LTI maps abstract flat transaction operations to the actual physical operations provided by the DBMS. Further, it maps logical transaction identifiers to physical transaction channels used for communication with the DBMS. With Oracle as database platform, the Oracle Call Interface (OCI) [Mc96] is used for this purpose [Gr97].

6.2 Global transaction support

The global transaction support (GTS) subarchitecture consists of a Global Transaction Manager (GTM) module and Global Transaction (GT) objects (see Figure 5). Each global transaction is managed by a GT object that is dynamically created at the start of the global transaction. The GT object is signaled by the workflow engine about events that may change the state of a global transaction, e.g. start and end of a global transaction step. The fact that a global transaction can have multiple active branches and iterative constructs implies that the process context of signaled events needs to be passed to the GT object as well. The main task of the GTM is to construct compensating global transactions as discussed in Section 5.2. The GTM is activated by the workflow engine when the engine raises a global rollback event. It uses the appropri-

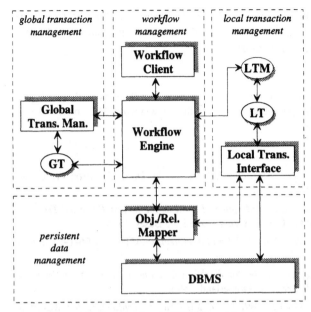

Figure 5: Integration in FORO architecture

ate GT object to obtain information on the current status of the global transaction, most notably the current execution graph and the compensating counterparts of executed steps. After the compensating global transaction has been constructed, it is passed to the GT object, which makes the information persistent.

Because a single GTM can serve multiple workflow engines at possibly remote sites, both GTM and GT objects are implemented as CORBA objects [OM95]. In this distributed objects approach, placement and clustering of processes can be handled transparently. The fact that the GTM routes all data access through the appropriate GT objects enables independent allocation of GTM processes and DBMS.

7. Conclusions

In designing a transaction model for workflow management, one is confronted with conflicting requirements. On the one hand, most transaction models are too heavily database-oriented to be non-restrictive to process requirements [Al96]. On the other hand, reliable data processing as obtained by the use of database-oriented transaction models is required in business applications. We have addressed this problem with a process-oriented upper layer providing flexibility towards process management and a database-oriented lower layer providing reliability towards data management. The 'interface-level' between the two layers can be chosen freely on an application-dependent basis.

Although the WIDE transaction support is presented in the context of workflow management, it is certainly not limited to this purpose. The transaction management architecture can easily be used in other environments where complex process support is important. The orthogonality of global and local transaction support allows the modification of one layer without affecting the other layer, or even omission of one layer if so required.

Most of the transaction support presented in this paper is at the time of writing this paper being implemented in the WIDE Version 1 system (except for the intra-transaction local concurrency control). After completion, it will undergo a thorough functional test at the end user sites in the WIDE consortium. In the WIDE Version 2 system, we plan to add support for distributed global transactions, handling of asynchronous global transaction aborts, a persistent local transaction mechanism and intra-transaction concurrency control for local transactions.

Acknowledgments

All members of the WIDE project are acknowledged for their contributions to the work presented in this paper. Special thanks go to Stefano Ceri of the Politecnico di Milano and Gabriel Sánchez of Sema Group at Madrid.

References

[Al96] G. Alonso et al.; *Advanced Transaction Models in Workflow Contexts*; Procs. Int. Conf. on Data Eng., 1996.

[Ba95] R. Barga, C. Pu; *A Practical and Modular Method to Implement Extended Transaction Models*; Procs. 21st Int. Conf. on Very Large Data Bases, 1995.

[C96a] F. Casati et al.; *WIDE: Workflow Model and Architecture*; CTIT TR 96-19; Univ. of Twente, 1996.

[C96b] F. Casati et al.; *Deriving Active Rules for Workflow Enactment*; Int. Conf. on Database and Expert System Appls.; Zürich, Switzerland, 1996.

[Ce97] S. Ceri, P. Grefen, G. Sánchez; *WIDE - A Distributed Architecture for Workflow Management*; Procs. 7th Int. Worksh. on Research Issues in Data Eng., 1997.

[Ch94] P.K. Chrysanthis, K. Ramamritham; *Synthesis of Extended Transaction Models using ACTA*; ACM Trans. on Database Systems, 19-3, 1994.

[Da91] U. Dayal, M. Hsu, R. Ladin; *A Transactional Model for Long-Running Activities*; Procs. 17th Int. Conf. on Very Large Databases, 1991.

[El92] A.K. Elmagarmid (Ed.); *Database Transaction Models for Advanced Applications*; Morgan Kaufmann; USA, 1992.

[Ga87] H. Garcia-Molina, K. Salem; *Sagas*; Procs. 1987 ACM SIGMOD Int. Conf. on Management of Data; USA, 1987.

[Gr97] P. Grefen, J. Vonk, E. Boertjes, P. Apers; *Two-Layer Transaction Management for Workflow Management Applications;* CTIT TR 97-07; Univ. of Twente, 1997.

[Lo93] D. Lomet (Ed.); *Special Issue on Workflow and Extended Transaction Systems*; IEEE Data Eng. Bull., June 1993.

[Mc96] D. McClanahan; *Oracle Developer's Guide*; Osborne McGraw-Hill, USA, 1996.

[OM95] Object Management Group; *The Common Object Request Broker: Architecture and Specification, Version 2.0*; Object Management Group, 1995.

[Re95] A. Reuter, F. Schwenkreis; *ConTracts - A Low-Level Mechanism for Building General-Purpose Workflow Management Systems*; IEEE Data Eng. Bull., 18-1, 1995.

Crash Recovery in an Open and Safe Nested Transaction Model

Sanjay Kumar Madria, School of Computer Sciences, University Sains Malaysia, Penang, Malaysia, skm@cs.usm.my. **S.N. Maheshwari**, Department of Computer Science and Engineering, IIT Delhi, India, snm@cse.iitd.ernet.in. **B.Chandra**, Department of Mathematics, IIT Delhi, India, bchandra@maths.iitd.ernet.in. **Bharat Bhargava**, Department of Computer Sciences, Purdue University, IN-47907, bb@cs.purdue.edu.

Abstract. In this paper, we present an open and safe nested transaction model and discuss the crash recovery issues. We introduce the notion of a recovery point subtransaction in a nested transaction tree. We introduce prewrite operations to increase concurrency. Our model is open and safe as prewrites allow early reads (before database writes on disk) without cascading aborts. The systems restart and buffer management operations are modeled as nested transactions to exploit possible concurrency during restart. Our model is useful in handling long-duration transactions.

1 Introduction

In a nested transaction model [Ma] a subtransaction may contain operations to be performed concurrently, or operations that may be aborted independent of their invoking transaction. Such operations are considered as subtransactions of the original transaction. This parent-child relationship defines a nested transaction tree and transactions are termed as nested transactions [Ma]. Failure of subtransactions may result in the invocation of alternate subtransactions that could replace the failed ones to accomplish the successful completion of the whole transaction. The model [Ma] uses only normal read and write operations. Each transaction has to acquire the respective lock before accessing a data object. A subtransaction's effect cannot be seen outside its parent's view. A child transaction has access to the data locked by its parent. When a transaction writes a data object, a new version of the object is created. This version of the object is stored in volatile memory. When the subtransaction commits, the updated versions of the object are passed to its parent. If the transaction aborts, the new version of the object are discarded. A parent commits only after all its children are terminated. When the top-level transaction commits, the current version of each object is saved on stable storage.

The intentions-list and undo-logging recovery algorithms given in ([FLMWa], [FLMWb], [FLW]) handle recovery from transaction aborts in the nested transaction environment by exploiting the commutative properties of the operations. The intentions-list algorithm works by maintaining a list of operations for each transaction. When a transaction commits, its list is appended to its parent; when it aborts, the intentions list is discarded. The undo-logging algorithm has been presented in [FLW]. When a transaction aborts, in contrast to intentions-list algorithm, all operations executed by its descendants on the object are undone from its current state and are subsequently removed from the log. In both intentions-list and undo-logging algorithms, an incomplete transaction is allowed to make uncommitted updates visible to those transactions that perform a commutative operation. This is restricted to the transactions at the same level of abstraction.

To exploit layer specific semantics at each level of operation nesting, Weikum presented a multi-level transaction model ([WI], [WBHM]). The model takes into account the commutative properties of the semantics of operations at each level of data abstraction to achieve a higher degree of concurrency. A subtransaction is allowed to release locks before the commit of higher level transactions. When a high level transaction aborts, its effect is undone by executing an inverse action which compensates the completed transaction. Recovery from system crashes is provided by executing undo actions at the upper levels and redo actions at the leaf level. Each level is provided with a level-specific recovery mechanism. This model has also been studied in the framework of object oriented databases in ([MRWBH], [RAA]).

In [Mb], a crash recovery technique similar to shadow page has been suggested in nested transaction environment based on undo/redo log methods. In terms of logging, both undo/redo logs are used. Mohan et al. ([MHLPS], [MOR]) has also discussed "write ahead logging" based crash recovery algorithm using conventional nested transaction model. This undo/redo type of recovery model exploits semantics of nested transactions.

In these nested transaction models ([Ma],[BBG],[WI]) if a transaction aborts, all its descendants effects are discarded either by restoring pre-images or by executing compensatory actions. Also, a committed subtransaction is made permanent only when its top-level transaction commits. The non-strict execution is provided by exploiting the commutative properties of the semantics of operations at the same level of data abstraction. The leaf level locks are released early only if the semantics of the operations is known and the corresponding compensatory actions defined. In many applications, the semantics of transactions may not be known and hence, it is difficult to provide non-strict executions. In real time situations, there are other classes of operations that cannot be compensated. These are the operations that have an irreversible external effect, such as handing over huge amounts of money at an automatic teller machine. Such operations have to be deferred until top-level commits, which restricts availability (i.e., increases response time).

We present a nested transaction recovery model in the environment of normal read and write operations to remove the deficiencies as stated above and to further improve availability. We assume that semantics of transactions at various levels of nesting are not known. There are two basic motivations behind our model. First, it is desirable that long-lived transactions should be able to release their locks before top-level transactions commit. Second, it may not be desirable or possible to undo or compensate the effects of one or more of the important committed descendants after the failure of a higher level transaction due to abort or a system crash.

2 Motivating Example and Overview of Our Nested Transaction Model

Consider the part of nested transaction tree for fund transfer operation from a group of accounts to another account. In the transaction tree, let T_s be a transaction on whose behalf T_{s1} invokes various subtransactions to collect (access) funds from different accounts. Once T_{s1} is committed, T_s invokes T_{s2} which finally credits the funds collected into another account. Suppose after a subtransaction T_w has withdrawn all the amount, T_s commits. If any transaction situated above T_s aborts then it is desirable for the transaction to complete successfully on transaction revival. This is because it is not possible to undo or correct the failed transaction's action by some compensatory actions. Another possibility is to delay the actual commit of T_s until its top-level transaction commits which restricts availability. For example, a balance transaction has to wait until the commit of the top-level transaction.

Our nested transaction model can handle the situations where a committed lower level subtransaction's effect cannot be undone or compensated in case of a higher level transaction's failure. A transaction's semantics may be such that beyond a certain point, it cannot rollback entirely or its effect should not be lost. We achieve this by introducing the concept of "recovery point subtransaction" of a top-level transaction in a nested transaction tree. It is essentially a subtransaction after whose commitment, its ancestors are not allowed to rollback. In case a superior transaction aborts or system fails after the commit of its recovery point subtransaction, the failed transaction has to complete on system revival. Such a transaction execution permits a recovery point subtransaction to reveal its result to other transactions at any level of nesting before its superior transactions commit. A recovery point subtransaction's effect is made durable before its top-level transaction's commit. This results in the relaxation of the isolation property [HR] of the transaction.

To avoid undo actions and the consequent cascading aborts and to increase the availability, we assume that each transaction issues a prewrite operation ([M],[MB]) before a write for the object it intends to write. Each prewrite operation contains the value that a user-visible transaction wants to write and precedes the associated final write. A prewrite operation actually does not change a data object's state but only announces the value the data object will have after the associated write is performed. The advantage of prewrite is that a read operation of another transaction can get the value before a data object's state is updated on stable storage and hence, results in increasing the availability of new data values. Prewrite operations are particularly helpful in the engineering design applications [KLMP], CAD [KKB], large software design projects [KS] etc where transactions are long.

A subtransaction that initiates different prewrite access subtransactions at leaf level for different data objects is defined to be the recovery point subtransaction. These announced prewrite values are made visible to other subtransactions after the commit of recovery point subtransaction. Our nested transaction tree consists of normal operations, system restart's analysis and redo operations, and buffer management operations. All these operations are specified in terms of nested transactions to exploit the concurrency further. However, in this paper we concentrate only on the recovery algorithm.

2.1 Requirements of Our Crash Recovery

System crash requires reviving of the database state of those data objects which do not contain their last committed values with respect to the execution upto the system failure. It also involves the problem of reviving the prewrite values (kept in prewrite-buffers) of the data objects which have been announced by the committed recovery point subtransaction before system failure. In order to identify such data objects, the dirty object table has to be revived. The dirty object table is used to keep track of those data objects whose finally written values are inconsistent with the stable database values. This table also keeps information about those data objects whose prewrite values, announced by the committed recovery point subtransactions, have not been subsequently written on the database before a system crash.

A system crash creates an additional problem of accomplishing the completion of those top-level transactions whose recovery point subtransactions have been committed before system crash. They have to reacquire the locks held by them at the time of failure before new transactions acquire such locks. To do this, the transaction and lock tables have to be revived. The transaction table keeps a list of all active transactions in the system at any time. The revived transaction table will recognize those active top-level transactions (and their active descendants) whose recovery point subtransactions have been committed before failure. The lock table contains the type of locks held by the transactions on different data objects at any time. The revived lock table will help in reacquiring the locks held by active top-level transactions and their descendants at the time of failure. New top-level transactions can be initiated as soon as the dirty object, transaction, and lock tables and consistent states of prewrite- and write-buffers of dirty data objects are re-established.

The dirty object table is required to be checkpointed periodically by transferring a copy of it to the stable storage during normal processing. The prewrite values and after-images are logged on stable storage during the execution of transactions to build the consistent dirty object table in case a system failure occurs before the next checkpoint is taken. A transaction is not permitted to complete its commit processing until the redo portion of that transaction has been written to stable storage. The redo portion of a log record provides information on how to redo changes performed by the committed transactions. The prewrite values are logged on the commit of the recovery point subtransaction. During system restart, the dirty object table is recovered with the help of most recent checkpointed copy of the dirty object table and is modified with the help of log stored after the last checkpoint.

The transaction and lock tables are checkpointed by transferring a copy of each of them to the stable storage periodically during normal processing. Whenever a subtransaction is made active or when any transaction acquires or releases a lock, the information is also logged to build a consistent state of these tables. However, such information may not be logged for read-only and prewrite access subtransactions as these transactions are to be discarded in case of a system failure. If a checkpoint is taken during restart recovery then the contents of transaction and lock tables will also be included in checkpoint. The entries corresponding to all other transactions except those which are to be restarted are removed from the transaction and lock tables. To do so, we need to find whether the stable storage contains the commit state of the recovery point subtransaction of each active top-level transaction. The commit states information is transferred to the stable storage during the commit of those subtransactions whose effects cannot be undone or lost in case of a failure.

The commit state information contains, besides associated variables, private data and other information, the identifier of the committed subtransaction as well as of its parent transaction. A commit state information of a subtransaction T_1 defines the state of its parent transaction T_2 at the time of commit of T_1. The commit state information helps in re-establishing the restart state of a top-level transaction in order to complete its remaining execution. No subtransaction whose effects cannot be undone in case of failure can be considered complete until its commit state information and all its data are safely recorded on stable storage. If the stable storage does not contain the commit state of the recovery point subtransaction of an active top-level transaction then all the entries corresponding to it and all its subtransactions are removed from the table. Otherwise, the top-level transaction has to complete its remaining execution on revival.

To revive the contents of write-buffer of a dirty data object, we copy the value of the data object from the stable-db to the write-buffer. However, the stable database version of the data object may not contain some or all the updates of committed transactions. It involves redoing those committed transactions after-images which have not been transferred to the stable-db before the failure. The redo of after-images will re-establish the state of the database in the write-buffer at the time of failure. Similarly, to recover the prewrite-buffers corresponding to dirty data objects, we redo the prewrite values logged on stable storage after the last checkpoint which have not subsequently been written. This re-establishes the states of prewrite-buffers of dirty data objects as they exists at the time of failure. The contents of prewrite- and write-buffers are recovered using the non-volatile storage version of the database, dirty object table and the log. There is at the most one prewrite log corresponding to a data object since once the associated write values are written, the corresponding prewrite log entry is removed from the stable storage as well as from the dirty object table.

To complete the active top-level transactions whose recovery point subtransactions have been committed before system failure, the scheduler has to decide the restart states to reinitiate such transactions. If the recovery point subtransaction's commit is the only commit record in the stable log then its active top-level transaction restarts from this commit state. Otherwise, the scheduler finds out the last commit state logged after the commit of recovery point subtransaction prior to system crash in order to restart the transaction from the last commit state. Once the restart state is established, the scheduler reacquires the type of locks the active top-level transaction and all its active descendants were holding at the time of failure. Once the locks are reacquired, the execution of a top-level transaction restarts from the restart state.

3 Nested Transaction Recovery Model and System Configuration

Our nested transaction database system model formally consists of transaction managers (TMs), recovery managers (RMs) and data managers (DMs). The data objects are modeled by the data managers (DMs). Each data manager keeps a copy of the data object in the secondary storage, called stable-db. The prewrite and write values of each object are kept in the respective buffers at the corresponding DMs. These are called prewrite- and write-buffers, respectively. Physically, only a subset of these DMs will have prewrite and write values of the data objects in the corresponding buffers. A read operation gets the value of the referenced data object from the prewrite-buffer (if any) otherwise it gets the value from the write-buffer. If the DM does not have a copy of the data object in the write-buffer, the read operation gets the value from the stable-db copy of the data object. The write-buffer's contents of a data object are transferred periodically to stable storage. Also, each DM maintains a log corresponding to the data object. Each DM also shares a common log.

Considering the above configuration, our model has four different transaction managers (TMs) for performing read (read-TM), write (write-TM) and system restart's analysis (analysis-TM) and redo (redo-TM) operations. Of these, read- and write-TMs are initiated by the user-visible transactions. Analysis-TMs and redo-TMs are invoked by an external agent such as the operating system. A hidden daemon transaction is associated with each write- and redo-TM transaction to co-ordinate the buffer management operations; i.e., the transfer of a data object's value to stable-db during the normal and system restart operations. To achieve the notion of spontaneity and transparency of buffer management operation, the daemon transaction wakes up and commits with respect to its associated transaction.

TMs are situated at one level below user-visible transactions. Next level of transaction hierarchy has six different recovery managers for co-ordinating read (read-RM), prewrite (prewrite-RM), write (write-RM), transfer (transfer-RM) and system restart's analysis (analysis-RM) and redo (redo-RM) operations. These RMs are made active by the corresponding TMs. During the span of daemon transaction, a daemon can initiate many transfer-RMs. This will help the transfer process to be made active during redo operations. These RMs initiate access subtransactions situated at the leaf level. Each read-, prewrite- and write-RM initiates read, prewrite and write access subtransactions, respectively. A read access reads the value either from the prewrite- or the write-buffer of the data object whereas a write subtransaction accesses only the write-buffer component of the data object. A transfer-RM initiates a transfer access (like read access but returns no value) to transfer the contents of write-buffer of the data object to the stable-db. The analysis-RM initiates copy, read, write and read-analysis access subtransactions. A copy transaction reinitializes the tables in the volatile memory whereas read accesses read the log entries after the last checkpoint record and write accesses update tables to bring their state as existing at the time of failure. A read-analysis subtransaction returns information about the objects dirty at the time of system failure. It also returns a list of active transactions (and their restart states) to be restarted on system restart. A redo-RM initiates copy, read, prewrite and write access subtransactions. Here, a copy transaction places the stable-db copy of the object in its write-buffer. A read access initiated by redo-RM reads a log entry corresponding to a data object logged after the last checkpoint record. A prewrite (write) access makes a prewrite-buffer's (write-buffer's) value consistent. The nested transaction tree structure is shown in Fig.1 (for normal operations) and Fig.2 (for system restart operations).

We assume that each user transaction knows its write-set before initiating a write-TM in order to write all the data objects. A write-TM first initiates a prewrite-RM which further initiates prewrite access subtransactions in order to announce prewrites for all the data objects contained in the write-set. This value for each data object is written in the prewrite-buffer allocated in the volatile memory. Modeling prewrites at leaf level provides user transparency to the prewrite operations.

We formally specify the prewrite-RM as the recovery point subtransaction of the top-level transaction. Once the prewrite-RM has committed, the prewrite values become visible outside its parent's view at any level of nesting without necessarily requiring the commit of all its superior transactions. After the prewrite-RM's commit, the write-TM initiates a write-RM to update all the data objects whose prewrite values have been announced before. The final updates are written in the write-buffers allocated in the volatile memory at each DM. With the invocation of each write-TM automaton, a daemon transaction is initiated automatically which further initiates transfer-RMs. A transfer-RM initiates a transfer access subtransaction to transfer the write-buffer's value to the stable-db. The write-buffer's contents can be transferred without the commit of the top-level transaction because write-values, once written, cannot be undone or lost.

To meet transaction and data recovery guarantees, the system maintains a log corresponding to each data object at the respective DM. The system maintains a common log (shared by all DMs) which keeps information about the progress of transactions and its associated data, their lock holding information etc. Our algorithm asserts that the log records representing changes to some data must already be on stable storage before the changed data is allowed to replace the previous version of that data on non-volatile storage. The log record corresponding to each data object is assigned a unique log sequence number (LSN) at the time the record is appended to the log. The LSNs are assigned in ascending order. Whenever a prewrite value is announced, the LSN of the prewrite log record to be written is placed in the LSN field of the prewrite value in the prewrite-buffer. Similarly, when the data object's value is updated in the write-buffer, the LSN of the log record is placed in the LSN field of the updated data object in the write-buffer. This value of LSN will be more than the value of LSN associated with the prewrite value of the same data object. The LSN with each prewrite and write value in the associated LSN field keeps track of the data object's state. Also, when a write-buffer's value is transferred to the stable-db, the after-image's LSN is placed in the LSN field of the stable-db. This tagging of LSN allows precise tracking of the states of the object with respect to logged updates of the data object for system restart purpose. Each write-buffer is also associated with a stableLSN field. The stableLSN field is the LSN of the stable-db copy of the object. A write-buffer's value is transferred to the stable storage if the stableLSN of the write-buffer is greater than the write-buffer's LSN. This will avoid accessing the stable-db's LSN to check whether the transfer of the object's value to the stable storage is required or not.

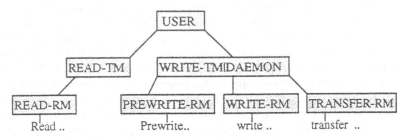

Fig. 1. Nested Transaction Tree for Normal Operations

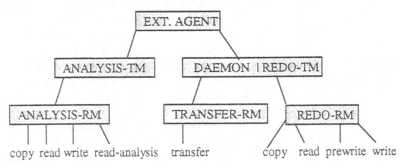

Fig. 2. Nested Transaction Tree for System Restart Operations

3.1 System Restart Operations

System restart has to perform two passes of the log: analysis pass and the redo pass. After the analysis pass of log records, the transaction table will contain the list of transactions active at the time of failure, the lock table will have lock entries corresponding to active transactions, and the dirty object table will contain the list of data objects which were dirty at the time of failure. The redo activity is performed in second pass in order to restore the dirty data objects to the values consistent with the information kept in the stable log.

The analysis pass is modeled as an analysis-TM which initiates an analysis-RM. The analysis-RM further initiates a copy access which reinitializes the lock, transaction and the dirty object tables by placing their stable storage copies in the buffer after the last checkpoint record. Next, it invokes read accesses to read the log records from the corresponding DMs after the last checkpoint record. The analysis-RM with the help of write accesses updates these tables as follows. If a log record corresponding to transaction table is encountered whose identity does not already appear in the table, then an entry is made in the table. The transaction table is modified to track the active transactions at the time of failure. Similarly, a log record corresponding to dirty object table is entered with the current LSN in the dirty object table if it is not already there. In a similar fashion, the lock table is also updated. Whenever a commit record is encountered, a list of commit records is made. This helps in establishing the restart states of the transactions to be re-executed. A read-analysis returns a set of min RecLSN (min LSN of log records from where redo recovery has to restart, called RedoLSN): one for each dirty data object with respect to write operations and a set of min RecLSNs (greater then the max RecLSNs of the corresponding data object) for each dirty data object with respect to prewrite operations. It also returns a list of active transactions and their restart states. The above information will be the output of an analysis-TM. A checkpoint is taken at the end of the analysis pass.

The redo activity is performed using the prewrite values and after-images logged on the stable storage. The redo activity can be skipped if there is no dirty data object. The transaction hierarchy for redo activity consists of a redo-TM for each object, a redo-RM at the next level and access subtransactions at the leaf level. Each redo-TM initiates a redo-RM which further triggers copy, read, prewrite and write access subtransactions to redo the operations present in the stable log corresponding to the data objects after the last checkpoint record. A copy transaction reinitializes the write-buffer by copying the contents of the stable-db to the write-buffer. Read operations read the write and prewrite log entries one by one after the last checkpoint. A prewrite access will reinitialize the prewrite-buffer with the help of prewrite log record value if the value of LSN associated with the prewrite log record is greater than LSNs of all the after-images logged on stable storage. A write access substitutes the value (after-image) of the data object read from the log in the allocated write-buffer of the data object if the data object's LSN in the write-buffer is found to be less than the log record's LSN. These log records will be those whose effects are not yet in the non-volatile storage version of the data object. The daemon transaction associated with the redo-TM initiates transfer-RMs to transfer the contents of the write-buffer to the stable-db. After the commit of redo-TM, a checkpoint is taken.

The analysis and redo activities in the form of nested transactions provide faster recovery since a redo-TM for each data object can be initiated in parallel. Also, if a system crash occurs during the execution of an analysis- or redo-TM, the corresponding new TM can be triggered on system restart. All the actions of previously committed subtransactions of the failed TM are not required to be discarded in case of a system failure. Similarly, in case of a normal transaction abort of any of these TMs, RMs, or their subtransactions, a corresponding new transaction can be initiated without discarding the effects of the aborted transaction and their descendants (if any). This helps in relaxing the atomicity property of such subtransactions since neither the actions of previously committed subtransactions are undone nor the failed TM or RM is retried until their completion on revival.

3.2 Buffer Management Operations

The transfer of a data object's value from the write-buffer to the stable storage is initiated with the help of a daemon transaction associated with each write-TM and redo-TM. The daemon transaction invokes a transfer-RM transfers the value of the data object from its write-buffer in the volatile memory to the stable-db on secondary storage. For the sake of uniformity, and in order to model correct atomicity requirements, transfer-RMs are modeled as transactions and placed as children of write- and redo-TMs in the transaction tree. One would like to permit transfer operations to take place with the intention that their invocations are not controlled by these TMs. They are intended to run spontaneously and transparently. Therefore, we have associated a daemon transaction with each write- and redo-TM so that these TMs do not have to be aware of the invocations of transfer-RMs. A daemon transaction commits with the commit of its associated TM. Therefore, it is possible to invoke many transfer-RMs during its span and these transfer-RMs may not have committed before their parent transaction's commit. However, we know that the sequence of transfer operations for a read-write data object from the write-buffer to stable-db is the same as transfer of last write. This enables the daemon transaction to initiate many transfer-RMs and to commit without the commit of all its transfer-RM subtransactions. The daemon transaction achieves the spontaneous and transparent behavior of the periodic transfer of the data from the volatile memory to stable storage and is failure-atomic.

The transfer of write-buffer to the stable-db takes place if the stableLSN of the write-buffer is greater than the LSN of the write-buffer. Once the transfer of the value along with LSN is completed, the corresponding log entry from the stable log is removed and the stableLSN of the write-buffer is set to the LSN of the write-buffer.

4 Data Structures

Some of the fields present in different types of log records are as follows.

LSN: This gives the address of the log record in the log address space. It is a monotonically increasing value. It is present in log records of the type "data". This may be included in other type of log records also but is not mandatory.

Transaction-id: Identifier of the transaction involved in the log record.

Object-id: Identifier of the object involved in the log record. It is present in log records of "data" and "lock" types.

Value: This is the redo data that describes the update that was performed. This also includes the committed prewrite value.

Active: Present in the log record written during the activation of a transaction.

Commit State: Present in the log record written during the commit of a subtransaction. This includes the private data, local variables, etc. of the committed subtransaction.

Lock: This is present in the log record which is logged when a subtransaction acquires or releases any lock. This includes information whether the lock is "retained" or "held" by the transaction.

Log records can be of the following types :

"Data" type of log records have the following structure:
<LSN, transaction-id, object-id, Prewrite or write value>.

"Transaction" type of log records are the form <transaction-id, status>. Note that status takes either the value "Active" or "Commit".

"Lock" type is of the form <transaction-id, lock type, object-id>.

We refer the whole log record structure by <log record> along with its type information.

<END-CHK-POINT> is a record to identify the end of a checkpointing activity.

4.1 Transaction and Lock Tables

To distinguish between different transactions and to know their status (active or not) in the system, we need to maintain the transaction-id and status of each transaction using a transaction table. Furthermore, to reflect the transaction tree, each transaction-id is such that it contains the identifier of its own as well as the identifier of its parent transaction. This type of transaction-id helps the scheduler in informing the commit or abort of a subtransaction to its parent. In addition, an abort request also contains identifiers of all its inferiors.

For the scheduler to know whether a transaction is active or not, it is sufficient that a transaction may keep only one status namely "active". Since the parent-child relationship of committed subtransactions are to be stored in the log separately by linking the log records of committed subtransactions to their parents, the transaction table need not keep information about committed subtransactions. A subtransaction enters the "active" status as soon as it is initiated and remains "active" until it commits or aborts. When a subtransaction commits, its entry is removed from the transaction table. After the commit of the recovery point subtransaction, the status of its upper level subtransactions remains "active" even in case of aborts at higher level because they have to complete their remaining execution on revival. On system revival, once such "active" top-level transactions are decided, all other "active" top-level transactions and their "active" descendants are removed from the table.

The lock table keeps the information about the locks held by all active transactions in the system at any time. Each entry of the table keeps information about the transaction-id, type of lock held and the object-id. When a transaction acquires a lock on a data object, an entry is made in the lock table. When a transaction commits or aborts, the corresponding transaction entry is removed from the table. A new entry is made about the transaction which inherits the lock from the committed or aborted transaction.

4.2 Dirty Data Object Table

Each entry in the dirty data object table consists of field's object-id, RecLSN (Recovery log sequence number) of prewrite and write operations. The value of RecLSN of write operation indicates in the log there may be updates which are, possibly, not yet in the non-volatile version of the data objects. The minimum of RecLSN values in the table gives the starting point for redo activity. All the write log records whose LSNs are greater than the min RecLSN are, possibly, required to be redone as these log records effects might not have been transferred to the stable-db. The min RecLSN of all prewrite operations which is greater than the max RecLSN of all write operations gives the starting point for redoing the prewrite operations. All the prewrite log records whose LSNs are greater than the min RecLSN are required to be redone as these are the prewrite log records whose associated write operations are not performed. Therefore, these prewrite log records need to be redone. Whenever the write values are announced, the corresponding prewrite entries from the dirty object table are removed. Similarly, whenever the data objects are written back to the non-volatile storage, the corresponding entries are removed from the table.

5 Checkpointing of Tables and Information Logging

The log information is written when an entry is made in the transaction table (except for read-only and prewrite access subtransactions) or when a transaction acquires or releases locks. Whenever a write-lock is acquired by a write access subtransaction, the information is recorded in the lock table as well as logged before the commit. Also, the log records written on behalf of subtransactions are always linked to the last record of their parents which reflects the transaction tree in the log.

The contents of the transaction, object and lock tables are included in the checkpoint that is taken during normal processing as well as during analysis and redo passes. During the restart recovery, these tables are initialized from the most recent checkpoint and are modified with the help of log records written after the last checkpoint. The entries corresponding to transactions, other than those whose recovery point subtransactions have been committed, are removed from the transaction table. Similarly, the locks holding information of the corresponding subtransactions are also removed from the lock table.

5.1 Commit Logging and Early Writing

Whenever a prewrite access subtransaction commits, its commit information and prewrite values are passed to its parent transaction which is the recovery point subtransaction. When the recovery point subtransaction decides to commit, its commit state information and its associated prewrite values are required to be logged. This commit state informs the scheduler that from this point of time, the committed subtransaction's effect cannot be lost under any circumstance. The commit of recovery point subtransaction occurs only after all its prewrite access subtransactions have been committed and therefore, the recovery point subtransaction's commit state has the effect of all its committed prewrite access descendants. Hence, the commit state of recovery point subtransaction is the first commit entry in the stable log. If system crashes immediately after the commit of its recovery point subtransaction, the scheduler will restart its active top-level transaction from the logged commit state onwards.

Whenever a write access subtransaction at leaf level decides to commit, its commit state and write value are logged. The commit information is passed to its parent transaction which helps in the termination of the parent transaction. The process of logging the commit state will continue till the top-level transaction commits. In case of failure, these logs will help in completing an active top-level transaction on revival. The process of transferring a transaction's commit state or prewrite or write values to the stable log is called transaction checkpointing (early writing). It is required in order to keep track of commit states, prewrite and write values of various subtransactions which helps in completing an active top-level transaction's re-execution. Transaction checkpointing will keep track of all logical committed states as well as prewrite and write values which cannot be lost. Read-only transactions require no early writing as they do not change a data object's state.

6. Conclusion

An open and safe nested transaction recovery model is presented in this paper. We have introduced the concept of a recovery point subtransaction in a nested transaction tree. The model provides increased concurrency and efficient failure tolerance. Our model will be particularly helpful in the management of long-duration transactions since the prewrite values are made visible before the commit of the transaction. The concurrency control algorithm is not discussed here to separate the issues involved in recovery. We have already worked out the details of concurrency control algorithm and its proof of correctness [M] based on I/O automaton model [LM]. We have also completed the proof of the recovery model based on I/O automaton model. These are available from the authors.

References

[BBG] Beeri, C., Bernstein, P.A. and Goodman, N., A Model for Concurrency in Nested Transaction System, Journal of the ACM, Vol. 36, No. 1, 1989.

[FLMWa] Fekete, A., Lynch, N., Merrit, M. and Whiel, W., Atomic Transactions, Morgan-Kaufmann, 1993.

[FLMWb] Fekete, A., Lynch, N., Merrit, M. and Weihl, W.E., Commutativity-Based Locking for Nested Transactions, Journal of System Sciences, Vol. 41, No. 1, pp. 65-156, Aug., 1990.

[FLW] Fekete, A., Lynch, N., and Weihl, W.E., A Serialization Graph Construction for Nested Transactions, In Proceedings of the 9th ACM Symposium on Principles of Database Systems, 1990.

[HR] Haerder, T. and Reuter, A., Principles of Transaction Oriented Database Recovery, ACM Computing Surveys, Vol. 15, No. 4, PP. 287-378, 1983.

[KKB] Korth, H.F., Kim, W., Bancilhon, On Long-Duration CAD Transactions, Information Science, 46, pp.73-107, Oct.1990.

[KLMP] Kim, W., Lorie, R., Mcnabb, D. and plouffe, W., A Transaction Mechanism for Engineering Design Databases, in Proceedings of the 10th International Conference on Very Large Databases, pp. 355-362, 1984.

[KS] Korth, H.F., and Speegle, G., Long Duration Transactions in Software Design Projects, in 6th International Conference on Data Engineering, IEEE, New York, pp.568 - 574, 1990

[LM] Lynch, N. and Merrit, M., Introduction to the Theory of Nested Transactions, Theoretical Computer Science, Vol. 62, pp. 123-185, 1988.

[M] Madria, S.K., Concurrency Control and Recovery Algorithms in Nested Transaction Environment and Their Proofs of Correctness, Ph.D. Thesis, Indian Institute of Technology, Delhi, India, 1995.

[Ma] Moss, J.E.B., Nested Transactions and Reliable Distributed Computing, Second Symposium on Relaibility in Distributed Software and Database Systems, pp.33-39, July,1982.

[Mb] Moss, J.E.B., Log-Based Recovery for Nested Transaction, COINS, Technical Report, University of Massachusetts at Amberest, pp. 87-98, Sept., 1987.

[MB] Madria, S.K., Bhargava, B., Improving Availability in Mobile Computing Using Prewrite Operations, CSD-TR-32, Department of Computer Sciences, Purdue University, IN, June,1997.

[MHLPS] Mohan, C., Haderle D., Landsay, B., Pirahesh, H. and Scwartz, P., Aries : A Transaction Recovery Method Supporting Fine-Granularity Locking and Partial Rollbacks using Write-Ahead Logging, ACM Transaction on Database Systems, Vol. 17, No. 1, March, 1992.

[MOR] Mohan, C. and Rothermel, K., Recovery Protocol for Nested Transaction Using Write-Ahead Logging, IBM Technical Disclosure Bulletin, Vol. 31, No. 4, Sept., 1988.

[MRWBH] Muth, P., Rakow, T.C., Weikum, G., Brossler, P., Hasse, C., Semantic Concurrency Control in Object-Oriented Database Systems, In proceedings of the 9th International Conference on Data Engineering, pp. 233-242, 1993.

[RAA] Resende, Rodolfo F., Agrawal, D., Abbadi, Amr El, Semantic Locking in Object Oriented Database Systems, *Technical Report TRCS 94-01*, University of California at Santa Barbara, 1994.

[WHBM] Weikum, G., Hasse, C., Brossler, P. and Muth, P., Multi-Level Recovery, In Proceedings of 9th ACM Symposium on Principles of Database Systems, Nashville, April, pp. 109-123, 1990.

[WT] Weikum, G., Principles and Realization Strategies of Multi-Level Transaction Management, ACM Transaction on Database System, Vol. 16, No. 1, March, 1991.

A Machine Learning Workbench in a DOOD Framework

Werner Winiwarter and Yahiko Kambayashi

Department of Information Science, Kyoto University,
Sakyo, Kyoto, 606-01 Japan

Abstract. In this paper we present a machine learning workbench, which we have developed by making use of deductive object-oriented database (DOOD) technology. It provides a comfortable environment for performing a large variety of machine learning tasks. By deriving full benefit of the available powerful logic and object-oriented programming language, we have implemented an easily extendable representative collection of machine learning algorithms. As realistic case study for the feasibility of the workbench we applied it to the automatic acquisition of linguistic knowledge within a natural language database interface.

1 Introduction

Despite the long tradition of *machine learning*, only recently its integration with database technology has become a focus of attention. This is mainly due to the emergence of the new area of *knowledge and data discovery (KDD)*, which confronts database research with new challenges [5].

However, so far most current KDD systems offer only isolated discovery features and cannot be embedded into larger applications. Therefore, we felt the need to develop a machine learning workbench that is integrated into a deductive object-oriented database system. With this, we give the user a convenient tool, which assists him in applying machine learning algorithms to his data collection stored in the same database. Besides this, we also support the easy modification of existing algorithms as well as the creation of new techniques.

We use as implementation platform the DOOD *ROCK & ROLL* [2], which enables the efficient implementation of a large variety of different machine learning algorithms. As basic collection we supply several algorithms for instance-based learning, prototype-based learning, decision trees, and rule-based learning.

To test the feasibility of the workbench we applied it to a case study, a *natural language database interface* for a production planning and control system. The learning task was to select the correct command class based on semantic features extracted from the user input. To show that the learned knowledge is language-independent, we trained the system on a large number of German sentences and used German, English, and Japanese sentences as test cases.

The rest of the paper is organized as follows. First, we briefly introduce the system architecture of the workbench before we discuss the implemented machine learning algorithms in more detail. Finally, we explain the set-up of the case study and present the achieved results from evaluation.

2 System Architecture

Machine learning (ML) algorithms construct a theory from training data that can then be used to classify unseen test data. All machine learning algorithms in Sect. 3 perform *supervised learning*, i.e. each training case has to be labeled with the correct class.

We use the system architecture shown in Fig. 1 for our machine learning workbench. The collection of *training data* is first *encoded*, which transforms the training cases into vectors of *feature* values. Features can be either pre-defined or derived from the data. The feature vectors are then used as input to the *training* module. It computes mappings from feature values to classes and stores them as *learned knowledge*.

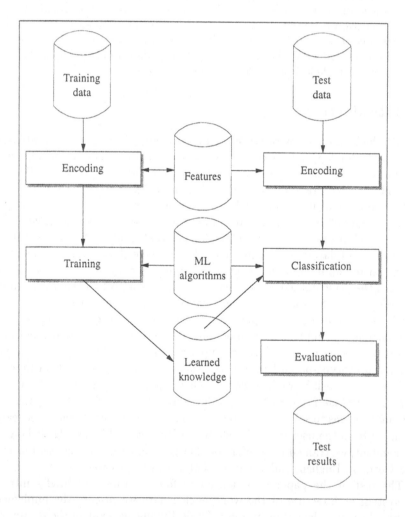

Fig. 1. System architecture

After the successful learning process, the theory can be tested based on a collection of *test data*. We transform the test data into feature vectors and *classify* them according to the learned classification rules. The classification module always produces not only one solution but a ranked list of classes.

The *evaluation* module compares the computed classifications with the correct classes and calculates *test results*. The two measures used for our case study in Sect. 4 are the *success rate*, i.e. the proportion of correctly classified test cases, and the proportion of cases for which the correct classification is among the first three computed classes (*top-3 rate*).

3 Machine Learning Algorithms

3.1 Instance-based Learning

Instance-based approaches represent the learned knowledge simply as collection of training cases or *instances*. A new case is then classified by finding the instance with the highest similarity and by using its class as prediction. Different instance-based algorithms vary in how they assess the similarity (or distance) between two instances. Two very commonly used methods are *IB1* [1] and *IB1-IG* [3]. Whereas IB1 applies the simple approach of treating all features as equally important, IB1-IG uses the *information gain* [7] of the features as weighting function.

We have developed the algorithm *BIN* for the special case of *binary features*, i.e. the value of all features is either 0 or 1. It calculates the distance between a new case X and a training case Y as sum of the distances between the values of the ith feature in X and Y:

$$\Delta(X,Y) = \sum_{i=1}^{n} w_i \cdot \delta(x_i, y_i) \quad \text{with} \quad \delta(x_i, y_i) = \begin{cases} 0 \text{ if } x_i = y_i \\ 1 \text{ otherwise} \end{cases} . \quad (1)$$

As weighting function w_i we use the following formula:

$$w_i = \frac{1}{c} \cdot \sum_{j=1}^{c} 1 - 4 \cdot p(D_i, j) \cdot [1 - p(D_i, j)] . \quad (2)$$

D_i indicates those instances that have value 1 for feature i and $p(D_i, j)$ denotes the proportion of instances in D_i that belong to class j to the number of cases for j. The term under the summation symbol calculates the selectivity of the feature i for a certain class j. It equals 1 if either all or none of the cases have value 1 for this feature. In other words, all instances for class j then either possess or do not possess this feature, which makes it a very discriminative characteristic. The other extreme is that $p(D_i, j)$ equals 50 %. In that case, this feature allows for no prediction of the class and the term becomes 0.

The weighting function assigns different weights to the individual features but it is insensitive concerning different feature values and classes. As an example of an asymmetric treatment of the values of binary features, we apply the following formula *BIN-S*. It replaces the calculation of the distance between X and Y by a similarity measure, which emphasizes the occurrence of the value 1 in both instances:

$$\text{SIM}(X, Y) = \sum_{i=1}^{n} w_i \cdot \sigma(x_i, y_i) - \Delta(x_i, y_i) \text{ with } \sigma(x_i, y_i) = \begin{cases} 1 \text{ if } x_i = 1 \wedge y_i = 1 \\ 0 \text{ otherwise} \end{cases}.$$

(3)

Finally, we also consider class-dependent weighting in that we introduce the following formula *BIN-SC*:

$$\text{SIM}(X, Y) = \sum_{i=1}^{n} p(D_i, C_Y) \cdot w_i \cdot \sigma(x_i, y_i) - \sum_{i=1}^{n} p(D_i, C_Y) \cdot w_i \cdot \delta_Y(x_i, y_i) - \\ \sum_{i=1}^{n} [1 - p(D_i, C_Y)] \cdot w_i \cdot \delta_X(x_i, y_i).$$

(4)

In this formula C_Y indicates the class of the training case Y. δ_Y and δ_X are calculated as follows:

$$\delta_Y(x_i, y_i) = \begin{cases} 1 \text{ if } x_i = 0 \wedge y_i = 1 \\ 0 \text{ otherwise} \end{cases} \quad ; \quad \delta_X(x_i, y_i) = \begin{cases} 1 \text{ if } x_i = 1 \wedge y_i = 0 \\ 0 \text{ otherwise} \end{cases}.$$

(5)

so that the second sum in (4) is rated higher for a larger number of occurrences of the ith feature for class C_Y whereas the third sum is rated lower. This means that if the training case Y contains a certain feature and the new case X does not, then we rate this difference the stronger the more often the feature occurs for class C_Y. On the other hand, for features appearing in the new case X but not in Y the opposite is true.

We have implemented all above-mentioned algorithms for binary features in ROCK & ROLL in that we store the instances as objects and assign to them the features as ordered lists sorted by the feature numbers. The calculation of the distance or similarity is then realized as method invocation on the feature list.

3.2 Prototype-based Learning

This can be regarded as subtype of instance-based learning. It differs from pure instance-based learning in that a *prototype* for each class is created. Those prototypes are then used for the comparison with new cases. A simple similarity function is *PRO-O*; it only considers features contained in the new case X for testing the similarity to a certain class C:

$$\text{SIM}(X, C) = \sum_{f \in X} p(D_f, C) \cdot w_f.$$

(6)

As weighting function w_f, we use again (2). A drawback of this formula is that it does not take account of important features for the class C that are missing in the new case X. To correct this shortcoming we extend (6) in that we rate occurring and missing features equally (*PRO-E*):

$$\text{SIM}(X,C) = \sum_{f \in X} p(D_f,C) \cdot w_f - \sum_{f \notin X} p(D_f,C) \cdot w_f \ . \qquad (7)$$

Finally, we refine this idea by giving more emphasis to features that are present in X in that we multiply the first sum in (7) by $|D_C|$, the number of cases for class C (*PRO-N*). The implementation in ROCK & ROLL is performed by creating an object for each prototype and by invoking the associated method for calculating the similarity to a new test case.

3.3 Decision Trees

Decision trees are among the most prominent representatives of *model-based* approaches. In contrast to instance-based algorithms, model-based techniques represent the learned knowledge in a theory language that is richer than the language used for the description of the training data. Such learning methods construct explicit generalizations of training cases resulting in a large reduction of the size of the stored knowledge base as well as the cost of testing new test cases.

The main difference between the various methods of constructing decision trees is the selection of the feature for splitting a node. Two main groups can be distinguished:

1. *static splitting:* selects the best feature for splitting always on the basis of the complete collection of instances,
2. *dynamic splitting:* re-evaluates the best feature for splitting for each node based on the current local set of instances.

Therefore, static splitting requires less computation effort because it performs the feature ranking only once for the construction process. However, it causes additional overhead to keep track of already used features and to eliminate features that provide no proper splitting of the set of instances. Besides that, dynamic splitting methods produce much more compact trees with fewer nodes, leaves, and levels. Thus, we result in a sharp reduction of the storage requirement as well as the number of comparisons during classification.

We have implemented decision trees for static (*BTF*) and dynamic splitting (*BTV*) by using the weighting function (2) as ranking scheme for the splitting criterion. In addition, we have also implemented the *IGTree* algorithm [4], which uses the information gain as static splitting criterion, and *C4.5* [8], which applies the information gain to dynamic splitting.

The decision trees are implemented in ROCK & ROLL by creating an object for each node and by linking the nodes according to the tree structure. The classification of a new case is then performed as top-down traversal of the tree starting from the root.

3.4 Rule-based Learning

Rule-based approaches represent the second large group of model-based techniques besides decision trees. They aim at deriving a set of rules from the instances of the training set. A *rule* is here defined as a conjunction of *literals*, which, if satisfied, assigns a class to a new test case. For the case of binary features, the literals correspond to *feature tests* with positive or negative *sign*. This means that they check whether a new case possesses a certain feature (for positive tests) or not (for negative tests).

The methods for deriving the rules originate from the field of *inductive logic programming* [6]. One of the most prominent algorithms for rule-based learning is *FOIL* [9], which learns for each class a set of rules by applying a separate-and-conquer strategy. The algorithm takes the instances for a certain class as *target relation*. It iteratively learns a rule and removes those instances from the target relation that are covered by the rule until no instances are left. A rule is grown by repeated specialization, adding literals until the rule does not cover any instances of other classes. In other words, the algorithm tries to find rules that possess some *positive bindings*, i.e. instances that belong to the target relation, but no *negative bindings* for instances of other classes. Therefore, the reason for adding a literal is to increase the relative proportion of positive bindings.

As weighting function for selecting the next literal, FOIL uses again the information gain. We have implemented FOIL, and in addition, we also use the algorithm *BR* with a class-dependent weighting function derived from (2). The test of rules is implemented as deductive method. The invocation of the method is a query with the feature list of the new case as parameter. The test returns those rules that are satisfied by the new case, resulting in corresponding assignments of classes to the new case.

4 Case Study: Natural Language Interface

As case study for investigating the effectiveness of the implemented machine learning algorithms we used the area of natural language interfaces. One of the main obstacles to their efficient use is the often required high amount of manual knowledge engineering. This time-consuming and tedious process is often referred to as "knowledge acquisition bottleneck". It may require extensive effort by experts highly experienced in linguistics as well as in the domain and the task.

Therefore, natural language interfaces are a domain that is very well suited for the application of machine learning algorithms to automate the acquisition process of linguistic knowledge. We have developed for that purpose the interface architecture displayed in Fig. 2. It represents a multilingual database interface for the languages English, German, and Japanese. First, the *language* of the user input is *detected* and the input is transferred to the corresponding language-specific *morphological and lexical analyzer*.

Morphological and lexical analysis performs the *tokenization* of the input, i.e. the segmentation into individual words or tokens. The input is then transformed into a *deep form list (DFL)*, which indicates for each token its surface

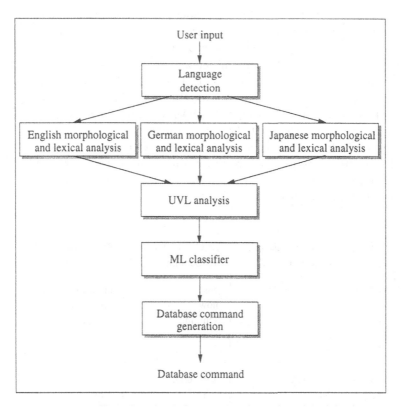

Fig. 2. Process model of natural language interface

form, category, and semantic deep form. As in database interfaces unknown values contained in the input possess particular importance for the meaning of a command, we treat them separately in the *unknown value list (UVL) analyzer*. This module checks the data type of unknown values and looks them up in the database whether they represent identifiers of existing entities. If this is the case, the entity type is indicated in the resulting UVL, otherwise the data type is used. DFL and UVL form the input to the *ML classifier* module realized by means of our machine learning workbench. The resulting classifications are then used to *generate* the appropriate *database commands*.

As application domain for the interface we have chosen a production planning and control system (PPC). During previous research we developed a German natural language interface based on 1000 example sentences that we mapped to 100 commands (10 for each command) [10]. The mapping was performed by elaborate semantic analysis; the development of the underlying rule base took several man-months.

Therefore, we were eager to see if we could replace this extensive effort by a machine learning component that learns the same linguistic knowledge automatically. We divided the 1000 sentences into 900 training cases and 100 test cases. Furthermore, we collected 100 Japanese and 100 English additional test sentences to see if the learned knowledge really operates at a semantic level that abstracts from language-specific phenomena.

For the encoding of the training set we only make use of the semantic deep forms contained in the DFL. We use as deep forms English concepts and map them to binary features that indicate whether a certain deep form is contained in the DFL or not. For the elements of the UVL we apply a more detailed encoding, which maps the number and the type to binary features. Figure 3 shows an example of the features derived from an English, German, and Japanese sentence for the update of the purchase price for a material. For the complete collection of 900 training sentences we resulted in the large number of 316 features, 289 for the DFL and 27 for the UVL.

Input	New purchase price of St 37 H is 1,7.	St 37 H kostet nun 1.7 Schilling	St37Hの購入代金を 1, 7に変えなさい。
DFL	new purchase price of be	cost now schilling	purchase price change
UVL	1 material 1 real	1 material 1 real	1 material 1 real

Fig. 3. Example of feature encoding

Therefore, the learning task represents a realistic real-life application, which differs from many toy problems often used in machine learning research in that it consists of a large number of training cases, features, and classes. Furthermore, many of the classes are very similar and even for human experts very difficult to distinguish.

As first experiment we compared the success rate and top-3 rate for instance-based and prototype-based algorithms. As can be seen from the results in Table 1, the three BIN algorithms produce results of comparable quality and clearly outperform IB1 and IB1-IG. Concerning the prototype-based techniques, we achieved the best results for PRO-N. Despite the much more condensed representation of the learned knowledge, the output for PRO-N is again of the same quality as the results for the BIN algorithms.

The comparison between the results for the individual languages shows that there is no advantage for the German test sentences. On the contrary the test results for German are inferior to that for English or Japanese. This may be partly due to a greater deviation of the German expressions and phrases used in the test set from the ones used in the training set. Besides this, the restriction

Table 1. Test results for instance-based and prototype-based learning

	GERMAN		ENGLISH		JAPANESE	
	Success	Top-3	Success	Top-3	Success	Top-3
IB1	82 %	94 %	98 %	99 %	94 %	98 %
IB1-IG	84 %	98 %	97 %	100 %	90 %	99 %
BIN	90 %	99 %	100 %	100 %	98 %	99 %
BIN-S	92 %	99 %	100 %	100 %	98 %	100 %
BIN-SC	94 %	100 %	99 %	100 %	99 %	100 %
PRO-O	86 %	99 %	96 %	100 %	95 %	100 %
PRO-E	89 %	99 %	88 %	99 %	87 %	99 %
PRO-N	95 %	100 %	97 %	100 %	97 %	100 %

of extracted features from the test set to those learned from the training set certainly performs an important filtering function because it removes language-specific syntactic particles that do not contribute to the meaning of the input.

The second part of the evaluation was the comparison of the algorithms for decision trees and rule-based learning. The test results in Table 2 indicate that trees with dynamic splitting are superior to those with static splitting and that C4.5 and BTV produce results of similar quality. Regarding rule-based techniques, BR outperforms FOIL with results similar to that for decision trees with dynamic splitting.

Table 2. Test results for decision trees and rule-based learning

	GERMAN		ENGLISH		JAPANESE	
	Success	Top-3	Success	Top-3	Success	Top-3
IGTree	80 %	94 %	92 %	100 %	86 %	97 %
BTF	86 %	97 %	95 %	100 %	90 %	96 %
C4.5	94 %	100 %	94 %	100 %	89 %	100 %
BTV	93 %	99 %	94 %	99 %	91 %	99 %
FOIL	85 %	97 %	92 %	97 %	88 %	96 %
BR	94 %	97 %	95 %	97 %	91 %	95 %

If we take a final look at Table 1 and Table 2, we can see that independent from the applied machine learning paradigm the achieved results reached for all four groups satisfactory quality. By considering the best representatives BIN-SC, PRO-N, C4.5, and BR, we obtained an average success rate for all three languages of 94.8 % and a top-3 rate of 99.1 %. This result is surprisingly high if one considers the complexity of the task at hand. In any case, we could show that machine learning represents a sound alternative to manual knowledge acquisition for the application in natural language interfaces.

5 Conclusion

In this paper we have presented a machine learning workbench, which aims at providing a new type of integrated environment for machine learning tasks. We have implemented a representative selection of machine learning algorithms by making use of deductive object-oriented database functionality.

The extensive case study for a natural language interface showed the feasibility of the approach in that linguistic knowledge is learned the acquisition of which normally takes a large effort of human experts. This case study shows that the workbench is a very useful tool for carrying out comparative studies of the performance of different machine learning algorithms for specific learning tasks.

Future work will concentrate on the extension of the provided machine learning algorithms, including unsupervised methods as well as connectionist and evolutionary techniques. Besides this, we also want to implement incremental learning techniques, which continue the learning process during the test phase. Finally, we intend to put more emphasis on the evaluation module in that we include statistical tests for the significance of the performance differences between different machine learning algorithms. We believe that our machine learning workbench represents a first promising step towards the important integration of the two research fields of database systems and machine learning.

References

1. Aha, D. W., Kibler, D., Albert, M.: Instance-based learning algorithms. Machine Learning **7** (1991) 37–66
2. Barja, M. L. et al.: An effective deductive object-oriented database through language integration. Proc. of the Intl. Conf. on Very Large Data Bases (1994) 463–474
3. Daelemans, W., van den Bosch, A.: Generalisation performance of backpropagation learning on a syllabification task. Drossaers, M., Nijholt, A. (eds): TWLT3: Connectionism and Natural Language Processing. Twente University Press, Enschede (1992) 27–37
4. Daelemans, W., van den Bosch, A., Weijters, T.: IGTree: Using trees for compression and classification in lazy learning algorithms. Artificial Intelligence Review (to appear)
5. Imielinski, T., Mannila, H.: A database perspective on knowledge discovery. Communications of the ACM **39:11** (1996) 58–64
6. Muggleton, S. (ed): Inductive Logic Programming. Academic Press, London (1992)
7. Quinlan, J. R.: Induction of decision trees. Machine Learning **1** (1986) 81–206
8. Quinlan, J. R.: C4.5: Programs for Machine Learning. Morgan Kaufmann, San Mateo, California (1993)
9. Quinlan, J. R., Cameron-Jones, R. M.: Induction of logic programs: FOIL and related systems. New Generation Computing **13** (1995) 287–312
10. Winiwarter, W.: The Integrated Deductive Approach to Natural Language Interfaces. Ph.D. thesis, University of Vienna (1994)

Examining Complex Objects
for Type Scheme Discovery

Takao MIURA and Isamu SHIOYA

SANNO College, Kamikasuya 1573, Isehara, Kanagawa 259-11, JAPAN
E-mail: { miura,shioya }@sanno.ac.jp

Abstract. We propose a heuristic paradigm to *mine* schemes for complex objects semi-automatically by examining current schemes and the
instances. Based on an *instance-based* data model, we will look for scheme
alternatives where each instance is classified into at most k (least general) intentions with respect to some semantic ordering.

1 Motivation

Database design is the process to clarify, analyze and define what users mean. Since a
database design phase is inherently non-deterministic, interactive processing should be
involved for sophisticated decision supports. Until now we don't establish full methodologies for design and redesign.

The process assumes that the world of interests can be classified *in advance* into a
form of scheme, and that data can be manipulated *independent of* problem-domains. By
utilizing them, the world of interests is described and manipulated by *sequences of primitive* features provided by data models. This framework is called *database paradigm*[11].
In this paradigm each instance is considered as a fact, and a scheme as a knowledge
description of the instances. It is the paradigm by which both users and the systems
can validate what users intend and how to optimize the way to obtain desired information. The foundation of suitable and efficient processing to massive data is due to
the paradigm.

However the paradigm has severe deficiencies, that is, there is no general way to
follow changes dynamically that arise very often during life-cycle of databases. Then
we have to determine a database scheme first and *then* populate it. This leads to the
fact that scheme description might not model *current* world of interest correctly nor
appropriately.

Traditionally the research topic as *scheme evolution* means how to obtain *flexible*
mechanism of databases at re-design in a top-down manner. Clearly we need more
substantial technologies that capture feed-back from database states to obtain database
schemes suitable for *current* databases.

When analyzing the description, we might generate new types. Such knowledge
discovery process considered databases as description of the meaning is called *knowledge
discovery in databases* (KDD). This topic is now focused by many researchers[2, 4, 5,
7, 17, 18]. KDD processes could be captured as both general framework for meta-
model manipulation[6] and the intersection between database design and knowledge
acquisition[9]. Then very ambitious paradigm might be established and applied to wide
range of applications.

We have proposed simplification and mining algorithms so far to obtain type
schemes[13, 14] and predicate schemes[16] based on an instance-based data model *AIS*.

In this investigation, we develop our theory for complex values (i.e., data structure instances) based on our general paradigm for scheme discovery[15], and this work complements our previous works stressing on discovery of schemes for complex values and complex objects. We will explore heuristic methods in such a way that each complex value is classified into at most k (least general) intentions with respect to some semantic ordering. Semantic orders are introduced and extended for scheme discovery of complex objects.

Some aspects of *specific* constructors such as recordof and setof have been analyzed in *nested relational model*[1], *Object-Oriented model*[8] and semantic data models[3]. However, to our best knowledge, there has been no approach proposed so far for discovery of complex objects schemes of *general* constructors.

Section 2 contains definitions of several notions used in this work. In section 3 we show our scenario of mining schemes while in section 4 we introduce semantic orders. Section 5 contains discovery of schemes for complex objects based on the orders.

2   An Instance-based Data Model

2.1   Primitive Definitions

This work discuss our investigation mainly based on *AIS* data model since the lessons described have wider applicability [10]. An *entity* is a surrogate of an object in the real world and we denote a set of entities by $\mathcal{E}$. An *entity type* is an intentional concept to capture common properties among objects, and we denote a set of entity types by $\mathcal{T}$ and a set of entities of a type $t \in \mathcal{T}$ by $\Gamma(t)$. One entity may have more than one types. We assume a special type @E which represents all the entities in a database instance.

An *association* is a representation of a relationship among objects, so one relationship corresponds to one association. Common properties among associations are captured as *predicates*. Each association of a predicate p among entities $e_1, .., e_n$ is denoted by $p(e_1...e_n)$. We assume a predicate has a set of entity types called *defined-types*. If p has $t_1, .., t_n$ as defined types, then $e_i \in \Gamma(t_i)$. The value n is called an *arity* of p. We denote a set of associations of p by $\Gamma(p)$, so $\Gamma(p) \subseteq \Gamma(t_1) \times ... \times \Gamma(t_n)$. Sometimes p is also denoted by p^n.

An *attribute* is a predicate $f(t_1 t_2)$ that has functional correspondence between two types, t_1 and t_2. The predicate f can be seen as a function $t_1 \rightarrow t_2$, and we call t_2 is an attribute of t_1.

A complex object consists of pairs of entity and data structure values (called *complex value*). The latter is a kind of implementation of information structure for efficient computer processing. Complex values are assumed to obey structural constraints called *complex types* as defined later. For a complex type d, we denote a set of complex values as $\Gamma(d)$. In an interpretation, correspondence of entities and complex values are explicitly related (called *type structure*) by $\lambda_d(e) = v$ where e is an entity of a type t, v a complex value that obeys a complex type d. A pair $e : v$ is called a *complex object*[11]. Then λ_d can be seen as a predicate over t, d.

EXAMPLE 1 Let us consider *Project Activity* database as our our running example. Here we assume several entity types: Project, Authority, Committee, LeadersCommittee, OperatorGroup, ExpertList, Checker, CommitteeMember, Worker, QualifiedPerson, Leader, Chair, Person and Experience. Their meanings are self-explanatory. Each type may have some of attributes such as Project carrying Goal and Content, Committee having Chair and Name, OperatorGroup having Leader. There are 4 predicates evaluate (Project, Autority), supervise (Project, Committee), work (Project, Operator Group) and nominate (Project, ExpertList) where the meanings are again self-explanatory. In this work, we don't utilize predicates any more but readers may understand the roles of the types through these predicates.

Figure 1 contains *AIS* diagram that represents part of our database scheme: circles means types, diamonds mean predicates and edges mean predicate definitions. By arrows we mean attribute relationships. Inclusion of circles says about ISA relationship as described later. By overlapping circles, sometimes we put a stress on a fact that the entity sets of the types could share some entities. □

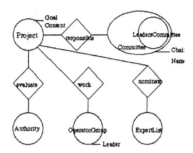

Fig.1. Project Activity Database Diagram

Each entity holds its own types and such model is called an *instance-based* model. Let $\tau(e)$ be the set of types that e has: $\tau(e) = \{t \in T \mid e \in \Gamma(t)\}$ that is called a *type scheme* of e. Remember an entity e of a type t may have other types. Every $\tau(e)$ is assumed to be finite. All the $\tau(e)$ represent typing information of the database and we call them a type scheme of a database.

When we have large sets of entities and huge number of type occurrences of $\tau(e)$, it seems hard to utilize scheme knowledge efficiently since we have to manage $\tau(e)$ individually. We believe knowledge control over types should be introduced and a unified mechanism for the simplification is indispensable.

One of the typical mechanisms to control types is *generalization* or ISA. For types t_1 and t_2, t_2 is the generalization of t_1 (or t_1 ISA t_2) if $\Gamma(t_1) \subseteq \Gamma(t_2)$. Applying generalization many times, we have the reflexive and transitive closure called ISA hierarchy. The hierarchy assures that we can infer ISA correctly: by t_1 ISA t_2 and t_2 ISA t_3 we can imply t_1 ISA t_3. Given two types t_1 and t_2, t_2 is called a *direct* generalization of t_1 if t_1 ISA t_2 and if there exists no t_3 (in a current database scheme) such that t_1 ISA t_3 and t_3 ISA t_2. Note ISA is really semi-order.

If an entity e has a type t and if t ISA t', e must have t', in other words, if $t \in \tau(e)$ and t ISA t' hold, $t' \in \tau(e)$ must be true. This is the condition that each type scheme keeps correct, called *type consistency* of databases. We always assume the consistency everywhere in databases.

EXAMPLE 2 In example 1, we have many ISA constraints. As in figure 1 , we have LeadersCommittee ISA Committee which means every committee consisting of the leaders must be an official committee. Here are other ISA constraints that are assumed for our discussion:

Leader ISA QualifiedPerson   Leader ISA CommitteeMember
Chair ISA CommitteeMember   QualifiedPerson ISA Worker
Checker ISA Worker   Worker ISA Person
CommitteeMember ISA Person

By inferring these ISA, we can have **Leader ISA Person** for instance. Figure 2 contains **ISA** hierarchies which describe the situation above. Here are **Person** entities with the complex type schemes as below (**Person** does not appear).

entity	types
Beethoven	Leader,CommitteeMember, QualifiedPerson, Worker
Brahms	Leader,CommitteeMember, QualifiedPerson,Worker
Bruckner	Worker, QualifiedPerson, CommitteeMember
Chopin	Worker
Liszt	Worker
Puccini	Leader,CommitteeMember, QualifiedPerson,Worker
Schumann	Worker
Schubert	Worker
Sibelius	CommitteeMember
Verdi	Leader,CommitteeMember, QualifiedPerson,Worker
Wagner	Checker,CommitteeMember, QualifiedPerson,Worker

□

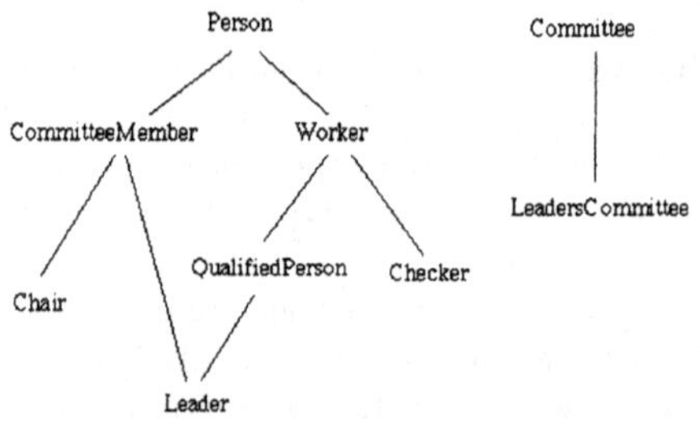

Fig.2. ISA Hierarchies in Project Activity

2.2   Complex Types and Type Schemes

Let $\mathcal{D}_U$ and $\mathcal{V}_U$ be sets of all the possible data structures and data structure instances respectively. When we say *data structures*, we mean a finite set of *constructors* $\mathcal{C}$ by which we define the exact structures. In the following, we will define complex types with respect to $\mathcal{C}$, denoted by $\mathcal{D}(\mathcal{C})$ or just $\mathcal{D}$. A constructor η for a data structure can be seen as a map from $\mathcal{D}_U^n$ to $\mathcal{D}_U$ where n is called an *arity* of η. Typical examples are setof, recordof(n) and arrayof(n) where the semantics are self-explanatory. We don't consider an *id* which maps a type to itself as a constructor in $\mathcal{C}$ but as special. For $\eta, \eta_1, .., \eta_n \in \mathcal{C}$ where $\eta : \mathcal{D}_U^n \to \mathcal{D}_U$ and $\eta_i : \mathcal{D}_U^{k_i} \to \mathcal{D}_U, i = 1, .., n$, the composition of the constructors $\eta(\eta_1 ... \eta_n)$ can be seen as a new constructor from $\mathcal{D}_U^{k_1 + .. + k_n}$ to $\mathcal{D}_U$, and the composition is called a *construction*.

Whenever we say a data structure instance, we mean a *data structuring operator* ζ over $\mathcal{V}_U$ to describe the semantics of the data structure. Typical examples are a collection of *records* consisting of elements of the form $[v_1, .., v_n]$ where n is common, a collection of *arrays* containing elements of the form $(v_1, .., v_n)$ where n is a common value, a collection of *sets* of which elements are of the form $\{v_1, .., v_n\}$ and $n \geq 0$ depends on each element, and boolean combinators such as $\cap, \cup$ of complex value sets. An *identity* is a special operator in $\mathcal{C}'$ which maps a value to itself. Note the constructors are maps over $\mathcal{D}_U$ but not over complex values $\mathcal{V}_U$.

Given a finite set of constructors $\mathcal{C} = \{\eta_1, ..., \eta_k\}$ over $\mathcal{D}_U$, a set of *complex types* $\mathcal{D}(\mathcal{C})$ is defined formally as follows:

(1) Every type $t \in \mathcal{T}$ is in $\mathcal{D}(\mathcal{C})$.
(2) For $\eta \in \mathcal{C}$ of an arity n and $t_1, .., t_n \in \mathcal{D}(\mathcal{C})$, $\eta(t_1...t_n)$ is in $\mathcal{D}(\mathcal{C})$.
(3) For every η_i, η_j, if $\eta_i(t_1...t_{n_i}) = \eta_i(s_1...s_{n_j})$, then $i = j$ and $t_k = s_k$ for $k = 1, .., n$. That is, every complex type has a unique construction.

To separate $\mathcal{T}$ from $\mathcal{D}(\mathcal{C})$, types $t \in \mathcal{T}$ are called *primitive* types while types in (1) and (2) are called *complex* types. By (3) we mean every construction has *free interpretation* in a sense that we explore just syntactical properties whatever constructors are interpreted.

In a similar manner we assume *data structuring operators* $\mathcal{C}' = \{\zeta_1, ..., \zeta_n\}$ where ζ_j has an arity n_j. A set of complex values by $\mathcal{C}'$, denoted by $\mathcal{V}(\mathcal{C}')$, is defined as follows:

(1) $\mathcal{E} \subseteq \mathcal{V}(\mathcal{C}')$.
(2) For $\zeta \in \mathcal{C}'$ of arity n and for $V_i \subseteq \mathcal{V}(\mathcal{C}')$ where $i = 1, .., n$, $\zeta(V_1...V_n) \subseteq \mathcal{V}(\mathcal{C}')$.
(3) For all constructions ζ_i, ζ_j containing no *identity*, there exists no common value in $\zeta_i(V_1...V_{n_i})$ and $\zeta_j(U_1...U_{n_j})$. That is, every complex value has a unique construction.

Entities in (1) are sometimes called *primitive* values while ones of (1) and (2) are called *complex* values. In the (2) above, $v \in \zeta(V_1...V_n)$ must be constructed from $v_i \in V_i$ or $v_i \subseteq V_i, i = 1, .., n$. Then we note v could be expressed as $v(v_1, .., v_n)$ in a sense that v is not a function but just a ζ-*vehicle* for the description of components. Because of (3), this expression is uniquely determined. We assume that v_i appears in every vehicle $v(v_1..v_n)$ where $i = 1, .., n$. For example, a set value $v \in 2^V$ consisting of $a_1, .., a_m \in V$, $v_1 = \{a_1, .., a_m\}$, is expressed as $v(v_1)$. Another example is a value v where $v \in V_1 \cap V_2$. Then v is described by v itself. The *identity*-vehicle is called a *trivial* vehicle. Note the number of vehicles corresponds to the number of operators.

Let us define the interpretation of $\mathcal{D}(\mathcal{C})$. Given constructors $\mathcal{C}$ and operators $\mathcal{C}'$, we assume $\zeta \in \mathcal{C}'$ for each $\eta \in \mathcal{C}$ where ζ is called the semantics of η. Then we define the *interpretation* $\Gamma(t)$ for $t \in \mathcal{D}(\mathcal{C})$:

(1) for a primitive type $t \in \mathcal{D}(\mathcal{C})$, $\Gamma(t)$ is the interpretation of *AIS*.
(2) for a complex type $t = \eta(t_1...t_n)$, $\Gamma(t)$ is defined as $\zeta(\Gamma(t_1), .., \Gamma(t_n))$.

By means of a notions of ζ-vehicle, $v \in \Gamma(\eta(t_1...t_n))$ is described as $v(v_1, .., v_n)$ where $v_i \in \Gamma(t_i)$ or $v_i \subseteq \Gamma(t_i), i = 1, .., n$.

In this work, we will discuss several constructors. For instance, a constructor `setof` maps t to a set type of t where the interpretation of `setof`(t) is all the possible subsets of $\Gamma(t)$. A `listof` is defined in a similar manner. A constructor `recordof(2)` maps t_1, t_2 to a record type consisting of values in $\Gamma(t_1) \times \Gamma(t_2)$ where the interpretation is all the possible pairs of $\Gamma(t_1)$ and $\Gamma(t_2)$.

constructor	vehicle	semantics
unionof(t_1, t_2)	*trivial*	$\Gamma(t_1) \cup \Gamma(t_2)$
intersectionof(t_1, t_2)	*trivial*	$\Gamma(t_1) \cap \Gamma(t_2)$
differenceof(t_1, t_2)	*trivial*	$\Gamma(t_1) - \Gamma(t_2)$
setof(t)	$\{v_1, .., v_n\}$	$2^{\Gamma(t)}$
listof(t)	$\langle v_1, .., v_n \rangle$	all the lists over $\Gamma(t)$
arrayof(n)(t)	$(v_1, .., v_n)$	$\Gamma(t) \times .... \times \Gamma(t)$ (n times)
recordof(n)($t_1, .., t_n$)	$[v_1, ..., v_n]$	$\Gamma(t_1) \times .... \times \Gamma(t_n)$
treeof(n)($t, t_1, .., t_n$)	$[v; v_1, ..., v_n]$	$\Gamma(t) \times \Gamma(\text{listof}(t_1)) \times .... \times \Gamma(\text{listof}(t_n))$ unique on $\Gamma(t)$

A set of constructors $\mathcal{C}$ depends on how AIS is implemented and not on the model itself. We recall complex values are classified into complex types. Each complex type $t \in \mathcal{D}$ corresponds to a set $\Gamma(t)$ of complex values: $\Gamma(t) = \{v \in \mathcal{V}(\mathcal{C}') \mid v \text{ of a type } t\}$. A complex value v may carry several complex types and let $\tau(v)$ be the set of complex types that v has: $\tau(v) = \{t \in \mathcal{D}(\mathcal{C}) \mid v \in \Gamma(t)\}$ that is called a *complex type scheme* of v. Note that Γ can be defined by using τ and vice versa.

$\Gamma(t)$ and $\tau(v)$ may be infinite even if there exist finite primitive types, finite constructors and finite entities. For example, a `listof` constructor causes infinite number of complex values from finite number of entities, and successive application of `listof` causes infinite number of complex types. If we also have unionof, a complex value e of a type t must other types unionof(t, t_1), unionof(t, t_2), ... and $\tau(e)$ is infinite.

EXAMPLE 3 In our example 1, there are several complex types to describe details. A complex object `Committee` is a pair of a `Committee` entity and a `setof` (`CommitteeMem ber`) entity which means a committee's organization. We describe this type of complex objects by `Committee` $\equiv$ `setof` (`CommitteeMember`). Thus $e : \{e_1, .., e_n\}$ means that a committee e consists of a collection of committee-members $e_1, .., e_n$. Here are some examples of the definitions:

`OperatorGroup` $\equiv$ `setof` (`Worker`)
`Authority` $\equiv$ `setof` (`Checker`)
`LeadersCommittee` $\equiv$ `setof` (`Leader`)
`ExpertList` $\equiv$ `listof`(`recordof(2)`(`QualifiedPerson, Experience`))
Figure 3 contains a diagram for the description of complex objects. Arrows with $\equiv$ show the complex objects while other arrows describe the constructions of complex types.

Complex values of a complex type `setof(Worker)` consist of workers. We are not interested in all the collections and we assume there are some complex values that appear in complex objects with the type schemes below.

complex value	complex types
{ Beethoven, Brahms }	setof(Leader), setof(Worker), setof(CommitteeMember), setof(QualifiedPerson)
{ Puccini, Verdi }	setof(Leader),setof(Worker), setof(CommitteeMember) setof(QualifiedPerson)
{ Sibelius, Brahms }	setof(CommitteeMember)
{ Wagner }	setof(Checker), setof(Worker), setof(CommitteeMember), setof(QualifiedPerson)
{ Chopin, Liszt }	setof(Worker)
{ Schumann, Schubert }	setof(Worker)
{ Brahms, Bruckner }	setof(CommitteeMember), setof(QualifiedPerson)

□

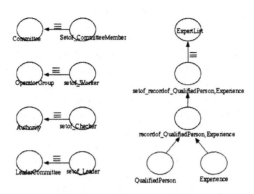

Fig.3. Complex Objects in Project Activity

3 Scenario of Scheme Discovery

In this section, we describe our scenario to mime complex type schemes in an intuitive manner based on a general paradigm of discovery[15]. In a database scheme, we assume some *semantic ordering*, say $\leq$, organized into DAG (directed acyclic graph) structures. In the case of primitive types, readers might think about ISA as a typical example and the very top as @E, but in the case of complex types, it is just the issue what kind of order we apply. In the next section, we will introduce several orders to adjust schemes appropriately. A notion of type consistency is still valid in the case of complex types but the exact semantics varies according to $\leq$.

Let S be a database scheme $(\mathcal{I}, \mathcal{E}, \leq, \Gamma, \tau)$ where $\mathcal{I}$ means a set of intentions (complex types in this case) and $\mathcal{E}$ a set of extensions (complex values). A scheme discovery is a problem to obtain better schemes. In this work, we propose two criterions *simplicity* and *appropriateness* as the better conditions for discovery of schemes. Intuitively a simple scheme means that classification by (complex) types is not complicated (not coarse) while an appropriate scheme means that the classification is effective (not sparse).

Formally, we say a scheme τ is *simple* of order k if $\forall v \in \mathcal{E}$ $|\tau(v)| < k$ for a fixed k. Readers migt think about *mutually disjoint* sets of complex values where all of τ schemes become singleton. But there is severe deficiency: huge (or sometimes infinite) number of new types are generated because one complex values may have more than one types and possibly more than exponential number of types are required. Given a complex value v and a semi-order, it is not hard to obtain a set of *least general* intentions $LG(v) = \{t_1, ...\}$ from $\tau(v)$, thus each intention set (i.e.,$\tau(v)$) becomes simpler. This approach is rather intuitive, users may design and examine schemes easily. Here in this work, we explore finite $LG(v)$ though $\tau(v)$ is not[1], since otherwise we can't *compute*.

The second criterion *appropriateness* is necessary to obtain suitable and efficient processing. Possibly $\Gamma(\tau(v))$ may be rather small. Then query parsing, type-checking and optimization should take much times yet few profit of massive-processing is obtained, very fine schemes increase the substantial overhead to deduce intentions based

---

[1] We will discuss the *finiteness* property of LG sets in section 5.

on our order and too many intentions must cause users to make query formulation hard. Thus we say that Γ is *appropriate* of h for a given h if $|\Gamma(\tau(v))| > h$. The value h is called a *threshold*. Otherwise, we say $\Gamma(\tau(v))$ is not appropriate, i.e., it is too fine.

It is not straightforward to obtain schemes that satisfy *both* criteria. Assume $LG(v)$ is not simple, i.e., $n \geq k$. Let $\wedge LG(v)$ a new intention whose extension is $\Gamma(t_1) \cap \ldots$. Note $\wedge LG(v)$ is a refinement of all the relevant intentions called a *conjunctive* intention. Because v has only one new intention $\wedge LG(v)$, a new $LG(v)$ must be simple but generally it has rather small number of extensions, i.e., not appropriate.

Our solution in this investigation is *unification* of intentions. It means that, if non-simple intentions remain or they have sets of instances of the cardinality less than the threshold h, we would change some intentions. It causes a loss of information.

Thus we propose a paradigm to discover simple and appropriate schemes as follows. For given values k and h, we utilize the order $\leq$ to obtain simple and appropriate schemes, i.e., τ (or Γ). We apply two strategies to do that: (1) we remove a type t from $\tau(v)$ if there exits $t' \in \mathcal{I}$ such as $t' \leq t$, and (2) we unify some of intentional descriptions if they are not appropriate.

Schemes are simplified by unifying types t_1 and t_2 using the order. More specifically, we find a least general type t_0 such that $t_1 \leq t_0$ and $t_2 \leq t_0$. The we replace t_1 and t_2 by t_0 thus we can unify the two. But such t_0 could be not determined uniquely nor finitely so that we utilize a semantical measure (or metric) that is introduced by the order. Important is the order since it plays essential roles to reduce and unify intentions.

4 Semantic Orders on Complex Types

4.1 ISA Hierarchy on Complex Types

Our first attemp is to extend ISA using general constructors of data structure. Since ISA is defined by means of set inclusion, it seems straightforward to start with *inclusion semantics*. Given two (complex) types t_1, t_2 in $\mathcal{D}(\mathcal{C})$, an ISA constraint (or generalization) over $\mathcal{D}(\mathcal{C})$ is a statement of the form t_1 ISA t_2 as usual. We say t_1 ISA t_2 holds in a database if $\Gamma(t_1) \subseteq \Gamma(t_2)$.

Very often we can *deduce* other ISA over $\mathcal{D}_U$ from others. For instance, assume t_1 ISA t_2 holds. Then setof(t_1) ISA setof(t_2) holds, since $2^{\Gamma(t_1)} \subseteq 2^{\Gamma(t_2)}$ because of $\Gamma(t_1) \subseteq \Gamma(t_2)$, however differenceof($t_0, t_1$) ISA differenceof($t_0, t_2$) does not. These don't come from t_1, t_2 but from the constructors. Thus we have to examine the properties of constructors of data structures.

In the definition of complex types, constructors can be seen as maps from $\mathcal{D}_U^n$ to $\mathcal{D}_U$. We say a constructor $\eta : \mathcal{D}_U^n \to \mathcal{D}_U$ is *monotonic* if η preserves inclusion, i.e, if, for every $t_1, ..., t_n \in \mathcal{D}_U$ and every $s_1, ..., s_n \in \mathcal{D}_U$ such that $\Gamma(t_i) \subseteq \Gamma(s_i)$ where $i = 1, ..., n$, $\Gamma(\eta(t_1, ..., t_n)) \subseteq \Gamma(\eta(s_1, ..., s_n))$.

THEOREM 1 setof, recordof(n), arrayof(n), listof, treeof(n), unionof and intersectionof are monotonic.

Note differenceof is not monotonic as shown above.

THEOREM 2 For $\eta : \mathcal{D}^n \to \mathcal{D}$ and $\eta_i : \mathcal{D}^{k_i} \to \mathcal{D}$ where $i = 1, .., n$, if all η, η_i are monotonic, then the construction $\eta(\eta_1, .., \eta_n)$ is also monotonic.

THEOREM 3 Assume a constructor $\eta : \mathcal{D}_U^n \to \mathcal{D}_U$ is monotonic, then η preserves ISA. That is, for $t_1, ..., t_n \in \mathcal{D}_U$ and $s_1, ..., s_n \in \mathcal{D}_U$, if t_i ISA s_i for $i = 1, ..., n$, then $\eta(t_1, ..., t_n)$ ISA $\eta(s_1, ..., s_n)$.

(Proof) Note t_i ISA s_i means $\Gamma(t_i) \subseteq \Gamma(s_i)$ and the result is trivial. $\square$

The above property says, if we have t_1 ISA t_2, then we also have another rule setof(t_1) ISA setof(t_2), that means we have setof(setof(t_1)) ISA setof(setof(t_2)) and so on. Given a finite number of ISA rules over primitive types, we must have infinite number of rules over complex types so we can't discuss finite implication any more.

EXAMPLE 4 In the example 2, there appear only setof, listof and recordof constructors which are monotonic (and inverse-monotonic as shown later). Then we can deduce ISA hierarchies from the example 2. In fact, figure 4 shows the hierarchies of our interests, readers can see the correctness of the new ones. $\square$

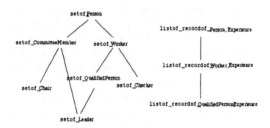

Fig.4. ISA Hierarchies in Project Activity

Although $\eta(t_1, ..., t_n)$ ISA $\eta(s_1, ..., s_n)$ holds, t_i ISA s_i does not always hold. A simple counter example is $\eta(t) = t \cup t_0$ where t_0 is a type. In fact, $\eta(t_0)$ ISA $\eta(t)$ but it is not ways true that t_0 ISA t. We say a constructor η is *inverse-monotonic* if $\Gamma(\eta(t_1, ..., t_n)) \subseteq \Gamma(\eta(s_1, ..., s_n))$ means $\Gamma(t_i) \subseteq \Gamma(s_i)$ for $t_i, s_i, i = 1, ..., n$.

THEOREM 4 Each of recordof(n), setof, listof and arrayof(n) are inverse-monotonic constructors.

Neither of unionof, intersectionof is not inverse-monotonic.

Monotonicity and inverse-monotonicity depend on the semantics of constructors. And if the both properties hold, for instance, in the case of complex types consisting of setof and recordof, ISA hierarchy on complex types is in one to one manner obtained from the primitive types. The two properties pose additional restriction on type consistency. If η is monotonic with the interpretation ζ, $t_i \in \tau(v_i)$ and t_i ISA s_i for $i = 1, .., n$, then $\tau(\zeta(v_1...v_n))$ contains both $\eta(t_1...t_n)$ and $\eta(s_1...s_n)$. Similarly, if η is inverse-monotonic, $\tau(\zeta(v_1...v_n))$ contains both $\eta(t_1...t_n)$ and $\eta(s_1...s_n)$ where $\eta(t_1...t_n)$ ISA $\eta(s_1...s_n)$, then $\tau(v_i)$ contains both t_i and s_i for $i = 1, .., n$.

4.2 Embeddable Complex Types

In this subsection, we discuss correspondence among *constructions* as well as complex types. Assume we have two complex types recordof(2)(t_1, t_2), recordof(3)(t_1, t_2, t_3). Because of the difference of recordof(2) and recordof(3), no ISA can hold between the two. However we can regard a complex value $(v_1, v_2) \in \Gamma(\texttt{recordof}(2)(t_1, t_2))$ as a value of $\Gamma(\texttt{recordof}(3)(t_1, t_2, t_3))$ by complementing a special value in $\Gamma(t_3)$, say $\perp$, and by regarding (v_1, v_2) as $(v_1, v_2, \perp)$. Since the former value appears physically as a part of the latter, it seems that $\texttt{recordof}(2)(t_1, t_2)$ is embedded into $\texttt{recordof}(3)(t_1, t_2, t_3)$. In a similar manner, a type t can be seen as $\texttt{setof}(t)$ by regarding a value $v \in \Gamma(t)$ as a singleton $\{v\} \in \Gamma(\texttt{setof}(t))$. But a set $\Gamma(\texttt{listof}(t))$ can't be injectively mapped to $\Gamma(\texttt{setof}(t))$ because of the difference of the cardinalities. Such a technique to translate constructions is called *embedding*.

Formally we say a function α from $\Gamma(\eta_1(t_1..t_n))$ to $\Gamma(\eta_2(t_1..t_n s_{n+1}..s_m))$ is an η_1-*embedding* if α is both *total*[2] and injective, and if each t_i-value v_i appears in $v(v_1..v_n)$ expressed by η_1-vehicle also appears as a component in $\alpha(v)$. We say a type $\eta_1(t_1...t_n)$ is η_1-*embeddable* to another type $\eta_2(t_1...t_n s_{n+1}...s_m)$, if there is an η_1-embedding from $\Gamma(\eta_1(t_1...t_n))$ to $\Gamma(\eta_2(t_1...t_n s_{n+1}...s_m))$. We will denote the embedding by $\eta_1(t_1...t_n) \hookrightarrow \eta_2(t_1...t_n s_{n+1}...s_m)$. For instance, $\texttt{recordof}(2)(t_1, t_2) \hookrightarrow \texttt{recordof}(3)(t_1, t_2, t_3)$. Intuitively, if a type t is η-embeddable to another s, we can rewrite the η-part to obtain s-values in an injective manner, and we will identify $v \in \Gamma(t)$ and $\alpha(v) \in \Gamma(s)$, and each value constituting $\Gamma(t)$ becomes a part of $\Gamma(s)$ (through α).

Let η_1 and η_2 be two constructions of the arities n and m respectively where $n \leq m$. We say η_1 is *embeddable* to η_2 (or $\eta_1 \hookrightarrow \eta_2$) if $\eta_1(t_1...t_n)$ is η_1-*embeddable* to another type $\eta_2(t_1...t_n s_{n+1}...s_m)$ for any types $t_1, .., t_n$ and some special values on $s_{n+1}, .., s_m$. For instance, $\texttt{recordof}(2) \hookrightarrow \texttt{recordof}(3)$.

For two types $t = \eta_1(t_1...t_n)$ and $s = \eta_2(t_1...t_n s_{n+1}...s_m)$, $t \hookrightarrow s$ can be seen as a special kind of ISA according to injection semantics since $\alpha(\Gamma(t)) \subseteq \Gamma(s)$ holds and every t_i-value appears as a component in the corresponding s value in an injective manner.

THEOREM 5 Given constructors $\eta_i, \xi_i \in \mathcal{C}, i = 1, .., k$ such that $\eta_i \hookrightarrow \xi_i$, $\eta(\eta_1..\eta_k) \hookrightarrow \eta(\xi_1..\xi_k)$ for any construction η of an arity k.

(Proof) Assume $\eta_i(t_1^i..t_{n_i}^i) \hookrightarrow \xi_i(t_1^i..t_{n_i}^i s_{n_i+1}^i..s_{m_i}^i)$. We show $\eta(\eta_1(t_1^1..t_{n_1}^1)..\eta_k(t_1^k..t_{n_k}^k)) \hookrightarrow \eta(\xi_1(t_1^1..t_{n_1}^1 s_{n_1+1}^1..s_{m_1}^1)..\xi_k(t_1^k..t_{n_k}^k s_{n_k+1}^k..s_{m_k}^k))$. Given an embedding α_i from $\Gamma(\eta_i(t_1^i..t_{n_i}^i s_{n_i+1}^i..s_{m_i}^i))$ to $\Gamma(\xi_i(t_1^i..t_{n_i}^i s_{n_i+1}^i..s_{m_i}^i))$, let $v \in \Gamma(\eta(\xi_1(t_1^1..t_{n_1}^1 s_{n_1+1}^1..s_{m_1}^1)..\xi_k(t_1^k..t_{n_k}^k s_{n_k+1}^k..s_{m_k}^k)))$ and $v(v_1..v_k)$ an expression in η-vehicle.

We define a new map β as $\beta(v(v_1..v_k)) = v(\alpha(v_1)..\alpha(v_k))$ and we show β is injective. If $v(\alpha(v_1)..\alpha(v_k)) = v(\alpha(v_1')..\alpha(v_k'))$ holds, all the data structure operators are identical, and $\alpha_i(v_i) = \alpha_i(v_i')$, since complex values have unique expressions. This means $v_i = v_i'$ since α_i is injective. $\square$

THEOREM 6 (1) If t ISA s, then $t \hookrightarrow s$ by id.
(2) $\eta_1 \hookrightarrow \eta_2$ and $\eta_2 \hookrightarrow \eta_3$ imply $\eta_1 \hookrightarrow \eta_3$.
(3) Assume t_1 ISA t_2 and $t_2 \hookrightarrow t_3$, then $t_1 \hookrightarrow t_3$ holds. By introducing another kind of *pseudo-equality*, denoted by $\doteq$, we can regard $\hookrightarrow$ as an order.

THEOREM 7 A constructor $id \hookrightarrow$ each of $\texttt{setof}$, $\texttt{listof}$, $\texttt{recordof}(n)$, $\texttt{arrayof}(n)$, $\texttt{treeof}(n)$ and $\texttt{unionof}$.

(Proof) Let us show some of them. $t \hookrightarrow \texttt{setof}(t)$ by $\alpha(v) = \{v\}$, $t \hookrightarrow \texttt{listof}(t)$ by $\alpha(v) = \langle v \rangle$, $t \hookrightarrow \texttt{recordof}(n)(t, t_2, .., t_n)$ by $\alpha(v) = [v, \perp, ..., \perp]$, $t \hookrightarrow \texttt{treeof}(n)(t, s_1, .., s_n)$ by $\alpha(v) = [v, \langle \rangle, .., \langle \rangle]$ and $t \hookrightarrow \texttt{unionof}(t, t_0)$ by $\alpha(v) = v$. $\square$

---

[2] That is, for each value v, $\alpha(v)$ is defined.

THEOREM 8 The followings hold:

(1) setof $\hookrightarrow$ listof.

(2) listof $\hookrightarrow$ treeof(1).

(3) recordof(n) $\hookrightarrow$ recordof(m), arrayof(n) $\hookrightarrow$ arrayof(m) and treeof(n) $\hookrightarrow$ tree of(m) where $n \leq m$.

(4) Both recordof(n) $\hookrightarrow$ arrayof(n) and arrayof(n) $\hookrightarrow$ recordof(n) hold. In other words, arrayof(n) $\doteq$ recordof(n).

(5) recordof(n) $\hookrightarrow$ treeof(n).

(6) arrayof(n) $\hookrightarrow$ listof.

(7) arrayof(n) $\hookrightarrow$ treeof(n).

(8) intersectionof $\hookrightarrow$ *id* and differenceof $\hookrightarrow$ *id*, but the converse are not true.

(Proof) Let us show only (2). listof $\hookrightarrow$ treeof(1) because $v \in \Gamma(\text{listof}(t))$ can be mapped to $[\bot, v] \in \Gamma(\text{treeof}(1)(t_0, t))$. $\square$

An important example is *tree embedding*. It holds that $\text{treeof}(n)(t, t_1, ..., t_n) \hookrightarrow \text{treeof}(m)(t, t_1, ..., t_n, ..., t_{n+m})$ by giving an embedding as $\alpha([e, \langle a_1..\rangle, ..., \langle b_1...\rangle]) = [e, \langle a_1..\rangle, ..., \langle b_1...\rangle, \langle\rangle, , , \langle\rangle]$.

We have discussed $\hookrightarrow$ between constructors and types so far. But sometimes we have $\hookrightarrow$ between constructions which can't be derived from the ones of constructors. For example, it is clear that $\text{recordof}(n+1) (t_1, .., t_{n+1}) \doteq \text{recordof}(2) (\text{recordof}(n) (t_1, .., t_n), t_{n+1})$ and $\text{arrayof}(n+1) (t) \doteq \text{recordof}(2) (\text{arrayof}(n) (t), t)$. A non-trivial example is the correspondence between $\text{setof}(\text{unionof} (t_1, t_2))$ and $\text{recordof}(2)$ $(\text{setof}(t_1), \text{setof}(t_2))$ by regarding $\{v_1, v_2, .., v_n\}$ as $[\{a_1, ..., a_k\}, \{b_1, .., b_m\}]$ where all the t_1-values in $\{v_1, v_2, .., v_n\}$ are grouped together into $\{a_1, ..., a_k\}$ and all the t_2-values into $\{b_1, .., b_m\}$. It is easy to see $\text{setof}(\text{unionof} (t_1, t_2)) \hookrightarrow \text{recordof}(2) (\text{setof} (t_1), \text{setof} (t_2))$ by this function. We note this property does not depend on t_1, t_2 but on the expressions setof(unionof) and recordof(2) (setof, setof).

THEOREM 9 Following properties hold.

(1) recordof(n+m) $\doteq$ recordof(2)(recordof(n),recordof(m))

(2) setof(unionof) $\hookrightarrow$ recordof(2)(setof, setof)

EXAMPLE 5 In the example 4, the followings hold:

setof(Worker) $\hookrightarrow$ listof(Worker)

listof(Worker) $\hookrightarrow$ listof(recordof(2)(Worker,Experience))

setof(CommitteeMember) $\hookrightarrow$ listof(Person)

listof(Person) $\hookrightarrow$ listof(recordof(2)(Person,Experience))

recordof(2)(QualifiedPerson,Experience) $\hookrightarrow$

listof(recordof(2)(QualifiedPerson,Experience))

By combining ISA hierarchies, figure 5 contains the new relationship among the complex types. Note the type schemes in example 3 become infinite. For example, a set value { Beethoven, Brahms } now contains setof (Worker), setof (setof (Worker)), ..., listof (Worker), listof (setof(Worker)), listof (listof (setof(Worker))), ..., listof(listof(Worker)), ..., listof (recordof(2) (Worker, Experience)), listof (listof (recordof(2) (Worker, Experience))), ..., listof (recordof(2) (Person, Experience)), listof (listof (recordof(2) (Person, Experience))), ... $\square$

A notion of $\hookrightarrow$ can be utilized to *rewrite* constructions for embedding of complex objects since we must unify two complex types consisting of different constructions. But not all the rules can be generated mechanically, so we assume the rules are explicitly given to the process of scheme discovery.

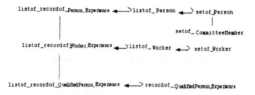

Fig.5. Embeddability in ISA Hierarchies

5 Discovering Complex Type Schemes

In this section, we discuss our main issue, how can we avoid complex type schemes that are infinite, and how to unify types to obtain simple and appropriate intentions. We denote an order by $\leq$ in this section.

Here we assume a set of constructors that satisfy (1) testing embeddability ($\eta_1 \hookrightarrow \eta_2$) can be decided in a finite time, (2) an *id* constructor is embeddable to all the constructors, and (3) for every construction η_1 of which vehicle is trivial, there exists a distinct construction η_2 such that $\eta_2 \hookrightarrow \eta_1$. The assumption (1) means we can translate constructions for unification of different types. The second says that each value can be seen of any types by supplying some values and that the more complicated constructions have, the wider the extensions have. For examples, intersectionof does not satisfy this property. An example of the last assumption is that unionof has a trivial vehicle and $t \hookrightarrow \text{unionof}(t, s)$ while intersectionof does not.

5.1 Polymorphic Nulls

Let setof(t) be a set type. Then because of the definition of the interpretation, $\Gamma(\text{setof}(t))$ may have an *empty* ϕ. This is true for all types t, so ϕ contains all the set types and $\tau(\phi)$ must be infinite. We define Φ as a type of which interpretation contains only ϕ. By definition, we must have Φ ISA s for all the set types s. and, because $\Gamma(\Phi)$ contains a set-value, Φ must be setof(t_0) where t_0 is an element type, and $LG(\phi) = \{\Phi\}$. Since setof is inverse-monotonic, t_0 ISA t holds for all types t. In other words, t_0 is the *smallest* type among all the complex types. Note ϕ is not identical to $\{\phi\}$. We have a similar story to listof with a special list ρ.

In the case of treeof (n), we sometimes imagine a *null* tree instance $[\perp, \rho, .., \rho]$ where $\perp$ means there exists *no element*, i.e., $\perp \in \Gamma(t_0)$. Other cases such as recordof (n) and arrayof (n) have similar special values like $[\perp, .., \perp]$ and $(\perp, ..., \perp)$. Note t_0 ISA t for every primitive type $t \in \mathcal{T}$ because of the smallest property, and is called $\perp$ if no confusion arises. The $\perp$ value is called a *null*, and it has all the types, while ϕ means $\{\perp\}$ and ρ means $\langle \perp \rangle$.

Generally, for a constructor $\eta : \mathcal{D}_U^n \to \mathcal{D}_U$, all the intersection of the interpretations of $\eta(t_1...t_n)$ contains a unique η-null which does not depend on types $t_1, ..$ but only on the constructor. For example, ϕ is setof-null and ρ listof-null. There are only finite constructor-dependent nulls because $\mathcal{C}$ is finite. But, for instance, $\{\{\}\}$ is the value which is included in all the setof(setof) constructions.

Since we have $\hookrightarrow$ mechanism, these nulls becomes identical. In fact, since $t \hookrightarrow$ setof(t), $\perp$ can be seen as $\{\perp\}$,i.e., ϕ. Then setof-null becomes $\perp$. We have $\perp = \{\perp\} = \{\{\perp\}\} = ...$ and a setof-null disappears. Generally, because we assume *id* $\hookrightarrow$ any constructor, all the constructor-dependent nulls become $\perp$.

5.2 Finiteness of Least General Sets

Now let us talk about *finiteness* property of least general sets. In the previous subsection it becomes clear that $\hookrightarrow$ is indispensable to avoid null problems.

Recall that we assume all of $\mathcal{T}$, $\mathcal{C}$, $\mathcal{E}$ and $\hookrightarrow$ rules are finite, and that the number of *stored* complex values is also finite. For a complex value v and a complex type scheme $\tau(v)$, we can generate the set of least general types with respect to an order $\leq$, denoted by $LG(v)$: For t_1, t_2 such that $t_1 \in LG(v)$, $t_1 \leq t_2$ or $t_1 \hookrightarrow t_2$, and $t_1 \in LG(v)$, then $t_2 \notin LG(v)$. Because of the type consistency, $\tau(v)$ and $LG(v)$ carry exactly same meaning. However, $\tau(v)$ may be infinite, and if $LG(v)$ is also infinite, we couldn't compute and simplify suitable type schemes because of the lack of finiteness. Null problems just come from this point.

We show $LG(v)$ is finite for given a complex value v. If $v = \phi$, $LG(v)$ is finite and we assume v is a *real* value. We recall that testing embeddability is finitely decidable, an *id* constructor is embeddable to all the constructors and that for every construction η_1 of which vehicle is trivial, there exists another construction η_2 such that $\eta_2 \hookrightarrow \eta_1$.

Let $t = \eta(t_1...t_n)$ be a complex type in $LG(v)$ where $v \in \Gamma(t)$ and $t_i \in \mathcal{T}$ ($i = 1, .., n$). Note v has the unique expression by ζ-vehicle, $v = \zeta(v_1, .., v_m)$, where each v_i is a primitive value or a set of primitive values. Let T_i be all the primitive types that some value in v_i has. T_i is finite since $\mathcal{T}$ is.

If there exists a constructor in η of which vehicle is trivial, some type becomes embeddable to t, a contradiction. Since η is interpreted into a sequence of data structuring operators η' of which vehicle is ζ. Now ζ can't contain an identity. Then, because of the finiteness of T_i, all the constructions from η and $T_1, .., T_n$ must be finite.

We have a finite set of $\mathcal{C}$ and $\mathcal{C}'$, that means only finite number of constructors can be interpretated into each constructor in ζ. That concludes $LG(v)$ must be finite.

EXAMPLE 6 According to the properties of ISA and embeddability, the type schemes become infinite as readers see. But by the finiteness of LG sets, we must have all the finite LG sets as belows. Here are LG sets appeared in example 3.

complex values	LG set
{ Beethoven,Brahms },{ Puccini, Verdi }	setof(Leader)
{ Sibelius, Brahms }	setof(CommitteeMember)
{ Wagner }	setof(CommitteeMember), setof(QualifiedPerson), setof(Checker)
{ Chopin, Liszt },{ Schumann,Schubert }	setof(Worker)
{ Brahms,Bruckner }	setof(CommitteeMember), setof(QualifiedPerson)

For each LG set T, there are some complex values that have T *directly* or *indirectly*. For instance, `setof(Worker)` is a LG set which is shared by all the set values except { Sibelius, Brahms }. The following is the summary of cardinalities.

LG set	complex values
setof(Leader)	2
setof(CommitteeMember)	5
setof(CommitteeMember), setof(QualifiedPerson), setof(Checker)	1
setof(Worker)	6
setof(CommitteeMember), setof(QualifiedPerson)	4

□

5.3 Unification of Type Schemes

To obtain simple schemes from an initial type scheme and the instances, we unify two type schemes. First of all, let us describe the basic idea informally[13]. Given two values e_1, e_2, let $LG(e_1) = \{t_1, t_2\}$ and $LG(e_2) = \{t_1, t_2\}$ be the least general sets respectively. In the case of primitive types, we define $t_2 \vee t_3$ as the least common ancestor of t_2, t_3 in ISA hierarchy [3]. Then we replace $LG(e_1), LG(e_2)$ by $\{t_1, t_2 \vee t_3\}$, and both are unified. $LG(e_1)$ is changed from $\{t_1, t_2\}$ to $\{t_1, t_2 \vee t_3\}$ or the type scheme becomes *weaker*.

Let us discuss complex types. If both t_2, t_3 are of η-type, say $\eta(s_1..s_n)$ and $\eta(u_1...u_n)$ respectively, then by obtaining the least general $v_i = s_i \vee u_i$ for $i = 1, .., n$, we define $\eta(s_1..s_n) \vee \eta(u_1...u_n)$ as $\eta(v_1...v_n)$. It is well-defined if η is monotonic and inverse-monotonic; if $\eta(s_1..s_n)$ ISA $\eta(w_1...w_n)$, $\eta(u_1..u_n)$ ISA $\eta(w_1...w_n)$ and $\eta(w_1...w_n)$ ISA $\eta(v_1...v_n)$, then s_i ISA w_i, u_i ISA w_i and w_i ISA v_i hold, which contradicts the definition of v_i.

If η is monotonic but not inverse-monotonic, the least general $v_i = s_i \vee u_i$ for $i = 1, .., n$ do not always lead to the least common type, i.e, $\eta(s_1..s_n) \vee \eta(u_1...u_n)$ ISA $\eta(v_1...v_n)$ but not equal. In this case, since we don't have any way to obtain least common types, the unification result depends on the constructor.

If η is neither monotonic nor inverse-monotonic, the least general $v_i = s_i \vee u_i$ for $i = 1, .., n$ do not always lead to the common type so that unification can't be defined. We don't discuss such constructors any more.

Assume t_2, t_3 have different constructors, say $\eta_1(s_1..s_n)$ and $\eta_2(u_1..u_m)$ respectively. Then by examining $\hookrightarrow$ rules, we try to find an embeddable type $\eta(w_1...w_p)$ for t_2 and t_3. If we find such a type, we rewrite t_2, t_3 to have the common constructor, and do the unification process as above. If not, it is no way to *harmonize* the two and we stop the unification.

Let us generalize the idea above. For every pair of types t, t' such that t ISA t', assume we have a sequence of types $t_0 = t, t_1, .., t_N = t'$ where each t_i is a direct generalization of t_{i-1}, $i = 1, .., N$. We may have more than one sequences from t to t'. Then the minimum N is called a *distance* between t and t', denoted by $dist(t, t')$. Given two types t_1 and t_2, t is called a *least general type* of t_1, t_2 denoted by $t_1 \vee t_2$, if (1) t is a common ancestor of t_1, t_2, (2) there exists no t' such that t' ISA t and t' is also a common ancestor of t_1, t_2, and (3) t gives the minimum value of $dist(t_1, x) + dist(t_2, x)$ where x satisfies (1) and (2). If a constructor is not inverse-monotonic, (2) has *less general* meaning.

EXAMPLE 7 Let us show some examples of unification of two complex types. setof (QualifiedPerson) $\vee$ setof (Leader) becomes setof (QualifiedPerson) since in the ISA hierarchy there is just 1 distance. Similarly setof (QualifiedPerson) $\vee$ setof (Checker) becomes setof (Worker) with the distance 2. The result of setof (Leader) $\vee$ setof (Checker) is setof (Worker) with the distance 3.

Let us describe more complicated unification. listof (QualifiedPerson) $\vee$ setof (Checker) cannot be made directly because of the difference of constructors. Since setof is embeddable to listof, we translate setof (Checker) to listof (Checker) and unify the two, then the result becomes listof (Worker) with the distance 3. Similarly, listof (recordof (2) (QualifiedPerson, Experience)) $\vee$ setof (Checker) becomes listof (recordof (2) (Worker, Experience)) with the distance 4 through two kinds of embeddings, setof $\hookrightarrow$ listof and id $\hookrightarrow$ recordof (2). $\square$

---

[3] When we have several candidates, select the appropriate under some rule such as alphabetical order.

Let $T_1 = \{t_1, ..., t_n, s_1, .., s_m\}$ and $T_2 = \{t_1, .., t_n, u_1, .., u_k\}$ be two sets of complex type schemes of some values where $n, m, k \geq 0$ and $t_1, .., s_1, .., u_1, ...$ are distinct. If $m > 0, k > 0$, we define $T_1 \vee T_2$ as $\{t_1, ..., t_n, s_i \vee u_j\}$ in which the s_i, u_j gives the minimum distance of $s_i \vee u_j, i = 1, .., m, j = 1, .., k$ and $dist(T_1, T_2)$ as $dist(s_i, u_j) - n$. The cardinality of unified schemes is reduced if $m > 1, k > 1$. If $m = 0$, we define $T_1 \vee T_2 = T_1$ and $dist(T_1, T_2) = k - n$. Similarly if $k = 0$, we define $T_1 \vee T_2 = T_2$ and $dist(T_1, T_2) = m - n$.

EXAMPLE 8 In example 6, let us unify a LG set T: { setof(CommitteeMember), setof(QualifiedPerson), setof(Checker) }.

Unifying T with setof (Leader), the result becomes setof (QualifiedPerson) with the distance 1. This is because the distance between setof(Leader) and setof (QualifiedPerson) is 1 and no common type appear. Similarly when we unifying T with setof (Worker), the result becomes setof(Worker) with the distance 1 too.

Unifying T with setof (CommitteeMember), the result becomes setof (Committee Member) with the distance 1, because there are two different types and one common type.

Finally, unifying T with { setof (CommitteeMember), setof (QualifiedPerson) } , the result becomes { setof (CommitteeMember), setof (QualifiedPerson) } with the distance -1. □

Assume that we have a complex value v where $LG(v)$ whose size is greater than k or $\Gamma(\wedge LG(v))$ whose size is less than h. Given $LG(v)$ we choose another $LG(v')$ that has the minimum distance from $LG(v)$ and unify them. Every value v'' in $\Gamma(\wedge LG(v))$ and $\Gamma(LG(v'))$ must be changed to have the new type scheme : $LG(v'') = LG(v) \vee LG(v')$.

We repeat this process until such v cannot be found any more or no change arises. Eventually we get to either of two situations. One is the case that every type scheme $LG(v)$ is simple and $\Gamma(\wedge LG(v))$ has the cardinality greater than v, another is the case *no change* that every type scheme contains more than k *common* types. In the latter case, we generate $\wedge LG(v)$ as a new type so every type scheme becomes simple. This process can be generalized as the algorithm UNIFY [15].

EXAMPLE 9 Let us continue the unification process in example 6. Let k and h be 2. Then we have only one exceptional complex value { Wagner }. By the unification of the LG set, we can conclude the LG set should be unified with the one of { Brahms,Bruckner }. In other words, setof(Checker) aspect of { Wagner } should be ignored to obtain both simple and appropriate type scheme. Here is the final result:

complex values	LG set
{ Beethoven,Brahms },{ Puccini, Verdi }	setof(Leader)
{ Sibelius, Brahms }	setof(CommitteeMember)
{ Wagner },{ Brahms,Bruckner }	setof(CommitteeMember), setof(QualifiedPerson)
{ Chopin, Liszt },{ Schumann,Schubert }	setof(Worker)

□

6 Conclusion

In this work, we presented scheme discovery for complex object by which database schemes could be evolved after the population. To achieve the goal, we have developed a rather theoretical framework that provides us with the solid foundation to construct and reconstruct type schemes. The unification of complex type schemes can be considered as an application of *knowledge discovery* to databases.

Here we assumed ISA and embeddability as the *second* ISA, i.e, $t_1 \hookrightarrow t_2$ has the weaker connection than t_1 ISA t_2. But, because all these orders are consistent, we can say semantical priorities might be posed differently on them. Such decision can't be made mechanically and more consideration could be done.

Acknowledgement

The authors thank Prof. B. Thalheim (Technical Univ. of Cottbus, Germany), Prof. S. Navathe (Georgia Institute of Technology, USA) and Prof. T. Bench-Capon (Univ. of Liverpool, UK) for their encouragement and useful comments to us.

References

1. Abiteboul, S., Fischer, P.C. and Schek, H.-J. (ed): Nested Relations and Complex Object in Databases, *Springer LNCS* 361 (1987)
2. Agrawal, R., Srikant, R.: Fast Algorithms for Mining Association Rules, *VLDB* (1994), 487-499
3. Arisawa, H. and Miura, T.: On the Properties of Extended Inclusion Dependencies, *VLDB* (1986), 449-456
4. Han, J., Cai, Y. and Cercone, N.: Knowledge Discovery in Databases : An Attribute Oriented Approach, *VLDB* (1992), 547-559
5. Han, J. and Fu, Y.: Discovery of Multiple-Level Association Rules from Large Databases, *VLDB* (1995), 420-431
6. Imielinski ,T. and Mannila, H.: A Database Perspective on Knowledge Discovery, *CACM* 39-11, 1996, 58-64
7. Kietz,J.U. and Morik, K.: A Polynomial Approach to the Constructive Induction of Structural Knowledge, *Machine Learning* 14 (1994), 193-217
8. Kim, W.: Introduction to Object Oriented Databases, *MIT Press* (1990)
9. Mannila, H.: Scheme Design and Knowledge Discovery, *ER Conference* (1996)
10. Miura, T., Arisawa, H.: Logic Approach of Data Models - *Data Logic, Future Database Systems* (1990), 228-259
11. Miura,T: Database Paradigms Towards Model Building, *Object Roll Modelling* (1994), 228-258
12. Miura,T. and Shioya, I.: Strategy Control for Database Queries, *Conference and Workshop of DEXA* (1995), 231-240
13. Miura, T. and Shioya, I.: Mining Type Schemes in Databases, *Conference and Workshop of DEXA* (1996), 369-384
14. Miura, T. and Shioya, I.: Knowledge Acquisition for Classification Systems, proc. *ICTAI* (1996), 110-115
15. Miura, T. and Shioya, I.: Paradigm for Scheme Discovery, proc.*CODAS* (1996), 101-108, World Scientific
16. Miura, T. and Shioya, I.: Differentiation for Scheme Discovery, to appear in *Intn'l Database Workshop (IDW)* (1997)
17. Ng, R. and Han, J.: Efficient and Effective Clustering Methods for Spatial Data Mining, *VLDB* (1994), 144-155
18. Piatetsky-Shapiro, G. and Frawley, W.J. (ed.): Knowledge Discovery in Databases, *MIT Press* (1991)

A Framework for Algebraic Optimization of Object-Oriented Query Languages

Issam Abbas, Omar Boucelma

Université de Provence, LIM
39, rue Joliot-Curie, 13453 Marseille Cedex 13
E-mail:<Firstname>.<Lastname>@lim.univ-mrs.fr

Abstract. Efficient query processing is still a challenging task, despite the emergence of the ODMG'93 standard. What we need is both an algebra-to perform algebraic optimization- and an intermediate language that could be used as a target language for OQL-like query compilers.

In this paper, we present an algebra that extends Backus's FP algebra by means of a set of powerful functionals. Our algebra has many important features. First, the number of equivalence rules is limited since one rule models many equivalence rules previously described in the context of an FP algebra. Second, many laws and heuristics described in the literature for both relational and object query optimization are represented by means of a reduced set of parametrized functionals. Finally, we believe that this algebra is a kernel of an appropriate target language for OQL-like query compilers.

1 Introduction

One advantage of the relational data model is the existence of a formal calculus and algebra to model and optimize database queries. As one moves to the OODBMS world, the problem becomes more complex. First, an object query language must deal with various kinds of constructs : bulk data types, nesting of type constructors, methods, etc. Second, despite of the emerging ODMG standard [5], there is still a need for an *effective* formalism to model object query languages.

In this paper, we present a framework for querying efficiently collections of objects. Our framework consists of an algebra and a kernel of a functional execution model. The algebra is an extension of LIFOO [9, 3], a functional query language that we designed for O_2[6]. The functional execution model is an extension of Backus' FP algebra with functionals and equivalence rules that help address algebraic query optimization. The extensions we devised for LIFOO are twofold : (a) develop an optimization framework, and, (b) design and implement a complete intermediate database language that could be considered as an appropriate target language for OQL-like query compilers.

The work we describe in this paper has some similarities with other works that have adopted a functional style for object query languages. Beeri and Kornatzy [2] extends FP [1] and FQL [4] providing an extensible set of data collections. Fegaras and Maier [7] suggest an "effective calculus" based on *monoid comprehensions*. In [10], FP equivalence rules are classified by their intended purpose and not solely by the kinds of functional forms that occur in the rule. OFL [8] is a language for querying abstract collections of complex objects (i.e, extents, multivalued attributes, etc). OFL is also intended to be a target language for OQL-like compilers. Our claim is that we provide a formalism that covers major issues that need to be addressed when designing an object oriented query language: expressiveness, algebraic optimization and compilation into efficient intermediate code.

This paper is structured as follows. Section 2 gives an overview of LIFOO and its algebra of programs. In Section 3 we describe some equivalence rules that we use in the optimization process. Finally, Section 4 concludes the paper.

2 Our Data Model and Query Language

2.1 The Functional Object Data model

Definition 1. Our data model consists of *functions* that capture the semantics of objects and values. As in most object-oriented databases, a value is either atomic (i.e., an integer, a float, a character, a string, true, false), or structured (tuple, array, list, set, bag). As a result, a value has a type that is either atomic or structured. An object x of type T is a pair $< n, v >$ where n is a name, v a value, and T the type of v. When there is no ambiguity, we use the term *element* to denote either an object or a value.

Definition 2. Given a function f, an object x of type T, an *application rule* is denoted as follows :

- $f : T \rightarrow T_f$, a function that applies to an object of type T and returns an element of type T_f.

- $f :\rightarrow T_f$, a function that applies to an object of any type, and returns an object of type T_f.

- $f : x$ is the object retuned when applying f to x.

- A function may return the null object denoted $\perp$. As a result, for any function f, $f : \perp = \perp$.

Definition 3. A *database schema* is a triple of sets :
$types : T_1, \cdots, T_m,$
$named\ objects : \{f_i :\rightarrow T_i,\ i \in (1..p)\}$, and
$methods : \{f_j : T \rightarrow T_j,\ j \in (1..q)\}$

Figure 1 illustrates a sample database schema.

$companies :\rightarrow set(Company)$ $Company = [name : string, city : string]$

$persons :\rightarrow set(Person)$

$employees :\rightarrow set(Employe)$ $Person = [name \quad : string,$

$name : Company \rightarrow string$ $address: [street: string,$

$city : Company \rightarrow string$ $city \quad : string]]$

$ceo : Company \rightarrow Person$ $Employee\ ISA\ Person = [\ company: Company,$

$safeway :\rightarrow Company$ $salary \quad : integer]$

$name : Person \rightarrow string$

$salary : Employe \rightarrow integer$

$employees : Company \rightarrow set(Employe)$

$address : Person \rightarrow [street : string, city : string]$

Fig. 1. A Sample Database Schema

Definition 4. A function has one of the following forms :

- A *named* object n :
  $n :\rightarrow T_n$
  $n : x =$ object referred by n.
- A *method* m :
  $m : C \rightarrow T_m$
  $m : x =$ message passing m to the object x.
- A *constant* :
  $"Michael" :\rightarrow string$
  $"Michael" : x = "Michael"$, for any x.
- A *primitive*
  $id : T \rightarrow T$
  $id : x = x$.
- A *Functional Form* is a function that combines other functions. Functional forms used in the sequel of the paper are described in Table 1.

Definition 5. A query q is a function that applies to an empty string value, and returns an answer of type T_q. A query is strongly typed : the type of a query is inferred by the typing rules corresponding to the various subqueries that compose the query. Note that we allow overloading of operators. Examples of queries are given below.

Example 1. Where is located safeway?

    $city \circ safeway$

Example 2. Give the sum salaries of all employees that work for *safeway*.

    $sum(salary) \circ employees \circ safeway$

Example 3. Give the pairs [ceo of each company, companies located in Marseille].

    $[\Pi_{ceo} \circ companies, \sigma_{(city \circ address)='Marseille'} \circ companies]_{Ceo,Com}$

Operator	Typing Rule	Reduction Rule
composition	$g \circ f : T \to T_g$ *if* $f : T \to T_f$ *and* $g : T_f \to T_g$	$g \circ f : x = g : (f : x)$
identity	$id : T \to T$	$id : x = x$
conditional	$cond_{p,f,g} : T \to T\prime$ *if* $p : T \to boolean$ *and* $f : T \to T\prime$ *and* $g : T \to T\prime$	$cond_{p,f,g} : x = if \ p : x$ $then \ f : x \ else \ g : x$
tuple *constructor*	$[f_1, \cdots, f_k]_{n_1, \cdots, n_k} :$ $T \to [n_1 : T_1, \cdots, n_k : T_k]$ *if* $\forall i \in \{1, \cdots, k\}, n_i \ is \ an$ *identifier and* $f_i : T \to T_i$	$[f_1, \cdots, f_k]_{n_1, \cdots, n_k} : x =$ $[n_1 : (f_1 : x), \cdots,$ $n_k : (f_k : x)]$
field	$\#n : [\cdots, n : T, \cdots] \to T$	$\#n : [\cdots, n : x, \cdots] = x$
project	$\Pi_f : c(T) \to c(T_f)$ *if* $f : T \to T_f$	$\Pi_f : c(x_1, \cdots, x_n) =$ $c(y_1, \cdots, y_n) \mid y_i = f : x_i$
select	$\sigma_p : c(T) \to c(T)$ *if* $p : T \to boolean$	$\sigma_p : c(x_1, \cdots, x_n) =$ $c(x_i \mid p : x_i, i \in \{1, \cdots, n\})$
sum	$sum(f) : c(T) \to numeric$ *if* $f : T \to numeric$	$sum(f) : c(x_1, \cdots, x_n) =$ $f : x_1 + \cdots + f : x_n$
existential *quantifier*	$\exists(f, p) : T \to boolean$ *if* $f : T \to c(T\prime)$ *and* $p : T\prime \to boolean$	$\exists(f, p) : x = \exists y \in f : x, p : y$
universal *quantifier*	$\forall(f, p) : T \to boolean$ *if* $f : T \to c(T\prime)$ *and* $p : T\prime \to boolean$	$\forall(f, p) : x = \forall y \in f : x, p : y$
set *constructor*	$\{f_1, \cdots, f_n\} : T \to set(T\prime)$ *if* $\forall i \in \{1, \cdots, n\}, f_i : T \to T\prime$	$\{f_1, \cdots, f_n\} : x =$ $set(f_1 : x, \cdots, f_n : x)$

Table 1. A Sample of Operators

2.2 The Algebras

In adopting a FP language as a basis for our query language, we seamlessly provided our query language with the whole set of FP equivalence rules as described in [1].

To enhance the optimization process, we extended our original algebra in supplying a set of useful functionals such as *reduce*, *join*, *until*, and *combine* denoted R, J, U, and C respectively.

- R, the *eager* collection iterator, is a generic operator that models iterators over collections that use the whole list of their arguments.
- U is the *lazy* collection iterator. This operator is useful in the context of a lazy traversal of a collection, i.e., that we do not need to build the whole collection.
- J is the *Nest-Join* operator. Operator J combines two operators: *join* of several sets of objects, and *unnest* of nested structures.

– C - *combine* and *unnest* - allows the aggregation of a list of objects (e.g., nodes in a path) with a set of objects (e.g., nodes in a subtree). This results in many paths as the number of nodes in the subtree.

Table 2 summarizes the main operators of our extended algebra.

Operator	Typing Rule	Reduction Rule
reduce	$R_{n_1,n_2}(f,g,h) : c(T) \to T_f$ if n_1, n_2 are identifiers and $f : T \to T_f$, $g : T \to T_g$ and $h : [n_1 : T_f, n_2 : T_g] \to T_f$	$R_{n_1,n_2}(f,g,h) : c() = R_0$ $R_{n_1,n_2}(f,g,h) : c(x_1, ..., x_n) = R_n$ with $R_0 = f : ""$ and $R_{i+1} = h : [n_1 : R_i, n_2 : (g : x_{i+1})]$
until	$U_{p_1}^{p_2} : c(T) \to boolean$ if $p_1 : T \to boolean$ and $p_2 :\to boolean$	$U_{p_1}^{p_2} : c() = False$ $U_{p_1}^{p_2} : c(x_1, .., x_n) =$ $\begin{cases} p_2 : "" & if\ p_1 : x = p_2 : "" \\ U_{p_1}^{p_2} : c(x_2, .., x_n) & otherwise \end{cases}$
join	$J_{n_1,\cdots,n_k}(f_1, \cdots, f_k) :$ $T \to set([n_1 : T_1, \cdots, n_k : T_k])$ if $n_1, \cdots, n_k$ are identifiers and $f_1 : T \to c(T_1), \cdots, f_k :$ $[n_1 : T_1, \cdots, n_{k-1} : T_{k-1}] \to c(T_k)$	$J_{n_1,\cdots,n_k}(f_1, \cdots, f_k) : x =$ $c([n_1 : y_1, \cdots, n_k : y_k] \mid$ $y_1 \in f_1 : x \wedge \cdots \wedge y_k \in$ $f_k : tuple(n_1 : y_1, \cdots, n_{k-1} : y_{k-1}))$
combine	$C_{n_1,\cdots,n_k}(f_1, \cdots, f_k) :$ $T \to set([n_1 : T_1, \cdots, n_k : T_k])$ if $n_1, \cdots, n_k$ are identifiers and $f_1 : T \to T_1, \cdots, f_{k-1} : T \to T_{k-1}, f_k :$ $[n_1 : T_1, \cdots, n_{k-1} : T_{k-1}] \to c(T_k)$	$C_{n_1,\cdots,n_k}(f_1, \cdots, f_k) : x =$ $c([n_1 : y_1, \cdots, n_k : y_k] \mid$ $y_1 = f_1 : x \wedge \cdots \wedge y_{k-1} = f_{k-1} : x$ $\wedge y_k \in f_k : [n_1 : y_1, \cdots, n_{k-1} : y_{k-1}])$
zero	$zero :\to c(T)$	$zero : x = c()$
unit	$unit : T \to c(T)$	$unit : x = c(x)$
merge	$merge(f,g) : T \to c(T\prime)$ if $f,g : T \to c(T\prime)$	$merge(f,g) : x = f : x + g : x$

Table 2. The Target Algebra

3 Algebraic Optimization

In this section we illustrate the optimization process through a sample of algebraic rules. This process consists of three main components:

1. A set of FP equivalence rules that act as lemmas for the extended equivalence rules.
2. A set of transformation rules that provide a detailed semantics of an operator, as illustrated in Table 3. In addition, these rules explicits an execution

model for operators that share a common property. For instance, Π and σ are both iterators; they can be modeled by means of the same operator R.

3. A set of equivalence rules expressed in a functional-style, without the need for head and body routines. Each law is a specification of an optimization algorithm whose goal is to refine the optimization process.

$$\Pi_f \equiv R_{n_1,n_2}(zero, f, merge(\#n1, unit \circ \#n2))$$
$$\sigma_g \equiv R_{n_1,n_2}(zero, cond_{g,id,zero}, merge(\#n1, unit \circ \#n2))$$
$$sum(f) \equiv R_{n_1,n_2}(0, f, \#n1 + \#n2)$$
$$\exists(f,p) \equiv U_p^{True} \circ f$$
$$\forall(f,p) \equiv U_p^{False} \circ f$$

Table 3. The Transformation Rules

3.1 Law for Pipelining Iterations

Law (1) below avoids the generation of unuseful intermediate structures. This law is similar to the *homomorphism fusion* law [7] which merges two piped monoid homomorphisms into a nested one. However, our law is more general in the sense that we do not impose restrictions on every parameter used in R. This law also is a generalization of some algebraic laws described in [2]. Examples of such laws are: *cascade of apply-to-all*, *cascade of filters*, and *combining apply-to-all with pump*.

$$R_{n_1,n_2}(f_1, g_1, h_1) \circ R_{m_1,m_2}(zero, g_2, merge(\#m_1, unit \circ \#m_2)) \equiv$$
$$R_{n_1,n_2}(f_1, g_1 \circ g_2, h_1) \qquad (1)$$

To illustrate the expressiveness of this law, let us consider query (2) below which computes the sum of salaries of employees working for SAFEWAY.

$$sum(salary) \circ (\sigma_{(name \circ company)='SAFEWAY'} \circ employees) \qquad (2)$$

The application of the transformation rules described in table 3 leads to:

$$R_{n_1,n_2}(0, salary, \#n1 + \#n2) \circ$$
$$(\sigma_{(name \circ company)='SAFEWAY'} \circ employees) \Longrightarrow$$
$$R_{n_1,n_2}(0, salary, \#n1 + \#n2) \circ$$
$$R_{n_1,n_2}(zero, cond_{(name \circ company)='SAFEWAY',id,\perp},$$
$$merge(\#n_1, unit \circ \#n2)) \circ employees$$

The expression above is a composition of two iterations: the rightmost one is a selection over the set E of all employees that verify the predicate $name \circ company =' SAFEWAY'$. The leftmost iteration applies the function $salary$ to each element of E and performs the sum as well.

Applying law 1 leads to the following expression:

$$R_{n_1,n_2}(0, salary \circ cond_{(name \circ company)='SAFEWAY',id,\perp}, \#n_1 + \#n_2) \circ$$
$$employees$$

whose computation is much more efficient. Indeed, to evaluate the expression above we need only one iteration over the set of all employees.

3.2 Law for Independent Iterations

In many cases, a query performs two or more iterations over the same collection. At a first glance, since those iterations seem to be orthogonal, it is hard to perform a factorization.

Law (3) below merges two iterations - over the same collection - into one iteration over the same collection.

$$[R_{n_1,m_1}(f_1, g_1, h_1), R_{n_2,m_2}(f_2, g_2, h_2)]_{n,m} \equiv R_{n,m}(F, G, H) \qquad (3)$$

$F = [f_1, f_2]_{n_1,n_2}$
$G = [g_1, g_2]_{n_1,n_2}$
$H = [h_1(\#n_1 \circ \#n, \#m_1 \circ \#m), h_2(\#n_2 \circ \#n, \#m_2 \circ \#m)]_{n,m}$

As an example, let us consider query (4) below

$$[\Pi_{ceo} \circ companies, \sigma_{(city \circ address)=Marseille} \circ companies]_{Ceo,Com} \qquad (4)$$

which returns [{ceo of a company}, {company located in Marseille}].

The transformation laws give:

$[R_{n_1,n_2}(zero, ceo, merge(\#n_1, unit \circ \#n_2)) \circ companies,$
$R_{n_1,n_2}(zero, cond_{((city \circ address)=Marseille,id,\perp)}, merge(\#n_1, unit \circ \#n_2)) \circ$
$companies]_{Ceo,Comp}$

In applying factorization rule (5) below,

$$[f \circ h, g \circ h]_{n_1,n_2} \equiv [f, g]_{n_1,n_2} \circ h \qquad (5)$$

we obtain the following expression:

$[R_{n_1,n_2}(zero, ceo, merge(\#n_1, unit \circ \#n_2)),$
$R_{n_1,n_2}(zero, cond_{((city \circ address)=Marseille,id,\perp)}, merge(\#n_1, unit \circ \#n_2))$
$]_{Ceo,Comp} \circ companies$

In applying rule 3, we obtain:

$$R_{Ceo,Com}(\ [zero, zero]_{n_1,n_2}, [ceo, cond_{((city \circ address)=Marseille, id, \perp)}]_{Ceo,Com},$$
$$[merge((\#n_1 \circ \#ceo), (\#m_1 \circ \#Com)),$$
$$merge((\#n_2 \circ \#Ceo), (\#m_2 \circ \#Com))]_{Ceo,Com})\ \circ companies$$

In the expression above, we ended in computing one loop instead of two. The set of companies located in Marseille, and the set of all ceo are computed with one iteration over the set of all companies.

3.3 Law for Lazy R

We are interested in a lazy evaluation of an R-expression. Law 6 below avoids the generation of a whole collection $c(x_1, \cdots, x_n)$, to test if one of the x_i satisfies a predicate $p_1 = p_2$.

$$U_{p_1}^{p_2} \circ R_{n_1,n_2}(zero, g, merge(\#n_1, unit \circ \#n_2)) \equiv U_{p_1 \circ g}^{p_2} \tag{6}$$

Let's illustrate the generic law above through law 7, which is one of its instances.

$$\exists(\Pi_f \circ g, p) \equiv \exists(g, p \circ f) \tag{7}$$

Law 7 avoids the calculation of f for all the elements of g, because we stop the calculation when the predicate p is satisfied.

3.4 Law for Lazy J

We are interested in evaluating a J−expression with form 8 that involves a predicate Q in conjunctive (or disjunctive) normal form.

$$U_Q^q \circ J_{a_1, \cdots, a_n}(f_1, \cdots, f_n) \tag{8}$$

Expression 8 has the following semantics: perform a calculation loop over a J-expression until the condition $Q = q$ is reached. To perform this calculation, we came up with seven canonical forms for Q, together with their corresponding laws.

As an example, let us consider predicate Q below,

$$Q = Q_1(\#a_i)\ op\ Q_2(\#a_{j_1}, \cdots, \#a_{j_m}),\ 1 \le i \le j_1 \le j_m \le n\ ,\ op \in \{\wedge, \vee\}$$

with its corresponding law 9:

$$U_{(Q_1(\#a_i)\ op\ Q_2(\#a_{j_1}, \cdots, \#a_{j_m}))}^{q} \circ J_{a_1, \cdots, a_n}(f_1, \cdots, f_n) \equiv U_1 \tag{9}$$

$$U_k = U^q_{U_{k+1}} \circ C_{a_1, \cdots, a_k}(\#a_1, \cdots, \#a_k, f_{k+1}) \quad k \in (1, \cdots, i-1)$$
$$U_i = U^q_{Q_1(\#a_i) \, op \, U_{i+1}} \circ C_{a_1, \cdots, a_i}(\#a_1, \cdots, \#a_{i-1}, f_i)$$
$$U_{i+1} = U^q_{Q_2(\#a_{j_1}, \cdots, \#a_{j_m})} \circ J_{a_1, \cdots, a_{j_m}}(\{\#a_1\}, \cdots, \{\#a_i\}, f_{i+1}, \cdots, f_{j_m})$$

To explicit the role of this law, let's consider the following query

$$U^{true}_{(salaryo \, ceoo \, \#com)=(salaryo \, \#emp)\wedge(salaryo \, ceoo \, \#ent)>20000^{\circ}}$$
$$J_{com,emp}(companies, employees \circ \#com)$$

whose semantics is: (a) unnest the grouping (company, employees), then (b) check if there exists an element that satisfies the predicate.
Let:

$$Q_1(\#com, \#emp) = (salary \circ ceo \circ \#com) = (salary \circ \#emp)$$
$$Q_2(\#com) \qquad\;\; = (salary \circ ceo \circ \#com) > 20000$$

Our query becomes:

$$U^{true}_{Q_1(\#com,\#emp)\wedge Q_2(\#com)} \circ J_{com,emp}(companies, employees \circ \#com)$$

To enable application of law 9, we sort the predicates in U:

$$U^{true}_{Q_2(\#com)\wedge Q_1(\#com,\#emp)} \circ J_{com,emp}(companies, employees \circ \#com)$$

In applying law 9 we obtain expression U_1 where:

$$U_1 = U^{true}_{Q_2(\#com)\wedge U_2} \circ C_{com}(companies)$$
$$U_2 = U^{true}_{Q_1(\#com,\#emp)} \circ J_{com,emp}(\{\#com\}, employees \circ \#com)$$

The evaluation of U_1 is performed as follows:

1. Get an element c in the set *companies*.
2. IF c does not satisfy the predicate $Q_2(\#com)$ THEN GOTO (1), ELSE evaluate U_2 on c, i.e., :
   (a) Unnest the grouping company-employees for the company c
   (b) Get an element (c, e) in the resulting set.
   (c) IF (c, e) satisfies $Q_1(\#com, \#emp)$ THEN STOP ELSE GOTO (b).

4 Conclusion

In this paper we presented a framework for object-oriented query language optimization. First we described a query language based on Backus' FP algebra. Then we focused on the target algebra, i.e., the extensions we added to the initial algebra. Finally, we demonstrated our query optimization process by means of a set of selected laws that hold in the target algebra.

As illustrated in Section 3, the optimization process is driven by a small set of functionals, hence minimizing the search space. We also described how an equivalence rule in our algebra captures rules and heuristics that are widely used in many optimization algorithms described in the literature.

We believe that the target algebra described in this paper can be used as a kernel for an intermediate database language suitable for OQL-like query compilers. As a result, our future plan is to demonstrate the effectiveness of our algebra for object oriented query optimization. First, we need to implement the core optimization engine. Then we need to implement an OQL translator.

References

1. J. Backus. Can functional programming be liberated from the von Neuman Style? A Functional Style and its Algebra of Programs. *Communications of the ACM*, pages 613–641, 1978.
2. C. Beeri and K. Kornatzky. Algebraic Optimization of Object-Oriented Query Languages. In *Proc. of Intl. Conf. on Very Large Data Bases*, pages 411–422, Paris, France, December 1990.
3. O. Boucelma and J. Le Maitre. An extensible functional query language for an Object-Oriented Database System. In *Proceedings of the Second International Conference On Deductive and Object-Oriented Database System, DOOD'91*, Munich, Germany, 16-18 Décembre, 1991. Springer Verlag, LNCS 566.
4. O.P. Buneman, R. E. Frankel, and R. Nikhil. An Implementation Technique for Database Query Languages. *ACM Trans. on Database Systems*, 7(2):164–186, 1982.
5. R.G.G. Cattell. *The Object Database Standard: ODMG-93, Version 1.1*. Morgan Kaufmann, 1993.
6. O. Deux. The Story of O2. *IEEE Transaction on Knowledge and Data Engineering*, 2(1), March 1990.
7. L. Fegaras and D. Maier. Towards an Effective Calculus for Object Query Languages. In *Proc. ACM SIGMOD Symp. on the Management of Data*, 1995.
8. G. Gardarin, F. Machuca, and P. Pucheral. OFL: A Functional Execution MOdel for Object Query Languages. Technical report, Université de Versailles/Saint-Quentin, 1994.
9. J. Le Maitre and O. Boucelma. LIFOO: un langage d'interrogation fonctionnel pour une base de données orientée objet. In *Cinquièmes journées BD avançées*, Genève, Suis se, 23-26 Septembre 1989.
10. Hennie J. Steenhagen and Peter M.G. Apers. Implementation of the Object-Oriented Data Model TM. In J. C. Freytag, D. Maier, and G. Vossen, editors, *Query Processing For Advanced Database Systems*, part 10, pages 273–303. Morgan Kaufmann, San Mateo, 1994.

A Library Application on Top of an RDBMS: Performance Aspects

O. Balownew[1], T. Bode[1], A.B. Cremers[1],
J. Kalinski[1], J.E. Wolff[1], H. Rottmann[2]

[1] Institute of Computer Science III, University of Bonn,
Römerstr. 164, 53117 Bonn, Germany
{ *oleg,tb,abc,cully,jw* } *@cs.uni-bonn.de*

[2] HBZ, Classen-Kappelmann-Str. 24, 50931 Köln, Germany
rottmann@hbz-nrw.de

Abstract. Applications which require a combination of structured data with unstructured text fields are becoming of increasing practical interest. But whereas structured data are usually stored in a relational database, large text collections are maintained by proprietary text or information retrieval systems. The synthesis of both areas is still a topic of intensive research. We describe one such application, namely maintaining library catalogues, and study the efficiency of two implementation alternatives both based on RDBMS technology. In the first alternative word occurrence information is encoded using bitlists. The other chooses a direct implementation within the relational model. Performance tests are done which are based on real world data and real world user transactions. They demonstrate that the problem of the bitlist implementation is caused by conversions which are necessary to combine them with structured data. In contrast, our direct implementation benefits from today's sophisticated RDBMS technology and performs promisingly well.

1 Introduction

During the last decades research in the areas of text retrieval systems and relational database management systems (RDBMS) has developed in rather separate ways. Early studies concerning the suitability of RDBMS for text retrieval applications had come to negative results, the typical argument being that the 'flat' structure of relational databases is conceptually inadequate as well as inefficient (see Schek [11], Freitag et al. [5]). Since its introduction the relational data model has not only undergone fundamental theoretical analyses, but has also found its way into convincingly powerful commercial products. Standardization efforts have led to a high degree of information interchangeability and portability.

As Kaufmann and Schek [7] are pointing out in a recent paper, it is especially the advent of client-server architectures and the development of parallel query evaluation algorithms on SMP and MMP platforms that call for a second assessment of text search with RDBMS. Furthermore, RDBMS providers are increasingly becoming aware of the importance of 'unstructured' data in addition to 'structured' data as stored in relational tables. ORACLE, for example, offers TextServer3 [10] (formerly SQL*TextRetrieval, which was considered in Kaufmann and Schek's study) as a tool which implements text retrieval functionality on top of their RDBMS.

Document acquisition for library catalogues is an application where structured and unstructured data coexist and where both are typically combined in librarians' queries. The central bibliographic database of a library network has to serve several hundred librarians working on millions of documents. First generation systems have reached critical internal restrictions and capacity limits. Recent proposals by the German Research Council [3] recommend a client-server architecture based on standard operating systems, interfaces and database management systems for next generation systems. In cooperation with the University Library Center of the State of North-Rhine-Westfalia (HBZ in Cologne) we carried out a performance study in order to answer the following questions:

– Is ORACLE TextServer3 a suitable tool for implementing text search functionalities of such a library system? [1]
– Are relational DBMS sufficiently powerful to meet the performance requirements of HBZ with respect to retrieval and update operations?

Section 2 discusses the application in some more detail. Technical aspects of the performance test are sketched in Section 3, while Sections 4 and 5 present the results of the performance test of ORACLE7 Server and TextServer3. Section 6 compares different direct implementations which are solely based on the RDBMS as alternatives to TextServer3. Section 7 briefly reviews earlier studies and related work. Finally, Section 8 gives some concluding remarks.

2 The HBZ Library Catalogue

2.1 System Requirements

Document acquisition in German libraries is based on rather sophisticated rules[2]. For example: Every document can have several titles each playing a different role (e.g. original book title and the title of a German translation). It can have more than one ISBN, because both the correct as well as incorrect numbers must be stored. Authors may have several names (e.g. pseudonyms, different transcriptions). Authors may be persons as well as corporate bodies. A person can be related to a book as its author, translator, editor and so on.

It turns out that the majority of data is structured (e.g. ISBN and publication year for documents, date of birth for persons). In fact the only complex text fields are document titles, names of corporate bodies and keyword sequences.

---

[1] It must be stressed that TextServer3 implementations with comparable requirements and magnitude do not exist.

[2] *Regeln für die alphabetische Katalogisierung (RAK)* which can be compared with *Anglo-American Cataloguing Rules (AACR2)*.

The current HBZ system has reached critical internal restrictions and capacity limits. As the number of libraries connected to HBZ is expected to increase and as HBZ wishes to provide a number of additional functionalities, the need for a new system has arisen. The German Research Council [3] recommends a client-server architecture based on standard software. This is why HBZ is interested in finding out whether this new system can be realized on top of a relational database management system.

Our view of relational DBMS is in the line of Kaufmann and Schek's [7] that

> *increasingly, relational database systems are being used as storage managers, upon which sophisticated object managers and application-oriented tools are built.*

We do not claim that our performance tests are able to assess the general suitability of RDBMS technology for text retrieval. But they provide clear guidelines for a relational database tailored to the special needs of library catalogue administration which are completely different from a library user's needs.

2.2 Test Design

The HBZ wishes that — in contrast to existing library systems — documents (6 mio.), document titles (7.5 mio.), persons (1.5 mio.), their names (1.8 mio.) and many more should be stored explicitly and non-redundantly by entities with numerous attributes and relationships between them. For each retrieval operation the exact number of documents satisfying the selection condition (hits) should be computed in about a second. Additionally, bibliographic data for the first twenty hits are to be presented to the user (for details see [1]).

Table 1. HBZ transactions

transaction		percentage	
deletion		0.2%	
insertion		8.1%	
correction		8.1%	
retrieval		83.6%	
	documents		24.3%
	corp. bodies		1.3%
	persons		4.8%
	browsing		34.3%
	navigation		14.5%
	other		4.4%

The performance test was to measure response times for 'real' user transactions on 'real' data. For this purpose HBZ provided a protocol of all user activities of a whole day. The protocol revealed that in the average there are five new transactions every second with a peak of eleven. Table 1 shows that a quarter of all user transactions are document or corporate body retrievals. Nearly all of these retrievals consist of words occurring in the title resp. in the name possibly in combination with some other condition, i.e. these retrievals involve text search operations.[3]

3 Technical Aspects of the Performance Test

The entire data (a total of nearly 5 GB) of the major part of the application and the HBZ protocol built the basis for our performance test which took place at the SEQUENT test center in Munich. During the whole test we enjoyed considerable support from a SEQUENT specialist and ORACLE tuning experts. The test configuration was as follows:

- Server: SEQUENT Symmetry 5000 SE 60
- Clients: five SUN Sparc Station 20
- Software: ORACLE DBMS Version 7.2, TextServer3

The server was equipped with 16 pentium CPU's, 1.5 GB main memory and a total of 50.4 GB hard disc space, half of which was reserved for database tables, index structures, temporary and rollback segments, and the other half for mirroring these data.

During the performance test we varied the number of CPU's (6, 8 or 16), the amount of main memory (768 MB or 1.5 GB) and the load (20 or 50 new transactions per second).

4 Results for ORACLE7 Server

4.1 SQL–Queries

In the first test series we examined the ORACLE database server. The tests therefore included only standard SQL–queries (a total of 24,851) without any updates or text retrieval transactions. We ran three tests with different hardware configurations each generating a load of 20 new transactions per second.

In a configuration with 16 CPU's and 1.5 GB main memory (400,000 buffers, block size 2KB) the average response time was always under 1 second with an overall average of 120 milliseconds for each query. Halving the number of CPU's to 8 even improved the response times, so that all of the queries (with the exception of one query type) could be answered in less than 0.5 seconds and an average response time of 95 msec was achieved. The third test was run with 8 CPU's and 768 MB main memory (150,000 buffers). The average response time deteriorated, sometimes over one second and the average response time increased to 245 msec.

The excellent response times are caused by the fact that librarians' queries were very precise. They have the books right on their desks, they know *exactly*

---

[3] A browsing operation is a request for the long output format of a given entity. Navigations follow associations between given entities.

what they are looking for and they just intend to check whether the book or its author have already been registered in the database. As a consequence more than 99% of the queries had less than 50 hits, and approximately 7% of the queries had no results at all.

4.2 SQL–Updates

The excellent results for standard SQL–queries showed that the load was far from being critical. When extending the queries by update operations we therefore generated an increased load of 50 new transactions per second. We ran two different tests with 6 resp. 8 CPU's and 1.5 GB main memory.

The table definitions included primary key, uniqueness and foreign key constraints. Furthermore, there were some triggers for the computation of derived attribute values. In most cases we had to run more than one SQL–statement to perform the update transaction and subsequent operations to preserve referential integrity. The update transactions, namely corrections, insertions and deletions did not cause any problems. In every case the average response time of all query and update transactions was less than 1 second.

5 Results for TextServer3

5.1 Design Decisions

In some way or the other a text retrieval system has to represent a word occurrence matrix B_{ij}, where $b_{ij} = 1$, if and only if search term w_i occurs in document title t_j. The TextServer3 stores the rows of this matrix in compressed format. Index support guarantees fast access to the bit vector associated with every search term. Results for queries with two or more search terms are obtained by Boolean operations on bit vectors. But typically, HBZ queries involve both title words as well as additional selection conditions on non-text fields. For illustration consider a query which combines a title word with the publication year.

According to agreement with ORACLE we decided to make use of so-called hitlist tables. In a first step the text retrieval component of a query is executed by means of TextServer3 API-procedures (see [6]). These procedures also perform a conversion of bit vectors into hitlist table entries. If bit j is set in the result vector and title t_j belongs to document d_k, then the hitlist table contains a row with document ID d_k. The remaining query can now be executed in standard SQL combining the hitlist table with base tables.

5.2 First Test

In a single–user test with 16 CPU's and 1.5 GB main memory nearly half of the 13 tested queries each of a different type[4] took longer than 30 seconds. In

---

[4] In this first run we tested queries with one title word, with one title word and a person's name or a year or a specific document type, and queries with 1 to 5 words in a corporate body's name.

the worst case a query with one title word and an additional SQL–condition took about 15 minutes. The queries were precisely formulated and quite typical for the librarians. The intermediate results computed by the TextServer3 API procedures were not very large: With the exception of two queries all the others had less than 240 hits.

The TextServer3 API procedures act as follows: In a first step a query is parsed, in a second step the bit vectors are combined (execute–phase) and finally the results are converted and written into hitlist table entries. A closer investigation showed, that the parse–and–execute phases always took about 3–5 seconds. The remaining response time was needed for building up hitlist tables. TextServer3 is most efficient, if large text tables are horizontally decomposed into tables each consisting of 500,000 tuples. This has been taken into account by the definition of 16 non-overlapping views. But parallel insertions into the views seem to cause write conflicts. Therefore we tried an alternative way to combine TextServer3 results with SQL–conditions.

5.3 Second Test

In the second test only the parse–and–execute steps were left to the TextServer3. By calling appropriate API procedures these intermediate results were then loaded into main memory and put into IN–clauses of standard SQL–queries. We thereby circumvented the need for hitlist tables.

Summarizing the results we can say that the parse–and–execute steps always took at least 3 to 5 seconds when searching a title word. Loading ID's into main memory, counting and fetching of the final records depended very strongly on the number of hits. In our test the loading phase took 2 seconds in the average and the fetching phase about 3 more seconds, although 83% of the queries had less than 100 hits.

In a nutshell, the performance test in the SEQUENT test center ended with following result: The relational RDBMS is overwhelmingly fast and neither HBZ retrievals nor updates are critical, as long as they do not involve text search operations. TextServer3, however, suffers from a serious bottleneck in the conversion of bitlists into ID-values, and in the HBZ-application such conversions must constantly be done.

The HBZ application that is characterized by a huge number of short text objects. We expect that TextServer3 performs much better on the same data volume, when there are fewer but larger text objects.

6 Retrieval without Bitlists

6.1 Test Configuration

As the use of compressed bit vectors does not pay off, one may ask, how a direct representation of the word occurrence matrix behaves. In the current section every word occurrence is represented by one tuple (word ID, document

ID, title ID) stored in the database table InvList having more than 48 mio. rows. Furthermore, there is a table Keyword collecting all the title words together with their Frequency-value.

Below we will compare different ways to implement the hit count for HBZ 'pure text retrieval queries', i.e. for those queries which exclusively consist of a set of keywords from document titles without further selection conditions. The HBZ protocol contains 4313 such queries most of them consisting of two or three words.

The tests have been performed at the University of Bonn in single-user mode on a SPARCstation 10 under Solaris 2.5 and ORACLE 7.3.2 with 5,000 buffers (block size 2KB).

6.2 Test Result

It has already been pointed out in Sect. 2.1 that librarians' retrievals are extremely selective, because they know exactly what they are looking for. This also holds for pure text retrieval queries. Although 95% of these queries consist of no more than four words, 93% of text retrieval queries have less than 50 hits. In the average a query has 76 hits. Curve A in Fig. 1 illustrates the number of queries in dependency from query hits: Point (x, y) states that $y\%$ of all text retrieval queries have less than x hits.

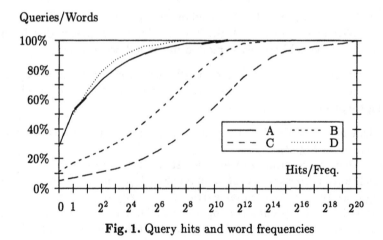

Fig. 1. Query hits and word frequencies

Now, although the number of query hits tends to be small, the single query words may fail to be selective. In fact, only one quarter of all query words have a frequency of less than 50, only half of them less than 1,000, and for fifteen percent the frequency exceeds 10,000 (curve C in Fig. 1). In the average a query word has 29,636 hits.

Fortunately, every query also has one less frequent word: 88% of all queries contain a word with frequency smaller than 1,000 (average frequency of the most selective query words: 524). In curve B in Fig. 1 a point (x, y) denotes that for $y\%$ of all queries their most selective word has a frequency smaller than x. It can be seen that the frequency distribution of all query words (curve C) is completely different from the frequency distribution of all title words (curve D).

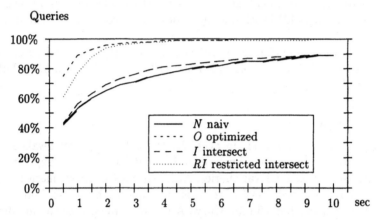

Queries

Fig. 2. Performance of evaluation strategies

In a first implementation only 65% of all queries are answered within the first two seconds (naive case N in Fig. 2). But the unbalanced frequency distribution of query words can be deliberately exploited in the following way:

- First **Frequency**-values are selected for all query words from table **Keyword**.
- Then the text retrieval query is rearranged such that words occur with decreasing frequency.

In this implementation 96% of all queries are answered within two seconds (the optimized case O in Fig. 2).

Of course, there are alternative evaluation strategies. Implementation I makes use of the **INTERSECT**–operator. Kaufmann and Schek [7] already mentioned that ORACLE ignores the fact that index entries are already ordered and thus performs additional time-consuming sort operations. They propose to intersect the inverted lists of infrequent words[5] only, then read in the entire selected titles and filter out the final result. Under the restricted intersection strategy RI words with **Frequency** $> 10,000$ are ignored during evaluation. But then the correct hit count will be computed for only 74% of all queries!. Transmission of ID lists and inspection of documents in order to detect 'false drops' thus seems to be too expensive.

It turns out that strategy O is superior not only with respect to average response times. It also has the advantage that its runtimes are nearly independent from the number of query words.

---

[5] In their terms infrequent words appear in at most 0.1% of all documents.

7 Related Work

DeFazio et al. [2] summarize experimental results when text indexing is not done by the DBMS, but remains in the responsibility of the application (i.e. text retrieval) software. They implemented a prototypical extension of ORACLE Rdb with alternative access methods and tables structured as indexes (index-only tables). On small text collections the prototype achieved promisingly efficient for both retrievals and updates.

In a recent article Macleod [8] compares the strengths and weaknesses of both the relational and the text model. He points out that the former is more flexible and is to be preferred, when relationships among data cannot be mapped onto predefined relations of the text model.

Kaufmann and Schek [7] compare the information retrieval system BASIS-Plus with SQL*TextRetrieval (the predecessor of TextServer3) and a DBMS-based implementation resembling that of Sect. 6. The major difference between SQL*TextRetrieval and TextServer3 is that in the former most work is done on the client side, whereas the latter works directly on the database server. The amount of data loaded into Kaufmann and Schek's test configuration as well as the generated load are significantly smaller than that of our performance tests. Furthermore, Kaufmann and Schek did not have 'real world' queries, and had to simulate all user activities.

Many optimized methods for storing and retrieving text documents are known today (see e.g. Frakes and Baeza–Yates [4]) which are often evaluated against some kind of test collections like TREC [9] to allow comparable result studies. But usually such tests concentrate on information retrieval aspects: Documents are large, and queries are to express an information need rather than the request for a specific document.

8 Conclusions

In the course of a performance test, initiated by the University Library Center of the State of North-Rhine-Westfalia (HBZ), we examined the suitability of an RDBMS for a specific library application, namely librarians' retrievals and updates during document acquisition. We performed the test with ORACLE7 DBMS Server and TextServer3 on the basis of almost the entire HBZ data and 'real' user transactions of a whole day.

Summarizing the results we can say that both standard SQL-queries and updates could be processed with excellent performance. Every transaction took less than 1 second even with a load 10 times higher than that of the actual HBZ system. On the other hand, there was a severe bitlist conversion problem, when text search operations performed by TextServer3 had to be combined with standard SQL-conditions.

We therefore examined a different representation of the word occurrence matrix for 'pure text retrieval queries' and showed that in the HBZ application a direct approach seems to be more promising than a bitlist representation. An optimized nested loop evaluation performs surprisingly well, when query words are rearranged according to their frequency values.

ORACLE has by now integrated TextServer3 functionalities into the database kernel (ConText Option). It will be interesting to see, in how far the HBZ application can benefit from this new approach and how it compares with the implementation alternatives studied in our paper.

Finally, we remark that after the performance test a call for tenders for the new HBZ system has been announced, which states that it should be built on top of an RDBMS.

9 Acknowledgements

We would like to thank the HBZ team engaged in the project and the performance test for the cooperation and helpful discussions. We gratefully acknowledge the contribution of ORACLE and SEQUENT.

References

1. O. Balownew, T. Bode, A.B. Cremers, J. Kalinski, J.E. Wolff, and H. Rottmann. Maintaing Library Catalogues with an RDBMS — A Performance Study —. Technical Report IAI-TR-96-13, University of Bonn, November 1996.
2. S. DeFazio, A. Daoud, L.A. Smith, and J. Srinivasan. Integrating IR and RDBMS using cooperative indexing. In *Proc. of the 18th Annual Int. SIGIR Conf. on Research and Development in Information Retrieval*, pages 84–92, 1995.
3. Deutsche Forschungsgemeinschaft — Bibliotheksausschuß. Empfehlungen zur Migration der deutschen Bibliotheksverbünde. *ZfBB*, 42(2):105–136, 1995.
4. W.B. Frakes and R. Baeza-Yates, editors. *Information Retrieval — Data Structures and Algorithms*. Prentice Hall, 1992.
5. Jürgen Freitag, Horst-Dieter Werner, and Wolfgang Wilkes. Strukturierte Attribute in Relationen zur Unterstützung von IR-Anwendungen. In *GI 12. Jahrestagung, Informatik-Fachberichte 57*, pages 623–647. Springer, 1982.
6. Graham Hoare. *Oracle TextServer3 — Workbench C Guide*. Oracle Corp., 500 Oracle Parkway, Redwood City, CA 94065, 1995. Version 1.0, Part No. A22190-1.
7. H. Kaufmann and H.-J. Schek. Text Search Using Database Systems Revisited — Some Experiments —. In C.A. Goble and J.A. Keane, editors, *Proc. of the 13th British National Conference on Databases (BNCOD 13)*, pages 204–225. Springer, LNCS 940, 1995.
8. Ian A. Macleod. Text retrieval and the relational model. *Journal of the American Society for Information Science*, 42(3):155–165, 1991.
9. National Institute of Standards and Technology. *Proceedings of the Fourth Text REtrieval Conference (TREC-4)*, Gaithersburg, Md., November 1995.
10. J. Newton and D.Y. Brenman. *Oracle TextServer3 — Administrator's Guide*. Oracle Corp., 500 Oracle Parkway, Redwood City, CA 94065, 1995. Version 3.0, Part No. A22191-1.
11. Hans-Jörg Schek. Methods for the administration of textual data in database systems. In R.N. Oddy, S.E. Robertson, C.J. van Rijsbergen, and P.W. Williams, editors, *Information Retrieval Research*, pages 218–235. Butterworths, 1981.

Analysis of Nearest Neighbor Query Performance in Multidimensional Index Structures

Guang-Ho Cha

Dept. of Multimedia Engineering, Tongmyong University of Information Technology,
Pusan, South Korea

Ho-Hyun Park, Chin-Wan Chung
Dept. of Computer Science, Korea Advanced Institute of Science and Technology,
Taejon, South Korea

Abstract

A frequently encountered type of query in geographic information systems and multimedia database systems is to find k nearest neighbors to a given point in a multidimensional space. Examples would be to find the nearest bus stop to a given location or to find some most similar images when an image is given. In this paper, we develop an analytic formula that estimates the performance for nearest neighbor queries and characterize the efficiency of multidimensional index structures for nearest neighbor queries. The developed formula can be used directly in the query optimizers and the characteristics of efficiency will become the basis for the design of the index structure. Experimental results show that our analytic formula is accurate within some acceptable error range. It is exhibited that the efficiency of the index structure depends on the storage utilization and the directory coverage of it.

1. Introduction

A great variety of applications require to find near neighbors in a multidimensional space. For example, typical applications are: finding the nearest MRI brain scans to an given image in medical image databases, retrieving video shots containing the frame similar to a given image in video databases, finding near hotels from a given location in geographic information systems, finding similar DNA's from a large genetics databases, etc.

Efficient processing of nearest neighbor queries requires an efficient index structure which capitalizes on the similarity of the objects to focus the search on the potential neighbors. In recent years, some index structures and algorithms have been developed for fast retrieval of near neighbors in a multidimensional space [1, 3, 7]. However, no attempt has been made to analyze the performance of the nearest neighbor queries on index structures as far as we know. The focus of most analyses [4, 6, 9] has been on the performance of range queries. In this paper, we develop an analytic formula to predict the performance of the nearest neighbor query in multidimensional index structures and investigate the factors that influence the performance of the nearest neighbor query. The developed formula can be used directly in the query optimizers and the investigated performance factors will be used for the basis of the design of multidimensional index structures.

2. Background

2.1 Basic Concepts of Multidimensional Index Structures

Most of multidimensional index structures have a tree structure which consists of internal and leaf nodes. A *leaf node* contains at most C_l entries of the form

$$(oid, R)$$

where C_l is the capacity of a leaf node, *oid* is a pointer to the object in the database, and R is a representative of the real object, e.g., it is a minimum bounding rectangle for the R-tree [5] or an n-dimensional feature vector for image databases [2, 3]. An *internal node* contains at most C_n entries of the form

$$(ptr, R)$$

where C_n is the capacity of an internal node, *ptr* is a pointer to the child node, and R is a bounding device that encloses all objects at lower levels, e.g., it is a minimum bounding rectangle in the R-tree or a minimum bounding interval in the HG-tree [2].

2.2 Basic Definitions

Let n be the dimensionality of the data space, $W_i = [0,1)$, $1 \leq i \leq n$, and $W = W_1 \times W_2 \times \ldots \times W_n$ be the n-dimensional unit data space in which all data objects are defined. Let us assume that for storing N data objects the index structure consumes m nodes s_1, $s_2, \ldots, s_m$, each corresponds to one disk page. The *directory region, $DR(s_j)$* of node s_j is a minimal n-dimensional bounding rectangle enclosing all objects in s_j. This corresponds to the node entry component R described in the above subsection. We assume that $DR(s_j)$ is represented by $[l_1, r_1] \times \ldots \times [l_n, r_n]$, $l_i, r_i \in W_i$, $l_i \leq r_i$ for $1 \leq i \leq n$. The *directory coverage, $C_d(T)$*, of the index structure T is defined by the union of the directory regions of all leaf nodes in the index structure [2]:

$$C_d(T) = \bigcup_{i=1}^{k} DR(s_i), \text{ where } k \text{ is the number of leaf nodes in the index structure.}$$

The *storage utilization* (U) of an index structure can be defined as follows [2]:

$$U = \frac{1}{m} \sum_{i=1}^{m} \frac{F_i}{P_i}$$

where F_i is the number of entries in node i, the P_i is the maximum number of entries that a node i can have, and m is the total number of nodes in the index structure.

Let D be a distance function defined in n-dimensional data space. Given a point $(x_1, x_2, \ldots, x_n)$ and a positive integer k, the k-nearest neighbor query finds the k nearest neighbors on $(x_1, x_2, \ldots, x_n)$ with respect to the distance function D. The typical way to compute the distance between two points is using the Euclidean distance. Let $X = (x_1, x_2, \ldots, x_n)$ and $Y = (y_1, y_2, \ldots, y_n)$ be two points in an n-dimensional space. Then the Euclidean distance, $D_2(X,Y)$ between X and Y is as follows:

$$D_2(X,Y) = \left[\sum_{i=1}^{n} |x_i - y_i|^2 \right]^{1/2}$$

3. Analysis of Index Structures for Nearest Neighbor Queries

In this section we develop an analytic formula to evaluate the average response time for k-nearest neighbor queries. For the performance measure of the query processing, we will use the number of disk accesses necessary to perform k-nearest neighbor query because the average query cost is dominated by disk accesses. And we will use the Euclidean distance as the (dis)similarity measure.

Nearest neighbor search algorithms should focus on eliminating unlikely candidates rather than pin-pointing the targets directly to find the k nearest neighbors, because a data object is not the nearest neighbor only when the index subsystem declares that it is not [3]. Thus it is not clear how to estimate the performance of nearest neighbor queries as compared with range queries in which a specific query region is given and only the nodes overlapping the regions are necessary to be inspected. Contrary to the range queries where the query region is fixed, the query region for the k-nearest neighbor query is widely variable depending on the query location and the data distribution. These problems make the analysis of the nearest neighbor query performance difficult, and may cause the relative errors of the performance analysis to be fluctuated.

At first, we provide an example to get an intuition for the analysis of the nearest neighbor query performance.

Example 1. Fig. 1 shows a collection of directory regions numbered 1 to 12 on a normalized 2-dimensional unit domain space, organized in a multidimensional index structure with fanout = 3. Let us assume that we want to find 5 nearest neighbors from the query location denoted by + in Fig. 1. Then the dotted circle will be the minimal search area of the 5-nearest neighbor query, i.e., all 5 nearest points are within the dotted circle. The directory regions numbered by 1, 3, 5, 10, 11 should be inspected.

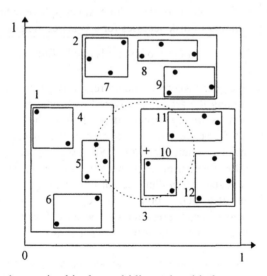

Fig. 1. Data (bullets) organized in the multidimensional index structure with fanout = 3.

Considering this observation, we can catch an insight that the smallest area needed to process the k-nearest neighbor query is the n-dimensional sphere containing the k nearest objects from the query location. Therefore, in the index structure, we can estimate the cost necessary to process the k-nearest neighbor query by computing the number of nodes that intersect the n-dimensional sphere. Then the expected number

DA of disk accesses needed to perform *k*-nearest neighbor query *Q* is given by

$$\sum_{i=1}^{m} Probability\,(\,R(k)\,\cap\,DR\,(\,s_i\,))\qquad\qquad(1)$$

where $R(k)$ is the expected query region covered by Q and m is the total number of nodes in the index structure. Formula (1) says that every node s_i whose directory region $DR(s_i)$ is overlapping the query region $R(k)$ must be inspected. The $R(k)$ becomes the volume $S_n(r)$ of the n-dimensional sphere containing k nearest objects. We will call it *hyper-volume*. We can get the size of each directory region $DR(s_i)$ from the index structure or can compute from the characteristics of the data set [9]. Table 1 gives the summary of symbols and their definitions that will be used in the paper.

Symbols	Definitions
n	number of dimensions
N	number of data points in the index structure
m	number of nodes in the index structure
s_i	i-th node in the index structure
$DR(s_i)$	directory region of node s_i
k	number of neighbors to find
$R(k)$	area covered by k objects
α	value to correct the area covered by k objects
$B(n)$	n-dimensional sphere
r	radius of the n-dimensional sphere
$S_n(r)$	hyper-volume of the n-dimensional sphere with radius r
DA	number of disk accesses for a k-nearest neighbor query

Table 1.   Summary of symbols and Definitions

Contrary to the range query where the query region is given directly, in the nearest neighbor query, determining the area $R(k)$ covered by k objects is an important problem because the area $R(k)$ is widely variable depending on the query location and the data distribution. Since the shape of the area covered by the k-nearest neighbor query is determined by n-dimensional sphere, i.e., $R(k) = S_n(r)$, we must compute $R(k)$ and $S_n(r)$.

Assumed that N uniformly distributed points are stored in a multidimensional index structure and the domain space is n-dimensional unit data space $[0,1)^n$, the area $R(k)$ covered by k points out of a total N points will be k/N. However, this value of $R(k)$ would sometimes lead to inaccurate estimations because $R(k)$ is widely variable depending on the query location and data distributions. Let us consider Examples 2 and 3.

Example 2. Fig. 2 shows two 3-nearest neighbor queries Q_1 and Q_2 in which their query locations are at + and ×, respectively. All data points are clustered within the area denoted by A. The query locations of Q_1 and Q_2 lie outside and inside A, respectively. Two areas covered by Q_1 and Q_2 to include 3 nearest neighbors show significant difference.

The $R(k)$ is also dependent on the data distribution. For example, in uniform distribution, the size of area $R(k)$ may be independent of the query location. On the other

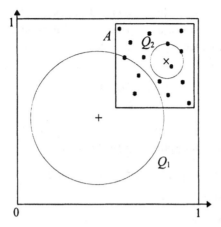

Fig. 2 Two 3-nearest neighbor queries with query points located in + and ×

hand, the influence of the query location on the size of $R(k)$ may be severe in skewed distribution. In particular, when the area covered by the whole data set is smaller, the effect of the query location to the size of $R(k)$ is severer. We give the next example to illustrate the effect how the area covered by the data set influences the size of $R(k)$.

Example 3. Fig. 3 illustrates two sample data distributions on a 1-dimensional space. The bullets on line segments represent data points. We assume that the whole data space is 8 units. Assuming that the search direction is restricted to only one direction, the number beneath each line segment represents the area (= the number of units) that must be searched to find 1-nearest neighbor when the query location lies in that segment. Summing up the results of 1-nearest neighbor query at each line segment, the sums of areas that must to be searched are 12 (= 1+2+1+2+1+2+1+2) units and 18 (= 5+4+3+2+1+1+1+1) units in (a) and (b), respectively.

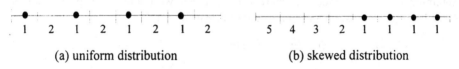

(a) uniform distribution   (b) skewed distribution

Fig. 3 Two sample data distributions on a 1-dimensional line

From the above example, we can get the knowledge that the area that must be searched to find k nearest neighbors tends to increase as the area covered by the data set becomes smaller when the query location is uniformly distributed. Based on the above observation, we correct the area $R(k)$ as follows:

$$R(k) = \frac{k}{N\alpha} \qquad (2)$$

where α is a heuristic value in $(0,1]$ to correct $R(k)$. When the data set has a uniform-like random distribution, α becomes 1. As the area covered by the data set is smaller, we make the α smaller. Smaller area covered by the data set makes it lower that the probability of laying the query location inside the area covered by the directory regions, and thus it tends to increase the size of $R(k)$.

Now, let us find the hyper-volume $S_n(r)$ and radius r of the n-dimensional sphere $B(n)$. Starting from 2-dimensional data space, we will generalize them to n-dimension. In the case of 2-dimension, we have the area $S_2(r) = \pi r^2$ of the circle $B(2)$ and can get the radius r from $\pi r^2 = R(k)$:

$$r = \sqrt{\frac{R(k)}{\pi}}$$

Generalizing the problem to n-dimension, we can compute recursively the hyper-volume S_n of the n-dimensional sphere $B(n)$ as follows:

$$S_n(r) = \int_{-r}^{r} S_{n-1}(f(x))\,dx, \; n \geq 2 \tag{3}$$

$$S_1(r) = 2r,$$

$$f(x) = \sqrt{r^2 - x^2}$$

For $n=2$ and $n=3$, $S_2 = \pi r^2$ and $S_3 = (4/3)\pi r^3$, respectively. We can compute the radius r of an n-dimensional sphere from Eq. 2 = Eq. 3. The hyper-volume of this n-dimensional sphere $B(n)$ with radius r is the estimator of the area covered by the k nearest neighbors from the query location.

Our goal is to estimate the expected number of disk accesses by finding the probability that the n-dimensional sphere $B(n)$ with radius r intersects a directory region $DR(s_i)$. To simplify the situation, we start from 2-dimensional space and then generalize it to n-dimension. As an example, see Fig. 4. $W = [0,1)^2$ is a 2-dimensional unit data space. A square DR is a directory region. Circle C with radius r represents the search area $R(k)$ including the k nearest neighbors, whose center is a query location. The probability that the directory region DR intersects the query circle C becomes the probability that the directory node may be accessed in the nearest neighbor query. We get

$$Probability(C \cap DR) = area(P) = area(DR) + perimeter(DR) \cdot r + area(C)$$

Summing it up to the index structure with m nodes, we obtain the expected number $DA(2)$ of disk accesses on a 2-dimensional space using Eq. 1:

$$DA(2) = \sum_{i=1}^{m} Probability(C \cap DR(s_i))$$

$$= \sum_{i=1}^{m} area(DR(s_i)) + r \sum_{i=1}^{m} perimeter(DR(s_i)) + area(C) \cdot m$$

Generalizing it to n-dimension we derive the following formula for DA:

$$DA(n) = \sum_{i=1}^{m} hypervolume_n(DR(s_i)) + r \sum_{i=1}^{m} hypervolume_{n-1}(DR(s_i))$$

$$+ \sum_{i=1}^{m} (\sum_{j=2}^{n} \frac{1}{2^j} hypervolume_{n-j}(DR(s_i)) \cdot S_j(r)) \tag{4}$$

This the estimator to evaluate the number of disk accesses necessary to perform the k-nearest neighbor query on n-dimensional data space. By the function $hypervolume_n(x)$ we refer to the hyper-volume of an n-dimensional solid x. For example, $n=3$, $n=2$, $n=1$, and $n=0$, $hypervolume_3(x) =$ volume of x, $hypervolume_2(x) =$ area of x, hy-

$pervolume_1(x)$ = perimeter of x, and $hypervolume_0(x)$ = number of vertices of x, respectively. $S_j(r)$ is the hyper-volume of the j-dimensional sphere with radius r.

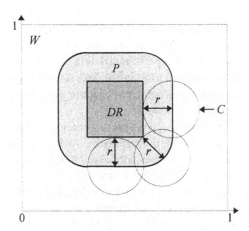

Fig. 4   Probability P that the directory region DR intersects the query circle C

We can make several comments related to the above formula. The performance of the nearest neighbor query relies on three factors: the total number of nodes in the index structure, the hyper-volumes of the directory regions, and the area covered by k nearest objects, which are represented by m, $hypervolume_j(DR(s_i))$, and $S_j(r)$, respectively, in Eq. 4. The size of m is mainly affected by the *storage utilization* of the index structure. Higher storage utilization reduces the total number of nodes, m, in the index structure. The $hypervolume_n(DR(s_i))$ is defined by the *directory coverage* of the index structure. Smaller directory coverage decreases the size of the $hypervolume_n(DR(s_i))$. In addition, all of the j-th hyper-volume $hypervolume_j(DR(s_i))$ are also important factors. The search area $S_j(r)$ is a j-dimensional sphere defined by the required number of objects out of a total number of objects.

4.   Experimental Results and Analysis

In order to evaluate our analysis we carried out several experiments on various data distributions. We employed the HG-tree [2] and the buddy-tree [8] as underlying multidimensional index structures for our experiments, but other structures such as R-tree can be used. The nearest neighbor search is based on the algorithm given by Roussopoulos et al. [7]. During each experiment, the 100,000 4-dimensional points from the data space $[0,1)^4$ has been inserted into the initially empty HG-tree and buddy-tree. In order to achieve statistically significant results the node size was set to 512 bytes which is at the lower end of realistic node sizes [8]. For our tests we used four groups of data sets as in [8]: uniform distribution, clustered distribution, bit distribution, and diagonal distribution.

We based our tests on the number of nodes (= pages) retrieved by k-nearest neighbor query. In Figs. 5 to 8 we see the average of 1,000 queries for each of several different number of nearest neighbors. In each experiment, we used the following heuristic value of α:

$$\alpha = \text{(the area covered by the data set)}^{1/n}$$

where n is the dimensionality of the data space. In practice, we approximated the area covered by the data set by the directory coverage of the index structure.

In the experiments, we used two groups of nearest neighbor queries. In one group of queries, query locations are distributed uniformly. Query locations of the other group follow the distributions similar to the data set. The experimental result of the former group is represented by Experimental1 and that of the latter group is represented by Experimental2 in Figs. 6 to 8. In the data set with uniform distribution, only the uniformly distributed queries were tested because the query locations of these queries follow the distributions of the data set.

The observation of the results in uniform distribution is that the analytical estimate is close to the actual result: the relative error is below 9%. In clustered distribution, on the other hand, the errors in the queries with small number of neighbors are relatively large compared with those of the uniform distribution. However, the average errors are within an acceptable range (less than 14%). In the bit distribution, all relative errors are below 16%. The errors in the diagonal distribution are large. However, when the distribution of the query locations is similar to the distribution of the data set, the average error is acceptable (less than 19%).

In the case that the ratio of the area covered by the data set to the whole data space is very small, which is the case of our diagonal distribution, the relative errors tend to be large. In this case, assuming that query locations are uniformly distributed, the probability that the query locations lie close to the desired data points or directory regions is very low. Therefore, the area $R(k)$ is very large, and thus it may cause the difference between the estimated area $R(k)$ and the actual area covered by k points to be high. Compared to the analysis of the range query performance [4, 9], the reason that the error rates in the analysis of the nearest neighbor query performance are somewhat high is because the fluctuation of the area $R(k)$ is relatively high depending on the query location and the data distribution. However, since we may make an optimistic assumption that the query locations given by users are not so far away from desired data objects, we may expect that the actual error rates are lower than those in the experimental results. For example, in content-based image databases, users may provide an query image similar to what they want to retrieve.

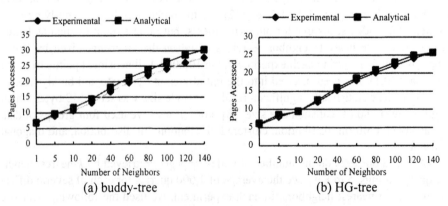

Fig. 5 Experimental vs. analytical results in uniform data distributions

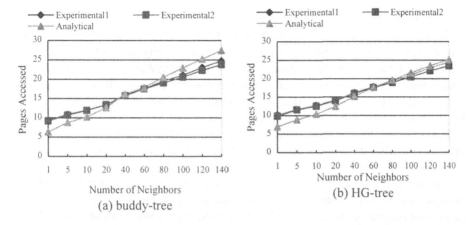

Fig. 6   Experimental vs. analytical results in clustered distributions

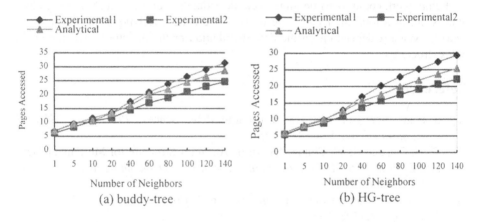

Fig. 7   Experimental vs. analytical results in bit distributions

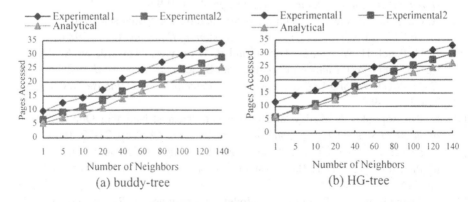

Fig. 8   Experimental vs. analytical results in diagonal distributions

5. Conclusions

There are two contributions in this work. First, we derived an analytic formula that can be used as a good estimate for the cost of nearest neighbor query performance. Using it we estimated the performance of the nearest neighbor query on various data distributions and showed that the analysis is applicable for prediction of the nearest neighbor query performance. Experimental results show that the estimation errors are within an acceptable range in most case, the average error is usually around 5%-20%. Even in the case that the area covered by the data set is extremely small, the average error is below 19% if the query distribution is similar to the data distribution.

Second, we showed that the storage utilization, the directory coverage, the hyper-volume of the directory region, and the area covered by the required k data objects are the major factors that influence the performance of the nearest neighbor query. These factors will become the basis for the design of multidimensional index structures. Up to now, it has not yet been well known what are the critical factors that influence the nearest neighbor query performance.

Future work could focus on more accurate estimation of the area $R(k)$covered by k objects out of a total of N data objects. Here we need a technique for adjusting the heuristic value α depending on the data distribution or the directory coverage of the index structure.

References

[1] S. Brin, "Near Neighbor Search in Large Metric Spaces," *Proc. of the 21th Int'l. Conf. on VLDB*, pp. 574-584, 1995.

[2] G.-H. Cha and C.-W. Chung, "HG-tree: An Index Structure for Multimedia Databases," *Proc. of the IEEE Int'l. Conf. on Multimedia Computing and Systems*, pp. 449-452, June 1996.

[3] T. Chiueh, "Content-Based Image Indexing," *Proc. of the 20th Int'l. Conf. on VLDB*, pp. 582-593, 1994.

[4] C. Faloutsos and I. Kamel, "Beyond Uniformity and Independence: Analysis of R-trees Using the Concept of Fractal Dimension," *Proc. of the 13th ACM Symposium on Principles of Database Systems*, pp. 4-13, 1994.

[5] A. Guttman, "R-trees: a dynamic index structures for spatial searching," *Proc. of the ACM SIGMOD Int'l. Conf. on Management of Data*, pp. 47-57, 1984.

[6] B.-U. Pagel, H.-W. Six, H. Toben, and P. Widmayer, "Towards an Analysis of Range Query Performance in Spatial Data Structures," *Proc. of the 12th ACM SI-GACT-SIGMOD-SIGART Symposium on Principles of Database Systems*, pp. 214-221, 1993.

[7] N. Roussopoulos, S. Kelley, and F. Vincent, "Nearest Neighbor Queries," *Proc. of the ACM SIGMOD Int'l. Conf. on Management of Data*, pp. 71-79, 1995.

[8] B. Seeger and H.-P. Kriegel, "The Buddy-Tree: An Efficient and Robust Access Method for Spatial Data Base Systems," *Proc. of the 16th Int'l. Conf. on VLDB*, pp. 590-601, 1990.

[9] Y. Theodoridis and T. Sellis, "A Model for Prediction of R-tree Performance," *Proc. of the 16th ACM SIGACT-SIDMOD-SIGART Symposium on Principles of Database Systems*, pp. 161-169, 1996.

A Query Language and Interface for Integrated Media and Alphanumeric Database Systems*

Jia-Ling Koh*, Arbee L.P. Chen, Paul C.M. Chang, James C.C. Chen

Department of Computer Science
National Tsing Hua University
Hsinchu, Taiwan 300, R.O.C.
Email : alpchen@cs.nthu.edu.tw

Abstract. In this paper, we consider a multidatabase system which consists of media databases and traditional *alphanumeric databases*. The *semantic relationships* which may exist among the objects in the media databases and alphanumeric databases are introduced. By applying the semantic relationships, the related information in the system can be integrated. Therefore, more powerful querying capabilities and a higher degree of information sharing can be achieved. A query language IMAQL is designed for querying the integrated system. A graphic query interface is also presented to facilitate user-friendly querying in the system.

1   Introduction

Due to rapid development of electronic devices and computer technologies, more and more information is represented in various types of media. Databases for managing media data have been individually developed, including image databases, audio databases, and video databases [1] [4] [7]. Content-based retrieval of media data has become an important research issue. [17] provides strategies to detect shot changes in a video to extract the key frame of each shot for content-based retrieval and browsing. The QBIC system [6] supports querying-by-example on image and video databases. A logic-based language considering spatial and temporal descriptions was designed to support a visual query interface on image sequences [2]. [8] proposed a data model, in which the metadata of the media content were used to provide similarity browsing of multimedia data.

In our previous work, the problems of content-based indexing and querying capabilities for various types of media databases were studied. A content-based video query language (CVQL) [13] was proposed for querying video data. The relative position between symbols and the motion of symbols in a video can be specified by CVQL. Furthermore, an indexing strategy based on *chord* was proposed for querying music data by giving a piece of music [5].

---

* this work was partially supported by the Republic of China National Science Council under Contract No. NSC 86-2213-E-007-017.
[1] Dr. Koh is now an assistant professor in the Department of Information and Computer Eduation at National Taiwan Normal University.

The development of computer networks in recent years has made data sharing among databases important. We have proposed the strategies for schema integration and query processing in a multidatabase system which consists of object databases [10, 11, 12]. Assume a multidatabase system which consists of individually developed media databases and traditional *alphanumeric databases*. More powerful querying capabilities can be achieved by integrating the information in the media databases and alphanumeric databases. For example, the users may want to retrieve the movies whose directors have ever won the Oscar award. Since the predicative condition cannot be derived from the video content directly, the query cannot be processed in a video database. However, it is possible that an existing alphanumeric database contains the personal information of the directors. In such a environment, two kinds of *semantic relationships* among objects may exist. The first one is the *identity relationship* which implies that the involved objects represent the same real-world entity. These objects are named *identical objects*. Another kind of relationship is the *composition relationship* which denotes that the data for representing one object are included in the content of another object. In this paper, we present a system named IMADS(Integrated Media and Alphanumeric Database System) which is being developed to achieve a more powerful querying capability and a higher degree of information sharing. A query language IMAQL is designed for this purpose. The two kinds of semantic relationships are used to integrate the related information in the multidatabase system. The identical objects are integrated to an *entity* in IMADS, which represents a real-world entity. The queries in IMAQL are specified based on the entities. The desired entities can be retrieved by giving predicates on the related entities of different types through the composition relationships.

The work on multimedia databases mainly focuses on designing a database to manage media and alphanumeric data. In order to manage media data in an alphanumeric database [16], a *pseudo attribute* was proposed to denote the features of the media data in the alphanumeric database. The users can therefore specify restrictions on media data by giving predicates on the pseudo attributes in an alphanumeric form. [15] designed a content-based retrieval engine for multimedia data, where the similarity, fuzzy, and text retrieval functions were provided. However, in these approaches, only information in single media data can be used to specify query predicates.

In our approach, we use the concept of entity and the relationships among entities to specify query predicates in a multidatabase system consisting of multiple media and alphanumeric databases. [9] proposed a multimedia query language for retrieving multimedia documents which consist of multiple media segments. The users can specify the content of each segment as well as spatial and temporal predicates among multiple media segments. However, the entity-level information was not considered in the content of each segment. A data modeling strategy called *media abstraction* was illustrated in [3] to provide a unified interface for integrating media data of different types. Although a language was proposed, the language was logic-based which was difficult for the users to use.

This paper is organized as follows. The next section clarifies the basic assumptions of the integrated environment. Various kinds of semantic relationships among objects in media and alphanumeric databases which contribute to the enhanced query capabilities are also introduced. Section 3 presents the syntax of the query language IMAQL. A graphic query interface for helping users to query the integrated system is shown in Section 4. Finally, section 5 concludes this paper with a discussion of the future works.

2 IMADS and the Semantic Relationships

2.1 The Integrated Environment

Assume IMADS consists of various types of media databases and an object-oriented database with alphanumeric data. Let a *media object* denote a data item in a media database, such as a movie in a video database. The symbols, voice, or words which can be extracted from a media object are named *symbol objects*. For example, a car appearing in a movie is a symbol object. In addition, a data item in an alphanumeric database is named an *alphanumeric object*. All the involved media databases in the system provide the content-based querying capabilities. That is, the symbol objects in a media object can be detected, and the indices on the features of the symbol objects are constructed. The classifications for categorizing the media and symbol objects respectively are also provided.

2.2 The Semantic Relationships

In IMADS, the *composition* or *identity* relationships may exist among media, symbol, or alphanumeric objects. Such kinds of relationships are called the *semantic relationships*, which are divided into the following five kinds.

1. The composition relationship between a media object and a symbol object: For example, the voice of a person appearing in an audio results in this kind of relationship between the audio and the voice of the person.
2. The composition relationship between two media objects: For example, a movie in a video database contains a song which is also represented as a media object in an audio database.
3. The identity relationship between two symbol objects: For example, a symbol object in an image and another in a video represent the same house.
4. The identity relationship between a media object and an alphanumeric object: For example, the director of a movie in a video database is represented by an object in an object-oriented database.
5. The identity relationship between a symbol object and an alphanumeric object: For example, John is represented as a symbol object in a video and also as an alphanumeric object in class **Person**.

The composition relationships can be added with descriptions in order to better represent the semantics of the relationships. For example, if a song is the main title of a movie, "main title" represents the semantics of the composition relationship.

Suppose objects **o1** and **o2** have a semantic relationship. The information concerning **o2** can thus be used in the predicates for retrieving **o1**. Furthermore, the predicates for retrieving **o1** can involve the information of object **o3** if **o2** and **o3** also have a semantic relationship.

The real-world entities represented in IMADS are divided into three kinds: *media entities, symbol entities,* and *alphanumeric entities.* A media entity is represented by a media object in the media databases combined with its possible identical alphanumeric object. The media entities are further divided into video, image, audio, and document types. The symbol entities are the symbol objects together with their possible identical alphanumeric objects. Those alphanumeric objects which have neither identical media objects nor identical symbol objects belong to alphanumeric entities.

3 Query Language IMAQL

3.1 Basic Features of IMAQL

An IMAQL query mainly includes two parts:

    Retrieve *Target-clause*;

    From *R-P-clause.*

Target-clause The *Target-clause* specifies the result to be retrieved by the query, which has one or a list of notation v or $v.P$ separated by commas. v is a variable bound to entities in the *R-P-clause*, and P is a *path expression* proposed in object-oriented databases for denoting a property of the candidate entities.

R-P-clause The *R-P-clause* following the keyword **From** denotes the searching ranges and predicates of the query, which consists of two parts:

    Range-clause

    Predicate-clause.

The *Range-clause* defines the searching range for the following *Predicate-clause*. It has the following form: *entity-type(classification):* e,

where the *entity-type* denotes the type of entities being evaluated. The *entity-type* can be one of the media types as specified by **Video, Image, Audio,** or **Document.** It also can be the symbol type denoted by **Symbol** or the alphanumeric type by **AlphaNum.** According to the specified entity type, the users can further specify a specific classification of the type to be the searching space. The entities in the specified range are called *candidate entities* of the *Predicate-clause.* e is a variable bound to the candidate entities.

The *Predicate-clause* specifies the restrictions on the associated candidate entities. It is defined as a boolean combination of predicates by using the logical connectives **and** and **or**. A predicate can be one of the following forms.

1. *containment predicate*

    A containment predicate restricts the candidate entities to those which contain a specific entity.

A *simple containment predicate* has the form: **contain** {*Component*}, where *Component* is denoted as: [*r-semantics*] *Sub-R-P-clause*. The *r-semantics* is used to specify the semantics of the composition relationship between a candidate entity and the component entity. The *Sub-R-P-clause* specifies the searching range and the predicates on the component entity.

A *complex containment predicate* has the following form:

> **contain** {*Component 1, Component 2, ..., Component n*}
> **where** { *S-T-predicates* },

where *Component i* ($1 \leq i \leq n$) has the same form as the *Component* in a simple containment predicate. A complex containment predicate restrains the candidate entities to those which contain a specific set of entities. In addition, the temporal and/or spatial relationships among the set of entities are specified in the *S-T-predicates*. The keyword **where** and the following *S-T-predicates* are omitted if no temporal or spatial predicates should be specified.

In this paper, three primitive functions are provided for denoting simple spatial and temporal predicates.

- **OMove**(*v*) *xy-expression*

  This function is used to specify predicates on the movement of a symbol entity. *v* is a variable bound to an entity. The *xy-expression* has the form: [**x** α 0, **y** α 0], where α is one of the comparators <, =, and >. It denotes the movement on the horizontal and vertical directions. For example, it represents that the entity moves to the right if **x** > 0 is specified in the *xy-expression*. **y** < 0 denotes that the entity moves down.

- **RP**(*v1, v2*) *xy-expression*

  The **RP** function specifies the relative position between two entities. *v1* and *v2* are variables bound to entities. The *xy-expression* has the same form as that in the **OMove** function except that it denotes the relative position from *v1* to *v2*. As an example, [**x** < 0, **y** > 0] denotes that *v1* is located on the upper-left side of *v2*.

- **RT**(*v1, v2*) *t-expression*

  The **RT** function specifies the predicate on the relatively appearing time of two entities. *t-expression* has the form: [**t** α 0]. α can be <, =, or >. If **t** < 0, *v1* appears before *v2*. **t** > 0 denotes that *v1* appears after *v2*. Otherwise, two entities appears at the same time.

The *S-T-predicates* is a sequence of these temporal and/or spatial predicates connected by logical connectives **and** and/or **or**.

2. *similarity predicate*

   A similarity predicate is used to denote the similarity retrieval by giving an example query, which is specified as: **similar-to**(*f-name*),

   where *f-name* is the name of a file which stores a media object. The similarity degree between a candidate entity and the given media instance is computed by a similarity function. The predicate is evaluated to be *true* if the degree is less than a threshold value.

3. *appearing-in predicate*

An appearing-in predicate restrains the candidate entities to those appearing in a specific entity. A *simple appearing-in predicate* has the form:

appear-in {*Composition* }.

The *Composition* has the form: [*r-semantics*] *Super-R-P-clause.*

The *r-semantics* denotes the semantics of the relationship between the candidate entity and the specified composition. The searching range and the predicates on the composition are specified in the *Super-R-P-clause.*

4. *property predicate*

A property predicate is used to specify predicates on the property of the candidate entity. It has the form: **with**(*P*):*p* {*P-clause*},

where *P* is a path expression denoting a property of the candidate entities. *p* is a variable bound to the value of the property of a candidate entity one at a time, which can be omitted. The entities representing the values of the property become the candidate entities of the *P-clause*. If no predicate is specified on the property, {*P-clause*} is omitted.

Q1:
Retrieve M;
From Video(Movie): M
      contain{[main title]**Audio**(Music):
             similar-to(ex_music)}

Q2:
Retrieve P;
From Video(Movie):
      contain{**Symbol**(Person): X
         appear_in{**Image**(Picture): P},
         Symbol(Car):C}
     where{**RP**(X,C)[x=0,y>0]
       and OMove(X)[x>0,y<0]
       and OMove(C)[x<0,y=0]

Fig. 1. The example queries

Another kind of predicates called *primitive predicates* are of the form: θ t, where t is a constant, and θ is one of the *primitive comparators*: $<$, $\leq$, $=$, $\geq$, or $>$. The primitive predicates are used when the associated candidate entities belong to string or integer type.

In the examples shown in Figure 1, **Video**(Movie) is a searching range, followed by the predicates on the searching range. The containment predicate in **Q1** specifies that the interested movies contain a specific music. The [main title] in the predicate denotes that the music should be the main title of the movies. Similarly, the containment predicates in **Q2** restrict the symbols in the interested movies. The clause following the keyword **Where** specifies the relative positions and motions of these symbols in the movies. Since a media entity may consist of various components, the searching ranges for each component should be separately specified. For example, **Audio**(Music) in **Q1**, **Symbol**(Person) and **Symbol**(Car) in **Q2** are the searching ranges of the components. Furthermore, predicates can be specified on the components. Take **Q1** as an example, the contained music is restricted to be similar to a given example by the similarity predicate: **similar-to**(ex_music). In **Q2**, the contained symbol person is

Q3:
Retrieve Y.name;
From **Video**(Movie):
    with(title):{="die hard"}
  and contain{**Symbol**(Person): X
        with(name):{="Bruce Willis}
      and with(height): h,
      Symbol(Person): Y
      with(height):{>h}}

Q5:
Retrieve n;
From **Video**(Movie):
    with(title):{="die hard"}
  and contain{**Symbol**(Man):
      with(height): h}
  and contain{**Symbol**(Man):P
      with(height):{ $\geq$ **all** h}
      and with(name):n}

Q7:
Retrieve M;
From **Video**(Movie):M
    contain{**Symbol**(Person): P}
  and all P **with**(height):{<160}}

Q4:
Retrievei X;
From **Video**(Movie): X
      with(director): P
  and contain{**Symbol**(Person): P,
      Symbol(Car): C}
    where{**RP**(P,C)[x=0,y$\geq$0]
    and OMove(C)[x>0,y=0]
    and OMove(P)[x>0,y=0]}

Q6:
Retrieve n;
From **Symbol**(Person):
      with(name):n
  and appear_in{**all Video**(Movie):
  with(director.name){="Jackie Chen"}}

Q8:
Retrieve count(M);
From **Video**(Movie):M
      contain{**Symbol**(Male):P}
  and with(director):P

Q9:
Retrieve M;
From **Video**(Movie):M
      contain{**Symbol**(Person):P}
  and Is-Class(P)**group-by**(M)="Female"}

Fig. 2. Example queries **Q3** to **Q9**

restrained to appear in certain picture. Therefore, an *R-P-clause* has a nested structure; that is, there can be another *R-P-clause* in a predicate. This nested structure also applies to the appearing-in and property predicates.

3.2 Extended Features

Join There are two ways for denoting the joins. The first way relates the entities by comparing their values. A join is also used to denote the identity of entities by assigning the same variable to bind the entities. For example, query **Q3** in Figure 2 retrieves the names of persons who appear in the movie "die hard" and are taller than the person named **Bruce Willis** also appearing in the movie. As another example shown in Figure 2, the movies whose directors also act in the movies by standing on top of a car running toward right are retrieved by **Q4**.

Quantifier The default quantifier for the predicates is the existential quantifier. The universal quantifier on the predicates should be specified explicitly by using the keyword **all**. The situations where the universal quantifier can be specified in a predicate are illustrated as the following.

- Applied in primitive predicates.
  For example, the example query **Q5** in Figure 2 shows how to retrieve the name of the tallest man in movie "Die Hard."
- Applied in containment/appearing-in predicates.
  For example, query **Q6** retrieves the names of persons who appear in all the movies directed by Jackie Chen.

In another situation, the users may require that a specific set of entities all satisfy some restrictions. As the example **Q7** shows, it retrieves the movie in which all the persons are shorter than 160cm.

Aggregation Functions The usage of an aggregation function is as in the form: *Function-name*(u)**group-by**(v), where u and v are variables bound to entities. For each entity bound by v, the entities bound by u and satisfying the associated predicates are placed in a group for the computation of the aggregation function. The **group-by**(v) is an option, which can be omitted.

The aggregation functions can be specified in the *Target-clause* and also in the predicates. According to the type of entities, different aggregation functions are provided. The example query **Q8** retrieves the number of movies whose directors are male and also as actors in the movies. The **Is-Class** function returns the minimum common classification for the set of involved entities. For example, the movies which only have actresses can be retrieved by example query **Q9**.

4   Query Interface

A query interface is designed for providing a user-friendly interface to query the IMADS system. For simplifying the usage of the query interface, the extended features proposed by IMAQL have not been provided in the interface. Suppose we would like to retrieve the pictures of a person who appears in a movie. In addition, the movie contain two specifiable shots. In the beginning of the movie, a person jumps down from a car and the background includes some flowers on the right and a tree on the left. After a period of time, a subway appears and a song is playing at the same time. Furthermore, the song is sung by Madonna. The query is specified by the query interface as Figure 3(a) to 3(f).

The query interface is shown as in Figure 3(a) when beginning a new query. The users use a mouse to choose one of the querying domains in order to specify the type of entities being searched. Then a new window appears and the classification of the specified domain can be selected. In our example, the classification **Picture** of image entities is selected. The menu item labeled by **Predicate** is used to select the kind of predicates to be specified. The item **Contain** listed in the **Predicate** menu is selected and a *containment-predicate window* appears as in Figure 3(b). The contained entities and their spatial relationships in the searched picture are described in the containment-predicate window. As figure 3(b) shows, it denotes that a person appears in the specified position of the searched picture. At the same time, a window captioned by **Global View of Query** shows all the specified entities in the query as shown in Figure 3(b). More predicates can be specified on the entities contained in **Picture x** by selecting the associated items in **Global View of Query** window. In order to specify predicates on entities in which the person appears, the **Appear in** item in the **Predicate** memu is selected and an *appearing-in-predicate* window appears. We can specify that the person in the picture also appears in a movie as shown in

Figure 3(c). Similarly, the containment predicates can be specified on the movie as Figure 3(d). Since a movie is a video entity, the time issue should be considered in the predicates. The *relative time bar* is used for specifying the temporal relationships be tween the contained entities. The button on the time bar can be moved left or right to denote the relatively appearing time of the contained entities in a time sequence. In addition, the motion of a symbol can be specified by giving the direction and offset. As Figure 3(d) shows, it denotes that a person jumps down from a car and the background includes some flowers on the right and a tree on the left. By moving the button on the time bar right, another shot which appears after the previous shot in the movie is described by Figure 3(e). In the shot, a subway appears and a song is playing at the same time. In order to specify predicates on properties of the song, the **Property** item in the **Predicate** memu is selected and a *property-predicate* window shows the properties of a song. As Figure 3(f) shows, the name of the singer is specified to be Madonna.

We have implemented the query interface by the *Java* language [14] in the environment of Window95 operating system. The interface can be accessed and used via the internet browsers by linking to the following URL: http://piggy.cs. nthu.edu.tw/imadbs/imadbs.html. Efficient query processing strategies are currently under development. Integrating the video database and the music database, which we have independently implemented, in IMADS is also being conducted.

5 Conclusion

In this paper, a multidatabase system which consists of media databases and traditional alphanumeric databases is discussed. The two kinds of semantic relationships, identity and composition relationships, among objects are introduced for integrating the information in these databases to construct an integrated system IMADS. A query language IMAQL is proposed to provide powerful querying capabilities in IMADS. The identical objects in the multidatabase system, which denote the same real-world entity are integrated and represented by an entity in IMADS. The information of all the identical objects are considered to be the features of the associated entity. The queries in IMAQL are based on the entities. IMAQL provides the capabilities for specifying predicates on various types of media data and alphanumeric data. Moreover, the desired entity can be retrieved by giving the predicates on the related entities of different types through composition relationships and properties. The join operations, quantifiers, and aggregation functions are also proposed. Finally, a user-friendly query interface is presented which provides the facilities of incrementally querying IMADS and browsing the results.

It is difficult to automatically detect the semantic relationships. Developing a tool by combining the knowledge databases and the techniques of pattern recognition to semi-automatically detect these relationships is an important research issue, which is currently under our consideration.

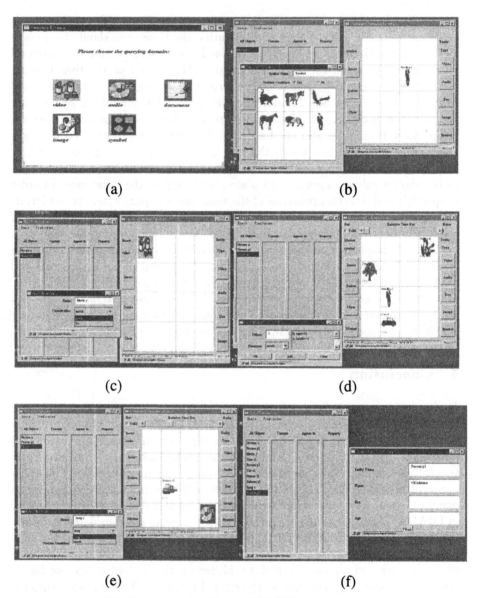

(a)   (b)

(c)   (d)

(e)   (f)

Fig. 3.   Query interface of **IMADB**

References

1. Y.A. Aslandogan et al., Design, Implementation and Evaluation of SCORE (A System for COntent based REtrieval of pictures), *Proc. IEEE Intl. Conf. Data Engineering*, (1995) pp.280-287.
2. A.D. Bimbo, E. Vicario, and D. Zingoni, Symbolic Description and Visual Querying of Image Sequences Using Spatial-Temporal Logic, *IEEE Trans. Knowledge and Data Engineering*, 7(4) (1995) pp.609-621.
3. A. Brink, S. Marcus, and V.S. Subrahmanian, Heterogeneous Multimedia Reasoning, *IEEE Computer*, Sep. (1995) pp.33-39.
4. S.K. Chang and A. Hsu, Image Information Systems: Where Do We Go From Here?, *IEEE Trans. Knowledge and Data Engineering*, 4(5) (1992) pp.431-442.
5. T.C. Chou, A.L.P. Chen, and C.C. Liu, Music Databases: Indexing Techniques and Implementation, *Proc. IEEE International Workshop on Multi-Media Database Management Systems* (1996), pp.46-53.
6. M. Flickner et al., Query by Image and Video Content: The QBIC System, *IEEE Computer*, Sep. (1995) pp.49-56.
7. Gibbs, C. Breiteneder and D. Tsichritzis, Audio/Video Databases: An Object-Oriented Approach, *Proc. IEEE Intl. Conf. Data Engineering*, (1993) pp.381-390. *IEEE Multimedia*, 1 (1) (1994) pp.12-24.
8. W.I. Grosky, F. Fotouhi, and I.K. Sethi, Using Metadata for the Intelligent Browsing of Structured Media Objects, *ACM SIGMOD RECORD*, 23 (4) (1994) pp.49-56. *Proc. the 20th VLDB Conference*, (1994) pp.297-308.
9. N. Hirzalla and A. Karmouch, A Multimedia Query Specification Language, *Proc. International Workshop on Multimedia Database Management Systems*, (1995) pp.66-73.
10. J.L. Koh and A.L.P. Chen, Integration of Heterogeneous Object Schemas, *Lecture Notes in Computer Sciences : Entity-Relationship Approach-ER '93*, Vol. 823, Springer-Verlang: Berlin, (1993) pp.297-314.
11. J.L. Koh and A.L.P. Chen, A Mapping Strategy for Querying Multiple Object Databases with a Global Object Schema, *Proceedings of IEEE the fifth International Workshop on Research Issues in Data Engineering*, (1995) pp.50-57.
12. J.L. Koh and A.L.P. Chen, Query Execution Strategies for Missing Data in Distributed Heterogeneous Object Databases, *Proceedings of IEEE the 16th International Conference on Distributed Computing Systems*, (1996) pp.466-473.
13. T.C.K. Kuo and A.L.P. Chen, A Content-Based Query Language for Video Databases, *Proceedings of IEEE International Conference on Multimedia Computing and Systems* (1996), pp.209-214.
14. Sun Microsystems, Inc., JavaSoft, 1995.
15. J.K. Wu, A.D. Narasimhalu, B.M. Mehtre, C.P. Lam, Y.J. Gao, CORE: a Content-Based Retrieval Engine for Multimedia Information Systems, *ACM Multimedia Systems*, 3 (1) (1995) pp.25-41.
16. A. Yoshitaka, S. Kishida, M. Hirakawa, and T. Ichikawa, Knowledge-Assisted Content-Based Retrieval for Multimedia Databases, *IEEE Multimedia*, 1 (4) (1994) pp.12-21.
17. H.J. Zhang, C.Y. Low, S.W. Smoliar, and J.H. Wu, Video Parsing, Retrieval and Browsing: An Integrated and Content-Based Solution, *Proc. ACM Multimedia*, (1995) pp.15-24.

An Algebraic Query Language for Object-oriented Data Models

Kazem LELLAHI*   Rachid SOUAH°   Nicolas SPYRATOS°

* LIPN, U.R.A. 1507 du C.N.R.S
Université Paris 13, Institut Galilée,
93430 Villetaneuse France.
E-mail: kl@ura1507.univ-paris13.fr

° LRI, U.R.A. 410 du C.N.R.S
Université Paris 11, Centre Orsay,
91405 Orsay cedex France.
E-mail: {souah, spyratos}@lri.lri.fr

Abstract. We introduce an object-oriented data model with a purely algebraic query language. In our model, a class attribute is seen as a partial function over the class extension. The query language has two components, a functional and an algebraic. The functional component is an algebra of functions expressed by rules. The algebraic component is an algebra of classes expressed by algebraic operations. Distinctive features of our query language are (1) it manipulates aggregate functions and algebraic computations at the same level as attributes, and (2) it allows the construction of path expressions in two ways: sequential, by function composition, and parallel by function pairing.

1   Introduction

In the relational model, data is structured in the form of sets of tuples with atomic values [Ull88]. This simple structuring is adequate for business-oriented applications, but cannot capture the semantics of complex applications. Nevertheless, this simple structuring is at the basis of a prominent feature of the relational model: the existence of an algebraic query language. A major advantage of such a language is that it allows to develop optimizers that are transparent to the end users. A major disadvantage is that it does not allow computations on data, hence the importance of languages such as SQL and its extensions.

In object-oriented data models [Kim95], data is structured in the form of objects, and objects can have a very complex structure. The rich structuring of objects, is quite adequate to capture the semantics of complex applications. On the other hand, the rich structuring of objects makes it difficult to define an algebraic query language, in the style of the relational model. To our knowledge, none of the languages proposed recently for object-oriented data models OQL[Cat94], O2SQL[BCD92], XSQL [KKS92] has the algebraic flavor of the relational algebra. Collection languages on the other hand [BNTW95] [BBN91] [Lel94] are based on an algebra of functions, and are strongly influenced by category theory and the theory of monads. The functional character of these languages however, is quite far from the relational style.

One important advantage of object-oriented data modeling is its computing power. However, computation in a query language seems to require a calculus different in nature than the classical λ-calculus [BNTW95] [LT97] [FD95].

The objective of this paper is two-fold: (i) define an object-oriented data model and (ii) define a *purely algebraic* query language for this model.

The basic tool that we use is the attribute-as-function approach. Although an attribute is often seen as a function *implicitly* (for example, an attribute is often seen as a method), the notion of an attribute-as-function has never been used *explicitly* in the definition of an object oriented data model (except in some non-object-oriented data models, such as DAPLEX[Shi81] and FQL[BF79]).

In our approach, a class is seen as a set of functions on the same set of objects, and the values of an object are seen as the results of simultaneously applying these functions on the object. We note that this viewpoint corresponds to that adopted in [LS91] [LS92] from which the present paper is inspired.

The query language that we will present manipulates finite sets of objects (the class extensions) on the one hand, and functions (the attributes and the type operations) on the other. As our language is algebraic, it also manipulates functions through algebraic operations. Although these operations are inspired by category theory [BNTW95], the present paper makes no explicit use of that theory.

In the present paper, because of lack of space, we only present the main ingredients of the model and its query language. We do this using a simplified version of the model, with no set-valued attributes. The complete model and its query language are presented in the full paper [LSS97].

2 The Model

2.1 The Database Schema

We begin with two denumerable, nonempty and disjoint sets: the set of *attribute names* and the set of *class names*, and a finite set β of basic types:

$$\beta ::= int \mid float \mid char \mid bool \mid string \mid \cdots$$

Later on, we shall complete β so that it becomes an adequate type system.

Definition 1 *We call attribute any triple (c, a, t), where c is a class name, a is an attribute name, and t is either a type or a class name; we call c the source and t the target of the attribute. If the target is a class name then the attribute is called an object-attribute, otherwise it is called a value-attribute.*

Definition 2 *We call class any finite nonempty set of attributes with the same source, such that no two attributes have the same name.*

Definition 3 *A database schema S is a finite nonempty set of classes such that:*
— The class names in S are all distinct, and
— for every attribute (c, a, t) in S, if t is a class then there is a class c' in S such that $t = c'$.

The first condition allows to identify uniquely a class of S by simply giving its name. The second condition requires that the target of every object attribute in S must be a class name of S.

We note that our definition of database schema allows overloading of attribute names.

Example 1 (Running Example) *Consider a database schema, that we shall call AGENDA, consisting of the following classes:*

$Pers(name : string;\ first\_name : string;\ spouse : Pers;\ addr : Addr)$
$Addr(num : int;\ street : string;\ zip : Zip)$
$Zip(code : int;\ city : string;\ state : string)$
$Tel(num : int;\ name : Pers;\ addr : Addr)$

In the above notation, a class with attributes $(c, a_1, t_1), \ldots, (c, a_n, t_n)$ is denoted by $c(a_1 : t_1, \ldots, a_n : t_n)$, and referred to as "the class c".

2.2 The Database instances

In order to define a database instance, we need the concept of *concrete type*. We shall assume that each basic type t is associated to a denumerable set $|t|$ which we shall call the concrete type of t. We shall also assume that two distinct types are associated to disjoint concrete types.

Additionally, we assume that each class name c is associated to a denumerable set $|c|$. Intuitively, $|c|$ is the set of all real-world objects that belong to the class c. We shall come back to the type system, in more detail, shortly.

Definition 4 *Let S be a database schema. An instance of S is a function δ that associates:*

- *each class c of S to a finite subset $\delta(c)$ of $|c|$, and*
- *each attribute (c, a, t) of S to a partial function $a_\delta : |c| \longrightarrow |t|$ such that:*
  - *$def(a_\delta) \subseteq \delta(c)$, and*
  - *if t is a class name then $range(a_\delta) \subseteq \delta(t)$.*

Here $def(a_\delta)$ denotes the domain of definition of the partial function a_δ, and $range(a_\delta) = \{a_\delta(x) \mid x \in def(a_\delta)\}$.

We shall call $\delta(c)$ the *extension* of c, and each object of $\delta(c)$ a c-object. Intuitively $\delta(c)$ is the set of all objects of $|c|$ that are currently of interest. Roughly, what Definition 4 says is that: every attribute of c is a partial function whose domain of definition is contained in the extension of c; additionally, if the attribute is an object-attribute then the range of the function must be contained in the extension of the target.

3 The query Language

The prominent characteristic of our query language is that it is purely algebraic. That is, it does not use variables but algebraic operations, on functions on the one hand, and on finite sets of objects on the other.

3.1 Functional Terms

Let S be a database schema, and let $c_1, \ldots, c_n$ be the class names of S. We associate S with a *type system* on the one hand, and with a *query language* on the other. The type system is constructed according to the following grammar:

$$\beta ::= int \mid char \mid float \mid bool \mid string \mid \cdots$$
$$\gamma ::= c_1 \mid \cdots \mid c_n$$
$$\tau ::= \beta \mid unit \mid \tau \times \tau \mid \gamma \mid set \ \tau$$

Here, *unit* is a particular type whose associated concrete type is a set with a single element. Note that the type system does *not* have the function constructor.

The query language associated with S manipulates two kinds of functions: the type operations, and the attributes. This is done using the following rules:

$$1. \quad \frac{}{id : t \longrightarrow t} \qquad 2. \quad \frac{f : t_1 \longrightarrow t_2 \qquad g : t_2 \longrightarrow t_3}{f.g : t_1 \longrightarrow t_3} \qquad 3. \quad \frac{}{ter : t \longrightarrow unit}$$

$$4. \quad \frac{}{fst : t_1 \times t_2 \longrightarrow t_1} \qquad 5. \quad \frac{}{snd : t_1 \times t_2 \longrightarrow t_2} \qquad 6. \quad \frac{f_1 : t \longrightarrow t_1 \qquad f_2 : t \longrightarrow t_2}{< f_1, f_2 > : t \longrightarrow t_1 \times t_2}$$

In fact, these rules express the universal properties of product, in the sense of category theory. Concretely, $t_1 \times t_2$ denotes the Cartesian product of two factors t_1 and t_2, *unit* denotes the Cartesian product of zero factors, and $set \ t$ denotes the set of finite subsets of t.

In our approach, all functions are partial. However, *id*, *fst*, *snd*, and *ter* are interpreted as total functions and have their usual definitions: *id* is the identity function, *fst* and *snd* are "first projection" and "second projection" of the product of two factors, and *ter* is the unique function that associates each element of t to the unique element of *unit*. Moreover, $f.g$ is interpreted as the composition $g \circ f$ of partial functions; and $< f_1, f_2 >$ is interpreted as the *pairing* of f_1 and f_2, defined as follows:

$$< f_1, f_2 > (x) = \begin{cases} (f_1(x), f_2(x)) \ if \ f_1(x) \ and \ f_2(x) \ are \ defined \\ undefined \qquad otherwise \end{cases}$$

As we shall see, the above interpretation of $< f_1, f_2 >$ imposes certain restrictions on the query language.

We assume that each basic type is equipped with its usual operations $(+, -, *, etc.)$. We also assume that each basic type is equipped with the comparators $\leq, =, \neq, <, \geq$ et $>$. We use also a comparator θ in its prefix notation $\underline{\theta} : t \times t \longrightarrow bool$. Every constant k of a basic type t is seen as a function $k : unit \longrightarrow t$; i.e. the function that associates the unique element of *unit* to k.

In our type system every class name of a database schema S is a type. We assume that each such type is equipped with the comparators $=$ and $\neq$ that perform purely syntactic comparison. These comparators allow to test if two objects of a class are the same object. Moreover, we assume that each attribute (c, a, t) of a class c is an operation $a : c \longrightarrow t$ for the type c.

In order for our query language to be able to express queries that require aggregate functions, we assume that some of the basic types are equipped with such built-in functions. In general, an aggregate function on a type t is a function $agg : set \ t \longrightarrow t$, verifying certain conditions [LT97]. Examples of aggregate functions are:

$Max, Min, Avg : set \ int \longrightarrow int$ $\qquad Max, Min, Avg : set \ float \longrightarrow float$

$And, Or : set \ bool \longrightarrow bool$ $\qquad Concat : set \ string \longrightarrow string$

Definition 5 *Let S be a database schema. A S-functional term (or simply functional term, when S is understood) is defined recursively as follows:*
- *The operations of basic types, the comparators, the operations of classes (i.e. the attributes) and the aggregate functions are functional terms.*
- *Any expression obtained by the application of rules 1 to 6 above on functional terms is a functional term.*

Given a functional term $e : t \longrightarrow t'$, we call t the *source* and t' the *target* of e.

Definition 6 *Let S be a database schema. We call S-condition on a type t (or simply condition on t, when S is understood), any S-functional term cond with source t and target bool.*

For example:
- If (c, a_1, t) and (c, a_2, t) are two attributes with common target t, and θ is a comparator on t, then $a_1 \; \theta \; a_2$ is a condition on c.
- If $cond_1$ and $cond_2$ are two conditions on t, then $cond_1$ *and* $cond_2$, $cond_1$ *or* $cond_2$, *not* $cond_1$ are conditions on t.
- If $e : t \longrightarrow t'$ is a functional term and k is a constant of t', and if θ is a comparator on t', then $< e, ter.k > .\theta : t \longrightarrow bool$ is a condition on t denoted $e\theta k$.

As these examples show, the selection conditions of the relational algebra are just special cases of conditions as defined in this paper.

3.2 Query Syntax

Let S be a database schema. Informally, a query over S is an expression obtained by combining classes and functional terms using algebraic operations. Each query is accompanied by a type that we shall call the *support* of the query. Intuitively, the support of a query is the type of the values that belong to the answer of the query. Formally, a query expression (or a query for short) and its support are defined as follows:

Definition 7 1. A class name c of S is a query and $supp(c) = c$.
2. if Q is a query and $f : supp(Q) \longrightarrow t$ is a functional term then $map(f, Q)$ is a query and $supp(map(f, Q)) = t$.
3. If Q is a query and $cond$ is a *condition on* Q, then $Q[cond]$ is a query and $supp(Q[cond]) = supp(Q)$.
   A condition on Q is defined as follows:
   - every condition on $supp(Q)$ is a condition on Q, and
   - if $f : supp(Q) \longrightarrow supp(Q')$ is a functional term, where Q' is a query, then f *in* Q' is a condition on Q.
4. If Q_1, Q_2 are queries, then $Q_1 \times Q_2$ is a query and $supp(Q_1 \times Q_2) = supp(Q_1) \times supp(Q_2)$.
5. If Q_1, Q_2 are queries such that $supp(Q_1) = supp(Q_2) = t$, then $Q_1 \; op \; Q_2$, where $op \in \{\cap, \cup, \backslash\}$, is a query, and $supp(Q_1 \; op \; Q_2) = t$.
6. If Q is a query and if $f : set(supp(Q)) \longrightarrow supp(Q)$ is a functional term, then $f(Q)$ is a query and $supp(f(Q)) = supp(Q)$.

Note that the operation *map* in the above definition is a two-argument operation of the query language, whereas in [BNTW95] this operation is a one-argument operation of the type system. As we mentioned in the introduction, for the purposes of this paper, we assume that the attribute functions are single-valued. Therefore, clause 6 of the above definition can only be applied for aggregate functions.

3.3   Query Semantics

Evaluation of a functional term Let S a database schema, δ an instance of S, and f a functional term. The evaluation of f on δ, denoted $eval(f, \delta)$, is a partial function obtained by replacing:
- each class operation $a : c \longrightarrow t$ by the partial function $a_\delta : |c| \longrightarrow |t|$
- each operation of a basic type by its implementation
- all other components (such as: fst, snd, id, etc.) by their interpretations, as in Section 3.1.

Evaluation of a query Let S be a database schema and δ an instance of S. The evaluation of a query Q on δ, denoted by $eval(Q, \delta)$, is a subset of the support of Q, and is defined recursively as follows:
1. For each class name c of S, $eval(c, \delta) = \delta(c)$
2. For each query Q, and for each functional term $f : supp(Q) \longrightarrow t$,

$$eval(map(f, Q), \delta) = \{eval(f, \delta)(x) \mid x \in eval(Q, \delta), \text{ and } eval(f, \delta)(x) \text{ is defined}\}$$

3. For each query Q, and for each condition of the form $cond : supp(Q) \longrightarrow bool$,

$$eval(Q[cond\,], \delta) = \{x \in eval(Q, \delta) \mid cond_\delta(x) \text{ is defined and } cond_\delta(x) = true\}$$

   where $cond_\delta = eval(cond, \delta)$.
4. For each query Q, and for each condition of the form f in Q',

$$eval(Q[f \text{ in } Q'\,], \delta) = \{x \in eval(Q, \delta) \mid f_\delta(x) \text{ is defined and } f_\delta(x) \in eval(Q', \delta)\}$$

   where $f_\delta = eval(f, \delta)$.
5. For all queries Q_1 and Q_2, $\quad eval(Q_1 \times Q_2, \delta) = eval(Q_1, \delta) \times eval(Q_2, \delta)$
6. For all queries Q_1 and Q_2,

$$eval(Q_1 \text{ op } Q_2, \delta) = eval(Q_1, \delta) \text{ op } eval(Q_2, \delta), \text{ where } op \in \{\cap, \cup, \backslash\}$$

7. For each query Q, and for each function $f : set(supp(Q)) \longrightarrow supp(Q)$,

$$eval(f(Q), \delta) = \{ f_\delta(eval(Q, \delta)) \}, \text{ where } f_\delta = eval(f, \delta).$$

Example 1 (continued) Let us enrich our AGENDA schema, by adding the following class:

Emp(ident : Pers; salary : int; commission : int; local : Addr; rank : string)

The following examples of queries give an indication of the expressive power of our query language:

1. Give all persons : *Pers*
2. Give the states of all persons : *map(addr.zip.state, Pers)*
3. Give the names and first names of all persons that live in the 14th district of Paris :
   map(< surname, name >, Pers[(addr.zip.city = Paris) and (addr.zip.code = 75014)])
4. For every person whose name is "Hercules", give the street, city and state where he lives :
   map(< addr.street, < addr.zip.city, addr.zip.state >>, Pers[name = Hercules])
5. Give all married couples that do not live at the same address :
   (Pers × Pers)[(fst.spouse = snd) and (fst.addr ≠ snd.addr)]
6. Give all persons that live in Paris but do not have a telephone :
   Pers[addr ∈ Addr[zip.city = Paris]] \ map(name, Tel)
7. Are there employees that live in Paris and work at Orsay :
   Or(map((local.addr.zip.city = Orsay) and (ident.addr.zip.city = Paris), Pers))
8. Give all annual income (salary plus commission) of each employee :
   *map(< ident.name, (salary + commission) * 12 >, Emp)*
9. Give the employees earing the maximum salary :
   Emp[salary in Max(map(salary, Emp))]

The answers to queries 1, 2 and 6 are sets of identities (thus non-printable). Queries 7 and 9 use aggregate functions. Query 8 performs arithmetic computations using constructors of the language. Indeed, the expression
*(salary + commission) * 12* is an abbreviation of the functional term
<< salary, commission > .add, ter.12 > .mul, where *add* and *mul* are, respectively, the operations "+" and "*" in prefix notation. Query 7 is of special interest : by identifying a singleton with the single element it contains, the answer obtained is a boolean!

4 Comparison with other query languages

4.1 Simulating the Relational Algebra

The table below shows through examples, how the basic operations of the relational algebra can be simulated in our query language.

Tables/Classes	Relational algebra	Our query language
$R(A, B, C)$	R $\pi_A(R)$ $\pi_{A,B}(R)$	$map(< A, < B, C >>, R)$ $map(A, R)$ $map(< A, B >, R)$
$R(A, B)$	$\sigma_{cond}(R)$	$map(< A, B >, R[cond])$
$R(A, B)$ $S(B, C)$	$R \times S$ $R \bowtie S$	$map(< A, B >, R) \times map(< A, B >, S)$ $map(< fst.A, < fst.B, snd.C >>,$ $(R \times S)[fst.B = snd.B])$
$R(A, B)$ $S(A, B)$	$R \cup S$ $R \cap S$ $R \setminus S$	$map(< A, B >, R) \cup map(< A, B >, S)$ $map(< A, B >, R) \cap map(< A, B >, S)$ $map(< A, B >, R) \setminus map(< A, B >, S)$

4.2 Comparison with SQL

In this section, we compare our query language with SQL-2 [MS95]. We are interested with queries that use nested selections, arithmetic expressions and aggregate functions. We show all such queries can be expressed in our query language. To this end, we use a relational version of the class *Emp*, namely:

$$Employee(name, salary, commission, state, rank)$$

- **Arithmetic expression Query**: Give the salary, commission and annual income for every engineer. In SQL-2:

  Select name, salary, commission, (salary + commission) * 12
  From   Employee   Where   rank ='engineer';

  In our query language:

  $map (< name, < salary, < commission, (salary+comission)*12 >>>, Employe[rank =' engineer'])$

- **Aggregate function Query**: What is the maximum salary earned by an engineer.

  In SQL-2:   Select Max(salary)   From   Employee   Where   rank ='engineer';
  In our query language: $Max(map(salary, Employee[rank = engineer]))$

- **Nested selection Query**: what are the names of employees earing a salary greater than 10000.

  In SQL-2:

  Select name   From Employee
  Where salary   in   (Select   salary From Employee Where salary > 10000)

  In our query language:

  $map(nom, Employe[salary in map(salary, Employee[salary > 10000])])$

Note that the expression $salary in map(salary, Employee[salary > 10000])$ is a condition in our query language.

4.3 Comparison with OQL

In object oriented models, the attribute value of an object can be another object. Therefore, in order to retrieve information from the database, one can follow the links that exist between objects without performing explicit joins. This leads to the notion of "path" which is present in most object-oriented query languages XSQL [KKS92], O2SQL [BCD92], and in particular in OQL [Cat94].

In this section, we compare our query language with OQL. However, our comparison is incomplete, due to the restrictions imposed for the purposes of this paper.

Query: retrieve the state, for every person.

  In OQL: Select $x.addr.zip.state$ From x in pers

where **pers** is the entry point of *pers* and $x.addr.zip.state$ is a path expression.

  In our query language: $map(addr.zip.state, Pers)$

where, *addr.zip.state* is a functional term, interpreted as a partial function from the set of "persons" to the set of "states". Therefore, the functional terms of our query language play the role of path expressions of OQL.

There are however some major differences between functional terms of our model and path expressions of OQL, namely:

- The functional terms are constructed algebraically, using an algebra of functions; they do not use variables. In OQL, path expressions use variables.
- In OQL, path expressions are constructed *only* by composition (sequential), whereas in our query language functional terms are constructed by combining composition and pairing (sequential and parallel). For example, suppose we want to retrieve the city and state, for every person :

In OQL :   Select $struct(state : x.addr.zip.state, city : x.addr.zip.city)$
           From x in pers

where *struct* is a type constructor. In the above query, *struct* allows to bind together the informations retrieved by the two paths : $x.addr.zip.state$ and $x.addr.zip.city$. This kind of constructor, however, is *not* orthogonal to composition of attributes.

In our language, the above query can be written in three equivalent ways :

$$map(addr.zip. < state, city >, \; Pers), \qquad map(addr. < zip.state, zip.city >, \; Pers),$$
$$map(< addr.zip.state, addr.zip.city >, \; Pers)$$

Composition and pairing of attributes are two orthogonal operations in our language. This orthogonality allows us to have several equivalent retrieval strategies for the same query. Hence the possibility to develop optimisation techniques.

- Our language does not treat constants in the same way as OQL does. In our language, a constant *is* a functional term that can be combined with other functional terms. In fact, a constant k of type t is seen as the operation $k : unit \longrightarrow t$. In OQL, a constant is a term which is *not* a path expression. For example, to answer the query "give all persons that live either in Paris or in Lyon" in OQL, we write :

Select x From x in pers
Where $x.addr.zip.city = \text{``}Paris\text{''}$ or $x.addr.zip.city = \text{``}Lyon\text{''}$

The expression in the where clause is interpreted as a predicate, which is evaluated as true if either the path $x.addr.zip.city$ references Paris or the path $x.addr.zip.city$ references Lyon. In our query language, this same query is written :

$Pers[<< addr.zip.city, ter.Paris > .eq \, , < addr.zip.city, ter.Lyon > .eq > .\underline{or}]$

Where, *eq* and *or* are the prefix notations of $=$ and *or* respectively. Note that, the whole expression $(addr.zip.city = \text{``}Paris\text{''})$ or $(addr.zip.city = \text{``}Lyon\text{''})$ is considered as a single functional term.

Moreover, the functional term of the query can be "optimized" as follows :

$addr.zip. << city, ter.Paris > .eq \, , < city, ter.Lyon > .eq > .\underline{or}$

5   Perspectives and Conclusions

In this paper we have proposed an object-oriented data model and a purely algebraic query language. The data model is based on a view of attributes as functions, and the query language is algebraic, in the style of the relational model. We have seen how the basic concepts of the relational model and of the languages SQL-2 and OQL can be expressed in our language in a natural way.

We have reached our objectives, within the limits and restrictions imposed for the purposes of this paper. One important restriction of our query language is that the semantics of $< f, g >$ does not allow null values to appear in query answers. To solve this problem, we need a more elaborate type system. We currently investigate this research direction.

References

[BBN91] V. Breazu-Tannen, P. Buneman, S. Naqvi. *Structural recursion as a Query Language*. In Proc. of Database Programming Languages: Bulk Types & Persistant data, pages 1-19, 1991.

[BCD92] F. Bancilhon, S. Cluet, and C. Delobel. *A query language for O_2*. In François Bancilhon, Claude Delobel, and Paris Kanellakis, editors, *Building an Object-Oriented Data-base System, The Story of O_2*. Morgan Kaufmann, 1992.

[BF79] O. P. Buneman and R.E. Frankel. *FQL-a functional query language*. In ACM SIGMOD Intl. Conf. on Management of Data, pages 52-57, 1979.

[BNTW95] P. Buneman, S. Naqvi, V.Tannen, L. Wong. *Principle of Programming with Complex objects and Collection types*. TCS, 149:3-48, 1995.

[Cat94] R. Cattel. *The Object Databases Standard: ODMG-93*. Morgan Kaufmann, 1994.

[FD95] L. Fegaras, D. Maier. *Towards an Effective Calculus for Object query languages*. In Proc. of ACM SIGMOD International Conference on Management of Data, pages 47-58, 1995.

[Kim95] W. Kim. *Modern Database Systems. The Object Model, Interoperability, and Beyond*. Addison-Wesley company, 1995.

[KKS92] M. Kifer, W. Kim, and Y. Sagiv. *Querying Object-oriented databases*. In Proc. of the ACM SIGMOD Conference on Management of Data, 1992.

[Lel94] S.K. Lellahi. *Towards a Characterization of Bulk types*. Research Report No 94-01, Université Paris 13, 1994.

[LS91] S.K. Lellahi, N. Spyratos. *Towards a Categorical Data Model Supporting Structural Object and Inheritance*. LNCS N0 504, pp 86-105, 1991.

[LS92] S.K. Lellahi, N. Spyratos. *Categorical modelling of Database concepts*. Technical report Series, FIDE/92/38, University of Glasgow, 1992.

[LSS97] S.K. Lellahi, R. Souah, N. Spyratos. *An Object-Relational Model with a Purely Algebraic Query Language*, LRI. Research Report No 1106, 1997. Université Paris 11 (Orsay).

[LT97] S.K. Lellahi, V. Tannen. *A Calculus for Collections and Aggregates*. Proceedings of Category Theory in Computer Science, 1997 (To appear in LNCS).

[MS95] J. Melton, A. R. Simon. *Understanding the New SQL: A Complete Guide*. Morgan Kaufmann Publishers, 1995.

[Shi81] D. Shipman. *The Functional Data model and the Data Language DAPLEX*. ACM Transactions on Database Systems, 6(1), mars 1981.

[Ull88] J.D. Ullman. *Principle of Database and Knowledge-Base Systems, Vol. 1*. Computer Science Press, 1988.

The Development of Ordered SQL Packages for Modelling Advanced Applications

Wilfred Ng and Mark Levene
{w.ng,m.levene}@cs.ucl.ac.uk
Department of Computer Science
University College London

Abstract. The ordered relational model is an extension of the relational model which incorporates partial orderings into data domains. We have already defined and implemented a minimal extension of SQL, called OSQL, which allows querying over ordered relational databases. One of the important facilities provided by OSQL is that it allows users to capture the underlying semantics of the ordering of the data for a given application. Herein we demonstrate that OSQL aided with a package discipline can be an effective means to manage the inter-related operations and the underlying data domains of a wide range of advanced application such as: tree-structured information, temporal information, incomplete information and fuzzy information. We illustrate with examples the uses of some generic operations arising from these applications in the form of four OSQL packages called: OSQL_TREE, OSQL_TIME, OSQL_INCOMP and OSQL_FUZZY, respectively.

1 Introduction

Recently, database researchers have recognised that ordering is inherent to the underlying structure of data in many database applications [12, 11, 17, 15]. However, current Relational Database Management Systems (RDMSs), which are overwhelmingly dominating the commercial DBMS market, still confine the ordering of elements in data domains to only a few kinds of built-in orderings. SQL2 (or simply SQL) [8], for instance, supports three kinds of orderings considered to be essential in practical utilization: the *alphabetical ordering* over the domain of strings, the *numerical ordering* over the domain of numbers and the *chronological ordering* over the domain of dates [7]. Let us call these ordered domains *system domains* or alternatively, domains with *system ordering*.

There is strong evidence that the system orderings provided by current RDMSs are inadequate. This inadequacy results in loss of semantics and thus hinders the wider use of comparison predicates. For example, the semantics of the comparison EMPLOYEE_RANK < 'General Manager', which seems to be very natural, cannot be captured by any one of the system orderings. Thus, many orderings which are semantically meaningful in practical applications cannot be expressed via the system orderings provided by current RDMSs. In order to alleviate this problem, we have extended SQL to Ordered SQL (OSQL) by providing the facility of user-defined orderings over data domains [15], which we refer to as *semantic orderings*.

Herein we investigate the introduction of a package discipline into OSQL, which allows us to modularise a collection of generic operations on an ordered data domain. These operations can then be called from within OSQL whenever the package they belong to is loaded into the system. The package discipline makes it easier to formulate queries relating to the underlying ordered domains of the package and allows us to extend OSQL with powerful operations, which enhance its applicability and expressiveness. We demonstrate that OSQL aided with a package discipline is extremely powerful and has a very wide range of applicability.

The use of packages is very popular and successful in many existing software systems such as Mathematica [19], PL/SQL in Oracle [9] and most recently LATEX 2$_\varepsilon$ [10] and Java [1]. Similar to the usage of packages in other systems, OSQL packages, supported by OSQL language constructs, enjoy many of the benefits of using modularisation techniques as a management tool. For instance, a top-down design approach is adopted for the grouping of related operations in an OSQL package, within which constraints can be enforced and supported by a language construct called enforcement. Thus, operations in an OSQL package can be controlled in a more coherent manner. Moreover, OSQL packages can hide the implementation details of the code of their operations. The database administrator has the flexibility to decide whether an operation should be public or private.

The most recent version of SQL (SQL3) has the provision for a procedural extension of SQL [14], which allow users to define functions in abstract data types. However, the issue of ordering abstract data type instances in SQL3 is a non-trivial issue [14]. Overall, SQL3 is much more complex than SQL2, and the process of adding to SQL3 the facility of managing objects has proved to be extremely difficult. Some design problems have already been found in SQL3 due to incompatible features arising from the integration of object orientation into SQL [13]. In any case the publication of SQL3 as an official standard which will replace SQL2 is predicted to be no sooner than 1998. It is then reasonable to anticipate that the process of upgrading existing RDMSs in order to comply with the SQL3 standard will take a longer time.

We emphasise that our approach is novel in the sense that we regard partial ordering as a fundamental property of data which is captured explicitly in the ordered relational model. It results in more efficient operations than those using the programming approach to embed this property into an application program. Furthermore, our approach adheres to the principle of upwards compatibility, since OSQL packages are provided as additional utilities to be used rather than replacing any standard features of a RDMS. Thus, our approach provides maximum flexibility for users and allows the design of optimisation strategies for the execution engine of a RDMS.

2 A Package Discipline for Ordered Databases

In this section we briefly describe the ordered relational data model and its query language OSQL. We also demonstrate how OSQL packages can be applied to solve various problems that arise from many advanced applications under the framework of the ordered relational model.

2.1 The Ordered Relational Model

A basic assumption of this model is that elements in a data domain have no explicit relations amongst them. In the ordered relational model, however, partial orderings (or simply orderings when no ambiguity arises) are included as an integral part of data domains. Without an explicit specification by the user, we assume that the domains of databases have the system ordering attached to them, that is, the alphabetical ordering on strings, the numerical ordering on numbers and the chronological ordering on dates. For example, assume a domain consisting of three employee names: Ethan and Nadav being the subordinates of their boss Mark. Viewing this domain as a conceptual domain, all three elements are indistinguishable with respect to their ordering. On the other hand, viewing this domain as a system domain, the alphabetical ordering is imposed onto the conceptual domain resulting in a linear ordering of the three names. Finally, viewing this domain as a semantic domain, the boss-subordinate relationship can be explicitly captured. The three different views of this domain is depicted in the diagram shown in Figure 1.

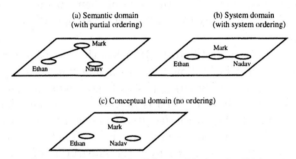

Fig. 1. Domains with different kinds of ordering

An important notion in our model is that given a conceptual domain, apart from the system ordering assumption, we can declare one or more semantic orderings which override the default system ordering. Furthermore, the orderings of domains can be extended to tuples so that tuples in an ordered relation are ordered according to the *lexicographical ordering* of the domains associated with the attributes present in the underlying relational schema. Therefore, any change in the order of attributes in a relational schema may affect the order of tuples in an ordered relation.

2.2 OSQL

Ordered SQL (OSQL) is an extension of the Data Definition Language (DDL) and Data Manipulation Language (DML) of SQL for the ordered relational model. In addition to the extended DDL and DML, OSQL provides a package definition language (PDL), which is detailed in Section 2.3

Herein we just describe the *SELECT* statement of the DML and the *CREATE DOMAIN* statement of the DDL; the detailed BNF for OSQL can be found in [15].

1. The DML of OSQL

SELECT ⟨ lists of attributes ⟩ *[ANY | ALL]* ⟨ levels of tuples ⟩ *[ASC | DESC]*
FROM ⟨ lists of ordered relations⟩
WHERE ⟨ comparison clause⟩

An *attribute list* above is a list of attributes similar to the usual one, except that it provides us with an option that an attribute can be associated with a semantic domain by the syntax *attribute name WITHIN domain name*. The purpose of declaring a *WITHIN* clause is to override the system ordering with semantic ordering specified by the domain name. When the *WITHIN* clause is missing then the system ordering will be assumed.

A *tuple level*, which is a set of positive numbers, with the usual numerical ordering, can also be written in some short forms [15]. As a set of tuples in a linearly ordered relation $r = \{t_1, \ldots, t_n\}$ is isomorphic to a set of linearly ordered tuples, we interpret each number i in a tuple level as an index to the position of the tuple t_i, where $i = 1, \ldots, n$ and $t_1 < \cdots < t_n$. An interesting situation to consider is when the output of a relation is partially ordered as a tree, having levels $\{l_1, \ldots, l_m\}$. In such a case we choose to interpret each number j in a tuple level as an index to a corresponding tree level l_j, where $j = 1, ..., m$ and $l_1 < \cdots < l_m$. Hence, a user can specify the retrieve of *ALL* the tuples or *ANY* one of the tuples in a specified level l_j. We note that in the case of a linearly ordered relation, the choice of using *ALL* or *ANY* has the same effect on the output since there is only one tuple in each level.

A *comparison clasue* follows the *FROM* keyword and a separated list of all relations used in a query. The meaning of the usual comparators $<, >, <=, >=$ is extended to include semantic comparison as we have mentioned earlier. A typical form of a semantic comparison is:
⟨ attribute ⟩ ⟨comparator⟩ ⟨ attribute ⟩ *WITHIN* ⟨ semantic domain ⟩

Without the optional *WITHIN* clause, the comparison is just the conventional one and is based on the relevant system ordering.

Example 1. Let us examine at the following OSQL statements:

(Q_1) *SELECT* (NAME, SALARY) (∗) *FROM* EMPLOYEE.
(Q_2) *SELECT* (SALARY, NAME) (∗) *FROM* EMPLOYEE.
(Q_3) *SELECT* ((NAME *WITHIN* EMP_RANK), SALARY) (∗)
　　　 FROM EMPLOYEE.

Note that the ordering of tuples in an output relation depends on two factors: firstly, on the ordering of domains of individual attributes, and secondly on the order of the attributes in an attribute list. The attribute list of the query (Q_1) is (NAME, SALARY), and thus tuples in the output answer are ordered by NAME first and only then by SALARY (see Figure 2(a)). Therefore the ordering of tuples is, in general, different to that of query (Q_2), whose list is specified as (SALARY, NAME), since the output of (Q_2) is ordered by SALARY first and then by NAME (see Figure 2(b)). It will also be different from that of (Q_3) whose list is ((NAME *WITHIN* EMP_RANK), SALARY), where the ordering of NAME is given by the semantic domain EMP_RANK shown in Figure 1 (see Figure 2(c)).

NAME	SALARY
Ethan	28K
Mark	27K
Nadav	28K

SALARY	NAME
27K	Mark
28K	Ethan
28K	Nadav

NAME	SALARY
Ethan	28K
Nadav	28K
Mark	27K

(a)   (b)   (c)

Fig. 2. An Employee relation EMPLOYEE with different ordering

2. The DDL of OSQL

The syntax of OSQL allows users to define semantic domains using the *CRE-ATE DOMAIN* command as follows:

CREATE DOMAIN ⟨ domain name ⟩ ⟨ data types ⟩
ORDER AS ⟨ ordering specification ⟩

The first part of the statement is similar to the SQL standard statement that declares a domain. Following the *ORDER AS* keywords is a specification of the ordering of a semantic domain. The basic syntax of the *ordering-specification* is: (⟨data-pair⟩, ⟨data-pair⟩, ...) where *data-pair* is of the form, *data-item* B < *data-item* A, if and only if *data-item* A is greater than *data-item* B in the semantic domain.

Example 2. The definition of the semantic domain shown in Figure 1(a) can be written as follows:

(Q_4) *CREATE DOMAIN* EMP_RANK *CHAR*(5) *ORDER AS*
    ('Ethan'<'Mark', 'Nadav'<'Mark').

For a large and complex domain, this syntax may be tedious. Thus OSQL provides a useful short forms {} and the keywords *OTHER* for those data items not mentioned explicitly to make the task of formulating queries easier (see [15] for detail). For instance, (Q_4) can be rewritten as follows:

(Q_5) *CREATE DOMAIN* EMP_RANK *CHAR*(5) *ORDER AS*
    ({'Nadav','Ethan'}<'Mark')

2.3 The Structure of OSQL Packages

An OSQL package is defined by the following statement.

PACKAGE ⟨ package name ⟩
    ⟨package body⟩
END PACKAGE

where the package body consists of a parameter component, a function component and an enforcement component. These three components are specified by the following six basic PDL *language constructs*:

1. Parameter constructs.
2. Function constructs.
3. OSQL constructs.
4. Program constructs.
5. Enforcement constructs.

The parameter component in an OSQL package is organized as a sequence of *parameter constructs* followed by the keyword *PARAMETER* as follows:

PARAMETER: parameter construct [parameter construct]...

where a parameter construct is of the form *package data type*: *variable names*, declaring global variables used in the function and enforcement components. For example, VARCHAR, INT and BOOL are package data types representing characters, integers and boolean values, respectively. After each package data type declaration there follows one or more variable names of the package data type. We use the symbol "$" to specify those variable names that are known to the system at compile time.

The function component in a package is organized as a sequence of *function constructs* followed by the keyword *FUNCTION*. A function construct is a block structure which is defined as follows:

⟨ function name ⟩ ⟨ input variables ⟩
    ⟨ parameter list ⟩
    DEFINE
    ⟨ function body ⟩
RETURN [⟨ output variables ⟩]

where *parameter list* is a sequence of parameter constructs and where the variables are local to the function. The *function body* describes the operation of the function consisting of an *OSQL construct* or a *program construct*. An OSQL construct is simply an OSQL statement such that its variables have been declared either within a function (i.e., local variables) or in the parameter component at the beginning of the package (i.e., global variables). A function in a package returns a list of zero or more values.

As the expressive power of OSQL is limited [16], we enhance OSQL with a *program construct* in OSQL, which is of the form *AS PROG program name*. The program name is the path location and the name of a program, which is written in C programming language, which allows SQL to be embedded in it. This program performs the operation of the function. For example, the program construct "AS PROG \usr\Prog\tree.root" in a function body specifies that the C program *tree.root* under the directory \usr\Prog\ implements the function.

The enforcement component in a package is organized as a sequence of *enforcement constructs* followed by the keyword *ENFORCEMENT*. An enforcement construct, which is similar to a function construct, is also a block structure as follows:

⟨ enforcement name ⟩
    DEFINE
    ⟨enforcement body⟩
END

where the body of an enforcement construct is formulated by a program construct which implements some constraints over the functions of an OSQL package. For example, an enforcement construct can be implemented to ensure that the identified domain is tree-structured. We reserve the enforcement,

ENFORCE_INIT, to be used by the system for the initialization of an OSQL package.

We refer to all functions and enforcements collectively as *operations*. There are two categories of operations such as is common in some programming languages: one is that of *public* operations, which are available to the users and another is that of *private* operations, which are only accessible by calling them from other operations within the package that they belongs to. We use the keywords *PUB* and *PRI* to label the operations as public and private, respectively. By default, whenever there is no such keyword labelling, we treat an operation as private. The public operations comprise the interface of a package to the database users, whilst the private operations are encapsulated and thus hidden from the users. For example, all enforcements are private because they are used by the system to ensure that the integrity of the domain and the consistency of the functions in a package.

3 OSQL Packages for Advanced Applications

We first show that how OSQL can be applied to solve various problems that arise in RDMSs involving applications of tree-structured information [2], incomplete information [6], fuzzy information [3] and temporal information [18] under the unifying framework of the ordered relational model. In order to make use the capabilities of OSQL in a more systematic manner, we define a variety of generic operations with respect to these advanced applications and classify them into four OSQL packages: OSQL_TREE, OSQL_TIME, OSQL_INCOMP and OSQL_FUZZY [16]. Using these packages, we then show how the mentioned queries can be formulated in a simpler manner by embedding the operations of the OSQL packages into OSQL.

Let us consider the following relation EMP_DETAIL shown in Figure 3.

NAME	SALARY	PREVIOUS_WORK	EDUCATION	SALARY_TIME
Ethan	12K	UNK	MSc	1994
Mark	10K	NI	MBA	1990
Mark	18K	NI	MBA	1996
Nadav	15K	Programmer	BA	1995

Fig. 3. An Employee relation EMP_DETAIL

Tree-structured Information:

Suppose that we have the domain EMP_RANK being declared by the statement (Q_4) (or equivalently (Q_5)) to describe the hierarchy of the employees in EMP_DETAIL. We can formulate the query of finding the name and salary of the common bosses of Nadav and Ethan as follows.

(Q_6) *SELECT* (*) (*) *FROM* EMP_DETAIL *WHERE* (NAME > 'Nadav' *WITHIN* EMP_RANK) *AND* (NAME > 'Ethan' *WITHIN* EMP_RANK).

Using the package OSQL_TREE, the query (Q_6) can be simplified as follows:

(Q_7) *SELECT* (*) (*) *FROM* EMP_DETAIL *WHERE* NAME *IN* COM_ANCESTOR('Nadav', 'Ethan').

Temporal Information:

We assume that SALARY_TIME is a time attribute whose values are times-tamps of the tuples in the relation EMP_DETAIL (for simplicity in presentation, we also assume that the time_stamping denotes *valid time* [18]). For instance, we can see that Mark had salary 10K in 1990 and his salary increased in 1996. Note that we do not record Mark's salary if there had been no change since the year it was last updated. We can use the keyword LAST to find the last time the tuple was updated, since the domain of the attribute SALARY_TIME is linearly ordered. With the following query, we show how to find the salary of Mark in 1993 as follows.

(Q_8) *SELECT* (SALARY_TIME, SALARY) (*LAST*) *FROM* EMP_DETAIL
  WHERE NAME = 'Mark' *AND* SALARY_TIME <= 1993.

Using the package OSQL_TIME, the query (Q_8) can be simplified as follows:

(Q_9) *SELECT* (SALARY) (*) *FROM* SNAPSHOT(EMP_DETAIL, 1993)
  WHERE NAME = 'Mark'.

Incomplete Information:

Suppose we have the domain INCOMPLETE_DOMAIN as in Figure 4 to capture the semantics of different null values; in this figure all known data values are more informative than the null symbol UNK (UNKnown), and UNK and DNE (Does Not Exist) are more informative than another null symbol NI (No Information)

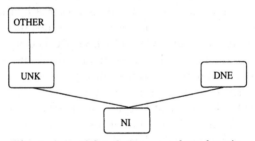

Fig. 4. A partial ordering on a data domain

Let us define a semantic domain called INCOMPLETE_DOMAIN for the attribute PREVIOUS_WORK as follows.

(Q_{10}) *CREATE DOMAIN* INCOMPLETE_DOMAIN *CHAR*(10) *ORDER*
  AS ('NI'<'DNE','NI'<'UNK'< *OTHER*).

We can now formulate the query which finds the name and previous work of those employees whose previous work is more informative than NI, as follows.

(Q_{11}) *SELECT* (NAME, PREVIOUS_WORK) (*) *FROM* EMP_DETAIL
  WHERE (PREVIOUS_WORK > 'NI' *WITHIN* INCOMPLETE_DOMAIN).

Using the package OSQL_INCOMP, the query (Q_{11}) can be simplified as follows:

(Q_{12}) *SELECT* (NAME, PREVIOUS_WORK) *FROM* EMP_DETAIL
  WHERE MORE_INFO(PREVIOUS_WORK, 'NI').

Fuzzy Information:

Suppose we have a semantic domain called QUALIFY to capture the semantic of the requirement "good science background in academic qualification" which is formulated as follows.

(Q_{13}) *CREATE DOMAIN* QUALIFY *CHAR*(10) *ORDER AS*
   ({'BA','MBA'}<'MSc') .

We can formulate the query of finding the name of an employee with good science background in academic qualification as follows.

(Q_{14}) *SELECT* ((EDUCATION *WITHIN* QUALIFY), NAME) (1) *DESC*
   FROM EMP_DETAIL.

Using the package OSQL_FUZZY, the query (Q_{14}) can be simplified as follows:

(Q_{15}) *SELECT* (IMPOSE_FUZZY(EDUCATION, QUALIFY), NAME) (1)
   FROM EMP_DETAIL.

The full reference of the details of OSQL packages can be consulted from [16]. Actually, the meaning of the operations are quite easy to understand. For instance, the operation COM_ANCESTOR in (Q_7) returns the names of all common bosses of Nadav and Ethan and the operation IMPOSE_FUZZY in (Q_{15}) returns the most appropriate tuple such that it satisfies the imposed fuzzy requirement "good science background in academic qualification". The above queries also demonstrate that there is an important difference between using an OSQL construct and a program construct in a function. The OSQL statement in an OSQL construct can be decomposed and restructured by the query execution engine of a RDMS for optimisation purposes. For instance, the query (Q_7), which uses the package function COM_ANCESTOR, is equivalent to the query (Q_6), which is an ordinary OSQL statement not using any functions. On the other hand, an external program specified in a program construct is "opaque" with respect to a RDMS, in the sense that its code can only be integrated into its associated OSQL statement at run time and thus allows no possibility of optimisation at compile time. As a result, operations defined by OSQL constructs are, in general, more efficient than those defined by program constructs.

4 Conclusions

We have presented a new query language, namely OSQL, for querying ordered relational databases and a modularisation package discipline which supports a wide spectrum of applications. An OSQL package has the advantage that it integrates all of the useful operations with respect to a particular application in a more coherent and systematic way as well as providing a basis which justifies its expressive power relative to its design requirements. OSQL provides us with new facilities to support the development of a package as well as to compare attributes according to semantic orderings, in addition to the usual system orderings. Thus, it allows us to capture the needed richer data semantics in advanced applications and it widens the applicability of the standard SQL.

In Figure 5, we show our design of the system architecture, which allows OSQL statements to be entered via the front end Unix interface, and then the OSQL precompiler generates a corresponding program consisting of a sequence of Oracle statements and calls a dynamic SQL handling routine. This routine pipes the program into the back end Oracle server for execution.

538

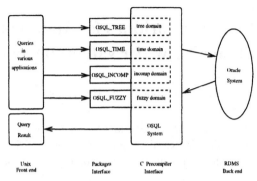

Fig. 5. Architecture of the OSQL system

References

1. E. Anuff. *The Java Sourcebook.* John Wiley & Sons, Inc., (1996).
2. J. Biskup. An Extension of SQL for Querying Graph Relations. *Computing Language* **15**(2), pp. 65-82, (1990).
3. B.P. Buckles and F.E. Petry. A Fuzzy Representation of Data for Relational Databases. *Fuzzy Sets and Systems* **7**, pp. 213-226, (1982).
4. M.A. Casanova, A.L. Furtado and L. Tucherman. A Software Tool for Modular Database Design. *ACM Transactions on Database Systems* **2**, pp. 209-234, (1991).
5. C.L. Chang. Decision Support in an Imperfect World. *IBM Research Report* RJ3421, IBM, San Jose, Dec, (1982).
6. E.F. Codd. Missing Information (Applicable and Inapplicable) in Relational Databases. *ACM SIGMOD record* **15**, pp. 53-78, (1987).
7. C.J. Date. *Relational Database Writings 1985-1989.* Addison-Wesley, (1990).
8. C.J. Date. *A Guide to the SQL Standard.* Addison-Wesley, 3rd ed., (1993).
9. S. Feuerstein. *Oracle PL/SQL.* O'Reilly & Associates, Inc., (1995)
10. H. Kopka and P. W. Daly. *A Guide to Latex2e.* Addion-Wesley, (1995)
11. L. Libkin. A Semantics-based Approach to Design of Query Languages for Partial Information In *Proceedings of the Workshop on Semantics in Databases,* pp. 63-80, (1995).
12. D. Maier and B. Vance. A Call to Order, In *ACM Symposium on Principles of Databases Systems.* pp. 1-16, (1993).
13. N. Mattos and L.G. DeMichiel. Recent Design Trade-Offs in SQL3. *ACM SIGMOD Record* **23**(4), pp. 84-89, (1994).
14. J. Melton. An SQL3 Snapshot, In *Proceedings of the International conference on Data Engineering.* pp. 666-672, (1996).
15. W. Ng and M. Levene. OSQL: An Extension to OSQL to manipulate Ordered Relational Databases. To appear in *Proceeding of the 3rd International Workshop on Next Generation Information Technologies and Systems,* Jerusalem, Israel, (1997).
16. W. Ng. *An Extension of the Relational Data Model to Incorporate Ordered Domains.* Ph.D. Thesis, Submitted, University College London, United Kingdom, (1997).
17. D. Raymond. *Partial Order Databases.* Ph.D. Thesis, University of Waterloo, Waterloo, Canada, (1996).
18. A. Tansel et al. *Temporal Databases: Theory, Design and Implementation.* The Benjamin/Cummings Publishing Company, Inc., (1993)
19. M. Trott. *Mathematica: A Detailed Introduction.* TELOS/Springer-Verlag, (1994).

Incremental Update Algorithms for Materialized Spatial Views by Using View Derivation Relationships[*]

Sang-Ho Moon, Bong-Hee Hong

Department of Computer Engineering, Pusan National University
30 Changjeon-Dong, Kumjeong-Ku, Pusan, 609-735, Korea
e-mail: {shmoon, bhhong}@hyowon.cc.pusan.ac.kr

Abstract. In spatial databases, it is necessary to provide spatial view modeling facilities in order to support a variety of user's perspective views on spatial objects. Because spatial views are usually derived by complex spatial queries, it is desirable to actually materialize spatial views as opposed to being computed on demand for offering improved query performance. A main obstacle to spatial view materialization is that materialized views must be maintained in a consistent state with respect to the updates of source spatial objects. This paper defines the semantics of updating materialized spatial views in terms of the cardinality constraints of view derivation relationships between spatial view objects and source spatial objects. We also present incremental update algorithms for keeping materialized spatial views consistent by using view derivation relationships.

1 Introduction

There have been a variety of user's needs of supporting different views of spatial objects in spatial databases. We use the term *spatial object* to refer to a collection of spatial primitives that represent the spatial characteristics of a geographic feature, such as house, road, and river. *Spatial primitives* mean elements used in describing the geometric attributes of a geographic feature. It should be able to view one geometric model for spatial objects with different geometric representation according to different user's perspectives[8]. For example, a traffic management system regards roads as a set of lines. On the other hand, a road management system sees roads as a set of areas.

We define a *spatial view* as a *virtual class* that is derived by a spatial query on one or more stored base classes which define spatial objects and/or other spatial views. The definition of a stored base class includes a list of spatial attributes and non-spatial attributes, a list of methods, and a list of superclasses. A virtual class in object-oriented databases is a class whose objects are not actually stored in the database.

There have been two approaches to view materialization that physically creates temporarily stored view objects when the view class is first queried: relational view materialization[2, 3] and object-oriented view materialization[6, 10]. The main difference between the two is whether or not to keep the object identifiers(OIDs) of its source objects on the materialized spatial view. Object identity is used to establish

---

[*] This work was supported in part by the Ministry of Science and Technology of Korea under the National GIS project and in part by Research Institute of Computer and Information Communication in Pusan National University.

a 1:1 relationship between view objects and source objects. We use the term *source objects* to mean the underlying base objects and/or views from which view objects are derived. By using a 1:1 relationship, it is possible to propagate the updates of source objects to materialized spatial views. On the other hand, it is not possible to establish a 1:1 relationship between view tuples and base tuples in materialized relational views, because object identities are not used in the relational database.

Two strategies have been proposed for realizing object-oriented view materialization. One is object-generating view materialization which replicates data on view materialization. The disadvantage of this approach is the time and effort required for view update propagation. The other is object-preserving view materialization which assigns the OIDs of source objects to the attributes of view objects instead of duplicating the attribute values of source objects. Object-preserving view materialization eliminates the value redundancy of relational views[6]. However, object-preservation requires additional accesses to source objects, and also the recomputation of materialized fields. As the other strategy, the deputy model[7] introduces the concepts of deputy objects, and allows an object to have multiple deputy objects which belong to different classes. Since deputy objects can be used as customized interfaces of source objects by selectively inheriting the attributes and methods from source objects, they can be used to realize object views. The deputy model approach is basically similar to object-preserving view materialization using OIDs.

To the best of our knowledge, MultiView might be the first work on the implementation of object-oriented materialized views[6]. Because MultiView employs object preserving operators to define virtual classes, thus its materialization is similar to object-oriented view materialization using the OIDs of source objects. MultiView has proposed incremental update propagation algorithms for materialized object-oriented views, where the effects of updates must be propagated to all classes affected by them[5]. MultiView's algorithms are incremental, and perform selective notification to the set of virtual classes directly affected by the update of a source object. These algorithms use a registration service by which virtual classes can register their interest in specific properties, and be notified upon modifications of those properties.

In order to keep the materialized spatial view consistent, it is important to incrementally update materialized view objects in response to the change to a source object. Figure 1 shows an example of updating a materialized spatial view object, SVO, which is directly affected by the update of a source object, A. The important point is how we can maintain consistency between source objects(A, B) and its materialized spatial view object(SVO).

There have been two kinds of approaches to view maintenance: re-materialization and incremental view maintenance[4, 6]. In re-materialization approach, a materialized view is maintained by recomputing it in response to the changes to the underlying data. In incremental view maintenance, the view objects are incrementally updated when the view's sources are updated[2, 3, 5]. Incremental view maintenance still has the problem of finding efficiently all the view objects directly affected by the updates of source objects. This paper mainly focuses on examining view derivation relationships between spatial view objects and source objects, and then on devising efficient incremental update algorithms for maintaining the consistency of materialized spatial view objects. To define the update semantics for each materialized spatial view object, we investigate the cardinality constraints of view derivation relationships according to 1:1, N:1, 1:N, and M:N relationship between spatial view objects and source objects.

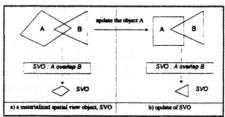

Fig. 1. Update propagation example for a materialized spatial view

This paper is organized into 6 sections. Section 2 defines a basic spatial model upon which our spatial views are based. Spatial view materialization is discussed in section 3, and view derivation relationships are introduced in section 4. We propose new incremental update algorithms to keep materialized spatial views consistent in section 5. Lastly, section 6 contains a conclusion and future works.

2 Spatial Views in Object-Oriented Spatial Databases

In this section, we first describe a spatial data model, and then propose a spatial view model before discussing the issues of spatial view materialization.

2.1 A Basic Spatial Data Model

The motivation of studying spatial view materialization is that the geometry of a spatial view might differ from that of source classes according to geometry mapping functions. We use the term *source classes* to refer to the underlying base classes and/or other view classes, from which spatial views are derived. For example, a source object with a line geometry may be translated into a spatial view object with an area geometry. As a result, the domain of an attribute in a spatial view may be different from that of the corresponding attribute of the stored base class. The slight differences between spatial views and object-oriented views are that 1)the domain of a geometry attribute in the spatial view may be different from that of the attribute of the source class, 2) methods specified in a spatial view may differ from those defined in a source class because of different geometry representation, and 3) spatial view materialization involves creating a temporarily stored spatial primitive class for representing the geometry of the spatial view. These differences lead to complicated implementation of spatial views.

Base classes include a specific attribute, named *Geom*, that represents spatial representation or geometry of a given spatial object. The domain of an attribute in a base class for representing geometry data is one of spatial primitive classes. Thus, the value of the attribute, *Geom*, is the OID of a spatial primitive object. Figure 2 shows an example of defining a base class for representing spatial objects, towns. An object,

T_{oid1}, of the class, Town, points to a spatial primitive object, PO_{oid1}, through the attribute, "*Geom*".

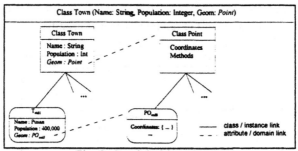

Fig. 2. Spatial object, Town

2.2 Definition of Spatial Views

The definition of a spatial view consists of schema elements and a view defining query. The schema elements include a list of view attributes, a derived geometry, and a list of methods. The list of view attributes means the non-spatial attributes of a spatial view. The derived geometry is a geometry attribute used to represent the geometry of a spatial view. The list of methods may be the same as the methods of source classes, or be newly defined for a spatial view. The query part of a spatial view definition involves projection and restriction operations. Figure 3 shows the syntax for defining a spatial view.

Spatial_View spatial-view-name (ViewAttributes, <u>Geom</u>)   // *schema elements*
    [Methods (methods_list);]
    AS   SELECT Attributes, *GeometryMappingFunction*   // *query description*
        FROM   *SourceClasses*
        [WHERE   *Predicates*]

Fig. 3. Syntax for defining spatial views

The geometry of a spatial view might be different from the geometries of its source classes. Based on geometry, we classify spatial views into two kinds of views: a *geometry preserving spatial view* and a *geometry generating spatial view*. We define these terms as follows. A *geometry preserving spatial view* is a spatial view that has the same geometry with its underlying source object. A *geometry generating spatial view* is a spatial view that has different geometry from its underlying source objects. To provide the geometry generating spatial view, the geometry of source objects should be able to be transformed into the different geometry.

3 Materialization of Spatial Views

To realize the materialization of spatial views, we decided to use the existing object-oriented view materialization which involves physical creation of the values of the attributes of a materialized view object when the view is first queried and keeping that value. The problem of this approach is that the database system must generate the virtual OID when each materialized view object is created.

From the point of view of materialization, two kinds of spatial views should be materialized differently. A geometry preserving spatial view does not replicate the geometries of its source objects. Instead, the spatial view object makes a reference to the same spatial primitive object, as shown in figure 4. Figure 4 shows that the materialization of a spatial view, Long_River, involves copying not the geometry of its source object, but the OID of the referenced spatial primitive object into the view object.

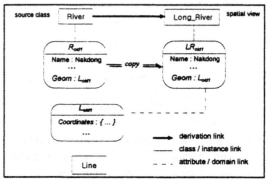

Fig. 4. Materializing geometry preserving spatial views

To materialize geometry generating spatial views, we have to create new spatial primitive objects for representing a new geometry which is derived from the geometries of source objects. The OIDs of newly created spatial primitive objects should be stored in the attribute, Geom, of a materialized spatial view object. Figure 5 shows a materialization example of geometry generating spatial views. A spatial view, Regions_Town_In_Highway, is defined by a spatial join between two source classes, Town and Highway. The geometry of a spatial view object, RT_{oid1}, is newly computed from that of a source object, PO_{oid1}, by a spatial operator, Buffer().

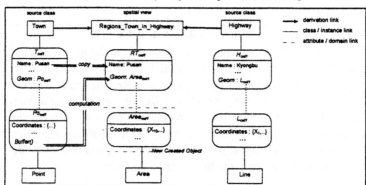

Fig. 5. Materializing geometry generating spatial views

4 View Derivation Relationships

In this section, we define the cardinality ratios and constraints of view derivation relationships in order to analyze update semantics of materialized spatial views.

4.1 Definition of View Derivation Relationships

To quickly find all the view objects related to the updated source object, we propose a *view derivation relationship* between spatial view objects and source objects. We assume that identifiers are generated for view objects when spatial views are materialized. Object identity of spatial views makes it possible to establish view derivation relationships. In general, if an one-to-one relationship can be established between view objects and source objects, it is possible to propagate the updates of a source object to the related materialized view objects.

A view derivation relationship type, VDR, is defined as a set of associations between materialized spatial view objects, SVO_m, and their source objects, SO_n^j, where j represents the index number of source classes. VDR is a set of relationship instances, VDR_i, where each VDR_i associates m SVO_m with n SO_n, and each SVO_m in VDR_i is a member of a spatial view class, SVO, and each SO_n^j in VDR_i is a member of source class, SO^j. Hence, a relationship type, VDR, can be defined as a subset of the cartesian product $SVO \times SO^1 \times SO^2, .., \times SO^n$. With above notation, the ith instance of view derivation relationships is formally defined as "$VDR_i = <SVO_m, SO_n^j >$".

If a spatial view object, SVO_m, is derived from only one source class, then the value of j becomes $1(j=1)$. In other words, SO_n^j is the set of objects of a source class, j, used to derive the view object, SVO_m. For example, if SVO_m is derived from two source classes, the instances of a view derivation relationship, VDR_i, are represented as "$VDR_i = <SVO_m, SO_{n1}^1, SO_{n2}^2 >$".

For example, consider a spatial view, Regions_Town_In_Highway, derived from two source classes: Highway and Town. Let SVO_m be a spatial view object, and T_{oidi} and H_{oidi} be a source object of Town and Highway, respectively. As shown in figure 6(a), we assume that four spatial view objects are given. At this time, a number of view derivation relationships are generated like figure 6(b). Now, we can define the view derivation relationship formally as "$VDR_i = <SVO_m, SO_{n1}^1, SO_{n2}^2 >$ where $SO_{n1}^1 = \{T_{oidi}\}$ and $SO_{n2}^2 = \{H_{oidi}\}$".

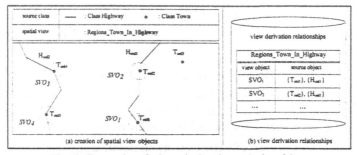

Fig. 6. Example of view derivation relationships

4.2 Cardinality Ratios of View Derivation Relationships

Relationship types usually have certain *cardinality constraints* that limit the possible combinations of view objects and source objects. In spatial views, these constraints are determined by geometry mapping functions. The number of relationship instances between spatial view objects and source objects is defined as *cardinality ratio*. Common cardinality ratios for binary relationships are 1:1, N:1, 1:N, and M:N. The reason for classifying view derivation relationships into four kinds of cardinality ratios is that the semantics of updating materialized view objects differ from each other according to cardinality ratios.

A 1:1 relationship means that a spatial view object is derived from only one source object. A spatial view, as shown in figure 7, is defined by an intersection of points with lines. The cardinality ratio of the view derivation relationship between Regions_Town_In_Highways and Towns is 1:1.

An N:1 relationship indicates that several spatial view objects are derived from one source object. The binary relationship between Regions_Town_In_Highways and Highways is of cardinality ratio N:1, as shown in figure 7(b). This means that each Highway can be related to numerous Regions_Town_In_Highways, but a Regions_Town_In_Highway can be related to only one Highway.

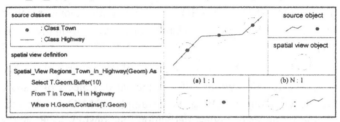

Fig. 7. Example of a 1:1 and an N:1 relationship

1:N relationship is opposed to N:1, and indicates that each view object is derived from several source objects, but a source object is only related to one view object. The relationship between Regions_Forest_Include_Towns and Towns, as shown in figure 8, is an example of a 1:N relationship.

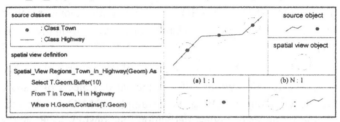

Fig. 8. Example of a 1:N relationship

An M:N relationship is a combination of both a 1:N and an N:1 relationship. That is, one spatial view object is derived from several source objects, and vice versa. The properties of an M:N relationship are not described here.

4.3 Cardinality Constraints of View Derivation Relationships

Let $Members(SO_{nk}^k)$ be a predicate which returns the number of participations of each object SO_{nk}^k, where $k \le j$, in VDR. Generally, a view derivation relationship, $VDR_i = <SVO_m, SO_{n1}^1, SO_{n2}^2, ..., SO_{nj}^j>$, implies that the number of source classes used for deriving SVO_m is j. For example, if j is equal to 1, the view derivation relationship becomes "$VDR_i = <SVO_m, SO_{n1}^1>$". In addition, if $Members(SO_{n1}^1)$ is equal to 1, it means that only one object in the source class SO^1 is used to drive the spatial view object, SVO_m. Hence, we classify the types of view derivation relationships, VDR_i, in terms of the number of source classes and the number of source objects used for deriving spatial views. Let j be the index number of each source class. We can formally define the cardinality constraints of view derivation relationships as follows.

If a spatial view is derived from only one source object, there is a 1:1 relationship between spatial view objects and source objects. The cardinality constraint of a 1:1 view derivation relationship can be expressed as "$(j =1)$ and $(Members(SO_{nk}^k) = 1)$".

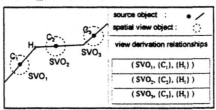

Fig. 9. Example of N:1 view derivation relationships

If a spatial view is derived by spatial joins, the cardinality ratio of view derivation relationships may be 1:1, N:1, 1:N, and/or N:M. At this point, a spatial view is derived from two or more source classes. One or more source objects of a given source class can participate in the view derivation relationship. For each view derivation relationship in figure 9, each source object, C_i, is used for deriving a specific view object. At the same time, there are many view objects derived from a given source object, H_1. The cardinality constraints of an N:1 view derivation relationship between view objects, SVO_m, and source objects, SO_{nk}^k, can be noted as follows.

$$(j \geq 2) \, and((Members(SO_{nk}^k) \geq 1)$$
$$and(for \ any \ VDR_i = <SVO_m, SO_{nk}^k >, Members(SVO_m) = 1))$$

Like an N:1 relationship, a materialized spatial view object participating in a 1:N relationship is derived from two or more source classes. In addition, a materialized spatial view object can be associated with one or more source objects of each source class. The cardinality constraint for a 1:N relationship between view objects, SVO_m, and source objects, SO_{nk}^k, can be expressed as follows.

$$(j \geq 2) \, and((Members(SVO_m) \geq 1)$$
$$and(for \ any \ VDR_i = <SVO_m, SO_{nk}^k >, Members(SO_{nk}^k) = 1))$$

Figure 10 shows an example of a 1:N relationship from the viewpoint of the materialized spatial view object.

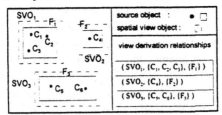

Fig. 10. Example of 1:N view derivation relationships

5 Incremental Spatial View Maintenance Algorithms

In this section, we define the semantics of updating materialized spatial views in terms of the cardinality constraints of view derivation relationships.

5.1 Update Semantics of Spatial View Objects

The difference of update semantics of materialized spatial view objects according to the cardinality constraints of view derivation relationships is an important consideration of maintaining materialized spatial views up to date. After updating the materialized spatial view objects, view derivation relationships will be changed. However, some updates of source objects can be processed by updating only view derivation relationships without changing materialized spatial view objects themselves.

An N:1 relationship

As shown in figure 11, the cardinality ratio of the relationships between spatial view objects, SVO_m, and source objects, H_i, is N:1. In this relationship, the update of H_i causes both the derived spatial view objects and the related view derivation relationships to be updated. Assume a source object, H_1, is deleted as shown in figure 11. To maintain the consistency of materialized spatial views, both the spatial view objects derived from H_1 and the corresponding view derivation relationships should be deleted.

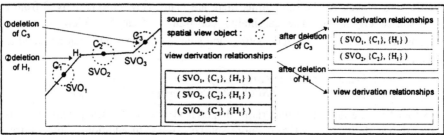

Fig. 11. Updating of view derivation relationships in a 1:1 and an N:1

A 1:N relationship

Compared to N:1 relationship, the update semantics of a 1:N relationship are not identical to an N:1 relationship. For 1:N, it is sufficient to update only the instances of view derivation relationships for propagating the update of a source object. Moreover, there is no necessity for updating the related spatial view object itself, since it might be derived from other source objects.

If a new source object is inserted, view derivation relationships should not be inserted but updated without inserting a new spatial view object. This is because the spatial view object related to a newly inserted source object would be already created. As shown in figure 12, an attempt to insert a new object, C_7 does not affect the materialized spatial view object, SVO_3. To find out the spatial view object, SVO_3 related to C_7, we should execute the related spatial view defining query with C_7. By using the result of executing the spatial view defining query, F_3 can be found which uniquely determines the spatial view object, SVO_3. Finally, the insertion of C_7 causes view derivation relationships to be updated, as shown in figure 12.

Deletion of source objects participating in a 1:N relationship causes the related view derivation relationships to be updated, like the insertion mentioned above. We omit to describe the update semantics of a 1:1 and M:N relationship due to space limitation.

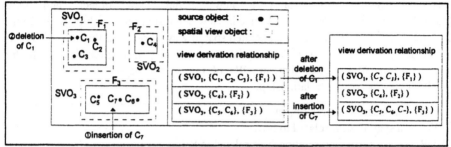

Fig. 12. Updating of 1:N view derivation relationships

5.2 Incremental Update Algorithms for Materialized Spatial View Objects

Update semantics for materialized spatial views mainly depend on update operations on source objects and the cardinality constraints of view derivation relationships. As shown in table 1, there are two cases of updating materialized spatial views in response to the insertion or deletion of a source object: one is to update both materialized spatial view objects and view derivation relationships. The other is to update only the related view derivation relationships without updating spatial view objects themselves.

update operations	cardinality constraints	1:1	N:1	1:N	N:M
insertion	spatial view objects	insert one object	insert one or more objects	no insertion	no insertion
insertion	view derivation relationships	insert one instance	insert one or more instances	update one instance (add an OID)	update one or more instances (add OIDs)
deletion	spatial view objects	delete one object	delete one or more objects	no deletion	no deletion
deletion	view derivation relationships	delete one instance	delete one or more instances	update one instance (delete an OID)	update one or more instances (delete OIDs)

Table 1. Classification of update semantics for materialized spatial views

Based on the update semantics in table 1, a view update algorithm for insertion of a new source object is devised. The main idea of incremental update algorithms is to use the cardinality constraints of view derivation relationships. Figure 13 shows a view update algorithm for propagating the insertion of a new source object.

We now explain briefly the sub-functions of a view update algorithm for insertion of a source object. First, *Search_DirectObj()* executes the related spatial view defining query for a newly inserted source object, and returns a set of source objects which determines spatial view objects related to the inserted source object. As mentioned before, the return value of this function varies with cardinality constraints between spatial view objects and source objects. In other words, while only one source object is returned in a 1:1 or a 1:N relationship, two or more source objects are returned in N:1 or N:M relationship. *Search_ViewDerRel()* retrieves the instances of view derivation relationships related to the retrieved source objects. *Create_SVObject()* also creates a new spatial view object, and then *Insert_ViewDerRel()* adds a new instance in view derivation relationships for defining a relationship between the newly generated spatial view object and the newly inserted source object. *Update_ViewDerRel()* updates view derivation relationships, where the "Insert" argument indicates that an OID of the source object is inserted to the specified view derivation relationship.

SO^{ins} := an inserted source object
SV   := a spatial view related to So_{ins}
VDR := view derivation relationships related to SV
VDR := { $VDR_i \in VDR$: VDR_i is a instance of VDR, i =1,...,n }
VDR_i = < SVO_m, SO_n^j > where j is the index of source classes

---

Procedure Update_Propagation_for_Insertion(SV, SO^{ins})
begin
      DirectSourceObjSet {SO_k^{direct}} := Search_DirectObj(SV, So^{ins})
      for each object SO_k^{direct} in DirectSourceObjSet {SO_k^{direct}}
      do
            InstanceSet {VDR_i} := Search_ViewDerRel(VDR, SO_k^{direct})
            if InstanceSet {VDR_i} == $\varnothing$ *// in case of a 1:1 or an N:1*
               SVO^{new} := Create_SVObject(SV, SO_k^{direct}, SO^{ins})
               Insert_ViewDerRel(VDR, SVO^{new}, SO_k^{direct}, SO^{ins})
            else   *// in case of a 1:N or an N:M*
               for each record VDR_i in RecordSet {VDR_i} **do**
                    Update_ViewDerRel(VDR, VDR_i, SO^{ins}, "Insert")
      endfor
end

Fig. 13. A view update algorithm for insertion of a new source object

Now, a complete set of incremental update algorithms to keep materialized spatial view objects in a consistent state was designed and being implemented on top of the Gothic which is an object-oriented GIS software[11]. Space limitation, however, prohibits detailed descriptions on the whole implementation and the results of performance evaluations.

6 Conclusion and Future Works

In this paper we have addressed the problem of spatial view maintenance which updates materialized view objects in response to the updates of underlying source objects. The main contribution of this paper is to examine the cardinality constraints of view derivation relationships between materialized spatial view objects and source objects, and to define the update semantics for materialized spatial view objects by using the cardinality ratios of view derivation relationships. Finally, we presented an incremental spatial view maintenance scheme, which involves temporarily materialized spatial view objects and keeping spatial views up to date.

As future works, we will study updatable spatial views which can update source objects through spatial views, and schema spatial view which represents virtual schema derived from underlying base schema.

References

[1] Serge Abiteboul, Anthony Bonner, "Objects and Views", Proc. of ACM-SIGMOD Int'l Conf. on Management of Data, pp 238-247, May 1991.

[2] Jose A.Blakeley, Per-Ake Larson, Fank Wm Tompa, "Efficiently Updating Materialized Views", Proc. of ACM-SIGMOD Int'l Conf. on Management of Data, pp 61-71, May, 1986

[3] Ashish Gupta, Inderpal Singh Mumick, V. S. Subrahmanian, "Maintaining Views Incrementally", Proc. of ACM-SIGMOD Int'l Conf. on Management of Data, pp 157-166, May, 1993

[4] Ashish Gupta, Inderpal Singh Mumick, "Maintenance of Materialized Views: Problems, Techniques, and Applications", Proc. of IEEE Int'l Conf. on Data Engineering, pp 3-18, 1995

[5] Harumi A. Kuno, Elke A. Rundensteiner, "Using Object-Oriented Principles to Optimize Update Propagation to Materialized Views", Proc. of IEEE Int'l Conf. on Data Engineering '96, 1996.

[6] Harumi A. Kuno, Elke A. Rundensteiner, "The MultiView OODB View System: Design and Implementation", Theory and Practice of Object Systems, vol. 2 no. 3, pp 203-225, 1996.

[7] Z. Peng, Y. Kambayashi, "Deputy Mechanisms for Object-Oriented Databases", Proc. of IEEE Int'l Conf. on Data Engineering '95, 1995.

[8] Robert Laurini, Derek Thompson, "Fundamentals of Spatial Information Systems", Academic Press, 1992.

[9] Giovanna Guerrini, Elisa Bertino, Barbara Catania, Jesus Garcia-Molina, "A Formal Model of Views for Object-Oriented Database Systems", Technical Report, DISI-96-2, 1996.

[10] C. Souza dos Santos, "Design and Implementation of Object-Oriented Views", Proc. of Int'l Conf. on DEXA '95, pp 91-102, 1995.

[11] Laser-Scan, "Writing and developing applications using GOTHIC ADE", Issue 2.0, 1995.

Incremental Maintenance of Materialized Views

Mukesh Mohania[*1] Shin'ichi Konomi[2] and Yahiko Kambayashi[3]

[1] ACRC, School of Computer and Information Science, University of South
Australia, The Levels 5095, Australia, Email: mohania@cis.unisa.edu.au
[2] Dept. of Information Science, Kyoto University, Sakyo, Kyoto 606-01, Japan,
Email: konomi@kuis.kyoto-u.ac.jp
[3] Dept. of Information Science, Kyoto University, Sakyo, Kyoto 606-01, Japan,
Email: yahiko@kuis.kyoto-u.ac.jp

Abstract. Materialized views are important in databases, particularly
in data warehouses, where they are used to speed up query processing
on large amounts of data. These views need to be maintained incrementally in response to database updates. In this paper we investigate the
problem of incremental maintenance of a materialized view in response
to changes to the base data. We show that a materialized view can be
maintained without accessing the view itself by materializing additional
relations. We firstly give an algorithm for determining what additional
relations need to be materialize in order to maintain a view incrementally. We then propose an algorithm for updating the materialized view
(and the additional relations) based on the optimized operator tree used
for evaluating the view as a query. A materialized view is updated by
propagating updates to the nodes of its operator tree in a bottom-up
fashion, where each node contains a relational algebraic operator and
computes an intermediate expression. Our algorithm derives the exact
update at every intermediate node in the tree, including the materialized view. Finally, we compare our incremental algorithm with the naive
algorithm that recomputes the view from scratch.

1 Introduction

Views define derived data which can be materialized in database systems. Materialized views are important for fast retrieval of derived data regardless of the
access paths and complexity of view definitions. When the underlying database
relations are updated, the materialized views must be recomputed to ensure the
correctness of answers to queries against them. The recomputation of the materialized views from scratch would be expensive. However, there is a need to
maintain materialized views incrementally. Incremental maintenance means that
changes to the base relations are used to compute the changes to the materialized views. In recent past, many incremental view maintenance methods have
been proposed in the literature [1, 2, 3, 4, 5, 7, 10, 11].

In this paper we investigate the problem of incremental maintenance of a materialized view in response to database updates. We consider views that contain

---

* Part of work done while visiting Kyoto University and supported by JSPS.

traditional relational algebraic operators and can be represented by an operator tree [6]. An operator tree is a binary tree, where leaf nodes represent database relations and non-leaf nodes represent relational algebraic operations. We show that a materialized view can be maintained efficiently by maintaining and materializing additional results, called auxiliary relations, which are derived from the intermediate results of the view computation. We maintain an auxiliary relation for each node in the optimized operator tree of that view. The key of an auxiliary relation is a foreign key that matches the primary key of each relation from which it has been derived; that is, a referential integrity is maintained between an auxiliary relation and the base relations. We give an algorithm for determining these auxiliary relations in order to maintain a view. These relations make it possible to maintain a materialized view without recomputing the intermediate results from scratch; therefore, the total computation cost can be reduced significantly. Another advantage of maintaining these auxiliary relations is that they may be used for answering ad-hoc queries in data marts environments. Since auxiliary relations also change in response to database updates, these relations need to be maintained along with the materialized view. We propose an algorithm that updates each auxiliary relation and materialized view incrementally in response to database updates. In the proposed algorithm, we make use of the optimized operator tree [6] that is used for evaluating the view as query, for maintaining the view. Updates to nodes in the operator tree are propagated in a bottom-up fashion. The update to each node are derived from the updates to its children nodes and the auxiliary relations materialized for them. Our algorithm derives the exact change at each intermediate node including the materialized view without accessing the view itself. That is, if a deletion of tuple t from the view is produced by the algorithm, then t is guaranteed not to exist in the new view, and likewise, if an insertion of tuple t to the view is produced by the algorithm, then t does not exist in the old view. The algorithm follows the approach of [1, 2] when tuples are inserted to base relations. In the case of deletion, the exact change to each intermediate node is derived from the auxiliary relations only. Finally, we compare our incremental algorithm with the naive algorithm that recomputes the view from scratch.

The rest of the paper is organized as follows. In Section 2, we introduce a motivating example. The evaluation of a view is represented by its operator tree; discussed in Section 3. To materialize the view, we maintain additional relations and they are discussed in Section 4. An efficient algorithm for view maintenance is presented in Section 5. In Section 6, we outline the previous work on view maintenance. Finally, Section 7 contains our conclusions and future plans.

2 An Example

In this section we give a running example for illustrating our view maintenance algorithm. Consider a database with four relations (the primary key in each relation is underlined).

- **EMP(E#, EName, D#)**; This gives the department of each employee.

- **DEPT(D#, DName, Area);** This gives the name of each department and its location.
- **RSCHR(E#, D#, Major);** This gives the department and major of each researcher. Since a researcher is an employee, relation **EMP** has a tuple for each researcher.
- **MNGR(E#, D#);** This gives the department of each manager. Since a manager is an employee, relation **EMP** has a tuple for each manager.

Consider the following query:
'Determine all employees who are neither researchers nor managers and work in 'East' area.

Since this query is often needed, it is profitable to store it as a materialized view, called **EastMiscEmp**. It is defined as a sequence of view definitions:

CREATE VIEW EastEmp(E#, D#) AS
$$(\pi_{E\#,D\#}(EMP)) \bowtie_{EMP.D\#=DEPT.D\#} (\pi_{D\#}(\sigma_{Area='East'}(DEPT)))$$

CREATE VIEW RschrOrMngr(E#, D#) AS $(\pi_{E\#,D\#}(RSCHR)) \cup MNGR$

CREATE VIEW EastMiscEmp(E#, D#) AS $EastEmp - RschrorMngr$

3 Operator tree

View evaluation can be represented by a tree, called an operator tree [6]. An operator tree is a binary tree, where the leaf nodes represent base relations and non-leaf nodes represent relational algebraic operations. Note that the operator tree has only binary operation nodes, unary operations such as selection and projection are associated with edges. A view (as a query) is optimized by the query optimizer before executing it. A query optimizer takes an operator tree as input and produces an output, called an optimized operator tree, which determines the internal sequence of operations for executing a query. Thus, an optimized operator tree defines a partial order in which operations must be performed in order to produce the result of the view. (Note that different query optimizers can determine different costs of evaluating the query.) We define the *depth d* of a node as max(*depth* of descendents)+1, where the *depth* of leaf nodes (i.e. database relations) is 0. The *height h* of the optimized operator tree is defined as the depth of its root.

The optimized operator tree for our running example is shown in Figure 1. Here, the nodes at leaf level are database relations and non-leaf nodes are operations. Each non-leaf node in the tree corresponds to a view defined in Section 2. We make use of the optimized operator tree for deriving auxiliary relations and for processing updates on the view. In the rest of the paper, we refer to the optimized operator tree as the 'operator tree'.

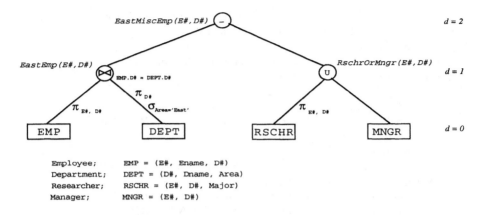

Fig. 1. An Operator Tree

4 Auxiliary relations and their maintenance

Given a materialized view to be maintained, it is possible to reduce the cost of view maintenance by materializing additional results, called auxiliary relations, of the view. Obviously there are overheads incurred by maintenance of these auxiliary relations, but their use can often significantly reduce the cost of computing the updates to the materialized view. By maintaining these relations, a view can be maintained incrementally without recomputing intermediate results from scratch and the exact change to every intermediate step can be derived from them. Another advantage of maintaining these auxiliary relations is that they can be used for answering ad-hoc queries in data marts environment where data warehouse contains a subset of data relevant to a particular domain of analysis or geographic region. Note that these relations are also maintained incrementally along with the materialized view; discussed in Section 5.

In this section we discuss an algorithm for determining, and then materializing, which auxiliary relations are needed for a given view. This algorithm always determines one set of auxiliary relations for materialization irrespective of which relation is updated. This is in contrast to the approach used in [9]. Since a view is represented by an optimized operator tree, the auxiliary relations are materialized in a bottom-up fashion. The contents of the auxiliary relations are computed while executing a view and they are derived from the intermediate results of the view. We maintain one auxiliary relation for each *join* and *union* operator, and two auxiliary relations for *difference* operator since it is not a commutative operator. In describing the algorithm, we use following notations.

Given a node i in the operator tree, its parent is denoted by $\uparrow i$, and $op(i)$ and $op(\uparrow i)$ are the operators associated with node i and $\uparrow i$, respectively. The children of node i are denoted by i' and i''. IR_i denotes the execution result of node i and AR_i denotes the auxiliary relation materialized for i. The keys

Input: operator tree of a view, intermediate results of the initial view computation.
Output: auxiliary relation for each node in the tree.
Algorithm MatAuxRel
    Determine height h of the tree and depth d of each node.
    for $d = 1$ to h **do**
      for each node i having depth d **do**
        Case 1 $(op(i) = \text{`} \bowtie')$:
          If $op(\uparrow i) \neq \text{`} \bowtie'$, then materialize $AR_i = \pi_{K_{i'} K_{i''}} (IR_{i'} \bowtie IR_{i''})$,
          else materialize $AR_i = IR_i$
        Case 2 $(op(i) = \text{`}-')$:
          Materialize both $AR_i^1 = IR_{i'} - IR_{i''}$ and $AR_i^2 = IR_{i''} - IR_{i'}$
        Case 3 $(op(i) = \text{`}\cup')$:
          If $op(\uparrow i) \neq \text{`} \bowtie'$, then $AR_i = \pi_{K_i}(IR_i)$ and augment CNT to AR_i,
          else materialize $AR_i = IR_i$ and augment CNT to AR_i.
      endfor
    endfor
end_algorithm

Fig. 2. An Algorithm for Materializing Auxiliary Relations

of $IR_{i'}$ and $IR_{i''}$ are denoted by $K_{i'}$ and $K_{i''}$, respectively. Let CNT denote the count attribute in the auxiliary relation where we need to store the count information. The algorithm **MatAuxrel** for materializing auxiliary relations is described in Figure 2. We now explain the intuition behind this algorithm.

If $op(i) = \text{`}\bowtie'$, then we have to access the results of both child nodes in order to compute the exact change to i. The reason is that the updated tuples in one child node can join with the tuples from the sibling node to produce tuples that are not in IR_i. This implies that if $op(\uparrow i) = \text{`}\bowtie'$, then we must materialize IR_i. If the $op(\uparrow i) \neq \bowtie$ then, as we will see next, we do not need to fully materialize IR_i in order to compute the change to $\uparrow i$. It suffices to materialize the key of IR_i in AR_i in order to compute the exact change to i and to $\uparrow i$.

If $op(i) = \text{`}-'$, then we materialize both $AR_i^1 = IR_{i'} - IR_{i''}$ and $AR_i^2 = IR_{i''} - IR_{i'}$, since '$-$' is not a commutative operator. The reason for materializing both AR_i^1 and AR_i^2 is that if there are updates to node i' (node i''), say $\delta i'(\delta i'')$, then the updates to i can be derived from $\delta i' - AR_i^2(\delta i'' - AR_i^1)$.

If $op(i) = \text{`}\cup'$ and $op(\uparrow i) \neq \text{`}\bowtie'$, then we materialize the key attributes of IR_i at i along with the count attribute, CNT. This attribute $CNT = 2$ if the tuple is in both children of i, and $CNT = 1$ if the tuple is in only one of the children. If there is a change in one child, then the incremental change to i can be derived from the auxiliary relation and the change to the child. In the case of an insertion, the incremental change to i will consist of those tuples in the change to the child whose key values are not present in AR_i. In the case of a deletion, we delete those tuples from AR_i whose the key value matches a key value in the change to the child. If $op(\uparrow i) = \text{`}\bowtie'$, then we materialize IR_i, rather than only its key values, along with the count attribute for the reason just discussed above.

The operator tree with resulting auxiliary relations is shown in Figure 3.

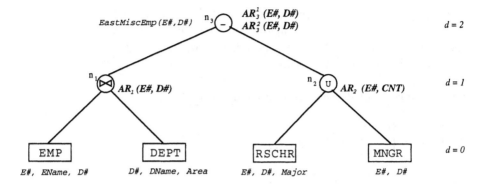

Fig. 3. An Operator Tree with Auxiliary Relations

We now show how auxiliary relations are used to compute the changes to the materialized view.

5 View Maintenance Algorithm

In this section we describe our view maintenance algorithm. The algorithm maintains a materialized view efficiently by materializing additional auxiliary relations; these relations are also maintained incrementally along with the materialized view. We use the operator tree for processing updates to the materialized view. Updates are propagated in a bottom-up fashion in the operator tree, i.e. we propagate updates all the way up to the root node. Our algorithm is characterized by the feature of the exact update to every intermediate node in the tree. The exact update to each node is derived from the updates to its children nodes and the auxiliary relations materialized for them. This feature of the algorithm allows to maintain statistics on intermediate expressions/views without accessing them.

5.1 Incremental Algorithm

We now present our incremental view maintenance algorithm based on materializing and maintaining a set of additional auxiliary relations. Our algorithm follows the approach of [1] and [2]. In [1], the authors have proposed two view maintenance algorithms (one for insertion and other for deletion of tuples) for maintaining a view defined by $\pi_{\bar{A}\bar{D}}(R \bowtie_{\bar{B}=\bar{C}} S)$, where the schema of R is $R(\bar{A}, \bar{B})$ and the schema of S $S(\bar{C}, \bar{D})$. These algorithms find the exact change to the view. The basic idea in these algorithms is to compute two sets of tuples in the updated relation (relation that is updated), say I_1 and I_2, and join them to the other relation, say the results are J_1 and J_2 after join. The exact change to the materialized view, say δV, is calculated by subtracting J_2 from J_1, i.e. $J_1 - J_2$. We rewrite the 'join' algorithm below. In the following algorithm, if the tuples are inserted, the δ will be replaced by $\triangle$ else $\triangledown$. The instance of a relation R, before and after an update is denoted by R^{old} and R^{new}, respectively.

Exact Incremental Change Algorithm for $R \bowtie S$

- let $I_1 = \{t \mid t \in \delta \}$;
- let $I_2 = \{t \in R^{old} \mid t[\bar{A}] \in \pi_{\bar{A}}(I_1) \}$;
- let $J_1 = \pi_{\bar{A}\bar{D}}(I_1 \bowtie_{\bar{B}=\bar{C}} S^{old})$;
- let $J_2 = \pi_{\bar{A}\bar{D}}(I_2 \bowtie_{\bar{B}=\bar{C}} S^{old})$;
- let $\delta V = J_1 - J_2$.

In the proposed algorithm, when tuples are inserted to base relations, the incremental change to the '$\bowtie$' node is calculated by the approach discussed in [1]. For other relational algebraic operator nodes, the exact change is calculated as discussed in [2]. In the case of deletion of tuples, the exact incremental change to each node is derived from the auxiliary relation associated with the node by deleting tuples having same key values as in the updates. Basically, since there is a referential integrity constraint between an auxiliary relation and base relations, we delete all references from the auxiliary relation that are deleted from base relations. Therefore, in this case, there is no need to recalculate intermediate expressions.

Let the base relations $R_1, \ldots, R_m$ be updated by the transaction T. We assume that a materialized view is updated for each update in the database relation. The incremental update algorithm proceeds as follows:

1. Determine the depth d of each node in the view operator tree using depth-first search algorithm [8].
2. Determine exact incremental updates to nodes in bottom-up fashion. It is always possible to derive the exact update to a node, since updates to its descendents by then would have been derived.

The algorithm **ViewMntAlg** is described in Figure 4. Note that when some of the base relations involved in the view definition are not updated, then there is no need to propagate updates along every path in the tree. In that case, it is not necessary to maintain and materialize auxiliary relations for all binary nodes in the tree.

5.2 Comparison with Naive Algorithm

In this section we compare our **ViewMntAlg** algorithm with the naive algorithm that recomputes the view from scratch. We believe that **ViewMntAlg** should perform better than the naive algorithm, since the former is an incremental maintenance algorithm where as the latter recomputes the view from scratch.

Input: Auxiliary relations, 'delta' relations, operator tree.
Output: updated auxiliary relations, updated materialized view.
Algorithm ViewMntAlg
  for each update in R_i do
    Find all ancestor nodes of R_i, say N, in the tree which are likely to be updated;
    for $d = 1$ to h do
      for each node i in N having depth d do
        If updates are insertion of tuples, then
          find exact change to i and update auxiliary relation associated with it.
        If updates are deletion of tuples, then
          find exact change to i by deleting those tuples from AR_i which
          are having same key values as in the updates, and also update AR_i.
        If i is a root node, then update materialized view.
      endfor
    endfor
  endfor
end_algorithm

Fig. 4. Incremental View Maintenance Algorithm

We now give an initial performance analysis of the **ViewMntAlg** and the **Naive** algorithms for our running example. We note that it is a very simple analysis since we do not consider many parameters such as storage cost, I/O cost, timing of the updates. We assume that the relations are indexed and tuple values are uniformly distributed over the domain. Let the cardinalities of **EMP**, **DEPT**, **RSCHR**, and **MNGR** relations be 10000, 10, 1000, and 100 respectively. Each department has many managers, and the departments in **DEPT** are located into two areas, namely, 'East' and 'West'. Let the cost of comparing and concatenating two tuples be 1 unit and the cost of updating one tuple in auxiliary relation or materialized view be 1 unit.

Let us suppose that 100 tuples are inserted in **EMP** relation, say $\triangle$ **EMP**. For this update, the incremental change to node n_1 and node n_3 needs to be computed since they fall along the path of update. Their corresponding auxiliary relations AR_1 and AR_3 also need to be maintained incrementally. The incremental change at n_1 is computed using exact change algorithm. To calculate the incremental change at node n_1 (say $\triangle n_1$), we compute I_1 and I_2 and join them with **DEPT**. The result would be $|I_1|=|\triangle$ **EMP**$|=100$, $I_2 = \{\}$ (since **E#** is a primary key in **EMP**), $J_1 = I_1 \bowtie (\sigma_{Area='East'}$**DEPT**$) = 250$ (note that we have assumed that tuple values are uniformly distributed), and $J_2=\{\}$). Therefore, the cost of computing incremental change at node n_1 would be 250 units, and cost of updating AR_1 by $\triangle n_1$ would be 250 units. The incremental change at n_3 (say $\triangle n_3$) is computed using algorithm discussed in [2]. The change at n_3 is derived from the $\triangle n_1$ and AR_2. In this case the cost of computing incremental change at node n_3 would be 250 units (since there will be at most 250 comparisons at n_3), and cost of updating AR_3 by $\triangle n_3$ would be 250 units (assuming none of them are researchers). (3) Finally, to maintain **EastMiscEmp**,

$\triangle n_3$ is to be inserted to the view. The cost would be 250 units. Hence, the total incremental cost of maintaining the view **EastMiscEmp** in response to update **EMP** by 100 tuples would be 1250. If the view is recomputed from scratch, then (1) To calculate node n_1, the cost is 25250 units. (2) To calculate node n_2, the cost is 10000 units. (3) To calculate node n_3 (final view), the cost is 25250 units. Therefore, the total cost of recomputing the view **EastMiscEmp** would be 60500 units. From this simple analysis we can see that the incremental algorithm reduces the maintenance cost significantly with respect to computing from scratch.

6 Related Work

The view maintenance problem in centralized databases has been studied by many researchers [2, 7, 3, 4, 5, 9, 11]. A recent survey of the view maintenance literature can be found in [4]. In all papers, except [9], views are defined as a subset of relational algebraic expressions, i.e. SPJ views, views with grouping/aggregation. In [9], the authors have proposed an exhaustive enumerative algorithm for maintaining a view and have shown that the view maintenance cost can be reduced by maintaining (and materializing) a set of additional views along with the original view. The choice of which additional views are finally selected from the expression DAG for materialization depends on the cost model and the relations that are updated. In [2], the authors have discussed many algorithms for different relational algebraic operators for maintenance of simple views. Their method is restricted to view definitions having only one relational algebraic operator. In [10], the authors have considered a problem of maintaining a collection of simple Select-Project views and they have developed a screen test procedure to filter out the tuples that need to be sent to remote sites. A more recent work on view maintenance in data warehousing has been given in [11, 7]. The algorithms in [11] are principally directed towards methods dealing with the control of concurrent updates and query requests between the warehouse and the source. In [7], the authors have proposed an algorithm for for making SPJ views self-maintainable. Their algorithm is based on pushing selections and projections to the base relations and make use of key and referential integrity constraints. In this paper, we improve upon the work reported in [7] by considering any view definition based on select, project, join, union, and difference operators.

7 Concluding Remarks and Future research

We have investigated the problem of incremental view maintenance in response to database updates. This problem is important for implementing SQL-92 assertions [9] and for many real-life database applications such as data warehousing, mobile computing, etc. We have shown that the cost of maintaining a materialized view can be reduced by materializing and maintaining additional results, called auxiliary relations, which may or may not contain intermediate results of the view. We have presented an efficient algorithm for maintaining a materialized view incrementally in the face of database updates. We use operator tree, used for evaluation of view, for propagating updates to the materialized view. In this operator tree, updates are propagated to the nodes in a bottom-up fashion, where the leaf nodes denote base relations and non-leaf nodes denote intermediate operations. Updates to a node are derived from the updates to its descendents and the auxiliary relations associated with them. Our algorithm derives the exact change to the auxiliary relation materialized for each node and to the final materialized view. Moreover, the auxiliary relations determined by our algorithm are independent of the relations that are updated.

In the future we plan to study a detailed performance analysis of our algorithm vs. full recomputation of the view. We also plan to extend our algorithm to other data models such as the one described in [3]. In addition, we plan to investigate how constraints can help in maintaining views more efficiently.

References

1. James Bailey, Guozhu Dong, Mukesh Mohania, and X. Sean Wang. Distributed view maintenance by incremental semijoin and tagging. Technical Report 95/37, Computer Science Department, University of Melbourne, 1995.
2. G. Dong and Mukesh Mohania. Algorithms for view maintenance in mobile databases. In *1st Australian Workshop on Mobile Computing and Databases, Monash University*, 1996.
3. T. Griffin and L. Libkin. Incremental maintenance of views with duplicates. In *Proc. ACM SIGMOD Int. Conf. on Management of Data*, 1995.
4. A. Gupta and I. S. Mumick. Maintenance of materialized views: problems, techniques, and applications. *IEEE Data Engineering Bulletin, Special Issue on Materialized Views and Warehousing*, 18(2), 1995.
5. A. Gupta, I. S. Mumick, and V. S. Subrahmanian. Maintaining views incrementally. In *Proc. ACM SIGMOD Int. Conf. on Management of Data*, pages 157–166, 1993.
6. Henry F. Korth and Abraham Silberschatz. *Database System Concepts*. McGraw-Hill, 1986.
7. Dallan Quass, Ashish Gupta, Inderpal Singh Mumick, and Jennifer Widom. Making views self-maintainable for data warehousing. In *Proc. of International Conference on Parallel and Database Information Systems*, 1996.
8. Elaine Rich. *Artificial Intelligence*. McGraw Hill, New York, 1983.
9. K.A. Ross, D. Srivastava, and Sudarshan S. Materialized view maintenance and integrity constraint checking: Trading space for time. In *Proc. ACM SIGMOD International Conference on Management of Data, Montreal, Canada*, 1996.
10. A. Segev and J. Park. Maintaining materialised views in distributed databases. In *Proceedings of the IEEE International Conference on Data Engineering*, 1989.
11. Y. Zhuge, H. Garcia-Molina, J. Hammer, and J. Widom. View maintenance in a warehousing environment. In *Proc. ACM SIGMOD Int. Conf. on Management of Data*, pages 316–327, 1995.

Federated Information Management for Cooperative Virtual Organizations*

Hamideh Afsarmanesh
University of Amsterdam
Kruislaan 403, 1098 SJ Amsterdam, The Netherlands, hamideh@wins.uva.nl

Luis M. Camarinha-Matos
New University of Lisbon
Quinta da Torre - 2825 Monte Caparica, Portugal, cam@uninova.pt

Abstract: A new emerging area of research and technological development, set forward by the requirements of today's progressive industries is the paradigm of virtual organizations. A virtual organization, is primarily an interoperable network of pre-existing enterprises with a common goal, where the enterprises can together function as a single real organization. This paradigm has the potential of representing the basic architecture needed in many multifaceted application domains. Early analysis of virtual organizations and their potential member organizations (nodes), identify a large number of main characteristics, and certain functional and information management requirements in this environment. Although the advanced Information Technology provides the necessary basic tools to support virtual organizations, there are many unresolved issues involved in the development of such cooperative architecture and system. This paper addresses many difficult issues in virtual organizations domain, but it mainly focuses on the management of information in this paradigm. Both the reference model for virtual organization's requirement specification, and the federated information management architecture that we claim to be essential for design of a system to support this paradigm, are the novel features presented in this paper.

Keywords: *virtual enterprises, cooperative information management, federated databases, multi-agent systems*

1 Introduction

Cooperative Virtual Organizations represent a new area of research and technological development enabled by recent advances in computer networks and telecommunication systems. Under this paradigm a number of pre-existing enterprises or organizations with some common goals can come together forming an interoperable network that acts as a single organization.

Although computer networks represent the enabling element, there are a large number of challenges and open issues left, such as the definition of a flexible reference architecture, information management, and supporting tools for the whole life cycle of the virtual organization. Among other characteristics describing this paradigm, we can mention: heterogeneity and autonomy of pre-existing nodes, possible loose- and tight-coupling among the nodes, proprietary vs. sharable node information, order negotiation and order status monitoring among the nodes, virtual organization coordination, need for appropriate supporting tools for specific file transfer (e.g. STEP files for product data), and supporting tools and mechanisms for data exchange and networking. In addition, the

---

* This research is partially supported by the ESPRIT project-22647, PRODNET II of the European Commission. This project involves the following partners: CSIN, New University of Lisbon, University of Amsterdam, ESTEC, Uninova, Lichen Informatique, CIMIO, Federal University of Santa Catarina and Fred Jung.

virtual organization's life-cycle phases, namely its creation, operation, need for dynamic reconfiguration, and dissolution, must be handled.

In *Section 2*, we introduce the virtual organization concept and exemplify it. In *Section 3* a simple cooperation supporting platform is defined for industrial virtual entreprise (VE). Furthermore, the federated database approach is addressed, and in specific, the PEER federated system is briefly described. In *Section 4*, a detailed description of a reference model is provided that facilitates the analysis of functional and information management requirements of different phases of life-cycle of virtual enterprise. Finally, in *Section 5*, we address the features available in the PEER federated system that properly support the information handling of VEs and specify the missing features that require extensions to the PEER system.

2 The Virtual Organization Concept

The need for particular associations among pre-existing organizations linked by computer networks, that can act in a close and more coordinated fashion or even define new forms of cooperation, is emerging in many various domains. With mutual interest among participating organizations, and provision of adequate support technology for their cooperation, this network can appear to the outside world as a single entity, called a Virtual Organization. However, a virtual organization is without a physical headquarter, a management hierarchy, or a vertical supervision or integration. Namely, the member nodes in this cooperation network remain autonomous, but join their skills and resources to provide better quality products and services or to become more competitive in an open and global economy.

Among the various cases of sectoral virtual organizations, the Virtual Enterprise - VE, and particularly the industrial virtual enterprise, is the most represented one. In fact, the paradigm of virtual enterprise nowadays represents a predominant area of research and technological development for today's progressive industries [Browne et al, 94], [Rabelo, Camarinha-Matos, 96], [Walton, Whicker 96]. In virtual enterprises, manufacturers do not produce complete products in isolated facilities. They operate as nodes in a network of suppliers, customers, engineers, and other specialized service functions. Virtual enterprises materialize by selecting skills and assets from different firms and synthesizing them into a single business entity. Virtual enterprises can be classified through many different perspectives. Here we address three fundamental characteristics of Duration, Configuration, and Coordination as the base for this classification.

i. Duration. There are alliances made for a single business opportunity and which are dissolved at the end of such process. On the other hand, there are also long term alliances that last for an indefinite number of business processes or for a specified time span.

ii. Configuration. The most common case is perhaps the variable/dynamic configuration, in which enterprises (non strategic partners) can dynamically join or leave the alliance according to the phases of the business process or other market factors. But in many sectors there are supply chains with an almost fixed structure (little or no variations in terms of suppliers or clients). Another facet related to the configuration is the possibility of an enterprise participating either simultaneously in various networks, or being exclusively committed to a single alliance.

iii. Coordination. In some sectors, as typified by the automobile industry, there is a dominant company "surrounded" by a relatively fixed network of suppliers (a star-like structure). The dominant company defines "the cooperation rules" and imposes its own information exchange protocol and standards. Similar examples can be found in the agribusiness sector. A different organization can be found in some supply-chains, without a dominant company (democratic alliance), in which all nodes cooperate on an equal basis, keeping their autonomy while joining their core competencies. However, once a successful alliance is formed, companies realize the mutual benefits of having some common management of resources and skills and they tend to create certain common coordination structure (a real federation). Besides the industrial enterprises case, similar situations start to emerge in other areas.

3   A Supporting Platform for VE

Many existing enterprises run legacy systems, that are not designed with the idea of directly connecting to corresponding systems in other enterprises. The situation is thus one of great heterogeneity and requires adaptation of existing production planning and control systems (PPC) running at the enterprises, their engineering tools, etc., to the VE's electronic linking. One approach to handle this situation is proposed in the ESPRIT PRODNET project and we have described it in [Camarinha-Matos et al, 1997]. In this paper, we have taken that same approach as the base, and defined the cooperation architecture on top of it. Nodes in the network can play the role of Suppliers, Producers, Final Consumers, etc. So, each SME is represented by a node in the network. Every node consists of two main components: the "Internal Module" and the "Cooperation Layer (CL)" as represented in *Figure 1*.

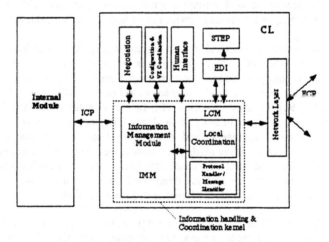

Figure 1: PRODNET Cooperation Layer

The Internal Module of a node represents the autonomous unit of a particular enterprise. It includes both the company's information management systems, and its internal decision making processes / enterprise activities; namely its internal PPC and engineering systems. The Cooperation Layer of a node consists of all the functionalities necessary for the inter-operation between this node and other nodes in the network and consists of several modules. The CL represents the communication and cooperation components, and works as the interlocutor of the company within the net.

As the members of a VE may be quite heterogeneous in terms of requirements, installed functionalities, and management policies it is necessary to specify the desired cooperation behavior (for each enterprise) in an explicit plan (special workflow plan) that will be "executed"/controlled by the Local Coordination Module (LCM). The LCM handles all Cooperation Events according to the specified rules for the particular enterprise. These events are of asynchronous nature and are provoked either by other nodes of the VE, by the Internal Module of the enterprise, or by the Human Interface. To support the interactions between nodes of the VE, two different protocols are necessary: Internal Communications Protocol (ICP) and External Communications Protocol (ECP).

The ICP supports all interactions between the CL and the Internal Module of the enterprise and includes various classes of messages: Configuration, Management, EDI and orders-related, STEP, Quality, IMM queries, unformatted messages, etc. The ECP supports all interactions between the CL and other nodes of the VE (and also between the CL and other organizations not belonging to the VE). This protocol handles the relevant classes of messages included in the ICP plus some additional messages to support negotiation and high level coordination.

Within the CL, two modules together, the Information Management Module (IMM) and the Local Coordination Module (LCM), have the intermediary/nucleus position for any exchange of information and message passing within and through the cooperation layer. Within IMM, the information will be modeled using a common data model, and will be accessed (queried and updated) using a common access language. The design of IMM is based on the PEER federated architecture.

3.1 PEER federated system

PEER is a fully federated, object-oriented information management system [Afsarmanesh et al, 93], [Tuijnman, Afsarmanesh, 93], [Afsarmanesh et al, 94]. Namely, it supports the sharing and exchange of information among cooperating autonomous and heterogeneous nodes, while both the information and the control are distributed within the network. The PEER federated architecture consists of a network of tightly/loosely interrelated nodes. The interdependencies between two nodes' information are established through the schemas defined on their information; thus there is no need to store the data redundantly in different nodes. Every node is represented by several schemas (see *Figure 2*): a local schema (LOC), several import schemas (IMP), several export schemas (EXP) and an integrated schema (INT) [Tuijnman, Afsarmanesh, 93]. The local schema is the schema that models the data stored locally. The various import schemas model the information that is accessible from other databases. An export schema models some information that a database wishes to make accessible to other nodes (usually, a node defines several export schemas). The integrated schema presents a coherent view on all accessible local and remote information. The integrated schema can define a particular classification of objects which are classified differently by the schemas in other nodes.

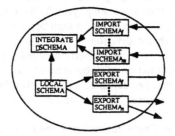

Figure 2: PEER schemas' representation

The local schema is the private schema defined on the physical data in a node. Derived from the local schema there are export schemas, each one defining a particular view on some local objects. For every export schema, the exporter node manages the information on the nodes who can access it, by keeping their node-id, their access rights on the exported information, and the agreed schema modification conditions, to notify the nodes who use this export schema of its changes. To obtain access to data in another node's export schema, a node has to input it as import schema. An import schema in one node is an export schema in another node. Originally, a node's integrated schema is derived from its local schema and various import schemas. In later stages of integration, instead of the local schema, the previous integrated schema will be used as a base. At the level of the integrated schema, the physical distribution of information becomes hidden, and the contributing nodes are no longer directly visible to the end user. Different nodes can establish different correspondences between their own schema and other nodes' schemas, and thus there is no single global schema for the network. A prototype implementation of the PEER system is developed in the C language in UNIX environment, and includes two user interface tools [Afsarmanesh et al, 94], a Schema Manipulation Tool (SMT) and a Database Browsing Tool (DBT).

3.2 Modeling IMM with PEER

The goal of the design of IMM architecture is three-fold: (i) Support for management of information exchanged among different components within the cooperation layer; (ii) Support the exchange of information between the enterprise's Internal Module and its Cooperation Layer; (iii) Support for information sharing and inter-operation between every two nodes in the virtual enterprise. Using PEER as the base federated architecture, the design of the IMM functionalities can support a number of features that are identified to be necessary for information handling in CL. The IMM can support: availability of a part of enterprise information for public access (EXP); provision of information for other VE members (EXP); availability of enterprise information for a sister company (EXP); directory of relevant other enterprises (IMP); access to data from other VE members (IMP); access to data from another sister company (IMP); federated query processing.

4 Reference Model for Management of Information

4.1 Cooperation architecture

From the information management point of view, the problem of designing the necessary architecture to allow the proper flow of data and control information across the virtual enterprise network, is challenging. The Information Management System must provide a high degree of interaction between physically distributed nodes. Clearly, every node in the network can take either the role of a member or a coordinator in several VEs simultaneously. Therefore, both the division of tasks and the information to be shared with the members of each VE need to be properly handled in the VE. Namely, access to every part of the enterprise information must be secured and only available to authorized nodes. Three kinds of nodes can be identified as described below. *Figure 3* represents the general structure of the Enterprises Network and its diverse nodes.

i. VE Member Enterprise node. Every enterprise in the network, may officially take part as a member in a VE. In addition to performing its production/services tasks as a VE member, its information management related functionalities include:
  - Establish contact and interact with other nodes,

- Share and exchange the information required for monitoring of the order-status and task performance, and
- Manage its public information (self, acquaintance, and joint information), and share and exchange its public information with other authorized network nodes.

The information handled within the IMM of the VE member (here called the public information), consists of all the information that is important to be exchanged with others to support the cooperation of enterprises in the network. Therefore, the enterprise can freely decide to hide its "private" part of the local information at the PPC, by not including it within its IMM in CL. The public information can be categorized into three parts. Self Information contains the local enterprise information, that can be shared in parts with different other enterprises; this information is physically stored in the IMM. Acquaintance information that consists of other enterprises information; this information is mostly accessible through the remote access to other enterprises, but also be partially duplicated and stored physically in the IMM. Joint information that provides the access to joint workspaces, for inter-working among this enterprise and other enterprises in the network.

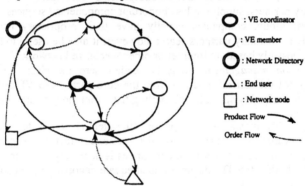

Figure 3: Network of enterprises

ii. VE Coordinator node . An enterprise in the VE network can take the coordination role in a VE. As a coordinator, the enterprise has the role of VE's configuration/reconfiguration, and continuous monitoring of its performance. Furthermore, its information management functionalities include:
- Establish contact and interact with other nodes,
- Share and exchange the common VE information with all VE members, and
- Manage all order-status monitoring and other evaluation data from all VE members, in order to determine the VE job performance at all times.

iii. Network Directory node. One or more nodes in the network may act as the directory nodes. Here network refers to a general wide area network such as Internet to which a large number of enterprises have access. Various VEs may be nodes on this network and, of course, not all network nodes belong to a given VE. Typically, a directory node is a read-only environment that also sells some of its information.

4.2 Identification of functional and information handling requirements

4.2.1 Creation/configuration phase of a VE

The creation/configuration support functionalities are naturally important in the case of "single business opportunity" type of VEs, but also in the case of long term alliances. In the latter case, although part of the network remains relatively stable, non-strategic nodes are dynamically added / removed according to the current business opportunities and the current state of each business process. The creation/configuration phase needs tools for partners search, and for decision support to help the negotiation process and all the dynamics associated to the joining / leaving of enterprises. Some of these steps are defined below:

i. *Search for partners.* The process of creation of the VE involves the search and selection of partners to be members of the consortium. The problem of finding partners can be decomposed in two groups:
   - core partners, responsible for critical components / services;
   - subsidiary partners, supplying less important components / services.

For the first group, companies usually have their proprietary list of potential suppliers. For subsidiary partners search however, it may be useful to have some IT-based tools, possibly based on Internet or other specialized networks.

For information management, what is needed here includes: the support for export/import of the self-information from the core partners to VE coordinator, and the import of (preferably specialized) mailing lists from the network directory.

ii. *Negotiation / agreements.* At this phase, all potential candidates must send their proposals towards the tender, to the caller/contractor. Additionally some complementary interactions between enterprises is necessary in order to reach a final agreement by both sides. The design of an adequate negotiation protocol and decision support tool is necessary.

For information management, what is needed here includes: the support for a framework/mechanism that can be used by two nodes as a joint workspace. Such a framework is currently not supported in PEER.

iii. *Contract awarding and management.* There are two stages here that need attention, one is the preliminary contracts signed between partners to write the tender, and the second is the real contract of work that is signed after the tender is selected by the investor. In both cases the following functionality is required. Once the enterprises are selected for a VE, they are entitled to become an official member of that VE. This process involves the contract negotiation between that enterprise and the VE coordinator.

For information management, what is needed here includes: the support for at least the import of information from the VE coordinator to the member enterprise. But there is in fact also the need to redundantly store the contract information in both places, a feature that is not at present properly supported by PEER.

iv. *Tender formation.* After the preliminary contracts are signed, the VE members will cooperate and jointly write a tender. In the tender the role, responsibilities, and the financial conditions for each enterprise need to be agreed and negotiated by the enterprise and the VE coordinator.

For information management, what is needed here includes: the support for an agreement environment between the VE coordinator and the VE members, that at present is not supported by PEER.

4.2.2 Operation phase of a VE

We now assume that a VE is established and started its operational phase. Various levels of interactions among the VE members must be supported. Notice, that here the PPC of an enterprise is augmented with a supporting layer (e.g., the cooperation layer described in *section 2*) that supports the enterprise's functionalities as a VE member.

i. Basic information exchange interactions. The minimal level of services required in a VE supporting platform are the followings:
- Information exchange mechanisms; to support the exchange of shared/public commercial data (e.g. contract-related interactions), technical data (e.g. product models and quality information), general information (e.g. market statistics and catalogues of products/services), etc.
- Interoperability between standards; to support the use of available and emerging diverse information modeling standards. For instance, the EDIFACT and STEP. Protocols and message formats that can combine different standards are necessary. For instance, an order (represented in EDIFACT) may reference products whose technical specifications are attached as a STEP model. As a member of a VE, an enterprise must be able to receive, interpret, and generate such multi-standard formatted messages.
- Order status monitoring; mostly to support the coordination of the VE, but also to support the other node-to-node coworking. For instance, a node (here a client), may need to know the status of processing of an order at its current stage in another node (here a supplier) in order to prevent any difficulties for itself.

For information management, what is needed here includes: the support for import/export of information between enterprises and the integration of the imported information with the local information. However, the order-status-reports require a feature stronger than simple import/export of information that PEER presently does not support. What is needed is the update-notification sent from the VE member to the VE coordinator on the order-status-report, that needs to further integrate into job-status, and perhaps to be redundantly stored in several nodes.

ii. Events/exception handling. As a member of a VE, an enterprise needs to act as an event driven system. Namely, it needs to handle asynchronous events and exceptions either generated inside the company or by other nodes in the network.

For information management, what is needed here includes: special support for urgent/important query handling, which is not at present supported in PEER.

iii. Advanced coordination. To properly support the functionality of a VE, and independent of the size of the VE, there is a need for a VE coordinator. The main task of the VE coordinator is the monitoring of the job status and comparing it to the VE plans as described in the contracts. In case, an enterprise fails to perform its duties, the VE must be reconfigured to replace the failing enterprise with another one, as the process is described in *Section 4.2.1*.

For information management, what is needed here includes: the support for the import/export of some proprietary information between the VE coordinator and other enterprises, as well as the joint workspaces that is presently not supported in PEER.

4.2.3 Material/services related aspects

It is important to support functionalities necessary to represent and monitor the flow of products and services through the VE network. Some required functionalities include:
- Materials/services flow management. Identification, representation and monitoring of all materials/services flows within the network.
- Logistics. Transportation, inventory and warehousing planning. This includes route planning, vehicles / crew assignment, distribution sequencing, etc., i.e. all activities which provoke materials/services flow between a point of origin and a point of consumption/destination [Pfohl 96], including the subsets supply logistics, production logistics, distribution logistics and waste logistics.
- Forecasting. The use of electronic links to transmit information from points of sale to production units and suppliers, combined with historic data, will allow the implementation of forecasting functions.
- Specific information flows related to product (bar coding, POS). In particular, it is important to understand and coordinate the interactions between materials/services flows and information flows and the multiple bar codes used.

For information management, what is needed here includes: the support for some import/export of information, as well as the joint workspace, that is presently not supported by PEER.

4.2.4 Enterprise cooperation aspects

Here, a number of information handling mechanisms and interaction protocols that are required to support the cooperation among the VE members are identified.
- Maintenance of public and shared information in the CL, assuring its link to the internal IS of the company;
- Maintenance of various cooperation spaces at each node;
- Maintenance of directories of access rights for members of a VE;
- Supporting information exchange, public/shared information query and update;
- Supporting the standards for data exchange (e.g. EDI and STEP);
- Federated information management for higher levels of coordination;
- Supporting cooperation of heterogeneous and highly autonomous agents;
- Supporting contingency cases (with time outs, redundancy, etc.); and
- Supporting negotiation mechanisms.

For information management, what is needed here is partially known (the import/export of information among nodes), and partially to be determined later.

4.2.5 New emerging services

It is important to notice that the VE paradigm is not an isolated phenomenon. Many new other services are rapidly being proposed over the network and some of them contribute to the functionalities required for virtual enterprises. One important related area is the Electronic Commerce that proposes solutions on important issues such as:
- Organization and publication of electronic catalogues and related mechanisms;
- Security mechanisms, namely to support interchange of payments related information;
- Advanced and customizable search engines, some of them based on mobile software agents; and
- Legal issues related to electronic-based business transactions.

For information management, what is needed here is partially known (the import/export of information among nodes), and partially to be determined later.

5 Using PEER for Information Management of a VE

In this section, first we list the existing features of PEER that adequately support the VE coordination aspects. Then in *Section 5.2* a list of necessary extensions to PEER is provided, in order to fully support the requirements set in *Section 4*.

5.1 Support for VE enterprises coordination

For simplicity reasons, here we only list the necessary IMP, EXP, and INT components for each kind of node.

(i) VE member enterprise node. The following represents the information modeling constructs necessary to support an enterprise as the member of only one VE. Clearly, similar frameworks have to be repeated if the enterprise is involved in more than one VE. The necessary constructs include: (1) an IMP for the network directory, to read announcements; (2) several IMPs for the call for tender (summary or extended); (3) an IMP for tender information (related to the node); (4) an IMP for the contract information; (5) an IMP for specific VE coordinator announcements; (6) an EXP for order-status-report; (7) an EXP for exception-problems-report.

(ii) VE coordinator node. Similar to the member enterprise case, here also the framework will be repeated if the enterprise is the coordinator of more than one VE. The necessary constructs include: (1) an IMP for network directory, to receive enterprise categories and mailing lists; (2) one IMP for every VE member to read order-status-reports; (3) one IMP for every VE member to read Exception-problems-report; (4) several EXPs for call for tender information (summary and extended); (5) an EXP for the tender; (6) one EXP for every contract (with every VE member); (7) an EXP for specific VE announcements; (8) an INT for Job-status-report (from all order-status-report IMPs).

(iii) Network directory node. The necessary constructs include: (1) several EXPs for call for tenders announcements; (2) several EXPs for mailing list of enterprises, perhaps also with classifications on their product/services.

5.2 Necessary extensions to PEER

Many extensions to the PEER federated system are required to properly support VEs. Following, we describe a few of these extensions.

1- Update notification mechanism. In several cases, when the data stored remotely in another enterprise is of great importance to this enterprise, e.g. the importance of the "regular status report" of the VE members to the VE coordinator, then the enterprise requires to be informed immediately about any modification / update to such data. In order to support this feature, the PEER system needs to be extended with the update notification mechanism. Clearly, the provision of update notification on certain data must be agreed bilaterally and certain notification rights must be assigned the authorized nodes. The notification rights here may follow the same structure as the object deletion rights defined for shared objects in [Tuijnman, Afsarmanesh 93].

2- Automatic updated information submission. Further to the necessity of update notification mechanism described above, in certain cases, for instance in the case of "exceptional problem report" from a VE member, there is a need for the VE coordinator to have immediate access to some remote information as soon as they are updated or available. Namely, it is not enough to receive the update notification only, rather the notification must accompany the exact data itself. One approach to support this capability in PEER, is to provide the possibility of one node (e.g. the VE coordinator) asking another node (e.g. a VE member) to run a local event (e.g. to process coordinator's query on certain data) in the case of an update (e.g. an update on the exceptional problem report). It is clear that handling the automatic transfer of updated information must be agreed bilaterally. This feature together with the update notification warning, provides enough immediate information for the VE coordinator to act, in an exceptional situation raised at a VE member enterprise.

3- *Handling redundant information updates.* A lot of information needs to be "redundantly stored" in different nodes on the network. One reason for redundancy is the traditional case of safe-keeping. Another reason is to provide more reliability in the case where the nodes are not always active and connected to the network. But, in addition to these cases, there is a need in VE to represent certain common information in several locations. Some examples in this category includes the need to store a part or all of the information in: contracts, order-status, final tenders, etc. For instance, at an enterprise, for every VE in which it is involved, its contract with the VE coordinator, a history of its order-status reports, and a part of the final tender needs to be stored locally in its CL. While at a VE coordinator also, all contracts made with VE members, all order-status reports from VE members (in versions), and the entire final tender document is needed to be stored locally in its CL. To solve the update problem for redundantly stored information, an update notification mechanism or the automatic updated information submission can be requested.

4- *Joint workspace.* For some kinds of cooperation, such as the contract negotiation, coworking in concurrent engineering, or reaching other kinds of agreements, the involved enterprises need to work on the same information at the same time. For instance, the conditions set in a contract can be simultaneously worked on by two or more partners during its development. To support this kind of information exchange, a new modeling feature is required to be developed in PEER, to provide a "joint workspace" for coworking of several partners. For example, a modeling construct that can be used and viewed for a contract workspace between two nodes, is a side-by-side representation of two contract forms; while each represent the last stage of the conditions agreed by each partner. Namely, at any time, each partner can automatically see the last stage of both its own and the other node's conditions side-by side, in order to decide on certain modifications. And the negotiation will end when both sides of the contract contain the same conditions. A feature similar to a part of this joint workspace construct, namely the necessary remote reference to the other node, for making its up-to-date contract available at this node, is already addressed in [Wiedijk, et al 96].

6 Conclusions

The paradigm of cooperative virtual organization represents a very important research area with a large growing potential, but facing many challenges and open questions. Among others, the open issues that need to be addressed include: better understanding of its behavior and requirements, design of a comprehensive reference model, information management policies and architecture, and supporting decision making tools. This paper contributed to the following areas:

- Characterization and understanding of the virtual organization concept in its various facets;
- Identification of its main functional and information management requirements;
- Proposal for a reference architecture;
- Proposal for information management strategies.

Here, the main emphasis was on the information management perspective. Federated databases demonstrate a large potential in handling the open issues in virtual organization domain, as identified by many contributing features of PEER federated architecture and systems, in this paper. However, there is a definite need for extensions to federated architecture, namely to support the features originated in the multi-agents system area. The main required aspects were also identified in the paper and an approach to handle PEER extensions is provided.

References

[1] Afsarmanesh, H; Tuijnman, F.; Wiedijk, M.; Hertzberger, L.O. (1993) - Distributed Schema Management in a Cooperation Network of Autonomous Agents. Proc. of the 4th Int. Conf. on Database and Expert Systems Applications (DEXA'93), Lecture Notes in Computer Science 720, Springer-Verlag, Sept 93.

[2] Afsarmanesh, F.; Wiedijk, M.; Hertzberger, L.O. (1994) - Flexible and Dynamic Integration of Multiple Information Bases. Proc. of the 5th Int. Conf. on Database and Expert Systems Applications (DEXA'94), Lecture Notes in Computer Science 856, pages 744-753, Springer-Verlag, Sept 94.

[3] Afsarmanesh, H.; Wiedijk, M.; Hertzeberger, L.O.; Negreiros Gomes, F.; Provedel, A.; Martins, R.C.; Salles, E.O.T. (1995) - A Federated Cooperation Architecture for Expert Systems Involved in Layout Optimization. in Balanced Automation Systems, L.M. Camarinha-Matos and H. Afsarmanesh (Eds.), Chapman & Hall, Jul 1995.

[4] Browne, J.; Sackett, P.J.; Wortmann, J.C (1994) - The system of manufacturing: A prospective study, Report to the DG XII of the CEC.

[5] Camarinha-Matos, L.M.; Afsarmanesh, H.; Garita, C.; Lima, C. (1997) - Towards and architecture for Virtual Enterprises, 2nd World Conference on Intelligent Manufacturing Processes and Systems, Budapest, Hungary, June 1997.

[6] Camarinha-Matos, L.M.; Carelli, R.; Pellicer, J.; Martin, M. (1997) - Towards the virtual enterprise in the food industry, ISIP'97 - OE/IEEE/IFIP Int. Conf. on Integrated and Sustainable Industrial Production, Lisbon, May 1997.

[7] Pfohl, H.-C. (1996) - Logistics. State of the art. Proceedings of the Esprit - Copernicus Symposium on Quality, Logistics and Technology Management, Budapest, Hungary, 9-10 Sept 1996.

[8] Rabelo, R.; Camarinha-Matos, L.M. (1996) - Towards agile scheduling in extended enterprise, in Balanced Automation Systems II, L.M. Camarinha-Matos, H. Afsarmanesh (Eds.), Chapman & Hall, Jun 1996.

[9] Tuijnman, F.; Afsarmanesh, H. (1993) - Management of shared data in federated cooperative PEER environment. Int. Journal of Intelligent and Cooperative Information Systems (IJICIS), 2(4): 451-473, Dec 1993.

[10] Walton, J.; Whicker, L. (1996) - Virtual Enterprise: Myth & Reality, Journal of Control, Oct 96.

[11] Wiedijk, M.; Afsarmanesh, H.; Hertzberger, L.O. (1996) - Co-working and Management of Federated Information-Clusters. 7th Int. Conf. on Database and Expert Systems (DEXA'96), Lecture Notes in Computer Science 1134, pp 446-455. Springer Verlag, Sept. 96.

Extending a View Mechanism to Support Schema Evolution in Federated Database Systems

Zohra BELLAHSENE

LIRMM UMR 9928 CNRS - Montpellier II
161 rue ADA 34392 Montpellier Cedex 5, France
e-mail : bella@lirmm.fr

Abstract. This paper discusses the impact of autonomy requirement on schema design in tightly coupled federated database systems. In a federated database system, an important feature of a schema evolution strategy should be how the conceptual autonomy can be preserved. The conceptual autonomy requirement states that evolution of a local schema should not affect the remote schemas. In this paper we propose a view mechanism enhanced with import/export facilities to support schema evolution enforcing the autonomy requirement. More precisely, some schema evolution operations having ability to entail incompatibility of existing programs with regard to the new schema will not actually performed but simulated by creating specific views. Our approach is concerned with preserving both remote schema from schema changes arising on a local schema and maintaining compatibility for local and remote existing programs.

Keywords: Federated database systems, conceptual autonomy, view mechanism, schema evolution, virtual class.

1 Introduction

A federated database system (FDBS) is a collection of cooperating but autonomous component database system [19]. In federated database systems, distribution is due to the existence of multiple database systems (DBSs) before the federation is built. The three-level schema architecture describing the architecture of a centralized DBS has been extended to support the three dimensions of federated database system-distribution, heterogeneity, and autonomy [10]. The main schemas appearing in this architecture are : the local schema as the conceptual schema of local database, the component schema as the translation of the local schema into a common model, the federated schema as the integration of multiple exported schemas, forming the global conceptual schema and lastly the external schema as a special view of the global schema, customized for a group of federated users. For simplicity, we assume single global (i.e. federated) schema for the entire tightly coupled FDBS.

The schema changes arise for many reasons: changed real world domain, reusability and extendibility of classes or cooperation with other systems, etc. [22]. Two schema evolution approaches strategies have been proposed. The first strategy called *conversion or instances adaptation* restructures the affected instances to conform to the structure of their modified classes [2] and [9]. In an object-oriented database, the effects of the schema changes can be particularly disruptive to the other users, because changes to the properties of a class must be propagated to the all subclasses of the class. The primary disadvantage of *conversion* approach is its lack of support for program compatibility since the former schema is discarded. The second approach, called *emulation*, is based on a class versioning rather than modifying the schema and converting the instances [11], [8]. Each class version evolution entails a new version of the class. This approach is more appropriate for evolution management notably it allows the continued support of old programs.

Recently some work has been done to show how schema evolution can be captured through views in object database systems [6], [21], [17] [5]. Schema evolution is supported by simulating each change operation by a specific view. In this paper, we discuss the extension of a view mechanism enhanced with import/export facilities to support schema evolution in distributed databases. The main concern of our approach is enforcing the conceptual autonomy requirement and maintaining compatibility for existing local and global application programs. When a schema change (entailing a risk of incompatibility) arises, a new virtual schema reflecting its changes, is assigned to the user, while the old one is maintained by the system, as long as other application programs continue to operate on it.

This paper is organized as follows. In section 2, we present the specific terms that we use in our proposition. Section 3 describes the functionalities provided by a view mechanism in federated database systems. A general update strategy is presented in section 4. How local schema can be updated is discussed in section 5. Related work is presented in section 6. Finally, section 7 contains concluding remarks.

2 Preliminaries

We assume that data model concepts such as database state, database schema, class, inheritance are familiar to the reader [12], etc. Our approach is independent from the Database System (DBS). However, the environment of our study is the O2 DBS. Thus, the examples described in this paper are based on the O2 data model [13].

2.1 Naming

The O2 data model does not provide class extension at the logical level. However, the class extension can be simulated by creating a named collection of objects which is a root of persistency. Names are entry points in the database. From these entry points, other objects can be reached through navigation.

2.2 The Sample Schema

Figure 1 describes an example of two object-oriented database schemata which will be used in this paper for defining and updating local schemas. This schema is inspired from the one presented in [22]. The first schema named SalesDB stores information about articles and customers. While the second schema, named ProdDB, stores information about materials and their suppliers. The schema description with the object data description language (ODDL) [16] is as follows:

```
Create schema SalesDB;
Class Article                              Class Customers
type tuple (anum: integer, price: float,   type tuple (name: string,
            bought_by: list  (Customer))              addr: string,
end;                                                   bought: set (Article))
                                           end;


Create schema ProdDB;                      Class Supplier
Class Material                             type tuple(name: string,
type tuple (matnum: integer, weight: float,           addr: string,
            type: string, suppl_by: Supplier)         supplies: set (Material))
end;                                       end;

name The_Articles: set(Articles); /* this is a root of persistency and a database
                                 entry point */
name The_Materials: set(Material); /* this is another root of persistency */
```

Fig.1. Example of local schemata.

2.3 Virtual Class

A virtual class VC_i is defined by a couple (P_v, Q_v)
where Q_v is a query allowing to compute the extent of VC_i and P_v, is a set of specific properties (non-derived attributes and methods).
This definition shows that a virtual class may own both properties derived from the root class (trough the query) and specific properties. This feature allows to simulate schema extension and schema modification operations.

Example 2.3. We imagine that the database administrator (DBA) wants to provide users with a view, providing a special treatment for computer materials. The query defining such a view is expressed as follows:
Virtual class Computers
query : Select x
        From x in The_Materials
        where x->type = "computer";
end;

3 Views in Federated Databases

A view mechanism can be used at several levels for information design in a federated database. First, views can be defined to support customization and access control on local databases by specifying the exported part of data. That is only visible properties are included in a virtual class which will be exported.

Example 3. Suppose that the local Database Administrator (i.e. DBA) of SalesDB schema, wants to share only a part of its schema, for instance, some properties (anum, price) of the class Article. While the ProDB local administrator wants to export only a part of the class Material (type, weight, supplier's name). He (she) can do so by creating virtual classes including only those properties allowed to be exported. First, he (she) has to specify virtual classes and then exports it with our view definition language [5] as follows:

Create virtual class Public_Articles
query : Select x
         From x in The_Articles; /* persistent set of the class Article instances */
         Hide bought_by;
end;

Create virtual class Public_Materials
query : Select x
         From x in The_Materials;
         Hide matnum;
end;

Export virtual class Public_Articles;
Export virtual class Public_Materials;

Within the federated level, in the context of a loosely coupled FDBS, views can be used to build a uniform, virtual interface over multiple databases [15], [7]. Finally, a view mechanism can be used to specify a subset of information in the federation that is relevant to the users of external schemas. Furthermore, views may provide access control to the data managed by the federation.

4 A Schema Update Strategy for a Federated Database

4.1 The General Strategy

We classified the set of schema modifications in two categories according their impact on the existing application programs. The former concerns the extending operations which augment the schema content. The second category includes the update operations corresponding to the delete and modify operations. The main difference between the two categories lies in the fact that the extending operations do not entail a risk of incompatibility of existing application programs with regard to the new schema. The operations belonging to the second category will not actually performed but simulated by creating specific views. This kind of operations can entail structural or semantic conflicts with regard to the global schema. The problem of structural and semantic conflicts are out the scope of this paper, see related work in [3][20][18].

4.2 Schema Consistency

Any schema change must ensure the schema consistency. In the context of an object database system, structural consistency is provided by using a set of invariants that define the consistency requirements of the class hierarchy. In our approach, two kinds of invariants have to be taken into account. The first kind of invariants concerning the class hierarchy is inspired from ORION ODBS [2]. We propose a new invariant enforcing the conceptual autonomy property. These invariants providing the basis of the semantics specification of schema updates propagation, have to ensure both the preservation of existing application programs and the schema consistency.

Conceptual Autonomy Principle
A federated database system provides *conceptual autonomy* if the specification and the semantics of the remote local schemas are not affected by any local schema change.

5 Local schema evolution

The schema evolution strategy we propose is independent from the data model. However, in this paper, we will illustrate it through an object-oriented schema evolution. Our virtual schema update language includes the basic schema changes [23] and more sophisticated modifications such as nest and unnest operations, affecting the aggregation links [5]. However, due to space limitations these schema changes will not be described here.

5.1 Add an Attribute to a Class

The semantics of the add attribute operation is to augment the type of a class. A relevant issue concerns the visibility of the added property for the remote databases and the existing derived classes if the specified class is a root derivation class The visibility of the added attribute should be specified in the Add command. The syntactic form of the add attribute command is :
Add Attribute <attribute specification><visibility> to <class name>;

The value of the visibility should be *private* or *public*. The default value is private.
Here is an algorithm for add an attribute. Let C_{exp} be a set of exported classes.
Add_Attribute(A: T, visibility, C) /* add an attribute A with a type T to C*/
If A exists then reject the operation
Else Add Attribute A: T to class C;

If $(C \, \varepsilon \, C_{exp})$ Then
    If (visibility = public) /* A will be added to the global schema */
      Add Attribute A: T to the global schema;
   If (V = (derivation root class)) and (visibility = private) then
   For i=1, k   /* k is the number of derived virtual classes from V */
    Hide Attribute A in view V_i
end Else;
End Add_attribute;

5.2 Delete a Property

Before propagating a delete operation, we need to know if the related property is currently used by application programs in the local database or in the remote databases. We define a function named "fused(p)" which returns a Boolean (true if p is currently used and false otherwise). This kind of function is also provided by programming language, for instance Smalltalk. Figure 2 summarizes the different cases arising when a property is deleted in a local schema.

position of p	p is used	Action to perform
exported	globally used	The deletion will not actually performed but simulated since p is used in remote programs
exported	locally used	The deletion will not actually performed but simulated since p is used in local programs.
exported	not used anywhere	Delete p in the local and the global schemata.
imported	locally not used	Delete p in the local schema only.
imported	globally not used	The deletion will not actually performed but simulated since p is imported.
imported	locally used	The deletion will not actually performed but simulated since p is used in local programs.
imported	globally used	The deletion will not actually performed but simulated since p is used in remote programs.

Fig. 2. Deletion strategy in a federated database.

The general syntactic form of a delete operation is :
Delete Attribute <property name> in < class name>;
The semantics of the delete operation is to remove the specified attribute from the type of the class C in the current local schema and affects the global schema only if the related attribute is not currently referenced by an application program in the remote databases. Let C_{exp} be a set of exported classes and let C_{imp} be a set of imported

classes. The algorithm dealing with the delete operation is described by the following procedure:

Delete_property (p, C) /* delete a property p in a class C */
If not(fused(p)) and C<>derivation root
    Then /* p is not used in existing programs and C is not a derivation root */
        If (C ε C$_{imp}$) Delete p in class C; /* p is deleted in the local schema */
        If (C ε C$_{exp}$) Then delete p in class C in the global schema
    end then
Else /* create a new version of C in which p will be hidden */
    create virtual class C' from C
    query : select x from x in C_extent;
    Hide p ;
    end;
    Rename C' as C;
End Delete_property;

Example 5.2. We imagine that the local DBA wants to delete the attribute weight in the class Material. The deletion operation is expressed as follows:
Delete Attribute weight in class Material;

Now suppose this attribute is referenced by an existing program then the deletion of this attribute will be not actually performed but simulated by creating a virtual class as follows:
create virtual class Material_V1 from Material
        query : select x from x in The_Materials;
        Hide weight;
        end;
Rename Material_V1 as Material;

5.3 Modify a Property

The semantics of this operation consists in modifying the type of an attribute or the code of a method. Adopted strategy is very closed to the strategy of the delete operation. Here is an algorithm to modify an attribute.

Modify_Attribute (A: T, C) /* Modify A in class C with a new type T */
If not(fused(p)) and C <> derivation root
        Then Modify A in class C in local schema;
          If (C ε C$_{exp}$) Then Modify A in class C in the global schema;
        end then
    Else /* the modification is not actually performed but simulated */
        create virtual class C' from C
        query : select x

```
        from x in C_extent;
        Hide A;
        Add Attribute A : T /* A has the new type T */
        end;
        Rename C' as C;
End Modify_Attribute;
```

6 Related Work

The original idea of using the view mechanism to support schema evolution has been published in [6]. Schema evolution is supported by using a view definition language allowing capacity-augmenting views. However no solution was provided to managing the specific attributes introduced by capacity-augmenting views.

In [21], the simulation process is enhanced and included in an external schema definition. An external schema is defined as a subset of base classes and a set of views corresponding to the schema modifications.

More recently, the Multi-view system is enhanced with schema evolution support [17]. However, the proposed view definition language does not allow the virtual classes derived from several base classes. On contrary, our method still works for composite virtual classes.

Another work [22] attempts to define a variable architecture of a federated database based on three schema transformation processors : (i) schema extension, (ii) schema filtering and (iii) schema composition.

An approach based on schema versioning and instance multifaceting to support program compatibility in distributed object database systems has been proposed in [8]. The originality of this work lies in pointing out similarities between schema evolution and heterogeneous schema integration. However, the taxonomy of proposed evolution operations do not include operations including more than one class.

7 Conclusion

This paper describes a view mechanism enhanced with import/export facilities to support schema evolution enforcing the conceptual autonomy requirement in tightly coupled federated database systems. More precisely, our approach consists in maintaining virtual versions of local schema so that local and global applications and remote schemas are unaffected by local schema changes. However, a version of the original schema is created only if the schema evolution operation entails a risk of incoherence of existing views and remote schemas or application programs. Thus, this strategy has as primarily advantage to avoiding the proliferation of view versions occurring in the other view based approaches [6], [17].

The feasibility of our approach is confirmed by an experimentation on a centralized database. A small prototype named SETV has been developed on top of the O2 DBS [14], [5].

References

1. ABITEBOUL S., BONNER A. ,"Objects and Views", in Proc. ACM SIGMOD, Conference on Management of Data, pp 238-247, Denver, Colorado, May, 1991.

2. BANERJEE J., KIM W., KIM K.J., KORTH H., "Semantics and Implementation of Schema Evolution in Object-oriented databases", in Proc. ACM SIGMOD Conference on Management of Data, San Francisco, 1987.

3. BATINI C., LENZIRIN M. et NAVATHE S., "A Comparative Analysis of Methodologies for Database Schema Integration", ACM Computer Surveys 18(4), pp. 323-364, December, 1986.

4. BELLAHSENE Z., PONCELET P.,TEISSEIRE M., " Views for Information Design without Reorganization", in Proc. of CAiSE'96, International Conference on Advanced Information System Engineering, Crete 20-24 May, Lecture Notes in Computer Science, Springer-Verlag, May, 1996.

5. BELLAHSENE Z., "Views for Schema Evolution in Object-oriented Database Systems", British National Conference on Database BNCOD-14", Lectures Notes in Computer Science, Springer Verlag, Edinburgh, July, 1996.

6. BERTINO E., "A View Mechanism for Object-oriented Database", 3rd International Conference on Extending Database Technology, March 23-24, Vienna (Austria),1992.

7. BERTINO E, "Integration of Heterogeneous data repositories by using object-oriented views", in Proc. of the first International Workshop on Interoperability in Multidatabase Systems, April, 1991.

8. CLAMEN S.M., "Schema Evolution and Integration", Journal of Distributed and parallel Databases 2 (1994), pp. 101-126.

9. FERRANDINA F., MEYER T., ZICARI R., G. FERRAN G., MADEC J., "Schema and Database Evolution in the O2 Object Database System", in Proc. of VLDB Conference, Zurich, Switzerland, september, 1995.

10. HEIMBIGNER D., D. McLEOD, "A Federated Architecture for Information Management", ACM Transactions on Office Information Systems, 3(3), pp. 253-278, July, 1985.

11. KIM W., CHOU H.T., "Versions of Schema for Object-Oriented Databases", in Proc. of the 14th VLDB Conf., L.A., California, pp 148-159, 1988.

12. KIM W., "Introduction to Object-Oriented Databases", MIT Press, Cambridge, Massachusetts, London, England, 1990.

13. LECLUSE C., RICHARD P., VELEZ F., "O$_2$, An Object Oriented Data Model", in Proc of the ACM SIGMOD Conference on Management of Data, Chicago, June, 1988.

14. LUCATO G., "Evolution de schema au travers des vues", Rapport de DEA, University of Montpellier II, June 1995.

15. MOTRO A., "Superviews: Virtual Integration of Multiple Databases", IEEE Trans. on Software Engineering, Vol. SE-13, N°7, July 1987, PP. 785-798.

16. The O2 User Manual, O2Technology, 1994.

17. RA Y.G., E. A., "A transparent object-oriented Schema Changes Approach Using View Evolution", IEEE Int. Conf. on Data Engineering, Taipei, Taiwan, 1995.

18. SIEGEL M., MADNICK S., "A Metadata Approach to Resolving Semantic Conflicts. In Proceedings of the 17th VLDB Conference, Barcelona, September, 1991.

19. SHETH A.P, LARSON J.A., "Federated Databases Systems for Managing Distributed, Heterogeneous, and Autonomous Databases", ACM Computer Surveys, 22(3):183-236, September, 1990.

20. SPACCAPIETRA S., PARENT C., DUPONT Y., " View integration: A Step Forward in Solving Structural Conflicts", IEEE Transaction on Knowledge and Data Engineering, October, 1992.

21. TRESCH M., SCHOLL M.H., "Schema Transformation without Database Reorganization", in SIGMOD Record, 22(1), March 1993.

22. TRESCH M., SCHOLL M. H., " Schema Transformation Processors for Federated Object Bases", in Proc. 3rd International Symposium on Database Systems for Advanced Applications (DASFAA), Daejon, Korea, April 1993.

23. ZICARI R., "A framework for O2 Schema updates", in Proc. of 7th IEEE International Conference on Data Engineering, PP. 146-182, April 1991.

On the Query Treatment in Federated Systems

Yangjun Chen   Wolfgang Benn

Department of Computer Science, Technical University of Chemnitz-Zwickau
09107 Chemnitz, Germany

Abstract. In this paper, a systematic method for evaluating queries issued to an federated relational database system is presented. The method consists of four phases: syntactic analysis, query decomposition, query translation and result synthesis, which all can be done automatically based on the metadata built in the system, even if the structure conflicts among the local databases exist.

1. Introduction

With the advent of applications involving increased cooperation among systems, the development of methods for integrating pre-existing databases becomes important. The design of such global database systems must allow unified access to the diverse and possibly heterogeneous database systems without subjecting them to conversion or major modifications [1, 10, 11]. One important issue in such a system is the query treatment, which has received much attention during the past several years. In [16], a query processing method is proposed based on the concept of "virtual function dependency" to derive reasonable values for *null values* which occur due to the integration. In [14], a query decomposition strategy has been developed based on a simple one-to-one concept mapping. Several earlier papers such as [12, 13] belong to special case studies. No systematic method has been suggested at all. Especially, in the case of structure conflicts, no idea on it emerges. (Although in [15] such problems are discussed, the method proposed there, based on the concept of *superrelations*, can not be automated.) The other researches reported in [2, 5, 6, 9] are mainly concerned with optimization.

In this paper, we address this problem and try to develop a systematic method for the (select-project-join) query evaluation in a (relational) heterogeneous environment. Our method consists of four steps: syntactic analysis, query decomposition, query translation and result synthesis. If the medadata are well defined, all of them can be performed automatically. First, the query decomposition can be done by using correspondence assertions. Secondly, the query translation can be automated based on the relation structure terms and the corresponding derivation rules, which are higher order logic concepts for accommodating complicated semantic heterogeneities. The last step: result synthesis is merely a simple process, by which the local answers are combined together.

The remainder of the paper is organized as follows. In Section 2, we show our system architecture and the data dictionary used for storing meta information. Then, in Section 3, the query treatment is discussed in detail. Finally, we set forth a short summary in Section 4.

2. System architecture and metadata

Before we discuss the main idea of our method for evaluating queries submitted to a federated system, we simply describe our system architecture and the metadata used to resolve the semantic conflicts among the component databases.

2.1 System architecture

Our system architecture consists of three-layers: FSM-client, FSM and FSM-agents as shown in Fig. 1 (here FSM represents "Federated System Manager".)

The work reported here is supported by DFG (Deutsche Forschungsgemeinschaft) under grant No. Be1786/1-1.

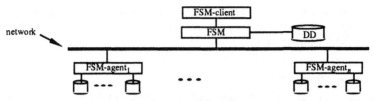

Fig. 1. System architecture

The task of the FSM-client layer consists in the application management, providing a suite of application tools which enable users and DBAs to access the system. The FSM layer is responsible for the mergence of potentially conflicting local databases and the definition of global schemas. In addition, a centralized management for the data dictionary (DD) is supported at this layer. The FSM-agent layer corresponds to the local system management, addressing all the issues w.r.t. schema translation and export as well as local transaction and query processing.

In term of this architecture, each component database is installed in some FSM-agent and must be registered in the FSM. Then, for a component relational database, each attribute value will be implicitly prefixed with a string of the form:

<FSM-agent name>.<database system name>.<database name>.<relation name>.<attribute name>,

where "." denotes string concatenation. For example, *FSM_agent1.informix.Patient-DB.patient_records.name* references attribute "name" from relation "patient_records" in an informix database named "PatientDB", installed in "FSM_agent1".

2.2 Metadata classification

In this subsection, we discuss the meta information built in our system, which can be classified into three groups: structure mappings, concept mappings and data mappings, each for a different kind of semantic conflicts: structure conflict, concept conflict and data conflict.

2.2.1 Structure mappings

In the case of relational databases, we consider three kinds of structure conflicts. They are,

1) when an attribute value in one database appears as an attribute name in another database,
2) when an attribute value in one database appears as a relation name in another database, and
3) when an attribute name in one database appears as a relation name in another database.

As an example, consider three local schemas of the following form:

DB_1:   faculty(name, research_area, income),

DB_2:   research(research_area, name$_1$, ..., name$_n$),

DB_3:   name$_1$'(research_area, income),

            ... ...

            name$_m$'(research_area, income).

In DB_1, there is one single relation, with one tuple per faculty member and research area, storing his/her income. In DB_2, there is one single relation, with one tuple per research area, and one attribute per faculty member, named by his/her name and storing its income. Finally, DB_3 has one relation per faculty member, named by his/her name; each relation has one tuple per research area storing the income.

If we want to integrate these three databases and the global schema R is chosen to be the same as "faculty", then an algebra expression like $\pi_{name,\ research\_area}(\sigma_{in-}$

$_{come>1000}(R))$ has to be translated so that it can be evaluated against different local schemas. For example, in order to evaluate this expression against DB_3, it should be converted into the following form:

> **for** each $y \in \{name_1', name_2', ..., name_m'\}$ **do**
>
> $\{\pi_{research\_area}(\sigma_{income>1000}(y))\}$.

A translation like this is needed when a user of one of these databases wants to work with the other databases, too.

In order to represent such conflicts formally, and accordingly to support an automatic transformation of queries in case any of such conflicts exist, we introduce the concept of *relation structure terms* (RST) to capture higher-order information w.r.t. a local database. Then, for the RSTs w.r.t. some heterogeneous databases, we define a set of derivation rules to specify the semantic conflicts among them.

Relation structure terms

In our system, an RST is defined as follows:

$$[re_{\{R_1, ..., R_m\}} | a_1: x_1, a_2: x_2, ..., a_l: x_l, y: z_{\{A_1, ..., A_n\}}],$$

where re is a variable ranging over the relation name set $\{R_1, ..., R_m\}$, y is a variable ranging over the attribute name set $\{A_1, ..., A_n\}$, $x_1, ..., x_l$ and z are variables ranging over respective attribute values, and $a_1, ..., a_l$ are attribute names. In the above term, each pair of the form: $a_i: x_i$ $(i = 1, ..., l)$ or $y: z$ is called an attribute descriptor (see [3]). The purpose of RSTs is to formalize both data and metadata. Therefore, it can be used to declare schematic discrepancies. In fact, by combining a set of RSTs into a derivation rule, we can specify some semantic correspondences of heterogeneous local databases exactly. For convenience, an RST can be simply written as $[re | a_1: x_1, a_2: x_2, ..., a_l: x_l, y: z]$ if the possible confusion can be avoided by the context.

Derivation rules

For the RSTs, we can define derivation rules in a standard way, as implicitly universally quantified statements of the form: $\gamma_1 \& \gamma_2 ... \& \gamma_l \Leftarrow \tau_1 \& \tau_2 ... \& \tau_k$, where both γ_i's and τ_k's are (partly) instantiated RSTs or normal predicates of the first-order logic. For example, using the following two rules

$r_{DB1\text{-}DB3}$: $[y | research\_area: x, income: z] \Leftarrow$

$\qquad$ ["faculty" $|name: y, research\_area: x, income: z], y \in \{name_1', name_2', ..., name_m'\}$,

$r_{DB3\text{-}DB1}$: ["faculty"$|name: x, research\_area: y, income: z] \Leftarrow$

$\qquad [x | research\_area: y, income: z], x \in \{name_1'', name_2'', ..., name_l''\}$,

the semantic correspondence between DB_1 and DB_3 can be specified. (Note that in $r_{DB3\text{-}DB1}$, $name_1''$, $name_2''$, ..., and $name_l''$ are the attribute values of "name" in "faculty".)

In the same way, we can establish the semantic relationships between DB_1 and DB_2, as well as those between DB_2 and DB_3 using similar derivation rules (see [3]).

In the remainder of the paper, a conjunction consisting of RSTs and normal first-order predicates is called a c-expression (standing for "complex expression"). For a derivation rule of the form: $B \Leftarrow A$, A and B are called the antecedent part and the consequent part of the rule, respectively.

2.2.2 Concept mappings

The second semantic conflict is concerned with the concept aspects, caused by the different perceptions of the same real world entities.

[18, 19] proposed simple and uniform correspondence assertions for the declaration of semantic, descriptive, structural, naming and data correspondences and conflicts (see

also [7]). These assertions allow to declare how the schemas are related, but not to declare how to integrate them. Concretely, four semantic correspondences between two concepts are defined in [19], based on their *real-world states* (*RWS*). They are equivalence ($\equiv$), inclusion ($\supseteq$ or $\subseteq$), disjunction ($\varnothing$) and intersection ($\cap$). Borrowing the terminology from [19], a correspondence assertion can be informally described as follows:

$$S_1 \bullet A \equiv S_2 \bullet B, \text{ iff } RWS(A) = RWS(B) \text{ always holds,}$$
$$S_1 \bullet A \subseteq S_2 \bullet B, \text{ iff } RWS(A) \subseteq RWS(B) \text{ always holds,}$$
$$S_1 \bullet A \cap S_2 \bullet B, \text{ iff } RWS(A) \cap RWS(B) \neq \phi \text{ holds sometimes,}$$
$$S_1 \bullet A \varnothing S_2 \bullet B, \text{ iff } RWS(A) \cap RWS(B) = \phi \text{ always holds.}$$

Experience shows that only the above four assertions are not powerful enough to specify all the semantic relationships of local databases. Therefore, an extra assertion: derivation ($\rightarrow$) has to be introduced to capture more semantic conflicts, which can be informally described as follows. The derivation from a set of concepts (say, $A_1, A_2, ..., A_n$) to another concept (say, B) means that each occurrence of B can be derived by some operations over a combination of occurrences of $A_1, A_2, ...,$ and A_n, denoted $A_1, A_2, ..., A_n \rightarrow B$. In the case that $A_1, A_2, ...,$ and A_n are from a schema S_1 and B from another schema S_2, the derivation is expressed by $S_1(A_1, A_2, ..., A_n) \rightarrow S_2 \bullet B$, stating that $RWS(A_1, A_2, ..., A_n) \rightarrow RWS(B)$ holds at any time. For example, a derivation assertion of the form: $S_1(parent, brother) \rightarrow S_2 \bullet uncle$ can specify the semantic relationship between *parent* and *brother* in S_1 and *uncle* in S_2 clearly, which can not be established otherwise.

2.2.3 Data mappings

As to the data mappings, there are different kinds of correspondences that must be considered.

1) (exact correspondence) In this case, a value in one database corresponds to at most one value in another database. Then, we can simply make a binary table for such pairs.

2) (function correspondence) This case is similar to the first one. The only difference being that a simple function can be used to declare the relevant relation.

3) (fuzzy correspondence) The third case is called the fuzzy correspondence, in which a value in one database may corresponds to more than one value in another database. In this case, we use the fuzzy theory to describe the corresponding semantic relationship (see [4] for a detailed description.)

2.3 Meta information storage

All the above meta information are stored in the data dictionary (which itself is implemented as an object-oriented database) and accommodated into a *part-of* hierarchy of the form as shown in Fig. 2.

The intention of such an organization is straightforward. First, in our opinion, a federated schema is mainly composed of two parts: the export schemas and the associated meta information, possibly augmented with some new elements. Accordingly, classes "*export schemas*" and "*meta information*" are connected with class "*federated schema*" using part-of links (see Fig. 2). In addition, two classes "*new elements*" and "*new constraints*" may be linked in the case that some new elements are generated for the integrated schema and some new semantic constraints must be made to declare the semantic relationships between the participating local databases. It should be noticed that in our system, for the two local databases considered, we always take one of them as the basic integrated version, with some new elements added if necessary. For example, if $S_1 \bullet person \equiv S_2 \bullet human$ is given, we may take *person* as an element (as a relation name or an attribute name) of the integrated schema. (But for evaluating a query concerning *person* against the integrated schema, both $S_1 \bullet person$ and $S_2 \bullet human$ need to be considered.) However, if

$S_1 \bullet faculty \cap S_2 \bullet student$ is given, some new elements such as $IS_{faculty,\ student}$, $IS_{faculty\cdot}$, $IS_{student\cdot}$ and $student$ will be added into S_1 if we take S_1 as the basic integrated schema, where $IS_{faculty,\ student} = S_1 \bullet faculty \cap S_2 \bullet student$, $IS_{faculty\cdot} = S_1 \bullet faculty \cap \neg IS_{faculty,\ student}$ and $IS_{student\cdot} = S_2 \bullet student \cap \neg IS_{faculty,\ student}$. On the other hand, all the integrity constraints appearing in the local databases are regarded as part of the integrated schema. But some new integrity constraints may be required to construct the semantic relationships between the local databases. As an example, consider a database containing a relation $Department(name, emp, ...)$ and another one containing a relation $Employee(name, dept, ...)$, a constraint of the form: $\forall e(\text{in } Employee) \forall d(\text{in } Department)(d.name = e.Dept \rightarrow e.name \text{ in } d.emp)$ may be generated for the integrated schema, representing that if someone works in a department, then this department will have him/her recorded in the emp attribute. Therefore, the corresponding classes should be predefined and linked according to their semantics (see [4] for a detailed discussion).

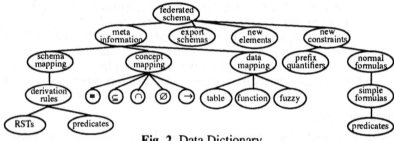

Fig. 2. Data Dictionary

Furthermore, in view of the discussion above, the meta information associated with a federated schema can be divided into three groups: structure mappings, concept mappings and data mappings. Each structure mapping consists of a set of derivation rules and each rule is composed of several RSTs and predicates connected with "," (representing a *conjunction*) and "⇐". Then, the corresponding classes are linked in such a way that the above semantics is implicitly implemented. Meanwhile, two classes can be defined for RSTs and predicates, respectively. Further, as to the concept mappings, we define five subclasses for them with each for an assertion. At last, three subclasses named "*table*", "*function*" and "*fuzzy*" are needed, each behaving as a "subset" of class "*data mapping*".

3. Query treatment

Based on the metadata built as above, a query submitted to an integrated schema can be evaluated in a four-phase method (see Fig. 3).

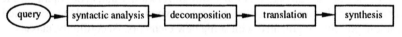

Fig 3. Query treatment

First, the query will be analyzed syntactically (using *LEX* unix utility). Then, it will be decomposed in terms of the correspondence assertions. Next, we translate any decomposed subquery in terms of the derivation rules so that it can be evaluated in the corresponding component database. At last, a synthesis process is needed to combine the local results evaluated. In the following, we discuss the last three issues in 3.1, 3.2 and 3.3, respectively.

3.1 Query decomposition

We consider the select-project-join queries of the following form:

$$\pi_{A_1...A_l}(\sigma_{sc_1...sc_m}(R_1 \underset{jc_1}{\bowtie} R_2 ... R_n \underset{jc_n}{\bowtie} R_{n+1})),$$

where $A_1, ..., A_l$ are attributes appearing in $R_1, ...,$ and R_{n+1}, sc_i ($i = 1, ..., m$) is of the form: $B \alpha v$, or $B \alpha C$ (called the selection condition), and jc_k ($k = 1, ..., n$) is of the form: $B \alpha C$ (called the join condition), with B and C representing the attributes in $R_1, ...,$ and R_{n+1}, v representing a constant and α being one of the operators: $=, <, \leq, >, \geq, \neq$. Then, the query decomposition can be done in an iteration process, in which each element (a relation name, an attribute name or a constant) appearing in the query is checked against the data dictionary.

First of all, we notice that if we use a pairwise integration strategy (see [4]), we need only to consider the case that a global query is decomposed into two ones for a loose co-operation (which is called a binary decomposition hereafter) and there is no mixing appearances of local relations in a decomposed query. (But for a close cooperation, the mixing appearance of local relations should be handled; which is beyond the scope of the paper.) Then, for the integration involving more than two component databases, we do the binary decomposition of a query recursively until all the decomposed queries can be evaluated locally. A second point we should pay attention to is that for a binary decomposition at most two decomposed subqueries can be generated.

We have the following definition.

Definition An *intermediate query* is a (global) query changed so that at least one relation name in it is replaced with a local one.

Accordingly, a binary decomposition is a process to generate (two) intermediate queries, following a series of substitution operations to replace each element with its local counterparts. For a relation name appearing in a global query, we distinguish among four cases:

(1) there is an equivalence assertion is associated with it,
(2) there is an intersection assertion is associated with it,
(3) there is a derivation assertion is associated with it and
(4) there is no assertion is associated with it at all.

In terms of different cases, four decomposition strategies are developed.

Formally, it can be described as follows.

Algorithm *binary_decomposition(q)*   (*q is a select-project-join query.*)
   begin
      generate_intermediate_queries(q);   (*see below*)
      let q_1 and q_2 be two intermediate queries generated by *generate_terminal_queries(q)*;
      for each q_i ($i = 1, 2$) **do**
         substitution(q_i);   (*see below*)
   end

In the following, we mainly discuss the implementation of *generate_intermediate_queries(q)*. *substitution(q_i)* works almost in a same way.

Algorithm *generate_intermediate_queries(q)*
   begin
      label := False;   (*label is used to control the **while-do** loop.*)
      r := the first relation name appearing in q;
      while *label* = False **do**
         {**if** there exists an equivalence assertion associated with r in the assertion set **then**
            {let the assertion be of the form: $r_1 \equiv r_2$;
            generate two queries q_{r1} and q_{r2} by replacing all the r's appearances in q with r_1 and r_2, respectively;

```
        label = True; }
    if there exists an intersection assertion associated with r in the assertion set then
        {let the assertion be of the form: r₁ ∩ r₂;
```

$label = True; \}$

if there exists an intersection assertion associated with r in the assertion set **then**

{let the assertion be of the form: $r_1 \cap r_2$;

generate two queries q_{r1} and q_{r2} by replacing all the r's appearances in q with r_1 and r_2, respectively;

let *new_element* be the new element constructed for $r_1 \cap r_2$;

(*note that *new_element* can be found in class "*new elements*" in the data dictionary; see [4]*)

for each select or join condition *Con* in q **do**

{let a be an attribute involved in *Con*;

if a appears in *new_element* and is involved in some "*method*" defining a "*global*" attribute **then**

remove *Con* from q_{r1} and q_{r2}, respectively; (*The reason for this can be seen from Example 1.*)

insert a into q_{r1} and q_{r2} as project attributes, respectively;}

$label = True; \}$

if there exists a derivation assertion associated with r in the assertion set **then**

{let the assertion be of the form: $r_1, ..., r_n \rightarrow r$;

generate q_{r1} by replacing r's appearances in q with $r_1, ..., r_n$

(also the corresponding join conditions among r_is should be added to q_{r1}); (*see Example 5*)

generate q_{r2} by replacing r's appearances in q with r; (*That is, q_{r2} is simply a copy of q.*)

$label = True; \}$

if there is no equivalence, intersection or derivation assertion associated with r **then**

$r := next(r); \}$ (*in this case, the next relation name will be checked.*)

end

Note that in the above algorithm, $\emptyset$ and $\subseteq$ are not considered for the decomposition of a select-project-join query, since if two concepts are associated with $\emptyset$ or $\subseteq$, only one of them is involved in the query each time. (But they should be considered for the new integrity constraints.) Further, for the intersection assertion, a select or a join condition will be removed from q_{r1} and q_{r2} if at least one attribute appearing in it is involved in the definition of some new (also global) attribute for the integrated schema (see 2.3). The reason for this is that the check of the condition can not be made until the corresponding local attribute values are available and computed in terms of the definition of the new attribute. Thus, such removed conditions are neglected only for the time being and should be considered once again during the synthesis process (see 3.3). Accordingly, the corresponding attributes are shifted to the project-range (as the project attributes) in the query.

Example 1. Consider a global query: $q = \pi_{name, income}(\sigma_{income>1000 \wedge research\_area='informa-tik'}(faculty))$, where *faculty* is a global relation with three attributes: "name", "income" and "research_area". If an assertion of the form: $S_1 \bullet faculty \cap S_2 \bullet student$ is declared and the corresponding new element is constructed in the data dictionary as discussed in [4] and the values of "income" are computed as follows,

$$g(x, y) = \begin{cases} \frac{x+y}{2} & \text{if there exist tuple } t_1 \in faculty \text{ and tuple } t_2 \in student \text{ such that } t_1.name = t_2.name \\ & \text{(in terms of data mappping), and } x = t_1.income \text{ and } y = t_2.study\_support; \\ Null & \text{otherwise.} \end{cases}$$

then two intermediate queries: $q_1 = \pi_{name, income}(\sigma_{research\_area='informatik'}(faculty))$ and $q_2 = \pi_{name, income}(\sigma_{research\_area='informatik'}(student))$ will be generated by *generate_intermediate_queries(q)*. Note that for them select condition "income>1000" is eliminated and "income" is accordingly moved to the project-range to get the relevant local values.

Example 2. Assume that we have an assertion of the form: $S_1(parent, brother) \rightarrow S_2 \bullet uncle$ stored in the data dictionary. Consider a global query: $q = \pi_{name}(\sigma_{nephew='John'}(uncle))$. If the relation schemas of *parent* and *brother* are *parent*(name, children) and *brother*(bname, brothers), then q_1 (the query against S_1) will be of the form: $\pi_{bname}(\sigma_{children='John'}(parent \bowtie_{name=brothers} brother))$, while q_2 (the query against S_2) is the same as q. We notice that to generate a query like q_1 automatically, we have to make the join conditions among the relations appearing in the left-hand side of "→" and the correspondences of the attributes of the both sides available beforehand. Therefore, they should be stored along with the corresponding derivation assertions in the data dictionary.

After the first decomposition step, two intermediate queries are produced and a substitution process (*substitution*(q_i), where q_i represents the query issued to DB_i; see [3]) will be executed to replace each "integrated" element in them with the corresponding local one. Obviously, this can be done in a similar way to that in *generate_intermediate_queries*(q).

3.2 Query translation

If the relevant RSTs and derivation rules are stored in the data dictionary, a query submitted to an integrated schema can be translated automatically. In the following, we sketch the corresponding method briefly.

3.2.1 Translation of simple algebra expressions: $\pi(\sigma(R))$

The translation of a simple query of the form: $\pi(\sigma(R))$, which contains no join operations, can be pictorially illustrated as shown in Fig. 4.

Fig. 4. Illustration for query translation process

This process consists of two functions. With the first function, we generate an extended substitution (ES) by matching the algebra expression to be translated with the corresponding rule's antecedent part (see [3]). With the second function, we derive a set of new algebra expressions in terms of the ES and the rule's consequent part. These two functions can be defined as follows:

the first function: *substi-production*: $P \times A \to S$,
the second function: *expression-production*: $P \times S \to A$,

where P, A and S represent the set of all c-expressions, the set of all algebra expressions and the set of all extended substitutions, respectively. (See [3] for a detailed discussion.)

3.2.2 About the translation of queries containing joins

Based on the technique described briefly in 3.2.1, a simple but efficient method for translating queries involving joins can be developed as follows. Consider the algebraic expression $\pi_{A_1 \ldots A_t}(\sigma_{sc_1 \ldots sc_m}(R_1 \underset{jc_1}{\bowtie} R_2 \ldots R_n \underset{jc_n}{\bowtie} R_{n+1}))$ again. It can be rewritten into a set of expressions of the following form:

$$T_1 = \pi_{A_{i_1} \ldots A_{i_r}}(\sigma_{sc_{j_1} \ldots sc_{j_s}}(R_1)),$$
$$T_2 = \pi_{A_{k_1} \ldots A_{k_t}}(\sigma_{sc_{l_1} \ldots sc_{l_u}}(R_2)),$$
$$\ldots \ldots$$
$$T_{n+1} = \pi_{A_{m_1} \ldots A_{m_w}}(\sigma_{sc_{n_1} \ldots sc_{n_v}}(R_{n+1})),$$
$$T = \pi_{A_1 \ldots A_t}(\sigma_{sc_1 \ldots sc_m}(T_1 \underset{jc_1}{\bowtie} T_2 \ldots T_n \underset{jc_n}{\bowtie} T_{n+1})),$$

where each T_i represents a subquery involving only one R_i, and therefore contains no joins.

Note that this rewriting is completely consistent with the traditional optimal technique

[8] and can be implemented without difficulty. Then, we apply the technique described in 3.2.1 to each T_i and subsequently make a series of join operations between T_i's. In this way, each local result can be obtained correctly and efficiently.

3.3 Synthesis process

From the query decomposition discussed in 3.1, we see that a synthesis process is needed to get the final result of a query. The main reason for this is the existence of new elements for an integrated schema, which can not be computed until some local values are available. Therefore, during the query decomposition phase, the relevant select or join conditions are removed to avoid any incorrect checks. But now they should be considered. For example, global query $q = \pi_{name, income}(\sigma_{income>1000 \wedge research\_area='informatik'}(faculty))$ may be decomposed into $q_1 = \pi_{name, income}(\sigma_{research\_area='informatik'}(faculty))$ and $q_2 = \pi_{name, income}(\sigma_{research\_area='informatik'}(student))$ during the decomposition phase. Further, q_1 may translated into

> **for** each $y \in \{name_1, name_2, ..., name_n\}$ **do**
> $\{$**if** $\pi_y(\sigma_{y>1000}(research))$ **then**
> $\{print(y)\}\}$.

if the local database is like DB2. Assume that the returned results from the local databases are stored in s_1 and s_2. Then, s_1 is a set of pairs of the form: (a, b), where a represents a faculty member whose research area is informatik, and b is his income. Similarly, s_2 is also a set of pairs of the form: (a', b'), where a' and b' represent a student's name (whose study area is also informatik) and his financial support, respectively. In terms of the corresponding method defined on income, condition "income>1000" can be rewritten to $g(b, b') > 1000$ (see Example 1 for g's definition). Applying this condition to s_1 and s_2, we can get part results s to $\pi_{name, income}(\sigma_{income>1000 \wedge research\_area='informatik'}(faculty))$, which belong to "faculty" and "students" simultaneously. The other part results belong to $IS_{faculty-} = (S_1 \bullet faculty \cap \neg IS_{faculty, student})$, which can be obtained by applying the condition "income>1000" to $s_1 - s$. In addition, we notice that if no new element is involved in the query evaluation, the final results are the union of those from local databases. In terms of the above analysis, we give our synthesis algorithm.

Algorithm *synthesis*
begin
  let s_1 and s_2 be two local results;
  if no new element is involved during the query decomposition **then**
     $s := s_1 \cup s_2$;
  else
     for each $t_1 \in s_1$ **do**
        for each $t_2 \in s_2$ **do**
           for each $con(a_1, ..., a_n) \in Cons$ **do**
              $\{$let b_i and c_i $(i = 1, ...n)$ be the two local counterparts of a_i;
              let m_i be the method defined over b_i and c_i;
              apply $con(m_1(b_1, c_1), ..., m_n(b_n, c_n))$ to t_1 and $t_2;\}$
     let s' be result;
     $s := s_1 - s'$ (or $s := s_2 - s'$, depending on which local database the relation name belongs to);
     apply $con(b_1, ..., b_n)$ to s (or apply $con(c_1, ..., c_n)$ to s if $s := s_2 - s'$);
     let s'' be the result;
     $s := s' \cup s''$;
end

In the algorithm *Cons* represents set of all the select and join conditions removed during the query decomposition) and $con(a_1, ..., a_n)$ represents a select or a join condition involving attribute names $a_1, ..., $ and a_n.

4. Conclusion

In this paper, a systematic method for evaluating queries submitted to a federated database is presented. The method consists of four phases: syntactic analysis, query decomposition, query translation and result synthesis. If the meta information are well defined, the entire process can be done automatically. Especially, in the case of structure conflicts, the query translation can be made based on the relation structure terms and the corresponding derivation rules. The query decomposition is based on the correspondence assertions. In addition, a new assertion: derivation assertion is introduced, which enables us to get a semantically more complete integrated schema, i.e., more complete answers to a query issued to an integrated database can be obtained.

Reference

1. Y. Breitbart, P. Olson, and G. Thompsom, "Database integration in a distributed heterogeneous database system," in *Proc. 2nd IEEE Conf. Data Eng.*, 1986, pp. 301 - 310.
2. Y. Chen and W. Benn, "On the Query Optimization in Multidatabase," in *Proc. of the first Int. Symposium on Cooperative Database Systems for Advanced Application*, Kyoto, Japan, Dec. 1996, pp. 137 - 144.
3. Y. Chen and W. Benn, On the Query Translation in Federative Relation Databases, in: *Proc. of 7th Int. DEXA Conf. and Workshop on Database and Expert Systems Application*, Zurich, Switzerland, Sept. 1996, pp. 491-498.
4. Y. Chen and W. Benn, "A systematic Method for Query Evaluation in Federated Relational Databases," Technical Report, the Computer Science Department, Technical University of Chemnitz, Germany, 1997.
5. W. Du and M. Shan, "Query Processing in Pegasus," in: O. Bukhres, A.K. Elmagarmid (eds): *Object-oriented Multidatabase Systems: A Solution for Advanced Applications*. Chapter 14. Prentice Hall, Englewood Cliffs, N.J., 1996.
6. W. Du, M. Shan and U. Dayal, "Reducing Multidatabase Query Response Time by Tree Balancing", in *Proc. 15th Int. ACM SIGMOD Conference on Management of Data*, San Jose, california, 1995, pp. 293 - 303.
7. Y. Dupont, "Resolving Fragmentation conflicts schema integration," in *Proc. 13th Int. Conf. on the Entity-Relationship Approach*, Manchester, United Kingdom, Dec.
8. R. Elmasri and S.B. Navathe, *Foundamantals of Database Systems*, The Benjamin/Cummings Publishing Company Inc. New York, 1989.
9. C.J. Egyhazy, K.P. Triantis and B. Bhasker, "A Query Processing Algorithm for a System of Heterogeneous Distributed Databases", *Int. Journal of Distributed and Parallel Databases*, 4, 49 - 79, Dec. 1996.
10. W. Klas, P. Fankhauser, P. Muth, T. Rakow and E.J. Neuhold, "Database Integration Using the Open Object-oriented Database System VODAK," in: O. Bukhres, A.K. Elmagarmid (eds): *Object-oriented Multidatabase Systems: A Solution for Advanced Applications*. Chapter 14. Prentice Hall, Englewood Cliffs, N.J., 1996.
11. W. Litwin and A. Abdellatif, "Multidatabase interoperability," *IEEE Comput. mag.*, vol. 19, No. 12, pp. 10 - 18, 1986.
12. E. Lim, S. Hwang, J. Srivastava, D. Clements and M. Ganesh, "Myriad: design and implementation of a federated database prototype", *Software-Practice and Experience*, Vol. 25(5), 533 - 562, May 1995.
13. E. Lim, J. Srivastava and S. Hwang, "An Algebraic Transformation Framework for Multidatabase Queries," *Distributed and Parallel Databases*, Vol. 3, 273 - 307, 1995.
14. L. Liu and C. Pu, "Issues on Query Processing in Distributed and Interoperable Information Systems," in: *Proc. of the first Int. Symposium on Cooperative Database Systems for Advanced Application*, Kyoto, Japan, Dec. 1996, pp. 218 - 227.
15. C. LEE and M. Wu, "A Hyperrelational Approach to Integration and Manipulation of Date in Multidatabase Systems," *Int. Journal of Cooperative Information Systems*, Vol. 5, No. 4 (1996) 395-429.
16. I. Nishizawa, A. Takasu and J. Adachi, "A query Processing Method for Integrated Access to Multiple Databases," in: *Proc. of the first Int. Symposium on Cooperative Database Systems for Advanced Application*, Kyoto, Japan, Dec. 1996, pp. 385 - 399.
17. W. Sull and R.L. Kashyap, "A self-organizing knowledge representation schema for extensible heterogeneous information environment," *IEEE Trans. on Knowledge and Data Engineering*, vol. 4, No. 2, 185 - 191, April 1992.
18. S. Spaccapietra and P. Parent, and Yann Dupont, "Model independent assertions for integration of heterogeneous schemas", *VLDB Journal*, No. 1, pp. 81 - 126, 1992.
19. S. Spaccapietra and P. Parent, "View integration: a step forward in solving structural conflicts", *IEEE Trans. on Knowledge and Data Engineering*, vol. 6, No. 2, 258 - 274, April 1994.

Query Processing and Transforming for a Federated Database System

Xuequn Wu

Deutsche Telekom AG, Technologiezentrum
Postfach 10 00 03, D-64276 Darmstadt, Germany
eMail: wu@tzd.telekom.de

Abstract. During an industrial research project of the German Telekom we have designed and developed the system VHDBS, which is a federated database system for integrating information from pre-existing and legacy databases. It offers an object-oriented data model and a common query language in the SQL/OQL style. In this paper we discuss the query processing and transforming for VHDBS. We show how a query against the federated database is split up into subqueries for different local databases, and how the results of the subqueries are synthesized to form the final result for the federated database. The corresponding algorithms are introduced. Moreover, we will also introduce the repository concept that serves as the basis for formulating and processing federated queries.

1. Introduction

During an industrial research project of the German Telekom we have designed and developed the system VHDBS, which provides a way to integrate the pre-existing as well as legacy database systems in a distributed and heterogeneous environment, and fills the data modeling gap between applications and distributed heterogeneous database systems. An object-oriented data model is used as common data model, that is more adequate to integrate heterogeneous data. A CORBA Object Request Broker [OMG96] is included in the system architecture and used to support the communication between client applications and database servers. Several mapping layers of the architecture allow for an open system, which provides a high degree of scalability.

In this paper we discuss the query processing and transforming for VHDBS. To support federated queries, the repository concept is introduced into the data model of VHDBS. A repository provides an object view to support the combining of information from different local databases, and serves as the basis for formulating federated queries. We designed a common query language called FQL. We are using FQL as both the query language and the specification language for repositories. Rather than inventing yet another query language, FQL adopts SQL and OQL of ODMG-93 [CAD+94] as the base language, making adaptations and extensions. These extensions result from our particular effort for cooperative use of databases in a distributed and heterogeneous environment, while ODMG-93's focus is on the standardization of logical centralized object-oriented database systems.

A query against the federated database will be decomposed and transformed to a set of subqueries oriented to local databases and a so called remaining federated query. Since FQL is independent of query languages used by local databases, an intermediate structure is employed by the transformation. The subqueries will be submitted to local databases and executed there. For that purpose, the mappings of the federated concepts, the federated data types, and the federated query language to those of local databases have to be defined and carried out. The results of these subqueries will be synthesized and serve as the basis for the remaining federated query. The remaining federated query replaces the original federated query and supplies the final result for the original federated query. The algorithms for these different steps to process queries will be presented.

The paper is organized as follows: Section 2 describes briefly the basic concepts of the VHDBS data model and the system architecture. Section 3 introduces the repository concept, which is the basis to combine information from different databases and the basis for the formulation of federated queries. Then in section 4 we discuss the query processing for VHDBS in detail. Finally, section 5 presents the conclusions.

2. Data Model and System Architecture Overview

Some basic concepts of the data model used by VHDBS are summarized in this section. We proposed an object-oriented data model (ODM) [Wu96], and such a data model offers a high level of abstraction by the data modeling. This model provides the most necessary and needed concepts for modeling different data, so that it is easy to map data models of existing database systems and database applications to ODM and vice versa. By the design of the data model we take the ODMG-93 [CAD+94] object model as a basis and are closely related to the InORM project [Wu91a] [Wu91b], which uses an object-relational data model to model relational and multimedia databases. Some adaptations and extensions are made to the ODMG-93, which are necessary for cooperative use of distributed databases in a heterogeneous environment, as ODMG-93's focus is on the standardization of logical centralized object-oriented database systems, and is therefore different from ours. Such extensions are for example the repository concept, the federated view concept and the metadata.

Repositories are the first class constructs of the system VHDBS, and the objects are organized as well as stored into repositories. The queries are always formulated on the basis of the repositories, and the results of the queries are put into repositories. Thus, repositories are the storage of the objects (virtual or logical storage on the federated level) and the entry points to reach the objects. The repositories are also the anchor to browse objects at the graphical interface FGRAPH [WN97]. By means of the repositories,

VHDBS provides users the views on the objects. These objects are actually stored in local databases.

The schema of the VHDBS system consists of two parts:
- The type system including all defined types and the graph of types according to inheritance. These types may be related to different local databases.
- The schemas of the repositories, each of which groups some types defined in the type system.

In [Wu96] the multi-layered architecture of VHDBS was described, including the interfaces, the federated server, the database servers and the local database systems, the metadata server and its metadatabase, as well as the CORBA component (Orbix [Ion95]). VHDBS is accessible through interactive and programmatic interfaces. Currently, two interactive interfaces are supported. One interactive interface is a command-line interpreter for FQL. The other one is the graphical interface FGRAPH. It allows the user to retrieve the database with graphical displays. VHDBS supports a C++ programming interface (VHDBS API), by which FQL can be used as a embedded language within C++.

The federated server mainly consists of the global object management component, the query processing subsystem, the type system and the metadata management component (metadata server). Using the type system a type graph is defined and maintained. The type graph consists of the system types and the types imported or mapped from the local schemas of the local databases, and it defines the inheritance relationships between the types. The metadata server manages the metadata, which is used to provide the information about the definitions of the types and the repositories of the system, as well as the locations of the data. The metadata plays an important role for supporting cooperative use of distributed and heterogeneous local databases. With the aid of the metadata server, the query processing subsystem establishes an execution plan for a query. A uniorm interface for database servers includes typical server operations that can be used commonly by different applications to access the data within any local database. CORBA, an industrial standard for distributed object computing, is included in the architecture, to support distribution of all components of the architecture. Our system is developed using IONA's Orbix.

3. Repository

Repositories are virtual or logical storage on the federated level, and they provide users the views that combine and integrate the information from different local databases. Repositories are the entry points to reach the objects. The queries are always formulated against repositories.

3.1 Mirror and Combi-Repositories

There are two kinds of repositories: mirror repositories and combi-repositories (combi-repository stands for combined repository). By means of mirror repositories the definitions (not the contents) of physical repositories of local databases will be mirrored to the federated level. Physical repositories are storage units of local databases, which are for instance relations in relational databases and database entries by some object-oriented databases. There is a one-to-one relationship between a mirror repository and a physical repository, i.e. a physical repository will be reflected to exactly one mirror repository.

With the following example we define two mirror repositories:
 DEFINE Persons OF Person
 FROM People IN O2:db2;
 DEFINE Pictures OF Picture
 FROM Photos IN Oracle:db1;
With the first definition we define a mirror repository called Persons. Its objects belong to the type Person. The corresponding physical repository is called People and is stored in the database db2 of the local database system O2. Similarly, the second definition defined a mirror repository called Pictures. The corresponding physical repository is Photos that is stored in the database db1 of the local database system Oracle.

Combi-repositories are defined through combining some existing repositories, which could be mirror repositories or themselves combi-repositories. Thus, a combi-repository can be used to define a rather complex relationship between the objects, which are stored as well as managed in some local databases. To specify such a relationship, restrictions and conditions should be given. Therefore, combi-repositories are defined and formulated with queries (combi-repositories are therefore also called query repositories). The queries are formulated in FQL.

The following example defines a combi-repository:
 DEFINE PERS PersonPicture AS
 SELECT p.name, b.picture
 FROM p in Persons, b in Pictures
 WHERE p.ssn=b.ssn;
With this simple example a combi-repository called PersonPicture is defined. It provides a view that combines the objects in the repositories Persons and Pictures. The key word "PERS" is a definition mode and specifies that the definition of this repository is persistent. If a repository is temporary, the definition of the repository will be removed after the current session. The example also shows that the essential part of the definition is a query of FQL. The repository will not be materialized (i.e. will not be filled with objects) until the first access to the repository is carried out. Note that the first line of the definition ("DEFINE ...AS") is optional. Thus, a query alone defines (implicitly)

also a repository. The result of the query will be put into this implicit repository. The default definition mode for such a repository is temporary. Through the name "LAST_QUERY" such a repository can be used in the next query.

3.2 Deriving and Determining of Types

VHDBS is based on the object-oriented data model ODM. All things are modeled as objects that belong to some types. Thus, types have also to be determined and assigned to repositories, regardless whether they are defined explicitly or implicitly. With regard to the deriving of types, there are again two kinds of repositories: single value repositories and collection repositories. A single value repository corresponds for example to a tuple, an integer, or a string variable. As the latter ones are mostly used, we discuss here only the deriving and determining of types for the collection repositories.

In general, a repository is of type CollectionType<ElementType>. ElementType may be arbitrary types and CollectionType is Set, Bag, List, or Collection. Repositories are usually defined with a query. The type for the repository is derived from its select-project part:

$$Rep_T = SELECT\ r1.X_{TX},\ r2.Y_{TY},\ ...$$
$$FROM\ r1\ in\ Rep1,\ r2\ in\ Rep2,\ ...$$

The types for Rep1 and Rep2 can be traced easily by means of metadata, because they are either mirror repositories or combi-repositories. As explained, a combi-repository is defined recursively, and the base for the recursive definition consists of some mirror repositories managed by the metadata. Therefore the types of the project parts (the dot notations) in the select clause are determinable. They are denoted as TX and TY. The repository Rep has now the implicit type T=CollectionType(ElementType). The ElementType is determined as a tuple type (TX, TY, ...). The CollectionType is derived from the CollectionTypes of the participating repositories. The derivation is made according to a lattice given in Fig. 1 (This lattice is in a simplified form by omitting the most types of single value repositories).

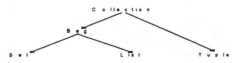

Fig. 1. Type Lattice for Deriving types of Repositories

The following example shows how a new collection type is derived according to this lattice:

Set, Set, List → Bag

4. Query Processing

FQL is the common query language of VHDBS. We are using FQL as both the query language to formulate the end-user queries and the specification language for repositories. A query against the federated database will be decomposed and transformed to a set of subqueries, which are to be submitted to different local databases. A query against the federated database has the following form. For simplicity, the discussion is restricted to two databases that are indexed with numbers. However, by this restriction we do not lose generality.

SELECT X1, [X2], ... FROM ... R1, ... R2, ... R12, ... WHERE C

A query consists of three parts that will be decomposed separately:

- The SELECT part determines the structure of the query result. The attributes in the SELECT part may come from both databases, but may also come only from one of them. Since the recursively defined combirepositories are based on the mirror repositories, every single term X1, X2 can be resolved and related to only one mirror repository, and consequently to only one local database, regardless how complex the term is constructed. Therefore, the decomposing of the SELECT part according to the local databases is trivial.
- The FROM part consists of aliases of repositories and components of repositories. For example, R1 is a repository from a database DB1, R2 from another database DB2, and R12 is related to both databases. The decomposing here is again trivial.
- The WHERE part contains the condition and the information about how the objects as well as the information from these two databases are combined. Some attributes of the objects from both databases appear in the condition C. These attributes in the condition can be combined arbitrarily. Therefore, the decomposing here is not trivial.

The result of the subquery submitted to DB1 is a set of X1 values that meet the part of the condition C, which is related to DB1. The same principle holds for the subquery submitted to DB2. The part of C, which is related to both databases, cannot be treated until the results of both subqueries are returned back to the federated level. Since this part has to be treated on the federated level, it is called remaining federated condition. The corresponding subquery based on the remaining federated condition is called remaining federated query. Thus, C will be decomposed into C1 and C2 for participating databases and CFED that is only treatable on the federated level. Both subqueries based on the subconditions produce results that have to be filtered through CFED.

4.1 Algorithm for Processing Federated Queries

Before describing the algorithm for processing of federated queries, we have to introduce the concept of query tree very briefly. The query language FQL is independent of any query languages used by local databases. If a federated query were transformed directly to a local query according to the syntax and semantics of the query language, the federated database would be dependent of that local database. Therefore, a federated query will be transformed to an intermediate structure called query tree.

A query tree is a attributed syntax tree [ASU86] and a binary tree at the same time. A node of the tree contains the following information: The concerned operation that may be any binary or unary operator such as AND, OR, NOT, and EQUAL TO, or any global function such as CARD and AVG; The kind of the node, which may be a FQL key word, an operation, or a content. Only a leaf has a content, and in that case the type of the content has to be indicated (e.g. string, integer and media); And the left and right son, and the father of the node.

The discussion of the algorithm is based on the following form of federated queries. Without losing generality, we assume again that these queries are related to two databases DB1 and DB2:

SELECT X1, [X2], ... FROM ... R1, ... R2, ... WHERE C

The queries taking this form are processed as follows:
1. Parse the query. As result a query tree will be produced.
2. Classify and mark the query tree for different local databases and for the federated database.
3. Establish subqueries for local databases.
4. Hand over the subqueries to local databases. The subqueries will be mapped to the queries of the local databases and be executed on the local databases.
5. Treat the remaining federated query. Based on the results of step 4, the remaining federated query will be established, and then executed.

In the following we will discuss steps 2, 3, and 5 in detail. Step 4 will be briefly discussed in section 4.5.

4.2 Classifying and Marking of Query Trees

Based on the analysis at the beginning of section 4, by the discussion for step 2 of the algorithm we consider only the condition in the WHERE part. Goal of this step is to decompose the condition C into terms C1, ..., Ci, ..., CFED. CFED is the remaining federated condition, and Ci is a subcondition that will be evaluated by a local database system. There may be more than one subcondition, which will be evaluated by one local database system.

A query tree is classified and marked in a bottom up way. Actually, the calcifying of a node follows the post order tree tracing. A node will be marked with one of the following values:

Marks:= {FED, DB1, ..., DBn, CON}

FED is used to mark a subtree that will be treated on the federated level, while DBi-subtree will be treated in the database DBi. There is such a mark for every local database. A CON-subtree contains only constants, which can be evaluated in any local databases. A CON-mark in subtrees can be replaced (rewritten) with a FED or a DBi mark. A node will also be with FED marked, if its content only exists in the federated database.

The classifying and marking of a query tree is carried out as follows:
• In case of a leaf (the leaves are attributes or constants):

- if the leaf contains a constant then it will be marked with CON.
- if the leaf contains an attribute,
  - if the corresponding repository has a physical mirror in the database DBi, then the leaf will be marked with DBi.
  - if the corresponding repository belongs to a temporary repository and does not have physical mirror in local databases, then the leaf will be marked with FED.
- In case of a node with one son (e.g. the negation operator or a global FQL function):
  - the same mark as that of the son will be used to mark the node.
- In case of a node with two sons (e.g. a logic connection or a comparison operator):
  - if both sons are marked with the same database DBi, or if one son with DBi and the other with CON, then the node will be marked with DBi.
  - if one of the sons is marked with FED, or if the two sons are marked with different database name DBm and DBn (DBm ≠ DBn), then the node will be marked with FED.

4.3 Establishing Subqueries for Local Databases

In order to establish a subquery for a local database DBi, a complete tree with SELECT, FROM, and WHERE part has to be produced:

- The SELECT part consists of the elements that are in the original SELECT part of the federated query and are related to different database DBi. In addition, the SELECT part will be extended to include all those variables in CFED, which are related to DBi. The values of these variables will be used on the federated level for the final evaluation of the original federated query.
- The FROM part consists only of those elements, which are related to DBi.
- The WHERE part is the DBi-subtree.

An example is given as follows:

```
SELECT r1.x, r2.y, r1.z
FROM r1 in DB1, r2 in DB2
WHERE r1.k = r2.m AND r1.x > r1.z AND r2.y LIKE "S*";
=>
DB1: DEFINE F1 AS
        SELECT r1.x, r1.z, r1.k
        FROM r1 in DB1
         WHERE r1.x > r1.z;

DB2: DEFINE F2 AS
        SELECT r2.y, r2.m
        FROM r2 in DB2
        WHERE r2.y LIKE "S*";
```

In this example a federated query is transformed to a DB1 and a DB2 subquery according to the algorithm given above. In form of query trees, these subqueries will be handed over to the corresponding databases. They will be executed in the local databases, and the query results will be put into the intermediate repositories F1 and F2 respectively.

4.4 Processing of Federated Remaining Queries

After that the subqueries return the results to the federated level, the remaining federated query will be established, which will supply the final result for the original federated query. A federated remaining query is established as follows:

- The SELECT part is the same as that of the original federated query, however, it will be evaluated on the intermediate repositories (in our example, the intermediate repositories are F1 and F2).
- Correspondingly, the repositories in the FROM part of the original query will be replaced with these intermediate repositories.
- In the WHERE part, the condition CFED will be applied, which is produced according to the corresponding query tree similar to that shown in Fig. 3.

The federated remaining query for the example given in section 4.1.1.2 is produced according to the above algorithm and it is given as follows:

FED: SELECT r1.x, r2.y, r1.z
FROM   r1 in **F1**, r2 in **F2**
WHERE **r1.k = r2.m**;

The AND operator of the original query is expressed now through the FROM part. The SELECT part produces the combination of the objects from F1 and F2, for which the additional condition r1.k = r2.m holds.

4.5 Mapping of Queries

For the sake of the limited space, we discuss the mapping for the step 4 of the algorithm given in section 4.1 very briefly. A more detailed discussion will be given in another paper. The subqueries established by the query processing subsystem will be mapped and transformed to the queries of the corresponding local database systems. For this purpose the mapping and transforming of the federated concepts, data types, and the constructs of FQL to those of the query languages of the local database systems have to be defined. For example, for the concept mapping the type (concept) will be mapped to the *class* of O2, the *class* or *collection type* of ObjectStore, or the schema definition of Oracle. The federated types have to be transformed to the types or classes of the local database systems. For example, *String* of VHDBS will be transformed to *string* of O2, *char** of ObjectStore, or *char* or *string* of Oracle. A subquery is transformed at first to a query tree, and then will be transformed as well as mapped to the query of the corresponding local database system. For that the mapping of the FQL constructs to those of the local database systems have to be done.

5. Conclusion

In this paper we presented our approach to the query processing and transforming for VHDBS, which has been developed by an industrial research project and is a federated database system for integrating information from pre-existing and legacy databases. The advantage of our approach is that the repository employed by VHDBS can be used to describe the association as well as combination of objects from distributed and heterogeneous databases or to transparently retrieve data from the local databases using the object-oriented view. The algorithms for processing and transforming queries in such a federated database system were introduced. We discussed how a query against the federated database is decomposed into subqueries for different local databases, based on the intermediate structure called query tree and the marking as well as classifying of the query tree. We discussed also how federated data model concepts, data types and query constructs are mapped to those of the local databases, and how the results of the subqueries are synthesized to form the final result for the federated database, using a sophisticated query transformation technique to produce the federated remaining query.

References

[ASU86]   A.V. Aho, R. Sethi, and Ullman. Compilers - Principles, Techniques and Tools. Addison-Wesley Publishing Company, 1986.

[CAD+94]   R. G. G. Cattell, T. Atwood, J. Duhl, G. Ferran, M. Loomis, and D. Wade. The Object Database Standard: ODMG-93. Morgan Kaufmann Publishing Inc., September 1994.

[CAD+94]   C.W. Chung. DATAPLEX: An access to heterogeneous distributed databases. Communications of the ACM, 33(1), 1990.

[Ion95]   IONA. Orbix Programming Guide. IONA Technologies Inc., Dublin, Ireland, 1995.

[OMG96]   OMG. The Common Object Request Broker: Architecture and specification. Object Management Group, Inc., Revision 2.0, Updated July 1996.

[WN97]   X. Wu and N. Weißenberg. A graphical Interface for cooperative access to distributed and heterogeneous database systems. To appear in Proceedings of IDEAS, IEEE Computer Society Press, 1997

[Wu91a]   X. Wu. A type system for an object-oriented database system. In Proceedings of the Fifteenth Annual International Computer Software & Applications Conference, pages 333-338, Tokio, Japan, September 11-13 1991. IEEE Computer Society Press.

[Wu91b]   X. Wu. A query interface for an object management system. In Proceedings of the 2nd International Conference on Data Base and Expert Systems Applications, Berlin, Springer Verlag, 1991

[Wu96]   X. Wu. An architecture for interoperation of distributed heterogeneous database systems. In Proceedings of the 7th International Conference on Data Base and Expert Systems, Zurich, Springer Verlag, 1996

Valid or Complete Information in Databases
—A Possibility Theory-Based Analysis—

Didier Dubois and Henri Prade

Institut de Recherche en Informatique de Toulouse (IRIT) – CNRS
Université Paul Sabatier, 118 route de Narbonne
31062 Toulouse Cedex 4 – France
Email: {dubois, prade}@irit.fr

Abstract: The validity of the information stored in a database may be guaranteed or not, according to the family of items which is considered. The information available in the database may be complete or not, as well, for a given type of items. The paper discusses how these forms of uncertainty can be represented in the framework of possibility theory, and how queries to a database where information is neither necessarily complete and nor valid, can be handled using possibilistic logic. One benefit of the possibilistic modelling is to allow for the use of graded levels of validity, and of graded levels of certainty that the information is complete.

1 Introduction

The validity of the information stored in a database can be often asserted, but not always, depending on the reliability of the sources which are feeding the database. Dually, the information available on a given topic may be known as complete in the sense that all the true information pertaining to this topic is stored in the base, i.e., no missing items can be true; but often the completeness of the information cannot be asserted.

Demolombe (1996a) gives the following illustrative example:

> "Let us take an example where a database contains information about flights which is represented by the relation schema: F(#Flight, Departure-city, Arrival-city, Company, Day). Assume that the information about validity is: *all the tuples in the relation F corresponding to flights whose departure city or arrival city is Paris, represent true facts of the world*, and the information about completeness is *all the true facts of the world corresponding to flights whose company is Air France are represented by a tuple in the relation F*."

As pointed out, already a long time ago, in the database literature (e.g., Motro, 1986, 1989), it might be desirable to inform the user about the validity and completeness of the retrieved information, when answering a given query. Thus, considering the previous example, Demolombe (1996a) writes

> "Now, if one asks the standard query: *what are the flights from Paris to London?*, the answer to the corresponding validity query is: *all the tuples in the answer are valid,*

and the answer to the completeness query is the answer is complete for all the tuples where the company is Air France."

Several modelling frameworks have been proposed for handling various types of uncertainty in databases; see (Motro and Smets, 1997) for introductions to these different approaches. Possibility theory (Dubois and Prade, 1988) has been shown of particular interest for modelling partially-known attribute values (whose precise values are pervaded with imprecision and uncertainty), as well as standard null values (e.g., Bosc and Prade, 1997). Moreover, the modelling of uncertainty provided by possibility theory can remain purely qualitative and is suitable for the representation of partial ignorance. It is thus tempting to investigate how validity and completeness issues could be captured in the framework of possibility theory.

The paper is organized in the following way. Section 2 discusses the representation of validity and completeness information using possibility theory, where validity and certainty of completeness can be easily graded according to the sources providing the pieces of data stored in the base. Section 3 suggests how possibilistic logic can handle queries w.r.t. to validity and completeness information. Section 4 briefly outlines directions for further research.

2 Representing Validity and Completeness Information

2.1 Possibility Theory

In possibility theory, the assessment of uncertainty is based on a $[0,1]$-valued measure of possibility Π and an associated measure of necessity N. Π and N are supposed to be defined on a set of classical propositions closed under negation, conjunction and disjunction. Π and N are such that the following duality relation holds,

$$N(\varphi) = 1 - \Pi(\neg\varphi). \tag{1}$$

This relation expresses that the more impossible '$\neg\varphi$', the more certain (or necessary) 'φ' is. Besides, N satisfies the min-decomposability characteristic properties

$$N(\varphi \wedge \psi) = \min(N(\varphi), N(\psi)) \tag{2a}$$
and
$$N(\bot) = 0 \tag{2b}$$

where $\bot$ denotes the contradiction. Moreover, it enables the user to introduce intermediary states between the three basic epistemic states: φ is true, i.e., $N(\varphi) = \Pi(\varphi) = 1$; φ is false, i.e., $N(\varphi) = \Pi(\varphi) = 0$, and φ is unknown, i.e., $N(\varphi) = 0$ and $\Pi(\varphi) = 1$. These intermediary states are

• φ is believed, or accepted: $N(\varphi) > 0$ and $\Pi(\varphi) = 1$
   (since $\min(N(\varphi), N(\neg\varphi)) = 0$, due to (2a-b), and due to (1) $N(\neg\varphi) = 0 \Rightarrow \Pi(\varphi) = 1$),

• φ is disbelieved: $\Pi(\varphi) < 1$ and $N(\varphi) = 0$
   (since $N(\neg\varphi) > 0 \Rightarrow N(\varphi) = 0$ and $N(\neg\varphi) > 0 \Leftrightarrow \Pi(\varphi) < 1$).

A possibility measure Π can be defined from a possibility distribution π on the set of interpretations of the language under consideration, in a finite setting. Namely, we have

$$\Pi(\varphi) = \max_{\omega \models \varphi} \pi(\omega) \quad \text{and} \quad N(\varphi) = \min_{\omega \not\models \varphi} (1 - \pi(\omega)).$$

The possibility distribution π rank-orders the interpretations according to their plausibility. The use of the real interval $[0,1]$ is not compulsory; any discrete, linearly ordered, scale of the form $1 = \alpha_1 > \ldots > \alpha_n = 0$ can be used as well, where 1 (resp. 0) denotes the top (resp. bottom) element of the scale (then the complementation to 1 in (1) is replaced by the order-reversing operation n of the scale defined by $n(\alpha_i) = \alpha_{n-i+1}$, $\forall i = 1,n$).

2.2   Graded Validity and Completeness

Let $s(x)$ be a statement corresponding to a potential or existing tuple x of the relational database R under consideration (e.g., in the example of the introduction, $s(x)$ pertains to the description of a flight x in terms of the attributes "Flight_number", "Departure_city", "Arrival_city", "Company" and "Day"). Let $R(x)$ denotes the fact that the corresponding tuple is stored in the database, i.e., belongs to the relation R.

   Then, it is reasonable to admit that what is stored in the database corresponds to accepted beliefs, while what is not stored in the database is somewhat disbelieved. Formally speaking, we have

$$R(x) \Rightarrow N(s(x)) > 0 \tag{3}$$

and
$$\neg R(x) \Rightarrow \Pi(s(x)) < 1 \tag{4}$$

where $N(s(x)) > 0$ (resp. $\Pi(s(x)) < 1$) expresses that the statement $s(x)$ corresponding to x is believed to be true (resp. is somewhat disbelieved, i.e., is believed to be false due to (1)). Thus, (3) and (4) express how the presence, or the absence, of a tuple x w.r.t. the database is understood. (3) and (4) are interpretative constraints which are supposed to hold. Moreover, since $s(x)$ represents a tuple information, it can be seen as the conjunction of elementary pieces of information $s_i(x)$ corresponding to the different attributes, namely $s(x) \equiv s_1(x) \wedge \ldots \wedge s_t(x)$. Then, note that $N(s(x)) > 0$ is equivalent to $\forall j = 1,t, N(s_j(x)) > 0$ due to (2), while $\Pi(s(x)) < 1$ expresses that *altogether* $s_1(x)$ and… and $s_t(x)$ is somewhat impossible.

   Some tuples in the database are asserted as being fully valid. By that, we mean that these tuples are not just believed to be true, but that their truth is fully guaranteed. This means that the person who enters the information corresponding to $s(x)$ in the database considers that this information is fully reliable, taking the source which provides it, and its area of competence, into account. It is also supposed that it is checked that $s(x)$ does not violate any integrity constraint, as any tuple entered in the database. Let Val be the property describing the tuples whose validity is fully guaranteed, then we have for those tuples x

$$R(x) \wedge Val(x) \Rightarrow N(s(x)) = 1 \tag{5}$$

which expresses that if the tuple appears in the database and belongs to a family of tuples asserted as valid, then it is completely certain that it represents true information.

   Expression (5) can be also equivalently written $Val(x) \Rightarrow (R(x) \Rightarrow N(s(x)) = 1)$, which somewhat parallels Demolombe (1996a)'s view of validity which in its simplest form, can be represented under the form $Val(\phi) \Rightarrow (B\phi \Rightarrow \phi)$, which expresses that if a formula ϕ is valid and if ϕ is believed by the database (which is expressed by $B\phi$ where B is a belief modality), then ϕ is true. In fact, Demolombe (1996a) uses a slightly more sophisticated definition of validity, namely $RV(p(x)) =_{def} K(\forall x \ (Bp(x) \rightarrow p(x))$ where K is a modality pertaining to the knowledge of an agent.

For other tuples, described as satisfying a property Comp, the information, is guaranteed to be complete; it means that

$$\neg R(x) \wedge Comp(x) \Rightarrow \prod(s(x)) = 0 \qquad (6)$$

i.e., if x is a tuple which satisfies Comp and which does not appear in the database, then it is false since the database is supposed to contain all the true tuples which satisfy Comp (e.g., in the example of the introduction, the predicate 'Comp' corresponds to the property of being an Air France flight).

Thus we can distinguish between i) statements which are surely true (since the corresponding information is in the database and is validated), ii) statements which are believed although they might be false (they correspond to pieces of information in the database whose validity is not fully guaranteed), iii) statements which are disbelieved although they might be true (since the corresponding information is not in the database), and iv) statements which are surely false (since they do not correspond to a piece of information stored in the base and the base is known to have a complete information on the topic under consideration).

In the possibility theory framework, it is easy to grade the levels of certainty, or the levels of possibility. Indeed, (3) and (4) can be modified into

$$R(x) \Rightarrow N(s(x)) \geq \alpha > 0 \qquad (7)$$
and
$$\neg R(x) \Rightarrow \prod(s(x)) \leq \beta < 1 \qquad (8)$$

for expressing that our level of certainty that a tuple in database corresponds to a true statement, is at least α, and the level of possibility that a tuple x not in the database corresponds to a true statement, is upper bounded by β (i.e., the certainty that the statement corresponding to x is false is at least equal to $1 - \beta$). As already said at the end of Section 2.1, a discrete linearly ordered scale is enough for assessing possibility and necessity degrees, so that α (resp. β) is, in practice, nothing more than the label of the minimal confidence in any information in the database (resp. the maximal possibility that an information not in the database is true), even if these labels are numerically encoded. It is only required that α is strictly greater than 0 (0 is the bottom element of the scale, i.e., the confidence is nonzero), and β is strictly less than 1 (1 is the top element of the scale), although β can be as "close" to 1 as it is meaningful in the scale. The inequality $\beta < 1$ expresses that any information outside the database is (at least slightly) less possibly true than a piece of information inside the database (since $N(s(x)) > 0 \Rightarrow \prod(s(x)) = 1$).

Besides, the reliability of the stored information depends on the sources which provide it. Thus, (5) can be generalized into

$$R(x) \wedge Val_i(x) \Rightarrow N(s(x)) \geq \alpha_i > 0, i = 1,k \qquad (9)$$

where the tuples which satisfy the property Val_i are validated by source i whose level of reliability is α_i. It is assumed that the sources can be rank-ordered according to their reliability and that there exists a more reliable source which provides pieces of information which are completely certain, i.e., $\alpha_1 = 1 \geq \alpha_2 \geq \ldots \geq \alpha_k > 0$. For the sake of coherence, it is assumed that $\min_{i=1,k} \alpha_i = \alpha_k = \alpha$ where α appears in (7). Indeed, any information in a database is at least as certain as the certainty level attached to the information provided by the least reliable source which feeds the database. Clearly, the reliability of a source may be topic-dependent. In such a case, we shall divide the source in several fictitious sources corresponding to each topic.

Similarly for completeness information, (6) is generalized into

$$\neg R(x) \wedge Comp_j(x) \Rightarrow \Pi(s(x)) \leq \beta_j < 1, j = 1, \ell \tag{10}$$

where the tuples which satisfy the property $Comp_j$ are assumed to be complete in the database with a certainty level at least equal to $1 - \beta_j$. The β_j's are supposed to be rank-ordered such that $\beta_1 = 0 \leq \beta_2 \leq \ldots \leq \beta_\ell < 1$, with $\max_j \beta_j = \beta_\ell = \beta$ for the sake of coherence with (8).

This enables us to distinguish between sets of pieces of information which are more or less certainly valid, or more or less certainly complete.

3 Processing Queries in Possibilistic Logic

3.1 Possibilistic Logic

The reader is referred to Dubois, Lang and Prade (1994a, b) for introductory and detailed presentations respectively. In the following, we only recall some basic points.

A possibilistic logic formula (φ, α) is an ordered pair constituted of a (first order or propositional) classical logic formula φ and a weight α belonging to a totally ordered scale, e.g., $[0,1]$, or a finite scale. (φ, α) is semantically interpreted as a constraint of the form $N(\varphi) \geq \alpha$ where N is a necessity measure. Then the following resolution rule is in agreement with this semantics in terms of necessity measure:

$$(\varphi, \alpha), (\psi, \beta) \vdash (Resolvent(\varphi, \psi), \min(\alpha, \beta)).$$

A particular case of the resolution rule is the cut rule for the propositional case:

$$\frac{(\neg\varphi \vee \psi, \alpha)}{(\varphi \vee \theta, \beta)}{(\psi \vee \theta, \min(\alpha, \beta))}.$$

Refutation can be extended to this framework. Let K be a possibilistic knowledge base made of a set of possibilistic logic formulas put under clausal form (this can be always done thanks to the min-decomposability property of necessity measures w.r.t. conjunction). Then, proving (φ, α) from K, which can be written symbolically $K \vdash (\varphi, \alpha)$, amounts to prove $(\perp, \alpha)$, where $\perp$ denotes the empty clause, by applying the resolution rule to $K \cup \{(\neg\varphi, 1)\}$ repeatedly. Moreover we have, $(\varphi, \alpha') \vdash (\varphi, \alpha)$ iff $\alpha \leq \alpha'$; besides, if $K \vdash (\varphi, \alpha)$ and $K \vdash (\varphi, \alpha')$, then $K \vdash (\varphi, \max(\alpha, \alpha'))$. So we are looking for the refutation which provides the greatest lower bound. This syntactic machinery is sound and complete with respect to a semantics in terms of a possibility distribution encoding an ordering on the interpretations, in agreement with the understanding of (φ, α) as $N(\varphi) \geq \alpha$.

Let us assume that a possibilistic knowledge base contains the two formulas $(\neg\varphi \vee \psi, \alpha)$, $(\neg\varphi \vee \neg\varphi' \vee \psi, \alpha')$ with $\alpha' > \alpha$. Then if we add the information $(\varphi, 1)$, we can infer that (ψ, α), while if we have both $(\varphi, 1)$ and $(\varphi', 1)$, we can infer a more certain conclusion, namely (ψ, α') using the more "specific" clause $(\neg\varphi \vee \neg\varphi' \vee \psi, \alpha')$, since $\alpha' > \alpha$.

Besides, in possibilistic logic it is always possible to move literals from the formula slot to the weight slot. Indeed, it can be shown that there is a semantic equivalence between $(\neg\varphi \vee \psi, \alpha)$ and $(\psi, \min(\alpha, \varphi[\omega]))$ for instance, where $\varphi[\omega]$ denotes the truth-value (1 for 'true', 0 for 'false') of φ for an interpretation ω. It means that saying that $\neg\varphi \vee \psi$ is at least α-certain is semantically equivalent to say that ψ is α-certain provided that φ is true (i.e., provided that we are in a situation ω which makes φ true). This remark can be exploited when some literal cannot be eliminated in the resolution process, and more generally in hypothetical reasoning.

3.2 Application to query evaluation

The machinery briefly recalled in Section 3.1 can be applied to querying a database w.r.t. to validity and completeness issues. Let $W(x)$ be a predicate expressing that the information reported in tuple x is indeed true in the real world. Then the validity and completeness information can be encoded by the following possibilistic knowledge base:

$$\{(\neg R(x) \vee W(x), \alpha),$$
$$(\neg R(x) \vee \neg Val_i(x) \vee W(x), \alpha_i) \text{ for } i = 1,k,$$
$$(R(x) \vee \neg W(x), 1 - \beta),$$
$$(R(x) \vee \neg Comp_j(x) \vee \neg W(x), 1 - \beta_j) \text{ for } j = 1,\ell\}.$$

It expresses that

- if a tuple x appears in the (relational) database (i.e., $R(x)$ holds), then this information is true in the world with certainty α;
- if moreover x satisfies the validity condition Val_i, it is certain at degree $\alpha_i \geq \alpha$ that it represents a true information, for $i = 1,k$; in particular for $i = 1$, the validity is completely guaranteed ($\alpha_1 = 1$);
- if a tuple x does not appear in the base, it is not true in the world with certainty $1 - \beta$;
- if moreover x satisfies the completeness condition $Comp_j$, it is certain that it is not a true information with certainty degree $1 - \beta_j \geq 1 - \beta$; for $j = 1$, it is totally certain that the information x in the base, such that $Comp_1(x)$ is true, is complete ($\beta_1 = 0$).

Let us go back to the example of Section 1. It writes,

$$K = \{ \quad (\neg R(x) \vee W(x), \alpha),$$
$$(\neg R(x) \vee \neg Depart(x, Paris) \vee W(x), 1),$$

$(\neg R(x) \vee \neg Arriv(x, Paris) \vee W(x), 1),$
$(R(x) \vee \neg W(x), 1 - \beta),$
$(R(x) \vee \neg Comp(x, Air\ France) \vee \neg W(x), 1)\}.$

Then, let us consider a flight which flies from Paris, i.e., it corresponds to tuples which are described by the possibilistic formula

$$f = (Depart(x, Paris), 1).$$

If we are asking for what is the valid information, i.e., the x's such that $W(x)$ is true, we proceed by refutation, adding the formula

$$(\neg W(x), 1)$$

to $K \cup \{f\}$. Then by applying the resolution principle repeatedly and moving literals in the weight slot when necessary, we get the empty clause

$$(\bot, R(x)[\omega])$$

which means that we are certain that the information about flight x is valid provided that it is in the base. Note that there is another way to get the empty clause but with a smaller weight, namely $(\bot, \min(\alpha, R(x)[\omega]))$ by using the general rule $(\neg R(x) \vee W(x), \alpha)$ only.

Assume we are looking for the flights for which the information is valid, i.e., we are interested in the x's such that $\neg R(x) \vee W(x)$ is true with a certainty as great as possible. So we add to K the two clauses $(R(x), 1)$ and $(\neg W(x), 1)$ and we get $(\bot, \max(\alpha, Depart(x, Paris)[\omega]), Arriv(x, Paris)[\omega])$, i.e., we obtain that the information about flights leaving from or arriving in Paris is valid, and to a less extent (certainty α) that any information in the database is valid. More generally, we obtain $(\bot, \max(\alpha, \max_{i=1,k} \min(\alpha_i, Val_i(x)[\omega])))$, which expresses that the items which satisfy $Val_i(x)$ are indeed valid with certainty degree α_i (since $\forall i, \alpha_i \geq \alpha$).

If we now ask what are the tuples in the base for which the information is complete, these tuples x are such as $\neg W(x) \vee R(x)$, i.e., if x is true in the world, it is in the base. Thus, proceeding by refutation from K, we add

$$(\neg R(x), 1)$$
and $\quad\quad\quad\quad\quad\quad (W(x), 1)$

to K, and we get by resolution (with the two last clauses of K)

$$(\bot, \max(1 - \beta, Comp(x, Air\ France)[\omega]),$$

i.e., we obtain the Air France flights (and by default, if $Comp(x, Air\ France)[\omega]) = 0$ any information is complete with certainty degree $1 - \beta$).

Remark: Let us consider an example where we know that flight information in the database is valid both for the flights leaving from Paris or those leaving from London, and where we have a flight x_0 for which we do not know if it leaves from Paris or London. It writes

$$K' = \{ \ (\neg R(x) \vee \neg \text{Depart}(x, \text{Paris}) \vee W(x), 1),$$
$$(\neg R(x) \vee \neg \text{Depart}(x, \text{London}) \vee W(x), 1),$$
$$(\text{Depart}(x_0, \text{Paris}) \vee \text{Depart}(x_0, \text{London}), 1) \ \}.$$

Then, wondering if the information about x_0 is valid, we add the formula $(\neg W(x_0), 1)$ to K', and we obtain $(\perp, R(x_0)[\omega])$, i.e., the information about x_0 stored in the database is valid. Let us imagine now that the validity information is itself imprecise, and only asserts that flight information about Paris departing flights *or* flight information about London departing flights is valid. In such a case, we should not conclude that the flight information about x_0 is valid. Moreover, it raises a technical problem since we would have to deal with a *disjunction* of possibilistic logic formulas (namely here $(\neg R(x) \vee \neg \text{Depart}(x, \text{Paris}) \vee W(x), 1)$ *or* $(\neg R(x) \vee \neg \text{Depart}(x, \text{London}) \vee W(x), 1))$ which cannot be handled inside standard possibilistic logic (however here, by reasoning case by case on the possible actual contents of the knowledge base, it can be seen that indeed we cannot conclude that the information about x_0 is valid). It is however possible in the general case to compute a possibilistic logic knowledge base which is semantically equivalent to the disjunction of possibilistic knowledge bases; see (Benferhat et al., 1997) on this point.

4 Concluding Remarks

We have suggested a simple way for modelling validity and completeness information in the possibility theory framework, in this preliminary study. A careful comparison with the modal logic-based approach proposed by Demolombe (1996a, b) is still to be done. However possibility theory-based logic have connections with conditional modal logic (e.g., Fariñas del Cerro and Herzig, 1991), so we should not be too much surprised by the existence of a possibilistic logic approach to the handling of valid and/or complete information in databases.

One benefit of the possibilistic approach is to allow for graded level of certainty. Due to the inference mechanism of possibilistic logic, the most certain conclusions with respect to the available information, can be obtained. It would be also possible to keep explicitly track of the sources providing the information. This can be done by dealing with generalized possibilistic formulas of the form $(\varphi, (\alpha^1 / s_1, \alpha^2 / s_2, ..., \alpha^m / s_m))$ with the following intended meaning: φ is true with certainty α^1 according to source $s_1, ...,$ with certainty α^m according to source s_m. Thus, all the information provided by a source has not necessarily the same level of reliability (a source may be more reliable on some topics than others), and the certainty labels associated with formulas are now only partially ordered. However, the basic possibilistic machinery can be extended to this framework; see (Dubois, Lang and Prade, 1992) for details. See also Demolombe (1997) for another approach where, in a modal logic framework, the author can model that a source s_0 is as much as reliable as some other source s_i (belonging to a set of sources used as references), by expressing that if an information is valid and believed by s_0, then it is also believed by s_i.

The validity information can be also easily incorporated into the framework proposed by (Prade and Testemale, 1984) for handling ill-known attribute values. Indeed in this approach the available information about attribute values in a tuple is represented by means of possibility distributions on the attribute domains. Asserting the validity of a tuple, as being certain at least at level α, then amounts to modifying each possibility distribution π into $\pi' = \max(\pi, 1 - \alpha)$ (since there is a possibility $1 - \alpha$ that the information is not valid and thus that the value of the attribute is outside the (fuzzy) set of values restricted by π). Then, the evaluation of queries is made in terms of possibility and necessity measures, $\prod$ and N, that each tuple satisfies the requirement. It can be easily checked that if $\prod(Q)$ and N(Q) are the evaluations of a query Q based on π, the evaluation incorporating the validity assessment (based on π') are given by $\max(\prod(Q), 1 - \alpha)$ and $\min(N(Q), \alpha)$ respectively. The latter expresses that, even if N(Q) is high (which means that according to the information represented by π we are certain that Q is satisfied), we cannot be more certain of the relevance of the tuple w.r.t. the query than its validity degree α.

Obviously, these ideas have also to be experimented in real databases still, in order to check if they provide a satisfactory handling of the problem, at the practical level.

Acknowledgements

The authors wish to thank Patrick Bosc and Robert Demolombe, as well as two anonymous reviewers, for their comments, suggestions and indications of some misprints about a previous version of this paper (reproduced in the Bulletin BUSEFAL, Université Paul Sabatier, Toulouse, No. 69, March 1997, pp. 163-171).

References

Benferhat S., Dubois D., Prade H. (1997) Syntactic combination of uncertain information: A possibilistic approach. In: Qualitative and Quantitative Practical Reasoning (Proc. of the 1st Inter. Joint Conf. ECSQARU/FAPR'97, Bad Honnef, Germany, June 9-12, 1997) (D.M. Gabbay, R. Kruse, A. Nonnengart, H.J. Ohlbach, eds.), Lecture Notes in Artificial Intelligence, Vol. 1244, Springer Verlag, Berlin, 30-42.

Bosc P., Prade H. (1997) An introduction to the fuzzy set and possibility theory-based treatment of flexible queries and uncertain or imprecise databases. In: Uncertainty Management in Information Systems — From Needs to Solutions (A. Motro, P. Smets, eds.), Kluwer Academic Publ., Boston, 283-324.

Demolombe R. (1996a) Answering queries about validity and completeness of data: From modal logic to relational algebra. In: Flexible Query-Answering Systems (Proc. of the 1996 Workshop FQAS'96, Roskilde, Denmark, May 22-24, 1996) (H. Christiansen, H.L. Larsen, T. Andreasen, eds.), Roskilde University, Denmark, 265-276.

Demolombe R. (1996b) Validity queries and completeness queries. In: Foundations of Intelligent Systems (Proc. of the 9th Inter. Symp. ISMIS'96, Zakopane, Poland, June 1996) (Z.W. Ras, M. Michalewicz, eds.), Lecture Notes in Artificial Intelligence, Vol. 1079, Springer Verlag, Berlin, 253-263.

Demolombe R. (1997) Formalizing the reliability of agent's information. 4th ModelAge Workshop on Formal Models of Agents, Sienna, Italy, Jan. 15-17.

Dubois D., Lang J., Prade H. (1992) Dealing with multi-source information in possibilistic logic. Proc. of the 10th Europ. Conf. on Artificial Intelligence (ECAI'92) (B. Neumann, ed.), Vienna, Austria, Aug. 3-7, 38-42.

Dubois D., Lang J., Prade H. (1994a) Automated reasoning using possibilistic logic: semantics, belief revision and variable certainty weights. IEEE Trans. on Data and Knowledge Engineering, 6(1), 64-71.

Dubois D., Lang J., Prade H. (1994b) Possibilistic logic. In: Handbook of Logic in Artificial Intelligence and Logic Programming, Vol. 3 (D.M. Gabbay, C.J. Hogger, J.A. Robinson, D. Nute, eds.), Oxford University Press, 439-513.

Dubois D., Prade H. (with the collaboration of Farreny H., Martin-Clouaire R., Testemale C.) (1988) Possibility Theory — An Approach to Computerized Processing of Uncertainty. Plenum Press, New York.

Fariñas del Cerro L., Herzig A. (1991) A modal analysis of possibility theory. Proc. of the Inter. Workshop on Fundamentals of Artificial Intelligence Reserch (FAIR'91) (P. Jorrand, J. Kelemen, eds.), Smolenice Castle, Czechoslovakia, Sept. 8-12, 1991, Lecture Notes in Computer Sciences, Vol. 535, Springer Verlag, Berlin, 11-18.

Motro A. (1986) Completeness information and its application to query processing. Proc. of the 12th Inter. Conf. on Very Large Data Bases, 170-178.

Motro A. (1989) Integrity = validity + completeness. ACM Trans. on Database Systems, 14(4), 480-502.

Motro A., Smets P. (Eds.) (1997) Uncertainty Management in Information Systems — From Needs to Solutions. Kluwer Academic Publ., Boston.

Prade H., Testemale C. (1984) Generalizing database relational algebra for the treatment of incomplete/uncertain information and vague queries. Information Sciences, 34, 115-143.

Handling Imperfection in Databases:
A Modal Logic Approach

Michinori Nakata[1], Germano Resconi[2], and Tetsuya Murai[3]

[1] Department of Information Science, Chiba-Keizai College,
4-3-30 Todoroki-cho, Inage-ku, Chiba 263, Japan, nakata@chiba-kc.ac.jp
[2] Dipartimento di Matematica, Universita Cattolica,
Via Trieste 17, Brescia, Italy, resconi@mbox.vol.it
[3] Division of Systems and Information Engineering,
Graduate School of Engineering, Hokkaido University,
Kita 13, Nishi 8, Kita-ku, Sapporo 060, Japan, murahiko@hokudai.ac.jp

Abstract. An extended relational data model that can deal with various kinds of imperfect information is shown under a modal logic approach. This gives a new direction to deal with imperfect information. In our extension various kinds of imperfect information can be handled simultaneously, although an extended relational model has been related with one kind of imperfect information so far. This is because our extended data model has a uniform expression and the same operations to various kinds of imperfect information. Moreover our model can support flexible queries as well as conventional queries. Thus, our approach gives an important basis to integrate different kinds of databases handling different sorts of imperfect information.

Keywords: Extended relational databases, Imperfect information, Uncertainty theories, Modal logic.

1 Introduction

A database is a model of the real world. We realize some aspects of the real world in database systems by using information obtained from the real world. In the process we encounter various kinds of imperfect information with uncertainty and imprecision. We cannot always obtain information without imperfection from the real world, because we cannot always recognize the real world within a short period. Moreover the real world in itself may have aspects pervaded with imperfection.

Thus far, several extended versions of relational models have been proposed to deal with a kind of imperfect information. The first is based on fuzzy set theory and possibility theory[11, 15, 17]. The second is based on probability theory[3, 9, 18]. The third is based on Dempster & Shafer theory[2, 7]. The last is based on rough set theory[1]. These extended relational models can deal with only one kind of imperfect information. As a matter of fact, we sometimes encounter plural kinds of imperfection simultaneously, when we make databases under the real world. This leads us to studying how to model various sorts of imperfection in a single framework. Recently Resconi et al. have developed a new approach to interpret several kinds of uncertainty theories in a framework[12, 13, 14]. For the time being this approach, based on modal logic, gives a framework to integrate probability theory, Dempster & Shafer theory, possibility theory, and fuzzy set theory[5, 6, 12, 13, 14]. This gives us a common framework to deal with various kinds of imperfect information. In the present paper we give the outline of an extended relational database based on their approach and show how various kinds of imperfect information are handled in the common framework from the viewpoint of modal logic.

2 Treatment of imperfection

2.1 Modal logic

Modal logic is an extension of classical propositional logic. Its language consists of the set of atomic propositions or propositional variables, logical connectives $\neg$, $\wedge$, $\vee$, $\rightarrow$, $\leftrightarrow$, modal operator of necessity $\square$ and possibility $\diamond$, supporting symbols $($, $)$, $\{$, $\}$, ... The objects of interest are formulas:

- an atomic proposition is a formula.

- if p and q are formulas, then so are $\neg p$, $p \wedge q$, $p \vee q$, $p \rightarrow q$, $p \leftrightarrow q$, $\square p$, and $\diamond q$.

The meaning of a formula is its truth value in a given context. Various contexts are usually expressed in terms of modal logic. A model M of modal logic is the triple $\langle \mathcal{W}, \mathcal{R}, \mathcal{V} \rangle$ where $\mathcal{W}$, $\mathcal{R}$, and $\mathcal{V}$ denote a set of possible worlds, a binary relation on $\mathcal{W}$, and a set of value assignment functions, respectively. One for each world in $\mathcal{W}$, by which truth(t) or falsity(f), is assigned to each atomic proposition. Value assignment functions are inductively extended to all formulas in the usual way. The only interesting cases are:

$\nu_i(\square p) = t$ iff for all $w_j \in \mathcal{W}$ $\langle w_i, w_j \rangle \in \mathcal{R}$ implies $\nu_j(p) = t$,
and
$\nu_i(\diamond p) = t$ iff there is some $w_j \in \mathcal{W}$ such that $\langle w_i, w_j \rangle \in \mathcal{R}$ and $\nu_j(p) = t$.

A relation $\mathcal{R}$ is usually called an accessibility relation; we say that a world w_j is accessible from a world w_i when $\langle w_i, w_j \rangle \in \mathcal{R}$. It is convenient to represent the relation $\mathcal{R}$ by an $n \times n$ matrix $\mathcal{R} = [r_{ij}]$, where $r_{ij} = 1$ if $\langle w_i, w_j \rangle \in \mathcal{R}$, $r_{ij} = 0$ if $\langle w_i, w_j \rangle \notin \mathcal{R}$ and to define $T(\nu_i(p)) = 1$ if $\nu_i(p) = t$, $T(\nu_i(p)) = 0$ if $\nu_i(p) = f$ for each world $w_i \in \mathcal{W}$ and each formula p.

2.2 Expressions of imperfection

We address imperfection at three different levels. In our approach, a possible world is characterized by that a proposition is true.

2.2.1 Imperfection at the level of elements and sets

Imperfection at the level of elements in a set is concerned with the concept of belongingness. Given a universe of discourse $\mathcal{X}$, propositions that are relevant to vaguely defined sets, typically fuzzy sets, have the form "a_x : an element x belongs to a given set A," where $x \in \mathcal{X}$ and A denotes a subset of $\mathcal{X}$ that is based on a vague concept. The vagueness involved in defining A can be captured by a model based on multiple worlds of some modal logic, in which a proposition a_x for some x is valued differently in different worlds. In other words, the proposition a_x is true for a world w_i, but false for another world w_j. We have a conflict situation, which is the origin of the membership value for the element x to the set A[12, 14]. Given a model with n worlds and proposition a_x, the model produces a valuation vector $\nu(a_x) = \langle \nu_1(a_x), \nu_2(a_x), \ldots, \nu_n(a_x) \rangle$. The set A may then be viewed as a vaguely defined set whose membership function, μ_A, which means a degree of belongingness, is defined for all $x \in \mathcal{X}$ by the formula $\mu_A(x) = \sum_{i=1}^{n} T(\nu_i(a_x))/n$.

Next, we consider imperfection at the level of sets. Propositions that are relevant to vaguely defined sets have a general form "a_S: A set S is included in a given set A," where we assume the logical value of a_S is true or false, given the set S and the set A. In the modal logic some possible worlds are associated with a set S. In a possible world associated with a set S, $a_{S'}$ is true if $S' \subseteq S$, otherwise false. Conversely, a set associated with a possible world corresponds to the largest set among S where a proposition a_S is true in that possible world. Thus, we can establish the relationship between worlds and sets S. In fact, for different worlds we can have different sets in a_S or the same set; namely, the relationship of possible worlds to sets is many to one.

2.2.2 Imperfection at the level of values

Imperfection at the level of values means how they are imprecise. To model a basic probability assignment in terms of modal logic, we employ propositions of the form "e_A: A given incompletely characterized element ε is classified in a set A," where $\varepsilon \in \mathcal{X}$ and $A \in \mathcal{P}(\mathcal{X})$. Because of the inner structure of these propositions, we can consider as atomic propositions(or propositional variables) only propositions $e_{\{x\}}$, where $x \in \mathcal{X}$. Propositions e_A are then defined by the formulas $\forall\, A \neq \emptyset\ e_A = \bigvee_{x \in A} e_{\{x\}}$ and $e_\emptyset = \bigwedge_{x \in \mathcal{X}} \neg e_{\{x\}}$. Here, for each world $w_i \in W$, it is assumed that $\nu_i(e_{\{x\}}) = \mathrm{t}$ for one and only one $x \in \mathcal{X}$. Each possible world is associated with one single element, rigorously speaking, one set with one element.

When we obtain a value in the form of a probability distribution, or a basic probability assignment, or a possibility distribution, we show how it is transformed into a uniform expression $\langle \mathcal{W}, \mathcal{R}, \mathcal{V} \rangle$. By reference [5] the following theorem is proved.

Theorem[5]

Let m_M denote the basic probability assignment that is produced by a given model M. For every rational-valued basic probability assignment m, there exists a model $M = \langle \mathcal{W}, \mathcal{R}, \mathcal{V} \rangle$ such that $m_M = m$.

By this theorem we can obtain $\langle \mathcal{W}, \mathcal{R}, \mathcal{V} \rangle$ when a rational-valued basic probability assignment m is given. m can be expressed as $m(A) = \alpha_A/\beta_A$ for every $A \in \mathcal{P}(\mathcal{X})$, where α_A and β_A are some nonnegative integers and $\beta_A \neq 0$. We can transform these numbers to obtain $\beta_A = \beta$ for every $A \in \mathcal{P}(\mathcal{X})$ and some constant β that is common to all A. We suppose that $\alpha_A \geq |A|$ for all $A \in \mathcal{P}(\mathcal{X})$. This can always be satisfied by multiplying m by γ/γ for some positive integer γ. We can determine the minimum integer β satisfying $\alpha_A \geq |A|$ for all $A \in \mathcal{P}(\mathcal{X})$ and α_A for each A. This β is the number of possible worlds; namely, $\mathcal{W}$ consists of β worlds $w_1, \ldots, w_\beta$. α_A is the number of possible worlds related with A that are expressed by $\mathcal{W}_A = \{w_{A1}, \ldots, w_{A\alpha_A}\}$. These possible worlds are accessible only to each other; namely the part of $\mathcal{R}$ is expressed by an equivalence relation. Finally, $\mathcal{V}$ is specified such that in each world belonging to $\mathcal{W}_A$ for only an element $x \in A$ the proposition $e_{\{x\}}$ is true. If it is only the specification that the same proposition is true for all worlds composing an equivalence relation, the equivalence relation is equivalent to an identity relation; namely, each world can be regarded as isolated.

First, we suppose that a value is given in the form of a probability distribution; for example, $((u, 0.5), (v, 0.5))$. From the probability distribution we have a basic probability assignment $(m(\{u\}) = 0.5, m(\{v\}) = 0.5)$, which gives $\beta = 2$. For possible worlds, $\mathcal{W} = \{w_1, w_2\}$. $\mathcal{R}$ is an identity relation; namely,

$$\mathcal{R} = \begin{pmatrix} 1 & 0 \\ 0 & 1 \end{pmatrix}.$$

$\mathcal{V}$ is a set of 2 valuation functions, ν_1 and ν_2, defined by atomic propositions which they valuate as true: $\nu_1(e_{\{u\}}) = $ t and $\nu_2(e_{\{v\}}) = $ t. As is shown in the example, each possible world is associated with a set consisting of a single element.

Second, we suppose that a value is expressed by a basic probability assignment $(m(\{a\}) = 0.2, m(\{b, c\}) = 0.4, m(\{c, d\}) = 0.4)$, which gives $\beta = 5$. For possible worlds, $\mathcal{W} = \{w_1, w_2, \ldots, w_5\}$. $\mathcal{R}$ is a relation that partitions $\mathcal{W}$ into three equivalence classes: $\{w_1\}, \{w_2, w_3\}, \{w_4, w_5\}$; namely,

$$\mathcal{R} = \begin{pmatrix} 1 & & & & \\ & 1 & 1 & & \\ & 1 & 1 & & \\ & & & 1 & 1 \\ & & & 1 & 1 \end{pmatrix}.$$

$\mathcal{V}$ is a set of 5 valuation functions with $\nu_1(e_{\{a\}}) = $ t, $\nu_2(e_{\{b\}}) = $ t, $\nu_3(e_{\{c\}}) = $ t, $\nu_4(e_{\{c\}}) = $ t, and $\nu_5(e_{\{d\}}) = $ t. Plural possible worlds correspond to the same set; namely, the relationship of possible worlds to sets is many to one. Possible worlds corresponding to the same set are not always linked to each other by an accessibility relation, but belong to different equivalence classes. For example, two possible worlds w_3 and w_4 are associated with the same set $\{c\}$, but are not linked to each other.

When a value is given by a normal possibility distribution, the possibility distribution is transformed into a corresponding basic probability assignment. Let a possibility distribution $\pi(x)$ be given by $\pi(x_1)/x_1 + \pi(x_2)/x_2 + \cdots + \pi(x_n)/x_n$ with $\pi(x_1) = 1$ and $\pi(x_i) \geq \pi(x_j)$ if $i > j$. A basic probability assignment $m(A_i) = \pi(x_i) - \pi(x_{i+1})$ is assigned to a set $A_i = \{x_1, \ldots, x_i\}$ for $i = 1, n$. Suppose that a value is $\pi(x) = 0.5/20 + 1/30$. This possibility distribution corresponds to a basic probability assignment $(m(\{30\}) = 0.5, m(\{20, 30\}) = 0.5)$, which gives $\beta = 4$. For possible worlds, $\mathcal{W} = \{w_1, w_2, w_3, w_4\}$. $\mathcal{R}$ is a relation that partitions $\mathcal{W}$ into three equivalence classes: $\{w_1\}, \{w_2\}, \{w_3, w_4\}$; namely,

$$\mathcal{R} = \begin{pmatrix} 1 & & & \\ & 1 & & \\ & & 1 & 1 \\ & & 1 & 1 \end{pmatrix}.$$

$\mathcal{V}$ is a set of 4 valuation functions with $\nu_1(e_{\{30\}}) = t$, $\nu_2(e_{\{30\}}) = t$, $\nu_3(e_{\{20\}}) = t$, and $\nu_4(e_{\{30\}}) = t$.

We always adopt symmetrical accessibility relations, although we have the possibility to reduce the number of possible worlds from the most simple and expensive ones. This means that imperfect information is dealt with in modal system S5.

As is understood from the mentions so far, when all possible worlds are associated with the same set, there is no imprecision; namely, this case corresponds to that the value is obtained as a singleton. In our approach, imperfection at the level of values is expressed by that some possible worlds are associated with different sets as well as imperfection at the level of elements and sets. Thus we can deal with not only various kinds of imperfection at the level of values but also imperfection at the level of elements and sets under the same framework.

3 Extended relational model

First, we address the framework of the extended relational model, and then describe select operators that are most frequently used in query processing.

3.1 Framework

The uniform expression to various kinds of imperfect information at the level of values is obtained by the approach based on modal logic, as is shown in the previous section. This is very significant, because we have to use different operators to different kinds of imperfect information in queries when we do not obtain a uniform expression.

Definition

A extended relational scheme R consists of a set of conventional attributes $\mathcal{A} = \{A_1, A_2, \ldots, A_n\}$ and a membership attribute μ; namely, $R = \mathcal{A} \cup \{\mu\} = \{A_1, A_2, \ldots, A_n, \mu\}$.

Definition

The value $t[A_i]$ of an attribute A_i in a tuple t is represented by:

$$\langle \mathcal{W}, \mathcal{R}, \mathcal{V} \rangle_{t[A_i]} = \langle \mathcal{W}_{t[A_i]}, \mathcal{R}_{t[A_i]}, \mathcal{V}_{t[A_i]} \rangle,$$

where $\mathcal{W}_{t[A_i]}$, $\mathcal{R}_{t[A_i]}$, and $\mathcal{V}_{t[A_i]}$ denote, respectively, a set of possible worlds, an accessibility relation, and a set of valuation functions for $t[A_i]$.

When we get values in the form of a probability distribution or a basic probability assignment, or a possibility distribution, we transform it into this expression, as is shown in the previous section. A tuple value $t[\mathcal{A}]$ that is a sequence $\langle t[A_1]t[A_2]\cdots t[A_n]\rangle$ of attribute values is also expressed by $\langle \mathcal{W}, \mathcal{R}, \mathcal{V}\rangle_{t[\mathcal{A}]} = \langle \mathcal{W}_{t[\mathcal{A}]}, \mathcal{R}_{t[\mathcal{A}]}, \mathcal{V}_{t[\mathcal{A}]}\rangle$.

In addition to the above extension, we introduce a membership attribute, as is done in data models handling a kind of imperfect information[7, 8, 16].

Definition

Each tuple value $t[\mathcal{A}]$ has its membership value $t[\mu]$ in a base relation r which is expressed by $(t[\mu_\Box], t[\mu_\Diamond])$, where $t[\mu_\Box]$ (resp. $t[\mu_\Diamond]$) is the degree in necessity(resp. in possibility) that a tuple value $t[A]$ belongs to r; namely,

$$r = \{\langle t[A], (t[\mu_\Box], t[\mu_\Diamond])\rangle \mid t[\mu_\Diamond] > 0\}.$$

As is addressed in the definition, a relation is an extended set having tuple values as elements. Every tuple value is expressed by $\langle W, R, V\rangle$. Hence, every relation also has its corresponding $\langle W, R, V\rangle$. A possible world is associated with a set consisting of plural elements at the level of database relations. The number of elements of a set associated with a possible world in a database relation is equal to or less than the number of tuples that compose the database relation.

Definition
The degree that a tuple value belongs to a base relation is a compatibility degree of that tuple value with imposed integrity constraints on the base relation.

The membership attribute expresses imperfection at the level of tuples. At the level of attributes integrity constraints specify a set of values that each attribute can take. At the level of tuples they specify a set of values allowed as tuple values. Now each tuple value $t[A]$ is expressed by $\langle W_{t[A]}, R_{t[A]}, V_{t[A]}\rangle$. When a tuple value contains imperfection at the level of attributes; namely, imprecise values in attributes, the number of possible worlds is plural and generally different possible worlds are associated with different sets. Sets associated with some possible worlds are contained in a set of tuple values specified by integrity constraints, but other sets with different possible worlds do not so. Thus the value of membership attribute is not always equal to 0 or 1. Moreover some possible worlds are associated with another one by an accessibility relation. This leads to that the value of membership attribute is obtained in a pair of values in necessity and possibility. As a result, when we allow imperfection at the level of attributes, imperfection also appears at the level of tuples. Imperfection at the level of attributes cannot be detached from that at the level of tuples.

The membership value is calculated, but not given in the present framework. Suppose that $t[A]$ is expressed by $\langle W_{t[A]}, R_{t[A]}, V_{t[A]}\rangle$ and $|W_{t[A]}| = n$. A compatibility degree of a tuple value $t[A]$ with integrity constraints C is:

$$Nec(C|t[A]) = T(\Box(C|t[A]))/n, \; Pos(C|t[A]) = T(\Diamond(C|t[A]))/n,$$

where $T(\Box(C|t[A]))$ (resp. $T(\Diamond(C|t[A]))$) is the number of worlds in which a tuple value $t[A]$ is compatible with the integrity constraints C in necessity (resp. in possibility):

$$T(\Box(C|t[A])) = \sum_i T(\nu_i(\Box(C|t[A]))), \; T(\Diamond(C|t[A])) = \sum_i T(\nu_i(\Diamond(C|t[A]))),$$

where $T(\nu_i(\Box(C|t[A])))$ and $T(\nu_i(\Diamond(C|t[A])))$ are the compatibility degrees of a tuple value $t[A]$ in a possible world w_i with the constraint C in necessity and in possibility.
For each possible world $w_i \in W_{t[A]}$,

$$\nu_i(\Box(C|t[A])) = t \equiv \forall w_j \in W_{t[A]} \; \langle w_i, w_j\rangle \in R_{t[A]} \Rightarrow \nu_j(C|t[A]) = t.$$

This formula means that for each possible world $w_i \in \mathcal{W}_{t[\mathcal{A}]}$, $\nu_i(\Box(C|t[\mathcal{A}])) = \mathrm{t}$ if and only if $\nu_j(C|t[\mathcal{A}]) = \mathrm{t}$ in all possible worlds w_j that are accessible from the possible world w_i. Similarly,

$$\nu_i(\Diamond(C|t[\mathcal{A}])) = \mathrm{t} \equiv \exists w_j \in \mathcal{W}_{t[\mathcal{A}]} \, \langle w_i, w_j \rangle \in \mathcal{R}_{t[\mathcal{A}]} \wedge \nu_j(C|t[\mathcal{A}]) = \mathrm{t}.$$

This formula means that for each possible world $w_i \in \mathcal{W}_{t[\mathcal{A}]}$, $\nu_i(\Diamond(C|t[\mathcal{A}])) = \mathrm{t}$ if and only if $\nu_j(C|t[\mathcal{A}]) = \mathrm{t}$ in at least one possible world accessible from the possible world w_i. Thus, $Nec(C|t[\mathcal{A}])$ (resp. $Pos(C|t[\mathcal{A}])$) is the number ratio of possible worlds that are compatible with the integrity constraint C in necessity (resp. in possibility).

Example 1
We suppose that a relation, an instance of an extended relational scheme $R = \{A_1, A_2, A_3, \mu\}$, has a tuple t and its attribute values are given by $t[A_1] = ((\{u\}, 0.5), (\{v\}, 0.5))$, $t[A_2] = 0.5/20 + 1/30$, and $t[A_3] = ((\{a\}, 0.2), (\{b, c\}, 0.4), (\{c, d\}, 0.4))$, respectively. Each expression $\langle \mathcal{W}, \mathcal{R}, \mathcal{V} \rangle$ for these attribute values is already obtained in subsubsection 2.2.2. We suppose that imposed integrity constraints C consists of only a constraint: *When A_1 is $\{u, v\}$, $A_3 = \{b, c\}$*. For this tuple value $t[\mathcal{A}]$, we obtain $Nec(C|t[\mathcal{A}]) = 2/5$ and $Pos(C|t[\mathcal{A}]) = 4/5$.

Tuples with low values of membership attributes may appear in database relations. We use a pair of values $(t[\mu_{\Box,r}], t[\mu_{\Diamond,r}])$ as a membership attribute value for a tuple t in a relation r. These values are degrees in necessity and in possibility that t belongs to the relation. From the degrees we can obtain degrees $(t[\mu_{\Box,\bar{r}}], t[\mu_{\Diamond,\bar{r}}])$ that t does not belong to r; namely, $t[\mu_{\Box,\bar{r}}] = 1 - t[\mu_{\Diamond,r}]$, and $t[\mu_{\Diamond,\bar{r}}] = 1 - t[\mu_{\Box,r}]$. We set the criterion $t[\mu_{\Box,r}] \geq t[\mu_{\Box,\bar{r}}]$, which is equivalent to $t[\mu_{\Diamond,r}] \geq t[\mu_{\Diamond,\bar{r}}]$, for accepting a tuple t in a relation r. This means that $t[\mu_{\Box,r}] + t[\mu_{\Diamond,r}] \geq 1$. The tuple that does not satisfy this criterion is discarded.

3.2 Query evaluations
We address how to extract desired information from our extended relational database. A query is performed by using select operations in relational databases, where it is evaluated to what degree a data value is compatible with a select condition $\mathcal{F}$. $\mathcal{F}$ consists of elementary formulas and logical operators *and, or,* and *not*. Elementary formulas are "A_k *is* m", "$A_k \, \xi \, A_h$ *is* m", "$t_i[A_k] \, \theta \, t_j[A_l]$" and their negation, where m, ξ, and θ denote a predicate, any one of arithmetic operators $+$, $-$, $\times$, $/$, and any one of comparators $=$, $<$, $>$, respectively. The predicate or the comparator may be flexible ones; for example, a fuzzy predicate or a fuzzy comparator, as is shown in the reference[11].
The compatibility degree of a tuple value $t[\mathcal{A}]$ with a select condition $\mathcal{F}$ is expressed by a pair of a degree $Nec(\mathcal{F}|t[\mathcal{A}])$ in necessity and a degree $Pos(\mathcal{F}|t[\mathcal{A}])$ in possibility that denote to what extent the tuple value is compatible with $\mathcal{F}$. Suppose that $t[\mathcal{A}]$ is expressed by $\langle \mathcal{W}_{t[\mathcal{A}]}, \mathcal{R}_{t[\mathcal{A}]}, \mathcal{V}_{t[\mathcal{A}]} \rangle$ and $|\mathcal{W}_{t[\mathcal{A}]}| = n$.

$$Nec(\mathcal{F}|t[\mathcal{A}]) = T(\Box(\mathcal{F}|t[\mathcal{A}]))/n, \; Pos(\mathcal{F}|t[\mathcal{A}]) = T(\Diamond(\mathcal{F}|t[\mathcal{A}]))/n,$$

where $T(\Box(\mathcal{F}|t[\mathcal{A}]))$ and $T(\Diamond(\mathcal{F}|t[\mathcal{A}]))$ are evaluated by the same method as addressed in the previous subsection.

The results of select operations are database relations having the same structure as the original ones. A membership attribute value for a tuple t in a derived relation is $(Nec(\mathcal{F}|t[\mathcal{A}]) \times t[\mu_\square], Pos(\mathcal{F}|t[\mathcal{A}]) \times t[\mu_\lozenge])$, where $(t[\mu_\square], t[\mu_\lozenge])$ is a membership attribute value in the original relation and $\times$ is arithmetic product, because the compatibility degree is the number ratio of possible worlds that are compatible with $\mathcal{F}$.

Queries can be classified into atomic ones and compound ones. Atomic queries are ones in which their select condition is expressed by one among elementary formulas. We show an example for an atomic query.

Example 2

We go back to example 1. Suppose a select condition $\mathcal{F}$: A_2 is $\{30, 40\}$; namely, A_2 is equal to 30 or 40. We calculate the compatibility degree of the tuple value $t[\mathcal{A}]$ with the select condition. Possible worlds that are necessarily and possibly compatible with the select condition are $i = 1, 2$ and $i = 1, 2, \ldots, 4$, respectively(See subsubsection 2.2.2). So, we get $Nec(\mathcal{F}|t[\mathcal{A}]) = 2/4$ and $Pos(\mathcal{F}|t[\mathcal{A}]) = 4/4$. Considering the membership attribute value in the original relation, a membership attribute value $(t[\mu_\square], t[\mu_\lozenge])$ is: $t[\mu_\square] = 2/4 \times 2/5 = 1/5$, $t[\mu_\lozenge] = 4/4 \times 4/5 = 4/5$.

When we use a flexible select condition; for example, it is expressed by using a fuzzy set like *the price of parts is about 30* where *about 30* is modeled by a fuzzy set $\{0.3/10, 0.7/20, 1/30, 0.7/40, 0.3/50\}$, the element associated with each possible world is contained with a degree between 0 and 1 in the specified set by the select condition. Suppose that a select condition $\mathcal{F}$ contains a fuzzy set $S = \{\mu(s_1)/s_1, \mu(s_2)/s_2, \cdots, \mu(s_n)/s_n\}$. We obtain $\alpha - level$ sets S_α: $S_\alpha = \{s|\mu(s) \geq \alpha\}$. When $\mathcal{F}_\alpha$ expresses the select condition corresponding to S_α, the compatibility degree of a tuple value in a possible world w_i with the select condition $\mathcal{F}$ is:

$$\begin{aligned} T(\nu_i(\square(\mathcal{F}|t[\mathcal{A}]))) &= \sup(\alpha|\nu_i(\square(\mathcal{F}_\alpha|t[\mathcal{A}]) = t)), \\ T(\nu_i(\lozenge(\mathcal{F}|t[\mathcal{A}]))) &= \sup(\alpha|\nu_i(\lozenge(\mathcal{F}_\alpha|t[\mathcal{A}]) = t)). \end{aligned}$$

Example 3

In example 1 we suppose a select condition $\mathcal{F}$: A_2 is about 30. We obtain $\mathcal{F}_1 : A_2$ is $\{30\}$, $\mathcal{F}_{0.7} : A_2$ is $\{20, 30, 40\}$, $\mathcal{F}_{0.3} : A_2$ is $\{10, 20, 30, 40, 50\}$. Thus, $Nec(\mathcal{F}|t[\mathcal{A}]) = (2 \times 1 + 2 \times 0.7)/4 = 0.85$, $Pos(\mathcal{F}|t[\mathcal{A}]) = (4 \times 1)/4 = 1$.

Compound queries have a select condition $\mathcal{F}$ containing logical operators $and(\wedge)$ or $or(\vee)$. We suppose that the select condition $\mathcal{F}$ is composed of elementary formulas f_1 and f_2 in a compound query. If f_1 and f_2 is noninteractive to each other; in other words, they do not contain common attributes at all, the compound query can be calculated by the evaluation of two atomic queries; namely,

$Nec(f_1 \wedge f_2|t[\mathcal{A}]) = Nec(f_1|t[\mathcal{A}]) \times Nec(f_2|t[\mathcal{A}])$,
$Pos(f_1 \wedge f_2|t[\mathcal{A}]) = Pos(f_1|t[\mathcal{A}]) \times Pos(f_2|t[\mathcal{A}])$,
$Nec(f_1 \vee f_2|t[\mathcal{A}]) = Nec(f_1|t[\mathcal{A}]) + Nec(f_2|t[\mathcal{A}]) - Nec(f_1|t[\mathcal{A}]) \times Nec(f_2|t[\mathcal{A}])$,
$Pos(f_1 \vee f_2|t[\mathcal{A}]) = Pos(f_1|t[\mathcal{A}]) + Pos(f_2|t[\mathcal{A}]) - Pos(f_1|t[\mathcal{A}]) \times Pos(f_2|t[\mathcal{A}])$.

Example 4
We suppose a select condition $\mathcal{F}$: A_2 *is* $\{about\ 30\}$ *and* $A_3 = \{b, c\}$ in example 1. We obtain $Nec(\mathcal{F}|t[\mathcal{A}]) = 0.85 \times 2/5 = 0.34$, $Pos(\mathcal{F}|t[\mathcal{A}]) = 1 \times 4/5 = 0.8$.

When the elementary formulas f_1 and f_2 composing $\mathcal{F}$ are interactive; for example, f_1 is A_2 *is* $\{20, 30\}$ and f_2 is A_2 *is* $\{30, 40\}$, the compatibility degree of a tuple value with $\mathcal{F}$ cannot be calculated by using those of the tuple value with f_1 and with f_2. This is not characteristic of our extended relational model, but is common to those allowing imprecise values in attributes(for example, see [10]). Suppose that f_1 is A_i *is* S_1 and f_2 is A_i *is* S_1. We calculate the compatibility degree by resetting such that $\mathcal{F}$ is A_i *is* $S_1 \cap S_2$ in the case of $\mathcal{F} = f_1 \wedge f_2$ and by resetting such that $\mathcal{F}$ is A_i *is* $S_1 \cup S_2$ in the case of $\mathcal{F} = f_1 \vee f_2$.

4 Concluding remarks

We have developed an extension of relational databases from the viewpoint of modal logic interpretation to imperfection. This gives a new direction to deal with imperfect information in databases. In our extension various kinds of imperfect information can be handled simultaneously, although an extended relational model has been related with one kind of imperfect information so far. This is because our extended data model has a uniform expression and the same operations to various kinds of imperfect information. Moreover our model can support flexible queries as well as conventional queries. Thus our approach also gives an important basis to integrate different types of databases handling different sorts of imperfect information. The present work is limited to situations with no inconsistency. The next step is to extend our approach so as to deal with situations with inconsistency.

References

[1] Beaubouef, T., Petry, F. E., and Buckles, B. P. [1995] Extension of the Relational Databases and Its Algebra with Rough Set Techniques, Computational Intelligence, 11:2, 233-245.

[2] Bell, D. A., Guan, J. W., and Lee, S. K. [1996] Generalized Union and Project Operations for Pooling Uncertain and Imprecise Information, Data & Knowledge Engineering, 18, 89-117.

[3] Barbará, D., Garcia-Molina, H., and Porter, D. [1992] The Management of Probabilistic Data, IEEE Transactions on Knowledge and Data Engineering, 4:5, 487-502.

[4] Dey, D. and Sarkar, S. [1996]A Probabilistic Model and Algebra, ACM Transactions on Database Systems, 21:3, 339-369.

[5] Harmanec, D., Klir, G. J., and Resconi, G. [1994] On Modal Logic Interpretation of Dempster-Shafer Theory of Evidence, International Journal of Intelligent Systems, 9, 941-951.

[6] Klir, G. and Harmanec, D. [1994] On Modal Logic Interpretation of Possibility Theory, International Journal of Uncertainty, Fuzziness and Knowledge-Based Systems, 2:2, 237-245.

[7] Lee, S. K. [1992]Imprecise and Uncertain Information in Databases: An Evidential Approach. in Proceedings of the 8th International Conference on Data Engineering, IEEE 1992, pp. 614-621.

[8] Nakata, M. [1996] Unacceptable Components in Fuzzy Relational Databases, International Journal of Intelligent Systems, 11:9, 633-647.

[9] Pittarelli, M. [1994] An Algebra for Probabilistic Databases, IEEE Transactions on Knowledge and Data Engineering, 6:2, 293-303.

[10] Prade, H. [1984] Lipski's Approach to Incomplete Information Data Bases Restated and Generalized in the Setting of Zadeh's Possibility Theory, Information Systems 9:1, 27-42.

[11] Prade, H. and Testemale, C. [1984] Generalizing Database Relational Algebra for the Treatment of Incomplete or Uncertain Information and Vague Queries, Information Science, 34, 115-143.

[12] Resconi, G., Klir, G. J., and Clair, U. S. [1992] Hierarchical Uncertainty Metatheory Based upon Modal Logic, International Journal of General Systems, 21, 23-50.

[13] Resconi, G., Klir, G. J., Clair, U. S., and Harmanec, D. [1993] On the Integration of Uncertainty Theories, International Journal of Uncertainty, Fuzziness and Knowledge-Based Systems, 1:1, 1-18.

[14] Resconi, G., Klir, G. J., Harmanec, D., and Clair, U. S. [1996] Interpretations of Various Uncertainty Theories Using Models of Modal Logic: A Summary, Fuzzy Sets and Systems, 80, 7-14.

[15] Umano, M. [1982] FREEDOM-O: A Fuzzy Database System, in Fuzzy Information and Decision Processes, M. M. Gupta and E. Sanchez, eds., North-Holland, Amsterdam, pp. 339-347.

[16] Umano, M. [1983] Retrieval from Fuzzy Database by Fuzzy Relational Algebra, in Proc. IFAC Symposium, Fuzzy Information, Knowledge Representation and Decision Analysis, E. Sanchez, ed., (Marseille, July 19-21), Pergamon Press, pp. 1-6.

[17] Zemankova, M. and Kandel, A. [1984] Fuzzy Relational Databases–A Key to Expert Systems, Verlag TÜV Rheinland, Cologne, 1984.

[18] Zimányi, E. [1997] Query Evaluation in Probabilistic Relational Databases, Theoretical Computer Science, 171, 179-219.

Text Knowledge Engineering
by Qualitative Terminological Learning

Udo Hahn & Klemens Schnattinger

ⓒⒻ Computational Linguistics Lab – Text Knowledge Engineering Group
Freiburg University, Werthmannplatz 1, D-79085 Freiburg, Germany
http://www.coling.uni-freiburg.de/

Abstract. We propose a methodology for enhancing domain knowledge bases through natural language text understanding. The acquisition of previously unknown concepts is based on the assessment of the "quality" of linguistic and conceptual evidence underlying the generation and refinement of concept hypotheses. Text understanding and concept learning are both grounded on a terminological knowledge representation and reasoning framework.

1 Introduction

Text knowledge engineering is a research area in which, on the one hand, natural language processing technology is applied for the automatic acquisition of knowledge from textual documents and, on the other hand, knowledge acquired from texts is integrated into already existing, yet underspecified domain knowledge bases. A constructive update of such knowledge repositories is performed according to formal constraints underlying proper knowledge base management and heuristic principles guiding knowledge engineering. Such a task is unlikely to be solved by simply plugging in off-the-shelf components. This is due to the vivid interactions between text analysis and knowledge acquisition processes. By this we mean the initial creation of various hypotheses upon the first mention of an unknown concept, the continuous refinement of and discrimination among competing hypotheses as more and more knowledge becomes available and, finally, the convergence on the most plausible hypothesis. Hence, the learning mechanism we describe proceeds incrementally, in a bootstrapping fashion, and is fairly knowledge-intensive, as we provide a classification-based reasoning scheme for the assessment of the different forms of evidence being encountered.

Two types of evidence are taken into account for continuously discriminating and refining the set of concept hypotheses — the type of linguistic construction in which an unknown lexical item occurs and conceptually motivated annotations of concept hypotheses reflecting structural patterns of consistency, mutual justification, analogy, etc. in the knowledge base. These forms of initial evidence are represented by a set of quality labels. Concept acquisition can then be viewed as a *quality-based decision task* which is decomposed into three constituent parts: the continuous generation of quality labels for single concept hypotheses (reflecting the *reasons* for their formation and their significance in the light of other

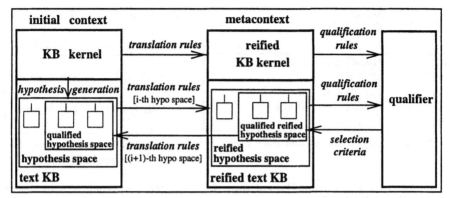

Fig. 1. Quality-Based Concept Acquisition System

hypotheses), the estimation of the overall *credibility* of single concept hypotheses (taking the available set of quality labels for each hypothesis into account), and the computation of a *preference order* for the entire set of competing hypotheses based on these accumulated quality judgments.

2 System Architecture

The methodology and corresponding system architecture (cf. Fig. 1) we propose serves the representation of quality-based assertions about certain propositions and the reasoning about characteristic properties and relations between these assertions. The text understanding processes use a terminological model of the underlying domain, the knowledge base *(KB) kernel*, on the basis of which the parser [6] generates a conceptual interpretation of the text in the *text KB*. Whenever an unknown lexical item occurs during the text understanding process, and this item is considered relevant for learning according to distributional criteria, conceptual hypotheses are generated [5]. These take linguistic criteria (mirrored by the assignment of corresponding *linguistic* quality labels) as well as conceptual conditions into account. Multiple concept hypotheses for a single lexical item are organized in terms of a corresponding hypothesis space as part of the text KB, each subspace holding different or further specialized concept hypotheses.

In order to reason about the credibility of these hypotheses a mirror image of the *initial context* which combines the KB kernel and the text KB is generated — the so-called *metacontext*. This is achieved by a truth-preserving mapping which includes the reification of the original terminological assertions from the initial context [13]. These reified representation structures are then submitted to conceptual *qualification rules* which determine purely conceptual indicators of credibility of the associated hypotheses and assign corresponding *conceptual* quality labels to them in the *reified hypothesis space*. A classifier extended by an evaluation metric for quality-based selection criteria, the *qualifier*, then determines the most credible concept hypotheses [11]. Only those will be remapped from their reified to the original terminological form by way of (inverse) translation rules, and thus become available again for the text understanding process.

Syntax	Semantics
$C \sqcap D$	$C^{\mathcal{I}} \cap D^{\mathcal{I}}$
$C \sqcup D$	$C^{\mathcal{I}} \cup D^{\mathcal{I}}$
R^{-1}	$\{(d,d') \in \Delta^{\mathcal{I}} \times \Delta^{\mathcal{I}} \mid (d',d) \in R^{\mathcal{I}}\}$
$R \sqcap S$	$R^{\mathcal{I}} \cap S^{\mathcal{I}}$
$c\mid R$	$\{(d,d') \in R^{\mathcal{I}} \mid d \in C^{\mathcal{I}}\}$
$R\mid c$	$\{(d,d') \in R^{\mathcal{I}} \mid d' \in C^{\mathcal{I}}\}$
$(R_1,..,R_n)$	$R_1^{\mathcal{I}} \circ .. \circ R_n^{\mathcal{I}}$

Table 1. Some Concept and Role Terms

Axiom	Semantics
$A \doteq C$	$A^{\mathcal{I}} = C^{\mathcal{I}}$
$a : C$	$a^{\mathcal{I}} \in C^{\mathcal{I}}$
$Q \doteq R$	$Q^{\mathcal{I}} = R^{\mathcal{I}}$
$a\, R\, b$	$(a^{\mathcal{I}}, b^{\mathcal{I}}) \in R^{\mathcal{I}}$

Table 2. Axioms for Concepts and Roles

Thus, we come full circle. The entire cycle is triggered for each new evidence that becomes available for a concept to be learned as the text understanding process proceeds.

In the following, we will illustrate the working of this architecture in more detail based on processing the example phrase (1) *".. the case of the PS/2-57SX .."* as the first learning step for the unknown item *"PS/2-57SX"*. Other learning steps are based on statement (2) *".. the PS/2-57SX with 4MB .."*, and (3) *".. the PS/2-57SX is equipped with a 3.5 inch disk drive .."*.

2.1 Terminological Logics

We use a concept description language (for a survey, cf. [8]) with a standard set-theoretical semantics (the interpretation function $\mathcal{I}$). The language has several constructors combining *atomic* concepts, roles and individuals (see Table 1). By means of *terminological axioms* a symbolic name can be defined for each concept and role term; concepts and roles are associated with concrete individuals by *assertional axioms* (see Table 2). Consider the following example:

(P1) *case*-01 : CASE
(P2) *PS/2-57SX* HAS-CASE *case*-01
(P3) HAS-CASE $\doteq$ (COMPUTER-SYSTEM $\sqcup$ DEVICE) $\mid$HAS-PART$\mid$CASE

The assertions P1 and P2 read as: the instance *case*-01 belongs to the concept CASE and the tuple $\langle PS/2\text{-}57SX, case\text{-}01 \rangle$ belongs to the binary relation HAS-CASE, respectively. The relation HAS-CASE is defined as all HAS-PART relations which have their domain restricted to the disjunction of the concepts COMPUTER-SYSTEM or DEVICE and their range restricted to the concept CASE.

2.2 Quality Labels

Linguistic quality labels reflect structural properties of phrasal patterns or discourse contexts in which unknown lexical items occur — we here assume that the type of grammatical construction exercises a particular interpretative force on the unknown item and, at the same time, yields a particular level of credibility for the hypotheses being derived. As a concrete example of a high-quality label, consider the case of APPOSITION. This label is generated for constructions such as *".. the printer @A@ .."*, with *"@..@"* denoting the unknown item. The apposition almost unequivocally determines *"@A@"* (considered as a potential noun)[1] to denote a PRINTER. This assumption is justified independent of further conceptual conditions, simply due to the nature of the linguistic construction being used. Still of good quality but already less constraining are occurrences of the unknown item in a CASEFRAME construction as illustrated by *".. @B@ is equipped with a 3.5 inch disk drive .."*. In this example, case frame specifications of the verb *"equip"* that relate to its PATIENT role carry over to *"@B@"*. So *"@B@"* may be anything that is equipped with a 3.5 inch disk drive, e.g., a computer system.

Conceptual quality labels result from comparing the conceptual representation structures of a concept hypothesis with already existing representation structures in the underlying domain knowledge base from the viewpoint of structural similarity, incompatibility, etc. The closer the match, the more credit is lent to a hypothesis. For instance, a very positive conceptual quality label such as M-DEDUCED is assigned to multiple derivations of the same concept hypothesis in different hypothesis (sub)spaces. Still positive labels are assigned to terminological expressions which share structural similarities, though they are not identical. For instance, the label C-SUPPORTED is assigned to any hypothesized relation $R1$ between two instances in case another relation, $R2$, already exists in the KB involving the same two instances, but where the role fillers occur in "inverted" order (note that $R1$ and $R2$ need not necessarily be conceptually inverse relations such as with *"buy"* and *"sell"*). This rule captures the inherent symmetry between concepts related via quasi-inverse conceptual relations.

2.3 Hypothesis Generation

Depending on the type of the syntactic construction in which the unknown lexical item occurs different hypothesis generation rules may fire. In our example *(1)*: *".. the case of the PS/2-57SX .."*, a genitive noun phrase places only few constraints on the item to be learned. In the following, let *target* be the unknown item *("PS/2-57SX")* and *base* be the known item *("case")*, the conceptual relation of which to the target is constrained by the syntactic relation in which their lexical counterparts co-occur. The main constraint for genitives says that the target concept fills (exactly) one of the n roles of the base concept. Since it cannot be decided on the correct role yet, n alternative hypotheses have to be opened (unless additional constraints apply) and the target concept is assigned as a filler of the i-th role of base in the corresponding i-th hypothesis space. As a consequence, the classifier is able to derive a suitable concept hypothesis by specializing the target concept (initially TOP, by default) according to the value restriction of the base concept's i-th role. Additionally, this rule assigns a syntactic quality label to each *i-th* hypothesis indicating the type of syntactic construction in which target and base co-occur.

---

[1] Such a part-of-speech hypothesis can directly be derived from the inventory of valence and word order specifications underlying the dependency grammar model we use [6].

In the given KB kernel, for our example five roles must be considered for the base concept CASE. Three of them, HAS-WEIGHT, HAS-PHYSICAL-SIZE, HAS-PRICE, are ruled out due to the violation of a simple integrity constraint (*"PS/2-57SX"* does not denote a measurable unit). Hence, two hypotheses remain to be made, one treating *"PS/2-57SX"* as a producer of hardware

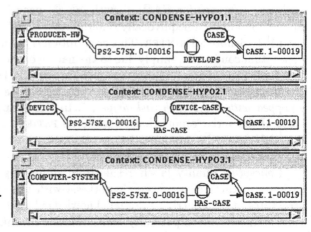

Fig. 2. Three Hypothesis Spaces

via the role DEVELOPS in the hypothesis space 1.1, the other one stipulating that *"PS/2-57SX"* may be a kind of HARDWARE via the role HAS-CASE in the hypothesis spaces 2.1 and 3.1, respectively (cf. Fig. 2).[2]

2.4 Conceptual Qualification

Quality annotations of the conceptual status of concept hypotheses are derived from qualification rules. For instance, one of the rules applies to the case where the same assertion is deduced in at least two different hypothesis spaces (cf. *H* and *H'* in Fig. 3). We take this quasi-confirmation as a strong support for the hypothesis under consideration. Hence, the very positive conceptual quality label M-DEDUCED is derived (for a formal specification of several qualification rules, cf. [4]).

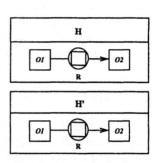

Fig. 3. A Conceptual Qualification Scenario

Considering our example, for *"PS/2-57SX"* the concept hypotheses COMPUTER-SYSTEM and DEVICE were both derived independently of each other in different hypothesis spaces. Hence, HARDWARE as their common superconcept has been multiply derived by the classifier in each of these spaces, too.

2.5 Quality-Based Classification

Whenever new evidence for or against a concept hypothesis is brought forth in a single learning step the entire set of concept hypotheses is reevaluated. First, a

---

[2] As the classifier aggressively pushes hypothesizing to be maximally specific, two distinct hypotheses are immediately stipulated for HARDWARE, namely DEVICE and COMPUTER-SYSTEM.

THRESH1	$\doteq$	HYPO $\sqcap$
		MAX(APPOSITION *term*)
THRESH2	$\doteq$	THRESH1 $\sqcap$
		MAX(CASEFRAME *term*)

Table 3. Threshold Levels

CRED1	$\doteq$	THRESH2 $\sqcap$
		MAX(M-DEDUCED *term*)
CRED2	$\doteq$	CRED1 $\sqcap$
		MAX(C-SUPPORTED *term*)

Table 4. Credibility Levels

selection process eliminates weak or even untenable hypotheses from further consideration. The corresponding quality-based selection among hypothesis spaces is grounded on threshold levels as defined in Table 3 (in Section 3 this selection level will be referred to as **TH**). Their definition takes mostly linguistic evidence into account and evolved in a series of validation experiments. At the first threshold level, all hypothesis spaces HYPO with the maximum of APPOSITION label are selected. If more than one hypothesis is left to be considered, at the second threshold level only concept hypotheses with the maximum number of CASE-FRAME assignments are approved. Those hypothesis spaces that have fulfilled these threshold criteria will then be classified relative to two different credibility levels as defined in Table 4 (in Section 3 this selection level will be referred to as **CB**). The first level of credibility contains all of the hypothesis spaces which have the maximum of M-DEDUCED labels, while at the second level (again, with more than one hypothesis left to be considered) those are chosen which are assigned the maximum of C-SUPPORTED labels. Threshold and credibility criteria make use of composed roles, a specific domain and range restriction on roles (in Tables 3 and 4 abbreviated as "X *term*"), and a new constructor MAX for the path computation. A complete terminological specification is given in [11].

To illustrate the use of threshold criteria, consider phrase *(3): ".. the PS/2-57SX is equipped with a 3.5 inch disk drive .."*, for which a CASEFRAME assignment is triggered in those hypothesis spaces where the unknown item is considered a COMPUTER-SYSTEM or DEVICE (or a specialization of any of them).[3] Therefore, the hypothesis space associated with the PRODUCER-HARDWARE reading (cf. hypothesis space 1.1 in Fig. 2) is ruled out by THRESH2 in the third learning step. As far as the sample phrase *(1)* is concerned, three hypothesis spaces are generated two of which stipulate a HARDWARE hypothesis. As the quality label M-DEDUCED has been derived by the classifier, the processing of the first sample phrase already yields a preliminary ranking with these two HARDWARE hypotheses preferred over the one associated with PRODUCER-HARDWARE (cf. Fig. 2). Note that only in the third learning step this preference leads to an explicit selection (as discussed above) such that the PRODUCER-HARDWARE hypothesis is actually ruled out from further consideration.

3 Evaluation

In this section, we briefly discuss some data from an empirical evaluation of our concept acquisition system (more detailed results are presented in [12]). We

---

[3] The PRODUCER-HARDWARE hypothesis cannot be annotated by CASEFRAME, since a hardware producer cannot be equipped with a 3.5 inch disk drive.

Step	Phrase	Semantic Interpretation
1.	the case of the PS/2-57SX ..	(GenitiveNP,Case.1,case-of,PS/2-57SX)
2.	the PS/2-57SX with 4MB ..	(PP-Attach,PS/2-57SX,has-degree,MB-Degree.1)
3.	the PS/2-57SX is equipped .. .. with a 3.5 inch disk drive	(CaseFrame,equip.1,patient,PS/2-57SX) (CaseFrame,equip.1,co-patient,DiskDrive.1) ↦ (PS/2-57SX,has-disk-drive,DiskDrive.1)

Table 5. Semantic Interpretation of a Text Fragment Featuring *"PS/2-57SX"*

focus here on its learning accuracy and learning rate. Due to the given learning environment, the measures we apply deviate from those commonly used in the machine learning community. For instance, conceptual hierarchies naturally emerge in terminological frameworks. So, a prediction can be more or less precise, i.e., it may approximate the goal concept at different levels of specificity. This is captured by our measure of *learning accuracy* which takes into account the conceptual distance of a hypothesis to the goal concept of an instance, rather than simply relating the number of correct and false predictions as is usually done in machine learning environments. Furthermore, in our approach learning is achieved by the refinement of *multiple* hypotheses about the class membership of an instance. Thus, the measure of *learning rate* we propose is concerned with the reduction of hypotheses as more and more *information* becomes available about one particular new instance, rather than just considering the increase of correct predictions as more and more *instances* are being processed.

We investigated a total of 101 texts from a corpus of information technology magazines. For each of them 5 to 15 learning steps were considered. A learning step is operationalized here by the representation structure that results from the semantic interpretation of an utterance which contains the unknown lexical item. In order to clarify the input data available for the learning system, cf. Table 5. It consists of three single learning steps for the unknown lexical item *"PS/2-57SX"* already discussed. Each learning step is associated with a particular natural language phrase in which the unknown lexical item occurs and the corresponding semantic interpretation in the text knowledge base (the data also incorporate the type of syntactic construction in which the unknown item occurs – this indicates the kind of linguistic quality label to be issued; "↦" provides the results from the application of verb interpretation rules).

Learning Accuracy. First, we investigated the *learning accuracy* of the system, i.e., the degree to which the system correctly predicts the concept class which subsumes the target concept under consideration. Learning accuracy (LA) is a path-sensitive measure for concept graphs. It relates the distance, i.e., the number of node being traversed, between those parts of a concept prediction which are correct and those which are not (cf. [12] for a technical treatment).

Fig. 4 depicts the learning accuracy curve for the entire data set (101 texts). The evaluation starts at LA values in the interval between 48% to 54% for **LA -**, **LA TH** and **LA CB**, respectively, in the first learning step. In the final step, LA rises up to 79%, 83% and 87% for **LA -**, **LA TH** and **LA CB**, respectively. The pure terminological reasoning machinery (denoted as **LA -**) which does not incorporate the qualification calculus always achieves an inferior level of learning

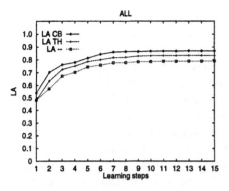

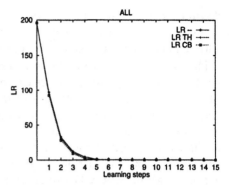

Fig. 4. Learning Accuracy (LA) for the Entire Data Set

Fig. 5. Learning Rate (LR) for the Entire Data Set

accuracy (and also generates more hypothesis spaces) than the learner equipped with the qualification calculus. Furthermore, the inclusion of conceptual criteria (**CB**) supplementing the linguistic criteria (**TH**) helps a lot to focus on the relevant hypothesis spaces and to further discriminate the valid hypotheses (on the range of 4% of precision). Note that an already significant plateau of accuracy is usually reached after the third step *viz.* 67%, 73%, and 76% for **LA -**, **LA TH**, and **LA CB**, respectively, in Fig. 4. This indicates that our approach finds the most relevant distinctions in a very early phase of the learning process, i.e., it requires only a *few* examples.

Learning Rate. The learning accuracy focuses on the predictive power of the learning procedure. By considering the *learning rate* (LR), we turn to the step-wise reduction of alternatives of the learning process. Fig. 5 depicts the mean number of transitively included concepts for all considered hypothesis spaces per learning step (each concept hypothesis denotes a concept which transitively subsumes various subconcepts). Note that the most general concept hypothesis in our example denotes OBJECT which currently includes 196 concepts. In general, we observed a strong negative slope of the curve for the learning rate.

After the first step, slightly less than 50% of the included concepts are pruned (with 93, 94 and 97 remaining concepts for **LR CB**, **LR TH** and **LR -**, respectively). Again, learning step 3 is a crucial point for the reduction of the number of included concepts (ranging from 9 to 12 concepts). Summarizing this evaluation experiment, the quality-based learning system yields competitive accuracy rates (a mean of 87%), while at the same time it exhibits significant and valid reductions of the predicted concepts (up to two, on the average).

4 Related Work

Our approach bears a close relationship to the work of [3], [9], [10], [15], and [7], who aim at the automated learning of word meanings from context using a knowledge-intensive approach. But our work differs from theirs in that the need to cope with *several competing* concept hypotheses and to aim at a *reason-based selection* is not an issue in these studies. Learning from real-world textual input usually provides the learner with only sparse and fragmentary evidence so that multiple hypotheses are likely to be derived requiring subsequent assessment.

The work closest to ours has been carried out by Rau *et al.* [9]. As in our approach, concept hypotheses are generated from linguistic and conceptual data. Unlike our approach, the selection of hypotheses depends only on an ongoing discrimination process based on the availability of these data but does not incorporate an inferencing scheme for reasoned hypothesis selection. The difference in learning performance – in the light of our evaluation study in Section 3 – amounts to 8%, considering the difference between **LA** - (plain terminological reasoning) and **LA CB** values (terminological metareasoning based on the qualification calculus). Hence, our claim that we produce competitive results.

Note that the requirement to provide learning facilities for large-scale text knowledge engineering also distinguishes our approach from the currently active field of information extraction (IE) [2]. The IE task is defined in terms of a *fixed* set of *a priori* templates which have to be instantiated (i.e., filled with factual knowledge items) in the course of text analysis. In particular, no *new* templates have to be created. This step would correspond to the procedure we described in this contribution. As far as the field of knowledge engineering from texts is concerned, i.e., text understanding and knowledge assimilation, our system represents a major achievement, since the problem has so far only been solved by either hand-coding the content of the textual input [14], or providing semi-automatic devices for text knowledge acquisition [16], or using simplistic keyword-based content analysis techniques [1].

5 Conclusion

We have presented a concept acquisition methodology which is based on the incremental assignment and evaluation of the quality of linguistic and conceptual evidence for emerging concept hypotheses. The principles underlying the selection and ordering of quality labels are general, as are most conceptual quality labels. The concrete definition of, e.g., linguistic quality labels, however, introduces a level of application-dependence. Nevertheless, as quality criteria are ubiquitous, one may easily envisage quality labels coming from sources other than linguistic and conceptual knowledge (e.g., a vision system may require quality labels which account for different degrees of signal distortion, 2D vs. 3D representations, etc. in order to interpret visual scenes in the course of learning new gestalts). No specialized learning algorithm is needed, since learning is a (meta)reasoning task carried out by the classifier of a terminological reasoning system. However, heuristic guidance for selecting between plausible hypotheses comes from the different quality criteria. Our experimental data indicate that given these heuristics we achieve a high degree of pruning of the search space for hypotheses in very early phases of the learning cycle.

Acknowledgements. We would like to thank our colleagues in the CLIF group for fruitful discussions and instant support, in particular Joe Bush who polished the text as a native speaker. K. Schnattinger is supported by a grant from DFG (Ha 2097/3-1).

References

1. R. Agarwal and M. Tanniru. Knowledge extraction using content analysis. *Knowledge Acquisition*, 3(4):421–441, 1991.
2. D. Appelt, J. Hobbs, J. Bear, D. Israel, and M. Tyson. FASTUS: A finite-state processor for information extraction from real-world text. In *IJCAI '93 – Proc. of the 13th Int'l. Joint Conf. on Artificial Intelligence*, pages 1172–1178, 1993.
3. F. Gomez and C. Segami. The recognition and classification of concepts in understanding scientific texts. *Journal of Experimental and Theoretical Artificial Intelligence*, 1:51–77, 1989.
4. U. Hahn, M. Klenner, and K. Schnattinger. Learning from texts: A terminological metareasoning perspective. In S. Wermter, E. Riloff, and G. Scheler, editors, *Connectionist, Statistical and Symbolic Approaches to Learning for Natural Language Processing*, pages 453–468. Berlin: Springer, 1996.
5. U. Hahn, M. Klenner, and K. Schnattinger. A quality-based terminological reasoning model for text knowledge acquisition. In N. Shadbolt, K. O'Hara, and G. Schreiber, editors, *EKAW '96 – Proc. of the 9th European Knowledge Acquisition Workshop*, pages 131–146. Berlin: Springer, 1996.
6. U. Hahn, S. Schacht, and N. Bröker. Concurrent, object-oriented natural language parsing: The PARSETALK model. *International Journal of Human-Computer Studies*, 41(1/2):179–222, 1994.
7. P. Hastings. Implications of an automatic lexical acquisition system. In S. Wermter, E. Riloff, and G. Scheler, editors, *Connectionist, Statistical and Symbolic Approaches to Learning in Natural Language Processing*, pages 261–274. Berlin: Springer, 1996.
8. B. Nebel. *Reasoning and Revision in Hybrid Representation Systems*. Berlin: Springer, 1990.
9. L. Rau, P. Jacobs, and U. Zernik. Information extraction and text summarization using linguistic knowledge acquisition. *Information Processing & Management*, 25(4):419–428, 1989.
10. U. Reimer. Automatic acquisition of terminological knowledge from texts. In *ECAI '90 – Proc. of the 9th European Conf. on Artificial Intelligence*, pages 547–549. London: Pitman, 1990.
11. K. Schnattinger and U. Hahn. A terminological qualification calculus for preferential reasoning under uncertainty. In *KI '96 – Proc. of the 20th Annual German Conf. on Artificial Intelligence*, pages 349–362. Berlin: Springer, 1996.
12. K. Schnattinger and U. Hahn. Intelligent text analysis for dynamically maintaining and updating domain knowledge bases. In *IDA '97 – Proc. of the 2nd Int'l. Symposium on Intelligent Data Analysis*. Berlin: Springer, 1997.
13. K. Schnattinger, U. Hahn, and M. Klenner. Terminological meta-reasoning by reification and multiple contexts. In *EPIA '95 – Proc. of the 7th Portuguese Conf. on Artificial Intelligence*, pages 1–16. Berlin: Springer, 1995.
14. D. Skuce, S. Matwin, B. Tauzovich, F. Oppacher, and S. Szpakowicz. A logic-based knowledge source system for natural language documents. *Data & Knowledge Engineering*, 1(3):201–231, 1985.
15. S. Soderland, D. Fisher, J. Aseltine, and W. Lehnert. CRYSTAL: Inducing a conceptual dictionary. In *IJCAI '95 – Proc. of the 14th Intl. Joint Conf. on Artificial Intelligence*, pages 1314–1319, 1995.
16. S. Szpakowicz. Semi-automatic acquisition of conceptual structure from technical texts. *International Journal of Man-Machine Studies*, 33:385–397, 1990.

A Tesseral Approach
to N-Dimensional Spatial Reasoning

F.P.Coenen, B. Beattie, T.J.M.Bench-Capon, B.M.Diaz and M.J.R.Shave

Department of Computer Science, The University of Liverpool,
Chadwick Building, P.O. Box 147, Liverpool L69 3BX, England.
Tel: 0151 794 3698 Fax: 0151 794 3715 email: frans@csc.liv.ac.uk

Abstract. A qualitative multi-dimensional spatial reasoning system is described founded on a tesseral representation of space. Spatial problems are presented to this system in the form of a script describing the nature of the N-dimensional space (the *object* space), the spatial objects of interest and the relations that are desired to exist between those objects. Objects are defined in terms of classes and instances of classes with locations and shapes defined as sets of tesseral addresses. Relations are expressed in terms of topological set relations which may be quantified through the application of tesseral *offsets*. Solutions to spatial problems are generated using a heuristically guided constraint satisfaction mechanism. The heuristics are directed at limiting the growth of the search tree through a constraint selection strategy applied at each stage of the satisfaction process. The general advantages of the system are that it is conceptually simple, computationally effective and universally applicable to N-dimensional problem solving.

1. Introduction

An N-dimensional spatial reasoning system is described that combines a reasoning mechanism, founded on set relations, with quantitative input and output data is described. The approach is designed for incorporation into systems which use raster encoded data, particularly Geographic Information Systems (GIS), so that a spatio-temporal reasoning capability can be attached to those systems. Particular GIS end-user applications that have been investigated by the authors include optimal site location scenarios, noise pollution investigations and nautical chart interaction. Other end applications that have been considered include N-dimensional scheduling and timetabling scenarios, well known AI "puzzles" such as the 8-queens problem and multi-dimensional shape fitting tasks. The last named are used to illustrate this paper.

The system is founded on a tesseral representation of space and uses a heuristically guided constraint satisfaction mechanism to resolve spatial problems defined in the form of a script. The heuristics are directed at the effective selection of constraints so as to minimise the growth of the solution tree and the pursuit of unsuccessful branches within that tree. Scripts comprise object definitions (in terms of classes and instances of such classes) and constraint definitions describing the relations that are desired to exist between objects. Object locations and shapes are defined in terms of sets of tesseral addresses and may be generated through interaction with existing spatial data formats. Output can be in a number of file or graphical formats as directed by the user.

2. Representation

Tesseral representations are well established and a substantial literature exists concerning the nature of such representations (for example [3] and [4]). Broadly such representations are founded on ideas concerning the hierarchical subdivision of N-dimensional space into isohedral sub-spaces down to a predefined resolution. The resulting sub-spaces are then referenced using some addressing system which has the effect of linearising the tessellated space. Such systems can have an arithmetic associated with them which provides translation through the space, and rotation of objects within that space. A 2-D illustration of the tesseral representation used to support the reasoning mechanism is given in Figure 1. Note that addresses increase in steps of 256 in the Y direction. This *base* has been chosen for the benefit of this document, but any other base could equally well have been selected. Objects of interest are considered to exist only in the positive quadrant of the representation, referred to as the *object space*. However the remaining quadrants need to be referenced to support the arithmetic associated with the representation.

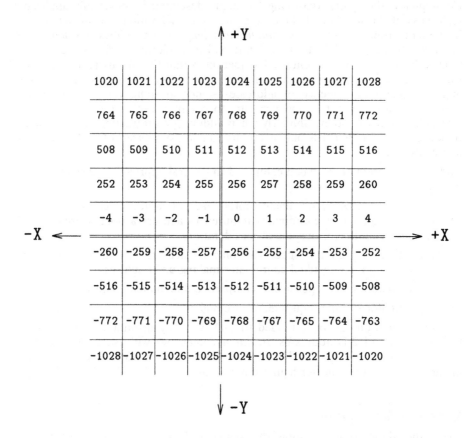

Figure 1: *Referencing for 2-D space*

The distinctive features of this representation, compared with other tesseral representations are:

1) The resulting linearisation is intuitively obvious and predictable (i.e. given any sub-space the addresses of all the physically adjacent sub-spaces can always be predicted). This is not the case with most other tessellations which follow a "Z" linearisation often referred to as the Morton sequence ([7]).

2) Translation and rotation algorithms are implemented using integer arithmetic. For example (with reference to figure 1) to move one tile in a "north-easterly" direction we add the address 257 to a "current" address, regardless of the physical location of that current address (to move to (say) the north-west we would add 255 and so on). Rotation is implemented using the standard approach taken from complex number theory. Consequently more efficient manipulation of objects is achieved than that supported by traditional tesseral arithmetics which, to be effective, required specialised tesseral processors.

The principal benefit of the linearisation (a feature of all tesseral addressing systems) is that N-dimensional space can be manipulated in one dimensional terms. Consequently the spatial reasoning technique described is universally applicable regardless of the number of dimensions under consideration. A further feature of tesseral representations is *runline encoding* which allows sequences of addresses to be stored in terms of start and end addresses. Knowledge of the relative location of runline encoded sequences within the linearisation then provides for effective comparison of sequences of addresses. For example to determine whether one sequence of addresses stands in some relation to another sequence of addresses it is not necessary to compare each address in one with each address in the other. Similarly when adding (or subtracting) one sequence of addresses to another it is only necessary to add (or subtract) the start and end addresses.

Cartesian representations, when compared to tesseral approaches, display the following general disadvantages:

1) Addresses (X-Y-Z-T coordinate tuples) are not uniform across the dimensions, the number of coordinates required to address a point increases with the number of dimensions under consideration.

2) Translation through the space can only be achieved by incrementing and decrementing the individual coordinates making up an address.

3) It is computationally expensive to compare and manipulate addresses.

4) The computer storage requirements are higher.

The representation can be extended to 3-D by applying multiples of a further base to the set of 2-D addresses. In this document we will use a base of 65536 (256^2) to define 3-D space. The representation can be extended in a similar manner to encompass further higher dimensions.

3. Object description

Using the above representation the shape and/or location of quantitatively defined spatial objects can be described in terms of a set of tesseral addresses. Using the system scripting language such objects are defined in terms of classes and instances of such classes using a syntax of the following form (single quotes surround literals and punctuation):

```
<CLASS>      : 'class(' CLASSNAME ',' OBJECTTYPE ').'
             | 'class(' CLASSNAME ',' OBJECTTYPE, SHAPE ').'
             ;

<INSTANCE>   : 'instance(' INSTANCENAME ',' CLASSNAME ').'
             | 'instance(' INSTANCENAME ',' CLASSNAME ','
                        LOCATIONSPACE ').'
             | 'instance(' INSTANCENAME ',' CLASSNAME ','
                        MODIFIERS ').'
             | 'instance(' INSTANCENAME ',' CLASSNAME ','
                        LOCATIONSPACE ',' MODIFIERS ').'
             ;
```

A number of types of object are recognised:

1)   Fixed objects: Objects which have a known location and consequently a known shape.

2)   Free objects: Objects that have a known shape but no specific location other than a general *location space* within which the object is known to exist.

3)   Shapeless objects: Objects that have no known shape or location (other than a general *location space* within which the object is known to exist).

In the case of a fixed object there is no requirement to define its shape as this will be given by its location. In the case of a free object, where the shape definition is omitted, the shape is assumed to comprise a single address. Where a location definition is omitted this is assumed, by default, to extend to the entire object space. The nature of locations (and shapes) can be augmented by the addition of "modifiers", for example we may include a `rotate` modifier indicating that the shape may be rotated.

4. Spatial relations

Using the proposed tesseral representations, relationships (constraints) between objects can be expressed using standard set relations (e.g. = - Equals, $\neq$ - notEquals, $\cap$ -Intersection, $\bar{\cap}$ - not intersection, $\subseteq$ - Subset, etc.). With respect to the scripting language a relationship between two spatial objects can is expressed as follows:

```
<CONSTRAINT> : 'constraint(' OPERAND1, OPERATOR, OPERAND2 ').'
             | 'constraint(' OPERAND, OPERATOR ').'
             ;
```

where the operands are single instances, lists of instances or entire classes of instances. Where a constraint comprises only one operand this is a shorthand for expressing a set of constraints where the operator links all possible instance pairs defined by the operand (in this case, of course, the operand must describe at least two instances). Using the above format standard topological relations can be expressed. To increase the expressiveness of the range of set operators available *offsets* may be applied to locations associated with either operand so that the existing set of relations can be augmented with directions and/or distances. As a result we can formulate relations such as `toTheNorthOf`, `disjoint(N)` (disjoint by a distance `N`), `toTheNorthOf(N)` (to the north of by a distance `N`) and so on. Further discussion on the application of offsets can be found in [1].

The ontology used to develop the spatial scripting language used here can be found in [5].

5. One-dimensional scenario

To illustrate the system's operation we will consider three shape fitting scenarios of increasing complexity commencing with a 1-D example (this section), and progressing to 2-D and 3-D in the following two sections. This provides a clear demonstration of how the same technique is applied irrespective of the number of dimensions.

In Figure 2(a) two discontinuous 1-D shapes are presented, labelled A and B. They are defined in terms of a set of 1-D tesseral addresses (the set of addresses incorporating the 0 address and running immediately parallel to the X-axis in Figure 1). Let us assume: (1) that these two shape definitions are associated with two classes of free object, (2) that there are two instances of each of these classes, a1, a2, b1 and b2, and (3) that we wish to fit these instances into a 1-D object space, comprising 20 addresses, in such a manner that no part of one instance's location coincides with that of another. Let us also assume that there is nothing that prevents us from rotating these objects (if only through 180°). We can express this problem in the form of a script as follows:

```
space([19]).

class(A, free, [0..2, 6, 8]).
class(B, free, [0..3, 5]).

instance(a1, A).
instance(a2, A, rotation).
instance(b1, B, rotation).
instance(b2, B, rotation).

constraint([a1, a2, b1, b2], notIntersection).
```

This script comprises four basic constructs: `space`, `class`, `instance` and `constraint`. The first is used to declare the object space we wish to work with. The second defines the classes of objects we are interested in and the third is used to declare instances of those classes. Note that, to reduce the amount of processing required, one of the instances is not rotated. Note also that the unary (one operand) constraint expression is a shorthand method of defining the following set of constraints:

```
constraint(a1, notIntersection, a2).
constraint(a1, notIntersection, b1).
constraint(a1, notIntersection, b2).
constraint(a2, notIntersection, b1).
constraint(a2, notIntersection, b2).
constraint(b1, notIntersection, b2).
```

When this script is passed to the tesseral spatial reasoning system two possible solutions are generated, these are illustrated in Figure 2(b).

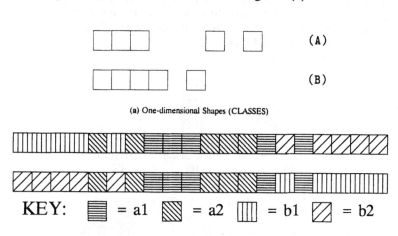

(a) One-dimensional Shapes (CLASSES)

KEY: ☰ = a1   ⊠ = a2   ⫴ = b1   ⊘ = b2

(b) Solutions
Figure 2: *One-dimensional shape fitting scenario.*

6. Two-dimensional scenario

Without requiring any change to the representation or the underlying constraint satisfaction mechanism the system can equally well be applied to two dimensional shape fitting problems. In Figure 3(a) a number of two dimensional shapes (Classes) are presented. Assuming one instance of each class and a 6x6 object space a script can be derived which will cause the spatial reasoning system to place these instances into this object space in such a manner that no instance overlaps any other. The script is as follows:

```
space(6,6)

class(A, free, [0..4, 259, 514..515]).
class(B, free, [0..2, 257, 259]).
class(C, free, [0..2, 258..259, 514]).
class(D, free, [-255, 0..3, 257]).
class(E, free, [0..2, 256, 258..259]).
class(F, free, [0..2, 256]).
```

```
instance(a1, A).
instance(b1, B, rotation).
instance(c1, C, rotation).
instance(d1, D, rotation).
instance(e1, E, rotation).
instance(f1, F, rotation).

constraint([a1, b1, c1, d1, e1, f1], notIntersection).
```

The definition of these shapes can be confirmed by reference to the 2-D "object space" given in Figure 1. Note that, to reduce the amount of work required to produce a result, one of the instances is again not rotated. The solution, on completion of the script, is given in Figure 3(b).

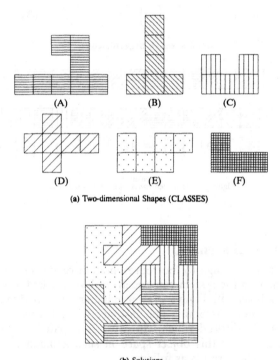

(a) Two-dimensional Shapes (CLASSES)

(b) Solutions
Figure 3: *Two-dimensional shape fitting scenario.*

7. Three dimensional scenario

A similar scenario can be designed with respect to a 3-D object space. Consider the seven shapes (classes) given in Figure 4(a). Assuming a 4x4x4 object space, and one instance of each class, we can write a script designed to fit these instances into the object space (without overlap) as follows:

```
space(4,4,4)

class(A, free, [-65535, -255, 0..2, 65537, 131073, 131329]).
class(B, free, [0..1, 257, 513, 65537, 66049, 131073..131074,
                131329, 131585]).
class(C, free, [0, 65536, 131072, 131074, 196607..196610]).
class(D, free, [0..2, 257..258, 65537..65538, 65793..65794]).
class(E, free, [0, 255..256, 511, 766..768, 65536, 65792,
                66302, 131328]).
class(F, free, [0, 256, 512, 767..768, 65536, 65792, 66304,
                131328, 196864]).
class(G, free, [0, 255..256, 65536, 65792, 66046..66048]).

instance(a1, A).
instance(b1, B, rotation).
instance(c1, C, rotation).
instance(d1, D, rotation).
instance(e1, E, rotation).
instance(f1, F, rotation).
instance(g1, G, rotation).

constraint([a1, b1, c1, d1, f1, e1,  g1], notIntersection).
```

Again, for reasons of efficiency, rotation is not permitted for one of the instances - if we allow rotation of instance a this will simply produce 24 different views of the same result. There is one solution to this problem as demonstrated in Figure 4(b).

Although it may be argued that the 1-D and 2-D shape fitting scenarios given in the foregoing two sections may be considered to be relatively simple in that the number of possible combinations in each case is "small" (346112 in the 1-D scenario and 7077888000 in 2-D scenario), the above example is significantly more taxing. We can carry out some rough calculations to indicate that there are in the region of 6×10^{13} location combinations for the above scenario. The fact that the system can successfully resolve such problems using standard computer hardware is an indication of the strength of the approach, particularly the representation on which it is founded, but also the heuristically guided constraint satisfaction technique currently used to resolve scripts describing tesserally defined spatial problems. The foregoing sequence of examples also clearly illustrates that the system can successfully operate in any number of dimensions without requiring any alteration to the basic representation or the operation of the system. Because of space limitations we can not present a 4-D shape fitting scenario here, however, the system has proved itself successful at resolving such scenarios.

8. Conclusions

A spatio-temporal reasoning mechanism has been described founded on a tesseral representation and linearisation of space. The mechanism offers the following significant advantages:

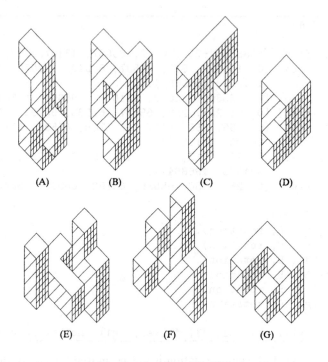

(A)   (B)   (C)   (D)

(E)   (F)   (G)

(a) Three-dimensional Shapes (CLASSES)

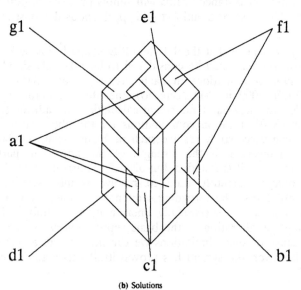

(b) Solutions

Figure 4: *Three-dimensional shape fitting scenario.*

1) It is universally applicable regardless of the number of dimensions under consideration.

2) It is fully compatible with Raster data representations rendering it suited to a wide range of applications, e.g. image analysis, reasoning for GIS and map interaction.

3) It is conceptually simple and computationally effective.

The approach has been incorporated into a spatial reasoning system, the SPARTA system, which has been tested against a great many application scenarios including environmental impact assessment and noise pollution (see [2] and [6]) for further detail). Current work is focused on noise pollution modelling and assessment in the city of London, and marine electronic chart interaction.

9. References

1. Beattie, B., Coenen, F.P., Bench-Capon, T.J.M., Diaz. B.M. and Shave, M.J.R. (1995). Spatial reasoning for GIS using a tesseral data representation, in N. Revell and A.M. Tjoa, A.M. (Eds), *Database and Expert Systems Applications, (Proceedings DEXA'95)*, Lecture Notes in Computer Science 978, Springer Verlag, pp207-216.

2. Beattie, B., Coenen, F.P., Hough, A. Bench-Capon, T.J.M., Diaz, B.M. and Shave, M.J.R (1996). Spatial reasoning for environmental impact assessment, *Third International Conference on GIS and Environmental Modelling*, Santa Barbara: National Centre for Geographic Information and Analysis, WWW and CD.

3. Bell, S.B.M., Diaz, B.M., Holroyd, F.C. and Jackson, M.J.J. (1983). Spatially referenced methods of processing raster and vector data, *Image and Vision Computing* 1(4) 211-220.

4. Diaz, B.M. and Bell, S.B.M. (1986). Spatial data processing using tesseral methods, *Natural Environment Research Council publication*, Swindon, England (1986).

5. Coenen, F.P., Beattie, B., Bench-Capon, T.J.M., Shave, M.J.R. and Diaz, B.M. (1996). An ontology for linear spatial reasoning, in R.R. Wagner and H. Thomas (Eds), *Database and Expert Systems Applications, (Proceedings DEXA'96)*, Lecture Notes in Computer Science 1134, Springer Verlag, 718-727.

6. Coenen, F.P., Beattie, B., Bench-Capon, T.J.M., Diaz, B.M. and Shave, M.J.R. (1996). Spatial reasoning for geographic information systems. *Proceedings 1st International Conference on GeoComputation*, School of Geography, University of Leeds 1 121-131.

7. Morton, G.M. (1966). A computer oriented geodetic data base, and a new technique in file sequencing, *IBM Canada Ltd.*.

Guidance for Requirements Engineering Processes

Samira Si-Said and Colette Rolland
email {sisaid, rolland}@univ-paris1.fr
Université Paris-1 Sorbonne, CRI, 17, rue de Tolbiac, 75013 Paris, FRANCE

Abstract *Guidance plays a crucial role in requirements engineering as this task is both ill defined and highly intellectual. Guidance can be provided once the goal to be achieved has been identified. Two kinds of guidance are proposed, point and flow guidance. The former supports the fulfillment of goals whereas the latter helps in goal identification. Guidance is driven by guidelines which we have modelled as processes instantiated from a process meta-model just as any other, normal process is. Finally, guidelines are modular. This makes possible the rapid modification of guidelines. The paper presents the two types of guidance, the corresponding guidelines and the tool environment which supports the enactment of guidelines.*

Introduction

Process engineering is considered today as a key issue by both the Software Engineering (SE) community and the Information Systems Engineering (ISE) community. Process engineering is a rather new research area. Consequently there is no consensus on, for example, what would be a good formalism to represent processes in, or, even, on what the final objectives of process engineering are [ABGM, 93]. However, there is already considerable evidence for believing that there shall be both, improved productivity of the software systems industry and improved systems quality, as a result of improved development processes [Dow, 93], [ABGM, 93], [JPRS, 94].

Guidance plays a crucial role in the Requirements Engineering RE process [RoPr, 94], [RSM, 95]. This is due, first, to the nature of these processes. RE is a highly intellectual and creative activity. Thus, guidance has to be far more knowledge-intensive than in other activities. The required support is based, for example, on suggestions on how to proceed in a certain situation, or on providing alternatives for achieving a goal. It is clearly beyond the simple automated control of sequences of activities provided by most methods in practice and by process software engineering environments. Second, it is very difficult, if not impossible, for the RE process to progress without guidance. Requirements engineers need to be guided and advised, locally to handle the particular situation they are faced to, and globally, to monitor the flow of decisions they have to make.

Existing CASE tools supporting current ISE methods and SE centred software environments are unable to provide today the kind of heuristics and experience based guidance required in the early phases of system development. CASE tools help in capturing, storing and documenting IS products but do not support RE engineers in their creative development activities [MRTL, 93]. Process-centred software development environments essentially enforce the process performance that conforms to some prescriptive process definition [Dow, 93].

Our guidance approach consists of supporting the RE engineers according to some pre defined process models called ways of working (wow). Ways of working are described by the instantiation of a process meta model which has been developed within the NATURE[1] project. The basic characteristics of this approach is the decision

---

[1] NATURE stands for Novel Approaches to Theories Underlying Requirements Engineering (ESPRIT Basic Project N° 6353).

orientation and the strong association between the decision and the situation in which the decision can be made. The process meta model as well as a product meta model are briefly presented in section 1 of the paper.

The second section is dedicated to the detailed presentation of our guidance approach. This approach is implemented in a process centered CARE environment called MENTOR presented in section 3, before concluding.

1. Overview of the process and the product meta models

1.1. Process modeling: a contextual notation

We consider that RE processes are essentially decision oriented. To take into account this characteristics, we have chosen to emphasise the contextual aspect of decisions [RoGr, 94], [Rol, 94]. Our process modelling approach strongly couples the context of a decision named *situation* to the decision itself. It makes the notion of a context, the coupling of a *situation* and the *intention of decision,* central to process modelling (see Fig. 1.).

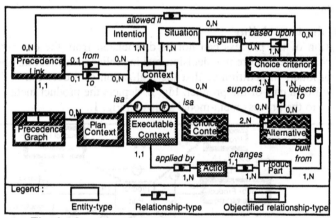

Fig. 1. :Overview of the process meta-model concepts

We distinguish three types of contexts : executable contexts, plan contexts, and choice contexts. This distinction is necessary to handle different granularity levels of contexts. A situation exists at different levels of granularity. Furthermore, decisions have consequences which differ from one granularity level to another. A complete understanding of the notion of a context can thus be gained by articulating the consequences of making the decision of a context on the product under development. We present here a brief description of each of the three contexts.

Executable context

At the lowest level, the RE process can be seen as a set of transformations performed on the product under development. Each transformation results from the execution of a deterministic action which, in turn, is a consequence of a decision made in a certain context. This leads to the introduction of the concept of an *executable context.*

An *executable context* expresses the realization of an intention by an action. This action modifies the product under development and eventually generates a new situation subject to new decisions.

Choice context

During requirements engineering processes, engineers may have several alternative ways to fulfill a decision. In order to represent such situations, we introduce the specialization of context into *choice context*. A *choice context* allows the exploration of alternative solutions represented in turn as contexts. Each alternative is associated to a set of supporting or objecting statements named *arguments* which are combined into *choice criteria* to support the selection of the appropriate alternative.

Plan context

The last kind of context correponds to decisions which need to be decomposed into more detailed ones. A *plan context* is an abstraction mechanism by which a context viewed as a complex issue can be decomposed in a number of sub-issues. Each sub-issue corresponds to a sub-decision working on a sub-situation.

The ordering of the component contexts, within a plan, is defined by a graph named *precedence graph* (Fig. 1.). There is one graph per plan context. The nodes of this graph are contexts while the links -called *precedence links*- define either the possible ordered transitions between contexts or their possible parallel enactment. Based on *arguments*, a *choice criterion* defining when to perform the transition is assigned to a precedence link.

1.2. Product modeling

The description of the process can not be dissociated from the description of the product. We have seen before that decision-making relies on a situation observed on a part of the product. In addition to that the realization of a decision is done by the transformation of a part of the product. Fig. 2. depicts the product meta-model [Sch, 93] connected to the process meta-model shown in Fig. 1..

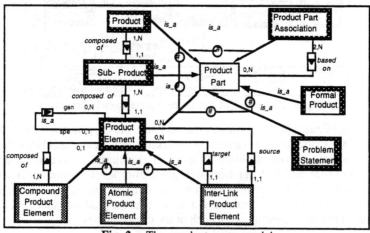

Fig. 2. : The product meta model

The central concept of the product meta-model is that of *Product Part*. It allows the representation of any piece of the product including the whole product, represented by *Product* in the figure as well as pieces of it, represented by *Sub Product* and *Product Element*. It also allows the construction of views on the product through the concept of *Product Part Association*. A *Product Element* can be an *Atomic Product Element*, if it can not be decomposed or a *Compound Product Element* if it can be described using other product elements. Product elements can be related to each others using the concept of *Inter Link Product Element*. Finally, a Product Part can be either a *Formal Product Part* or an informal *Problem Statement*.

The guidelines supporting the way-of-working of the RE process will be represented as hierarchies of contexts (see [RolGro94] for examples).

2. The guidance approach

As the process is decision-oriented, guidance assumes that there is an intention to be achieved and that help is needed to fulfill it. Our approach proposes two kinds of help (a) help in the satisfaction of an intention and, (b) help in selecting the next intention to make the process proceed. We refer to the former as *point guidance* and to the latter as *flow guidance*. These forms of guidance are governed by *guidelines* which are expressed as *hierarchies of contexts* (refer to Fig. 1.). In the rest of this section we develop point and flow guidance respectively.

2.1. Point guidance

Point guidance is associated to *guidance points*. A guidance point p_i represented by a couple (*situation$_i$; decision$_i$*) expresses that a RE engineer focuses on a product part (the situation) corresponding to the decision. The set of guidance points represent all situations in which point guidance can be provided.

In order to identify the guidance points we need both the identification of a set of product parts *P,* and a set of related intentions *I*. The set of guidance points will be the set of all meaningful combinations from *P*I*.

Let us construct some guidance points for the Object Model of the OMT [RBPEL, 91] methodology. A partial set of product parts is given in Fig. 3.. These product parts are obtained by the instantiation of the product meta model.

Complementarily, we have identified a set of generic intentions for RE methodologies. These are   - *Identify* : for identifying a product part.
- *Attach:* for attaching a property to a product part
- *Describe*: for attaching a constraint to a product part
- *Construct* : for refining a product part by associating its components.
- *Validate* : for validating a product part.
- *Complete* : for completing a product part

The set of meaningful guidance points is now generated from these intentions and the product parts identified. A sample of these is given below:

<(Pb. St.); *Identify_Class*>; < (Pb. St); *Identify_ Attribute* >etc.

<(Attribute); *Attach*> etc.

<(Class); *Describe*>; <(Association); *Describe*>; <(Attribute); *Describe*> etc.

<(association); *Validate* >; <(Class); *Validate*>; <(Attribute); *Validate*> etc.

A guideline is associated to each guidance point. It is a hierarchy whose root is the guidance point, that is, the context c_i = < situation$_i$; decision$_i$>. The hierarchy will be progressively constructed by successive refinements of c_i. The leaves of the hierarchy are executable contexts which cause product transformation. Fig. 4. illustrates the guideline associated with the guidance point <(Association); Validate>.

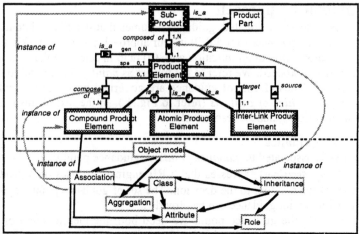

Fig. 3.: Instantiating product parts

The hierarchy refining the context <(Association); Validate> expresses the fact that validation is a complex decision for which several solutions are possible. In our example, there are three alternatives (a) for confirming the association if it is valid (b) for deleting it, if it is invalid and (c) for transforming it to make it valid.

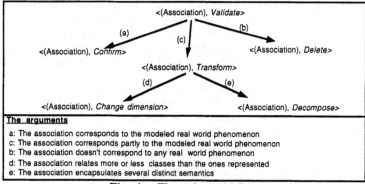

Fig. 4. : The point guideline

The transformation decision is itself complex and thus can be refined into two other decisions : The decomposition allowing the explosion of an association into several associations and the change of related classes. Each hierarchy is able to provide local guidance according to the situation described in the guidance point. This guidance is provided by the enactment of the hierarchy of contexts constituting the guideline. At the end of the enactment, a new guidance point has to be selected in order for the process to proceed further. This leads us to introduce the second form of guidance.

2.2.   Flow guidance
Flow guidance provides support to progress from one guidance point to another under a *strategy* of development.
A strategy - generally opposed to tactics- is concerned with the way to progress in a process. A stratgey is domain specific. In the software engineering and information system engineering domains, we can find a set of common design strategies like Top down, Bottom up, Inside out strategies [BCNa, 92]. Flow guidance is performed by guidelines based on a number of different startegies. These guidelines help in the selection of the decision to make in the next step before it is resolved.

Flow guidelines are expressed using the same notation introduced in section 1.1. They are hierarchies of contexts. The enactment of a flow guideline supports the RE engineer in the selection of a new guidance point.

An example of a flow guideline is shown in Fig. 5.. It describes how to progress after the identification of an attribute in OM of OMT using the inside out strategy.

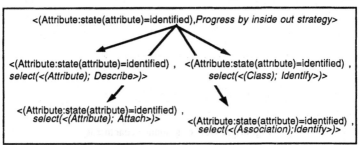

Fig. 5. : A flow guideline

The context in Fig. 5. is a choice context with four alternatives. Each of the alternatives proposes the selection of a new guidance point . The choice criteria associated to the alternatives are not shown here.

Every flow guideline corresponds to a possible guidance flow. The identification of guidance flows can be done in two steps :

- first, the set of strategies needs to be identified. Let S be this set.

- second the set of targets, T, of all guidance points has to be identified. The target is the product part resulting from the transformation performed by the point guideline. For instance, for the guidance point, <(Pb. St.), Identify_Class> the target is the Class identified.

$T = \sum (target(GP_i))$, where GP_i is a guidance point, $1 \leq i \leq N$, and N is the number of guidance points.

The set of flow guidelines is the meaningful sub set obtained from $T \times S$. It expresses the possible transitions between the guidance points using the several identified strategies. The example depicted in Fig. 5. expresses the possible transitions from the guidance point <(Pb. St.); *Identify_Attribute*> using the inside out strategy.

2.3. Guidance enactment : a spiral view

Guidance of RE processes is obtained by the enactment of guidelines. The two types of guidance are performed in turn to provide continuous support to the RE engineers. To illustrate the enactment, we adopt a spiral view as depicted in Fig. 6..

Requirements engineering proceeds by the repeated use of the following cycle:

- choose a guidance point,

- enact the corresponding point guideline,

- select the next guidance point.

The selection of the next guidance point is supported by the flow guideline. The two inter-linked forms of guidance are viewed as two intertwined spirals (see Fig. 6.).

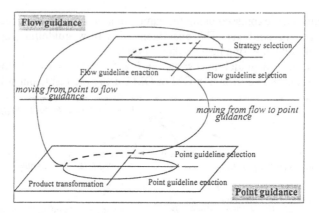

Fig. 6. : A view of guidance enactment

Enactment of flow guidance is viewed as a progression through the four quadrants of a spiral.

During the *first quadrant*, it is suggested that the RE engineer could select a strategy from a set of suggested strategies. The selection of a strategy will lead to the selection of a guidance flow.

The *second quadrant* consists of retrieving the flow guideline to support the engineer in the application of the strategy.

The *third quadrant* aims at enacting the flow guideline to select a guidance point.

The *fourth quadrant* aims at moving to the first quadrant of the lower level, interetwined spiral. This is to provide guidance in the enactment of the selected guidance point.

Enactment of point guidance, is also viewed as a progression through the four quadrants of a spiral.

In the *first quadrant,* the guideline associated with the selected guidance point is identified.

The *second quadrant* aims at the enactment of the point guideline. This results in the identification of executable contexts.

The *third quadrant* transforms the product by executing the executable contexts obtained in the second quadrant.

The *fourth quadrant* aims at moving to the first quadrant of the higher-level, intertwined spiral. This is to provide flow guidance to select the next guidance point to be enacted.

We have implemented our two level guidance approach in the process centered Computer Aided Requirements Engineering (CARE) environment (section 3).

3. A process centered CARE environment

Fig. 7. illustrates the different components of the Computer Aided Requirements Engineering (CARE) environment MENTOR. It provides guidance to both method engineers and application engineers. We will concentrate in this paper on the enactment mechanism : the *guidance engine*. In addition to its guidance facilities, the environment includes tool such as editors and viewers. In this respect, MENTOR includes the functionality offerred by existing Meta CASE tools (e.g. MetaEdit [SLTM, 91], RAMATIC [BBDG, 89], etc.).

As shown in Fig. 7., the environment is organized in four main components :
-the repository to store both ways-of-working and product models (see Fig. 8).
-the method engineer environment for guiding method engineers.
- the application engineer environment for guiding application engineers.
-the guidance mechanism composed of the guidance engine as the kernel for the whole CARE environment, and the session manager to co-ordinate access to all tools.

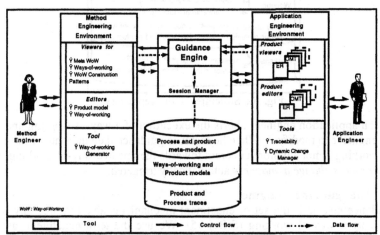

Fig. 7.: MENTOR : general architecture

3.1. The repository

The repository uses the O2 O.O.D.B.M.S. to store and manage data.

As shown in Fig. 8., it is structured in three levels :

-the meta level corresponding to the implementation of both process and product meta models as O2 classes.

-the model level corresponding to ways-of-working and product models related to different methodologies.

-the work space level, composed of ways-of-working and product under development.

The Application engineering environment includes a set of specific graphical *product editors* and *product viewers* to develop specifications. A *traceability* tool and a *process change manager* are also available.

A *product viewer* allows a RE engineer to display the current state of a product in a window whereas a *product editor* provides him means to directly modify the product under development (in the current version of the prototype, tools are available for ER and static OMT specifications, these can easily be extended).

The *traceability tool* offers means for keeping track of product and process traces. The generated trace can be used for documentation purposes but can also be used as the raw material necessary for later improvement of ways--of-working.

The *process change manager* aims at keeping coherent the elements used during the enactment of a way-of-working after modifications of the way-of-working.

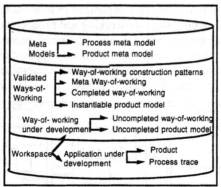

Fig. 8.: Structure of the repository

Assume an application engineer aborts the execution of a way-of-working and asks a method engineer to modify it. When he resumes guidance then the state of the enacted way-of-working is not anymore coherent towards the updated way-of-working. In this case, the *process change manager* is automatically triggered.

3.2. The guidance engine

The guidance engine is the set of enactment mechanisms able to guide any process governed by a way-of-working [SiBe, 95]. We use the term enactment, as in the software community, to refer to the fact that the process is performed not only by machines but by the symbiosis of human beings and computers [ABGM, 93]. However whereas software centered environments look at process enactment as *program execution* we take the view of process enactment being *model interpretation*. This provides more flexibility in human-machine interaction and permits non-determinism.

The guidance engine interacts with the process agent to whom it provides guidance based on the process knowledge stored in the way-of-working. In so doing, it controls the incremental construction of the product under development. The guidance engine can be viewed as an active object which interacts with three other kinds of objects : the product under development, the process agent and the process model.

The guidance engine is generic in the sense that it can guide the enactment of any process modeled in terms of the process meta-model we propose. For example, the process leading to the construction of a way-of-working (represented in a meta way-of-working) is guided in the same way as the process for constructing a specific application. Obviously the objects interacting in each case are different. During the process of constructing a specific application, the guidance engine interprets the way-of-working to provide advice to the RE engineer (the agent) and to support the construction of the requirements specification. The input is a way-of-working and the output is the RE specification. An example of a guided session within MENTOR environment can be found in [SRG, 96].

4. Conclusion

Our work is directed towards providing guidance in the ill-structured task of requirements engineering. Our claim is, first, that guidance can be provided once the goal to be achieved has been identified. Point guidelines support the fulfillment of such goals. Secondly, we believe that guidance can also be provided for identification of goals. This corresponds to flow guidance and the use of a strategy. Guidance is driven by guidelines which we have modelled as processes instantiated from the same meta-model as any other process. Thus, conceptually, there is no difference between, for example, the guideline as a process and the RE process itself. Finally, guidelines are modular. This makes possible the rapid modification of guidelines. .

We are now working on the extension of the guidance approach and the CARE environment to take into account multi-agent processes.

References

[ABGM, 93] P. Armenise, S. Bandinelli, C. Ghezzi, A. Morzenti, "*A survey and assessment of software process representation formalisms*", Int. Journal of Software Engineering and Knowledge Engineering, Vol. 3, No. 3, 1993.

[BCNa, 92] C. Batini, S. Ceri, S. Navathe, "*Conceptual Data Base Design : an ER approach*", Benjamin/Cummings (Pub.), 1992.

[BBDG, 89] P. Bergsten, J.A. Bubenko, R. Dahl, M. Gustafsson L.A. Johasson : "*RAMATIC - a CASE Shell for Implementation of Specific CASE Tools*", Tech. report SISU, Stockholm, Sweden, 1889.

[Dow, 93] M. Dowson : *Software Process Themes and Issues*. In Proceedings of the second International Conference on the Software Process, February 1993.

[FeHu, 93] P. H. Feiler, W. S. Humphrey, "*Software Process Development and Enactment : Concepts and Definitions*", Proc. 2nd Int. Conf. on "Software Process", 1993.

[JPRS, 94]. M. Jarke, K. Pohl, C. Rolland, J. R. Schmitt, "*Experience-Based Method Evaluation and Improvement : A Process Modeling Approach*", Int. IFIP WG8. 1 Conference in CRIS series : Method and associated Tools for the Information Systems Life Cycle", North Holland (Pub.), 1994.

[MRTL, 93]. P. Martiin, M. Rossi, V-P. Tahvainen, K. Lyytinen, "*A comparative review of CASE shells - a preliminary framework and research outcomes*", published in Information and Management, 25, 1993, pp11-31.

[RoGr, 94] C. Rolland, G. Grosz : *A General Framework For describing a Requirements Engineering Process*. In proceedings of the Int. conf. on man systems and cybernetics, ICMSC94, san Antonio, Texas USA, October 1994.

[Rol, 94]. Rolland C., "*A Contextual Approach to modeling the Requirements Engineering Process*", SEKE'94, 6th International Conference on Software Engineering and Knowledge Engineering, Vilnius, Lithuania, 1994

[RoPr, 94] C. Rolland, N. Prakash, "*Guiding the Requirements Engineering Process*", in the Proceedings of the IEEE Asia-Pacific Software Engineering Conference (APSEC), 1994

[RSM, 95] Rolland C., Souveyet C., Moreno M. "*An Approach for Defining Ways-Of-Working*", to appear in the Information Systems Jounral in 1995.

[RBPEL, 91] J. Rumbaugh, M. Blaha, W. Premerlani, F. Eddy, W. Loresen : "*Object-oriented modeling and design*", Prentice Hall international, 1991.

[Sch, 93] J.R. Schmitt : *Product Modeling for Requirements Engineering Process Modeling*. IFIP WG 8.1 Conf. On Information Systems Development Process 1993.

[SiBe, 95]. Si-Said S. Ben Achour C. : "*A Tool for Guiding the Requirements Engineering Process*", in Proceedings of the 6th Workshop on the Next Generation of CASE Tools, Jyvaskyla, Finland, pp 23-42,1995.

[SRG, 96] S. Si-Said, C. Rolland, G. Grosz : " *MENTOR :A Computer Aided Requirements Engineering Environment*", in Proceedings of CAiSE' 96, Crete, GREECE, May 1996.

[SLTM, 91] K. Smolander, K. Lyytinen, V.P. Tahavanainen, P. Martiin : "*MetaEdit : A Flexible Graphical Environment for Methodology Modelling*", in Proceedings of CAiSE' 91, LNCS N° 498, pp168-193, Tomdheim, Norway, 1991.

Repository Based Software Cost Estimation

Andreas Henrich

Praktische Informatik, Fachbereich Elektrotechnik und Informatik,
Universität Siegen, D-57068 Siegen, Germany,
e-mail: henrich@informatik.uni-siegen.de

Abstract. One important problem with software development projects is to get an early and nevertheless accurate estimation of the software development costs. In the literature various methods have been developed for this purpose. The most popular examples are Boehm's *COCOMO*, Albrecht's *function-point method* or Sneed's *object-point method*. The two last-named methods are based on early results of the analysis phase, whereas COCOMO is based on an a priori estimation of the software size in *"lines of code"*. On the other hand, modern software development environments usually employ the object management facilities of a repository to store the documents created and maintained during software development. Hence, software cost estimation methods like the *object-point method*, which are based on early analysis results, can be implemented easily on top of the repository. In this paper we present such a repository based realization of software cost estimation methods.

1 Introduction

Most software development projects represent a considerable investment. Therefore it is essential to estimate the corresponding costs and benefits in advance, to decide whether the project should be realized or not and to control the project budget. With respect to the benefits different types of projects have to be distinguished. There are projects aiming for rationalization, projects aiming for a competitive edge, and projects necessary due to legislative regulations, to mention only a few possibilities. On the other hand, each project causes costs. The principal components of project costs are [11]: (1) hardware costs, (2) travel and training costs, and (3) effort costs (the costs for paying software engineers). Whereas a quantitative estimation of the project benefits depends on the concrete situation, hardware costs as well as travel and training costs are relatively easy to estimate. However, effort costs are harder to estimate, but fortunately various techniques for their estimation have been proposed:

1. *Percentage methods:* Cost estimation techniques falling into this category are based on some type of waterfall model assuming that the software development process is made up of a number of stages such as requirements specification, software design, and so on. The basic assumption is that the distribution of the effort costs over the phases is nearly constant, at least for projects dealing with systems of a similar type. This *"constant"* distribution

can be exploited to calculate an estimate of the effort for the whole project when the actual effort of the first phase is known.

2. *Techniques based on the size of the software product:* Two prominent representatives of this category are *Putnam's cost estimation model* [8] and *COCOMO* [2] (COCOMO = COnstructive COst MOdel). The basis for CO-COMO, for example, is the formula Effort = $c_1(\text{KDSI})^{c_2}$, where KDSI is the number of thousands of delivered source instructions and c_1 and c_2 are constants which vary depending on the type of the project. To refine the estimation, a series of multipliers can be applied which take into account factors such as product reliability, database size, execution and storage constraints, personnel attributes and the use of software tools.

3. *Techniques based on analysis results:* In 1979 the *function-point method* was proposed by Albrecht [1] as an alternative to using code size as the basis for the cost estimation. The *function-point method* is based on an analysis of the functionality of the software rather than on its size. In the course of the stronger emphasis on the maintained data in analysis methods in 1990 Sneed proposed the so called *data-point method* [9]. This method is essentially based on the information contained in an entity-relationship diagram. Finally in 1996 Sneed presented the *object-point method* [10], which is based on the information gathered applying object-oriented analysis techniques.

For the applicability of these software cost estimation techniques a corresponding tool to automate the application of the techniques is needed. To this end, the cost estimation techniques can be realized based on the functionality of a repository. Roughly spoken a repository is a database system underlying a software development environment. The intention is that all tools store the documents created and maintained during software development in this open repository. In the present paper we describe the realization of a software cost estimation system based on a repository. This system employs the *percentage method* for first rough base estimations (cf. section 3) and the *object-point method* for a more sophisticated estimation (cf. section 4). We selected these techniques because — in contrast e.g. to COCOMO — most of the information needed for their application can be derived directly from documents in the repository. Before actually describing this cost estimation system, we have to introduce the repository underlying our considerations.

2 The Repository

The ideas presented in this paper have been developed and implemented based on a concrete environment consisting of H-PCTE [6] (an implementation of the OMS of PCTE) and the query language P-OQL [4].

PCTE (*Portable Common Tool Environment*) is the ISO and ECMA standard for a public tool interface (PTI) for an open repository [7]. As one of its major components PCTE contains a structurally object-oriented object management system (OMS). The data model of the PCTE OMS can be seen as

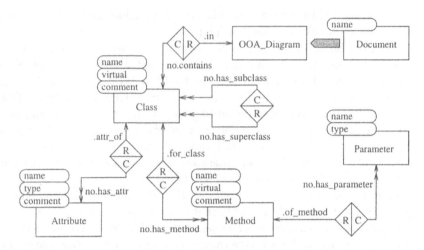

Fig. 1. Simplified example schema for OOA-diagrams

an extension of the binary Entity-Relationship Model. The object base contains objects and relationships. Relationships are normally bi-directional. Each relationship is realized by a pair of directed links, which are reverse links of each other, i.e. point into opposite directions.

The type of an object is given by its name, a set of applied attribute types and a set of allowed outgoing link types. New object types are defined by inheritance.

A link type is given by a name, an ordered set of attribute types called key attributes, a set of (non-key) attribute types, a set of allowed destination object types, and a category. PCTE offers five link categories: *composition* (defining the destination object as a component of the origin object), *existence* (keeping the destination object in existence), *reference* (assuring referential integrity and representing a property of the origin object), *implicit* (assuring referential integrity) and *designation* (without referential integrity).

Let us consider the example schema for OOA-diagrams in figure 1. As usual, object types are given in rectangles, attribute types are given in ovals, and link types are indicated by arrows. A double arrowhead at the end of a link indicates that the link has cardinality *many*. Links with cardinality many must have a key attribute. In the example the numeric attribute *no* is used for this purpose. For example the link type *contains* from *OOA_Diagram* to *Class* has such a key attribute and is hence described as *"no.contains"*. Therefore an instance of this link type can be addressed by its link name which consists of the concrete value for the key attribute and the type name separated by a dot – e.g. *"3.contains"*. A 'C', 'E', or 'R' in the triangles at the center of the line representing a pair of links, indicates that the link has category *composition*, *existence*, or *reference*.

Finally the schema contains a subtype relationship between the object types *Document* and *OOA_Diagram* which is indicated by a broad shaded arrow.

P-OQL [4, 5] is an OQL-oriented [3] query language for PCTE. A query in P-OQL is either a select-statement, or the application of an operator like *sum*.

Assume that we search for the name and the applicable methods of all classes in the OOA-diagram named *"Clearing"*. This corresponds to the P-OQL query:

```
select C:name, normalize C:[_.has_superclass]*/_.has_method/->name
   from D in OOA_Diagram, C in (D:_.contains/->.)
   where D:name = "Clearing"
```

In the **from-clause** of this query two base sets are defined: Base set D addressing all OOA-diagrams and base set C addressing all objects which can be reached from the actual object of base set D via a path matching the regular path expression "D:_.contains/->.". In this path expression the prefix "D:" means that the actual element of base set D is used as the starting point of the definition. "_.contains" means that exactly one link of type *contains* must be traversed. Here the underscore ("_") is used as a wildcard denoting that arbitrary key attribute values are allowed. "/->" is used to address the destination object of the path. In addition "->" can be used to address the last link of the path. The "." at the end of the regular path expression means that the object (or link) under concern is addressed. It is also possible, to address an attribute – which is for example the case in the target-clause of the above query – or a tuple of values (see [4] for more details).

The **select-clause** of the example query states that a multi-set of pairs is requested. Each pair consists of the name of the class and a set containing the names of the methods which can be applied to instances of the class. Since methods defined for superclasses of the class under concern can also be applied to instances of the class, we have to address these methods as well. To this end, the regular path expression "C:[_.has_superclass]*/_.has_method/->name" is used in the query. The starting point of this expression is the actual element of base set C. The meaning of "[_.has_superclass]*" is that zero or more links matching the link definition "_.has_superclass" have to be traversed. Alternatively P-OQL knows the iteration facilities [*path_definition*]+ to indicate that a path matching *path_definition* has to be traversed at least once and [*path_definition*] to indicate that a path matching *path_definition* is optional. After traversing an arbitrary number of *has_superclass* links, exactly one link of type *has_method* is traversed using the link definition "_.has_method". Finally the *name* attribute of this method is addressed using "/->name". The resulting multi-set is transformed into a set using the unary operator `normalize`.

In addition to the link definitions used in the above example P-OQL allows the specification of a set of link categories with the meaning that all links having one of the given categories fulfill this link definition. E.g. the expression "[{c, e}]+/->." addresses all objects which can be reached via a path consisting only of links with category *composition* or *existence*.

3   Implementation of the Percentage Method

To apply the percentage method the schema given in figure 1 has to be extended. Figure 2 illustrates these extensions. Whereas the introduction of an object type

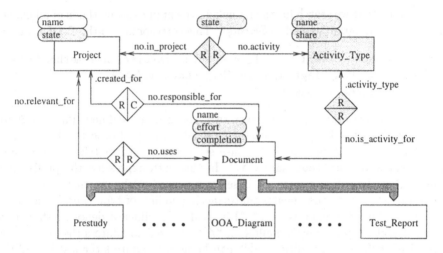

Fig. 2. Schema for the application of the percentage method

Project with corresponding link types is necessary for arbitrary project oriented cost estimation techniques, the densely shaded object types, link types and attributes are specific for the percentage method.

To represent the different activities (or phases) in a software development project the object type *Activity_Type* is introduced. The objects of this type represent the stages of the waterfall model on which the percentage method is based. Each activity type (such as prestudy or requirements analysis) has a *name* and a *share*. The *share* represents the average portion of the effort spend for the activity. The link type *activity* from *Project* to *Activity_Type* has a non-key attribute *state* representing the state of the activity in the project. Each document is linked to exactly one activity type by a link of type *activity_type*. Furthermore, for each document the *effort* spend up to now and the degree of *completion* (0 to 100 %) are maintained. Finally the *state* attribute for projects represents the state of the project as a whole.

To apply the percentage method for a concrete project we first have to fill the *share* attributes for the *Activity_Type* objects. If there are no finished projects in our repository, the corresponding values can be estimated by experts. Otherwise they can be extracted from the repository applying the following query:

```
select AT:name, AT:.,
       (sum (select Doc1:effort
             from Doc1 in (AT:_.is_activity_for/->.)
             where Doc1:.created_for/->state = FINISHED)
       / sum (select Doc2:effort
             from Doc2 in Document^
             where Doc2:.created_for/->state = FINISHED))
   from AT in Activity_Type
```

For each activity type this query yields a triple with the name of the activity type, an object reference for the corresponding object in the repository, and the average share. The object reference is requested using a dot as the second component in the select-clause of the query. This object reference can be used to set the value of the attribute *share* of the activity type. The average share is calculated employing two sub-selects. The first sub-select yields the effort for all documents in finished projects which are associated with the activity type under concern. To this end, in base-set `Doc1` all documents are addressed which can be reached from the activity type under concern via a link of type *is_activity_for*. In the where-clause of the sub-select these documents are restricted to those contained in finished projects. Finally the `sum` operator is applied to the result of the sub-select summing up the efforts dedicated to the activity type under concern. The second sub-select does very much the same, but the base-set here addresses all documents irrespective of the associated activity type.

When the share attributes for the activity types are set, the effort of all projects with at least one finished activity can be estimated by the following P-OQL query:

```
select P:name,
       (sum (select Doc:effort
               from Doc in (P:_.responsible_for/->.)
               where Doc:.activity_type/->name
                  <= (select Act1:/name
                        from Act1 in (P:_.activity->.)
                        where Act1:state = FINISHED))
       / sum (select Act2:/share
                from Act2 in (P:_.activity->.)
                where Act2:state = FINISHED))
    from P in Project
    where P:state = RUNNING
      and 0 < sum (select Act3:/share
                     from Act3 in (P:_.activity->.)
                     where Act3:state = FINISHED)
```

In base-set P the query considers all running projects for which the share of at least one finished activity is greater than zero. This second condition is necessary to prevent divisions by zero in the select-clause of the query. To state this condition, we employ a sub-select addressing the finished activities of the project under concern. To be more precise, in base-set `Act3` we address the links of type *activity* originating from the project under concern by the regular path expression "`P:_.activity->.`". In the where-clause of the sub-select we check whether the *state* attribute applied to the link has the value FINISHED, and in the select-clause we address the share attribute of the destination object by the expression "`Act3:/share`". Finally these *share* values are summed up.

For each project fulfilling the conditions the name and the estimated effort are reported. The estimated effort is again calculated employing two sub-selects.

In the first sub-select the documents associated with the project under concern are addressed in base-set Doc using the regular path expression

"P:_.responsible_for/->.". In the where-clause of the sub-select we check if the document under concern is associated with an activity type which is already finished for the project under concern. This test is performed applying a further sub-select, which determines the names of all activities which are finished for the project. In this case the relation "<=" stands for the subset relation, because it is applied to (multi-)sets.

The second sub-select is exactly the same as the sub-select used in the where-clause of the query.

4 Implementation of the Object-Point Method

The *object-point method* uses so called *object-points* as a measure for the size of object-oriented software, and hence, as a measure for the effort costs caused by the development of this software. Sneed bases his method on three sub-models: an object model, a communication model and a process model. The estimation of the effort costs is then performed in three steps:

A measure for the *coding effort* is derived from the classes in the object model. To this end, for each class the number of attributes, the number of relations, the number of methods and the novelty are considered. The coding effort is estimated by so called *class-points*:

Class-Points = ((attributes) + (relations × 2) + (methods × 3)) × novelty

For the estimation of the *integration effort* the message exchange described in the communication model is considered. For each message the number of parameters, the number of sources, the number of destinations, the complexity (*low* = 0.75, *medium* = 1.0 or *high* = 1.25), and the novelty are considered:

Message-Points = ((parameters) + (sources × 2) + (destinations × 2))
× complexity × novelty

Finally, the process model is employed for the estimation of the *system testing effort*. System processes (multiplier 6), batch processes (2), online processes (4), and realtime processes (8) are distinguished. In addition the complexity, and the number of variants is considered for each process:

Process-Points = (process type + variants) × complexity

The aggregate effort measure *object-points* is derived as follows:

Object-Points = Class-Points + Message-Points + Process-Points

The effort estimation derived in this way is then refined by considering a range of factors representing the quality requirements (such as reliability, time efficiency, or portability) and project attributes (such as the technical support, the reliability of the network, or the employed methods). Let QRM represent the multiplier for the quality requirements and PAM represent the multiplier for the project attributes. Then the *adjusted-object-points* can be determined as follows:

Adjusted-Object-Points = Object-Points × QRM × PAM

According to Sneed, one Adjusted-Object-Point corresponds to a development effort of approximately 0.25 person-days. Of course this relation has to be verified and customized for each company.

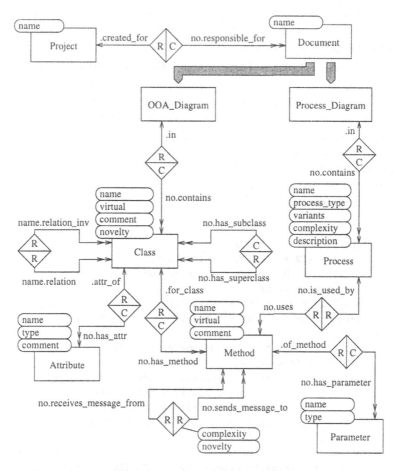

Fig. 3. Schema for the application of the object-point method

In the following we assume that the employed software development environment contains tools to create and edit the object model, the communication model and the process model, and that these tools store the data in the repository in accordance to the schema depicted in figure 3. In this schema classes have an additional attribute *novelty*, which is 1.0 for classes which are completely new and 0.0 for classes for which approved implementations exist. In addition instance relationships between classes are represented by links of the type *relation*.

To represent Sneed's communication model, we have introduced the link types *sends_message_to* and *receives_message_from* for methods. Analogously to Sneed links of type *sends_message_to* have an enumeration attribute *complexity* and a float attribute *novelty*. However, in contrast to Sneed in our data model a message is always considered in the context of a sending and a receiving method. As a consequence a message has always exactly one source and one destination.

Messages which would have multiple sources or destinations in Sneed's model correspond to multiple links in our model. Hence, for our schema Sneed's formula for the Message-Points simplifies to

Message-Points $= ((\text{parameters}) + 4) \times \text{complexity} \times \text{novelty}$

Finally, in our schema the process model is represented by a further subtype of the object type *Document*. From this subtype *Process_Diagram* the process descriptions can be reached via links of type *contains*. The objects of type *Process* have associated attributes *name, process_type, variants, complexity* and *description*. Furthermore the relationship to the employed methods is represented by links of type *uses*.

Based on this schema the following P-OQL query determines the object-points for a project named *"Clearing"*.

```
(sum                                              // add Class-Points
    (select ((count C:_.has_attr->.
              + ((2 * count C:*.relation->.)
                + (3 * count C:_.has_method->.)))
            * C:novelty)
      from P in Project, C in (P:[{c}]+/->.)
      where P:name = "Clearing" and C:. is of type Class)
  + (sum                                          // add Message-Points
      (select ((count M:/_.has_parameter->. + 4)
              * (M:novelty
                * (case M:complexity = LOW      ==> +0.75,
                        M:complexity = MEDIUM  ==> +1.00,
                        M:complexity = HIGH    ==> +1.25)))
        from P in Project, M in (P:[{c}]+/_.sends_message_to->.)
        where P:name = "Clearing")
    + sum                                         // add Process-Points
        (select ((((case Pc:process_type = SYSTEM   ==> 6,
                         Pc:process_type = BATCH    ==> 2,
                         Pc:process_type = ONLINE   ==> 4,
                         Pc:process_type = REALTIME ==> 8)
                  + Pc:variants)
                * (case Pc:complexity = LOW      ==> +0.75,
                        Pc:complexity = MEDIUM  ==> +1.00,
                        Pc:complexity = HIGH    ==> +1.25))
          from P in Project, Pc in (P:[{c}]+->.)
          where P:name = "Clearing" and Pc:. is of type Process)))
```

In this query the results of three sub-queries determining the class-points, the message-points and the process-points are added up. In each sub-query a base-set P addressing all Projects is used. In the where-clause this base-set is restricted to the project named *"Clearing"*.

In the sub-query determining the **class-points** all components of the project under concern are addressed via the regular path expression "P:[{c}]+/->." in a second base-set C. In the where-clause this base set is restricted to classes. For each class the number of attributes, the number of relations, and the number of methods are determined counting the outgoing links of the corresponding types. The numbers derived in this way are weighted according to Sneed's formula and multiplied by the *novelty* of the class.

To calculate the **message-points** all *sends_message_to* links in the complex object forming the project under concern are addressed in a base-set M. To this end, the regular path expression "P:[{c}]+/_.sends_message_to->." is used. This path expression starts traversing one or more composition links. Finally a link of type *sends_message_to* has to be traversed and this link itself is addressed using the notation "->.". For the messages represented by these links the number of the parameters of the destination method it determined using the expression "count M:/_.has_parameter->.". The number determined in this way is then multiplied with the novelty and the complexity of the message. To convert the enumeration type attribute *complexity* into a numerical value, the case statement of P-OQL is used.

Finally the **process-points** are determined analogously to the class-points.

In principle the query described above is used in our software cost estimation tool which proceeds as follows: (1) The user of the tool has to enter the name of the project. (2) The object-points are determined by a P-OQL query corresponding to the above query except that the project name *"Clearing"* is replaced by the actual project name. (3) The result of the query is presented in a result window. In this window the user can add the quality requirements and the project attributes needed to calculate the adjusted object-points. (4) The adjusted object-points are calculated when a corresponding button is pushed.

References

1. A.J. Albrecht. Measuring application development productivity. In *Proc. Application Development Symposium*, pages 83–92, Philadelphia, Penn., USA, 1979.
2. B. Boehm. *Software Engineering Economics*. Prentice-Hall, 1981.
3. R. Cattell, editor. *The Object Database Standard: ODMG-93*. Morgan Kaufmann, San Mateo, Cal., USA, 1993.
4. A. Henrich. P-OQL: an OQL-oriented query language for PCTE. In *Proc. 7th Conf. on Software Engineering Environments*, pages 48–60, Noordwijkerhout, 1995.
5. A. Henrich. Document retrieval facilities for repository-based system development environments. In *Proc. 19th Annual Intl. ACM SIGIR Conf. on Research and Development in Information Retrieval*, pages 101–109, Zürich, 1996.
6. U. Kelter. H-PCTE: A high-performance object management system for system development environments. In *Proc. 16th Annual Intl. Computer Software and Applications Conf.*, pages 45–50, Chicago, Ill., USA, September 1992.
7. Portable Common Tool Environment - Abstract Specification / C Bindings. Standards ECMA-149/-158, 3rd edition and ISO IS 13719-1/-2, 1994.
8. L.H. Putnam. A general empirical solution to the macro software sizing and estimating problem. *IEEE Transactions on Software Engineering*, 4(4):345–361, 1978.
9. H.M. Sneed. Die Data-Point-Methode. *ONLINE, ZfD*, (5):48, May 1990.
10. H.M. Sneed. Estimation of the development costs of object-oriented software. *Informatik-Spektrum*, 19(3):133–140, 1996. in German.
11. I. Sommerville. *Software Engineering*. Addison-Wesley, 4th edition, 1992.

Using a Generic Approach to Support the Construction of Methods

Veronique Plihon
GECT, Université de Toulon et du Var
BP 132
83957 La Garde Cedex
plihon@univ-tln.fr

Colette Rolland
CRI, Université Paris I Sorbonne
17 rue de la Sorbonne
75005 Paris
rolland@univ-paris1.fr

Abstract

The new emerging field of Method Engineering acknowledges the need for rapid construction of methods. In this paper, we propose to define a method as a set of method chunks which contains guidelines for supporting the development process. There are two types of guidelines. One type supports decisions leading to a transformation of schema elements, whereas the second one helps in controlling the flow of decisions.

In order to improve efficiency in the construction of methods, we propose to derive the method chunks from a set of generic patterns, obtained by abstracting out the commonalties from a set of current methods.

This paper presents the approach we propose to build a method. It focuses on the generic knowledge first and then presents an example of method construction based on the approach. Finally we exemplify the use of a method to model an elevator control system.

I Introduction

Most development projects need to have their own specific methods in order to deal with the specific situations they are faced to. Thus, there is a felt need to build new methods to deal with these new situations [Hidding94]. However, defining a new method is time consuming. Thus, the Method Engineering community has tried to provide solutions for supporting fast method construction. There are two broad approaches to do this :

• The *situational method approach* proposed by Harmsen [Harmsen94], Welke [Welke91] and Saeki [Saeki94] is based on the concept of reusability. This approach is centred around a method base in which method fragments (either process or product fragments) are stored. These fragments are part of existing methods, but they can serve as a basis for building new methods. The underlying process of this approach calls for the selection and subsequent assembly of method fragments in order to create the new method. Proposals have been made to facilitate selection of method fragments using contingency factors [Slooten96] or descriptors [Rolland96a] which characterise them. The assembly of fragments can be done by using techniques similar to schema integration [Batini92].

• *Meta-modelling approaches* have also been proposed to improve the productivity of method engineers. These approaches propose to derive new methods by instantiation of a meta-model. In [Grundy96], Grundy proposes to use the COCOA meta-model to derive methods whereas in [Lyytinen89] method construction is based on the instantiation of the GOPRR meta-model.

In both these approaches to speed-up method construction, the aspect of the way-of-working adopted by the method engineer is de-emphasised. We believe that considerable speed-ups shall result if this aspect is taken into account. In this paper, we propose a way to do this.

Within the CREWS [1] project, our approach aims at discovering the generic behaviour patterns of method engineers, representing them in a method independent way, and making them available in a library for repeated use. As a result, knowledge about 'what must be done' is augmented with knowledge about 'how it can be done' thereby facilitating the task of the method engineer. Under our approach, the construction of a method consists of applying the generic patterns to the product model of a specific method. This is done automatically. Given the product model of the method under construction, the process model is automatically generated by applying the generic patterns. The product model of a method is itself obtained by instantiating the product meta-model [Plihon96].

The generic patterns stored in the library belong to two different kinds of method knowledge : some patterns (called *guidance point chunks* or *point chunks* for short) describe the way to achieve product transformations whereas others (referred to as *control process flow chunks* or *flow chunks* for short) allow to control the overall process flow. A chunk supporting the construction of a product element in a schema, for instance, belongs to the *point chunk* category. On the contrary, a chunk providing different alternative ways to select the next process step to be executed is an example of a *flow chunk*.

The layout of the paper is as follows. In the next section we focus on the generic knowledge associated with point chunks and then show how it can be used to construct the product transformations part of object-oriented methods. In section three we look at generic knowledge associated with flow chunks and show how it can be used to build the process flow part of object-oriented methods. Finally in section four, we show that the new method constructed by us is specially suited to the elevator control problem.

II Presentation of the Point Chunks

Early method engineering approaches [Welke91], [Harmsen94] assume that method construction is an assembly process of methods fragments. These method fragments are method specific and can be product or process parts of existing methodologies. One can draw an analogy between such method fragments and reusable classes in object oriented approaches.

However, our belief is in the existence of a corpus of generic *method construction knowledge* which has not been looked for, identified and described yet. We have used a bottom-up approach to identify objects, rules and constraints which are common among different methods. This approach is qualified as 'bottom-up' because it starts from the study of several methods and results in a unique generic method. For instance, let's consider the E/R and the OMT methods. In the E/R [Chen76] method, it is suggested to *refine an entity-type* by (1) introducing its attributes, (2) refining its

[1] This work in partly supported by the ESPRIT project CREWS (n° 21.903) which stands for Cooperative Requirements Engineering With Scenarios.

attributes by defining (2.1) its domain, and (2.2) its valuation, and finally (3) by specifying a key for the entity-type.

In the OMT [Rumbaugh91] method, the *definition of a class* consists of (1) adding attributes to the class, (2) defining the attributes by defining (2.1) their domain and (2.2) their valuation, (3) adding operations to the class, (4) defining the operations by defining (4.1) its type and (4.2) its parameters.

In both cases, the underlying intention (the goal you want to fulfil) is the same and it can be abstracted by the following sequence, which is generic: assuming that an element can be characterised by concepts (concept participating to its description), properties and constraints; for *describing an element*, one should (1) attach its concepts, (2) describe its concepts (when it is needed), (3) attach its properties and (4) attach its constraints (if any).

Figure 1 shows that the guidelines provided by the E/R and by the OMT method (left part of the figure) are equivalent to the guidelines derived from the generic one (right part of the figure).

Knowledge of the Specific Methods	Knowledge Derived from a Generic Method Pattern
Refine Entity-Type : (1) Introduce Attributes, (2) Refine Attributes ((2.1) Define Domain, (2.2) Define Valuation), and (3) Specify Key	**Describe Entity-Type :** (1) Attach Attributes, (2) Describe Attributes ((2.1) Attach Domain, (2.2) Attach Valuation), and (3) Attach Key
Define Class: (1) Add Attributes, (2) Define Attributes ((2.1) Define Domain, (2.2) Define Valuation), (3) Add Operations, (4) Define Operations ((4.1) Define Type, (4.2) Define Parameters)	**Describe Class:** (1) Attach Attributes, (2) Describe Attributes ((2.1) Attach Domain, (2.2) Attach Valuation), (3) Attach Operations, (4) Describe Operations ((4.1) Attach Type, (4.2) Attach Parameters)

Figure 1: Comparison of the knowledge available in specific methods to the one derived from generic method patterns

• For *describing an Entity-Type* (right part of figure 1) we assume that an attribute is its concept which is, itself characterised by two properties, its domain and its valuation, whereas the key is considered as a constraint.

• For *describing a class* we assume that the attributes and the operations are concepts of the class, respectively characterised by two properties: the domain, the valuation on one hand and the type and parameters on the other hand.

The same abstraction mechanism has been applied on many other parts of method processes to identify other generic intentions. The list of generic intentions we have identified is presented in figure 2, in a hierarchical manner.

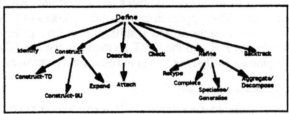

Figure 2 : Hierarchy of generic method intentions

• The *Define* root represents the intention assigned to any method. *Identify*, *Construct*, *Describe*, *Check*, *Refine* and *Backtrack* are six sub-intentions of the *Define* intention.

• *Construct in Top Down* (*Construct-TD* for short), Construct in Bottom-Up (*Construct-BU* for short) and *Expand* are three sub-intentions of the *Construct* intention.

• *Retype, Complete, Specialise/Generalise, Aggregate/Decompose* are four sub-intentions of the *Refine* intention.

• All the leaves of the tree presented in figure 2 are primitive intentions in the sense that they act upon the product that they modify.

Let's overview the role of each primitive intention:

• The *Identify* intention leads to the creation of a product element.

• The *Construct-TD* intention is associated with the construction of a complex product element, i.e. an element which is built upon other elements. The Top-Down approach suggests to identify the complex element (for instance the RT) before its components (for instance the ETs).

• For constructing a complex product element, the *Construct-BU* intention suggests to identify the components of the complex element (for instance the ETs) before the complex component itself (for instance the RT).

• The *Expand* intention is associated with the construction of a complex product element following a spreading-out approach. Applied on an ET it leads to the creation of a RT with all the (not already existing) ETs the RT is based on.

• The *Attach* intention allows us to connect a descriptive property (for instance the valuation) to a product element (for instance the attribute).

• The *Retype* intention aims to transform a product element (for instance a RT) into another one (for instance an ET).

• The *Complete* intention allows us to add missing features (for instance an attribute) to an existing product element (for instance a class).

• The *Specialise* intention is associated to product elements which encapsulate several representations of real world phenomena sharing common characteristics. For instance, in the OMT object model, a class can be specialised into several classes inheriting from a class containing the common features.

• The *Generalise* intention is used to gather common features of several sub-types elements (for instance classes) in a super-type (for instance a super-class).

• *Aggregate* means group several product elements having strong semantic relationships into a unique element.

• The *Decompose* intention is used to precise the semantic of a product element encapsulating several independent real world phenomena.

• The *Check* intention aims at verifying that quality rules are satisfied.

• The *Backtrack* intention aims at undoing one or several actions which have been done. Achieving the backtrack intention requires a process trace which keeps track of what has happened in the process and when.

Although this hierarchical classification of intentions is powerful for describing processes within methods, there is need to add a product dimension to cover the overall aspects of methods. Thus we introduce the notion of *situation* which represents the product the intention can be applied on. Consequently, a chunk can be characterised by a couple <(*situation*), *intention*> [Rolland94].

Some intentions can be directly realised as transformations of a product, whereas others need to be decomposed or refined to be executed. To differentiate between them, we have identified three different types: when an intention is executed by a transformation of the product under development, it is called *executable*, when an intention can be achieved in different alternatives ways, it is denoted as *choice intention*, and finally, when an intention should be decomposed before being executed, it is called *plan intention*.

Figure 3 presents some of the generic point chunks available in the library.

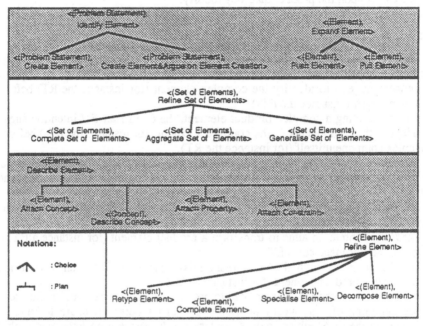

Figure 3 : Some patterns associated to the generic intentions

The chunks presented in figure 3 are qualified as *generic* because the product parts they are related to are method independent.

II.1 Obtaining Point chunks
From the generic patterns stored in the library of reusable knowledge it is possible to construct point chunks of new methods.

Their construction consists of instantiating the generic method patterns stored in the library, on the specific product the method is composed of. In the rest of the section, we generate the point chunks of the new object-oriented method which we shall use to build the elevator control system in section 4.

Our method uses the triplet of concepts <class-operation-event> which is present in almost all Object Oriented methods nowadays, OOA&D [Martin92], OMT [Rumbaugh91], TOOM [Souveyet96] O* [Brunet93], among others and was earlier introduced in systemic methods such as REMORA [Rolland88].

Since the product of our method is composed of *classes*, *operations* and *events*, the construction of the method consists in instantiating the chunks on these three concepts.

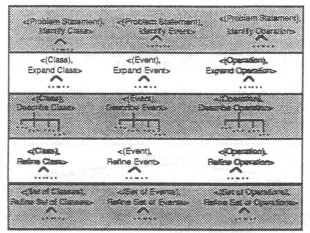

Figure 4: Instantiation of generic patterns for the construction of an OO method

Figure 4 presents some of the point chunks resulting of the instantiation process.

The most interesting chunks participating to the construction are the one which are dedicated to the *Expand* intention. As a matter of fact, the *Expand* pattern suggests a new and flexible way of constructing an element by exploiting mental connections to identify one element which is part of the environment of another one, and then repeating the process for the identified element. We present the *Expand* pattern in the following.

II.2 Detailing the Expand Point Chunk
As mentioned in the beginning of this section, we identify three major concepts common to most OO methods: *class*, *event* and *operation*. The common view is that of an event being a "noteworthy state change of a class" (OOA&D) which "triggers operations" [Martin92]. Since an operation "modifies the state of an object in a class" (OMT), there is a causal relationship among the three concepts which explains that the cause of change (event) generates changes (object state changes induced by operations) which can in turn be events.

This semantic relationship among the three concepts may be exploited by the way-of-working especially when using a spreading-out strategy; e.g. operations can be derived from the triggering event, events can be derived from the class, classes can be derived from the operations performed on them...etc. Vice-versa, events can be derived from the operations they are triggering, operations can be derived from the classes they modify, and classes can be derived from events. These relationships are summarised in figure 5.

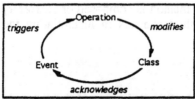

Figure 5 : The causality relationships between the major OO concepts

Consider Figure 6. There are two different choices available for expanding a class. These choices suggest the expansion of a class using the causal connection that the class maintains with the operation and the event.

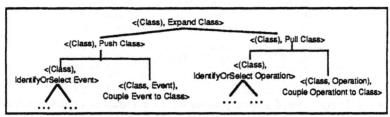

Figure 6: The Expand Class Chunk

The intention associated to a causality relationship (Figure 6) is called *Push* when the arc is traversed in the direction of the arrow, and the reverse one is called *Pull* when the arc is traversed in the opposite direction of the arrow. The *Pull Class* serves to introduce the operations of a class whereas the *Push Class* is used to identify the event acknowledged as a state change of an object of the class.

The same reasoning has been applied for the expansion of an operation (resp. an event). *Pull Operation, (resp. Pull Event)* will end up in identifying the event which triggers the operation, (resp. the class it is acknowledged on). Similarly, the software engineer could choose *Push Operation (resp. Push Event)* in order to identify the embedding class (resp. the operation triggered by it).

III The Chunks Controlling the Process Flow

The method chunks which control the process flow are derived from generic patterns of process flow. Figure 7 presents three of these generic patterns.

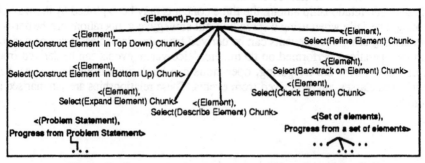

Figure 7 : Some generic patterns controlling the process flow

• The *Progress from Problem Statement* pattern allows to progress in the construction of the schema by identifying its elements from the description of the problem statement.

• The *Progress from Element* pattern proposes seven ways to progress from an element in the schema construction. Each alternative selects a point chunk applicable to a specific product element. Therefore, there should be at least one product element in the product under development.

• The *Progress from a set of elements* pattern allows the checking and refinement of elements. To be applied, the product must contain several elements of the same type.

The generic patterns presented above are also part of the same generic library which contains the point chunks. The generic flow chunks can be instantiated on the product of specific methods to generate the chunks. In the following we are focusing on the instantiation of the generic flow chunks done on our OO methods.

• In the OO methods, the *<(Problem Statement), Progress from Problem Statement>* has three alternatives *(<(Problem Statement), Select (Identify Class) Chunk>; <(Problem Statement), Select (Identify Operation) Chunk>; <(Problem Statement), Select (Identify Event) Chunk>)*.

• The *<(Element), Progress from Element>* is instantiated on the class, the operation and the event. As an example figure 8 shows the instantiation of this generic pattern on a class. Each alternative allows to select a point chunk to be executed.

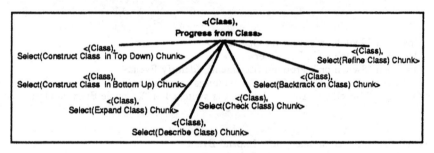

Figure 8 : The *Progress from Class* Chunk

As before, the *<(Set of elements), Progress from a set of elements>* chunk is instantiated on the three concepts of our OO method. Thus, three chunks are generated out of this generic pattern, one for the classes, one for the operations and one for the events. The *<(Set of classes), Progress from a set of classes>*, for instance, has three alternatives namely *<(Set of classes), Select (Check set of classes) Chunk>*, *<(Set of classes), Select (Backtrack on set of classes) Chunk>*, and *<(Set of classes), Select (Refine set of classes) Chunk>*.

IV Application of the OOM [Deneckere96] Method to an Elevator Control System

This section presents the step by step trace of the process followed to elaborate the schema of an elevator control system, using the OO point chunks and flow chunks we introduced in the foregoing sections. The Description of the problem statement for the functioning of an elevator system that we use is described in [Grosz94].

In the trace of the process presented below, the steps for finding the point chunk to execute and the one representing its execution are shown. To differentiate the use of flow chunks from the use of point chunks, we have used a grey pattern for the flow chunks. The impact the steps have on the product is shown in figure 9.

The process starts with the choice of the *Progress from Problem Statement* chunk, then, it is entirely based on the application of the *Progress from Element*.

* <(Problem Statement), Progress from Problem Statement>
* <(Problem Statement), Select (Identify Class) Chunk>
- <(Problem Statement), Identify Class>
- <(Problem Statement), Create Class "Button">
* <(Class "Button"), Progress from Class>
* <(Class "Button"), Select (Expand Class) Chunk>
- <(Class "Button"), Expand Class>
- <(Class "Button"), Pull Class>
- <(Class "Button", Problem Statement), Identify Operation>
- <(Problem Statement), Create Operation "Switch on">
- <(Class "Button", Operation "Switch on"), Couple Operation to Class>
* <(Operation "Switch on"), Progress from Operation >
* <(Operation "Switch on"), Select (Expand Operation) Chunk>
- <(Operation "Switch on"), Expand Operation>
- <(Operation "Switch on"), Pull Operation>
- <(Operation "Switch on", Problem Statement), Identify Event>
- <(Problem Statement), Create Event "A button is switched on">
- <(Operation "Switch on", Event "A button is switched on"), Couple Event to Operation>
* <(Event "A button is switched on"), Progress from Event>
* <(Event "A button is switched on"), Select (Expand Event) Chunk>
- <(Event "A button is switched on"), Expand Event>
- <(Event "A button is switched on"), Pull Event>
- <(Event "A button is switched on", Problem Statement), Identify Class>
- <(Problem Statement), Create Class "Passenger">
- <(Event "A button is switched on", Class "Passenger"), Couple Class to Event >

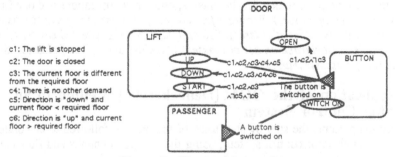

c1: The lift is stopped
c2: The door is closed
c3: The current floor is different from the required floor
c4: There is no other demand
c5: Direction is "down" and current floor < required floor
c6: Direction is "up" and current floor > required floor

Figure 9 : The resulting product

Figure 9 summarises the execution of the above steps together with the use of the seven others point chunks.

VI Conclusion

We have presented a new approach for improving the efficiency of method construction. This approach proposes to derive new methods from generic method knowledge which is stored in a library of reusable patterns. Methods are composed of a set of chunks which contain guidelines for supporting the development process. Through an example we have introduced the difference between the knowledge which provides guidance for achieving transformations on the product from the one allowing the selection of the next possible step to execute in the process.

In order to validate this approach, we are building an electronic handbook that we plan to put on a web server in order to make it accessible to many potential users and to receiving comments and feedback from them.

VII References

[Batini92] : Batini C., Ceri S. Navathe S. B., "Conceptual Database Design, An entity-relationship approach", Benjamin/cummings Eds., 1992.

[Brunet93] : Brunet, J., "Analyse Conceptuelle orientée-objet", PhD thesis, University of Paris 6, France, 1993.

[Chen76] : Chen P. P. S., "The Entity-Relationship Model : Towards an unified view of data", ACM Transactions on Database Systems, Vol 1, N°1, March 76.

[Deneckere96]: Deneckere R., Souveyet C. , Rolland C. , "Hanbook for the OO methods", Internal Report, TOOBIS Project, 1996.

[Grosz94]: Grosz G., Rolland C., "The case study of the elevator system with O*",deliverable 2 Andersen Consulting, June 1994, (38 pages).

[Grundy96]: Grundy J. C., Venable J. R., "Towards an integrated environment for method engineering", Proceedings of the IFIP TC8, WG8.1/8.2 Working Conference on Method Engineering, Atlanta, USA, 26-28 August 1996.

[Harmsen94]: Harmsen F et al, "Situational method engineering for informational system project approaches", in Method and Associated Tools for the Information Systems Life Cycle, Verrijn-Stuart and Olle (eds.), North Holland, pp169-194, Maastrischt, The netherlands, 1994.

[Hidding94] : Hidding G.J. , "Methodology information : who uses it and why not?" Proc. WITS-94, Vancouver, Canada, 1994.

[Lyytinen89] : Lyytinen K., Smolander K., Tahvainen V-P., "Modelling CASE Environments in sytems Work", CAISE'89 conference papers, Kista, Sweden, 1989.

[Martin92] : Martin J., Odell J. J., "Object-oriented Analysis and Design", Prentice-Hall, 1992.

[Plihon96] : Plihon V., "Un environnement pour l'ingénierie des méthodes", Ph'D thesis, University Paris I-Sorbonne, January 1996.

[Rolland88] : C. Rolland, O. Foucault, G. Benci, "Conception des systèmes d'information : La méthode REMORA", Eyrolles, 1988.

[Rolland94] : Rolland C., Grosz G., "A General Framework for Describing the Requirements Engineering Process", C. IEEE Conference on Systems Man and Cybernetics, CSMC94, San Antonio, Texas, 1994.

[Rolland96a] : Rolland C., Prakash N., "A proposal for context-specific method engineering", Proceedings of the IFIP TC8, WG8.1/8.2 Working Conference on Method Engineering, Atlanta, USA, 26-28 August 1996.

[Rolland96b] : Rolland C., Plihon V. : Using Generic Method Chunks to Generate Process Models Fragments, Proc of the Third International Conference on Requirement Engineering (ICRE'96) Conference, 1996.

[Rumbaugh91] : J. Rumbaugh, M. Blaha, W. Premerlani, F. Eddy, W. Loresen : "Object-oriented modeling and design", Prentice Hall international, 1991.

[Saeki94] : Saeki M., Wenyin K., "PCTE based Tool for Supporting Collaborative Specification Development", Conference PCTE'94, San Francisco, Dec. 1994.

[Slooten96] : van Slooten K., Hodes B.; "Characterizing IS Development Projects" ; Proceedings of the IFIP TC8, WG8.1/8.2 Working Conference on Method Engineering, Altanta, USA; 26-28 August 1996.

[Souveyet96] : Souveyet S., "Méthode orientée objet dédiée aux aspects temporels dans les systèmes d'information (TOOM)", Submitted paper, 1996.

[Welke91] : Welke R, and Kumar K., "Method engineering : a proposal for situation-specific methodology construction", in Systems Analysis and Design : A Research Agenda, Cotterman and Senn(eds), Wiley, 91.

The Role of Structural Events in Behaviour Specification

Dolors Costal, Maria-Ribera Sancho, Antoni Olivé and Anna Roselló

Universitat Politècnica de Catalunya, Departament LSI
Jordi Girona Salgado, 1-3, E-08034 Barcelona -- Catalonia
e-mail: [dolors l ribera l olive l rosello]@lsi.upc.es

Abstract. An important challenge of the Information System research field is to facilitate the designer the task of conceptual specification. Our aim is to contribute in this direction by facilitating the behavioural specification component of this task. Our approach is based on providing a set of semantically enriched structural events for a given Information Base schema and using them to simplify the definition of the Information Base transition schema.

1. Introduction

An Information System conceptual specification is a formal model of the Universe of Discourse (UoD) considered from a structural point of view, that is, the Information Base schema as well as from a behavioural point of view, that is, the Information Base transition schema. An important challenge of the Information Systems research field is to facilitate the designer the task of conceptual specification. The aim of this paper is to contribute in this direction by facilitating the behavioural specification component of this task.

Our approach is inscribed in the context of the ongoing ROSES (Rules, ObjectS and EventS) project, whose aim is to explore the concept of event and knowledge base management systems. However, we believe that the approach is general and that it might inspire some ideas helpful in other contexts or languages.

In ROSES, there is an object model that provides the concepts needed to define the Information Base schema [CBC+96] while the Information Base transition schema is defined by an event model [BCC+96].

ROSES object model is based on the well known concepts of generalisation/specialisation hierarchies, single valued and multivalued attributes, derived attributes, integrity constraints, keys, etc. In this paper, we do not include aspects related with generalisation/specialisation hierarchies because they are out of its scope. ROSES object model provides, additionally, new features that allow to define, in a simple way, common dynamic constraints of objects and attributes.

ROSES event model includes the external event classes which determine the Information Base behaviour. An external event class has a certain structure and defines a certain effect on the Information Base (IB). As mentioned before, our purpose is to facilitate this behavioural specification. We accomplish this objective by using *structural events*.

Conceptual specification languages provide (either implicitly or explicitly) a set of structural events based on its IB schema. Such events allow common changes such as inserting or deleting an object instance, changing the value of attributes, and so on. In ROSES we have elaborated a little bit more the concept of structural event. We take into account, in its definition, the dynamic features (as well as the common static features) specified in the object model. We also determine, automatically, the set of possible structural events. Each structural event has associated a set of constraints and effects on the IB. We argue that these elaborated structural events contribute to external event specification because either an external event class directly coincides with an structural event class or its specification can be easily made in terms of structural event classes.

This paper is organised as follows. Next section reviews, in short, the ROSES object model. Section 3 presents the event model and the role of structural events in its specification. Section 4 is devoted to the description of the structural event automatic obtention. Finally, section 5 gives our conclusions and points out further work.

2. Object Model

The object model provides the concepts needed to define the IB structure. More specifically, it allows to describe the object classes which are relevant to the Information System.

The object model definition in ROSES includes some elements which are usually found in many object-oriented specification languages: generalisation/specialisation hierarchies, single valued and multivalued attributes, derived attributes, integrity constraints, keys, etc. On the other hand, it adopts the temporal approach in which object existence and attribute values depend on time. Additionally, it incorporates the specification of features which describe some of the dynamic constraints of object classes and their attributes: population features and attribute features. This is one of the innovative concepts of ROSES with respect to previous languages.

In the following, we illustrate the object model definition in ROSES through an example. We do not include aspects related with generalisation/specialisation hierarchies because they are out of the scope of this paper.

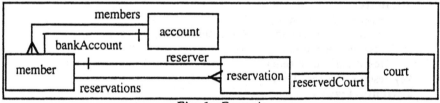

Fig. 1. Example

We have chosen an example which corresponds to a subset of a tennis club information system. Figure 1 shows its object classes and the attributes relating them. The graphical notation has been adapted from [MaO92]. There are four object classes in the example: *member, account, reservation* and *court*. The object class *member* represents the members of the tennis club. Each member has a bank *account* to make payments. Also, each member is able to *reserve* one or more *courts* of the club.

To illustrate object class specification in ROSES, consider in more detail object classes *member* and *reservation*. Figure 2 includes their specification.

```
create base object class member with
    population features non-permanent instances;
    attributes
        number: integer;
        name: string(20);
        address: string(20);
        telephone: integer;
        lastYearReservations: integer derived;
        bankAccount: account;
        reservations: set of reservation;
    key number;
    attribute features
        number, name:
            single permanent existence interval,
            always initially valued, non-modifiable;
        address, telephone, bankAccount:
            single permanent existence interval,
            always initially valued, modifiable;
        reservations:
            never initially valued, size between 0 and N,
            insertions allowed, deletions not allowed;
    attribute rules
        Self.lastYearReservations (at T) = N if
            member(Self) (at T), A = year(T) - 1,
            N = count (Res where
                reservation(Res) (at T), Res.reserver= Self,
                Res.reservedDate (at T) = D,  year(D) = A);
end

create base object class reservation with
    population features permanent instances;
    attributes
        reservedCourt: court;
        reserver: member inverse of reservations;
        reservedDate: date;
        reservedHour: integer;
    key reserver, reservedDate;
    attribute features
        reservedCourt, reserver, reservedDate, reservedHour:
            single permanent existence interval,
            always initially valued, non-modifiable;
    constraints
        notAvailable(reserver:M, reservedDate:D, reservedHour:H, time:T) if
        reservation(Self) (at T), reservation(R) (at T), R≠Self, Self.reserver=M,
        Self.reservedCourt (at T) = C, R.reservedCourt (at T) = C,
        Self.reservedDate (at T) = D, R.reservedDate (at T) = D,
        Self.reservedHour (at T) = H, R.reservedHour (at T) = H;
end
```

Fig. 2. Specification of object classes *member* and *reservation*

When an object is created in a class, the system automatically assigns an object identifier (oid) to it. The oid is used to make reference to the objects of the class.

Object attributes are defined in the **attributes** clause. They can be single valued (such as *number, name* and *address* of class *member*) or multivalued (such as *reservations* of class *member*). The latter case is indicated with the keywords **set of**.

Attribute type can be predefined (integer, string, real, etc.) or can be an object class. For example, in class *member*, attributes *bankAccount* and *reservations* are defined over object classes *account* and *reservation*, respectively.

For attributes defined over object classes, ROSES permits the specification of inverse attributes with the clause **inverse of**. For an attribute *a* of object class *A* taking value over an object class *B*, the designer may define in *B* an attribute *b* being the inverse of *a*. The implicit meaning is that an instance of *B* references through *b* all the instances of *A* which reference *B* through *a*. In our example, attribute *reservations* of *member* object class has an inverse attribute *reserver* in the *reservation* object class.

Additionally, ROSES allows the definition of derived attributes. They have an associated derivation rule which is included in the **attribute rules** clause. This is the case of *lastYearReservations*. Its derivation rule states that the value of this attribute for a given member (Self) at a given time instant T is the number of reservations made by the member with a *reservedDate* corresponding to the year previous to the year of T.

In this paper, we do not include a description of the syntax and semantics of ROSES different types of rules (attribute, constraint and event rules) [BCC+96]. Instead, we give their intuitive meaning which is sufficient for our purposes.

Object classes may have associated integrity constraints which are defined in the **constraints** clause by means of inconsistency rules. For the object class *reservation* there is a constraint *notAvailable* forbidding to reserve a court for a date and hour which is already occupied.

As mentioned above, the proposed object model incorporates the specification of features which describe usual dynamic constraints of object classes and their attributes.

Dynamic constraints of object classes are specified in the **population features** clause. We define an object class as of **permanent instances** if its instances exist forever once they are created. Otherwise, we define it as of **non-permanent instances**. In our example case, class *member* has non-permanent instances while class *reservation* has permanent instances.

Temporal features of attributes are declared in the **attribute features** clause. They allow to specify the attribute dynamics during the object life: the moment of value acquisition, the expected existence intervals and the modifiability.

For initial value acquisition, an attribute may be **always/sometimes/never initially valued** depending on whether it takes value always, sometimes or never, respectively, at the moment of the object creation. For example, attribute *number* must take value when a member is created and, thus, it is defined as **always initially valued**.

The formulation of expected existence intervals is relevant only for single valued attributes. According to this, a single valued attribute may be declared as: **multiple existence interval, single permanent existence interval** and **single non-**

permanent existence interval. **Multiple existence interval** states that the attribute may have value during several discontinuous time intervals. **Single permanent existence interval** indicates that if the attribute takes a value, it will keep on having value until the object deletion. **Single non-permanent existence interval** means that the attribute may have value during a single time interval although it may lose its value before the object deletion. For example, attribute *address* of class *member* is declared as **single permanent existence interval** to prevent a member from losing the value for attribute *address*.

The specification of modifiability depends on whether the attribute is single valued or multivalued. For single valued attributes, **modifiable/non-modifiable** means that the attribute is modifiable or not, respectively. In the case of multivalued attributes, modifiability comes down to the following features: modifiability by insertion of values (**insertions allowed/not allowed**) and modifiability by deletion of values (**deletions allowed/not allowed**).

The combination of features for a given attribute describes its dynamics. Attribute *address* of our example is: **always initially valued, single permanent existence interval** and **modifiable**. This implies that a member has an address from its creation till its deletion although this address can change in the meantime.

3. Event Model

The event model provides the concepts needed to define the evolution of the IB. More specifically, it includes the external event classes which determine the IB transitions from one state to another.

An external event corresponds to a change in the UoD that occurs at a given time instant and which is not induced by the Information System itself. External events of our example case could be the insertion of a new member, the reservation of several courts made by a member, etc.

External event classes group those external events that notify the same kind of change in the UoD. When the system receives an external event, it assigns an identifier (eid) to it and adds the event to the corresponding external event class.

An external event class has a certain structure and defines a certain effect on the IB. The structure of an external event class corresponds to the information given to the system when the external event occurs. The effect of the external event describes the changes that it induces in the IB.

The difficulty of specifying external event classes is threefold. First, the designer must capture their structure taking into account the user requirements. This structure can be, in some cases, quite complex. Secondly, he must describe the effect of the external event on possibly several object classes and their attributes. Finally, he must take into account that this effect has to preserve the constraints and dynamic features specified in the object model.

3.1 Facilitating External Event Specification with Structural Events

In order to partially overcome the difficulties mentioned above, one of the main objectives of the ROSES system consists on facilitating the task of external event class definition. In ROSES, external events do not have a direct effect on the IB. This is accomplished by structural events. This kind of events reflects the basic changes that may occur in each object class of the IB.

An important aspect of the ROSES system is the ability to automatically obtain the set of structural event classes corresponding to a concrete object model. The singularity of ROSES structural events comes from the fact that the object model includes the specification of features which describe the dynamic constraints of object classes and their attributes. The consideration of all these features allows the obtention of richer structural event classes. In this paper we explain that this enrichment presents many advantages for external event specification because part of this specification is already embedded in the automatically obtained structural events.

In the following, we introduce the structural events of the ROSES system and, after that, we illustrate its usefulness for external event specification.

3.1.1 Structural Events

In ROSES, the IB evolves as a consequence of the occurrence of structural events. An structural event is an instance of an structural event class. This concept can be seen as parallel of that of basic update operations used conventionally. An structural event class would correspond to an operation and an structural event would correspond to the invocation of the operation. From now on, in cases in which the context is unambiguous, we refer to structural event classes simply as structural events.

We consider five kinds of structural events, depending on their effect on the IB: object insertion, object deletion, attribute insertion, attribute update and attribute deletion.

The effect of an object insertion structural event is, basically, the addition of an instance in an object class at the time instant when the event occurs. In a similar way, the effect of an object deletion structural event is, basically, the removal of an instance from an object class at the time instant when the event occurs.

The effect of an attribute insertion structural event consists, mainly, on the addition of an attribute value to an instance of an object class at the time instant when the event occurs. Similarly, the effect of an attribute update/deletion structural event consists, mainly, on the update/deletion of an attribute value of an object class instance.

The structural event enrichment that we propose in this paper comes down to three aspects. In first place, only the necessary structural events classes will exist (e.g. it may happen that an object class has not an object deletion structural event class). Secondly, structural event classes have exactly the parameters which are strictly necessary (e.g. an object insertion structural event class may not include all object class attributes as parameters). Finally, when an object class has an attribute defined over another object class, structural events may have additional effects to those already described (e.g. an attribute insertion structural event may have the additional effect of adding an instance to an object class). As explained above, this enrichment has been possible thanks to the dynamic features specified in the object model.

Taking the tennis club example of figure 2 the following structural event classes will exist: *insert_member, delete_member, update_member_address,*

update_member_telephone,update_member_bankAccount, insert_member_reservations
and *insert_reservation*. Figure 3 shows structural event classes *insert_member* and
insert_reservation that will be used in the rest of the paper.

```
structural event class insert_member with
    attributes
        number: integer;
        name: string(20);
        address: string(20);
        telephone: integer;
        bankAccount: account optional;
        new_bankAccount: subevent sub_insert_bankAccount optional;
        time: time;
        subevent class sub_insert_bankAccount with
        attributes
            accountNumber: integer;
        end
    constraints
        exclusive(time:T) if
            insert_member(X), X.time=T,
            ((X.bankAccount = nil, X.new_bankAccount=nil) or
            (X.bankAccount ≠ nil, X.new_bankAccount≠nil));
end
structural event class insert_reservation with
    attributes
        reservedCourt: court;
        reserver: member;
        reservedDate: date;
        reservedHour: integer;
        time: time;
end
```

Fig. 3. Structural event classes *insert_member* and *insert_reservation*

In ROSES, an event class definition consists, basically, on the specification of its
attributes and on the constraints associated to the events of the class. Event attributes
are described in the **attributes** clause and constraints in the **constraints** clause.

Consider structural event class *insert_member*. There is a *time* attribute indicating
the time instant when the event occurs and is communicated to the system. The rest
of attributes contain values for *member* attributes that can take initial value. Note that
attribute *reservations* is not present because its definition in the object class *member*
establishes that it will never take value at the member insertion. Attribute
bankAccount is declared as **optional** because it may or may not take initial value.

The effect of an occurrence of an *insert_member* event is similar to the invocation
of an insertion operation in conventional models but taking into account the dynamic
features. That is, a new instance of class *member* with the values given for its
attributes will exist from the time instant indicated by attribute *time*. The system will
assign an oid to the new object. This instance will continue existing until a
delete_member event occurs. The initialised attributes will keep their values until an

attribute update structural event occurs for any of them (*update_member_address*, *update_member_telephone* and *update_member_bankAccount*).

Note that the attribute *new_bankAccount* is itself a subevent. It can only have value if attribute *bankAccount* has not a value, as specified by the constraint of the event class. The subevent causes the additional effect of inserting a new occurrence in the class *account*. This is an example of an additional effect caused by the existence of an attribute defined over an object class. Intuitively, when a new member is added, its attribute *bankAccount* has to be initialised. Then, two possibilities arise: either the value for bankAccount already exists or it has to be added as a new object of class *account* and assigned to the attribute *bankAccount* of the new member. These cases have to be considered in the structural event obtention process.

The structure and effect of event *insert_reservation* is hopefully straightforward.

In next subsection, the use of structural events for external event specification will be illustrated. The usefulness of structural events comes from the fact that they consider all the aspects already specified in the object model (temporal features of the population, moment of value acquisition, expected existence intervals and modifiability).

3.1.2 External Events and Event Rules

As mentioned above, ROSES external events do not have a direct effect on the IB. This goal is accomplished by structural events. Therefore, the effect of external events is defined in terms of structural events. We use event rules to establish the relation between ones and the others. Then, external event effect definition is simplified because part of it is already embedded in the automatically obtained structural events.

Two possible external event classes of our tennis club example can be the insertion of a new member (*add_member*) and the reservation of several courts made by a member (*reserve*). In the following, we illustrate the impact of having structural events on the definition of external events by means of these examples.

Consider the external event class *add_member*. The goal of this event is to add a new member and initialise its attributes. It can be seen that this is, precisely, the goal accomplished by the structural event *insert_member*. ROSES allows structural events to be external at the same time. Therefore, in this case the designer does not have to specify neither the structure of the external event nor the event rules that give its effect. We argue that this correspondence happens frequently in most conceptual domains. This is because ROSES structural events model the basic changes that may happen in the real world while taking into account all the dynamic features specified in the object model.

Something different happens with the external event class *reserve*. The goal of this event is to register several reservations (five at most) made by a single member at the same time. In this case, there is not any correspondent structural event because *reserve* affects several instances of the same object class. For this reason, the external event *reserve* must be defined and its effect must be specified in terms of event rules that relate it with the suitable structural events. Figure 4 includes this specification.

In the definition of external event class *reserve*, attribute *reserver* indicates the member that makes the reservations while attribute *reservations* communicates the set of reservations to be made. *Reservations* is multivalued because the member should be able to make several reservations simultaneously. Its domain is a set of subevents. Each occurrence of subevent *oneReserve* corresponds to the reservation of one court for a given date and hour.

```
create base external event class reserve with
    attributes
        reserver: member;
        reservations: set of subevent oneReserve size between 1 and 5;
        time: time;
    subevent class oneReserve with
        attributes
            reservedCourt: court;
            reservedDate: date;
            reservedHour: integer;
    end
end
create rule newReservations
    insert_reservation(reservedCourt: C, reserver: M,
                    reservedDate: D, reservedHour: H, time: T) if
        reserve(R), R.time = T, R.reserver = M,
        OneRes in R.reservations, OneRes.reservedCourt = C,
        OneRes.reservedDate = D, OneRes.reservedHour = H.
end
```

Fig. 4. External event class *reserve* and event rule *newReservations*

The effects of this external event class *reserve* are defined with a single rule *newReservations*. Intuitively, an occurrence of structural event *insert_reservation* with suitable attribute values has to be induced for each occurrence of the subevent *oneReserve*. This is accomplished through the literal 'OneRes in R.reservations' that instantiates variable *OneRes* as many times as subevents components has the occurrence of *reserve* external event (referred as R in the rule).

In this case, although there is not a direct correspondence between *reserve* and any structural event, its specification is considerably simplified by the availability of structural events. The designer can focus the problem of making several reservations simultaneously but he can ignore the problems associated to make a single reservation. For example, he can ignore the inconsistencies that may arise for not taking into account the features specified in the object model such as not giving value to attribute *reservedDate* that is **always initially valued**, reserving a previously non-existent *court*, etc. Additionally, the effect of the external event is implicitly specified because the event rule relates it with structural events that have a predefined effect. Finally, the availability of the structure of *insert_reservation* (that creates a single reservation) facilitates the designer the task of capturing the structure of external event *reserve* (that creates several reservations).

We argue that the examples presented above are representative of the difficulty associated to external event specification and of the advantages of enriched structural event provision: either the external event directly coincides with an structural event or its specification can be easily made in terms of structural events.

It is relevant to mention that a few practical cases have been experienced with the following specification languages: Yourdon Systems Method [You93], Syntropy [CoD94] and ROSES. The conclusions of the comparison in which refers to the behaviour specification indicate that, using ROSES, there is a drastic reduction of time investment and specification length with respect to the other two languages.

The strengthness of our approach relies on the fact that the ROSES system is able to automatically generate the structural events corresponding to a given object model. This automatic obtention is described in next section.

4. Automatic obtention of structural event classes

For space reasons, the procedure for structural event obtention will be described in an informal way. A more detailed explanation can be found in [CSR97]. This procedure does not consider generalisation/specialisation hierarchies wich are one objective of our further work. [CSR97] also presents a formalisation of structural event effects.

In order to simplify the explanation of the automatic obtention of structural event classes, we divide this process in two parts. The first one is devoted to the deduction of which structural event classes must exist (4.1). The second one obtains their attributes and constraints (4.2). We illustrate this procedure with an example in 4.3.

4.1 Structural event existence

Let C be a class of the object model, then there exists an object insertion structural event named *insert_C*. If class C has been declared as of **non-permanent instances**, there also exists an object deletion structural event named *delete_C*.

Let attr be a non-derived attribute defined on an object class C. Taking into account the feature defining its initial value acquisition, if attr is **sometimes initially valued** or **never initially valued**, there exists an attribute insertion structural event named *insert_C_attr*.

We now consider the expected existence intervals of attr. If attr has been defined as **multiple existence interval**, then there exist structural events *insert_C_attr* and *delete_C_attr*. In case of being **single non-permanent existence interval**, there exists an structural event *delete_C_attr*.

Considering the specification of its modifiability three cases arise. If attr is **modifiable** then there exists an structural event *update_C_attr*. If attr has been declared as **insertions allowed**, then there exists an structural event *insert_C_attr*. If attr has been declared as **deletions allowed**, then there exists an structural event *delete_C_attr*.

4.2 Structural event attributes and constraints

Attributes and constraints that compose an structural event depend on the features defined for object classes and their attributes. If an object class has an attribute defined over an object class, this attribute has an inverse attribute (either implicit or explicit) in the second object class. If the designer has not defined the inverse attribute explicitly, a set of default features for it is assumed by ROSES. The features of the inverse attribute influence the structural events corresponding to the direct attribute and its object class. Depending on these features, when a value for the direct attribute is inserted, either this value already exists as an object or it has to be inserted as such, simultaneously.

Three kinds of attributes appear depending on the features of their inverses. An attribute is **value always existent on insertion** when at the insertion of a value for the attribute this value already exists as an object. It is **value never existent on insertion** when at the insertion of a value for the attribute this value never exists as an object. It is **value sometimes existent on insertion** when at the insertion of a value for the attribute this value may or may not exist as an object. This can be seen as a derived feature of the direct attribute. In [CSR97] the definition of these derived features in terms of the inverse attribute features can be found.

4.2.1 Object insertion structural events

Let C be an object class. Its corresponding insertion structural event *insert_C* contains the time attribute and additional attributes that depend on the definition of class C.

Let attr be an attribute defined in class C over a predefined type t and declared as **always initially valued**. Then, *insert_C* contains an attribute "attr: [**set of**] t". The **set of** option (between brackets) should be applied only if attr is multivalued. We follow this convention from now on.

Let attr be an attribute defined in class C over a predefined type t and declared as **sometimes initially valued**. Then, *insert_C* contains an attribute "attr: [**set of**] t optional".

Let attr be an attribute defined in class C over an object class C1. The following three cases arise:

1) attr is **value always existent on insertion**
   This case is similar to that of predefined type attributes. The only difference is that the domain of the event attribute is C1.

2) attr is **value never existent on insertion**
   If attr is declared as **always initially valued**, *insert_C* contains an attribute "new_C1_attr: [**set of**] **subevent** sub_insert_C1". The subevent *sub_insert_C1* has the same attributes as the object insertion structural event *insert_C1*.
   If attr is declared as **sometimes initially valued**, *insert_C* contains a similar attribute with the optional clause.

3) attr is **value sometimes existent on insertion**
   If attr is declared as **always initially valued**, *insert_C* contains the following two attributes: "attr: [**set of**] C1 optional" and "new_C1_attr: [**set of**] **subevent** sub_insert_C1 optional".
   If attr is single valued then the event contains the constraint *exclusive*. If it is multivalued, it contains the constraint *mandatory*:

> exclusive(time:T) **if** insert_C(X), X.time=T,
> ((X.attr=nil, X.new_C1_attr=nil) **or**
> (X.attr≠nil, X.new_C1_attr≠nil)).
> mandatory(time:T) **if** insert_C(X), X.time=T,
> X.attr=nil, X.new_C1_attr=nil.

If attr is declared as **sometimes initially valued**, *insert_C* contains the same attributes as in the previous case. If it is single valued it also contains the *singlevalue* constraint:

singlevalue(time:T) **if** insert_C(X), X.time=T,
X.attr≠nil, X.new_C1_attr≠nil.

4.2.2 Object deletion structural events

Let C be an object class. Its corresponding deletion structural event contains only attributes: "c: C" and "time: **time**". Attribute *c* indicates the occurrence of object class C that is affected by the deletion.

4.2.3 Attribute insertion/update structural events

Let attr be an attribute defined in object class C. Its corresponding insertion/update structural event contains attributes: "c: C" and "time: **time**".

Attribute *c* indicates the occurrence of object class C that is affected by the insertion/update. As can be seen this event is not complete. Apart from attributes *time* and *c*, we have additional attributes that depend on the features of attribute attr as explained in the following paragraphs.

If attr takes value over a predefined type t, the event contains the attribute "attr: **t**"
If attr takes value over an object class C1 three cases arise:

1) attr is **value always existent on insertion**
   This case is similar to that of predefined type attributes. The only difference is that the event attribute domain is C1.

2) attr is **value never existent on insertion**
   Insert/update_C_attr contains an attribute "new_C1_attr: **subevent** sub_insert_C1". The subevent *sub_insert_C1* has the same attributes as the object insertion structural event *insert_C1*.

3) attr is **value sometimes existent on insertion**
   Insert/update_C_attr contains the following two attributes: "attr: C1 **optional**" and "new_C1_attr: **subevent** sub_insert_C1 **optional**". The event also contains the constraint *exclusive* defined as follows:

exclusive(time:T) **if** insert/update_C_attr(X), X.time=T,
((X.attr=nil, X.new_C1_attr=nil) **or**
(X.attr≠nil, X.new_C1_attr≠nil)).

4.2.4 Attribute deletion structural events

Let attr be an attribute defined in object class C. Its corresponding deletion structural event contains attributes "c: C" and "time: **time**". Attribute *c* indicates the occurrence of object class C that is affected by the deletion.

If attr is multivalued, this event has an additional attribute that depends on the domain of attr. If attr takes value over a predefined type t, the event contains the attribute "attr: **t**". If attr takes value over an object class C1, the event contains the attribute "attr: C1".

4.3 An Example

In this section we apply the described obtention process to the object class *member* and its attributes.

In first place, we determine which structural event classes exist. There exists an structural event class *insert_member*. *Member* has been declared as of **non-permanent instances**, then there also exists an structural event class *delete_member*. Given that attribute *reservations* is **never initially valued**, there exists an structural event class *insert_member_reservation*. Attributes *address*, *telephone* and *bankAccount* are **modifiable**, then there exist structural event classes *update_member_address*,*update_member_telephone* and *update_member_bankAccount*.

Secondly, we show how to obtain the attributes and constraints for the case of the structural event *insert_member*. This structural event is initially declared as follows:

> **structural event class** insert_member **with**
>   **attributes**
>   ...
>   time: **time**;
> **end**

We complete this event by taking into account attribute features. Attributes *number, name, address* and *telephone* are defined over a predefined type, single valued and declared as **always initially valued**. Then, four attributes will be added to the structural event *insert_member* : "number: **integer**", "name: **string**(20)", "address: **string**(20)" and "telephone: **integer**".

Attribute *bankAccount* has been defined over object class *account*. We assume that it is of **value sometimes existent on insertion**. *BankAccount* is also **always initially valued** and single valued, then the event contains two attributes: "bankAccount: account **optional**" and "new_bankAccount: **subevent** sub_insert_bankAccount **optional**". It also contains an exclusive constraint

This completes the process of *insert_member* structural event obtention and the final result coincides with that shown in figure 3.

5. Conclusions and Further Work

In this paper we have studied the role of structural events in behaviour specification. It has been illustrated that the specification of dynamic features in the object model allows an enrichment of structural events. It has been argued that the so obtained structural event classes considerably simplify the specification of external events that describe the IB behaviour. We have also presented a procedure for the automatic obtention of enriched structural event classes. This approach has been experienced in several practical cases and the results are, for the moment, promising.

We plan to continue this work in, at least, two points. On one hand, we want to extend our approach to the treatment of generalisation/specialisation hierarchies. On the other hand, we would like to define a methodology that guides the designer in the process of taking advantage of structural events for behaviour specification.

Acknowledgements

We would like to thank the members of the ROSES group and the anonymous referees for their helpful comments. This work has been partially supported by PRONTIC CICYT program project TIC95-0735.

References

[BCC+96]   Barceló,M.; Costa,P.; Costal,D.; Olivé,A.; Quer,C.; Roselló,A.; Sancho,M.R. *El llenguatge ROSES. Part I*. Report LSI-96-55-R

[CBC+96]   Costa,P.; Barceló,M.; Costal,D.; Olivé,A.; Quer,C.; Roselló,A.; Sancho,M.R. "Las clases de objetos en ROSES". *Primeras Jornadas de investigación y docencia en Bases de Datos*. La Coruña, Junio 1996, pp. 98-108.

[CoD94]   Cook, S.; Daniels, J. *Designing Object Systems. Object-Oriented Modelling with Syntropy*, Prentice-Hall, 1994.

[CSR97]   Costal,D.; Sancho,M.R.; Roselló,A. *Structural Events in ROSES*, ROSES internal report, 1997.

[MaO92]   Martin, J.; Odell, J.J. *Object-Oriented Analysis and Design*. Prentice-Hall, 1992.

[You93]   Yourdon, E. *Yourdon Systems Method*, Yourdon Press, 1993.

AUTHOR INDEX

Lecture Notes in Computer Science

For information about Vols. 1–1229

please contact your bookseller or Springer-Verlag